Morocco

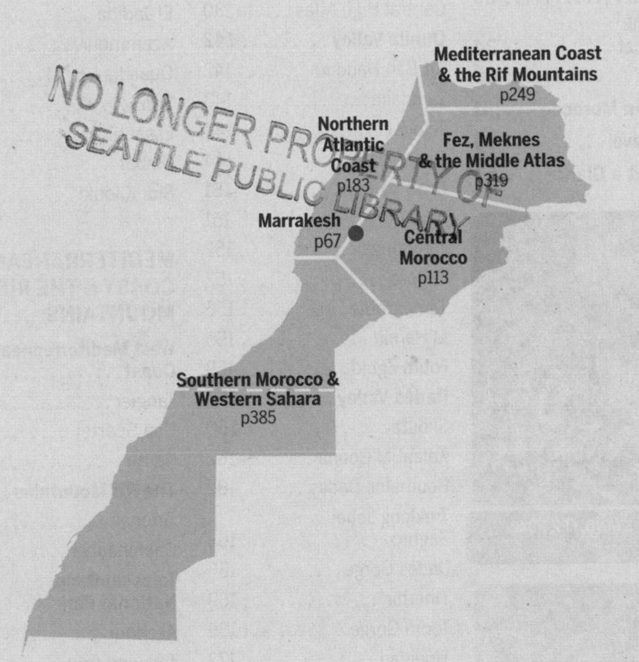

Stephen Lioy, Joel Balsam, Stephanie d'Arc Taylor, Sarah Gilbert,
Zora O'Neill, Lorna Parkes, Helen Ranger

PLAN YOUR TRIP

SNAIL STAND, FEZ P342

JULIAN LOVE/LONELY PLANET ©

PRICKLY PEAR, TAFRAOUTE P407

SIMON URWIN/LONELY PLANET ©

ON THE ROAD

Contents

UNDERSTAND

SURVIVAL GUIDE

COVID-19

We have re-checked every business in this book before publication to ensure that it is still open after the COVID-19 outbreak. However, the economic and social impacts of COVID-19 will continue to be felt long after the outbreak has been contained, and many businesses, services and events referenced in this guide may experience ongoing restrictions. Some businesses may be temporarily closed, have changed their opening hours and services, or require bookings; some unfortunately could have closed permanently. We suggest you check with venues before visiting for the latest information.

Right: Glaoui Kasbah (p144), Telouet

CORNFIELD/SHUTTERSTOCK©

WELCOME TO

Morocco

I fell in love with Morocco from the first sip of sweet mint tea, poured from a great height in a Tangier cafe. I was almost within touching distance of Europe and yet it felt so thrillingly different. Almost 20 years and countless visits later, I still feel that same sense of wonder, whether I'm dodging donkeys in the labyrinth of the Fez medina, meeting artists and designers in Marrakesh, enjoying oasis life among the palms or watching the catch of the day being unloaded in Essaouira. For me, Morocco really does have it all.

By Sarah Gilbert, Writer
@SarahGTravels sarahgtravels
For more about our writers, see p528

Morocco

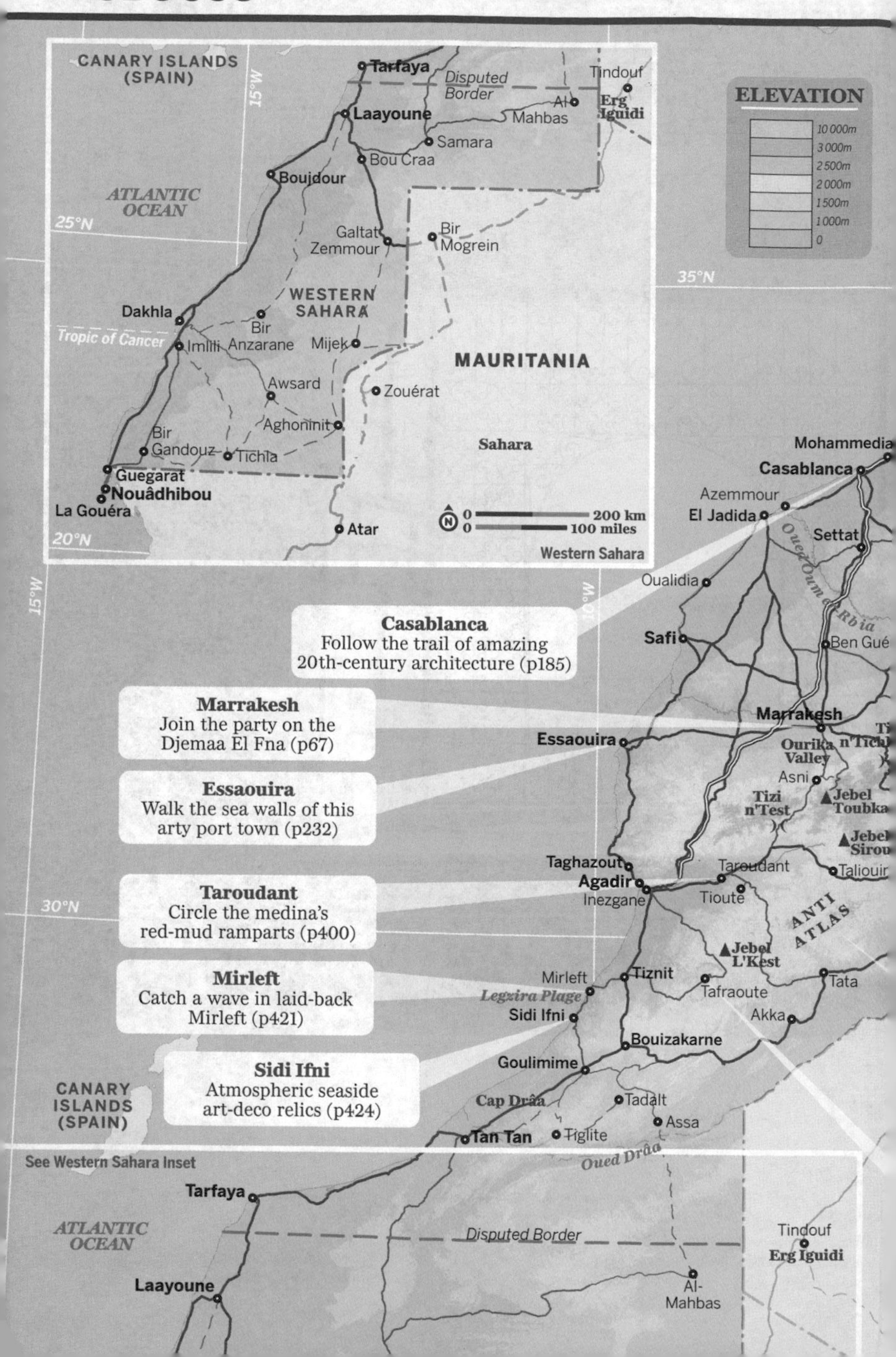

CANARY ISLANDS (SPAIN)
Tarfaya
Disputed Border
Tindouf
Al Mahbas
Erg Iguidi
Laayoune
Samara
Bou Craa
Boujdour
ATLANTIC OCEAN
25°N
15°W
Galtat Zemmour
Bir Mogrein
WESTERN SAHARA
Dakhla
Tropic of Cancer
Bir Anzarane
Imlili
Mijek
MAURITANIA
Awsard
Zouérat
Aghouinit
Bir Gandouz
Tichla
Sahara
Guegarat
Nouâdhibou
La Gouéra
20°N
Atar
0 200 km
0 100 miles
Western Sahara
ELEVATION
10 000m
3 000m
2 500m
2 000m
1 500m
1 000m
0
35°N
Mohammedia
Casablanca
Azemmour
El Jadida
Settat
Oued Oum er Rbia
Oualidia
10°W
Casablanca
Follow the trail of amazing 20th-century architecture (p185)
Safi
Ben Gué
Marrakesh
Join the party on the Djemaa El Fna (p67)
Marrakesh
Essaouira
Ourika Valley
Asni
Essaouira
Walk the sea walls of this arty port town (p232)
Tizi n'Test
Jebel Toubka
Jebel Sirou
Taghazout
Agadir
Inezgane
Taroudant
Tioute
Taliouir
Taroudant
Circle the medina's red-mud ramparts (p400)
30°N
ANTI ATLAS
Jebel L'Kest
Mirleft
Catch a wave in laid-back Mirleft (p421)
Mirleft
Legzira Plage
Tiznit
Tafraoute
Tata
Sidi Ifni
Akka
Bouizakarne
Sidi Ifni
Atmospheric seaside art-deco relics (p424)
Goulimime
CANARY ISLANDS (SPAIN)
Cap Drâa
Tadalt
Assa
Tan Tan
Tiglite
See Western Sahara Inset
Oued Drâa
Tarfaya
ATLANTIC OCEAN
Disputed Border
Tindouf
Erg Iguidi
Laayoune
Al-Mahbas

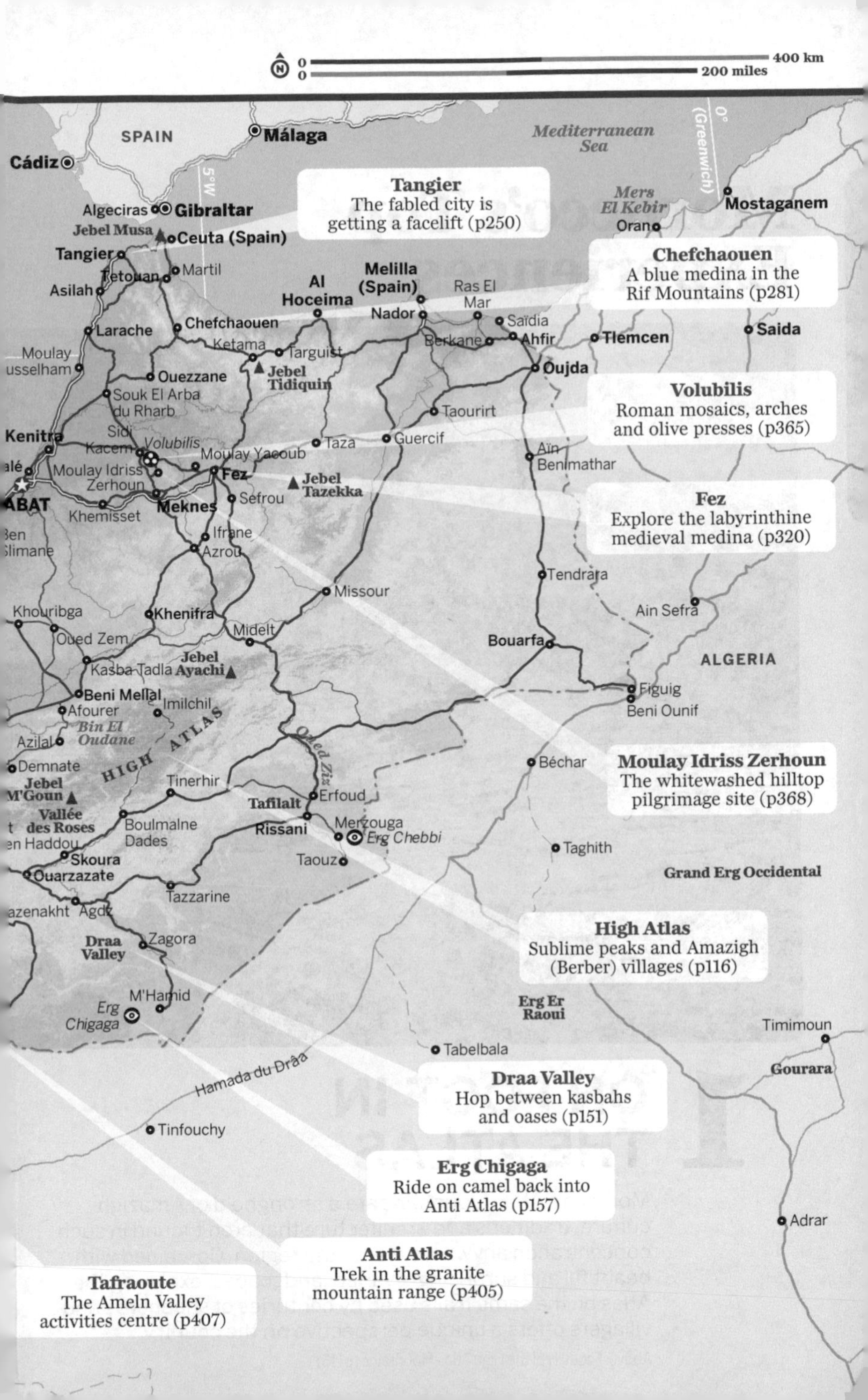

0
0
400 km
200 miles
SPAIN
Málaga
Cádiz
Mediterranean Sea
0° (Greenwich)
5°W
Tangier
The fabled city is getting a facelift (p250)
Algeciras
Gibraltar
Jebel Musa
Ceuta (Spain)
Mers El Kebir
Oran
Mostaganem
Tangier
Tetouan
Martil
Asilah
Al Hoceima
Melilla (Spain)
Ras El Mar
Chefchaouen
A blue medina in the Rif Mountains (p281)
Nador
Chefchaouen
Saïdia
Larache
Ketama
Targuist
Berkane
Ahfir
Tlemcen
Saida
Moulay Bousselham
Jebel Tidiquin
Oujda
Ouezzane
Souk El Arba du Rharb
Volubilis
Roman mosaics, arches and olive presses (p365)
Taourirt
Kenitra
Sidi Kacem
Volubilis
Taza
Guercif
Moulay Yacoub
Aïn Benimathar
Salé
Moulay Idriss Zerhoun
Fez
Jebel Tazekka
RABAT
Sefrou
Fez
Explore the labyrinthine medieval medina (p320)
Khemisset
Meknes
Ben Slimane
Ifrane
Azrou
Tendrara
Missour
Khouribga
Khenifra
Ain Sefra
Oued Zem
Midelt
Bouarfa
Jebel Ayachi
Kasba Tadla
ALGERIA
Beni Mellal
Imilchil
Figuig
Afourer
Beni Ounif
Bin El Oudane
Azilal
HIGH ATLAS
Oued Ziz
Demnate
Béchar
Moulay Idriss Zerhoun
The whitewashed hilltop pilgrimage site (p368)
Jebel M'Goun
Tinerhir
Erfoud
Tafilalt
Vallée des Roses
Boulmalne Dades
Rissani
Merzouga
Erg Chebbi
Skoura
Taouz
Taghith
Ouarzazate
Grand Erg Occidental
Tazzarine
Agdz
Draa Valley
Zagora
High Atlas
Sublime peaks and Amazigh (Berber) villages (p116)
M'Hamid
Erg Chigaga
Erg Er Raoui
Timimoun
Tabelbala
Gourara
Hamada du Drâa
Draa Valley
Hop between kasbahs and oases (p151)
Tinfouchy
Erg Chigaga
Ride on camel back into Anti Atlas (p157)
Adrar
Anti Atlas
Trek in the granite mountain range (p405)
Tafraoute
The Ameln Valley activities centre (p407)

Morocco's Top Experiences

1 ON FOOT IN THE ATLAS

Morocco's Atlas Mountains are a stronghold of Amazigh culture, traditions and architecture that aren't found in such concentration anywhere else in the region. Combined with beautiful and surprisingly varied landscapes, exploring the Atlas on the same trails used by centuries of shepherds and villagers offers a unique perspective on the country.

Above: Foothills of the High Atlas Mountains (p116)

LUKAS HODON/SHUTTERSTOCK ©

Toubkal Circuit

Though it shares the final summit push to North Africa's highest peak with the popular two-day Toubkal Summit hike, the week-long Toubkal Circuit spends far more time in remote shepherds' pastures and out of the way villages for a taste of local culture in addition to the sweeping views. Read up on mandatory guide requirements before setting off. p121

PERRA JEAN-MICHEL/SHUTTERSTOCK ©

STREETFLASH/SHUTTERSTOCK ©

M'Goun Traverse

Trekking below ruined *kasbahs* and overnighting in villages tucked away up rocky defiles, the rugged trails and pristine landscapes of the M'Goun Traverse draw nature lovers and culture enthusiasts in equal measure. p137

Jebel Saghro

Just south of the High Atlas, the desert trails of Jebel Saghro are starkly beautiful by contrast. Well off popular travel routes and accessible in winter when the higher mountains are snowed under, it's a great alternative option for adventure seekers on an active holiday. p163

2 ROCK THE KASBAH

Restored *kasbahs* (fortresses) define the layout of many Moroccan towns and have shaped the history of the country, from sultans and soldiers to the Glaoui family and French occupation. These iconic structures have largely been converted into museums, luxury hotels and the occasional sprawling restaurant – most visitors take every chance they can to stop in and explore.

POSZTOS/SHUTTERSTOCK ©

HENK VRIESELAAR/SHUTTERSTOCK ©

ROB CRANDALL/SHUTTERSTOCK ©

Telouet Kasbah

The formerly glorious Glaoui fortress in Telouet is slowly crumbling back into the desert, but the ornately tiled 2nd-floor reception rooms speak to the prestige of the family at its peak. p144

Kasbah Bab Ourika

Kasbah-inclined visitors looking for a splurge should head to this restored fortress turned luxury hotel in the Ourika Valley. It has a stunning hilltop location and plenty of activities in the surrounding mountains. p128

Top: Ourika Valley (p126)

Draa Valley

Seemingly every other village in the Draa Valley features mighty *kasbahs* in various stages of disrepair, but don't miss a walk through the Kasbah des Caids in Tamnougalt or an overnight at the Kasbah Timidarte. p151

Above: Kasbah des Caids (p152), Tamnougalt

3 CATCHING WAVES

With over 1835km of coastline along the Mediterranean and Atlantic, there are no end of beaches and breaks for visitors who come to Morocco to ride the waves. Plenty of small towns on the Atlantic coast have gained a reputation as water-sports hideaways, and if you can make it to them you'll find plenty of likeminded company as the next set rolls in.

Windsurfing in Essaouira

Ride the famous *taros* (coastal winds) in Morocco's most blustery city, known as the 'Windy City of Africa', with conditions suitable for beginners and experts alike. p236

Below right: Windsurfing competition, Essaouira

SADIK YALCIN/SHUTTERSTOCK ©

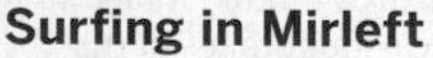

Surfing in Mirleft

The undisputed star among Morocco's southern beaches, the quiet town of Mirleft offers some of Morocco's best surfing conditions and all the board rentals and surf camps you could ever need. p421

Kitesurfing in Dakhla

Reliable year-round wind conditions and calm lagoon waters make Dakhla (pictured right) prime kitesurfing territory – so much so that even the Moroccan royal family gave it a go in 2016. p435

4 IMMERSIVE AMAZIGH MUSEUMS

DEL BOY/SHUTTERSTOCK©

While visitors to Morocco can experience Amazigh life all across the country, it's worth searching out one of the handful of excellent museums that present the traditional lifestyles and cultural artefacts of Amazigh culture. These spaces offer a well-curated and easy to understand holistic overview of the community that can be difficult to pull together from day-to-day interactions.

Ecomusée Berbère

The restored *ksar* of Tafza village now hosts a thorough introduction to traditional Amazigh daily life – including a series of fascinating short documentaries filmed in rural mountain areas of Morocco in the 1940s and '50s. p127

Musée des Arts et Traditions

This small museum in the Draa Valley city of Zagora highlights traditional lifestyles in the region with unique cultural treasures and excellent explanations in French and English. p153

Musée Berbère

Inside the Jardin Majorelle, the tiny Musée Berbère's collections of textiles and jewellery highlight the artistic heritage of the Amazigh community. p84

Above: Exterior of Musée Berbère at Jardin Majorelle

5 FEEL THE MUSIC

Every step in Morocco is set to a background beat – whether a *muezzin's* call to prayer or the musical calling cards of peddlers winding through the medina lanes. The sounds of the streets build to a crescendo matched only by the bounty of festivals the country hosts – everything from the traditional and divine to electronica and rap is on the playbill, if only you know where to listen.

Below: Gnaoua musicians (p463)

Festival of World Sacred Music

Fez plays host to this popular festival, an eclectic gathering of everyone from Tibetan monks and Latin American shamans to Sufi mystics and Harlem gospel choirs. p336

Gnaoua World Music Festival

For four days each summer, Essaouira is fully devoted to the sounds of the Gnaoua World Music Festival, dedicated to the unique eponymous musical tradition. p27

Festival Mawazine

More commonly known as the 'Rhythms of the World' festival, Rabat's Festival Mawazine sees a mix of international superstars and emerging local artists. p205

6 MOVIE MAGIC

RYZHKOV OLEKSANDR/SHUTTERSTOCK ©

Ouarzazate Film Studios

Though it's not the only show in 'Ouallywood', Atlas Film Corporation Studios is the best place to see famous cinema sets. Wander through Tibetan temples and Egyptian throne rooms and into the massive fortress from *Kingdom of Heaven*. p145

GC PHOTOGRAPHER/SHUTTERSTOCK ©

Aït Ben Haddou

Featured in an impressive list of Hollywood blockbusters – *Gladiator* and *Alexander* to name a few – the popularity of the restored Aït Ben Haddou *ksar* (fortified village) boomed after featuring as the cities of Yunkai and Pentos in the popular HBO series *Game of Thrones*. p142

Some of Morocco's most picturesque sights have become particularly popular with tourists after featuring in big-budget movies and television series – two of the most famous are just south of the Atlas Mountains on the edge of the Sahara. In locations that evoke a hint of magic, ambling around the sets of favourite movie scenes is enough to transport visitors to a whole other – if somewhat scripted – world.

7 AMAZING MEDINAS

If you pause for a moment in the twisting, turning heart of the medina, stepping out of the stream of shoppers, you can watch Morocco's very essence flash by. These ancient, crowded quarters – the walled old city with winding lanes, dead ends, boutique riad hotels, mounds of spices, *djellaba*-clad traders, tea drinkers and a sensory assault around every corner – offer a strong dose of Morocco's famous Maghrebi mystique.

Chefchaouen

Charming Chefchaouen's blue-washed medina walls (pictured below right) live up to the hype, with a photo opportunity at every corner. p281

MAURIZIO DE MATTEI/SHUTTERSTOCK©

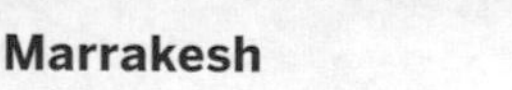

Marrakesh

Marrakshis rush between souqs and Djemaa El Fna within the medina's ramparts. Follow in their tracks to battle donkey carts amid the crowds or dive into alley offshoots to wherever they may lead. p68

Above: Metalwork stall

Fez

The world's largest living medieval medina is a car-free tangle of more than 9000 atmospheric alleyways in which to get lost, and nearly as many traditional crafts shops. p320

Right: Chouara Tannery (p322)

8 ADVENTURE SPORTS

FRANCOIS SEURET/SHUTTERSTOCK©

Opportunities for adventure sports abound in Morocco – and a frenzy of young new tour operators have begun to offer guiding services and organisational assistance for activities such as rock climbing, kayaking, mountain biking and much more. Whether on a self-powered mountain-bike traverse of the Anti Atlas or high on a multi-pitch looking for the key to an unsolvable problem, the only real limit to adventure these days is your imagination.

Rock Climbing in Zaouiat Ahansal

The village of Taghia deep in the heart of the High Atlas has slowly climbed in popularity among avid athletes in recent years. p132

Rafting & Kayaking

Morocco Adventure & Rafting (p103) takes guests on the water for everything from beginners' skills clinic on Bin el Ouidane to multiday excursions across the High Atlas. p50

Mountain Biking in Toubkal

Local operators and aficionados organise High Atlas routes, from easy day tours to hardcore traverses, from their base at the heart of Toubkal National Park in Imlil. p116

Above: Mountain biking, Atlas Mountains

Need to Know

For more information, see Survival Guide (p487)

Currency

Moroccan dirham (Dh)

Language

Moroccan Arabic (Darija), Tamazight (Berber), French

Visas

Nationals of 68 countries, including those from the UK, EU, US, Canada, Australia and New Zealand, can enter Morocco visa-free for up to 90 days.

Money

ATMs are widely available. Credit cards are usually accepted at top-end accommodation, large tourist-orientated restaurants and shops but often incur a surcharge of around 5%.

Mobile Phones

If you have an unlocked mobile phone, you can buy a prepaid Moroccan mobile SIM card.

Time

Western European Time (GMT/UTC plus one hour). Morocco does not observe daylight saving time.

When to Go

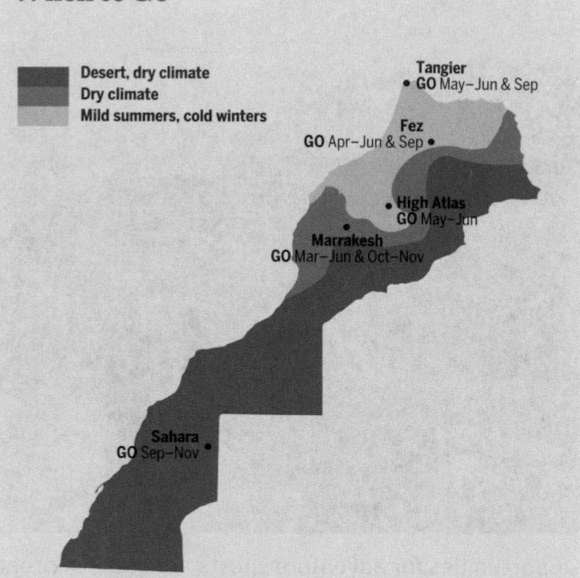

High Season

(Nov–Mar)

- Spring and autumn are the most popular times to visit.
- Marrakesh and the south are popular at Christmas and New Year, but the north of the country can be chilly and wet.
- Domestic tourism means peak prices in July and August on the Atlantic coast.

Shoulder

(Apr & Oct)

- Spring sandstorms in the Sahara and persistent rain in the north; balmy temperatures in most parts of the country.
- Accommodation prices and demand jump around Easter time.

Low Season

(May–Sep)

- Accommodation is discounted as inland cities sizzle.
- In 2022, Ramadan will begin in April, and it will start in March from 2023 to 2025.

Useful Websites

Visit Morocco (www.visitmorocco.com) Website of the Moroccan National Tourist Office.

The View from Fez (http://riadzany.blogspot.com) News and opinions.

Morocco World News (www.moroccoworldnews.com) Moroccan news portal.

Why Morocco (https://mandyinmorocco.com/podcast) A podcast from Mandy Sinclair, a Canadian in Marrakesh.

Lonely Planet (lonelyplanet.com/morocco) Destination information, hotel bookings, traveller forum and more.

Important Numbers

Always dial the local four-digit area code even if you are dialling from the same town or code area.

Ambulance	☎15
Fire	☎15
Gendarmerie (police outside cities)	☎177
Police (city)	☎19

Exchange Rates

Australia	A$1	Dh6.6
Canada	C$1	Dh7.3
Europe	€1	Dh10.7
Japan	¥100	Dh8.9
New Zealand	NZ$1	Dh6.1
UK	£1	Dh12.4
USA	US$1	Dh9.6

For current exchange rates, see www.xe.com.

Daily Costs

Budget: Less than Dh600

- Dorm bed: from Dh100
- Basic double room with shared bathroom: from Dh150
- Soup or sandwich: Dh4–30
- Local bus trip: Dh6

Midrange: Dh600–1400

- Admission to sights: Dh10–70
- Double room in a city riad: Dh450–1000
- Group day tour: from Dh300
- Dinner main: Dh70–150

Top end: More than Dh1400

- Private day tour: from Dh700
- 4WD hire and driver per day: from Dh1200
- Three-course set menu: from Dh350
- High-end double room in a city riad: from Dh1200

Opening Hours

Morocco follows the Monday-to-Friday working week for business purposes. Friday is the main prayer day, so many businesses take an extended lunch break on Friday afternoon or don't open at all. During Ramadan office hours shift to around 10am to 3pm.

Banks 8.30am to 6.30pm Monday to Friday

Bars 6pm until late

Government offices 8.30am to 6.30pm Monday to Friday

Post offices 8.30am to 4.30pm Monday to Friday

Restaurants noon to 3pm and 7pm to 10pm (cafes generally open earlier and close later)

Shops 10am to 7pm Monday to Saturday

Arriving in Morocco

Mohammed V International Airport (Casablanca) Trains run to Casa Port station (Dh43, 45 minutes) at 4am, hourly from 6am to 10pm, and again at 11.45pm; grands taxis to central Casablanca cost Dh300, though fares can end up being much more.

Tanger Med ferry terminal Shuttle buses run hourly to Tangier's main bus station (Dh20, 45 minutes).

Menara Airport (Marrakesh) Airport bus 19 to central Marrakesh (Dh30) runs every 30 minutes between 6.15am and 9.30pm. Petits taxis charge inflated rates into the centre; it's worthwhile booking a transfer through your accommodation (Dh150 to Dh200).

Getting Around

Train Reasonably priced, with good coverage and frequent departures between the major cities, but no lines in the south or along the Mediterranean coast.

Car Somewhat expensive but useful for travelling at your own pace or for visiting regions with minimal public transport. Cars can be hired in every town or city, but navigating the big cities can be hair-raising.

Bus Cheaper and slower than trains, ranging from modern coaches to rickety local affairs. Useful for destinations not served by trains.

Taxi *Grands taxis* run set routes between nearby towns and cities. Cheap but cramped.

Air Royal Air Maroc and Air Arabia offer internal flights.

For much more on **getting around**, see p500

First Time Morocco

For more information, see Survival Guide (p487)

Checklist

➡ Check airline baggage restrictions – you may be packing a rug on your return journey.

➡ If it's your first visit and you're staying in a medina riad, book a pick-up through your accommodation to avoid getting lost.

➡ Book tickets to popular sights in advance, such as Jardin Majorelle in Marrakesh.

What to Pack

➡ European-style two-prong electrical adaptor.

➡ Comfortable footwear for exploring cities on foot and hiking in the mountains.

➡ A reusable shopping bag; Morocco banned plastic bags in 2016.

➡ A stash of euros can be useful for paying your riad bill.

Top Tips for Your Trip

➡ Morocco is a much bigger country than you think. Don't over-stuff your itinerary and allow plenty of time to travel between destinations.

➡ Many Moroccans speak French, but try learning a few words of Darija (Moroccan Arabic). Locals will reward you for your efforts.

➡ Haggling in the souqs is best thought of as a performance rather than a zero-sum game.

➡ Shared taxis (grands taxis) are a quick way of getting between towns. Buy all six seats if you want to travel solo.

➡ If you get lost in a medina, follow the flow of people until you get back to a main thoroughfare or ask a shopkeeper for directions.

What to Wear

Morocco's brand of Islam is pretty relaxed, but life in rural towns and ancient medinas remains more traditional. For both men and women, it's best to not wear shorts, sleeveless tops or revealing clothing in these areas. If you do, some people will be embarrassed for you and the family that raised you and avoid eye contact. So if you don't want to miss out on some excellent company – especially among older Moroccans – dress modestly.

Sleeping

Bed down in everything from a stylish riad to a swanky resort or a beachfront hostel, a mud-brick kasbah turned boutique hotel to a nomad-style tent.

Riads Morocco has become famous for its traditional medina homes converted into boutique guesthouses.

Hotels These range from the most basic to five-star resorts.

Camping There are plenty of camping sites around the south for those with camper vans or tents. Trekkers can access mountain refuges in some areas.

Photography

Morocco is a photographer's dream, but never point your camera at anything that's vaguely military or strategic, including airports, bridges, government buildings, members of the police or armed forces, and checkpoints in and near the Western Sahara.

It is common courtesy to ask permission before taking photographs of people – women, older people and rural folk often don't want to be photographed.

Bargaining

Bargaining or haggling is part and parcel of the Moroccan experience, especially for tourist goods and services. If you want to avoid it, many tourist shops have fixed prices.

Tipping

Tipping is an integral part of Moroccan life; almost any service can warrant a tip. Although you shouldn't feel railroaded, the judicious distribution of a few dirham for a service willingly rendered can make your life a lot easier.

Cafes Leave Dh2.

Car park attendants Dh2 to Dh5; Dh10 for overnight.

Hotel porters Dh3 to Dh5 is standard.

Restaurants 10% is standard.

Guides Dh70 to Dh150 per half/full day (unless they've taken you to unrequested shops).

Private drivers Dh150 to Dh200 per day.

Trekking porters Add on Dh20.

Language

Moroccan Arabic (Darija) and Tamazight (Berber) are Morocco's two official languages, although French is also widespread as a language of government and law. You'll frequently find English speakers in main tourist destinations and the larger cities. Spanish is widespread in Tangier, south to Larache and along the Mediterranean coast and Rif Mountains.

There are courses in Arabic – both modern standard and Moroccan (Darija) – in most major cities in Morocco, with a high concentration in Fez, Rabat and Casablanca, where long- and short-term programmes are offered.

Etiquette

Morocco is a tolerant country, but following a few rules of etiquette will make your travels smoother and avoid embarrassment.

Greetings Handshakes are followed by lightly touching your heart with your right hand. Men should wait for Moroccan women to offer handshakes.

Attire Both men and women should cover their shoulders and knees.

Eating The left hand is considered unclean as it's used for toilet duties. Don't handle food with your left hand, particularly if eating from a communal dish such as a tajine.

Eating

Moroccan cuisine is a lot more than just couscous and tajines. From cooked vegetable salads and slow-cooked meats to fresh fruits and flaky pastries laced with orange-flower water, the flavours on offer are mouth-watering.

Midrange restaurant menus can be stuck in a three-tajine rut, so to get more variety you need to go low and feast on street food, or high and dine at one of the increasing number of creative fusion restaurants. But they say the best Moroccan food is cooked at home, so your riad might be the next best option. *B'saha,* here's to your health.

An important dining tip: pace yourself. Moroccan meals can be lengthy and generous, and they might seem a bit excessive to an unyielding waistband. Take your time and you should make it to dessert, perhaps a *bastilla* (multilayered pastry) with toasted almonds, cinnamon and cream. Your Moroccan hosts may urge you on like the audience in a pie-eating contest, but obey your instincts and quit when you're full with a heartfelt *alhamdulillah!* (praise be to God!).

What's New

While Morocco appears timeless to the wide-eyed visitor, recent decades have brought massive changes to both daily life and the national stage. Massive economic growth has driven standards of living by leaps and bounds, and the country continues to shine culturally as an inspiration in arts, fashion and food globally.

Al Boraq

Africa's first high-speed TGV-style train whizzes between Tangier and Casablanca in just over two hours, hitting top speeds of 320km/h.

Grand Théâtre de Casablanca

Adding to Casablanca's architectural treasure trove, this ubercontemporary, multidisciplinary art space (p197) is the largest theatre in Africa.

Tanja Marina Bay

Morocco's first urban marina (p254) sits at the start of Tangier's crescent-shaped Corniche, with space for superyachts and restaurants such as La Table du Marché.

Fez Fanadiq

Four *fanadiq* (inns once used by travelling caravans) have been restored to their former glory and are now one-stop shopping spots (p324) for handicrafts, including women's cooperatives and disappearing artefacts.

Jardin Majorelle

The YSL Foundation has expanded the gardens (p83) by opening up the section containing Villa Oasis, where Pierre Bergé lived until his death in 2017.

Dar Shâan

Rabat's most stylish boutique riad (p208) has just opened in the medina, mixing up Andalusian stone columns and

LOCAL KNOWLEDGE

WHAT'S HAPPENING IN MOROCCO

Stephen Lioy, Lonely Planet writer

Morocco's popularity with travellers continues to grow, though it remains unclear whether targets to join the world's top 20 tourism destinations will be met. Improved transport infrastructure (high-speed trains between Tangier and Casablanca as well as new sealed roads reaching to remote High Atlas villages) and government-funded renovations of crumbling medina architecture in Marrakesh, Salé, Tetouan, Fez and Essaouira give increasing numbers of visitors more reasons to stay longer and explore further. It appears to be working, with incoming visitors growing 8% to 10% year-on-year, even despite the tragic terrorism-linked murder of two foreign hikers on the slopes of Jebel Toubkal in December 2018 that made media headlines around the world.

Long unresolved, the political conflict in Western Sahara continues to simmer as Rabat invests increasingly heavily here as well. A US$1 billion port construction project in Dakhla announced in 2019, and proposed EU-backed green-energy projects, are just the latest in what the Moroccan government claims to be over US$7 billion of investment in the region since 2015.

contemporary art, heavy wooden doors and retro furniture; there's a rooftop pool, too.

Mandala Society

This newcomer (p240) to Essaouira's increasingly sophisticated dining scene has arty decor, an organic plant-based menu and top-notch coffee – plus it's plastic-free.

1-54

The new Marrakesh edition of the international and influential Contemporary African Art Fair (p91) acts as a platform for dozens of emerging and established artists from across the continent.

Riad Zitoun El Kedim

This street in Marrakesh has become a new outpost for style hunters in search of more refined Moroccan design, fashion and beauty products.

Badia Palace

Marrakshi storks have always loved it, but now there's more reason than ever to visit the 16th-century ruins of Badia Palace (p82), fresh from a renovation that has added interesting exhibitions.

Marrakech Yoga Studio

An airy riad home has been converted into the medina's first yoga studio (p96), and within its walls is the only vegan lunch venue in the area.

Couscous as World Heritage

Couscous (p38), the ubiquitous staple of Amazigh cuisine, has been added to UNECSO's list of intangible world heritage in December 2020.

COVID-19 Impact on Tourism

The Moroccan government estimates that 57% of companies across all sectors suspended operations as a result of the COVID-19 pandemic, rising to as high as 89% in hospitality, with fears that many small and family-owned business will not reopen at the end of the pandemic.

LISTEN, WATCH & FOLLOW

For inspiration and up-to-date news, visit www.lonelyplanet.com/morocco/travel-tips-and-articles.

Morocco World News (https://www.moroccoworldnews.com/) Independent news source on developments in Morocco and the MENA region.

Journey Beyond Travel (www.journeybeyondtravel.com/blog) Instructive blog on all things tourism in Morocco from a Tangier-based tour operator.

Why Morocco (https://mandyinmorocco.com) Mandy Sinclair, a Canadian in Marrakesh, talks to Moroccans and expats about everything from architecture to filmmaking for her podcast.

The View from Fez (http://riadzany.blogspot.com) An informative blog from Australian expat Sandy McCutcheon, with news and views on developments around the country.

FAST FACTS

Food trend 'French' tacos

World's largest exporter sardines

Rank among African countries for nominal GDP 5th

Pop 34 million

population per sq km

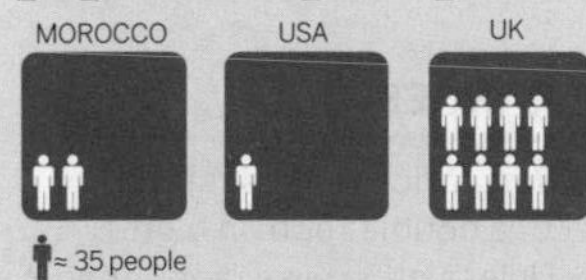

Western Sahara Stabilized

Increasing international recognition of Moroccan authority over Western Sahara, including the early-2021 groundbreaking of a US Consulate in Dakhla, may presage an opening to even further international business and tourism investment in the long-neglected region.

Accommodation

Find more accommodation reviews throughout the On the Road chapters (from p65)

Accommodation Types

Riads Morocco is renowned for its traditional medina homes that have been turned into boutique guesthouses.

Hotels Range from the most basic budget rooms to exclusive five-star resorts.

Hostels Stylish privately run hostels with kitchens and roof terraces are opening up in places like Marrakesh, Fez, Essaouira and Mirleft.

Camping Plenty of camping sites exist in southern areas for travellers with camper vans or tents. Hikers can access mountain refuges in some areas.

Glamping There are increasingly luxe glamping options in the desert, and Morocco's first boho-chic yurt has just opened on a deserted sweep of beach south of Sidi Kaouki.

Gîtes d'étape Homestays or hostels that offer basic accommodation around popular trekking routes in the Atlas and Rif Mountains.

Mountain Refuges Swiss-chalet-style accommodation, usually in dormitories with communal showers and often including a lively communal dining-living room.

Homestays Many won't have running water or electricity, but you'll find warmth and hospitality. You should be prepared to pay what you would in *gîtes d'étape*.

PRICE RANGES

The following price ranges refer to the cost of a double room in high season. Unless otherwise mentioned, prices exclude breakfast.

€ less than Dh400

€€ Dh400–Dh800

€€€ more than Dh800

Exceptions to these price ranges are Casablanca, Essaouira, Fez, Marrakesh, Rabat and Tangier. For these places, these price ranges apply:

€ less than Dh600

€€ Dh600–Dh1200

€€€ more than Dh1200

Best Places to Stay

Best on a Budget

Budget accommodations are plentiful throughout Morocco, from hostels in the cities and on the coasts to *gîtes d'étape* in mountainous rural areas, and while facilities can vary by location the common theme throughout is a warm welcome and sincere hospitality. That money you saved on a bed will come in handy as you plan trips around the common room table.

- Rodamón (p93), Marrakesh
- Aftas Beach House (p423), Mirleft
- MIA Hostel (p223), Asilah
- Medina Social Club (p337), Fez
- Lunar Surf House (p396), Tamraght
- Hostel Baraka (p284), Chefchaouen

Best for a Splurge

For travellers looking to splash out a little, Morocco offers excellent value high-end options that are often a destination unto themselves. Spend a few nights at any of these, and you'll leave impressed.

- Riad Laaroussa (p339), Fez
- Riad L'Orangeraie (p94), Marrakesh
- Dar Al Hossoun (p403), Taroudant
- Kasbah Bab Ourika (p128), Ourika Valley
- La Sultana (p229), Oualidia

Best for Families

With so many overnight choices in Morocco offering the warmth of a family home, it's no surprise that there are excellent options for those travelling with children. On-site activities to enjoy, treasured antiques to admire, and winding kasbah lanes to explore are just the start. After just a few nights, you may well feel like part of the extended family.

- Le Jardin des Biehn (p338), Fez
- Kasbah Timdaf (p141), Demnate
- L'Ma Lodge (p161), Skoura
- Touda Ecolodge (p136), Zaouiat Oulmzi
- Ali & Sara's Desert Palace (p178), Merzouga

Best for Solo Travellers

Along with Morocco's hostels, many of the country's *gîtes d'étape* are built around a communal lifestyle that makes it easy to find groups to share adventures (or at least trip costs) and build parties for trekking or climbing outings, while still allowing dedicated misanthropes to sink into a good book on a rooftop terrace or under a village shade tree.

- Gîte Taoujdat (p134), Zaouiat Ahansal
- Gîte Le Toubkal (p119), Aroumd
- Gîte Timit (p136), Timit
- Gîte Le Cathédrale (p132), Tamga

Best for Scenery

From scenes of snowy Atlas peaks to endless waves (of both the desert and ocean varieties), Morocco offers plenty of places to kick up your feet and enjoy the views. Many of these are also near the trailheads of the country's best outdoor adventures, which makes them the perfect places to relax after all the excitement.

- Auberge Le Festival (p171), Todra Gorge
- Dar Ahansal (p133), Zaouiat Ahansal
- Azalai Desert Lodge (p155), Zagora
- El Malara (p409), Tafraoute
- Kasbah Azul (p152), Agdz

Kasbah Bab Ourika (p128) gardens

Booking

Accommodation in Morocco is affordable compared to Europe or North America, and the value for money is often much higher. You should book ahead during high season (November to March), as well as the period around Easter.

Airbnb (www.airbnb.com) Search online for homes, apartments and other private accommodation with real-time availability.

Booking.com (www.booking.com) A vast range of hotels and other accommodation.

Lonely Planet (lonelyplanet.com/hotels) Find independent reviews, as well as recommendations on the best places to stay – and then book them online.

Month by Month

TOP EVENTS

Marathon des Sables, March

Fes Festival of World Sacred Music, June

National Festival of Popular Arts, July

Marriage Moussem, September

January

Moroccan winter: the north is wet, and snow makes many mountains impassable for trekkers and even motorists. Marrakesh and the south receive the most tourists, especially around New Year.

Marrakesh Marathon

The year-round Djemaa El Fna carnival acquires a sporty dimension with this annual road race, when 5000 marathoners cross the finish line on the grand square. The route follows the city ramparts and alleys of palms, orange and olive trees. (p91)

February

Winter continues: the weather is generally poor, although drier, balmier spots, such as Marrakesh and Agadir, are bearable. Apart from overlanders and city-breakers, few visitors are spotted.

1-54

The Marrakesh edition of this Contemporary African Art Fair founded by Touria El Glaoui – it's also held in London and New York – began in 2018. Held at the iconic La Mamounia hotel, it acts as a platform for dozens of emerging and established artists from across Africa and its diaspora. (p91)

March

The country wakes up with the beginning of spring, when the mountains thaw and wildflowers and almond and cherry trees blossom. Winds begin to disturb the desert and Souss Valley, continuing through April.

Almond Blossom Festival

This pretty festival is held in the Anti Atlas in spring, when the Tafraoute area is awash with blossoms. Traditionally about celebrating the harvest in Morocco's almond capital, the festival is now also about local folklore, with singing, dancing, theatre and storytelling. (p409)

Beat Hotel

Launched in 2019, Beat Hotel mixes film, talks and lifestyle workshops with four days of poolside grooving, sunset DJ sets and late-night dance parties. It's held at the Fellah Hotel south of Marrakesh. (p92)

Marathon des Sables

Starting and finishing in Morocco's movie town, Ouarzazate, the Saharan ultramarathon is as epic as films made in 'Ouallywood'. The gruelling seven-day challenge, held in March or April, crosses 243km of desert. Water is provided. (p147)

April

Spring continues: the country is lush and green, and temperatures are now reliably hot nationwide. Tourist numbers are high, particularly around Easter, when prices jump. In 2022 Ramadan will start in April.

Printemps Musical des Alizés

A must for classical music lovers, this three-day spring festival of chamber music in Essaouira draws world-class musicians from around the globe to play free concerts at small venues across the city, such as Dar Souiri. (p237)

Jidar Street Art Festival

Rabat turns in to an open-air art gallery every year, with local and international street artists leaving their monumental art works on the walls. (p205)

Casamémoire Heritage Days

Discover Casablanca's extraordinary 20th-century architecture on a free guided tour around downtown, Quartier Habous and the medina with this nonprofit of architects and artists. (p190)

May

Prices drop in hotels and souqs as the tourist season ends, although the heaviest summer heat is yet to come; the average daily temperature in Marrakesh is about 28°C. Ideal for mountain trekking.

Festival of the Roses

In the Dadès Valley, garlands and mountains of petals come out for Kalaat M'Gouna's festival to celebrate the rose harvest. (p162)

June

Summer is hotting up although High Atlas peaks are still snowy. Northern Morocco and the coast are good places to be.

Fes Festival of World Sacred Music

Fez's successful world-music festival has hosted everyone from Youssou N'Dour to Björk. Equally impressive are the concerts by Moroccan *tariqas* (Sufi brotherhoods); fringe events include exhibitions, films and talks. Held at the end of May or beginning of June; book accommodation far in advance. (p336)

Festival Mawazine

This popular and free music festival in Rabat grows every year and attracts big names from the Arab, African and Western spheres. Expect everyone from Elton John to Afrobeat and Lebanese divas. (p205)

Gnaoua World Music Festival

A passionate celebration held in Essaouira in late June, with concerts featuring international, national and local performers, plus art exhibitions. A great chance to hear some bluesy gnaoua, a musical genre developed here by freed sub-Saharan enslaved people. (p237)

July

Snow melts from the mountains, and the High Atlas is scorching, hovering around 30°C. The beaches are breezy, but busy with domestic and European tourists in the north. In 2022 the Islamic holiday of Eid Al Adha falls in July.

Asilah Festival

At this annual month-long cultural festival, everyone from Japanese artists to Sufi chanters, plus spectators, descend upon the whitewashed medina. Events include workshops, concerts, exhibitions and artists painting the town. (p222)

Jazzablanca

Casablanca's popular jazz festival has been taking over the city for more than a decade. Expect the best local and international names to hit the stage. (p190)

National Festival of Popular Arts

This street-theatre festival is a typically colourful Marrakshi event, highlighting the best of Moroccan traditional and popular culture. Djemaa El Fna is even more anarchic than usual during the opening night parade, featuring 500-plus performers. (p92)

August

This month is a scorcher with an average of 40°C in Marrakesh, and it can easily exceed that in the interior. Head to southern Atlantic beaches to avoid the crowds.

Moussem of Moulay Idriss

During Morocco's largest *moussem* (festival), picturesque whitewashed Moulay Idriss fills with *fantasias* (musket-firing cavalry charges), markets and music. Five pilgrimages to this *moussem* are said to equal one to Mecca. (p370)

September

With autumn, Morocco is once again prime territory for foreign travellers. Beaches empty of local holidaymakers and even the desert is pleasant with the scent of dates and gentle breezes.

Sidi Yahia Moussem

Thousands of pilgrims head east to the Sidi Yahia Moussem in Oujda, which includes a *fantasia*. (p313)

Marriage Moussem

At this famous three-day festival in the Middle Atlas village of Imilchil, local Imazighen (Berbers) search for a partner. Everyone looks their best, sporting woollen cloaks, white *djellabas* (traditional full-length hooded garments) and elaborate jewellery. (p167)

TANJAzz

Attracting an ever-growing roster of international and local musicians, Tangier's annual jazz festival is a great way to take in the cosmopolitan side of Morocco's music scene. (p255)

Jazz au Chellah

Going strong for nearly three decades, this popular festival features collaborations between European and Moroccan jazz musicians staged in the atmospheric surrounds of the Chellah. (p206)

Moussem of Moulay Idriss II

Fez's Moussem of Moulay Idriss II sees a musical procession showered with orange-blossom water parade through the medina. (p336)

October

October is a popular month to visit, although rain is beginning to set in north of the Middle Atlas.

Moussem of Sidi Ben Aïssa

One of Morocco's largest *moussems* takes place at the mausoleum of Sidi Ben Aïssa, a Sufi saint, outside Meknes' medina walls. Public displays of glass-eating, snake bites and ritual body piercing are no longer allowed, but *fantasias*, fairs and the usual singing and dancing are. (p359)

Toubkal Marathon

Test yourself against North Africa's highest peak on this challenging 42km ascent and descent of Jebel Toubkal. (p120)

Festival of Sufi Culture

This Fez festival hosts events including films, lectures and concerts with Sufi musicians from around the world in historical settings throughout the imperial city. (p336)

November

A busy time in Marrakesh and further south, with more people heading to the desert or trekking nearby. Birdwatchers stake out wetlands.

Festival du Safran

This festival in Taliouine celebrates all things saffron, the world's most expensive spice, with tours of the town's cooperatives, as well as music and dancing in the streets. (p406)

Visa for Music

Billed as the first festival to focus on African and Middle Eastern music, Visa for Music brings in around 50 acts over four days at venues across Rabat. (p206)

December

The country is busy at the end of the month with Christmas holidaymakers. Snow closes High Atlas passes, but the white blanket is good news for skiers.

Itineraries

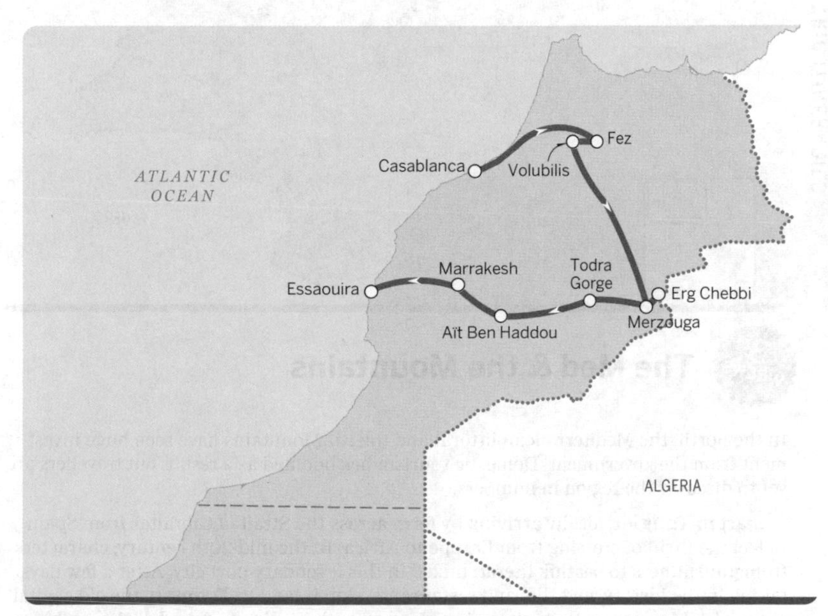

Essential Morocco

Morocco is a big country, but in two weeks you can still comfortably cover a lot of ground and explore the best of what it has to offer, from imperial cities to mountains and desert.

Touch down in **Casablanca**, the commercial capital, and start with a tour of the stupendous Hassan II Mosque and its showstopping 20th-century architecture. Take the train to venerable **Fez**, with its ancient yet thriving medina.

Next, cross the Middle Atlas via the Roman city of **Volubilis**, south to the Ziz Valley oasis for your first taste of Moroccan kasbah culture, continuing all the way to **Merzouga**, a gateway to the Sahara. Saddle up your camel and sleep under the stars amid the perfectly sculpted dunes of **Erg Chebbi**.

Shadowing the High Atlas as you head west brings you to the **Todra Gorge** for a day's hiking amid the canyons and *palmeraies* (palm groves). From here, head past Ouarzazate to **Aït Ben Haddou**, with its fairy-tale 11th-century *ksar* (fortified village).

En route to the Atlantic, check into a riad in **Marrakesh**, and spend as many sunsets as possible on the theatrical Djemaa El Fna square. Don't stop until you reach the artsy seaside medina and fishing port of **Essaouira**.

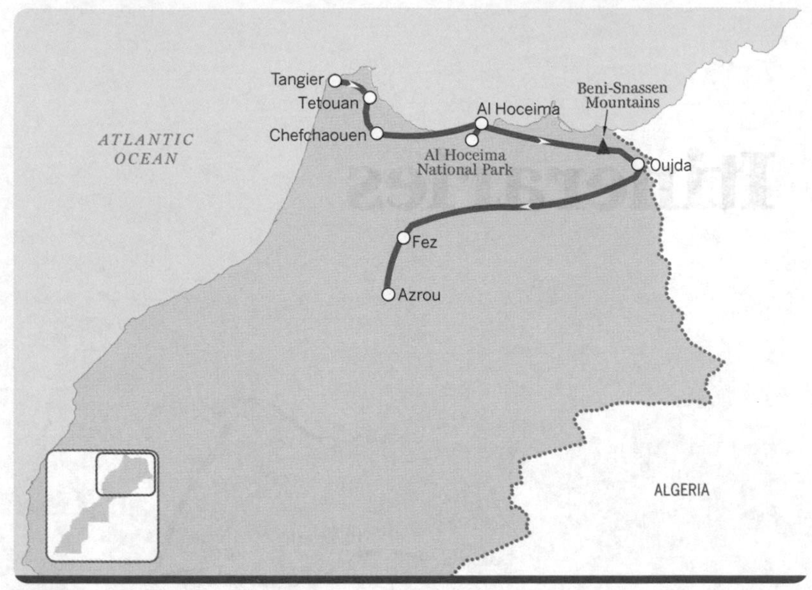

3 WEEKS The Med & the Mountains

In the north, the Mediterranean littoral and the Rif Mountains have seen huge investment from the government. Domestic tourism has boomed as a result, but travellers are yet to discover the region in numbers.

Start in **Tangier**, ideally arriving by ferry across the Strait of Gibraltar from Spain to feel the thrill of crossing from Europe to Africa. In the mid-20th century, characters from gunrunners to beatnik literati mixed in this legendary port city. After a few days taking in the history, nightlife and restaurants, skip inland to **Tetouan**, the old capital of Spanish Morocco, with its charming blend of Arab medina and Andalusian architecture. The Spanish left a lighter imprint on nearby **Chefchaouen**, nestled in the Rif Mountains with its gorgeous blue-painted core. It's tempting to spend a string of sunsets listening to the minarets chorus each other's call to prayer, but Chaouen is also a good trekking spot. You can head deep into the mountains on a four-day trek via riverside Akchour to Taourarte, visiting Amazigh (Berber) villages, breathtaking waterfalls and unbelievable geological formations along the way.

Continue east along the coast to the proud, modern seaside resort of **Al Hoceima**, gateway to the dry canyons and limestone cliffs of the **Al Hoceima National Park**. Walk to the park along the coast or book a memorable tour that includes hiking or mountain biking and a homestay with an Amazigh family. En route to the Algerian border, there's more fine scenery in the **Beni-Snassen Mountains**, which you can enjoy in a swimming pool with mountain views or at a 300-year-old rural lodge. With its gorges, caves, mesa and Barbary sheep, this verdant area is far removed from classic images of Morocco and was once home to some of the oldest discovered Homo sapiens.

From here, head to **Oujda** to refresh yourself with some city comforts, before taking the train to that grandest of imperial cities, **Fez**. Dive into the medina and relax in a riad, but if you find yourself missing the countryside, you can make an easy day trip into the cedar-clad Middle Atlas around the market town of **Azrou**.

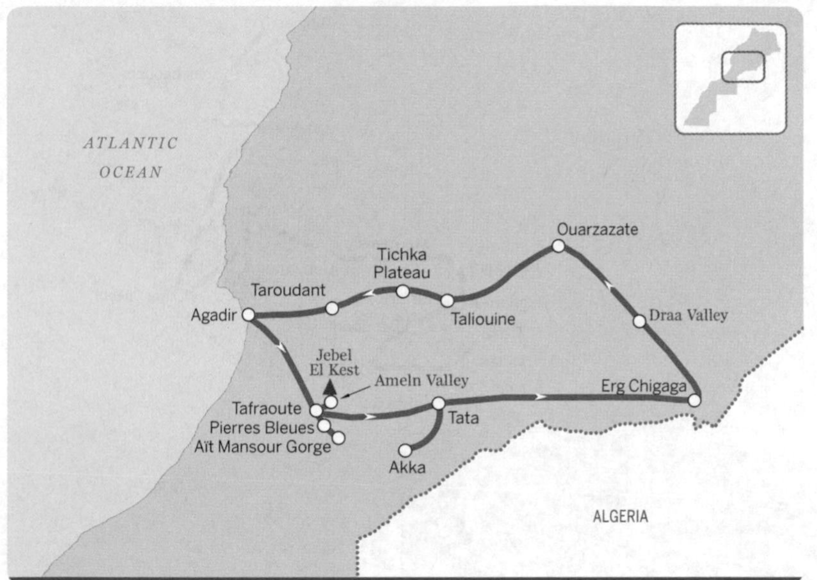

Circling the South

This itinerary takes you deep into the south for wild mountain and desert landscapes, far from clicking cameras and with plenty of activities to stimulate the mind and body.

Agadir is a handy entry point, but adventurers will want to leave quickly. Head to the Amazigh heartland of tiny **Tafraoute**, surrounded by beautiful Anti Atlas scenery such as the **Ameln Valley**, with its lush *palmeraies* (palm groves) and pink-hued houses. Spend a few days trekking through the valley and up Jebel El Kest, bike past rock formations and engravings to the surreal **Pierres Bleues**, known as the Painted Rocks, and continue south through the **Aït Mansour Gorge**. At the gorge's far end, where the spectacular landscape belies the ancient slave routes that passed this way, stay in the Afella-Ighir oasis.

By now, you'll have developed a taste for Morocco's secluded southern corners. Once back in Tafraoute, wind east through the Anti Atlas and descend to the equally silent and epic Sahara. The last stop before Jebel Bani and a whole lot of *hamada* (stony desert), **Tata** makes a convenient base for exploring the oases, kasbahs, fortified granaries and rock engravings in remote spots such as **Akka** (best discovered with a guide). A dusty journey to the east, the yellow-gold dunes of **Erg Chigaga** are more remote and less visited than Merzouga. In nearby M'Hamid, find yourself a camel to lead you north into the kasbah-littered **Draa Valley**.

At the top of valley, head back towards the mountains. Commandeer a bike (mountain or motor), horse, mule or dromedary in film favourite **Ouarzazate**, where the stony desert landscape has been a celluloid stand-in for Tibet, Rome, Somalia and Egypt. Return to the coast via **Taliouine**, where you can buy the world's most expensive spice in Africa's saffron capital. Pause here, or in **Taroudant**, for a trekking reprise in a mountainous area such as the **Tichka Plateau**. With its red walls and backdrop of snow-capped peaks, Taroudant has hassle-free echoes of Marrakesh. Its souqs and squares are pleasant places to relax, and it's handy for Agadir Al Massira International Airport.

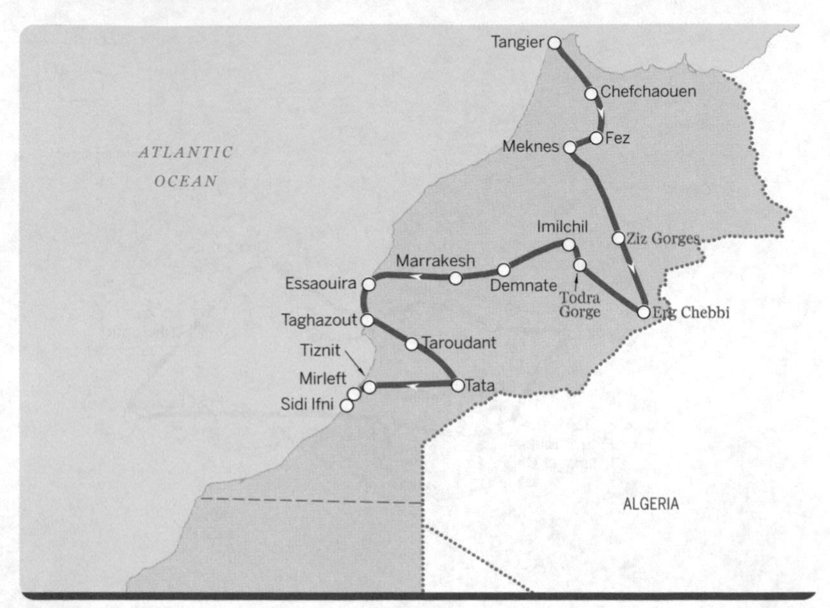

Highlights & Hidden Gems

Given six weeks, you can really dive deep into Morocco, exploring its big-ticket destinations while still having plenty of time to discover its more hidden corners and getting off the beaten track, or just taking more time to soak up the country.

Start in famously decadent **Tangier**, with its Europe-facing medina, before heading into the Rif Mountains and the blue-washed medina of charming **Chefchaouen**, a worthy Instagram star. Further south, the magnificent medinas in **Fez** and **Meknes** reveal the grandeur of Morocco's imperial cities.

After a few days of labyrinthine lanes and dye pits, you'll be ready for more mountains. Wind through the Middle Atlas and the barren landscape of the **Ziz Gorges**, punctuated with a verdant palm grove. It's now just a few dusty hours to **Erg Chebbi**, the achingly beautiful expanse of rolling dunes, which you can explore on a camel or sandboard.

Brush off the sand and return to the High Atlas at **Todra Gorge**. Hike between the enclosing rock walls and then jump in a market-bound truck through tiny villages and deeper into the mountains. **Imilchil**, surrounded by red rock and turquoise lakes, is the site of a wedding *moussem* (festival) in September.

Descend through the High Atlas and turn southwest, pausing to refuel in Amazigh foodie and cultural hub **Demnate**. The next stop is **Marrakesh**, with its famous riad hotels, designer shopping and the wild square of Djemaa El Fna. Hit the wild west coast at hippie-turned-boutique hang-out **Essaouira** and then head south to laid-back **Taghazout**, Morocco's premier surf spot. Take the N10 to **Taroudant**, the Souss Valley's prettiest market town with its mud-walled medina and kasbah.

Travel barren mountains and empty roads to **Tata**, a Saharan gateway where blue-robed guides can show you the desert. The road back to the Atlantic passes oases, *palmeraies*, kasbahs, fortified granaries and rock carvings. Near the coast, detour north to the **Tiznit** jewellery souq, particularly if it's a Thursday (market day). Arcing west and south, you arrive in **Mirleft**, with its pink and blue arches and wild beaches, and **Sidi Ifni**, a jumble of wind-whipped art-deco relics surrounded by coastal walks.

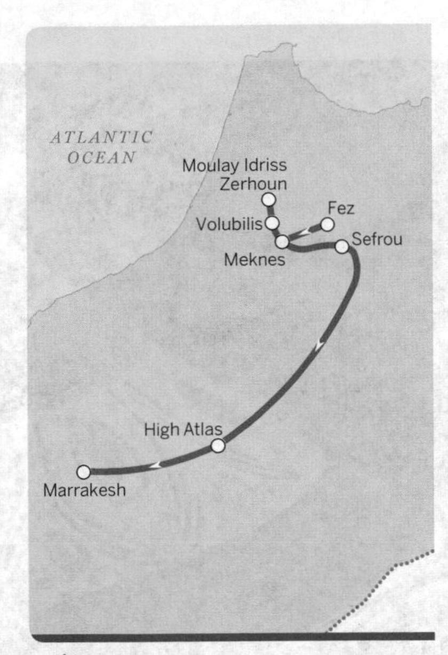

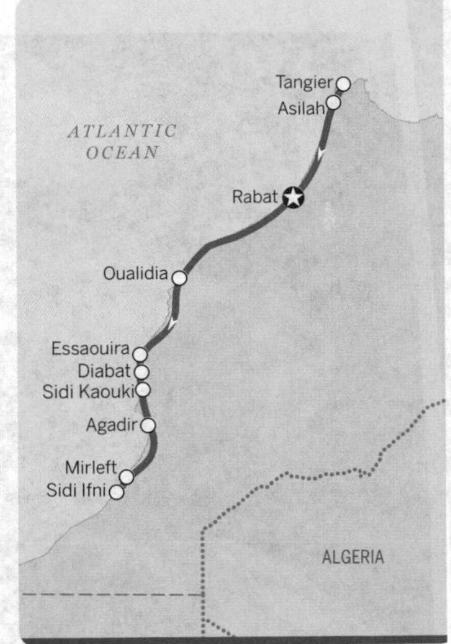

10 DAYS Empire & Atlas

This short route gives a fast-paced introduction to Morocco: its storied cities, ancient medinas and the mighty Atlas Mountains that ripple down the length of the country.

This itinerary begins in two cities once ruled by time-honoured dynasties. Modern Morocco and its rich past jostle for space in the extraordinary medieval medina of **Fez**. Next, catch your breath in nearby **Meknes**, often bypassed by travellers despite its echoes of Sultan Moulay Ismail's glory days.

A detour north takes you to **Volubilis**, Morocco's best-preserved Roman ruins, and testament to the Roman Empire's astonishing breadth. Nearby **Moulay Idriss Zerhoun**, with the mausoleum of the founder of Morocco's first imperial dynasty, is another wonderful antidote to urban clamour.

Head south into the Middle Atlas, stopping at the Amazigh town of **Sefrou**, with its charming medina. From here, take the cross-country route via Beni Mellal, skirting the edge of the **High Atlas Mountains** to the iconic Red City, **Marrakesh**. The city's souqs, street performers and imperial architecture create an intoxicating mix.

3 WEEKS Atlantic Adventure

Morocco's Atlantic seaboard takes you from the clamour of the north to the quieter coastline of the south where cities give way to dramatic sea cliffs, long sandy beaches and picturesque fishing ports.

Take the ferry from Spain to **Tangier**, at once quintessentially Moroccan and a decadent international outpost. Catch the train south, first to chilled-out **Asilah**, with its art-filled medina, and then on to **Rabat**, with its colonial architecture and palm-lined boulevards. Follow Casablanca's suburbanites on the spectacular ocean road to oyster capital **Oualidia** and a perfect crescent-shaped lagoon.

Further south, breezy **Essaouira** beckons with a laid-back medina, renovated riads and windsurfing schools. When you've eaten your fill at the outdoor fish grills, follow the spirit of Jimi Hendrix and surfers-in-the-know to the peaceful beaches at **Diabat** and **Sidi Kaouki**.

Past more surf spots, **Agadir** is a modern, tourist-friendly seaside resort, but the wild beaches and guesthouses of **Mirleft** are more appealing, along with the Spanish art-deco treasures of **Sidi Ifni**.

Vegetable tajine with almond and chickpea cousco

Plan Your Trip

Eat & Drink Like a Local

There's a lot more to Moroccan cuisine than couscous and tajines. From cooked vegetable salads and slow-cooked meats to fresh fruits and flaky pastries, the flavours on offer are mouth-watering. Mid-range restaurant menus tend to repeat the same old tajines, so to get more variety, feast on street food or try one of the growing number of creative fusion restaurants. Home-cooking is often the best, so eating at your riad (guesthouse) might be another good option.

TATIANA BRALNINA/SHUTTERSTOCK ©

The Year in Food

Morocco is the archetypal Slow Food destination, and there's never a bad time to visit. Its myriad fruits and vegetables are often bound for Europe, but head to any medina market to find local, seasonal produce piled high on market stalls and wooden carts.

Spring (March–May)

It's time for avocados, apricots and oranges, as well as strawberries, delicious in fresh juices.

Summer (June–August)

Fruits, such as watermelon, tomatoes, peaches, figs, grapes and prickly pear, have ripened, and mid-June brings the Cherry Festival (p352) in Sefrou.

Autumn (September–November)

Autumn sees grapes and pomegranates (mentioned in the Quran as being one of the fruits of paradise), along with the date harvest – it's said that Morocco has more than 100 varieties.

Winter (December–February)

The cooler months bring clementines, onions, beetroots, carrots and potatoes, as well as omnipresent oranges.

Food Experiences

Meals of a Lifetime

Tajines and couscous may be the quintessential must-eat dishes, but Morocco has other treats in store.

Bastilla A Fassi speciality, this savoury-sweet pie is made up of wafer-thin *warqa* (filo-like pastry) traditionally layered with pigeon, cooked with caramelised onions, lemon, eggs and toasted sugared almonds and then dusted with cinnamon and powdered sugar.

Tanjia This Marrakesh dish has been dubbed the bachelor's dish, as it was originally cooked by single men who would put chunks of meat, onions, preserved lemon, garlic and cumin into a terracotta pot and take it to the local communal oven or hammam to slow cook in the hot coals.

Mechoui Traditionally a whole lamb, marinated with spices and slow-roasted for hours in an underground oven until it falls off the bone and melts in the mouth. Perfect for groups, although it's possible to get a smaller portion of shoulder or leg. Often needs to be booked in advance.

Amlou The 'Moroccan Nutella' is an addictively sweet spread from the south – a mix of argan oil, honey and almonds – and delicious with warm *msemen* (flaky, pan-fried flatbread).

Cheap Treats

Merguez sandwich This spicy lamb or beef sausage is grilled and tucked into bread, and sometimes topped with *harissa* (hot chilli sauce) for extra fire. Popular countrywide.

Tacos A newcomer to the snack scene, the Moroccan take on tacos bears little resemblance to its Mexican cousin: a toasted tortilla wrapped around meat – perhaps chicken nuggets – and chips slathered in a lurid cheesy sauce.

Pastries You can't move for super-sweet Moroccan pastries. *Chebakia* – deep-fried dough, coated in a honey and rosewater syrup and sprinkled with sesame seeds – is particularly calorific. You can find them everywhere, but it's said that the finest are made in Fez.

Sardines In Essaouira, buy your sardines at the fish souq and then have them grilled at a neighbouring cafe. They can be found everywhere marinaded with tangy *chermoula* – a mix of herbs, garlic and spices – dusted with flour and deep fried.

Bissara This thick fava bean or broad bean soup is especially popular for breakfast, served topped with a generous drizzle of olive oil, a sprinkling of cumin and a freshly baked *khobz* (flatbread).

Dare to Try

Nothing goes to waste in Morocco, and those with a strong stomach should try these popular dishes, available from markets and food stalls across the country.

Snail soup Pluck the earthy-tasting snails from their shells and then drink the flavoursome broth or opt for the broth sans snails; this mix of more than 10 spices is reputedly good for your digestive system.

Camel spleen Think more camel sausage. The spleen is stuffed with camel meat, spices and hump fat and then baked, sliced, grilled and served up in a gamey-tasting sandwich.

Sheep's head Watching a sheep's head being charred over hot coals isn't for the squeamish, but Moroccans have their favourite parts, perhaps a soft chunk of cheek. The brain is probably bubbling away in a rich sauce nearby.

Tripe The stomach lining of a sheep, goat or cow is mixed with stewed white beans and cooked with lashings of garlic and cumin.

Cow's feet In this gelatinous dish, cow's feet are stewed with chickpeas and raisins in a spice-filled sauce.

Traditional bakery, Fez

What to Eat

Always on the Menu

Eat your way across Morocco and you'll always find variations of these dishes on the menu.

Tajine The quintessential Moroccan dish is a stew cooked in a conical earthenware pot that keeps the ingredients exceptionally moist and tender. The most common tajines are chicken with preserved lemons and green olives, lamb or beef with prunes, and *kefta* (spiced meatballs of ground lamb and/or beef) interspersed with eggs, all in a zesty tomato sauce. You'll find them everywhere, from the fanciest restaurants, served on linen tablecloths and eaten with heavy silverware, to roadside eateries where they'll be pulled straight off a *kanun* (earthenware brazier) and plonked down on a rickety table with a hunk of *khobz* (flatbread) serving as a utensil. Here you'll be able to pick your tajine; point to one that's been bubbling away for a while, with nicely caramelised onions and well-reduced sauce. Don't let appearances fool you, this could be one of the best tajines you'll eat.

Couscous Morocco's national dish – aka *seksu* – is traditionally served on Fridays at home; although restaurants now dish it up every day of the week. The age-old process is time consuming: durum wheat is ground into fine granules and then rolled by hand. Salted water and flour is added, after which it can take up to five hours to steam to light and fluffy perfection. Couscous is served with an array of vegetables – perhaps seven, à la *seksu bedawi* that hails from Casablanca, including cabbage, carrots, courgettes, onions, potatoes, pumpkin and squash – or a mix of meat or chicken and vegetables, all accompanied by a flavoursome broth that soaks in to the couscous.

Brochette Moroccan kebabs are a firm favourite, rubbed with salt and spices, grilled on a skewer and served with *khobz* and *harissa* (hot chilli paste), cumin and salt. Among the most popular varieties are lamb, chicken, *kefta* and the flavourful 'mixed meat' (usually lamb or beef plus heart, kidney and liver).

Salad Less elaborate than mezze, simple salads are often served as a starter. Smoky *zaalouk* is made with grilled aubergines, mixed with tomatoes and seasoned with garlic, cumin, chilli and coriander, and *taktouka* is a cooked salad combining roasted peppers and tomatoes. A fresh Moroccan salad – a mix of tomatoes, cucumbers, onion and parsley – makes the perfect partner to a hearty tajine.

PRICE RANGES

The following price ranges refer to the cost of an evening main course.

€ less than Dh70

€€ Dh70–Dh150

€€€ more than Dh150

Pastries, Tangier

Argan Oil Vitamin-rich Moroccan argan oil is popular as a cosmetic but also as a gourmet treat: the toasted-hazelnut flavour makes an intriguing dipping oil and salad dressing.

Harissa If you want to spice up your tajine, ask for *harissa* (hot chilli sauce). It's not always on the table as it is in Tunisia, but most restaurants have it, and you can find it at the olive souqs.

Ras el hanout (literally meaning 'head of the shop') is Morocco's ubiquitous spice mix. Each spice shop makes up its own particular blend, but cumin, coriander, cinnamon, cloves and ginger all feature. Popular spice-based sauces include:

➡ *mhammar*: paprika, cumin and butter

➡ *mqalli*: saffron, oil and ginger

➡ *msharmal*: saffron, ginger and a dash of pepper

➡ *qadra*: fermented butter with vegetable stock, chickpeas and/or almonds

Al Ftour (Breakfast)

Even if your days back home begin with just coffee, it would be a culinary crime to skip breakfast in Morocco. Whether you grab yours on the go in the souq or sit down to a leisurely repast, you are in for a treat. Breakfasts are rarely served before 8am in guesthouses and hotels, so early risers in immediate need of coffee will probably have to head to a cafe or hit the souqs.

As a guest in a Moroccan home, you'd be treated to the best of everything, and the best guesthouses uphold this Moroccan tradition each morning. You'll carb-load like a Moroccan marathoner, with a combination of some of the following to jump-start your day.

Ahwa (coffee) *Ahwa* is one option, but also *nus-nus* (half coffee, half milk), *chai b'na na* (mint tea) or *chai wa hleb* (tea with milk), *wa* (with) or *bla* (without) *sukur* (sugar).

Aseer limoon Orange juice.

Bayd (egg) Cooked in omelettes or tajines, with a dash of *kamun* (freshly ground cumin).

Beghrir Moroccan pancakes with an airy, spongy texture like crumpets, best with honey or jam.

French pastries Croissants, pain au chocolat and others.

Khobz Moroccan flatbread, usually served with butter and jam or olive oil and *zaatar* (a Lebanese or Syrian blend of spices that includes hyssop, sumac and sesame).

Spice stall, Marrakesh

Msemen Flaky, pan-fried Moroccan flatbread. Sometimes known as *rghaif*.

Sfenj Moroccan deep-fried doughnuts, sprinkled with sugar or drenched in honey.

Sidewalk cafes and kiosks put a local twist on the continental breakfast with Moroccan pancakes and doughnuts, French pastries, coffee and mint tea. Follow your nose and rumbling stomach into the souqs, where you'll find tangy olives and local *jiben* (fresh goat's or cow's milk cheese) to be devoured with just-baked *khobz*.

In the souqs, you can't miss vendors with their carts piled high with fresh fruit. You'll never know how high oranges can be stacked or how delicious freshly squeezed *aseer limoon* can be until you pay a visit to a Moroccan juice vendor's cart.

El Ghda (Lunch)

Lunch is traditionally the biggest meal of the day in Morocco and is followed by a nice nap through the heat of the day. The lunch hour is really a three- to four-hour stretch from noon to 3pm or 4pm, when most shops and facilities are closed, apart from those catering to tourists.

For speed eaters, this may seem inconvenient, but, especially in summer, it's best to do as the locals do and treat lunchtime as precious downtime. Tuck into a tajine, served à la carte with crusty bread, or upgrade to a prix fixe (set price) three-course menu. Afterwards, you'll have a whole new appreciation for mint tea and afternoon naps.

Heavenly Couscous

Imazighen (Berbers) call it *seksu*, a *New York Times* food critic called it one of the dozen best dishes in the world, and when you're in Morocco, you can call couscous lunch. You know that yellowish stuff that comes in a box, with directions on the side instructing you to add boiling water and let stand for three minutes? That doesn't count. What Moroccans call couscous is a fine, pale, grain-sized, hand-rolled pasta, lightly steamed with aromatic broth until toothsome and fluffy, served with a selection of vegetables and/or meat or fish in a delicately flavoured reduction of stock and spices.

Since preparing and digesting couscous takes a while, Moroccans usually enjoy it on Fridays when many have the day or the afternoon off after Friday prayers. Couscous isn't a simple side dish but rather the main event, whether it's in the age-old Casablanca-style with seven vegetables, heaped with lamb and vegetables à la Fez or served with tomatoes, fish and fresh herbs in Essaouira.

Many delicious couscous dishes are vegetarian, including the pumpkin couscous of Marrakesh and a simple High Atlas version with stewed onions. But scrupulous vegetarians will want to inquire in advance as to whether that hearty stock is indeed meat-free. Sometimes a couscous dish can be ordered à la carte, but usually it's the centrepiece of a multicourse lunch or celebratory *diffa* (feast), and when you get a mouthful of the stuff done properly, you'll see why.

Snack Attack

If you're still digesting your lavish guesthouse breakfast come lunchtime, try one of the many small restaurants offering lighter fare. Many hard-working locals do not take afternoon siestas and instead eat sandwiches on the go. At the risk of stating the obvious, always join the queue at the stall thronged with locals: Moroccans are picky about their food, preferring the

Above: Snail stall, Djemaa El Fna (p72), Marrakesh

Right: Vegetables cooked in a tajine

LUCKY BUSINESS/SHUTTERSTOCK ©

cleanest establishments that use the freshest ingredients. Here's what you'll find on offer at snack bars.

Merguez Hot, spicy, delicious homemade lamb sausage, not to be confused with *teyhan* (stuffed spleen; like liver, only less bitter and more tender). *Merguez* is usually reddish in colour while *teyhan* is pale.

Pizza Look out for wood-fired ovens and try tasty local versions with olives, onions, tomatoes, Atlantic anchovies and wild thyme.

Shawarma Spiced lamb or chicken roasted on a spit and served with *tahina* (sesame sauce) or yoghurt, with optional onions, salad, *harissa* and a dash of sumac (a tart, pickle-flavoured purple spice; highly recommended).

The Moroccan Power Lunch

Some upscale Moroccan restaurants that serve an evening *diffa* (feast) to tourist hordes serve a scaled-down menu at lunch, when waitstaff are more relaxed and the meal is sometimes a fraction of the price you'd pay for dinner. You might miss the live music and inevitable belly dancing that would accompany a fancy supper – but then again, you might not. Three courses may seem a bit much for lunch, but don't be daunted: what this usually means is a delightful array of diminutive vegetable dishes, followed by a fluffy couscous and/or a small meat or chicken tajine, capped with the obligatory mint tea and biscuits or fruit.

BEST EATING

Umia (p241) Stylish dining in a contemporary space in Essaouira's medina.

Restaurant Brasserie La Bavaroise (p196) Franco-Moroccan brasserie in classy Casablanca surroundings.

Restaurant Villa Mandarine (p208) Mediterranean-inspired dining in a gorgeous garden in Rabat.

Djemaa El Fna Food Stalls (p73) Open-air eating in Marrakesh that's as much street theatre as food.

Ruined Garden (p332) Intimate green oasis in the Fez medina offers sophisticated Moroccan dishes.

Populaire Saveur de Poisson (p261) Lively and rustic seafood restaurant in Tangier.

L'Asha (Dinner)

Dinner in Morocco doesn't usually start until 8pm or 9pm, after work and possibly a sunset stroll. Most Moroccans eat dinner at home, but you may notice young professionals, students and bachelors making a beeline for the local *snak* (kiosk) or pizzeria. In winter, you'll see vendors crack open steaming vats of *harira*, a hearty soup with a base of tomatoes, onions, saffron and coriander, often with lentils, chickpeas and/or lamb. Dinner at home may often be *harira* and lunch leftovers, with the notable exception of Ramadan and other celebrations.

With enough hard currency and room in your stomach, you might prefer restaurants to *snak* fare for dinner. Most upscale Moroccan restaurants cater to tourists, serving an elaborate *prix fixe* Moroccan *diffa* (feast) in a palatial setting. This is not a dine-and-dash meal, but an evening's entertainment that often includes live music or belly dancing and wine or beer.

Your meal may come with a side order of kitsch. Many palace restaurants appear to have been decorated by a genie, complete with winking brass lamps, ornate mirrors, swagged tent fabric and tasselled cushions as far as the eye can see. Often it's the ambience you're paying for rather than the food, which can vary from exquisitely prepared regional specialities to mass-produced glop. Here's a rule of thumb: if the place is so cavernous that your voice echoes and there's a stage set up for a laser show, don't expect personalised service or authentic Moroccan fare.

Food Quality

The food you find in Morocco is likely to be fresh, locally grown and homemade rather than shipped in, microwaved and served semithawed. Most Moroccan ingredients are cultivated in small quantities the old-fashioned way, without GMOs (genetically modified organisms), chemical fertilisers, pesticides or even mechanisation. These technologies are far too costly an investment for the average small-scale Moroccan farmer, as is organic certification and labelling. Though you may not see a label on it to this effect, much of the Moroccan produce you'll find in food markets is chemical- and GMO-free.

Flatbread stall, Marrakesh

Meats

Carnivores and sustainably minded eaters can put aside their differences and enjoy dinner together in Morocco. As you may guess from watching sheep and goats scamper over mountains and valleys in Morocco, herds live a charmed existence here – at least until dinnertime. Most of the meat you'll enjoy in Morocco is free-range and antibiotic-free and is raised on a steady diet of grass and wild herbs. If you wonder why lamb and mutton is so much more flavourful in Morocco than the stuff back home, you'll find your answer scampering around the High Atlas foothills.

Produce

The appearance, fragrance and flavour of Moroccan market produce leaves supermarket fare in the shade. There's a reason for this: Moroccan produce is usually harvested by hand when ripe and bought directly from farmers in the souqs. Follow the crowds of Moroccan grandmothers and restaurant sous-chefs to the carts and stalls offering the freshest supplies. Be sure to peel, cook or thoroughly wash produce before you eat it.

Vegetarians: Your Moroccan Menu

Breakfast Load up on Moroccan pastries, pancakes, fresh fruit and fresh-squeezed juice. Goat's cheese and olives from the souq are solid savoury choices with just-baked *khobz* (bread). *Bissara* is a delicious bean soup that's typically meat-free, but steer clear of bubbling roadside vats – they may contain snails or sheep's-head soup.

Lunch Try the mezze of salads, which come with fresh bread and may range from delicate cucumbers in orange-blossom water to substantial herbed beets laced with kaffir lime. Vegetarians can sometimes, but not always, order a vegetable tajine or couscous with seven vegetables. Ingredients are bought fresh daily in small quantities, and the chef may not have factored vegetarians into the restaurant's purchases, so call ahead if you can. Pizza is another widely available and inexpensive menu option, best when topped with local herbs and olives.

Snacks Market stalls feature cascades of dried figs, dates and apricots alongside towering cones of roasted nuts with salt, honey, cinnamon, sugar or hot pepper. Chickpeas and other pulses are roasted, served hot in a paper cone with cumin and salt, and are not to be missed. Tea-time menus at swanky restaurants may feature *briouats*, triangular pastries stuffed with herbs and goat's cheese or an egg, plus finger sandwiches, pastries and cakes. If that's not enough, there's always mint tea with cookies or nuts.

Dinner For a hearty change of pace from salads and couscous, try a vegetarian pasta (anything with aubergine is especially tasty) or omelette (usually served with thick-cut fries). If you're staying in a Moroccan guesthouse, before you leave in the morning you can usually request a vegetarian tajine made to order with market-fresh produce.

Vegetable couscous

When to Eat

Seasonal Variations

If there is one food you adore or a dish you detest, you might want to plan the timing of your visit to Morocco accordingly. Morocco offers an incredible bounty of produce, meats and fish, but these vary seasonally, which means that if you're visiting in autumn, you may have to enjoy fresh figs instead of kiwi fruit.

When you consider your menu options, you'll also want to think about geography. Oualidia oysters may not be so fresh by the time they cross mountain passes to Ouarzazate, and Sefrou cherries can be hard to come by in Tiznit. If your vacation plans revolve around lavish seafood dinners, head for the coasts; vegetarians visiting desert regions in autumn should have a high tolerance for dates.

Eating During Ramadan

During Ramadan, most Moroccans observe the fast during the day, eating only before sunrise and after sunset. Dinner is eaten later than usual, and many wake up early for a filling breakfast before dawn. Another popular strategy is to stay up most of the night, sleep as late as possible, and stretch the afternoon nap into early evening. Adapt to the local schedule, and you may thoroughly enjoy the leisurely pace, late-night festivities and manic feasts of Ramadan.

Although you will not be expected to observe the fast, eating in public is still frowned upon. Hence many restaurants are closed during the day until *iftar*, the evening meal when the fast is broken – though if you call ahead to restaurants in tourist areas, you may have luck. Plan ahead: load up on snacks in the market to eat indoors, make arrangements for breakfast or lunch in the privacy of your guesthouse and ask locals about a good place to enjoy *iftar*.

Iftar comes with all the traditional Ramadan treats: *harira* (a hearty soup made of tomatoes, onions, saffron and coriander, often with lentils, chickpeas and lamb), dates, milk, *shebbakia* (a sweet, coiled pastry that's guaranteed to shift your glucose levels into high gear) and *harcha* (buttery bread made of semolina and fried for maximum density). You may find that *harira* is offered free; even Moroccan McDonald's offers it as part of their special Ramadan Happy Meal.

Where to Eat

Morocco has a wide range of eating options. Reservations are only necessary at higher-end places.

Restaurants A lot of smaller restaurants stick to a limited roster of standard tajine dishes, with couscous served on Fridays.

Tajine stall, Marrakesh

Cafes Simple breakfasts are usually available in cafes, along with pastries.

Riads Many excellent restaurants are found inside riads, which open their doors (and tables) to nonguests. Alcohol may be served.

Drinking in Morocco

Morocco has a cafe culture rather than a drinking culture. Alcohol is available, but often bars are smoky male-dominated affairs, and women – if they're allowed in at all – shouldn't go unaccompanied. Marrakesh has a thriving nightclub scene, followed by Casablanca, and Tangier has some great bars, but elsewhere in Morocco, there's a paucity of nightlife. Top-end hotels, restaurants and some riads offer the most relaxed drinking options if you're looking for something stronger than mint tea.

Alcohol

Yes, you can drink alcohol in Morocco without offending local sensibilities, as long as you do it discreetly. Serving alcohol within Moroccan medinas may be frowned upon, and liquor licences an expensive bureaucratic nightmare, but some Moroccan guesthouses and restaurants get around these hurdles by serving booze out of sight indoors or on a terrace, or suggesting you BYO. If you're in the mood for a beer and don't find it on the menu, you might want to ask the waiter in a low voice, speakeasy-style.

One note of caution: quality assurance is tricky in a Muslim country where mixologists, micro-brewers and licensed sommeliers are in understandably short supply, and your server may not be able to make any personal recommendations from the wine menu. Since wines are subject to unpredictable heat exposure in transit and storage, be sure to taste your wine before the server leaves the table – red wines are especially subject to spoilage. Don't hesitate to send back a drink if something about it seems off; your server will likely take your word for it.

Wine

Moroccan wine has come a very long way in the last 15 years. Most of the vineyards are in the Meknes region, where the climate in

THANOSQUEST/SHUTTERSTOCK ©

Mint tea

the Middle Atlas foothills provides moderate rainfall and plenty of sunshine. Add the heavy, rocky clay soil and an elevation of 580m to 700m, and you get some exceptional vineyards.

Started by the Romans (or possibly before) and developed by the French, the industry fell into the doldrums after independence but has since been revitalised with new vineyards and brands coming onto the market.

However, there remains a dichotomy around wine production in Morocco. It is *haram* (forbidden) in Islam, there is no advertising within the country and many vineyards are tucked away behind olive trees. Only a handful of supermarkets and independent shops stock alcohol. And yet, some 90% of the wine made in Morocco is drunk in the country and not all of it by tourists. The industry provides a large number of jobs as well as taxes for the government.

➡ There are no boxed wines, and all wine bottles have corks rather than screwtops. If you intend to buy wine for consumption during your stay, bring your own corkscrew.

➡ Locally produced kosher wines are available.

➡ Cellars or *caves* at supermarkets have an entrance separate to the main store. They stock wines from other countries as well as beer and spirits.

➡ Alcohol shops close a few days before Ramadan and reopen a few days after Eid.

➡ Most upmarket establishments serve wine and perhaps beer and cocktails.

➡ There are very few places that allow you to bring your own wine (or other alcoholic drinks); ask first. Be discreet.

Red Wine

Red is by far the most successful wine produced in Morocco. Grapes used are cabernet sauvignon, syrah, merlot, tempranillo, grenache and mourvèdre.

From the Meknes region, look out for the Domaine de la Zouinas smooth Epicuria and Volubilia Classic, and the full-bodied – and only AOC wine – Coteaux de l'Atlas from Celliers de Meknes Château Roslane (p362).

Ouled Thaleb vineyard on the coast between Casablanca and Rabat produces organically grown wines such as Ait Souala and Médaillon.

The red wines from Domaine du Val d'Argan (p241) near Essaouira include Gazelle, Val d'Argan and Orian.

Southeast of Rabat, La Ferme Rouge produces a wide range of wine including the reasonably priced La Cuvée du Terroir from carignan, merlot and cinsault, and more expensive wines such as Ithaque (90% syrah, 10% tempranillo).

White Wine

If reds are the most successful, then whites are the least. They are often oxidised and too heavy. But there are a few vineyards getting it right: Domaine de la Zouina's Volubilia (chardonnay, sauvignon and vermentino grapes) is pleasant, while the Val d'Argan Blanc (viognier, roussane) is flavourful. Ouled Thaleb makes a blend as well as a single-grape sauvignon.

Gris

Gris is probably the wine for which Morocco is best known, and it is a refreshing choice for a hot summer day. It comes in a number of shades of palest pink with a greyish tinge, depending on the grapes used: syrah and muscat for Val d'Argan's Perle Grise, and caladoc, mourvèdre and marselan for Domaine de la Zouina's elegant Volubilia, for example.

Rosé

Syrah, muscat, cabernet sauvignon, tempranillo, cinsault and grenache are used in Moroccan rosés. Some of these wines are very pink and can be oversweet.

Sparkling

Sparkling One méthode champenoise wine is made by Celliers de Meknes (p362), La Perle du Sud Blanc de Blanc Brut.

Wine Tasting & Tours

Tours and tastings are rare, but around Meknes you can taste the wines of Celliers de Meknes (p362) and the smaller Domaine de la Zouina (p362). It tends not to be the genteel affair you might find in other wine-producing countries. Generous amounts of wine are poured, and you're expected to drink it rather than spit. You can also do some tasting at the Domaine du Val d'Argan (p241) estate near Essaouira when you have lunch in their restaurant.

Beer

Morocco's main breweries are found in Casablanca, Tangier and Fez. Casa is a fine local pilsner beer, and other popular brands are Flag Spéciale and Stork.

Spirits

Mahia, a Moroccan spirit distilled from figs, is around 80% proof, with a flavour somewhere between Italian grappa and Kentucky moonshine. You won't find it on most menus because it's usually made in home distilleries for private consumption. If you're staying at a guesthouse, your hosts may know where you can get some, but they may try to warn you off the stuff – *mahia* hangovers are legendary.

Juice

Freshly squeezed orange juice is one of the delights of a Moroccan breakfast, but it's not all that's on offer. In season, you can sip mango, strawberry and pomegranate juice, and look out for sugar cane, date and avocado drinks.

Mint Tea

Mint tea is the national drink and a hallmark of Moroccan hospitality, so don't expect to rush it. Dubbed 'Berber whiskey', it's poured from a metal teapot into a glass from a great height – the resulting bubbles are thought to make it more appealing to the eye – and served piping hot to encourage the guest to linger. You can opt to have it with sugar or without, but the default is sweet.

Coffee

Most coffee is made with a cafetière (French press) and will deliver a caffeine hit to propel you through the souqs. Moroccans tend to take their coffee thick and black; ask for *nus-nus* (half and half) to have it mixed with steamed milk.

Surfing, Taghazout (p39

Plan Your Trip

Activities

Morocco's diverse landscapes mean endless options for adventure. Hike through North Africa's highest mountain ranges, trek by camel into the Sahara or surf the Atlantic rollers. The lack of light pollution in mountain villages and desert dunes allows for spectacular stargazing.

Top Activity Spots

Atlas Mountains & Jebel Saghro

Hoist yourself up here for rock climbing, from bouldering to mountaineering; downhill skiing and ski trekking; wildlife spotting, including monkeys, sheep and leopards, all of the Barbary variety; trekking; mountain biking; and white-water rafting.

Merzouga & M'Hamid

Hotfoot it to the Sahara to take part in camel treks, moonlight dune hikes and sandboarding, and to look out for wildlife – including desert warblers and the bat-eared fennec fox – and sleep in a Berber-style tent.

Essaouira & Oualidia

Hit the beach for surfing, windsurfing, kitesurfing, kayaking and canoeing; and for marine mammals and birdlife such as the endangered bald ibis.

Birdwatching

Morocco is a birdwatcher's paradise. A startling array of species inhabits the country's diverse ecosystems and environments, especially the coastal wetlands.

Around 460 species have been recorded in the country, many of them migrants passing through in spring and autumn when Morocco becomes a way station between sub-Saharan Africa and breeding grounds in Scandinavia, Greenland and northern Russia. Other birds fly to Morocco to avoid the harsh northern European winters. The lagoon at Merja Zerga National Park in Moulay Bousselham is the best site in the country for migratory birds.

Souss-Massa National Park (p395) is another favourite of twitchers, and a visit can be facilitated by guides at both of the sleeping options in the park; **La Dune** (☎0666807824; www.ladune.de; Sidi R'bat; s/d Dh350/400, tents from Dh250; 🅿) will appeal to independent travellers.

There's excellent birdwatching in the desert of Western Sahara as well; tours can be organised by the knowledgable **Dakhla Rovers** (☎0636808515, 0636808514; www.dakhla-rovers.com).

A pleasant time for birdwatching is from March to May when the weather is comfortable and a wide variety of species is usually present. Winter (December to February) is also a particularly active time in the wetlands and lagoons.

In addition to local birdwatching guide **Hassan Dalil** (☎0668434110; hassandalil873@gmail.com; tour Dh300), who offers boat tours of the Merja Zerga lagoon, the following companies offer birding tours around Morocco:

Birdfinders (www.birdfinders.co.uk)

Birding Tours Morocco (www.birdingtoursmorocco.com, based in Merzouga)

Naturetrek (www.naturetrek.co.uk)

Wild Insights (www.wildinsights.co.uk)

Camel Treks

Exploring the Sahara by camel – whether on an overnight excursion or a longer desert safari – is one of Morocco's signature activities and most rewarding wilderness experiences.

Morocco's most evocative stretches of Saharan sand are Erg Chebbi, near Merzouga, and Erg Chigaga, near M'Hamid and Zagora.

Only consider doing your camel trek in autumn (September and October) or winter (November to early March). Outside these months, the desert experiences gruelling extremes of heat plus sandstorms in the spring.

Prices start at around Dh210 for a sunrise or sunset tour and Dh420 for an overnight stay in a tented camp, but rates vary depending on the number of people, the length of the trek and your negotiating skills.

Organising a Camel Trek

Travellers with time to spare can organise a guide and provisions in the main desert gateways of M'Hamid and Merzouga. This benefits the local community and counters the trend towards young guides leaving home to look for work in the more popular tourist centres.

M'Hamid is probably the more hassle-free of the two destinations, although the choice is wider in Merzouga and Zagora, 96km to the north. Try to get recommendations from other travellers.

It's quicker and easier, involving less negotiations and waiting around, to organise a trip in advance – either through an international tour operator or a Morocco-based company, such as **Wild Morocco** (☎0655778173; www.wildmorocco.com) or **Desert Candles** (☎0673267893; www.desert-candles.com; ⏲8am-8pm).

Men's hammam, Marrakesh

Hammams

Visiting a public hammam (traditional bathhouse) is infinitely preferable to cursing under a cold shower in a cheap hotel. They're busy, social places where you'll find gallons of hot water and staff available to scrub you clean for a small fee.

Every neighbourhood has at least one hammam, often with separate spaces for men and women, others open to either sex at different hours or on alternate days.

You'll need a hammam kit of flip-flops, towel and a plastic mat (to sit on), as well as a spare pair of underwear and your shampoo and soap. You can also bring your own *savon beldi* (black soap made from olive resin), *kessa* (coarse scrubbing mitt) and *ghassoul* (clay mixed with herbs), that you can pick up at the souqs. You'll be given a bucket and scoop; remember to use the communal bucket when filling yours with water. Most hammams have showers.

Nudity is common in some public hammams, but etiquette differs among neighbourhoods: if unsure, ask an attendant. Some may ask both men and women to keep their underpants on; however, it's acceptable to wear your swimsuit if this makes you feel more comfortable.

Local hammam admission is typically around Dh10 (more in tourist areas), plus the optional extras of *gommage* (scrub) and massage. Ask your hotel for a tourist-friendly recommendation.

Midrange and top-end hotels often have private hammams offering more expensive steam, scrubs and massages, usually alongside other spa treatments, such as wraps and facials.

Rock Climbing

There is a growing climbing scene in Morocco, with some sublime routes. Anyone contemplating climbing should have plenty of experience and be prepared to bring all their own equipment.

The Anti Atlas and High Atlas offer everything from bouldering to very demanding mountaineering routes that shouldn't be attempted unless you have a great deal of experience.

Des Clark's guidebook *Mountaineering in the Moroccan High Atlas* (2011), subtitled 'walks, climbs and scrambles over 3000m' covers some 50 routes and 30 peaks in handy pocket-sized, plastic-covered form, with plenty of maps, photos and practical information. Another excellent guide is Mo-

Rockclimbing, Todra Gorge (p169)

rocco Rock (www.moroccorock.com), which is particularly good on the Anti Atlas. The authors run an active Facebook community.

The Todra Gorge is also prime climbing territory, and a good local operator is **Aventures Verticales** (☎0524895727; www.climbing-in-morocco.com; Km 14, Tizgui; half-/full day per person Dh125/200).

Zaouiat Ahansal is an increasingly popular rock-climbing destination, and *Taghia et Autres Montagnes Berbères* by Christian Ravier and Ihintza Elsenaar is a good local resource.

The Royal Moroccan Ski & Mountaineering Federation (www.frmsm.ma) has lists of climbing routes. A good local climbing tour operator is **Climb Morocco** (http://climbmorocco.com).

Skiing

Skiing is viable from November to April although Morocco's ski stations are somewhat ramshackle. For more information, including local ski clubs, contact the Royal **Moroccan Ski & Mountaineering Federation** (www.frmsm.ma).

Downhill Skiing

The popular resort of Oukaimeden (p129), about 70km south of Marrakesh, has North Africa's highest ski lift and equipment for hire. **Michlifen** (⊙Nov-Mar), near Fez, is the place to ski in the Middle Atlas, with drag lifts on both slopes and places to hire gear, although some seasons the snow is thin on the ground.

Ski Trekking

Ski randonnée is increasingly popular, especially from late December to February. The Ait Bougmez Valley (p134) has prime routes for experienced, self-reliant skiers with their own gear.

Surfing, Windsurfing & Kitesurfing

With thousands of kilometres of coastline, the Moroccan Atlantic is a fine, if underrated, destination for surfing, windsurfing and kitesurfing. Lessons, equipment hire and surfing safaris are all available.

ALTERNATIVE ACTIVITIES

Looking for an unusual way to experience Morocco's outdoors beyond the traditional trekking, camel tours and rock climbing? Here are some lesser-known options to experience the country's natural beauty.

Horse Riding

Southern Morocco is popular for horse riding, along beaches such as Diabat to hills, mountains, valleys, gorges and the desert.

Specialist travel companies offer guided horse-riding tours, including **Club Farah** (0535548844; www.clubfarah.com; hour/half-day/full-day rides Dh120/350/600) near Meknes, **Equi Evasion** (0666780561; www.equievasion.com; rides 1hr/3hr €15/€35) in Diabat and **Unicorn Trails** (www.unicorntrails.com), a UK-based operator offering four expeditions in the High Atlas, Sahara and Essaouira areas.

Mountain Biking

Ordinary cycling is possible in Morocco, but mountain biking opens up the options considerably. For the very fit, the vast networks of *pistes* (dirt tracks) and footpaths in the High Atlas offer the most rewarding biking. The Anti Atlas, the Jebel Saghro plateau and the Draa Valley also offer excellent trails.

Travel agencies, hotels and shops hire out mountain bikes, for example in Tafraoute, but the quality isn't really high enough for an extended trip. Adventure tour companies cater to serious cyclists:

Freeride Morocco (www.freeridemorocco.com) Vehicle-supported mountain bike tours in the High Atlas from a Marrakesh-based operator. Offers set departures and custom trips.

AXS (0524400207; www.argansports.com; Rue Fatima Al Fihria, Sidi Youssef Ben Ali; half-day city tours from Dh350, bike hire per 24hr from Dh200;) Marrakesh-based cycling operator running mountain bike tours in the High Atlas and providing bike hire.

Saddle Skedaddle (www.skedaddle.co.uk) UK-based tour operator operating vehicle-supported cycling tours of Morocco, for all abilities.

White-Water Rafting & Kayaking

Although white-water rafting and kayaking are underdeveloped in Morocco, the rivers in the High Atlas near Bin El Ouidane have stunning scenery. **Water By Nature** (www.waterbynature.com) is a specialist rafting operator running tours in Morocco.

Northern & Central Morocco

North of Rabat, Mehdiya Plage has strong currents but reliable year-round breaks. Moving south, Plage des Nations and Témara Plage (Témara), both within 20km of Rabat, are also good for surfing. Sidi Bouzid and the beaches around El Jadida (p225) also attract surfers.

Oualidia (p228) has a longstanding surf camp and the sheltered lagoon has the perfect conditions for beginners. En route to Safi, the Lalla Fatna beach has some of Morocco's best breaks: one of the world's longest tubular right-handers has drawn many of surfing's big names.

Southern Morocco

Essaouira (p232) has been singled out by some surfers, although the 'Wind City of Africa' is even better for windsurfing and kitesurfing year round.

Nearby Sidi Kaouki (p246) is an upcoming destination for all three of these sports.

Near Agadir, the Taghazout (p397) area has some of Morocco's best surfing beaches and numerous businesses catering to surfers. Other surf-centric destinations to consider are Agadir (p386) and Mirleft (p421).

Jebel Toubkal (p120)

Plan Your Trip

Trekking in Morocco

Morocco is home to some of Africa's most beautiful mountains, and it's a year-round trekking destination. In summer, head to Jebel Toubkal. In winter, when snow closes the High Atlas, there's Jebel Saghro to explore, while the Anti Atlas and Rif Mountains are ideal for the seasons in between.

Trekking Regions

High Atlas

Tackle North Africa's highest peak, Jebel Toubkal, and meet Imazighen (Berbers) on the longer Toubkal Circuit. Escape the crowds and be inspired by the remote M'Goun Massif's spectacular valleys and beautiful remote villages.

Jebel Saghro

Head southeast to some of Morocco's most rugged and stunning scenery, perfect for winter walking.

Rif Mountains

Take a gentler path through little-visited cedar forests in the Talassemtane National Park near Chefchaouen.

Anti Atlas

Visit a few of the Ameln Valley's 26 villages en route to an ascent of the 'amethyst mountain', Jebel El Kest. Enjoy serious trekking and stark beauty among the remote villages and tremendous gorges beneath volcanic Jebel Siroua.

Where to Trek

Some trailheads are off the beaten path as far as public transport goes. You might need to factor in the cost of hiring a grand taxi to get you to where you can start walking, or of an extra day's walking along mountain *pistes* (dirt tracks) to reach the start of trails.

Toubkal Circuit

An ascent of Jebel Toubkal, North Africa's highest peak (4167m), is Morocco's most iconic trek. The two-day hike starts at Imlil near Marrakesh; those wanting more can hire mules to make a Toubkal Circuit trek of a week or more.

M'Goun Massif

Despite the sometime fearsome reputation of the M'Goun Massif, this three-day trek is suitable for most levels of fitness. The landscape is both varied and spectacular, from dry gorges to lush valleys, but be prepared to get your feet wet hopping or wading across shallow rivers if hiking in spring.

Rif Mountains

Morocco's lowest mountain range is ideal for springtime trekking, when the Rif's oak forests are in their greenest leaf and the slopes carpeted with wildflowers. Trek through the Talassemtane National Park, past Amazigh (Berber) villages to arrive at the audacious natural rock formation of God's Bridge.

Jebel Saghro

This trek of four to six days threads a path between the High Atlas and the Dadès Valley. The traverse of Jebel Saghro is arid but starkly beautiful, and it's a prime winter trek when other mountain trails are inaccessible because of snow.

Anti Atlas

The Anti Atlas is where Morocco's ripple of mountains finally peter out into the Sahara. In these much-overlooked mountains, hardcore trekkers can take a week to tackle the volcanic peak of Jebel Siroua or hike for five days through the villages of the Ameln Valley to Jebel El Kest. David Wood's *Walks and Scrambles in the Anti Atlas* is an excellent resource for the region.

What to Pack

Clothing & Equipment

The way you dress is important, especially among remote mountain people, who remain conservative. In villages, wear buttoned shirts or T-shirts and not sleeveless vests, which villagers use as underwear. Above all, trousers should be worn rather than shorts. This applies equally to men and women.

The importance of dress in the villages cannot be overemphasised (as many a frustrated and embarrassed trekking tour leader will affirm). However much you might disagree with this conservatism, respecting local traditions will bring great rewards, not least by way of contact, hospitality and assistance.

All year round, you will need to pack strong, well-broken-in walking boots.

Trekking Areas

You will also need a waterproof and windproof outer layer. It's amazing how quickly the weather can change, so you'll also need a sunhat, sunglasses and high-factor sunscreen.

In summer (June to August) light, baggy cotton trousers and long-sleeved shirts are musts, and because nights can still get cold even at lowish altitudes, you should also bring a fleece or jumper.

When trekking during winter (November to March), always pack warm clothing, including a woollen hat and gloves for High Atlas hikes. You should be prepared for cold weather wherever you trek in the country.

Sleeping Bags

Whether you are camping or staying in houses, a four-season sleeping bag is essential for the High Atlas and Jebel Saghro from September to early April, when temperatures as low as -10°C are not unknown.

In lower ranges, even in high summer, a bag comfortable at 0°C is recommended. A thick sleeping mat or thin foam mattress is a good idea since the ground is extremely rocky. Guides can usually supply these, and all homestays will proactively offer them.

Food

The choice of dry rations is limited in rural Morocco. You cannot be sure of finding much beyond powdered milk, a range of dried fruit, sachets of soup, biscuits, some tinned fish and dates. Supermarkets in larger towns and cities are a much better option, and if you take a mule, you will be able to plan a more varied diet.

Bread, eggs, vegetables and basic supplies (eg tea and tinned tuna) may be available in some mountain villages, but don't count on it. Meals can also be arranged in some villages (Dh50 to Dh70 per person is standard), especially at *gîtes* (hostels)

TREKKING MAPS

Morocco is covered by a 1:100,000 and also a 1:50,000 topographical map series.

Some of the 1:50,000 series are unavailable to the public; travellers exploring wide areas are advised to stick to the 1:100,000 series.

Although marked in Cyrillic script, 1:100,000 maps of Morocco made by the Soviet military are as topographically accurate as any available.

The best place in Morocco to buy maps is **Direction de la Cartographie** (☎0660102683; www.ancfcc.gov.ma; cnr Aves My Youssef & My Hassan I) in Rabat, which lists the maps it sells online. Maps and photocopies are also available at other bookshops around Morocco, as well as at stalls around **Djemaa El Fna** (off Place de Foucald) in Marrakesh and, as a last resort, on the approaches to the Atlas trekking routes.

A variety of maps is available for sale online.

and *refuges* (chalet-style accommodation), although they usually need to be ordered in advance. Do not rely on local suppliers as your only source of food unless you have made previous arrangements.

Change money in the nearest major town and ensure that you have plenty of small notes. If you do get stuck, euro notes may be accepted at disadvantageous rates.

Stoves

Most *gîtes* have cooking facilities, but you will want to bring a stove if you are camping. Multifuel stoves that burn anything from aviation fuel to diesel are ideal.

Methylated spirits are hard to get hold of, but kerosene is available. Pierce-type butane gas canisters are also available but not recommended for environmental reasons. Your guide will be able to offer advice.

Tents

The key decision when planning a route is whether to sleep in a tent or rely on *gîtes* and homestays. A good tent opens up endless trekking possibilities and will get you away from the crowds.

You can hire tents from tour operators and guides, and in larger trailhead towns like Imlil.

Other Equipment

Bring a basic medical kit as well as water-purification tablets, iodine drops or a mechanical purifier. All water should be treated unless you take it directly from the source.

To go above 3000m between November and May, you need experience in winter mountaineering and cold-weather essentials including crampons, ice axes and snow shovels. This equipment is available for hire at major trailheads.

If you are combining trekking with visits to urban areas, consider storing extra luggage before your trek rather than lugging around unwanted gear. Most hotels will let you leave luggage, sometimes for a small fee. Train stations in larger cities have secure left-luggage facilities.

Guides

However much trekking and map-reading experience you have, we strongly recommend that you hire a qualified guide, if for no other reason than to be your translator (how is your Tashelhit?), plus *faux guides* (unofficial guides) won't come near you if you are with a guide.

Good guides will enhance your cultural experience. They will know local people, which will undoubtedly result in invitations for tea and food, and richer experiences of local lifestyles.

If something goes wrong, a local guide will be the quickest route to getting help. Every year foreigners die in the Moroccan mountains. Whatever the cause – a freak storm, an unlucky slip, a rock slide – the presence of a guide would invariably have increased their chances of survival.

Choosing a Guide

A flash-looking, English-speaking *faux guide* from Marrakesh is no substitute for a gnarled, old, local mountain guide who knows the area like the back of his hand.

Official guides carry photo-identity cards. Guides should be authorised by the Fédération Royale Marocaine de Ski et Montagne or L'Association Nationale des Guides et Accompagnateurs en Montagne du Maroc. They should be credited as *guides de montagne* (mountain guides), which usually requires study for at least six months at the Centre de Formation aux Métiers de Montagne, a school for mountain guides at Tabant in the Ait Bougmez Valley.

Accompagnateurs (escorts) will have had only one week's training and will not be insured to lead mountain trips; *guides de tourisme* (tourist guides) are not qualified to lead treks.

Official mountain guides have been trained in mountain craft, including first aid. In times of uncertain weather or in an emergency, they will be infinitely more efficient than a cheaper guide lacking proper training. If a guide is reluctant to show a photo card, it probably means they either don't have one or it has expired (they should be renewed every three years).

Some *guides de montagne* have additional training in rock climbing, canyoning and mountaineering and will charge extra for these services. Most guides speak either French or English, and some also speak Spanish or German. Several young Moroccan female guides, who have succeeded in breaking into the previously all-male world of mountain guiding, are in high demand.

Hiking, Atlas Mountains foothills, Ouirgane (p129)

Hiring a Guide

Accredited mountain guides in Morocco can be found through private tour operators or the *bureaux des guides* in Imlil, Setti Fatma and Chefchaouen.

The minimum rate for official guides is Dh400 per day (per group, not per person), but it can vary according to season and location. The price does not include food and accommodation expenses.

Guides generally get free accommodation in *refuges* and *gîtes,* but you may be asked to cover their meals. If you walk a linear route, you'll also be expected to pay for their return journey.

Negotiate all fees before departure and count on giving at least a 10% tip at the end unless you have been unhappy with the service.

If your guide is organising your trip (rather than a tour operator), be sure to go through all aspects of the trek ahead of time. Discuss where each day will start and end; whether tents will be shared (most guides have a tent and/or sleeping bag); how many mules will be hired; who will be cooking (if there are enough of you, the guide may insist on hiring a cook, usually for about Dh100 a day); food preferences; water provision; and the division of food and equipment among the group.

Hiring a Mule

Mules (and the odd donkey) are widely used in Morocco for transporting goods through the mountains, and you can easily hire one to carry your gear.

If you are relying on heavy local supplies or are in a large group, hiring a mule makes especially good sense. As a rough guide, mules can carry up to 90kg – or up to four sets of gear. If the route is very steep or demanding, the muleteer may insist upon carrying less.

Some trekking routes are not suitable for mules, although detours (for the mule) are often possible. If high passes are covered in snow, porters may have to be used instead of mules (one porter can carry up to 18kg).

There is usually a standard charge for a mule and muleteer of about Dh130 per day. As with guides, if you trek a linear route, you'll also be expected to pay for the muleteer's return journey.

Top: Amazigh desert camp, Merzouga (p176)

Bottom: Pack donkeys

Where to Sleep

If you would rather not carry a tent, you can often stay in *refuges* and in villages at either *gîtes d'étape* (basic homestays or hostels) or *chez l'habitant* (in someone's home). Especially in remote areas, village rooms may only have a mattress on the floor, although in places such as Imlil they often come with the luxury of a bed.

The bulk of trekking accommodation options in the High and Middle Atlas are *gîtes*. In the Rif and Anti Atlas, *gîtes* are uncommon, and accommodation is more often in local homes or in tents.

Camping

Vegetation at high altitude is highly sensitive. When camping, minimise your impact on the environment by not removing or disturbing the vegetation around your campsite. Sufficient fodder (barley) for all baggage mules and donkeys should be brought in.

Gîtes d'Étape

Gîtes provide basic accommodation, often offering little more than a foam mattress in an empty room, or on a roof terrace or balcony. They have basic bathrooms and toilets, although the better ones have hot showers. Given notice, the proprietor can rustle up a tajine.

The standard rate is Dh50 per person per night, although prices can vary according to season and location. Meals are extra (usually Dh30 to Dh50 per person), as are hot showers (usually Dh10 to Dh15 per shower).

The more upmarket, privately owned *gîtes* typically charge up to Dh200 per person for half-board, while rooms at a luxury kasbah in Imlil cost up to Dh280.

Refuges

Club Alpin Français operates three rustic *refuges* – built of stone and wood with very basic shared facilities – in Oukaimeden, Tazaghart and Toubkal. *Refuges* are often packed in July and August.

Members of CAF and Hostelling International get the cheapest price for a bed. Members of affiliated and recognised alpine organisations (eg the UK's Alpine Club) and children under 16 are also eligible for discounts.

BOOKS FOR THE TRAIL

- Trailblazer's *Moroccan Atlas – the Trekking Guide* by Alan Palmer. An indispensable guide for serious trekkers to the High Atlas, Jebel Saghro and M'Goun Massif.
- *Great Atlas Traverse* by Michael Peyron. The two-volume work by the Morocco-based British writer is the definitive text for the great traverse, but it is quite old, and the level of detail will be less useful for the casual trekker.
- *The Atlas Mountains: A Walking and Trekking Guide* by Karl Smith. Published by the walking specialist Cicerone, this book has route descriptions and information on subjects such as ski-touring, although it gets mixed reviews.
- *Mountaineering in the Moroccan High Atlas* by Des Clark. Also published by Cicerone, this guide – subtitled 'walks, climbs and scrambles over 3000m' – covers some 50 routes and 30 peaks in handy pocket-sized, plastic-covered form, with plenty of maps, photos and practical information.
- *The Mountains Look on Marrakech* is Hamish Brown's atmospheric narrative account of a 96-day trek across the mountains.

Responsible Trekking

Morocco is being developed as a walking destination, but many regions are still remote – and susceptible to the cultural and environmental impact of tourism. Many travellers return home warmed and heartened by Amazigh hospitality, but as visitor numbers increase so too does the pressure on locals. In response, travellers should adopt an appropriate code of behaviour.

Erosion

Hillsides and mountain slopes, especially at high altitudes, are prone to erosion. Stick to existing tracks and avoid short cuts that bypass a switchback. If you blaze

Jebel Siroua (p416)

a new trail straight down a slope, it will turn into a watercourse with the next heavy rainfall, eventually causing soil loss and deep scarring.

First-Aid Courses

Those heading to very remote areas may like to do a first-aid course, such as those offered by the American Red Cross and St John's Ambulance. Particularly if you're going trekking, you could take a wilderness medical training course, such as that offered by the Royal Geographical Society (www.rgs.org).

Human Waste Disposal

It's important to avoid contamination of water sources. Where there is a toilet, use it; where there is none, bury your waste. Dig a small hole 15cm deep and at least 60m from any watercourse – an important point to remember, given how many trekking routes follow rivers and streams. Consider carrying a lightweight trowel: in the arid Atlas Mountains, digging without one can be difficult. In snow, dig down to the soil; otherwise, your waste will be exposed when the snow melts.

Use toilet paper sparingly; burn it when possible or carry it out. Cover the waste with soil and a rock.

Local Hospitality

Invitations for tea and offers of food are common in the mountains. By taking a guide who may have friends in many villages, you'll open yourself up to even more offers of genuine hospitality.

While these offers are unconditional, it is worth bearing in mind that the mountain economy is one of basic subsistence farming. No one has large supplies, and in outlying villages there may be no surplus food. Offering your hosts some tea or sugar (preferably in cones) is a welcome gesture. Dried fruits are also appreciated, as is a taste of any imported food you may have.

For this reason, it is important to be generous when buying provisions for yourself and guides.

Low-Impact Cooking

Don't depend on open fires for cooking: cutting wood for fires has caused widespread deforestation in Morocco. Ideally, cook on a

Ameln Valley (p412)

lightweight multifuel or kerosene stove and avoid those powered by disposable butane gas canisters. If you do make a fire, ensure it is fully extinguished after use.

Medicine

In remote areas, people along the way will often ask for medicine, from disinfectant and bandages to painkillers or cream for dry skin (which many children have). It's hard to recommend this to travellers with no background in medical assessment, but if plaintive requests convince you to do so, always make sure the guide explains what to do with what you offer – how often to take it and so on.

Rubbish

Carry out all your rubbish; never bury it or burn it (Western-style packaging never burns well) or allow your guide to hurl it over a cliff.

Don't rely on bought water in plastic bottles when filtering options are available, as disposal of these bottles is creating a major problem in Morocco. Instead, purify locally sourced water.

Washing

Don't use detergents or toothpaste in or near watercourses, even if they are biodegradable. For personal washing, use biodegradable soap and wash at least 50m away from any watercourse. Disperse the waste water widely to allow the soil to filter it fully before it makes its way back to the watercourse. Use a scourer, sand or snow to wash cooking utensils rather than detergent.

Words to Trek By

Even just a few words in the local Tamazight (Berber) language can make a big difference to your experience. The following terms will be helpful when trekking. Note that some Amazigh terms are borrowed from Moroccan Arabic and understood by both linguistic groups.

adfel – snow

adrar – mountain (plural *idraren;* also *jebel*)

afella – summit

agdal – pasture (also *almu*)

aghbalu – water spring

aman – water

anzar – rain

aryaz– man

asserdoun – mule

assif – watercourse, river valley

azaghar – plateau (also *izwghar*)

azib – seasonal shelter for shepherds

chaba – ravine

iferd – lake (also *tamda*)

ifri – cave (plural *ifran*)

kerkour – cairn

taddart – house

talat – dried-up ravine or watercourse

tigm – house

tizi – mountain pass

Plan Your Trip
Family Travel

A storybook echo of mischievous jinns and legendary warriors permeates the medinas and kasbahs of Morocco, its desert dunes and opulent palace gardens – this North African country has plenty to capture a child's imagination. Child-adoring locals and a range of excellent hotel options add to the appeal for families.

Keeping Costs Down

Accommodation

Many hotels will not charge for children under two years of age. Some, but not all, hotels can provide cots, so enquire before booking or bring your own. For children between two and 12 years sharing a room with their parents, it's often at least 50% off the adult rate.

Eating

Portions are huge, and it's rare for restaurants to have kids menus. Count on ordering one or two dishes for the entire family to share, and start slowly with picky eaters on the diverse array of spices and sauces in traditional Moroccan dishes.

Transport

Travellers with children can buy discount cards for rail travel. Grands taxis can be a real squeeze with young children who have to sit on your lap, though this does save travel funds. Hiring a vehicle is well worth the extra expense if you want to really explore, but you are often better off hiring through your hotel, which can often book a car with driver, seatbelts and air-con for barely more money than a regular taxi (and far less hassle).

Children Will Love...

Active Adventures

Inside Morocco Travel (☎0524430020; www.insidemoroccotravel.com; 4th fl, 29 Rue de Yougoslavie, Marrakesh; ⏲8.30am-6pm) Family-friendly trips to find waterfalls and fragrant forests on accessible trails through the High Atlas (from Marrakesh) or Middle Atlas (from Fez or Meknes).

AXS (☎0524400207; www.argansports.com; Rue Fatima Al Fihria, Sidi Youssef Ben Ali, Marrakesh; half-day city tours from Dh350, bike hire per 24hr from Dh200; 👪) Cycling adventures exploring back roads and mountain life on a family-friendly biking trip into the High Atlas Mountains.

Merzouga (p176) Organise trips into the Sahara desert, starting with a half-day camel ride into the dunes and then a night around the campfire with music and sleeping under the stars.

Taghazout (p397) Surf's up! April to October is the best time for kids as the swells are smaller and the water is warmer.

Terres d'Amanar (☎0661926529; www.terresdamanar.com; Douar Akli, Tahanaoute; activities from Dh100; 👪), Ziplines, obstacles courses and horse rides cater to families looking for a little adventure outside of Marrakesh.

Outdoor Entertainment

Oualidia (p228) The lagoon has safe, calm waters and a wide, sandy beach.

Parque Marítimo del Mediterráneo (☎0956517491; www.parquemaritimo.es; Avenida Compañía del Mar, Ceuta; adult €1-6, child free-€4.50; ⏲11am-8.30pm & 9.30pm-1.30am Tue,

Wed & Sun, to 2.30am Fri & Sat Jun-Sep;) Children enjoy this creative maritime park with pools surrounded by restaurants and cafes.

Ouasiria (0524380438; www.oasiria.com; Km 4, Route d'Amizmiz, Marrakesh; adult/child Dh250/150; 10am-6pm;), A large modern water park with shuttle transfers from central Marrakesh – perfect for summer cool-downs.

Agadir (p386) Morocco's premiere coastal resort is home to all-inclusive resorts, but also clean waters, a beach promenade and perfect sands for castle building.

Anima Garden (0524482022; www.anima-garden.com; Douar Sbiti, Ourika Valley; adult/child Dh120/60; 9am-6pm), Striking sculptures will delight kids at this park in the foothills of the High Atlas Mountains.

Culture & Education

Creative Interactions (0524421687; www.creative-interactions.com; Apt 47, Immeuble El Khalil Bldg, Ave des Nations Unies; 2hr private/2-3 people €40/36 per person, 3½hr €65/59) Family-friendly Marrakesh Explorer medina tours, henna workshops and short intros to Moroccan Arabic and local culture.

Atlas Film Corporation Studios (0524882212, 0524882223; Ouarzazate; Dh80; 8.30am-7.30pm), Hands-on exploration of sets and props from famous films made in the area.

Volubilis (adult/child Dh70/30; 8.30am-sunset) Trace the Roman history of North Africa at this ancient city in the Middle Atlas where kids will love scrambling across ruins punctuated by lonesome columns.

Cafe Clock (0535637855; www.cafeclock.com; Derb El Magana, Talaa Kebira, Fez; mains Dh60-85; 9am-11pm;) Bite-sized 6pm concerts on Sundays, covering everything from Amazigh trilling to gnaoua drumming; perfect for kids to enjoy over an early dinner. There are additional branches in **Marrakesh** (0524378367; www.cafeclock.com; 224 Derb Chtouka; mains Dh60-90; 9am-11pm;) and **Chefchaouen** (0539988788; www.cafeclock.com; 3 Derb Tijani; mains from Dh70; 9am-11pm;) .

Region by Region

Marrakesh

Marrakesh has the country's best range of family-friendly hotels, including semirural options with pools on the city outskirts; dazzling souqs, kid-friendly restaurants, *calèche* (horse-drawn carriage) rides and the nightly circus action on Djemaa El Fna. While occasionally overwhelming, the constant stimulation of the Red City means families never need find themselves lacking for entertainment.

Central Morocco

Tour Ouarzazate's film studios and kasbah, then head to the desert for dunes and dromedary rides. Sleeping in an Amazigh tent amid the towering sand dunes of the Sahara is a quintessential Morocco experience for families.

In the High Atlas mountains snow-covered peaks, waterfalls, cooler summer days and family-friendly kasbah accommodation options are all within a couple of hours of Marrakesh's international airport. Active families may enjoy the variety of day-hikes available from Imlil or Aït Bougmez; for a more laid-back holiday, Ouirgane and the Ourika Valley.

Atlantic Coast

The Atlantic Coast offers plenty of beaches, water and wind sports. Agadir's long, sandy beach is popular; mix it with somewhere more colourful such as relaxed Essaouira, with its fun-to-explore ramparts and medina. Add to that freshly-caught seafood and a rich history ranging from Phonecian to Portugese, and there's plenty to recommend the area.

Mediterranean Coast & the Rif

The pastel blue medina of Chefchaouen is equally enchanting for visitors young and old, while rarely explored national parks at Al Hoceima and Talassemtane provide an opportunity to get up close and personal with local birdlife and Barbary apes.

Fez, Meknes & the Middle Atlas

The Imperial Cities of Fez and Meknes and the Roman ruins of Volubilis all give younger visitors the chance to experience a (literally) hands-on visit to ancient history. The Middle Atlas is home to pleasant hikes in rolling hills compared to the more challenging High Atlas peaks to to south, perfect for families that want to test themselves with more active outdoors holidays.

Southern Morocco & Western Sahara

Southern Morocco's beach towns retain much of the appeal of the rest of the Atlantic coast, with the lower elevations of the Anti Atlas mountains making for a less intense alternative to the steep climbs and long descents of the High Atlas further north.

Less-developed transport links and long bumpy journeys, along with a notable security presence, make Western Sahara one of the least attractive regions of Morocco for young travellers; however, those families looking to experience kitesurfing or with a taste for rugged desert adventure will find the area hard to resist.

Good to Know

Look out for the icon for family-friendly suggestions throughout this guide.

Local attention Locals grow up in large families, so children help break the ice and encourage contact with Moroccans. Moroccans love children so much that you may want to bring a backpack to carry smaller kids, in case they grow tired of the kissing, hugging, gifts and general adulation.

Breastfeeding Feeding in public is acceptable in Morocco, though mothers are expected to cover with a shawl or similar.

Shopping Families will struggle to find Western baby products in the medinas of Moroccan cities, but the villes nouvelles (new towns) are usually a safe bet to pick up supplies – particularly the big Carrefour supermarkets.

Animal encounters Encourage children to avoid dogs and other mammals because of the risk of rabies and other diseases – although there isn't likely to be a risk on camel rides in the desert or with donkeys and mules working in places like Fez medina.

Useful Resources

Lonely Planet Kids (lonelyplanetkids.com) Loads of activities and great family travel blog content.

Maroc Mama (marocmama.com) Expat mother Amanda's take on the country based on 15 years of living and raising children in Morocco.

Wild Junket (wildjunket.com) A mum making her way to every country in the world – featuring a detailed 'Morocco with Kids' guide.

Kids' Corner

Say What?

Hello	Assalaamu alaykum
Goodbye	Bsslaama/ Ma'a ssalaam
Thank you	Shukran
My name is ...	Smeetee ...

Did You Know?

- Moroccan goats climb argan trees to eat the fruit.
- Many Moroccans don't have baths at home – they go to hammams instead.

Have You Tried?

Bastilla
Pigeon, lemon, eggs, onions and almonds baked in a pie.

Regions at a Glance

Marrakesh

Shopping
History
Food

Souqs & Boutiques

Marrakesh can satisfy even the most ardent shopaholic, from its warren of souqs to chic boutiques. Homegrown and expat designers are giving traditional crafts a contemporary twist.

Palaces

Marrakesh's rulers have left their mark on this most lavish of imperial cities. Explore the grand ruins of Badia Palace.

Dining Out

Marrakesh might be the best place in Morocco to eat out. There's the fantastic street food on Djemaa El Fna, lavish riad dining and international cuisine. Wash it all down with a glass of local wine.

p67

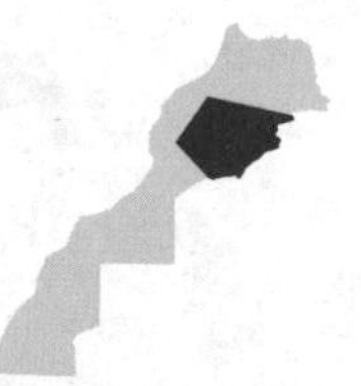

Central Morocco

Adventure
Architecture
Landscapes

High Atlas Trekking

The High Atlas mountains are a destination tailor-made for trekking. Hike for an afternoon or a week, or tackle Mt Toubkal, North Africa's highest peak.

Kasbahs & Ksour

Central Morocco is known for the kasbahs that dot the Draa Valley. Nkob is home to 45 of them, and both crumbling and restored *ksour* (fortified villages) line the road from Rissani to Zagora.

Desert Exploration

The days of the great caravans to Timbuktu are done, but you can still saddle up your camel and trek into the great sand sea of the Sahara and sleep under the stars in a traditional Imazighen (Berber)-style encampment.

p113

Northern Atlantic Coast

Beaches
Architecture
Outdoors

Sand & Surfing

This encompasses Paradise Beach and Sidi Kaouki, a top surfing and windsurfing spot. Laid-back Oualidia has a sand-fringed lagoon while Moulay Bousselham has a gorgeous stretch of golden sand.

Moorish Architecture

Gems include Essaouira, a fortified town with wave-lashed ramparts. Art deco meets neo-Moorish in Casablanca, and Rabat has a stunning kasbah.

Birdwatching

Beaches and coastal wetlands offer excellent birdwatching, particularly around Moulay Bousselham, where the protected Merja Zerga (Blue Lagoon) attracts thousands of birds, from plovers to pink flamingos.

p183

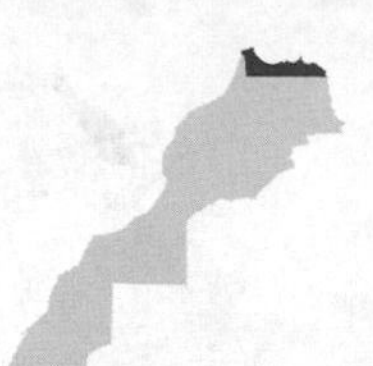

Mediterranean Coast & the Rif Mountains

Coast
Nature
Mountains

Beaches

From beaches near Tangier – such as Plage Robinson – the Mediterranean coast ripples east. Top beaches are found in M'Diq, Cala Iris, Al Hoceima and Saidia, all undiscovered in comparison with Europe's Mediterranean beaches.

National Parks

Two national parks offer the best of the region. Talassemtane encompasses green mountains, tiny villages and the God's Bridge rock formation. Al Hoceima's great mesas, dry canyons and thuja forests lead to limestone sea cliffs.

Trekking in the Rif Mountains

Hiking through the Rif Mountains in Talassemtane National Park is superb, and the park is largely uncharted compared with High Atlas routes.

p249

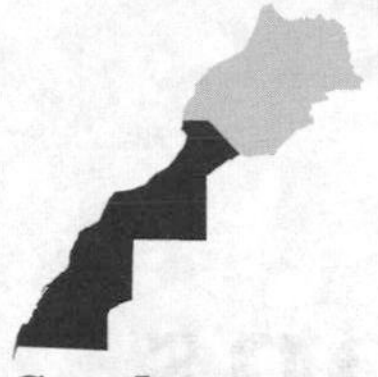

Fez, Meknes & the Middle Atlas

Souqs
History
Food

Handicraft Shopping

Fez is a place to shop pottery collections and leather tanneries while watching pieces being made. Meknes' souqs are devoted to textiles, jewellery, carpets and embroidery.

Minarets & Mosaics

Fez El Bali is the world's largest living medieval medina, its spiritual heart the Kairaouine Mosque. Volubilis was a Roman outpost, with many preserved mosaics, while Moulay Idriss Zerhoun boasts Morocco's only cylindrical minaret.

Fassi Cuisine

Fez's cuisine is Morocco's finest, with sublime *bastilla* (savoury-sweet pies) and pastries. The Middle Atlas is the place to seek out Sefrou cherries and fine Meknes wines.

p319

Southern Morocco & Western Sahara

Remote
Oases
Activities

Coastal Hideaways

Remote seaside escapes offer dilapidated charm. Mirleft is a favourite with its cafes and wild beaches. Art deco Sidi Ifni is as perfectly faded as a sepia photo, and Tan Tan Plage comes with a sweeping beach.

Palmeraies

Beneath ochre cliffs, palms worthy of *One Thousand and One Nights* nestle in the Aït Mansour Gorge and Ameln Valley, refreshing Saharan travellers around Tata and Tighmert.

Sand & Surf

Taghazout is Morocco's premier surf spot while Agadir, Mirleft and Sidi Ifni offer wind- and water sports. Inland, Dahkla is an emerging desert excursion destination.

p385

On the Road

Mediterranean Coast
& the Rif Mountains
p249
Northern
Atlantic
Coast
p183
Fez, Meknes
& the Middle Atlas
p319
Marrakesh
p67
Central
Morocco
p113
Southern Morocco &
Western Sahara
p385

AT A GLANCE

POPULATION
993,400

FOUNDED
1062 CE

BEST DRINK WITH A VIEW
Grand Balcon du Café Glacier (p99)

BEST HAMMAM EXPERIENCE
Le Bain Bleu (p88)

BEST MOROCCAN SWEETS
Patisserie Al Jawda (p95)

WHEN TO GO

Mar–May A great time for medina escapades with temperatures hovering around 30°C.

Jun–Aug Brings scorching heat along with the National Festival of Popular Arts.

Sep–Nov Ideal for souq exploring and sightseeing without sweating profusely.

A souq in the medina (p100)

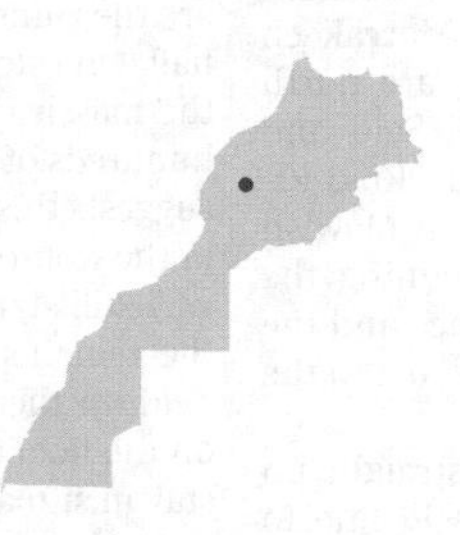

Marrakesh

مراكش

Marrakesh is most people's first taste of Morocco and what an introduction it is. Somewhere between the souq action, the tilework and marble monument overload, and the hundredth time you find yourself lost amid the medina's doodling alleyways, this great city of the Maghreb will work its magic on you. But when you've finally found your way out of the old city, Marrakesh is a jumping-off point to some of Morocco's most stunning landscapes, set against the soaring peaks of the Atlas Mountains.

INCLUDES

Sights

Marrakesh knows how to put on a show. Its heady sights and sounds dazzle, frazzle and enchant, as they have done for almost a millennia.

Most monuments are inside the medina ramparts (a 19km circuit). The medina's main souqs, as well as Musée de Marrakech and Maison de la Photographie, are north of Djemaa El Fna, while Dar Si Said and Bahia Palace are south along Rue Riad Zitoun El Jedid towards the Mellah (Jewish quarter). The Kasbah area, containing the gilded Saadian Tombs, Badia Palace and the royal palace (closed to visitors), is just to the south.

It's a 20- to 25-minute stroll straight up Ave Mohammed V from Djemaa El Fna to the central Gueliz district of the Ville Nouvelle (new town). The main sight in the new town is Jardin Majorelle, but Gueliz is also home to a clutch of art galleries, most significantly MACMA for vintage photography and Comptoir des Mines for contemporary Moroccan art.

The souqs are generally open 10am to 8pm, though many stalls are closed on Friday afternoon.

Djemaa El Fna & Southern Central Medina

Djemaa El Fna and its nightly carnival is the beating heart of the medina. All the action is overlooked by the serene minaret of the Koutoubia Mosque, just a short hop away. There's also a couple of excellent museums to the south, off Rue Riad Zitoun El Jedid.

Djemaa El Fna SQUARE

See p72.

★Koutoubia Mosque MOSQUE

(Map p74; cnr Rue El Koutoubia & Ave Mohammed V; closed to non-Muslims) Five times a day, one voice rises above the Djemaa din as the muezzin calls the faithful to prayer from the Koutoubia Mosque's minaret. The tower is a monumental cheat sheet of Moorish ornament: scalloped keystone arches, jagged merlon The tower is a monumental cheat sheet of Moorish ornament: scalloped keystone arches, jagged merlon crenellations and mathematically pleasing proportions; the square dan Amazigh trademarkcrenellations and mathematically pleasing proportions; the square dan Amazigh trademark. This 12th-century 75m-high tower was the prototype for the Giralda in Seville, Spain. In the 19th century, booksellers clustered around its base – hence the name, from *kutubiyyin* (booksellers).

On the northwestern side of the minaret are the ruins of the mosque's original prayer hall. One story goes that it collapsed during the massive 1755 Lisbon earthquake, killing hundreds of people as it crumbled. Research suggests this could be plausible. To the north of the Koutoubia minaret, the original doorway still stands. On the far wall of the ruins the remains of the arches that would have held up the ceiling are visible. The stumps on the floor are the hall's columns, and they stay in situ as a memorial.

In Arabic, *djemaa* means congregation as well as gathering, and one theory is that the true translation of Djemaa El Fna is not 'assembly of the dead', but 'mosque of the dead', a legacy of the tragic event that occurred here.

Stretching out behind the mosque are the **Koutoubia Gardens** (Map p84; Ave Mohammed V; 8am-8pm), a palm-tree-dotted swathe of greenery which is a favourite Marrakshi spot for strolling and relaxing on park benches.

★Dar Si Said MUSEUM

(Map p84; 0524389564; www.fnm.ma; Derb Si Said, Rue Riad Zitoun El Jedid; adult/child Dh30/15; 10am-6pm Wed-Mon) Si Said, the original owner of this 19th-century medina mansion, a monument to Moroccan *mâalem* (master artisans), was brother to Grand Vizier Bou Ahmed, who lived at Bahia Palace.

It is now home to the well-presented **National Museum of Weaving and Carpets**, which sends visitors on a journey through the history and social significance of the many different forms of Moroccan carpet-making, from rural weavings to urban looms. Architectural highlights include the spectacularly decorated 1st-floor wedding chamber and peaceful riad garden.

Musée Tiskiwin MUSEUM

(Map p84; 0524389192; www.tiskiwin.com; 8 Rue de la Bahia; adult/child Dh30/10; 9.30am-12.30pm & 2.30-6pm) Travel to Timbuktu and back again via Dutch anthropologist Bert Flint's art collection, crammed inside this ornate medina riad. Each room represents a caravan stop

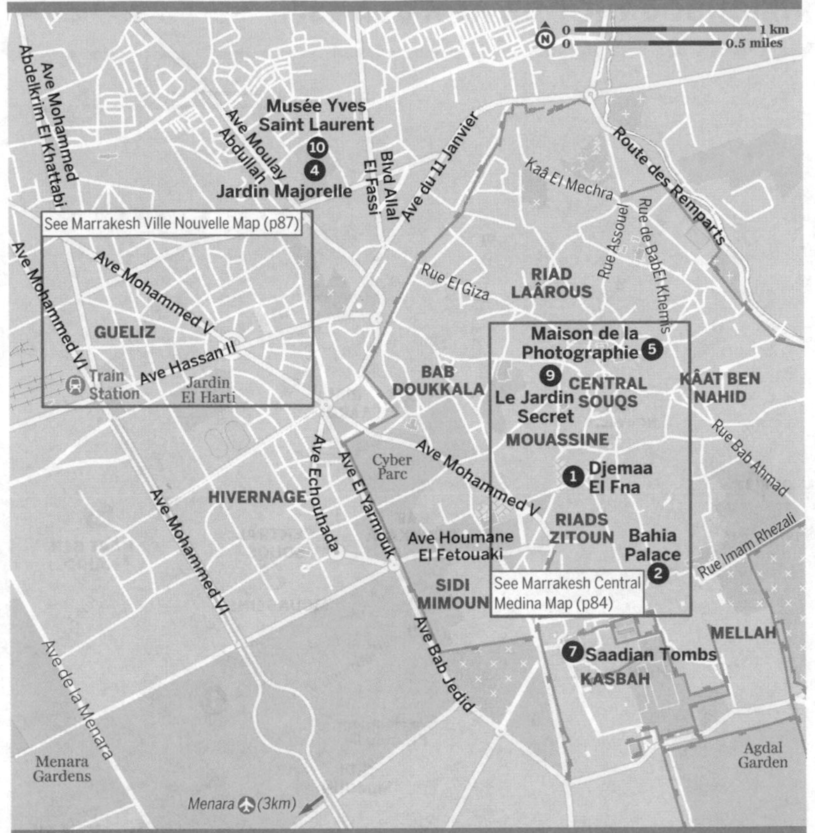

Marrakesh Highlights

❶ **Djemaa El Fna** (p72) Diving into the chaos of snake charmers and brass bands.

❷ **Bahia Palace** (p78) Living like an emperor at the city's most ornate palace.

❸ **Medina Maze** (p80) Wandering aimlessly through the winding alleys of Marrakesh's oldest quarters.

❹ **Jardin Majorelle** (p83) Strolling the psychedelic desert gardens of this once-private artist's vision.

❺ **Maison de la Photographie** (p77) Looking into the past at a curated vision of Morocco.

❻ **Foodie Adventures** (p91) Biting off more than you can chew on a food tour.

❼ **Saadian Tombs** (p82) Gilding the lily at this paean to the Saadian royalty.

❽ **Hammams** (p88) Scrubbing away the dust of travel days and souq wanders.

❾ **Le Jardin Secret** (p75) Escaping the medina chaos in a restored 400-year old riad.

❿ **Musée Yves Saint Laurent** (p79) Worshipping at the temple of a global high-fashion icon.

along the Sahara-to-Marrakesh route, presenting indigenous crafts from Tuareg camel saddles to High Atlas carpets. The museum's displays and explanatory texts are eccentric, but Tiskiwin's well-travelled artefacts offer tantalising glimpses of Marrakesh's trading-post past.

NEIGHBOURHOODS AT A GLANCE

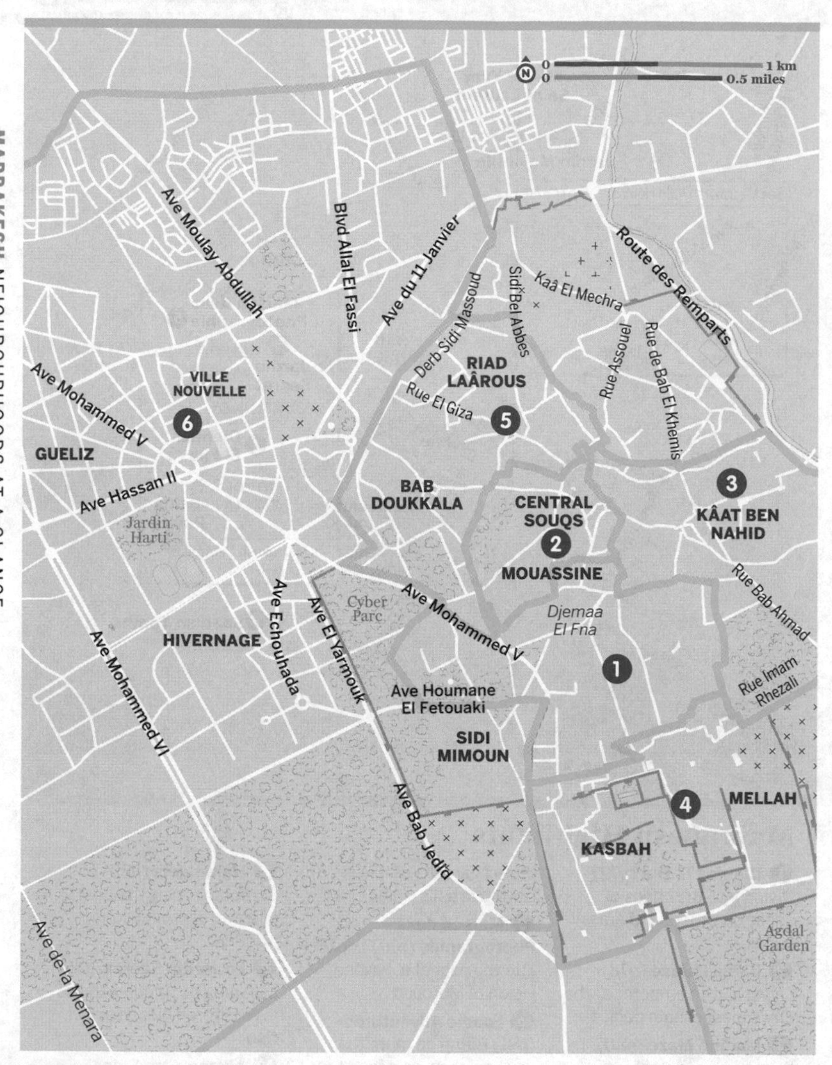

❶ Djemaa El Fna & Southern Central Medina (p68)

If there's one thing you can't miss in Marrakesh it's the reeling, free-wheeling nightly circus that is Djemaa El Fna. This chaotic square is the heart and soul of Marrakesh, where snakes are charmed by day, music troupes shimmy and shake at night and hordes of hungry revellers come to chow down at food stalls. Heading south, the parallel Riad Zitoun roads and surrounding alleyways sway to an entirely different tune, offering welcome respite from the northern souqs.

❷ Mouassine & Central Souqs (p75)

The lanes that spool north from Djemaa El Fna sum up the push and pull between old and new in Marrakesh. This atmospheric area is home to the city's biggest concentration of souqs and *qissariat* (covered markets), where shafts of sunlight strike through palm-frond roofing and hawkers bid you hello in 10 languages. But then you hit Mouassine – a showcase of the medina's changing face, where a fresh breed of boutiques, Mediterranean-inspired rooftop restaurants and lounge-style cafes are making their mark.

❸ Kâat Ben Nahid & Bab Debbagh (p77)

Along with Mouassine, Kâat Ben Nahid is the core of the old medina, with scrawls of close-knit alleyways hiding sumptuous 17th-century riads. On its western edge is the Mnebhi Palace, now the Musée de Marrakech. This is also where you'll find Ali Ben Youssef Medersa (closed at the time of writing for a massive refurb), a clutch of excellent museums and, to the east, one of the medina's poorest districts, home to the malodorous Bab Debbagh tanneries.

❹ Kasbah & Mellah (p82)

When the Almoravids founded Marrakesh in 1062, the Kasbah area was where they set up camp. Kasbahs (fortresses) were erected for the glory and protection of warmongering sultans, and it was here that Morocco's early dynasties were forged and later floundered. Many of Morocco's top historical sites lie in this area of the medina, but tour groups rarely linger, and the atmosphere is a little more mellow than in the northern souqs. Adjoining the Kasbah is the Mellah – the old Jewish quarter, with its quiet alleys, synagogues and whitewashed cemetery.

❺ Bab Doukkala & Riad Laârous (p83)

Bab Doukkala and Riad Laârous are the shrinking violets of the medina: quiet neighbourhoods with few visitor attractions and still enough local residents to outnumber tourists. But therein lies their charm. Bab Doukkala in particular is a wonderful window into authentic Marrakshi life without the tourist trappings. Its name comes from the Doukkala tribe that centuries ago would have used this gate to enter Marrakesh on trade forays.

❻ Gueliz & Ville Nouvelle (p83)

Gueliz is the yang to the medina's yin, and here you'll find broad European-style boulevards with art deco history, designer shopping and French-influenced cafe, restaurant and bar culture. It is the traffic-clogged heart of the Ville Nouvelle, the area to the west of the medina walls where the French put down roots when Morocco became a protectorate in 1912. On its edge is the popular Jardin Majorelle, but don't just come for the gardens: delve a little deeper, and you'll find modern Moroccan life just as authentic as the medina hubbub.

PAVLIHA/GETTY IMAGES©

TOP SIGHT
DJEMAA EL FNA

Roll up, roll up for the greatest show on earth. Everywhere you look in Marrakesh's main square, you'll discover drama in progress. It's been this way for almost a millennia: a hypnotic dance of hoopla, *halqa* (street theatre) and food stalls, set to the tune of gnaoua drums and snake charmers with their racing *pungi* flutes.

History

Djemaa El Fna sprang into life in the 11th century, around the time that the city of Marrakesh was founded by the Almoravids. Historians and locals will argue over whether the square got its name from the fact that public executions were likely held here: one translation is 'assembly of the dead'. Another translation is 'mosque of the dead', which could be a nod to the partial collapse of neighbouring Koutoubia Mosque in the 18th century (p68), burying worshippers inside.

For centuries, the square was used as a giant food market, with traders flooding down from the mountains to set up under canvas tents each day. Early photos of this era can be seen in Maison de la Photographie (p77). The present boundaries of the square were imposed by the French, as all the buildings surrounding the Djemaa were erected during the protectorate era.

Morning Quiet

Stroll Djemaa as it wakes up to catch the plaza at its least frenetic. At this point, the stage is almost empty. Orange-juice

TOP TIPS

- Keep a stock of Dh1 coins on hand. You'll need them for tipping the performers. A few dirhams (a little more if you took photos) is all that's necessary when the hat comes around.
- Stay alert to motorbikes, cars and horse-drawn-carriage traffic before 2pm, as well as pickpockets and rogue gropers.
- Be warned that you will see chained monkeys dressed in football kit paraded for tourists, and the practices of the snake charmers are ethically questionable. We advise avoiding both.

PRACTICALITIES

- Map p84
- off Place de Foucald

vendors are first on the scene, along with the snake charmers and their baskets of cobras. Eager dentists, potion sellers and henna-tattoo artists start setting up makeshift stalls under sunshades.

Night-Time Carnival

Cars are banned from the square after 2pm, and local food stalls start setting up for the nightly dinner scrum around 4pm. At sunset the Djemaa finds its daily mojo as Amazigh (Berber) troupes and gnaoua musicians start tuning up and locals pour into the square. The hullabaloo doesn't knock off for the night until around 1am. To view it from a different perspective, head to one of the rooftop cafes ringing the square.

Dinner at Djemaa

Spicy snail broth, skewered hearts, bubbling tajines, flash-fried fish: the Djemaa food stalls are a heaving one-stop shop for Moroccan culinary specialities, and they're not to be missed. Despite alarmist warnings, your stomach should be fine. Clean your hands before eating, use bread instead of utensils and stick to filtered water.

Stalls have numbered spots and are set up on a grid. The snail chefs are in a line on the eastern side. For fried fish and calamari, pull up a pew at stall 14. Look for a lovely lady called Aicha who runs stall 1 in the southwestern corner for *brochettes* (kebabs), tajines and *harira* (a cheap, hearty soup made of tomatoes, onions, saffron and coriander with lentils and chickpeas).

After dinner, join locals at the row of copper tea urns on the southern edge of the stalls. The speciality here is warming ginger tea called *khoudenjal* with cinnamon, mace and cardamom, served with a dense, sticky and similarly spicy scoop of cake – a pit stop at No 71 Chez Mohammed's is the perfect way to round out your meal.

CULTURAL COLLAPSE

Djemaa El Fna has been a protected urban landmark since 1922 and Unesco-inscribed since 2001 as a place of unique cultural exchange. Yet Unesco has flagged the square as a space under 'serious threat' from urbanisation and cultural assimilation.

For centuries, Djemaa has been a stage for gnaoua dance troupes, whispering fortune tellers, cartwheeling acrobats and, above all, *hikayat* (storytellers). Today, the last of the storytellers have gone and with them many of the square's traditional performers. Djemaa is still the throbbing heart of the medina, but like its inhabitants, it's moved with the times. Live music and local food are its 21st-century trademarks.

TAKE A BREAK

If you feel your energy flagging, head to the terrace of Grand Balcon du Café Glacier (p99) for a mint tea.

For serious munching, follow your nose to Hadj Mustapha (p97), a basic canteen that dishes up some of the best *tanjia* in town.

Marrakesh

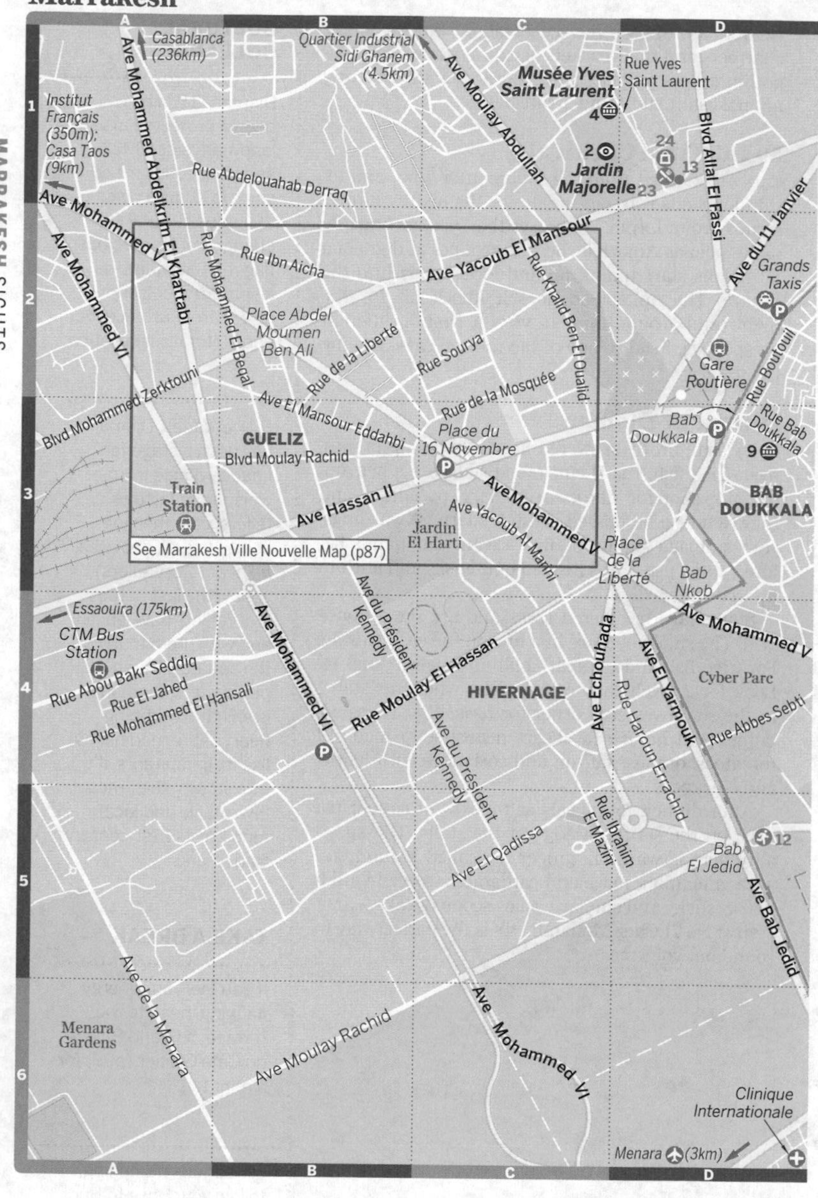

Moroccan Culinary Arts Museum MUSEUM

(Map p84; ☎0524427177; Rue de la Bahia, Riad Zitoun El Jedid; adult/child Dh40/free; ⏰9am-6pm) Claiming to be the first of its kind in Morocco, this large riad museum opened in late 2019 and should be the first stop in Marrakesh for food lovers. Set over three floors, exhibitions are neatly separated into different types of local cuisine, covering everything from soups to pastries and street food. English-language displays bring the history and culture surrounding Morocco's distinguished food heritage to life.

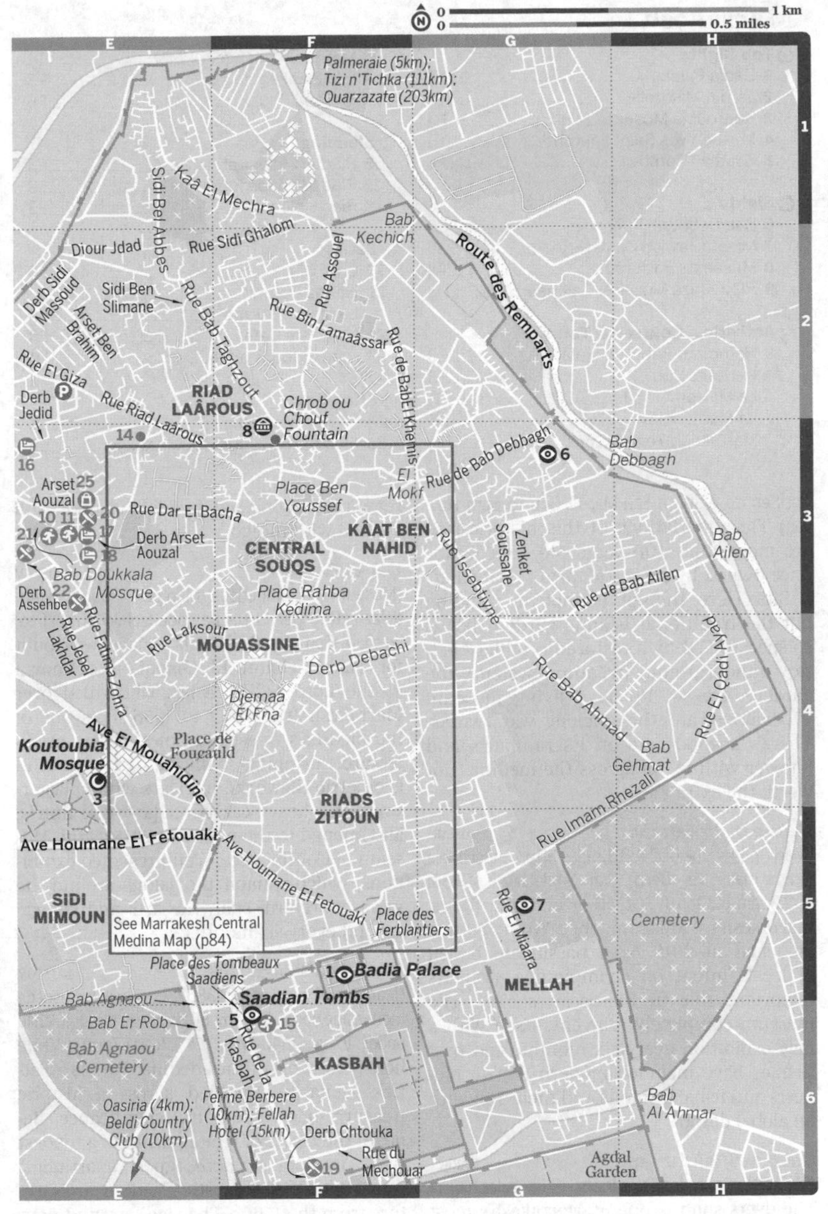

Mouassine & Central Souqs

Mouassine and the central souqs is one of the oldest areas of the medina, and as such, there's a high concentration of museums, *fanadiq* and palaces. You could easily spend a couple of days here, soaking up the history and dipping in and out of attractions between souq shopping.

★Le Jardin Secret MUSEUM
(Map p84; ☎0524390040; www.lejardinsecretmarrakech.com; 121 Rue Mouassine; adult/7-24 yr Dh50/40, tower Dh35/20; ⏲9.30am-7.30pm

Marrakesh

Top Sights
1 Badia Palace ... F5
2 Jardin Majorelle ... C1
3 Koutoubia Mosque ... E4
4 Musée Yves Saint Laurent ... C1
5 Saadian Tombs ... F6

Sights
6 Bab Debbagh Tanneries ... G3
7 Miaara Jewish Cemetery ... G5
8 Musée du Parfum ... F3
9 Riad Kniza Musée & Galerie ... D3

Activities, Courses & Tours
10 Hammam Bab Doukkala ... E3
11 Heritage Spa ... E3
La Maison Arabe ... (see 21)
12 La Mamounia ... D5
Marrakech Yoga Studio ... (see 22)
13 Mountain Voyage ... D1
14 Pikala Bikes ... E3
15 Sultana Spa ... F6

Sleeping
16 Riad Al Massarah ... E3
17 Riad El Youssoufi ... E3
18 Riad Helen ... E3

Eating
19 Cafe Clock ... F6
20 Henna Cafe ... E3
21 La Maison Arabe ... E3
22 Namaste Cafe ... E3
23 Pause Gourmande ... D1

Shopping
24 33 Rue Majorelle ... D1
25 Mustapha Blaoui ... E3

Apr-Sep, to 6.30pm Feb-Mar & Oct, to 6pm Nov-Jan) The foundations of this historic riad are more than 400 years old, and it was once owned by powerful *qaid* (local chief) U-Bihi. Here, though, it's not the building but the traditional Islamic garden that is so special. Fed by a restored original *khettara* (underground irrigation system), the gardens are set up as a living museum to demonstrate the ancient waterworks. There's a good cafe on its ramparts and a tower with views across the medina (not worth the extra fee).

Musée de la Femme MUSEUM
(Map p84; 0524381129; http://museedelafemme.ma; 19 Derb Sidi Abdelaziz; Dh30; 9.30am-6.30pm) Spread over three floors, Marrakesh's Museum of Women was launched in 2018 by a passionate bunch of locals intent on championing women's important role in Moroccan society. The museum completely reinvents itself with a new exhibition every six months, and past themes have included modern female pioneers and tribal fashions and their influence on global design.

Souq des Teinturiers MARKET
(Map p84; Souq des Teinturiers; irregular hours) The dyers souq is one of Marrakesh's most colourful markets, with skeins of coloured wool draped from the rafters above stalls. However, very little remains of its original purpose. Seek out shop number 19 (there's a sign above the doorway, but it may be partially obscured), which has the souq's only remaining dying vat inside the door, still stained with indigo.

Dar El Bacha MUSEUM
(Museum of Confluences; Map p84; Route Sidi Abdelaziz, Rue Dar El Bacha; adult/child Dh60/free; 10am-6pm Tue-Sun) This palace was built for Pacha Thami El Glaoui, also known as the Lord of the Atlas, who ruled over Marrakesh from 1912 to 1956. It is one of the medina's finest examples of riad architecture, dripping with *zellige* (colourful geometric tilework), intricate white plasterwork and heavy carved cedar-wood lintels, and opened to the public in 2015 as the Museum of Confluences. Well-presented exhibitions, which inhabit the salons around the main courtyard, span the arts and change around every six months.

Musée de Mouassine MUSEUM
(Map p84; 0524385721; www.museedemouassine.com; 5 Derb El Hammam; adult/child under 15 yr Dh40/free; 9.30am-7pm) While house-hunting in the medina, Parisian Patrick Menac'h stumbled across a historic treasure of great cultural significance. Beneath the layers of white plaster of a modest riad's 1st-floor *douiria* (guest apartment) was a jewel of domestic Saadian architecture from the 1560s. The riad's ground-floor rooms hold a small collection of Amazigh artefacts and temporary photography exhibitions, but the painstakingly restored interior of the upstairs salons are the true star of this charming museum. There's also a small rooftop cafe.

Kâat Ben Nahid & Bab Debbagh

Plenty of Marrakesh's big-hitting sights are scattered through the dense quarter of Kâat Ben Nahid. Skip the tanneries if you don't have a strong stomach for persistent touts and hassle (or hire a guide). There's enough to keep visitors busy for at least a day – and a busy one, at that.

★Maison de la Photographie MUSEUM
(Map p84; ☎0524385721; www.maisondelaphotographie.ma; 46 Rue Souq El Fassi; adult/child Dh50/free; ⏲9.30am-7pm) When Parisian Patrick Menac'h and Marrakshi Hamid Mergani realised they were both collecting vintage Moroccan photography, they decided to open a photography museum to show their collections in context. Together they 'repatriated' 4500 photos, 2000 glass negatives and 80 documents dating from 1870 to 1950; select works on view here fill three floors, organised by region and theme, and include a rare, full-colour 1957 documentary shot in Morocco. Most works are editioned prints from original negatives, and are for sale.

After your visit, head up to the rooftop terrace for a coffee or pot of tea. If you're heading to Ourika Valley, be sure to check out their second venture, the Ecomusée Berbere (p127).

★Musée de Marrakech MUSEUM
(Map p84; ☎0524441893; www.museedemarrakech.ma; Place Ben Youssef; adult/child Dh50/30; ⏲9am-7pm, to 6pm Oct-Mar) The Musée de Marrakech exhibits a collection of Moroccan art forms within the decadent salons of the Mnebhi Palace. The central internal courtyard, with its riot of cedar archways, stained-glass windows, intricate painted door panels and, of course, lashings of *zellige*, is the highlight, though don't miss the display of exquisite Fez ceramics in the main room off the courtyard, and the palace's hammam. This is one of Marrakesh's oldest museums and looks dated compared with some others.

Orientalist Museum MUSEUM
(Map p84; https://theorientalistmuseumofmarrakech.business.site; 5 Derb El Khamsi; adult/child under 12 Dh50/free; ⏲10am-7pm) Opened in 2019 as a sister museum to MACMA (p86) in Gueliz, this small private gallery beautifully displays the big guns of Orientalist painting inside a 17th-century riad. The impressive collection of 19th- and 20th-century European artists who fell for Morocco's landscapes and peoples include Henri Le Riche, Edy Legrand and, of course, Jacques Majorelle – he of garden fame. There's even a Salvador Dalí in here. Complete your tour with a coffee in the tranquil rooftop cafe.

MARRAKESH'S FANADIQ

Fanadiq (inns once used by caravans – the singular is *funduq*) once dotted the important stopover towns on Morocco's caravan routes. Since medieval times, these creative courtyard complexes provided ground-floor stables and workshops, and rented rooms for desert traders and travelling merchants upstairs. From this flux of artisans and adventurers emerged the inventive culture of modern-day Marrakesh. As trading communities became more stable and affluent, though, most *fanadiq* were gradually replaced with private homes and storehouses.

Only 140 *fanadiq* remain in the medina, many of them now converted into artisan complexes. Most retain shreds of fine original woodcarving, romantic balconies and even some stucco work, and there has been a recent drive to restore them, part of a citywide push to upgrade historic sites. The best to poke your head into, to admire their well-travelled, shop-worn glory, are found on **Rue Dar El Bacha** and **Rue Mouassine**.

Well-preserved **Funduq El Amri** (Map p84; Rue Dar El Bacha) would have once been the staging post for medieval merchants selling sugar and tea.

Slightly decrepit **Funduq El Ouarzazi** (Map p84; Place Bab Fteuh; ⏲10am-7pm) is a dream come true for shoppers who enjoy poking about in pursuit of treasure.

Funduq El Mizen (Map p84; Rue Dar El Bacha) *Mizen* means balance in Arabic, and this is where traders would have come to weigh goods for sale. Today it houses artisan workshops.

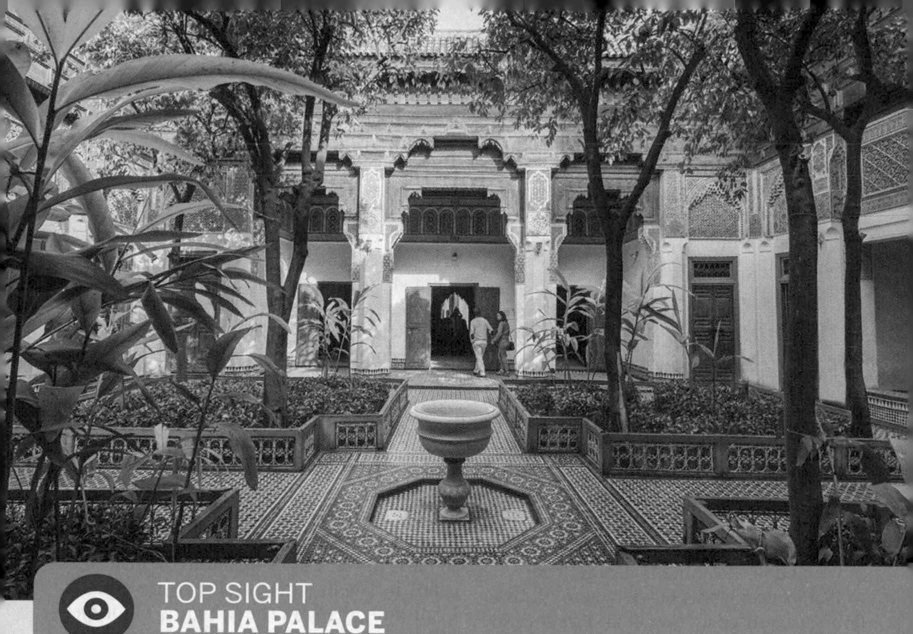

TOP SIGHT
BAHIA PALACE

Imagine the pomp and splendour you'd dream up with Morocco's top artisans at your beck and call, and here you have it. La Bahia (The Beautiful) is an 8000-sq-metre floor-to-ceiling extravagance of intricate marquetry, plasterwork and *zouak* (painted wood), begun by Grand Vizier Si Moussa in the 1860s but expanded by his son and successor Abu 'Bou' Ahmed.

Petit Riad

Closest to the entrance, the single-storey Petit Riad is similar in layout and size to traditional houses of the medina, but it's notable for the ornamentation of its salons. Its walls of intensely elaborate white plasterwork are inscribed with verses from the Quran.

Cour d'Honneur

Sandwiched between the Petit Riad and the Grand Riad, you'll pass through two courtyards. The first is relatively plain, but the second, called the Grand Cour or Cour d'Honneur, is the undisputed heart of the palace and one of the most spectacular open spaces ever to be conceived in Morocco. It is 1500 sq m in size and was restored to its original brilliance in 2018.

Grand Riad

Step through the doorway from the Cour d'Honneur into the large courtyard of the Grand Riad, studded with fountains and lush foliage and sound-tracked by birdsong. This is the oldest part of the complex, completed in 1867.

TOP TIPS

- Tour groups descend throughout the day, so come for opening or later afternoon if you can.
- Leave plenty of time to admire the site, so that you can pause and wait for passing groups to dissipate – large tours can overrun whole rooms.
- The palm-shaded entry garden is a great place to stop for a minute and get your map bearings before heading back onto the street.

PRACTICALITIES

- Map p84
- ☎ 0524389564
- Rue Riad Zitoun El Jedid
- adult/child Dh70/30
- 🕒 9am-5pm

DAN GLASSER ©

TOP SIGHT
MUSÉE YVES SAINT LAURENT

Yves Saint Laurent's love affair with Marrakesh began in 1966 – by the end of his first visit, he'd acquired the deeds to a house in the medina. The Algerian-born French fashion designer (1936–2008) was fascinated by the artistry and palette of Morocco. In 2017 this museum opened as a homage to his work and the inspiration he drew from his second home.

Daring Architecture

The museum was designed by Studio KO and was the brainchild of Yves Saint Laurent's partner Pierre Bergé (1930–2017), who wanted a space that was 'profoundly Moroccan'. To this end, the building was designed without external-facing windows, to emulate this traditional feature of Marrakesh's riads. The terracotta colour of the exterior brickwork mirrors the dominant hue of Morocco's 'Red City'.

Main Exhibition

The core of the museum is a permanent display of his sketches, rotating haute-couture fashions and colour-themed accessories. The backdrop is entirely black – a key colour in YSL's designs – creating a cavernous cocoon pierced only by audiovisuals of the designer's catwalk shows and recordings of him speaking. On the right as you enter, the exhibition starts with a biography of Yves Saint Laurent, including a letter sent by YSL to French Vogue's editor-in-chief Michel de Brunhoff in June 1954 at the age of 17. Top-quality temporary exhibitions, which change two or three times a year, are held in a smaller adjacent room.

TOP TIPS

➡ Combined tickets covering Jardin Majorelle, Musée Berbère and Musée Yves Saint Laurent can be bought directly from the Musée Yves Saint Laurent ticket counter, avoiding lengthy queuing time at Jardin Majorelle (note that you must start your visit at Musée Yves Saint Laurent if you buy your ticket here).

➡ Tickets can be bought online.

PRACTICALITIES

➡ Map p74

➡ ☎ 0524298686

➡ www.museeysl marrakech.com

➡ Rue Yves Saint Laurent

➡ Dh100

➡ ⏲ 10am-6pm Thu-Tue

Marrakesh Medina

A HALF-DAY TOUR OF THE MEDINA

To discover the medina's hidden treasures, begin this leisurely stroll at ❶ **Dar Si Said**, a model of restrained 19th-century elegance now home to the National Museum of Weaving and Carpets. Next, head north up Rue Riad Zitoun El Jedid and emerge into ❷ **Djemaa El Fna**, from where you can see the iconic minaret of ❸ **Koutoubia Mosque**. Cross the plaza to Place Bab Fteuh in the northwest corner. On your right is **Bab Fteuh Funduq**, where artisans create jewellery and trays.

Follow Rue El Mouassine north past the Mouassine mosque and duck down a small *derb* (alleyway) beside the monumental ❹ **Mouassine Fountain** to marvel at the 16th-century splendour of ❺ **Musée de Mouassine**, with its finely restored Saadian-era *douiria* (guest apartment) and interesting cultural exhibits in the downstairs salons. Emerge dazzled into the sun and continue north.

At the next arched junction, head left along Rue Dar El Bacha and you'll spot grand courtyard *fanadiq* (inns once used by caravans), such as ❻ **Funduq El Amri** and **Funduq El Mizen**. Some date back to the 16th century, and most are populated by artisan workshops. Retrace your steps to the junction and head north for lunch in the tranquil shaded courtyard of ❼ **Le Jardin**.

Refuelled, turn right out of Le Jardin and right again after the small arch onto Rue Amesfah, which takes you eastwards past the Ben Youssef Mosque, Ali Ben Youssef Medersa and onwards into Kâat Ben Nahid. Follow signs to the ❽ **Orientalist Museum**, where a 17th-century riad houses works by the masters of Orientalist art. Finish the tour amid vintage photographs of the medina and a spectacular sunset view from the rooftop of ❾ **Maison de la Photographie**.

Fanadiq
These medieval caravanserai once provided lodging and stabling for desert traders visiting the souqs. Of the 140 remaining in the medina, many have now been converted into artisan workshops and are being restored.

Mouassine Fountain
Built in the mid-16th century by Abdallah El Ghalib, the Mouassine Fountain is one of 80 original medina fountains. Its installation was a pious act, providing water for people and animals.

Djemaa El Fna
The beating heart of the medina for almost a millennia, Djemaa El Fna is still a hypnotic dance of hoopla, *halqa* (street theatre) and fire-fuelled food stalls, set to the tune of gnaoua drums that compete with the whine of snake charmers' flutes.

Koutoubia Minaret
This 12th-century, 73m-high tower is the architectural prototype for Seville's La Giralda, and it's a monumental cheat sheet of Moorish ornamentation: scalloped keystone arches, jagged merlons and mathematically pleasing proportions.

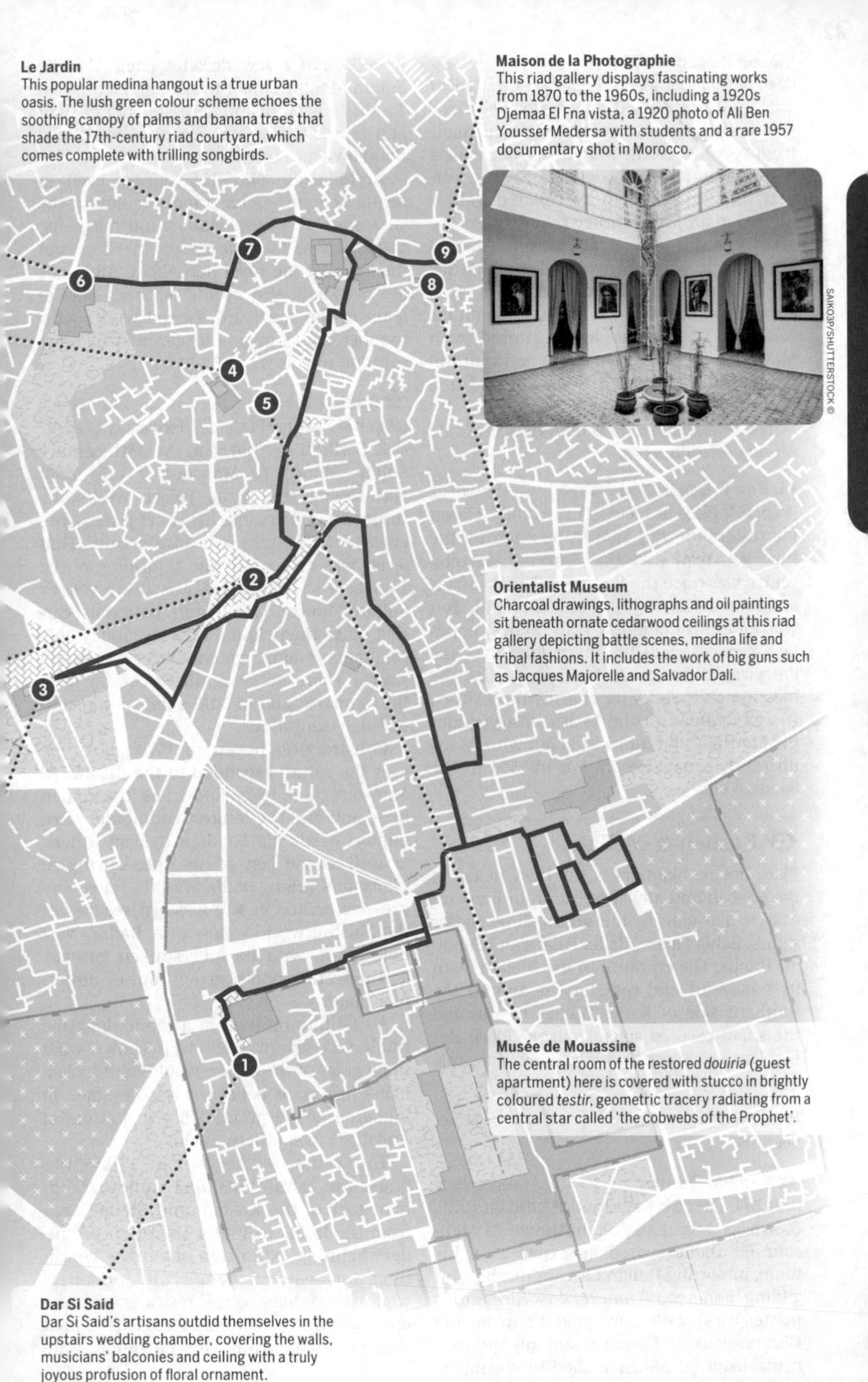
Le Jardin
This popular medina hangout is a true urban oasis. The lush green colour scheme echoes the soothing canopy of palms and banana trees that shade the 17th-century riad courtyard, which comes complete with trilling songbirds.
Maison de la Photographie
This riad gallery displays fascinating works from 1870 to the 1960s, including a 1920s Djemaa El Fna vista, a 1920 photo of Ali Ben Youssef Medersa with students and a rare 1957 documentary shot in Morocco.
SAIKO3P/SHUTTERSTOCK ©
Orientalist Museum
Charcoal drawings, lithographs and oil paintings sit beneath ornate cedarwood ceilings at this riad gallery depicting battle scenes, medina life and tribal fashions. It includes the work of big guns such as Jacques Majorelle and Salvador Dalí.
Musée de Mouassine
The central room of the restored douiria (guest apartment) here is covered with stucco in brightly coloured testir, geometric tracery radiating from a central star called 'the cobwebs of the Prophet'.
Dar Si Said
Dar Si Said's artisans outdid themselves in the upstairs wedding chamber, covering the walls, musicians' balconies and ceiling with a truly joyous profusion of floral ornament.
1
2
3
4
5
6
7
8
9

Musée Boucharouite MUSEUM

(Map p84; ☎0524383887; Derb El Cadi; adult/child Dh40/free; ⏰9.30am-6pm Mon-Sat, closed Aug) Berber *boucharouites* (rag rugs made from recycled cloth) may be a poor cousin to the famous jewel-toned Moroccan carpets, but this beautifully collated gallery housed in an 18th-century riad displays the artistry of this lesser-known craft. The museum is the work of avid collector Patrick de Maillard, who lives on site and is often around to animatedly talk you through his collection.The rooms are scattered with Moroccan popular art, from agricultural implements to painted doors, in addition to the *boucharouites*.

The terrace upstairs is a lovely secret cafe serving refreshments.

Ali Ben Youssef Medersa ISLAMIC SITE

(Map p84; Place Ben Youssef) Currently closed for restoration but should be open by the time you read this, this Quranic learning centre was once the largest in North Africa and remains among the most splendid. 'You who enter my door, may your highest hopes be exceeded' reads the inscription over the entryway, and after almost six centuries, the blessing still works its charms on visitors. It was founded in the 14th century under the Merinids, but fully kitted out with its exuberantly ornate decoration in 1565 in the Saadian era.

Kasbah & Mellah

Place des Ferblantiers is the busy nexus of the Kasbah and Mellah area. From here, it's easy to navigate to the area's three major sights: Bahia Palace, Badia Palace and Saadian Tombs. The entrance to the Mellah, with its synagogue and cemetery, is around the southern side of Bahia Palace, or through the small covered spice souq off Place des Ferblantiers. There's loads to see in this area, so plan to spend a day here.

Bahia Palace PALACE

See p78.

★ **Saadian Tombs** HISTORIC SITE

(Map p74; Rue de la Kasbah; adult/child Dh70/30; ⏰9am-5pm) Saadian Sultan Ahmed Al Mansour Ed Dahbi spared no expense on his tomb, importing Italian Carrara marble and gilding honeycomb *muqarnas* (decorative plasterwork) with pure gold to make the **Chamber of 12 Pillars** a suitably glorious mausoleum. Al Mansour died in splendour in 1603, but a few decades later, Alaouite Sultan Moulay Ismail walled up the Saadian Tombs to keep his predecessors out of sight and mind. It was the French who opened them up again in 1917.

Al Mansour played favourites even in death, keeping alpha princes handy in the **Chamber of Three Niches** and relegating to garden plots some 170 chancellors and members of the royal household. All tombs are overshadowed by his mother's mausoleum in the courtyard, carved with poetic, weathered blessings and guarded by stray cats and tortoises.

★ **Badia Palace** HISTORIC SITE

(Map p74; behind Place des Ferblantiers; adult/child Dh70/30; ⏰9am-5pm) As 16th-century Sultan Ahmed Al Mansour (r 1578-1603) was paving the Badia Palace with gold, turquoise and crystal, his court jester wisecracked, 'It'll make a beautiful ruin.' That jester was no fool: at the beginning of the 18th century, the place was destroyed by Sultan Moulay Ismail and materials carried off to then-capital Meknes. Today only remnants remain, watched over by nesting storks. There are magnificent views from the ramparts, and in 2018 a renovation added some exhibitions.

Construction began in 1578, the same year the sultan ascended to the throne. Al Mansour came to be known as 'the golden king' and was the longest-ruling and most famous of all the Saadian dynasty rulers, as well as the last of his line. During Al Mansour's reign, Badia was the most impressive palace in the western reaches of the Muslim world – now only Badia's vast **courtyard**, with its four sunken gardens and reflecting pools, give a hint of its former majesty.

A CGI film on loop in a room along the ruin's far eastern back wall shows what some areas of the palace would have looked like – historians believe it was designed in imitation of the grand Moorish palaces of Andalusia in southern Spain.

The ruin's **subterranean chambers** house two exhibitions, one a photographic history of the Kasbah and Mellah area from the 1920s to 1950s, the other an underwhelming exhibition about the conditions for enslaved people and prisoners who would have once resided in these underground caverns. Across the vast courtyard (opposite the entrance), the

MUSEUMS OF BAB DOUKKALA

Bab Doukkala and Riad Laârous are busy local neighbourhoods, and there are just a couple of small museums in this area. The real attraction is the Bab Doukkala market strip running northwest from the mosque to Bab Doukkala gate, thronged by local shoppers.

Riad Kniza Musée & Galerie (Map p74; ☎0689849400; www.riadkniza.com; 34 Derb L'Hotel; ⏲noon-3pm & 7pm-midnight) This private museum has been a labour of love for owner Mohammed, who used to run the respected Al Badii antique shop in Gueliz. When his family closed the shop, the big question was what to do with his overflowing collection of Moroccan antiques. The answer was this lovely little museum, which is split into rural and urban culture, displaying High Atlas carpets, tribal jewellery and clothing, decorative Fez pottery dating to the 17th century and a wonderful collection of Amazigh sugar hammers.

Musée du Parfum (Map p74; Derb Chérif; adult/child Dh40/free; ⏲9am-6pm) Formerly the Musée de l'Art Vivre, this small perfume museum explores Morocco's love affair with essential oils. Rooms cover topics such as hammam rituals, the cosmetic benefits of argan and prickly pear oils, and the role of aromatherapy, herbs and spices in Moroccan culture. If you're into olfactory, you can even sign up for a workshop to create your own perfume (Dh400 to Dh600). The shady courtyard cafe is a relaxing place for a pot of tea.

Khayzuran Pavilion houses temporary contemporary art exhibitions.

Just west of the pavilion, a highlight is the room housing the **Koutoubia minbar** (prayer pulpit). Once the minbar of the Koutoubia Mosque (p68), its cedar-wood steps with gold and silver calligraphy were the work of 12th-century Cordoban artisans headed by a man named Aziz – the Metropolitan Museum of Art restoration surfaced his signature.

To reach the palace entrance, head through Place des Ferblantiers and turn right along the ramparts.

Lazama Synagogue SYNAGOGUE

(Map p84; Derb Manchoura; Dh10; ⏲9am-7pm Sun-Thu, to 6pm Fri, closed Jewish holidays) Only a couple of synagogues in the Mellah are still used by Marrakesh's dwindling Jewish community, including this one, which doubles as an interesting museum of Jewish life in Morocco. It was originally built in 1492 by Jews expelled from Spain, but its blue-and-white interior is a much later iteration. The synagogue is on the right-hand side of the pretty internal courtyard – note the Star of David motif in *zellige*.

On the left-hand side, a series of rooms explores 2000 years of Moroccan Jewish history. Marrakesh's Mellah was established in 1557, and by the 19th century the population had swelled to become the largest Jewish community in Morocco.

Miaara Jewish Cemetery CEMETERY

(Map p74; Rue El Miaara; Dh10; ⏲9am-7pm Sun-Thu, to 5pm Fri, closed Jewish holidays) Muslim burial grounds in Morocco are typically closed to visitors, but this sprawling walled Jewish cemetery of whitewashed tombs admits all who wish to pay their respects. It was established in 1537, narrowly predating the Mellah (Jewish quarter), but it's still well maintained by Marrakesh's small Jewish community – you'll see rocks of remembrance on top of some of the tombs.

Gueliz & Ville Nouvelle

Compared with Marrakesh's medina, the neighbourhood of Gueliz still feels quite off the beaten track for tourists, yet it has a couple of worthwhile museums, and its contemporary shops, cafes and restaurants are a good place to survey the pulse of modern Morocco. Jardin Majorelle and the Musée Yves Saint Laurent are on the edge of Gueliz; it's worth extending your time in the area to explore further.

Musée Yves Saint Laurent MUSEUM

See p79.

★**Jardin Majorelle** GARDENS

(Map p74; ☎0524313047; www.jardinmajorelle.com; Rue Yves Saint Laurent; adult/child Dh70/free, incl Musée Berbère Dh100, incl Musée YSL Dh200; ⏲8am-6pm May-Sep, to 5.30pm

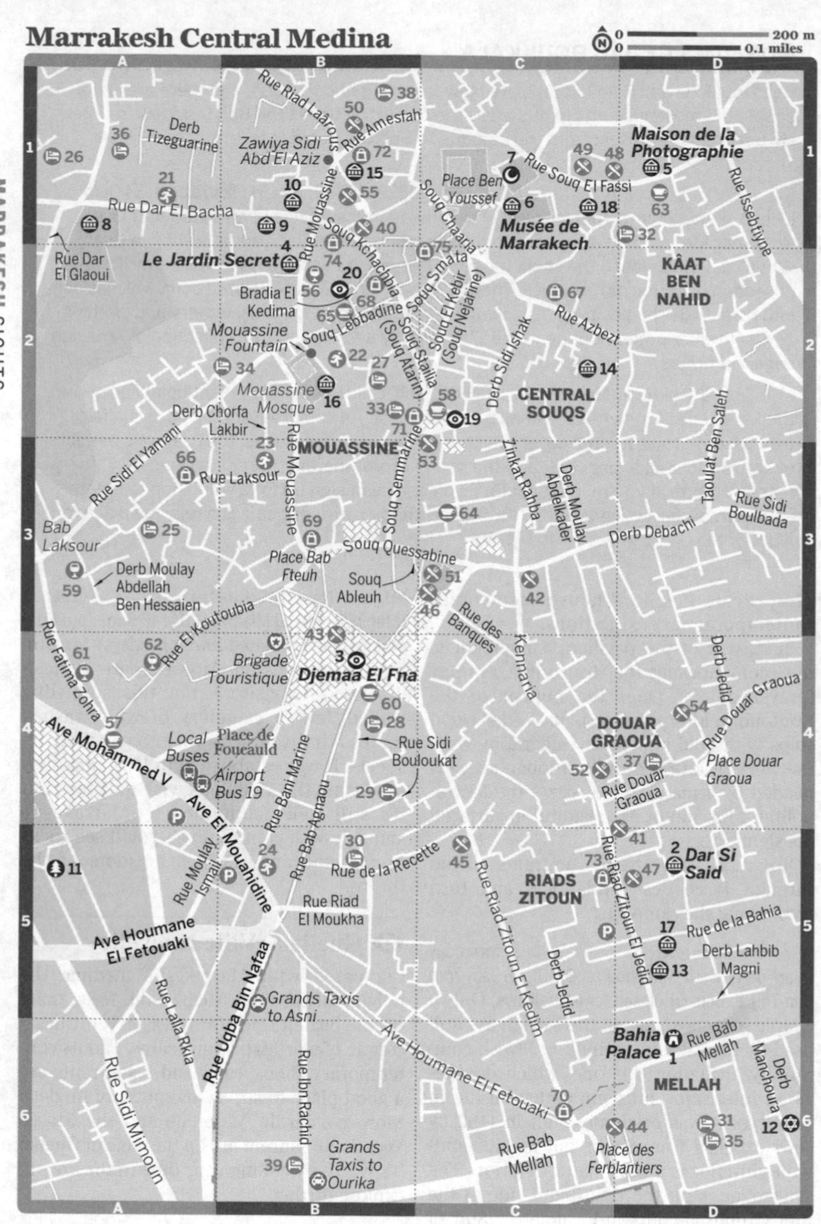

Oct-Apr, Musée Berbère closed Wed) French fashion designer Yves Saint Laurent and his partner Pierre Bergé bought Jardin Majorelle in 1984 to preserve the vision of its original owner, French landscape painter Jacques Majorelle, and keep it open to the public. The garden, started in 1924, contains a psychedelic desert mirage of 300 plant species from five continents. At its heart lies Majorelle's electric-blue art deco studio, home to the **Musée Berbère**, which showcases the rich panorama of

Marrakesh Central Medina

Top Sights

1	Bahia Palace	D6
2	Dar Si Said	D5
3	Djemaa El Fna	B4
4	Le Jardin Secret	B2
5	Maison de la Photographie	D1
6	Musée de Marrakech	C1

Sights

7	Ali Ben Youssef Medersa	C1
8	Dar El Bacha	A1
9	Funduq El Amri	B1
10	Funduq El Mizen	B1
11	Koutoubia Gardens	A5
12	Lazama Synagogue	D6
13	Moroccan Culinary Arts Museum	D5
14	Musée Boucharouite	C2
15	Musée de la Femme	B1
16	Musée de Mouassine	B2
17	Musée Tiskiwin	D5
18	Orientalist Museum	C1
19	Rahba Kedima	C2
20	Souq des Teinturiers	B2

Activities, Courses & Tours

21	Hammam de la Rose	A1
22	Hammam Mouassine	B2
23	Le Bain Bleu	B3
24	Marrakech Roues	B5

Sleeping

25	Dar Attajmil	A3
26	Dar Baraka & Karam	A1
27	Equity Point Hostel	B2
28	Hôtel Cecil	B4
29	Hotel du Trésor	B4
30	Le Gallia	B5
31	Riad Azoulay	D6
32	Riad Berbère	D1
33	Riad Le J	B2
34	Riad L'Orangeraie	B2
35	Riad Noos Noos	D6
36	Riad Tizwa	A1
37	Riad UP	D4
38	Rodamón	B1
39	Villa Verde	B6

Eating

40	Beats Burger	B1
41	BlackChich	D5
42	Corner Cafe	C3
43	Djemaa El Fna Food Stalls	B4
44	Earth Cafe	D6
45	Earth Café	C5
46	Hadj Mustapha	C3
47	La Famille	D5
48	Le Foundouk	C1
	Le Jardin	(see 15)
49	Le Trou Au Mur	C1
50	Max & Jan	B1
51	Mechoui Alley	C3
52	Naranj	C4
53	Nomad	C3
54	PepeNero	D4
55	Souk Kafé	B1

Drinking & Nightlife

	Bacha Coffee	(see 8)
56	Café Arabe	B2
57	Café El Koutoubia	A4
58	Chichaoua	C2
59	El Fenn	A3
60	Grand Balcon du Café Glacier	B4
61	Kabana	A4
62	Les Jardins de la Koutoubia	A4
63	Maison de la Photographie Terrace	D1
64	Riad Yima	C3
65	Terrasse des Teinturiers	B2

Shopping

66	Al Nour	A3
67	Anamil	C2
	Arganino	(see 74)
68	Cooperative Artisanale des Femmes de Marrakesh	B2
69	Funduq El Ouarzazi	B3
70	Kaftan Queen	C6
71	L'Art du Bain Savonnerie Artisanale	B2
72	Max & Jan	B1
73	Naturom	C5
	Sissi Morocco	(see 71)
74	Souq Cherifia	B1
75	Souq Haddadine	C2

Morocco's indigenous inhabitants through displays of some 600 artefacts.

In recent years the site has become incredibly popular and now ranks as Morocco's most visited tourist attraction, with around 900,000 visitors a year. Helping to alleviate the funnel of bodies, in December 2018 the YSL Foundation expanded the gardens by opening up the section containing **Villa Oasis** (10am-6pm Fri-Mon), where Bergé lived until his death in 2017.

Jardin Majorelle also houses a pretty courtyard cafe, a small book and photography shop, and a chic boutique selling Majorelle blue slippers, textiles and Amazigh-inspired jewellery influenced by YSL designs. All areas of the site are wheelchair and pram accessible.

Musée Yves Saint Laurent (p79) is next door to the gardens, and combined tickets can be bought for both attractions; plan to spent the best part of a day between

JARDIN MAJORELLE TIPS

- In peak season, expect to queue from 15 minutes to an hour to get in. Arrive before 10am, and ideally for opening at 8am, for best chances of quick entry.
- Visit Friday to Monday when tickets include entry to the Villa Oasis gardens.
- Don't miss the Musée Berbère; it's well worth the extra Dh30 cost.

the two. Tickets can now be purchased online, which is highly recommended; otherwise, expect to queue 15 minutes to one hour.

★Comptoir des Mines GALLERY
(Map p87; ☎0663010191; www.comptoirdesminesgalerie.com; 62 Rue de Yougoslavie; ⏲3-7pm Mon, 10am-1pm & 3-7pm Tue-Sat) FREE Once the home of a mining corporation, this 1932 building now houses Marrakech Art Fair founder Hicham Daoudi's latest project: a contemporary gallery. Restored to its original art deco glory, the sweeping staircases, terrazzo flooring, crystal-shaped wall sconces and furniture make this spot worth a visit in itself. Rotating art exhibitions over three floors profile leading and up-and-coming artists from Morocco and the rest of Africa. Hassan Hajjaj, called the Andy Warhol of Morocco, has a dedicated gallery space here too.

MACMA GALLERY
(Musee d'Art et de Culture de Marrakech; Map p87; ☎0524448326; 61 Passage Ghandouri, Rue de Yougoslavie; adult/child under 12 Dh70/free; ⏲10am-7pm Mon-Sat) In 2019 MACMA's painting archive was moved to its sister venue, the Orientalist Museum (p77), and this modern gallery shifted its focus to photography, beautifully arranged around a smattering of decorative arts. Images, captured mostly by roving European photographers, span 100 years from 1870 to 1970 and offer an intriguing insight into different facets of Moroccan life, from the chiefs of the High Atlas to urban craftspeople and the women of the northern Rif. Info boards are in English and French.

Combined tickets for MACMA and the Orientalist Museum cost Dh100 (Dh70 for students), and in our view both are equally worth your time.

David Bloch Gallery GALLERY
(Map p87; ☎0524457595; www.davidblochgallery.com; 8 bis Rue des Vieux Marrakchis; ⏲10.30am-1.30pm & 3.30-7.30pm Tue-Sat, 3.30-7.30pm Mon) One of Gueliz's most upmarket private galleries, David Bloch exhibits provocative international contemporary art in a striking black-and-white setting. The selection often veers towards the abstract and usually includes some Moroccan works.

Gallery 127 GALLERY
(Map p87; ☎0524432667; www.galerie127.com; 2nd fl, 127 Ave Mohammed V; ⏲2-7pm Tue-Sat) Channelling New York gallery fashions, this one is up a dim, once-grand staircase in an industrial-chic chamber with the obligatory exposed brick-and-concrete wall. It exhibits a range of new and vintage works by international photographers (mostly Mediterranean). Shows vary from straightforward travel photography to more interpretive works.

Theatre Royal ARCHITECTURE
(Map p87; Ave Hassan II) Begun in the 1970s by Tunisian architect Charles Boccara, this grand edifice is a focal point for cultural shows in Marrakesh, despite remaining unfinished. If the front door's open, the caretaker may offer to show you around (for a tip). Check out the domed ceiling and woodwork flourishes that merge Moroccan and European styles. The 1200-seater open-air theatre hosts ballets and musicals.

Palmeraie & Outskirts

★Musée de la Palmeraie MUSEUM
(☎0661095352; off Route de Fez; adult/child Dh40/free; ⏲9am-5.30pm) There's no comprehensive archive of modern Moroccan art in central Marrakesh: it's out here, hidden in the Palmeraie, and it's well worth travelling for. Set in a sprawling Andalusian garden of adobe houses, the Musée de la Palmeraie displays an outstanding collection of photography, painting and sculpture. Its 20th-century watercolours, drawings, prints and oil paintings, by Marrakshi artists such as Hicham Benohoud, Abderrahim Iqbi and Larbi Cherkaoui, are particularly strong and demonstrate how local artists have been inspired by Moroccan life and Islamic culture.

Follow signs from here to **Musée Farid Belkahia** (☎0524328959; http://fondationfaridbelkahia.com; off Route de Fez; adult/child

Marrakesh Ville Nouvelle

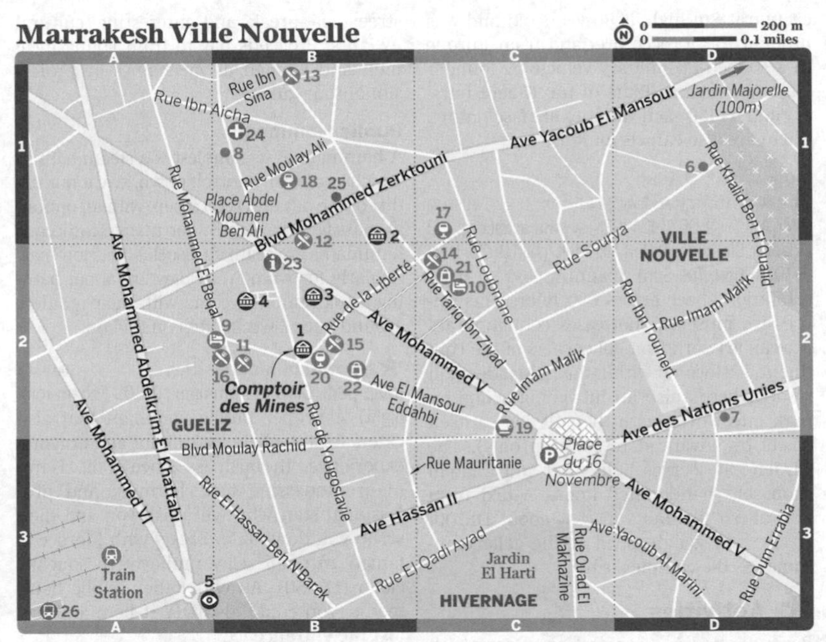

Marrakesh Ville Nouvelle

Top Sights
1 Comptoir des Mines.......B2

Sights
2 David Bloch Gallery.......B1
3 Gallery 127.......B2
4 MACMA.......B2
5 Theatre Royal.......A3

Activities, Courses & Tours
6 Centre for Language & Culture.......D1
7 Creative Interactions.......D2
8 Inside Morocco Travel.......B1

Sleeping
9 Blue Sea Le Printemps.......B2
10 Hôtel Toulousain.......C2

Eating
11 +61.......B2
12 Al Fassia.......B1
13 Amal Center.......B1
14 Kilim.......C2
15 Patisserie Al Jawda.......B2
16 Pâtisserie Amandine.......B2

Drinking & Nightlife
17 68 Bar à Vin.......C1
18 Barometre Marrakech.......B1
Café du Livre.......(see 10)
19 Grand Café de la Poste.......C2
20 Kechmara.......B2

Shopping
21 Atelier 44.......C2
22 Some Slow Concept Store.......B2

Information
23 Office Regional Marocain du Tourisme.......B2
24 Polyclinique du Sud.......B1

Transport
25 KAT.......B1
26 Supratours.......A3

Dh50/30; 9am-6pm) for works by one of the most well-known figures in 20th-century Moroccan art, housed in his former villa.

Cactus Thiemann GARDENS
(0661614901; www.cactusthiemann.com; Km 10, Route de Casablanca; Dh150; by appointment only Mon-Sat;) If you think a cacti garden isn't worth travelling across the bumpy lunar pistes of outer Marrakesh for, think again. Cactus Thiemann is one of North Africa's largest cacti farms, with fields of giant aloe, agave and prickly pear. The largest

cactus, at 8m high, is 80 years old and was brought to Morocco overland from Europe in a souped-up military vehicle by founder Hans Thiemann. Tours of the 17-acre nursery and its 150 cacti varieties are fascinating. There are also camels for kids.

Museum of African Contemporary Art Al Maaden MUSEUM
(MACAAL; ☎0676924492; www.macaal.org; Al Maaden, Sidi Youssef Ben Ali; adult/child Dh70/free; ⊙10am-6pm Tue-Sun) Spanning 900 sq m of exhibition space across two floors, this impressive museum showcases contemporary African artwork from all corners of the continent. It's located within the Al Maaden golf resort: there's also an intriguing sculpture park interwoven with the golf course itself (visits by advanced reservation only). The garden cafe serves light food and a small shop sells handcrafted items. A taxi from Marrakesh medina will cost about Dh100; ensure you get dropped at the gallery entrance as the complex is big.

Activities

Beyond medina exploration, Marrakesh offers opportunities for everything from mountain-biking day trips into the Atlas Mountains to steaming yourself to perfection in a hammam. Cooking classes are popular and allow you a small window on Marrakshi culture.

Cycling

★AXS CYCLING
(☎0524400207; www.argansports.com; Rue Fatima Al Fihria, Sidi Youssef Ben Ali; half-day city tours from Dh350, bike hire per 24hr from Dh200; 👪) Get on a bike and discover Marrakesh's sights on a classic city ride, glide through the Palmeraie, or munch through street stalls between rides on the tasting tour. Those up for adventure can mountain-bike in the Atlas or cycle to Essaouira. High-quality Giant road bikes, mountain bikes (including kids' bikes) and helmets are provided.

★Pikala Bikes CYCLING
(Map p74; ☎0684913915; www.pikalabikes.com; Riad Laârous; 2½hr tour Dh250, 24hr bike hire Dh80) This Dutch-funded nonprofit organisation is a community project on a mission to get young Marrakshis to ditch motorbike aspirations in favour of good old-fashioned cycling. Group cycling tours depart from its Riad Laârous garage most mornings at 9.30am and include a back-street tea break and interesting cultural insights. Proceeds pay to train young local men and women as mechanics or professional tour guides.

Public Hammams

A hammam at its simplest is a steam bath in which you wash yourself down, sweat out the dirt of the day and then scrub, with an optional massage afterwards. For many Moroccans hammams are as much a social occasion (particularly for women) as they are about bathing. Children often come with their mothers around once a week, often on Fridays.

★Hammam Mouassine HAMMAM
(Map p84; Derb El Hammam; Dh10; ⊙5am-midnight) A proper public hammam that also caters for travellers looking for an authentic experience. In business since 1562, Hammam Mouassine has charming and professional staff who will wash you and then scrub you down *(gommage)* with Morocco's famed *rhassoul* clay until you're squeaky clean (Dh150). As with other public hammams, you could also DIY it here and pay just the entrance fee.

Hammam Bab Doukkala HAMMAM
(Map p74; Rue Bab Doukkala; adult/child Dh12/5; ⊙women noon-7pm, men 8.30pm-midnight) This 17th-century hammam in the southeast corner of Bab Doukkala Mosque has heated *tadelakt* (waterproof limestone plaster) floors in good repair, a high cedar-wood stepped ceiling in the changing area and a cavernous hot room topped by a burgundy cupola. Staff speak little English; this is a real-deal, mellow hammam busy with locals, particularly from 5pm for women.

Private Hammams

A private hammam might sound decadent, but it's one of the best deals in Marrakesh. Note, you need to choose your venue carefully – some hammams are so over-subscribed they're anything but relaxed.

Le Bain Bleu SPA
(Map p84; ☎0524383804; www.lebainbleu.com; 32 Derb Chorfa Lakbir; hammam & gommage Dh200, with massage from Dh600; ⊙10am-9pm) Relaxation pools are usually reserved for Marrakesh's luxury spas, but Le Bain Bleu sets itself apart from the competition with a lovely lounging pool courtyard, as well as a rooftop for post-pampering sun snoozes, airy petal-strewn rest room and rooftop bar-restaurant called Dar Justo. Couples

hammam packages, facials, manicures and pedicures are available. It's well signposted off Rue El Mouassine.

Sultana Spa SPA
(Map p74; ☎0524388008; www.lasultanamarrakech.com; off Rue de la Kasbah; hammam & scrub Dh400; ⊙10am-8pm) La Sultana's opulent spa is one of the most luxurious and professional in the medina. Signature body scrubs and facial treatments use spices plus argan and prickly-pear oils, and the spa also offers a high-end traditional hammam experience. The icing on the cake is the column-flanked indoor pool room with Jacuzzi and fireplace, dripping with Moroccan lanterns. Book ahead.

Heritage Spa HAMMAM
(Map p74; ☎0524384333; www.heritagespamarrakech.com; 40 Derb Arset Aouzal; hammam & scrub from Dh290; ⊙10am-8pm) Forget any illusions of authentically local hammams: bliss out in this private spa-hammam with a detoxing black-soap and bitter-orange scrub or hot herbal massage. It's housed in a traditional riad with comfy nooks for treatments, free-flowing mint tea and good-quality, 100% natural products.

Hammam de la Rose SPA
(Map p84; ☎0524444769; www.hammamdelarose.com; 130 Rue Dar El Bacha; hammam & scrub Dh250, massage from Dh250; ⊙10am-8pm) This atmospheric private hammam gets the thumbs-up for its superprofessional staff and squeaky-clean premises. There's a range of beauty treatments you can add, from rose facial masks and clay cleansing to a host of massage options.

La Mamounia SPA
(Map p74; ☎0524388600; www.mamounia.com; Ave Bab Jedid; day pass Mon-Sat/Sun Dh1600/2000; ⊙9am-8pm) If you want to pretend you're a visiting celebrity, Mamounia's spa is the place to go. Its opulence, fused with Moroccan design, justifies the high price: get a load of the subterranean relaxation room with pool illuminated by giant lanterns, and the cavernous indoor swimming pool where an overwater lounging throne sits beneath a hand-painted cedar-wood ceiling that took three years to complete.

Horse Riding

Les Cavaliers de L'Atlas HORSE RIDING
(☎0661157620; www.lescavaliersdelatlas.com; Route de Casablanca; half/full day €50/90) Run by passionate equestrian Sophie Chauvat, this is a professional stable with a mix of Arab, Anglo-Arab and Berber horses and Welsh and Shetland ponies. Options range from half-day rides through the Palmeraie to multiday horse treks in the Atlas. All equipment is provided, including riding caps, half-chaps and body protectors for children. Transport costs an extra Dh100.

The centre is located 10 minutes north of Marrakesh, just off the Route de Casablanca (N9) and is clearly signposted on the road. For those who want to make their holiday all about riding, their guesthouse **Dar Guerris** (double/suite €90/150) is on site.

HAMMAM TIPS

- Public hammams are usually open for women during the day and men during the evening, though there are some exceptions to the rule.
- In public hammams, bring your own towels (in a waterproof bag), a plastic mat or something to sit on, flip-flops, and a change of underwear.
- Many private hammams offer package deals for couples. Book ahead.

Swimming

★**Beldi Country Club** SWIMMING
(☎0524383950; www.beldicountryclub.com; Km 6, Route de Barrage 'Cherifa'; adult/child pool day-pass Dh200/100, incl lunch Dh390/250; ⊙10.30am-6.30pm; 👪) Located just 6km south of the city centre, the Beldi feels a million miles away from the dust and chaos of the medina. Lie back and smell the 15,000 roses at Dominique Leymarie's eco-chic paradise with its pools (including one for kids), spa, hammam, curated souq shopping and restaurant (serving alcohol). Transfers cost Dh100 each way from the medina, or Dh120 to the airport.

Oasiria WATER PARK
(☎0524380438; www.oasiria.com; Km 4, Route d'Amizmiz; adult/child Dh250/150; ⊙10am-6pm; 👪) All-day family fun whizzing down kamikaze and cobra slides, playing in wave pools and pirate lagoons, plus river tubing, Jacuzzis, restaurants and an on-site infirmary to ensure everyone stays safe. Free shuttles run from Djemaa El Fna and Gueliz throughout the day.

TOURING THE TANNERIES

Leather working is one of Morocco's medieval trades, and the **Bab Debbagh Tanneries** (Association Sidi Yacoub; Map p74; Rue de Bab Debbagh; ⏲ Sat-Thu) – ideally situated next to the river from where they draw water to pummel animal hides – have been in use for hundreds of years. The largest cooperative, Association Sidi Yacoub, is down a lane just inside the gate, on the southern side of Rue de Bab Debbagh – you'll know you've reached it when the acrid smell assaults your nose. Beware that scams are rife around the tanneries; hassle is guaranteed.

The Association Sidi Yacoub is open to visitors and free to visit, but it's likely you'll be accosted by a 'guardian' at the entrance telling you otherwise. Try to ignore them or fob them off with a small tip of Dh10 to Dh20, and insist upon entering without a 'guide' (which will cost you dearly). If you're not up for this battle, go with an official guide as part of a medina tour; this is the only way to ensure you skip the hassle.

The pungent smell comes from the use of ammonia in the troughs that's used to soften the leather and strip it of its animal hairs. Unlike at the tanneries in Fez, you won't see a rainbow of dyes used; here the tanneries only work the natural leather, and dyeing is done elsewhere. Surrounding the roughly hewn troughs of clay, you'll find the leather-workers' workshops, which have been handed down from generation to generation. It's hard, dirty work and exclusively a male industry.

The best time to come is in the morning when you'll usually be able to see tanners at work, transforming stinking animal skins that are dropped off by donkey carts into supple leather ready to be tailored into goodies for the souqs.

In exchange for a tip, you'll usually also be offered to see the tanneries from above, from one of the houses near the Bab Debbagh gate. The bird's-eye views offer a completely different perspective, but be aware that many of the 'houses' are actually leatherware shops, and touts can be pushy. Don't feel pressured into having to buy something if you don't want to.

Also beware the young men on foot or motorbikes who will follow you from the central souqs and then may insist upon entering with you for an extortionate fee. Because these touts are so persistent and at times aggressive, we recommend getting a taxi to the outside of Bab Debbagh and walking *into* the medina, as the tanneries are only just inside the gate.

Courses

★ Ateliers d'Ailleurs ARTS & CRAFTS

(☎0662166026; www.ateliersdailleurs.com; workshops €35-69) Engaging a handpicked network of professional artisans who work with pottery, *tadelakt*, woodwork, *zellige*, brassware and more, these ateliers (studios) are good value for what you get: a unique insight into traditional craft techniques and the opportunity to chat with the artisan one-on-one. Workshops are private and hands-on, running for either three or five hours.

★ Atelier Chef Tarik COOKING

(☎0674902427; www.atelier-chef-tarik.com; Km 22, Route d'Amizmiz; cooking class €75;) Farm-to-table cooking is at the heart of this rural culinary school a half-hour drive from Marrakesh, where rustic adobe houses and relaxed kilim-cushion garden seating give way to a bucolic organic farm and cooking tent. If you don't fancy buying caged chickens from a Marrakesh souq, chef Tarik's class is an excellent alternative. The price includes transfers.

La Maison Arabe COOKING

(Map p74; ☎0524387010; www.lamaisonarabe.com; 1 Derb Assehbe; 1hr workshop Dh300) Bab Doukkala's legendary Maison Arabe (p97) restaurant also runs this slick cookery school. Longer classes with high-tech demonstration screens can feel a little impersonal, but this school is one of the only places in Marrakesh where tourists with limited time can book in to punchy one-hour courses. Participants cook one dish, accompanied by plenty of interaction with the hosting chef, and then eat together after.

Amal Targa COOKING

(☎0524493776; http://amalnonprofit.org; Harouchi, Sofia, Targa; adult/child under 10 Dh350/200) Gueliz's favourite nonprofit restaurant (p95) now runs good-value cooking and baking classes on the western outskirts of Marrakesh. Morning classes focus on the secrets of Morocco's classic tajine, cooked over charcoal, while the afternoon baking course encourages participants to perfect one sweet treat, such as gazelle horn pastries or *msemen* (fried flaky flatbread). Transport is not included.

Study Arabic in Marrakech LANGUAGE
(☎0672869036; www.studyarabicmarrakech.com; off Route de Casablanca; private/group lessons per hr Dh100/80) Has both short-term programmes for travellers wanting to pick up some Darija (Moroccan Arabic) along with tips on local etiquette, and long-term courses in both Darija and modern standard Arabic. Private classes are available, and if you have a group of six or more, it can be arranged for the class to take place at your hotel.

Creative Interactions LANGUAGE
(Map p87; ☎0524421687; www.creative-interactions.com; Apt 47, Immeuble El Khalil Bldg, Ave des Nations Unies; 2hr private/2-3 people €40/36 per person, 3½hr €65/59) Creative Interactions offers Moroccan Arabic classes designed for short-term travellers. These fun and friendly workshops allow even visitors on a short stay a chance to learn the basics. Classes include tips on how to deal with hassle and how to haggle. The 3½-hour sessions come with a cooking demonstration and lunch; two-hour classes include a tea-making lesson.

Centre for Language & Culture LANGUAGE
(Map p87; ☎0524447691; www.clcmorocco.org; cnr Rues Sourya & Khalid Ibn El Oualid) American and Moroccan teachers with years of experience offer summer language courses in Modern Standard Arabic with homestay hook-ups. Lessons are immersive, and the school applies the Communicative Language Learning (CLL) technique in its Arabic classes.

Tours

Should you hire a guide to tour the medina? The answer depends on what you want to achieve. Guided tours of the medina will help you cover specific landmarks in an hour or two without getting lost and will ensure you don't receive any hassle in the medina: think of your guide as your shield. They can provide context to sights where free information is (almost always) lacking, but be aware that not everything they say should be taken as gospel and often their historical knowledge is poor. Also don't expect sweet souq deals: guides get commissions on whatever you buy.

Hotels, riads and travel agencies can arrange guides, or you can book official guides directly via the tourist office in Gueliz for Dh300/600 for a half/full day. This rate is pretty standard, but generally the cost reflects the quality: the city's five-star guides may charge a little more.

City Tour Marrakech BUS
(☎0663527797; www.marrakech.city-tour.com; 48hr pass adult/child Dh190/95;) Save your feet by signing up for this hop-on, hop-off electric bus tour to whizz you between Marrakesh's furthest-flung sights: far more convenient than haggling for taxis. The ticket covers two routes. The historic itinerary includes the Kasbah, Dar Si Said museum, Menara Gardens, Mamounia and Gueliz, while the garden route ticks off Jardin Majorelle and the Palmeraie.

Marrakech Food Tours FOOD & DRINK
(☎+1-800-656-0713; www.marrakechfoodtours.com; US$65) Munch your way through the medina: weave through the souqs tucking into *tanjia* (slow-cooked stew) and sampling Marrakshi street food, or try the mixed walking tour that includes sit-down restaurant stops. Local hosts take groups of up to six participants on a whirlwind tour of Marrakshi flavours, or let them whisk you to an Atlas Mountains village for a local meal. Bring your appetite.

Festivals & Events

Marrakesh hosts an annual programme of festivals befitting its self-proclaimed role as Morocco's cultural capital. From contemporary art and film to traditional song and dance, Marrakesh loves to get its glad rags on and play host. Tickets to events can generally be bought beforehand through festival websites or at official ticket outlets in town.

Marrakesh Marathon SPORTS
(www.marathon-marrakech.com; half-/full-marathon fee €50/70; ⏲Jan) Run like there's a carpet salesman after you – from Djemaa El Fna square to the Palmeraie and back – for this annual marathon.

1-54 ART
(Contemporary African Art Fair; www.1-54.com; La Mamounia; ⏲Feb) Taking over where the now-defunct Marrakech Biennale left off,

the city's Contemporary African Art Fair attracts around 6000 visitors each year. It's held at La Mamounia and acts as a platform for dozens of emerging and established artists from across Africa and its diaspora.

Beat Hotel MUSIC
(www.beat-hotel.com; Fellah Hotel; Mar) Launched in 2019, Beat Hotel mixes film, talks and lifestyle workshops with four days of poolside grooving, sunset DJ sets and late-night dance parties. It's held at the **Fellah Hotel** (0525065000; www.fellah-hotel.com; Km 13, Route de l'Ourika, Tassoultante; d/ste from €85/100;) south of Marrakesh.

National Festival of Popular Arts PERFORMING ARTS
(Jul) The only thing hotter than Marrakesh in July is this free-form folk fest. Amazigh musicians, dancers and street performers from around the country pour into Marrakesh to thrill the masses.

Sleeping

Room rates are the highest in Morocco, but Marrakesh has it all: you can sleep anywhere from the funkiest fleapit to palaces straight out of some North African Hollywood fantasy. Booking ahead is crucial for medina riads due to the limited number of rooms. Note that unmarried couples can't get a room together if one person is Moroccan.

Medina

★Le Gallia HOTEL €
(Map p84; 0524445913; www.hotellegallia.com; 30 Rue de la Recette; s/d/tr Dh350/550/850;) Madcap Djemaa El Fna is around the corner, but Le Gallia maintains the calm and grace of another era with comfortable, clean-as-a-whistle rooms, all with air-con, heating and reliable hot water, arranged around a courtyard trimmed with colourful tiles and shaded by orange trees. Run by the French Galland family since 1929, it's often packed with repeat visitors. Good for solo travellers.

Hôtel Cecil HOTEL €
(Map p84; 0524442203; Rue Sidi Bouloukat; s/d/tr Dh250/330/440, with shared bathroom Dh150/230/330;) Cecil's twin courtyards framed by fat pink pillars and comfy sofas offer digs minutes from Djemaa El Fna. Rooms with bathroom have more pizzazz, thanks to hand-painted furniture and the addition of air-con. For those sharing bathrooms there are clean toilets and showers on each floor; several rooms can accommodate three to four people.

Hotel du Trésor RIAD €
(Map p84; 0524375113; 77 Derb Sidi Bouloukat; s/d/ste from €42/50/80;) This good-value riad brims with whimsy and rock-and-roll style from the mod Panton chairs beside the plunge pool to the snug rooms chock-a-block with eclectic razzle dazzle. Behind painted doors are walls of vintage mirrors reclaimed from the Mamounia, crystal chandeliers over a red-velvet-padded bed, and in the terrace Blue Suite, a soaking tub and fireplace.

Villa Verde BOUTIQUE HOTEL €
(Map p84; 0601606538; www.facebook.com/villaverdemarrakech; Rue Ibn Rachid; dm/s/d from €12/30/55;) This stylish and immaculately clean budget hotel has been cleverly kitted out to look like a riad, with wooden shutters, *zellige* and a courtyard of potted palms. The Moroccan owner and his staff hail from the southern deserts near Merzouga, and they also run tours there. Room configurations will suit groups, solo travellers and families, and there's direct road access.

Equity Point Hostel HOSTEL €
(Riad Amazigh; Map p84; 0524440793; www.equity-point.com; 80 Derb El Hammam; 8-/6-/4-bed dm €12/15/18, tw €68;) Courtyard pool – yep. Cushioned salon nooks filled with *zellige*, brass lanterns and carved cedar door trimmings – yep. Hammam and cooking classes – yep. Usual riad price-tag – nope. Equity Point converted this labyrinthine old mansion into a wallet-friendly backpackers boutique with a roof terrace bar-restaurant and dorms (both mixed and female-only), which come with air-con, small lockers and ensuite bathrooms.

★Riad UP RIAD €€
(Map p84; 0665367936; www.riadup.com; Derb Boutouil 41, Kennaria; d/ste €90/130;) Mediterranean chic meets medina living. Mallorcan owner Elsa Bauza oversaw every aspect of her riad's renovation, retaining its handsome central courtyard, installing a plunge pool in the patio and giant fireplace in the salon, while stripping rooms down to their elegant essentials to create tranquil, minimalist spaces that deserve a spread in *Architectural Digest*. Elsa is usually on site, and service is excellent.

★**Riad Helen** RIAD €€
(Map p74; ☎0524378611; www.riadhelen.com; 138 Derb Arset Aouzal; r from €75; 📶) This stylish *dar* (traditional house), down funky Derb Arset Aouzal with its alley-wall mural art, is run by Parisians Celine and Fabian and offers six rooms. Inside there are lashings of white-trim, sea-green shuttered windows and French doors to keep things light and airy. Good-sized 1st-floor rooms are dressed in soft pastels, and there's one on the roof that can sleep three.

★**Riad Berbère** RIAD €€
(Map p84; ☎0524381910; www.leriadberbere.com; 23 Derb Sidi Ahmed Benacer; d from €85; ❄📶) Besides having one of the most romantic garden courtyards in the medina, beloved by cats, it's the service and special little touches like free cucumber water and petals on the pillows that put classy Riad Berbère in its own stratosphere. The riad dates to the end of the 17th century, but rooms favour a refreshing white aesthetic and have designer appeal. Breakfasts are unmissable.

★**Riad Noos Noos** RIAD €€
(Map p84; ☎0524386825; www.riadnoosnoos.com; 8 Derb Jamaa Kebir; s €55-65, d €90-110, f €100-110; ❄📶) There's lots to love about Riad Noos Noos, starting with its mellow location in the Mellah, stork-viewing roof terrace and kooky retro style. Online deals usually make its double/twin rooms – with premium comfy beds – a total bargain. There's a small hammam, pool table and bar off the shady central courtyard, and the riad has a great-value family suite.

★**Rodamón** HOSTEL €€
(Map p84; ☎0524378978; www.rodamonhostels.com; Diour Saboun, 32 Rue Amesfah, Bab Taghzout; 8-/6-/4-bed dm Dh170/185/200, d/f from Dh750/1150; ❄📶🏊) Marrakesh's best hostel is this Spanish-owned riad complex deep in the souqs. The 100-year-old interior was gutted and reimagined to create a contemporary Moroccan feel, and boy did they do an excellent job. There's a pool, bar and roof terrace, but it's the ensuite dorms that deserve applause: giant lockers, comfy beds with curtains for privacy, and niches with plug sockets and lamps.

Riad Le J RIAD €€
(Map p84; ☎0524391787; www.riadlej.com; 67 Derb El Hammam; r €75-100; 📶) What do you get if you cross Italian furniture designers with Marrakshi craftsmanship? An achingly cool hideaway where art deco Mamounia mirrors meet eclectic art, and *zouak* (painted wood) ceilings merge with retro lamps. There are just four spicy rooms on offer – Mint, Saffron, Pepper and Cinnamon – and the welcome is as genuine and personal as the interiors are beautiful.

Riad Tizwa RIAD €€
(Map p84; www.riadtizwa.com; 26 Derb Gueraba, Dar El Bacha; r €75-140; 📶) The Scottish Bee brothers bring their signature style to Marrakesh with this intimate hideaway, sister to their property in Fez. Pops of colour add a modern freshness to the six generously sized rooms, which still have original stucco and antique tiling. Beds are so comfortable you won't want to get up, and you don't have to: breakfast is served whenever you please.

Dar Attajmil RIAD €€
(Map p84; ☎0524426966; www.darattajmil.com; 23 Rue Laksour; r €90-110; 📶) Italian owner Lucrezia and her attentive staff offer a warm welcome and an even warmer rooftop hammam at this relaxed and elegant riad of blush-pink *tadelakt* walls, cosy lounging salons and banana-tree shaded courtyard. Just four rooms – home to softly sumptuous furnishings and wood ceilings – guarantee a personal touch. Its location, right on a main medina thoroughfare, is perfect.

Dar Baraka & Karam RIAD €€
(Map p84; ☎0524426463; www.marrakech-riads.com; 11 & 18 Derb Halfaoui; s/d/ste from Dh450/750/1300; ❄📶🏊) Guests get two riads in one at Dar Baraka and Dar Karam, two interconnected houses with equally bright woodwork colour themes – one red, one turquoise – offset by naked white walls for an arresting aesthetic. The configuration gives lots of privacy and a sense of space, making it a peaceful retreat. There's also a hammam and a good-value single room (though it's missing air-con).

Riad El Youssoufi RIAD €€
(Map p74; ☎0524376170; www.riadelyoussoufi.com; 188 Arset Aouzal; d €64-79; ❄📶🏊) With such a warm welcome from Moroccan-Belgian owner Asma and her house manager Karim, it's little wonder this intimate riad gets repeat visitors. There are just five unfussy, well-designed rooms off the leafy courtyard, a comfy roof terrace where you can sip wine, cosy nooks for relaxing, and mint tea with Moroccan pastries on arrival.

★Riad L'Orangeraie RIAD €€€

(Map p84; ☎0661238789; www.riadorangeraie.com; 61 Rue Sidi El Yamani; r/ste €150/180; 📶🏊) From Moroccan sweets and fresh flowers in your room to top-notch personal service, Riad L'Orangeraie gets all the finer details right. The layout is perfect: shaded sofas on the rooftop for breakfast, a cosy lounge with open fire where guests can curl up with wine at night and a generous pool with loungers in a discrete courtyard.

★Riad Azoulay RIAD €€€

(Map p84; ☎0524383729; www.riad-azoulay.com; 3 Derb Jamaa Kebir; d €110-135, ste from €150; ❄📶🏊) The restoration of this 200-year-old mansion, once home to the wealthy Azoulay family, advisors to the royal family, was a labour of love for Italian owner Sandro. The result is a haven of casual luxury where original cedar ceilings and plasterwork decor sit comfortably alongside modern art and coloured kilims. Suites (two of which sleep four) have fridges.

Riad Al Massarah RIAD €€€

(Map p74; ☎0524383206; www.riadalmassarah.com; 26 Derb Jedid; d Dh950-1550; 📶🏊) 🍃 The ultimate feel-good getaway: British-French owners Michel and Michael redesigned this old riad sustainably to maximise comfort and sunlight, and minimise electrical and water waste. It now has Green Key eco certification. Each of the six guest rooms (all of which can be converted to twins) is distinct, with original art, handmade textiles, and some have wood-burning stoves.

🛏 Ville Nouvelle & Palmeraie

Medina hotels beat those in the Ville Nouvelle hands down for atmosphere, but if you prefer a more contemporary sleep, Gueliz has plenty of options. This is where you'll find the international hotels, aimed at the package-holiday market. It's no better value to stay here, but most hotels have on-site bars and larger pools than you'll find in the medina, and for travellers with limited mobility there's a lot less dragging of luggage.

Hôtel Toulousain HOTEL €

(Map p87; ☎0524430033; www.hoteltoulousain.ma; 44 Rue Tariq Ibn Ziyad; new s/d Dh300/400, old Dh250/300, with shared bathroom Dh150/220; 📶) Toulousain is an old, easy-going 30-room hotel arranged around a shady courtyard and run by a kind Moroccan-American family in a prime Gueliz location. There's a variety of rooms that come in a highly confusing number of configurations, including some with private showers but shared toilets; the pick of the bunch is the new 'traditional-style'.

Blue Sea Le Printemps HOTEL €€

(Map p87; ☎0524432992; www.blueseahotels.com; 19 Blvd El Mansour Eddahbi; d/ste from Dh600/1500; P📶🏊) This 114-room hotel, run by the Spanish Blue Sea Hotels Group, is a winner for families and travellers seeking full facilities and a larger pool. Rooms feel contemporary, and they come with fridges and most have balconies. There are plenty of twin rooms and two-bedroom family suites. Check the website for offers; rooms are often half-price.

★Riad Bledna RIAD €€

(☎0661182090; www.riadbledna.com; off Route de Ouarzazate; d €65, f €80-95; P🏊) 🍃 Welcome to the garden villa of the Moroccan-British Nour family, who pamper visitors as if they are favourite house guests. With eight rooms of spice-toned *tadelakt* walls and traditional *tataoui* ceilings (made from reeds woven into intricate patterns), a filtered pool and delicious home cooking (with produce from their organic five-acre garden), this is a peaceful and thoroughly homey country pad.

Casa Taos GUESTHOUSE €€€

(☎0661200414; www.casataos.net; Km 8, Route de Targa; r €175-235; P📶🏊) Hicham and family ladle out lashings of hospitality at this colourful villa with beautiful rooms and a two-bed family pavilion, all kitted out in an eclectic fusion melding modern and traditional Moroccan design with art deco. Wipe off the medina dust and loll by the large pool under swaying palm trees. At mealtimes, feast on innovative Mediterranean menus made from this foodie family's organic garden produce.

Jnane Tamsna RESORT €€€

(☎0524329423; www.jnane.com; Douar Abiad, Palmeraie; d €160-420; 📶🏊) 🍃 Sustainability meets jet-setting style at Meryanne Loum-Martin's country pad. Paths thread through landscaped gardens (planted by her ethnobotanist husband, Gary) leading to swimming pools, tennis courts and large rooms scattered with antiques, art and Moroccan textiles. Expect organic cuisine from the family farm, craft cocktails, endless activity options and lazy days lapping up the secluded beauty of the nine-acre palm-fringed property.

Eating

Marrakesh's culinary scene has improved considerably with a flurry of new restaurants opening in both the medina and Gueliz. That said, as traditionally Marrakshis don't eat out often, most medina restaurants are aimed squarely at the tourist market, and meals can be hit-and-miss. In middle-class Gueliz, there's more of a local dining vibe with both Moroccan and international restaurants.

Medina

★Djemaa El Fna Food Stalls MOROCCAN €
(Map p84; Djemaa El Fna; mains Dh30-50; ⌚sunset-1am) Grilled meat and tajines as far as the eye can see, plus snail soup, sheep's brains and skewered hearts: eating amid the mayhem of the Djemaa food stalls is not to be missed. Follow the locals to find the stalls with the freshest produce. Our recommendations are number 14 for fried fish and number 1 for *brochettes* (kebabs) and tajines.

★Amal Center MOROCCAN €
(Map p87; ☎0524446896; http://amalnonprofit.org; cnr Rues Allal Ben Ahmad & Ibn Sina; mains Dh45-70; ⌚noon-3.30pm; 📝) 🍃 So many restaurants in Marrakesh reflect poorly on local cuisine, but here you get the real home-cooking deal. And, happily, it's all for a good cause: the Amal Center is a nonprofit association that supports and trains disadvantaged Moroccan women in restaurant skills. Meals are served in a leafy courtyard garden, and the service is warm.

The menu changes daily, but there are usually three choices of starters, mains and dessert, including at least one vegetarian option; on Friday, couscous is always the star of the show. Prices are locally focused, so the clientele is a happy mix of local families, expats and in-the-know tourists. If the spicy zing of your tajine has your tastebuds craving more, the centre runs cooking classes (p90).

★Henna Cafe MOROCCAN €
(Map p74; www.hennacafemarrakech.com; 93 Arset Aouzal; mains Dh40; ⌚11am-7.30pm; 📶📝) 🍃 Herbal teas, detox juices, henna tattoos, book exchange, Darija classes, good conversation…they're all on the menu at this intimate upstairs cafe, where a local *nquasha* (henna artist) draws intricate designs on hands and feet, and you can munch on salads, falafel and *khleer* (cured lamb) sandwiches on the covered rooftop. All profits go to local residents in need.

Prices for henna tattoos start at Dh50 for a small design and climb up to Dh500. Only organic brown henna is used at the cafe; the catalogue of designs has been donated by top henna artists from around the world and are the best you'll find in Marrakesh.

The cafe runs education programmes for locals (its teaching room is below the cafe) and is always looking for volunteers willing to teach French, Spanish and English classes. Check its website for details.

Mechoui Alley MOROCCAN €
(Map p84; east side of Souq Ableuh; roast lamb Dh45-70; ⌚11am-2pm) Just before noon, the vendors at this row of stalls start carving up steaming sides of *mechoui* (slow-roasted lamb). Very little English is spoken, but simply point to the best-looking cut of meat, and ask for a *nus* (half) or *rubb* (quarter) kilo. The cook will hack off falling-from-the-bone lamb and hand it to you with fresh-baked bread, cumin and salt.

Patisserie Al Jawda SWEETS €
(Map p87; ☎0524433897; 11 Rue de la Liberté; ⌚8am-8pm) Care for a pastry, or perhaps 200 different ones? Moroccan patissier Hakima Alami can set you up with sweet and savoury delicacies featuring figs, orange-blossom water, desert honey and other local, seasonal ingredients. Her shop is a lovely, old-fashioned affair where well-heeled Gueliz residents drop by for treats. You pay by weight; just point at what you want.

★Cafe Clock CAFE €€
(Map p74; ☎0524378367; www.cafeclock.com; 224 Derb Chtouka; mains Dh60-90; ⌚9am-11pm; 📶📝) Little sister to the Fez original, Cafe Clock is housed in an old school with sunset views over the Kasbah from its rooftop. The food, including vegie options like quiche and seasonal couscous, is decent – tourists delight in the signature camel burger. However, its popularity rests on its packed calendar of cultural performances, which also attracts many young Marrakshis.

As well as ad hoc art exhibitions and live Amazigh and gnaoua concerts on Saturday and Sunday respectively, Cafe Clock hosts weekly sessions of *hikayat* (storytelling), inviting Djemaa El Fna's last traditional storyteller to weave his magic while teaching a new generation this dying oral art form. Sessions are held in a mix of Darija and English.

The cafe also runs a variety of cultural workshops. Sign up for a 101 session on Marrakshi culture and language, stir up some Moroccan flavours on a cooking course, learn how to make your pen dance across the page during a calligraphy course or master the basics of playing the oud.

★ Naranj LEBANESE €€

(Map p84; 0524386805; www.naranj.ma; 84 Rue Riad Zitoun El Jedid; mains Dh60-155; 11.30am-10.30pm Mon-Sat;) Naranj's ultraslick interior of *khamsa* (hand-shaped amulet) mirrors, low-hanging copper lamps and bar seating is quite a scene change on Riad Zitoun El Jedid. It wouldn't look out of place in a hipster 'hood in Beirut, which is the point, because the menu is a contemporary take on Lebanese. Head straight up to the lovely split level terrace and order anything with falafel.

★ Le Jardin MOROCCAN €€

(Map p84; 0524378295; https://lejardinmarrakech.com; 32 Derb Sidi Abdelaziz; mains Dh80-160; 11am-11pm;) Entrepreneur Kamal Laftimi transformed this 17th-century riad in the medina's core into a contemporary, oh-so-pretty oasis where you can lunch beneath a canopy of banana trees, serenaded by songbirds, as tiny tortoises inch across the floor tiles. The menu's modern edge shines through in dishes like beef *tanjia* (stew), with pickles and stuffed seabream with preserved lemon sauce. Booking recommended.

★ Nomad MEDITERRANEAN €€

(Map p84; 0524381609; www.nomadmarrakech.com; 1 Derb Arjan; mains Dh100-130; 11am-11pm;) Nomad's multitiered rooftop is one of the medina's buzziest venues, particularly at night when its lanterns twinkle over Rahba Kedima. The small menu adds contemporary twists to North African ingredients and flavours, creating dishes such as Agadir calamari in a cumin-infused anchovy sauce or whole organic chicken with house-made harissa and *chermoula*. Vegetarian and vegan dishes, like cauliflower in ras-el-hanout spice and turmeric butter, are excellent.

Beats Burger BURGERS €€

(Map p84; 0666994789; www.beatsburger.com; 35 Souq Jeld Kemakine; mains Dh55-115; noon-9pm;) It's a sign of the times in Mouassine to find a gourmet burger joint sitting snug amid the souqs. This neat French-owned restaurant, with floor-to-ceiling windows for prime souq-noseying and a tiny four-table roof terrace, serves juicy prime beef patties (or chicken or fish) with tongue-in-cheek, music-themed names such as 'Notorious Beats' and 'Let it Beat'.

Namaste Cafe VEGAN €€

(Map p74; 0661082041; www.marrakechyogastudio.com; 37 Derb Raouia, Dar Anis; set menu Dh150; 11.30am-4.30pm Mon-Sat;) The only spot in the medina dedicated to vegan food, this simple organic cafe inside **Marrakech Yoga Studio** (yoga class Dh200; 8.30am-6.30pm Mon-Sat) serves one set menu daily, but it's guaranteed to be fresh, packed with goodness from Moroccan farms, and full of flavour. Expect inventive feasts like onion and olive cake, followed by rice salad with saffron-infused radish, and banana ice cream with chocolate and peanut-butter crunch.

Souk Kafé MOROCCAN €€

(Map p84; 0664172456; 11 Derb Sidi Abdelaziz; mains Dh75-120; 11am-11pm;) Climb to the rooftop, doff your sunhat to the giant rattan tea pot and plonk down on a cushion ready to stay a while: this is authentic local food worth savouring. The Moroccan mezze of six cooked vegetable dishes qualifies as lunch for two – but wait until you get a whiff of the aromatic Marrakshi *tanjia*, with its slow-cooked, perfectly falling-apart beef.

La Famille MEDITERRANEAN €€

(Map p84; 0524385295; 42 Rue Riad Zitoun El Jedid; mains Dh85-95; noon-4pm Mon-Sat;) Stepping through the alleyway into La Famille is like emerging through a Narnia wardrobe: it's a different world inside this leafy garden cafe, cocooned from the dusty souq outside. The wholesome menu is vegetarian, inventive and changes daily. Expect dishes like brussels sprout gnocchi with Parmesan, orange zest and dried fig, or barley salad with garlic cheese, salted chickpeas and pear.

Corner Cafe MOROCCAN €€

(Map p84; 0524428307; www.cornercafe.ma; 18 bis Kennaria; mains Dh70-90; 10am-10pm

Tue-Sun; ❄📶🖊) Squeeze yourself up the stairs and onto the teeny Med-inspired mezzanine of this pocket-sized cafe and prepare for a treat. Corner Cafe's simple menu of tajines, couscous, kebabs and burgers (with an equivalent vegetarian menu) leaves diners unprepared for the beautifully presented dishes that emerge from the kitchen. Even the fruit salad has a wow factor.

Hadj Mustapha MOROCCAN €€

(Map p84; east side of Souq Ableuh; stew with bread Dh75; ⏲noon-11pm) The eastern side of Souq Ableuh is known as '*mechoui* alley' for its lunchtime lamb feasts, but the alley's southern entrance is most famous for Hadj Mustapha. The speciality here is the paper-sealed crockpots of *tanjia*, Morocco's famed 'bachelor's stew'. Use bread as your utensil to scoop up the butter-soft meat, sprinkle with cumin and salt, and then chase with olives.

BlackChich AFRICAN €€

(Map p84; ☎0654850600; 1 Derb Nakouss, Riad Zitoun El Jedid; mains Dh70-90; ⏲noon-10.30pm) Housed in a former English church (hence the bell in the logo), laid-back, multilevel BlackChich is a great option for lesser-known African dishes and Senegalese plates. Portion sizes are generous, and the views of the medina from its rooftop are picturesque. Try the Egyptian dukkah-crusted chicken with honey and mint, paired with a date and banana milkshake or homemade lemonade with fresh mint.

Earth Café VEGETARIAN €€

(Map p84; ☎0661289402; 2 Derb Zouak; mains Dh70; ⏲10am-10pm; 📶🖊) Now for something completely different. The Earth Café, right in the heart of the souqs, is small, but its veggie culinary ambitions are great. You'll have no problem getting your five-plus a day here with the choice of veggie burgers, stir-fry-style dishes and vegan plates, served in a colourful house of nooks and terraces.

There's a second branch on **Place des Ferblantiers** (Map p84; Rue Bab Mellah; mains from Dh70; ⏲10am-10pm; 🖊).

★La Maison Arabe MOROCCAN €€€

(Map p74; ☎0524387010; www.lamaisonarabe.com; 1 Derb Assehbe; mains Dh160-250; ⏲7.30pm-midnight; 📶🖊) La Maison Arabe's reputation precedes it: this was the first restaurant set up to cater to foreigners in the medina, in the 1940s. It was a favourite of Winston Churchill, and once you experience the service, you'll see why. A long list of local wines accompanies the menu of international dishes and refined Moroccan classics. Complete your feast with *amlou* (argan-nut butter) tiramisu.

★Le Trou Au Mur GASTRONOMY €€€

(Map p84; ☎0524384900; http://letrouaumur.com; 39 Derb El Farnatchi, Rue Souq El Fassi; mains Dh100-200; ⏲noon-3pm & 6.30pm-midnight Wed-Mon; ❄📶) The menu at this classy yet laid-back contemporary restaurant is on the money with its mix of little-seen Moroccan dishes, fusion food and international crowd pleasers. Stay cool in the mod dining room or head to the rooftop for giant martinis, Berber shepherd's pie, mac and cheese or the house speciality of *mechoui* (slow-roasted lamb).

★PepeNero ITALIAN €€€

(Map p84; ☎0524389067; www.pepenero-marrakech.com; 17 Derb Cherkaoui; mains Dh120-220; ⏲7.30-11.30pm Tue-Sun; 📶🖊) Housed in part of Riad Al Moussika, Thami El Glaoui's one-time pleasure palace, this dreamy Italian-Moroccan restaurant is one of the finest in the medina. The show-stealer is its fresh house-made pasta, including imaginative vegie options like celeriac ravioli with chive sauce. Request a table beside the courtyard pool, rimmed by citrus trees, to make the most of the occasion. Reservations required.

Le Foundouk MOROCCAN €€€

(Map p84; ☎0524378190; www.foundouk.com; 55 Rue Souq El Fassi; mains Dh100-210; ⏲7pm-midnight Thu-Tue; 📶) A spidery iron chandelier lit with candles sets the mood for fine dining, with Moroccan and international menus. Portions aren't huge, but great care is taken to present dishes beyond the run-of-the-mill tourist options, such as tajine with squid and chermoula (herb, garlic and spice marinade), confit leg of lamb with garlic, saffron and pears, and seven-cereal couscous with fish and artichokes.

Gueliz & Ville Nouvelle

Pause Gourmande CAFE €

(Map p74; ☎0524290215; 1 Rue Yves Saint Laurent; mains Dh60-105; ⏲8am-6.30pm; ❄📶) Eating choices around Jardin Majorelle are limited, but this comfy, two-storey cafe with outside seating stands out for its youthful buzz and efficient staff. The coffee is good, and there's an extensive menu of usual suspects (pizza, *bastilla*, tajine, sandwiches, salads) if you need a meal.

Pâtisserie Amandine SWEETS €
(Map p87; ☎0524449612; www.amandinemarrakech.com; 177 Rue Mohammed El Beqal; sweets & desserts from Dh10; ⊙7.30am-9pm) If you're in need of a coffee break while touring Gueliz, this French-influenced update on a Moroccan patisserie shop is a good bet. We defy you to resist its cake counter, where rich custard mille-feuille, rainbow macarons and zesty lemon tarts sit alongside sticky Moroccan pastries.

★**Kilim** MOROCCAN €€
(Map p87; ☎0524446999; Rue de la Liberté; mains Dh60-130; ⊙7am-midnight;) This airy spot is the work of Kamal Laftimi, who launched the popular Nomad restaurant in the medina in 2014. It's his first foray into Gueliz, and he brings a contemporary take on Moroccan ingredients that's surprisingly lacking here. The menu skips from the likes of watermelon, feta and olive salad to crispy chicken sandwich with harissa mayo and fries.

+61 AUSTRALIAN €€
(Map p87; ☎0524207020; https://plus61.com; 96 Rue Mohammed El Beqal; sharing plates Dh50-130; ⊙noon-4pm & 7-10pm Mon-Sat) The menu is constantly evolving at stylish +61, where Australian chef Andrew Cibej aims to capture the laid-back culture of his country in a thoroughly modern way. Dishes are designed to share, put together with locally sourced ingredients and have a strong focus on seasonal greens. The simplicity of the food is matched by the neutral colour palette of the dining room.

Al Fassia MOROCCAN €€€
(Map p87; ☎0524434060; www.alfassia.com; 55 Blvd Mohammed Zerktouni; mains Dh110-175; ⊙noon-2.30pm & 7.30-11pm Wed-Mon) In business since 1987 and renowned for its all-female team, this stalwart of the Marrakesh dining scene is still considered one of the best. The menu champions the classics of Moroccan cuisine, including lesser-known tajines such as lamb with aubergine and beef with almonds and eggs, though we've had reports that service can be hit and miss. Reservations are essential.

Drinking & Nightlife

Marrakesh doesn't have a huge nightlife scene, but in recent years, a few trendy bars have opened in Gueliz. The medina has only a handful of restaurants and bars licensed to serve alcohol, but many riads sell beer and wine to guests in the privacy of their inner courtyards. Sipping mint tea is the main nightlife drinking action for locals.

Solo women should be aware that some clubs can have a sleazy atmosphere.

Medina

★**Kabana** ROOFTOP BAR
(Map p84; ☎0808510684; www.kabana-marrakech.com; Rue Fatima Zohra; ⊙11am-2am;) It feels like there's a bit of Bali and a bit of Senegal in this lively yet relaxed rooftop bar with views of Koutoubia Mosque. Vintage furniture, natural materials and palm prints give the terrace a chic boho feel. Staff give out blankets on colder nights, and there's indoor seating beneath a forest of lanterns for rainy days. Try the signature travel-themed cocktails.

★**Café El Koutoubia** CAFE
(Map p84; Ave Mohammed V; ⊙10am-7pm;) The street terrace at this charmingly old-fashioned cafe with wrought-iron balustrades has cracking views of the Koutoubia Minaret across the road. Despite its touristy position, it's a favourite hang-out for both elderly gentlemen clad in *djellaba* (traditional hooded robes) and suited businessmen – plus the occasional Marrakshi hipster – giving it a properly local ambience.

★**Bacha Coffee** CAFE
(Map p84; Route Sidi Abdelaziz, Rue Dar El Bacha; ⊙10am-6pm Tue-Sun;) Tucked within the chambers of the Dar El Bacha museum (p76), this fancy salon cafe intends to bring coffee connoisseurship back to Marrakesh. Prepare to scrape your jaw off the floor when you see the opulent rooms (a throwback to the early 20th-century colonial French-protectorate era), the 23-page menu of 100% arabica coffees and the prices (pot of coffee from Dh40).

★**El Fenn** COCKTAIL BAR
(Map p84; ☎0524441210; www.el-fenn.com; Derb Moulay Abdellah Ben Hussain, Bab Laksour; ⊙1-10pm;) The best place to see the Koutoubia Mosque's nightly illumination is this achingly hip rooftop bar set up by Richard

Branson's sister. Here, Marrakesh's movers and shakers converge for the medina's best cocktails and relaxed DJ sets. Skip the disappointing, overpriced restaurant, but do plan for an evening sipping martinis under cushion-strewn Berber tents.

Chichaoua TEAHOUSE
(Map p84; ☎0524338470; 69 Place Rahba Kedima; ⌚11am-7pm; 📶) See the black door left ajar, leading to an ascending tiled staircase, just west of Café des Épices on Rahba Kedima? That's the entrance to Chichaoua, the secret tea room launched by Nomad restaurant across the square. Ask for a rundown of its house blends, including the signature sweet orange tea, before reclining on the Barbie-pink midcentury sofa for a sophisticated cuppa.

Café Arabe BAR
(Map p84; ☎0524429728; www.cafearabe.com; 184 Rue Mouassine; ⌚10am-11pm; 📶) Gloat over souq purchases with cocktails on the roof of this bar-restaurant popular with artists, designers and expats. Prices are reasonable for such a stylish place, and you can order half bottles of decent Moroccan wines. The rooftop is divided into two sections, one reserved for diners (the Italian food is surprisingly good), the other for drinkers.

Les Jardins de la Koutoubia BAR
(Map p84; ☎0524388800; www.lesjardinsdelakoutoubia.com; 26 Rue El Koutoubia; ⌚3-11pm) This 1920s hotel offers drinkers double trouble. At sunset, head straight up to the Sky Bar, a secret haven of stylish, shady day beds and trickling fountains, with a shisha menu. When night falls, move downstairs into the classiest gin joint in the medina, with powerful long drinks delivered to leather club chairs beneath cedar ceilings.

To find the Sky Bar, take the lift in the northwest corner (behind the pool) up to the 3rd floor.

Riad Yima TEAHOUSE
(Map p84; www.riadyima.com; 52 Derb Aarjane; ⌚10am-7pm Sun-Thu, to 1.30pm Fri; 📶) Acclaimed Moroccan artist and photographer Hassan Hajjaj created this kitsch-crammed tearoom, boutique and gallery. Here, all your preconceived notions of Moroccan restaurants and riads, with their *Arabian Nights* fantasy of candlelit lanterns, arches and belly dancers, are revamped with a tongue-in-cheek sense of humour, accompanied by a traditional glass of mint tea, of course. It's signposted from Rahba Kedima.

Grand Balcon du Café Glacier CAFE
(Map p84; Djemaa El Fna; ⌚9am-11pm) Yes, it's a total tourist trap, but the roof terrace here is *the* place on the Djemaa to get a good overall view of the carnival of life below. Head straight upstairs, buy a drink (you can't enter without buying something) and get your camera ready for panoramic plaza views.

Terrasse des Teinturiers CAFE
(Map p84; ☎0524391252; 8 Souq Sebbaghine; ⌚10am-9pm) Souqs exhausting you? Climb up the stairs to find a little rooftop oasis high above the haggling din, with colourful skeins of wool hanging from the rooftop pagoda. There's cold juice and coffee, as well as tajines and couscous (from Dh60) if you're hungry.

Gueliz & Ville Nouvelle

★Barometre Marrakech COCKTAIL BAR
(Map p87; ☎0524379012; www.facebook.com/barometremarrakech; Rue Moulay Ali; ⌚6.30pm-midnight Mon-Sat; 📶) Step into a mad professor's underground lab where apothecary jars and brewery piping line the dimly lit bar. Barometre is a first for Marrakesh: an experimental cocktail bar that wouldn't look out of place in Paris or New York. Eschew the classics for a house special; try the Marrakesh Market with whisky, cinnamon, orange and saffron, or a Moorish Coffee with honey, cinnamon and nutmeg.

★Grand Café de la Poste CAFE
(Map p87; ☎0524433038; cnr Blvd El Mansour Eddahbi & Rue Imam Malik; ⌚8am-1am; 📶) Restored to its flapper-era glory, this landmark bistro oozes colonial decadence. Prices run high for food, but you can't beat the atmosphere if you want to be transported back to the art deco era when French diplomats built Gueliz. Lap up the old-world ambience of dark wood, fans and potted palms with a coffee, Darjeeling tea or wine in hand.

68 Bar à Vin WINE BAR
(Map p87; ☎0524449742; 68 Rue de la Liberté; ⌚6pm-2am) A hip and ultralively little wine bar that packs in a nice mixed crowd of Moroccans and foreign residents. There are both European and Moroccan wines on offer as well as beer. Staff are on the ball and

friendly. When it gets too smoky later in the evening, escape to the patio bench seating out the front.

Kechmara BAR
(Map p87; ☎0524422532; www.kechmara.com; 3 Rue de La Liberté; ⏰9am-1.30am; 📶) Want to hang out with the Marrakshi cool kids? Head straight to the covered rooftop bar at Kechmara after sunset and watch it pack out with a buzzing young crowd who lounge on sofas sipping wine and cocktails. Quirky installations, a riot of foliage and flickering candles create a memorable garden-in-the-sky feel. Drinks come with complimentary extras like tapas and spicy juice shots.

Café du Livre CAFE
(Map p87; ☎0524446921; www.facebook.com/cafedulivremarrakech; 44 Rue Tariq Ibn Ziyad; ⏰10am-11pm Mon-Sat; 📶) This upstairs cafe-bar is a chilled-out spot with draft beer, coffee, bar snacks, cushy seating and walls of books to browse and buy. Come for happy hour (6pm to 8pm Tuesday to Saturday) for some of the cheapest beer (from Dh25) and wine (bottles from Dh120) in town. When the after-work crowd descends, it takes on a lively neighbourhood pub atmosphere.

Shopping

Marrakesh is one of the world's great shopping destinations. The full gamut of Moroccan crafts – both traditional and contemporary – can be found here, and few travellers return from a trip empty-handed. In the souqs, haggling is the name of the game, but some medina boutiques and all the Gueliz design shops have fixed prices.

Medina & the Souqs

Running in parallel south from the Djemaa El Fna, Rues Riad Zitoun El Jedid and Riad Zitoun El Kedim are both excellent places to shop. You can get most of the same artisan wares on these streets as in the northern souqs, but the sellers are more laid-back, and there are fewer tour groups here. Recently Riad Zitoun El Kedim has also acquired a cluster of upmarket, fixed-price shops selling contemporary Moroccan homewares, clothes and beauty products.

★**Naturom** COSMETICS
(Map p84; ☎0524383784; 213 Rue Riad Zitoun El Jedid; ⏰9am-8pm) 🍃 Naturom's neatly packaged and keenly priced argan, verbena and orange-blossom beauty products are all 100% certified organic, using pure essences and essential oils to ensure everything is hypoallergenic. With its own medicinal and herbal garden, it has full traceability of most raw materials. Staff speak excellent English and can guide you through the range, including anti-ageing prickly pear oil and hammam *gommage* (exfoliating scrub).

★**Sissi Morocco** FASHION & ACCESSORIES
(Map p84; http://sissimorocco.com; Rahba Kedima; ⏰11am-6pm) This memorable Marrakesh brand has taken old sepia photos of Amazigh tribal women and incorporated them into hand-embroidered and printed bolster cushions, tote bags, purses and t-shirts. The results are striking, and the quality is top notch. French designer Silvie Pissard has her main boutique in Sidi Ghanem (p102), but this petite branch is more conveniently located, in **Rahba Kedima** (Place des Epices; Map p84).

★**Max & Jan** FASHION & ACCESSORIES
(Map p84; ☎0524375570; www.maxandjan.com; 14-16 Rue Amesfah; ⏰10am-7pm) Brace yourself for the future of Marrakesh: Belgian-Swiss design duo Jan Pauwels and Maximilian Scharl have taken over multiple premises to create this giant temple to contemporary Moroccan design. One side is all about quirky jewellery, colour-pop ceramics, posters and cheeky slogan T-shirts, while the other features jazzy caftans, slouchy active-wear and outrageously embellished jackets that wouldn't look out of place on the catwalk.

Pass the camel graffiti, keep heading back and you'll find an artfully arranged collection of rugs and throws in a courtyard that leads up to a popular roof-terrace **cafe** (Map p84; ☎0524427645; https://maxandjan.com; 16 Rue Amesfah; mains Dh100-170; ⏰noon-10pm). Max & Jan may have a global edge, but it's firmly rooted in Morocco: Max was born here, and Jan has lived in Morocco for 15 years. The products sold here are all locally made.

★**Souq Cherifia** DESIGN
(Map p84; Souq Kchachbia; ⏰10am-7pm) Short-circuit souq fatigue and head straight for this converted *funduq* (inn once used by caravans) where younger local designers congregate on the 1st floor in the Carré Créateurs (Artisan Sq). Pick up hand-

embroidered hessian accessories from **Khmissa**, snazzy Berber-design *babouches* (leather slippers) with chunky soles from **Tilila**, and top-quality argan oil, *amlou* (argan-nut butter) and beauty products from **Arganino** (Map p84; 15 Souq Cherifia, Derb Sidi Abdelaziz; ⏲10am-8pm).

L'Art du Bain Savonnerie Artisanale COSMETICS
(Map p84; ☎0666572707; Rahba Kedima; ⏲9.30am-6.30pm) Art du Bain's biodegradable, pure olive oil soaps carry the scent of Marrakesh in them: honey, orange blossom, jasmine, eucalyptus – there's even a chamomile milk version for children – plus scrubs and *ghassoul* clay for the hammam. Soaps come packaged in recycled paper with a contemporary monotone geometric design. The Hand of Fatima soap dishes make great souvenirs.

Al Nour ARTS & CRAFTS
(Map p84; ☎0524390323; www.alnour-textiles.com; Rue Laksour 57; ⏲9.30am-2pm & 3-7.30pm) This smart cooperative run by local women with disabilities is where you can find fabulous neutral household linens, embroidered garments and top-quality accessories. All the textiles can be made to measure, and it's a popular place for stylish hand-stitched Marrakesh-mod tunics, dresses and shirts for men, women and kids. Purchases pay for salaries, training programmes and healthcare.

Anamil ARTS & CRAFTS
(Map p84; 48 Derb Sidi Ishak, Rue Azbezt; ⏲10am-6pm) If you're looking for a unique Moroccan woollen rug or high-quality local souvenirs, Abdess Anamil can help. His small shop is crammed with beautiful things, some of which he has cherry-picked from the workshops of Marrakesh artisans or hunted out in antiques shops, while the dishwasher-safe ceramics and textiles are his own designs. He also speaks excellent English.

Mustapha Blaoui HOMEWARES
(Map p74; ☎0524385240; www.facebook.com/blaouimustapha; 144 Arset Aouzal; ⏲10am-6pm) Treasure hunters rejoice: this is a one-stop shop for all things artisanal. Moroccan lanterns drip from the ceilings of this grand emporium that features well-made delights collected by owner Mustapha Blaoui. Concealed behind an inconspicuous wooden door with no sign, the large space offers a relaxed shopping experience amid several chock-a-block rooms holding everything from cushions and carpets to tables and teapots.

Souq Haddadine ARTS & CRAFTS
(Blacksmith's Souq; Map p84) The blacksmith's souq is full of busy workshops where the sound of the metalworkers' hammers provides a staccato background beat. If you've been tempted by some of those lovely Moroccan lamps for sale throughout the souqs, buying direct here will probably get you the best price. It's difficult to find: follow the noise.

Kaftan Queen FASHION & ACCESSORIES
(Map p84; ☎0524375132; www.facebook.com/Kaftanqueen; Rue Riad Zitoun El Kedim; ⏲10am-1pm & 3-7pm Mon-Sat) Kaftan Queen is light and airy with a changing room fit for royalty, with Syrian mirrors and elegant chandeliers. Everything is reasonably priced, from caftans made for everyday wear to delicately beaded *babouches* in colourful suedes and a range of kimonos. Clutch bags made from locally sourced fabrics and tassels make for a perfect Marrakesh souvenir.

Gueliz & Ville Nouvelle

★**Sidi Ghanem** DESIGN
(Route de Safi; ⏲Mon-Sat) Modern Moroccan design fanatics head 4km out of the central city to the industrial district of Sidi Ghanem to scour local designer factory outlets and showrooms. Negotiate a taxi set rate of Dh150 to Dh250 for the round-trip ride from the medina, and score a map of the quarter at an open showroom.

Be aware that opening hours of shops vary, but some close Saturday afternoon and nearly all are closed on Sunday. Bus 15 goes to Sidi Ghanem from Djemaa El Fna.

★**33 Rue Majorelle** FASHION & ACCESSORIES
(Map p74; ☎0524314195; www.33ruemajorelle.com; 33 Rue Yves Saint Laurent; ⏲9am-7pm) More than 60 designers, mostly from Morocco, are represented in this two-floor emporium, and co-owner Yehia Abdelnour dedicates much of his time to sourcing up-and-coming local talent. Quality is high and the prices can be too, but it's still easy to find lovely threads for under Dh1000. Star buys include silk harem pants, cotton children's smocks and billowing caftans.

SAFETY IN MARRAKESH

Marrakesh is, in general, a safe city, but hustlers and touts are part and parcel of the medina experience. Keep your wits about you and be prepared for a fair amount of hassle.

➡ Pickpockets work on Djemaa El Fna and, to a lesser extent, around the medina. Carry only the minimum amount of cash necessary.

➡ Be particularly vigilant if walking around the medina at night.

➡ Hustlers and unofficial guides hang around the medina. They can be persistent and sometimes unpleasant. Maintain your good humour and be polite when declining offers of help.

Atelier 44 CONCEPT STORE
(Map p87; ☎0524201489; www.facebook.com/atelier44marrakech; 44 Rue Tariq Ibn Ziyad; ⏲10am-8.30pm Mon-Sat) Locals from Casablanca and Rabat make the trek to Marrakesh to shop at Atelier 44's collection of fine contemporary Moroccan designers who are keen to showcase their handmade goods in the Red City. The spa downstairs offers a range of treatments, and the owner's background in the cosmetic industry means only the finest products are used (and also line the shelves for sale).

Sissi Morocco HOMEWARES
(☎0615226520; http://sissimorocco.com; 366 Quartier Industriel Sidi Ghanem; ⏲9am-6pm Mon-Fri, by appointment Sat) The enviable apartment-style showroom creates the perfect ambience for shopping for homewares and textiles. Sissi is known for its bolsters featuring sepia images of Amazigh women and Moroccan scenes mixed with coloured textiles in various textures, a perfect contemporary souvenir from Morocco. The similarly styled bucket bags and t-shirts are equally powerful. All are French-designed, Marrakesh-made.

Some Slow Concept Store HOMEWARES
(Map p87; ☎0524433372; www.facebook.com/someslowconcept; 76 Blvd El Mansour Eddahbi; ⏲10am-7pm Mon-Sat) In a spacious 1936 villa, the Some Slow Concept Store blends the artisanal heritage of Marrakesh with modern-day tastes and trends. Six cosy rooms spread across two floors showcase quality homeware ranges of chic crockery, textiles, lighting and objets d'art. A kitchen pantry selling gourmet artisanal food items leads to a secret vegetarian cafe in a tranquil sunken courtyard.

ℹ Information

EMERGENCY NUMBERS

Ambulance (☎150)
Police (☎190)
Tourist Police (Brigade Touristique; ☎0524384601)

MEDICAL SERVICES

French and Arabic are the most common languages in hospitals, pharmacies and medical clinics.

Clinique Internationale (Map p74; ☎appointments 0524369545, emergencies 0524369595; www.clinique-internationale-marrakech.com; Bab Ighli, off Ave Guemassa) is a central private hospital that's recommended by Marrakesh's foreign residents. It's located east of the Menara Gardens, just off the road to the airport.

Polyclinique du Sud (Map p87; ☎0524447999; 2 Rue de Yougoslavie) is a well-regarded private hospital in Gueliz.

TOILETS

Public toilets are scattered throughout the medina. Most are decently clean and are manned by attendants who expect Dh1 or Dh2 as a tip. Look for the 'WC' signs. Otherwise, head to a cafe.

Public toilets and toilets in cafes and restaurants often have no toilet paper, so keep a supply with you.

Don't throw the paper into the toilet as the plumbing is often dodgy; instead discard it in the bin provided.

TOURIST INFORMATION

Office Regional Marocain du Tourisme (Map p87; ☎0524436179; Place Abdel Moumen Ben Ali; ⏲8.30am-4.30pm Mon-Fri) Offers pamphlets but little in the way of actual information.

Most hotels and riads provide free maps of the city.

TRAVEL AGENCIES

Tawada Trekking (☎0618244431; www.tawadatrekking.com; Hay Ezzaitoun) Multiday trekking tours, rafting and 4x4 trips and cultural immersion are the speciality of this small, professional company run by one of the first Moroccan female licensed mountain guides.

Morocco Adventure & Rafting (www.rafting.ma; half-day rafting trip €80) This company has been leading rafting expeditions (March to mid-May) in the Atlas for more than two decades, with a team of local and international guides all with a minimum of five years' guiding experience. Excursions range from a half-day whitewater trip to Ourika to a three-day rafting excursion in the Ahansel Valley.

Climb Morocco (http://climbmorocco.com) Marrakesh-based operator offering climbing instruction and tours. Guides have more than 20 years of climbing experience.

Insiders Experience (☎0669699374; www.insidersexperience.com; tours from Dh1500) Hop in a vintage motorbike sidecar with a friendly and informative resident expat guide on these off-the-beaten-track tours of the city, desert and Atlas Mountains, or combine a ride with a hot-air balloon excursion.

Inside Morocco Travel (Map p87; ☎0524430020; www.insidemoroccotravel.com; 4th fl, 29 Rue de Yougoslavie; ⊙8.30am-6pm) Specialises in trekking trips into the High Atlas and combined 4x4 excursions exploring the desert and mountains. Its day trip visiting the Agafay Desert, Lalla Takerkoust and hiking around Imlil (from €60 per person) is worthwhile if you're short of time. Can cater for families.

Desir du Maroc (☎0661163585; www.desirdumaroc.com) Abdelhay Sadouk has 30 years' experience introducing visitors to Morocco, leading history and culture tours around Marrakesh's lesser-known sites and further afield to the coast, desert and mountains.

Freeride Morocco (www.freeridemorocco.com) Vehicle-supported mountain bike tours in the High Atlas from a Marrakesh-based operator. Offers set departures and custom trips.

Mountain Voyage (Map p74; ☎WhatsApp 0667611259; www.mountain-voyage.com; 18 Ave Yacoub El Mansour; ⊙9am-1pm & 3-7pm) This British-owned company provides licensed English-speaking guides for tailor-made Marrakesh tours, sustainable tourism excursions in the Middle Atlas, and High Atlas excursions with stays at the Kasbah du Toubkal.

Morocco Exchange (www.moroccoexchange.org) A nonprofit organisation (part of Crossing Borders Education) offering students short-term exchange and travel programmes with a focus on cross-cultural education through visiting cities and rural villages. The programme aims to be different by encouraging participants to engage in discussions and share ideas with young English-speaking Moroccans.

ℹ Getting There & Away

AIR

Small, modern **Marrakech Menara Airport** (☎0524447910; www.marrakesh-airport.com; 📶) is located 6km southwest of town. Because of the growing number of international and charter flights serving Marrakesh, the airport is expanding, and a second terminal is now open.

In the arrivals hall, you'll find currency exchange, ATMs, an information desk and phone providers where you can equip yourself with a Moroccan SIM card. The currency exchange office stays open until the last flight for the night has arrived. There's free wi-fi throughout the airport.

BUS

If you're heading to a more far-flung destination in the south or east, check bus schedules the day before, as there's usually only a couple of services daily at most. For all early-morning bus departures, get tickets the day before, as morning buses fill quickly on holidays and weekends. Essaouira is the most popular destination by far and the one route where you can guarantee services will get booked up, so you should buy tickets at least a couple of days before travelling.

There is little to choose between the main two bus companies, CTM and Supratours. All buses are comfortable, have air-con and abide by set departures (unlike the buses that leave from the *gare routière*, which often hang around if they're not full). To popular destinations such as Agadir, Casablanca and Essaouira, CTM and Supratours offer a more expensive 'comfort plus/premium' service on slightly smaller, nicer buses with toilets.

Both CTM and Supratours have websites, but online booking functionality is extremely poor, and very few visitors have any success booking this way – it's recommended to book in person or to ask your riad to do it for you.

Marrakesh's **Gare Routière** (Map p74; Bab Doukkala; ⊙6am-10pm) is just outside the city walls next to Bab Doukkala, a 15-minute walk northeast of Place du 16 Novembre in Gueliz or a 20-minute walk from Djemaa El Fna.

Inside, a variety of private local bus companies have their ticket booths for regular services to Agadir, Casablanca, Essaouira, Fez and Meknes; and a couple of services daily to Errachidia and Zagora. Buses are of similar quality to CTM and Supratours, but services rarely stick to their timetables. Prices are marginally cheaper, but note that this station is full of persistent touts who take commission on bookings – you may well get quoted three different prices for the same trip.

CTM's Essaouira buses also pick up and drop off here, which makes it the most convenient company to book with if you're heading to Essaouira and staying in the medina. There's a CTM ticket office inside the station.

There are plans afoot to move the station out of the central city.

CAR & MOTORCYCLE

If you're coming into town with your own wheels, try to arrive during daylight hours. Driving through the busy, chaotic traffic at night is stressful for first-time visitors. At all times be alert for scooters, horse carriages, donkeys, pedestrians and other drivers who rarely obey road rules.

Local car hire companies often offer more competitive deals than international operators, with quoted rates starting at around Dh250 per day with air-con and unlimited mileage; prices rise to about Dh450 for larger cars. For 4WD hire, count on Dh1000 to Dh1300 per day with minimal insurance; the priciest options are for the largest vehicles, which can carry up to seven people. You should be able to negotiate a 10% to 20% discount in low season (July to September and mid-January to mid-February).

International agencies Avis, Hertz, Europcar and Budget all have desks at the airport. **KAT** (Map p87; ☎0524430175; 68 Blvd Mohammed Zerktouni; per day from €24, 4x4 €125; ⊙8am-9pm) is a recommended English-speaking local agency.

If you're feeling brave and/or foolhardy, you might join the fray on a scooter or motorcycle. Rentals are available from **Marrakech Roues** (Map p84; ☎0663061892; www.marrakech-roues.com; Imm Roux, 3 Rue Bani Marine; bicycle per half-/full-day Dh80/120, motorbike per day from Dh500; ⊙9am-7pm Mon-Sat).

TAXI

Grands taxis are larger taxis that can carry up to seven people and are licensed to travel outside the city. They can be a good option for low-cost group travel but rarely come with functioning seatbelts so are not a great choice for families who want to use car seats (you're better off booking a private car through your hotel). You can book grands taxis as private cars, or buy a seat in a *collective*. They don't leave until they are full, which can mean a lot of waiting around at the car park, depending on the popularity of your destination. The prices quoted below are for a seat in a *collective*.

Grands taxis to **Asni** (Map p84; Rue Uqba Bin Nafaa; Dh20) and some other High Atlas destinations depart from Rue Uqba Bin Nafaa, alongside the medina wall, a short walk from Djemaa El Fna. Those departing for **Ourika Valley and**

CTM BUS SERVICES FROM MARRAKESH

The **CTM bus station** (Map p74; ☎0522541010; www.ctm.ma; Rue Abou Bakr Seddiq; ⊙6am-10pm) is located southwest of the train station (about 15 minutes on foot). There's not much at the station in the way of facilities beyond a smoky 24-hour cafe with stuttering wi-fi. You can buy tickets at the station, at the CTM counter in the *gare routière* at Bab Doukkala and from the CTM ticket office in Gueliz on Blvd Mohammed Zerktouni.

A taxi from the station to Djemaa El Fna shouldn't cost more than Dh20, but it's virtually impossible to get that rate – drivers will often quote Dh50. Note that if you have a large suitcase, you will need a grand taxi, and they charge more (Dh50 is about right). Your best bet for a decent fare is to walk as far away from the station as possible and hail a petit taxi from the road.

DESTINATION	PRICE	DURATION (HR)	FREQUENCY (DAILY)
Agadir	regular/premium Dh115/140	3½-4	19
Casablanca	regular/premium Dh90/130	3½	20
Errachidia	Dh175	10	1
Essaouira	Dh80	3½	2
Fez	regular/premium Dh180-190/250	8-9	6
Laayoune	Dh365	14-15½	7
Ouarzazate	Dh90	4	6
Tan Tan	Dh225	9	8
Tiznit	Dh145	5½	13
Zagora	Dh155	7½	2

SUPRATOURS BUS SERVICES FROM MARRAKESH

Supratours (Map p87; www.supratours.ma; Ave Hassan II) is located west of the train station, in the old station building. The station has a cafe. Bus services connect to train departure and arrival times. Larger bags incur an extra Dh5 charge, which needs to be paid for at the room to the left of the main entrance, signposted as 'Enregistrement Bagages', before boarding.

Taxis wait in the Supratours parking lot.

DESTINATION	PRICE	DURATION (HR)	FREQUENCY (DAILY)
Agadir	regular/comfort plus Dh110/130	3½	11
Dakhla	Dh490	23	2
Essaouira	regular/comfort plus Dh80/110	3	6
Laayoune	Dh360	15	6
Ouarzazate	Dh90	4½	3
Merzouga	Dh240	12	1
Zagora	Dh140	7¾	1

Setti Fatma (Map p84; Rue Ibn Rachid; Dh30-35) cluster around Rue Ibn Rachid, one road to the east.

Grands taxis (Map p74; off Ave du 11 Janvier) serving destinations further afield, including those bound for Agadir (Dh120), Demnate (Dh50), Essaouira (Dh100), Ouarzazate (Dh120) and Taroudant (Dh120), gather at a car park just north of Bab Doukkala, beyond the bus station. Prices can fluctuate by Dh10 to Dh20 depending on demand.

TRAIN

Marrakesh's modern **train station** (www.oncf.ma; cnr Ave Hassan II & Blvd Mohammed VI; 🛜) is big, organised and convenient, with ATMs, cafes and fast-food outlets. There's free wi-fi and limited seating. Buy tickets at the staffed counter or from multilingual self-service kiosks. At the latter, you can also pick up tickets pre-booked online – the ONCF online booking system is actually pretty good. Prices are the same online and at the station, and payment can be made with cash or card.

Taxis wait just outside. To Djemaa El Fna, it's no more than Dh20 on the meter (Dh30 at night), but drivers are notorious for not putting the meter on. Usually you'll be offered a grand taxi if you are carrying large luggage, which costs more – around Dh50. City bus 10 (Dh4) heads down Ave Hassan II and Ave Mohammed V to Djemaa El Fna roughly every 20 minutes between 6am and 10pm.

ℹ Getting Around

Compact and flat, Marrakesh was made for walking. The medina's skinny maze of souqs and alleys can only be explored on foot. They're usually shady and would make for very pleasant ambling were it not for the speeding motorbikes – walking anywhere in the medina requires vigilance, as there's plenty of local traffic (also people, carts, donkeys etc) even along car-free streets.

Gueliz is laid out like a European city, with pavements for walking, but the lack of shade can make it a hot place to wander around, particularly in summer.

TO & FROM THE AIRPORT

Airport bus 19 (Map p84; Place de Foucauld; one way/return Dh30/50; ⏱6.15am-9.30pm) runs a circular route, every 30 minutes, between the airport and central Marrakesh. From the airport, it stops at Place de Foucauld (a one-minute walk to Djemaa El Fna) and then runs along Ave Mohammed V via Bab Nkob (alight for Bab Doukkala) to Gueliz (passing Place du 16 Novembre and the train station) before heading back to the airport.

A petit taxi to central Marrakesh from the airport (6km) should be no more than Dh70 on the meter, but you will most likely have extreme difficulty convincing the driver to take you for this fare. Late at night, with no other transport available, drivers will typically quote between Dh120 and Dh150.

For journeys to the airport from the medina, all taxis drivers will quote the same rate of Dh150 to Dh200, depending on which area of the medina you're in.

BICYCLE

This pancake-flat city is good terrain for cyclists, but traffic is a major problem: you'll need to be a confident rider to stomach the medina hubbub. Good-quality bicycles and helmets can be hired from AXS (p88) and Pikala Bikes (p88).

TRAIN SERVICES FROM MARRAKESH

The last Tangier train travels overnight. Sleeping-car compartment tickets cost from Dh499; book at least two days in advance.

DESTINATION	PRICE 1ST/2ND CLASS	DURATION (HR)	FREQUENCY (DAILY)
Casablanca	Dh150/120	2¾	hourly
Fez	Dh290/215	6	hourly
Meknes	Dh266/198	5¾	hourly
Rabat	Dh197/152	4	9
Tangier	Dh327/216	9½	7

In 2016 Marrakesh became the first city in Africa to introduce a bike-sharing scheme. **Medina Bike** (☎0612644734; www.medinabike.ma; 1-/7-day pass Dh50/150) has kiosks at Koutoubia Mosque, Place de la Liberté in Gueliz and Jardin Majorelle. Register for the service through the app or website.

BUS

Local buses are run by **Alsa** (Map p84; www.alsa.ma; Place de Foucauld; fare Dh4). There's a semi-helpful route map on Alsa's website and at the main medina bus stop at Place de Foucauld in front of Djemaa El Fna. Services start around 6am and finish between 9.30pm and 10pm, with buses on most routes running every 15 to 20 minutes. Tickets cost Dh4; buy on board using small change.

Key bus lines include the following:

Bus 1 Djemaa El Fna–Gueliz–Bab Doukkala

Bus 10 Djemaa El Fna–train station

Bus 11 Bab Doukkala–Djemaa El Fna–Menara Gardens

Bus 12 Bab Doukkala–Jardin Majorelle–Gueliz–Hivernage

Bus 15 Djemaa El Fna–Gueliz–Sidi Ghanem

Bus 16 Djemaa El Fna–Bab Doukkala–Gueliz–northwest suburbs

CALÈCHES

These green horse-drawn carriages congregate at Place de Foucauld next to Djemaa El Fna and around Jardin Majorelle. They're a pleasant way to get around if you avoid the rush hours (8am, noon and 5.30pm to 7.30pm). Bargain hard on the cost: a good rate would be around Dh150 for a 1½ hour tour, but many tourists end up paying double that. You can dictate the route to an extent, but a typical tour might run from Jardin Majorelle to the Kasbah and Mellah via Djemaa El Fna, and around the ramparts.

Check the condition of the horse before haggling for a ride as some are better cared for than others. Animal welfare charity SPANA (www.spana.org) works with Marrakesh's *calèche* drivers, monitoring horse welfare and maintaining water troughs along popular carriage routes.

CAR & MOTORCYCLE

Driving in Marrakesh is not for the faint-hearted. Drivers rarely stay in lane and don't indicate, and you'll have to contend with taxis that stop in awkward places, crowds, *calèches*, donkey carts…you get the picture. We don't recommend it. If you are driving around Morocco and need to park up in Marrakesh while visiting the city, we recommend picking accommodation in Gueliz or on the outskirts of the medina close to a public car park.

In the medina there are guarded car parks on Rue Fatima Zohra (near Djemaa El Fna), Rue Riad Zitoun El Jedid (near Bahia Palace), Rue Berrima (south of Bahia Palace) and Rue El Adala (by Bab Doukkala). In Gueliz there's a secure underground car park on Ave Mohammed V, opposite the post office. Expect to pay Dh20/40 during the day/per 24 hours.

In Gueliz, some roads have parking meters (Dh2 per hour). If you find street parking without a meter, a guardian will expect a Dh10 tip for keeping an eye on your car; look for the person in the blue coat or high-vis jacket and pay your tip afterwards.

TAXI

There are no useful ride-hailing apps in Marrakesh, and getting a taxi can be a stressful experience. All drivers will insist their meter is 'broken' and will quote prices up to 10 times the metered rate – avoid getting taxis wherever possible, but particularly those waiting at stands that get a lot of tourist business (the airport, train station, Jardin Majorelle and virtually all those around the medina gates). You can usually get a better price by flagging a taxi down from the street.

If your party numbers more than three, you must take a grand taxi, which are a little harder to find on the roads but not impossible. Note that taxis take multiple fares at the same time (never mind how they work out who owes what), though it's common for drivers to insist tourists take a private journey to justify the fare hike you'll be shafted with.

If you're trying to hail a taxi from the road, you can theoretically flag down any taxi as long as it has fewer than three passengers already inside. The driver will ask where you're going, and if it's in the same direction as the other passengers, he should let you jump in.

MASSIMO PIZZOTTI/GETTY IMAGES ©

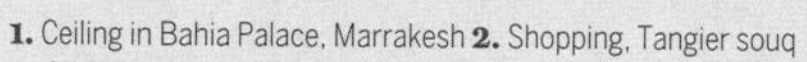
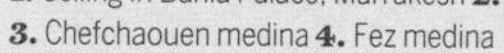
1. Ceiling in Bahia Palace, Marrakesh **2.** Shopping, Tangier souq
3. Chefchaouen medina **4.** Fez medina

GERT-JAN VAN VLIET /SHUTTERSTOCK©

Winding Lanes

You could happily spend days in the best medinas of Morocco – getting lost, drinking tea, and getting lost again. The serendipity of chance discoveries are all part of the charm. Magical medinas are found in every part of the country, each with its own special flavour – here are some of the most atmospheric.

Marrakesh Medina

Inside 19km of ramparts, the theatrical Djemaa el Fna (p72) is the beating, back-flipping heart of the Marrakesh medina. Follow crazy lanes – or thoroughfares if you forgot your compass – to sights such as Bahia Palace (p78).

Tangier Medina

Europe is just across the Strait of Gibraltar, but it feels a world away among the kasbah and souqs of the Tangier medina (p250). Spots like Petit Socco have been given a fresh coat of paint as part of the city's makeover.

Chefchaouen Medina

High in the Rif Mountains, Chefchaouen medina (p281) is painted a delightful Andalucian blue, fringed with terracotta tiles and green hills. You won't get too horribly lost in this compact mini-maze.

Essaouira Medina

In the salty embrace of Morocco's Atlantic sea, the fortified walls of Essaouira's laid-back medina (p233) trace the coastline and seagulls swarm overhead. It still has all the classic hallmarks: narrow twisty lanes, souqs and the aroma of spices – but here they combine with the damp sea air, smell of fish guts and crashing waves.

Fez Medina

Old Fez (p323) is Morocco's largest intact medina and embodies over 1200 years of history. Even old hands get lost in this maze of souqs and tanneries – you might chance upon a craft museum or a 14th-century *medersa* (theological college).

1. Erg Chebbi (p176) **2.** Aït Mansour Gorge (p411) **3.** *Palmeraie*, Nkob (p180) **4.** Paradise Valley (p399)

CORNFIELD/SHUTTERSTOCK ©

Deserts & Oases

Morocco sits on the edge of the great Sahara, and its dunes and oases are a huge draw for travellers. Follow the paths of the old camel caravans that once trekked across the desert, carrying salt and gold from Timbuktu.

Erg Chebbi & Erg Chigaga

The dunes at Erg Chebbi (p176) and Erg Chigaga (p157), respectively rising to 160m and 300m, are Morocco's greatest desert sights. These are the places to disappear into the desert, accompanied by a camel and blue-robed guide, to see the sand sea by moonlight and sleep in a nomad camp.

Desert Valleys

Coming from Marrakesh, there are more accessible glimpses of the desert in the Draa Valley (p151), where a sign once advised desert caravans that Timbuktu was only 52 days away, and oases remain the region's lifeblood. In Ouarzazate (p144) the desert stretches to the foot of the Atlas, and palms can be spotted through slit windows in the Taourirt kasbah.

The Deep South

Largely overlooked by travellers, the *hammada* (flat, stony desert) of the far south runs through the Western Sahara. It's a stark environment, mainly crossed by overlanders en route to Mauritania.

TOP OASES

Figuig (p172) Seven traditional desert villages amid 200,000 date palms.

Nkob (p180) Mudbrick castles overlook the *palmeraie* (palm grove).

Skoura (p160) The Unesco-protected 'Oasis of 1000 Palms'.

Ameln Valley (p412) Village *palmeraies* beneath Jebel L'Kest.

Tata (p413) Treetops are a welcome sight in this Saharan outpost.

Paradise Valley (p399) *Palmeraies*, oleanders and beehives line the gorge.

AT A GLANCE

POPULATION
Errachidia: 92,374

TALLEST WATERFALLS
Cascades d'Ouzoud (p131)

BEST OASIS ESCAPE
Auberge La Terrasse des Délices (p150)

BEST WEEKEND RETREAT
Riad Cascades d'Ouzoud (p131)

BEST SAHARAN FUSION
Relais Saint Exupéry (p149)

WHEN TO GO

Mar & Apr Mountains thaw; desert blooms. Skip Easter holidays when prices jump.

May & Jun Ideal High Atlas hiking: hot, not scorching. Accommodation and souq bargains.

Oct & Nov Prime desert time; gentle breezes, dates galore.

Cascades d'Ouzoud (p131)
ALBERTSAOVO/GETTY IMAGES ©

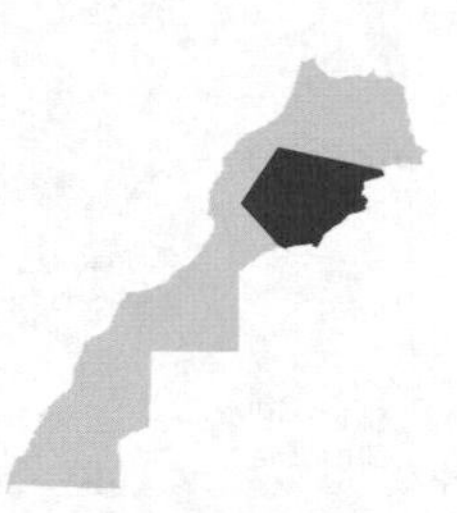

Central Morocco

وسط المغرب

Against the soaring peaks of the Atlas mountains, picturesque Amazigh (Berber) villages, palm-filled oases and undulating desert landscapes set the stage for an extraordinary range of adventures. There's hiking along craggy clifftops in the M'Goun and Toubkal Massifs or the stunning Todra and Dadès Gorges, and desert wanders by camel amid the sand dunes surrounding Merzouga and M'Hamid.

Amazigh culture is the region's real treasure. Family-run guesthouses and lavish kasbahs roll out the welcome mat, spread decadent feasts and introduce out-of-towners to the great wonders of Atlas living. Speaking of wonders, central Morocco has them in spades, from thundering waterfalls and fossil-strewn plateaus to ancient citadels and snowy mountain passes, plus North Africa's highest ski slopes.

INCLUDES

Central Morocco Highlights

❶ **Zaouiat Ahansal** (p132) Getting off the beaten track by hiking, rafting or climbing.

❷ **Erg Chigaga** (p157) Enjoying breathtaking sunsets and star-filled nights amid the rolling dunes of the Sahara.

❸ **Jebel Toubkal** (p116) Standing atop North Africa's highest peak as the sunrise lights the horizon.

❹ **Ait Bougmez Valley** (p134) Walking through Morocco's stunning and secluded Shangri-La.

❺ **Draa Valley** (p151) Following desert caravan routes from kasbah to kasbah.

❻ **Tin Mal Mosque** (p130) Beholding the last remnants of the Almohid empire's great mountain stronghold.

❼ **Dadès Gorge** (p166) Spotting crag-top villages and extreme geological formations.

❽ **Skoura** (p160) Slowing down and strolling amid swaying palm trees in this Unesco-protected oasis.

❾ **Glaoui Kasbah** (p144) Witnessing a troubled history and impeccable artistry at this historic site in Telouet.

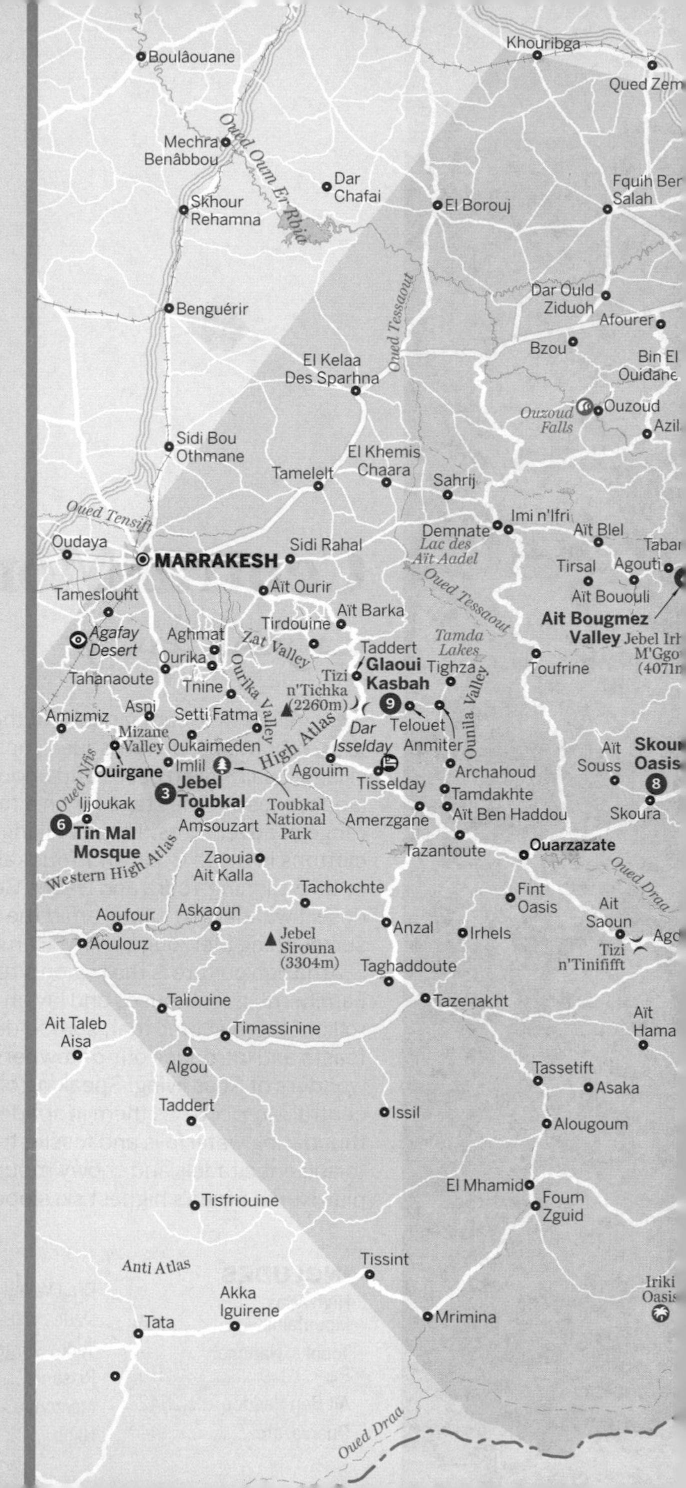

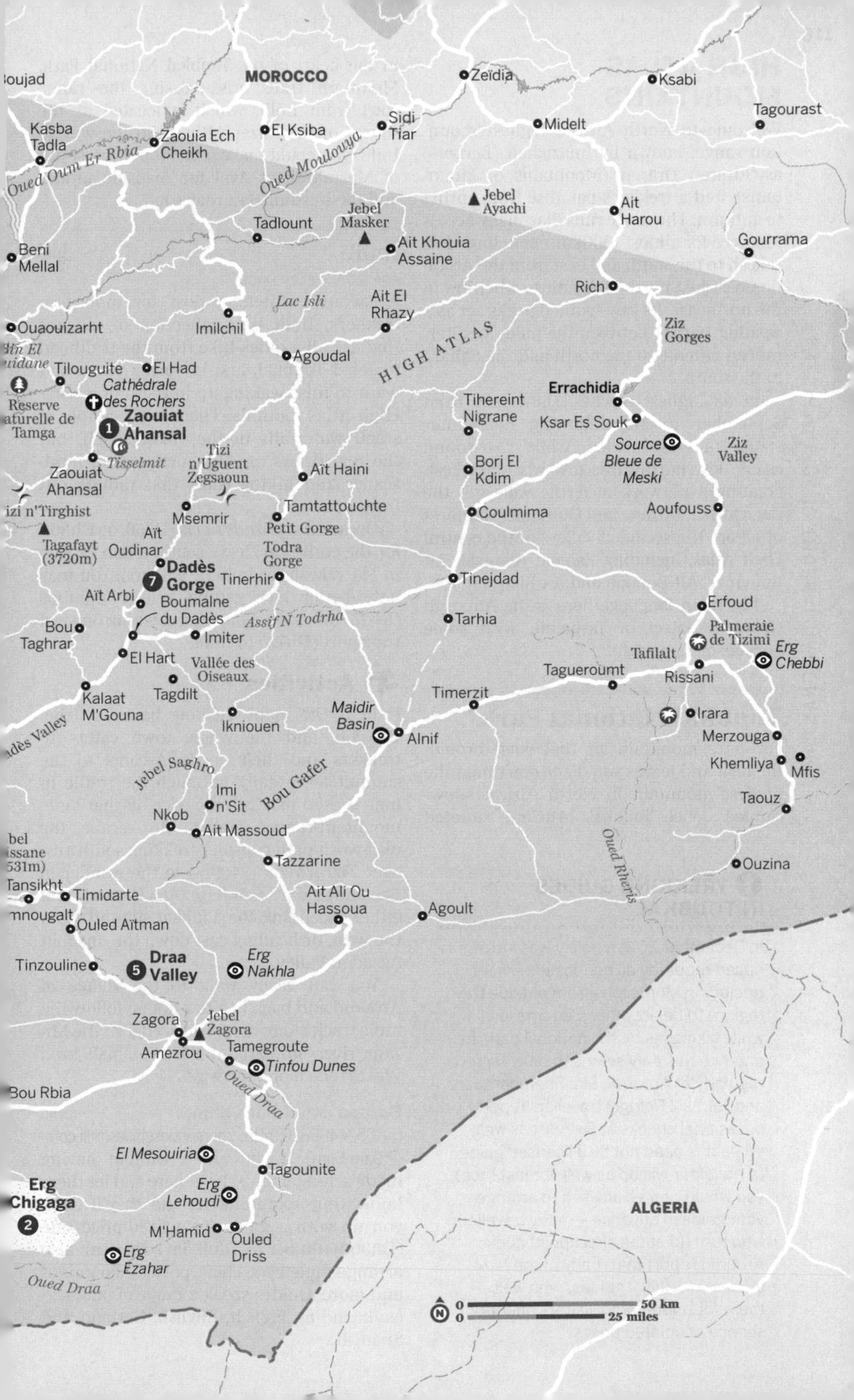

MOROCCO
Zeïdia
Ksabi
Tagourast
Kasba Tadla
Zaouia Ech Cheikh
El Ksiba
Sidi Tiar
Midelt
Oued Oum Er Rbia
Oued Moulouya
Jebel Ayachi
Ait Harou
Jebel Masker
Tadlount
Beni Mellal
Ait Khouia Assaine
Gourrama
Rich
Lac Isli
Ait El Rhazy
Ouaouizarht
Imilchil
Ziz Gorges
Agoudal
HIGH ATLAS
Tilouguite
El Had
Cathédrale des Rochers
Reserve
Errachidia
Tihereint Nigrane
Ksar Es Souk
Zaouiat Ahansal
Source Bleue de Meski
Ziz Valley
Tizi n'Uguent Zegsaoun
Tisselmit
Borj El Kdim
Aït Haini
Zaouiat Ahansal
Tamtattouchte
Msemrir
Aoufouss
Coulmima
Petit Gorge
Aït Oudinar
Tagafayt (3720m)
Todra Gorge
Dadès Gorge
Tinerhir
Tinejdad
Aït Arbi
Boumalne du Dadès
Erfoud
Bou Taghrar
Assif N Todrha
Tarhia
Imiter
Palmeraie de Tizimi
El Hart
Tafilalt
Erg Chebbi
Vallée des Oiseaux
Tagueroumt
Rissani
Tagdilt
Timerzit
Kalaat M'Gouna
Maidir Basin
Irara
Iknioun
Alnif
Merzouga
Jebel Saghro
Bou Gafer
Khemliya
Mfis
Imi n'Sit
Taouz
Nkob
Ait Massoud
Oued Rheris
Tazzarine
Ouzina
Tansikht
Timidarte
Ait Ali Ou Hassoua
Agoult
Ouled Aïtman
Tinzouline
Draa Valley
Erg Nakhla
Jebel Zagora
Zagora
Amezrou
Tamegroute
Tinfou Dunes
Bou Rbia
Oued Draa
El Mesouiria
Tagounite
Erg Chigaga
Erg Lehoudi
ALGERIA
M'Hamid
Ouled Driss
Erg Ezahar
Oued Draa
0 50 km
0 25 miles

HIGH ATLAS MOUNTAINS

Welcome to North Africa's highest mountain range, known by Imazighen (Berbers) as 'Idraren Draren' (Mountains of Mountains), and a trekker's paradise from spring to autumn. The range runs diagonally across Morocco for almost 1000km, encircling Marrakesh to the south and east from the Atlantic Coast just north of Agadir to Khenifra in the northeast. Its saw-toothed peaks act as a weather barrier between the mild, Mediterranean climate to the north and the Sahara to the south.

In its highest reaches, snow falls from September to May, allowing for winter sports in Oukaimeden, while year-round rivers flow northwards towards Marrakesh creating a network of fertile valleys – the Zat, Ourika, Mizane and Ouirgane. Happiest of all are the secluded valleys of the central High Atlas, including Zaouiat Ahansal, Ait Bougmez, Ait Bououli and Ait Blel.

The main language here is the Amazigh (Berber) dialect of Tashelhit, with some pockets of Tamazight.

Toubkal National Park

For pure mountain air that cuts through the heat and leaves you dizzy, don't miss the highest mountain in North Africa: snow-capped Jebel Toubkal (4167m), situated in the heart of the Toubkal National Park. Mountain trails criss-crossing the range start from Imlil, which is located at the source of the Mizane River. On the way to Imlil, you could make a pit stop 47km south of Marrakesh at Asni for roadside tajines and the bustling Saturday souq.

TREKKING GUIDES IN TOUBKAL

In December 2018 a policy was introduced requiring all non-local trekkers (including Moroccans from outside the region) to be accompanied by a local while hiking inside the national park. In practice this only seems to be enforced regularly at Aroumd, Sidi Shamharoush and Toubkal Refuge; travellers report occasional checks at Tachdirt as well. While this need not be a licensed guide (a muleteer will do as well, for instance) you would be well advised to arrange your guide in advance – many travellers who turn up at the checkpoint above Aroumd report that many of the *faux guides* (unofficial guides) who wait there for unprepared visitors offer poor service at inflated prices.

Imlil إمليل

POP 5100 / ELEV 1740M

A favourite hitching post for mountain trekkers, Imlil is a collection of villages that are all a quick hike from the trailhead to Jebel Toubkal, and in spring you won't want to miss waking up in these flowering High Atlas foothills. There are a couple of small waterfalls in the village itself, but the real draws are the surrounding landscapes and hiking trails that radiate out from here.

Occasional *grands taxis* (Dh50, or Dh300 for the entire car) leave south of Bab Er Rob in Marrakesh for Imlil (2½ hours). You may have better luck getting a local minibus (Dh25) or taxi to Asni, then catching onward transport (Dh7.5) to Imlil.

Activities

Imlil is the main trekking base for Jebel Toubkal, and the whole town caters to trekkers and their needs. Ascents to the summit leave daily, although the traffic in high season may rub the edge off that lone-mountain-ranger fantasy. To escape the well-worn path consider trekking southwest over Tizi n'Mzik (2489m) to the wonderful **Cascades d'Irhoulidene** (Azib Tamsoult) and either ascending the Toubkal summit from the west, or heading east down the unspoilt Azzadan Valley.

You can easily walk to the village of Aroumd and back in a few hours; follow the mule track along the western edge of the Mizane river, stopping at the two small **Imlil Waterfalls** along the way.

Bureau des Guides d'Imlil HIKING
(☎0524485626; http://bureaudesguidesimlil.com; ⊙9am-6pm) If you arrive without having made arrangements, head here and let them know your requirements and they'll hook you up with a guide for a fixed-price rate (Dh300/400 per half/full day); they can also arrange muleteers, chefs, porters, ski guides and more. Guides speak a range of languages, including French, English, German and Spanish.

Trekking maps (Dh80) and free wi-fi are available, and you can leave luggage here (Dh20).

Toubkal Guide TREKKING
(☎0671157636, 0661417636; ⏲9am-6pm Mon-Sat) Run by one of the four co-owners of Mountain Travel Morocco (with whom they share an Imlil office just below the main junction and bridge), Jamal's extensive history in the trekking and tourism sectors means he has a fairly good understanding of what foreign clients expect, and is able to provide it.

Mountain Travel Morocco TREKKING
(☎0524485784; ⏲9am-6pm Mon-Sat) Established by four of Imlil's most-experienced trekking guides, Mountain Travel Morocco is Imlil's first fully registered, private guiding outfit offering treks to suit all levels. Guides are also trained in first aid and are experienced in dealing with altitude sickness. To ensure you can undertake the trek you want when you want to complete it, book in advance.

Mountain Bike Morocco MOUNTAIN BIKING
(☎0668766245; https://mountain-bike-morocco.com) Run by a group of avid local bikers, this well-equipped outfit uphill from the Bureau des Guides offers a range of itineraries criss-crossing the Atlas. Routes range from relaxed day tours to an epic nine-day Atlas traverse from Marrakesh to Jebel Saghro.

Sleeping

Imlil is packed with *gîtes* (basic homestays or hostels) and small hotels, but it's generally a good idea to book ahead; some places close between November and February. Additional options are available in nearby Aroumd, but the village has minimal facilities by comparison.

★ **Riad Atlas Toubkal** GUESTHOUSE €
(☎0662058251; www.riadatlastoubkal.com; d/tr/ste Dh300/400/600; P wi-fi) This appealing guesthouse has eight cosy rooms with large picture windows that catch mountain breezes and boast views as fine as those at the kasbah; three rooms also have balconies. Piles of board games and books keep idle hours filled. Guest showers for sweaty trekkers, panoramic views from the restaurant and parking complete the excellent service.

LAST-MINUTE TREK NEEDS

Although small, **Atlas Extreme** (☎0661601590; https://atlasextreme.com; Imlil; ⏲9am-7pm) carries an impressive variety of trekking and climbing equipment, including hard-to-find butane canisters for camping stoves and a small selection of maps.

Imlil Lodge GUESTHOUSE €
(☎0671157636; https://toubkalguide.com; Tamatert; r €35-40; wi-fi) Run by Jamal Imrehane, owner of Toubkal Guide, this friendly stone-faced guesthouse looks out over Imlil and the Mizane Valley from Tamatert. Arranged around an internal courtyard, riad-style rooms come with fancy stucco ceilings, brass lanterns and stripey Asni blankets. Several rooms have balconies and one also has a fireplace.

Needless to say, with one of the most experienced local guides as your host, all your trekking needs are covered here. Just up the hill is the **Kasbah Imlil** (☎0661417636; www.kasbah-imlil.com; Tamatert; r €30-40; wi-fi), a similarly nice choice run by the same owner.

Riad Atlas Prestige GUESTHOUSE €
(☎0666494954; www.atlas-prestige.com; d €20-30, tr €35; wi-fi) This pleasant six-room guesthouse has an appealing riad-style layout, with an open courtyard and several terraces for taking in the views. Rooms are comfortably furnished with handsome tiled floors, and the best have balconies. Dinners cost Dh80 per person. It's a steep 10-minute uphill walk from the centre of Imlil.

Riad Ouassaggou RIAD €
(☎0667491352; www.guesthouseouassaggou.com; Douar Aït Soukka; s/d/tr Dh200/250/300; wi-fi) A walnut orchard shades the valley paths surrounding this eight-room guesthouse, where visitors are received like long-lost relatives by Houssein, an English-speaking mountain guide. Cosy, comfortable bedrooms have en suites, one with a *tadelakt* (waterproof-plaster) tub. The terrace is ideal after a morning trek, and they can also arrange meals.

Imlil Refuge HOSTEL €
(☎0661873771; dm Dh100) Imlil Refuge offers the cheapest lodging in town with 10 simple but clean rooms that share bathrooms. There's a sitting room with fireplace, a roof terrace and a shared kitchen. It's a fine bunkhouse for trekkers before or after making the big ascent.

WORTH A TRIP

A DAY AMONG THE DUNES: AGAFAY DESERT

Though the stony hills of the Agafay Desert may lack the towering dunes of the Sahara, High Atlas panoramas and proximity to Marrakesh make the area's rough dry expanse a popular glamping getaway from the city. In spring wheat and wildflowers predominate; in summer and autumn it really does look like the desert.

Luxury desert retreats are the name of the game here. They're all set up for relaxing, unwinding and making the most of the harshly beautiful surrounding countryside. If you're looking to explore the area on the cheap, it's better to make a day trip from Marrakesh.

Because of the rural, isolated nature of most retreats and resorts in this area, most travellers eat in their accommodation. Those just passing through or with their own wheels can find a handful of tajine and fast-food joints at the main intersection in the centre of Lalla Takerkoust village on the north edge of the lake.

La Fleche Takerkoust (0694870066; https://laflechetakerkoust.com; Lalla Takerkoust; d/tr from Dh400/600;) The seven simple but comfortable rooms at La Fleche are pretty much the only option if you just need a room for the night without the luxury frills. It's just above the main intersection at the centre of Lalla Takerkoust village, on the north end of the lake.

La Pause (0610772240; www.lapause-marrakech.com; Douar Lmih Laroussiéne; tent/r €180/225, ste €250-400; P) Escape the grid at this luxury desert getaway where you can experience the stark, visceral beauty of Morocco's countryside. This is a chill-out zone extraordinaire, where electricity and smartphone checking is out, hammock swinging and nomad-tent dining is in, and you bed down in spacious bedroom tents or rustic-chic bungalows complete with candles, *tataoui* (woven reed) ceilings and Berber carpets. All rates include breakfast, and most guests will book half- or full-board. Chauffeured transport is available to and from Marrakesh for the 30km trip, as are helicopter transfers. It's also possible to arrange meals and activities without being an overnight guest.

Inara Camp (0524204973; www.inaracamp.com; tents incl half-board Dh2000-2800, ste Dh3500-4000; P) Luxury tents here are equipped with all the necessities, with more-expensive options boasting small terraces with sunrise views, and staff seem to be genuinely dedicated to making sure every day at the camp is unique and special for guests. A separate section of the camp is available for day-use guests, many of whom come to partake in activities like hiking and camel riding then stay for dinner to enjoy the night sky.

Terre des Étoiles (0524447375; www.terredesetoiles.net; s/d/tr incl half-board from Dh1711/1980/2855; P) Get away from it all at this peaceful spot amid the lunar terrain with fine views of the distant Atlas Mountains. Lodging is in spacious luxury tents complete with comfy mattresses, quality furnishings and en suite bathrooms. There's plenty of chic common spaces to relax in for the day, or guests can head out on excursions.

La Villa du Lac (Rive du Lac; 0661249900; www.lavilladulac-marrakech.net; Lalla Takerkoust; r Dh900-1200;) Trade in desert views and starry nights for lakefront sunsets beside the swimming pool. When Lalla Takerkoust lake is full the waters lap right up to the lower terrace here, but at any time of year the view to hillocks and villages on the opposite shore is sublime. Ask for one of the larger rooms, which are worth the extra charge.

Getting There & Away

Getting to Lalla Takerkoust village is no problem by bus or grand taxi from Marrakesh (Dh6) or Amizmiz (Dh6). But unless you have your own wheels, getting rides to and around the the desert camps is near impossible without getting massively overcharged. All the resorts in the area can arrange pick-up and drop-off transfers to and from Marrakesh.

Douar Samra RIAD €€
(☎0524484034; www.douar-samra.net; Tamartert; r per person incl half-board €47-59; 📶) At the eastern end of the valley in Tamartert, a trail zigzags among low-slung houses made of *pisé* (rammed earth); the triple-decker one is Douar Samra. Take the hewn stone steps to candlelit, wood-beamed guest rooms – one of which is in a tree house, which is a hit with child travellers.

Donkeys deliver luggage, there's wi-fi in the organic garden, and aperitifs with sunsets on the terrace. The overall vibe is idyllic.

Kasbah du Toubkal HERITAGE HOTEL €€€
(☎0524485611; www.kasbahdutoubkal.com; d €175-270, ste €365, villa €960; ❄📶) This converted historic kasbah, at 1800m, lords it over Imlil with grand views over the mountainous landscape. The 11 bedrooms range from quaintly cute to kasbah cool, and 'Berber Salons' (three/four people €145/175, €42 for each additional person) allow families and groups to bunk communally. Traditional hammam, mountain guides, board games and tasty meals (prix-fixe dinner €20) are on offer.

Minimum two nights in high season. A 5% community tariff has helped build several boarding schools and supply two ambulances. The kasbah is uphill through the forest from Imlil, but donkeys can be arranged for luggage.

Eating & Drinking

There are a few simple cafes and restaurants around town; the best meals, however, are served in the higher-end hotels, for which you'll need to book ahead.

As elsewhere in the Atlas Mountains, nightlife is unknown here.

Cafe Atlas Toubkal CAFE €
(mains Dh35-90, set menus Dh150; ⏱8.30am-9pm; 📶) Well-located above the Imlil Bridge, this cafe has a bit of everything: pizzas, *brochettes* (kebabs) and cakes. Head up to the roof deck for superb panoramas over the landscape – you'll have plenty of time to contemplate the view as you wait to be served. Also offers decent coffee.

Hôtel Les Etoiles de Toubkal MOROCCAN €€
(☎0524485618; pizzas around Dh60, meals Dh40-130; ⏱11am-midnight; 📶) Tiled tables in the garden of this downtown hotel offer a tranquil dining retreat. Aside from the standard selection of tajines and grilled meats, you can also order pizza. It's just uphill across from the Bureau des Guides (p116).

Aroumd

POP 1800 / ELEV 2000M

For Amazigh hospitality above the trekker fray, head up to the hilltop village of Aroumd (also called Armed). The 3km walking path up from Imlil passes a burbling stream, two waterfalls and shady orchards. There are no distinct tourist sites in the village, but the winding alleyways between stone houses make for pleasant wandering, and views from the top of the village back down the Imlil Valley are excellent.

If you're packing heavy luggage and plan to spend the night, contact your guesthouse, which can arrange private transport from Imlil. Otherwise, it's a lovely but uphill walk (3km from Imlil) through the walnut forests that separate the two – follow the path near Kasbah du Toubkal. You can also hire a donkey (Dh50).

Sleeping & Eating

There are a handful of restaurants along the waterway on the way up through the forest from Imlil. These make nice stops for a drink or the usual bubbling tajine. There are no restaurants in the village itself, though guesthouses can generally prepare meals for nonguests with advance notice.

Dar Imperial HOTEL €
(☎0636056052, 0671066381; www.darimperial.com; s/d/tr from Dh180/280/400, d/tr/q with shared bathroom Dh220/330/450; 📶) Book here for private rooms at the top of the village, with some of the best views of any guesthouse in the valley. In *gîte d'étape* (homestay) style, parties travelling together may be asked to share rooms if it's busy.

Gîte Le Toubkal GUESTHOUSE €
(Chez Hadj Omar; ☎0650928921; dm Dh100) Aroumd's original guesthouse remains popular among tour groups and independent travellers alike thanks to comfortable rooms and plenty of common spaces in which to stretch out and relax before or after a hike. The best feature is the tree-lined courtyard patio, which makes a fine place to unwind. However, the paucity of showers may be a problem when the house is full.

Half-board is available for an additional Dh100.

Gîte Atlas Toubkal GUESTHOUSE €
(☎0668882764; https://gite-atlas-toubkal-ma.book.direct; dm Dh100; 📶) Seventeen shared rooms with shared baths, all pleasantly decorated with local handicrafts. The terrace looking up into the valley is particularly nice for rest days after a long hike. Half-board is available for an additional Dh100.

It's towards the bottom of the main village, on the western face of the hill.

Jebel Toubkal Ascent

North Africa's tallest peak, **Jebel Toubkal** (4167m) doesn't require technical climbing experience. In summer, anyone in good physical condition can reach the summit. In early October, runners of the **Toubkal Marathon** (⏱early Oct) scamper 42km up and down Jebel Toubkal. For extreme ultramarathoners, the organisers tacked a 106km High Atlas trail onto the marathon, calling it the **Toubkal Trail**.

Although the 2247m ascent from Aroumd isn't technically difficult, challenges include Toubkal's fast-changing climate, steep slopes of scree and altitude sickness. Hikers should factor in sufficient time to ascend slowly and steadily. An ascent of Toubkal can be combined with satellite peaks, and some fit trekkers ascend **Ouanoukrim** (4088m) as well.

DAY 1: AROUMD TO TOUBKAL REFUGE

Duration 5-6 hours
Distance 10km
Ascent 1287m

TREK AT A GLANCE

Duration Two to three days

Distance 27km

Standard Hard

Start/Finish Aroumd village

Highest Point Jebel Toubkal (4167m)

Accommodation Camping or mountain *refuges* (cabins)

Public Transport Yes

Summary The most popular walk in the High Atlas, with magnificent views. The route is straightforward, but the trek up the scree slope is hard, and trekkers can be struck with altitude sickness. The trek is best in summer and autumn, but check conditions before departure – there can be snow even in June.

From south of **Aroumd**, where at the time of research a checkpoint has been erected to verify that all non-locals are trekking with local guides, cross the stony valley floor and follow the well-defined mule trail gradually uphill towards a very large rock above the eastern side of the Assif Reraya, which leads to the hamlet and shrine of **Sidi Chamharouch** (2330m). Beyond the shrine, to the left of the track, are cascades, pools and a prime picnic spot in the shady overhang of the rocks.

After crossing the river by the bridge at Sidi Chamharouch, the rocky path veers away from the river for 2km and zigzags steeply above the valley floor. It then gradually levels off, before rejoining the course of the river. The **Toubkal Refuge** and **Mouflon Refuge** are visible for an hour before you reach them, immediately below the western flank of Jebel Toubkal.

DAY 2: SUMMIT ASCENT & RETURN TO AROUMD

Duration 9 hours
Distance 17km
Ascent 960m
Descent 2247m

Set off as early as possible to avoid climbing in the sun – many hikers leave around 3am. There is no shade and nothing to block the wind, so be sure to dress warmly and pack extra water and snacks. If you've trekked here directly from Imlil, you may not be acclimatised, so walk at a steady, slow pace to avoid altitude sickness. If you experience severe headaches or vomiting, descend immediately. However tempting, do not lie down to sleep on the slope.

Two *cwms* (valleys formed by glacial activity) run down the western flank of Toubkal, divided by the west-northwest ridge, which leads down from the summit. The southern *cwm* is the more usual route and starts immediately above Toubkal Refuge to the left, where you cross the river and head eastwards to the scree slope.

Start to climb the well-defined path to the left of the slope, cross the field of boulders, and then follow the path that zigzags up to **Tizi n'Toubkal** (3940m), straight ahead on the skyline. From there the path turns left (northeast) and follows the ridge to the summit (4167m). Allow up to four hours to reach the top, depending on your fitness and weather conditions.

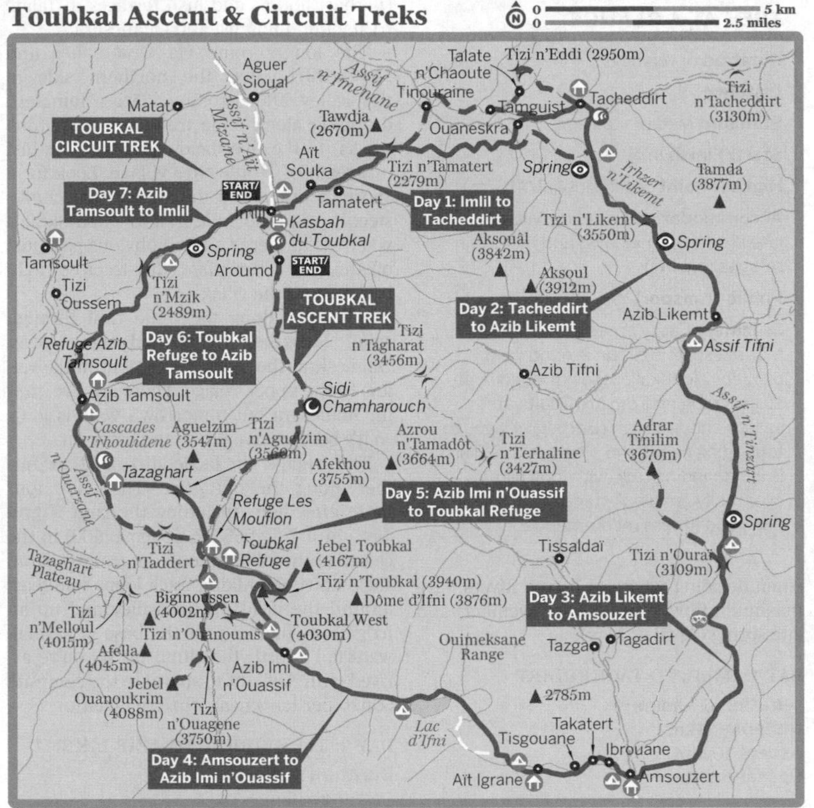

Stick to the same route coming down, bearing left when the *refuge* comes into view. The descent to the *refuge* should only take 2½ hours, after which you can return to Aroumd or Imlil. If you are planning on spending a second night at the *refuge*, you could come down the longer route via the Ihibi *sud* (south) circuit. It's a straightforward four-hour walk down to the *refuge* for well-earned congratulations and celebratory chocolate.

Trekking the Toubkal Circuit

Beyond the majestic peaks and fabulous views of Jebel Toubkal, this circuit offers fascinating glimpses into Amazigh (Berber) life in remote High Atlas villages. You will need camping gear for this route, though with short detours you could use basic village accommodation and mountain *refuges* (cabins) instead.

Since this trek is fairly strenuous, you might want an extra rest day. The ascent of Jebel Toubkal takes place on the fifth day, allowing four days of acclimatisation to altitude. Most of the route is above 2000m, with several passes over 3000m.

June to mid-October is the key season, with passes snowed-over and potentially dangerous outside this window unless you're prepared with ropes and crampons.

By early June daytime temperatures are pleasantly warm but nights may still be cold. Midsummer guarantees long daylight hours and snow-free passes (though not always a snow-free Toubkal), but in the lower valleys temperatures can be extremely hot and water nonexistent. July and August are the busiest months in the High Atlas, but trekking is best done early morning and later in the afternoon to avoid the heat.

Flash flooding can occur in summer after thunderstorms – something to bear in mind

TREK AT A GLANCE

Duration Seven days

Distance 79km

Standard Medium to hard

Start/Finish Imlil

Highest Point Jebel Toubkal (4167m)

Accommodation Camping, village *gîtes* (basic homestays) and mountain *refuges* (cabins)

Public Transport Yes

Summary Easily accessible from Marrakesh, this circuit around (and up) Jebel Toubkal passes through landscapes ranging from lush, cultivated valleys and Amazigh (Berber) villages to forbidding peaks and bleak passes. This is a demanding trek, with long climbs over rocky terrain. A guide is mandatory, and good fitness recommended.

when deciding where to camp. Rivers have maximum flow in autumn (November) and late spring (April or May).

DAY 1: IMLIL TO TACHEDDIRT

Duration 6-7 hours
Distance 14km
Ascent 1028m
Descent 381m

The first day's relatively gentle route follows the road linking **Imlil** (1740m) to the village of Tacheddirt (2400m). The road climbs gently eastwards from Imlil zigzagging up past **Aït Souka** and through **Tamatert** to the pass at **Tizi n'Tamatert** (2279m). From Imlil to the pass, following mule and hiking tracks and staying off the road as much as possible, is around 4.5km and 605m of elevation gain.

At the pass is a weather-beaten shop selling pricey soft drinks. To the northeast are great views of **Tizi n'Eddi** (2950m), the pass leading to Oukaimeden, and **Tizi n'Tacheddirt** (3230m). It's possible to follow an obvious pass behind the shop up to the peak of **Tawdja** (2670m), adding 2.5km to the day's journey, for nice views of Toubkal and the Imlil valley.

The path and tarmac meet at the pass, where the tarmac turns southeast and follows the ridge for 7km to the night's campsite; along this stretch you are treated to views across the valley to neat Amazigh (Berber) houses and lush terraces in Talate n'Chaoute, Tamguist and Ouaneskra.

The longer route via **Ouaneskra** and **Tacheddirt** takes the northern side of the valley after crossing Tizi n'Tamatert, dropping along mule trails and *piste* (dirt tracks) to the river below and crossing just upstream of **Tinouraine** village. Look for a shortcut just above the village that climbs steeply up to the mule trail to Ouaneskra; if you miss it, there's a more obvious path just off the first set of *piste* (dirt track) switchbacks above the village.

Continue along the mule trail through small **Tamguist** village and above lower Ouaneskra (the oldest settlement in the valley) to the upper village. There are five *gîtes* in Ouaneskra but tomorrow's walk is long, so it's best to have lunch and carry on.

The village of Tacheddirt is 2km further along the old *piste*. There are four more *gîtes* here, including the large **Tigmi Tacheddirt** (☎0662105169; dm Dh100) in the centre of the village (good for groups). From Tacheddirt, the hiking track loops southeast around the head up the valley and up an irrigation channel past the base of a small waterfall (worth the climb up if you've arrived with daylight to spare) to the campsite (Dh20 per tent) near Irhzer n'Likemt.

DAY 2: TACHEDDIRT TO AZIB LIKEMT

Duration 5-7 hours
Distance 9km
Ascent 1060m
Descent 923m

Leave camp early to make the climb up to **Tizi n'Likemt** (3550m), a vertical gain of 1060m, winding around the many switchbacks on a more gentle ascent instead of heading straight up the steep mule path. Though the walk is mostly shaded by mountain shadows in the morning, it's a long climb, getting progressively steeper from the 3000m mark.

Atop Tizi n'Likemt are views of verdant valleys and jagged peaks, including Oukaïmeden (to the north) and Jebel Toubkal (southwest) on clear days, though with typically strong winds here you may not find yourself lingering long to enjoy the panorama.

The rocky path leading down the other side (southeast) passes a semipermanent water source on the left after 30 minutes, and irrigated pastures above **Azib Likemt** after another hour. An *azib* is a summer settlement, and Azib Likemt (2650m) is occupied from May through October by local people growing crops on irrigated terraces and leading livestock up to higher pastures. Take time to admire the traditional stone houses in which families spend the summer.

You may be offered shelter or a place to pitch your tent in Azib Likemt. Otherwise, walk through terraces down to the **Assif Tifni**, turn right and walk upstream to a group of large boulders, where you'll find a flat campsite (Dh20 per tent) close to the river.

DAY 3: AZIB LIKEMT TO AMSOUZERT

Duration 5-6 hours
Distance 16km
Ascent 624m
Descent 1300m

From Azib Likemt, the well-worn trail leads south opposite the campsite, up the mountainside and into the tremendous gorge formed by **Assif n'Tinzart**. On the river's eastern bank, the trail snakes high above the river before descending close to the valley floor. Follow the river for about 6.5km past stunning cliffs and through wide pastures, until an obvious track leads up the valley to **Tizi n'Ouraï** (3109m, also known as Tizi n'Ououraïne) and brilliant views of the eastern face of Toubkal, Dôme d'Ifni (3876m) and the rest of the jagged Toubkal Massif.

Continue over the col, where the trail traverses the head of the valley to a spur and trail crossroads. Heading southwest, a trail leads down the ridge to **Tagadirt** (after 100m there's a fantastic viewpoint south to Jebel Siroua), but turn left (southeast) and follow the mule track south. Traverse the head of another valley and along the side of a spur to reach the ridge after 3km. After a further 1km, just before two pointed outcrops, the path forks. Turn right and continue descending to a large cairn. Descend southwest, then west down the end of the spur to **Amsouzert** (1797m) in about 2.5km.

Amsouzert is a prosperous village spread on both sides of the river. If you're planning a rest day, this is an excellent place to take it. You can stay at one of several guesthouse in the village, including the rustic **Gîte Himmi Omar** (☎0677330878; dm Dh100) (with a great common space) just east of the bridge or **Dar Amsouzert** (☎0673169299; dm Dh100) (with nicer stylish rooms) just west of the bridge. It may also

BEFORE YOU GO: JEBEL TOUBKAL CHECKLIST

Maps The 1:50,000 sheet map *Jebel Toubkal* covers the whole Toubkal Circuit and is sometimes available through the Bureau des Guides (p116) in Imlil. The four-sheet, 1:100,000 topographical *Toubkal Massif Walking Map* also covers the circuit, produced by the Division de la Cartographie (Moroccan Survey) and obtainable from their office in Rabat, in London at Stanfords (www.stanfords.co.uk) and in Marrakesh at Hotel Ali on Djemaa El Fna (Dh150). Government-produced 1:100,000 *Cartes des Randonnées dans le Massif du Toubkal* marks trekking routes but includes less topographical detail.

Guide Local guides are mandatory on the trails between Imlil and Toubkal summit, and this may be expanded in coming years to the entire Toubkal National Park. Engage licensed guides at Imlil's Bureau des Guides. Allow at least a day to hire a guide and make trekking arrangements – though if you have specific needs or are travelling in high season, it may take more time.

Mule Mountain guides can organise mules and muleteers for your gear, which is particularly important if you intend to climb directly to the summit of Jebel Toubkal on day five. Talk this through with your guide.

Food Basic food supplies are available in Imlil, and trail mixes, packaged soups and other light, portable food is stocked by Marrakesh supermarkets.

Water Purifying locally sourced water is a responsible alternative to bottled water, but in midsummer don't count on finding available water sources – bring your own supply.

Gear A stick or trekking pole is useful for long rocky descents.

Fuel Petrol, diesel and kerosene can be bought in Marrakesh or Asni.

Tent Your guide can arrange tents. The circuit may require some camping, but you could add detours to seek out lodging, or possibly do without tents in summer.

be possible to camp at **Camping Azerg** (☎0618986510; per tent Dh20) 200m west of the village bridge.

In Amsouzert, there are small shops, a couple of cafes west of the river and early morning transport to the N10 highway connecting Marrakesh and Ouarzazate. About 3km south of Amsouzert is another village called Imlil (not to be confused with the Imlil trailhead on the northern side of the range), which hosts a busy Wednesday souq.

DAY 4: AMSOUZERT TO AZIB IMI N'OUASSIF

Duration 6-8 hours
Distance 13km
Ascent 1524m
Descent 42m

From Amsouzert follow the well-used *piste* that continues westwards towards Lac d'Ifni above the north side of the village bridge. The path takes you through the villages of **Ibrouane**, **Takatert** and **Tisgouane** before reaching **Aït Igrane**, 3.7km beyond Amsouzert, where there are a couple of small cafes and **Gîte Belaïde** (☎0678390648; tent/dm/d Dh20/50/240), the nicest of the village's three small guesthouses. Make sure to try the local honey and olive oil, both of which are offered in the shop downstairs.

Follow the 4WD track along the riverbed west out of Aït Igrane, picking up the narrow rocky mule path where the 4WD track crosses the river then turns sharp left. The mule path leads around the north side of **Lac d'Ifni** (2295m), across sharp, rocky, barren, inhospitable terrain. The climb is steep at first, but it descends to the northeastern corner of Lac d'Ifni, an inviting expanse of green water (safe for swimming). The walk to the lake is around 3.5km from Aït Igrane. On the north side of the lake are several small shops where you may be able to buy water, soft drinks and, with any luck, a fresh-squeezed orange juice.

On the small beach on the northern shore are shady (if occasionally fly-filled) stone shelters. If it's rainy, camping nearer the next pass is treacherous, and you're better off finding a campsite above the lake.

From the northwestern side of the lake, the track crosses the wide, dry part of Lac d'Ifni before the long trudge up towards Tizi n'Ouanoums (3660m). The path climbs through a rocky gorge, keeping to the south side of the river. About 11.7km from Amsouzert you'll reach **Azib Imi n'Ouassif** (2891m), situated at a crossing of dramatic gorges.

Beyond this point the path climbs steeply to **Tizi n'Ouanoums**, with winds near the summit and small, frigid waterfalls. You'll find flat, rocky areas for pitching tents and shelters in surrounding cliffs long used by local shepherds. The last suitable campsite is a further 1.3km up at 3330m directly beside the path. If you're attempting the Toubkal summit the next day it's worth the extra hike now, but the site is small so consider how much upwards traffic you've seen throughout the day and whether there's likely to be space for your tent.

DAY 5: AZIB IMI N'OUASSIF TO TOUBKAL REFUGE

Duration 5-8 hours
Distance 7km
Ascent 798m
Descent 960m

The path to the summit of Tizi n'Ouanoums (3660m) climbs immediately west from the campsite. If you're carrying your own gear you'll need to continue over the pass and down to Toubkal Refuge along a steep 4km trail that takes roughly three hours. Several day-hike options exist from the *refuge*, or you may prefer to rest in preparation for the traditional summit ascent (p120) early the next morning.

However, if you've hired mules to carry the bulk of your gear and you have faith in your guide's navigational skills, it's also possible to climb from this campsite to Toubkal's summit and then down to the *refuge* directly. This route is only for fit and fleet-footed hikers, and includes some stretches of scrambling up and over large rocks, but the views are excellent and it's actually faster than the traditional route to the summit. Do not attempt this route if the weather is rainy or windy, or if you are an inexperienced hiker.

Continue up the main trail towards Tizi n'Ouanoums for around 800m, until the path climbs sharply to the left at around 3550m, where you'll spot a small side trail to the northeast. From here the way traverses 400m east before turning sharply northwest and climbing to 3930m on the western shoulder of Toubkal West (4030m). Traverse the north flank of Toubkal West for 600m to where the path joins the main route up Toubkal's primary (eastern) peak. After the rough trail from camp to here, the final 200m of elevation gain to the summit will seem almost easy by comparison.

MURDER IN THE MOUNTAINS: TERRORISM IN THE HIGH ATLAS

On the morning of 17 December 2018 residents of Imlil awoke to the shocking news of a double murder in the mountains above town. Two foreigners – Louisa Vesterager Jespersen of Denmark and Maren Ueland of Norway – had been brutally murdered where they slept alongside the trail from Sidi Shamharoush.

Four men were immediately arrested for the attack and an eventual total of 24 suspects – several of whom had recently published videos proclaiming allegiance to the Islamic State – were apprehended in connection with the crime and eventually charged with murder- and terrorism-related offences.

The government acted quickly to prevent a similar incident from reoccurring – establishing police checkpoints throughout the region and requiring all non-locals (including Moroccans from beyond the valley) to trek in the company of a local. Despite an immediate slump in visitors, numbers to the national park quickly rebounded and no reports of similar incidents have been received since.

From the peak of **Jebel Toubkal** (4167m), the highest point in North Africa, panoramic mountain vistas stretch out in every direction. After enjoying the accomplishment of reaching this point, wind back down from the summit along the same trail and then follow the obvious rocky descent for 3.5km (and a total of 960m of elevation loss) to the *refuges*.

CAF's **Toubkal Refuge** (☎0661695463; www.refugedutoubkal.com; dm from Dh100), sometimes labelled Neltner on maps, suffers from occasional overcrowding and a lack of facilities; however, there's 24-hour electricity. The newer **Refuge Les Mouflons** (Refuge Mouflon; ☎0663763713; www.refugelesmouflons.com; dm/r with shared bathroom incl half-board Dh280/820) provides better facilities and a better-stocked shop, though the lounge can be quite chilly even in summer. You can also camp just downstream from here.

With an extra day in base camp you could ascend the second-highest mountain in the region, **Jebel Ouanoukrim** (4088m, five to six hours return), or to cut the trip short you could head directly down to **Imlil** in four to five hours of walking.

DAY 6: TOUBKAL REFUGE TO AZIB TAMSOULT

Duration 4-5 hours
Distance 10km
Ascent 419m
Descent 1277m

From the Toubkal Refuge pick up the mule track that heads northwest then gently climbs north across the slope for about 1km. You will come to a fork near a small rounded wall, used as a sheepfold. Turn left, westwards, up the zigzagging mule path, which will bring you in roughly 3km to **Tizi n'Aguelzim** (3560m).

The alternate path via **Tizi n'Melloul** (3875m) offers a harder route to and from the Toubkal Refuge, but provides access en route to **Afella** (4045m) southeast of the pass and to the jagged ridge leading on north to **Biginoussen** (4002m).

Panoramic views await at Tizi n'Aguelzim pass: east to the Toubkal summit, northeast to the Imlil valley, northwest to Azzadene and west to the Tazaghart plateau. From here, the track twists in some 86 hairpin bends downhill. At the bottom, it crosses a stream beside a tiny campsite. One kilometre further on at a fork, take the left-hand track southwards for an additional 1km to where the track leads uphill to cosy **CAF Tazaghart Refuge** (Lepiney; ☎0667852754, Oukaimeden 0524319036; http://cafmaroc.ffcam.fr; dm Dh95), which sits beside a small waterfall.

There are mattresses for 22 people, gas-lights and a basic kitchen – half-board (DH105) is available as well with advance notice. The *gardien* (caretaker) is based in Tizi Oussem, so be sure to phone ahead to book a spot, or else try passing a message to him via muleteers or shepherds. Campers can pitch tents beside the *refuge*, or on flat ground above the falls.

The route down to **Azib Tamsoult** (2210m) passes the impressive Cascades d'Irhoulidene (p116), also the site of a small shop selling cold drinks and snacks, beyond which vegetation and tree coverage increases. A 1km walk from the falls brings you to a pleasant campsite (Dh20 per tent) and, just below, the newly built **Refuge Azib Tamsoult** (☎0661695463; www.refugetamsoult.com; dm/r Dh100/400). To reach the village, walk north for another 4km.

DAY 7: AZIB TAMSOULT TO IMLIL

Duration 4-5 hours
Distance 10km
Ascent 325m
Descent 565m

If you have made good time and you have the legs, you could continue over to Imlil at the end of day six. From the vegetable terraces of Azib Tamsoult, with the Assif n'Ouarzane down to the left, a mule track traversing the forested valley is visible to the north. Head towards it above the Tamsoult village and over the stream, and stay on it, avoiding left forks into the valley.

Climbing slightly and heading steadily northeast through the juniper forest you arrive at **Tizi Mzik** (2489m), where a sheep shed might serve as shelter and a small shop may have cold drinks. **Imlil** is a 4km descent along a well-worn mule track (there's a spring to the right of the trail after 40 minutes), but it's worth detouring south up the valley 1km to the Imlil waterfalls (p116), continuing down to Imlil or up to Aroumd via the pleasant paths through walnut forest to finish off the hike.

Western High Atlas

South of Marrakesh, this is the most frequently visited High Atlas region and has long been a key route south. The heavily touristed Ourika Valley deposits you at the trekking base of Setti Fatma, while the Mizane Valley leads you to the more atmospheric village of Imlil. The ski resort of Oukaimeden sits between the two. Further afield, Ijoukak and Zat Valley make for interesting trailheads with far fewer travellers, and both are home to interesting cultural attractions as well.

LOCAL KNOWLEDGE

WESTERN HIGH ATLAS SOUQS

In the valleys surrounding Jebel Toubkal, towns have market days featuring local crafts, fresh produce and donkeys on the following days:

Monday Tnine

Tuesday Tahanaoute, Aït-Ourir

Wednesday Tighdouine

Thursday El Khemis Ouirgane, Aghbalou

Friday Aghmat

Saturday Asni

Sunday Setti Fatma

Zat Valley

When Marrakesh is sweating it out, breezes are rippling through barley and swaying poplar trees along this charmed river valley. **Tighdouine's** Wednesday souq offers a look at valley life and the chance for roadside tajines, and the healing spring at **Source Sidi El Wafi** is culturally interesting.

Press on to Zat's true wonders: gardens built right into cliff faces, stone houses with bright blue doors, white-framed windows with families leaning out to say hello. This is all best appreciated on foot, ideally as part of a longer trek to Ourika or even Toubkal.

Three- to five-day walking tours are possible, wending their way up the rich valley (most of Marrakesh's potatoes, turnips, olives, figs and tomatoes come from here) to **Talatassat's** local potteries before continuing on to the red sandstone **Yaggour Plateau**, the location of an important concentration of prehistoric rock engravings. Beyond, **Tizi n'Rhellis** leads to the neighbouring Ourika Valley.

You'll want to pack a tent or perhaps hire a guide who can charm his way into an informal village homestay for you – the only formal accommodation options are down in Tighdouine and aren't much to write home about. The nondescript **Cafe Hotel** (s/d Dh100/200) at the north of the village is overwhelmingly adequate.

Grands taxis (Dh25) run between Marrakesh and Tighdouine regularly. On market days it may be possible to find a minibus ride to outlying villages as the souq is wrapping up, but otherwise you'll need to come with your own transport or be prepared to pay heavily for a ride.

Ourika Valley

Temperatures are cooler in the shadow of snowcapped High Atlas peaks, and this blooming valley a little south of Marrakesh is the city's escape hatch from the soaring summer heat. The valley is especially mood-altering from February to April, when almond and cherry orchards bloom and wildflowers run riot.

Ourika's beauty and easy accessibility have led to significant development, which now threatens to mar its mountain-valley vibe. From Aghbalou onwards, makeshift cafes and BBQ joints line the riverside strung together by flimsy rope bridges that allow day-trippers to cross the river, while at the end of the valley sits the summer resort and well-worn trekking base of Setti Fatma.

For High Atlas scenery with fewer tourist coaches and moped-mounted salesmen, you may prefer the Mizane or Zat Valleys.

TNINE

The main town of the Ourika Valley and home to a large **Monday souq**, Tnine (aka Tnin l'Ourika) makes a worthwhile detour for a visit to its lush saffron and botanical gardens. Nearby is one of the Ourika Valley's finest cultural museums, a good starting point for delving into its Amazigh (Berber) heritage.

Just outside Tnine along the road up the valley, the local **Centre d'Informations Touristique Ourika** (☎0668561784; ⏲8.30am-6pm, to 1pm Sun) sells a sheet map (Dh20) of valley vista points and provides updates on trekking conditions.

Grands taxis leave frequently for Bab Er Rob in Marrakesh (Dh10) and to Setti Fatma (Dh20), while the ponderously slow Bus 25 (Dh8) from Sidi Mamoun in Marrakesh and overcrowded minibuses (Dh15) to Setti Fatma make the same journeys for slightly lower costs.

It's possible to get to Asni from here for around Dh9, but doing so will require several transfers between short bus and grands taxis hops.

Sights

★Ecomusée Berbère MUSEUM

(☎Khalid 0610256734, Salah 0607598585; www.museeberbere.com; Douar Tafza, Km 37, Route de l'Ourika, Tafza; adult/child under 12 Dh40/free; ⏲9.30am-6pm) Four kilometres past Tnine, a discreet sign points up a dirt path into the Amazigh (Berber) village of Tafza, where the three-storey mud-brick *ksar* (fortified village) that once housed the local *qaid* (chief) is now a museum. Enthusiastic guided visits (in English, French or Spanish) cover every detail of household life, from symbols carved in door frames to silver dowry jewellery, and a 1½-hour loop of short documentaries show life in the High Atlas in the 1940s and '50s.

Call ahead to reserve meals on the terrace (Dh70), to arrange visits to Tafza pottery workshops, or for half-day excursions that take in community gardens, pottery workshops and village life.

WORTH A TRIP

ANIMA GARDEN

Nestled in the foothills of the High Atlas Mountains, **Anima Garden** (☎0524482022; www.anima-garden.com; Douar Sbiti; adult/child Dh120/60; ⏲9am-6pm) is a space designed by multimedia artist André Heller. Surprising sculptures referencing local and international themes are hidden among the shady pathways and flowerbeds filled with wildflowers, cacti, water features, palm trees and tall grass. The on-site **cafe** serves light food, sweets and an array of hot beverages.

There's a free shuttle service here from just behind Koutoubia Gardens in Marrakesh; seat preference is given to those with online reservations. Check the website for shuttle timings and detailed directions to the pickup point.

Safranerie de l'Ourika GARDENS

(☎0522484476; www.safran-ourika.com; Takatert; adult/child Dh20/free; ⏲8.30am-6pm; P) Almost anything thrives in Ourika's rich soil, including saffron, organically grown here from bulbs that are cultivated near Talouine. Saffron is a high-maintenance plant, with flowers harvested before dawn for maximum potency. Guided tours of the several-hectare fruit and saffron orchards are given by staff who reiterate key points on explanatory placards.

Tours end with a complimentary tea (a mixture of herbs grown in the garden) and a soft-sell of Safranerie saffron and estate-grown herbal teas (around Dh100). You can also watch the harvest take place during the first three weeks of November, although you'll need to arrange it in advance and get here by around 5am.

To get here look for the poorly signed turnoff about 700m west of the bridge, opposite a pharmacy.

Jardin Bio-Aromatique d'Ourika GARDENS

(Nectarôme; ☎0524482149; www.jardin-bioaromatique-ourika.com; Douar El Haddad; garden visits adult/child Dh20/10, with guide Dh70; ⏲9am-5pm, to 6.30pm Jun-Aug; P) The organic botanical gardens of a Franco-Moroccan bath-product company combining Amazigh (Berber) herbal remedies with modern aromatherapy make for pleasant wandering, and they certainly smell great. With reservations it's also possible to order meals (Dh70 to Dh120), with many ingredients plucked fresh from the gardens.

Just west of the bridge in Tnine, turn north along a dirt track at a poorly signed turnoff.

Sleeping & Eating

Fast food and tajine joints are dotted along the main street through Tnine – our clear favourite being **Almanzar** (tajines Dh80-120; 7am-10pm) on a curve in the road between the main roundabout and the Setti Fatma turnoff.

Kasbah Jad Auberge GUESTHOUSE €€
(0524482953; www.auberge-marrakech.com; Douar Akhlij Ourika; s/d/tr/ste Dh400/450/500/650; P) This appealing family-run place has much to recommend it, starting with attractively furnished rooms, all of which offer memorable views over the valley. Take the spiral staircase to the roof for more great views and a choice spot for meals on request. There's also an indoor pool (open year-round) and a hammam.

★ **Kasbah Bab Ourika** LODGE €€€
(0661634234; www.kasbahbabourika.com; d Dh2045-3035, ste Dh3970-7710; P) Occupying an outstanding hilltop location in the Ourika Valley, this rammed-earth kasbah provides understated luxury, including uninterrupted views of snowy Atlas peaks, top-quality meals, superbly finished interiors and massive gardens. You can relax beneath olive trees while admiring the view, float in the gorgeous pool or unwind in the hammam.

There are loads of activities on offer here: 4WD trips, camel treks, mountain biking and pleasant walks you can take from the guesthouse. Turn up a dirt road to the east of the souq and follow it for 3km to the signed final stretch that climbs to the hilltop kasbah.

OFF THE BEATEN TRACK

AMIZMIZ SOUQ

Historically one of the most important market towns in the High Atlas and still home to a busy **Tuesday souq**, Amizmiz remains a meeting point for plains and mountain communities, and the location tucked into the final foothills of the High Atlas makes it an appealing day-trip option from Marrakesh or the Agafay Desert. It's a good alternate trailhead for trekkers too, including to the little-visited Tichka Plateau.

Regular minibuses (Dh10) and grands taxis (Dh20) travel between Amizmiz and Marrakesh when full. For transport to mountain villages, turn up in the afternoons to see what's available, but your best bet will be on Tuesdays as the souq is starting to wind down.

SETTI FATMA ستي فاطمة

POP 22,283

This little village is a popular weekend escape for Marrakesh locals who scramble up to a series of seven cascading waterfalls or just soak their feet in the river down below. The village is neatly nestled in a canyon beneath the High Atlas mountains at the southern end of the Ourika Valley road. Prime times to visit are in early March when the cherry and almond trees are in bloom, or in August for the four-day *moussem* (festival) with its fair and market at the *koubba* (shrine) of Setti Fatma. In mid-summer the whole valley is clogged with visitors from Marrakesh, so consider heading to the splendidly untrammelled nearby valleys of Zat or Ouirgane instead.

Hiking to the waterfalls ranges from a steep 20-minute walk to the base of the lowest and largest, a near-vertical 10-minute scramble beyond to an eyrie-like overlook at the most spectacularly situated drink stall this side of Toubkal, and an athletic hour beyond to the base of the highest (and smallest) falls.

Ignore the *faux guides* (unofficial guides) and stick to the easily followed paths, or find a licensed guide to lead the way if you expect to need a hand on the more treacherous bits of the rocky ascent. The **Bureau des Guides** (0666746872; settifadmaguide@gmail.com; 9am-5pm) can hook you up, but you'll have to fight crowds of touts to make it that far.

From Aghbalou to Setti Fatima, both sides of the highway are lined with cafe-restaurants offering tajines priced to move. There are a couple of reasonable choices in Setti Fatma proper, but for the most part expect to overpay because of the location.

There are loads of basic, inexpensive guesthouses along both sides of the river in

Setti Fatma. Tucked down a pebble staircase about 1km before Setti Fatma is **Au Bord de l'Eau** (0661229755; www.obordelo.com; d Dh250-370, ste Dh450-500;). It's wonderfully secluded away from the tourist bustle, with just the sound of the rushing river to disturb dreams of summit ascents.

At **Hôtel les Jardins Setti Fatma** (0667848871; http://perso.menara.ma/oubna2010; s/d Dh100/150), rooms are large and clean and decorated with wonderful tilework, though oddly dim.

Basic and reasonably clean rooms with lumpy pillows and hot showers plus a restaurant downstairs serving well-caramelised tajines (from Dh70) make **Hôtel Asgaour** (0524485294; r DH200, with shared bathroom Dh170;) a reliable if not inspired option.

Grands taxis to Setti Fatma leave frequently from Bab Er Rob in Marrakesh (Dh30). You may also find less-frequent minibuses (Dh20) here. Minibuses, often dangerously overpacked, also travel regularly between here and Tnine (Dh15).

Oukaimeden اوكيمدن

POP 4400 / ELEV 2650M

This sleepy mountain village, perched at 2650m in the High Atlas, offers a peaceful escape from the hustle of Marrakesh 75km to the north. It's a fine year-round destination with hiking amid wildflower-strewn valleys in springtime and downhill skiing in winter. Aside from its beckoning outdoor adventures, however, there isn't much to Oukaimeden.

From December to April there are seven runs (nursery to black) totalling 10km at the **Oukaimeden Ski Base**, with seven tows and the highest ski lift in Africa (3268m). Gear, passes and lessons are available at prices that will delight those used to European rates. Cross-country skiing is also available.

Staff at the CAF Refuge can point you towards trekking trailheads, or in summer can show you around the open-air **petroglyph** FREE site at the entrance to the village.

There aren't many lodging choices here, so it's wise to reserve ahead in ski season. **CAF Refuge** (0524319036; http://cafmoroc.ffcam.fr; dm from Dh110;) has heated dormitories, a bar-restaurant and kitchen, library and wi-fi; but you'll need your own sleeping bag. At **Chez Juju** (0524319005; www.hotelchezjuju.com; d Dh900-1500;) you'll

LOCAL KNOWLEDGE

SETTI FATMA MOUSSEM

Locals call the four-day **Setti Fatma Moussem** (Aug) one of the most important festivals in all of Morocco. Though the central shrine itself is off-limits to non-Muslims, the whole event is just as much county fair as religious celebration, and visitors of all faiths are welcome to join in on the fun.

find a reliable restaurant with a bar, plus simple rooms with en suites.

If you're not travelling by hire car, your best bet is to arrange transport through CAF Refuge. Otherwise, you can charter a grand taxi from Marrakesh's Bab Er Rob (Dh400 to Dh600).

Ouirgane

POP 6916

When Marrakesh is baking and day trippers are swamping Ourika, Marrakshis sneak off to mellow Ouirgane for High Atlas breezes, peaceful hikes through quiet villages and romantic country retreats. For those crossing the Tizi n'Test between Taroudant and Marrakesh, Ouirgane makes an excellent stopover.

Lodging in the area tends toward the higher end, with beautifully landscaped boutique guesthouses, most with pools. The kitchens at Chez Momo II and Ouirgane Ecolodge are worth planning a stop around if you'll be passing through around meal times.

The handful of simple rooms at **Gîte du Lac** (0670405714; s/d with shared bathroom Dh200/350;) are clean and comfortable, but the setting along the highway on the west edge of the village lacks charm. It's a good choice for travellers just looking for a budget place to crash between short hikes to surrounding villages.

For a peaceful escape it's hard to fault the environmentally minded retreat at **Ouirgane Ecolodge** (0668760165; www.ouirgane-ecolodge.com; s/d/tr from Dh300/400/650;) . Rooms boast a warm Berber design, and the lounge is a fine place for a meal or to curl up with a good book.

Country living comes with Marrakesh style at **Chez Momo II** (0524485704; www.aubergemomo.com; Km 61, R203; s/d/ste Dh650/780/910;). Garden bungalows

DON'T MISS

SALT OF THE EARTH

Local villagers mine salt at **Marigha Salt Mine** using traditional methods that have been in use for generations, pulling buckets of mineral-rich water from wells up to 20m deep and pouring them into evaporating pans in which salt crystals slowly form. The mines are along the road between Marigha and Tinzert villages, around 3km southeast of the highway.

have *tadelakt* (waterproof-plaster) baths, pine-beam ceilings, kilim-upholstered armchairs, and panoramic patios; suites have fireplaces and extra beds for kids. The inn is also a weekend dining destination, and the restaurant offers three-course lunches and the occasional Saturday night barbecue.

Frequent local buses (Dh20, 1½ hours) and grands taxis (Dh20, one hour) leave south of Bab Er Rob in Marrakesh for Asni. From there, less frequent grands taxis make the further 16km journey between Asni and Ouirgane (Dh10, 35 minutes).

Ijoukak

POP 6641

At the wide-open confluence of the Nfis and Agoundis Valleys, the town of Ijoukak may not look like much now, but the region was once the heart of the Almohad Caliphate that spread across much of Northern Africa and the Iberian Peninsula.

Modern visitors come primarily to visit the last remaining monument to the Almohad era, the magnificent Tin Mal Mosque, en route to the deserts beyond. However, keen trekkers will find it a useful trail head to access the Tichka Plateau to the west or as an alternate starting point for hikes to Toubkal National Park to the east.

Hikes here range from half-day walks to neighbouring villages or multiday hikes across the Tichka Plateau to Imintanoute or Talmakante. This is fairly remote territory – expect local hospitality along the way, but also be prepared for self-sufficiency.

The Almohad-era **Tin Mal Mosque** (0618126514; suggested tip Dh10-20; 9am-5pm) was built in 1156 in honour of the dynasty's strict spiritual leader, Mohammed Ibn Tumart, and it remains an architectural wonder. The mosque is still used for Friday prayers, but on other days the guardian will usher you through its massive doors and rose-coloured archways into the serene prayer hall. The intricate geometry of the carved cedar ceilings has been preserved through painstaking restoration, and the soaring archways give a sense of solidity and grace.

The valley's small **Wednesday souq** (8am-4pm Wed) is also an interesting stop, and a good place to stock up on fresh supplies before a hike. A handful of restaurants work on souq day, and two small restaurants do a sluggish trade beside the main intersection in the centre of Ijoukak.

The only formal accommodation in the centre of Ijoukak is **Gîte Chez Imnir** (0666025512; r Dh150), which can also arrange trekking guides and mules, though you'll see signs for others along the trails to both Toubkal and the Tichka Plateau.

Grands taxis gather at Ijoukak's main intersection for Marrakesh (Dh40) via Ouirgane and Asni, and to Taroudant (Dh50) over the Tizi n'Test.

For a ride to neighbouring villages and trail heads, arrive in time for the last hours of the Wednesday souq, when shoppers head back with loaded trucks to their mountain homes.

Central High Atlas

The road less travelled lies to the east of Marrakesh in the central High Atlas, accessible through the regional hubs of Demnate and Azilal. Here a chalky mass of muscular mountains, weather-worn canyons and sculpted gorges (which provide the best climbing in the country) hide fertile valleys, many inaccessible to vehicles until a few years ago. Several peaks in the area exceed 4000m including Irhil M'Goun, which at 4071m is the highest point.

Ouzoud Falls

The Tissakht River drops 190m over just 2km to meet the canyon of Oued El Abid, creating multitiered falls, and the view only gets better as you descend into the cool of the canyon past the late-afternoon rainbow mists to the pools at the base of the largest of these. Along the way, Barbary apes clamour for attention – though a sign advises not to feed them. The falls are most dramatic from March to June.

The many-tiered **Cascades d'Ouzoud** are stunningly beautiful, with several distinct falls, the largest a massive 100m drop. The area is also one of the most popular day trips from Marrakesh, so be prepared to not have this natural idyll to yourself. On summer weekends the cafe-lined paths that lead down to the falls are filled with local families and tourists browsing souvenir stalls and taking pictures. Walk past the signs for Riad Cascades d'Ouzoud towards the precipice, where converging paths wind down towards the largest falls and beyond.

From the base you can hike to see the picturesque 800-year-old Amazigh (Berber) village of **Tanaghmelt** – follow the path by the lower pools past a farmhouse and up the slopes to the west for about 1.5km. For longer treks, follow the course of the river down to the **Gramaa Nakrouine caves** (two hours) and the **Gorges of Oued El Abid** (another two hours).

The welcoming **Camping Zebra** (☎0666328576; http://campingzebra.com; campsite per 2 people from Dh85; r DH400, with shared bathroom Dh250; P 📶) mixes tent sites alongside four garden rooms with shared bathroom and a mini kasbah with four en suites. A communal lounge where you can order meals livens the place up, and the staff can show you the way to Tanaghmelt. It's 1.3km south of the car park above the falls, in the direction of Azilal.

A simple guesthouse with colourful, reasonably priced rooms, **Hotel Chellal d'Ouzoud** (☎0523429180; www.hotelchellalouzoud.com; s/d Dh220/350; 📶) can be found on the path heading down to the falls (about 150m walk from the car park). If you're just looking for a patch of flat ground to pitch a tent for the night, **Camping La Nature** (☎0667634817; tent pitch per person Dh15) just off the car park above the falls is the most central thing around. Facilities are basic almost to the point of nonexistence. Full-day/overnight parking is also available for Dh10/20.

The stylish mud-brick **Riad Cascades d'Ouzoud** (☎0523429173; www.ouzoud.com; s Dh350, d Dh450-650; 📶) is located on the car park at the top of the cascades and offers the best accommodation in Ouzoud, along with quality meals and a range of activities in the surrounding area.

Cafes flanking the falls offer various set meals (generally a salad, tajine or grilled chicken, and chips) for Dh60 to Dh100. The menus and prices are largely the same, so choose based on the views. Guesthouses also generally serve meals on site.

It's easiest to get transport direct to Azilal, from where grands taxis run when full to Ouzoud (Dh30/180 per person/taxi), terminating at a car park just above the falls. Head back to Azilal before 4pm, when taxis become scarce and drive hard bargains. To avoid backtracking you can also jump off at the Ouzoud turn-off, 21km west of Azilal, and grab a taxi from here (Dh10/60 per person/taxi).

Azilal أزيلال

POP 30,000

The centre of Azilal province is mainly of interest to travellers as a handy transport hub between Demnate, the Cascades d'Ouzoud, and the Zaouiat Ahansal and Ait Bougmez Valleys. This is the last place you'll reliably be able to stock up on cash in the area; it's a good idea to get petrol here too if you're driving. There's a Thursday souq.

You'll find mostly budget hotels in Azilal, most of which are simple but fair value. Rooms are sufficient at **Hotel Assanfou** (Ave Hassan II; s/d/tr Dh120/160/180; 📶), and there are rare (for Azilal) en suite baths. One block southwest of the new square, **Ajabli** (☎0643966066; Hay Oued Edahab Rue 22; s/tw with shared bathroom Dh60/120; 📶) has simple spotless rooms, while a good-value option in the centre is **Hotel Ouzoud** (☎0523459153, 0678906856; Ave Hassan II; s/d with shared bathroom Dh70/120) with basic but pleasant rooms.

A profusion of tajine joints dot the main road (Ave Hassan II) in town of which **Ibnou Ziad** (meals Dh40-80; ⏲11am-8pm) is the most reliable, on the main avenue just southwest of the new square.

For a warm beverage, **Espace Belle Vue** (off Ave Hassan II; ⏲5am-11pm) has some of the best outdoor seating on the new square opposite the mosque.

Four daily buses run between Azilal and Marrakesh (Dh60, 3½ hours) via Demnate (Dh25, 1½ hours). There's also a 6pm bus to Agadir (Dh120, nine hours) via Marrakesh. Buses and taxis depart from a station behind the main mosque, which is itself just off the new square.

Plenty of grands taxis run from Marrakesh to Azilal (Dh80) and, less frequently, from Azilal to Demnate (Dh40). In the afternoon, when full, local minibuses depart from Azilal to Tabant (Dh30, three hours), the main town in Ait Bougmez, and to Zaouiat Ahansal (Dh65, four to five hours), some via Reserve Naturelle de Tamga (Dh35, three hours).

Reserve Naturelle de Tamga

The Reserve Naturelle de Tamga is a vast national reserve of over 8400 hectares of rolling forested mountains. Birdwatchers will have a field day (or several) observing 107 species of birds, including rare and endangered species; botanists will enjoy wandering mixed-forest slopes of pine, juniper, cedar and oak; while climbers will be left stunned by their first sight of the mountain.

However, this is very much territory for self-starters; there are no marked trails, no on-site signage or interpretation, and nobody to tell you where to go. Indeed there are no shops or restaurants in the area – load up on supplies before you come or plan to take all meals at your guesthouse.

The most-famous peak of the Reserve Naturelle de Tamga, **Cathédrale des Rochers** (Cathédrale Imsfrane) absolutely dominates the surrounding landscape – supposedly in the same manner great cathedrals dominate their cities, hence the name 'Cathedral of the Rocks'. Climbers looking for a serious challenge take on the 400m-plus cliffs, but mere mortals must be content to look up from below at these towering spires.

There are several simple guesthouses here, with **Gîte Le Cathédrale** (☎0661876401; dm Dh100; 📶) being the largest and best run.

Irregular minubuses between Zaouiat Ahansal (Dh30, two hours) and Ouaouizeght (Dh35, three hours) pass through the Reserve Naturelle de Tamga and the nearby village of Tilougguite, particularly on Saturdays for the small weekly market there.

Most travellers use their own vehicle to visit the area. The gravel and dirt road can be treacherous in both directions, and is particularly unsuitable for 2WD vehicles after heavy rains. Get the latest info at Zaouiat Ahansal or Ouaouizarht (if coming from the north) before setting out.

Zaouiat Ahansal

Fantastically remote and fiercely independent, Zaouiat Ahansal was founded in the 13th century by travelling Islamic scholar Sidi Said Ahansal, who, according to local legend, was instructed to establish a religious school wherever his cat leapt off his mule. Happily, that location sits astride a prominent crossroads between the Central High Atlas and the plains of Marrakesh and is blessed with fresh water and abundant grazing.

As a result, the region prospered materially and intellectually. Libraries, religious schools, saints' houses and highly decorative *ighirmin* (collective granaries) testify to this wealthy cultural heritage. Even today a significant number of pilgrims continue to visit the region during the Islamic month of Shawwal, bearing gifts of clothing and food for Sidi Said Ahansal and his descendants.

With the tarmac road from Azilal arriving in 2013, Zaouiat Ahansal has been making a name for itself among serious climbers and adventurous trekkers.

Sights

Four distinct villages spread across the valley offering the chance to explore the area's cultural and mountainous landscapes.

Amezray is perched above the valley, straddling the main road through the area. Two large 17th-century *ighirmin* stand above the village, including the restored **Ait Ben Hmad Igherm** (Amezray), as do several smaller 18th-century religious structures. It's a winding 4km drive down from here to the market area, but a level 2km footpath along the river makes things easier for walkers exploring the area.

At the bottom of the valley, where the Ahansal River turns sharply north and widens, is the home of the small **Monday souq**, local government services and a few small cafes, including **Au Bord du Fleuve** (🕐9am-6pm). From here, the valley road crosses a bridge and climbs towards the other three villages.

Agoudim, the largest and most culturally important village in Zaouiat Ahansal, is 1km up from the bridge. Four large *ighirmin* dominate the village, the smallest of which was constructed to shelter pilgrims visiting the 13th-century **tomb of Sidi Said Ahansal** just below. The largest, **Ait Sidi Moulay Igherm**, is home to the saint's descendants and still serves as a hostel to pilgrims.

Tighanimin, the smallest village in the area, is a further 2km beyond Agoudim. As you pass through, keep an eye out for the 18th-century *igherm* above the village.

Taghia is a further 5.5km upstream from a signed turnoff above Tighanimin, following a combination of under-construction *pistes* and old mule trails. The village is located at the base of a stunning limestone cirque, understandably popular with climbers. If you're travelling with an abundance of gear you may want to hire a mule from Tighanimin to reach it (Dh120 including muleteer).

Activities

Zaouiat Ahansal is blessed with an abundance of historical and natural sites: old saint's houses, places of pilgrimage and hand-tended community gardens. For a more in-depth tour, an Atlas Cultural Foundation (www.atlasculturalfoundation.org) staff member can be hired for a half-day (Dh350) or multiday tours of the region and their community projects.

To explore the region's dramatic scenery and sights, it's advisable to hire a local, licensed mountain guide (Dh300 to Dh400 per day). Guesthouse owners in Amezray and Taghia can generally arrange trekking and (more rarely) climbing guides with several days notice. Renowned international climbing guide **Kristoffer Erickson** (http://kristoffererickson.com; day climbs €500) is based part of the year in Agoudim, but you'll want to contact him far in advance to make plans.

Rock climbers love the valley's sheer cliff faces and multitude of routes – many local guesthouses are run by licensed mountain guides who can arrange trekking or climbing parties with a few days' notice. Independent climbing is also possible and popular – *Taghia et autres Montagnes Berbères* by Christian Ravier and Ihintza Elsenaar is an excellent and up-to-date print resource, but for much of the year there are enough climbers in the valley that it's also easy to just ask around for route recommendations.

An easy ramble leads to **La Source de Taghia**, where water cascades out of the cliff face and down a rocky hillside at these small springs just south of Taghia. It's often a good spot to sit and observe climbers slowly making their way up the sheer mountains.

For a more challenging trip, **Tagoujimt n'Tsouiannt** (the highest scalable cliff face) is also accessible by trek via the aptly named Tire-Bouchon (Corkscrew) Pass, as hikers must 'corkscrew' themselves through a tight and winding series of stone and wood steps to reach the top.

Climbers and trekkers are advised to bring basic medical supplies, as the small clinic in Agoudim has poor facilities. In the case of emergencies, there is a government ambulance that runs between Agoudim and the hospital in Azilal.

RESPONSIBLE TOURISM

The locals of Zaouiat Ahansal take immense pride in the natural beauty and traditional culture of their region and are making a collective effort to influence foreigners visiting this region to do so in an environmentally sustainable and respectful manner with the following suggestions:

- Pack out all rubbish and empty containers.
- Bring a water-treatment system rather than purchasing bottled water.
- Dress conservatively around locals and avoid wearing shorts or tank tops.
- Avoid drinking alcohol in front of, or with, locals.

Sleeping & Eating

Guesthouses in Amezray, Agoudim, and Taghia welcome travellers looking to explore the valley. Advance reservations are recommended from March to June, and in September and October, particularly for climbers and hikers hoping to base themselves in Taghia.

A handful of shops and restaurants above the marketplace work on irregular hours, but generally most visitors will take meals at their guesthouse.

Kasbah Amezray GUESTHOUSE €
(0666531002; www.kasbah-amezray.com; Amezray; r Dh200;) This 12-room guesthouse has cosy rooms (five with en suite) with exposed stone walls and wood-beam ceilings. It's set in front of a photogenic granary, which you can visit. Proprietor Youssef is good contact to arrange treks, rock climbing, 4WD trips and transfers to Marrakesh. Half-board is available for Dh150.

★ **Dar Ahansal** GUESTHOUSE €€
(0678962584; www.darahansal.net; Amezray; s/d incl half-board Dh380/560; P) Atop Amezray the impressive rock-hewn *dar* (small house) of mountain guide Youssef Oulcadi rises organically out of the tough mountain landscape, its terraces built around Aleppo pines and landscaped with blushing roses and oleanders. Inside, rooms are beautifully finished with terracotta floors, *zellige* (colourful geometric mosaic tiles) bathrooms and raffia-framed beds. Campsites (per person Dh50) also available.

Gîte Ahmed Amahdar GUESTHOUSE €
(0678538882; amahdar.ahmed@gmail.com; Agoudim; dm incl half-board Dh150) Bunk at the

ATLAS CULTURAL FOUNDATION

The Atlas Cultural Foundation (www.atlasculturalfoundation.org) is a registered US nonprofit organisation with the mission of helping under-served Moroccans, especially women and children, improve their quality of life through locally determined development projects focusing on cultural preservation, community and environmental health, and education. In partnership with the local Moroccan Association Amezray SMNID, they are responsible for the restoration of three historic saints' houses and the extraordinary communal granaries, which now form some of the major sights in the valley.

Another core component of ACF's work is its programmes run through Atlas Cultural Adventures (http://atlasculturaladventures.com). Participants assist in ACF's ongoing community development projects, work side by side with locals, and experience rural Moroccan village life. Programmes are focused on community leader capacity building, historic preservation, design and construction of small community projects, public health workshops and sustainable farming. Programmes are open to students or independent travellers and are from three days to five weeks in length.

guesthouse of village sheikh Sidi Ahmed Amahdar for hot showers, clean shared bathrooms and a family-style welcome from the folks who manage the place. It's set below a restored granary (ask son Mohammed to give you a tour inside) about 850m after crossing the bridge. Lunch is an extra Dh50.

Gîte Farid GUESTHOUSE €
(☎0661158857; yousseffarid87@gmail.com; Agoudim; dm incl half-board Dh155) Mountain guide Youssef Farid and family (including his English-speaking daughter) run this small guesthouse just off the *piste* as it approaches Agoudim. Showers are an extra Dh10, and half-board is available for Dh70 per person.

Gîte Taoujdat GUESTHOUSE €
(☎0694234195; https://climbingtaghia.com; Taghia; dm incl half-board Dh150) Trekking groups head up to this basic guesthouse at the home of guide Said Massaoudi and his son Mohammad. It consists of mattresses on wooden pallets accompanied by simple but tasty meals. Lunch is an extra Dh50.

Gîte Mohamed Amil GUESTHOUSE €
(☎0669261684; amilmohamed70@yahoo.com; Taghia; dm incl half-board Dh150) At the top end of Taghia (and thus closest to the mountains), this small guesthouse is popular with climbers and fills quickly.

Gîte Jamal GUESTHOUSE €
(☎0619003980; http://gite-jamal-taghia.com; Taghia; dm incl half-board Dh160) At the foot of Taghia just past the bridge, this small 12-bed, family-run guesthouse is a good choice for travellers who care more about exploring the village itself than immediate access to climbing routes.

ℹ Getting There & Away

Zaouiat Ahansal is accessible by two routes from Azilal. The quicker route south through Ait Mohammed across the Tizi n'Tselli-n-Imanain (2763m) and Tizi n'Illissi (2606m) is the way minivans from Azilal (Dh40, 3½ to four hours) will take, leaving Zaouiat Ahansal in the morning and returning from Azilal in the afternoon. Grands taxis only originate in Azilal and cost about Dh50 per person, but you may struggle to fill the vehicle.

Less direct but more scenic, daily minivans leave Zaouiat Ahansal for Ouaouizeght (Dh 50, six to seven hours) on the eastern side of Bin el Ouidane via the Reserve Naturelle de Tamga (two hours). If you're planning to self-drive this route, check locally on the state of the dirt and gravel roads north of Zaouiat Ahansal before departing; particularly after heavy rain, as they may be in a shockingly bad condition.

Ait Bougmez Valley

Paved roads have given unprecedented access to Morocco's 'happy valley' with its mud-brick towers and rich cultivated terraces. Scattered throughout the valley, 25 *douars* (villages) blend with their spectacular backdrops. In the hills you'll spot villagers collecting wild mountain plants to make herbal remedies and natural dyes, and in the broad alluvial valley are acres of lovingly tended fruit orchards.

The Y-shaped valley centres around the *zawiya* (shrine) of Sidi Moussa, which sits on a cone-shaped hill at the centre with the villages of Imelgas and Ikhf-n-Ighir to the northeast, Tabant to the southeast and Timit and Agouti to the west. Tabant, with its weekly Sunday souq, school and official mountain-guide training centre, is at the heart of the valley and the main transport hub. At the far eastern end, Zaouit Oulmzi is an alternative base for trekkers looking to make day hikes into the mountains and through rarely visited villages.

Although there are plenty of mountainous hikes in the region – with summit-baggers heading straight for **Irhil M'Goun** (4068m) – ambling between villages along the valley floor is enormously rewarding, with 40 local associations and cooperatives offfering their own brand of sustainable tourism and providing much needed education to future generations.

AGOUTI

Agouti is beloved by trekkers for scenic M'Goun views and down-to-earth Amazigh hospitality at several *gîtes d'étape* (basic homestays or hostels), as well as the picturesque ruined *kasbah* (fortress) above the village. It's also the starting point of the three-day M'Goun Massif (p137) hike.

There aren't any standalone restaurants in Agouti, but all lodging in the area offers half-board.

Though it may not look like much from the street, **Gîte M'Goun** (Chez Moha; ☎0661407478; mgounguest@gmail.com; s/d Dh100/200) has spacious rooms with en suite bathrooms and a warm welcome, making this one of the best options in Agouti. Moha can arrange local trekking guides with a few days' notice. It's at the village centre.

At **Gîte La Montagne Au Pluriel** (☎0661211093, 0661882434; s/d/tr/q Dh100/160/225/280), small but cosy rooms with low ceilings, most with shared bathrooms, are available at excellent prices. It's located on the main road through the village.

The first guesthouse on the western edge of the village, **Flilou** (☎0672709957; tamsilt@menara.ma; dm/s/d incl half-board Dh160/240/480, d incl half-board with shared bathroom Dh320; P) offers clean dorms and doubles, savoury meals and modern bathrooms. The mattresses are stiff, but the welcome is warm.

Minibuses to Azilal (Dh30, 2½ hours) leave when full throughout the day (though they often take all morning to fill up), and more frequently to Tabant (Dh20).

TABANT

The largest settlement in Aït Bougmez and home to the **Sunday souq** (⊙8am-2pm Sun), Tabant is the economic and transport hub of the valley. It does make a good base for exploring the surrounding countryside, though if you're looking for quiet village life perhaps consider staying elsewhere in the valley.

A few cafes operate along the main street near the souq, where your nose may well lead you to **Café des Amis** (meals Dh25-35; ⊙8am-6pm) of its own accord; a few more street stalls operate on Sundays during market hours. Most guesthouses can prepare meals with advance notice.

Staying in Tabant is an obvious choice if you're visiting the Sunday Souq, but the town's position at the centre of the Y-shaped valley also makes it an ideal base for day trips to surrounding villages.

Aït Bougmez's first boutique-style guesthouse, **Dar Si Hamou** (☎0667644862; s/d Dh250/310) is set around a pretty garden

ARTISANS ONLINE

Inhabitants of the Aït Bougmez Valley are a resourceful bunch, testament to which is the launch of Anou (www.theanou.com), a new artisan-managed online platform that enables illiterate artisans to sell their work independently.

Unlike Etsy or eBay, the resource isn't open to anyone, but rather is limited to locally recognised artisans peer-verified by Anou's leadership team, the benchmark being the quality of the products produced and the motivation of the artisans to expand and develop their product line.

Anou then assists artisans in creating a profile page with a biography of each member, photographs of their studio and tools, and GPS coordinates of their workshops. Each piece created is subsequently approved by Anou's administration team before being posted to the site, ensuring that every product you see is exactly the item that will be shipped to you. When products sell, artisans pop the purchased item in the post and, *voilà*, in two to three weeks your new handcrafted carpet, bag or sculpture will arrive on your doorstep.

It's a great resource for travellers, as Anou's primary buyers are, so far, conscientious tourists keen to ensure that they are buying direct from artisans. At the time of writing there were 200 artisans on the site and 35 cooperatives and associations now extending well beyond Ait Bougmez.

courtyard with mountain views, while **La Fibule Berbère** (☎0662655533; aitouchi@yahoo.fr; r Dh200;) has two floors of spacious rooms built around a dim central courtyard. Go 500m east past the souq.

A few minibuses leave each day for Azilal (Dh30, three hours), though if you're heading only as far west as Agouti or the turnoff for Aït Bououli (Dh20) or west to Zahouiat Oulmzi (Dh20), be sure to check which direction the driver is heading.

TIMIT

For a village-life alternative to nearby Tabant, the village of Timit offers a laid-back pace and the chance to wander village orchards and observe the rhythms of local life.

For a spectacular sunset, climb the steep but straightforward trail up to the *zawiya* of **Sidi Moussa**, a local *marabout* (saint), on a conical hilltop at the centre of the valley. The round structure served as a collective granary and has been restored through a community effort, with fitted-stone walls and weather-beaten wooden doors making a worthy photo backdrop. When it's open, locals charge Dh10 admission, which includes tea.

In the village centre is the simple but delightful **Gîte Timit** (La Maison Imazighne; ☎0673260438; gite.timit@hotmail.fr; dm/d Dh50/100), whilst in the surrounding countryside you'll find the stylish **La Kasbah du M'Goun** (☎0662778148; www.ecotours-ma.com; dm/s/d/tr Dh120/450/600/700;).

Timit is a little over 1.5km west of Tabant along the main road. Catching a ride to Tabant (around Dh5) or Agouti (around Dh10) 5km to the west generally isn't hard, though often vehicles are few and far between.

ZAOUIAT OULMZI

The handful of villages at the end of the Aït Bougmez Valley are small and remote even by local standards, and Zaouiat Oulmzi is literally the end of the line. East of here shepherds take their flocks to graze near seasonal Lac Izoughar and the twisting mountain valleys beyond that eventually lead all the way to Zaouiat Ahansal.

Lac Izoughar is a favoured watering hole for the nomadic Aït Atta tribe. Higher water levels make this most impressive in March and April, but the 11km walk from the village and back is pleasant hiking anytime.

Though ambitious plans for building a multilift ski resort beyond Lac Izoughar have never come to fruition, *ski randonnée* (alpine touring) remains popular among a select few visitors each year. Inquire about a guide at your accommodation.

The upscale **Touda Ecolodge** (☎0662144285; www.touda.fr; s/d/tr €60/70/90;) has a perfect combination of comfort and hospitality, making it one of the best options in the entire region, and the panoramic views from its hilltop position above the village certainly don't hurt either. For something a little more budget-friendly and still perfectly serviceable, the **Gîte Zawyat Oulmzi** (☎0678301332; gite.zawyat_oulmzi@yahoo.fr; dm/s/d/tr Dh80/100/180/230) also offers comfortable beds and warm meals.

From the turnoff on the main road 2km northwest of the village, occasional minibuses pass by en route to Tabant (Dh20) and Azilal (Dh50).

Ait Bououli Valley

The remote Aït Bououli Valley's scattered villages make prime short-hike territory for travellers looking to escape the beaten track, and trekkers prepared for longer journeys can use Sebt Aït Bououli as an alternate trailhead for the three-day trek over the M'Goun Massif.

From **Sebt Aït Bououli**, the valley centre and site of the Saturday souq, stunning mountain village **Rougoult** (due south 7.5km) and pretty **Abachkou** (2km to the southwest) are both day hike options. Along

EMPOWERING LOCAL WOMEN

The **Women's Cooperative of Aït Bououli** (☎0616247899, 0671419106; ⏲9am-5pm) is a 40-member cooperative that takes every aspect of carpet-making into its own hands: tending and shearing sheep; carding and spinning fluffy lambswool into yarn; and collecting plants to dye yarn rich hues. Look for a sign pointing just off the valley road around 2.5km west of Sebt Aït Bououli, below the village of Assameur.

The members also take turns minding the shop, so you'll be buying carpets from the woman who made it, her sister or her neighbour. If you find the door closed, which is likely as the opening hours are somewhat of a suggestion, just call the director and she'll come down from the village to open the small storeroom.

the valley road 2.5km east are a trio of tiny villages built right into a two-toned black and ochre bluff. On green terraces gambolling lambs are the valley's claim to fame: Bououli means 'those who keep sheep'.

The only formal guesthouse in the valley is the **Gîte Adrar Abachko** (☎0668523661; Sebt Aït Bououli; dm Dh50) just east of the centre of Sebt Aït Bououli, which can also arrange meals.

A handful of daily minibuses leave for Demnate (Dh35). Despite the proximity to Aït Bougmez, no public transportation connects the two. Travellers attempting to travel from here directly will need to hike or find local transport to the intersection of the Aït Mohammed–Aït Bougmez road about 13km east of Sebt Aït Bououli.

Trekking the M'Goun Traverse

While crowds flock to Jebel Toubkal, nature lovers head to the M'Goun Massif, where pristine landscapes and some of Morocco's highest peaks make for rewarding challenges for trekkers. This walk will suit all grades of trekkers, including families.

If you're going in spring, dress warmly and be prepared to get your boots wet: walking river gorges is one of the great pleasures of M'Goun. The M'Goun Traverse crosses a bevy of ravines with small streams, crests the mountain range, and then follows another river down into its valley.

The most reliable route to Agouti is from Azilal (Dh30, 2½ hours).

From Aït Ali n'Ito, infrequent collective taxis (Dh10) make the 8.5km trip to the junction with the new highway at Aït Alla, where it's possible to continue north to Demnate (Dh70) or south towards Ouarzazate (Dh50).

DAY 1: AGOUTI TO ROUGOULT

Duration 6-7 hours
Distance 20km
Ascent 776m
Descent 671m

From the trailhead in the centre of Agouti, follow a level *piste* for 2.7km southwest towards the village of Arous, turning opposite the first few small buildings onto a dirt path that curves around the south of the multihued rock outcropping that dominates this end of the village. Climb past a smattering of houses towards what appears to be a small pass, but is actually the beginning of a rocky traverse that ends with a climb to the 2429m Tizi n'Tafaniz, about 6km from the trailhead.

WHEN TO GO

➡ Wildflowers bloom across the M'Goun Massif from March to May, though snowmelt also makes river crossing more difficult.

➡ Trekking routes in the region remain open until the first snowfalls of winter, with the season typically ending in mid-October – though attempts at peaks at higher elevations may encounter snow even earlier in the year.

From the pass, angle southwest across a small plateau that drops gently towards a small streambed after 1.5km. Several trails diverge here; cross the streambed and begin clmbing immediately to the forested hillside just to the east. Follow the contours of the ridge for around 3km, descending at one point down a steep rocky trail, until a dramatic rocky ravine impedes easy progress to the south. Pick your way carefully down to and across the streambed here, climbing briefly up before continuing to traverse the ridge through successive small ravines to the obvious long ridge in the distance that slopes down northwards towards **Aït Bououli**.

The panorama of surrounding villages from the crest of this ridge is excellent, as is the view southwest towards the day's final short climb. Follow the obvious trail to an unnamed 2488m pass (almost exactly 15km from the start of the day's hike) and stay on the same trail as it curves down around the ridge and drops to the valley below.

If you need water, follow the curve of the path southeast and up the valley to the stream – if it's dry, continue 100m south along the ridge to a reliable spring on the path to Ifri n'Aït Kherfalla. Otherwise, look for a cutoff that descends to the southwest along a rocky and occasionally treacherous descent – be particularly careful on this steep section if you're carrying a heavy pack. Near the bottom of the descent, at a small saddle with stunning views of Rougoult's ruined kasbah, the trail angles to the southeast to join the piste for the final 1.5km to the village.

In **Rougoult** you'll find a shaded Tifra River campsite and sometimes informal homestays (per person Dh150 excluding breakfast) – ask around to see who has space.

An alternative to this hike is the fairly easy 7.5km *piste* straight up the Tifra river valley from Aït Bououli, but you'll miss some over the loveliest views and wildest landscapes of the trek by taking this option.

DAY 2: ROUGOULT TO AMEZRI

Duration 7-8 hours
Distance 16km
Descent 644m
Ascent 848m

For 8km, the morning walk follows the Tifra along a stony path criss-crossing the river. As the well-trodden mule path climbs, the landscape becomes more barren, occasionally leading above rocky gorges – but the path always follows the course of the river south. After about 8km is a serviceable campsite at **Ifri** pasture, and another a further 5km on at a small spring (the final reliable water source before the pass).

Beyond is a steep climb up the final 250m of vertical ascent to the pass of **Tizi n'Rougoult** (2900m). From the broad saddle beneath the pass, a path leads east to a ridge that climbs to Jebel Tarkeddid and the summit of Irhil M'Goun (4068m) – only 100m lower than Jebel Toubkal – due east. Our route up the well-worn Rougoult pass is straight ahead. In the near distance across the **Tessaout River**, exposed mountain slopes reveal great gashes of rust, green and grey rock.

TREK AT A GLANCE

Duration Three days

Distance 57km

Standard Medium

Start Agouti

Finish Aït Ali n'Ito

Highest point Tizi n'Rougoult (2900m)

Accommodation Camping or *gîtes*

Public transport Yes

Summary This walk traverses the northeastern slopes of the M'Goun Massif and then drops down into the Tessaout Valley; it will suit most trekkers, even younger ones. There's one long day of walking, but this varied trek crosses stunning mountain landscapes, and travels through river gorges and remote valleys.

From the Rougoult pass, the mule path is clearly marked, winding gradually downhill for 3.5km before reaching the village of **Tasgaïwalt** (2521m) and joining the *piste*. Curious village children may keep you company on the easy 2.5km walk along the *piste*, keeping the river to your left, to the village of **Amezri** (2250m). Just up the northwest river bank from the village bridge, **Gîte d'Étape Agnid Mohamed** (☎0671018649; dm Dh100) has several large rooms, some of which overlook the valley, with a rudimentary hot shower and toilets. Half-board is available (Dh100) and there's convenient camping (Dh25) too.

If you'd like to start or end the hike in Amezri, occasional collective taxis (Dh50) travel the rough 120km mountain road to and from Skoura, particularly on Mondays for the market there.

DAY 3: AMEZRI TO AÏT ALI N'ITO

Duration 5-6 hours
Distance 21km
Ascent 537m
Descent 714m

Follow the bitumen track to the west out of Ameri for 5.5km to where it overlooks the village of **Imi n'Ikkis**. While it's possible to follow this track all the way past Ichbaken to Aït Ali n'Ito (a total of around 22km), the far more interesting route crosses the river here and climbs northwest out of Imi n'Ikkis up a dry streambed for around 280 vertical metres to the bottom edge of the **Lota n'Tessaout** plateau. Climb gently through and beyond this popular grazing area for 9km, traversing the contours of the ridge when necessary, until Aït Ali n'Ito is visible in the low valley due west.

Instead of heading directly down to the northwest, however, curl southwest around the final rise of the low ridge and down an obvious path into the pretty village of **Tiftacht**. From the bottom of the village, it's an easy 3km down the *piste* to **Aït Ali n'Ito** and the excellent **Gîte d'Étape Assounfou** (☎0668968263; dm Dh200), the first and still by far the best in the Tessaout Valley with great views, electricity and hot showers.

DAY HIKES FROM AÏT ALI N'ITO

Several villages in and around the Tessaout Valley make nice day-hike destinations from Aït Ali n'Ito. The tarmac leads 3km west alongside the river to the lovely village of **Fakhour**, where houses scale the hillside.

M'Goun Traverse Trek

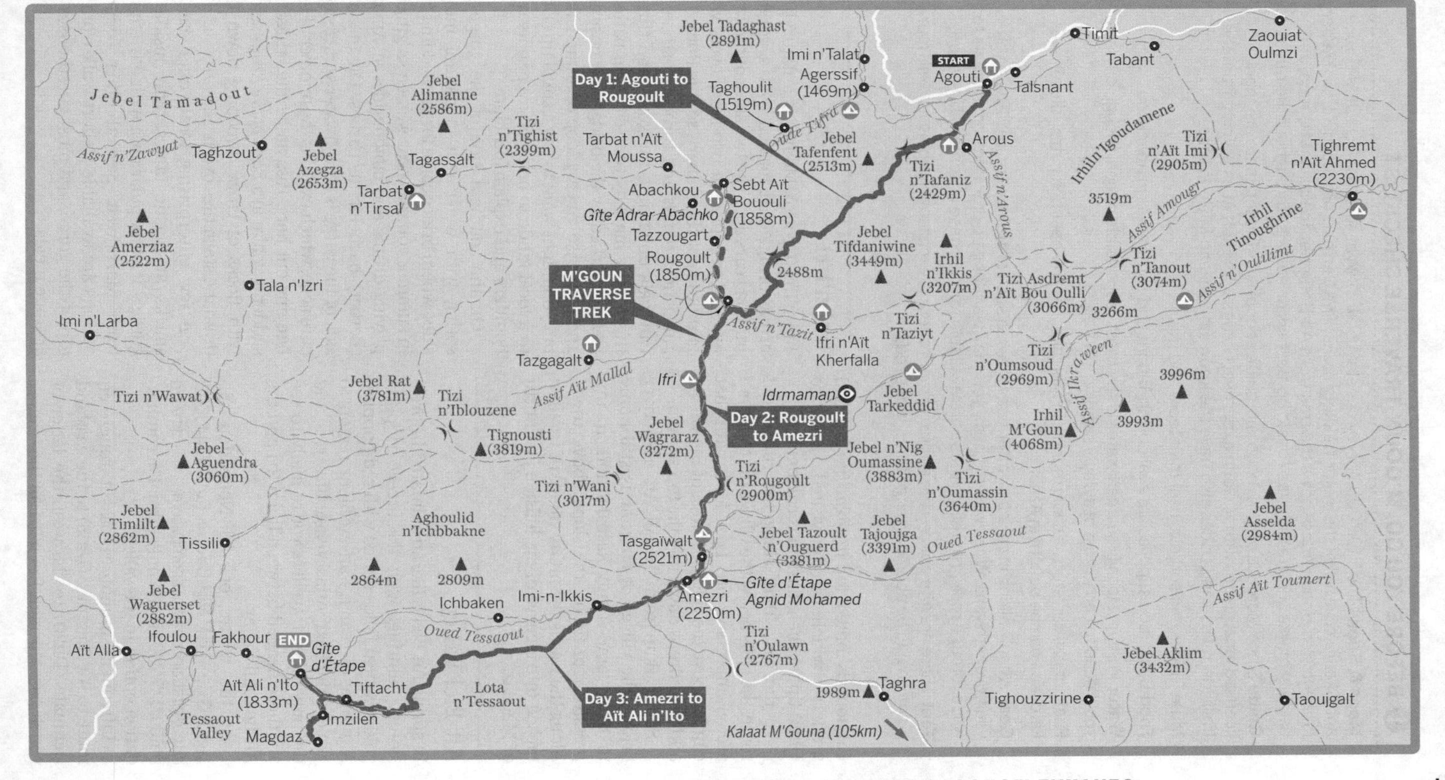

BEFORE YOU GO: M'GOUN TRAVERSE CHECKLIST

Maps & Books The 1:100,000 survey sheets *Azilal, Zawyat Ahannsal, Qalat M'Gouna* and *Skoura* cover all of the major trekking areas. The German-produced *Kultur Trekking im Zentralen Hohen Atlas* shows the trek from Ait Bougmez to Kalaat M'Gouna, and usefully marks and grades *gîtes* (basic homestays or hostels) throughout the range.

Guide Since Morocco's main mountain-guide school is in Tabant, there are many licensed local guides with M'Goun expertise. Guides with High Atlas training from the Imlil, Marrakesh and Dadès also have the know-how to lead M'Goun trips.

Mule Guides can sort out local muleteers and mules.

Food Basic food supplies are available in Tabant and sometimes in Abachkou.

Water Purifying locally sourced water is the most responsible option, though on day one you'll need to carry most of a day's supply.

Fuel For gas canisters, a supermarket in Marrakesh is the best bet. Petrol, diesel and kerosene can be bought in Azilal.

Gear When walking in spring or after heavy rain, a stick or trekking pole will help you vault over streams. When water is high, you may want plastic or waterproof sandals to wade through rocky riverbeds; these are available for purchase at some village shops.

Tent There are *gîte* options the entire trek, but there is excellent camping as well. Your guide should be able to arrange tents if desired.

Fakhour is noted for its *agadir* (fortified granary), which can be visited (Dh10 to Dh20 tip for the guardian is customary).

To the east 10km along the rutted old route, the cliffs below the village of **Ichbaken** are an impressive site. Look for a path that climbs above the ridge just west of the village and then drops down into the top section.

South 4km from the Aït Ali n'Ito river bridge, the village of **Magdaz** is still home to three large family kasbahs and an impressive *agadir* on the slope above town. Along the way is the pretty village of **Imzilen** tucked into a curve of the hillside just north of Magdaz.

Ait Blel Valley

In spring Aït Blel is like an animated Impressionist painting, with the breeze rippling golden wheat fields dotted with red poppies. Any time of year it's an excellent region to explore the High Atlas' village lifestyles, and the only other travellers you're likely to see are those headed between Imi n'Ifri and the Aït Bououli Valley.

At the centre of Tizi Noubadou village, **Gîte Tizi Noubadou** (☎0661443602; http://gitetizinoubadou.doomby.com; dm/s/d Dh100/125/250) is the only formal accommodation option in the valley.

Infrequent minibuses pass through en route to Aït Bougmez (Dh15) to the east and Demnate (Dh20) to the west, the latter of which pass through Imi n'Ifri on the way.

Imi n'Ifri

Imi n'Ifri (Grotto's Mouth) is a natural travertine bridge that formed over a gorge 1.8 million years ago. The two sides of the bridge are said to represent two local lovers whose families kept them apart, so this Romeo and Juliet held hands and turned to stone. You can walk down into the gorge and through this toothy maw by yourself – the paths are clearly marked by the bridge and post office and comprise an easy loop of around 1km – but you might want to pay a small tip (Dh20) to a local guide to help you over some tricky boulders and explain local lore.

On the southern side of the gorge is a spring with water rich in natural mineral salts, where brides come for prewedding rites; in summer you may hear women singing and playing drums and tambourines at Amazigh (Berber) bachelorette parties. On the other side of the gorge is a freshwater spring said to cure acne, which explains the number of teens hanging out here. Pass under the bridge, and suddenly you're in a *Lord of the Rings* setting, with flocks of crows swooping down from dramatic stalactites overhead.

A few enterprising locals offer tea and snacks at plastic tables right inside the gorge – it's a popular area with day trippers from Marrakesh. Several other (quieter) options are available a short walk from the top of the gorge, and most guesthouses can arrange meals.

A good budget option just 400m from the top of the gorge, the family-run **Gite Kasbah Imi n'Ifri** (Chez Thami; ☎0662105168; thamitrek1@hotmail.com; dm Dh150) has basic rooms with shared bathrooms. To get here, walk south from the junction.

Set into the hillside overlooking Demnate and shaded by flourishing gardens, **Tizouit** (☎0658346148; www.tizouit.ma; Aït Oumghar; r Dh700-900; P 📶 ❄) is a labour of love and it shows. Expect an idyllic escape in this superb ecolodge with its eight individual cottage rooms.

The splashy kasbah-hotel **Illy Kasbah** (☎0523508953; Route d'Imi n'Ifri; r €87-99, ste €135; P 📶 ❄), 5km from Demnate on the road to Imi n'Ifri, offers opulent rooms surrounding a riad-style courtyard and a small outdoor pool with sunset views.

If you're staying at a guesthouse near Imi n'Ifri, you'll be able to walk to the gorge. Buses and grands taxis stop at Demnate, where you'll need to take an onward taxi (Dh30) or shared minivan (Dh 4) the final 6km to Imi n'Ifri along the R307.

Demnate دمنات

POP 24,000

The once-grand Glaoui kasbah and mud-brick ramparts have been left to crumble, yet Demnate's fascinating interfaith heritage has survived, revealed by the former *mellah* (Jewish quarter) at the heart of town. It's a lively town to explore, though most visitors are only passing through to visit the Sunday souq or en route to the picturesque gorge of Imi n'Ifri to the east.

Demnate's Jewish population dates back to at least the 12th century, but the local *mellah* was only established in 1894 following local pogroms. Once home to artisans and wine merchants, mass emigration to Israel since the 1950s has resulted in the quarter now bearing very few indications of its former history. The entrance to the old neighbourhood is about 150m on the right after the town's main gate.

South of the bus station, the **Sunday souq** (⏲9am-4pm Sun) is an opportunity to taste-test local olives, olive oils and almonds, and to browse Demnate's local woodwork and yellow-glazed pottery painted in henna. **Produits Agricoles Naturelles** (☎0600050202; ⏲9am-9pm) sells a more limited version of the same tasty goods from its shop opposite the O'Libya petrol station.

The 100-year-old olive groves dotting hillsides around Demnate produce Morocco's best olive oil, with trace mineral salts, a golden colour and subtle woodsy flavours that compare favourably to Tuscan oils. Almonds are another renowned local product, and the flowering of the local orchards makes March a lovely time to visit. Visitors interested in traditional crafts can hunt down the potteries northeast of town in the village of **Boughlou**; turn right at the Espace du Kasbah Cafe and head 4km off-road.

Cafes with outdoor seating line the main street. Behind the *gare routière* (central bus station), you'll find a lively selection of open-sided eateries, serving up bubbling tajines and the latest football match playing overhead.

To overnight in Demnate, the **Marrakesh Residences** (☎0523506996; r with shared bathroom Dh100; 📶) is the best of a limited lot. Out of town, **Kasbah Timdaf** (☎0523507178; www.kasbah-timdaf.com; s/d Dh690/880; P 📶) is a much more enticing option, though you'll want your own wheels. This stone and mud-brick kasbah is built in the traditional local style with artful rooms warmed by vintage wood-burning stoves. It may seem palatial, but it is a working farm surrounded by almond and olive groves, providing inspired Mediterranean-Amazigh (Berber) meals (Dh210) on a vine-draped terrace with expansive views. Look for it 15 minutes down the road to Azilal.

Grands taxis to Marrakesh (Dh50) and Azilal (Dh40) leave from just west of the main gate in Demnate.

Buses leave for Marrakesh (Dh30, two hours) from 6am to 9pm and to Azilal (Dh12, one hour) from 7am to noon from the bus

OFF THE BEATEN TRACK

DINOSAUR FOOTPRINTS

Geologists claim that tracks imprinted in exposed rock in the village of Tabalout are in fact footprints of the Megalosauripus from the Middle to Upper Jurassic period, about 160 million years old. Look for a walled area just off the left side of the road; if the gate is locked, ask at the house just down the hill for the key.

Tabalout is about 7km east of Imi n'Ifri, on the road to Aït Blel.

FESTIVALS IN DEMNATE

Hundreds of Jewish families from Morocco, France, Israel, Canada and the US arrive each July for the **Jewish Moussem**, a week-long mystical event said to offer miracle cures.

Demnate has two *zawiyas* (Islamic religious shrines), making the annual **Hamdouchi Moussem** in September twice as raucous. Pilgrims visiting each *zawiya* dance to a different rhythm in an all-day music festival in the town centre before going their separate ways in three-hour parades to the *zawiyas*. Sometimes the *moussem* peaks in blood purification, with dancers cutting themselves on the scalp in dramatic acts of ritual cleansing.

station (take the road to the right before the town gate and turn left at the roundabout), with additional limited services to Rabat (Dh100, five hours).

To reach nearby Imi n'Ifri, you'll need to take a taxi (Dh50 for the whole taxi) or a minibus (Dh4) from the minibus stand, which also has departures for Aït Blel (Dh20) and Aït Bououli (Dh35).

OUNILA VALLEY

Follow the ancient caravan route through the High Atlas over the **Tizi n'Tichka** pass (2260m) and you'll find yourself descending from forested slopes into the flat, stony landscape of Morocco's pre-Sahara. Long an essential trade route, the prosperous Ounila Valley is today mostly strongly associated with the Glaoui clan's infamous rule from the family home of Telouet.

Though the French-built highway now bypasses Ounila for a more direct route to Ouarzazate, travellers with an eye for history still visit for the slowly crumbling Glaoui kasbah and the Hollywood-darling *ksar* of Aït Ben Haddou. Beyond the historical interest, mountain villages such as Anmiter (whose red-tower kasbah gives a glimpse of what Aït Ben Haddou may have looked like in its original state) and isolated lakes make the region attractive to nature lovers as well.

Aït Ben Haddou آيت بن حدو

POP 3000

With the help of some Hollywood touch-ups, the Unesco-protected red mud-brick *ksar* of Aït Ben Haddou seems frozen in time, still resembling its days in the 11th century as an Almoravid caravanserai. Movie buffs may recognise it from *Lawrence of Arabia*, *Jesus of Nazareth* (for which much of the *ksar* was rebuilt), *Jewel of the Nile* (note the Egyptian towers), *Gladiator* and more recently *Game of Thrones*.

Much of the *ksar* is now given over to souvenir shops, with most locals having relocated to the new village of Issiwide along the main road. A handful of families do still live in the *ksar* – one of which at the bottom of the village has opened their home as a small one-room 'museum' (Dh10), with a dusty collection of old door latches, swords, baskets and satchels. Wind your way through lanes up to a ruined *igherm* (fortified granary), towering above Aït Ben Haddou; it offers magnificent views of the surrounding *palmeraie* (palm grove) and unforgiving *hamada* (stony desert) that stretches out beyond the village.

Note that there is no official entrance fee to the *ksar*, despite the best efforts of several local 'entrepreneurs' with fake tickets to sell to unsuspecting tourists. Enter along the footbridge for the least hassle.

Sleeping

There are dozens of guesthouses in the area, some of which offer fine views of the *ksar*. Owing to intense competition, prices are quite reasonable.

Restaurants dot the main drag, though you may want to avoid the ones with big tour buses parked in front. You'll also find a few eateries along the lanes on the way down to the *ksar*.

Kasbah du Jardin GUESTHOUSE €
(0524888019; www.kasbahdujardin.com; campsite Dh40, s/d Dh250/350;) Decent, nicely equipped rooms set around a sparkling pool – book an upstairs one for better views. You can also pitch a tent here, but there's not much shade and you'll have to pay Dh40 to use the pool. Find it on the northwestern edge of the new village.

Etoile Filante d'Or GUESTHOUSE €
(0524884489; kasbah.yunkai@gmail.com; s/d Dh175/350;) Desert nights on the Etoile's

roof terrace lure guests out of 17 spacious rooms for inspiring *ksar* views. Guest rooms feature traditional touches such as *tataoui* (woven reed) ceilings and Amazigh (Berber) blankets. The guesthouse has a popular restaurant where you can enjoy Moroccan, Chinese and European fare; though things do occasionally get a bit loud with tour groups.

★ **Auberge Bagdad Cafe** GUESTHOUSE €€
(0524882506; https://hotel-ait-ben-haddou.com; s/d incl half-board Dh600/750; P) The friendly Bagdad Cafe is well known for its good food – a few, simple home-cooked dishes done to a high standard and complemented by a well-stocked bar – but it also has jaunty rooms decked out with rattan-framed beds, rag rugs and bright, modernist bed linens. You'll find it on the main drag just beside the large car park for the village.

Eating & Drinking

Cafe-Restaurant Tamlalte MOROCCAN €
(mains Dh25-50; 8am-9pm) Just on the new village side of the footbridge across from the *ksar*, this laid-back eatery serves up an unsurprising selection of soups, salads, tajines and couscous. The best reason to come here is for the views from the terrace.

Auberge Cafe-Restaurant Bilal MOROCCAN €
(0697564528; auberge.chezbilal@gmail.com; mains Dh30-60; 8am-9pm;) For lunch or tea with a magnificent view, pull up a patio chair and gaze at Aït Ben Haddou across the way. Options include omelettes, couscous and kebabs. There are also a handful of simple rooms available from Dh300.

La Terrazza ITALIAN €€
(0651172334; mains Dh50-140; 10am-11pm;) Find real espresso-based coffee, paninis and crepes, pizza and pasta and more at this unexpected Italian-run joint just uphill from the river on the new side of town.

Chez Brahim MOROCCAN €€
(0671816312; meals Dh100; 7am-10pm;) Seek out Brahim's place for fantastic *ksar* views from the rooftop terrace or the *pisé* (rammed-earth) salon, complemented by a set menu including salads, tajine and dessert. It's hidden in the backstreets of the new village – turn at the alley to the left of Bagdad Cafe and walk about 200m.

The same family also offers 10 pleasantly set rooms (doubles from Dh300) with fine views.

Tawesna TEAHOUSE
(0661330374; https://tablespaysannes.com; 8am-6pm) This small teahouse serves up a basic set menu (Dh25) of coffee or tea and a plate of homemade local sweets, the proceeds from which support the local Association for Rural Women and Solidarity. With advance notice, they can also prepare a range of Amizigh (Berber) set menu meals for group bookings. Find it just beyond the bridge in the old village.

Getting There & Away

Grands taxis run from outside Ouarzazate bus station when full (Dh20 per person) and from the turnoff 9km before Aït Ben Haddou (around Dh5 per person or Dh30 for the whole vehicle), dropping off passengers along the main road through the new village.

Tamdakhte

POP 6185

A beautifully ruined kasbah and hiking access to several surrounding gorges make Tamdakhte a pleasant alternative base to nearby Aït Ben Haddou, particularly for those who would prefer to escape the group tours there.

The magnificent unrestored **kasbah** (tip Dh15), a crumbling Glaoui construction still topped by storks' nests, is the centrepoint of the village. There's not much to see inside, but the sense of history alone is worth the visit. You'll need the *gardien* (caretaker) to get inside but, don't worry, they'll find you.

There are a few guesthouses in Tamdakhate, which also provide meals. For a wider selection head back to Aït Ben Haddou.

In a grand setting, **Kasbah Ounila** (0662843001; www.kasbah-ounila.com; r incl half-board from DH440;) has jaw-dropping views of the kasbah from its terrace, and the energetic staff can advise on walks and outings.

The *pisé* guesthouse **Kasbah Ellouze** (0524890459; www.kasbahellouze.com; s/d/ste incl half-board Dh700/900/1280;) blends in with the adjacent kasbah and makes for a fantastic retreat. The best rooms have orchard views (*luz* means almonds), or go for doubles by the heated pool.

No public transport originates here, but it is generally possible to flag down grands taxis between Telouet (Dh15) and Aït Ben Haddou (Dh15) or Ouarzazate (Dh35).

Telouet تيلويت

POP 14,211

Telouet occupied a privileged position as the birthplace of French collaborator and autocrat Pasha Glaoui until he was ousted in 1953 by the Moroccan independence movement. Legend has it that when the imposing doors of Telouet's Glaoui kasbah were thrown open at last, locals who had mysteriously disappeared years before stumbled dazed onto Telouet streets – they'd been locked in the pasha's basement.

In many ways Telouet seems arrested in time half a century ago, from the bustling Thursday Souq to the crumbling kasbah and the nearby remains of an ancient village once home to enslaved people. Salt mines are also still active in the area, and prized pink salt found along the nearby Oued Mellah (Salt River) was once accepted as currency – look for a sign to the '*mine du sel*' along the road before Anmiter.

Narrow river-valley oases east of Telouet are lined with crumbling Glaoui kasbahs, gorges riddled with caves, and ancient fortified villages such as Anmiter (11km east of Telouet), which has two well-preserved red kasbahs and a historic *mellah* (Jewish quarter) – though the Jewish population has long since left.

OFF THE BEATEN TRACK

RIAD KASBAH OLIVER

Owned by Tighza native Mohamed El Qasemy and his British wife Carolyn, **Riad Kasbah Oliver** (☎0668443040; www.homestaysmorocco.net; Tighza; r per adult/child under 12 yrs Dh300/100; 📶) is a labour of love. Built by hand from stone and earth by local village craftsmen, the result is simple, sustainable accommodation. Doors were fashioned in Telouet, furniture upcycled and hot showers are solar-powered.

Walking tours, overnight camping at Lac Tamda, salt-mine visits, souq trips, and homestays or tea with local villagers are just some of the many activities that can be arranged. You'll find the turnoff to Tighza 11km east of Telouet along the Ounila Highway, from where it is a 4.2km drive on a very rough *piste* (dirt track) to the village. Call directly to arrange transport.

The obvious highlight is the once-glorious **Glaoui Kasbah** (Dh20; ⏲9am-5pm), which has been left to crumble. The best indication of Telouet's former position as the centre of a trans-Saharan trading empire are the ornate 2nd-floor reception rooms. No less than 300 artisans worked on salons faceted with stucco, *zellige* (colourful geometric mosaic tiles) and painted cedar ceilings.

There are several simple guesthouses in town, with better options on the road to and in Aït Ben Haddou.

The simple but very welcoming family-run guesthous **Dar Aissa** (☎0670222247; daraissa@hotmail.fr; r per person Dh120) offers unfussy but colorful rooms with shared bathrooms set around a modest courtyard. Meanwhile, small but pleasant shared rooms and a large walled garden plus a friendly welcome make **Maison d'Hotes Afoulki** (☎0524891314; hafoulki@yahoo.fr; dm incl half-board Dh200; 📶) the best bet in Telouet, and the location just north of the weekly souq is the most convenient in town.

A few restaurants around Telouet's central square serve good-value tajines (Dh40) and Amazigh (Berber) omelettes (with tomato, olives and herbs; Dh30). The few options directly beside the kasbah entrance are generally high-cost and low-value, aimed mostly at group tours, and best avoided.

Grands taxis to Marrakesh are around Dh60 per seat, but you may well get stuck paying for all six seats. There are no buses from Ouarzazate, only taxis, which charge around Dh35 per seat and also stop in at Aït Ben Haddou (Dh15).

Ouarzazate ورزازات

POP 69,420

Strategically located Ouarzazate (*war*-zazat) has gotten by largely on its wits instead of its looks. For centuries people from the Atlas, Draa and Dadès Valleys converged to do business at Ouarzazate's sprawling Taourirt Kasbah, and a modern garrison town was established here in the 1920s to oversee France's colonial interests. The movie business gradually took off in Ouarzazate after the colonial French protectorate left in the 1950s, and 'Ouarzawood' movie studios have built quite a resume providing convincing backdrops for movies supposedly set in Tibet, ancient Rome, Somalia and Egypt.

There are only a handful of tourist sites in and around the city, but with scores of

THAMI EL GLAOUI: LORD OF THE ATLAS & PASHA OF MARRAKESH

With the signing of the Treaty of Fez in 1912 the French government found itself not only the proud owner of a new protectorate in Morocco but also a staunch, if questionable, new friend: Thami El Glaoui.

His family having nearly come to ruin under Sultan Moulay Hafid, Thami El Glaoui took the opportunity offered by the Treaty of Fez to throw his lot in with the French – a move seen both at the time and by modern historians as a sellout of his native Morocco, with Glaoui himself helping to orchestrate the eventual exile of Sultan Mohamed V and Glaoui's troops regularly used to enforce French rule in Marrakesh and the Atlas. The trade paid off, however, with El Glaoui eventually appointed Pasha of Marrakesh.

From the Glaoui ancestral home in Telouet the family controlled and taxed vast trade networks between the Sahara and Marrakesh, and soon after joining forces with the French the family business allegedly began to extend into kidnapping, prostitution, and more. By the early 1950s he was believed to be one of the richest men in the world. Whatever the source of his funds, the Pasha was well-received among the international community and (in)famous for throwing lavish parties in his Marrakesh and Telouet palaces.

Much of the family's wealth was confiscated by the state upon Mohamed V's return from exile, including the string of Glaoui kasbahs that lie across the Atlas from Marrakesh to Ouarzazate and beyond, and today Telouet's Glaoui Kasbah – constructed with the ideal of making it the most beautiful palace in the Muslim world – stands as a crumbing reminder of both the family's former dominance and troubling legacy in the region.

Gavin Maxwell's *Lords of the Atlas* (1966) is considered one of the definitive works on the subject, and will add excellent historical context for travellers visiting the region.

agencies offering all variety of trips, this is an ideal launching pad for mountains, desert oases and gorges.

Sights

★Taourirt Kasbah HISTORIC BUILDING

(Ave Mohammed V; Dh20; 8.30am-6pm) Unlike other Glaoui-era kasbahs, Taourirt escaped ruin by moonlighting as a Hollywood backdrop (*Sheltering Sky, Gladiator, Prince of Persia*) and attracting the attention of Unesco, which has carefully restored small sections of the inner sanctum. Follow the maze of stairwells to the top floor, where you'll find a prayer room through keyhole archways, traces of stucco and an original *tataoui* (woven reed) ceiling.

Tifoultoute Kasbah HISTORIC BUILDING

(Dh20; 8am-6pm) Built in the 17th century and extended by the Glaoui clan in the 18th, this commanding hilltop kasbah has now been converted into a privately owned restaurant (open to diners till midnight), with tables scattered throughout the building. Though only the smaller 18th-century extension is open to visitors (the rest left to slowly return to the sands), several magnificently tiled rooms inside make it worth the trip.

Bus 4 (Dh4) runs here from past the Ouarzazate souq and bus station, ending directly in front of the kasbah. From here it's a 4km walk to Atlas Studios, an easy option to combine visits to the two if it isn't too hot out.

Atlas Film Corporation Studios FILM LOCATION

(0524882212, 0524882223; Dh80; 8.30am-7.30pm) The first 'Ouarzawood' studio, established by Mohammed Belghimi in 1983, displays sets and props from movies filmed here, including *Jewel of the Nile, Kingdom of Heaven* and *Kundun*. Guided tours run every 20 to 40 minutes and take you through some of the stages, sets and workshops incorporated in the 11 hectare site, although you're also welcome to wander around on your own.

The studio is 5km west of town on the Marrakesh road and easily accessible on the green city buses 1 and 2 (Dh4) that run along Ave Mohammed V. A further half hour walk into the desert is what appears to be a complete fortress town – this is the *Kingdom of Heaven* set (combined entry with the studios Dh110).

Musée de Cinema MUSEUM

(0524890346; Ave Mohammed V; adult/student Dh30/15; 8am-6pm) This small cinema museum is housed in a former studio and exhibits a collection of old film sets, props

Ouarzazate

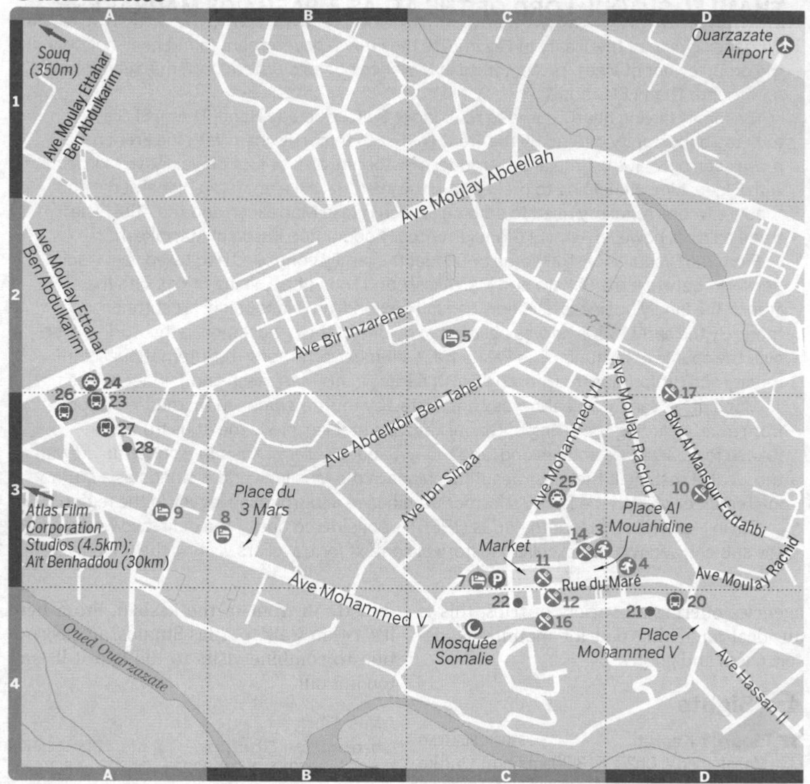

and cinematic equipment, which visitors are mostly encouraged to touch, play and pose with. Located opposite the Taourirt Kasbah, it is a convenient alternative if you can't get to the larger studios out of town.

Tours

Desert Majesty TOURS
(☎0524890765; www.desertmajesty.com; 18 Place Al Mouahidine; ⏰9am-8pm Mon-Sat) A highly recommended local agency offering trips to the High Atlas and the desert. Airport pick-ups, multilingual guides originating in Erfoud, Merzouga, M'Hamid and Taouz, and reassuringly safe drivers are offered at competitive prices. Booking queries are handled by Felicity, who is fluent in English, German, French and Darija.

Notably, they'll even go so far as to recommend other firms for itineraries beyond their expertise, a level of forthrightness we didn't often find in Ouarzazate.

Désert et Montagne TOURS
(☎0524854947; www.desert-montagne.ma; Dar Daïf, Douar Talmasla) Morocco's first female mountain guide and her company organise trips to meet Amazigh (Berber) families in the mountains, walking and 4WD trips in the desert and High Atlas, and longer trips following caravan routes.

The agency operates out of Dar Daïf in Douar Talmasla. To reach it, continue south on the N9 and cross the Oued (River) Ouarzazate, after which it is signposted to the left. The guesthouse is a lovely quiet retreat of plant-filled courtyards, but travellers without their own wheels will find the location inconvenient.

Maroc Experience TOURS
(☎0524883363; www.marocexperiencetours.com; 3-4 Place Al Mouahidine; ⏰9am-6pm Mon-Sat) Italian-owned agency that offers a wide range of tours as well as plane tickets and other travel essentials, and gets

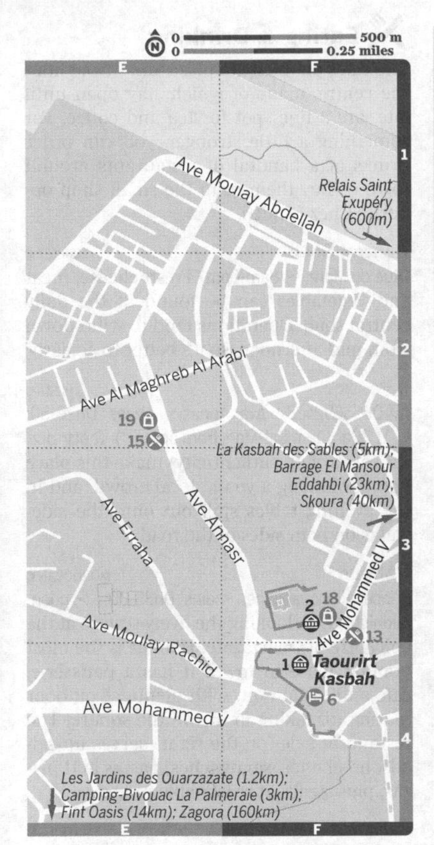

Ouarzazate

Top Sights
1 Taourirt Kasbah.......F4

Sights
2 Musée de Cinema.......F3

Activities, Courses & Tours
3 Desert Majesty.......C3
4 Maroc Experience.......D3

Sleeping
5 Dar Bergui.......C2
6 Dar Kamar.......F4
7 Hotel Amlal.......C3
8 Hotel Azoul.......B3
9 La Gazelle.......A3

Eating
10 Accord Majeur.......D3
11 Central Souq.......C3
12 Chez Dimitri.......C4
13 Douyria.......F3
14 Habous.......C3
15 Il Postino.......E2
16 Jardin des Arômes.......C4
Patisserie de Habous.......(see 14)
17 Restaurant du Goût Chinois.......D2

Shopping
18 Complexe Artisanal.......F3
Coopérative de Tissage.......(see 18)
19 Horizon Artisanat.......E2

Transport
20 CTM Bus Station.......D4
21 Desert Evasion.......D4
22 ESON Maroc.......C4
23 Gare Routière.......A3
24 Grand Taxi Stand.......A2
25 Grand Taxis to Tabount.......C3
26 Minibus Stand.......A3
27 Minibus to Demnate.......A3
28 Supratours Al Hizam.......A3

good reviews from travellers. Check in for last-minute discounts on upcoming tour departures.

Festivals & Events

Marathon des Sables SPORTS
(www.marathondessables.com; Mar-Apr) This gruelling seven-day, 250km desert ultra-marathon changes course each year, and is revealed when runners converge in Ouarzazate. It is considered to be among the world's most difficult ultras.

Moussem of Sidi Daoud CULTURAL
(Aug) The *moussem* honouring Sidi Daoud is held in Ouarzazate each August, with the usual religious processions and singing plus a small souq for craftsmen from the region.

Sleeping

Ouarzazate's hotel scene offers a good variety of midrange B&Bs and *maisons d'hotes* (small hotels) in the centre alongside larger, tour-group-oriented hotels such as the Ibis and Karam Palace which cluster near the Taourirt Kasbah and along the Route de Zagora.

★**Hotel Amlal** HOTEL €
(0524884030; www.hotelriadamlal.com; s/d/tr Dh200/300/400; P) With its zigzagging tilework and cool terrazzo floors, Hotel Amlal is an atmospheric option. Its 28 air-con rooms feature simple wood and wrought-iron furnishings, narrow beds and snug, tiled bathrooms. Although the place is showing its age, the location is excellent, with good dining options a short stroll away.

PROTECT THE DESERT

Though many agencies and hotels still offer them, quad bikes cause considerable damage to the fragile desert ecosystem and are not recommended. On motorbikes and bicycles, riders are advised to stay on well-marked trails to minimise displacement of native species.

La Gazelle HOTEL €

(0524882151; https://hotel-lagazelle.com; Blvd Mohammed V; s/d/tr Dh150/180/270;) Despite feeling like a '60s throwback, the spacious grounds and pleasant pool won us over to this budget-friendly motel near the centre of town. Rooms are a touch on the small side, but cozy for that, and friendly staff tip the scales.

Hotel Azoul HOTEL €€

(0524883015; Ave Mohamed V; s/d/ste Dh340/460/660;) This good-value place has attractive rooms painted in neutral tones, with silky striped bed covers, carved dark-wood furniture and decent lighting (plus extras like electric kettles, minifridges and flat-screen TVs). Rooms at the front are brighter with small balconies, but also noisier.

Dar Bergui GUESTHOUSE €€

(0668675164; www.darbergui.com; Sidi Hussain Ben Nacer; s/d/tr Dh500/660/880;) Located within walking distance of the Place Al Mouahidine, this sleek *pisé* (rammed-earth) villa with crenellated turrets is the home of Jean-Michel and Martine. The six villa bedrooms arranged around the courtyard swimming pool are simply and tastefully furnished and offer good value for money, especially considering the bountiful breakfast of pancakes, homemade yoghurt, fruit and cake.

Dar Kamar GUESTHOUSE €€€

(0524888733; www.darkamar.com; 45 Kasbah Taourirt; s Dh765-1020, d Dh900-1200, ste Dh1360-1900;) Once a stern 17th-century Glaoui courthouse, this cosy *pisé* (rammed-earth) guesthouse has a sense of humour: upturned tajines serve as sinks and sewing-machine tables are repurposed as desks. Local iron-workers went wild decorating the en suites, though showers are poorly ventilated – a fine excuse to use the in-house hammam and massage room.

Eating & Drinking

The cafes on the main plaza and throughout the centre, many of which stay open until late, are a fine spot for tea and coffee. For something a little stronger, you can order drinks at a handful of restaurants around town or buy them from the small shop opposite Chez Dimitri.

Central Souq MARKET €

(Rue du Maré; 8am-6pm) Fresh cheese, meat and vegetables can be found at the daily central souq. Operations tend to wind down from mid-afternoon, so it's better to go early.

Il Postino PIZZA €

(0653692428; Ave Annasr; pizzas Dh20-50; 11.30am-1am Sat-Mon, from 5pm Fri) Tasty pizzas (of varying authenticity) make this place popular among a young local crowd, and in the evening tables spill out onto the sidewalks on both sides of the road.

Habous MOROCCAN €

(Place Al Mouahidine; mains Dh35-80; noon-midnight) Overlooking the lively square at the epicentre of Ouarzazate, Habous is the most popular place in town. It has a patisserie, cafe and restaurant, with plenty of outdoor seating for taking in life on the square. The restaurant side (on the right) serves up salads, brochettes, sandwiches, pastas and pizzas, plus steaks at reasonable prices.

Patisserie de Habous PASTRIES €

(0524882699; Place Al Mouahidine; breakfasts Dh20-40; 7am-11pm;) On balmy evenings, all strolls lead here for French éclairs, croissants and Moroccan pastries. In the morning, grab a seat on the terrace for coffee and people-watching as you order a *msemen* (square fried pancake-like bread) or set menu breakfast.

★ **Douyria** MOROCCAN €€

(0699917827; www.restaurant-ouarzazate.net; 72 Ave Mohammed V; mains Dh60-110; 11.30am-7pm, closed Wed;) One of the best eateries in town, Douyria wows diners with its rooftop terrace (though without kasbah views), candlelit tables and cushion-lined nooks perfect for sipping a cocktail. You can feast on richly flavoured local dishes, including unusual options like tajine of roasted goat basted in argan oil or an excellent pigeon *bastilla* (pie).

Vegetarians should go for the flavour-rich vegetarian *bastilla*. For dessert, there's house-made date or saffron ice cream.

Jardin des Arômes MOROCCAN €€
(☎0524888802; 69 Ave Mohammed V; mains Dh100-150; ⏰10am-2.30pm & 7-10pm Tue-Sun) Step off busy Ave Mohammed V and climb the steps up to this peaceful garden, with white leather chairs, thick curtains and a tent-like interior overlooking the greenery. Start off with the Lebanese mezze, such as *tabbouleh* (salad of tomatoes, parsley, onions and bulgur), baba ganoush, or hummus before moving onto a hearty tajine or a plate of roasted lamb with raisins and almonds.

Chez Dimitri FUSION €€
(☎0524883334; Ave Mohammed V; mains Dh60-160; ⏰11am-11pm) This spot has been around since 1928, when Chez Dimitri played a pivotal role as petrol station, transport hub, restaurant and even dance hall in the fledgling city. You can contemplate the past – old sepia prints line the walls – while dining on warm goat's cheese salad, lamb chops or the house speciality of moussaka.

Restaurant du Goût Chinois CHINESE €€
(☎0696901119; mains Dh48-196; ⏰11.30am-9.30pm) If you're looking for something completely different after too many days in the desert, a Hunanese owner and chef here ensures that you get an authentic 'taste of China', and the mostly Chinese clientele proves the point. The menu is in French and Chinese only.

La Kasbah des Sables FRENCH €€€
(☎0524885428; www.lakasbahdessables.com; 195 Hay Aït Kdif; meals Dh200-340; ⏰noon-2pm & 7-11pm Tue-Sun; P) Conceived by owner Brigitte Babolat, this Moorish fantasy palace – a medley of cosy lounges and nooks arranged around a series of patios – took three years to create. The centrepiece is an enormous shallow pool backed by a wall of jewel-coloured lights and surrounded by romantic, candlelit tables where you are served a mix of primarily Moroccan and French dishes.

Afterwards lounge in cushion-lined cubbyholes filled with objets d'art crafted in Ouarzazate and Marrakesh. In the morning you'll have to shake yourself and wonder if you didn't dream the whole experience. It's located 5km west of central Ouarzazate, in the old neighbourhood of Al Kdif.

Relais Saint Exupéry FUSION €€€
(☎0524887779; www.relais-ouarzazate.com; 13 Blvd Moulay Abdellah; mains Dh115-170; ⏰11.30am-2.30pm & 6.30-10pm) The Relais serves creative dishes featuring local ingredients such as Talouine saffron and Saharan salt. Try flaky *bastilla* (savoury pie) of fish, or dromedary meat in a Mali-inspired sauce of garlic, cumin, ginger and paprika. It may seem odd to find adventurous gastronomy near the Ouarzazate airport, but this airport was an inspiration to *Little Prince* author and pilot Antoine de Saint-Exupéry.

Accord Majeur FRENCH €€€
(☎0524882473; www.restaurant-accord-majeur.com; Rue Al Mansour Ad Dahbi; mains Dh95-150; ⏰7-10pm Mon, noon-2pm & 7-10pm Tue-Sat; 📶) After a week of desert dining, you may find yourself sleepwalking to this French bistro opposite the Berbère Palace. Here, in cosy nooks lit by a mellow, yellow glow from dozens of brass wall lamps, Aurélie and Charlie serve an impressive menu of confit du canard, foie gras, smoked salmon, beef carpaccio and even homemade ice cream.

Shopping

Horizon Artisanat ARTS & CRAFTS
(☎0524886938; Ave Annasr; ⏰9am-6.30pm) Henna-painted pottery, hand-painted tea glasses, and silver filigree rings are sold at reasonable fixed prices, supporting Horizon's programmes to provide vocational training for adults with disabilities and integrate disabled children and adults into the community. The association supports some 2500 people, including 53 permanent staff members. With prior arrangement, it's also possible to tour the facility and meet the craftsmen.

Complexe Artisanal ARTS & CRAFTS
(Ave Mohammed V; ⏰9.30am-6pm Mon-Sat) Opposite the kasbah, this sprawling complex of state-run showrooms (only of few of which seem to be open at any given time) features elaborately woven tapestries, local stone carvings, inlaid daggers, metal lanterns and embroidered linens.

The **Coopérative de Tissage** (Weaving Cooperative; ☎0662610583; Complexe Artisianal, Ave Mohammed V; ⏰9.30am-6pm Mon-Sat) is the obvious standout.

Getting There & Around

AIR

Ouarzazate Airport (☎0522435858; www.onda.ma) is located 2km north of town. Royal Air Maroc (www.royalairmaroc.com) has multiple directly weekly flights to Marrakesh and Casablanca as well as a once-weekly direct

OFF THE BEATEN TRACK

FINT OASIS

The fairy-tale setting of the Oasis de Fint – lush palm groves along a languid river, with towering black rocks as a background – makes it a popular side trip from Ouarzazate. There's not a ton to do here, but that's much of the appeal. Stroll the village's dirt tracks, walk barefoot along the river bed up and down the oasis, or just linger poolside and watch it all unwind from above.

A handful of small family-run guesthouses cluster in the centre of the village, while on the outskirts are a couple of higher-end options that feel more like hotels.

Auberge Tissili (☎0653989137, 0637890415; www.oasisfint.com; s/d with shared bathroom Dh250/300) This family compound in the centre of the village is full of the sounds of domestic life, though guests can retreat to two-person tents in a side courtyard.

Auberge La Terrasse des Délices (☎0668515640; www.terrassedesdelices.com; s/d/tr incl half-board Dh400/700/950; ❄) Expect a warm welcome at this idyllic guesthouse, whose pleasant rooms are set around an interior courtyard and a picturesque terrace.

No public transportation serves the Fint Oasis. The best option for most travellers will be to hire an entire grand taxi from the Ouarzazate taxi stand for around Dh200 for the 15km journey. Guesthouses and tour agents can also arrange private transfers.

service to Paris-Orly, while Ryanair (ryanair.com) operates services to Madrid, Bordeaux and Marseilles.

During the annual hajj pilgrimage and popular events such as the Marathon des Sables, there are extra flights.

There is no bus into town; taxis to/from the airport cost between Dh50 and Dh80 depending the time of day.

BUS

CTM (☎0524882427; Ave Mohammed V; ⏲4.30am-midnight)'s bus station is right in the centre of town, with a choice of buses that serve Marrakesh (Dh90 to Dh95, five daily), Casablanca (Dh650, 8½ hours, four daily) and Zagora (Dh60, three daily) via Agdz (Dh30), along with one daily bus to each of Agadir (Dh145, 7½ hours, one daily), Errachidia (Dh95, six hours) and Zagora (Dh60, three hours, two to three daily). During local holidays and busy periods, book your tickets at least a day in advance.

The main local **bus station** (Mahta) is 1km northwest of the town centre off Ave Moulay Abdellah. Several buses a day leave from here to Marrakesh (Dh60 to Dh70), Boumalne Dades (Dh30, two hours) via Kelaat M'Gouna (Dh20, 1½ hours), Taroudant (Dh80, five hours), Tazenakht (Dh20, three hours), Foum Zguid (Dh40, four hours), Tata (Dh80, five hours) and M'Hamid (Dh70, seven hours) via Zagora (Dh50, four hours).

The **Supratours** (☎0661082656; www.supratours.ma; N° 66, Lot Al Hizam; ⏲7.30am-10.30pm) office just southeast of the bus station operates buses from Marrakesh (Dh90, five hours, four daily) and two daily services to Zagora (Dh60, 2½ hours) via Agdz (Dh35, 1½ hours) as well as Boumalne Dades (Dh50) via Kalaat M'Gouna (Dh40), along with one daily departure to each of Errachidia (Dh110) and Merzouga (Dh155, eight hours).

CAR

For desert detours you might want to hire a car (from Dh350 per day); car hire with a driver costs Dh900 (car) to Dh1250 (4WD). There are dozens of agencies in town and international outfits have booths at the airport. Local operators with 4WDs include **Desert Evasion** (☎0524888682; www.desert-evasion.net; Imm El Ghifari, Ave Mohammed V; ⏲8.30am-12.30pm & 2.30-6.30pm) and **ESON Maroc** (☎0666890899; www.eson-maroc.com; Ave Mohammed VI; ⏲9am-6pm), though all operators seem to insist on a hired driver for 4WD trips.

TAXI

Grands taxis leave when full from outside the main bus station to Aït Benhaddou (Dh20), Telouet (Dh40), Agdz (Dh30), Boumalne Dades (Dh35), Marrakesh (Dh100), Kalaat M'Gouna (Dh30), Skoura (Dh15), Tinerhir (Dh60) and Zagora (Dh80). For the Fint Oasis you'll almost certainly have to hire an entire car (Dh200) to make the trip.

MINIBUS

From the minibus stand just west of the bus station services run to Aït Benhaddou (Dh20), Telouet (Dh25) and Skoura (Dh15). Across from the Supratours office, a single daily 9am minibus departs for Demnate (Dh70) via the mountain road.

LOCAL TRANSPORT

Local Buses 1 and 2 (Dh4) run down Ave Mohamed V and on to Atlas Studios, while Bus 4 (Dh4) runs from the bus station through Tabount, a suburb across the river, to the Tifoultoute kasbah.

Petits taxis run up and down Ave Mohammed V for flat rates of Dh5 per person during the day and Dh7 at night (based on three people sharing). A small grand taxi stand just north of the central square runs nearly around the clock to Tabount (Dh25).

DRAA VALLEY وادي درعة

One of Morocco's most scenic stretches, the Draa Valley winds its way from Ouarzazate over the jagged peaks of the Jebel Saghro to the Sahara Desert. Its historical richness is evident in its prehistoric rock engravings and ancient kasbahs and *ksour* (fortified villages), where community-run museums tell the story of nomadic tribes, caravan routes and trading between Amazigh (Berber), African, Jewish and Christian merchants. And you can drop in on idyllic *palmeraies* dotted with rural villages where life has barely changed for centuries.

Agdz اكدز

POP 9700

Travellers who whizz straight from Ouarzazate to Zagora and M'Hamid are missing out on Agdz (ag-*dz*), a classic caravanserai oasis with a still-pristine *palmeraie* studded with ancient mud-brick kasbahs. As you approach the town, you'll see the tajine-shaped peak of Jebel Kissane on the horizon, and spot mountain bikers heading off to the 1660m Tizi n'Tinififft pass, some 20km away. The mountains glisten with what looks like snow, but that's a mirage: it's sunlight bouncing off deposits of reflective mica.

Agdz crafts traditions include carving, pottery and basket-weaving, and you might spot a few prime examples outside shops downtown or at the Thursday souq.

None of Agdz's key attractions are apparent from the main road. The historic centre is east of the N9, about 1.5km along a dusty *piste,* so has been largely bypassed by mass-tourism development. For that very reason, an unusual number of authentic mud-brick kasbahs have been preserved. Overnight visitors might also take a morning stroll through the vast Agdz *palmeraie*, just north of the village.

The 170-year-old **Caïd's Kasbah** (0524843640; Dh30; 10am-5.30pm) that once belonged to the *qaid* (local chief) of Agdz is still run by his descendants. Stop at the reception of **Casbah Caïd Ali** (0524843640, 0698906550; Rue Hassan II; campsite for 2 people Dh60, d/tr/q Dh240/350/400;) next door for admission to the mud-brick structure, and explore a maze of rooms spread over three storeys. The play of light and shade in the ancient kasbah could keep photographers entertained for hours, but best of all are the rooftop views over the neighbouring oasis.

Agdz makes a great base for exploring the area, with some atmospheric lodging options, including several kasbah-style guesthouses.

Dar Jnane (0673181314; www.darjnane-location-sud-maroc.com; d Dh390) has three attractive rooms set amid peaceful tree-filled gardens roughly 1km (well-signed) off the main road. You can hire mountain bikes and Lahcen and Dominique can advise on scenic walks in the area. The bijoux guesthouse **Dar Sofar** (0644009006; www.darsofar.com; d/tr Dh650/750; P) has just four spacious rooms, all brightly decorated in local crafts and fabrics, leading on to a pretty patio garden and a luminous pool lined with green Tamegroute tiles. Owner Pierre has a long

THE IDEAL DATE

For prime date selection, head to **Tinzouline**, about 56km south of Agdz, during the September to November date season. You're getting close when you spot vendors with dates overflowing from palm-frond baskets along the Zagora road. You may run into traffic for the Monday souq, where you'll be elbow to elbow with local grandmothers vying for the finest local speciality, boufeggou dates. This is a date to remember: nicely caramelised outside by the desert sun, and tender and savoury-sweet inside.

If you're not visiting the valley in autumn, you still have a year-round date in **Timidarte**, where local dates are turned into jams and syrups at **Cooperative Kasr Al Hamra** (0661932242; Maison Ougarane; 9am-6pm).

ROCK THE KASBAHS IN TIMIDARTE

If you want to (all together now) rock the kasbahs, stop to check out the prime specimens in the village of Timidarte, down a dirt road north of the N9 between Agdz and Tamnougalt. The finest example dates from the 17th century and has been converted by Timidarte's tourism association into an authentic **kasbah guesthouse** (☎0668680047; www.kasbahtimidarte.com; s/d incl half-board Dh300/460, with shared bathroom Dh260/320) , with part of the profits going towards community projects.

There isn't much regular transport passing through Timidarte, though you should be able to arrange a morning grand taxi to Agdz and continue from there.

history in hospitality and can help you organise all manner of activities.

Ensconced in lush greenery, contemporary eco-friendly **Kasbah Azul** (☎0524843931; www.kasbahazul.com; d Dh990-2585; P) has nine beautifully furnished bedrooms as well as several stylish salons and a marble hammam.

Buses from Ouarzazate (Dh30, 1¼ hours) and Zagora (Dh35, 1½ hours) stop in the Grand Place; the CTM office is in the northeast corner of the square. You can also pick up grands taxis here for Ouarzazate (Dh30 to Dh40), Zagora (Dh40) and Nkob (Dh30). The N12 to Rissani meets the N9 29km east of Agdz.

Tamnougalt

Perched on a hill 8km from Agdz is one of the star attractions of the Draa Valley: Tamnougalt's 16th-century mud-brick *ksar* is one of the oldest still standing and still inhabited.

Tour the maze of rooms at the **Kasbah des Caids** (Musée du Tamnougalt, Chez Hassan; ☎0667345602; www.kasbah-des-caids.com; Dh20, optional guide around Dh100; ⊙08.30am-sunset) with one of the descendants of the original *qaid*, including his office and hammam, light-filled courtyards and dark secret passageways. It's attached to the *ksar* where 300 families once lived, including 35 Jewish families – just 20 remain – along a warren of alleyways lit by skylights. If Hassan isn't there, local guides hang around the entrance to the kasbah, including **Abdel Jalil** (☎0673618400; Dh50-100), who can also arrange *palmeraie* tours and overnights in the village.

More luxe options await out of town and in Zagora, but for an authentic experience book a room in the *ksar*.

At **Chez Yacob** (☎0524843394; r per person incl half-board Dh300; P), eight en suite rooms sit round a soaring courtyard, all capped by a scenic terrace overlooking the *palmeraie*. This is also a popular lunch spot.

The ecofriendly bungalows in a walled organic farm at **Bab El Oued** (☎0660188484; www.babelouedmaroc.com; d/tr/ste from Dh825/1320/1815; P) are built with local design in mind. The French- and English-speaking owners grow 60 types of plants, including herbs and vegetables for farm-to-table Moroccan-Mediterranean meals (lunch/dinner Dh176/210).

There's no reliable public transport here.

Zagora زاكورة

POP 34,851

The original, iconic 'Tombouctou, 52 jours' (Timbuktu, 52 days) sign, featuring a nomad with a smirking camel, may have been swept away in an inexplicable government beautification scheme, but Zagora's fame as a desert outpost remains indelible. The Saadians launched their expedition to conquer Timbuktu here in 1591, and desert caravans passing through Zagora gave this isolated spot cosmopolitan character.

These days Zagora remains a trading post and meeting place, hosting a regional souq on Wednesday and Sunday and putting on a variety of lively festivals.

Sights

★Amezrou VILLAGE

Zagora's desert-crossroads culture can be glimpsed in the neighbouring village of Amezrou, where the historic mud-brick *mellah* (Jewish quarter), was once home to around 400 Jewish households, is part crumbling, part restored. Along its labyrinthine alleyways you can peek inside a small rammed-earth synagogue (Dh10), watch builders at work up ramshackle ladders and meet the artisans soldering metal good-luck charms with Amazigh (Berber),

African, Jewish and Muslim designs. A local will offer to show you the sights (tip around Dh50).

★**Musée des Arts et Traditions de la Valleé du Draa** MUSEUM
(☎0667690602; Ksar Tissergate; Dh25; ⏰8.30am-7pm) Follow the signs to this fascinating small museum, where three floors are dedicated to traditional life in the Draa Valley. Look out for tribal jewellery and wedding garb, the intriguing birthing room and tea glasses thought to shatter on contact with poison. All exhibits come with excellent explanations in French and English, or take a tour with a local guide.

Jebel Zagora MOUNTAIN
This spectacular mountain rises over the Draa River – worth climbing for the views, provided you have stamina, water and sunblock and set off in the early morning. The round trip to Jebel Zagora takes about three hours on foot, or 45 minutes by car along the *piste* to the right beyond Camping de la Montagne. Halfway up are the faint ruins of an 11th-century Almoravid fortress, but the military installation at the summit is off limits.

Tours

Almost every visitor to Zagora is heading for the desert and some plan their trips here rather than waiting to get to the desert gateway of M'Hamid, a three-hour drive further south. While Erg Chigaga is the big draw (56km off-road southwest of M'hamid), closer – but far less spectacular – dunes include Tinfou (p156; 25km south beside the N9).

Practically all hotels and campsites can fix you up for a dromedary ride and desert excursions, and, in some cases, they may offer better deals if combined with accommodation. As always, it pays to compare costs as prices can go up or down depending on time of year and demand.

★**Wild Morocco** TOURS
(☎0655778173; www.wildmorocco.com) This Amazigh (Berber)-Anglo partnership run by M'Hamid-native Yahya and corporate-escapee Emily distinguishes itself by its professionalism and passion, with well-planned itineraries that promote desert culture. Adventurers can join three- to six-day desert treks following nomadic migration routes, as well as overnight at Camp El Koutban in the shadow of Erg Chigaga. Longer excursions combining trekking in the Atlas Mountain are also possible.

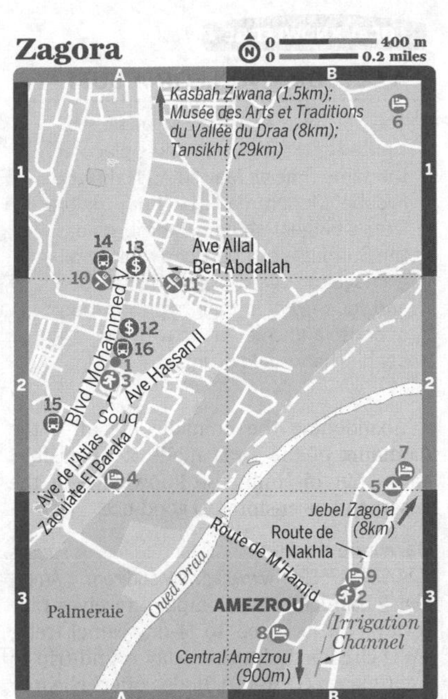

Zagora

Activities, Courses & Tours
1 Caravane Desert et Montagne ... A2
2 Caravane du Sud ... B3
3 Caravane Hamada Draa ... A2

Sleeping
4 Auberge Restaurant Chez Ali ... A2
5 Camping Auberge Oasis Palmier ... B2
6 Dar Pienatcha ... B1
7 Riad Dar Sofian ... B2
8 Riad Soleil du Monde ... B3
9 Villa Zagora ... B3

Eating
10 Boulangerie & Patisserie Draa ... A2
11 Hôtel-Restaurant La Rose des Sables ... A2
Restaurant Chez Ali ... (see 4)

Information
12 Banque Populaire ... A2
13 BMCE ... A1

Transport
14 Bus Station & Grands Taxis ... A1
15 CTM Bus Station ... A2
16 Supratours ... A2

LOCAL KNOWLEDGE

A CELEBRATION FOR A SUFI

The **Moussem of Sufi Moulay Abdelkader Jilali**, which takes place at the same time as Mawlid An Nabi (the Prophet Muhammad's birthday), is the Draa's biggest shindig. Members of the Sufi Jilala brotherhood make a pilgrimage to Zagora to pay their respects, and you may hear their hypnotic music of praise and celebration with the bendir (hand-held drum).

Abandoning the nomadic life after the damming of the Draa made it unfeasible, Yahya put his immense knowledge of the desert and its customs to good use.

Caravane du Sud TOURS
(0524847569; www.caravanesud.com; Amezrou; 8am-7pm) This company receives rave reviews for its three- to 14-day camel treks, 4WD circuits and a three-day round-trip to Erg Chigaga (Dh1900). It also offers cheaper departures from M'Hamid. You'll find it on the roundabout in Amezrou.

Discovering South Morocco TOURS
(0524846115; www.zagora-desert.info) The highly regarded English- and French-speaking, Zagora-born guide, Mohamad Sirirou, garners rave reviews for his multi-night desert expeditions with dromedaries.

Caravane Hamada Draa TOURS
(0661328106; www.hamadadraa.com; Blvd Mohammed V) This professional outfit offers treks to nomadic camps by licensed English-speaking guides and native nomad Youssef M'Hidi.

Caravane Desert et Montagne TOURS
(0611153766; http://caravanedesertetmontagne.com; 112 Blvd Mohammed V) This outfit partners with local nomads to create off-the-beaten-camel-track adventures for individuals and small groups.

Sleeping & Eating

The city of Zagora and the neighbouring village of Amezrou have accommodation to suit all budgets. Many of the more atmospheric options are around the *palmeraies*.

Hotels provide set meals (Dh100 to Dh150) to guests and nonguests by prior reservation. Auberge Restaurant Chez Ali is a standout for quality and freshness, and you can join off-duty desert guides at **La Rose des Sables** (0524847274; Ave Allal Ben Abdallah; meals Dh40-60). Cafes and *laterie* (juice shops) cluster around the intersection of Boulevard Mohammed V and Ave Allal Ben Abdallah and serve a good selection of staples like roast chicken, tajine and pizza for Dh20 to Dh35.

For something sweet, stop at the **Boulangerie & Patisserie Draa** (Blvd Mohammed V; snacks Dh5-7; 7am-10pm) off the main plaza.

★ **Auberge Restaurant Chez Ali** INN €
(0524846258; http://chezali.net; Ave de l'Atlas Zaouiate El Baraka; d Dh200-400, with shared bathroom Dh70-90;) The peacocks stalking around the gorgeous garden may be aloof, but otherwise the welcome here is warm. Sky-lit upstairs rooms have simple pine furnishings, bathrooms and balconies, and 'traditional' rooms have mattresses on carpets and shared bathrooms. Enjoy delicious traditional dishes (Dh65) in the garden, a pool and overnight trips to the desert run by English-speaking guides Mohamed and Yusuf.

The menu in the house **restaurant** (0524846258; http://chezali.net; Ave de l'Atlas Zaouiate El Baraka; mains Dh65; 11am-10.30pm;) is short but perfectly formed, and with fresh dishes like Ali's Garden Salad and seven-vegetable couscous, it's perfect for vegetarians. For Dh50 diners can take a dip in the tempting pool.

Camping Auberge Oasis Palmier CAMPGROUND €
(pixameharee@hotmail.com; Route de Nakhla; camping per person/tent/car Dh20/30/15;) Just north of Amezrou, this campsite has a mixture of palm-shaded pitches, Berber-style tents and a few rooms. It also has a cafe, free wi-fi, hot showers (Dh10) and electric hook-ups (Dh20) and they even deliver fresh bread to your tent. Unsurprisingly, it's often full of happy campers, so book in advance.

★ **La Dune Blanche** CAMPGROUND €€
(0667966464; www.bivouac-laduneblanche-zagora.com; per person incl half-/full board Dh370/450) Surrounded by low dunes 20km south of the village of Tagounite, accommodation here is in *pisé* (rammed-earth) cottages dressed with fabric to mimic the feel of a tent. Salah meets you at Tagounite gas station with a 4WD to take you the remainder of the way.

Each 'tent' has a different colour and is furnished with comfortable beds dressed in natural woollen blankets, carpets and cut-metal lanterns, which cast swirling patterns on the walls. From here, any number of excursions are possible. Given the location, it is necessary to book in advance.

Dar Pienatcha GUESTHOUSE €€
(☎0645956570; darpienatcha@hotmail.fr; d €55, incl half-board €65; P ❄ 📶 🏊) In the midst of a peaceful palm grove, this bijoux French-family-owned guesthouse mixes up European style and desert design. Rooms come with smooth *tadelakt* (waterproof plaster) walls, open fires, and bathrooms lined with Tamegroute-green tiles. A palm-fringed pool with plenty of lounging space, hospitable staff and garden dinners (€15) under the stars all add to its appeal. Cash only.

Kasbah Ziwana GUESTHOUSE €€
(☎0661348388, 0671519055; http://kasbahziwana.com; Ksar Tissergate; s/d incl half-board Dh300/600) This rammed-earth building in a 400 year-old *ksar* on the edge of a palm grove 7km north of Zagora comes with attractively furnished rooms. Relax in the peaceful courtyard or on the panoramic roof terrace, and get plenty of local insight from host Naaji, a guide with many years of experience.

Riad Soleil du Monde GUESTHOUSE €€
(☎0661687131; www.riadzagora.net; Amezrou; d Dh330-540; P 📶 🏊) Tucked down a narrow dirt road near Amezrou, this pretty four-room guesthouse has striking rooms with coloured glass light fixtures, *pisé* (rammed-earth walls) and decorative moulding. The pool, fringed by towering date palms and pomegranate trees, makes a fine retreat on hot days. The warm welcome and idyllic location in the *palmeraie* adds to the appeal.

Villa Zagora GUESTHOUSE €€
(☎0524846093; www.mavillaausahara.com; Route de Nakhla, Amezrou; d from €50, tent per person €15; 📶 🏊) This converted country home makes desert living look easy. French doors reveal plush Moroccan rugs, soaring ceilings and an eclectic art collection. Staff fuss over you like the Moroccan relations you never knew you had, and decadent alfresco dinners (menus €15) feature oasis-fresh ingredients. If you're travelling in a group, the six-room villa can be all yours.

★**Azalai Desert Lodge** BOUTIQUE HOTEL €€€
(☎0661164394; www.azalailifeexperience.com/en/azalai-desert-lodge-2; Tissergate; s/d incl half-board from Dh1400/1600) On the edge of the palm grove, the eight super-stylish rooms at this modern-Moroccan lodge are all individually decorated – think Paul Bowles' battered leather suitcases. If you can tear yourself away from the pool and the garden hammocks, borrow a bike to explore oasis life or walk to Ksar Tissergate's excellent museum (p153), before enjoying a gourmet Moroccan meal under the stars.

★**Riad Dar Sofian** BOUTIQUE HOTEL €€€
(☎0524847319; www.riaddarsofian.com; Route de Nakhla, Amezrou; tent/s/d/tr Dh220/680/880/1100; P 📶 🏊) This super-stylish desert oasis exudes understated luxury. The fabulous *pisé* (rammed-earth) edifice was constructed by a team from Skoura, while craftsmen from Fez executed the acres of tilework inside and the modern Moroccan decor mixes up antique furnishings, traditional details and contemporary comforts. There's a new sumptuous suite and an organic garden for farm-to-fork fare.

ℹ Getting There & Away

Zagora has a small airport, southwest of town off the N12, that has four weekly flights from Casablanca with Royal Air Maroc (www.royalairmaroc.com).

The **CTM bus station** (☎0524847327; Blvd Mohammed V) is at the southwestern end of Mohammed V, while the local **bus station** (Blvd Mohammed V) is beside the mosque, where grands taxis also depart. **Supratours** (☎0524847688; Blvd Mohammed V), near the Banque Populaire, offers a 6am bus to Marrakesh (Dh140, seven hours) and Ouarzazate (Dh60, 2½ hours). There is also a CTM bus to M'Hamid (Dh40, 2¾ hours) and three daily CTM buses to Ouarzazate (Dh60, three hours), two of which continue to Marrakesh (Dh135, 8½ hours).

Other companies, which are based at the local bus station, have at least one run a day to Marrakesh (Dh120) and Ouarzazate (Dh55, three hours). There are buses to Rissani (Dh100, six

ℹ AN ATM OASIS

Stock up on cash at one of the last ATMs you'll find before you hit the Sahara. There are branches of **Banque Populaire** (Blvd Mohammed V) and **BMCE** (Blvd Mohammed V).

hours) via Nkob (Dh20, two hours) and Tazzarine (Dh35, 2½ hours) three times a week. A bus passes through Zagora to M'Hamid (Dh35, three hours) in the morning. More frequent minibuses run to M'Hamid (Dh30) throughout the day when full.

Grands taxis (p155) can be found in the centre of town beside the new mosque. They are more regular early in the morning. Destinations include Tamegroute (Dh10, 20 minutes), Agdz (Dh35, 1½ hours), Ouarzazate (Dh80, three hours), M'Hamid (Dh35, 1½ hours) and Nkob (Dh50 to Dh60, 1½ hours).

Tamegroute تامكروت

POP 6000

This earthen village was once an important centre of Islamic learning and spiritual healing. Today there are two reasons to visit on your way to or from the desert: a small but fascinating library filled with priceless ancient manuscripts, and the family-run potteries that still produce distinctive green-glazed ceramics in the age-old way.

The shrine of the **Zawiya Nassiriyya** (suggested donation Dh20; ⌚ morning & late afternoon Sat-Thu) is said to cure anxiety and high blood pressure, thanks to the post-mortem calming influence of Sidi Mohammed Ben Nassir – founder of the influential and learned Nassiri brotherhood, who were famed for their ability in settling Draa Valley disputes in the 17th century, and it's still a place of pilgrimage for the sick, as well as a working Quranic school. The annual *moussem* is held a month after Eid Al Adha.

While the mausoleum is closed to non-Muslims, the remarkable library inside the adjacent Quranic school is open to all – providing the keyholder's around. Among the 4000 ancient manuscripts that remain on the glassed-in shelves – there used to be around 50,000 – are maps with precise details, exquisite calligraphy and a Quran written on gazelle hide dating back to 11th-century Cordoba. Find it through an arch in the northwest corner of the main square.

Walk through the local pottery-making process at **Maison de Poterie** (☎0666663166; ⌚8am-6pm Mon-Fri). Oxidised copper in the clay yields the rich green glaze, and the technique originated when the Nassiri brotherhood invited craftsmen from Fez to settle in the village. Seven families remain, turning out everything from portable bowls and plates to outsized vases.

The **Tinfou Dunes**, around 7km south of Tamegroute, seem like a child's sandbox compared to the great sand seas of M'Hamid and Merzouga, but it's fun to climb and run down the big dunes. To stay out in the dunes, contact **Stargazing Hotel SaharaSky** (☎0524848562; www.saharasky.net/hotel; Tinfou Dunes; s/d from Dh490/780; P @ 🛜 ❄).

There's not much in the way of lodging in the village, and the best option is opposite the main square at the **Auberge-Restaurant Jnane Dar Daifa** (☎0661348149; s/d Dh300/380, with shared bathroom from Dh180/220), which is also the best place to drop in for a meal.

There aren't many regular buses passing through Tamegroute, but you will able to arrange a grand taxi to Zagora and continue from there.

M'Hamid محاميد

POP 7500

Once it was a lonesome oasis, but these days M'Hamid is a wallflower no more. Border tensions between Algeria (which lies just 40km south), Morocco and the Polisario (a rebel national liberation movement, aiming to get Morocco out of the Western Sahara) had isolated this caravan stop until the 1990s, when accords allowed M'Hamid to start hosting visitors again.

It doesn't take long to reach the dunes from here – some nuzzle right up against guesthouses on the western side of town – but to be enveloped by large dunes, you'll have to head out across the *hamada* (hard-packed rocky desert) by dromedary or 4WD.

Sights

Erg Chigaga is the big draw here, its dramatic dunes and rippling expanse are large enough to give each camp a secluded feel.

Away from the desert, M'Hamid encompasses two towns and five different ethnic groups: the Harratine, Amazigh (Berber), Chorfa, Beni M'Hamid and the fabled nomadic 'Blue Men'. M'Hamid Jdid, the prematurely aged 'new' town, has a mosque, roadside cafe-restaurants, small budget hotels and a Monday **souq** (⌚6am-noon Mon). There's a frontier-town feel here, with tough guys in *shesh* (turban) and sunglasses hanging around dusty cafes, swapping stories.

The old kasbah sits in the *palmeraie* (palm grove), 3km away across the Draa River. Another worthwhile stop is the

Ksar Ouled Driss, 5km before M'Hamid, which includes a small **ethnographic museum** (Dh20; ⌚hrs vary) displaying traditional household objects in a mud-brick courtyard.

A string of villages stretch south along a single road from M'Hamid to Taouz – literally the end of the road – and well worth a stop.

There are overnight camel treks to Erg Lehoudi and El Mesouiria. You can get there by *piste* off the main road 18km before M'Hamid, but a guide is advisable. The highlight is a camel trek to Erg Chigaga.

Other further-flung destinations include Erg Ezahar and the Iriki Lake, and an epic 12-day camel trip to Foum Zguid.

★Erg Chigaga — DUNES

The area's star attraction is the misnamed Erg Chigaga, not a single dune *(erg)* but an incredible stretch of golden sand sea some 56km southwest of M'Hamid. It is the largest sand sea in Morocco, snaking along the horizon for 40km and bordered to the north and south by mountain ridges. The best way to get here is in classic movie style: by camel (from Dh500 to Dh600 per day), which takes between five and seven days round-trip.

To reach the area in just a few hours, a 4WD costs from Dh1000 to Dh1300 per day with insurance, plus another Dh350 to Dh500 for the camp.

This sea of golden crescents, which peak at 300m, hides small, semipermanent camps in its troughs. As a result, the desert experience here is quiet and enveloping, offering spectacular night skies illuminated by the enormous arc of the Milky Way.

Erg Ezahar — DUNES

This tall 'screaming' dune set amid a sea of smaller dunes wails eerily when the wind kicks up. Located 65km southwest of M'Hamid, it takes three days to reach it by camel, passing an old *marabout* (saint's shrine) and the flat plain of Bousnaïna, where artefacts from a long-disappeared village are sometimes uncovered. There are no fixed camps here.

El Mesouiria — DUNES

Located just 8km northwest of M'Hamid, El Mesouiria is an option for an easy overnight camel trek. Dunes range between 60m and 80m in height and are characterised by their white sand and a smattering of tamarisk trees.

Erg Esmar — DUNES

This collection of small dunes, rising to just 80m, are well off the main radar with no permanent camps. With its mixture of red and white dunes, it's particularly photogenic at sunset.

Erg Lehoudi — DUNES

(Dunes of the Jews) The 100m-high Erg Lihoudi, located 8km northeast of M'Hamid, are some of the most easily accessible dunes in the area. Characterised by their white river sand because of their proximity to the Draa, they are frequented by a higher number of day-trippers and some of the semipermanent camps are in need of attention.

☞Tours

Treks on foot, by camel or 4WD to Erg Chigaga can be arranged in Marrakesh, Zagora or M'Hamid. Sales ploys come with the territory, so don't be reeled in by scare tactics

ℹ BOOKING ERG CHIGAGA EXCURSIONS: TOP TIPS

Book ahead Given the considerable logistics of desert travel (and the fact that top guides are often booked in advance through Marrakesh agencies), it's always best to book ahead. It also gives you time to nail down the details of your camp and itinerary.

First time? Keep it short As any Sufi mystic will attest, being alone with your thoughts in the desert can be an illuminating, uplifting experience – but those not accustomed to such profound isolation may get bored quickly.

Camel riding or camel trekking Be aware that not all camels are for riding. In fact, most dromedaries are used for transporting luggage and food. If you want to ride your camel, you need to specify that at the outset, and it may cost more if additional animals are needed.

Before you commit to a longer trip, get names The guide (and the guide's language ability) can make or break your experience. Ask for the name of the guide with whom you'll be travelling, do an internet search for reviews, and solicit feedback.

DJS & DUNES

Sahara Music Festival (www.facebook.com/saharamusicfestival; Erg Chigaga; ⏲ Apr) is a new electronic music festival mixing up DJs and dunes, international stars and local Gnaoua musicians, and camel rides and pool parties. Check Facebook for details.

from *faux guides* (unofficial guides). Prices are fairly standard: overnight camel treks are around Dh350 per person per day, treks to Erg Chigaga around Dh500. Also bear in mind that many desert tour operators only accept payment in cash.

★**Desert Candles** TOURS
(☎0673267893; www.desert-candles.com; ⏲8am-8pm) A tie-up between M'Hamid native and former-nomad Abdellah Hajja, and Solveig Gromholt from Norway, Desert Candles' professionally run tours include everything from sandboarding excursions and camel rides to multiday wild-camping desert tours, all led by multilingual guides. They also have a highly rated – and budget-friendly – desert camp in the Erg Chigaga dunes that's fun for all ages.

Caravane de Rêve TOURS
(☎0670020033; www.caravane-de-reve.com/en; 2-night tour Dh1000) The Caravan of Dreams team is made up of multilingual Saharaoui nomads and German, Monika Diefenbach. A popular option is their two-night tour departing M'Hamid by dromedary on the two-hour journey to Erg Lihoudi, spending the first night in their traditional nomad-style tents; the next day you're taken by 4WD to their second camp at Erg Chigaga for sandboarding and stargazing.

Bivouac Sous Les Étoiles TOURS
(☎0644777405; www.bivouacsouslesetoiles.org) Expert and friendly 4WD excursions and camel treks led by the personable Hassan and a team of M'Hamid locals. Operates several desert camps costing between €30 and €135 per person, which employ locals and respect the desert environment.

Zbar Travel TOURS
(☎0668517280; www.zbartravel.com) This locally owned company comes highly recommended, offering overnights at an Erg Chigaga encampment, sleep-outs under the stars, sandboarding and dromedary treks.

Sleeping & Eating

There are some good boutique hotels in and around M'Hamid but most visitors use the town as a jumping-off point for overnighting at camps in the desert.

Auberge Kasbah Dar Sahara GUESTHOUSE €
(☎0667853317; http://darsaharatour.com; s/d/q €25/40/50; P 📶) A big draw for budget travellers, this small, very welcoming place has rustic rooms with shared facilities, relaxing common areas and outdoor space where you can unwind and contemplate the peace of the desert. To get there, head west all the way through town and look for the sign leading up to the left.

Auberge La Palmeraie GUESTHOUSE €
(☎0668729851; www.aubergelapalmeraie.com; r per person incl half-board Dh200) Located across the Draa River in the shade of the palm grove is the Laghrissi brothers' budget-friendly camp. It provides simple accommodation, mixing traditional goat-hair Berber tents and modest *pisé* (rammed-earth) rooms with mattress beds on flat-weave carpets. Showers and toilets are basic, with the latter being of the squat variety. Experienced guides, they offer well-priced excursions.

Turn left at the mosque as you enter M'Hamid, and you'll find it just past Hamada du Draa.

Dar Azawad BOUTIQUE HOTEL €€
(☎0524848730; https://darazawad.com; Ouled Driss; d from Dh660; P ❄ 📶) This contemporary kasbah is all smooth *tadelakt* (waterproof plaster) walls, vibrant rugs and mosaic tiles, with spacious rooms and suites scattered around a garden bursting with desert basil, date palms and tamarisk trees. The restaurant serves up traditional Moroccan dishes around the Insta-worthy pool or in the cosy salon, and you can be steamed, scrubbed and massaged at the marble hammam.

Dar Sidi Bounou GUESTHOUSE €€
(☎0677291310; www.darsidibounou.com; tent/r from Dh220/350; P 📶) A desert dream: dunes in the backyard, sand hammams, Saharawi music jam sessions and *mechoui* (whole roast lamb) feasts on starry terraces. Retreat to Amizigh (Berber) tents or mud-brick huts that sleep six to eight, sleep on the roof, or curl up between crisp cotton sheets in the main house. Three-course lunches and dinners (Dh130) available, plus lighter options (Dh80).

Instead of the usual sandy pool, Dar Sidi Bounou offers desert immersion experiences such as landscape-painting, cooking or belly-dancing classes. It's 4km beyond Ouled Driss.

★ **Camp Al Koutban** TENTED CAMP €€€
(0655778173, 0613036972; https://wildmorocco.com/camping-morocco/camping-morocco-berber; Erg Chigaga; s/d €80/130, transfers from €120; Sep–mid-Jun) Wild Morocco's secluded desert camp is just a 90-minute round-trip hike from Erg Chigaga's tallest dune. Hike – or let a camel take the strain – sandboard and stargaze. The 150km off-road return journey is all part of the experience, as you bounce over *hamada* (rocky desert) studded with acacia and tamarisk, stopping for panoramic vistas and tea with seminomadic desert dwellers.

★ **Erg Chigaga Luxury Desert Camp** TENTED CAMP €€€
(0656563385; www.desertcampmorocco.com; tent per person incl full-board Dh2500) A pebble's throw from Erg Chigaga's highest dune, this luxurious tented camp has 13 sumptuous tents furnished with wall-to-wall carpets, handcrafted beds and high thread-count linens. And it's ecofriendly, with solar-powered lighting, chemical toilets and traditional showers. Expect camel rides, guided walks, chill-out zones, board games and magical evenings filled with Gnaoua ballads – the experience here is second to none.

Camp Adounia TENTED CAMP €€€
(0661215062; http://campadounia.com; Erg Birtam; per person incl full-board €150) Spacious, minimalist tents come with ecofriendly, en suite sand toilets, while a Berber-carpet trail leads to shady lounging spots. Sunset camel rides (Dh300) are a must, then try sandboarding, dune meditation or a Saharan cooking class. The camp also hosts holistic and yoga retreats (see www.moroccoretreats.com), and can arrange transfers from Marrakesh with a stopover in Aït Ben Haddou (Dh1000 return per vehicle).

The extra-large tents and proximity to M'hamid – it's only 40 minutes from the main road – means that the camp is great for children.

Getting There & Away

A CTM bus leaves M'Hamid at 6am for Zagora (Dh40, 1½ hours), Ouarzazate (Dh85, five hours) and Marrakesh (Dh160, 10 hours). Local buses and taxis leave for Zagora (Dh35) throughout the day. Buses and taxis all depart from the main square in M'Hamid.

Foum Zguid وادي دادس

POP 8986

This diminutive oasis town in Tata Province boasts the largest *palmeraie* for miles, studded with crumbling *ksour* (fortified villages).

Heading south, it's strictly 4WD territory, bumping over *hamada* to **Iriqui National Park**, 65km away, with its salt lake and short-lived desert wetlands that are a magnet for migratory birds, before arriving in the desert proper and the sweeping sand sea of Erg Chigaga.

There are a handful of places to stay around Foum Zguid. The restaurant at **Maison d'Hôtes Hiba** (0663613408; d €50, incl half-board €80;) serves restorative meals of tajine, salad and fruit on the scenic terrace or in the air-conditioned salon, while comfortable grotto-style rooms have en suites. **Bab Rimal** (0528216278; www.marocdesert.com; d from €70, incl half-board from €90; P) is complex of faux *pisé* cottages. It's a popular lunch stop for tour groups, who relish a few hours by the flower-fringed pool on the long drive.

For meals, **Restaurant Chegaga** (mains Dh40-70; 8am-9pm) is a popular restaurant on the eastern side of the main town square with outdoor seating, barbecued *brochettes* (kebabs) and monster sandwiches.

Daily buses depart Foum Zguid heading west along the N12 to Tata (2½ hours) and east to Zagora (3½ hours), along with the carpet-weaving town of Tazenakht, 1½ hours north, which sits at the crossroads between Ouarzazate and Agadir and is something of a transport hub.

Without your own 4WD transport and desert navigation skills, travelling south to Erg Chigaga is impossible from Foum Zguid, but if you are driving yourself, fuel up in Tazenakht as the two gas stations further south don't have a reliable supply of petrol.

DADÈS VALLEY سداد يداو

Swaying palms, mud-brick kasbahs and rose-filled valleys – even on paper, the Dadès Valley fires the imagination. From the daunting High Atlas to the north to the rugged Jebel Saghro range to the south, the valley is dotted with oases and ancient castles, giving the region its fairy-tale nickname: Valley of a Thousand Kasbahs.

Paved roads from Tinerhir east to Errachidia, then north up the N13 to Meknes, allow travellers to connect easily with Middle Atlas itineraries, and south to Merzouga and the desert.

But some of the best views are glimpsed when travelling on foot, along hidden trails between the Dadès and Todra Gorges and nomad routes across the Saghro.

Skoura سكورة

POP 4332

By the time caravans laden with gold and spice reached Skoura, the camels must've been gasping. After a two-month journey across the Sahara, blue-robed Tuareg desert traders offloaded their cargo at this oasis town, where Middle Atlas mountaineers packed it onto mules headed to Fez.

Ouarzazate, 40km west, is now the region's commercial centre, but Skoura's historic mud-brick kasbahs and its gorgeous green palm oasis remain, and desert traders throng to the Monday and Thursday souqs brimming with intensely flavourful desert produce. When market days are done and palm-tree shadows stretch across the road, no one seems in a hurry to leave.

Sights

Navigating the maze-like network of dirt tracks in Skoura's vast *palmeraie* is challenging; online maps are unreliable so hotels will send directions if you're self-driving, and invest in a guide (Dh50 per hour) if you're on foot. Most hotels offer their own excursions.

★Palmeraie AREA

(Palm Grove) Skoura's beautiful Unesco-protected *palmeraie* has been dubbed 'Oasis of 1000 Palms'. Under the green canopy, a 15-mile patchwork of plots are watered by an ingenious, centuries-old *khettara* (underground irrigation system) of canals, levers and locks. More than 100 bird species flourish here, as well as more than 20 date varieties. Overnight in a *pisé* (rammed-earth) guesthouse and explore the *palmeraie* on foot or bicycle. A guide will help make the most of your explorations, and stop you getting lost.

Kasbah Amridil HISTORIC BUILDING

(☎0524852387; with/without guide Dh60/10; ⏲8am-7pm) One of Morocco's grandest kasbahs, this 17th-century marvel once appeared on the Dh50 note. Signposted just a few hundred metres from the main road, this living museum showcases traditional kasbah life over the centuries, with hand-carved door locks, an olive oil press, still-functioning bread ovens and stalls where animals were once kept. The kasbah has been split into two, each with its own entrance – the part on the right has retained a more authentic feel and has the higher terrace.

The part on the left has been restored and altered to feature a garden in the middle, a design not native to the region but imported from Marrakesh.

Musée Memoire de Ouarzazate MUSEUM

(Kasbah Dar Bahnini; ☎524852368; www.facebook.com/darbahnini; Dh20; ⏲8am-sunset) This kasbah-turned-museum showcases the history and traditions of Southern Morocco's Imazighen (Berbers). Anthropologist Abdelmoula El Moudahab will explain the exhibits, including a marriage document written in saffron, an assortment of primitive but effective door locks and drawings revealing how a kasbah is put together, as well as sharing the region's fascinating folklore. It doubles as a **performance space**, so check for events.

Tours

Toufiq Mousaoui TOURS

(☎WhatsApp 0611723005; tmousaoui0@gmail.com) One of Skoura's top guides, Toufiq has a wealth of knowledge about the region's history and culture. Arrange walking or biking tours through the palm grove, lunch with a local family and try a donkey trek (good for kids). And if you don't have time to get to the desert proper, he has a nearby camp that's the next best thing.

Nomad Attitude TOURS

(☎0524852281; www.nomadattitude.com) Run by the owners of L'Ma Lodge, this top-notch outfit offers a wide range of excursions both near and far. You can arrange 4WD trips, multiday treks, desert bivouacs and more.

Sleeping & Eating

Skoura is a wonderfully peaceful place to overnight, with the best accommodation hidden in the *palmeraie*. Most places here tend towards the higher end of the budget, but they're absolutely worth it.

Given this is a small oasis, there are no real restaurants, so hotels offer full board, or half-board with some light lunch options. If you're just passing through, you may be able to book lunch (depending on numbers), but you'll need to reserve ahead.

Sawadi Ecolodge GUESTHOUSE €€
(☎0524852341; www.sawadi.ma; Douar Tajanate; s/d/ste €60/70/85; P 🛜 ≋) An oasis within an oasis, 4 acres of organic gardens and a working farm make a bucolic setting for rammed-earth bungalows, with produce used to prepare delicious dinners (around €16). After visits to local artisans or kasbah tours, unwind with a steamy hammam or chilled white wine by the pool. They sell their own first-pressed olive oil and conserves too.

Follow white triangle markers from the road into the northern end of the oasis.

Auberge Restaurant Chez Talout GUESTHOUSE €€
(☎0524852666; www.cheztalout.com/en; Oulad Arbia; d/ste €70/80; P) This good-value, family-owned guesthouse has large, comfortable rooms, most with multiple beds, and all traditionally decorated. After a dusty day's exploring, the pool is the perfect place to cool off and its breezy hilltop location means 360-degree views over the *palmeraie* from three rooftop terraces. The restaurant serves up Moroccan salads, *brochettes* and tasty tajines (lunch/dinner €10/12).

★**L'Ma Lodge** GUESTHOUSE €€€
(☎0666647908; www.lmalodge.com; r/ste €105/150; ⊙closed Jul; 🛜 ≋) This gorgeous lodge has seven spacious, light-filled rooms and suites, decorated with antiques, elegant furnishings and artwork from Morocco and beyond. There's a tree-filled garden – the organic fruits feature in jams and juices, and you can swing in hammocks, swim in the heated pool, play a few rounds of pétanque or arrange a massage. There's also a kids' play area.

The restaurant serves excellent, creative vegetarian-friendly dishes, and the affable hosts have a wealth of information on making the most of the area. To get there, look for the marked turn-off on the N10, just east of Skoura, and then follow the signs. Reserve well ahead.

★**Les Jardins de Skoura** GUESTHOUSE €€€
(☎0524852324; www.lesjardinsdeskoura.com; Palmeraie de Skoura; s/d/ste from €85/95/135; 🛜 ≋) Low-key, high-romance, Skoura style: this garden guesthouse offers eight intimate rooms and three spacious suites, all with nooks carved from rammed-earth walls, decorative rugs and original art. Explore the palm grove by bike, nap beside the pool, then dine (€21) under the stars surrounded by twinkling candles or in front of the open fire in the cosy salon. Follow the orange triangle markers from the main road.

Kasbah Aït Ben Moro HERITAGE HOTEL €€€
(☎0661440885; http://kasbahaitbenmoro.com; r €70-100; P 🛜 ≋) An 18th-century kasbah has been given a stylish makeover that remains true to its desert roots, complete with original palm-beam ceilings, moody low-lit passageways and water-conserving cactus gardens. The three tower rooms are the sweetest deals, with shared bathrooms and oasis views; ask for one with a fireplace. It's located on the N10, 2km west of Skoura.

Shopping

★**La Poterie Chez La Famille Kabor** CERAMICS
(☎0678560702; Ouled Arbia; ⊙8am-sunset) Down the hill, 1km from Chez Talout, three generations of the same family handcraft earthen bread ovens and elegant urns, along with easier-to-transport cups, bowls and plates. Super-friendly Mohamed demonstrates the ancient process, from vigorously crushing the clay with a wooden bat to working the wheel with the heel of his foot. A fun experience for all ages.

Skoura Cultural Centre ARTS & CRAFTS
(☎0524852392; ⊙hours vary) At this small space, Skoura residents sell items made with palm fronds, sustainably harvested without harming the trees. For travellers who've admired one of Morocco's most majestic palm groves, these sun hats, bread baskets, mats and lanterns make meaningful mementos, while purchases support the centre's palm preservation efforts. It's 300m on the left after the Skoura crossroads to Toundoute.

Getting There & Away

There are infrequent buses from Ouarzazate (Dh20, 45 minutes) and Tinerhir (Dh44, two hours) to the centre of Skoura, which lies just off the N10 at the eastern end of the oasis. *Grands taxis* from Ouarzazate (Dh20) and Kalaat M'Gouna (Dh25) stop just after the crossroads.

Kalaat M'Gouna قلعة مكونة

POP 14,190

Although it takes its name from the nearby M'Goun Mountain, the small town of Kalaat M'Gouna is famous for roses and daggers. Around 50km from Skoura, small pink Damask roses – brought to Morocco by the French in the 1930s – start peeking through dense roadside hedgerows, and you can't miss the bottles of local rosewater for sale in town.

During the town's annual rose festival, you'll see rose garlands everywhere. And at the Wednesday souq you can load up on dried roses to make your own potpourri.

To stop and smell the roses on a nature walk book official guides through your accommodation (around Dh350 per day). The **Bureau des Guides** (☎0661796101; Kasbah Assafar, Vallée des Roses; ⏰8am-6pm) is another option.

There aren't any decent lodging options in the town itself, though there are several memorable guesthouses just outside.

On a striking clifftop perch, **Kasbah Itran** (☎0524837103; www.kasbahitran.com; d incl half-board Dh600, with shared bathroom Dh400; 📶) is a maze of terraces and salons. Hiking excursions are also available. It's 2km northwest of Kalaat M'Gouna; minivans pass en route to Tourbiste village (Dh10).

At the tranquil **Kasbah Iswan** (☎0524891771; www.kasbah-iswan.com; Tazroute; r per person incl half-board Dh375) nights are filled with friendly conversation and delicious couscous while days can be spent hiking through spectacular scenery. It's 7km north of Kalaat M'Gouna, in the small village of Tazroute.

Buses run between Ouarzazate and Tinerhir via Kalaat, but are often full. You can catch buses and grands taxis from the centre of Kalaat, where they pull up beside the road. Taxis serve Ouarzazate (Dh35, 1½ hours), Skoura (Dh20, 45 minutes), Boumalne Dades (Dh10, 40 minutes) and Tinerhir (Dh35, 1½ hours).

Boumalne Dades بومالن دادس

POP 12,238

Twenty-four kilometres northeast of Kalaat M'Gouna you reach a fork: the main road continues over the river to the hillside town of Boumalne Dades while the left-hand road leads into stunning Dadès Gorge. Boumalne itself doesn't have much to offer, aside from being a base to explore the nearby gorge. However, it's worth stopping off during the lively Wednesday and Sunday souqs.

Most visitors pass through en route to guesthouses in the more atmospheric setting of the gorge. In town, the best options include **Casbah d'Hôte La Jeanne Ecolodge** (☎0667415697; s/d/tw/tr €45/55/65/70; 📶), a family-run guesthouse offering spacious traditional rooms along with the warm welcome of the owner Moha, who can give you lots of tips on exploring the region. Follow signs leading north off Ave Mohammed V. Morocco meets sub-Saharan Africa at **Hotel Xaluca Dadès** (☎0535578450; www.xaluca.com/en/hotel/hotel-xaluca-dades; s/d/ste from Dh740/900/1460; P📶🏊), a 1970s convention centre turned hotel, atop a hill, north of the centre. There's a hammam (Dh100), bar,

THE ROSE CITY

Villagers flock to Kalaat M'Gouna to celebrate the rose harvest at the three-day **Festival of the Roses** (⏰late May or early Jun). Expect much singing, dancing and feasting, along with a beauty pageant culminating in the crowning of the Queen of the Roses, and parades through mounds of fragrant rose petals. The town's hotels fill up quickly, so book early or come on a day trip.

Coming from Skoura, **Unité de Distillation de Rose** (☎0661348177; ⏰8am-5.30pm) is located on the right 500m before the town. A cooperative of five farms, every element of the rose is used to make rose oil, rosewater for cosmetics and cooking and petals for potpourri. The adjoining shop offers a full range of products, including rosewater used as a face tonic and perfume.

The rose-infused lotions and potions at **Boutique Riyaad Al Ward** (☎0668886333; ⏰9am-7pm) are certified organic, with roses purchased directly from local farmers. You'll find everything from simple rosewater to highly concentrated rose oil and hydrating rose-scented face cream.

BEFORE YOU GO: JEBEL SAGHRO CHECKLIST

Maps The 1:100,000 *Boumalne* and *Tazzarine* maps cover the region, but a more detailed trekking map with history and information on the back is 1:100,000 *Randonnée culturelle dans le Djebel Sarhro*, by Mohamed Aït Hamza and Herbert Popp, written in French and available in Morocco, including at hotels in Boumalne and Nkob.

Guide You can find a licensed local guide directly through a *bureau des guides* in any of the three main Saghro trekking centres: Kalaat M'Gouna, Boumalne (p167) and Nkob (p180). Expect to pay Dh350 a day for a guide and Dh150 for a mule.

Water Dehydration is common any time of the year, so pack extra water.

Food Stock up in Ouarzazate or Boumalne de Dadès. The three Saghro departure towns all have tea, tinned fish, biscuits and bread, and you may find eggs, dates, almonds, bread and tinned sardines in some villages.

Mule Given the amount of water you must carry, mules are a worthwhile investment.

Gear Bring a sleeping bag. You won't need a tent unless you'd rather camp than stay at *gîtes* (basic homestays or hostels).

pool table and a panoramic terrace swimming pool with a hot tub.

For a quick meal, local favourite **Restaurant Oussikis** (Place de Souk; mains Dh40-100; 8am-3pm) sits inside the souq plaza to your left, where chef Fadil Faska transforms fresh, local ingredients into savoury tajines, flaky *bastilla* and more.

Supratours (0524830326) offers a daily service to Ouarzazate (Dh50, 2¼ hours), Tinerhir (Dh30, 45 minutes), Marrakesh (Dh125, seven hours) and Merzouga (Dh115, six hours). Buses stop opposite the ticket office, near to the Banque Populaire.

Cheaper private buses also leave daily to Ouarzazate (Dh30), Tinerhir (Dh10) and Marrakesh (Dh100), and multiple times daily to Errachidia (Dh40).

Pick up a grand taxi around the Banque Populaire. You may have to wait a while for it to fill up, but they do go to Ouarzazate (Dh40), Tinerhir (Dh20) and Aït Oudinar (inside the Dadès Gorge; Dh12).

Trekking Jebel Saghro

Comparatively few tourists venture into the starkly beautiful Jebel Saghro (aka Jebel Sarhro or Djebel Sahro) as most of the flat-topped mesas, volcanic pinnacles and deep gorges dotted with palm groves are only accessible on foot and lack the attention-catching elevations of the High Atlas peaks. This arid, isolated territory is home turf to the seminomadic Aït Atta, legendary warriors famous for their 1933 stand against the French here, on **Jebel Bou Gafer**.

Jebel Saghro is accessed from three trekking hubs: Kalaat M'Gouna and Boumalne Dades on the north side of the range, and the southern village of Nkob. The most scenic routes head through the heart of the range, between Igli and Bab n'Ali, though much of this has now been converted to tarmac roads and isn't very hiker-friendly.

Collective taxis run from Boumalne Dades to Tagdilt (Dh15), departing in the afternoon and returning to Boumalne early the next morning. From Imi n'Isimdal collective taxis (Dh10) run early most mornings (around 6am) to Kalaat M'Gouna, returning the opposite direction in mid-afternoon, providing the option to skip the final day and 14km of walking.

Day 1: Tagdilt to the Assif Ouarg Valley

Duration 5 hours
Distance 16km
Ascent 566m
Descent 32m

Tagdilt is a quiet village with a useful trailhead, a daily collective taxi from Boumalne and three *gîtes* (homestays) – including the spacious **Tagdilt Gîte** (Chez Brahim Bourig; 0661776708; gitetagdilt@gmail.com; dm Dh100), whose owner can also arrange hired mules. For 11km you could follow the *piste* used by vans crossing the mountain to Nkob, or veer onto the track that occasionally strays to the side, until you arrive at the village crossroad of **Imi n'Ouarg**.

Here the path leaves the main *piste* (which continues to the mines at Tiouit) and turns right (southwest) beside the village school, marked by a Moroccan flag, to continue on a smaller *piste* up the winding Assif Ouarg valley beneath the summit of **Jebel Kouaouch** (2592m). En route you'll pass through the small village of Imsoual.

After about 4.5km the *piste* finally ends and the way continues along a mule trail that climbs 2km further to the end of the valley. There are several potential campsites both here and beyond the next pass, and a lovely family **homestay** (☎0661082321; dm Dh100, tents Dh30) just up the first winding set of switchbacks at 2273m.

If you end the day with time to spare, head just to the east, where views from the 2365m **Tizi n'Ouarg** pass are particularly enjoyable as the setting sun casts dramatic shadows all down the Assif Ouarg.

Day 2: Assif Ouarg Valley to Irhazzoun n'Imlas

Duration 7-8 hours
Distance 20km
Ascent 507m
Descent 1436m

The most memorable walk on this trek is also the most difficult, starting with a 200m climb towards the moon-like landscape of a 2479m plateau behind **Jebel Kouaouch**, the highest of a row of peaks straight ahead. While it isn't essential to climb the 2595m peak, views from the summit to the High Atlas and across Jebel Saghro to the Sahara are exceptional and the way up is a straightforward walk until the last 20m or so, which require a bit of light scrambling. Return down via the same summit path to continue along the main trail.

The path drops steeply down ahead, but our track veers right (southwest) across the valley's shoulder and over another ridge, with views south to the palms and kasbahs of Nkob. **Igli** is due south over a series of slopes. You'll pass several campsites with constant springs as you continue towards the hamlet. Three low buildings form a **gîte** (dm Dh100) with a toilet and wood-fired hot showers. There's no electricity or sleeping mats here, but the friendly *gardien* (caretaker) runs a shop selling trekkers' necessities, including mule shoes. Sunsets from here are breathtaking, and if you wanted to add an extra day to the itinerary this might be a good place to break up the trip.

Continuing southwest over a small ridge and down a lonely windswept valley (turn around for excellent views of the cliffs above Igli), turning west towards the junction visible in the mid-distance where the path joins a desert *piste* that runs towards Irhazzoun n'Imlas just below the odd rock formation known as the **Tête de Chameau** (Camel's Head) all alone in a wide valley.

Follow the *piste* below the long, dramatic cliffs of the **Needles of Saghro** for nearly 3.5km until just before it curves around the last small hill on the plateau and drops towards Irhazzoun n'Imlas. Before the *piste* drops along the western slope of the hill, look for a faint mule trail on the eastern slope that winds down through the black-rock hills and then down through the riverbed past stands of palms and oleander to the village of **Irhazzoun n'Imlas** where there are several spaces where camping is possible on the east side of the riverbed.

TREK AT A GLANCE

Duration Five to six days

Distance 95km

Standard Medium

Start Tagdilt

Finish Kalaat M'Gouna

Highest Point Kouaouch peak (2595m)

Accommodation Camping and *gîtes* (basic homestays or hostels)

Public Transport Yes

Summary A great alternative to the classic north–south traverse of Saghro, showcasing the staggering and varied beauty of the range. Given long days of walking, you might add another night to the route.

Day 3: Irhazzoun n'Imlas to Assaka n'Aït Ouzzine

Duration 5-6 hours
Distance 21km
Ascent 531m
Descent 239m

From Irhazzoun n'Imlas the path joins a *piste* that runs left to Nkob and right towards the Dadès Valley. Take the right track (northwest) towards a sheer cliff on the left, with the rocky path leading beneath it and up to a broadening valley. The *piste* loops

Jebel Saghro Trek

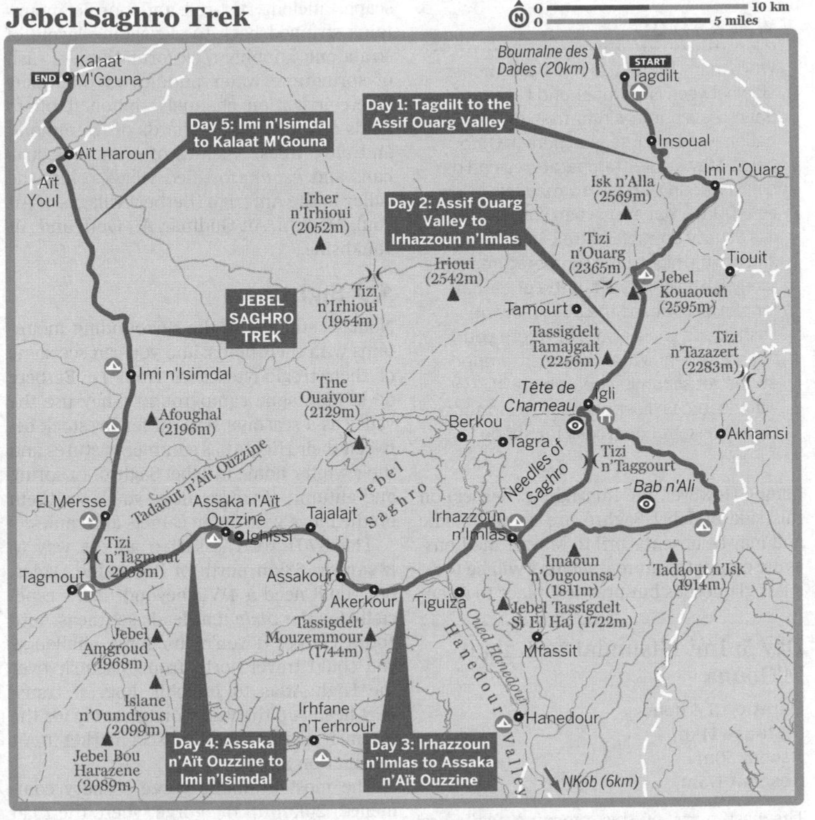

around the north side of **Jebel Tassigdelt Si El Haj** (1722m) and then south again towards **Tiguiza** village, intersecting another *piste* that leads right (west) to **Akerkour** village, into a narrowing valley dotted with palms, past the picturesque hillside village of **Ighissi** and up an incline to **Assaka n'Aït Ouzzine** (1584m), a beautiful old village with a crumbling centuries-old *agadir* (fortified granary). There's a free campsite on the riverbed and it might be possible to stay in a home in the village (with meals) for around Dh100, though this is best arranged through a guide.

Day 4: Assaka n'Aït Ouzzine to Imi n'Isimdal

Duration 7-8 hours
Distance 24km
Ascent 600m
Descent 529m

From Assaka, the *piste* leads out of the valley into a rocky, windy steppe. The track runs for 9km, wedged between 2000m ridges, to **Tagmout** (also called Amgroud after one of the mountains overlooking the village) and a well-kept **gîte** (Chez Mohamed Elouich; ☎0691274263; dm Dh100; ⏲Oct-Mar) with electricity, mattresses, blankets and possibly lunch (around Dh60).

From Tagmout the *piste* leads northwest to Kalaat M'Gouna and south to Nkob, with transport headed to Nkob's Sunday souq. The trek heads northeast, climbing over 300m to **Tizi n'Tagmout** (2038m) for stunning views north to the M'Goun Massif. Just north of the pass is the pasture of **El Merssе** (1922m), where shade and a year-round spring facilitate camping.

The track continues due north, mostly in gentle descent, but with occasional climbs. Nearly 11km after the pass is the tiny hamlet of **Imi n'Isimdal**, where it may be possible to overnight *chez l'habitant* (in someone's

WHEN TO GO

While many High Atlas trails are impassable between November and February, Saghro is a prime winter trekking destination – the ideal season here is October to May. Winter temperatures can dip below freezing, and snow may fall as low as 1400m – but even when it does snow, it is usually possible to trek. In autumn and spring, night-time temperatures rarely fall below zero, but the potential for rain also means the possibility of flash floods so be aware of where you pitch your tent. When summer temperatures get scorching hot (above 40°C), water sources disappear, and even scorpions hunker under rocks for shade.

home). However, the Imazighen (Berber) on this side of Jebel Saghro are seminomadic and may be absent April to May. If the houses are empty, the animal shelters will be too – a less glamorous but practical place to sleep.

Day 5: Imi n'Isimdal to Kalaat M'Gouna

Duration 3-4 hours
Distance 14km
Ascent 50m
Descent 175m

The best parts of this morning walk are the beginning and end. The *piste* west out of Imi n'Isimdal reveals occasional M'Goun and Siroua views in between rolling hills. Continue north, occasionally northwest, on a well-worn track that leads down a gully towards the Dadès Valley. As you get closer, you will see the villages of **Aït Youl** on your left, **Aït Haroun** on the right, and a valley studded with old kasbahs. Head for Aït Haroun, where there is a bridge over the Dadès River. The Boumalne–Kalaat M'Gouna road is nearby, but long after you return to the modern world, Saghro's seminomadic spirit stays with you.

Dadès Gorge وادي دادس

As the local saying goes, the wind has a son who lives in Boumalne, which is why he rips down this valley to visit him in winter. Sitting in the rain shadow of the Central Atlas, the Dadès Gorge presents a dramatic landscape: ancient rust-red and purple mountains stripped back to zigzagging layers of strata and knobbly rock formations. A rush of springtime water puddles in the valley where irrigation channels siphon it off to fields of wheat and orchards of fig, almond and olive trees. A series of crumbling kasbahs and *ksour* (fortified villages) line the valley in the Amazigh (Berber) villages of Aït Youl, Aït Arbi, Aït Oudinar, Aït Ouffi and Aït Toukhsine.

Sights

Nomads still live in the surrounding mountains with their herds, and you can see some of their troglodyte caves from Le Berbère de la Montagne campground. They use the valley as a seasonal stop-off for livestock between their High Atlas summer pastures and their winter home in Jebel Saghro. In spring and autumn, if you're lucky, you'll see them on the move with laden camels and mules.

The R704 road is sealed all the way to **Msemrir**, 63km north of Boumalne Dades, but you'll need a 4WD beyond that – especially for the *piste* that leads southeast into Todra Gorge. If you're up for a challenge, you could travel north from Msemrir over the High Atlas to Imilchil. Lots of transport heads up the valley on Saturday for the Msemrir market. There's also a market in Aït Oudinar on Sunday.

The most dramatic gorge scenery commences 26km up the gorge where the road crosses the river and starts to climb through an extraordinary series of hairpin bends (see www.dangerousroads.org). When the road flattens out again, you might take that as your cue to turn around: you've covered the best gorge scenery you can see without a 4WD or good hiking shoes.

There's a good trekking trail heading northwest, beginning just across the river, 28km from Boumalne Dades. The energetic could cover the distance from Dadès and Todra Gorges on foot (a two- to three-day walk). Most hotels in the gorge and Boumalne Dades can arrange hiking guides (around Dh300 per day), 4WD trips to the Todra Gorge (Dh1500 to Dh2000 per day) and bicycle hire (around Dh100). Contact the **Bureau des Guides** (☎0671310923; atlasguide3@gmail.com) for more details.

Aït Youl HISTORIC BUILDING

Those art-deco tourism posters you'll see all over Morocco showing a red-and-white kasbah in a rocky oasis aren't exaggerating: just

6.5km into the gorge, the old Glaoui kasbah of Aït Youl is set against a lush backdrop of almond and fig trees. A local kid will offer to show you around for a small tip (Dh20). A couple of kilometres past Aït Youl, the road crosses a river valley that offers a sneaky back way to Kalaat M'Gouna on foot.

Tamellalt Valley NATURAL FEATURE
Eighteen kilometres from Boumalne you'll find these extraordinary red rock formations that look like wax, melting right into the green carpet of the *palmeraie* below Aït Arbi. They're known locally as *Les Doigts de Singes* (Monkey's Fingers) given their bizarre wind-worn shapes. A little further on is the more colourfully named 'Valley of Human Bodies', where famished travellers are said to have died of hunger and been turned to stone.

Gorge de Miguirne GORGE
(Sidi Boubar Gorge) Cresting over a small pass, 14km from Boumalne, is the hidden gem of Gorge de Miguirne, which joins the Dadès Gorge from the south. It offers a fine half-day hike amid its springs, rock pools and stunning rock formations, sculpted by time and the elements. Ask at your guesthouse for a guide.

Festivals & Events

Marriage Moussem CULTURAL
(Imilchil; Sep) Just another striking Middle Atlas Amazigh (Berber) village most of the year, Imilchil is flooded with visitors during its three-day marriage *moussem* in September. At this huge festival, local Imazighen (Berbers) scope the scene for marriage material. Women strut their stuff in striped woollen cloaks and elaborate jewellery, and boys preen in flowing white *djellabas* (full-length hooded garments with long sleeves).

The festival usually runs Friday to Sunday in the third or fourth week of September; dates are posted at tourist offices throughout the country. Organised tours to the event are available from cities throughout Morocco, and newly paved roads from Rich and Aït Haini to Imilchil have brought busloads of tourists to see romance blossom. With hustlers, *faux guides* and souvenir stalls eyeing the tourists, onlookers are beginning to outnumber the young lovers – but there's no denying the voyeuristic fascination of the event.

During the festival, the area is covered in tented accommodation. Otherwise, there is basic hotel accommodation at Chez Bassou.

To get to Imilchil from Marrakesh, head northeast by bus or grand taxi to Kasba Tadla, and onward by grand taxi to El Ksiba. At El Ksiba there is a daily bus to Aghbala. The turn-off for Imilchil is near Tizi n'Isly, about 10km before Aghbala. From the turn-off, 61km of paved road leads south to Imilchil. You may also find local grands taxis or trucks Imilchil-bound for Friday and Sunday souqs.

It's possible to reach Imilchil (a breathtaking 160km by 4WD or souq-bound lorry) from Boumalne Dades or more easily along paved road from Tinerhir. Minibuses leave Tinerhir for Imilchil (Dh40, 2½ to three hours) daily around 9am (also returning around 9am).

Sleeping

Accommodation options have exploded along the gorge and there's something for all budgets. Most of it is within 28km of Boumalne Dades.

Chez Bassou HOTEL €
(0668564475; Imilchil; d incl half-board Dh500;) This 20-room guesthouse in Imilchil – a Middle Atlas town around a four-hour drive north from Boumalne Dades – has a fine location in the mountains. Rooms are small but clean and comfortable, with adequate blankets for cold Atlas nights. Meals are available at the good on-site restaurant.

Le Berbère de la Montagne GUESTHOUSE €
(0524830228; https://berbere-montagne.com; Km 34; campsites Dh80, r per person incl half-board Dh250-300; P) At this peaceful spot, tent pitches overlook the river and come with a kitchen, laundry facilities, hot showers and toilets. The guesthouse sits within a few metres of the narrowest point of the gorge, where nine rooms are decorated

BIRDWATCHING IN THE DADÈS

Horned lark, wheat-ears, sand grouse, buzzards and eagle owls are just some of the species you may spot in the aptly named **Vallée des Oiseaux** (Valley of the Birds), along with a healthy reptile population and small herds of Edmi gazelle and Addax antelope. Organise trips with the knowledgeable Hamou Aït Lhou at the **Bureau des Guides** (0623774463; hamou.aitlhou57@yahoo.fr; Ave Mohammed V).

with *tataoui* ceilings (made from reeds woven into intricate patterns), terracotta tiled floors and pine beds heaped with warm blankets.

It's perfectly located for hikes into the Petit Gorge and up into the hills to visit nomad encampments and secret caves hung with stalactites; guides from Dh200 per day.

Chez L'Habitant Amazigh GUESTHOUSE €
(☎0670714551; zaid.azul@hotmail.fr; Km 20, Aït Arbi; s/d incl half-board Dh300/500;) Spend a night at the Tair family home, and you'll get a warm introduction to Amazigh (Berber) life, with evening discussions of history and culture, followed by family music jams. Cheerfully decorated pink *pisé* (rammed-earth) rooms and exuberantly furnished salons can't compete with first-class terrace views over the river and valley rock formations. It's also a good place to arrange treks around the gorge.

★**Chez Pierre** INN €€
(☎0524830267; www.chezpierre.org; Km 26, Aït Ouffi; s/d/tr/q Dh550/680/850/950, half-board per person Dh235;) At this chic retreat, 11 light-filled rooms and two, two-bedroom apartments are notched right into the gorge wall, with contemporary Moroccan decor, plant-filled terraces and a poolside sun deck. A rosy gorge sunset is the prelude to a drink at the bar and spectacular six-course dinners (Dh250) where Mediterranean cuisine meets seasonal Moroccan produce beside the snug wood-burning stove.

Les 4 Saisons du Dades GUESTHOUSE €€
(☎0524831755; www.chambresdhotesdades.com; Km 24, Aït Oudinar; s/d incl half-board Dh330/500) Book early for one of the four 'seasonal' rooms at Youssef Azrarag's welcoming guesthouse, where Amazigh hospitality, vintage French furniture and bright local decor blend seamlessly. All the rooms overlook the lovely patio garden where numerous varieties of mountain mint and verveine perfume the air. After tough treks, collapse on Moroccan cushions in the large open-plan kitchen.

Kasbah de Mimi GUESTHOUSE €€€
(☎0671523855; mimi.kasbah@laposte.net; Km 12, Aït Ibriren; r per person incl half-board €50;) Staying at this painstakingly restored cliff-side bolthole is like being in the home of a friend with excellent taste: original artwork on the walls, antique furniture and a grand piano in the well-stocked library. Outside, there's a swimming pool, sun-filled patios and flower-filled terraces.

The 500m cliffhanger of a road to reach it is harrowing, but village kids will cheer your arrival.

Eating

The best dining is at Chez Pierre. Other than that there are a few casual eateries along the valley. To snap that iconic image of the road snaking up the valley, stop for coffee or a snack on the terrace of **Hotel Restaurant Timzzillite** (mains Dh40-80; 10am-8pm).

Le Jardin de Source MOROCCAN €
(☎0670019030; Km 11, Aït Ibrirne; mains Dh40-100; 11am-9pm;) Leisurely lunches at this pretty garden restaurant near the mouth of the gorge include flavourful vegetarian options, omelettes and vegetable tajines and marinated turkey kebabs. Several good-value rooms (€18 per person, including half-board) are also available.

★**Chez Pierre Restaurant** MEDITERRANEAN €€
(☎0524830267; www.chezpierre.org; Km26, Aït Ouffi; mains Dh125, six-course menu Dh250; 7pm-9pm) Mediterranean flair meets Moroccan market-fresh produce on the daily-changing menu at this restaurant attached to the Inn of the same name. Perhaps roast beetroot and goat's cheese and chicken in an almond crust, rounded off with an indulgent chocolate fondant. There's a good wine list too. On balmy nights, dine alfresco under a canopy of stars. Reservations recommended.

Shopping

Association Gorge du Dadès ARTS & CRAFTS
(☎0666396949, 0677909670; Km 24, Aït Oudinar; 2-5pm Mon-Sat) Tufted carpets are made at this weaving cooperative, but soft kilim blankets made with undyed, extra-fluffy lambswool are signature pieces. The women are introducing nonchemical dyes made from local walnut shells (brown), onion skins (yellow) and poppies (black). Items are sold at fixed prices and the weaver is paid directly.

Getting There & Away

Grands taxis and minibuses run up the gorge from Boumalne to the cluster of hotels in Aït Oudinar and Aït Ouffi (Dh10) and to Msemrir (Dh30, 1½ to two hours). To return, flag down a passing vehicle. You can also hire a taxi for a half-day trip (around Dh250) into the gorge. Minibuses run frequently up to Msemrir; the last one back to Boumalne leaves at about 4pm.

Tinerhir تنغير

POP 42,044

Charm falls a distant third to dust and hustle in Tinerhir (aka Tinghir), a busy mining town and transit hub recently benefiting from a rash of expansion and construction thanks to an administrative upgrade to independent provincial capital. If you need a break after the 51km drive from Boumalne Dades, head to the eastern edge of town, where a palm oasis unfolds like a ribbon of green. Under the canopy, you'll discover crumbling kasbahs, the abandoned 19th-century Medersa Ikelane (look for the whitewashed mud-brick cupola) and, to the north of town, the ruins of Ksar Asfalou, where Muslim and Jewish students once studied under the same roof.

A souq is held 2.5km west of the centre on Monday, and there's a Saturday livestock souq in town.

Most people prefer to lodge in more charming accommodation in the Todra Gorge. One of the best options here is **Kasbah Petit Nomade** (0668495838; http://kasbah-petitnomade.com; Douar Ichmarine; r per person incl half-board Dh275; P 📶) , which lies north of town and has three simple rooms decked out in bold colours around an internal courtyard. The food here is made with flair and features a bounty of fresh produce sourced from local farms. Tours of the *palmeraie* and nearby villages provide fascinating insights, and hiking, climbing or horse riding excursions in the gorge can easily be arranged. You'll find it signed off the highway some 2km north of Tinerhir, at the start of the gorge in the village of Ichmarine.

Hôtel Tomboctou (0524835191; www.hoteltomboctou.com; 126 Ave Bir Anzarane; s/d/tr incl half-board Dh570/750/1030;) has quirky, cosy rooms with en suites in a renovated kasbah built in 1944 for the local *qaid* (chief). There's also a good on-site restaurant (menu Dh130), plus oasis walking tours and bicycle trips can be organised.

Eating options are limited but simple grill restaurants line Ave Mohammed V and Ave Hassan II, with the **Central** (Ave Hassan II; mains Dh30-50, three-course set menu Dh60; 11am-7pm) a standout. To stock up on supplies (including alcohol), stop by **Chez Michele Supermarket** (Ave Mohammed V; 9am-9pm, closed Fri & Ramadan).

Buses leave from Place Principale, off Ave Mohammed V. Supratours stops in Tinerhir en route to Boumalne Dades (Dh30, one hour), Ouarzazate (Dh65, three hours), Marrakesh (Dh135, seven hours) and, heading in the other direction, Errachidia (Dh55, three hours), Erfoud (Dh80, four hours) and Merzouga (Dh90, five hours). You'll find the ticket office to the right of the bus lot in front of the mosque.

On other lines, there's frequent service from Tinerhir to Marrakesh (Dh130) via Ouarzazate (Dh40), and to Erfoud (Dh40), Meknes (Dh110) and Boumalne Dades (Dh20).

Grands taxis to Ouarzazate (Dh60), Alnif (Dh25) and Errachidia (Dh45 to Dh70) leave from Place Principale, where you'll also find minivans or pick-up trucks into Todra Gorge (Dh10) and beyond to Tamtattouchte (Dh18) and Imilchil (Dh40). Grands taxis to Tamtetoucht (Dh18), Aït Haini (Dh20) and Imilchil (Dh40) leave between 9am and 1pm.

Todra Gorge مضيق تودغا

Being stuck between a rock and a hard place is a sublime experience in the Todra Gorge, where a 300m-deep fault splits the orange limestone into a deep ravine at some points just wide enough for a crystal-clear river and single-file hikers to squeeze through. The road from Tinerhir passes through green *palmeraies* and Amazigh (Berber) villages until, 15km along, sky-high walls of pink and grey rock close in around the road.

Visit in the morning, when sunlight illuminates the gorge. Souvenir sellers and tour buses clog the centre in the afternoons, until it suddenly turns dark and bitterly cold. But the road continues past this point, from where there's little traffic, and winds its way for 18km to Tamtetoucht village and on to Imilchil some 95km beyond.

There are no banks in the gorge and limited connectivity and phone coverage, so carry enough cash.

Activities

The gorge offers hiking for all abilities, from easy rambles through *palmeraies* to multiday treks over rough *piste* all the way to the Dadès Gorge. Or let a horse do the hard work and book a ride with Auberge Cavaliers.

Todra Gorge & Tinerhir

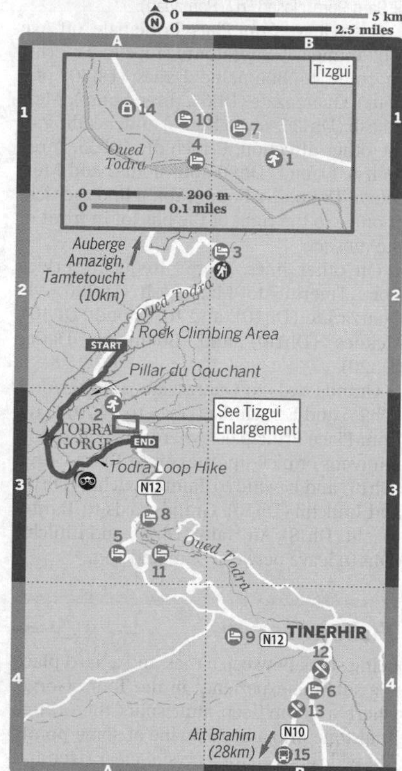

Todra Gorge & Tinerhir

Activities, Courses & Tours

1 Auberge Cavaliers B1
2 Aventures Verticales A3

Sleeping

3 Auberge Le Festival B2
4 Dar Ayour A1
5 Hôtel Camping Le Soleil A3
6 Hôtel Tombctou B4
7 Hotel Valentine B1
8 Kasbah Amazir A3
9 Kasbah Petit Nomade B4
10 Maison La Fleur A1
11 Palmeraie Guesthouse A3

Eating

12 Café Restaurant Central B4
13 Chez Michele Supermarket B4

Shopping

14 Berber Carpets A1

Transport

15 Bus Station B4
Grands Taxis (see 15)

Hiking Todra Loop

For a vigorous morning hike, try a three-hour loop from north of the gorge to Tizgui, south of the gorge. A 30-minute walk beyond the main gorge is the **Petite Gorge**, where you'll find a trailhead near Auberge Le Festival. Take the track leading uphill to the left (southwest) – regular donkey and mule traffic keep this path well defined. Head to the pass, and from there, ascend southeast to the next pass. This would be a good place to stray from the main route to look over the rim of the gorge, but be careful, as the winds are powerful up here.

From the second pass, descend to the Amazigh (Berber) village of **Tizgui**, where you can stroll through the *palmeraies* back to the gorge.

Rock Climbing

Todra's vertical rock faces offer sublime rock-climbing routes (French grade 5 to 8), some of them bolted. Many of the routes are over 25m long, although there is some spectacular multipitch climbing where routes run over 300m. For experienced climbers **Pillar du Couchant**, near the entrance to the gorge, offers classic long climbs, while the **Petite Gorge** is better for novice climbers, with good short routes. Few of the routes are mapped, although many hotels keep logbooks detailing current information on local routes. Otherwise, internationally certified guides and reliable equipment can be hired from Aventures Verticales.

Tour Operators

Aventures Verticales CLIMBING

(☎0524895727; www.climbing-in-morocco.com; Km 14, Tizgui; half-/full day per person Dh125/200) This professional outfit has internationally certified guides offering climbing, alpinism and trekking excursions for all levels. The small shop in Tizgui also stocks top gear for hire and sale, including Rock Pillar climbing shoes, Petzl helmets and Beal ropes, plus tents and sleeping bags.

Auberge Cavaliers HORSE RIDING

(☎0618530790; www.facebook.com/equestriantrep; Km 14, Aït Baha Tizgui; per hr €15) This guesthouse organises professional horse-riding adventures in the gorge and beyond for all ages and abilities. Book in advance for overnight horse treks with guide and food.

Sleeping & Eating

Most visitors take their meals at their guesthouses. Beyond packing a picnic, the best lunch spots are at **Camping Le Soleil** (☎0524895111; Km 8; campsites per person/tent/car €2.50/2.50/3, r per person €20, incl half-board €25; P 📶 🏊) and the restaurants in the small village of Aït Baha Tizgui.

★ **Auberge Amazigh** GUESTHOUSE €
(☎0610127555; Km 34, Tamtetoucht; campsite per person Dh50, r per person Dh180, incl half-board Dh250; P 📶) Located 17km past the gorge in the village of Tamtetoucht, Auberge Amazigh has just four cosy rooms, each with traditional *pisé* (rammed-earth walls) carved with Amazigh (Berber) motifs and sporting mosquito nets and colourful throws, all topped with a pretty roof terrace. Hamid and his family make hospitable hosts, serving up moreish meals and plenty of local knowledge.

Hotel Valentine GUESTHOUSE €
(☎0524895225; www.hotel-valentine.net; Km 14, Aït Baha; s/d Dh200/300, incl half-board Dh250/400; 📶) In the village of Aït Baha Tizgui, about 800m before the gorge, Hotel Valentine rolls out the welcome mat with thoughtful service and remarkably budget-friendly rooms. Accommodation is on the small side, and only two of the eight rooms have views, but you can head up to the roof terrace for a splendid panorama over the village, *palmeraie* and chiselled mountains beyond.

Maison La Fleur GUESTHOUSE €
(☎0670404369; www.maison-lafleur.com; Km 14, Aït Baha Tizgui; dm/d incl half-board Dh150/400; P 📶) Run by a Japanese expat named Noriko, this surprising spot on the main road in Aït Baha Tizgui has six simple rooms (including a five-bed dorm) painted in muted colours, plus a great open terrace. It's an easy 700m walk to the gorge, and probably the only spot in the Atlas mountains where you'll find miso soup on the menu.

★ **Auberge Le Festival** INN €
(☎0661267251; www.aubergelefestival-todragorge.com; Km 22; r per person incl half-board from Dh350; P) 🍃 Get back to nature in romantically lit cave rooms dug right into the hillside and finished in moulded *tadelakt* (waterproof plaster), or rock-walled, solar-powered tower rooms surveying the Petit Gorge. After self-guided treks and climbs (Dh300 per hour) arranged by the multilingual owner, relax on the panoramic terrace or help harvest vegetables in the organic garden for dinner.

★ **Palmeraie Guesthouse** GUESTHOUSE €€
(☎0524895209; www.palmeraieguesthouse.com; Km 7; s/d incl half-board Dh350/500; 📶) Just inside the *palmeraie*, this delightful guesthouse has a series of pretty terraces draped with flowering vines and attractive rooms set with Berber carpets, vintage travel posters and original artwork. Rachid and Doreen give a warm welcome, and this is a great base for exploring the *palmeraie* – ask to take Jack the donkey for a stroll.

Kasbah Amazir GUESTHOUSE €€
(☎0524895109; http://kasbahamazir.com; Km 10; s/d Dh250/400, incl half-board Dh400/600; P 📶 🏊) This reliable place hits all the right notes, with bright rooms – some with small balconies – a riverside location and friendly service. Some rooms are bigger than others and have better views, so check a few out before committing.

Dar Ayour GUESTHOUSE €€
(☎0524895271; www.darayour.com; Km 13; s/d incl half-board €35/60; P 📶) Riads have arrived in Todra at this warm, artsy five-storey guesthouse that's all Middle Atlas rugs, sparkly *handiras* (Moroccan wedding blankets) and colourful abstract paintings. Fall asleep to the sounds of the river rushing past. All 10 rooms have en suites and fine views over the valley; four have balconies. There's also a roof terrace with 360-degree views.

Shopping

Berber Carpets ARTS & CRAFTS
(☎0668763091; Auberge Royal Palmas, Aït Baha Tizgui; ⏲8am-6pm) This cooperative in the Auberge Royal Palmas sells a range of handmade carpets, from simple kilims to more elaborate pieces that took many months to create. You can watch the women weavers in action, and there's little pressure to buy. Prices range from Dh500 to more than Dh15,000. Credit cards accepted and shipping available.

Getting There & Away

The now paved road from Aït Haini north to Imilchil and the intersection of the N8 Beni Mellal–Fez road is accessible to normal vehicles. Grands taxis run up the gorge from Tinerhir to

Imilchil (Dh40, 2½ hours), and there's usually one transit minivan heading up the gorge every day, with more on Wednesday for Aït Haini's Thursday market and on Friday for Imilchil's Saturday market. Your lodging can advise on when the next public transport is scheduled.

Tinejdad

POP 44,000

Once a stop-off on the caravan trail, the sprawling town of Tinjedad – 'nomad' in Tamazight – is now home to two fascinating museums. Amazigh (Berber) and Saharan peoples would quench their thirst at the Sources de Lalla Mimouna natural springs, which is now an ethnographic museum. And an ancient *ksar* has been restored and made liveable once more, in a sustainable project involving the community and help from international architects.

There are limited lodging options in the area, though there's one atmospheric **guesthouse** (☎0535880355; www.elkhorbat.com; Ksar El Khorbat; s/d/tr Dh475/530/625;) in the *ksar* that's well worth an overnight stay.

Grands taxis run from the main market in the centre of town to Goulmima (Dh25, 45 minutes), Errachidia (Dh50, 1½ hours) and Tinerhir (Dh20, one hour).

Sights

Tinejdad's crossroads culture remains remarkably intact just off the N10. The Lalla Mimouna springs museum is signposted to the north 3km before town, and the green line of the Ferkla Oasis begins on the southwest edge of town, where you'll spot towering Ksar Asrir.

To see what treasures you can find from desert traders, hit the Sunday and Wednesday souqs on the western side of town.

★ Musée des Sources de Lalla Mimouna MUSEUM

(☎0535786798; Dh50; 8am-sunset; P) This indoor/outdoor private museum is the passion project of Tinejdad native Zaid Abbou, built around the fizzing, magnesium-rich springs of Lalla Mimouna. Artefacts collected over 40 years – including ceramics, agricultural tools, jewellery and illuminated books – give an insight into oasis life, housed in a series of unfolding spaces across a garden dotted with literary quotations about valuing nature, particularly water.

At Zaid's converted home you'll find the **Galerie d'Art Chez Zaid** (8.30am-6pm), with Tinejdad-made ceramics in the courtyard, sand-worn bracelets in the salon and well-patched nickel silver teapots in the kitchen, alongside his beautiful calligraphy.

★ Musée de Oasis MUSEUM

(Ksar El Khorbat; www.elkhorbat.com/en.museum.htm; Dh20; 8am-6pm) Inside the Ksar El Khorbat, this award-winning museum traces tribal migrations through 22 rooms of carefully curated artefacts of seminomadic life: saddles worn shiny, contracts inscribed on wooden tablets in Arabic and Hebrew, ceramic urns for water and preserved butter, heavy silver jewellery and inlaid muskets and handcuffs to protect it all from would-be thieves.

Ksar El Khorbat VILLAGE

(☎0535880355; www.elkhorbat.com) This spectacular example of a mid-19th-century fortified village was crumbling to dust when it underwent a major restoration using traditional techniques and materials, as well as adding a few contemporary comforts. Today, around half of the dwellings are still inhabited, while others have been turned into a 22-room museum, a guesthouse, a restaurant and a women's craft workshop. The aim is to preserve the history and culture of the *ksar* through sustainable tourism while benefiting the whole community.

Ferkla Oasis AREA

Take a bike (hire one for Dh80) and tour the Ferkla *palmeraie* with a local guide (Dh200) from El Khorbat. You'll explore the Ksar Asrir, once the economic hub of the oasis, with a substantial *mellah* (Jewish quarter) and a mosque dating back to the Almoravids. You'll stop off at a Sufi shrine with an unusual earthen minaret and learn about the *khetteras*, underground water channels that fed the oasis.

FIGUIG

POP 10,872

In the days of cross-border tourism with Algeria – the border's been closed since 1994 – Figuig (fig-eeg) was popular with travellers, but few people make it here now, mainly just hardcore bikers in search of an end-of-the road feel. That's a shame because it's one of Morocco's loveliest oasis towns, with seven traditional desert villages amid 200,000 date palms fed by artesian wells. Once a historic way station for pilgrims travelling to Mecca, Figuig now sleeps, only waking for the autumn date harvest.

Figuig has an upper and lower town. The main road, Blvd Hassan II, runs through the upper (new) town, where there are ATMs and pleasant municipal gardens.

Where the road passes the Figuig Hotel, it drops downhill towards the lower town – the basin of palms and *ksour* (fortified villages) that make up the old part of Figuig. This ridge provides a handy landmark as well as views over the *palmeraie* and into Algeria: the best views are from Azrou, where the path leads towards Ksar Zenaga, and from the terrace of the Figuig Hotel.

The seven *ksour* that make up the town each control an area of *palmeraie* and its all-important water supply.

The crumbling state of many *ksour* lets you see their clever construction: palm-tree trunks plastered with *pisé,* and ceilings made of palm fronds. It's cool and dark and often eerily quiet. It's easy to get lost but children will happily guide you for a few dirham.

The largest of the town's seven *ksour* is **Ksar Zenaga**, south below the ridge splitting the oasis. Take the paths following irrigation channels, then suddenly you're among a warren of covered passages. As you tunnel between houses, look out for some marvellous, ancient wooden doors and – watch out – you may find yourself in someone's backyard.

Close to the upper part of town, west of the main road, **Ksar Oudaghir** boasts a lovely 11th-century octagonal minaret. It's known as the *sawmann al hajaria* (tower of stone) and its design echoes the minarets of Mauritania and the Sahel (a semiarid zone between the Sahara and the Sudanian Savanna) rather than Morocco.

There's a limited number of accommodation options in Figuig. Ask at **La Maison de Nanna** (☎0536897570; www.maison-dhote-nanna-figuig.com; Rue Ouled Sellam, Ksar Zenaga; s/d incl full-board Dh300/600), a family home built of *pisé* in a *ksar*.

Always check transport options the day before travelling as schedules and availability of services can change. There's a daily CTM bus north to Oujda (Dh110, 5½ hours). All stop at Bouarfa (Dh40, two hours), where you can change for connections to Errachidia. You can't cross over to Algeria.

ZIZ VALLEY & THE TAFILALT

Snaking down through the dramatic Ziz Gorges from Rich, the Ziz River brings to life the last southern valley of the Ziz and the Tafilalt oases before ebbing away in the rose-gold dunes of Merzouga. Starting just south of the Middle Atlas town of Rich and about 30km north of Errachidia, the tremendous Ziz Gorges provide a rocky passage south through the Tunnel du Légionnaire (built by the French in 1928). To the south, the valley widens, presenting a spectacular sight: a dense canopy of palms wedged between ancient striated cliffs, which date to the Jurassic period. It's worth taking some time here to explore the rich, untouristed *palmeraies.*

The provincial capital is located in Errachidia, a convenient pit stop for those travelling north along the N13 to Midelt, Meknes and on to Fez.

Errachidia الرشيدية

POP 92,374

Established as a military garrison for the French Foreign Legion, the provincial capital of Errachidia is still home to a sizeable military population stationed here to keep an eye on the nearby border with Algeria. Much like Ouarzazate, it is an expanding modern town staking out ever-larger residential suburbs thanks to a significant injection of development funds. For those travelling north along the N13 to Midelt and Meknes, it can make a convenient lunch stop. Market days are Sunday, Tuesday and Thursday.

Despite its regional importance, Errachidia has a limited number of decent hotels, so you may want to push north for camping options at Meski and along the road south to Aoufous, or hold out for Merzouga.

If you're on your way to/from the Middle Atlas, Ismail's rural seven-room guesthouse **Gîte Luna del Fuego** (☎0632229501; www.lunadelfuego.info; Ksar Ifri; s/d €10/20) makes a perfect place to spend a night. It's 30km north of Errachidia, just off the N13. On the outskirts of Errachidia, the contemporary kasbah **Auberge Tinit** (☎0535791759; http://auberge-tinit.info; s/d/tr Dh300/500/700, incl half-board Dh350/600/800; wi-fi) was made with traditional materials and comes with 17 spartan but spotless en suite rooms, built around a swimming pool.

Errachidia has a few popular restaurants on the main road near the bus station, the best of which is **Restaurant Zerda** (Ave Moulay Ali Cherif; mains Dh30; ⏲9am-10pm).

Errachidia's Moulay Ali Cherif Airport is located about 4km northeast of the city centre. Royal Air Maroc (www.royalairmaroc.com) flies six times a week to/from Casablanca.

Buses operate out of the central **bus station** (Rue M'Daghra). CTM (www.ctm.ma) has daily and overnight services to Marrakesh (Dh170, 10 hours) and Meknes (Dh140, 7½ hours), and an overnight to Fez (Dh130, 7½ hours).

Private buses run to Ouarzazate (Dh75, six hours, three daily), Marrakesh (Dh150, 11 hours, three daily), Fez (Dh95 to Dh110, five daily), and Rissani (Dh25, two hours, nine daily) via Erfoud (Dh20).

Grands taxis depart three blocks northeast of the main bus station. Destinations include Erfoud (Dh30, one hour), Meknes (Dh120, five hours), Fez (Dh130, five hours), Tinerhir (Dh60, 1½ hours), Rissani (Dh30, 1½ hours) and Merzouga via Rissani (Dh35, 1½ hours).

Meski & Aoufous

Driving south along the N13 to Erfoud, you pass the origins of the Ziz River at Meski, 17km south of Errachidia. From here the road crests a desert plateau to a striking viewpoint over the Ziz *palmeraie* before descending to the town of Aoufous, 40km south of Errachidia, midway to Erfoud. Formidable *ksour* (fortified villages) line the route, peeking above the palm tops, and Aoufous has some stunning *pisé* (rammed-earth) buildings and an impressive ruined kasbah as well as useful services such as petrol and money.

The origins of the Ziz River can be found at **Source Bleue de Meski** (Meski), where warm, natural springs bubble to the surface beneath the Ksar Meski's picturesque remains. Downstream and across the river is an abandoned *ksar* fabulous for sunset views. The spring is signposted around 1km west of the main road.

To taste the fruits of the local date palms, visit the **Cooperative Al Ouaha** (Aoufous; Dh20; ⏲9am-noon Tue, Thu & Sat), signed on the main road past the village mosque on the left, next to the village commune.

For a contrast to the deserts of Merzouga, spend the night in one of the good-value guesthouses near the Ziz *palmeraie*, which also provide meals.

The welcoming **Maison d'Hôte Zouala** (☎0672144633; r per person incl half-board Dh300; 📶) makes a great base for exploring the palm grove. Hamid is a wealth of information on Ziz Valley culture and can arrange visits to the village school and a women's cooperative as well as excursions. It's located about 47km north of Erfoud. Look for a signed turn-off on the N13.

For gorgeous valley views above the swaying palms, head straight to the poolside terrace at **Maison Vallée de Ziz** (☎0661835151; www.facebook.com/MaisonValleeDuZiz; s/d incl half-board Dh250/600; 📶🏊). It makes a good lunch stop (Dh80) and guides Mohammed and Said can arrange excursions.

The palm-shaded **Camping Tissirt** (☎0662141378; http://campingtissirtziz.free.fr; per person/car/tent/caravan Dh15/15/15/30, bungalows Dh130; 📶) has three simple rammed-earth bungalows (shared bathrooms) at the edge of the palm grove 12km north of Aoufous. Showers (Dh10) and electricity (Dh25) are extra. They can arrange excursions and bicycles are also available for hire.

Public buses travel from Errachidia to a terminal above the Source Bleue spring (Dh5, 7am to 9pm). Any bus or grand taxi to Erfoud or Aoufous can drop you at the turn-off. When leaving, flag down a grand taxi from the main road.

Rissani الريصاني

POP 20,469

Rissani is where the Ziz River quietly ebbs away, but between the 14th and 18th centuries it was the location of the famed desert capital, Sijilmassa, where fortunes in gold and enslaved people were traded via caravans crossing the *sahel* (the zone between the Sahara to the north and the Sudanian savanna to the south). In fact Rissani was so strategic that the Filali (ancestors of the ruling Alaouite dynasty) staged their epic battle here to supplant the Saadians.

Today, Rissani is a dusty shadow of its former self. Barely a quarter of the population live in the 17th-century *ksar* (fortified granary) while the modern town constitutes a single street and one square. Still, echoes of the past can be heard in the epic haggling

WORTH A TRIP

FOSSILS IN ERFOUD

Erfoud lies in the heart of Morocco's fossil beds, and the Paleozoic strata south of the highway between Erfoud and Alnif are a prime hunting ground for diggers. Kilometres of shallow trenches have been hand-dug by Amazigh (Berber) miners in their search for trilobite fossils. Few of them are found in perfect condition so diggers take broken trilobites to 'prep' labs, where they are restored. Trilobite replicas can be made from plaster, plastic or auto-body putty, and can be hard to distinguish from real fossils.

For a good introduction to Morocco's fossils head to **Tahiri Museum of Fossils & Minerals** (☎0535576874; www.facebook.com/tahirimuseum; Route de Rissani; ⏱8am-7pm), Brahim Tahiri's private museum. Scientifically important specimens are exhibited beside their lesser cousins for sale in the boutique. Brahim's efforts at raising awareness of Morocco's rich geological heritage have even been recognised internationally with the naming of his very own trilobite, *Asteropyge tahiri.* You'll find the museum around 11km from Erfoud along the Rissani road – easily spotted by the life-size replicas of dinosaur skeletons out front. Prize fossils in museum display cases aren't for sale, but they do have some rare specimens for purchase and you can buy objects studded with more common trilobite and ammonite fossils.

CTM (☎0535576886; Place de FAR) runs to Errachidia (Dh30, 1¼ hours) and Rissani (Dh20, 25 minutes). **Supratours** (Place de FAR) has services to Merzouga (Dh40, one hour). **Grands taxis** (Place de FAR) run to Merzouga (Dh35, one hour), Rissani (Dh10, 20 minutes), Errachidia (Dh30, one hour) and Tinerhir (Dh65, five hours). All depart from Place des FAR.

over sheep and goats at Sunday, Tuesday and Thursday souqs.

With the dunes barely 35km further south, few people choose to spend the night in Rissani, visiting on a day trip from Erfoud or Merzouga. If you do need to stay, the **Hôtel Sijilmassa** (☎0535575042; hotel-sijilmassa@menara.ma; Place Al Massira Al Khadra; d with/without air-con Dh220/120; ❄📶) has clean air-conditioned rooms with cramped en suites at a convenient location near the bus and taxi stations, with cafes near here and the souq.

CTM (Place Al Massira) has an office in the centre of town. It runs one bus a day at 8pm to Meknes/Fez (Dh150/165, eight to nine hours) via Erfoud (Dh20, 30 minutes) and Errachidia (Dh40, 1¾ hours).

Supratours runs an evening service to Meknes (Dh140) and Fez (Dh140) via Errachidia (Dh40), a morning service to Marrakesh (Dh190, 12 hours) and an early morning and evening service to Merzouga (Dh30, 30 minutes).

Local buses leave from the central bus station, 400m north of the square on the road to Erfoud. There are services to Fez (Dh140, 13 hours) via Meknes (Dh110, nine hours) and to Marrakesh (Dh190, 10 hours). Buses run occasionally to Tinerhir (Dh40, six hours); check at the station for departures. There are six buses a day to Errachidia (Dh30, two hours) via Erfoud.

Grands taxis run frequently from opposite Hôtel Sijilmassa to Erfoud (Dh10), Errachidia (Dh30), Tinerhir (Dh75), Merzouga (Dh20) and occasionally Taouz (Dh30).

Sights

The ruins of Sijilmassa and the Circuit Touristique (Landmark Loop) are both signed off the N13 to the west of the town centre. More mud-brick *ksour* (fortified villages) flank the road to Merzouga, including Dar El Beidha and Ksar Haroun; look for signposts on your left leaving town.

Dune-bound visitors may be tempted to zoom through Rissani, but photographers, history buffs and architecture aficionados could spend a day exploring decrepit *ksour* (fortified villages) and artfully crumbling kasbahs on this 21km 'Landmark Loop'. It's best tackled in a clockwise direction from the regal ruins of **Ksar Abbar** – a favourite palace in exile for sidelined members of the Alaouite dynasty – past half a dozen crumbling *ksour* to the still-inhabited **Ksar Tinheras** situated on a rise offering spectacular views over the Tafilalt.

Also of note en route are **Zawiya Moulay Ali Ash Sharif** (⏱8am-6pm) FREE, the shrine built to honour the Alaouite dynasty's founder, and the royal **Ksar Oulad Abdelhalim**, a glorious 19th-century ruin with huge ramparts.

The circuit is signed 1.5km west of Rissani along the N13.

Sijilmassa RUINS

Little remains of the once-great city of Sijilmassa – just two decorated gateways and a handful of semi-collapsed structures. But go back to the 8th century and it was a major staging post for trans-Saharan trade, when caravans of up to 20,000 camels would depart for the salt mines of what is now modern-day Mali, then continue to Niger and Ghana, where a pound of Saharan salt was traded for an ounce of African gold.

Ksar El Fida HISTORIC BUILDING

(suggested donation Dh10; ⌚8am-7pm) This enormous, restored Alaouite kasbah (1854–72) served as the palace for the local *qaid* (chief) right up until 1965, after which it housed a museum of archaeology. Now only the son of the former owner remains and is happy to give you a short guided tour in French or Arabic.

Merzouga

POP 4150

When a wealthy family refused hospitality to a poor woman and her son, God was offended and buried them under the mounds of sand called Erg Chebbi. So goes the legend of the dunes rising majestically above the twin villages of Merzouga and Hassi Labied, which for many travellers fulfil Morocco's promise as a dream desert destination.

But Erg Chebbi's beauty coupled with Merzouga's accessibility has its price. Paved roads across the Middle Atlas from Midelt and east from Ouarzazate mean that desert tourism is booming and camps have sprung up like date palms in an oasis. In high season (spring and autumn) convoys of 4WDs churn up huge dust clouds as they race across the desert for sunset camel rides, and purists lament the encroachment of hotels flanking the western fringes of the dunes – although there's no denying the spectacular dune views from rooms and terraces.

Sights & Activities

The classic Merzouga excursion is to head into the desert and overnight in nomad-style tents. Plan on sunset camel rides, fireside music jams and star-filled nights, followed by an early morning walk to the tallest nearby dune to watch the sunrise. Invasive quads (dune buggies), which level dunes and disturb residents and wildlife, are not recommended.

★**Erg Chebbi** DUNES

Shape-shifting over 28km from north to south and reaching heights of 160m, the great sand sea of Erg Chebbi is extraordinarily scenic. The rose-gold dunes rise dramatically above a pancake-flat, grey *hamada* and turn stunning shades of orange, pink and purple as the sun sets.

Lac Dayet Srij BIRDWATCHING

(Merzouga Lake; Tamzgidat) At the southern end of Erg Chebbi, near Tamzgidat village, between November and May, you'll find this seasonal lake. It's one of the best areas in Morocco for spotting desert birds, including Egyptian nightjars, desert warblers, fulvous babblers and blue-cheeked bee-eaters, but in recent years the lake has been drier than normal.

Sleeping

Merzouga has a range of accommodation from simple family-run guesthouses to lavish kasbah-style hotels, between Hassi Labied to the north and Merzouga to the south; book in advance and check the exact location of your hotel. Bring warm clothing for overnight trips to the desert, as it can get very cold.

★**Chez Youssef** GUESTHOUSE €

(☎0666367174; www.chezyoussef.com; Merzouga Village; d/tr Dh420/580, incl half-board Dh540/760; 📶) Affable Youssef's simple *pisé* (rammed-earth) home offers four rooms arranged around a courtyard shaded by a single palm. The oasis-inspired decor is spare, but its spotlessly clean and the food is home-cooked. Also on offer are good-value camel treks and overnight stays in a peaceful camp far from the crowds (Dh600 per person), with a maximum of four people.

Chez Julia GUESTHOUSE €

(☎0535573182; www.chez-julia.com; d from Dh180; ❄📶) Pure charm in the heart of Merzouga village: seven simply furnished rooms (and three shared bathrooms) are decorated in sun-washed colours (rose, lemon, blue) with straw-textured *pisé* (rammed-earth walls), antique mantelpieces and white-tiled shared bathrooms, plus a furnished family apartment (Dh400 to Dh800). Ask about

Rissani & Merzouga

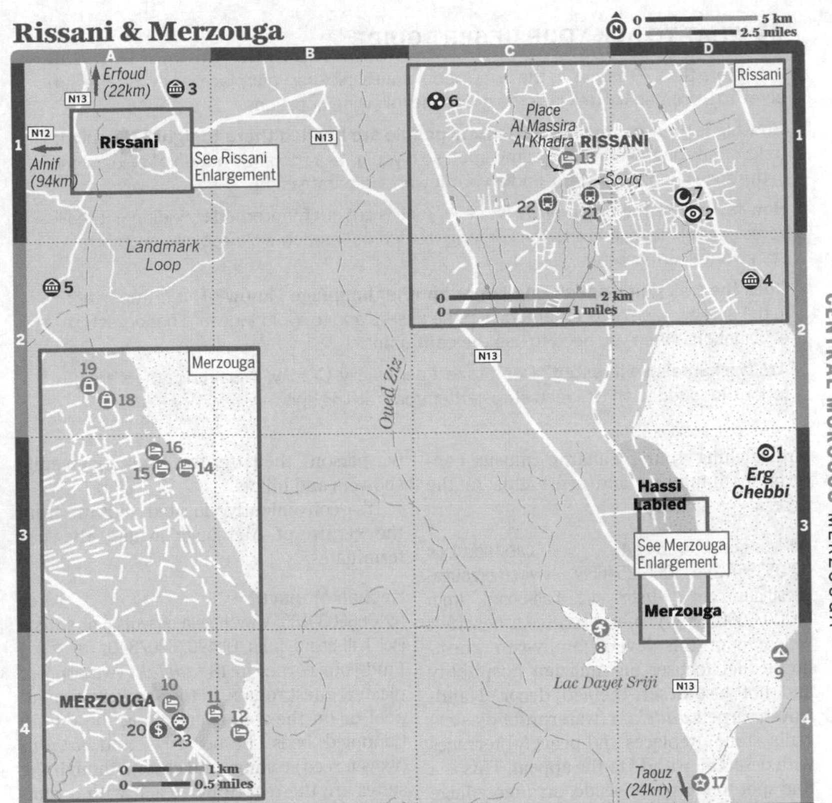

Rissani & Merzouga

Top Sights
1 Erg Chebbi D3

Sights
2 Ksar Abbar D1
3 Ksar El Fida A1
4 Ksar Oulad Abdelhalim D2
5 Ksar Tinheras A2
6 Sijilmassa C1
7 Zawiya of Moulay Ali Ash Sharif D1

Activities, Courses & Tours
8 Lac Dayet Srij C4

Sleeping
9 Ali & Sara's Desert Palace D4
10 Chez Julia A4
11 Chez Youssef A4
12 Hotel Riad Ali B4
13 Hôtel Sijilmassa C1
14 Kasbah Kanz Erremal A3
15 Kasbah Mohayut A3
16 Maison Merzouga A3

Entertainment
17 Dar Gnaoua D4

Shopping
18 Depot Nomade A2
19 La Dune Doré A2

Information
20 Al Barid Bank A4

Transport
21 CTM C1
22 Gare Routière C1
Grands Taxis .... (see 13)
23 Grands Taxis A4
Supratours Bus Stop .... (see 23)

WHAT TO ASK YOUR DESERT GUIDE

With more than 70 camps in the Erg Chebbi dunes, picking your place is key. Before you agree to a dromedary trek, ask the guide the following questions.

How big is your camp, and how many people are headed there tonight? Overnight treks often congregate in the same spot, so if you have a romantic notion of being alone in the dunes under the stars, find an outfit with a separate camp.

How far is it to the camp site? Not everyone is cut out for dromedary-riding – it makes some seasick, and others chafe. For long treks, bring motion-sickness pills and cornstarch or talcum powder.

Does the trek guide speak English or another language I know? This is important in the unlikely case of an emergency in the desert, and to avoid awkward hand-gesture explanations when you need to use the bathroom.

Are the camels well rested? Don't take it personally. Cranky, overtired camels are notorious for sudden shifts, dead stops and throat-rattling spitting.

birdwatching tours, Saharan music concerts, fossil-hunting and overnights in the desert.

★ Maison Merzouga GUESTHOUSE €€
(0535577299, 0661254658; www.merzouga-guesthouse.com; d/ste incl half-board from Dh700/1000;) Guests receive a heartfelt welcome at this lovely family-run guesthouse that focuses on Amazigh hospitality and not just desert-themed decor. Handwoven carpets, *tadelakt* (waterproof plaster) walls, stone fireplaces and peaceful terraces with desert views add to the appeal. This is a fine spot to lounge poolside, arrange village trips or set off to explore the desert with an in-the-know local.

Kasbah Kanz Erremal HOTEL €€
(0535578482; www.kanzerremal.com; d/tr/q Dh480/720/950;) Eschewing the rustic vibe of many other Merzouga hotels, Kanz Erremal favours understated style. Cushioned banquets line the airy, central courtyard while rooms with desert views are swathed in cool, white linens and gauzy curtains. Best of all is the wide terrace that almost touches the desert and a sleek infinity pool with dreamy dune views.

Hotel Riad Ali GUESTHOUSE €€
(0670624136; www.hotelriadali.com; s/d Dh450/650;) A mod kasbah provides instant relief from the white-hot desert with 11 guest rooms in Majorelle blue and lemon arranged around a shimmering courtyard pool. Overnight dromedary trips are led by an experienced, local official tour leader and includes standard, high-end or luxury bivouac accommodation (Dh450 to Dh1100 per person), the latter two boasting en suite showers and toilets.

It's conveniently located 600m from the centre of Merzouga where the bus terminates.

Kasbah Mohayut INN €€
(0666039185; www.hotelmohayut.com; s/d/ste incl half-board from Dh490/620/840;) Find your corner in 18 *tadelakt* (waterproof plaster) guest rooms, in the shade by a small pool or on the roof overlooking the dunes. Canopied beds, Berber rugs and *tataoui* (woven reed) ceilings add charm, though the suites are the real draw – each with a rooftop terrace complete with a cafe, well placed for taking in the desert views.

★ Merzouga Luxury Desert Camp TENTED CAMP €€€
(0661776766; http://merzougaluxurydesertcamps.com; d incl half-board Dh4100) Surrounded by towering dunes a mere 10km from Merzouga, this luxury desert camp offers spacious safari tents, complete with carved-wood furniture, top-quality mattresses and an en suite. Sunset camel rides, Amazigh (Berber) whisky round the campfire and a bountiful meal is followed by music and stargazing using the high-tech telescope. Arrive and depart by dromedary; a 4WD transfer is Dh600.

★ Ali & Sara's Desert Palace CAMPGROUND €€€
(0668950144; thedesertpalace@hotmail.com; per person all-inclusive Dh1000;) Make friends with Romeo, George and Casanova – no they aren't cheeky local lads, but your trusty dromedaries – as you head out from

Merzouga nomad-style. Husband-and-wife team, Ali and Sara, have crafted a personalised experience that stays true to Amazigh (Berber) culture and traditions, with authentic tents and stunning sunset views over the high dunes before a feast around the campfire.

Entertainment

★Dar Gnaoua LIVE MUSIC

(Khamlia; 9am-sunset) The hypnotic rhythms of Gnaoua may be associated with Essaouira but in the tiny enclave of Khamila, 6km south of Merzouga, people have stayed true to their sub-Saharan African culture and traditions. Dar Gnaoua is home to the Bambara group; just drop in, there are always musicians on hand to perform to an enthusiastic crowd. A CD (Dh100) makes a great souvenir.

Shopping

Chez Les Artistes ART

(0667412187; Khamlia; 9am-7pm Mon-Sat) Creative French-Amazigh (Berber) couple, Johanne and Lahcen, have set up a small, rammed-earth art gallery and cafe in the village of Khamlia. Her work is figurative, drawing inspiration from desert peoples, while he creates vibrant abstracts incorporating Amazigh symbols. They serve good coffee, too.

Depot Nomade ARTS & CRAFTS

(648886706; Hassi Labied; 8am-sunset) This tardis-like, rammed-earth store is a seemingly never-ending series of interconnected rooms that's a one-stop shop for Moroccan arts and crafts. You'll find everything from tightly woven kilim, to inlaid mirrors, studded leather bags and tribal jewellery. They also support the local initiative to encourage visitors not to give money to school-age children and to get them back in education.

La Dune Doré COSMETICS

(8am-7pm) Opened in 2016, this welcoming shop in Hassi Labied stocks high-quality products made in Morocco, including oils made from argan, almond, prickly pear and saffron – all of which offer alleged health benefits, ranging from improved circulation to cellulite reduction. Prices are fixed, so no hard bargaining required. You can also get henna painting on your hands (around Dh70).

OFF THE BEATEN TRACK

BEYOND THE END OF THE ROAD: OUZINA & ALNIF

People head to Taouz for that edge-of-the-world feel, and to spot mineral formations and possibly dinosaur bones where the desert swallows the road.

Instead of turning back at Taouz, you could take the *piste* (dirt track) by 4WD about one hour (30km) southwest towards the 2km stretch of dunes at **Ouzina**, a seldom-visited desert destination known only to Sahara savants. Here you'll find **Kasbah Ouzina** (0668986500; www.kasbahouzina.com; Ouzina; s/d incl half-board from €45/60), a small auberge with mercifully sand-free beds. At Ouzina the *piste* turns west toward the Draa Valley, heading 45km to **Mharje village**, where you can turn north onto a well-graded *piste* to Alnif, where it intersects with the tarmac road to Zagora. Otherwise, you could follow a bumpy *piste* from Taouz west towards the Draa Valley south of Zagora. Either way, the Taouz–Zagora journey takes at least seven hours, and you'll need a 4WD, GPS, plenty of water, petrol, food, a spare tyre, a mobile phone and a Sahara-savvy guide.

To visit local fossil sites around **Alnif** contact geologist Mohand Ihmadi, who leads short trips (Dh200 for the afternoon) from the **Ihmadi Trilobites Centre** (0666221593; alnifearth@gmail.com). Arrange a trek by phone or email, or stop off at his museum-cum-shop (9am to 5pm) on Alnif's main street to marvel at his collection.

Much of Morocco's Anti-Atlas Mountains are built of Paleozoic rocks, dating back to between 245 and 570 million years. When these rocks were deposited, a shallow sea covered the region. Trilobites scuttled along the sea floor, and huge schools of Orthoceras, squid-like nautiloids with cone-shaped shells, swam above. When they died, their shells were preserved in the region's slimy mud, awaiting resurrection as the polished curios that now fill Alnif's roadside shops. Prices depend on rarity, condition and the quality of the workmanship, and can range from a few dirhams to tens of thousands of dirhams for museum-quality specimens.

OFF THE BEATEN TRACK

DESERT PETROGLYPHS

The small desert town and oasis of Tazzarine is located in the heart of the Aït Atta tribal area, midway between Alnif and Nkob. Despite many years of drought, the palm groves and henna fields are still a pretty sight. Although there is little to stop for in the small straggling town, a few kilometres southwest you'll find the prehistoric site of **Aït Ouazik** (Aït Waaziq; 9am-sunset) with its wonderful petroglyphs clearly depicting images of elephants, giraffes, buffaloes and antelope. They date from about 5000 BCE when the area had a savannah-like character. It's close to Tazzarine but around 20km off road. Also south of Tazzarine is the small, but picturesque and rarely visited dunefield of Foum Tizza, an area of sand contrasting with blue-black rocks.

Local buses ply the road between Rissani and Zagora (six hours), via Alnif, Tazzarine and Nkob. More reliable, though, are grands taxis from Tazzarine to Alnif (Dh30, 1½ hours) and Ouarzazate (Dh75, four hours).

Getting There & Away

The N13 runs from Rissani to Merzouga. Most hotels are some distance from the road on marked *pistes* (dirt tracks); though these tracks are usually OK in a standard 2WD, don't head off-road as you're likely to get stuck in the sand. Minibuses will pick up or drop off in Hassi Labied – your hotel can make arrangements. Minivans run from Merzouga between 7.30am and 9.30am in high season (spring and autumn).

Supratours has a 7pm bus to Fez (Dh200, 9¼ hours). The bus stop is on Merzouga's main street, just off the highway leading north to Rissani.

Grands taxis leave from Merzouga centre heading north to Rissani (Dh15). Transport is harder to come by for Taouz to the south; you might have to hire out all six places (Dh100).

NKOB نقوب

POP 7209

Rather than retracing the N10 back to Marrakesh via Tinerhir and Ouarzazate, adventurous desert travellers opt for the N12, which links the Tafilalt with the Draa Valley. The road, which sees little traffic and few tourists, traces the southern foothills of Jebel Saghro via Alnif, Tazzarine and Nkob winding through dramatic, rocky landscapes as it passes through prime fossil-hunting territory. It joins the N9 to Marrakesh at Tansikht, 61km north of Zagora and 101km south of Ouarzazate. Kasbah-studded Nkob is the most atmospheric place to stay and provides a good base for Jebel Saghro treks and exploration.

One of Morocco's best-kept secrets is the Amazigh (Berber) oasis of Nkob (Nkoub), where 45 rammed-earth kasbahs make you stop and stare. The town has a dusty, bustling thoroughfare (which is also the main road leading in and out of town), where you can still find traditional craftsmen at work – but no banks.

The name Nkob comes from a cave in the area that once served as a lodging of sorts for Aït Atta nomads. Beyond town lie the deep green palms of the oasis and the looming mountains of Jebel Saghro.

Pass through for the **Sunday souq**, or visit **Aït Atta Chassures** (6am-9pm) opposite the post office for a wardrobe-sized emporium where cobblers bang out traditional walking sandals with coloured leather, rope and used tyre treads – more comfortable than they sound and surprisingly stylish.

For hikers, Nkob is a gateway for the five-day loop across Jebel Saghro along with shorter hikes to the spectacular rock pinnacles of Bab n'Ali. Also possible is a spectacular, white-knuckle off-road drive over the Tizi n'Tazazert pass (2283m) and through the swirling rock formations of the Taggourt Plateau before dropping down to Iknioun and the Dades Valley. Ask for info at the **Bureau des Guides** (WhatsApp 0667487509; mohamed_moroccotrek@hotmail.fr).

This is a great place to overnight, with good-value kasbah hotels scattered around town. Aside from a few basic places along the main road, dining options are limited and travellers eat where they're lodging.

Around 1km west of Nkob, **Auberge-Camping Ouadjou** (0524839314; www.ouadjou.com; r incl half-board from Dh250, campsite incl shower Dh100; P) offers welcome comforts for desert-weary travellers: small courtyard rooms with hot showers in en suite bathrooms, or camper van and tent pitches in the garden. Visitors ordering lunch can use the pool (around Dh100).

The beautifully restored **Kasbah Baha Baha** (☎0524839763; www.kasbahabaha.com; s/d/tr from Dh380/500/690, with shared bathroom Dh250/370/500; P 📶 🏊) comes with a gorgeous garden and striking oasis views. Gourmet meals (breakfast/dinner from Dh40/120) are served poolside. Rooms range from simple with shared bathrooms to pretty duplexes with private terraces, all attractively designed with local materials.

The friendly, well-priced **Kasbah Ennakhile** (☎0524839719; www.kasbah-nkob.com; s/d incl half-board Dh400/560; 📶 🏊) comes with all the essential creature comforts and multilingual staff. The expansive terrace and adjoining pool offer unobstructed views over the *palmeraie* and village. It's on the road leading east out of town, about 800m past the main square.

Rebuilt to *pisé* perfection, **Kasbah Hôtel Aït Omar** (☎0652030102; www.kasbah-hotel-aitomar.com; s/d €50/90; P 📶 🏊) has a 120-year-old crenellated rooftop and descending terraces offering unparalleled village views. Zigzagging staircases reveal private patios and 11 individually decorated rooms come with traditional touches. The separate Petite Kasbah offers simpler rooms with shared bathrooms (€30 to €40).

Key transit hubs are Rissani and Zagora, with buses in both directions on the road between the two. You'll also find grands taxis to/from Ouarzazate (Dh50), and a 7am CTM bus to Ouarzazate (Dh45, three hours) and on to Marrakesh (Dh135, 7½ hours).

AT A GLANCE

POPULATION
Casablanca: 3.36 million

LARGEST MOSQUE IN MOROCCO
Hassan II Mosque (p185)

BEST UNIQUE BOUTIQUE HOTEL
Villa Mandarine (p208)

BEST SURF-BUM HIDEAWAY
Hotel Le Kaouki (p246)

BEST SHELLFISH FEASTS
La Table de la Plage (p230)

WHEN TO GO

Mar–May Observe huge flocks of migrating birds on lagoons along the coast.

Jun Join world-music devotees at Essaouira's world-famous Gnaoua festival.

Sep Hit the beaches after the Moroccan tourists leave, while the weather's still good.

Hassan II Mosque (p185), Casablanca

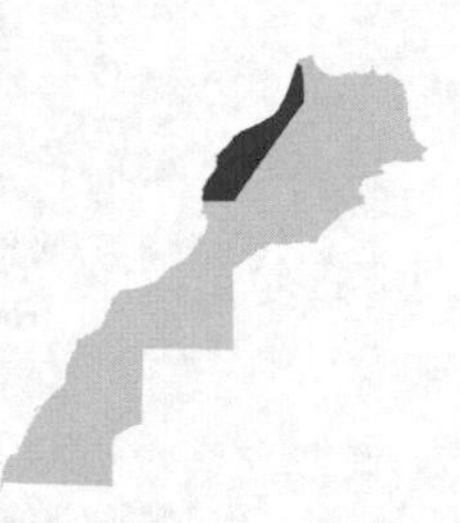

Northern Atlantic Coast

الساحل الأطلسي الشمالي

This windswept coast is home to Morocco's cultured capital, Rabat, and its economic hub, Casablanca. The refined Moorish architecture and liberal attitudes on display in both cities are a far cry from the medieval medinas and conservative lifestyles of cities such as Fez and Marrakesh.

There's more to see than these big cities, though. Vast swathes of golden sand, small fishing villages, historic ports built by the Portuguese and fortified towns with vibrant medinas are scattered along the ocean's edge. Outside the towns, farmland rolls gently down to the sea and wetland reserves showcase rich birdlife in autumn and spring. The region is bookended by Asilah and Essaouira, famed for their medinas and surrounding beaches.

INCLUDES

Northern Atlantic Coast Highlights

1 Essaouira (p232) Wandering through the oceanside medina and watching traditional wooden boats being constructed in the bustling port.

2 Rabat (p200) Exploring the historic walled medina and evocative kasbah.

3 Oualidia (p228) Feasting on freshly shucked oysters next to a tranquil lagoon.

4 Casablanca (p185) Admiring this cosmopolitan city's treasure trove of neo-Moorish, art nouveau and art deco architecture.

5 Merja Zerga National Park (p219) Spotting rare migrating birds from a boat on the marshy wetlands.

Casablanca الدار البيضاء

POP 3.36 MILLION

Morocco's economic and commercial hub, Casablanca is the best representation of the modern nation. This is where money is being made, where young Moroccans come to seek their fortunes and where business and the creative industries prosper.

The city's handsome 20th-century buildings, which often meld French-colonial design and traditional Moroccan style, are best admired in the downtown area. Visitors who spend time there, in the Quartier Habous and in the beachside suburb of Aïn Diab, are sure to get into the local swing of things and realise that this old pirate lair is looking towards the future, embracing the European-flavoured urban sophistication that has underpinned life here for the past century.

There's a large number of urban regeneration and construction projects underway, including the reinvention of L'Eglise du Sacré Coeur as a cultural centre and the opening of the largest theatre in Africa, the architecturally stunning Grand Théâtre de Casablanca.

History

The Phoenicians established a small trading port in the now-upmarket seaside suburb of Anfa in the 6th century BCE that by the early 15th century was a safe haven for pirates and racketeers. They became such a threat that the Portuguese sent 50 ships to subdue them and, in 1575, they arrived to stay, erecting fortifications and renaming the port Casa Branca (White House).

The Portuguese abandoned the colony in 1755 and nothing remains of their tenure, but by the mid-1800s a booming Europe turned to Morocco for increased supplies of grain and wool, and merchants flocked back to the city. The Spanish renamed it Casablanca, which stuck, and by the beginning of the 20th century the French had secured permission to build an artificial harbour.

Increased trade brought prosperity to the region, but the activities and influence of the Europeans also caused resentment. Violence erupted in 1907 when Europeans desecrated a Muslim cemetery. The procolonialist French jumped at the chance to send troops to quell the dispute and by 1912, Casablanca was part of the new French protectorate, and became its main port. It remains one of the largest in Morocco.

Sights

Casablanca is more concerned with business than tourism. Tourists are thin on the ground and there are remarkably few traditional attractions. Other than the impressive Hassan II Mosque, the city's main attraction lies in its neighbourhoods: the showstopping 20th-century architecture of the downtown area, the pretty Quartier Habous and the upmarket beachfront suburbs of Anfa and Aïn Diab.

★Hassan II Mosque MOSQUE

(Map p186; Blvd Sidi Mohammed Ben Abdallah; guided tours adult/child 4-12yr Dh120/30; tours 9am, 10am, 11am & 3pm) This opulent mosque, built at enormous expense, is set on an outcrop jutting over the ocean with a 210m-tall minaret that's a city landmark. It's a showcase of the finest Moroccan artisanship: hand-carved stone and wood, intricate marble flooring and inlay, gilded cedar ceilings and exquisite *zellige* (geometric mosaic tilework) abound. It's one of two Moroccan mosques open to non-Muslims; multilanguage guided tours are conducted outside prayer times for modestly clad visitors. There's also a small museum showcasing the craftwork involved.

One of the largest mosques in Africa, it can hold 105,000 worshippers – 25,000 inside, the rest on the outside courtyards. Built and partially funded by King Hassan II (the remaining funds were gathered through a somewhat controversial public subscription process), the mosque complex was designed by French architect Michel Pinseau, took six years to build and was completed in 1993.

Its dramatic location overhanging the ocean waves echoes verse from the Quran, which states that God's throne was built upon the water. Believers pray on a floor that can be heated when necessary, and can feel the breeze through the retractable roof in warmer months.

The size and elaborate decoration of the prayer hall is simply spectacular. A team of more than 6000 master craftspeople was assembled to work on the mosque, delicately carving intricate patterns and designs in fragrant cedar wood from the Middle Atlas and pink granite from Agadir. The gates were made from brass and titanium, and the ablution fountains in the basement, which are shaped like huge lotus flowers, were carved from local marble.

To see the interior, visitors must be 'decently and respectfully dressed' (knees and

Casablanca

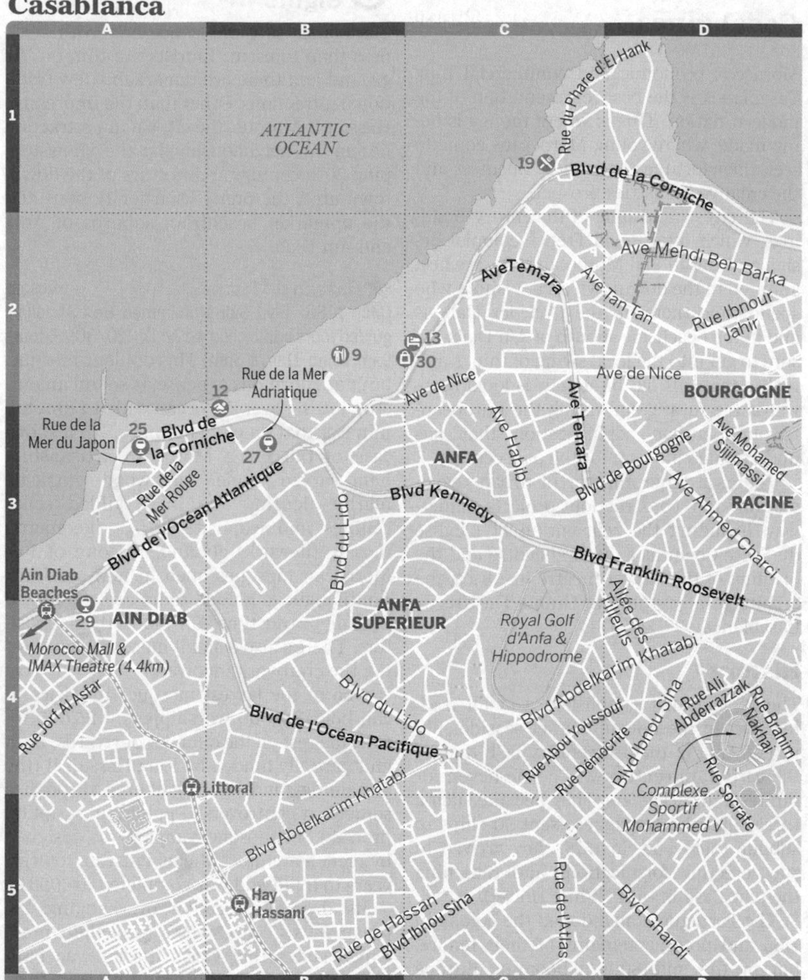

upper arms covered); women don't require a headscarf. Tours last around 45 minutes and are conducted in French, English, German and Spanish, and take in the prayer hall and subterranean ablutions rooms.

The **hammams** (Map p186; ☎0522472763; Dh50, treatments Dh90-450) have opened under private management and they're as stunning as you'd expect, with acres of marble, lofty domed ceilings and gilt fittings. There is a range of packages, from a simple scrub to more elaborate wraps and massage, though sadly the service doesn't quite live up to the setting.

West of the mosque, one of the city's major urban regeneration projects has turned the stretch of **seafront promenade** (Map p186) from the Hassan II Mosque to the El Hank lighthouse in to a sweeping public space, with gardens, cafes and endless ocean views.

Downtown

It's often said that Casablanca has no sights apart from the Hassan II Mosque, but the French-built centre is packed with grand examples of 20th-century architecture, some of which are being restored.

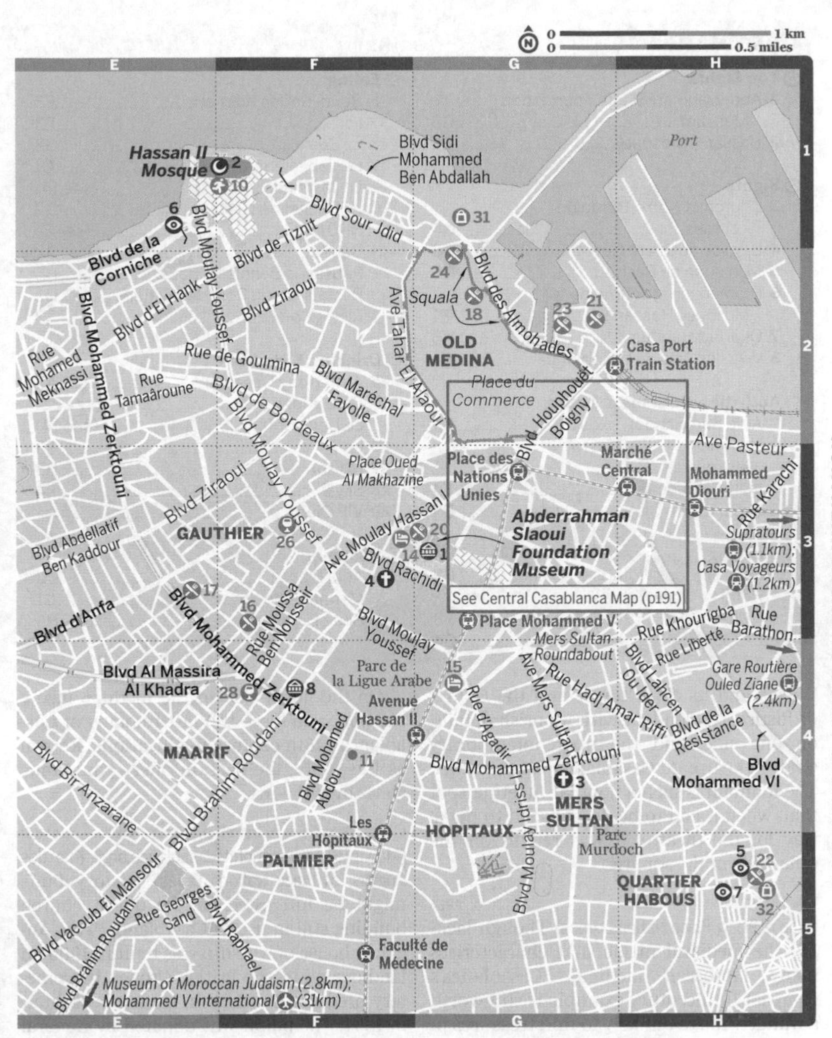

★ **Abderrahman Slaoui Foundation Museum** MUSEUM

(Map p186; ☎0522206217; http://musee-as.ma; 12 Rue du Parc; Dh60; ⏲10am-6pm Tue-Sat; 🚋Place Mohammed V) This privately owned house-turned-museum showcases Abderrahman Slaoui's outstanding collection of Moroccan decorative arts, from Orientalist travel posters to ornate Amazigh (Berber) jewellery encrusted with semiprecious stones, inlaid furniture (including pieces designed by Marrakesh-based Louis Majorelle), to exquisite perfume flasks. Take a sightseeing break with a mint tea at the terrace cafe.

Villa des Arts de Casablanca GALLERY

(Map p186; ☎0522295087; www.fondationona.ma; 30 Blvd Brahim Roudani; ⏲9.30am-7pm Tue-Sun; 🚋Avenue Hassan II) FREE Set in a beautiful art deco villa dating from 1934, this small gallery is operated by the nonprofit Fondation ONA. It stages interesting temporary exhibitions by contemporary Moroccan artists, and works to promote art and culture to schoolchildren and students.

Place Mohammed V SQUARE

(Map p191; Ave Hassan II; 🚋Place Mohammed V) This perpetually busy square is surrounded by striking public buildings, such as the

Casablanca

Top Sights
1 Abderrahman Slaoui Foundation Museum ... G3
2 Hassan II Mosque ... F1

Sights
3 Church of Notre-Dame de Lourdes ... G4
4 L'Eglise du Sacré Coeur ... F3
5 Mahakma du Pasha ... H5
6 Promenade Maritime de la Mosquée Hassan II ... E1
7 Quartier Habous ... H5
8 Villa des Arts de Casablanca ... F4

Activities, Courses & Tours
9 Anfa Surf School ... B2
10 Hammams of the Hassan II Mosque ... F1
11 Institut Français ... F4
12 Tahiti Beach Club ... B3

Sleeping
13 Four Seasons Hotel Casablanca ... C2
14 Hôtel Le Doge Relais & Châteaux ... F3
15 Le 135 Hôtel ... G4

Eating
16 Bondi Coffee Kitchen ... F3
17 Iloli ... E3
18 La Sqala ... G2
19 Le Cabestan Ocean View ... C1
Le Jasmine ... (see 14)
20 Le Rouget de L'isle ... G3
NKOA ... (see 8)
21 Ostréa ... G2
22 Pâtisserie Bennis Habous ... H5
23 Restaurant du Port de Pêche ... G2
24 Rick's Café ... G2

Drinking & Nightlife
25 Armstrong Casablanca ... A3
Cafe Imperial ... (see 22)
Le Doge Cafe ... (see 14)
26 Le Trica ... F3
27 Maison B ... B3
28 Sky 28 ... F4
29 VIP Club ... A4

Shopping
30 Anfa Place ... C2
31 Marina Shopping ... G1
32 Souq Habous ... H5

Wilaya and its clock tower and the Courts of Justice, resplendent with Moorish details, on one side, and the ubercontemporary Grand Théâtre de Casablanca on the other. The fountain is such a popular meeting spot that, when it had to be demolished to make way for the theatre, it was rebuilt on the other side of the square.

Old Medina AREA

(Map p191; Place Nations Unies) Though lacking the medieval magic that characterises many Moroccan medinas, Casablanca's compact 19th-century example is still worth a wander. You're unlikely to find treasures in its everyday shops (hardware stores, pharmacies and shops selling cheap clothing and shoes predominate), but its whitewashed crooked lanes, occasional tree-shaded square and buzzy local cafes make it a popular route for those walking between downtown Casablanca and the Hassan II Mosque.

The most heavily used entrances are through Bab Marrakech on Ave Tahar El Alaoui or through the gate next to the rebuilt **clock tower** (Map p191) at the northeast corner of Place des Nations Unies. The narrow lanes near these gates are where most shops are found; the rest of the medina remains largely residential.

On the north side of the medina, facing the port, you'll see the last remains of Casablanca's 18th-century fortifications. Known as the **sqala**, the bastion offers panoramic views over the sea.

Church of St John the Evangelist CHURCH

(Map p191; www.stjohnscasablanca.org; Rue des Anglais; Place Nations Unies) History buffs might be interested in the oldest church building still in use in Casablanca. This Anglican house of worship was built in 1906 on land owned by the British Crown. Its cemetery predates the church, having been built in 1864. The pulpit was donated by General George Patton, the WWII general who led Allied troops ashore at Safi in November 1942 as part of Operation Torch.

Church of Notre-Dame de Lourdes CHURCH

(Map p186; cnr Ave Mers Sultan & Blvd Mohammed Zerktouni; Avenue Hassan II) A striking example of European modernist architecture, this 1956 Catholic church is notable for its elongated concrete entrance and its stunning stained-glass windows, which were designed by noted French artist Gabriel Loire. It overlooks the Rond-point de l'Europe (aka Mers Sultan Roundabout). The church plays host to occasional concerts; check the notice board for details.

Quartier Habous (Nouvelle Medina)

Also known as Nouvelle Medina (New Medina), the **Quartier Habous** (Map p186), about 2.5km southeast of Place Mohammed V, is Morocco lite – an idealised version of a traditional medina with clean streets, attractive Moorish buildings and arcades, neat rows of shop stalls and even a small park. Built by the French in the 1930s, it was a unique experiment: a medina built to Western standards to accommodate the first rural exodus in the 1920s. Though undeniably ersatz, it blends Moroccan architecture with French ideals very successfully, and its tourist-centric souq offers excellent opportunities to source souvenirs.

The **Royal Palace** (closed to the public) is to the north of the district, while to the south is the old **Mahakma du Pasha** (Map p186; Blvd Victor Hugo), which has more than 60 rooms decorated with sculpted wooden ceilings, stuccowork, wrought-iron railings and tiled floors; although it's not always open to visitors.

Quartier Oasis

Museum of Moroccan Judaism MUSEUM
(0522994940; www.jewishmuseumcasa.com; 81 Rue Chasseur Jules Gros; Dh50; 10am-5pm Mon-Fri, 11am-4pm Sun; Gare de l'Oasis) The only Jewish museum in the Arabic-speaking world, this institution is set in an attractive garden villa that once functioned as a Jewish orphanage. It traces the 2000-year history of Jews in Morocco, focusing on Casablanca's Jewish community (most of the country's Jews live here). The thoughtfully curated and well-labelled collection includes ornate clothing, traditional tools and ritual objects. Photographs usually feature in the temporary exhibition space, and there's a reconstructed 1930s synagogue from Larache in an adjoining room.

The museum is 1km from the Gare de l'Oasis tram stop. From the tram stop, walk down Route de l'Oasis past the train station then turn right into Rue Abu Dhabi. Rue Chasseur Jules Gros is the sixth street to the left. A taxi from the city centre will cost Dh40, but note that most taxi drivers are unaware of the museum's existence so will need to be given directions. Also note that it is sensible to call ahead to check that the museum is open as it sometimes closes when the security situation is unsettled. Students are given free entry on Wednesday.

Courses & Tours

Casablanca has a multitude of language schools, including a French school with qualifications approved by the French Ministry of Education.

Institut Français LANGUAGE
(Map p186; 0522779870; https://if-maroc.org/casablanca; 121-123 Blvd Mohammed Zerktouni; 8.30am-6.30pm Mon-Sat, 10am-2pm Sun; Avenue Hassan II) This longstanding cultural centre has been putting on events, including

CASABLANCA IN...

One Day

Start your day by visiting the city's major landmark and tourist drawcard, the **Hassan II Mosque** (p185). Next, head to **La Sqala** (p195) for lunch, before wandering through the **Old Medina** (p188) and taking an architecture-focused stroll around the downtown area. In the evening, pay homage to a cinematic classic by dining at **Rick's Café** (p195) or head to the beachside suburb of Aïn Diab to enjoy the Morocco-meets-Mediterranean menu at ultrachic **Le Cabestan** (p196).

Two Days

With another day to enjoy the city, start in the Quartier Habous, where you can pick up some souvenirs at the souq and buy a selection of Moroccan pastries at **Pâtisserie Bennis Habous** (p194) – enjoy them with a good coffee at **Cafe Imperial** (p195). In the afternoon, pop into the **Abderrahman Slaoui Foundation Museum** (p187) to admire its collection of Moroccan decorative arts, check out an exhibition at the **Villa des Arts de Casablanca** (p187) and then finish the day by enjoying an excellent French dinner at old-fashioned favourite **Restaurant Brasserie La Bavaroise** (p196) followed by a drink and a dance at **La Bodéga** (p195).

ARCHITECTURE OF CASABLANCA

The first French resident-general, Hubert Lyautey, hired French architect and urban planner Henri Prost to redesign Casablanca in the early 20th century as the economic centre of the new protectorate and the jewel of the French colonies. In turn, Prost enlisted the help of some of Europe's top architects; his wide boulevards and modern urban planning still survive, as does much of the rich architectural heritage of the era, a unique mix of art deco, and neo-Moorish design.

Lyautey underestimated the success of his own plans and the city grew far beyond his elaborate schemes. By the end of WWII, Casablanca had a population of 700,000 and was surrounded by heaving shanty towns. These have only recently been demolished – often controversially – and their residents rehoused on the outer urban edge of the city.

To really understand the significance of Casablanca's 20th-century buildings, take a private tour with a local architect from **Casamémoire Architecture Tours** (☎0522474333; visites.casamemoire@gmail.com), a nonprofit organisation that's spearheading a campaign for the city to be recognised by Unesco. Tours last around three hours and there are four areas to choose from; free, but donations welcome (suggested donation per person around Dh150). Email to book at least 10 days in advance. It also holds annual **heritage days** (☎0522474333; ⌚Apr) with free architecture tours around different areas of the city.

films and concerts, and offering French-language courses of various lengths for more than 50 years. And it's the only place in the city with qualifications approved by the French Ministry of Education.

Taste of Casablanca Food Tour FOOD & DRINK

(☎0630847014; https://tasteofcasablanca.com; tours from US$90) Get a taste of Casablanca through its food. Go off the tourist trail on a three-hour street-food tour, trying out different breads, pastries and juices, enjoy a seafood feast at the Marché Central, or explore the coast and experience a Moroccan-style BBQ with *kefta* (meatballs) and *brochettes* (kebabs). This highly recommended outfit also offers dining with a family and cooking classes.

Festivals & Events

Sbagha Bagha Casablanca Street Art Festival ART

(www.sbaghabagha.ma; ⌚Jul) This festival sees street artists from Morocco and around the globe adorning the city's white-walled apartment blocks with vibrant monumental murals. The programme includes exhibitions and a graffiti battle. Watch this art space.

Jazzablanca MUSIC

(www.jazzablanca.com; ⌚Jul) This longstanding festival mixes up famous and up-and-coming jazz – along with pop, rock, blues and funk – artists from Morocco and around the globe. More than 40 concerts are spread over nine days and two venues – the Casa-Anfa racecourse plays host to the main stage, while the Village also holds workshops on food and fashion. Check the website for dates.

L'Boulevard Festival of Casablanca CULTURAL

(http://boulevard.ma; Stade du R.U.C.; ⌚Sep; Hay Andia) This 10-day music and arts festival celebrates Morocco's urban culture with an impressive line-up of local and international artists from a host of musical genres. There's also a battle of the bands competition for young musicians, with the winners getting to share the stage with big-name acts.

Sleeping

Occupancy rates and prices are higher here than in most other Moroccan cities, so it's always a good idea to book your accommodation in advance.

Budget hotels here are almost uniformly poor value – check for cleanliness before booking in – and good midrange options are few and far between. Top-end options predominantly cater to business travellers.

Hotel Guynemer HOTEL €

(Map p191; ☎0522275764; hotelguynemer@yahoo.com; 2 Rue Mohammed Belloul; s/d Dh350/450, ste s/d Dh450/650; P; Place Mohammed V) Cheap and cheerful, the Guynemer has

Central Casablanca

Central Casablanca

Sights

1	Central Market Post Office	C2
2	Church of St John the Evangelist	A2
3	Main Post Office	A3
4	Old Medina	A1
5	Place Mohammed V	A4

Sleeping

6	Hôtel Astrid	B4
7	Hotel Guynemer	B3
8	Hôtel Les Saisons	C1
9	Hôtel Maamoura	C3
10	Hyatt Regency Casablanca	A2

Eating

11	Dar Beida	A2
12	La Bodéga	D2
13	La Taverne du Dauphin	C1
14	Marché Central	D2
15	Restaurant Brasserie La Bavaroise	D2

Drinking & Nightlife

16	Café Alba	B3
17	Petit Poucet	C2

Entertainment

18	Cinéma Rialto	C3
19	Grand Théâtre de Casablanca	A4

Transport

20	Avis	D1
21	Budget	C2
22	Bus 10 to Gare Routière Ouled Ziane	B2
23	CTM Bus Station	D2
24	Petits Taxis	C2

survived several renovations with many of its original 1930s features intact. Regular rooms are comfortable but slightly cramped, especially the bathrooms; suite rooms are better sized. All have double-glazed windows, satellite TV and comfortable beds.

Hôtel Astrid HOTEL €

(Map p191; ☎0522277803; hotelastrid@hotmail.com; 12 Rue 6 Novembre; s/d excl breakfast Dh330/440; wi-fi; tram Place Mohammed V) Though it's in need of a revamp, this dated budget option is worth considering as it's clean, offers good wi-fi and the staff are helpful. Cash only; breakfast an extra Dh35.

★**Hôtel Les Saisons** HOTEL €€

(Map p191; ☎0522490901; www.hotellessaisonsmaroc.ma; 19 Rue El Oraïbi Jilali; s/d/ste Dh675/875/1140; wi-fi; tram Place Nations Unies) In a central location in downtown, this small and efficiently run modern hotel offers good-sized, clean and comfortable rooms, a decent breakfast and an in-house restaurant serving alcohol. Friendly and helpful staff are always on hand to offer travel tips.

Hôtel Maamoura HOTEL €€

(Map p191; ☎0522452967; www.hotelmaamoura.com; 59 Rue Ibnou Batouta; s/d/tr Dh450/600/700; P wi-fi; tram Marché Central) Popular with small tour companies and regular visitors to the city, this well-priced hotel offers clean and spacious rooms, a good breakfast and helpful staff. Wi-fi can be patchy.

★**Four Seasons Hotel Casablanca** HOTEL €€€

(Map p186; ☎0529073700; www.fourseasons.com/casablanca; Blvd de la Corniche, Anfa; d excl breakfast from Dh2666; P wi-fi pool) This contemporary seaside hotel pays homage to local craftsmanship with beaten brass doors and polished plasterwork. Rooms are light-filled and stylish, there's a modern Moroccan restaurant and ocean views from fish restaurant Bleu (no alcohol). When not lounging by the heated pool, guests are often found in the luxe spa or around the fire pit on the terrace.

★**Hôtel Le Doge Relais & Châteaux** BOUTIQUE HOTEL €€€

(Map p186; ☎0522467800; www.hotelledoge.com; 9 Rue Docteur Veyre; r Dh1750-2100, ste Dh2600-3000; P wi-fi; tram Place Mohammed V) This downtown 1930s villa has been lovingly restored to its art deco splendour, with 16 individually decorated rooms dressed in period furnishings, and a showstopping spiral staircase leading to a rooftop-terrace restaurant with views over the city. There's also an atmospheric Moroccan restaurant – beautifully decorated with stained glass and wood panelling – and a small spa with a marble hammam.

City Walk Downtown Casablanca

START L'EGLISE DU SACRÉ COEUR, BLVD RACHIDI
END PLACE DU 16 NOVEMBRE
LENGTH 3KM; ONE HOUR

Central Casablanca has a rich architectural heritage, dominated by a style of architecture commonly known as neo-Moorish (neo-Mauresque in French). Developed in the 1920s and 1930s, this blend of French-colonial design and traditional Moroccan style was heavily influenced by the art deco and art nouveau movements – hallmarks include ornate wrought-iron balconies, rounded exterior corners and decorative facades and friezes. These were incorporated alongside traditional Moroccan features such as arches, cupolas, columns, *mashrabiyas* (wooden-lattice screens), *muqarnas* (decorative plaster vaulting) and richly coloured *zellige* (geometric mosaic tilework).

This walking tour identifies some of the most notable examples in the downtown precinct, along with a few art deco and art nouveau gems.

Start on the northwest edge of the Parc de la Ligue Arabe at the unusual white **1 L'Eglise du Sacré Coeur** (Map p186; Blvd Rachidi; tram Place Mohammed V), an extraordinary architectural meld of the art deco, Moorish and neo-Gothic styles, with twin towers that resemble minarets and decorative aperture-style windows. Closed at the time of research, it was set to reopen as a cultural centre.

Continue southeast along Blvd Rachidi to **2 Place Mohammed V** (p187) surrounded by impressive administrative buildings, with the 1930s **3 Wilaya** (old police headquarters, now governor's office) dominating the south side. Though topped by a modernist clock tower, the upper-storey detailing of the Wilaya has pronounced Gothic and Islamic echoes, making it a true architectural oddity.

The **4 Tribunal de Premiere Instance** (*palais de justice* or law courts) dates from 1925. Its main entrance, with its stucco and tile detailing, was inspired by the Persian *iwan*, a vaulted hall that opens into the central court of the *medersa* (school) of a mosque.

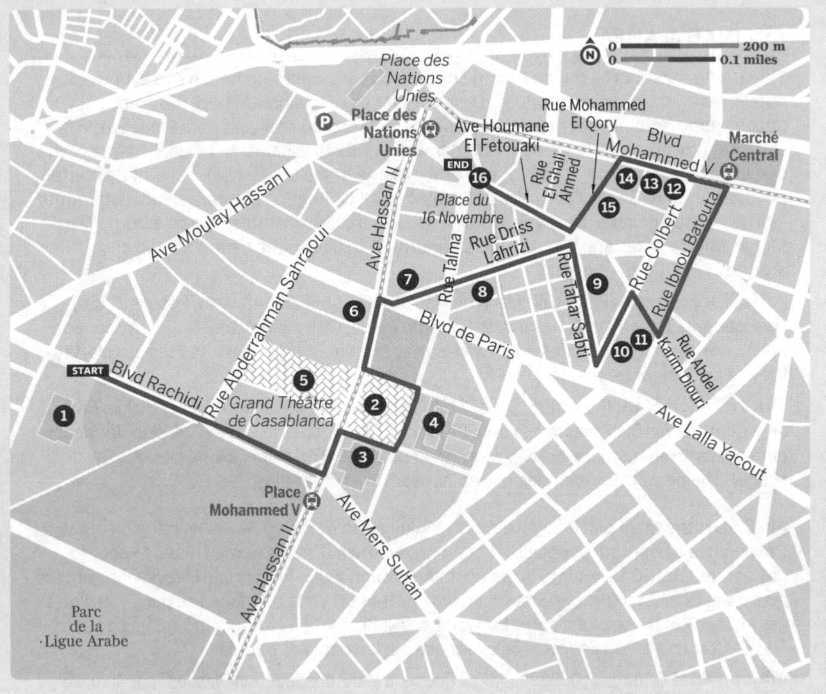

Dominating the western side of the square is the dazzlingly white, ultra contemporary **5 Grand Théâtre de Casablanca** (p197) designed by a Pritzker Prize–winning architect. The largest theatre in Africa, it's a multidisciplinary art space including two halls that can hold up to 2400 people, and a music space for 300.

To the north of the square is Casablanca's **6 main post office**, built between 1918 and 1920, fronted by arches and stone columns and decorated with art nouveau–style mosaics. The carved stucco on the facade of the nearby **7 Banque Al Maghrib** on Blvd de Paris, and the ornate main door with its *mashrabiya*-style detailing, reference traditional Moroccan architecture, although the building's form is decidedly modern. From here, walk east on Rue Driss Lahrizi, where impressive facades line both sides of the street. The most striking of these is **8 La Princière Salon de Thé**, with its huge stone crown on the roofline.

Next, turn right into Rue Tahar Sabti, which is lined with colonial buildings that are now apartments, hotels and offices. The most impressive of these is the art deco **9 Hotel Amouday** at No 51, with its distinctive ocean-liner-style design.

Take a V-turn left into Rue Colbert and look for **10 Hôtel Transatlantique**, a handsome building dating from 1922. The filigree-like detailing surrounding the main entrance is quite striking. Then turn right into Rue Abdul Karim Diouri to find **11 Hotel Volubilis** with its recessed balcony, burnished-gold detailing and art nouveau signage.

Turn left up Rue Ibnou Batouta and continue to the corner of Blvd Mohammed V. Next, turn left and look out for an array of wonderful facades along the street's south side. The **12 Central Market Post Office**, with its delicate motifs, and **13 Le Matin/Maroc Soir**, with its classic style, are two of the most impressive.

At the end of this block, on the corner of Rue Mohammed El Qory, is **14 Petit Poucet** (Map p191; 9am-10pm), a bar-cafe once frequented by Antoine de Saint-Exupéry, Édith Piaf and Albert Camus, but now past its prime. Turn left here into Rue Mohammed El Qory to find the **15 Cinéma Rialto** (p197), a hardly changed art deco gem where the 1942 film *Casablanca* is still occasionally screened. Continue south to the junction with Ave Houmane El Fetouaki and turn right to reach **16 Place du 16 Novembre**, home to plenty of art deco buildings.

AÏN DIAB & ANFA

These affluent suburbs on the Atlantic beachfront are lined with beach clubs, upmarket hotels, restaurants, bars and clubs. Long the city's entertainment hub, the area is now equally popular for its shopping, courtesy of the Morocco Mall and Anfa Place (p198).

The sandy beach at Aïn Diab is popular with young locals but isn't clean, so those who can afford to do so tend to pay for day entry to one of the beach clubs. One of the better ones is the Tahiti Beach Club, with swimming pools, loungers, umbrellas and restaurants.

The Casablanca tramway goes to Aïn Diab, where it terminates. The ride from Place Mohammed V takes approximately 35 minutes. A taxi from the centre should cost around Dh35 (Dh70 at night).

Anfa Surf School (Plage Lalla Meryem; Map p186; ☎0668289148; Anfa; lessons Dh150) Upscale Anfa Beach stretches in front of Anfa Place, with a palm-tree-lined promenade and some international cafes – the waves may not be as impressive as Essaouira's, but they're perfect for beginners.

Tahiti Beach Club (Map p186; ☎0522798025; www.facebook.com/Tahitibeachclub; Blvd de la Corniche, Aïn Diab; adult/child from Dh150/50; ; Aïn Diab Plage) This popular beach club offers three restaurants, two swimming pools, a gym, a spa, a kids club and a surf school. The entry price includes use of loungers and umbrellas.

Aïn Diab is the main place for late-night drinking and dancing. However, hanging out with Casablanca's beautiful people for a night on the town doesn't come cheap. Expect to pay at least Dh150 to get into any club and as much again for a drink. Heavyset bouncers guard the doors and practise tough crowd control – if you don't look the part, you won't get in. Many of these clubs cater for well-heeled Gulf Arabs (a Saudi prince has a palace on the Corniche), and Egyptian or Lebanese performers are popular.

Maison B (Map p186; ☎0698999442; 5 Rue de la Mer Adriatique, Aïn Diab; 7pm-4am) As glam as Casa's club scene gets, this spot near the Anfa Place has a restaurant serving Mediterranean and Asian food. It's particularly popular in the warmer months, when its terrace area is invariably packed on weekends. The music is good with international DJs, the service less so.

Armstrong Casablanca (Map p186; ☎0613086045; 1 Rue de la Mer du Japon, Aïn Diab; 11pm-4am) One of the few clubs in town where you can dance to live music, with a different theme every night – Tuesday is open mic night, Wednesday is Afro Jam and Friday night is party night with DJs as well as live bands.

Le 135 Hôtel HOTEL €€€
(Map p186; ☎0522279112; www.le135hotelcasablanca.com; 135 Ave Hassan II, Ville Nouvelle; s/d/tr excl breakfast Dh1400/1800/1900; P; Avenue Hassan II) The 13 bright rooms at Le 135 come with comfortable beds and all mod cons. Breakfast costs Dh80 per person, and parking is Dh40 per night.

Hyatt Regency Casablanca HOTEL €€€
(Map p191; ☎0522431234; https://casablanca.regency.hyatt.com; Place des Nations Unies; r Dh2200-2600, ste Dh3900-27,000; P; Place Nations Unies) Its central location means that this five-star hotel is a popular meeting place for Casablancais, who enjoy lunch at Café M, a coffee or drink in the foyer, or a meal at swish Moroccan restaurant **Dar Beida** (mains Dh190-270; 7pm-2am;). Rooms are spacious, businesslike and well equipped; facilities include a fitness centre and an outdoor pool. Service is both polished and friendly.

Eating

The city has everything from fast-food joints to fine-dining fusion restaurants, and plenty of fresh fish and seafood on offer.

★**Pâtisserie Bennis Habous** BAKERY €
(Map p186; ☎0522303025; 2 Rue Fkih El Gabbas, Quartier Habous; pastries Dh5; 8am-9pm) Secreted in a lane in the Souq Habous, this famous patisserie deserves a dedicated visit. Make your choice of traditional Maghrebi pastries such as *cornes de gazelle* (crescent-shaped cookies stuffed with almond paste and laced with orange-flower water) or *akda aux amandes* (almond

macaroons) and then head to nearby **Cafe Imperial** (Map p186; Quartier Habous; ⊙8am-10pm) to order a coffee and scoff your bounty.

Marché Central MARKET €

(Map p191; meals from Dh40; ⊙9am-6pm; Marché Central) The Marché Central is a great place to have lunch after exploring the market – the cross-shaped fish market is particularly impressive. Tables from a dozen simple eateries are crammed with diners feasting on huge platters of fish, grilled vegetables, bread, salads and seafood soup. Cheap, filling and perfect for people watching.

★**NKOA** INTERNATIONAL €€

(Map p186; 0663572406; www.facebook.com/nkoafood; 11 Abou Kacem Chab, Quartier Gauthier; mains from Dh95; ⊙noon-3pm & 7.30-10.30pm Tue-Sun;) This supercool spot takes its inspiration from global flavours, mixing them with Moroccan produce and European culinary techniques. The result is creative dishes that taste as good as they look – such as Zulu, a black-bread burger with fig sauce. There's plenty for vegetarians too, all washed down with delicious juices. The soundtrack is an equally fabulous fusion.

★**Rick's Café** MEDITERRANEAN €€

(Map p186; 0522274207; www.rickscafe.ma; 248 Blvd Sour Jdid, Old Medina; mains Dh100-180; ⊙noon-3pm & 6.30pm-1am) Immerse yourself in Bogart and Bergman's *Casablanca* at this reimagining of Rick's celluloid cafe. The art deco interiors, the strains of 'As Time Goes By' and fez-clad bartenders will transport you to the famed gin joint, while you enjoy classic French and Moroccan dishes, accompanied by a live jazz soundtrack from 9.30pm. Book in advance and note the dress code.

★**La Bodéga** TAPAS €€

(Map p191; 0522541842; www.restopro.ma/bodega; 129 Rue Allah Ben Abdellah; mains Dh80-160; ⊙noon-3pm & 7pm-2am Mon-Sat, 7pm-2am Sun; ; Marché Central) Local partygoers of all ages love this hybrid tapas bar-restaurant where meaty dishes are served accompanied by a soundtrack of loud – and often live – music (everything from salsa to Arabic pop). Spanish vino flows freely and the dance floor is packed after 10pm on weekends. At other times there may be football on the big screen or even flamenco performances.

Bondi Coffee Kitchen CAFE €€

(Map p186; 0651687707; www.facebook.com/bondicoffeekitchen; 31 Rue Sebou, Quartier Gauthier; mains from Dh60; ⊙10am-9pm;) This cool contemporary cafe is a Moroccan-Australian enterprise aiming to bring healthy yet delicious eating to Casa. Think salmon poke and mango pickle, or prawn spaghetti with roasted cherry tomatoes and rocket. There are lots of vegie options too, along with raw pressed juices. And the top-notch coffee goes perfectly with the moreish carrot cake.

Restaurant du Port de Pêche SEAFOOD €€

(Map p186; 0522318561; Le Port de Pêche; mains Dh90-135; ⊙noon-2.30pm & 7-10.30pm) Packed to the gills at lunch and dinner, this tried-and-trusted restaurant on the upstairs floor of a building in the middle of Casablanca's port serves the city's freshest and finest seafood. Fish can be enjoyed fried or grilled, plain or meunière, and there are oysters and other shellfish on offer. Note that smokers on nearby tables are inevitable.

La Sqala MOROCCAN €€

(Map p186; 0522262029; www.facebook.com/lasqala; Blvd des Almohades; mains Dh75-170; ⊙8am-11pm) Tucked in to and named after the ochre walls of an 18th-century fortified bastion on the edge of the old medina, this pretty garden restaurant is a tranquil escape from the downtown bustle. Particularly popular for breakfast, it also serves *briouates* (stuffed pastries), tajines, *bastillas* (savoury-sweet pies) and *brochettes*. No alcohol, but a good selection of fresh juices.

La Taverne du Dauphin FRENCH €€

(Map p191; 0522221200; www.facebook.com/TaverneDuDauphin; 115 Blvd Houphouët Boigny; mains Dh40-85, set menu Dh115; ⊙noon-11pm Mon-Sat; Place Nations Unies) A Casablanca institution, this staunchly traditional restaurant near Casa Port has been serving up *fruits de mer* (seafood) since it opened in 1958 and is particularly busy at lunchtime. Service is friendly, there are dedicated smoking and nonsmoking sections and the three-course set menu is a bargain.

★**Le Jasmine** MOROCCAN €€€

(Map p186; 0522467800; www.hotelledoge.com; 9 Rue Dr Veyre; mains from Dh190; ⊙7-11pm) This fine-dining Moroccan restaurant is set in an exquisite space at the art deco Hôtel Le Doge (p192). With its red-velvet chairs, ornate stained-glass ceiling, marble floors and

CASABLANCA WITH CHILDREN

Casablanca is a sprawling and noisy city, so many families travelling with young children choose to retreat from the chaos of the city centre and hang out at the beach or in their hotel. The Four Seasons Hotel (p192) is on the beach in Aïn Diab and has a swimming pool, as does the Hyatt Regency (p194) downtown. Alternatively, the beach clubs in Aïn Diab have pools, playgrounds and attached terrace cafes specialising in ice cream.

Next to Aïn Diab, the upmarket suburb of Anfa is home to the enormous Morocco Mall (p198), which has a giant aquarium and an IMAX Theatre in addition to shops and a food court and makes a good choice for teens.

sparkling chandeliers, it's like stepping into the 1930s. Perfectly prepared dishes include a lightly spiced shrimp and monkfish tajine and a sinful chocolate fondant.

★Le Cabestan Ocean View MEDITERRANEAN €€€

(Map p186; ☎0522391190; www.le-cabestan.com; 90 Blvd de la Corniche; mains Dh140-290; ⏰noon-3pm & 7pm-midnight) Perched beneath the lighthouse, this stylish restaurant has a French Riviera feel and Mediterranean-inspired menu. Opt for just-caught fish and seafood, perhaps salt-baked sea bass, and wash it down with a creative cocktail or Casablanca beer. Reservations essential; request a table on the terrace or next to a panoramic window. There is a hearty snack menu between 3pm and 7pm.

★Restaurant Brasserie La Bavaroise FRENCH €€€

(Map p191; ☎0522311760; www.restopro.ma/bavaroise; 133 Rue Allah Ben Abdellah; mains Dh160-230; ⏰noon-midnight Mon-Fri, from 7pm Sat; 🚊Marché Central) Down a dishevelled street behind the Marché Centrale, La Bavaroise has been serving an ultraloyal local clientele since 1968 and shows no sign of losing its popularity. The speciality is grass-fed beef from the Atlas served in the form of steak with pommes frites, green salad and French-style sauces. Other highlights include oysters from Dakhla and decadent desserts.

Iloli JAPANESE €€€

(Map p186; ☎0608866633; https://iloli-restaurant.com; 33 Rue Najib Mahfoud, Quartier Gauthier; mains Dh140-490; ⏰12.30-2.30pm & 7.30-11.30pm Tue-Sat) This zen restaurant's ambition is to combine the best of Japan and Morocco and it works; the sushi, sashimi and dishes such as black cod with preserved lemons and turbot meunière with yuzu are sublime. Dine in or out, or around the open kitchen and watch the chefs at work.

Le Rouget de L'isle FRENCH €€€

(Map p186; ☎0522294740; 16 Rue Rouget de l'Isle; mains Dh180-220; ⏰noon-3pm & 7.30-11pm Mon-Fri, 7.30-11pm Sat; 🚊Place Mohammed V) Occupying a charming 1930s villa in a leafy street near the Abderrahman Slaoui Foundation Museum, this upmarket restaurant is known for its modern French cuisine served in a wonderful garden scented with night-blooming jasmine. It's a romantic spot for dinner in warm weather – in the cooler months guests eat in the intimate, art-adorned salon.

Ostréa SEAFOOD €€€

(Map p186; ☎0522441390; www.ostrea.ma; Le Port de Pêche; mains Dh120-260; ⏰noon-11.30pm) Head to this restaurant in the port for a taste of Oualidia's famous oysters, fresh from the restaurant's own oyster farm. Follow up with some just-caught fish.

🍷 Drinking & Nightlife

There are plenty of dive bars in the centre of town but they're off-limits to all females except prostitutes. The bars in the larger hotels – especially the Hyatt Regency (p194) or Sofitel Tour Blanche – or trendy restaurants such as Le Cabestan are far better options.

Le Doge Cafe BAR

(Map p186; ☎0522467800; www.hotelledoge.com; Hôtel Le Doge Relais & Châteaux, 9 Rue Docteur Veyre; ⏰7am-11.30pm; 📶) There aren't that many places to have a drink in downtown Casablanca but at the top of art deco Hôtel Le Doge's (p192) stunning spiral staircase is an open-sided terrace with city views, craft cocktails and a good wine list. Pair your drink with some tasty tapas from the Spanish chef's menu.

Sky 28 BAR

(Map p186; ☎0522978000; www.kenzi-hotels.com; 28th fl, Kenzi Tower Hotel, Twin Centre, Blvd

Zerktouni, Maarif; ⌚3pm-2am) This retro-looking lounge bar sits on the top of the Kenzi Tower Hotel, so grab a pricey cocktail and drink in the 360-degree views all the way to to the Hassan II Mosque from its floor-to-ceiling windows. They also have a tapas menu, including sushi (Dh160 for 12 pieces), Dakhla oysters (Dh150 for six) and burgers (Dh160).

Café Alba CAFE

(Map p191; ☎0522227154; 59-61 Rue Driss Lahrizi; ⌚6.30am-9.30pm; 🚊Marché Central) This cafe is worth a stop for its art deco–era elegance, female-friendly atmosphere and premium people-watching seats. The set breakfast deals offer the best value.

Le Trica BAR

(Map p186; ☎0522220706; 5 Rue El Moutanabi, Quartier Gauthier; ⌚6pm-1am) This American-style gastropub is set over two levels but still gets jam-packed on Friday and Saturday nights when the DJ spins techno. It's also a popular place to watch big football matches on the big screen or grab a drink after work (happy hour 6.30pm to 9pm). Don't miss the giant mojitos; the Trica burger (Dh95) is good too.

VIP Club CLUB

(Map p186; 12 Rue des Dunes, Aïn Diab; ⌚10pm-4am, to midnight Sun) On a hill next to the Aïn Diab tram terminus, this long-established and expensive venue has a more inclusive vibe than many clubs in the city, with a large dance floor and good DJs.

☆ Entertainment

Save for the Grand Théâtre de Casablanca there's not much in the way of entertainment for visitors. There are plenty of cinemas however, from art deco gems to mega theatres, but English-language films are dubbed in French, unless it specifically states *version originale*.

★Grand Théâtre de Casablanca THEATRE

(Map p191; http://casa-amenagement.ma/en/nos-projets/grand-theatre-de-casablanca; Place Mohamed V, Ville Nouvelle; 🚊Place Mohamed V) About to open at the time of research, this dazzlingly white, ubercontemporary structure designed by a Pritzker Prize–winning architect dominates one of Casablanca's most popular squares. The largest theatre in Africa, it's a multidisciplinary art space including two halls that will hold 2400 people, and a music space for 300. And it'll be inclusive of the wider community, with performances projected on to the Place Mohammed V.

Cinéma Rialto CINEMA

(Map p191; ☎0522262632; www.facebook.com/cinemarialto; Rue Mohammed El Qory; ⌚2-8pm; 🚊Marché Central) One of the city's must-see architectural gems, this two-tier cinema built in 1929 has been saved and restored to its former art deco splendour, including plush red seating. It's still a functioning single-screen cinema and popular concert venue, hosting everyone from classical orchestras to rock bands. Check the Facebook page to see what's on.

CASABLANCA: THE FILM

Memorable performances, a haunting signature song and a sensational script by Julius J Epstein, Philip G Epstein and Howard Koch make the 1942 film *Casablanca* one of Hollywood's greatest achievements. Inspired by Murray Burnett and Joan Allison's unproduced stage play *Everybody Comes to Rick's*, producer Hal B Wallis and director Michael Curtiz put together a stellar cast and crew and shot the film in just over two months at the Warner Bros studio in Burbank, California. No scenes were filmed in Casablanca itself, but it evoked the city and its cosmopolitan wartime population, and images of Rick's Café Américain, street cafes and the souq gave many cinema-goers their first-ever visual introduction to the Maghreb.

Watching the film today, it's both fascinating and sobering to consider how its story of refugees and lost souls stranded in a foreign place mirrors the contemporary geopolitical situation and the plight of refugees from Syria and other war-torn countries.

It has become almost obligatory for travellers visiting modern-day Casablanca to pop into Rick's Café (p195) on the edge of the old medina for a cocktail or meal while being serenaded by pianist Issam. When quizzed, Issam admits that he's lost count of how many times he's played 'As Time Goes By', but says he still enjoys doing so. Here's looking at him.

CHANGING STREET NAMES

Casablanca's French street names are slowly being replaced with Moroccan names. Our maps and directions use the names that were on street signs at the time of research, but these may change. It is also worth noting that many locals, including taxi drivers, have yet to make the transition.

Shopping

Although not an artisan centre, Casablanca has a good choice of traditional crafts from around Morocco. The best place to shop for these is in the Quartier Habous, south of the centre. There are also craft shops of varying (usually low) quality along Blvd Houphouët Boigny on the edge of the old medina aiming to attract the tourist dirham.

Souq Habous MARKET

(Map p186; Quartier Habous) Shopping isn't a highlight of Casablanca, but those wanting to snaffle a few souvenirs should head to the attractive but touristy souq in the streets east of the central roundabout in the Quartier Habous. Shops sell everything from leather *babouches* (slippers), to shaggy rugs, spices and ceramics. Be prepared to haggle.

Morocco Mall MALL

(www.moroccomall.net; Blvd de la Corniche, Anfa; 10am-9pm, to 10pm Fri & Sat) Morocco's fanciest shopping destination, and the second-largest mall in Africa, has stores galore, from luxe international designer brands to a dedicated 'souq' area selling traditional Moroccan goods. Take a shopping break to gawp at the two-storey-high aquarium, and fill up in the multinational food court. There's also an IMAX cinema showing Hollywood blockbusters.

Marina Shopping SHOPPING CENTRE

(Map p186; www.marinashopping.ma; 10am-9pm, to 10pm Fri & Sat) In the traditionally no-shop zone between Casa Port train station and the Hassan II Mosque, this new mall is part of the regeneration of the port area, with a mix of local and international brands, a supermarket, food court (til 11.30pm) and a terrace overlooking the ocean.

Anfa Place MALL

(Map p186; 0522954646; http://anfashopping.com; Blvd de la Corniche, Aïn Diab; 10am-9pm, to 10pm Sat & Sun;) On the waterfront in Aïn Diab, this Norman Foster–designed shopping mall is a good place to stock up on provisions, with a supermarket, a pharmacy and plenty of retail outlets. Free wi-fi too. It's also home to Megarama, the plushest cinema in town with four comfortable theatres that are usually packed.

Orientation

The medina – the oldest part of town – is tiny and sits in the north of the city close to the port. To the south of the medina is Place des Nations Unies, a large traffic junction that marks the heart of the city. The city's main streets branch out from here: Ave des Forces Armées Royales (Ave des FAR), Ave Moulay Hassan I, Blvd Mohammed V and Blvd Houphouët Boigny.

Ave Hassan II leads to Place Mohammed V, easily recognised by its grand art deco administrative buildings. Quartiers Gauthier and Maarif, west and southwest of the Parc de la Ligue Arabe, are home to upmarket housing, restaurants, cafes and retail outlets.

To the southeast is the Quartier Habous (also known as the Nouvelle Medina) and to the west is Aïn Diab, the beachfront suburb whose Corniche is home to upmarket hotels, restaurants and nightclubs.

Information

ACCESSIBLE TRAVEL

Casablanca is more accessible than many Moroccan cities, with wide French-built boulevards and modern, business-oriented chain hotels with wheelchair-accessible lifts and ramps.

Travellers with vision or hearing impairment are poorly catered for, however. Hearing loops, Braille signs and talking pedestrian crossings are nonexistent.

For more information, download Lonely Planet's free Accessible Travel guide from https://shop.lonelyplanet.com/categories/accessible-travel.com.

DANGERS & ANNOYANCES

The medina, downtown, Anfa and Aïn Diab are generally safe, although avoid walking down dimly lit medina streets late at night. *Faux guides* (unofficial guides) may try to offer their services; deter them with a firm *'La, shukran'* ('No thanks'). As in all big cities, opportunistic pickpocketing can occur, so keep your valuables secure while you're sightseeing.

City centre traffic is heavy and chaotic and many *petits taxis* don't have functioning seatbelts, turning a rush-hour journey into a white-knuckle ride. Hotels and guesthouses often have preferred taxi drivers which they can summon for a small extra fee (around Dh15).

Getting There & Away

Casablanca is Morocco's major transport hub, with international and domestic air and bus links, as well as train links to many destinations throughout the country.

AIR

Casablanca's **Mohammed V International Airport** (☎0522435858; www.casablanca-airport.com) is 30km southeast of the city on the Marrakesh road. Regular flights leave from here for most European countries, as well as to West Africa, Algeria, Tunisia, Egypt, the Middle East and North America.

Internally, the vast majority of Royal Air Maroc's flights go via Casablanca, so you can get to many destinations in Morocco directly from the city.

BUS

The **CTM bus station** (Map p191; ☎0522541010; www.ctm.ma; 23 Rue Léon L'Africain; Marché Central) is close to Ave des FAR. There are daily CTM bus departures to destinations across the country. Destinations include nine daily services (Dh230, 7¼ hours) and two premium services (Dh275, 6½ hours) to Agadir; four services to Essaouira (Dh140, 7¼ hours); and seven daily services (Dh100, 3¼ hours) and two premium services (Dh130, 3¼ hours) to Marrakesh.

The main reason to trek out to the modern Gare Routière Ouled Ziane, 4km southeast of the centre, is for services to destinations not covered by CTM – almost all non-CTM services depart from here. A taxi here will cost about Dh25; alternatively take bus 10 (Map p191) from outside Cinema Rif on Ave des FAR.

Also on Rte Ouled Ziane, but more than 1km closer to town than Gare Routière Ouled Ziane, Supratours runs national buses of a similar standard to CTM, though to fewer destinations. Fares are slightly cheaper.

CAR

Casablanca is well endowed with car hire agencies, including **Avis** (Map p191; ☎0522312424; www.avis.com; Boulevard Zaid Ou Hmad; 8am-7pm, to noon Sun; Houph Boigny) and **Budget** (Map p191; ☎0522313124; www.budget.com; 5 Ave des FAR; 8.30am-noon & 3-6pm, 9am-noon Sun; Place Nations Unies), with offices downtown and at the airport.

TAXI

Grands taxis arrive at and depart from Gare Routière Ouled Ziane.

TRAIN

Casablanca has five train stations, but only two are of interest to most travellers.

Casa Port is located a few hundred metres northeast of Place des Nations Unies, in the port precinct. This is the station for trains to/from Rabat Ville (1st/2nd class Dh55/40, one hour, 10 daily) and Kenitra (1st/2nd class Dh97/55, 1¼ hrs, 10 daily). The train to/from Mohammed V International Airport also starts/ends here.

Casa Voyageurs is where long-distance trains to all national destinations except Rabat and Kenitra arrive and depart, including the Al Boraq high-speed train that launched in late 2018, linking Casablanca to Tangier in just two hours, with stops in Rabat Agdal and Kenitra. A tramline connects the station with other parts of the city including downtown and Aïn Diab.

Getting Around

Most areas of the city are reachable via the city's excellent modern tramway. Other than the tram, *petits taxis* are your best and fastest option for getting around Casablanca.

TO & FROM THE AIRPORT

Train services run between the Mohammed V International Airport and Casablanca's Casa Port

DESTINATIONS SERVED BY CASA VOYAGEURS

TO	1ST-CLASS FARE (DH)	2ND-CLASS FARE (DH)	TIME (HR)	FREQUENCY (DAILY)
Azemmour	46	33	1	8
El Jadida	53	37	1½	8
Fez	174	116	3¾	18
Marrakesh	148	95	2¾	11
Meknes	143	95	3	18
Nador	275	196	11	2 direct
Oujda	322	216	10¾	2 direct
Tangier	195	132	6	1 direct
Tangier (Al Boraq)	364	224	2	14
Rabat (Al Boraq)	90	50	45 mins	14

station at 4am and then on the hour from 6am to 10pm, with a final service at 11.45pm (1st/2nd class Dh64/43, 45 minutes). Trains stop at Oasis and Casa Voyageurs en route. You'll need to change at Casa Port for Rabat and Kenitra, and at Casa Voyagers for other major destinations. Trains leave from below the ground floor of Terminal 1. From Casa Port train station, the first train to the airport leaves at 3am and then every hour from 5am to 10pm.

The set price for a *grand taxi* between the airport and the city centre is Dh300, though drivers work an unofficial cartel, and fares can end up being much more at night or at times of high demand – consider booking an airport pick-up with **Vendôme Transport Touristique** (☎ 0522277619) to be sure of getting the official price. Note that some taxi drivers receive commissions if they bring clients to particular hotels and can be unscrupulous in orchestrating this – don't believe any driver who tells you your hotel of choice is closed.

BUS

Bus tickets cost Dh4. For details of designated routes and stops see http://mdinabus.ma/docs/Lignesbus.pdf for details. Visitors are likely to find the new tramway or *petits taxis* a better way to get around.

CAR & MOTORCYCLE

Traffic in downtown Casablanca is chaotic and often gridlocked, and only those born into it or with nerves of steel should attempt to drive.

Parking meters (Dh2 per hour, two hours maximum) operate from 8am to noon and 2pm to 7pm, except on Sunday and public holidays. If you don't pay, you may be fined or have your wheels clamped. On unmetered streets a guard will often request a tip for watching your car; it is common practice to pay Dh5.

TAXI

Casablanca's red **petits taxis** (Map p191) are hailed on the street, or your hotel can call one for a small extra charge (around Dh15).

The fare for a short trip starts at Dh15, and drivers sometimes stop to collect other passengers along the way. Drivers rarely use the meter; try and insist that they do, or negotiate the fare before getting into the taxi. Prices rise by 50% after 8pm.

Have plenty of small coins to hand, and check your change.

TRAM

The excellent **Casa Tramway** (www.casatramway.ma) makes getting across the city a simple and comfortable exercise.

The most useful section of line for travellers is from Casa Voyageurs train station to Place Mohammed V, via the Marché Central and Place des Nations Unies. Trams also go to Aïn Diab (about 35 minutes from central Casablanca).

Trams run every 15 minutes, with the first and last departures from the termini at 5.30am and 10.30pm.

Tickets are Dh6 for a single trip, bought from easy-to-use machines on the platforms (multiple-journey tickets are also available).

Rabat الرباط

POP 577,830

Morocco's capital since 1912, and its administrative and diplomatic hub, Rabat may be short on top-drawer tourist attractions, but it compensates with a relaxed pace and easy charm. There are a lot of restoration projects under way along the Ville Nouvelle's orderly palm-lined boulevards and it's relatively traffic-free – a blessed relief for those who have spent time in Casablanca. There's a clean central beach, an intact and atmospheric kasbah, and an attractive walled medina that is far less touristy than those in other large cities. All in all, the city is a good choice for a short sojourn.

History

The fertile plains inland from Rabat drew settlers to the area as far back as the 8th century BCE. Both the Phoenicians and the Romans set up trading posts in the estuary of the Bou Regreg River in Sala, today's Chellah. The Roman settlement, Sala Colonia, lasted long after the empire's fall and eventually became the seat of an independent Amazigh (Berber) kingdom. The Zenata tribes built a *ribat*, a fortress-monastery from which the city takes its name, on the site of Rabat's present kasbah. As the new town of Salé (created in the 10th century) began to prosper on the north bank of the river, the city of Chellah fell into decline.

The arrival of the Almohads in the 12th century saw the *ribat* rebuilt as a kasbah, a strategic jumping-off point for campaigns in Spain, where the dynasty successfully brought Andalusia back under Muslim rule. Under Yacoub Al Mansour (the Victorious), Rabat enjoyed a brief heyday as an imperial capital, Ribat Al Fatah (Victory Fortress). Al Mansour had extensive walls built, added the enormous Bab Oudaia to the kasbah and began work on the Hasan Mosque, intended to be the greatest mosque in all of the Islamic West, if not in all of the Islamic world.

Al Mansour's death in 1199 brought an end to these grandiose schemes, leaving the great Hassan Mosque incomplete. The city soon lost all significance, and it wasn't until the 17th century that Rabat's fortunes began to change.

As Muslim refugees arrived from Christian Spain, so did a band of Christian renegades, Moorish pirates and global buccaneers. Rabat and Salé became safe havens for corsairs – merciless pirates whom English chroniclers dubbed the Sallee Rovers. At one point, they even created their own pirate state, the Republic of Bou Regreg. These corsairs roved as far as the coast of North America seeking Spanish gold, and to Cornwall in southern England to capture Christian slave labour. The first Alaouite sultans attempted to curtail their looting sprees, but no sultan ever really exercised control over them. Corsairs continued attacking European shipping until well into the 19th century.

Meanwhile, Sultan Mohammed Ben Abdallah briefly made Rabat his capital at the end of the 18th century, but the city soon fell back into obscurity. In 1912 France strategically abandoned the hornet's nest of political intrigue and unrest in the traditional capitals of Fez and Marrakesh and instead shifted power to coastal Rabat, where supply and defence were more easily achieved. Since then, the city has remained the seat of government and official residence of the king.

Sights

Central Rabat

★Musée Mohammed VI Art Moderne et Contemporain MUSEUM
(Map p206; ☎0537769047; www.museemohammed6.ma; cnr Aves Moulay Hassan & Allal Ben Abdallah, Ville Nouvelle; adult/child under 12 Dh40/10; ⏲10am-6pm, closed Tue; 🚊Mohammed V/Gare de Rabat) Conceived and funded by the present king, this museum opened in 2014 as the country's first national museum of modern and contemporary art. Alongside a permanent display of Moroccan artists dating from the 1950s to the present day, it plays host to temporary exhibitions from big-name international artists.

★Kasbah des Oudaias FORTRESS
(Map p202; Rue Jamaa, Medina; 🚊Bab Chellah) Rabat's historic citadel occupies the site of the original *ribat* (fortress-monastery) that gave the city its name. Predominately residential, its narrow streets are lined with whitewashed houses, most of which were built by Muslim refugees from Spain. There are scenic views over the river to Salé and out to the ocean from the **Plateforme du Sémaphore**, its highest point. The pretty **Andalusian Gardens** (⏲sunrise-sunset) at its southern edge are a popular meeting spot for locals.

Rabat Medina AREA
(Map p206; 🚊Medina Rabat, Bab Chellah) When the French arrived in the early 20th century, this walled medina by the sea was the full extent of the city. Built on an orderly grid in the 17th century, it is small enough to be easily explored in half a day, but tangled enough to make getting lost inevitable. The main market street is **Rue Souika**, with local shopping on its western stretch and shops geared largely to tourists in the covered **Souq As Sebbat** (Map p202; ⏲9am-9pm; 🚊Bab Chellah) to its east.

The **Grande Mosquée de Rabat Medina** (Map p206; off Rue Bab Chellah, Medina; 🚊Bab Chellah), a 14th-century Merinid original that has been rebuilt in the intervening years, marks the start of the Souq As Sebbat. If you continue past the **Rue des Consuls** (so called because diplomats lived here until 1912), you'll come to the *mellah* (Jewish quarter) just before Bab El Bahr and the river. Turning north along Rue des Consuls, which is home to many jewellery shops, will take you to one of the more interesting areas of the medina, with *fanadiq* (ancient inns used by caravans) and some grand former diplomatic residencies. At its northern end the street terminates in an open area that was the setting for slave auctions in the days of the Sallee Rovers. From here you can make your way up the hill to the Kasbah des Oudaias.

Most eateries are on the major pedestrian thoroughfare of Ave Mohammed V, which runs between the Medina Rabat tram stop and Ave Laalou, the medina's northern boundary. Popular fast-food joints with street seating, budget-friendly Restaurant de la Libération (p209) and a parade of street vendors sell snacks such as *babbouche* (cooked snails) served in a fragrant and spicy soup, freshly squeezed sugar-cane juice, syrup-drenched pastries, freshly baked bread and whatever fresh fruit is in season.

The most dramatic entry is through the enormous Almohad gate of **Bab Oudaia**

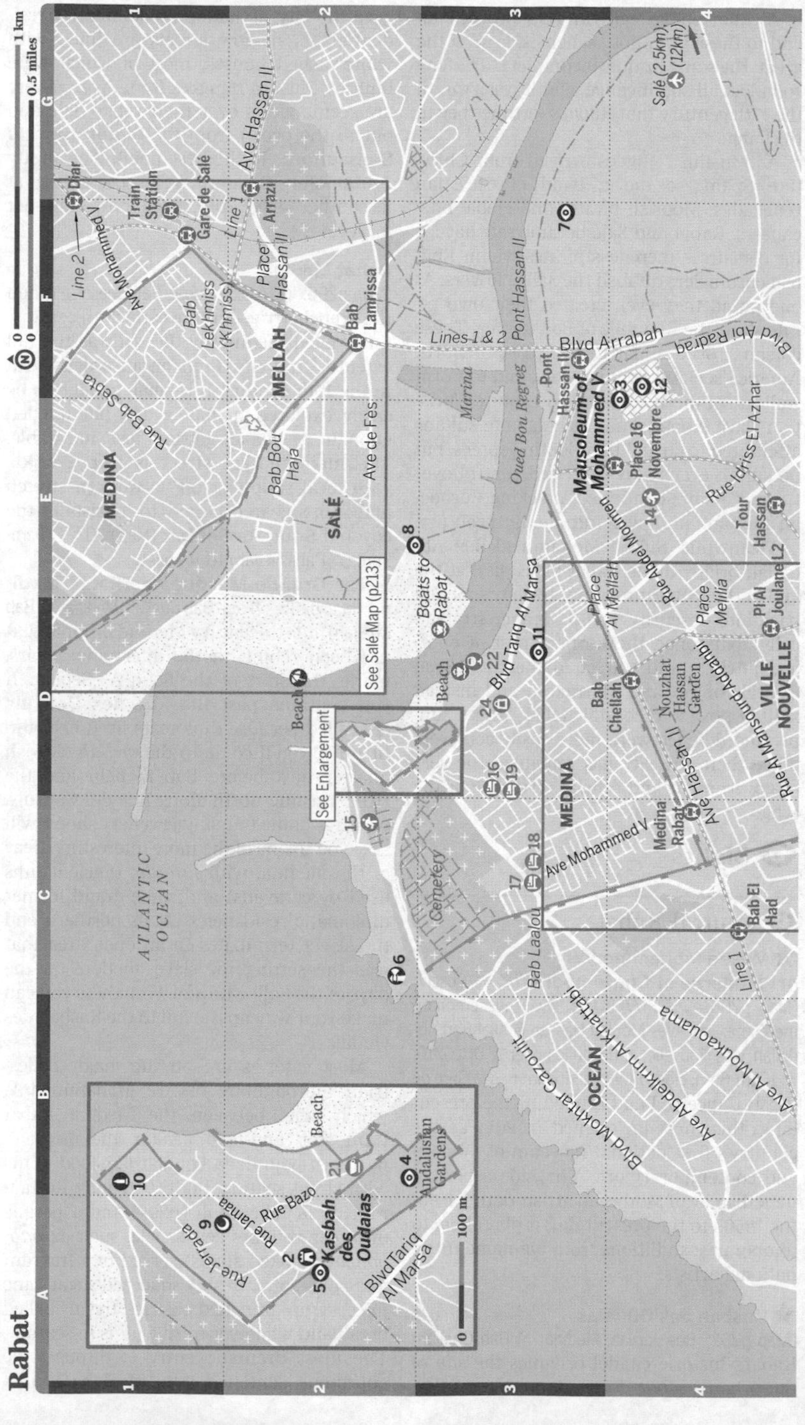

Rabat

0 1 km
0 0.5 miles
ATLANTIC OCEAN
Rue Jerrada
9
Rue Jamaa
Rue Bazo
2
5
Kasbah des Oudaias
Beach
21
10
4
Andalusian Gardens
Blvd Tariq Al Marsa
0 100 m
6
15
See Enlargement
Beach
See Salé Map (p213)
MEDINA
Rue Bab Sebta
Ave Mohammed V
Line 2
Diar
Train Station
Gare de Salé
Bab Lekhmiss (Khmiss)
Line 1
Arrazi
Ave Hassan II
Place Hassan II
Bab Bou Haja
MELLAH
SALÉ
Bab Lamrissa
Ave de Fès
8
Boats to Rabat
Beach
22
24
Cemetery
16
19
17
18
Bab Laalou
Blvd Tariq Al Marsa
11
Marina
Lines 1 & 2
Oued Bou Regreg
Pont Hassan II
Pont Hassan II
7
Blvd Arrabah
MEDINA
Ave Mohammed V
Mausoleum of Mohammed V
3
12
Place 16 Novembre
14
Bab Chellah
Place Al Mellah
Rue Abdel Moumen
Medina Rabat
Ave Hassan II
Nouzhat Hassan Garden
Place Melilia
Rue Al Mansour-Addahbi
Pl Al Joulane L2
VILLE NOUVELLE
Tour Hassan
Rue Idriss El Azhar
Blvd Abi Radrad
Salé (2.5km); (12km)
OCEAN
Blvd Mokhtar Gazoulit
Ave Abdelkrim Al Khattabi
Ave Al Moukaouama
Line 1
Bab El Had

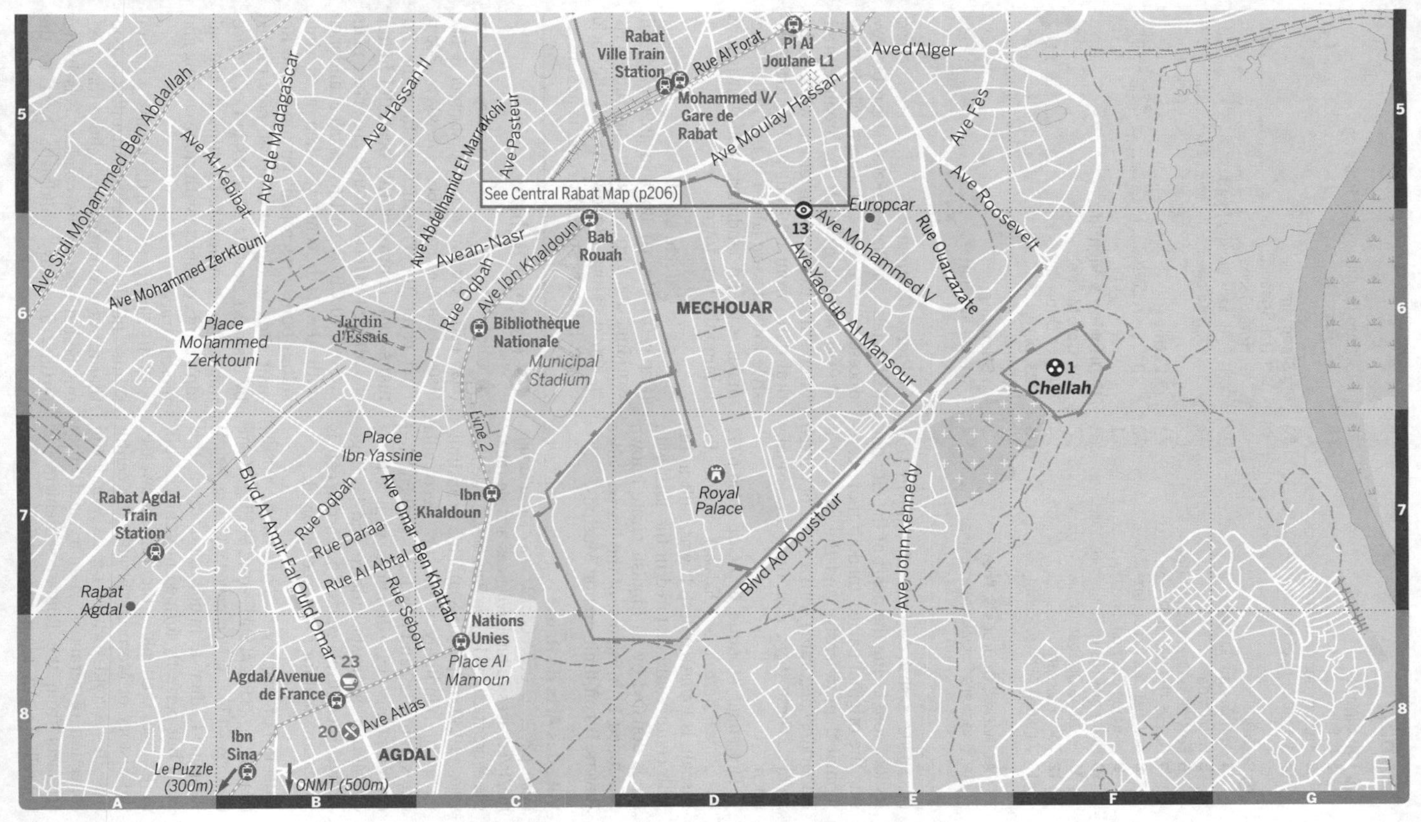

Rabat Ville Train Station
Rue Al Forat
Pl Al Joulane L1
Ave d'Alger
Mohammed V/ Gare de Rabat
Ave Moulay Hassan
Ave Fès
Ave Sidi Mohammed Ben Abdallah
Ave Al Kebibat
Ave de Madagascar
Ave Hassan II
Ave Abdelhamid El Marrakchi
Ave Pasteur
See Central Rabat Map (p206)
Europcar
13
Ave Mohammed V
Ave Roosevelt
Rue Ouarzazate
Ave Yacoub Al Mansour
Bab Rouah
Avean-Nasr
Ave Mohammed Zerktouni
Ave Ibn Khaldoun
Rue Oqbah
Bibliothèque Nationale
MECHOUAR
Place Mohammed Zerktouni
Jardin d'Essais
Municipal Stadium
1
Chellah
Line 2
Place Ibn Yassine
Royal Palace
Ibn Khaldoun
Blvd Al Amir Fal Ould Omar
Ave Omar Ben Khattab
Rue Oqbah
Rue Daraa
Rue Al Abtal
Rue Sebou
Rabat Agdal Train Station
Blvd Ad Doustour
Ave John Kennedy
Rabat Agdal
Nations Unies
Place Al Mamoun
23
Agdal/Avenue de France
20
Ave Atlas
AGDAL
Ibn Sina
Le Puzzle (300m)
ONMT (500m)

Rabat

Top Sights
1 Chellah F6
2 Kasbah des Oudaias A2
3 Mausoleum of Mohammed V F4

Sights
4 Andalusian Gardens B2
5 Bab Oudaia A2
6 Fort de la Calette Lighthouse C2
7 Grand Théâtre de Rabat F3
8 Le Quai Des Créateurs E2
9 Mosque El Atiqa A1
10 Plateforme du Sémaphore B1
11 Souq As Sebbat D3
12 Tour Hassan F4
13 Villa des Arts de Rabat D5

Activities, Courses & Tours
14 Chantiers Sociaux Marocains E4
15 Club Nautique de la Plage de Rabat C2

Sleeping
16 Dar Shâan D3
17 Hôtel Darna C3
18 L'Alcazar Luxury Ryad C3
19 Riad Kalaa D3

Eating
20 L'Entrecôte B8

Drinking & Nightlife
21 Café Maure B2
22 Le Dhow D3
23 Oliveri B8

Shopping
24 Marilyn Bottero D3

(Map p202; Kasbah des Oudaias), built in 1195. Its location, facing the heart of the city outside the original palace, made it more ceremonial than defensive and the gateway is elaborately decorated with a series of carved arches. These days, it is only occasionally open.

The small **Mosque El Atiqa** (Map p202; Rue Jamaa, Kasbah Les Oudaias), inside the kasbah, is Rabat's oldest. It was built in the 10th century and restored in the 18th with funds donated by an English pirate known as Ahmed El Inlisi, one of the feared Sallee Rovers. It's off-limits to non-Muslims.

Villa des Arts de Rabat ARTS CENTRE
(Map p202; ☎0537668579; www.fondationona.ma/fr/espaces-culturels/villa-des-arts-de-rabat/site-et-architecture; 10 Rue Beni Mellal, Ville Nouvelle; ⏲9.30am-7pm Tue-Sun) This beautifully restored, blindingly white art deco villa dates from 1929 and now holds well-curated contemporary art exhibitions with a focus on Moroccan artists, culture and heritage, alongside cultural events. The garden cafe is a pleasant spot for a sightseeing break.

Museum of History & Civilisation MUSEUM
(Map p206; 23 Rue Al Brihi Parent; Dh20; ⏲10am-6pm, closed Tue; Mohammed V/Gare de Rabat) Reopened after a major renovation, this small but perfectly formed museum is split in to two sections – the first showcases the history of Morocco through the centuries, the second focuses on its wonderful collection of ceramics, statuary and other artefacts from the Roman settlements at Volubilis (p365), Lixus and Chellah.

St Pierre Cathedral CHURCH
(Cathédrale Saint-Pierre de Rabat; Map p206; www.dioceserabat.org; Place Al Joulane, Ville Nouvelle; Place Al Joulane) With an architecturally interesting exterior, this bright white cathedral dates from 1919 but its two art deco-style towers were added in the 1930s. They make a useful landmark when navigating around the new town.

Fort de la Calette Lighthouse LIGHTHOUSE
(Map p202; Medina) Built in 1920 and still working, this 31m-tall, white lighthouse rises above natural stone walls and the rocks below. It looks especially striking at sunset.

Eastern Rabat

★**Chellah** ARCHAEOLOGICAL SITE
(Map p202; cnr Ave Yacoub Al Mansour & Blvd Moussa Ibn Nassair; Dh60; ⏲8.30am-5.30pm) First came the Phoenicians, then the Romans took control of this beautiful hilltop site above the fertile Bou Regreg river plain around 40 CE. From 1154, it lay abandoned until the 14th century, when a Merinid sultan built a necropolis on top of the Roman site. An elegant minaret, now topped by a stork's nest, is all that's left of a once-impressive mosque and behind it, the sultan's tomb, complete with stone carving and mosaic traces.

To its right (east) are the tombs of several saints and the Bassin aux Anguilles, a pool that attracts women who believe that feeding boiled eggs to its resident eels brings fertility and easy childbirth. Next to the minaret, at a lower level, is a small *medersa* (school for studying the Quran) with the remains of pillars, students' cells, a mihrab (niche indicating the direction of Mecca) and an ornamental pool. At the bottom of the site, on the slope beneath the tomb of Sultan Abu Al Hasan and his wife, is a shady walkway lined with flowers, palm trees and bamboo.

★Mausoleum of Mohammed V MAUSOLEUM
(Map p202; Blvd Mohammed Lyazidi, Quartier Hassan; ⊙sunrise-sunset; Pont Hassan II) FREE The present king's father (the late Hassan II) and grandfather were laid to rest in this marble mausoleum, which is decorated with exquisite examples of Moroccan craftwork, including colourful *zellige* (geometric mosaic tiles) and carved plaster. Its carved cedar ceiling is covered in gold leaf, and is quite magnificent. Royal guards wear traditional garb. Visitors must be respectfully dressed and can look down into the tomb from a gallery.

Tour Hassan HISTORIC SITE
(Hassan Tower; Map p202; Ave Tour Hassan, Ville Nouvelle; Pont Hassan II) Rabat's must-see sight – along with the neighbouring mausoleum – this iconic tower looms 44m above the Bou Regreg estuary. It was originally part of an ambitious Almohad project to build the world's second-largest mosque (after Samarra in Iraq), but its patron Sultan Yacoub Al Mansour died before it was completed. The mosque was destroyed by an earthquake in 1755, and today only this tower and a photogenic forest of shattered stone pillars remains in testament to his grand plan.

Activities

La Grande Piscine de Rabat SWIMMING
(Ave Moustapha Assayeh, Ville Nouvelle; Dh10; ⊙10am-8pm) The largest swimming pool in Africa has opened its doors in Morocco's capital, covering a vast area of the seafront, with four pools for different age groups and abilities and an army of staff. The low entrance fee means that it's accessible to all – and gets packed in summer and on sunny weekends.

Club Nautique de la Plage de Rabat WATER SPORTS
(Map p202; 0537261609; www.cnprabat.com; Plage des Oudaias) There's fun for all the family at one of Morocco's largest nautical clubs on Oudaias beach. Sailing, surfing, bodyboarding and sea kayaking rental, courses and lessons are on offer at both the beach and the Bou Regreg Marina on the Salé side of the river.

Chantiers Sociaux Marocains VOLUNTEERING
(Map p202; 0537732266; www.csmmorocco.org; 13 Rue Al Mouahidine) Rabat-based NGO engaged in nationwide health, education and development projects, taking international volunteers aged 18 to 35. They also offer month-long courses in Arabic, and hiking trips to the High Atlas and desert.

Center for Cross-Cultural Learning LANGUAGE
(CCCL; Map p206; 0537202365; www.cccl-morocco.com; Ave Hassan II, Bab El Had; Bab El Had) This private school comes recommended for its intensive short courses in Modern Standard Arabic and Darija (Moroccan Arabic); students can opt for a homestay, and have access to a library of 6000 books. It also organises a variety of cultural activities, including art exhibitions and concerts to promote cross-cultural understanding.

Festivals & Events

Jidar Street Art Festival ART
(Jidar Toiles du Rue; www.jidar.ma; ⊙Apr) Rabat is turning into an open-air art gallery, with local and international street artists leaving their monumental artworks behind, all thanks to the annual Jidar Street Art Festival, which brings 12 artists to the city to make their mark. Do your own self-guided street art trail, or if you're here in April, you can watch the artists at work.

★Festival Mawazine MUSIC
(Rythmes du Monde; www.festivalmawazine.ma; ⊙Jun) Showcasing eclectic musical genres, this long-standing festival mixes up the biggest names from the international pop music scene with established and emerging local artists. The nine-day festival is spread over four main stages including the international OLM Souissi arena in Agdal, the African stage in Bou Regreg, the beachfront stage focussing on Moroccan music and world music in the Chellah.

Rabat Biennale ART
(www.biennale.ma; ⊙Sep) Rabat's inaugural Biennale was held in September 2019, exhibiting work in a range of disciplines –

Central Rabat

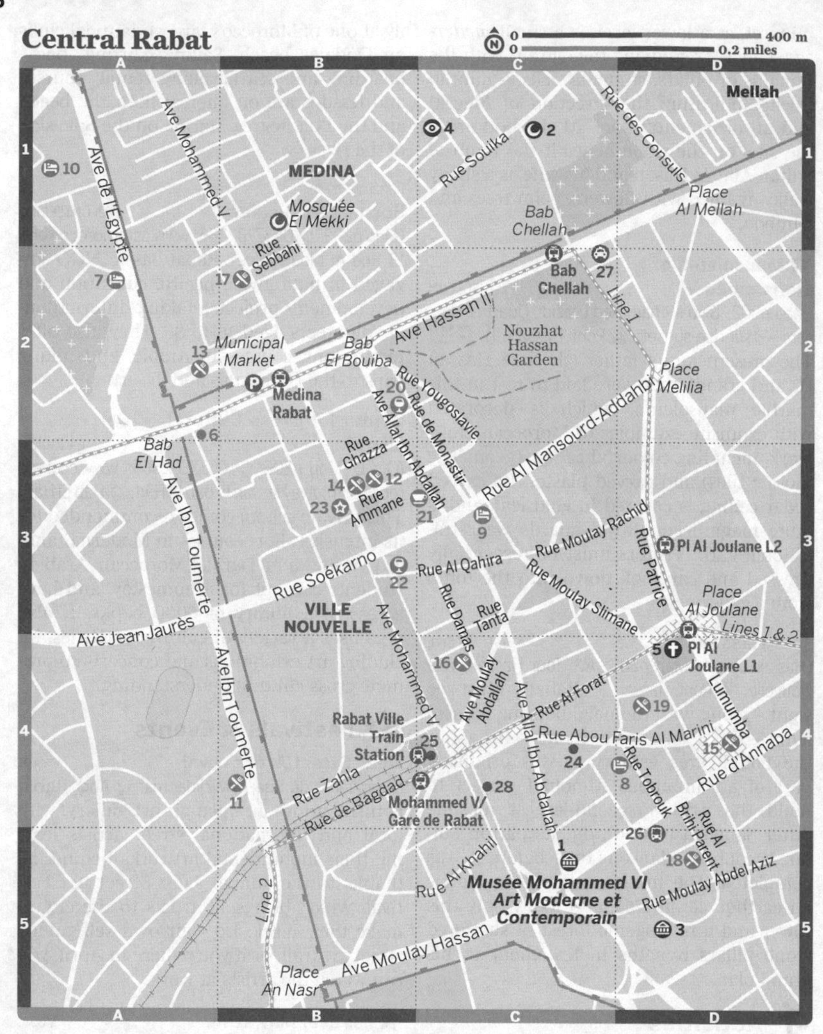

including visual, street and performance art – around the city. In 2019, the focus was firmly on women artists; watch this art space.

Jazz au Chellah MUSIC
(www.facebook.com/JazzauChellah; Sep) Going strong for nearly three decades, this festival features collaborations between European and Moroccan jazz musicians and is staged in the atmospheric surrounds of the Chellah (p204). Check its Facebook feed for programme details.

Visa for Music MUSIC
(https://visaformusic.com; Nov) Billed as the first festival to focus on African and Middle Eastern music; expect around 50 acts on three different stages over four days, from Morocco to Mozambique.

Sleeping

There are a growing number of atmospheric riads in the medina. In the Ville Nouvelle, low-budget options tend to be dives but there are also some comfortable midrange business hotels.

Central Rabat

Top Sights

1 Musée Mohammed VI Art Moderne et Contemporain ... C5

Sights

2 Grande Mosquée de Rabat Medina ... C1
3 Museum of History & Civilisation ... D5
4 Rabat Medina ... C1
5 St Pierre Cathedral ... D4

Activities, Courses & Tours

6 Center for Cross-Cultural Learning ... A2

Sleeping

7 Auberge De Jeunesse ... A2
8 Le Pietri Urban Hotel ... D4
9 ONOMO Rabat Médina ... C3
10 Riad Meftaha ... A1

Eating

11 Cosmopolitan ... B4
12 Cozy Cafe ... B3
13 Fruit & Vegetable Market ... A2
14 La Comédie ... B3
15 La Rive ... D4
Le Bistro du Pietri ... (see 8)
16 Le Petit Beur ... C4
17 Restaurant de la Libération ... B2
18 Restaurant El Koutoubia ... D5
19 Ty Potes ... D4

Drinking & Nightlife

20 Amnesia ... B2
Café Cinéma Renaissance ... (see 23)
21 Cafetéria du 7ème Art ... C3
22 Casa José ... B3

Entertainment

23 Cinéma Renaissance ... B3

Transport

24 Avis ... C4
25 Budget ... C4
26 Buses to Salé ... D5
27 Grands Taxis for Casablanca, Fez, Meknes & Salé ... C2
28 Hertz ... C4
Rabat Ville ... (see 25)

Ville Nouvelle

Le Piétri Urban Hotel HOTEL €€

(Map p206; ☎0537707820; www.lepietri.com; 4 Rue Tobrouk, Ville Nouvelle; s/d/ste from Dh617/728/1300; ; Mohammed V/Gare de Rabat) If only all the midrange hotels in the city lived up to the standard set by this small business hotel. On offer are reasonable prices, a central location, helpful bilingual staff and 35 spacious and bright rooms with good beds, satellite TV and double-glazed windows.

There's also an excellent restaurant, Le Bistro du Pietri (p209), with live jazz twice a week.

ONOMO Rabat Médina HOTEL €€€

(Map p206; ☎0537703074; www.onomohotel.com/en/hotel/11/onomo-hotel-rabat-medina; 2 Rue Ghandi, Ville Nouvelle; s/d/tr Dh888/976/1200; P; Place Al Joulane) Geared towards business people, this friendly modern hotel located a 10-minute walk from Rabat Ville (p211) train station offers well-maintained and attractive rooms with double-glazed windows, good beds, reading lamps, work desk and satellite TV; some also have balconies overlooking the park. Breakfast is served in the hotel's bright and cheerful lobby cafe.

Medina & Kasbah

Auberge De Jeunesse HOSTEL €

(Map p206; ☎0537725769; auberge.jeunes.rbt@hotmail.fr; 43 Rue Maressa Bab El Had, Quartier Bab El Had; dm Dh60; ; Medina Rabat) A peaceful courtyard garden is the main reason to stay in this old-style hostel, the second is its proximity to Bab El Had bus station. There are two 16-bed male dorms and one 20-bed female dorm; none have air-con or fans. The shared bathrooms (four showers for men, three for women) are clean but lack hot water.

★**Riad Meftaha** B&B €€

(Map p206; ☎0537721406; www.riad-meftaha.com; 15 Rue Iran, Quartier Marassa Océan; r Dh595-995; ; Bab El Had, Medina Rabat) Owner Franck is a friendly and helpful host, making this quiet riad just outside Bab Laalou an excellent choice. The rooms are nicely decorated but the pick of the bunch is undoubtedly the terrace suite. Note that double rooms lack air-conditioning; all have satellite TV. Breakfast is generous.

Hôtel Darna HOTEL €€

(Map p202; ☎0537734705; www.hoteldarna.ma; Ave Laalou, Medina; s/d/tr Dh350/550/650; ; Medina Rabat) This dated, dimly lit hotel has a good location on the edge of the medina, where small rooms come with

RABAT'S VILLA MANDARINE

Set in a gorgeous garden full of vibrant bougainvillea and orange trees, French-owned family-home-turned-boutique-hotel **Villa Mandarine** (0537752077; www.villamandarine.com; 19 Rue Ouled Bousbaa, Souissi; d from Dh2380; P) is filled with art, antiques and family heirlooms. No two of the 36 rooms are alike but all are beautifully decorated and come with private terraces. There's also a first-rate restaurant, swimming pool and hammam. It's a 15-minute drive from the centre.

If you're not staying at the hotel, it's worth jumping in a *petit taxi* to Rabat's embassy district for lunch or dinner in the gorgeous perfumed garden of **Restaurant Villa Mandarine** (0537752077; www.villamandarine.com; 19 Rue Ouled Bousbaa, Souissi; main Dh170-220; 12.30-2.30pm & 7.45-10.30pm). The menu mixes Moroccan ingredients and French fine dining, perhaps blue-lobster bisque with dill, or slow-roasted goat followed by the *trio de crèmes brûlées*.

double-glazed windows, reasonably comfortable beds and sketchy hot water. Breakfast comes with views over the medina.

★ **Dar Shâan** BOUTIQUE HOTEL €€€
(Map p202; 0537722020; http://dar-shaan.com; 24 Rue Jirari, Medina; d from €120) The medina's most stylish boutique is adorned with Andalusian stone columns and cool contemporary artwork, heavy wooden doors and 11 brightly painted rooms, decorated with retro furniture and fabulous flea-market finds. An elegant dining room serves sophisticated dinners (three-courses Dh250), plus there's a marble hammam and a small pool on the roof terrace with views over the medina to Salé.

★ **L'Alcazar Luxury Ryad** BOUTIQUE HOTEL €€€
(Map p202; 0537736906; www.lalcazar.com; 4 Impasse Ben Abdellah, off Ave Laalou, Medina; r Dh900-3000; P; Medina Rabat) In an easy-to-find spot on the edge of the medina, this stylish adaptation of a traditional riad comes with eight individually decorated rooms and sumptuous suites with comfortable beds and spacious bathrooms, a charming central patio and a multi-tiered rooftop terrace with expansive medina views. Amenities are top-quality, breakfast is delicious and service is friendly.

Riad Kalaa BOUTIQUE HOTEL €€€
(Map p202; 0537202028; www.riadkalaa.com; 3-5 Rue Zebdi, Medina; d from €105; ; Medina Rabat) This restored 19th-century riad has retained its traditional character, with 11 rooms and deluxe suites spread around a sky-high courtyard, with smooth *tadelakt* (waterproof limestone plaster) walls, tiled floors and comfortable beds. Up top, there's a roof terrace and pool, and the popular courtyard restaurant (open to nonguests) serves up typical Moroccan fare – salads, tajines and sticky desserts (three-course menu Dh280).

Eating

Considering Rabat's status as the nation's capital, its restaurant scene is low-key – but there are some first-class restaurants in the Ville Nouvelle. The part of Ave Mohammed V that runs the length of the medina is a good place to find fast food and cheap eats.

Ville Nouvelle & Agdal

★ **Cozy Cafe** CAFE €
(Map p206; 0537720506; www.facebook.com/cozycaferabat; 2 Rue Jeddah, Ville Nouvelle; main Dh40; 7am-11.30pm) This contemporary cafe mixes French pastries, Moroccan sweet treats and American pancakes, all made on the premises. For a light lunch, there's a menu of salads, sandwiches and pasta dishes, as well as a range of detox juices. There are 18 flavours of gourmet ice cream, too. Eat in or on the leafy terrace.

La Comédie CAFE €
(Map p206; 269 Ave Mohammed V, Ville Nouvelle; pastries from Dh10; 7am-10pm; Medina Rabat) Efficient staff serve excellent coffees and good pastries and gateaux at this popular cafe. Claim a table under the large trees and watch the passing parade on Ave Mohammed V.

La Rive CAFE €
(Map p206; 0537730001; Place Moulay Hassan, Ville Nouvelle; snacks from Dh10; 7.30am-midnight; Place Al Joulane) Modern and airy, this popular cafe-restaurant sits on a sunken plaza away from the traffic and bustle. The good-value menu is international, serving

up everything from tajines to steak frites and pizza, and there's a set menu for less than Dh100. One quibble: it can get a bit smoky.

Ty Potes FRENCH €€
(Map p206; ☎0537707965; http://typotes.com; 11 Rue Ghafsa, Ville Nouvelle; salads Dh70-85, tartines Dh65-95; ⏰noon-2.45pm Tue-Sat & 7-10.45pm Thu-Sat; 🚊Place Al Joulane) Head to the leafy street behind the St Pierre Cathedral to find this popular expat haunt. The menu features sweet and savoury crêpes and *galettes* (savoury pancakes), salads and *tartines* (open sandwiches), which are ideally enjoyed in the rear garden. The Sunday brunch (Dh120) is particularly popular. Both alcohol and charcuterie are served.

Le Petit Beur MOROCCAN €€
(Map p206; ☎0537731322; www.lepetitbeur.ma; 8 Rue Damas, Ville Nouvelle; menus from Dh80; ⏰11.30am-2pm & 7-11pm Mon-Sat; 🚊Mohammed V/Gare de Rabat) Known for its friendly waiters and fresh Moroccan food, this small restaurant offers an array of daily specials, tajines, *brochettes*, *briouates* (stuffed pastries) and *bastillas*. The set menu (Dh90) of salad, *brochettes* and water is excellent value. Lunchtimes are quiet, but it's wise to book for dinner, when an oud (lute) player serenades diners.

Restaurant El Koutoubia MOROCCAN €€
(Map p206; ☎0537701075; 10 Rue Pierre Parent, Ville Nouvelle; mains Dh80; ⏰noon-3pm & 7-10.30pm; 🚊Mohammed V/Gare de Rabat) It opened back in 1955, and this Moroccan restaurant, with attached bar (strictly for men), has managed to retain its clients and traditional decor over the decades. All the classic Moroccan dishes are available – tajines, *brochettes*, couscous and *bastillas* – and the helpful English-speaking owner is happy to translate the menu.

★Cosmopolitan FRENCH €€€
(Map p206; ☎0537200028; www.facebook.com/CosmopolitanRabat; cnr Ave Ibn Toumert & Rue Abbou Abbas El Guerraoui, Ville Nouvelle; mains Dh160-240; ⏰noon-2.30pm & 7.30-10.45pm; 🚊Mohammed V/Gare de Rabat) This gourmet place near Bab Ruach occupies a handsome art deco villa and is one of the only restaurants in town serving modern French cuisine. The menu changes daily and relies on market-fresh finds, with seafood taking pride of place. Dine in the front courtyard in warm weather and upstairs during the cooler months. Excellent wine list.

Le Bistro du Pietri FRENCH €€€
(Map p206; ☎0537737144; Le Piétri Urban Hotel, 4 Rue Tobrouk, Ville Nouvelle; mains Dh140-170, menu Dh220; ⏰7am-midnight, from 5.30pm Sat & Sun; 📶; 🚊Mohammed V/Gare de Rabat) We usually shy away from dining at restaurants in business hotels, but this one in the Le Piétri Urban Hotel (p207) is an exception. The predominantly French food is well prepared and tasty. There's a good wine list, a kids menu and live jazz most weekends and Tuesday nights.

L'Entrecôte FRENCH €€€
(Map p202; ☎0661155959; www.facebook.com/LentrecoteRabat; 74 Blvd Al Amir Fal Ould Omar, Agdal; mains Dh80-180; ⏰noon-11pm; 🚊Agdal/Ave de France) The menu at this old-school restaurant is classic French with occasional forays over the border into Spanish territory, and the result is popular with locals and tourists alike. Steak and seafood dishes dominate (there's little for vegetarians), and there's a good value two-course deal (Dh120).

Medina

Restaurant de la Libération MOROCCAN €
(Map p206; 256 Ave Mohammed V, Medina; mains Dh60; ⏰11.30am-10pm Mon-Sat; 🚊Medina Rabat) Cheap, cheerful and marginally more classy than the string of other places along this perpetually busy road, this basic restaurant does a steady line in traditional favourites. Friday is couscous day and a bowl of *harira* (a hearty soup made of tomatoes, onions, saffron and coriander, often with lentils, chickpeas and lamb) will set you back Dh6.

Fruit & Vegetable Market MARKET €
(Map p206; Ave Hassan II; ⏰8am-7pm Mon-Sat; 🚊Medina Rabat) The medina's indoor market has a good choice of fresh produce, dried fruits and nuts. You should be able to find everything else you need (including booze) at the surrounding stalls or along Rue Souika and near Bab El Bouiba.

Drinking & Nightlife

Rabat's nightlife is a lot more limited – and subdued – than Marrakesh's and Casablanca's, but there are a few bars and clubs worth visiting in the Ville Nouvelle and Agdal. Expect to pay around Dh200 to enter clubs, and the same for drinks.

Ville Nouvelle & Agdal

Casa José BAR

(Map p206; ☎0537201514; www.facebook.com/CasaJoseRabat; 279 Ave Mohamed V, Ville Nouvelle; mains from Dh70; ⊙noon-1am) Soak up the Andalusian vibe at this Moroccan chain of classy bars, complete with flamenco shows and Spanish tapas. Enjoy a glass or two of Moroccan wine with dishes such as paella, patatas bravas and tortilla.

Café Cinéma Renaissance CAFE

(Map p206; ☎0537723773; www.facebook.com/Cafecinemarenaissance; 266 Ave Mohammed V, Ville Nouvelle; ⊙8am-10pm; 📶) This cafe-bar above the namesake cinema has kept its art deco parquet flooring and sparkling chandeliers, and a terrace overlooking the action on Ave Mohammed V. Popular with digital nomads by day, at night it holds cultural events and music nights, including Monday Jam Sessions (Dh30), slam poetry nights on Thursday and music masterclasses. Check the Facebook feed for details.

Amnesia CLUB

(Map p206; ☎0612991190; www.facebook.com/AmnesiaRabat; 18 Rue de Monastir, Ville Nouvelle; ⊙11.30pm-4am; 🚊Medina Rabat) A Rabat institution (it opened in 1989), this huge, pricey and perennially popular club can accommodate more than 1000 patrons and sees plenty of action on its dance floor. Resident DJs have a fondness for house and R&B.

Oliveri CAFE

(Map p202; ☎0537777800; cnr Ave de France & Blvd Al Amir Fal Ould Omar; ⊙7am-11pm; 🚊Agdal/Ave de France) Oliveri has been serving up top-notch ice cream and superb sundaes since 1950, and this Agdal branch is just as popular today.

Medina & Kasbah

Café Maure CAFE

(Map p202; Rue Bazo, Kasbah Les Oudaias; ⊙9am-5pm; 🚊Bab Chellah) Sit back, relax and gaze out over the estuary to Salé at this open-air cafe spread across several tiled terraces above the Andalusian Gardens. Mint tea is the tipple of choice at this kasbah institution, and pastry sellers will pass by with trays of *cornes de gazelle* (almond-paste cookie laced with orange-flower water) and *ghriba* (almond cookies).

Cafetéria du 7ème Art CAFE

(Map p206; Ave Allal Ben Abdallah; ⊙9am-10pm; 📶; 🚊Medina Rabat) Set in a pretty garden, this buzzy outdoor cafe is popular with students, professionals and visitors. It serves a good breakfast and snacks such as pizza and sandwiches, and is a good spot for a coffee, juice or ice cream anytime.

Le Dhow BAR

(Map p202; ☎0537702302; https://ledhow.com; Quai de Bouregreg) This authentic wooden dhow (a traditional Arab sailing boat), permanently moored in the Bou Regreg, is the perfect spot for a sundowner overlooking Salé. Enjoy a cold beer, a chilled wine or a classic cocktail, then dine elsewhere.

☆ Entertainment

Cultural centres associated with Rabat's many foreign embassies often host music, dance, art and literary events. Most films are dubbed in French, unless marked as *version originale*.

Under construction at the time at research, the new **Grand Théatre de Rabat** (Map p202), designed by the late Zaha Hadid, will be the city's preeminent cultural and entertainment venue.

Cinéma Renaissance CINEMA

(Map p206; ☎0537722168; www.renaissance.ma; 360 Ave Mohammed V; adult/student Dh50/30; 🚊Medina Rabat) Built in the 1930s, this lovely art deco building was a theatre before being restored and turned in to a cinema, cultural space and cafe. It shows Hollywood flicks and art-house films, and plays host to cinema clubs and various art-related events.

Shopping

Bee on 6th CONCEPT STORE

(☎0537750079; www.facebook.com/pg/beeon6th; cnr Ave Mohamed Vi & Rue Sanbra, Souissi; ⊙10.30am-7pm, to 8pm Fri, closed Mon) Rabat's first concept store stocks a stylish range of homeware, clothes, jewellery and accessories by modern Moroccan designers, as well as international brands, including scented candles from Tanzania and Italian shoes.

Mega Mall SHOPPING CENTRE

(☎0537757575; Km 4.2, Ave Mohammed VI, Souissi; ⊙10am-9pm) If you need a shopping fix, head to the largest mall in Morocco's capital, where you'll find all the usual international suspects along with Moroccan brands and a host of cafes and restaurants, plus a skating rink, bowling alley and kids' play area.

Marilyn Bottero CERAMICS
(Map p202; Rue des Consuls, Medina; ⏰10am-6pm) You can buy Italian painter and ceramicist Marilyn Bottero's vibrant work at her small shop on the Rue des Consuls.

Information

ACCESSIBLE TRAVEL

Rabat is more accessible than many Moroccan cities, although narrow streets and uneven pavements in the medina and kasbah can make wheelchair access difficult. Business-oriented hotels outside the medina are more likely to have lifts and ramps.

Travellers with vision and hearing impairment are poorly catered for, however. Hearing loops, Braille signs and talking pedestrian crossings are nonexistent.

For more information, download Lonely Planet's free Accessible Travel guide from https://shop.lonelyplanet.com/categories/accessible-travel.com.

DANGERS & ANNOYANCES

Rabat is considered a generally safe city, although try to avoid dimly lit streets in the medina and kasbah late at night. *Faux guides* (unofficial guides) may try to offer their services; deter them with a firm *'La, shukran'* ('No, thanks'). As in all big cities, opportunistic pickpocketing can occur, so keep your valuables secure while you're sightseeing.

TOURIST INFORMATION

Direction de la Cartographie (☎0660102683; www.ancfcc.gov.ma; cnr Aves My Youssef & My Hassan I) Good place to buy hiking maps.

TRAVEL WITH CHILDREN

Other than the *plage* (beach) and the La Grande Piscine de Rabat (p205), which has a child-friendly pool, and the kids' play area at Mega Mall, there are few specific attractions in the city for younger visitors. Children may enjoy tram journeys and will almost certainly have fun crossing between Rabat and Salé on one of the commuter rowing boats. They will also enjoy exploring the Kasbah des Oudaias (p201), where they can pretend to be pirates or expend energy running around the Plateforme du Sémaphore and Andalusian Gardens.

Getting There & Away

AIR

Rabat-Salé Airport has seen increased traffic in recent years, with a number of international airlines arriving here. This makes it an option worth considering when flying into the country, especially as the immigration queues at Casablanca's Mohammed V International Airport are notoriously long and chaotic. Train services to and from the city are excellent, with frequent services to destinations including Casablanca, Tangier and Fez.

BUS

Intercity buses service Rabat, but you are much better off using the train.

Rabat has two bus stations – the main **Gare Routière Kamra** (☎0537795816; Blvd Hassan II/N1; 🚊Ibn Rochd), from where most buses depart and arrive, and the less chaotic **CTM bus station**, 500m south. To get to the town centre from Kamra, take bus 30 (Dh4) or a *petit taxi* (Dh30). The closest tram stop, Ibn Rochd, is a 1.3km walk east along Ave Ibn Rochd.

Note that some intercity buses pass through central Rabat rather than stop at Kamra.

CTM routes not covered by rail link include the following:

Agadir Dh250 to Dh260, 7 to 9½ hours, five daily

Errachidia Dh185, 8½ hours, one daily

Tetouan Dh140, 4 hours, three daily

CAR

Avis (Map p206; ☎0537721818; www.avis.com; 7 Rue Abou Faris Al Marini; ⏰8am-7pm, to noon Sun; 🚊Mohammed V/Gare de Rabat), **Budget** (Map p206; ☎0530200520; www.budget.com; Rabat-Ville Train Station; ⏰9am-noon & 3-7pm, to 6pm Sat, to noon Sun), **Europcar** (Map p202; ☎0537722328; www.europcar.com; 25 Rue Patrice Lumumba, Ville Nouvelle; ⏰7.30am-9pm Mon-Sat, 8.30am-7pm Sun) and **Hertz** (Map p206; ☎0537709227; www.hertz.com; 467 Ave Mohammed V; ⏰8am-noon & 2.30-6.30pm Mon-Fri, 9am-noon & 3-6pm Sat; 🚊Mohammed V/Gare de Rabat) all have offices at the airport, as well as in the Ville Nouvelle.

TAXI

Grands taxis (Map p206) leave for Casablanca, Fez, Meknes and Salé from a car park opposite Bab Chellah, next to the petrol station.

TRAIN

The train is the most convenient way to arrive in Rabat, as the **Rabat Ville** (Map p206) is in the centre of the Ville Nouvelle and within easy walking distance of the medina. The station has a food court and wi-fi, as well as Budget car-hire and Supratours offices.

Trains run every 30 minutes from 6am to 10pm between Rabat Ville and Casa Port train stations (1st/2nd class Dh69/37, 70 minutes). You can connect with trains to Casablanca's Mohammed V International Airport at Casa Port.

The fast and efficient Al-Boraq high-speed train, inaugurated in November 2018, arrives into **Rabat Agdal** (Map p202) train station; however, at the time of research this stretch of the line was not high-speed.

On all long-distance routes there's always one late-night *ordinaire* train among the *rapide* services. *Rapide* services include the following.

Fez 1st/2nd class Dh127/85, 2½ hours, hourly

Marrakesh 1st/2nd class Dh195/127, five hours, nine daily

Meknes 1st/2nd class Dh95/69, two hours, hourly

Oujda 1st/2nd class Dh285/190, 9½ hours, two daily

Tangier 1st/2nd class Dh153/101, four hours, eight daily

Getting Around

TO & FROM THE AIRPORT

ALSA buses operate between the city and the airport, departing from Rabat Agdal station every hour between 6am and 11pm, stopping at Rabat Ville around 15 minutes later and then direct to the airport. Tickets cost Dh25, and the journey takes approximately 30 minutes.

A *grand taxi* to the airport should cost Dh150 during the day and Dh200 at night, although you will need to bargain to get these prices.

BOAT

Commuter rowing **boats** (Map p202) cross the estuary between Rabat and Salé between sunrise and sunset (Dh2.50).

BUS

ALSA (www.alsa.com) took over bus services in Rabat and neighbouring Salé in 2019; the fleet is new and tickets (Dh5) can be purchased on board from conductors. Services to Salé depart Rabat from **Ave Moulay Hassan** (Map p206).

CAR & MOTORCYCLE

While Rabat's traffic is relatively tame, especially compared to the likes of Casablanca and Marrakesh, parking – especially during the week – can be problematic.

Blue lines around street car parks indicate that drivers must buy a ticket from a nearby machine (Dh2 per hour).

City-centre parking restrictions apply from 8am to noon and 2pm to 7pm Monday to Saturday; metered parking costs Dh2 per hour.

When there are no blue lines or machines, unofficial parking attendants will often help you park and expect a tip of Dh5 to Dh10.

TAXI

Rabat's blue *petits taxis* are plentiful, cheap and quick. A ride around the centre of town will cost between Dh15 and Dh30 – try to insist that the driver uses his meter. There's a petit-taxi rank near the entrance of the medina on Ave Hassan II and another at the train station. Note that *petits taxis* aren't allowed to drive between Rabat and Salé.

Larbi El Wardi (☎0661712017) is a friendly English-speaking taxi driver with a modern car, and can do short or long trips.

TRAM

The smart and efficient Rabat-Salé tramway (www.tram-way.ma) system is an excellent way to get around Rabat.

Line 1 runs along Ave Hassan II next to the medina, detouring past the Hassan Tower to Bab Lamrissa next to the Salé medina and then on to Hassan II.

Line 2 starts at Madinat Al Irfane, stopping at Agdal/Avenue de France, Mohammed V/Gare de Rabat in the Ville Nouvelle, Bab Lamrissa, Salé Ville train station and Hay Karima.

Fares are Dh6, bought from ticket machines on the platforms (multiple-journey tickets are also available).

Services run around every 15 minutes, from 6am to 10pm.

Salé سلا

POP 890,400

Salé is becoming a tale of two cities: the ancient, tourist-free medina where life appears unchanged for centuries, and the swanky new marina, its wide promenade lined with upmarket cafes and restaurants and Moroccan designer boutiques along Le Quai des Créateurs.

The city's development boom continues apace and its population explosion means that it's now considerably larger than its neighbour Rabat, on the opposite bank of the Bou Regreg River, and – joined by an efficient modern tram link, as well as the traditional rowing boats – it's functioning as an integrated part of the capital rather than the staid satellite town it once was.

History

People began to settle in Salé in the 10th century, and the town grew in importance as inhabitants of the older settlement at Sala Colonia began to move across the river to the new town. Warring among local tribes was still rampant at this stage, and it was the Almohads who took control of the

Salé

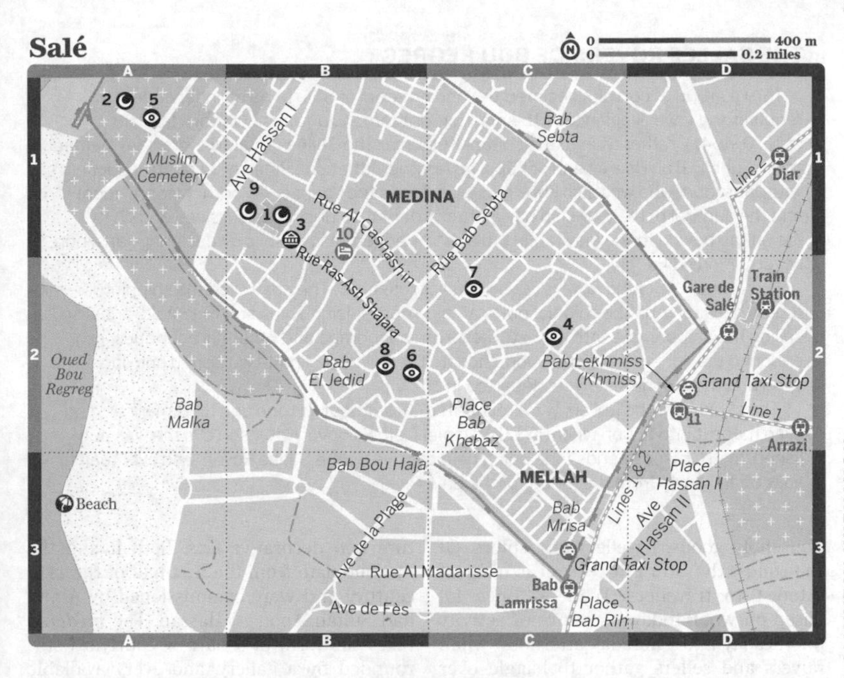

area in the 12th century, establishing neighbouring Rabat as a base for expeditions to Spain.

Spanish freebooters attacked in 1260; in response, the Merinids fortified the town, building defensive walls and a canal to Bab Mrisa to allow safe access for shipping. The town began to flourish and established valuable trade links with Venice, Genoa, London and the Netherlands.

As trade thrived so too did piracy, and by the 16th century the twin towns prospered from the activities of the infamous Sallee Rovers pirates.

By the 19th century, the pirates had been brought under control, Rabat had been made capital and Salé had sunk into an obscurity from which it is only now emerging.

Sights

Le Quai Des Créateurs AREA

(Map p202; 0537880589; www.facebook.com/lequaidescreateurs; Marina) Set on the banks of the Bou Regreg River, this low cubist structure hosts pop-up retail space for Moroccan designers, jewellers and artists. East along the wide promenade, cafes and bar-restaurants are opening up here, too.

Medina AREA

(Bab Lamrissa) Small and relatively easy to navigate, this 13th-century walled medina retains an almost medieval flavour. It's visited on a regular basis by the city's pious, who come to worship in the **Grand Mosque** and three important shrines, and local women for the souqs selling fresh produce, clothing,

THE SALLEE ROVERS OF BOU REGREG

In 1619 a group of corsairs declared the ancient port of Salé to be an independent republic and gave allegiance to their leader, Dutchman Jan Janszoon van Haarlem (c 1570–1641), rather than to the sultan. Known as the Sallee or Salé Rovers, they named their republic Bou Regreg and set up a government that consisted of 14 pirate leaders, with Janszoon, who was also known as Murat Reis the Younger, as both their president and the admiral of their 18-ship navy. After ordering an unsuccessful siege of the city, the sultan bowed to the inevitable and acknowledged the republic by declaring Janszoon governor in 1624.

Under the rule of the Rovers, Salé initially prospered. They patrolled the shipping routes between Atlantic colonial ports and Europe, seizing ships and their gold, and also selling the ships' crews into slavery. Fees from anchorage and other harbour dues also enriched the corsairs' coffers. Soon, though, the political climate worsened and Janszoon and most of his followers departed in 1627.

The exploits of the Rovers were recounted throughout Europe and the Americas, and even made it into fiction when, in 1719, Daniel Defoe's novel *Robinson Crusoe* was published. In it, Crusoe spends time being held captive by the Sallee Rovers and eventually sails off to liberty from the mouth of the Salé River.

household goods, jewellery and spices. Of the souqs, the **Souq El Ghezel** is of most interest to travellers. While it once focused on wool, today it's a hive of activity on Tuesday and Thursday afternoon when buyers and sellers gather to haggle over the price of all manner of items at auctions organised by women. Other marketplaces include **Souq El Merzouk**, which sells the woven grass mosque mats for which Salé is famous.

The main entrance to the medina is Bab Bou Haja, near the Bab Lamrissa tram stop on the southwestern wall. From here, walk left (north) to the souqs and the Great Mosque, 500m further northwest along Rue Ras Ash Shajara (also known as Rue de la Grande Mosquée). Alternatively, enter at Bab Lekhmiss (aka Khmiss), between the Bab Lamrissa and Gare de Salé tram stops, and walk straight ahead to find the souqs and mosque.

Souq El Kebir MARKET

(Medina; 🚊Bab Lamrissa) In the medina's main souq, hole-in-the-wall emporiums sell household goods, leather and wood. The spice souq is nearby, where you can pick up mounds of plump olives for a couple of dirham.

Medersa Abou Al Hassan HISTORIC BUILDING

(Médersa des Mérinide; Medina; Dh60; ⏲8.30am-5pm; 🚊Bab Lamrissa) Next to the Grand Mosque's (p213) magnificent entrance gate, this *medersa* (school for studying the Quran) is a showcase of Merinid architecture and decorative arts. Both it and the mosque date from the first half of the 14th century and were commissioned by Almohad Sultan Abou Al Hassan. The *medersa* takes the form of a narrow courtyard surrounded by a gallery, and every available surface is encrusted in intricate *zellige* (colourful mosaic tiles), carved stucco and carved cedar wood.

Small student cells surround the gallery on the upper floor, from where you can climb through an aperture to the flat roof, which has excellent views of Salé and across to Rabat. The guardian who shows you around will expect a small tip – around Dh50 for an hour.

Zawiya of Sidi Abdallah Ben Hassoun ISLAMIC SHRINE

(Rue Sidi Abdallah Ben Hassoun, Medina; 🚊Bab Lamrissa) Salé's patron saint, Sidi Abdallah Ibn Hassoun, was a 16th-century Sufi cleric and teacher. He's revered by Moroccan Muslims as a patron of travellers in much the same way as Catholics revere St Christopher. An annual candlelit pilgrimage and procession in his honour takes place on the evening of Mouloud (the Prophet's birthday), ending at this *zawiya* (Sufi shrine) behind the Grand Mosque. Only Muslims may enter.

Slave Prison NOTABLE BUILDING

(Ave Sidi Ben Achir; Dh20; 🚊Bab Lamrissa) Built by the dastardly Sallee Rovers pirates and recently restored, this slave prison next to the Muslim cemetery hadn't officially opened during our most recent visit, but should be open by the time of this guide's publication.

Koubba of Sidi Ben Ashir At Taleb ISLAMIC SHRINE
(cnr Aves Sidi Ben Achir & Abdelkader Al Harrati, Medina; Bab Lamrissa) This white *koubba* (shrine of a saint) at the edge of the medina was built to honour a 14th-century Spanish adherent and teacher of Sufism. The faithful come here to pray for cures to blindness and other ailments. Non-Muslims may not enter.

Sleeping & Eating

The tram has made Salé more accessible and in turn more accommodation is opening up, but still the choice is limited. There's a five-star Fairmont hotel under construction in the marina but the best option is Repose in the medina. There are plenty of hole-in-the-wall cafes in the medina and the lovely rooftop restaurant at Repose, as well as an increasing number of international restaurants around the marina.

★ **Repose** GUESTHOUSE €€
(0537882958; www.therepose.com; 17 Zankat Talaa, Ras Chejra, Medina; ste Dh450-750; ; Bab Lamrissa) Married couple Jan and Rachid have restored this traditional medina house with style, creating a delightful retreat. All seven rooms have vibrant decor, sitting areas and spacious bathrooms. There's a shaded roof terrace for leisurely breakfasts and vegetarian meals (dinner Dh200). They can arrange cooking classes and massages, tea with a family, and dispatch you to the neighbouring hammam fully equipped.

In-house restaurant **No 17** (three-course set dinner Dh200; 8pm) is an excellent choice to enjoy home-cooked vegetarian food and city views on the plant-filled roof terrace, or in the cosy salon; nonguests need to reserve ahead. The daily-changing menu makes the most of seasonal ingredients and flavours but gives them a modern twist – perhaps date, carrot and orange salad or stuffed aubergine served with couscous, rounded off with a divine lemon parfait.

Getting There & Away

Rowing **boats to Rabat** (Map p202; Dh5; sunrise-sunset) leave the marina when full.

The easiest way to travel between Salé and Rabat is by tram (Dh6) – the Gare de Salé stop is closest to the medina – or by *grand taxi* from Bab Lekhmiss or Bab Mrisa (Dh5 one-way if you share). Note that *petits taxis* are not permitted to travel between Rabat and Salé.

Trains run to/from Rabat, but the tram or *grands taxis* are probably the simplest options. Trains also run north to the transport hub of Kenitra (Dh16, 25 minutes) and to Fez (Dh85, 2¾ hours).

All-new buses, operated by Spanish-company ALSA, depart regularly for Rabat (Dh5).

Around Rabat & Salé

Témara Plage BEACH
(Témara) Wild and sandy Témara Plage, 15km south of the city, is popular with surfers and sunbathers in summer; there are dangerous rips so swimmers should be cautious. The beach can be reached on bus 33 from Bab Al Had in Rabat.

Plage des Nations BEACH
The clean, sandy strip of beach, around 25km north of Rabat, gets some serious wave action that's good for surfers, but the currents can be dangerous for swimming.

To get to the beach, drive north as far as the Musée Belghazi and turn left down a road known as Sidi Bouknadel. Bus 9 from Rabat or Salé will drop you at the turn-off, from where it's a 2km walk to the beach past huge developments of holiday apartments.

Jardins Exotiques GARDENS
(0537822756; www.jardinsexotiques.com; Bouknadel; adult/child/family Dh20/12/50; 9am-5.30pm, to 7.30pm spring & summer) Created by French horticulturist Marcel François in 1951, these gardens were declared a Natural Heritage site in 2003. Recently renovated, they're filled with exotic flora from Africa, Latin America and the Caribbean and make a popular day trip for residents of Rabat and Salé. The gardens are around 20km north of Rabat on the road to Kenitra. Take bus 9 from Bab Chellah in Rabat or from Bab Lekhmiss at the Salé medina.

Lac de Sidi Boughaba LAKE
This freshwater lake, part of the Lac Sidi Boughaba Parc National, is located in Mehdia, on the outskirts of industrial Kenitra. As a refuelling stop for thousands of birds migrating between Europe and sub-Saharan Africa, the lake provides some of the country's best birdwatching, especially between October and March. To get to the

lake follow the signposts from the beach road to Mehdiya Plage, 300m past the Cafe Restaurant Belle Vue. The lake is a 3.3km walk from the turn-off.

Larache العرائش

POP 125,010

Like most of the other towns on this stretch of the Atlantic, Larache is laid-back for most of the year but bursts into life in summer, when Moroccan tourists flock to nearby Ras R'mel beach. Occupied by the Spanish for most of the 17th century, the town developed a local industry building ships for the corsairs operating further south. It eventually became the main port of the Spanish protectorate in 1911.

While it retains some handsome Hispanic architecture, Larache gets far fewer tourists than Asilah, its northern neighbour. Come here for local flavour rather than headline sights – although the ruins of Lixus are well worth a visit – and don't expect a lot in terms of accommodation and eating options.

Sights

The Ville Nouvelle has some grand Hispano-Moorish architecture dating from the colonial era, particularly around lovely Place de la Libération (the former Plaza de España), and its living blue-and-white medina is well worth a wander. On weekends and in the early evening, the pedestrianised *balcón* (elevated platform) overlooking the Atlantic is a popular spot for a promenade. North of the River Loukos, on the outer edge of town, sit the ruins of ancient Lixus, the legendary site of the Garden of the Hesperides.

★Place de la Libération SQUARE

Built by the Spanish, who called it Plaza de España (some locals still do), this grand oval-shaped plaza is the town's focal point. Decorated with palm trees and a fountain, it's encircled by handsome Hispano-Moorish buildings where terrace cafes are a favourite haunt for locals. On the eastern side, the magnificent, glaze-tiled **Bab Al Khemis** is the centrepiece of an arched walkway and leads to the medina's marketplace.

The town's much-loved pedestrianised *balcón* is one block north.

★Medina AREA

Entered through the **Bab Al Khemis**, an imposing Hispano-Moorish structure, Larache's blue-and-white medina has changed little over the years. Mostly residential, it's arranged around the **Zoco de la Alcaiceria**, a colonnaded marketplace, where fresh produce and household goods are sold from open-fronted stores, wooden carts or straight off the cobbles. To the north is a maze of narrow lanes leading to the ruined **Saadian Fortress**. South, up the hill, is the handsome **Music Conservatory** (Conservatoire de Musique de Larache) and a scenic lookout.

Lookout VIEWPOINT

(Plaza Dar El Majzen; Plaza Dar El Majzen) With stunning views over the port and estuary, this lookout is a popular meeting spot. On the way you'll pass the crumbling 17th-century fortification **Kasbah de la Cigogne**, built by the Spaniards under Philip III, and the old town's landmark **mosque** (closed to non-Muslims).

Ras R'mel Beach BEACH

Larache has a small rubbish-strewn strip of sand below the town, but the best beach is across the Loukos Estuary, an 11km drive from the town centre. In summer, small boats ferry passengers across the estuary, from where the beach is a short walk across the dunes. You'll need to bargain with the boatman to get the best price (around Dh10). At other times a *petit taxi* from the town centre will cost around Dh25.

Galerie Lafnar GALLERY

(☎0654044810; 58 Assadr Alaadam, Medina; ⏲10am-1pm & 5-9pm) In an interesting old *funduq* (ancient inn used by caravans), this art gallery sells work by local artists, as well as staging occasional exhibitions. Just off the Zoco de la Alcaiceria in the heart of the medina.

Jean Genet's Grave LANDMARK

French literature buffs mays want to head to the old Spanish cemetery, the final resting place of Jean Genet (1910–86). If the gate is locked, ring the bell for the caretaker. A small tip is expected for showing you to the grave.

Sleeping

There are a couple of atmospheric riad guesthouses in the medina but accommodation options are predominantly in the budget category, catering to domestic tourism, with most hotels clustered along the streets just south of Place de la Libération.

★**Hôtel España** HOTEL €

(☎0539913195; www.hotelespanalarache.com; 6 Ave Hassan II; d/tw Dh330/380; P📶) Housed in a handsome Hispano-Moorish building, this old-school hotel is a safe and friendly accommodation choice. Rooms are clean, comfortable and well maintained, with satellite TV and double-glazed windows. The best are at the front, with balconies overlooking the action on Place de la Libération.

Hotel Hay Essalam HOTEL €

(☎0539916822; 9 Ave Hassan II; s/d/tw Dh116/133/166, with shared bathroom Dh90/116/140; ❄📶) The best of Larache's low-budget accommodation options, this simple place offers a variety of room types; some have basic bathrooms and air-con, others are little more than unadorned cubes. Those at the front are light but noisy – light sleepers should opt for one at the rear. No English.

Hôtel Somarían HOTEL €€

(☎0539910116; hotelsomarian@live.fr; 68 Ave Mohammed Zerktouni; s/d/tr Dh400/500/600; 📶) Housed in an unattractive modern building across the street from the covered central market, the Somarían offers colourful, comfortable rooms, all of which have spotless bathrooms.

La Maison Haute GUESTHOUSE €€

(☎0668340072; http://lamaisonhaute.free.fr; 6 Derb Ben Thami, Medina; s/d/tr from Dh350/450/550) Colourful, with bags of character – the same goes for polyglot owner, Hassan – this Hispano-Moorish house overlooking the Zoco de la Alcaiceria has six rooms, an apartment sleeping four and a roof terrace with views over the medina and estuary. A family-home-turned-guesthouse, it's filled with fascinating, dusty antiques, but in need of some TLC. Hot water is not guaranteed.

Sultana Larache B&B €€€

(☎0661191162; 8 Rue Halhoula, Medina; d from €80; 📶) Hidden away down one of the medina's winding lanes, this large house – said to have once been owned by a sultan – has been sensitively and stylishly restored. There are just three rooms with neutral-toned, smooth *tadelakt* walls and local touches, along with a breezy salon with medina views and a cosy salon with a log fire.

Eating & Drinking

Eating out in Larache is cheap and cheerful with plenty of little places around Place de la Libération. The Spanish influence lingers on in the paella and tortillas served in most restaurants. Cafes with outdoor terraces surround Place de la Libération and face the *balcón*. The town is almost entirely alcohol-free.

★**Gran Café Lixus** INTERNATIONAL €

(Place de la Libération; set breakfast Dh30; 🕒6.30am-11pm) A Larache institution, this

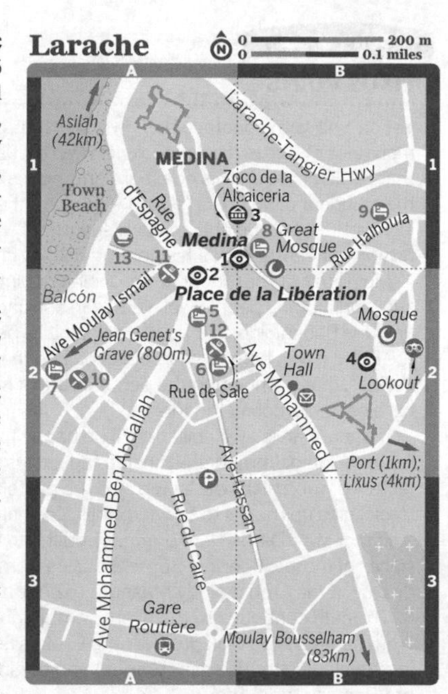

Larache

Top Sights
1 Medina ... B1
2 Place de la Libération ... A2

Sights
3 Galerie Lafnar ... B1
4 Music Conservatory ... B2

Sleeping
5 Hôtel España ... A2
6 Hotel Hay Essalam ... A2
7 Hôtel Somarían ... A2
8 La Maison Haute ... B1
9 Sultana Larache ... B1

Eating
10 Casa Ché ... A2
11 Gran Café Lixus ... A2
12 Restaurant Puerta Del Sol ... A2

Drinking & Nightlife
13 Café Balcón Atlantico ... A1

DON'T MISS

LIXUS RUINS

Set on a hill with spectacular views over the Loukos Estuary, the Carthaginian and Roman ruins of **Lixus** (Larache-Tangier Hwy/N1; Dh60; ⊙8am-7pm) are evocative reminders that settlements on this coast are among the oldest in the country. And while it lacks the grandeur of Volubilis (p365) – much of the ruins have been eroded by time and the elements – you'll be able to wander without the crowds. And now there's a contemporary visitor centre with a fascinating display charting what's known of the site's history.

Megalithic stones found in the vicinity point to it originally being inhabited by a sun-worshipping people well versed in astronomy and mathematics. Then little is known until the Phoenicians set up the colony Liks here in about 1000 BCE. According to Pliny the Elder, it was here that Hercules picked the golden apples of the Garden of the Hesperides, thus completing the penultimate of his 12 labours. The golden apples could well have been Moroccan tangerines.

If a guardian is available, they'll be happy to show you around – a tip (around Dh100) is appreciated. Immediately inside the gate is the lower town, with the remains of *garum* factories where fish was salted and the paste so beloved by the Romans was produced. A track leads up the hill to the acropolis, passing a steep amphitheatre built by the Romans along the way. Baths were originally built into the side of the amphitheatre, with some traces of mosaic flooring. Some mosaics from the site were removed and are now on display at the Archaeology Museum (p276) in Tetouan.

The path continues to the overgrown acropolis, which straddles the crest of the hill. From here you can look out over the Loukos Estuary and salt fields below. The civic buildings (including temple sanctuaries) and original city ramparts are here, as are traces of pre-Roman structures.

In the 6th century BCE, the Phoenician Atlantic colonies fell to the Carthaginians. Lixus remained a trading post, principally in gold, ivory and enslaved people and, by 42 CE, had entered the Roman Empire. Its primary exports soon changed to salt, olives, wine and *garum*, and its merchants also grew rich from the export of wild animals for use in the Empire's amphitheatres.

The colony at Lixus rapidly declined as the Romans withdrew from North Africa, and was abandoned completely in the 5th century, after the collapse of the Roman Empire. Later, the site became known to Muslims as Tuchummus.

Lixus is approximately 5.5km north of Larache on the road to Tangier and the main gate is just off the highway, by the road running in front of the estuary. A *petit taxi* costs Dh20 one-way, but you may have trouble flagging down a bus or taxi for your return trip; it's best to organise for the driver to pick you up at an agreed time.

old-world cafe has occupied a prime perch on the Place de la Libération since 1920. Take a look at the art deco interior with its soaring columns, grand piano and photo-filled walls, then sit at a terrace table, perfect for people watching, over a crêpe and juice at breakfast, pizza in the evening and mint tea any time.

Restaurant Puerta Del Sol MOROCCAN €
(☎0539913641; 5 Rue Ahmed Chaouki; mains Dh25-40; ⊙noon-10pm Mon-Sat) Join the locals enjoying Moroccan staples, including tajines and *brochettes,* along with Spanish favourites such as paella and tortilla at this cheap-and-cheerful indoor-outdoor eatery close to Place de la Libération.

★**Casa Ché** SEAFOOD €€
(☎0677830200; 87 Ave Mohammed Zerktouni; mains Dh70; ⊙noon-3pm & 7-10pm Mon-Sat) This clean and simple place near the covered central market is bedecked with portraits of Che Guevara and popular with both locals and visitors for its Mediterranean, Moroccan and Basque dishes, with an emphasis on fresh fish and seafood. Try the tajine de boquerones (anchovies).

Café Balcón Atlantico CAFE
(cnr Rue de Casablanca & Rue Tarik Ibnou Ziad; ⊙8am-11pm) Overlooking the *balcón* and Atlantic beyond, this bright, bustling cafe has plenty of breezy outdoor seating and good coffee. It's one of the best spots in town for a relaxed breakfast or a sightseeing break.

Getting There & Around

The **bus station** (Rue Ibnou Khaldoun) is an easy walk south of Place de la Libération, off Ave Mohammed Ben Abdallah. Most major destinations are covered by CTM, including the following.

Agadir Dh315, 9¾ hours, one daily

Casablanca Dh100, four hours, six daily

Fez Dh85, 4¾ hours, five daily

Marrakesh Dh210, 8 hours, two daily

Tangier Dh35, 1¼ hours, five daily

Grands taxis run from outside the bus station to Souk El Arba (Dh40), Tangier (Dh35) and Kenitra (Dh50). Those heading to Asilah (Dh20) usually leave from outside the municipal produce market on Ave Malek Ben Marhal.

Petits taxis charge Dh20 to Lixus and Dh25 to Ras R'mel Beach.

Moulay Bousselham مولاي بوسلهام

POP 7370

Though inundated by local holidaymakers in high summer, the small town of Moulay Bousselham is blissfully tranquil for the rest of the year. The sweeping golden sand beach is one of the most attractive on the North Atlantic coast, although strong currents and crashing waves can prove dangerous. With a car, it makes a relaxed base for day trips to Rabat and Casablanca to the south and Asilah to the north.

The town is named after a 10th-century Egyptian saint who is commemorated in one of the *koubbas* (shrines) that line the slope down to the sea, guarding the mouth of the river.

And a 15-minute walk south of the main road into town is the protected Merja Zerga lagoon, one of the country's most important bird habitats, attracting birdwatchers from around the globe.

Sights & Activities

Merja Zerga National Park NATIONAL PARK

Don't miss a boat trip on the Merja Zerga (Blue Lagoon), roughly 1km south of town. Part of a 70 sq km namesake national park (4 sq km of water, the rest marshland) it attracts myriad migrant birds, including flamingos, making it one of Morocco's prime birdwatching habitats and North Africa's most important wetlands. Best times to visit are spring and autumn, but there are about 75 species year round. Enlist an expert guide; they'll pick you up from your hotel.

You'll see herons, ibises, spoonbills, plovers, egrets and more. Slender-billed and Audouin's gulls are regular visitors, as are shelducks, teals, terns, marsh harriers and peregrine falcons.

The lagoon is between 50cm and 4m deep depending on the tide. Most of the water comes from the sea, but 10% is freshwater from the Dredr River, south of the lagoon.

There are five other villages around the lake, four of which depend on agriculture, one other on fishing. Many of the fishers take tourists around the lake as a sideline. Boat trips with the local boaters are easily arranged if you wander down to the small port where boats are moored. Expect to pay about Dh100 per hour for the boat. If possible, contact Hassan Dalil or Khalil Fachkhir in advance for a specialised birding tour; both have their own boats and speak English.

Hardcore birdwatchers may also want to explore Merja Khaloufa, an attractive lake about 8km east of Moulay Bousselham and part of the park, which offers good viewing of a variety of wintering wildfowl.

★**Hassan Dalil** BIRDWATCHING

(☎0668434110; hassandalil873@gmail.com; tour Dh300) Eagle-eyed Hassan has more than 30 years of experience spotting the native and migratory birdlife of the Merja Zerga lagoon. As well as pointing out the plethora of bird species, he'll throw in some history and culture too. He also takes avid birders to spot marsh owls to the south of the lagoon.

You can also contact him via Restaurante Milano (p220).

Khalil Fachkhir BIRDWATCHING

(☎0663095358; nidlehibou@yahoo.com; tours per boat Dh250-300) Recommended English-speaking guide who knows the lagoon and its birds extremely well. He has his own boat and the tour usually lasts around 1.5 to 2 hours, but times are flexible.

Sleeping

Most visitors stay in private villas (many wealthy city-dwellers have holiday villas here), but there's also a campground and a couple of hotels and B&Bs. The prime location is on the Front de Mer (seafront).

Villa Nora B&B €€

(☎0537432071; Front de Mer; s/d incl breakfast Dh370/400; 📶) The sprawling whitewashed villa comes with stunning views over the ocean. Furnishings (including beds) are dated and creature comforts, such as hot water, can't be taken for granted. But it's clean, the staff are friendly and the grassy terrace is the perfect spot to kick back.

★ Vila Bea BOUTIQUE HOTEL €€€
(☎0537432087; www.vilabea.com; 41 Front de Mer; d from Dh1375; ⏱closed Jan; P❄📶🏊) Many guests barely leave this superstylish beachside retreat thanks to the large and luxurious rooms, spacious lounge filled with retro-chic furnishings, stunning pool terrace and the best restaurant in town (three-course set dinners Dh270). Four of the eight rooms have sea views – two have private terraces – and showstopping sunset views, along with direct access to the beach.

Eating & Drinking

The pickings are slim when it comes to dining out, so most visitors self-cater or eat in their guesthouse. Note that alcohol isn't officially available in the town.

Restaurante Milano MOROCCAN €
(mains Dh30-60; ⏱11am-4pm & 6-10pm) In a prime position on the main street, this bustling place is popular with both tourists and locals. Decent sandwiches, pasta and pizza are on offer, as well as tajines. No alcohol.

★ Cafe Restaurant Izaguirre SEAFOOD €€
(☎0537432445; Rue du Port; mains Dh50-200; ⏱8am-10pm) Next to the sea-blue fishing boats moored in the lagoon, this clean and cheerful restaurant specialises in the catch-of-the-day and is universally acknowledged to be the best restaurant in town. Head up the stairs to the blue-and-white terrace, where friendly waiters are rushed off their feet in the summer months. No alcohol.

Cafe Atlantico CAFE
(⏱8am-9pm) Perched above the beach, the terrace of this small cafe has sweeping views over the Atlantic from all sides. Have a coffee break or sip on a strawberry juice while you take in the showstopping sunsets.

Getting There & Away

Moulay Bousselham is about 40km due south of Larache. To travel between the two towns by public transport, you'll need to detour to the little town of Souk El Arba (*grand taxi* from Larache Dh40, 45 minutes), from where there are frequent *grands taxis* (Dh20, 45 minutes) to Moulay Bousselham. A private *grand taxi* will cost Dh250.

Grands taxis between Moulay Bousselham and the city of Kenitra – from where you can make your way to Rabat, Casablanca, Meknes or Fez from the Kenitra-Medina train station – charge Dh50 for the 1½-hour trip; a private taxi is Dh350.

Asilah أصيلة

POP 31,150

With a bite-sized, impossibly picturesque medina, a relaxed vibe and a string of beautiful beaches close by, Asilah makes an easy introduction to Morocco's Atlantic Coast.

Founded by the Phoenicians around 1500 BCE, it was invaded by the Carthaginians, Romans, Normans and Portuguese, among others. And the tortilla, paella and Rioja wine served in most of its restaurants are reminders that it was Spanish territory for a long time.

The town is sleepy for most of the year, but in the summer months its population triples and the streets and town beach are crammed with sun-seeking Moroccan and Spanish families, many of whom have holiday homes here. The best time to visit is in spring or autumn when it's still warm but the tourist hordes have left.

History

This small but strategic port has had a turbulent history ever since it began life as the Carthaginian settlement of Zilis. During the Punic Wars the people backed Carthage, and when the region fell to the Romans, the locals were shipped to Spain and replaced with Iberians. From then on, Asilah was inexorably linked with the Spanish and with their numerous battles for territory.

As Christianity conquered the proponents of Islam on the Iberian Peninsula in the 14th and 15th centuries, Asilah felt the knock-on effects. In 1471 the Portuguese sent 477 ships with 30,000 men, captured the port and built the walls that still surround the medina, a trading post on their famous gold route across Africa. In 1578 King Dom Sebastian of Portugal embarked on an ill-fated crusade from Asilah. He was killed, and Portugal (and its Moroccan possessions) passed into the hands of the Spanish, who remained for a very long time.

Asilah was recaptured by Moulay Ismail in 1691. In the 19th century, continuing piracy prompted Austria and then Spain to send their navies to bombard the town. Its most

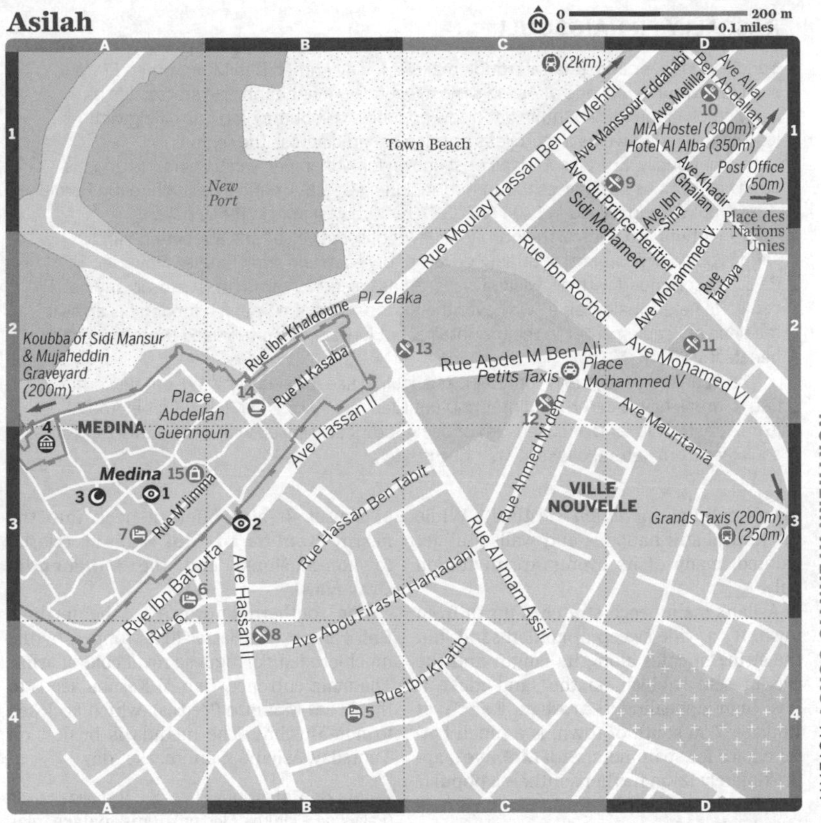

Asilah

Top Sights

1 Medina A3

Sights

2 Bab Homar B3
3 Great Mosque A3
4 Palais de Raissouli A3

Sleeping

5 Christina's House B4
6 Dar Azaouia A3
7 Dar Manara A3

Eating

8 Ali Baba B4
9 Casa García D1
10 La Perle d'Asilah D1
11 Marché Central D2
12 Restaurant Dar Al Maghrebia C2
13 Restaurante Oceano Casa Pepe C2

Drinking & Nightlife

14 Al Madina B2

Shopping

15 Bazar Atlas A3

famous renegade was Er Raissouli (p222), one of the most colourful bandits ever raised in the wild Rif Mountains. Early in the 20th century, Er Raissouli used Asilah as his base, becoming the bane of the European powers. Spain made Asilah part of its protectorate from 1911 until 1956.

Sights

Asilah has long had a reputation as a city of the arts. It all started in 1978 when several Moroccan artists were invited to literally paint the town, holding workshops for local children and leaving murals on the whitewashed medina walls as part of the

RASCALLY ER RAISSOULI

Bandit, kidnapper and general troublemaker, Moulay Ahmed Ben Mohammed Er Raissouli (or Raisuni) was one of Asilah's most legendary inhabitants. He started life as a petty crook in the Rif Mountains and saw no problem in bumping off unwilling victims, leading to his renown as a merciless murderer, feared across the region.

Internationally, Er Raissouli was best known for kidnapping westerners. He and his band held various luminaries to ransom, including Greek-American billionaire Ion Perdicaris, who was ransomed in 1904 for US$70,000, a vast sum in those days.

In an attempt to control the unruly outlaw, consecutive sultans appointed him to various political positions, including governor of Asilah and later Tangier. However, Er Raissouli continued with his wicked ways, amassing great wealth in whatever way he could. He held considerable sway over the Rif tribes and the Spanish funded his arms in the hope of keeping order in the mountains, but Er Raissouli often used them against his benefactors.

The Spaniards eventually forced Er Raissouli to flee Asilah after WWI, but he continued to wreak havoc in the Rif hinterland until January 1925, when the Rif rebel Abd Al Krim arrested him and accused him of being too closely linked with the Spanish. Er Raissouli died from natural causes two months later.

town's cultural *moussem* (festival). While the festival still happens and walls still get painted, many of its events are invitation only.

Asilah's main beach stretches north from town. It's a wide sweep of golden sand, but the string of cafes along its length and the ever-present rubbish on the sand make it less than appealing. **Paradise Beach** at Rmilate, 7km south of town, is a much better choice for swimmers. **Sidi Mghayet**, approximately 13km further south, is a popular surf beach and nearby **Rada Beach** has a busy beach cafe.

You'll need to take a taxi to out-of-town beaches, so ask your accommodation to suggest someone, or contact English-speaking **Mohamed Arabi** (☎0628448989, 0668019700).

★Medina AREA

Asilah's compact medina is surrounded by sturdy stone fortifications built by the Portuguese in the 15th century. Enter through the **Bab Al Kassaba** and wander along its warren of alleyways, where the brilliant-white buildings punctuated with blue paintwork that match the sea and sky – many of which have been bought and restored by foreigners – are dotted with boutiques and galleries. Colourful murals painted each year during the Asilah Festival, as well as by local schoolchildren, make it exceptionally photogenic.

Access to the ramparts is limited. The southwestern bastion is the best spot for views over the ocean and is a popular spot at sunset. It also offers a peek into the nearby **Koubba of Sidi Mansur** (closed to non-Muslims) and the **Mujaheddin Graveyard**.

The southern entrance to the medina, **Bab Homar** (Ave Hassan II), is topped by the much-eroded Portuguese royal coat of arms. The main entrance, Bab Al Kasaba, leads to the **Great Mosque** (Medina), which is closed to non-Muslims. The medina is busiest on Thursday, Asilah's main market day.

Palais de Raissouli HISTORIC BUILDING

(Palais de Culture; Medina) This palace was built in 1909 by Er Raissouli the pirate and stands as a testament to the sumptuous life he led at the height of his power. Beautifully restored, it is usually only open during the Asilah Festival. The building includes a main reception room with a glass-fronted terrace overlooking the sea, from where Er Raissouli forced convicted murderers to jump to their deaths onto the rocks 30m below.

Festivals & Events

Asilah Festival CULTURAL

(Moussem Culturel International d'Assilah; www.assilah.net; ⏰Jun-Jul) At this annual month-long festival, everyone from Japanese artists to Sufi chanters, plus spectators, descend upon the town. Events include workshops, public art demonstrations, concerts and exhibitions. Events centre on the Palais de Raissouli and Centre de Hassan II Rencontres Internationales.

Sleeping

There's a good selection of budget and midrange accommodation, but surprisingly few guesthouses inside the medina walls – although there's no shortage of Airbnb options. During high season (July and August) prices rise and the town is flooded with visitors; book well in advance if you have to travel at this time.

★ **MIA Hostel** HOSTEL €

(0539417894; www.miahostels.com; 55 Lot Minza; dm Dh106-160, d/tw Dh490/640;) Taking its name from owners Mehdi, Ismael and Ali, this excellent hostel does them proud. Dorms and rooms have comfortable beds, air-con, plenty of hot water in the bathrooms, and facilities include a TV lounge, a book exchange, bike and surfboard rental, a communal kitchen and a rooftop terrace for summer barbecues (Dh50 to Dh100).

Christina's House GUESTHOUSE €

(0610502026; www.christinashouseasilah.com; 26 Rue Ibn Khatib, off Blvd 16 Nov; s/d/tr €30/40/50;) A friendly guesthouse that feels more like a home than a hotel, with six colourful rooms with tiled floors and simple bathrooms. There's a comfortable lounge, communal kitchen and huge rooftop terrace with plenty of seating, perfect for the leisurely continental breakfast.

Hotel Al Alba BOUTIQUE HOTEL €€

(0539416923; www.hotelalalba.com; 35 Lot Nahil; s/d/ste from Dh570/700/925;) On the edge of the town centre, this small hotel has bright stylish rooms, decorated in blue and white in homage to the medina. The young, multilingual staff go out of their way to be helpful and the hammam (Dh315) is a real draw. The restaurant (three-course set menu Dh115) serves typical Moroccan and fish dishes; no alcohol.

Dar Manara GUESTHOUSE €€

(0539416964; www.asilah-darmanara.com; 23 Rue M'Jimma, Medina; r Dh700;) This Spanish-owned riad has been converted into an intimate guesthouse, one of the only such options in the medina. Rooms are small but nicely decorated and common areas include an elegant salon with an open fireplace and a roof terrace complete with traditional Moroccan seating. A communal breakfast is served at 9am sharp.

★ **Dar Azaouia** GUESTHOUSE €€€

(0672110535; www.darazaouia-asilah.com; 18 Rue 6, Quartier Moulay Idriss; s/d/tr/ste Dh650/850/1050/1300;) The hands-on Belgian owner has painstakingly restored this beautiful traditional house just outside the medina walls, artfully blending Moroccan tradition with contemporary European style. Local textiles, handicrafts and original artwork fill the five rooms and three suites, all with good beds and fireplaces. A cosy salon and a two-level roof terrace add to its charms. Book in advance.

Eating & Drinking

Aside from La Perle d'Asilah (p224), there's little in the way of fine dining here, but there are plenty of sun-filled terraces to feast on simple fish and seafood dishes, as well some fast-food joints with carbon-copy menus of pizza and tajines. Most drinking in town occurs in the Spanish restaurants, and there are no bars or clubs worthy of recommendation. Cafes are found on nearly every street corner in the blocks around Place Mohammed V, but many are male preserves.

★ **Restaurant Dar Al Maghrebia** MOROCCAN €

(0633662377; 7 Rue Al Banafsaje; mains Dh45-110; noon-4pm & 7-10pm) Deserving kudos for its bargain prices, tasty dishes and atmospheric surrounds, this small restaurant off Place Mohammed V offers a selection of *bastillas*, *brochettes*, *briouats* (stuffed pastries) and tajines in manageable portions. Dine in the charming dining salon or at one of street tables. No alcohol, but virgin cocktails and fruit juice are available.

Ali Baba MOROCCAN €

(0633580050; cnr Ave Abou Ferras El Hamadani & Ave Hassan II; dishes Dh20-50; noon-1am) Popular with locals, this impeccably clean place serves fresh and tasty *harira* (lentil soup), tajines, shawarma (meat sliced off a spit and stuffed in a pocket of pita-type bread), plus pizza and sandwiches. Eat in or get it to go.

Marché Central MARKET €

(Ave Mohamed VI; 8am-8pm) Asilah's small central market is a good place to source fresh fruit, vegetables, meat, fish and spices; the row of restaurants in its front arcade serve up fresh fish at bargain prices.

Restaurante Oceano Casa Pepe SEAFOOD €€

(0539417395; 8 Place Zellaka; mains Dh60-350; noon-5pm & 8pm-midnight) This Spanish restaurant has been serving customers since

AROUND ASILAH

An interesting trip from Asilah is a visit to the lively **Had Gharbia Souq** (Sun) in the village of Had Gharbia, 14km northeast of town, inland off the road to Tangier. Families come from far and wide to this outdoor market to haggle over vegetables, chickens, charcoal and plastic goods from China.

The mysterious **Monoliths of M'Soura** make an interesting half-day trip from Asilah. This prehistoric site consists of a large stone circle (actually an ellipse) of about 175 stones, thought to have originally surrounded a burial mound. Although many of the stones have fallen or been broken, the circle is still impressive, its strange presence heightened by the desolation of its location. The tallest stone reaches about 5.5m in height and is known as El Uted (The Pointer).

The stone circle is about 25km (by road) southeast of Asilah. To get there you'll need a sturdy vehicle. Head for the village of Souq Tnine de Sidi El Yamani, off highway R417, which branches east off the main Tangier–Rabat road. Veer left in the village and follow a poorly maintained, unsealed track 6km north to the site. It can be difficult to find so you may want to ask for directions or hire a guide in the village.

1914 and is still going strong. The original Pepe has passed away, the dimly lit interior is old-school tapas bar and the menu is overlong, but dine outside and stick to staples like octopus salad and fried fish, washed down with a robust vino, and you can't go too far wrong.

Casa García SPANISH €€
(0539417465; 51 Rue Moulay Hassan Ben El Mehdi; mains Dh50-125; noon-3pm & 7-11pm) Spanish-style seafood dishes are the speciality at this popular marine-themed restaurant a couple of streets back from the beach. Expect staples such as grilled sardines, seafood paella and deep-fried calamari, along with the catch-of-the-day. The restaurant is cavernous and can get noisy but the breezy terrace is a pleasant place to while away an evening with a bottle of wine.

★ **La Perle d'Asilah** FRENCH €€€
(0618556980; cnr Rue Allal Ben Abdallah & Ave Melilla; mains Dh120-250; noon-3pm & 7-10.30pm) At Asilah's finest dining option, the menu leans heavily on the Gallic, mixing in Asian and Spanish influences from the Moroccan owner-chef's experience in top restaurants around the globe. Surrounds are classy, the narrow terrace is lovely on a balmy evening and the set two- and three-course menus (Dh180 to Dh210) are outstanding value.

Al Madina CAFE
(Place Abdellah Guennoun, Medina; 9am-9pm) The main attraction of this simple little cafe in the medina is its sunny seating area in the square in front of El Khamra Tower. It's a great place to watch the world go by with a mint tea.

Shopping

Bazar Atlas ARTS & CRAFTS
(0661103345; 25 Rue de Commerce; 9am-9pm) There's a fine selection of carpets on offer at this two-storey shop, with piles of shaggy Beni Ouarain, tightly woven kilim and colourful Azilal upstairs, and distinctive green-glazed pottery from Tamegroute downstairs.

Getting There & Away

Few intercity buses stop in Asilah so most locals use the train or *grands taxis* when travelling to other Moroccan destinations.

The bus station is opposite the Shell petrol station on the Tangier–Rabat road, but few intercity buses stop here. The only useful and regular service is on local company Alsa to Tangier (Dh7).

Grands taxis to Tangier (Dh20) and Larache (Dh20) depart when full from a stand near the Shell petrol station on the Tangier–Rabat road. A taxi to Tangier's airport (only 26km from Asilah) costs Dh250.

The art deco–era train station is 2km north of the medina; petits taxis from the south side of Place Mohammed V will take you there for Dh10. Destinations include the following.

Fez 1st/2nd class Dh136/92, 3½ hours, four daily

Marrakesh 1st/2nd class Dh306/216, 9½ hours. One overnight train goes direct to Marrakesh, but this train originates in Tangier, so buy your ticket in advance.

Rabat 1st/2nd class Dh130/88, 4½ hours (one change), eight daily

Tangier 1st/2nd class Dh27/17, 30 minutes, eight daily

El Jadida الجديدة

POP 194,930

El Jadida's chief draw is its beautiful Unesco-protected, 16th-century Cité Portugaise, with its hulking honey-coloured bastions, subterranean cistern and distinctly European air. It's possible to explore it in a couple of hours on the way to or from Casablanca, but if you stay the night you'll be able to wander without the day trippers.

In July and August the town transforms into a heaving holiday resort, popular with Moroccan families.

History

The hulking fortress was built by the Portuguese in 1506 to protect their ships heading down the West African coast. They baptised it Mazagan, and it soon developed into the country's most important trading post. Sultan Sidi Mohammed Ben Abdallah seized Mazagan from the Portuguese following a siege in 1769, but the Portuguese blew up most of the fort before leaving. Most of the new settlers preferred to live in the new town, and the citadel remained a ruin until the early 19th century when Sultan Abd Er Rahman resettled some of the Jews of Azemmour in old Mazagan and renamed the town El Jadida, 'the New One' in Arabic.

The large and influential Jewish community soon grew rich on trade with the interior. Unlike most other Moroccan cities, in El Jadida there was no *mellah* (Jewish quarter); the Jews mixed with the general populace and an attitude of easy tolerance was established. During the years of the colonial French protectorate its port gradually lost out to Safi and Casablanca, but the town became an administrative centre and popular beach resort.

Sights

The beaches within and to the immediate north and south of town are packed in July and August, despite being quite filthy.

★Cité Portugaise HISTORIC SITE

(Portuguese City) FREE Head through the main entrance gate of the Unesco-protected Cité Portugaise off Place Mohammed Ben Abdallah, and on the left are the early 16th-century **Church of the Assumption** and the **Grande Mosquée de Mazagan** boasting a unique five-sided minaret. Stop off at the atmospheric vaulted cistern – **La Citerne Portugaise** (adult/child Dh60/25) – before scaling a steep slope up to the hefty ramparts, where the **Bastion de L'Ange** makes an excellent photo stop, with views out to the ocean and the port.

A stroll along the ramparts takes you to the Bastion de St Sébastian, passing a ruined synagogue still sporting a Star of David on its facade.

At the end of the main road is the Porte de la Mer, the original sea gate where ships used to unload their cargo. To the left, through an archway, is a communal bakery where women still bring their bread to be baked. And you might recognise the cistern, lit by a single shaft of light, as the location for the dramatic riot scene in Orson Welles' 1951 film *Othello*.

Sidi Bouzid BEACH

The golden crescent of Sidi Bouzid beach, 5km south of El Jadida, is more pristine than the town beach and popular with both sunbathers and surfers. The water's chilly but the sunsets are magnificent. To get here, take local bus 14 (Dh5) from Place Mohammed Ben Abdallah.

Sleeping

The most characterful small hotels are in the Cité Portugaise and the medina. The budget options in the Ville Nouvelle cater more to domestic tourism. You need to book ahead if visiting in summer.

Riad Les Maisons des Epices GUESTHOUSE €€

(☎0523392764; https://riadlamaisondesepiceseljadida.com; 16 Rue Ben Driss, Medina; d from €50;) Dating from 1912, this historic house was the first to be built in El Jadida's medina. The six rooms open on to a pretty patio and no two are alike, but they all have smooth *tadelakt* walls and lofty ceilings. Breakfast is served on the roof terrace with views

FESTIVAL INTERNATIONAL JAWHARA

Staged in the towns of El Jadida, Azemmour and Bir Jdid, the **Festival International Jawhara** (☎0523355221; www.festivaljawhara.ma; Aug) includes sport, theatre and visual arts, but it concentrates on music, staging performances by big-name Moroccan and African artists.

El Jadida

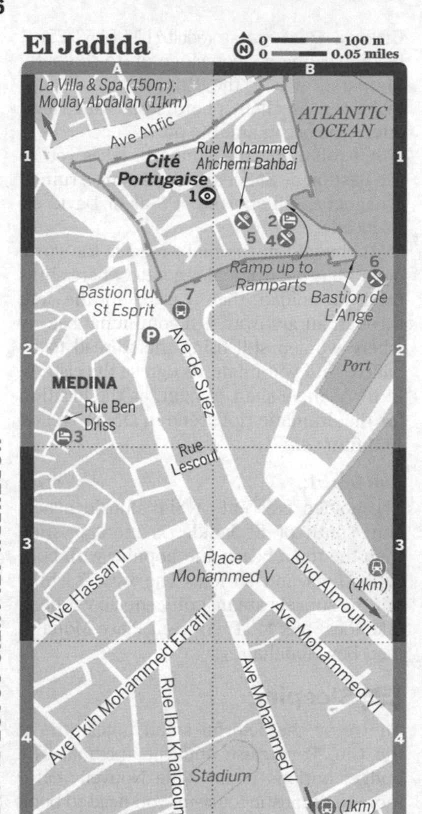

El Jadida

Top Sights

1 Cité Portugaise A1

Sleeping

2 L'Iglesia B1
3 Riad Les Maisons des Epices A2

Eating

4 La Capitainerie B1
5 Le Lokal B1
6 Restaurant du Port B2

Transport

7 Bus 14 to Sidi Bouzid A2

over the city, and dinner (two/three courses Dh150/200) is available on request.

★Mazagan Beach and Golf Resort RESORT €€€
(☎0523388080; www.mazaganbeachresort.com; Route de Casablanca; d from Dh1520; P❄📶🏊) This contemporary kasbah-style resort commands a vast stretch of beach, 16km north of El Jadida. It's so vast that even with 500 rooms it never feels crowded, and with 11 restaurants, two pools, a stables and water sports centre, there's no reason to leave.

There are lots of kid-friendly activities, while adults can enjoy the award-winning spa, bars, nightclub and casino.

★Dar Al Manar GUESTHOUSE €€€
(☎0523351645; www.dar-al-manar.com; r Dh800-1000) Five stylish and spacious rooms decorated in a contemporary Moroccan style await at this tranquil rural retreat near the Sidi M'sbah lighthouse, 7km from El Jadida. Guests enjoy relaxing in the lovely garden and downstairs lounge, and can dine on the terrace (set menus Dh200 to Dh250). The English- and French-speaking owner is both charming and helpful.

L'Iglesia BOUTIQUE HOTEL €€€
(☎0523373400; www.liglesia.com; Eglise St Antoine de Padoue, Cité Portugaise; d from Dh1500; 📶) A 16th-century Catholic church has been turned into a one-of-a-kind boutique hotel. The eight rooms mix up church architecture, vintage furniture and modern Moroccan design. There are five more rooms at the nearby La Capitainerie, a former harbour master's office that served as the American consulate until 1896, along with a great seafood-focused restaurant.

La Villa & Spa HOTEL €€€
(☎0523344423; http://lavilladavid.fr; 4 Ave Moulay Abdelhafid; r Dh860-1160, ste Dh1380; 📶🏊) A French-owned hotel just north of the Cité Portugaise, La Villa has sleek modern rooms with good beds, excellent bathrooms and satellite TV. There's a rooftop bar and dining area (dinner Dh300), the top terrace has a hot tub (Dh80 per hour) and massages are available in a dedicated downstairs room (Dh350 per hour).

✕ Eating & Drinking

El Jadida is short on decent restaurants and cafes. For a relatively cheap eat, pull up a seat at one of the popular fried-fish restaurants on Ave de Suez, opposite the port. These all serve fried fish, salad and bread for around Dh70.

The numerous sleazy bars around town are resolutely off-limits to women. In summer some of the licensed fish restaurants opposite the town beach and Sidi Bouzid morph into clubs after dinner and welcome a mixed crowd, but it's better for women not to go alone.

★Le Lokal CAFE €€
(☎0665085052; www.facebook.com/pg/LeLokalElJadida; Cité Portugaise; set dinner Dh80; ⏰10am-10pm; 📶) At this lovely, art-filled cafe you can sip on a fresh juice – perhaps avocado or date – or eat breakfast on one of the tiled terraces while gazing out over the old city. If you reserve in advance, they'll cook up a tasty tajine or couscous too. Look for the sign on the Cité Portugaise's main drag and head upstairs.

★La Capitainerie MEDITERRANEAN €€
(☎0523373400; www.liglesia.com; Cité Portugaise; mains Dh100, three-course set menu Dh290; ⏰noon-4pm & 7-10.30pm) In the annexe of L'Iglesia, the decor is retro, the plates and glasses are handmade and the à la carte and fixed-price menus change daily, with a focus on just-caught fish and seafood with a Moroccan twist – perhaps sardines or a fish tajine. The restaurant opens onto a large terrace shaded with olive and palm trees.

Restaurant du Port SEAFOOD €€
(☎0523342579; Port du Jadida; mains Dh90-130; ⏰noon-3pm & 7-10pm Mon-Sat, noon-3pm Sun) Head into the port and up the stairs to find this restaurant, which focuses on simple fish dishes and views over the harbour. It's one of the few restaurants in town serving alcohol, and the small bar in the main dining space can attract some rather raddled types so it's not great for solo women diners in the evening.

Sel de Mer SEAFOOD €€€
(☎0523388000; www.mazaganbeachresort.com/dining/sel-de-mer; Route de Casablanca; mains from Dh245; ⏰7pm-midnight Mon, Wed & Fri-Sun; P📶👪) Bathed in an ethereal blue light, this sophisticated restaurant located at the Mazagan Beach and Golf Resort focuses on the catch-of-the-day displayed on ice. Perhaps briny oysters from Oualidia, meaty turbot or sea bass with divine lobster ravioli, all washed down with a fine Moroccan wine. Service is polished but unstuffy. Reserve in advance and note the smart dress code.

Kids of all ages are welcome; there is a special menu.

Getting There & Around

The **bus station** (Ave Mohammed V) is a 20-minute walk from the medina and the fortress.

TO	COMPANY	FARE (DH)	TIME (HR)	FREQUENCY
Casablanca	CTM	50	2	6 daily
Essaouira	CTM	100	4½	1 daily
Marrakesh	STCR	55	4	hourly
Rabat	STCR	50	4	12 daily
Safi	CTM	60	2½	8 daily

Grands taxis for Azemmour (Dh10, 15 minutes) and Casablanca (Dh35, one hour) leave from Ave Mohammed V, next to the bus station.

El Jadida's train station is located 4km south of town. There are eight services a day to and from Casablanca's Casa Voyagers station (1st/2nd class Dh53/37, 80 minutes). A *petit taxi* to the centre will cost Dh15 to Dh20.

Local bus 14 for Sidi Bouzid (Dh5) leaves from Place Mohammed Ben Abdallah, near the fortress.

Azemmour أزمّور

POP 40,920

With a rich history of arts and crafts, Azemmour has inspired many artists over the decades, some who've chosen to live here and open small galleries, others who've left their modern mark on the 16th-century medina's crumbling walls. It may be close to the cosmopolitan arts hub of Casablanca but life here is sleepy and traditional and, despite its picturesque clifftop medina, it's still off the tourist trail and feels delightfully undiscovered.

Built by the Portuguese in 1513 next to the Oum Er Rbia (Mother of Spring River) and the ocean, as one of a string of trading posts along the coast, the town's most famous inhabitant was Estevanico the Black. Captured and made a slave, he later became one of the first four explorers to cross North America, from Florida to the Pacific.

Sights

★Medina AREA
An ochre-walled warren of winding streets, whitewashed houses and hole-in-the-wall shops, Azemmour's medina has yet to undergo an all-encompassing restoration. Built next to the banks of the Oum Er Rbia (Mother of Spring River) in the 16th century, its Portuguese heritage can still be seen in its ornate doorways and wooden balconies.

Residents have long been associated with arts and crafts – here you'll find traditional weavers, an impressive new artisan centre, and startlingly contemporary murals adorning crumbling walls.

Wandering around the tourist-free medina offers both a journey back in time and a glimpse of life in modern working-class Morocco. Enter through the large gate with its unusual semicircle-shaped arch; the ramparts can be accessed from here. Walk along the walls to see Dar El Baroud (the Powder House), a Portuguese gunpowder store of which only the tower remains. To the north of the medina is the *mellah* (Jewish quarter) with a still-standing synagogue painted in blue and white. Further on, you'll get wonderful views over the river.

Sleeping & Eating

There's a few simple eateries outside the medina walls in the new town, but none are worthy of recommendation. Most visitors eat at their lodgings.

Dar Nadia B&B €€

(0658090972; 3 Rue Souika El Malah, Medina; s/d €35/50;) A traditional, lovingly restored *dar* (traditional house) tucked away behind a blue door in the heart of the medina, Dar Nadia has a peaceful central courtyard and nicely decorated rooms, all with private bathrooms and soaring ceilings – a couple have fireplaces.

★L'Oum Errebia BOUTIQUE HOTEL €€€

(0523347071; www.azemmour-hotel.com; 25 Impasse Chtouka, Medina; s/d Dh600/800;) A showcase of contemporary Moroccan art and antiques, this French-owned boutique blends traditional craftwork with contemporary design. Each of the nine rooms feature sunken showers and *tadelakt* floors and walls; two have serene river views. There's a cosy lounge with a fireplace, two rooftop terraces, a small swimming pool and an in-house hammam. Book dinner (Dh250) in advance.

Shopping

Maison de l'Artisan ARTS & CRAFTS

(Ave Allal Ben Abdellah, Medina; 10am-6pm) This shiny new government-sponsored complex was created to preserve Azemmour's traditional crafts, and includes workshops, training rooms and space for the artisans to sell their wares. You can watch them chip away at stucco, carve wood and weld metal, then shop for well-priced leather sandals and the distinctive embroidery that's a speciality of the town.

Getting There & Away

Trains stop nine times daily at Azemmour Halte, 2km from the town centre. These link the town to El Jadida (1st/2nd class Dh27/16, 20 minutes) and Casablanca (1st/2nd class Dh46/33, one hour).

The town is also linked to El Jadida by *grand taxi* (Dh10) and bus (Dh5).

Oualidia الوالدية

POP 5830

Oualidia (wa-lid-ee-ah) is part delightful beach resort, part sleepy fishing village, spread around a gorgeous crescent-shaped lagoon fringed with golden sands and protected from the wild surf by a rocky breakwater.

With great fish and seafood – the town is renowned for its oysters – and a range of accommodation options, it's a popular weekend and summer retreat for Marrakshis and Casablancais, and the perfect destination for those in need of a break from the city hubbub.

Outside July and August it's quiet, with little more to do than relax, surf and gorge on shellfish. In spring and autumn, birdwatchers arrive to observe migrating pink flamingos, terns, egrets and more on the lagoon and surrounding coastal wetlands.

Sights

The town is named after the Saadian Sultan El Oualid, who built the kasbah, now atmospherically crumbling on the bluff overlooking the lagoon, in 1634. The lagoon also attracted Morocco's royalty, and the grand villa on the water's edge was Mohammed V's summer palace, now all but abandoned.

On Saturday, there's a traditional market when people from surrounding villages come to town to sell their wares.

Oualidia Lagoon NATURAL FEATURE

Oualidia's languid lagoon and coastal wetlands is a paradise for birdwatchers, playing host to many bird species, both native and migratory, especially in spring and autumn. Expect to see egrets, plovers, oystercatchers and curlews, and pink flamingos in season. Small wooden boats will take you puttering around its fringes for around Dh50.

Activities

The safe, calm waters of the lagoon are perfect for swimming, kayaking and paddleboarding, while the wide, sandy beach on either side of the breakwater is good for kitesurfing. It's also an under-the-radar surfing hotspot, with a long-established surf camp and waves to suit both novice and experienced surfers.

★ Surfland Surfcamp SURFING
(☎0661146461; www.facebook.com/surfland.surfcamp; surfing lessons adult/child Dh200/150) Veteran surfer Laurent Miramon started this surf camp for kids in 1991 and it's still going strong. It also offers professionally run surfing lessons for all ages and abilities, with equipment included. The gentle conditions of the protected lagoon are perfect for beginners, while experienced surfers can take on the more serious waves at Tomato Beach.

Dream Surf Oualidia WATER SPORTS
(☎0661817817; Oualidia Plage; equipment hire from Dh150; ⏲Apr–mid-Nov) Take advantage of the lagoon's calm waters and hire a paddleboard, bodyboard or kayak from this reputable beachfront shop. Surfboards, quad bikes and scooters are also available.

Sleeping

There are several accommodation choices near the beach – including one of Morocco's finest boutique hotels, the luxe La Sultana – and a few in the upper town. Properties on the water are understandably popular and should be booked well in advance, especially in summer.

★ Dar Beldi B&B €€
(☎0523366288; Douar Moulay Abdessalam; s/d Dh550/690; 📶) This charming B&B sits behind a rather unprepossessing entrance off the main street. Five clean and lovingly decorated rooms are surrounded by a gorgeous garden and there's plenty of lounging space on the sun-drenched terrace and in cosy salons. French owners Pierre-Yves and Guy make ebullient and helpful hosts, happy to offer advice and to arrange transport and activities.

L'Initiale Hotel-Restaurant B&B €€
(☎0523366246; initialhotel@gmail.com; Oualidia Plage; s/d/tr Dh450/500/600; 📶) This modern whitewashed hotel sits above a popular restaurant next to the beach, where six bright rooms come with tiny balconies. If you're an early-to-bed type, restaurant noise might be a problem, but it serves up reasonably priced fresh fish and seafood, along with pasta and pizza. A roof terrace was under construction on our last visit.

★ La Sultana HOTEL €€€
(☎0523366595; www.lasultanahotels.com/oualidia; Parc à Huîtres No 3; r Dh4400-7900; ⏲closed Jan; P📶🏊) Each of the 12 elegant suites comes with a fireplace, hot tub and terrace with lagoon views. When not picnicking on deserted beaches and visiting oyster farms, lucky guests spend their time lounging by the infinity pool, being pampered at the spa, sipping sundowners at the jetty bar and enjoying seafood feasts at the terrace restaurant. A lavish breakfast costs Dh230.

Hôtel L'Hippocampe HOTEL €€€
(☎0661221394; https://hippocampeoualidia.com; Rte du Palais; r incl breakfast/half-board from Dh850/1050; P📶🏊) At this longstanding hotel, rooms and family-sized suites are simple but comfortable. The big draws are the flower-filled garden and expansive terrace with magnificent lagoon views, along with a well-stocked bar, a restaurant with a fish and seafood focus, a seawater lap pool and access to a small private beach. Lounge around or get active, kayaking and surfing.

Eating & Drinking

For cheap eats, head to Ave Hassan II in the upper town, otherwise hotel restaurants are the way to go, with shellfish on every menu. Local nightlife is low-key; there's a pleasant lounge bar at Hôtel L'Hippocampe.

Snack Pedro MOROCCAN €
(☎0633186174; Ave Hassan II; mains Dh30; ⏲11am-9pm) The best of the budget-friendly fast-food joints on the main road: English-speaking Pedro serves up a top-notch octopus tajine (small/medium Dh40/70), or get a burger, sandwich or panini to take to the beach.

DON'T MISS

BEACHSIDE SHELLFISH

In the afternoon, head to the beachfront to buy freshly gathered shellfish from crates on the backs of fisherpeople's scooters. Oysters, clams, razor shells and sea urchins are shucked as fast as you can eat them and served with a squeeze of lemon for around Dh5 a shell. Divine.

La Table de la Plage SEAFOOD €€€
(☎0523366595; www.lasultanahotels.com/oualidia; La Sultana, Parc à Huîtres No 3; seafood platters Dh150-1250; ⏰noon-3.30pm; 📶) Even if you're not staying at La Sultana, consider indulging in a leisurely lunch at its terrace restaurant on the lagoon's edge. It specialises in fresh shellfish, which is kept in high-tech tanks. The oysters, clams and spider crabs are delicious, so are the just-caught fish, and organic veggies plucked from their own garden. Great wine list, too. Reservations recommended.

Ostréa II SEAFOOD €€€
(☎0523366451; www.ostrea.ma; Parc à Huîtres; 12 oysters Dh180-280; ⏰11am-10pm) Oualidia is famous for its oyster beds, which produce about 200 tonnes of oysters annually, and this waterfront restaurant attached to an oyster farm is a great place to slurp some bivalves. These come in three grades – the difference is the size. Order them grilled with cheese or chives, or au naturel. Paella and fried fish are also available.

The well-signed access road to the restaurant is off the main highway, at the entrance to town. It's an easy 15-minute walk from the roundabout in the upper town.

Getting There & Away

Grands taxis congregate on Ave Hassan II near the Banque Populaire and travel to/from Casablanca (Dh90, 2½ hours), El Jadida (Dh50, 40 minutes) and Safi (Dh50, 45 minutes). To Marrakesh, a taxi *complet* (*grand taxi* functioning as a private taxi) will cost Dh800. From the main road, it's a 10-minute walk down to the lagoon and beach – *grands taxis* will ask for an extra tip to drop you down here.

Safi آسفي

POP 308,510

An industrial city and thriving port, Safi is a lot less picturesque than other coastal towns. It holds little of interest for visitors – most people just stop here en route to or from Essaouira to visit the giant pottery that produces the brightly coloured Safi ceramics that can be found all over the country. Deter would-be guides with a *'La, shukran'* ('No, thanks').

The new town's tree-lined boulevards are pleasant enough but the alleys of the walled medina and fortified Portuguese-built medina are more atmospheric to stroll through.

History

Safi's natural harbour was known to the Phoenicians and the Romans, and in the 11th century, it was a port for the trans-Saharan trade between Marrakesh and Guinea, where gold, enslaved people and ivory were sold. In the 14th century, the town became an important religious and cultural centre when the Merinids built a *ribat* here. The Portuguese took the city for a brief spell from 1508 until 1541, when the Saadians took it back. They built the monumental Qasr Al Bahr fortress and generally expanded the town, but destroyed most monuments upon their departure.

In the 16th century Safi grew wealthy from the trade in copper and sugar, and European merchants and agents flocked to the city, but when the port at Essaouira was rebuilt in the 18th century Safi was largely forgotten.

Safi's real revival came in the 20th century when its fishing fleet expanded and huge industrial complexes were built to process the 30,000 tonnes of sardines caught annually. A major phosphate-processing complex was established south of the town and the city began to expand rapidly. Today, Safi is one of Morocco's largest ports.

Sights

Medina AREA
Safi's walled medieval medina is sliced in two by Rue du Souq, which runs northeast from Bab Lamaasa to Bab Chaaba and is lined with shops. On the southern side of this street, down a twisting alley, are the remains of the 16th-century **Cathédrale Portugaise** (Medina; Dh50; ⏰8am-noon & 2.30-6pm). The **Kechla**, another structure built by the Portuguese, is located in the medina's southeastern corner. Shops and street stands selling Safi's famous ceramics are clustered around Bab Chaaba.

Colline des Potiers LANDMARK
(Bab Chaaba) The earthen kilns and chimneys of Potters' Hill are clearly seen from Bab Chaaba at the edge of the medina. The skills used here are predominantly traditional and you can wander around the cooperatives and see the potters at work. If a potter invites you in to watch him at work, you'll be expected to give a small tip (Dh20 should suffice) or buy an item or two from the shop.

Qasr Al Bahr HISTORIC BUILDING
The ruins of Safi's once-impressive castle are located next to the crashing waves of the

ANDR

M

Thursday, March 16, 2023

Safi

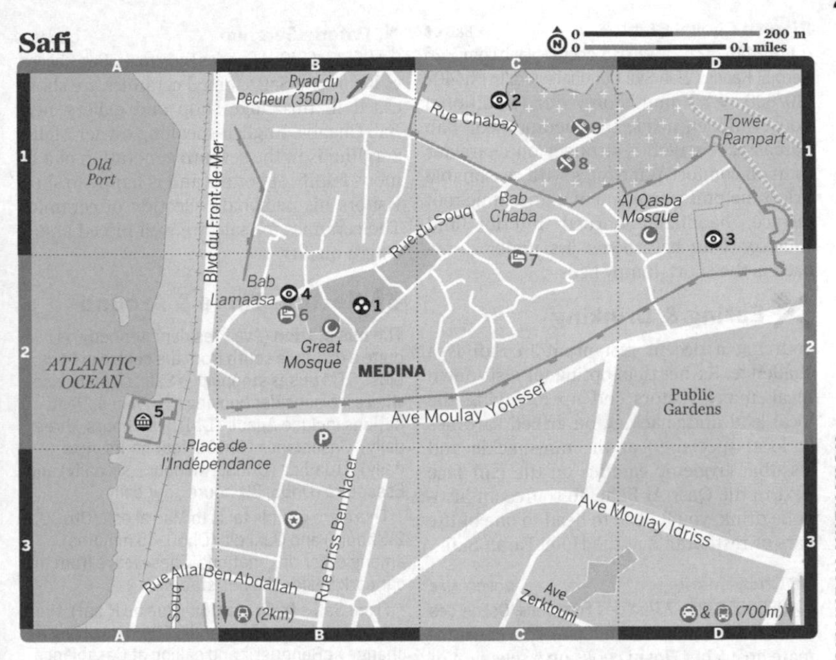

Safi

Sights

1 Cathédrale Portugaise B2
2 Colline des Potiers C1
3 Kechla D1
4 Medina B2
5 Qasr Al Bahr A2

Sleeping

6 Riad Le Cheval Blanc B2
7 Riad Safi C2

Eating

8 Café Restaurant Du Potier C1
9 Chez Hosni C1

Shopping

Poterie Serghini .... (see 8)

Atlantic. Built to enforce Portuguese authority, house the town governor and protect the port, the tower also once housed prisoners who were kept in the basement before being killed or shipped as enslaved people. Now in an appalling state of disrepair, the castle is closed to the public while it awaits a long-overdue restoration.

Sleeping

There are a couple of medina riads and a handful of decent midrange business-style hotels in Safi, but few of the budget options on offer are clean or comfortable.

★Riad Safi GUESTHOUSE €
(☎0655471180; www.riadsafi.com; 14 Rue de l'Eglise, Medina; d Dh400;) One of only two B&Bs in Safi medina, this traditional house has been tastefully restored, with just eight rooms decorated in local fabrics and crafts and a pretty roof terrace. Use it as a base to explore Safi's ceramics culture, take a guided tour of the medina or hike along the coast. Round off with a tasty homemade tajine (Dh70).

Ryad du Pêcheur HOTEL €€
(☎0671815570; www.ryaddupecheur.com; 1 Rue des Cretes; s Dh500, d Dh550-700, suite Dh700-900; P) The owner of this hotel is from a well-known family of local potters, so colourful tiles are everywhere. Clean and comfortable rooms and family-sized suites are set around the courtyard restaurant. Draws include the restaurant (p232) and a rooftop terrace with sweeping views over the port's ship-building yards.

Riad Le Cheval Blanc B&B €€
(☎0524464527; www.riad-cheval-blanc.com; 26 Derb El Kaouss, Bab Sidi Boudhab; s/d/tr Dh440/510/600;) A multistorey *dar* (traditional house) hidden inside the medina near Bab Lamassa, this B&B is stronger on character than on comfort, but comes with reasonable prices, helpful management, panoramic roof terrace, handicraft-adorned interior and squeaky-clean bathrooms. Its major drawback is the short, lumpy beds.

Eating & Drinking

Sourcing a decent restaurant in Safi is a challenge. Rather than opting for a sit-down meal, many visitors end up following the local lead and snacking on grilled sardines (a local speciality) at the ramshackle and less-than-hygienic eateries on the cliff face next to the Qasr Al Bahr. To source an alcoholic drink, you'll need to head to one of the bars or restaurants at the Hôtel Farah Safi.

★**Chez Hosni** MOROCCAN €
(☎0660052323; 7 Rue des Forgerons, Coline des Potier; mains Dh60; ⊙11am-10pm) A consummate host, chef Hosni cooks up a selection of moreish traditional tajines, but a standout is his sea-bream tajine. And if you're vegetarian, he'll happily adapt his recipes.

Café Restaurant Du Potier MOROCCAN €
(4 Rue des Forgeronts, Bab Chaaba; tajines Dh50-60; ⊙11am-10pm) You'll sit next to a tiled fountain under an orange tree and a fig tree if you choose to enjoy a simple Moroccan meal, glass of mint tea or fresh juice at this hotel's courtyard cafe near the Colline des Potiers. Owned by the Serghini family of potters, whose ceramics shop is attached, it's a pleasant place in which to while away some time.

Restaurant Ryad du Pêcheur MOROCCAN €€
(☎0524610291; www.ryaddupecheur.com; 1 Rue des Cretes; pastas Dh50-80, mains Dh70-135; ⊙7-11.30am, noon-6pm & 7-11pm) A nice spot for a meal in the warmer months, this courtyard restaurant at the eponymous hotel (p231) serves simple pasta dishes, tajines and fried fish in a garden setting. No alcohol.

Shopping

Safi is famed for its pottery, and you can find some great items here if you can handle the heavy sales pitch, as well as some awful tourist dross. Head to the Colline des Potiers (p230) or to Poterie Serghini.

★**Poterie Serghini** CERAMICS
(☎0661346910; 4 Rue des Forgeronts, Bab Chaaba; ⊙10am-7pm) Safi's famed ceramics are showcased in this huge shop and gallery near Bab Chaaba. English-speaking owner Mehdi Serghini is in the seventh generation of a famous family of potters and is happy to show visitors his personal collection of ceramics. The ceramics for sale are well priced and of a high quality.

Getting There & Around

The **bus station** (Ave President Kennedy) is quite a distance south from the centre of town. Most CTM buses stopping in Safi originate elsewhere, so consider booking in advance. Destinations include Agadir (Dh115, six hours, three daily), Casablanca (Dh105, four hours, nine daily), El Jadida (Dh65, two hours, six daily) and Essaouira (Dh55, 2¼ hours, four daily).

There are grands taxis to Marrakesh (Dh100, 2½ hours) and Oualidia (Dh50, 45 minutes), among other destinations. These leave from the car park beside the bus station.

From Safi's **train station** (Rue de R'bat), there are services at 8.15am and 5.10pm involving a change at Benguérir and calling at Casablanca (1st/2nd class Dh140/87, 4¼ hours), Rabat (1st/2nd class Dh208/132, 5½ hours) and Fez (1st/2nd class Dh311/209, 8¼ hours).

The main attractions can be explored on foot. Both the bus station and the train station are quite a distance south from the centre of town. A metered *petit taxi* from either will cost around Dh10. Local buses operate from just north of Place Driss Ben Nacer.

Essaouira الصويرة

POP 77,970

It is the beautifully named *alizee* (coastal winds), or *taros* in Amazigh (Berber), that has allowed Essaouira (*essa*-weera) to retain its traditional culture and character. For much of the year, the wind blows so hard here that relaxing on the beach is impossible, meaning that the town is bypassed by the hordes of beach tourists who descend on other Atlantic Coast destinations in summer.

It is known as the 'Windy City of Africa' and it attracts plenty of kitesurfers in April, May, July and August and pro surfers from September to March, although water sports are a draw year round for beginners. However, the majority of visitors come here in spring and autumn to wander through the spice-scented lanes of the fortified medina, browse the many art galleries and boutiques, relax in some of the country's best hotels and watch as fishing nets are mended and traditional boats constructed in the hugely atmospheric port.

Essaouira lies on the crossroads between two tribes: the Arab Chiadma to the north and the Haha Amazigh in the south. Add to that the Gnaoua, who came originally from sub-Saharan Africa, and the Europeans, and you get a rich cultural mix.

History

Most of Essaouira's medina and fortifications date from the 18th century, but the town has a much older history that began with the Phoenicians. For centuries, foreigners had a firm grip over the town, and although Moroccans eventually reclaimed it, the foreign influence lingers on in the way the town looks and feels today.

In 1764 Sultan Sidi Mohammed Ben Abdallah installed himself in Essaouira (then known as Mogador) so that his corsairs could launch attacks on the people of Agadir, who were rebelling against him. He hired a French architect, Théodore Cornut, to create a city in the middle of sand and wind, where nothing had previously existed. The combination of Moroccan and European styles pleased the sultan, who renamed the town Essaouira, meaning 'well designed'. The port soon became a vital link for trade between Timbuktu and Europe. It was a place where the trade in gold, salt, ivory and ostrich feathers was carefully monitored, taxed and controlled by a garrison of 2000 imperial soldiers.

By 1912 the French had established their protectorate, changed the town's name back to Mogador and diverted trade to Casablanca, Tangier and Agadir. It was only with Moroccan independence in 1956 that this sleepy backwater again became Essaouira. Since Orson Welles filmed *Othello* here and hippies chose it as a hang-out, the town has seen a steady flow of visitors – everyone from artists, surfers and writers, to European tourists escaping the hubbub of Marrakesh.

Sights

Although there aren't many formal sights in Essaouira, it's a wonderful place for rambling. The medina, souqs, ramparts, port and beach are perfect for leisurely discovery, interspersed with relaxed lunches and unhurried mint-tea breaks.

★Medina — AREA

Surrounded by dramatic, wave-lashed ramparts, the narrow streets, hassle-free souqs, street vendors and vibrant galleries of Essaouira's walled medina make it a wonderful place to stroll. Dating from the late 18th century and added to Unesco's World Heritage list in 2001, it was famously used in the opening scene of Orson Welles' 1951 film *Othello* and, more recently, *Game of Thrones*.

Unlike the maze-like medinas of Marrakesh and Fez, in breezy Essaouira's mellow medina it's hard to get lost. Take time to wander along the main thoroughfare, Avenue de l'Istiqlal, dipping in to the souqs that fan out around it, the sun-drenched squares and the skinny alleyways lined with white, blue-shuttered buildings, many of which house boutiques and galleries.

Skala de la Ville — FORT

(Medina) You might recognise the ramparts of the 18th-century Skala de la Ville. They, along with the hulking Bastion Nord, had a starring role in *Game of Thrones* as Astapor. In real life these ramparts protected the medina from the crashing Atlantic waves, and its row of 19 bronze cannons from a host of seafaring marauders. Today – tourists

JIMI HENDRIX: CASTLES OF SAND OR PIE IN THE SKY?

There are plenty of stories told about Jimi Hendrix in Essaouira. That the musician lived here on and off for a few years in the 1960s. That he owned a riad in which you can now stay, or maybe it's a restaurant in which you can eat. That he stayed in quite a few other riads, or a campervan, or perhaps a tent. That he tried to buy Île de Mogador and composed 'Castles Made of Sand' here. Even that he sired various children here and shared a room with Timothy Leary.

But it's just an urban myth. Hendrix visited Morocco for about a week in July 1969, and two or three days of this were spent in Essaouira. He didn't even bring his guitar, and it was 18 months after the album containing the song 'Castles Made of Sand' was released.

Essaouira

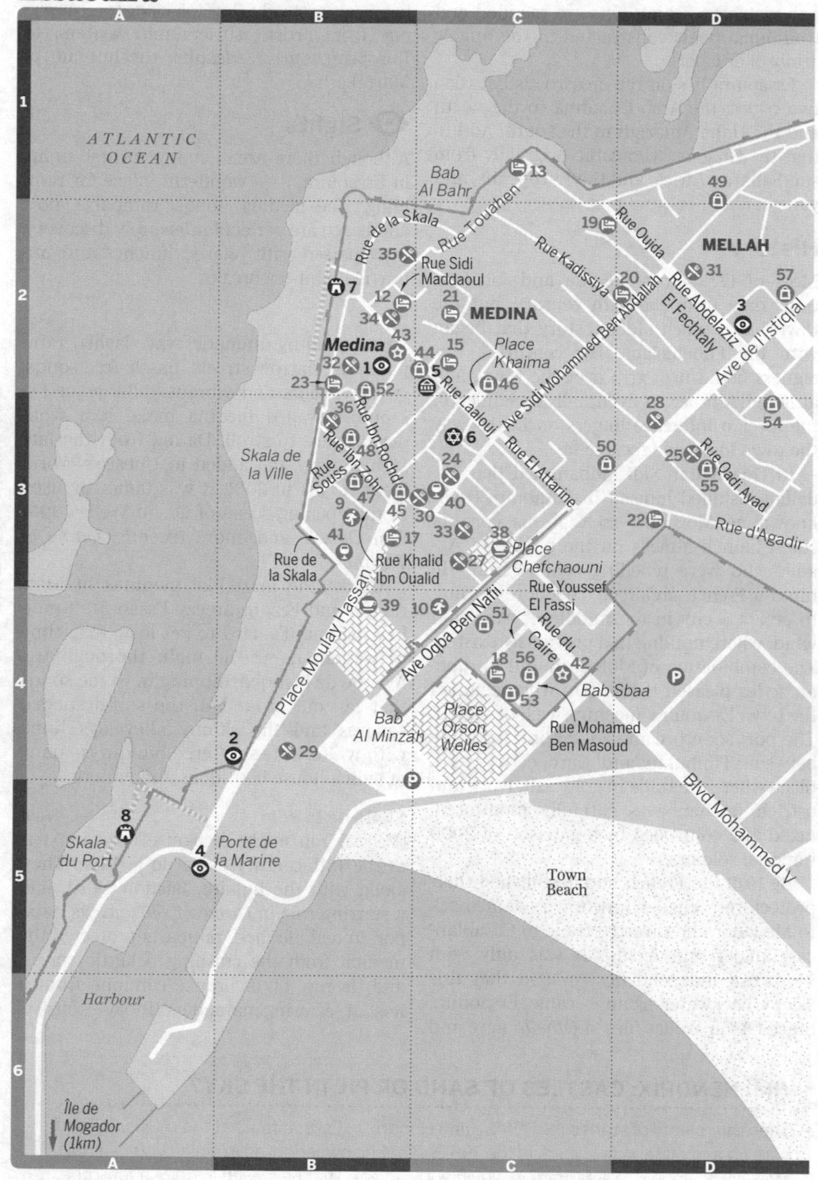

aside – it's a peaceful place to take in the ocean views and a prime sunset-watching spot.

Simon Attias Synagogue SYNAGOGUE

(Rue Ziry Ibn Atiyah, Medina) Behind the imposing wooden door (there's no sign) lies a beautifully restored 19th-century synagogue, filled with the scent of fragrant cedar wood. In the rooms off the main patio is a fascinating exhibition covering all aspects of Jewish culture in Essaouira, from clothes to religious artefacts.

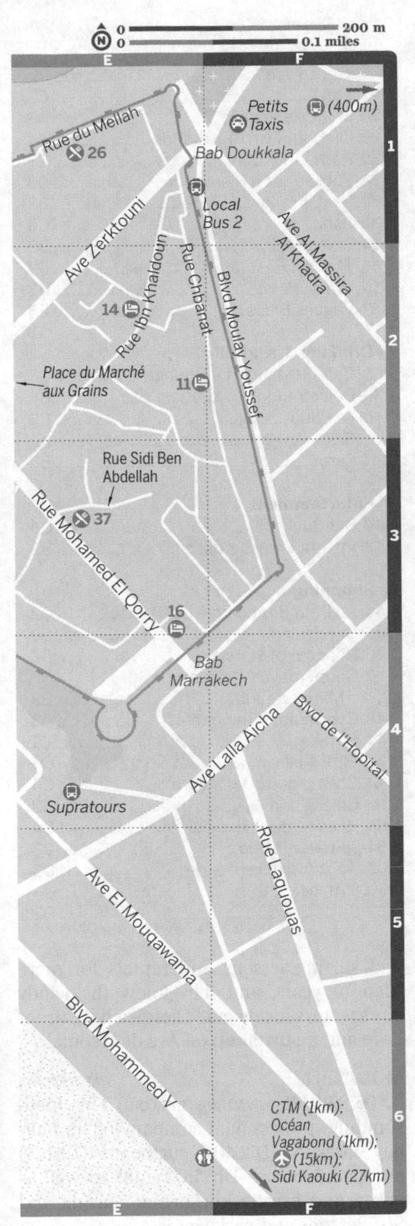

Sidi Mohammed Ben Abdellah Museum MUSEUM
(☎0524475300; musee_amba_ess@gmail.com; Rue Laâlouj, Medina; Dh70; ⏲8am-5pm, closed Tue) Housed in an old riad, this somewhat fusty museum has a small collection of jewellery, costumes, embroidery, woodcarving and weapons from the region. Its collection of ritual and musical instruments is interesting.

Essaouira Beach BEACH
Essaouira's wide, sandy beach is great for walking and kitesurfing, but sunbathing and swimming can be difficult when the winds are strong. For swimming, stick to the town stretch, as Plage Safi to the north has dangerous currents. Beach football is a popular weekend activity and camel owners ply the sands to the south. Bargain hard if you want to take a ride (under Dh50) but there are better camel encounters to be had in Diabat.

If you want to take a walk, head south across the Ksob River (impassable at high tide) to see the ruins of the Borj El Berod, an old fortress and pavilion that's partially covered in sand. From here you can walk inland to the village of Diabat or continue along the sands to the sand dunes of Cap Sim.

Skala du Port FORTRESS
(adult/child under 12yr Dh60/25; ⏲9am-5.30pm) This honey-coloured bastion looms over the picturesque harbour and its sea-blue fishing boats. Look back at the walled medina from here, through a curtain of screeching seagulls, and you'll get the same evocative image of the city that appears on all the posters. It appeared as Astapor in *Game of Thrones* too.

Port PORT
Essaouira's large working port is noisy, pungent and hugely atmospheric. Along with the flurry of sea-blue wooden boats arriving and departing, nets being repaired and the day's catch being landed, you can see traditional wooden boats being made. The boatbuilders supply fishing vessels for the entire Moroccan coast and even as far away as France, as the design is particularly seaworthy. It's also worth visiting the **fish auction**, which takes place in the market hall just outside the port gates.

Île de Mogador ISLAND
Just off the coast lies the Île de Mogador, which is actually two islands and several tiny islets. They are also known as the famed Îles Purpuraires (Purple Isles) of antiquity: the Romans used the purple dye extracted from molluscs plucked from the bay to dye their imperial togas. The uninhabited islands are a protected sanctuary for Eleonora's falcons,

Essaouira

Top Sights
1 Medina ... B2

Sights
2 Fish Auction ... B4
3 Fish Souq ... D2
4 Port ... A5
5 Sidi Mohammed Ben Abdellah Museum ... C2
6 Simon Attias Synagogue ... C3
7 Skala de la Ville ... B2
8 Skala du Port ... A5

Activities, Courses & Tours
9 Azur Art & Spa ... B3
L'Atelier Madada ... (see 56)
Le P'tit Spa de l'Heure Bleue ... (see 16)
10 Villa Maroc Oriental Spa ... C4

Sleeping
11 Dar 91 ... E2
12 Dar Afram ... B2
13 Dar Al Bahar ... C1
14 Dar Beida ... E2
15 Dar Emma ... C2
16 Heure Bleue Palais ... E3
17 Jack's Apartments & Suites ... B3
18 Madada Mogador ... C4
19 Riad Dar Maya ... C2
20 Riad Etoile d'Essaouira ... D2
21 Riad Malaika ... C2
22 Riad Nakhla ... D3
23 Salut Maroc! ... B2
Villa Maroc ... (see 10)

Eating
24 Adwak ... C3
25 Caravane Cafe ... D3
26 La Mouette Gourmande ... E1
La Table by Madada ... (see 18)
La Terrace ... (see 16)
27 Loft ... C3
28 Mandala Society ... D3
29 Outdoor Fish Grill Stands ... B4
30 Pâtisserie Driss ... C3
31 Pâtisserie La Bienvenue ... D2
32 Restaurante Les Alizés ... B2
33 Saha Kfé ... C3
34 Silvestro ... B2
35 Triskala Restaurant ... B2
36 Umia ... B3
37 Vagues Bleus ... E3

Drinking & Nightlife
38 Café Restaurant L'Horloge ... C3
39 Dolcefreddo ... B4
40 Le Patio ... C3
Salon Anglais ... (see 16)
41 Taros ... B3

Entertainment
42 Dar Souiri ... C4
43 Institut Français Essaouira ... B2

Shopping
44 Au Petit Bonhomme La Chance ... C2
45 Bendahhane ... B3
46 Boheme of Morocco ... C2
47 Coopérative Artisanale des Marqueteurs ... B3
48 Coopérative Tamounte ... B3
49 Corallo ... D1
50 Elizir Gallery ... C3
51 Galerie d'Art Damgaard ... C4
52 Galerie Jama ... B2
53 Histoire des Filles ... C4
54 Jewellery Souq ... D3
55 Koulchi Concept Store ... D3
56 L'Atelier ... C4
57 Spice Souq ... D2

which can be easily seen through binoculars from Essaouira beach – you can't land on the islands without special permission.

Activities

Essaouira – aka Africa's 'windy city' – has long been a haunt of surfers-in-the-know; now its omnipresent gusts of wind attract kitesurfers and windsurfers too. And there's plenty to hold visitors' attention on dry land, with endless stretches of golden sand, a lively, one-of-a-kind art scene, laid-back souq shopping and the chance to enjoy fine-dining fishy feasts.

★Explora WATER SPORTS
(☎0611475188; https://explorawatersports.com; from €30) This professional, family-run outfit has been offering kitesurfing, windsurfing and surfing lessons and rentals for more than 10 years, and they know the windy city's waters inside out. There's a beachfront **cafe** and a **surf shop** on Ave de l'Istiqlal.

MOGAsurf WATER SPORTS
(☎0618910431; www.mogasurf.com) This long-standing, professional company offers half-day kitesurf (Dh550), surfboard (Dh165) and paddleboard (Dh275) rental, as well as group and private kitesurfing, surfing and SUP lessons and packages.

Ecotourisme et Randonnées HIKING
(☎0662616678; www.essaouira-randonnees.com; half-/full-day tours Dh250/500) Frédérique has been offering hiking tours in the countryside around Essaouira for more than 10 years, including birdwatching, visits to local

argan groves, the Sidi M'Bark waterfall and the Ksob River.

Villa Maroc Oriental Spa HAMMAM
(☎0524476147; www.villa-maroc.com; 10 Rue Abdullah Ben Yassine, Medina; from Dh350) The lovely in-house hammam at Villa Maroc (p239), just inside the medina walls, offers a range of bath, massage and beauty treatments. The 'Traditional Beauty' package (Dh600) includes *gommage* (scrub), a *ghassoul*-clay body wrap and 10-minute argan-oil massage, using their own organic natural oils. Bookings essential.

Le P'tit Spa de l'Heure Bleue SPA
(☎0524783434; https://heure-bleue.com; Heure Bleue Palais, 2 Rue Ibn Batouta, Medina; hammam from Dh495) It's small but perfectly formed; at this beautiful dark marble hammam at the Heure Bleue Palais (p239) you'll be treated like a sultana or sultan. After being exfoliated with black soap and slathered in purifying *ghassoul* clay, you'll end with a massage with nourishing argan oil, among other pampering packages. You can even **dine** here after your treatment. Bookings essential.

Azur Art & Spa SPA
(☎0524785794; www.azur-spa-essaouira.com; 15 Rue Khalid Ben Walid, Medina; ⌚10.30am-7.30pm) This contemporary, spotlessly clean spa makes an excellent choice for a well-priced treatment in the dreamy dark *tadelakt* hammam. It offers a range of hammam-centric packages (from Dh120), including one with a gentle scrub option for hammam novices. And being Essaouira, it combines beauty treatments with a small art gallery.

Courses

★L'Atelier Madada COOKING
(☎0700189017; www.lateliermadada.com; Rue Mohamed Ben Masoud, Medina; incl lunch Dh500; ⌚10.30am-3pm & 3.30pm-7pm Mon-Sat) Set in a stylishly restored former almond warehouse and attached to one of Essaouira's best restaurants (p241), this cookery school offers places for eight people per session. Learn the secrets of tajines, couscous and *bastilla* after a trip to the souq (Dh500), or Moroccan pastry in the afternoons (Dh220). The courses are presented in English and French.

Festivals & Events

There's no shortage of eclectic events for music lovers, from classical concerts at the Printemps Musical Des Alizés to electronica-meets-gnaoua at MOGA and foot-stomping flamenco at the Festival des Andalousies Atlantiques. The city's most famous festival is undoubtedly Gnaoua World Music Festival, which sees bands including Les Pigeons du Sable (Pigeons of the Sand) filling the medina streets with their seductive sub-Saharan rhythms.

★Gnaoua World Music Festival MUSIC
(www.festival-gnaoua.net; ⌚late Jun) Essaouira overflows every year for this celebrated four-day festival. Gnaoua is a musical and spiritual tradition brought north by sub-Saharan enslaved people and here their ancient musical traditions are mixed with contemporary funk, blues and jazz. Concerts are free, but to avoid the crush invest in a VIP ticket that will give you access to space in front of the stage.

Printemps Musical des Alizés MUSIC
(www.facebook.com/Printempsmusicaldesalizes; ⌚Apr) A must for classical music lovers, this three-day spring festival of chamber music draws world-class musicians from around the globe to play free concerts at small venues across the city, such as Dar Souiri.

MOGA MUSIC
(www.mogafestival.com/en; ⌚Oct) This week-long showcase of Moroccan, African and international electronic artists brings in global DJs and pairs them with local talent, such as Gnaoua musician Maâlem Omar Hayat, dubbed the 'Jimi Hendrix of the *sintir*', a three-stringed lute-like instrument.

Le Nuits Photographiques ART
(https://essaouiranuitsphotographiques.com; ⌚Oct) The four-day festival celebrates photography, from sub-Saharan Africa to the Mediterranean, showcasing the work of around 50 emerging artists with three

KITESURFING IN ESSAOUIRA

Morocco's premier kitesurfing destination draws both pros and novices. The wind is stronger during the summer months, from April to September, and swells are bigger in winter, while a wetsuit is needed year-round. Beginners should take to the waves in the morning, as they get stronger in the afternoon. There's everything from two-hour lessons to intensive week-long courses available.

WORTH A TRIP

BBIO ORGANIC FARM

Idyllic **Bbio Organic Farm** (☎0667965386; https://castlesinthesand.com/bbio-organic-farm; Dh500; ⏰11am-5pm; 👪) makes a perfect day out or a pit stop on your way to Marrakesh. Tours (bookings essential) are with the owner Khalid, who will share his ingenious farming methods. Afterwards enjoy a leisurely alfresco lunch lounging on Berber rugs – expect fresh juices, hand-pressed olive oil, homemade bread, corn-fed chicken and bountiful salads of whatever's in season. Delicious. Return taxi is Dh300.

thematic exhibitions in public spaces around Essaouira, along with workshops open to photographers of all levels.

Festival des Andalousies Atlantiques MUSIC
(www.facebook.com/FestivalDesAndalousiesAtlantiques; ⏰late Oct) Now in its 17th year, this popular festival celebrates Andalusian music and dance, including heel-clacking flamenco shows and classical orchestras, with artists from Morocco, Spain and beyond.

Sleeping

Essaouira has a wonderful range of accommodation options catering for every taste and budget. Most of these are within the walls of the medina, so everything you need is within walking distance. In summer book ahead, or at least arrive early in the day to find a room.

Dar Emma RENTAL HOUSE €
(☎0667965386; https://castlesinthesand.com/dar-emma; Rue Laalouj, Medina; per week €850; 📶) The two-bedroom Dar Emma sleeps four and is perfect if you want your own place. This tall, skinny house, spread over four floors, has an artful mix of traditional Moroccan decor, vintage finds and contemporary touches, with a roof terrace for sunny days and a log fire for chilly evenings. Four-night minimum stays are possible in low season.

Riad Etoile d'Essaouira B&B €
(☎0524472007; 2 Rue Kadissiya, off Ave Sidi Mohammed Ben Abdallah; s/d/tr from Dh195/270/435; 📶) Comfortably appointed and brightly decorated with local fabrics, this B&B makes an excellent budget choice. English-speaking staff are friendly, and guests enjoy breakfast on the terrace.

★ **Jack's Apartments & Suites** APARTMENT €€
(Jack's Bohemian Suites; ☎0524475538; www.jackapartments.com; Place Moulay Hassan, Medina; d/apt from €58/95; 📶) Swiss traveller Jack came to Essaouira to windsurf and stayed, opening a business renting apartments and suites. In various locations around the medina, they sleep between two and eight people and are clean, stylish and well equipped; some have private terraces and others can access a rooftop terrace with sea views. The office is in Place Moulay Hassan.

Riad Malaika RIAD €€
(☎0524784908; www.riad-essaouira-malaika.com; d from €65; 📶) Tucked down a quiet medina street, this beautifully preserved 300-year-old riad is all ornate stucco, painted cedar wood and gleaming *zellige* (colourful geometric mosaic tilework), with 10 lofty-ceilinged rooms decorated with antique furniture. There are house-made breads and pastries every morning for breakfast on the terrace, and in the evening you can feast on market-fresh fare in an intimate salon.

Riad Nakhla B&B €€
(☎0524475230; www.riadnakhla.com; 12 Rue d'Agadir, Medina; d from €40; 📶) Ignore the unprepossessing passageway, inside is a lovely central courtyard surrounded by 16 clean and attractive rooms. All have good beds and satellite TV, some have seating alcoves and a few have sea views. Breakfast is served on the pleasant roof terrace. Ultra-friendly staff seal a great deal.

Dar 91 APARTMENT €€
(http://dar91.com; Rue Chbanat, Medina; from Dh370; 📶) This trio of serviced apartments is set in a tall, skinny 18th-century building along a quiet medina street. Light and bright, each one is different, filled with retro furniture and souq finds, with a fully equipped kitchen and seating. And you won't have to make breakfast; yoghurt, fruit, eggs and a baguette are left outside your door each morning.

Dar Afram B&B €€
(☎0524785657; https://hoteldarafram.jimdo.com; 10 Rue Sidi Magdoul, Medina; s/d/tr from Dh300/400/600; 📶) This extremely friendly guesthouse has seven simple rooms with a

funky vibe. The Aussie-Moroccan owners are musicians and an impromptu session often follows evening meals (Dh90) shared around a communal table. Guests love the summer BBQs held on the rooftop terrace with its sunloungers and sea view.

Dar Al Bahar B&B €€
(☎0524476831; www.daralbahar.com; 1 Rue Touahen; d/tr Dh550/825; 📶) The nine immaculately kept rooms at this lovely guesthouse, tucked under the ramparts near the Skala de la Ville (p233), are simple and stylish, featuring good beds and colourful tiled bathrooms. Local art adorns the walls and the views from the roof terrace overlooking the ocean are stunning.

★**Dar Beida** RENTAL HOUSE €€€
(☎0667965386; https://castlesinthesand.com/dar-beida; Rue Ibn Khaldoun, Medina; per week from €1080) In this 200-year-old medina mansion, retro-chic design meets Moroccan minimalism. There's a fully equipped kitchen and dining area, the living space comes with two egg-shaped log fires and there's a sun-drenched roof terrace. And the four-bedroom house may be white but it's filled with splashes of colour, such as a South African beaded chair and vibrant Azilal rugs.

★**Riad Dar Maya** BOUTIQUE HOTEL €€€
(☎0524785687; www.riaddarmaya.com; 33 Rue Oujda, Medina; d €120) Sleek and sophisticated, this riad-turned-boutique hotel is decorated with a mix of modern Moroccan crafts and souq finds. The five, neutral-toned rooms are spread over three floors; some come with private balconies and all have smooth *tadelakt* walls, deep tubs, underfloor heating and log fires. The rooftop terrace has a hot tub; there's even a small hammam.

★**Madada Mogador** BOUTIQUE HOTEL €€€
(☎0524475512; www.madada.com; 5 Rue Youssef El Fassi, Medina; r/ste from Dh1250/1850; 📶) If the definition of a boutique hotel is an establishment offering a chic interior, luxe rooms, quality toiletries and high levels of service, the Madada Mogador fits the bill. Nine rooms – some with sea views – are on offer, along with a stylish lounge and a spectacular roof terrace where drinks and tasty snacks are served.

★**Heure Bleue Palais** HOTEL €€€
(☎0524783434; www.heure-bleue.com; 2 Rue Ibn Batouta, Medina; d/ste from Dh1950/3340; 📶🏊) A decided hush falls as you walk through the doors of the Heure Bleue, one of Essaouira's top hotels. This swish riad has facilities galore – rooftop restaurant and swimming pool with 360-degree views, marble hammam, bar and restaurant. The rooms channel French-heritage-chic and oriental opulence, and the gorgeous courtyard comes complete with swaying palms.

Salut Maroc! BOUTIQUE HOTEL €€€
(☎0524475560; www.salutmaroc.com; 32 Rue Ibnou Rochd, Medina; d from €125) Lovers of minimalism look away now. This 18th-century medina mansion is a riot of vibrant colours and psychedelic patterns. Five of the 11 rooms have sea views, and some come with hand-painted murals while the others have dazzling mosaic tiles. Start the day with a breezy breakfast on the terrace and end it with sundowners and a Moroccan barbecue.

Villa Maroc HOTEL €€€
(☎0524476147; www.villa-maroc.com; 10 Rue Abdallah Ben Yassine, Medina; s/d/ste from Dh1050/1400/2100; 📶) Housed in a large converted 18th-century town house, the Villa Maroc is a model of restrained chic, with airy whitewashed rooms offset by tiled floors and colourful fabrics. The terrace offers great views, while the in-house spa (p237) is as well regarded for pampering as the restaurant is for intimate dining (set menu Dh250).

The same operators also have a countryside retreat 12km from the medina, complete with pool, barbecue and three guest rooms. A shuttle bus operates between 11am and 5pm (lunch Dh250).

DOES IT YURT?

A sleepover in Morocco's first yurt at **Petit à Petit** (☎0667965386; https://castlesinthesand.com/petit-a-petit-beach-yurt-luxury-glamping-essaouira; Sidi M'Barek; d incl half-board €328) means a wild Atlantic beach can be yours alone. Explore by camel, have a private surf lesson or just chill out, before feasting on a traditional tajine. Showstopping sunsets and stellar stargazing are guaranteed. Add on a delicious barbecue fish lunch and wash it down with a cold beer or organic rosé.

It's a 45-minute drive south of Essaouira; a return taxi is around Dh400.

ESSAOUIRA'S ART SCENE

Essaouira has developed into a hub for its own unique style of contemporary art, with many self-taught local artists producing colourful and primal work, sometimes dubbed *art brut*.

It was Danish collector Frederic **Damgaard** (☎0524784446; Ave Oqba Ben Nafii; ⏲9am-1pm & 3-7pm) that noticed similarities in their two- and three-dimensional work to the indigenous art of other cultures, and encouraged these Swiri fisherpeople and farmers to develop their artistic expression.

Born in 1959, Tabal is the undisputed godfather of the movement. Essaouira is the spiritual home of the Gnaoua, whose roots lie in sub-Saharan Africa and whose music mixes Islamic Sufism with African traditions. Their watchwords are rhythm, colour, trance and mysticism – all the elements that inspire Tabal's work.

Ben Ali, born in 1966, took his inspiration from his late father Ali who founded a community of junkyard artists back in the 1970s, before going on to develop his own style. A former fisher, he now upcycles found objects and creates vibrant art. You can buy his work at the Elizir Gallery (p243).

Bendahhane (☎0661347262; www.bendahhane.com; 3 Rue Hajjali, Medina; ⏲10am-9pm) also sells small, wallet-friendly pieces from the likes of Babahoum, who didn't begin to paint until he was 70, and whose perspective-free depictions of rural life are filled with fascinating detail and humour.

And you can see other artists, such as Azzedine, Baki, Fillali and Hader, at work in the Souq Joutiya (p243).

Eating

There's everything from fine-dining fusion to first-rate fish restaurants, traditional Moroccan to vegetarian-friendly cafes.

La Mouette Gourmande MOROCCAN €
(☎0662683519; Rue Mellah, near to Bab Doukkala, Mellah; mains from Dh40; ⏲1-3pm Mon-Fri) Set in Essaouira's ancient *mellah* (Jewish quarter), the Greedy Seagull is part restaurant, part social project, training women in culinary skills to help them find employment. Enjoy the fruits of their labour – tajines, couscous, grilled fish and *brochettes* – with a panoramic view over the ocean. Reserve by telephone at least three hours in advance.

Pâtisserie La Bienvenue CAFE €
(☎0677166241; 7 Rue Abdel Aziz El Fachtall, Medina; ⏲10am-8pm) Head to this small *salon de thé* (tea room) to sample some of the best Moroccan pastries in town, paired with a cup of tea or coffee. The *cornes de gazelle* (pastries stuffed with almond paste and laced with orange-flower water) are absolutely delicious.

Vagues Bleus ITALIAN €
(☎0611283791; 2 Rue Sidi Ben Abdellah, Medina; mains Dh45-50; ⏲noon-3pm & 6.30-9pm, closed Fri) At this tiny hole-in-the-wall restaurant, the Moroccan owner learnt to rustle up top-notch pasta from the former owner, an Italian chef, and then he taught his wife. Everything on the daily changing menu is fresh and very tasty.

Outdoor Fish Grill Stands SEAFOOD €
(port end of Place Moulay Hassan; fish, bread & salad from Dh40; ⏲11am-10pm) Eating at these alfresco food stands is one of the definitive Essaouira experiences. Servers can be pushy but choose a stall that looks busy, pick out your just-caught fish and shellfish and it'll be cooked on the spot and served with bread and salad. Agree on the price before you order.

Pâtisserie Driss PASTRIES €
(near Place Moulay Hassan, Medina; pastries from Dh4; ⏲8.30am-4.30pm) This icon of Essaouira opened way back in 1928, and its cafe with attached semihidden courtyard has many loyal regulars. Sadly, service can be as chaotic as the decor, but it's worth grabbing a sweet treat – from croissants to *cornes de gazelles* – to go.

★**Mandala Society** VEGETARIAN €€
(www.mandalamaroc.com; 46 Ave de l'Istiqlal, Medina; mains from Dh85; ⏲9.30am-5pm & 7-10pm; 📶🍷) 🌿 This newcomer on the medina's main drag quickly developed a loyal following for its arty decor, organic meat-free menu and top-notch coffee. Expect smoothies, avocado on sourdough bread, as well

as sinfully good homemade chocolate cake, generous salad bowls and hot specials, such as tofu wok. There's friendly staff and free wi-fi; it's plastic-free too.

★Triskala Restaurant MOROCCAN €€
(☎0643405549; 58 Rue Touahen, Medina; mains from Dh70; ⌚12.30-3.30pm & 6.30-10pm) This diminutive restaurant is a real gem, with a short menu that changes daily and puts a creative Moroccan spin on fish and vegetarian dishes, all locally sourced, fresh and organic, like smoked-sardine tart or pumpkin and artichoke tajine. The decor's as cool as the soundtrack, too.

★Restaurant Les Alizés MOROCCAN €€
(☎0524476819; 26 Rue de la Skala, Medina; set menus Dh129; ⌚noon-3pm & 6.30-10pm) Set in a 19th-century house, this popular place is run by a charming Moroccan couple. Expect delicious dishes, particularly the couscous with fish and the *boulettes de sardines* (sardine balls) tajine, and a warm welcome. It's a good idea to book ahead.

Caravane Cafe MEDITERRANEAN €€
(☎0524783111; www.facebook.com/CaravaneCafeArt; 2 Rue Du Qadi Ayad, Medina; mains from Dh125; ⌚11am-11pm Tues-Sun) This atmospheric riad-turned-restaurant is filled with diverse art and decor from vibrant canvases to neon Buddhas. The equally eclectic international menu can be a bit hit-and-miss but it's worth a visit for the nightly entertainment from musicians, magicians and fire-eaters.

The owner's new tapas bar, Le Love by Caravane, is on the other side of the street.

Adwak MOROCCAN €€
(2 Rue de Tetouan, Medina; menu from Dh75; ⌚noon-3pm & 7-10pm Mon-Sat) This cosy corner restaurant feels like you've stepped into someone's living room. Forget creative fusion dishes, this is traditional Moroccan at its best, with tajines, including a vegie version, couscous and fresh fish. Go early to get a table.

Saha Kfé CAFE €€
(☎0524783861; Place de l'Horloge, Medina; mains Dh75; ⌚8am-5pm) Tucked into a corner of the pretty Place de l'Horloge is an oasis of calm in the medina. Its outdoor tables are perfect for people watching over breakfast or a light bite – perhaps quinoa salad with goat's cheese – or indulge in homemade orange cake, coffee or a fresh juice.

Silvestro ITALIAN €€
(☎0524473555; 70 Rue Laalouj, Medina; pizza Dh70; ⌚noon-3.30pm & 7-10.30pm Tue-Sun) When you're tired of tajines, head to this popular Italian-run restaurant in the heart of the medina. Owner Pinot Silvestro's not afraid of a clashing pattern, pairing floral wallpaper with Moroccan tiles, but dishes up authentic pizza and pasta and a perfect panna cotta, all washed down with some local or Italian vino. Cash only.

Loft MEDITERRANEAN €€
(☎0524784462; 5 Rue Hajjali, Medina; mains Dh75-110; ⌚noon-10pm, closed Wed) The short menu at this tiny eatery near Place Moulay Hassan changes daily according to what's plentiful and good at the souqs, resulting in food that is fresh and full of flavour. Dishes are predominantly Mediterranean, but the tajines and couscous are delicious too. Decor is retro-funky and the English-speaking waiters are friendly. No alcohol.

★Umia MEDITERRANEAN €€€
(☎0524783395; umia.essaouira@gmail.com; 22 Rue de la Skala, Medina; mains from Dh180; ⌚6.30-11pm, closed Tue;) This sleek, contemporary restaurant is one of Essaouira's hottest, with both visitors and locals rushing to dine on the Mediterranean-influenced menu based around seasonal, Moroccan market finds. Perhaps a bowl of clams in a garlicky white-wine sauce, paired with a local wine and rounded off with an indulgent chocolate mousse.

★La Table by Madada MEDITERRANEAN €€€
(☎0524475512; www.latablemadada.com; 7 Rue Youssef El Fassi, Medina; mains Dh100-220; ⌚7-11pm, closed Tue;) Style meets substance

WORTH A TRIP

DOMAINE DU VAL D'ARGAN

In 1994 Charles Melia left Châteauneuf-du-Pape to create Morocco's southernmost winery, **Domaine du Val d'Argan** (☎0524783467; www.valdargan.com; Ounagha; ⌚11am-7pm), 20km from Essaouira; since then it's grown from five to 50 hectares. After a vineyard tour (tastings from Dh50), lunch on traditional dishes with a twist along with a tasting of five wines (Dh330), including Moroccan speciality gris, all with wonderful views over the countryside. Bookings essential.

at one of Essaouira's best fine-dining restaurants, housed in an old almond warehouse. The interior is a blend of traditional Moroccan and modern European, and the menu focuses on seafood and fish dishes, alongside contemporary riffs on local favourites such as tajines and *bastilla*. Service is friendly but can sometimes be leisurely. Reservations highly recommended.

La Terrace MEDITERRANEAN €€€
(☎0524783434; www.heure-bleue.com; Heure Bleue Palais, 2 Rue Ibn Batouta, Medina; three-course lunch Dh450; ⊙noon-3pm) This easy, breezy rooftop restaurant on top of the Heure Bleu Palais (p239) has a short chalkboard menu focussing on fresh salads, seafood and the catch-of-the-day. And don't miss the *tiramisou*, a Moroccan take on tiramisu with *amlou* (almonds, honey and argan oil). Afterwards you can work off the calories in the lovely pool.

The old-school British vibes of the **Salon Anglais** (⊙3pm-midnight) bar make it a popular place to sip on a classic cocktail or one of their bespoke creations (Dh160).

Drinking & Nightlife

There are a few places to have a drink but don't expect to party into the wee hours.

Beach & Friends BAR
(☎0524474558; www.facebook.com/Beachandfriends; ⊙11am-11pm; 📶) Smack bang on the beach, this colourful lounge-bar turns from a popular sunbathing spot into the place for sundowners. There's a list of classic cocktails (Dh80), live music and a tapas menu, with a daily specials board covering the catch-of-the-day.

Dolcefreddo CAFE
(Place Moulay Hassan, Medina; ⊙8am-11pm) Perfect for people watching from under a shady parasol, this alfresco cafe serves the best espresso in the medina, alongside top-notch gelato – or combine the two in an affogato. You can even bring your own pastry along to eat with their coffee, tea or freshly squeezed orange juice.

Taros BAR
(☎0524476407; Place Moulay Hassan; ⊙9am-midnight) This sprawling bar-cum-restaurant, where multilevel terraces come with views over the square and port, is a great place for a sundowner. There's often live music. It's also good for afternoon tea, or a drink at the bar.

Le Patio BAR
(☎0524474166; 28 Rue Moulay Rachid, Medina; ⊙7.30-11pm) This hip bar and restaurant is a seductively lit den with blood-red furnishings and a black mirror ball. You'll need to buy some tapas (Dh40) to just sit and drink. There's live music on Thursday, Friday and Saturday.

Océan Vagabond BAR
(☎0524783934; www.oceanvagabond.com/fr/essaouira-maroc; Essaouira Beach; ⊙9am-6pm) This laid-back beachfront place is the perfect spot to while away a lazy afternoon; it's open for lunch daily, and stays open for drinks and dinner on Friday and Saturday.

It also offers two-hour group surfing (adult/child Dh440/220), windsurfing ((adult/child Dh825/660) and kitesurfing (Dh825) lessons, and rents out the gear.

Café Restaurant L'Horloge CAFE
(Rue Abdellah Chefchaouni, Medina; ⊙noon-3pm & 7-10pm) Set in a pretty square near the clock tower, this longstanding cafe's outdoor tables make a good spot for a sightseeing break over a mint tea or *nus-nus* (half-and-half coffee).

Entertainment

Dar Souiri ARTS CENTRE
(☎0524475268; 10 Rue du Caire, Medina; ⊙9am-noon & 3-7pm Mon-Sat) This beautifully restored medina mansion is the headquarters of the Association Essaouira-Mogador, and plays host to regular art exhibitions, cultural events and concerts throughout the year, including around the Printemps Musical Des Alizés (p237) festival. It also offers Arabic and French lessons and has a superb library. Check the notice board outside for upcoming events.

Institut Français Essaouira ARTS CENTRE
(☎0524476197; http://if-maroc.org/essaouira; Derb Lâalaouj, 9 Rue Mohammed Diouri, Medina; ⊙Mon-Sat, closed Aug) This cultural centre hosts exhibitions, concerts and performances by Moroccan and French artists and musicians, along with art-house films. It also offers French-language courses for all abilities.

Shopping

Essaouira is famous for its woodworking, and particularly for products made from fragrant thuja wood, a medium to dark reddish-brown wood with plenty of knots. While it's not an endangered species, buying

THE SOUQS OF ESSAOUIRA

Essaouira's ancient souqs are still as much for locals as for visitors, and you can find everything from *djellaba* (full-length hooded garment with long sleeves) to *babouches* (pointed leather slippers) and bold Amazigh (Berber) jewellery studded with semi-precious stones, all jostling for space with made-in-China plastic buckets and faux trainers. The Fish Souq and the Spice Souq share a home. On one side, the catch-of-the-day is laid out on white slabs, eyed up by hungry felines and savvy seagulls. On the other side, as well as perfect pyramids of multihued spices, you'll find all your hammam needs, from black soap to scrubbing mitts.

Souq Joutiya Turn left outside the Bab Doukkala and around 15 minutes later you'll reach the industrial quarter's abandoned warehouses. Take a left past salvaged wooden doors and scrap metal and, before you reach the ocean, among the trash and treasure you'll find a row of ramshackle fisherpeople's huts turned studios – look out for artists Azzedine, Fillali and Hader. On Sunday the market along the main street means bargain hunters prepared to rummage can pick up a new wardrobe for Dh20.

Fish Souq (off Ave de l'Istiqlal) Join the locals and street cats picking up their fresh fish at this small market. For a cheap lunch, buy half a dozen sardines, and for around Dh10 one of the neighbouring cafes will grill them for you and serve them up with bread and a simple salad.

Jewellery Souq (Ave de l'Istiqlal; ⌚10am-8pm) Essaouira has long been a centre of jewellery making and trade; this bijoux collection of shops sells everything from heavy Berber jewellery to glittering gold and silver inlaid with semiprecious stones. It's sold by weight and workmanship, so be prepared to barter.

Spice Souq (Marche aux Epices; off Ave de l'Istiqlal, Medina; ⌚9am-8pm) You'll find all manner of potions, powders and pyramids of freshly ground spices in this aromatic souq, including *ras el hanout* (top of the shop: a classic mix of pungent spices used for stews and grilling), as well as cumin, turmeric, cinnamon, ginger, paprika and saffron that will help you create tasty tajines in your own kitchen.

Had Draa Souq (Had Draa; ⌚Sun) The Sunday market at Had Draa, 30km from Essaouira, is the largest in the region, where animals and produce have been traded for centuries. Early risers will be able to pick up anything from a long-lashed camel to a bleating goat and watch locals bartering over a donkey, doing the weekly shop and gossiping over mint tea. The epitome of farm-to-fork, it has a livestock area, an on-site halal abattoir and stalls selling grilled-meat kebabs.

anything made from thuja increases demand and therefore encourages illegal logging; if you do buy, make sure it's from a cooperative.

Shop for local specialities, including vibrant art, raffia shoes, thuja wood (buy from a cooperative such as Coopérative Artisanale des Marqueteurs) and Morocco's liquid gold – organic argan oil. Fixed prices at stylish concept stores such as Histoire des Filles, Koulchi and Minimal take the hassle out of haggling, while Elizir Gallery is a must for vintage lovers. And Amazigh (Berber) markets don't get more authentic than a Sunday morning spent sizing up sheep at Had Draa.

★ **Elizir Gallery** ANTIQUES
(22 Ave de l'Istiqlal, Medina; ⌚10am-9pm) Vintage lovers could happily while away a few hours here. Friendly owner Abdellatif has amassed a treasure trove of fabulous finds – perhaps a Vernor Panton lamp, long-forgotten film poster or antique Berber doors. He's also extremely knowledgeable about Essaouira's artists and sells their work in portable form, but he can ship anything big to anywhere in the world.

★ **Histoire des Filles** CONCEPT STORE
(☎0524785193; www.facebook.com/histoiredefilles; 1 Rue Mohamed Ben Masoud, Medina; ⌚10am-1.30pm & 3-7.30pm) Essaouira's first concept store – curated by Parisian Christelle Pailly – stocks a superstylish mix of Moroccan and Moroccan-based designers for women, men and kids, including Las Chicas caftans, Lalla bags, Luc Baille jewellery and Cote Bougie candles.

DANGERS & ANNOYANCES

For the most part, Essaouira is a safe, relaxed tourist town, but you should avoid the Mellah (Jewish quarter) after dark; there are problems with drugs and drinking north of Ave Mohamed Zerktouni and east of Ave Sidi Mohamed Ben Abdellah.

★Galerie Jama TEXTILES
(☎0670016429; www.galeriejama.com; 22 Rue Ibnou Rochd, Medina; ⏲10am-8pm Mon-Sat) If you don't know your Beni Ourain from your *boucharouite* (rag rug made from recycled cloth), this is the place to come. The extremely knowledgeable Mustapha has been working with Moroccan carpets for 35 years and specialises in top-quality, vintage pieces from around the country. It's a no-pressure experience and prices are fair but there's always some wiggle room. Antique textiles and pottery are downstairs.

Koulchi Concept Store CONCEPT STORE
(☎0666594554; 4 Rue Qadi Ayad, Medina; ⏲10am-9pm, cafe to 7pm) Topped by a roof-terrace café, this tall medina riad is filled with covetable Moroccan design: bags, blankets, carpets, ceramics and more.

Au Petit Bonhomme La Chance HEALTH & WELLNESS
(☎0666014502; 30 Rue Laalouj, Medina; ⏲10am-6pm) Stock up on everything you need for a DIY hammam visit – black soap, mineral-rich *ghassoul* clay, scrubbing mitts – alongside herbal tea blends, natural perfumes and henna.

Corallo JEWELLERY
(☎0610026492; 176 Ave Mohammed Ben Abdallah, Medina; ⏲11am-8.30pm) At his bijoux store, Stefano from Naples handcrafts one-of-a-kind pieces of jewellery from silver and natural stones, including pearl, topaz and turquoise.

L'Atelier HOMEWARES
(☎0700789017; www.facebook.com/lAtelier Essaouira; Rue Mohamed Ben Masoud, Medina; ⏲10am-6.30pm) This boutique-cum-cafe is a good place to take a break with a fresh juice or smoothie and a bite from the vegetarian-friendly chalkboard menu, before stocking up on homemade jams, organic olive oil and Sidi Yassine's ethical argan oil. It also stocks covetable homeware from the likes of La Verre Beldi and the cooperative Arts Tissage Tam's cushions and throws.

Boheme of Morocco HOMEWARES
(☎0642686563; www.facebook.com/bohemeofmorocco; Place Khaima, Medina; ⏲10am-7pm Mon-Sat) This wardrobe-sized, self-proclaimed 'Berber Concept Store' stocks a covetable collection of Moroccan-made homeware, from macramé wall hangings to raffia lampshades, mud-cloth cushion covers and recycled glassware.

Coopérative Tamounte ARTS & CRAFTS
(☎0524785611; www.tamounte-essaouira.com; 6 Rue Souss Essaouira; ⏲10am-8pm) Two cooperatives for the price of one, where the men make thuja-wood items and the women make top-quality argan-oil lotions and potions. It's down a dingy passageway and can be a bit hard to find – look for the sign hanging on the wall.

Coopérative Artisanale des Marqueteurs ARTS & CRAFTS
(☎0671737399; 6 Rue Khalid Ibn Oualid, Medina; ⏲10am-9pm) Come to this cooperative in an *impasse* (dead-end lane) off Place Moulay Hassan to watch the woodworkers in action, hand-turning the thuja wood with a lathe, and to browse an expansive range of wooden items, including inlaid work.

Getting There & Away

AIR

Essaouira-Mogador Airport (☎0524476704; www.onda.ma; Route d'Agadir) is 17km and around a 20-minute drive south of the medina. Flights include Ryanair from London Stansted, Transavia from Paris and Royal Air Maroc Express from Casablanca.

BUS

The **bus station** (Ave Ghazouat) is about 400m northeast of the medina, an easy walk to Bab Doukkala during the day but better in a *petit taxi* (Dh10) if you're arriving or leaving late at night. CTM buses leave from its dedicated **office**, (☎0522541010; www.ctm.ma; Place 11 Janvier, Lotissement Azlef) a Dh10 petit-taxi ride from the medina.

CTM destinations include Agadir (Dh70, 3¼ hours, three daily), Casablanca (Dh140, seven hours, four daily) via Safi (Dh55, two hours, four daily), El Jadida (Dh100, five hours, three daily) and Marrakesh (Dh80, 3½ hours, two daily).

Supratours (☎0524475317; www.supratours.ma; Bin Lassouar, off Ave Lalla Aicha) runs to Marrakesh train station (Dh80, three hours, six daily). There's also a daily departure to Agadir (Dh70, 3½ hours). Book in advance for these services, particularly in summer.

Local bus 2 to Diabat (Dh5) and Sidi Kaouki (Dh8) leaves from Blvd Moulay Youssef outside Bab Doukkala. There are about eight services a day.

TAXI

The grand-taxi rank lies immediately west of the bus station. Fares include Sidi Kaouki (Dh10, 15 minutes), Marrakesh (Dh90, 2½ hours) and Agadir (Dh80, two hours).

Getting Around

To get to the airport, take bus 2, which passes the airport turn-off (Dh10, 30 minutes, every two hours), or a *grand taxi* (Dh150 to Dh200). The blue petits taxis are a good idea for getting to and from the bus station (Dh10), but they can't enter the medina. If you're happy to walk but don't want to carry your bags, hire one of the many enterprising men with luggage carts who will wheel your bags directly to your hotel for about Dh20.

Diabat الديابات

The sleepy Amazigh (Berber) village of Diabat was once a dope-smoking colony popular with hippies. Jimi Hendrix, Cat Stevens and Frank Zappa may have strummed their guitars around a beach bonfire and some locals remain convinced that Hendrix's 'Castles Made of Sand' was inspired by the ruins of the Bordj El Berod watchtower – even though he wrote it before his visit.

It makes a good half-day trip from Essaouira for horse or camel rides or you can stroll there along the beach and taxi back. And golfers can tee off at the Golf de Mogador, with two golf courses designed by Gary Player.

Local bus 5 leaves from outside Essaouira's Bab Marrakech (Dh5, every two hours).

Activities

For something more serious than camel and horse rides and quad tours on the beach, several companies offer multiday rides and hikes along the coast and in the countryside around Essaouira.

★Equi Evasion HORSE RIDING
(☎0666780561; www.equievasion.com; rides 1hr/3hr €15/€35) This professional family-run outfit offers horse and camel treks for all ages and abilities, from one-hour rides to full days along the beach or through eucalyptus and argan forests, along with two- to eight-day treks for experienced riders; there's hiking along the Atlantic Coast, too.

Zouina Cheval HORSE RIDING
(☎0669807101; www.zouina-cheval.com; rides 1hr/3hr from €15/€32) This outfit is owned and run by Najib and Sophie, highly qualified and experienced instructors who cater for all levels, including children and beginners. Camel rides, longer horse trails and camping trips are also available.

Ranch de Diabat HORSE RIDING
(☎0524476382; www.ranchdediabat.com; 1hr horse or camel ride Dh150, half-day fishing trip Dh380) This longstanding, family-run ranch offers a host of activities, including horse and camel riding, quad excursions and fishing trips. Hikes and four- to six-day trail rides in the desert or along the coast (Dh6065 to Dh8800) are also on the menu. They'll pick you up in Essaouira if you can't make it to Diabat.

Family Adventure ADVENTURE
(☎608247905; www.familyadventure-essaouira.com; tours 1hr/4hr from €30/€70) Owned by three brothers from Diabat, Family Adventure organises professionally run, one- to four-hour quad-biking adventures that are perfect for families of all ages. Go at sunset when the beach and dunes are at their most beautiful. Horse rides are on offer too.

Sleeping

Auberge Tangaro BOUTIQUE HOTEL €€€
(☎0524784784; www.aubergetangaro.com; Zone du Golf; r €70-160; P 🛜 🏊) If you want to get away from it all, this early-20th-century villa makes a tranquil retreat. Set in a pretty garden, the 19 cottage rooms are simple but stylish and all have private terraces, plus there's a hammam, bar-restaurant and turquoise pool. Some public areas are looking time-worn but a refurb is in the offing, we're told.

Eating & Drinking

There are a number of restaurants and bars in the Sofitel. Alternatively, Essaouira is only a short-ish taxi ride away.

Jimi Hendrix Cafe CAFE
(Diabat; tea Dh10; ⊙9am-9pm) From Diabat to Woodstock. This low-key cafe is dedicated to all things Hendrix – who may or may not have hung out here back in the day – with

walls plastered in faded photographs and artistic renditions of the rock legend. Hum along to 'All Along the Watchtower' while you sip a mint tea.

Sofitel Essaouira Mogador Golf & Spa BAR

(☎0524479400; www.sofitel.com; Domaine Mogador, Diabat; ⏲9-4am) If you're out Diabet way, it's worth popping in to this swanky-looking resort for a drink poolside at the aptly named Le Pool Bar, or sundowners on the terrace of the indoor-outdoor Le Tiki So Bar, which shuts up shop at 1am. If you still have the energy, the two-floor So Lounge Mogador is jumping til 4am.

Sidi Kaouki سيدي كاوكي

POP 4580

Surfers in the know discovered the charms of Sidi Kaouki long ago, with its consistent waves, wild beaches, budget-friendly accommodation and simple cafes. Now it's developing into a hub for kitesurfers and windsurfers too, and you can bodyboard off the beach.

But even if you don't take to the water, it's a chilled escape from Essaouira. Away from the beaches you're more likely to find goats blocking the roads than cars.

The large building on the rocks, washed by the sea, is the final resting place of Sufi saint Sidi Kaouki, who was known for his healing abilities. Muslims still visit the shrine.

Activities

Surfing dominates during the winter months, and kitesurfing and windsurfing in the breezier summer months, although all three can be practised year-round. There are conditions to suit all abilities, but Essaouira is better for absolute beginners.

There are several places that rent equipment; you can also book lessons or longer surfing safaris that include the gear.

★Blue Morocco Surf Club SURFING

(☎0661203600; www.blue-morocco.org) This outfit offers surf courses for all levels, including longer surfing safaris with camping in the wild. Long-time surfer Azhar Joundi knows Essaouira's coastline like the back of his hand and where to find the best breaks. Lessons start at €25, a week-long course is €300 and all-inclusive with accommodation and food is €500.

OceanVibes KITESURFING

(☎0644707745; bojamalotfi@gmail.com) This locally run outfit, headed up by long-standing trainer Boujemaa, based in Essaouira and Sidi Kaouki, offers private and group kitesurfing, windsurfing and surfing lessons for all abilities, as well as gear rental and kitesurf packages. Surfing lessons from €15, windsurfing from €55 and kitesurfing from €60.

Sidi Kaouki Surf Station WATER SPORTS

(☎0672044016; www.sidi-kaouki.com) With a wide range of pro and beginner gear, this place offers surfboard rental (one day from €9), windsurfer rental (one day from €63) and kitesurf rental (one day €60), along with SUP rental (one day from €20). It also offers yoga-and-surf combos with accommodation and transport. Check the website for details.

Sleeping & Eating

Les Kiosques are a string of simple eateries around the main square, serving grilled fish, tajines and Friday couscous. But the best restaurant in town is at Hotel Le Kaouki.

Hotel Le Kaouki GUESTHOUSE €

(☎0524783206; http://sidikaouki.com; d incl full-board Dh660) This rustic beach retreat has just 10 blue-and-whitewashed rooms decorated with colourful rugs and throws, and shared facilities. With no electricity, it's candlelit at night, adding to its charm. Khadija rustles up the best tajines and grilled fish in town (dinner Dh130), served in the convivial salon or on the shady terrace. French owner Roro can arrange any activity.

Rebali Riads BOUTIQUE HOTEL €€€

(☎0654384119; www.rebaliriads.com; r/villa from €120/200; P 📶 ≋) Self-catering, boutique-hotel style. One- to five-bedroom villas, sleeping two to 10 people, come with outside space and shared or private pools, open-plan lounges and well-stocked kitchens; rooms share a kitchen. Breakfast is served on the terrace, and you can book for lunch and dinner. The hotel can also arrange classes with the chef.

Le Douar des Arganiers B&B €€€

(☎0613206042; www.douardesarganiers.com; Sidi Kaouki; r from Dh700; 📶) 🍃 An open-plan lounge and four expansive suites mix classic and contemporary Moroccan design, with bare stone walls and wooden beams, and a living space with a fireplace. Some have balconies, all have views over the countryside, as does the terrace, perfect for a leisurely breakfast. Solar panels create electricity and hot water, and wastewater takes care of the garden.

La Mouette et Les Dromadaire SEAFOOD €€

(☎0678449212; www.facebook.com/LaMouetteEtLesDromadaires; mains Dh110; ⏲10am-8pm, closed Tue) Simple yet stylish, this laid-back beach bar and restaurant flows directly on to the beach and is perfect for a leisurely brunch or lunch. The menu focuses on fish – John Dory tartare, swordfish, octopus salad, grilled calamari – so feast feet-in-the-sand or on the terrace to an ocean soundtrack, and chill out with a bottle of Moroccan wine or a cocktail.

Al Vent INTERNATIONAL €€

(☎0623836615; http://sidikaoukihotel.com; mains Dh40-125; ⏲8am-midnight; ☑) This Spanish-owned place opposite the beach is popular with the easy-going surfer crowd for its paella (fish, chicken or seafood), burgers and tajines. There are good options for vegetarians and vegans too. The owners also offer backpacker-style accommodation.

ℹ Getting There & Away

Sidi Kaouki is about 25km south of Essaouira. Bus 2 (Dh8) leaves from outside Bab Doukkala every two hours from around 7am to 6pm and takes around 40 minutes.

AT A GLANCE

POPULATION
Tangier: 1,083,460

SPANISH EXCLAVES IN MOROCCO
2

BEST 1920S ART DECO HOTEL
Hotel Villa Florido (p297)

BEST CANDLELIT KASBAH DINING
Chez Hicham (p288)

BEST BEER & TAPAS
La Cerveceria (p306)

WHEN TO GO

Apr Spring is perfect for trekking in the Rif and exploring national parks without the heat.

Jul Head to Tetouan for its annual festival promoting female artists.

Sep Mediterranean beaches await, without the crowds.

Grande Mosquée (p252) and city view, Tangier

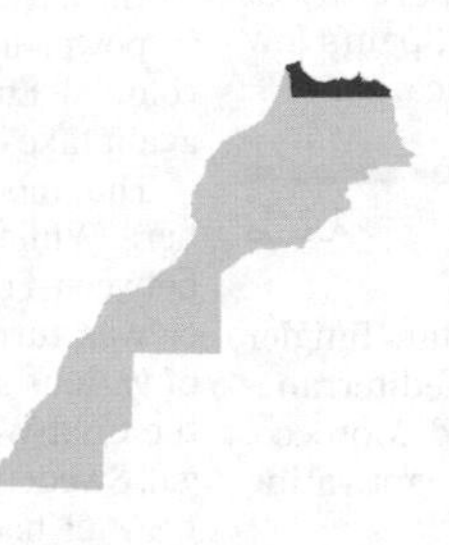

Mediterranean Coast & the Rif Mountains

Caught between the crashing waves of the Mediterranean and the rough crags of the Rif Mountains, northern Morocco is one of the most charming parts of the country. Tangier, the faded libertine of a port that links Africa and Europe, has shed its shady past to enjoy a rebirth as the fashionable Moroccan riviera. To the east, the coast is dotted with cliffs and coves; the area booms as a Moroccan holiday destination.

The pastel-blue medina of Chefchaouen deserves its reputation as a magnet for travellers, while Tetouan has the food and architecture of the Spanish protectorate era. Echoes of Spain continue with the medieval fortresses and modernist architectural treasures at the enclaves of Ceuta and Melilla.Inland, you can get away from everything with treks in the Rif and walking in the Beni-Snassen Mountains.

INCLUDES

WEST MEDITERRANEAN COAST

Morocco's west Mediterranean coast takes in the area around the storied port city of Tangier, as well as Ceuta, one of Spain's few remaining enclaves in North Africa.

Tangier طنجة

☎0539 / POP 1,083,460

Overlooking the Strait of Gibraltar, Tangier (*tan-ja*) dips its toes into the Mediterranean and the Atlantic, Europe and Morocco, beach life and city life, and a captivating past and an exciting future.

Shaded medina streets and whitewashed Ville Nouvelle alleyways reveal secrets of a shady drug-fuelled past when Beat Generation writers smoked hash and had boozy parties in ancient buildings beneath flapping seagulls.

While alive in myth, Tangier's sketchy days are long gone (though cannabis and liberal attitudes towards alcohol remain). King Mohammed VI's multi-billion-dirham port reinvigoration plan has given the city a facelift, and the TGV (high-speed rail) has enticed business interest.

Some worry Tangier is becoming a small Casablanca, but if the diehard expats have anything to say about it, the city of old won't disappear without a fight. There are far worse ideas than to sit in a Tangier cafe and watch the exciting transformation unfold.

History

Tangier's history is a continual tale of foreign invasion, much of it driven by the city's strategic location at the entrance to the Mediterranean. The area was first settled as a trading base by the ancient Greeks and Phoenicians, and named for the goddess Tinge, the lover of Hercules, who legendarily pulled Europe apart from Africa to form the Strait of Gibraltar. Under Roman rule, it was the capital of the province of Mauretania Tingitana. The Vandals attacked from Spain in AD 429, followed by the Byzantines, and then the Arabs, who invaded in 705 and suppressed the Amazigh (Berber) tribes. Tangier passed between various Arab factions before finally coming under Almohad rule in 1149. Then the Portuguese arrived, capturing the city on their second attempt in 1471, only to hand it to the British 200 years later as a wedding gift for Charles II. The English diarist Samuel Pepys lived here briefly, calling it 'the excrescence of the earth'. Morocco regained control of the city under Sultan Moulay Ismail in 1679, destroying much of the city in the process. They remained in power until the mid-19th century, when colonial European powers wanted to once again take over North Africa.

The modern history of Tangier begins here. While the rest of Morocco was divided between France and Spain, strategic Tangier was turned into an 'International Zone' of various sectors, similar to West Berlin in the Cold War. France, Spain, Britain, Portugal, Sweden, Holland, Belgium, Italy and the USA all had a piece of the pie, which was managed by the sultan, at least on paper. This situation lasted from 1912 until shortly after Moroccan independence in 1956, when the city was returned to the rest of the country. During this famous Interzone period, expats flooded in, forming half the population, and a wild, anything-goes culture broke out, attracting all sorts of people, for reasons both high and low. Socialites, artists, currency speculators, drug addicts, spies, sexual deviants, exiles, eccentrics – the marginalia of humanity all arrived, giving the city a particularly sordid reputation.

When the Interzone period ended, Tangier entered a long period of decline. As the economic base moved on, so did the cultural scene. The city became a dreary port, while retaining its criminality. King Hassan II hated the city and starved it of funding. Street hustlers multiplied, turning off tourists. The number of expats dwindled, until there were only a few thousand left.

Since 2007 Tangier has been the site of major development, most notably its new port, Tanger Med, marina, Tanja Marina Bay (p254), and the high speed TGV train line to Casablanca.

Sights

Medina & Kasbah

The **medina** (Map p256), the top attraction of Tangier, is a labyrinth of alleyways both commercial and residential and as charming as it is challenging. It's contained by the walls of a 15th-century Portuguese fortress, although most buildings are actually relatively new for a Moroccan medina. The place is full of travellers' treasures and offers glimpses of traditional living. Touts pining for lost tourists aim to extort tips or earn a

Mediterranean Coast & the Rif Mountains Highlights

1 Chefchaouen (p281) Getting lost in the blue-washed alleys of one of Morocco's most enchanting medinas.

2 Tangier (p250) Looking beyond this city's gleaming modern face to find traces of the artists, from Matisse to the Beat poets, who made it home.

3 Tetouan (p273) Taking in the art and history of this Riffian town's museums, its beautifully restored Spanish architecture and its lovable medina.

4 Melilla (p300) Wandering around the modernist buildings and imposing medieval fortress, before indulging in tapas for lunch or dinner.

5 Talassemtane National Park (p290) Trekking amid the forests and Amazigh (Berber) villages of the Rif Mountains.

6 Beni-Snassen Mountains (p311) Exploring the remote loquat-filled gorges and visiting some of the world's oldest human remains.

cut from the souqs, and even after a dozen visits, the medina can still leave you disoriented. Yet, there is beauty and history in these walls, where artists, spies and mafiosi roamed. No Tangier trip is complete without a visit.

★ Tangier American Legation Museum MUSEUM
(Map p256; ☎0539935317; www.legation.org; 8 Rue d'Amerique; Dh20, guided tour Dh50; ⏰10am-5pm Mon-Fri, to 3pm Sat) This museum, in an elegant five-storey mansion, is a must-see: Morocco was the first country to recognise the United States by opening its ports to the fledgling nation in 1777, and this was the first piece of American real estate abroad, as well as the only US National Historic Landmark on foreign soil.

★ Petit Socco SQUARE
(Place Souq Ad Dakhil; Map p256) This was once the most notorious crossroads of Tangier, the site of drug deals and all forms of prostitution. Today the facades are freshly painted, tourists abound, and it's a wonderful square for people watching over a mint tea.

★ Kasbah Museum of Mediterranean Cultures MUSEUM
(Map p256; ☎0539932097; Place de la Kasbah; adult/child Dh20/10; ⏰10am-6pm Wed-Mon) This recently refurbished museum is housed in the former sultan's palace of Dar El Makhzen. The focus is on the history of the area from prehistoric times to the 19th century. Exhibits are well-presented in French and Arabic only. Work your way anticlockwise around the first courtyard before heading inside to the rest of the displays, followed by a walk in the charming Andalusian garden.

Particular highlights are the **mosaic of Venus** from Volubilis and statuary, plus the **giant replica maps**. The first map tracks trade routes from the Phoenician trade in metals to the electronic goods of the 21st century; the second is a gorgeous map of the known world made in Tangier in 1154 (hint: it's upside down from the viewer's perspective). The museum is inside the medina – follow the perimeter all the way to the western end, to the highest part of the city, enter the Bab Kasbah gate and follow the road to the museum.

The museum is wheelchair accessible.

Nahon Synagogue SYNAGOGUE
(Map p256; ☎0539931633; 3 Rue Synagogue, cnr Rue Cheikh El Harrak; by donation; ⏰9am-6pm Sun-Fri) FREE Tangier once had 17 synagogues and 27,000 Jewish residents. That number has dwindled and the only synagogue open to the public is Nahon – but it's a beauty. Intricate bronze lanterns hang over the main sanctuary and wine-coloured drapes cover the Torah (Hebrew bible) on the *bema* (stage). Upstairs is an exhibit of *ketubah* (marriage contracts) from couples who were married here.

Musée de la Fondation Lorin MUSEUM
(Map p256; ☎0539930306; 44 Rue Touahine; by donation; ⏰11am-1pm & 3.30-7.30pm Sun-Fri) FREE This eclectic museum is housed in a former synagogue. Here you will find an open 2-storey room with an engaging collection of B&W photographs of 19th- and 20th-century Tangier on the walls. Meanwhile, a children's theatre production may be going on in the centre. The museum doubles as a workshop for disadvantaged kids, bringing life to the static display.

Grande Mosquée MOSQUE
(Map p256) From the Petit Socco in the medina, the route leading towards the sea leads east past this grand green-shingled mosque, which at one time housed a Portuguese church. Entry is prohibited for non-Muslims.

Tomb of Ibn Battuta TOMB
(Map p256) This modest tomb is purported to be the last resting place of Ibn Battuta, who was born in Tangier in 1304 and became the greatest traveller of the period – outpacing Marco Polo at an easy clip. The tomb remains locked and there's not much to see at the site.

Ville Nouvelle

With its Riviera architecture and colonial ambience, the stretch from Place de France along Blvd Pasteur still hints at the glamour of the 1930s. It's a popular place for an early evening promenade, or a few hours sipping mint tea in one of the many streetside cafes – particularly the venerable landmark Gran Café de Paris (p262), where you still might half-expect to bump into Truman Capote or Jean Genet.

★ Grand Socco LANDMARK
(Place du 9 Avril 1947; Map p256) The Grand Socco is the romantic entrance to the medina, a large, sloping, palm-ringed plaza with a central fountain that stands before the keyhole gate, Bab Fass. Once a major market,

Tangier

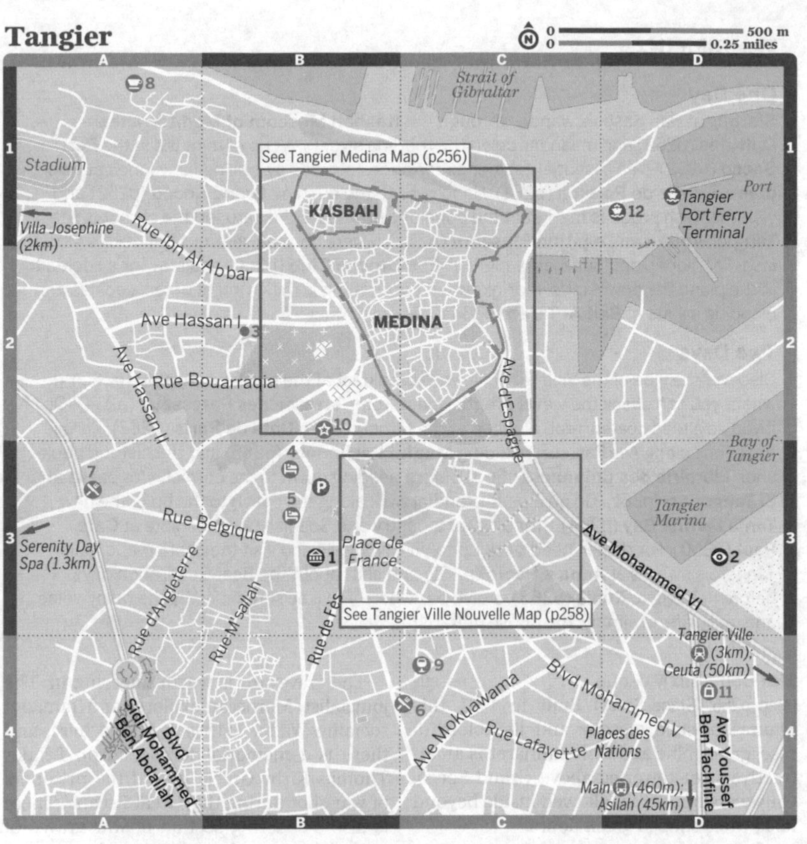

Tangier

Sights
1 Mohamed Drissi Gallery of Contemporary Art B3
2 Tanja Marina Bay D3

Activities, Courses & Tours
3 Blue Door B2

Sleeping
4 Grand Hôtel Villa de France B3
5 Pension Hollanda B3

Eating
6 Anna E Paolo C4
7 La Gelateria A3

Drinking & Nightlife
8 Cafe Hafa A1
9 La Bodega de Tanger C4

Entertainment
10 Beit Al Tarab B2

Shopping
11 Ibn Batouta Mall D4

Transport
12 Ferry Company Ticket Offices D1
FRS ..... (see 12)
Inter Shipping ..... (see 12)

its cobblestone circle is now the end of the line for taxis, the point at which the modern streets narrow into the past.

For the best ground-floor view, climb the steps at the highest point on the circle, across from the large tan building (the police station), to what locals simply call **La Terrasse**. There's a cafe up here where locals spend the day playing *parchís* (a widely popular Spanish board game). This is what you came for, one of those dreamy moments when you think you've entered a movie set.

TANGIER IN...

One Day

Starting at Bab Kasbah, wander through the **Kasbah Museum of Mediterranean Cultures** (p252) and meander down the medina streets. A cup of mint tea in the **Petit Socco** (p252) is an essential Tangier experience, followed by a filling fishy lunch at **Populaire Saveur de Poisson** (p261). Head over to the bustling **Grand Socco** (p252) and visit the fresh produce market at the edge of the medina. Just around the corner is the **Tangier American Legation Museum** (p252), where you can seek out Morocco's *Mona Lisa*. For dinner, opt for a classy night at **El Morocco Club** (p260) and stay for a cocktail in the piano bar downstairs. If drinking isn't your thing, a rockin' night of tea, cookies and clapping awaits at **Beit Al Tarab** (p264).

Two Days

Discover the vibe of the Ville Nouvelle with breakfast at the plush **La Giralda** (p260), where you can check the views over to Spain from **Terrasse des Paresseux** (p254). Or if you've already eaten, grab a coffee at the famous **Gran Cafe de Paris** (p262). Peruse the shops along Ave Pasteur including **Madini Parfumeur** (p265) and the historic bookshop **Librairie des Colonnes** (p265) before heading down to the corniche for paella at **El Tangerino** (p261). Go on a post-prandial walk along the beach to the tip of the new **Tanja Marina Bay** (p254), stopping for a pastry and Spanish hot chocolate at **Cafe Paul** (p260). For dinner, head back up to Ville Nouvelle and visit the charismatic Italian-Tangerois owners at **Anna e Paolo** (p261) and chat about the Beat Generation days before heading to **Rubis** (p263), a dive bar where you'll be serenaded by the raspy voice and jazzy riffs of Jimmy, the house guitarist.

Sidi Bou Abib Mosque MOSQUE
(Map p256; Grand Socco) Built in 1917, this Mauresque-style mosque and its colourful rose, green, blue and white minaret is an attractive sight towering above Grand Socco. Only worshippers are allowed inside beyond its keyhole-shaped green doors.

Mendoubia Gardens PARK
(Map p256) This large park is full of strolling couples and children playing football. The Mendoubia Gardens are flanked by an elegant line of colonial buildings, perhaps the most attractive of its kind in the city. At the top of the central hill is a monument flanked by cannons that contains the speech given by Mohammed V asking for independence.

St Andrew's Church CHURCH
(Map p256; 50 Rue d'Angleterre; by donation; ⏰10am-5pm Sat-Thu, services 8.30am & 11am Sun) St Andrew's Church is one of the more charming oddities of Tangier. Completed in 1894 on land granted by Sultan Hassan, the interior of this Anglican church is decorated in high Fassi style, with the Lord's Prayer in Arabic over the altar. Behind the altar is a cleft that indicates the direction of Mecca, with carved quotes from the Quran.

The graveyard is worth lingering in. The journalist, Moroccan explorer and Tanjaoui socialite Walter Harris is buried here, and there is a memorial for Squadron Leader Thomas Kirby Green, one of the prisoners of war shot during the 'Great Escape'. There is also a sobering section of war graves of entire downed aircrews, their headstones attached shoulder to shoulder. Caretaker Yassine is always on site and can offer you a tour.

Terrasse des Paresseux ARCHITECTURE
(Map p258) The aptly named 'Idlers' Terrace' provides sweeping views of the port, Spain and, on a really clear day, Gibraltar. A set of ancient cannons faces the bay, symbolically warding off usurpers (apart from the children who love to climb them).

Tanja Marina Bay MARINA
(Map p253; ☎0539331717; www.tanjamarinabay.ma; Ave Mohammed VI) King Mohammed VI's multibillion-dirham plan to reinvigorate Tangier's port is well under way, and his shiny new marina with space for 800 boats is complete. Jutting out into the Strait of Gibraltar, the marina includes a long boardwalk with several cafes and restaurants, an ice-cream parlour, an upmarket restaurant, a tapas bar and disco (p264).

Activities

Serenity Day Spa SPA
(☎0539372828; Rue Adolfo Fessere, Quartier California; hammam & scrub Dh400) Here is a chance for women to escape the all-too-male world of Morocco, at least for a few hours, and indulge the body in luxurious surroundings. This female-only hammam gets high marks from local customers. It's west of Place de Koweit, on the road to the golf course; take a cab.

El Minzah Wellness SPA
(Map p258; ☎0539333311; 85 Rue de la Liberté; pool Dh100, fitness room Dh200; ⏰9.30-11am & 7-11pm) Pamper yourself at the luxury spa, where there's a fully equipped gym (with superb views to the sea), hammam, sauna and Jacuzzi, as well as a range of massage and other therapeutic treatments.

M'nar Park AMUSEMENT PARK
(☎0539343831; www.mnarpark.ma; Cap Malabata; aquapark adult/child Dh200/100; ⏰10am-10pm pool Apr-Sep) Located south of Cap Malabata, with great views across the Bay of Tangier, this cliffside resort is a short escape from the city and gets packed with Moroccan families in summer. With a water park, arcade, karting, a small train, a mini-football field, paintball, restaurants and a cafe, there's plenty to do. Accommodation includes apartments, bungalows and luxury villas.

Blue Door COOKING
(Map p253; ☎0612020210; www.bluedoorcuisine.com; 38A Rue Al Mabarra; couscous €65, tajine €60, bread €35; ⏰10am-2pm & 4-8pm) Behind a big – you guessed it – blue door is this clean and spacious American-owned cooking school. Local women share their wisdom about making couscous, tajines and Moroccan bread, the latter of which is taken to a local oven to bake. You'll also visit a nearby spice shop. It's a fun, professional and worthwhile way to experience Moroccan cuisine.

Classes are in English, French and Spanish. Reserve at least one day in advance.

Festivals & Events

TANJAzz MUSIC
(www.tanjazz.org; ⏰Sep) This ever-popular festival with a good reputation for attracting leading names has been running for more than two decades and hosts concerts by local and international jazz musicians.

Festival du Court Métrage Méditerranéen FILM
(International Mediterranean Short Film Festival; www.ccm.ma; ⏰Oct) Week-long festival of short films from around the Mediterranean.

Sleeping

Many of Tangier's sleeping options are showing their age, but there are gems to be found. Palatial *dars* (traditional houses) are tucked into tiny medina streets along with budget hotels and a few hostels. Ville Nouvelle has a wide array of accommodation for all budgets. Note an extra tax per night and per guest may be added to the price.

Medina

★**Bayt Alice** HOSTEL €
(Map p256; ☎0539374315; 26 Rue Khatib Beni Idder; 4-/7-bed dm Dh100/130, s/tw/d

TANGIER ART GALLERIES

Tangier is filled with small galleries worth poking your head into. All of the following are free.

Mohamed Drissi Gallery of Contemporary Art (Map p253; 52 Rue d'Angleterre; ⏰10am-6pm Mon-Sat) FREE Housed in the fine grounds of the former British Consulate, this gallery hosts temporary exhibitions.

Galerie Conil (Map p256; ☎0534372054; 7 Rue du Palmier, Petit Socco; ⏰11am-1.30pm & 4-7pm Mon-Sat) FREE Split over three galleries in the medina; you'll find artwork, books and clothing.

Galerie Delacroix (Map p258; ☎0539932134; 86 Rue de la Liberté; ⏰2.30-9pm Tue-Sun) FREE Exhibition space of the Institut Français, featuring temporary exhibitions.

Centre Culturel Ibn Khaldoun (Map p258; ☎0662456897; 71 Rue de la Liberté; ⏰10am-1pm & 6-8.30pm Mon-Sat) FREE Contemporary art in a fine corner gallery. It's free.

Les Insolites (p265) Check out the photo gallery in the back of this welcoming bilingual bookstore.

Tangier Medina

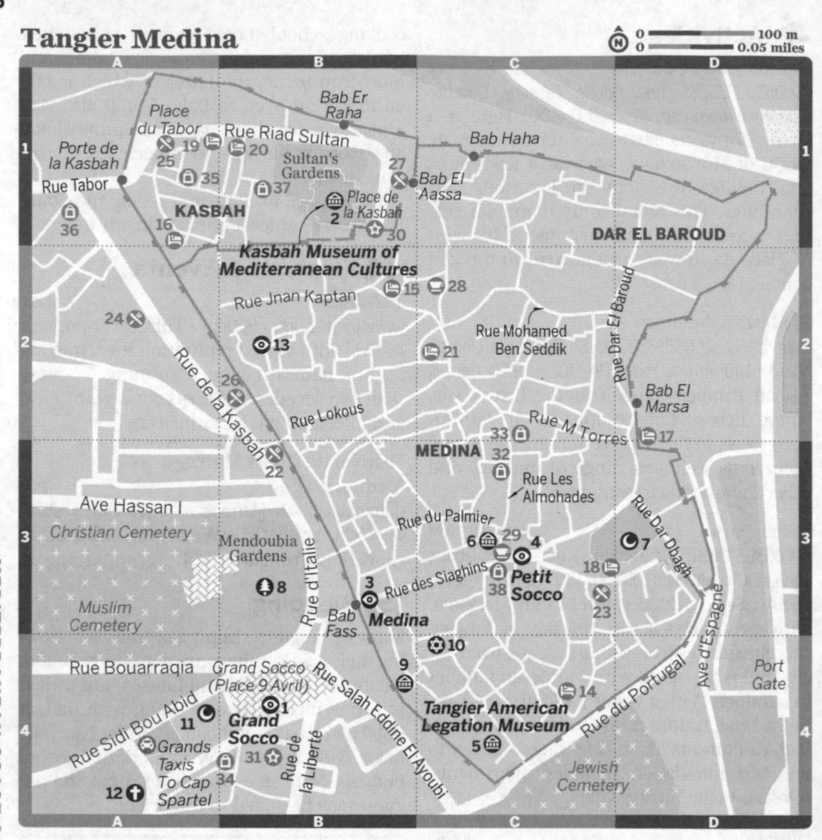

Dh280/350/400;) Designed by a French architect and named after her daughter, this medina hostel stands out from the pack. Over several floors in a pretty traditional home, the dorms and private rooms have eclectic decor, and staff are terrific. Moroccan breakfast is delish, with rich cheeses, olives and breads. Upstairs there's a terrace with panoramic views of the sea.

Riad Arous Chamel B&B €
(Map p256; 0665896903; 16 Rue Abdessadak; d small/large room Dh400/750;) A rare budget riad in the medina, Arous Chamel features ornate Moroccan decor with modern comforts. The seven rooms are cosy and picturesque, with stained glass doors and ceramic tile bathrooms. The building itself is over 250 years old, and was transformed into a guesthouse in 2008. Breakfast is served on the rooftop, with spectacular sea and medina views.

Hotel Mamora HOTEL €
(Map p256; 0539934105; 19 Ave Mokhtar Ahardan; s/d Dh200/300) This budget hotel near the Petit Socco was built in 1950, but just underwent renovations a few years ago. Rooms are clean and brightly coloured – you should have no trouble being alert in the morning with these shades. A new gold-coloured lounge with red retro couches has excellent views out to sea. A solid medina option.

★Dar Nour GUESTHOUSE €€
(Map p256; 0662112724; www.darnour.com; 20 Rue Gourna, Kasbah; d/ste from Dh650/1300;) This lovely peppermint-walled guesthouse has no central courtyard. Instead, rooms here branch off two winding staircases, creating a maze of dream-like rooms and salons, each more romantic than the last. Rooms are stylishly decorated with objets d'art and packed with books, creating a relaxed and homely atmosphere, while bath-

Tangier Medina

Top Sights
1 Grand Socco ... B4
2 Kasbah Museum of Mediterranean Cultures ... B1
3 Medina ... B3
4 Petit Socco ... C3
5 Tangier American Legation Museum ... C4

Sights
6 Galerie Conil ... C3
7 Grande Mosquée ... D3
8 Mendoubia Gardens ... B3
9 Musée de la Fondation Lorin ... B4
10 Nahon Synagogue ... C4
11 Sidi Bou Abib Mosque ... A4
12 St Andrew's Church ... A4
13 Tomb of Ibn Battuta ... B2

Sleeping
14 Bayt Alice ... C4
15 Dar Chams Tanja ... B2
16 Dar Nour ... A1
17 Hotel Continental ... D2
18 Hotel Mamora ... C3
19 La Tangerina ... A1
20 Nord Pinus Tanger ... B1
21 Riad Arous Chamel ... C2

Eating
22 Abo Tayssir ... B3
23 Ahlen ... C3
24 Café À l'Anglaise ... A2
25 El Morocco Club ... A1
26 Hamadi ... B2
27 Le Salon Bleu ... B1

Drinking & Nightlife
28 Cafe Baba ... C2
29 Café Central ... C3
Dar Nour ... (see 16)
Nord Pinus Tanger ... (see 20)

Entertainment
30 Casbah Social Club ... B1
31 Cinema Rif ... B4

Shopping
32 Bleu de Fes ... C3
33 Boutique Majid ... C2
34 DARNA, The Women's Association of Tangier ... B4
35 KM Couleurs ... A1
36 Las Chicas ... A1
37 Laura Welfling ... B1
38 Volubilis ... C3

rooms are lined with *tadelakt* (waterproof plaster). Some rooms have a private terrace.

La Tangerina GUESTHOUSE €€
(Map p256; 0539947731; www.latangerina.com; 19 Rue Riad Sultan, Kasbah; d Dh660-1650;) This is a perfectly renovated riad at the very top of the kasbah, with 10 rooms of different personalities. Bathed in light and lined with rope bannisters, it feels like an elegant, Berber-carpeted steamship cresting the medina. The roof terrace overlooks the ancient crenellated walls of the kasbah and commands one of the city's best views.

Hotel Continental HOTEL €€
(Map p256; 0539931024; hcontinental@menara.ma; 36 Rue Dar El Baroud; s/d Dh730/1030; P) This grand hotel overlooking the strait offers a fascinating taste of International Zone archaeology; parts of *The Sheltering Sky* were filmed here. There are 54 rustic rooms (75% face the sea), which all received the direly needed additions of air-conditioning, modern TVs and proper toilets. The hotel has a large, dusty craft shop.

Dar Chams Tanja B&B €€€
(Map p256; 0539332323; www.darchamstanja.com; 2 Rue Jnan Kabtan; tw/d Dh1360/1690;) This attractive seven-bed *maison d'hôte* (B&B) is only a decade old – a rarity in the medina – so everything is spic and span. Rooms are bright with intricate Moroccan-style, colour-coordinated bed frames and furniture. The rooftop is home to an exquisite view and has solar panels that heat the guesthouse's water. An in-house hammam and massage room are for guests only.

Nord Pinus Tanger GUESTHOUSE €€€
(Map p256; 0661228140; www.nord-pinus-tanger.com; 11 Rue Riad Sultan, Kasbah; d €190, junior/deluxe ste €230/290;) This is a very grand kasbah house with somewhat Gothic stone columns and staircase. Rooms are a delight, with eclectic decor and every comfort. Excellent meals are served in the opulent dining room or on the roof terrace (nonguests welcome). The bar on the terrace with a stunning sea view is a favourite for an aperitif.

Ville Nouvelle

Hotel El Muniria HOTEL €
(Map p258; 0539935337; 1 Rue Magellan; s/d Dh200/250;) This is your best budget option in the Ville Nouvelle, and is chock-full of Beat Generation history (William

Tangier Ville Nouvelle

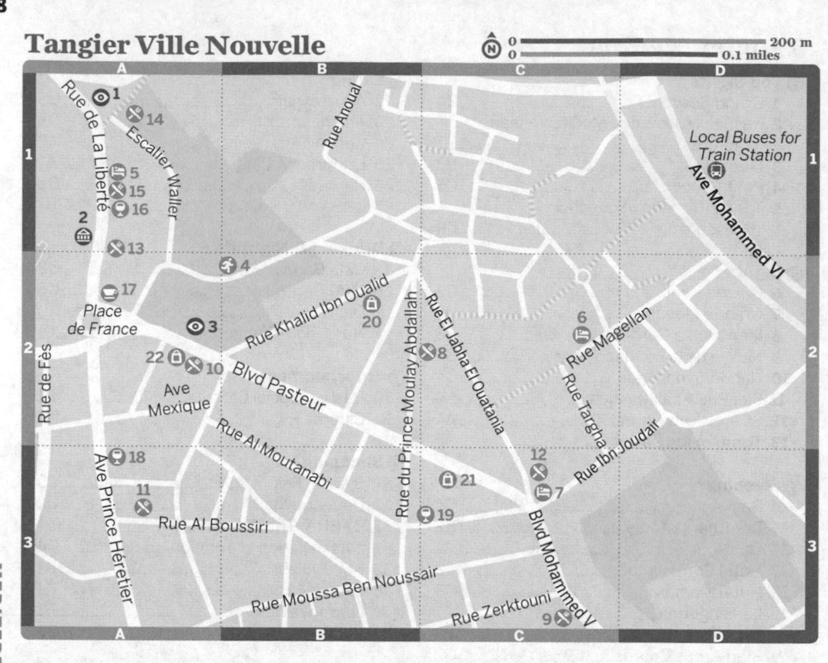

Tangier Ville Nouvelle

Sights
1 Centre Culturel Ibn Khaldoun A1
2 Galerie Delacroix A1
3 Terrasse des Paresseux A2

Activities, Courses & Tours
4 El Minzah Wellness B2

Sleeping
5 El Minzah A1
6 Hotel El Muniria C2
7 Hotel Rembrandt C3

Eating
8 Al Achab C2
9 Champs Élysées C3
10 La Giralda A2
11 Le Pagode A3
12 Number One C3
13 Patisserie La Española A1
14 Populaire Saveur de Poisson A1
15 Restaurant El Korsan A1

Drinking & Nightlife
16 Caid's Bar A1
17 Gran Café de Paris A2
18 Hole in the Wall Bar A3
Number One ......(see 12)
19 Rubis C3
TangerInn Pub ......(see 6)

Shopping
20 Les Insolites B2
21 Librairie des Colonnes C3
22 Madini Parfumeur A2

Burroughs lived here while writing *Naked Lunch*). Bright blue French windows set it apart, revealing the careful touch of a hands-on family operation.

Pension Hollanda HOTEL €
(Map p253; ☎0539937838; 139 Rue de Hollande; s/d Dh250/350, r with shared bathroom per person Dh150) Tucked away in a quiet street a short walk from Place de France, this former hospital has bright whitewashed rooms and high ceilings, with tiny bathrooms. All rooms have a TV and a sink; doubles come with a shower. For a budget steal, don't miss the loft rooms up the hidden spiral staircase.

Hotel Rembrandt HOTEL €€
(Map p258; ☎0539333314; cnr Blvds Mohammed V & Pasteur; s/d Dh700/900;) Rooms here are pretty standard and are in marked contrast to the elegant downstairs lobby, with its classic elevator and curving staircase echoing its 1950s roots. However, the glassed-in restaurant is good, the green

garden cafe is a tranquil spot to relax, and there's a reasonable pub for an evening drink. Rooms with a sea view cost around Dh100 extra.

★Grand Hôtel Villa de France HISTORIC HOTEL €€€
(Map p253; www.leroyal.com; Rue de la Liberté; s/d from Dh2000/2400, ste from Dh3000) Few hotels are as venerable as the gloriously refurbished Grand Hôtel Villa de France. French painter Eugène Delacroix stayed here in 1832; his compatriot, Henri Matisse, followed just before WWI. You can enjoy the still-spectacular views Matisse painted from his old room (35), decorated as it was in his day.

★El Minzah HOTEL €€€
(Map p258; 0539333444; www.leroyal.com; 85 Rue de la Liberté; d/ste from Dh2000/3500;) The classiest five-star hotel in Tangier proper, this beautifully maintained 1930s period piece offers three excellent restaurants, two equally good bars, a fitness centre, spa and even a babysitting service. It's shaped like an enormous hollow square, with a tremendous Spanish-Moorish courtyard, and has history oozing from its walls. Nonguests can use the pool for Dh200 or if they buy lunch.

Sashay past the doorman and glide down the stairs to the beautiful Andalusian courtyard where there are dozens of photographs of celebrity visitors around the walls. Most of the photos date from the 1950s and '60s. A suave Rock Hudson, Aristotle and Jackie Onassis, Winston Churchill, and glitzy Rita Hayworth are just some familiar faces that we spotted.

Outskirts of Tangier

★Villa Joséphine HERITAGE HOTEL €€€
(0539334535; www.villajosephine-tanger.com; r Dh3200-7800;) A mansion or a palace? It's hard to decide at this restored 1920s residence, once a summer retreat for Moroccan royalty and partying European diplomats. Everything about the 10 rooms here is sumptuous, from the period decor to the up-to-the-minute amenities and service. All have balconies or terraces looking out to sea.

Eating

Moroccan food is all over Tangier, but for the tajine-weary the international city has an array of options from around the world.

For groceries, street-side vendors are rarely out of sight and international items can be found at Carrefour Market inside **Ibn Batouta Mall** (Map p253; 0539942118; Ave Youssef Ibn Tachfine; 10am-10pm).

Medina

Ahlen MOROCCAN €
(Map p256; 0664123512; 8 Rue des Postes; mains Dh40-65; noon-11pm Tue-Sun;) Rachid, the owner of this affordable medina restaurant, is passionate about nutrition, so he makes all of his preservative-free tajines, soups and couscous with organic ingredients. He's so passionate, in fact, he may tease you for opting for a soft drink over a freshly squeezed orange juice. Jokes aside, the food here is delicious, especially for the price.

Abo Tayssir SYRIAN €
(Map p256; 0644660292; 14 Rue d'Italie; mains Dh40-70, set lunch Dh50; 10am-midnight, to 2am Jun-Aug;) Asma and Redwane serve Syrian food with a heart ten times larger than their heart-shaped falafel balls; it may be tough to eat and run without a chat over tea with the lovable couple. Set lunches include hot lentil soup, dippable kibbeh (meatballs), *tabbouleh* (parsley salad), baba ganoush (smoked aubergine dip) and hummus. Vegetarian lunch menus are also available (Dh40).

Le Salon Bleu MEDITERRANEAN €€
(Map p256; 0529271618; Place de la Kasbah; set menu Dh60-160; 10am-11pm;) This romantic cream and sea-blue restaurant winds up several rooms and rooftop terraces with idyllic views of the sea and kasbah below. Set menus include an array of tasty Mediterranean-style dips, soups and salads, accompanied by either fish or a tajine. Great for a date any day of the week.

Hamadi MOROCCAN €€
(Map p256; 0539934514; 2 Rue de la Kasbah; mains Dh80-Dh150; 11am-4pm & 7pm-midnight) Hamadi, an institution in Tangier for well over 50 years, has elegant red sofas and carpeted walls that may appear over the top, but the kitchen backs it up. Pie-slice-sized chicken *bastilla* (stuffed savoury-sweet pie) sprinkled with cinnamon is a menu standout, as is lamb tajine. Live traditional music attracts a crowd nightly, including plenty of tour groups.

MATISSE IN TANGIER

Of the many artists who have passed through Tangier, Henri Matisse is one of the most famous. The French impressionist and leading light of the early-20th-century Fauvist movement called Tangier a painter's paradise. His two visits to the city, in the spring of 1912 and again the following winter, had a profound influence on his work.

Inspired by the luminous North African light and the colour and harmony found in traditional Moroccan art, Matisse completed some 20 canvases and dozens of sketches during his time in Tangier. In them he honed the qualities that define his mature work: bold abstract lines, two-dimensional shapes and vibrant, expressive – as opposed to natural – colours.

Matisse mainly looked to the daily life of the medina for his themes. He produced several striking portraits of Zohra, a local prostitute, and a wonderful painting of a strong-featured Riffian woman sitting legs akimbo against an azure sky.

However, it is Matisse's renditions of the city that really strike a chord. Two of the most evocative are *Vue sur la Baie de Tanger* (View of the Bay of Tangier) and *La Porte de la Casbah* (Entrance to the Kasbah). Both are relatively subdued in their use of colour, but in *Paysage Vu d'une Fenêtre* (Window at Tangier) the artist hits full stride. The painting shows the view from his window in the Grand Hôtel Villa de France (p259), looking out over St Andrew's Church, with its squat tower, to the kasbah beyond. The overriding colour is a pure, sizzling Mediterranean blue.

Café À l'Anglaise MOROCCAN €€
(Map p256; 37 Rue de la Kasbah; mains Dh90-150; ⏲10am-10pm; 📶) Despite the name, you won't find English food here. Instead, there's delicious Moroccan Jewish cuisine heavy on garlic, including a variety of tajines and Moroccan salads. The cookies are tasty too.

★El Morocco Club MEDITERRANEAN €€€
(Map p256; ☎0539948139; 1 Rue Kashla, Kasbah; mains Dh140-195, tapas Dh40-90; ⏲noon-11.30pm; P📶) King Mohammed VI was seen dining here, which is as good a recommendation as any. A very smart renovation of this elegant building along the medina wall has resulted in an upmarket restaurant and atmospheric red-lit piano bar (from 8pm). The food fuses French and Moroccan flavours and is of the utmost quality.

Ville Nouvelle

Cafe Paul BAKERY €
(☎0539332379; www.paul-maroc.com; Tanja Marina Bay; pastries from Dh10, mains Dh60-160; ⏲9am-midnight, to 2am Sat & Sun; 📶) On Tangier's brand new marina with views of the yachts and sea, this cafe bakes flaky and irresistible pastries, perfectly dipped in a creamy Spanish-style hot chocolate. There's plenty more on the menu if you're in for a meal, including crêpes, burgers and pizza. A great place to stop when exploring the deceptively large marina.

La Gelateria ICE CREAM €
(Map p253; ☎0539332377; Ave Sidi Mohamed Ben Abdullah; ice cream scoop Dh16; ⏲7am-11pm) Find an anecdote to Tangier's heat at this airy cafe overlooking the Mohammed V Mosque. Go all out with the Romeo and Juliet, a divine six-scoop treat, or opt for something smaller, such as classic ice-cream flavours or sorbet in a cone.

Champs Élysées CAFE €
(Map p258; 6 Blvd Mohammed V; breakfast from Dh16; ⏲7am-11pm; 📶) This enormous whitewashed cafe is high on opulence, with a huge central chandelier and red velour upholstery. Breakfasts are decent and coffee is served in a ceramic cup and saucer, rather than the usual glass. Great sticky pastries.

Patisserie La Española PASTRIES €
(Map p258; 97 Rue de la Liberté; pastries from Dh10; ⏲7am-10.30pm, to 12.30am Jun-Sep) A heavily mirrored tearoom opened in 1959, this cafe tempts people off the street with its pretty arrangements of cakes and pastries. Everyone seems to come here – locals, foreigners, businesspeople, courting couples and more.

La Giralda CAFE €
(Map p258; ☎0539370407; 1st fl, 5 Blvd Pasteur; breakfast from Dh32; ⏲7am-midnight; 📶) This grand cafe overlooking the Terrasse des Paresseux has sumptuous, Egyptian-influenced decor and an intricately carved ceiling. Huge windows give great sea views.

A light menu of crêpes and paninis make it a good stop for breakfast or lunch.

★Anna E Paolo ITALIAN €€
(Map p253; ☎0539944617; 77 Rue Prince Héretier; mains from Dh80; ⏰noon-3pm & 8-11pm Mon-Sat) This is a genuine, family-run bistro with Italian Tangier-born owners; it feels like you've been invited for Sunday dinner. Expect a highly international crowd, lots of cross-table conversations about the events of the day, and wholesome food, including excellent charcuterie and pizzas, homemade pastas, meat and fish.

El Tangerino MEDITERRANEAN €€
(☎0539943973; 186 Ave Mohammed VI; mains Dh70-180; ⏰12.30pm-midnight; 📶) A classy nautical-themed restaurant on the corniche, El Tangerino serves heaping paella, pan and all, along with grilled fish, *pinchos* (tapas) and pizza. Upstairs has exquisite views of the sea and is ideally enjoyed with a drink and some tapas. Private wine-cellar seating is available by reservation.

RR Ice CAFE €€
(☎0539301039; www.facebook.com/RrIceTanger; Ghandouri, Malabata; mains Dh30-140; ⏰9am-1am) This cliffside cafe may have the best sea view in all of Tangier. It dishes out huge sundaes and crêpes, in addition to fish, burgers, pizza and juice cocktails. The garden sports resort-like tables and chairs, popular with families enjoying the unparalleled views and warm sun.

Number One MOROCCAN €€
(Map p258; ☎0539941674; 1 Ave Mohammed V; mains from Dh85; ⏰noon-3pm & 7-midnight) The orange walls and white windows in this renovated apartment provide the feel of a holiday cottage, while the red lighting, background jazz and exotic mementos lend it an intimate, sultry allure. The Moroccan-French cuisine gets high marks from locals, who have been coming here for decades. Alcohol is served.

Le Pagode CHINESE €€
(Map p258; ☎0539938086; Rue Al Boussiri; mains from Dh100; ⏰noon-2.30pm & 7-11pm Tue-Sun; 📶) If you're tired of tajines and pasta, this authentic Chinese fare is a decent alternative. La Pagode is an intimate and classy dining area, with lacquered furniture, white tablecloths and low lighting, paired with a classic Chinese menu. Alcohol is available.

★Populaire Saveur de Poisson SEAFOOD €€€
(Map p258; ☎0539336326; 2 Escalier Waller; fixed-price menu Dh200; ⏰1-5pm & 7-10.30pm Sat-Thu) This charming seafood restaurant is well worth the hype, offering an excellent, filling, four-course meal in rustic surroundings. First comes the fish soup, followed by inventive plates of fresh catch, olives and

21ST-CENTURY TANGIER

Times were that Tangier was exactly the sort of Moroccan destination you'd skip through – a rundown city full of hustlers trading on stories of a libertine past. Those days are long behind it, and Tangier entered the 2020s with a fresh face and a confident spring in its step.

Tangier's renaissance kicked off in 2017 when the main port was replaced by the Tanger Med facility, 48km along the coast, now the biggest port in Africa. The new port allowed investment to flow in, not least the Renault-Nissan and Peugeot car plants. Renault alone makes 400,000 vehicles a year at its plant near Tangier, exporting to the European Union as well as selling on the domestic market (the majority of *petits taxis* are now locally made Dacias, a Renault subsidiary). The plant is entirely fuelled by biomass from Morocco's olive oil industry – a neat fusion of ancient and modern Moroccan know-how.

The next step has been the Tangier Metropolis programme, a multi-billion-dirham plan to remodel the city's port, build a new marina and add a TGV high-speed rail line linking the city to Casablanca and Rabat. Much of the plan is already complete, and visitors can meander the sparkling new Tanja Marina Bay and ride its TGV line. But there's more to come, including an upmarket port community, a more orderly Medina and a series of cable-car lines connecting the old city to the port and Ville Nouvelle.

The plan is to make Tangier attractive to investors as a tech hub, and to bring the city to the forefront of Moroccan, Gulf and cruise-ship tourism. It remains to be seen whether all those dirhams will pay off, and whether all signs of the sordid Interzone days will disappear, but it's clear the city is on an upswing and worth lingering longer than a hop-over.

fresh breads. It's all washed down with a homemade juice cocktail made from a dozen fruits. Dessert is honey and almonds. Not just a meal, a whole experience.

Al Achab SEAFOOD €€€

(Map p258; ☎0539949389; 3 Rue du Prince Moulay Abdellah; set menu Dh160; ⊙1-5pm & 7-11pm; 📶) The Ville Nouvelle version of Populaire Saveur de Poisson (p261), but less expensive and with superb service. The set menu here will leave you stuffed, with seafood barley soup, breads with spicy *harissa* (chili paste), spinach, shrimp and swordfish tajine, white shark skewers and sea bass, all washed down with raisin, fig and date juice. Dessert is strawberry, nuts and honey.

Restaurant El Korsan MOROCCAN €€€

(Map p258; ☎0539935885; El Minzah Hotel, 85 Rue de la Liberté; mains around Dh160; ⊙1-3pm & 8-11pm; 📶) One of Tangier's top restaurants, this chic and classy place inside El Minzah Hotel offers a smaller, more-intimate version of the palace restaurant theme but without the bus tours. Well-presented Moroccan classics are served to soft live music and traditional dancing. Reservations are necessary, including one day's prior notice for lunch. Dress well.

Drinking & Nightlife

Finding a drink in much of Morocco can feel near impossible, but in Tangier there are drinking holes around almost every corner. Bars remain principally the domain of men, but there are a few more-westernised places where women can comfortably have a drink.

Tangier's clubbing scene picks up in the summer, when Europeans arrive on the ferries.

Cafes

Tangier's cafe culture is unlike anywhere else in Morocco and is clearly influenced by its neighbors to the north, Spain and France. Time goes by on Mediterranean time as many (mostly men) lounge all day, chairs turned outwards, drinking mint tea from transparent glasses, which is believed to be good for the body and soul.

★Gran Café de Paris CAFE

(Map p258; Place de France; ⊙6am-10.30pm) Gravity weighs upon the grand letters of the Gran Café de Paris, reminding us of its age at the crossroads of Tangier. Facing Place de France for almost a century, this is the most famous of the cafes along Blvd Pasteur and was a prime gathering spot for the Tangier literati.

Cafe Baba CAFE

(Map p256; ☎0602957448; 1 Sidi Hosni; ⊙10.30am-11.30pm) Opened in the Interzone days, this smoky medina cafe got its current name from the hippies who said 'Thank you, Baba' to the man who served their tea. Clients smoked *kif* (cannabis) then – the Rolling Stones' Keith Richards was photographed smoking a pipe here in 1966 – and students smoke *kif* now, as you'll smell. Tea and coffee are on offer.

Cafe Hafa CAFE

(Map p253; ☎0626687190; Rue Hafa; ⊙8.30am-11pm) A 10-minute walk west from the medina is this beloved sea-facing cafe with what many locals consider Tangier's best view. Opened in 1921, Cafe Hafa mainly serves tea and coffee, but spaghetti, pizza and burgers are also available (mains Dh30 to Dh60). Next to the cafe are cascading terraces where lovebirds young and old catch the sunset, tea in hand.

Café Central CAFE

(Map p256; Petit Socco; ⊙6am-11.30pm) The premier people-watching site in the medina, with tables on the pavement facing Petit Socco. See the local mafiosi arrive, watch odd specimens of humanity drift past, hear the strange shouts echo down the alleys and wonder what is going on upstairs. This historic cafe is the perfect place to sip your coffee.

Bars & Clubs

★Dar Nour ROOFTOP BAR

(Map p256; ☎0662112724; 20 Rue Gourna; ⊙6.30-11pm; 📶) After 6.30pm, the roof atop the outstanding Dar Nour guesthouse becomes one of the best cocktail parties in town, featuring flavourful mojitos, martinis and wines beneath the sunset and the stars. There's no better way to spend a warm Tangier evening.

Number One BAR

(Map p258; 1 Blvd Mohammed V; ⊙11am-midnight) Inside an apartment building, left after the entrance, this bar is perennially popular with expats. The decor is adorably funky, as is the bar's CD collection. The bar's owner, Karim, whose quotes hang above the tables, is lovable and hilarious. Cold beer, decent wine, spirits and tapas are on offer. Women are welcome.

TANGIER & THE BEAT GENERATION

The Beat Generation was a post-WWII American counterculture movement that combined visceral engagement in worldly experiences with a quest for deeper understanding. Tangier was a key location in its development. Writer Jack Kerouac and poet Allen Ginsberg both passed through, visiting another key figure in the movement, William Burroughs, who had moved here in 1953. Much of Burroughs' most famous work, *Naked Lunch*, was written in and directly inspired by Tangier. Burroughs' writing utilised the cut-up technique pioneered by the multitalented Brion Gysin, who also spent a significant part of his life here. Burroughs, along with Paul Bowles (who was not a fan of the Beat writers' work), inspired a coterie of local artists. The result was a mixed bag, from the heights of artistic creativity to the lows of moral depravity. Traces of Tangier's grimy literary history can still be found around town:

Hotel El Muniria (p257) The hotel where William Burroughs wrote *Naked Lunch*, holed up with a supply of typewriter ribbons and methadone.

TangerInn Pub (p263) A sleazy bar turned tourist and hipster hang-out, where Ginsberg, Kerouac and others drank: check the photos on the wall.

Café Central (p262) Burroughs' principal hang-out on the Petit Socco, where he sized up his louche opportunities.

Tangier American Legation Museum (p252) Houses a small section on the Beats.

Hotel Continental (p257) Scenes from the movie version of Paul Bowles' *The Sheltering Sky* were filmed here.

Gran Café de Paris (p262) The main post-WWII literary salon during the Interzone, it also drew Tennessee Williams and Truman Capote.

For more on the Beats and Tangier's other writers, read Josh Shoemake's essential *Tangier: A Literary Guide for Travellers*.

Nord Pinus Tanger BAR
(Map p256; Rue Riad Sultan, Kasbah; ⊙11am-midnight) On the top floor of this kasbah guesthouse is a bar and terrace, with fabulous views across to Spain. Sip a cocktail in the retro-chic lounge full of quirky chairs, Moroccan cushions and contemporary photography. A great place for a chilled-out drink.

TangerInn Pub BAR
(Le Tangerine; Map p258; ☎0610047227; 1 Rue Magellan, Hotel El Muniria; ⊙9am-2am Mon-Sat; 📶) The former hang-out for Beat writers William Burroughs, Jack Kerouac and Allen Ginsberg has been renovated to suit the next generation, and now teems with expats and young Moroccans. On weekends, house and R&B music blasts from the speakers. As in the 1950s, it remains a great place to drink beer.

Caid's Bar BAR
(El Minzah; Map p258; 85 Rue de la Liberté; ⊙10am-2am; 📶) Long the establishment's drinking hole of choice, this El Minzah landmark is a classy relic of the grand days of international Tangier, and photos of the famous and infamous adorn the walls. Women are more than welcome and the adjacent wine bar is equally good.

La Bodega de Tanger BAR
(Map p253; ☎0539945595; Rue Allal Ben Abdellah; ⊙noon-3pm & 5pm-3am; 📶) This hopping tapas bar feels like something you'd find in Europe or the US, not a country where drinking is widely frowned upon. No matter, drinks here flow from the well-stocked bar; wine and whisky collections are quite respectable. Live music and DJs liven up the party on weekends.

Rubis BAR
(Map p258; ☎0539931443; 3 Rue Ibn Rachid; ⊙noon-1am; 📶) Rubis would just be your average smoky bar if not for local legend Jimmy (real name Mohammed), a singer and guitarist who brings down the house nightly with his raspy voice and jazzy riffs. **Free tapas** of paella, potato salad, sardines and more are served with every drink. A **full menu** is available if the tapas don't fill you up.

PAUL BOWLES IN TANGIER

Perhaps the best-known foreign writer in Tangier was the American author Paul Bowles, who died in 1999, aged 88. Bowles made a brief but life-changing trip to Tangier in 1910, on Gertrude Stein's advice, then devoted the next 15 years to music composition and criticism back home. In 1938 he married Jane Sydney Auer, but they were never a conventional couple – he was an ambivalent bisexual, and she was an active lesbian. After WWII, Bowles took her to Tangier, where he remained the rest of his life. Here he turned to writing amid a lively creative circle, including the likes of William Burroughs and Mohammed Choukri. Visiting writers, from Jean Genet to Truman Capote, all sought out Bowles.

During the 1950s Bowles began taping, transcribing and translating stories by Moroccan authors, in particular Driss Ben Hamed Charhadi (also known by the pseudonym Larbi Layachi) and Mohammed Mrabet. He was also an important early recorder of Moroccan folk music.

Thanks partly to Bernardo Bertolucci's 1990 film, Bowles' best-known book is *The Sheltering Sky* (1949), a bleak and powerful story of an innocent American couple slowly dismantled by a trip through Morocco. His other works include *Let It Come Down* (1952), a thriller set in Tangier; *The Spider's House* (1955), set in 1950s Fez; and two excellent collections of travel tales, *Their Heads Are Green* (1963) and *Points in Time* (1982). *A Distant Episode: the Selected Stories* is a good compilation of Bowles' short stories.

There is a dark and nihilistic undercurrent to Bowles' writing. The Tangier American Legation Museum (p252) has a wing dedicated to Bowles' life and work.

555 CLUB
(Tanja Marina Bay; ⏲10am-3am; 📶) By day, the party's at Sky 5, a tapas bar and lounge restaurant with plenty of comfy seating on the new Tanja Marina Bay. After 11pm, the party moves over to the 555 nightclub on the marina's tip, where resident and visiting DJs can blast the tunes as loud as they please.

Hole in the Wall Bar BAR
(Map p258; Rue du Prince Héretier; ⏲11am-midnight) For chuckles only, walk up Rue Prince Héretier from the Terrasse des Paresseux (p254) one-and-a-half blocks and you'll see a swinging black door, Old West style. Welcome to the smallest bar in Tangier, if not the world. Beer only.

☆ Entertainment

The arts are alive and well in Tangier. Galleries around town often hold concerts, events and talks. Traditional Moroccan music can sometimes be heard at restaurants or cafes. Clap along and enjoy the show!

★Beit Al Tarab LIVE MUSIC
(Map p253; ☎0664672122; Rue Amérique du Sud; ⏲7-10pm) This red-brick teahouse is so gorgeous and well decorated it may indeed be a museum. The walls are adorned with striking artwork and instruments from the owner's personal collection – even the bathrooms are stunning. After 7pm, the place fills with locals drinking tea, eating organic cookies and clapping to traditional live music. Who needs alcohol to have fun anyway?

★Cinema Rif CINEMA
(Cinematheque de Tanger; Map p256; ☎0539934683; www.cinemathequedetanger.com; Grand Socco; ⏲9am-10pm Tue-Sun; 📶) The brightest light on Tangier's cultural scene, Cinema Rif is a combination art-house cinema, **cafe** and archive. Young locals come to soak up the ambience and use the free wi-fi in this well-restored art deco building. It shows both indie and mainstream films, mostly American, Moroccan, Spanish or French (with Spanish and American films often dubbed into Arabic).

Casbah Social Club LIVE MUSIC
(Map p256; ☎060829904; 1 Rue Ibn Abou; ⏲6-9.30pm) Steps from the Kasbah Museum is an unassuming tiny cafe, but every night the place gets rocking with a free concert by Arabo-Andalusian fusion band Les Fils de Detroit (Sons of the Strait) who jam out with their ouds (tear-shaped guitars) and tambourines. The only beverage on offer is sweet mint tea. Donations are appreciated.

Shopping

As the gateway to Morocco for those coming by ferry, Tangier has a good choice of beautiful Berber carpets, extravagant clothing and other trinkets and wares. Unfortunately, quality isn't what it used to be, but you can still land amazing finds. Bargaining is accepted in souqs, but some newer places such as DARNA and Las Chicas have fixed prices.

Medina

★Las Chicas ARTS & CRAFTS

(Map p256; ☎0539374510; 52 Kacem Guenoun, Bab Kasbah; ⏲10.30am-7pm Mon-Sat; 📶) Just outside the kasbah, this is an eclectic mishmash of a shop, stocking art pieces, homewares, cosmetics and some exquisite designer clothes. It also has a charming **cafe** (Dh70–150), serving innovative brunches and set menus. Offering a fun twist on the usual Moroccan style, this place is an absolute treat.

★Boutique Majid ANTIQUES

(Map p256; ☎0539938892; www.boutiquemajid.com; Rue les Almohades; ⏲10am-7pm) You can get lost for hours in this exotic antique shop, but the real gem is Majid himself. Straight out of central casting (including his red fez), Majid will regale you with stories of the Rolling Stones, Anthony Bourdain and other luminaries while showing you his amazing collection of Moroccan doors, jewellery, artefacts, clothing, fabrics and carpets.

Volubilis ARTS & CRAFTS

(Map p256; ☎0539931362; 15 Petit Socco; ⏲10am-1pm & 3-7.30pm) Mohamed's shop bordering Petit Socco sells curated capes, vests, shoes and leather goods made by cooperatives in Chefchaouen and Fez. Most notably, the shopkeeper sells his own artwork, including painted scenes of refugees on popsicle sticks or the last paper in a cigarette pack. Postcards (Dh10) made with Mohamed's drawings also make for a good keepsake or to send home.

Laura Welfling ARTS & CRAFTS

(Map p256; ☎0539949789; Place de la Kasbah; ⏲10.30am-2pm & 4-6.30pm Wed-Mon, from 4pm Tue) Next to the Kasbah Museum, this is a beautiful shop with some superb one-of-a-kind pieces designed by French artist Laura Welfling. You'll find eccentric handmade clothing, bags, decor items, notebooks, fans and ceramics.

Bleu de Fes ANTIQUES

(Map p256; ☎0539336067; www.bleudefes.com; 16 Rue les Almohades, Petit Socco; ⏲10am-7pm) Drool over stacks and stacks of Berber carpets from the Middle and High Atlas. Not seeing what you want? There are more floors and rooms to discover. Don't forget to negotiate.

KM Couleurs CLOTHING

(Map p256; ☎0539939505; 19 Rue Ben Ajiba, Bab Kasbah; ⏲10am-6pm Tue-Sun) Franco-Senegalese artist Karim LeGros sells beautiful handmade African-style textiles in this tiny boutique near the kasbah. There's bright clothing, petite shoes and delicate handbags, as well as perfumes and natural products.

Ville Nouvelle

Les Insolites BOOKS

(Map p258; ☎0539371367; 28 Rue Khalid Ibn Oualid; ⏲10am-6pm Mon-Sat) This cute bilingual bookstore and photography gallery is a modern reminder of the city's remarkable literary history. Books are curated by the staff, who'll be happy to offer a recommendation and chat about Tanjaoui life. The photo gallery includes exhibitions by Moroccan artists, and lectures are occasionally held.

Librairie des Colonnes BOOKS

(Map p258; ☎0539936955; 54 Blvd Pasteur; ⏲10am-8pm Mon-Sat) A famous landmark with wonderful architecture, this Tangier bookshop has a decent English section and carries classics from the city's literary past. There are frequent book readings and events, including author appearances. It was once the haunt of Paul Bowles, Jean Genet, Samuel Beckett and Marguerite Yourcenar, and is an institution in Tangier.

DARNA, The Women's Association of Tangier ARTS & CRAFTS

(Map p256; www.darnamaroc.com; Rue d'Angleterre; ⏲9am-6pm Mon-Sat) 🍃 The yellow building opposite the Grand Socco lookout point is a small complex housing a boutique with crafts, clothing and an inexpensive **restaurant** in a sunny courtyard. Crafts and cooking are undertaken by DARNA, a community house helping women in need.

Madini Parfumeur PERFUME

(Map p258; ☎0539375038; 5 Blvd Pasteur; ⏲10am-10pm Mon-Thu, from 4pm Fri) This perfume shop overlooking Terrasse des Paresseux (p254) has been bottling scents from around the region for over a century. A rainbow of coloured jars lines the walls filled with vanilla, musk, orange blossom, rose water and more. Tiny Moroccan-style bottles will remind you of your trip until you can make it back for a refill.

Information

ACCESSIBLE TRAVEL

Ville Nouvelle is reasonably accessible; all major hotels have elevators. The medina is far trickier, though it is possible to enter via both the kasbah and Grand Socco. The Kasbah Museum of Mediterranean Cultures (p252) is wheelchair accessible.

Download Lonely Planet's free Accessible Travel guides from https://shop.lonelyplanet.com/categories/accessible-travel.com.

DANGERS & ANNOYANCES

Tangier is far safer than it used to be.

- As in any big city, it's best to stick to the beaten path at all times, and to take cabs point to point at night.
- Solo women may be subject to being hassled after dark.
- Touts in the medina will offer to show you to shops, but they get a cut – and will likely want a tip. It's best to refuse and keep on your way.
- Street touts may also try to sell *kif* (cannabis).

TRAVEL WITH CHILDREN

For kids, M'nar Park (p255) is heaven. Located south of Cap Malabata, with great views across the Bay of Tangier, this cliffside resort offers a water park, an electronic game park, karting, a small train, a mini-football field, paintball, restaurants, a cafe and residential bungalows for families.

In town, tiny vehicles are available for rent along the corniche and there's a small amusement park, **Wafa Even Parc** (Ave d'Espagne; rides Dh10-20; 9-11pm), located beside Tanger Ville Station. Close to the Grand Socco is Mendoubia Gardens (p254), a park with grass and swings.

Getting There & Away

With a ferry port, international airport, TGV train station and buses, Tangier is possibly Morocco's best-connected city.

AIR

The **Ibn Batouta International Airport** (0539393720) is 15km southwest of the city centre. It serves a number of budget airlines (including EasyJet, Ryanair, Vueling and Air Arabia), as well as Iberia and Royal Air Maroc.

BOAT

Tangier effectively has two ports: **Tangier Port** (Map p253) (in the city) and the newer **Tanger Med** terminal, 48km east along the coast.

From Tangier Port, there are fast catamaran ferries run by **FRS** (Map p253; www.frs.es) and **Inter Shipping** (Map p253; www.intershipping.es) to Tarifa (Dh400, one hour). There are more than a dozen sailings a day, with the ferry companies leaving on alternate hours. The service includes a free bus transfer to Algeciras (50 minutes) on presentation of your ferry ticket.

Tickets are available online or from the company **ticket booths** (Map p253) outside the ferry terminal at Tangier Port; be sure to pick up an exit form so you can avoid hassles later.

Services from Tanger Med are primarily to Algeciras.

Book in advance during peak periods (particularly Easter, the last week in August and the last week in October). Allow an hour before departure to get tickets and navigate passport control. Remember the time difference with Spain (Morocco is one hour behind during daylight saving time, April to November). If you're arriving in Morocco, remember to get your passport stamped on the ferry.

BUS

CTM buses depart from the **main bus station** (0531063010; Place Jamaa El Arabia), about 2km south of the city centre by the Syrian mosque – the distinctly un-Moroccan-looking minarets are a useful nearby landmark. Destinations include the following.

DESTINATION	COST (DH)	DURATION (HR)
Casablanca	100	5½
Chefchaouen	45	3
Fez	115	6
Marrakesh	230	10
Meknes	95	5
Rabat	75	4
Tetouan	25	1

Cheaper bus companies also operate from the main bus station. There are regular departures for all the destinations listed for CTM, plus services to Al Hoceima (Dh40, 10 hours) and Tanger Med (Dh20, 45 minutes). A metered *petit taxi* to/from the town centre is around Dh10.

The main bus station has a left-luggage facility (per item 24hr Dh7/10).

CAR

The major international car-hire agencies are at the airport, as well as in town.

TAXI

The grand-taxi rank for places outside Tangier is across from the main bus station; taxis run to Tetouan (Dh30, one hour), Chefchaouen (Dh70, three hours), Asilah (Dh25, 30 minutes), Larache

(Dh40, 1½ hours) and Al Hoceima (Dh200, five hours). For Ceuta, travel to Fnideq (Dh35, one hour), 3km from the border. There are no direct taxis to the border (Bab Sebta). *Grands taxis* to Tetouan also frequently wait for arriving trains at Tanger Ville train station. For destinations on the outskirts of Tangier, such as the Caves of Hercules or Cap Malabata, use the **grand-taxi rank** (Map p256) on the Grand Socco.

TRAIN

Tangier's remodelled **train and TGV station** (www.oncf-voyages.ma) is modern and simple to navigate. Twenty TGV trains run daily to Casablanca (Dh206, two hours and 10 minutes). Prices are lower when purchased in advance but increase on weekends and holidays. TGV trains also stop in Kenitra (Dh116, 50 minutes) and Rabat (Dh157, one hour and 10 minutes).

Traditional train service runs throughout the day to Meknes (Dh90), Fez (Dh111), Rabat (Dh101), Casablanca (Dh132) and Marrakesh (Dh 216), including a night service with couchettes, the famed *Marrakesh Express*, which should be reserved in advance (single Dh690, double per person Dh470, Dh370 with couchette). During summer, a 12-hour train runs east to Oujda (Dh222, double bed Dh470). A *petit taxi* to/from Tangier centre should cost around Dh14.

Getting Around

TO & FROM THE AIRPORT

A *grand taxi* takes 25 minutes and costs Dh100 for the entire car (Dh150 after 10pm). To pick up a local bus from the airport, bus 17 and bus 70 run to the Grand Socco; you'll need to walk 2km to the main road.

TO & FROM TANGER MED

A shuttle bus (Dh20) runs every hour between Tanger Med and Tangier's main bus station (45 minutes). The driver will drop you off near the train station if you ask.

BUS

Buses aren't really necessary for getting around Tangier, but two potentially useful services are **bus 13** (Map p258), which runs from the train station via Ave Mohammed VI to Tangier Port gate, and bus 2, which links the train station and the main bus station.

TAXI

Ultramarine with a yellow stripe down the side, *petits taxis* do standard journeys around town, charging 50% more at night. It's fully acceptable (and encouraged) to flag down a taxi that has passengers but spare seats.

Cap Spartel راس سبارطيل

Just 14km west of Tangier lies Cap Spartel (*kap spar-tell*), the northwestern extremity of Africa's Atlantic coast. It's a popular day trip for locals and tourists alike. A dramatic drive takes you through La Montagne, an exclusive suburb of royal palaces and villas, and over the pine-covered headland to a lighthouse. The building is closed, but the views are what the crowds come for anyway. The beaches to the south are clean and quiet outside the summer season, so you can find your own private cove.

Grands taxis from Tangier are the best way of getting to Cap Spartel. A round-trip charter should cost around Dh200, including waiting time. Taxis leave from the rank in front of St Andrew's Church in Tangier.

Sights

Grottes d'Hercule CAVE

(Dh5; 9am-9pm) Legend has it that Hercules used his brute strength to rip Europe from Africa, and afterward he rested here. Grottes d'Hercule is comprised of two caves; one has waterfalls and painfully kitschy decor, the other is empty, and you can view the sea through a hole that looks like the map of Africa. The experience is touristy, yet somehow worth it, especially if accompanied with a walk along the beach to the south.

Sleeping & Eating

Cap Spartel is a short day trip from Tangier, so it's easiest to base yourself there, although it does have options for camping as well as a luxury hotel for those with bigger budgets.

There are several similar cafes and restaurants along the coastal road.

Camping Achakkar CAMPGROUND €

(0611582512; camping per person Dh25, plus per tent/car/campervan Dh25/20/45, bungalows Dh250-550;) Inland from the cave, this shady site has clean facilities and hot water (electricity Dh30, hot showers Dh20). It has a shop that stocks essentials and a cafe serving breakfast (Dh35), paninis, shawarma and pasta.

Le Mirage HOTEL €€€

(0539333332; www.lemirage.com; d from Dh2600;) One of the finest hotels in the Tangier area, with a dramatic location perched on the cliff beside the grotto, Le Mirage offers a view of miles of broad Atlantic

ROAD TRIPPING FROM TANGIER TO CEUTA

The scenic road from Tangier to Ceuta is worth taking: green patchwork fields, alluring mountain roads, rolling hills, rocky headlands and good sandy beaches reveal a different side to Morocco.

The road begins at Cap Malabata, the headland opposite Tangier. There's a corniche with expensive apartments, a golf course and the large M'nar Park (p255), a great place for children and with a restaurant that has views back towards Tangier.

There's no more development until Ksar Es Seghir, 25km further around the coast. This small fishing port, dominated by the remains of a Portuguese fort, has a yacht basin and a beach that's popular in summer. Just beyond you'll spot Tanger Med, the massive container facility and ferry port, 48km from Tangier.

The great crag of Jebel Musa, one of the ancient Pillars of Hercules, rises up 10km or so further on, and views along the pretty mountain road are spectacular.

beach. The bungalows are exquisite, as the price suggests, and there's a spa and piano bar. Nonguests can get a taste of the opulence in the immaculate restaurant (meals around Dh500), or just stop by for a drink beneath the pergola. From the sunny terrace you can see the Roman ruins of Cotta, where *garum* (fish sauce) was processed.

Cap Spartel Café & Restaurant MOROCCAN €

(☎0539933722; Cap Spartel Rd; breakfast Dh22, paninis Dh30; P 📶) This restaurant next to the lighthouse is popular on weekends. Set over a couple of buildings with a lovely garden in summer, it serves good juice, breakfast, savoury and sweet crêpes, paninis and pizza.

Ceuta سبتة

☎0952 / POP 85,140

Ceuta (*seyoo-tah*) is one of several Spanish possessions on the Moroccan coastline – a slice of Europe in Africa. Located on a peninsula jutting out into the Mediterranean, it offers a compact dose of Spanish-style architecture, decent museums, tapas bars and bracing nature walks. While it may be connected to Morocco, if you ask the locals here it's as Spanish as Madrid, and isn't disappearing from the map anytime soon.

If entering from Morocco, Ceuta's border is an eye-opener. Long lines of Moroccans queue to cross, many of them thick with duty-free goods taped under their *djellabas* (robes). Border guards don't seem to mind. Perhaps they're more focused on stopping migrants and refugees from squeezing into Europe, a pressing issue that has resulted in bodies tragically washing onto shore.

Ceuta has flights to Spain and connects with Algeciras by ferry.

History

Ceuta served as one of the Roman Empire's coastal bases; its Arabic name, Sebta, stems from the Latin *septem*. After a brief stint under the control of the Byzantine Empire, the city was taken in 931 CE by the Arab rulers of Muslim Spain – the basis for Spain's claim of historical rights to the land. For the next 500 years, however, this city at the tip of Africa was a prized possession, fought over and ruled successively by Spanish princes, Moroccan sultans and Portuguese kings.

Things began to settle down when Portugal and Spain united under one crown in 1580, and Ceuta passed to Spain by default. When the two countries split in 1640, Ceuta remained Spanish, and has been ever since.

Sights

★Plaza de África LANDMARK

This is the charming heart of Ceuta, with manicured tropical plantings, a square of freshly renovated cobblestone pathways and some of the city's finest architecture.

Moving clockwise from the oblong **Comandancia General**, a military headquarters closed to visitors, you encounter the striking yellow **Santuario de Nuestra Señora de África** (⏲9am-1pm & 5-8pm), the 19th-century **Palacio de la Asamblea** (☎0956528200), and finally the **Cathedral Santa Maria de la Asunción** (☎0956517771; ⏲9am-1pm & 6-8pm Tue-Sun, museum 10am-1pm Tue-Sat) with its museum.

The centre of the plaza contains a memorial to soldiers lost in the Spanish-Moroccan War of 1860, a conflict over the borders of Ceuta.

★ **Murallas Reales** ARCHITECTURE

(☎ 0956511770; Ave González Tablas; ⊙ 10am-2pm & 5-8pm Mon-Sat, 11am-2pm Sun) FREE The most impressive sight in Ceuta is the medieval Royal Walls, which date back over 1000 years and have been passed from Arab to Portuguese to Spanish hands. These extensive fortifications, of great strategic complexity, have been beautifully restored, with information boards in English.

Museo de los Muralles Reales (⊙ 10am-2pm & 5-8pm Tue-Sat) FREE lies within the walls themselves. This two-floor gallery houses temporary art exhibitions lasting four years each. Squeezed out of the fort's unforgiving architecture, it's a beautifully designed space with plenty of pieces to admire. Worth visiting irrespective of what's on. Recent highlights have included a superb collection of work by Spanish painter and Ceuta's former deputy mayor Mariano Bertuchi (1884–1955).

Museo de la Basilica Tardorromana MUSEUM

(20 Calle Queipo de Llano; ⊙ 11am-2pm & 6-9pm Tue-Sat) FREE This superbly executed underground museum is integrated into the architectural remains of an ancient basilica discovered during street work in the 1980s, including a bridge over open tombs, skeletons included. The artefacts become a means of branching out into various elements of local history. In Spanish, but definitely worth a lap through.

Museo de la Legión MUSEUM

(☎ 0956526219; Paseo de Colón; by donation; ⊙ 10am-1.30pm Mon-Sat) FREE This intriguing museum is dedicated to and run by the Spanish Legion, an army unit set up in 1920 that played a pivotal role in Franco's republican army. Loaded to the gills with memorabilia, weaponry and uniforms, not to mention glory, pomp and circumstance, it is a fascinating glimpse into the military culture that shaped the Spanish Morocco.

There's the imperious statue of fascist leader Franco, an explanation of how the legion's founder, Millan Astray, lost his right eye, and the history of the legion in cinema. All information is in Spanish.

Playa de la Ribera BEACH

Ceuta's urban beach is jam-packed during summer with nearly nude Spaniards and fully clothed Moroccan women. The beach is lined with cafes and bars perfect for whiling away an afternoon with a *cerveza*.

Playa del Chorillo BEACH

The bigger of Ceuta's two beaches, Playa del Chorillo is a little further from the city centre, but it's only slightly less busy. The water is a magnificent blue, but unfortunately, the sand is a bland grey.

Casa de los Dragones ARCHITECTURE

(House of Dragons; cnr Calle Camoens & Millán Astray) The Casa de los Dragones on Plaza de los Reyes is a fantastic dream that has entered the real world. This former home is an extraordinary example of eclectic architecture, with Moorish arches, polished brick facades, mansard roofs, fabulous balconies and the pièce de résistance, four enormous dark dragons springing from the roof. If only it were open to the public!

Plaza de los Reyes LANDMARK

With its green triumphal arch (inscribed 'a monument to coexistence') and fountain, this plaza borders the twin-towered yellow **Iglesia de San Francisco**. In the northwest corner, a statue of a man in a *capirote* (conical hooded hat) holding hands with a child is a tribute to Ceuta's holy week (it's not related to the notorious United States white supremacist group).

Museo de Ceuta MUSEUM

(☎ 0956517398; 30 Paseo del Revellín; ⊙ 11am-2pm & 5-9pm Tue-Sat Jun-Sep; 👪) FREE This ageing municipal museum has a small collection showing the peninsula's pre-Spanish history, with all labels in Spanish. The temporary exhibitions are of more interest.

Parque Marítimo del Mediterráneo PARK

(☎ 0956517491; www.parquemaritimo.es; Avenida Compañía del Mar; adult €1-6, child free-€4.50; ⊙ 11am-8.30pm & 9.30pm-1.30am Tue, Wed & Sun, to 2.30am Fri & Sat Jun-Sep; 👪) This creative maritime park is a real hit in the summer and perfect for families. One of several parks developed by the artist and architect César Manrique, it borrows the city-walls theme to construct a huge pool deck on the sea, including a grand lagoon and two other saltwater pools, surrounded by tapas bars, pubs, restaurants, cafes and a disco.

Baños Arabes HISTORIC BUILDING

(Plaza de la Paz) Accidentally discovered during street work, these ancient Arab hammams sit on a main road, an incongruous sight.

Ceuta

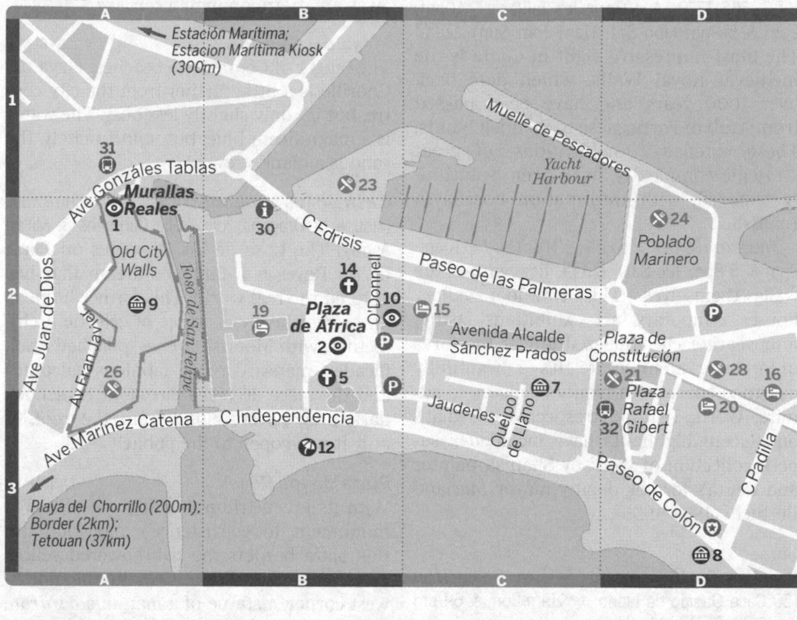

Ceuta

Top Sights
1 Murallas Reales ... A2
2 Plaza de África ... B2

Sights
3 Baños Arabes ... F2
4 Casa de los Dragones ... E3
5 Catedral Santa Maria de la Asunción ... B2
6 Museo de Ceuta ... E3
7 Museo de la Basilica Tardorromana ... C2
8 Museo de la Legión ... D3
9 Museo de los Muralles Reales ... A2
10 Palacio de la Asamblea ... B2
11 Parque Marítimo del Mediterráneo ... E2
12 Playa de la Ribera ... B3
13 Plaza de los Reyes ... E3
14 Santuario de Nuestra Señora de África ... B2

Sleeping
15 Hercules ... C2
16 Hostal Central ... D2
17 Hostal Plaza Ruiz ... E3
18 Hotel Ulises ... E3
19 Parador Hotel La Muralla ... B2
20 Pensión La Bohemia ... D3

Eating
21 Central Market ... D2
22 Charlotte ... E3
23 El Lucas ... B1
24 El Refectorio ... D2
25 El Ronquío ... F2
26 El Secreto de Yuste ... A2
27 Mesón El Cortijo ... E3
28 Vincentino Pastelería ... D2

Drinking & Nightlife
29 Dublin ... E2

Information
30 Main Tourist Office ... B2

Transport
31 Buses to Border ... A1
Buses to Border ... (see 32)
32 Local Bus Station ... D3

There are two of them, with barrel-vaulted roofs originally covered with marble – the high-tech spa of its time. You can do a lap around the historic building, but it isn't open to the public.

Monte Hacho HIKING

A walk around Monte Hacho is an option on a nice day; maps are available at the tourist office or you can wing it and follow the narrow coastal road. Since it's an uphill slog

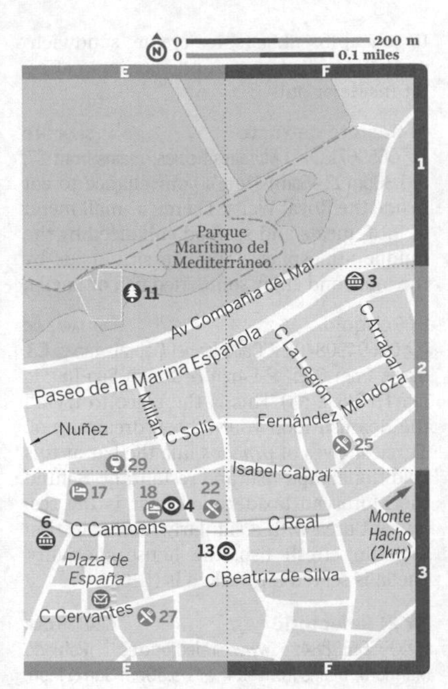

from town, a good option is to start by taking a cab (€15) to the **Mirador de San Antonio** two-thirds of the way up, which offers magnificent views over Ceuta and north to Gibraltar.

The summit of the peninsula is crowned by the massive **Fortaleza de Hacho**, a fort first built by the Byzantines, and still an active military installation. No visitors are allowed. Back down at the main road, you keep going clockwise until you reach the Museo Histórico Militar.

Museo Histórico Militar FORT
(Castillo del Desnarigado; ☎0956514066; Carretera del Monte Hacho; ⏲9am-2pm Mon-Fri, from 10am Sat & Sun Apr-Sep, closed Sun Oct-May) FREE Named after a noseless pirate who landed here in 1417, Ceuta's Desnarigado military museum is jam-packed with memorabilia from Ceuta's many battles. An Arab cast-iron cannon engraved in 1635 is a standout, as are German bazookas, WWI cavalry gear and Ceuta's first computer. There is a lighthouse above and a secluded beach below.

García Aldave SCENIC DRIVE
The García Aldave nature area can be crossed from coast to coast along the N354, either by car or on foot. The route contains a series of circular neomedieval watchtowers, closed to visitors, and military training bases. Several of these are visible from **Mirador de Isabel II**, which offers great views across the isthmus to Monte Hacho.

Sleeping

Ceuta has few sleeping options and they tend to fill up, especially in high season. Booking ahead is a good idea. More affordable options are *pensiónes* (guesthouses), some of which are identifiable by the large blue-and-white 'CH' plaque.

★ **Pensión La Bohemia** HOTEL €€
(☎0956510615; 16 Paseo del Revellín; per person €35; 📶) This well-run operation, one flight above a shopping arcade, offers a bright and spotless set of rooms arranged around a central courtyard. Bathrooms are shared, with plenty of hot water and communal showers. Rooms have small TVs and fans; some have internal windows only.

Hostal Plaza Ruiz HOTEL €€
(☎0956516733; www.hostalplazaruizceuta.com; 3 Plaza Ruiz; s/d €42/62, Fri & Sat €48/70; 📶) This good-value, two-star hotel in an excellent location has ultramodern decor and is very welcoming. Rooms are tiny but spotless, and all come with bathroom and fridge. Low-season discounts are available.

Hostal Central HOTEL €€
(☎0956516716; www.hostalesceuta.com; 15 Paseo del Revellín; s/d €45/52; 📶) This place is in a charming location and offers a warm welcome. Rooms are airy with nice pine furniture; the best have wrought-iron balconies overlooking the cafes of the plaza.

Parador Hotel La Muralla HOTEL €€€
(☎0956514940; www.parador.es; 15 Plaza de África; d from €110; ❄📶🏊) This spacious four-star hotel is perfectly situated on the Plaza de África (p268). Rooms are comfortable, but not luxurious, with simple wooden doors and plain ceramic tiles. Balconies overlook a pleasant garden overflowing with palm trees. A bar-cafe on the ground floor adds value.

Hercules BOUTIQUE HOTEL €€€
(☎0627183696; www.herculesboutiquehotel.com; 17 Calle Gómez Marcelo; s/d/ste €95/105/120; 📶) A fresh addition to Ceuta's ageing accommodation scene, Hercules hosts 11 clean rooms stacked over four floors. The rooms are tiny but manage not to feel squished and furniture is luxurious and modern. The sliding

glass door entrance sets the tone from the get-go. Breakfast is included.

The hotel gets its name from the Hercules Marina out front.

Hotel Ulises HOTEL €€€
(☎0956514540; www.hotelulises.com; 5 Calle Camoens; s/d €75/85;) This hotel is a decent deal, with an excellent location and parking nearby. The rooms aren't large, but some have balconies. The cafe spills out onto the pavement in view of Plaza de los Reyes (p269) and is perfect for people watching over a drink and a few tapas.

Eating & Drinking

Ceuta is packed with similar-looking traditional tapas bars, all serving an array of *pinchos*, *raciones* (a larger helping of tapas) and *bocadillos* (sandwiches). The best places to find tapas bars are around Calle Millán Astray. Finer seafood restaurants are along the western coast.

Ceuta is a relief for those who've spent time in Morocco and are craving a drink; a cheap *caña* (cup of beer) or glass of *vino* (wine) is never far off. There are numerous bars near Parque Marítimo del Mediterráneo and a small bar zone at Plaza Teniente Ruiz.

Central Market MARKET
(8am-3pm Mon-Sat) This cavernous market is the local spot for fresh meat and produce, and a vibrant experience as well.

★**Mesón El Cortijo** TAPAS €
(☎0956511983; 16 Calle Cervantes; tapas €2.80; 1-4pm & 8.30pm-midnight;) A classic neighbourhood gathering place that's heavy on tapas, *cerveza* (beer) and friendliness. Catch up on football, gossip and practise your *español*.

Charlotte CAFE €
(Plaza de los Reyes; breakfast €4, tapas from €2; 8am-11pm Mon-Thu, 9am-2pm Fri & Sat, 11am-2pm Sun;) This is the perfect place for just about anything at any time of day: it serves breakfast (with great hot chocolate), lunchtime sandwiches, beer, cocktails and tapas. Swift, efficient service and a prime people-watching spot on the square make it very popular.

Vincentino Pastelería CAFE €
(Calle Alférez Bayton; sandwiches €2-2.50; 8am-9.30pm) This traditional Spanish cafe buzzes all day with people clamouring for cheap breakfasts, ice cream, sandwiches, delicious patisserie and excellent coffee. Sit inside or out.

El Secreto de Yuste SPANISH €
(☎0659671814; 1 Muralles Reales; mains from €7; 1.30pm-12.45am) Here's your chance to eat inside the Royal Walls. There's a small menu of local meats and seafood enhanced by the unique atmosphere. You can sit outside by the moat and enjoy some fried fish or paella.

El Ronquío TAPAS €€
(☎0669490840; 2 Calle Isabel Cabral; tapas €3, mains from €12; 1-4pm & 8-11pm Sun-Thu, to 1am Fri & Sat;) This is the place to try all the Spanish food you've been dreaming of. Three shelves of *pinchos* line the bar at this traditional tapas bar and restaurant. Behind the Moroccan taxidermied boar is the restaurant area with a similarly huge selection including fresh fish, the house speciality. Paella is served on weekends (€10).

★**El Refectorio** SPANISH €€€
(☎0956513884; www.elrefectorio.es; Poblado Marinero; mains from €14; 1-5.30pm Sun & Mon, 8.30pm-midnight Tue-Sat) Considered by many to be Ceuta's best restaurant, El Refectorio has a good bar, and dining inside and out with magnificent sea views from the balcony. It excels at shellfish, fish and meats and has a good wine list.

El Lucas SEAFOOD €€€
(☎0956515525; Real Club Nautico; market; 2-5pm & 8.30-11pm Mon-Sat, 8.30-11pm Sun;) Choose your victim from the fish on ice as you enter this seafood restaurant in a prime location overlooking the yacht harbour. There's no formal menu, only whatever fresh catch was reeled in that day. The seating is banquet-style with large round tables and there's a great terrace in the warmer seasons.

Dublin PUB
(7 Calle Antioco; 3pm-3am) Live music blasts Thursday through Saturday at this Irish pub, which stays open for 365 thirsty days a year. No food here, only drinks. If the volume gets to you, you can escape to the square outside.

Go down the steps where Calle Delgado Serrano takes a 90-degree bend.

Information

MONEY

Euros are used for all transactions in Ceuta. ATMs are plentiful, though not all work with foreign debit cards. Outside banking hours, you can change money at the more expensive hotels. There are informal money-changers on both sides of the border, although it's technically illegal to take dirhams out of Morocco.

TELEPHONE

To phone Ceuta from outside Spain, dial 0034 first.

TIME

Ceuta is one hour ahead of Morocco during daylight saving time. Most businesses close in the afternoon for siesta time and are closed on Sunday.

TOURIST INFORMATION

Ceuta's history is outlined by the *ruta monumenta,* a series of excellent information boards in English and Spanish outside key buildings and monuments. The **main tourist office** (0856200560; Calle Edrisis, Baluarte de los Mallorquines; 8.30am-8.30pm Mon-Fri, to 2.30pm Sat & Sun) is friendly and efficient, with good maps and brochures.

Getting There & Away

FROM MOROCCO

Buses and *grands taxis* to Ceuta often land at Fnideq, rather than at the border (Bab Sebta). If so, the border is a further 1km walk, or Dh7 by taxi. Although the border is open 24 hours, public transport is sparse from 7pm to 5am.

On the Moroccan side, hustlers will try to sell you a departure form for €1, but you can pick one up for free at the passport window; grab one before queueing. If you're driving a rental car, you will be required to show proof of authorisation to take the vehicle out of the country. The 100m crossing is surprisingly disorganised, with multiple people asking for your passport. Pedestrians must frequently walk in the car lanes. Once across, Spanish authorities probably won't stamp your passport – that gets done on the mainland. Just make sure you get a stamp within 72 hours to avoid any hassles.

Collective *grands taxis* at Bab Sebta will take you to Tetouan (Dh25, 40 minutes), from where you can pick up onward transport. Taxis to Chefchaouen or Tangier are rare, so you'll likely need to hire a private vehicle (Chefchaouen, Dh300, 90 minutes; Tangier, Dh200, one hour). A good alternative is to take a *grand taxi* to Fnideq (Dh7, 10 minutes), just south of the border, from where transport to Tangier is more frequent (Dh35, one hour).

FROM MAINLAND SPAIN

There are 20 high-speed ferries daily to and from Algeciras operated by Balearia (www.balearia.com), Transmediterranea (www.trasmediterranea.es) and FRS (www.frs.es). Prices start at €30 for foot passengers and take about an hour.

Buy your tickets online or at the **ticket kiosk** (0956506275; 9am-9pm) in front of **Estación Marítima** (Ferry Terminal; Calle Muelle Cañonero Dato).

Getting Around

Bus 7 runs up to the border (*frontera*) every 10 minutes from Plaza de la Constitution (€1). If you arrive by ferry and want to head straight for the border, there's a bus stop on Ave González Tablas opposite the entrance to the ramparts. Local buses also stop on Ave González Tablas. There's a taxi rank outside the terminal building.

If you have your own vehicle, street parking is restricted to a maximum of two hours during the day (marked with white or blue lines). You cannot park within yellow lines. If you're staying longer, use the car park (Calle O'Donnell; per hr €1.40, per day €12) on Calle O'Donnell.

THE RIF MOUNTAINS جبال الريف

The Rif *(reef)* is the greenest and most northerly of Morocco's mountain chains. Packed with tall peaks, hospitable Amazigh (Berber) villagers, and yes, fields of cannabis (Morocco is the world's number-one cannabis producer thanks in large part to cultivation from this mountain range), the Rif is an excellent place to explore, especially on foot. There are plenty of good hikes, particularly in Talassemtane National Park.

Tucked inside the Rif Mountains is a tiny village with a big reputation – Chefchaouen, known as the 'blue pearl' because of its pastel-blue medina. Tetouan, the former capital of the Spanish protectorate and the Rif's largest city, has a long history of artisanship and a World Heritage–listed medina. On the Rif's rugged coastline are a number of beaches and the whitewashed city of Al Hoceima, perched atop the cliffs.

Tetouan تطوان

0539 / POP 402,120

Tetouan (*teh-twan*) is a jewel of a town in a striking location at the foot of the Rif Mountains, and just a few kilometres from the sea. It sees relatively few foreign visitors: there's an air of authenticity here that adds great value to a visit. The ancient medina, a Unesco World Heritage site, looks like it has not changed in several centuries. The modern centre that abuts it gleams in white,

Tetouan

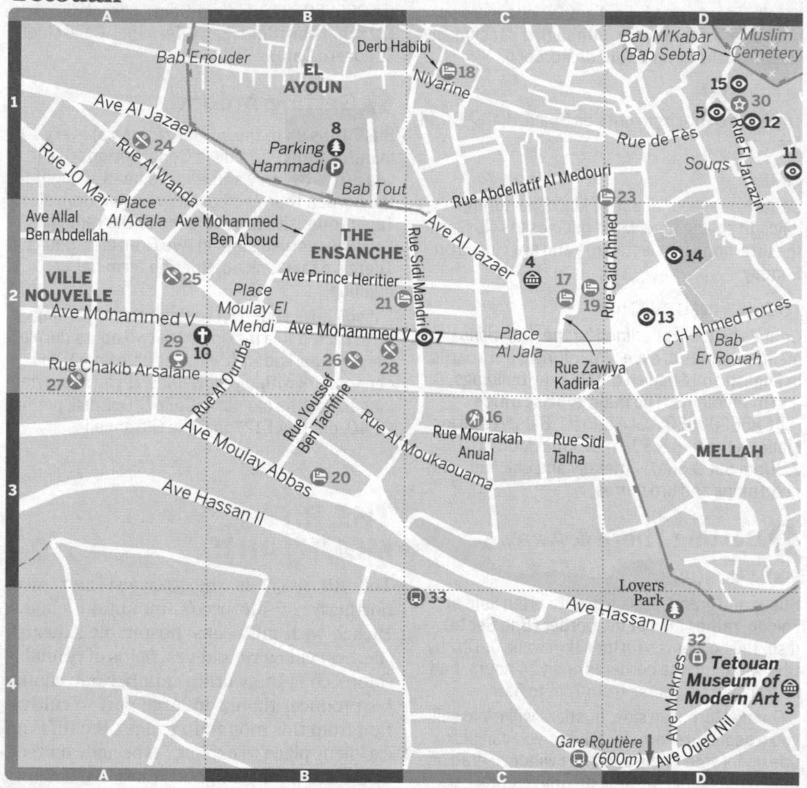

its Spanish facades given a recent facelift to seductive affect.

The Spanish influence dates from 1912–56, when Tetouan was the capital of the Spanish protectorate, which encompassed much of northern Morocco. The town's long relationship with Andalusia has left it with a Hispano-Moorish character that is unique in Morocco, as physically reflected in the white buildings and broad boulevards of the Spanish part of the city, known as the Ensanche (extension).

History

From the 8th century onwards, the city served as the main point of contact between Morocco and Andalusia. In the 14th century the Merinids fortified the city to serve as a base from which to control rebellious Rif tribes and to attack Ceuta, but it was destroyed by Henry III of Castille in 1399. After the Reconquista (the reconquest of Spain, completed in 1492), the town was rebuilt by Andalusian refugees. It prospered, due in part to their skills as well as thriving pirate activity.

Moulay Ismail built Tetouan's defensive walls in the 17th century, and the town's trade links with Spain developed. In 1860 the Spanish took the town under Leopoldo O'Donnell, who extensively Europeanised it, but upon recapture two years later, the Moors removed all signs of European influence.

At the turn of the 20th century, Spanish forces occupied Tetouan for three years, claiming it was protecting Ceuta from Rif tribes. In 1913 the Spanish made Tetouan the capital of their protectorate, which was abandoned in 1956 when Morocco regained independence. Lately the Andalusian government has provided a great cultural boost to the city by financing various restoration projects.

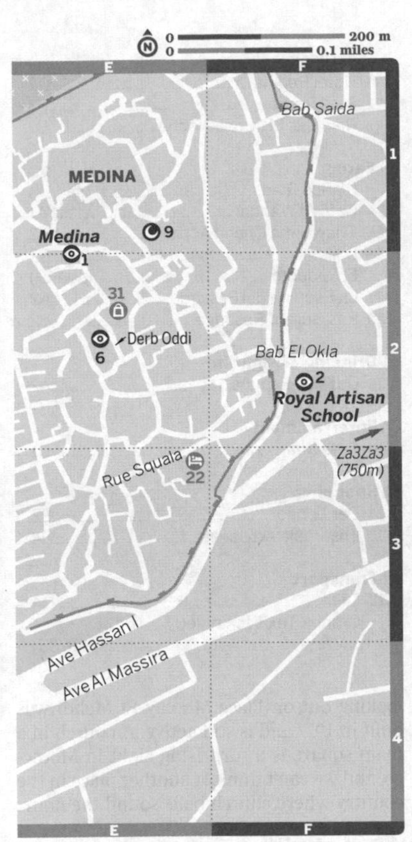

Sights

Medina

Tetouan's medina is an authentic time machine, with buildings that have witnessed centuries of history. The medina is also very traveller-friendly, with moped-free lanes, few street hustlers, amiable residents and a general lack of congestion. Luckily for you, it doesn't get the attention it deserves.

★Royal Artisan School NOTABLE BUILDING
(Dar Senaa; ☎0539972721; Ave Mohamed Ameziane; Dh50; ⏰8.30am-4.30pm Mon-Thu, to 1pm Fri) Just outside Bab El Okla is the best artisan centre in northern Morocco. This is a fascinating opportunity to see masters teaching apprentices traditional arts, including ornamental woodwork, silk costumes, carved plaster, intricate mosaics and decorative rifles. A fantastic central treasury holds the best of the best – don't miss the ceiling. Staff will open it upon request.

Dar El Oddi CULTURAL CENTRE
(☎0539721671; www.dareloddi.com; 5 Derb Oddi; Dh25; ⏰10am-6pm Tue-Sun) The wealthy El Oddi family graciously opened their sparkling family riad to the public as a cultural centre in 2018, celebrating their beloved Tetouan. Exhibits consist of pictures, maps and vibrant postcards and stamps from Tetouan's past, but the riad itself is the most fascinating part. Don't miss the traditional family kitchen on the ground floor.

Grande Mosquée MOSQUE
Built in 1808 on the ruins of a smaller mosque, the Grand Mosquée has one of the largest minarets in Tetouan – you'll have to tilt your head way up to see the top if you're in the medina street. Non-Muslims are not allowed to enter.

Feddan Park PARK
(Ave Alger) Feddan Park used to be what's currently known as Place Hassan II, but it was destroyed following the Spanish protectorate to make room for the Royal Palace. Locals who missed the park (some say they met their husband or wife there) were pleased when King Mohammed VI rebuilt it in its current location. Feddan is again a popular hang-out spot, with a huge cafe, playground and plenty of seating.

Place Hassan II LANDMARK
The broad and empty Place Hassan II, which is mostly roped off for security reasons, links the medina to the Ensanche. It looks like it houses the Wizard of Oz, with guards standing in front of the long flat facade of the **Royal Palace**, and four somewhat bizarre columns towering all around.

These are not minarets, as one might suppose, but art-nouveau light towers designed by Enrique Nieto, a student of modernist Spanish architect Antoni Gaudí, who lived in Melilla. The large decorations on the opposite wall are abstract Hands of Fatima, a common symbol used to ward off the evil eye.

The Ensanche

Restored to resemble the era when Tetouan was capital of the Spanish protectorate, the broad **Ensanche** along Ave Mohammed V from Place Al Jala to Place Moulayel-Mehdi

Tetouan

Top Sights
1 Medina E2
2 Royal Artisan School F2
3 Tetouan Museum of Modern Art D4

Sights
4 Archaeology Museum C2
5 Carpentry Souq D1
6 Dar El Oddi E2
7 Ensanche C2
8 Feddan Park B1
9 Grande Mosquée E1
10 Iglesia de Bacturia A2
11 Jewellery Souq D1
12 Leather Souq D1
13 Place Hassan II D2
14 Royal Palace D2
15 Tannery D1

Activities, Courses & Tours
16 Artisan Visit C3

Sleeping
17 Blanco Riad C2
18 Dar Rehla C1
19 El Reducto C2
20 Hotel Panorama Vista B3
21 Hotel Regina B2
22 Riad Darna E3
23 Riad Las Mil y una Noches D1

Eating
Blanco Riad .... (see 17)
24 Cafe Al Wahda A1
25 Chawarma Chand Acham A2
26 Dallas B2
El Reducto .... (see 19)
27 La Esquina del Pescado A2
28 Restaurant Restinga B2

Drinking & Nightlife
29 Casa de España A2

Entertainment
30 Cafe Kharrazin D1

Shopping
31 Dar Lebadi E2
32 Ensemble Artisanat D4

Transport
33 CTM C4
Grands Taxis to Fnideq & Martil .... (see 33)

is lined with bright Spanish colonial architecture with a few art-deco elements reminiscent of styles found in Casablanca and Larache. You'll find hotels, banks and places to eat here.

A few blocks from Place Al Jala is a small **Archaeology Museum** (Ave Al Jazaer; Dh10; ⏲10am-5pm Wed-Mon) with an excellent collection of pottery and mosaics mostly from the Roman ruins at Lixus, displayed both inside and in the gardens.

★ Tetouan Museum of Modern Art MUSEUM
(☎0666046081; www.gotetouan.com/museums.html; Ave Al Maki Al Naciri; ⏲9am-1pm & 2-5pm Tue-Sun) FREE Tetouan boasts one of only two schools of fine arts in Morocco (Casablanca has the other), so it's fitting that this museum should live here. The building itself is worth a visit: a magnificent Spanish-castle-like building that was once the railway station to Ceuta. It has been carefully renovated to protect the artworks and to provide ample light inside.

Iglesia de Bacturia CHURCH
(Iglesia de Nuestra Señora de la Victoria; Place Moulay El Mehdi; ⏲mass 7pm daily, 11am Sun) This bright yellow Roman Catholic church looking out on Place Moulay El Mehdi was built in 1917 and is still active. A church in a main square is a surprising sight in Morocco, and we can't think of another place in the country where church bells sound the hour.

Activities

Quad Discovery ADVENTURE SPORTS
(☎0610468462; www.facebook.com/tetouanquaddiscovery; El Malaliyine; 1hr/2hr Dh250/400; ⏲9am-7pm) A couple of young locals have taken it upon themselves to inject some outdoor fun into the Tetouan region. Zakaria and Hamza lead quad-bike (ATV) tours through the rolling countryside past donkeys, goats and dogs. The trip is messy, but fun, and can be extended to three-hour rides that include meeting villagers and trying local cuisine.

Artisan Visit WALKING
(☎0674358942; www.greenolivearts.com; 18 Ave Mohammed Ben Abderahman; 2 people Dh550, additional person Dh250; ⏲9.30am-1pm Mon-Sat) Green Olive Arts, an artist residency in Tetouan, hosts 3½-hour walking tours that visit Ensemble Artisanat (p279), Royal Artisan School and the souqs in the medina. The local guide sparks up conversations with the artisans while they're working and

translates questions visitors have about their work. The experience is informative, especially for those who don't speak Arabic.

Festivals & Events

Voix de Femmes ART
(Jul/Aug) Since 2008 this festival has highlighted female artists – both Moroccan and international – with expositions by artisanal cooperatives and concerts open to the public. It's a fine extension of Tetouan's artistic heritage and a rarity for the region.

Sleeping

Tetouan has some spectacular riads, many of which have opened in former family dwellings over the last few years. The Ensanche has some decent options, but with far less charm.

If you prefer to be nearer to the coast, the port of Martil is an inexpensive 15-minute cab ride away; M'Diq, the classier option, is twice that.

★Riad Darna HOSTEL €
(0667559571; www.riaddarna.com; 6 Ruelle Selloum; dm/d/f Dh155/495/770;) This bright and clean medina riad is one of the freshest you'll find in the region. Turquoise doors with handles shaped like *hamsas* (signifying the hand of God) hide comfortable dorms and suites over several floors. Dorm beds are divided by walls and curtains. Breakfast is served on the rooftop where there's a quality lounge and view.

Hotel Regina HOTEL €
(0539962113; 8 Rue Sidi Mandri; s/d Dh230/340;) One of the larger budget choices, the Regina uses Riffian fabrics to liven up its 56 rooms. Recent renovations have delivered new mattresses and a new restaurant on the 5th floor. Everything is sparklingly clean and the service is good, making the Regina a solid budget option.

★El Reducto GUESTHOUSE €€
(0539968120; www.elreducto.com; 38 Zanqat Zawiya; s/d from Dh400/550;) The spotless, palatial rooms are truly fantastic: big bathrooms with lots of Spanish glazed tiles (one has a Jacuzzi for two), quality furniture and beautiful silk bedspreads. Climb the spiral staircase to the roof terrace for spectacular views. Some rooms are above the excellent restaurant (p278) while others are in the annexe on the opposite side of the lane.

Riad Las Mil y una Noches RIAD €€
(0661485809; www.riad1001n.com; 65 Rue Caid Ahmed; s/d Dh500/600, ste Dh760-1045;) Count the chandeliers at this bright and decorative riad in the medina a short walk up from Place Hassan II (p275). The entire former family home is painted floor-to-ceiling with intricate hand-drawn designs. Manager Khan is eager to please and has a wealth of knowledge. The rooftop has some of the best in-medina views and is kept warm off season.

Dar Rehla RIAD €€
(0539711768; www.darrehla.net; 3 Derb Habibi; s/d Dh400/500;) You'll feel like one of the family at this six-room riad in a quiet alley off busy Niyarine above the Ensanche. The rooms are spacious and beautifully decorated with keyhole doorways, and there's a lovely terrace to enjoy in summer. Tip: pick up some sweets on the street and enjoy them with a pot of mint tea in your room.

Hotel Panorama Vista HOTEL €€
(0539964970; Ave Moulay Abbas; s/d Dh350/450;) Any place calling itself Panorama Vista has to be certain of its location, and, sure enough, rooms here offer dramatic views of the Rif Mountains. The rooms themselves are hotel-chain style without a lot of local ambience, but they're clean and everything works. This is the best value outside the medina. The cafe on the 1st floor offers a strong Moroccan-continental breakfast.

THE SOUQS OF TETOUAN

Next to Tetouan's **tannery** (Bab M'Kabar; 9am-5pm), where you can see how the cow hides get their shades, the **Leather Souq** features traditional Moroccan shoes, jackets and bags. Many of the products have been made with methods passed down over generations.

Tetouan is known for its artisans, and this **Jewellery Souq** is the spot in the medina where you'll find a collection of jewellery boutiques.

Best visited after going to the Artisanal School (p275), where you can see the detail and hard work that goes into making each piece, the **Carpentry Souq** is where you'll find Tetouan's famous carpentry for sale.

Blanco Riad GUESTHOUSE €€€
(0539704202; www.blancoriad.com; 25 Rue Zawiya Kadiria; d/ste from Dh550/1650;) This beautiful medina house with its typical Tetouan architecture has been carefully restored and furnished with a blend of modern and antique pieces. It offers large, comfortable rooms and a zen-like garden. One of the salons contains a good restaurant open to nonguests, and there's a boutique with a clothes designer doing clever things with traditional Riffian fabrics.

Eating & Drinking

Tetouan has figured out its riads, but is sadly lacking in the food department. It has the grilled fish thing down, but locals usually prefer fast food over Moroccan cuisine. A couple of medina riads are your best bet.

La Esquina del Pescado SEAFOOD €
(0539961001; 43 Rue Chakib Arsalane; mains from Dh60; noon-10pm) Just west of Place Moulay El Mehdi is this ocean-blue restaurant that serves a wide selection of grilled and fried fish. Portion sizes are excellent for the price and the *poisson friture* (fried fish platter) is a particularly good deal at Dh75. No alcohol.

Dallas PASTRIES €
(0533966069; 11 Rue Youssef Ben Tachfine; pastries from Dh4; 8am-11pm;) Yes, it is named after the TV show, but the moniker has no bearing on this place, a patisserie stacked to the rafters with plates of pastries. This is where local families come to load up on sweets and savoury pies.

Cafe Al Wahda CAFE €
(0533966794; 16 Rue Al Wahda; pastries from Dh4; 7am-9pm Sat-Thu, 7am-noon & 2-9pm Fri) A female-friendly cafe popular with locals, where sticky cakes are a speciality. It's a bit claustrophobic on the upper floor.

DON'T MISS

MEDINA CONCERTS

Every night starting around 8pm, young locals pull out their guitars and jam outside **Cafe Kharrazin** (Tarbiaa; 8pm-2am) in the heart of the medina. The ambience is vibrant and the music soulful. Order a tea and don't be shy about pulling up a chair. Find it near the tannery (p277) and northeastern Bab Mkabar gate.

Chawarma Chand Acham FAST FOOD €
(0533231158; 3 Rue 10 Mai; falafel Dh8, sandwich Dh20, pizza Dh40; noon-midnight) This little snack bar has a Syrian influence and does good falafel and shawarma, as well as inexpensive pizzas, burgers and sandwiches. There's a small seating area upstairs (handy if you're waiting for a pizza), or you can eat on the move. Don't forget to ask for garlic sauce.

★**Blanco Riad** MOROCCAN €€
(0539704202; 25 Rue Zawiya Kadiria; set menu from Dh155; noon-10pm) The menu at this elegant riad is a cut above the usual. A big change from the standard tajine menu, it features some innovative Moroccan dishes and is heavy on local seasonal produce. The garden is pleasant in summer, and the dining room has both Moroccan and western seating. Reservations essential; no alcohol.

El Reducto MOROCCAN €€
(0539968120; 38 Zanqat Zawiya; mains from Dh80; noon-11pm) Tuck into traditional Moroccan (and some Spanish) fare in the grand surroundings of this old house, which once belonged to a Moroccan vizier and is decorated with antique glazed Seville tiles. Desserts are particularly tasty and alcohol is served.

Restaurant Restinga MOROCCAN €€
(21 Ave Mohammed V; mains from Dh40; 9am-9pm) The open-air courtyard shaded by a huge ficus tree is this charming restaurant's primary attraction – along with the rare alcohol licence. A great place to duck out of the crowded boulevard for a rest and a beer, as well as some seafood from the coast.

Casa de España BAR
(Rue Chakib Arsalane; noon-11pm;) It looks like a living room, with a leather couch facing a fireplace, TV and football trophies, but in fact Casa de España is one of Tetouan's few bars. Plates of tapas come with every drink; if you're hungry, there's a grill restaurant in the adjoining room. Smoking is permitted, but the tall ceilings combat the smoke.

Shopping

Tetouan has a long history of expert artisans. Wood and leatherwork are the local specialities, but you'll also find carpets, *djellabas* and multicoloured *sheshias* (Rifian reed hats).

Dar Lebadi ARTS & CRAFTS
(☎0533973856; Jenoui section; ⏰9am-7pm) The shopping palace of the medina, this 200-year-old building, which was a former governor's house, has been meticulously restored. It is a clearing house for Berber artisans and Rabati carpets, and has friendly staff. It's worth a stop just to see the building, but be careful: you may be there for hours.

Ensemble Artisanat ARTS & CRAFTS
(Ave Hassan II; ⏰8am-8pm Mon-Sat) This government-sponsored emporium is a hive of activity, with carpet weavers, leatherworkers, jewellers and woodworkers all plying their trades. Prices are fixed.

ℹ Getting There & Away

BUS

From Tetouan's modern **bus station** (cnr Ave 9 Avril & Ave Meknes) you can get to any town in the north. There's a left-luggage office (medium/large bag Dh6/10). Local buses serve the following destinations.

Al Hoceima Dh115, six hours
Chefchaouen Dh120, 25 minutes
Fnideq Dh15, 50 minutes
Larache Dh45, two hours
Martil Dh6, 25 minutes

CTM (☎0539961688) has its own station; destinations include the following.

Casablanca Dh140, six hours
Fez Dh100, six hours
Marrakesh Dh235, nine hours
Rabat Dh120, four hours
Tangier Dh27, one hour

GRANDS TAXIS

Grands taxis leave from the main bus station for Al Hoceima (Dh150, four hours), Chefchaouen (Dh35, one hour), Larache (Dh50, 1½ hours), Asilah (Dh50, 1½ hours) and Tangier (Dh30, one hour).

Grands taxis leave from the CTM bus station for Fnideq (for Ceuta; Dh10, 40 minutes), Martil (Dh5, 15 minutes) and M'Diq (Dh7, 20 minutes).

PETITS TAXIS

Petits taxis are canary yellow; a ride around town should be around Dh10.

If you have your own vehicle, you can keep your car at the guarded **Parking Hammadi** (Ave Al Jazaer; per hr day/night Dh8/4).

DRINKING IN THE CRAZINESS

Once upon a time, a Tetouani came up with a hare-brained plan to blend avocado with fruit juice and top it with a mountain of fresh and dried fruit, nuts and honey. *Za3za3* (*zeh-zeh*, meaning 'craziness') was born; it was a hit and has since been copied in many variations. It can be found in pint glasses all over the medina, especially the *mellah* (Jewish quarter). Don't leave Tetouan without trying a glass.

The original **Za3Za3** (Ave Fes; juice Dh10-25; ⏰6.30am-12.30am) joint is a 10-minute walk from Bab Al Okla, but you'll need to walk much longer if you plan to burn off those calories.

Around Tetouan

M'Diq المضيق

☎0539 / POP 68,400

Tucked into the lee of the north side of Cabo Negro is the surprising town of M'Diq (*mdik*). Once a small fishing village, it has rapidly grown into a classy resort, with a grand entrance, a fine beach, good hotels, the enormous Port de Plaisance shopping centre with lots of restaurants, and the yacht club. Even King Mohammed VI vacations here.

There's really little to separate M'Diq from Florida, but if you're suffering from medina fatigue, it's the perfect stop and only 20 minutes from Tetouan.

Grands taxis and buses travelling between Tetouan and Fnideq (3km short of the border with Ceuta) pass through M'Diq. *Grands taxis* gather around the car park opposite the Golden Beach Hotel and go to Tetouan (Dh7, 15 minutes), Martil (Dh7, 20 minutes) and the border (Dh15, 30 minutes).

Sleeping & Eating

M'Diq's sleeping options tend to cater to the summer tourist trade and ignore the lower end of the price bracket. Ask for discounts outside the summer months.

There's no shortage of sweets to enjoy on a hot summer day. A string of cafes and fast-food options along the seafront serve sugary drinks and snacks as well as fish and burgers. The Port de Plaisance shopping centre has smoothies, pizza, ice cream and a few upmarket restaurants including the picturesque Lorizon.

Hotel Côte d'Or HOTEL €€

(0539663219; Corniche; s/d Dh360/490;) One of several hotels along the corniche, this one is fairly bland with simple, modern rooms. It is in a superb location opposite the beach, and there's a cafe and restaurant on the ground floor. Ask for a room with a sea view.

Golden Beach Hotel HOTEL €€€

(0539975077; www.golden-beachhotel.com; 84 Route de Sebta; s/d/ste Dh638/1389/1847;) This aptly named hotel is right on the sand and worth the splurge, especially outside of summer season when prices dip. It's short on charm but well run and has good facilities, including a restaurant, disco, pool and a piano bar with a most clever bar top: piano keys in marble.

High-season prices include breakfast and lunch or dinner.

Café Olas SEAFOOD €

(0539664433; Corniche; mains from Dh65; 7am-midnight;) You can't miss this waterfront landmark dressed up as a lighthouse, with a hopping downstairs cafe with beach-facing windows and huge plates of seafood. The decor is snappy and the rooftop views superb. You can also find *za3za3* (zeh-zeh; an avocado and fruit smoothie with fresh fruit and nuts on top) as well as crêpes and waffles.

Lorizon SEAFOOD €€

(0684444440; mains from Dh60, paella from Dh120; 1pm-midnight;) At the end of a causeway jutting out into the sea, this Asian-inspired thatched-roof restaurant comes as quite a surprise. The menu includes tapas, paella and other seafood, and the decor is nautical themed. Windows on three sides ensure both picturesque views of the sea and that seagulls can watch you while you eat. No alcohol.

Martil مرتيل

0539 / POP 81,960

Tetouan's port of Martil *(mar-til)* is one of the most popular beach towns in summer for Moroccan and regional tourists, but less so for foreign visitors. The long corniche is lined with cafes, ice-cream shops and fast-food restaurants serving similar fare. Many eat instead in the wind-battered apartment blocks and hotels that fill to the brim during summer. The town also has a golf course nearby and a pair of small shopping centres.

Stay here if you're craving the beach. If you're looking for a more traditional experience, choose a riad in Tetouan and take the 8km cab ride to the coast.

The coast road (Rocade) stretches from Fnideq along the Mediterranean coast to Saïdia in the far east. From Fnideq to Martil there's a spanking new corniche along the beautiful beach. While there are few hotels, a huge number of holiday apartment blocks have been completed along this stretch, and more are being built. There are resorts at Plage Riffiyenne and the Marina Smir, and the enormous Ritz-Carlton resort.

Local buses to Tetouan (Dh5, 15 minutes) leave from the bus station near the water tower at the southern end of the beach. You'll find *grands taxis* to Tetouan (Dh7, 10 minutes) near the big mosque.

Sleeping & Eating

Martil is chock-full of apartment rentals and resorts aimed squarely at local holidaymakers. They're decent, if a little bland. If you want something with more character, rest your head in nearby Tetouan.

The corniche is the place to go to eat, as there is a host of open-fronted restaurants facing the sea, as well as ice-cream parlours if you want a cone on your beach stroll. Cheap fast-food places are clustered in the streets near the bus station.

There are a couple of bars in Martil that serve alcohol. In the summer season there are frequent live music events on the corniche.

Hotel Etoile de la Mer HOTEL €

(Estrella del Mar; 0539979058; Ave Hassan II; s/d Dh200/350;) With its funky design – a central, plant-filled atrium criss-crossed by stairways – and good location one block from the beach, this is one of Martil's best sleeping options. Riffian textiles and green paint brighten things up. The best rooms have balconies overlooking the sea.

Camping Al Boustane CAMPGROUND €

(0539688822; Corniche; camping per person Dh20, per tent/car/camper Dh30/25/40, electricity Dh25; office 7.30am-noon & 7-11pm;) This secure campsite is one block from the beach, set in a pretty garden. Facilities are showing their age, but it does have a pool in summer.

There are serious drainage problems when it rains. Turn off the corniche at the fountain.

Le Guayana MOROCCAN €
(Corniche; mains Dh35-90; 10am-9pm;) This friendly beachside restaurant has an intriguing menu of salads, pizzas and paninis as well as Thai and rice dishes. Good for juice or a meal on a hot summer day.

Chefchaouen شفشاون

0539 / POP 45,870

Beautifully folded beneath the raw peaks of the Rif, Chefchaouen *(shef-shao-wen)* is one of the prettiest towns in Morocco: an artsy, blue-washed mountain village that feels like its own world. But it's no longer an off-the-beaten-track destination for artists and backpackers looking to score some *kif* (cannabis) – those days are long gone. While the *kif* hustlers remain, summertime can involve hoards of tourists chest-to-back waiting to take selfies with a flower pot. Yet somehow, the 'blue pearl' manages to still be worth it; with its blue-hued Andalusian-style buildings, red-tiled roofs and narrow lanes, there really is no place like it.

Aim for more than a day here, leaving time to relax, explore (and let's be honest, we all want an amazing Chefchaouen photo) and take a day trip or trek to neighbouring Talassemtane National Park.

History

Chefchaouen was originally known as Chaouen, meaning 'peaks'. Under Spanish occupation the spelling changed to Xaouen, and in 1975 the town was renamed Chefchaouen (Look at the Peaks). These days the names are used interchangeably.

Moulay Ali Ben Rachid founded Chaouen in 1471 as a base for Riffian Berber tribes to launch attacks on the Portuguese in Ceuta. The town expanded with the arrival of Muslim and Jewish refugees from Granada in the late 15th century, who built whitewashed Andalusian-style houses with tiny balconies, tiled roofs and patios (often with a citrus tree in the centre), that give the town its distinctive Spanish flavour. The pale-blue wash seen today came later, but exactly when it was first introduced remains a mystery.

The town remained isolated and xenophobic – Christians were forbidden to enter on pain of death – until occupied by Spanish troops in 1920. When the Spanish arrived, they were surprised to hear the Jewish inhabitants still speaking a variant of medieval Castilian. The Spanish were briefly thrown out by Amazigh (Berber) leader Abd Al Krim during the Rif War in the 1920s, but they soon returned and remained until independence in 1956.

Sights

Medina

Winding alleyways, cute doorways and charming plazas all in many shades of blue – this is what has attracted millions to this tiny village in the Rif Mountains, and there's no sign tourism will let up. Despite overcrowding, Chefchaouen's medina is still well worth the visit.

The heart of the medina is the shady, cobbled Plaza Uta El Hammam, dominated by the red-hued walls of the kasbah and the adjacent **Grande Mosquée** (Plaza Uta El Hammam). Towering over Plaza Uta El Hammam, the Grand Mosquée and its unusual octagonal minaret were built in the 15th century by the son of the town's founder, Ali Ben Rachid. Like all mosques in Chefchaouen, it is closed to non-Muslims.

Kasbah HISTORIC BUILDING
(0539986343; Plaza Uta El Hammam; Dh60; 9am-5.30pm Oct-May, to 6.30pm May-Sep) If you're getting tired of blue, Chefchaouen's 15th-century clay-brown kasbah contains a lovely Andalusian-style garden, a former prison, the small **Center for Research and Andalusian Studies** and even smaller **art gallery** (only open during exhibitions). One of the fortress' 13 spires, the Portuguese Tower, named after the Portuguese prisoners who built it, features plaques tracing Riffian history and provides exquisite views of the medina.

Horno Bab El Ain HISTORIC SITE
(Ave Hassan I; 9am-5pm) A traditional bakery; locals still bring their bread dough and *bastilla* to bake here.

Outside the Medina

Oued Ras El Maa WATERFALL
The waterfall of Ras El Maa is just beyond the far northeastern gate of the Chefchaouen medina. It's here, where the water comes gushing out of the mountain, that local women come to do their washing. The

Chefchaouen

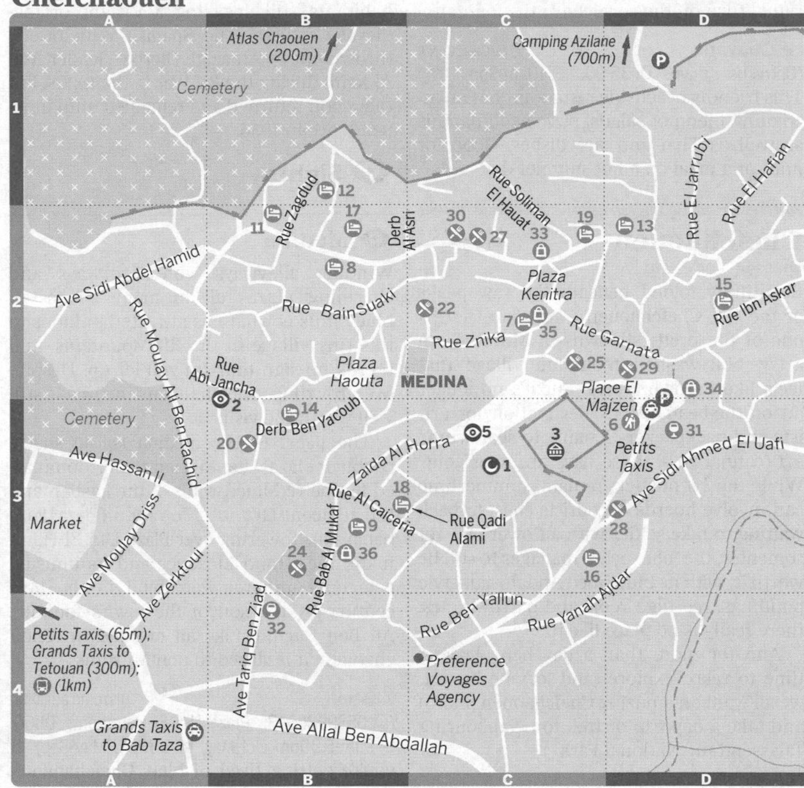

sound of the water and the verdant hills just beyond the medina wall provide a sudden, strong dose of nature.

Spanish Mosque MOSQUE

The mosque was built by the Spanish in the 1920s, but never used. It fell into disrepair and remains closed, but the grounds out front make for a perfect place to behold the blue city and watch the sunset dip behind the green hills with a freshly squeezed orange juice in hand.

Activities

Climbing Jebel El Kelaâ

Looming over Chefchaouen at 1616m, Jebel El Kelaâ might initially appear to be a daunting peak, but with an early start, it can easily be climbed in a day if you're in reasonably good shape.

The hike starts from behind Camping Azilane (p285), following the 4WD track that takes you to the hamlet of **Aïn Tissimlane**. Rocks painted with a red-and-white stripe indicate that you're on the right path. The initial hour is relatively steep as you climb above the trees to get your first views over Chefchaouen, before cutting into the mountains along the steady *piste* (track). You should reach Aïn Tissimlane within a couple of hours of setting out, after which the path climbs and zigzags steeply through great boulders for nearly an hour, before reaching a pass. Turn west along the track, which leads to the saddle of the mountain, from where you can make the final push to the summit. There's a rough path, although you'll need to scramble in places. The peak is attained relatively quickly, and your exertions are rewarded with the most sublime views over this part of the Rif.

It's straightforward and quick to descend by the same route. Alternatively, you can head north from the saddle on a path that

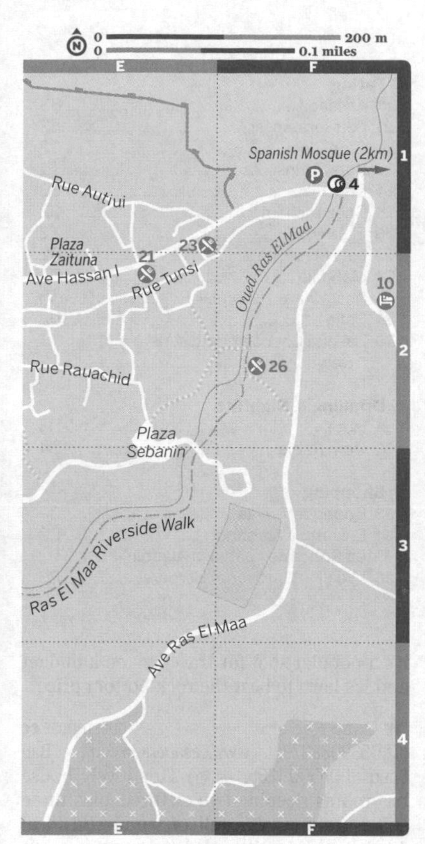

takes you to a cluster of villages on the other side of the mountain. One of these villages, **El Kelaâ**, has 16th-century grain stores and a mosque with a leaning minaret. From here, a number of simple tracks will take you back to Chefchaouen in a couple of hours.

Trekking

Just outside Chefchaouen is the massive Talassemtane National Park (p290), which contains a range of short and multiday hikes. A popular day trip is to take a *grand taxi* to Akchour and hike to either Akchour Waterfalls (p290) or God's Bridge (p291), a geological formation that you won't believe is natural.

Lesser visited, but no less beautiful, is **Bouhachem Regional Nature Reserve**, which lies between Tetouan, Chefchaouen and Larache. One of two parks in the Rif Mountains, Bouhachem is exceptionally beautiful and covers an enormous territory. The forest has various species of oak and maritime pine, and is home to an important number of birds, mammals (including the rare Barbary macaque) and reptiles. Hikers can trek to local villages and explore the mountains and forests. Several *gîtes* (rural hostels) are available for overnight stays.

Abdeslam Mouden TREKKING
(☎0661463905; rifwalks@gmail.com; guide Dh250-500) Abdeslam Mouden is an honest guide and passionate ecotourism advocate with a quarter-century of experience leading trips around the Rif. He and his team of 13 trained guides lead half-day and overnight treks for groups up to 12 in both Talassemtane and Bouhachem parks. WhatsApp him for pointers before tackling the trails yourself.

Chaouen Rural TREKKING
(☎0539987267, 0610210146; www.chaouenrural.org; Place El Mazjen; guide per day Dh400) Chaouen Rural offers multiday hikes to Tallesemtane and the coast as well as cooking, pottery and plant distillation courses inside Bouhachem. Travellers can also visit cooperatives that produce honey or couscous. Manager Khadija is quick to respond and all services are listed on the website – a rarity in Chefchaouen. Contact before visiting the office as the doors usually remain closed.

Courses

Chefchaouen Cooking Class COOKING
(☎0658036242; abdelghanirhani6543@gmail.com; per person Dh350) There are several cooking classes in Chefchaouen, but chef Rhani offers the most personal experience, cooking up Moroccan dishes in his apartment or at his clients' accommodation. Meals aren't traditional – Rhani adds his own spin with ingredients like white wine and soy sauce – but dang, they're delicious and the class feels like a dinner party among friends. Alcohol is available.

Groups up to six. Rhani is also a **certified guide** who hosts hiking tours and day trips to other cities.

Sleeping

It might be small, but Chefchaouen has hundreds of accommodation options – and they can all fill up, so book ahead. As the medina is what you come here for, it's the ideal place to stay. However, there are some good options outside the walls that are close by.

Chefchaouen

Sights
1 Grande Mosquée ... C3
2 Horno Bab El Ain ... B3
3 Kasbah ... C3
4 Oued Ras El Maa ... F1
5 Plaza Uta El Hammam ... C3

Activities, Courses & Tours
6 Chaouen Rural ... D3
Lina Ryad & Spa ... (see 19)

Sleeping
7 Casa Hassan ... C2
8 Casa Perleta ... B2
9 Dar Dadicilef ... B3
10 Dar Echchaouen ... F2
11 Dar Gabriel ... B2
12 Dar Meziana ... B1
13 Dar Terrae ... D2
14 Hostel Baraka ... B3
15 Hotel Koutoubia ... D2
16 Hotel Marrakesh ... C3
17 Hotel Riad Cherifa ... B2
18 Hotel Souika ... B3
19 Lina Ryad & Spa ... C2

Eating
20 Assaada ... B3
21 Baissara Ansar ... E2
22 Cafe Clock ... C2
23 Cafe Tounsi ... E1
24 Chez Aziz ... B3
25 Chez Hicham ... C2
26 El Jaleo ... F2
27 Lala Mesouda ... C2
28 Mandala ... D3
Restaurant Tissemlal ... (see 7)
29 Sofia ... D2
30 Zakaria Chocolat Patisserie Belge ... C2

Drinking & Nightlife
31 Hotel Parador ... D3
32 Oum Rabie ... B4

Shopping
33 Boutique Terrae ... C2
34 Ensemble Artisanat ... D2
35 La Botica de la Abuela Aladdin ... C2
36 L'Art De L'Artisanat Berbère ... B3

Medina

★Hostel Baraka GUESTHOUSE €
(☎0539882910; www.riad-baraka.net; 16 Rue Sidi Hmed El Bouhali; dm/d Dh100/275, d with shared bathroom Dh220; 📶) English-owned Hostel Baraka is a bright and cheery place to rest your backpack. The rooms are comfortable with clean facilities and there's a convivial terrace with amazing views. There are a handful of private rooms or dorms for four with bunk beds. Staff are happy to help orientate travellers in the medina.

Hotel Koutoubia GUESTHOUSE €
(☎0539988433; hotelkoutoubia@hotmail.fr; Rue Andalouse; r with medina/mountain views Dh250/350; 📶) This hotel does quality budget accommodation well, and has friendly and attentive management, a central location, traditional decor, spotless rooms and a closed-in roof terrace where you can have breakfast on those cold Chefchaouen mornings.

Hotel Souika HOSTEL €
(☎0539986862; Derb Hadi Alami; dm/d Dh60/140; 📶) A hostel by any other name, Souika has a series of dorms with bunk beds, plus a couple of double rooms. It's as basic as it gets, with adequate shared showers and toilets. Some rooms have mould on the walls. Still, it's a popular spot for travellers on a budget and it's hard to beat the rock-bottom price.

★Casa Perleta GUESTHOUSE €€
(☎0539988979; www.casaperleta.com; Bab Souq; d Dh500-1265; ❄📶) This lovely house has rooms sleeping two or three, plus three suites for four. It's full of wonderful local fabrics and furniture, and the white walls soothe after the blue medina. The cosy sitting room has a fireplace for chilly nights, and there's central heating in all rooms. Topping it off is a terrace with great views.

Dar Dadicilef RIAD €€
(☎0539882893; Derb Hadri; tw with shared bathroom Dh250, d Dh400-500, q Dh420; 📶) A friendly Moroccan family runs this conveniently located and well-kept blue riad near Bab El Ain. The larger doubles are luxurious with a spacious relaxing area and a huge tub in the bathroom. Moroccan-style breakfasts are delicious with soft sheep cheese and cakes. The rooftop is great for taking in the medina or having a snooze on the cushions.

Dar Gabriel GUESTHOUSE €€
(☎0539989244; www.dargabriel.com; Bab Souq; d Dh700; ❄📶) The warmth of natural brick paired with lots of local rugs and fabrics make this a comfortable option. The cosy lounge has a fireplace, there are three roof terraces and meals can be provided. Rooms

are simple and individually decorated. Excursions into the mountains are on offer.

Dar Terrae GUESTHOUSE €€
(☎0539987598; www.darterrae.com; Ave Hassan I; d/ste Dh480/600, s/d/tr with shared bathroom Dh280/380/500;) This cute guesthouse (known locally as 'Hotel Italiano') is hidden up and down a tumble of stairs and odd corners. Rooms are cheerful, and some have their own bathroom and fireplace. Breakfast is served on a cute terrace and you can have dinner by request (a restaurant is being built). Owners Bilal and Hanaa may be the sweetest people in Chefchaouen.

Dar Meziana GUESTHOUSE €€
(☎0539987806; www.darmezianahotel.com; Rue Zagdud; r Dh648-933;) Beautifully decorated, this boutique hotel has a unique angular courtyard, lush plantings, lots of light, the highest quality furniture and extraordinary ceilings. It's at the edge of the medina and not well signposted (follow the row of yellow planters), but it is lovely. The price of the room includes dinner and breakfast.

Lina Ryad & Spa GUESTHOUSE €€€
(☎0645069903; www.linaryad.com; Ave Hassan I; d Dh1550;) The upmarket Lina Ryad is opulent and impeccably turned out – a brand-new building made to look traditional. It has large, comfortable rooms with TV (and free movies) and helpful staff. The roof terraces have fabulous views. An internal courtyard holds a delightful heated pool that's surprisingly private, and there's a Moroccan restaurant (mains Dh100) only for hotel or spa guests.

The **spa** (hammam Dh300, massage Dh400; 11am-8pm) here is much more than a hammam, with an Instagram-worthy indoor pool and a sizeable list of pampering services. Traditional Moroccan hammams are 45 minutes, as are massages. Facials, waxing, manicures and pedicures are also available.

Hotel Riad Cherifa RIAD €€€
(☎0539986370; www.riadcherifa.com; 6 Derb Ahmed Laaroussi; d Dh700-1100, ste Dh1185-1400;) One of Chefchaouen's newest and finest luxury accommodations, Riad Cherifa houses 12 dazzling rooms and an outdoor pool beneath an exposed rock wall. The common areas are elegantly designed with just a hint of blue, turquoise ceramic steps, velvet chairs and an impressive chandelier. A hammam and massage room (Dh300 apiece) can be found near the entrance.

Casa Hassan GUESTHOUSE €€€
(Dar Baibou; ☎0539986153; www.casahassan.com; 22 Rue Targhi; s/d incl half-board from Dh700/850;) Don't be confused by the signs: Casa Hassan is now across the street from its sister restaurant of the same name. The move has much improved this long-established guesthouse – knocking together a couple of properties has provided airy, well-laid-out rooms, a couple of courtyards and a pleasant patio garden, as well as the obligatory roof terrace. A solid choice.

Outside the Medina

Hotel Marrakesh HOTEL €
(☎0539987774; Hotel.Marrakech1@hotmail.com; 41 Ave Hassan II; s/d with shared bathroom Dh150/220, d/tr with shower Dh250/320;) Slightly outside the medina but with good access, the Marrakesh is a hotel with a bit of cheer. Bright pastel rooms invite the fresh air in, and beds almost touch the ground. The common room attracts with its central fireplace, and the roof terrace has fine valley views. All rooms share toilets; the more expensive rooms have a shower.

Camping Azilane CAMPGROUND €
(☎0539986979; Hay Ouatman; camping per adult Dh30, plus per tent/car/campervan Dh20/20/35, electricity Dh15;) A shady setting with great views makes this site popular, although cleanliness is questionable. It's a stiff 20-minute walk from the medina. There's a

DON'T MISS

A RIVERSIDE STROLL

A walk along **Oued Ras El Maa** will provide excellent views of the city walls while supplying a healthy dose of natural calm just outside the medina madness. The route takes about 30 minutes and is an easy saunter downhill.

Exit the medina at **Bab El Ansar** and head over the bridge, crossing the river. Turn right and go down the stairs to the path on the eastern side of Ras El Maa. You'll walk past locals doing their laundry and cobblestone bridges, some of which date back to the city's founding in the 15th century. After dipping down into a the gorge, the path eventually meets Ave Allal Ben Abdallah, where you can hail a taxi or head back to the medina on foot.

shop that sells some essentials, but otherwise facilities are basic (hot showers Dh10). Fires only from December to May; alcohol is allowed if you bring it yourself.

★ **Auberge Dardara** INN €€
(☎0539707007, 0661150503; www.facebook.com/auberge.dardara; Route Nationale 2; d/tr Dh600/750;) This authentic French *auberge* (inn) in the Moroccan countryside offers large rustic suites with TVs and fireplaces and an excellent restaurant. The 10-hectare complex includes an active farm and gardens, a pool, a craft shop, a hammam, a fitness centre, fishing, biking, mule riding, trekking and treasure hunts. Guest programmes include crafts, gardening and more.

It's a 10-minute grand taxi ride south of town (Dh6). Find a cab at the stand (p290) with taxis for Bab Taza.

★ **Dar Echchaouen** GUESTHOUSE €€€
(☎0539987824; www.darechchaouen.com; 18 Ave Ras El Maa; d/ste from Dh690/890, bungalows Dh1300;) This gorgeous accommodation just outside the medina and near Ras El Maa is its own private paradise, with beautiful gardens and very comfortable, spacious rooms with spectacular views. A dip in the pool beneath the towering Rif cliffs is a summer delight. Echchaouen also features a spa, private hammam, massages and a restaurant.

Eating

The touristy cafes and restaurants on Plaza Uta El Hammam all serve pretty much the same exact food. Good meals can be found elsewhere, but you'll have to be selective.

★ **Sofia** MOROCCAN €
(☎0671286649; Place Outa Hammam, Escalier Roumani; mains Dh30-80; 12.30-5.30pm & 7-10.30pm) The only female-owned restaurant in Chefchaouen, Sofia (named after the owner's daughter) is a revelation in a city where restaurants have largely neglected what's on the menu. Chef Nuura's cinnamon-hinted *bastilla* rolls are to die for and the vegetarian couscous has to be the best in town. Seating is outdoors on a few tables across from the small kitchen.

★ **El Jaleo** MOROCCAN €
(☎0601403160; Rue Ras El Maa; Dh40-80; noon-5pm & 7-11pm Tue-Sun;) El Jaleo, meaning 'the mess', takes the best cooking in Chefchaouen – from Nuura of Sofia – to a wonderfully atmospheric restaurant above Oued Ras El Maa (p281). The menu is unique, including steamed lamb, aubergine lasagna, *pinchos* and tajines. The lush garden is perfect for beholding sunset over the blue city after a long day exploring.

Baissara Ansar SOUP €
(Ave Hassan I; soup Dh6; 8am-10pm) Little more than two tables, several chairs and Ahmed's friendly smile, this tiny soup joint with no sign serves just two things: *bissara* (bean soup with olive oil and a dash of cumin) and mint tea (Dh4). Fresh local bread is served on the side. Your stomach – and your wallet – will thank you.

Mandala ITALIAN €
(☎0539882808; mains from Dh35; 1-11pm;) Offering a welcome break from Chefchaouen's endless tajine parade, Mandala serves up some good pizzas and pastas, plus a serviceable steak. The seating is cosy and service is good. If you're feeling lazy, you can get delivery to your guesthouse.

Zakaria Chocolat Patisserie Belge DESSERTS €
(☎0679909871; Ave Hassan I; pastries Dh15; 8am-8pm) Zakaria moved to Chefchaouen with his young daughter for the 'easy life', stirring up hot chocolate and baking delicious pastries from his native Belgium. The shop is little more than a cubby hole, but it's great for a sweet break after exploring the medina. Belgian waffles are available from Sunday to Tuesday.

Lala Mesouda MOROCCAN €
(☎0539989133; Ave Hassan I; mains from Dh30; noon-10.30pm) A lively and cosy restaurant with fun fabrics and intimate seating – some chairs are handcrafted out of tree trunks. The food is traditional Moroccan, serving up affordable tajines and decent soups. It always seems to be packed, so be prepared to queue.

Assaada MOROCCAN €
(☎0666317316; Bab El Ain; mains from Dh30; 10am-10pm) This reliable cheapie tries hard to please. Located on both sides of the alley just before Bab El Ain, it offers better than average Moroccan cuisine (the *kefta* tajine with spiced meatballs is tasty) and good juices. The rooftop is a peaceful place to enjoy the sunset and soak in the call to prayer, while the street terrace is great for people watching.

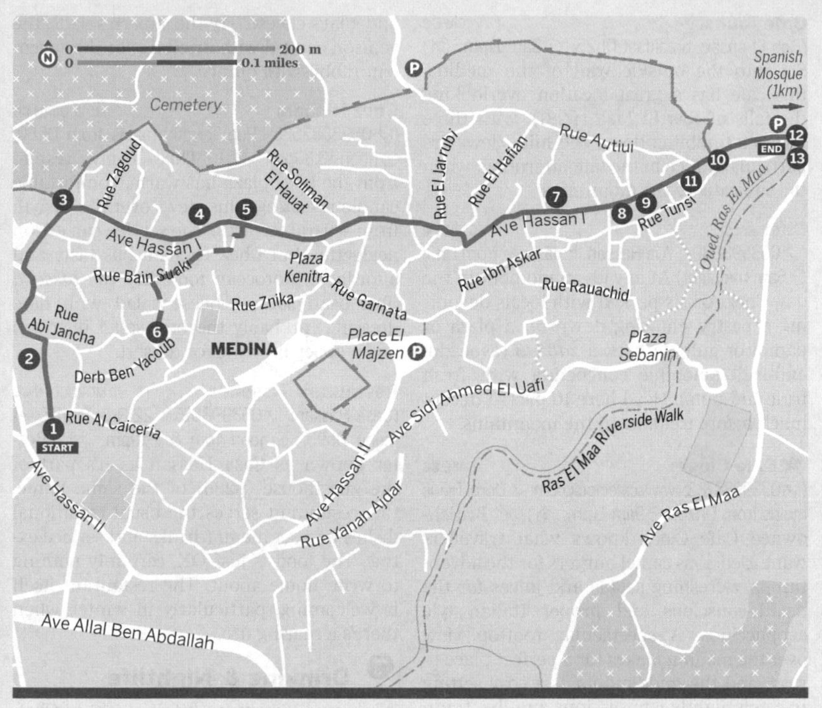

Town Walk
Medina Meander Made Simple

START BAB EL AIN
END BAB EL ANSAR
LENGTH 1KM; 45 MINUTES

This quick jaunt through the blue city will take you along one of the medina's main thoroughfares. Don't be afraid to stray up or down a blue staircase or two; Chefchaouen's medina is small and you won't get lost for long.

Start at the medina gate **1 Bab El Ain** and fill your reusable water bottle in the fountain; Chefchaouen has excellent mountain spring water that's safe to drink. Holding left, follow your nose to 16th-century oven **2 Horno Bab El Ain** (p281), where locals still bring their bread dough and *bastilla* (savoury-sweet pies) to bake.

Continue along Ave Hassan I past the **3 Bab Souq** gate; you may need to say 'excuse me' as you cut through a queue of amateur photographers at the colourful pots along **4 Derb El Asri**, a popular Instagram snap. Stop, if you wish, for a Belgian waffle and a hot chocolate at **5 Zakaria**.

Any alley to the right will take you down to **6 Plaza Haouta**, a peaceful square where men drink tea and play *parchís* (a Spanish board game widely popular in northern Morocco), but continuing along Hassan I will take you past a line of bazaar-style shops coaxing you to come in for tea (and a carpet).

Take a wee break on one of the two benches at **7 Place Zaituna** (Olive Square) and peer at the medina's oldest olive tree. Up ahead is **8 El Ansar Mosque**, which has a unique minaret that's layered like a cake (with blue circling the base, of course). A cheap snack along the way is waiting at tiny **9 Baissara Ansar** (p286), where Ahmed serves the local speciality soup with a dash of cumin for just Dh6.

If you haven't let a windy blue path lead you astray, you'll reach **10 Bab Al Ansar** where you may hang a right for a waterfall-side tea at **11 Cafe Tounsi** (p288), continue straight to the gushing **12 Oued Ras El Maa** (p281), take a hike up to the Spanish Mosque or opt for a **13 riverside walk** (p285) for an out-of-medina experience.

Cafe Tounsi CAFE €

(Bab El Ansar; breakfast Dh25; 8am-11pm;) Set into the outside wall of the medina, this cafe has a great location overlooking the falls of Ras El Maa (p281), with three terraces tumbling down the hill. Views are particularly nice in the late afternoon, when the sun catches the mountains.

Chez Aziz PASTRIES €

(0539988894; Ave Hassan II; pastries from Dh3; 6am-midnight) At any given moment in the day, Chez Aziz is packed with locals devouring a pastry, chowing down on a pizza or panini or gulping back a *za3za3* (avocado-and-fruit smoothie concoction with fresh fruit and nuts). Head here to pack a decent lunch before trekking in the mountains.

★Café Clock CAFE €€

(0539988788; www.cafeclock.com; 3 Derb Tijani; mains from Dh70; 9am-11pm;) British-owned Café Clock knows what travellers want. Delicious camel burgers for the adventurous, refreshing salads and juices for the health-conscious and proper Italian-style cappuccinos. A spectacular rooftop view over the medina makes for a perfect place to read, and the middle floor is a cosy setting to catch nightly jam sessions and live traditional Arabic music.

★Auberge Dardara Restaurant MOROCCAN €€

(0661150503, 0539707007; www.facebook.com/auberge.dardara; Route Nationale 2; mains from Dh80, dinner set menu Dh120; 8-11am, 1-4pm & 6-9pm) This is the best restaurant in the area and worth the 10-minute drive from town (Dh6). The Tanjaoui owner uses only the freshest ingredients from the garden, bakes his own bread and makes his own olive oil and goat's cheese. Try the superb salads, the venison cooked with dried figs or the succulent rabbit with quince.

Chez Hicham MOROCCAN €€

(0598882625; Rue Targhi; mains from Dh60; noon-10.30pm;) This lovely respite from the busy plaza has warm, comfortable candlelit seating, plus views over the kasbah from several terraces. The service can err on neglectful, but Chez Hicham has tasty and affordable Moroccan food. Try the *bissara* (fava-bean soup), cheese salad with date dressing (probably the best salad in town) and a gooey brownie for dessert.

Restaurant Tissemlal MOROCCAN €€

(Casa Hassan; 0539986153; 22 Rue Targhi; set menu Dh95; noon-4pm & 7-10pm;) Better known as Casa Hassan as it's part of the guesthouse (p285) of the same name, this restaurant serves the usual traditional dishes in a set menu (drinks and service extra). The food is just OK, certainly nothing to write home about. The restaurant itself is welcoming, particularly in winter when there's a roaring fire.

> **LOCAL KNOWLEDGE**
>
> **FARM-TO-TABLE FAVOURITES**
>
> The market off Ave Hassan II is excellent for fresh fish, meat, fruit and vegetables, and gets particularly busy on Monday and Thursday, when people come from outside Chefchaouen to sell produce.
>
> Several local specialities are worth checking out, particularly the fragrant mountain honey and soft ewe's cheese – both served at breakfast. Add fresh *dial makla* (a type of bread) and you have your picnic.

Drinking & Nightlife

While you'll likely see *kif* (hashish) in Chefchaouen, you're far less likely to see a beer.

Oum Rabie BAR

(0661204865; Ave Hassan II; 5pm-1am Tue-Sun) Smoky Oum Rabie manages to be the best bar in town, though the competition isn't exactly fierce (it's the only one not in a hotel). The two-floor establishment has character, with Moroccan-style furniture and neon lights overlooking a central bar area and TV. Flag Speciale beers are Dh20 and tapas are free.

Hotel Parador BAR

(0539986136; Place El Majzen; 11am-11pm) Hotel Parador's restaurant offers beer and wine with meals, which may be enjoyed poolside on the back terrace. But if you aren't hungry or are looking for something stronger, the hotel's tiny bar is well stocked. Drinks can be enjoyed at the bar or in the adjacent room on one of the hotel's comfortable couches.

Atlas Chaouen BAR

(0539986265; 9am-11pm) If you're desperate for a beer or glass of wine, the bar inside Hotel Atlas Chaouen will do – there's even a great view of the Rif Mountains through its big windows. But it's a tough hike up to get here and the bar is smoky and altogether soulless.

Shopping

Chefchaouen remains an artisan centre and, as such, is an excellent place to shop – especially for Riffian woven rugs and blankets in bright primary colours. The largest concentration of tourist shops is along Ave Hassan I.

La Botica de la Abuela Aladdin COSMETICS
(0631864386; 17 Rue Targi; 8am-11pm) Welcome to Chefchaouen's store of witchcraft and wizardry, where natural soaps and spices dangle from the ceiling like potions and elixirs at Hogwarts. The three-decade-old shop gets packed with customers mining for individual items, but the owners make things easy by stringing together kitchen- and bathroom-starter packs. Several copycat shops are around town, but this is the original.

Boutique Terrae FASHION & ACCESSORIES
(0539987598; Ave Hassan I; 9am-9pm) The tiny boutique below Dar Terrae (p285) stands out from the rest of Chefchaouen's bazaar-style shops, offering unique bags, charming bracelets, cute notebooks and fashionable summer shirts. Many of the items are made from camel-skin leather. Hotel-owner Bilal drives around Morocco to curate all the items himself.

Ensemble Artisanat ARTS & CRAFTS
(Place El Majzen; 9am-9pm) This place houses some of Chefchaouen's best artisans, selected by their peers. Poke your head into each room around the central courtyard to watch the creators hard at work on their craft.

L'Art De L'Artisanat Berbère TEXTILES
(0539986071; 23 Derb Bab El Moukaf; 9am-9pm) This cooperative lined wall-to-wall-to-wall with rugs and blankets may be a challenge to find down an alley near Bab El Ain, but it's worth the hunt. The not-so-pushy salesmen are a treat compared to what you might experience further south, and the products are of good quality. Co-operative profits are shared among 35 local families. Haggling encouraged.

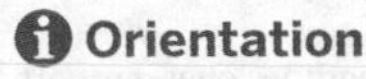

Orientation

Chefchaouen is split into an eastern half (the medina), and a western half (the *ciudad nueva*, or new city). The heart of the medina is Plaza Uta El Hammam, with its unmistakable kasbah (p281).

The principal route of the new city is Ave Hassan II (not to be mistaken for the medina's principal route, Ave Hassan I), which stretches from Plaza Mohammed V (a leafy square designed by artist Joan Miró) past the western gate of Bab El Ain, around the southern medina wall and into the medina itself. Here it dead-ends at Place El Majzen, the main drop-off point. The bus station is a steep 1.5km hike southwest of the town centre. The falls of Ras El Maa (p281) lie just beyond the medina walls to the northeast.

WHY SO BLUE?

Chefchaouen's locals spend painstaking hours keeping their city blue – chances are you'll see someone painting while you're there. But why blue? Surprisingly, the reason remains a mystery.

Some say it was the city's Jewish residents, who arrived after escaping the Spanish Inquisition, that painted the city blue, which signifies divinity in Judaism. It's also possible Jews painted only their *mellah* (neighbourhood) blue and the rest of town followed suit. Others say the blue deters mosquitoes and the sun's heat. Or maybe the blue represents Oued Ras El Maa (p281), the river that nourishes the villagers. The least appealing reason, though no less plausible, is that Chefchaouen is blue today because it attracts tourists and the powers that be want to keep it that way.

For one of the best views from inside the medina, head up to the top of Café Clock.

Information

DANGERS & ANNOYANCES

- The barrage of locals trying to sell *kif* is frustrating and relentless. Simply say no and keep walking.
- Some locals may invite you to visit a cannabis plantation. Going would be taking a risk as police could be waiting to arrest foreigners in possession of illegal contraband.
- Staring and catcalling remains an issue here, as elsewhere in Morocco.

TRAVEL AGENCIES

The helpful, English-speaking **Preference Voyages Agency** (0661967233; www.preferencevoyages.com; 39 Ave Hassan II; 9am-12.30pm & 3-6.30pm Mon-Fri, 9am-12.30pm Sat) has tourist information and organises mountain treks with registered guides.

Getting There & Around

BUS

Bus services from Chefchaouen originate elsewhere, so are often full on arrival. Buy the ticket for your onward journey on arrival in Chefchaouen to secure a seat.

The **bus station** (☎0539987669) is 1.5km southwest of the town centre at the far end of Ave Mohammed V (Dh10 in a *petit taxi* from Place El Majzen). CTM and all other buses use the same station.

CTM serves the following destinations.

DESTINATION	COST (DH)	DURATION (HR)
Casablanca	165	6
Fez	75	4
Nador	125	11½
Rabat	125	4½
Tangier	45	3

Other companies run a number of cheaper services to the same destinations.

CAR

The safe and convenient Hotel Parador **car park** (Place El Majzen; per night Dh20) can be used by nonguests.

GRANDS TAXIS

The fixed price for a *grand taxi* from Tangier airport to Chefchaouen is Dh650, and Dh600 from Tanger Med. Unless you can find several people to split the fare with you, it is far cheaper to go to Tangier first and then hop to Chefchaouen via Tetouan. Even if you buy two places, you will save more than Dh500 and add less than an hour.

Grands taxis northbound leave Chefchaouen from just below Plaza Mohammed V. Most just run to **Tetouan** (Dh35, one hour), where you must change for Tangier or Ceuta – direct taxis are rare.

Grands taxis headed south gather below the central market. Catch one to Ouezzane (Dh35, one hour), where you can pick up onward transport to Fez and Meknes.

There is very little transport heading east to the coast. The best option is to take a *grand taxi* to Dardara junction (Dh8, 15 minutes) or **Bab Taza** (Dh15, 30 minutes) and hope for the best from there.

PETITS TAXIS

Some of Chefchaouen's blue petits taxis congregate on Place El Majzen; others can be found near the market. They're unmetered; most fares shouldn't top Dh10.

TALASSEMTANE NATIONAL PARK

One can only wander Chefchaouen's medina for so long before yearning to do something else besides snap photos. Fortunately, a massive playground isn't far off.

Established in 2004 to protect the Moroccan fir forests from deforestation and added to Unesco's Mediterranean Intercontinental Biosphere Reserve in 2006, Talassemtane National Park *(tell-es-em-ten)* is a vast 580 sq km landscape blessed with magnificent ranges, gorges and valleys, carpeted in forests of cedar, cork oak and fir. Many come as a day trip to explore the sites around Akchour like God's Bridge, a geological feature seemingly carved by a higher being. Others opt for longer treks through Amazigh (Berber) villages, eating home-cooked meals and crashing on beds at *gîtes*.

Sure, this is *kif* country; cannabis plants cover over three-quarters of cultivable land here. But visitors have little reason to feel threatened, especially if travelling with a guide – growers tend to be genuinely interested and welcoming.

Akchour

Tucked amongst the towering cliffs and verdant valleys of Talassemtane National Park is the tiny village of Akchour *(ack-shor)*, an excellent base for exploring the park.

Akchour is largely built for tourism, with virtually all locals living in neighbouring villages. In recent years, the town has exploded with visitors, foreign and domestic, due to the freshly paved mountain road from Chefchaouen. The increase in tourism led to a serious garbage problem, with plastic bottles, bags and other trash often ditched along the river. But local authorities have taken note and have been doing a better job with clean-up.

Akchour's main strip has a few shops, a *gîte*, a couple of traditional restaurants and some street vendors. At the base of town is a dam where hikers split off to tackle either God's Bridge or Akchour Waterfalls.

Sights

Akchour Waterfalls WATERFALL

(Cascades d'Akchour) Cascading over smooth jagged rocks, the Akchour waterfall feeds into a turquoise pool. The view is breathtaking, especially when enjoyed with a fresh juice or tea supplied by vendors who make the two-hour trek here every morning.

Guides in Akchour will try and sell you a round-trip tour, but the path here is mostly flat and easy to navigate. Simply take a left at the dam and go up the hill along the well-trodden path. You'll pass a smaller waterfall at about 45 minutes. Tajine and beverage vendors are stationed every 10 to 15 minutes along the route.

God's Bridge BRIDGE

About 45 minutes from Akchour (1.5km), a huge reddish-brown stone arch towers 25m above the river Oued Farda. Unbelievably, the bridge wasn't carved by human hand, but rather by the river's flow over countless millennia. As the river carved a path deeper and deeper, it left the bridge high and dry.

To get here, go right at the Akchour dam and hug the steep mountainside all the way to the bridge. Alternatively, go down the canyon and follow along beside the river to look up at the bridge. The trip can be challenging either path you take. Don't try to descend to the water from where the bridge meets the mountain – loose rocks have been known to give way.

Small cafes along the water and at the bridge sell tea and tajines.

Sleeping & Eating

There is a simple *gîte* on the road above the main strip (meals are in the restaurant down below) and a campsite in town.

Restaurants and street stands are clustered at the bottom of the street near the dam. L'Ermitage's international restaurant with its seasonal menu is open to nonguests.

★L'Ermitage LODGE €€€

(☎0678998189; www.akchourermitage.com; d/cabin/ste Dh1450/1550/2300;) Downstream from the Akchour Waterfalls along 800m of private river is a spectacular family-owned ecolodge and wellness retreat. The 11 chalets and wood-and-stone cabins radiate a Scandinavian vibe and there's plenty of space to lounge by the water. Sustainability measures include composting, water recycling and a vegetable garden; the latter sustains the international restaurant's seasonal menu.

★Le Caiat LODGE €

(☎0666288715, 0671854997; www.caiat.com; RP 4105, Taghzoute; d per person from Dh160) The Portuguese owner of this charming mountain refuge some 20km from Chefchaouen is a keen environmentalist and rock climber who works with locals arranging treks in Talassemtane National Park. Trails of two hours to two days lead to cooling cascades, rock pools, challenging peaks and rare black pines. The restaurant has breathtaking views, but the food is a disappointment.

Getting There & Away

Grands taxis leave Chefchaouen from a stand on Ave Allal El Fassi across from the Olibya petrol station. *Grands taxis* leave when full, charging Dh25 for the 45-minute ride. Otherwise, the full car can be purchased for Dh150.

Parking in Akchour costs Dh10.

Trekking from Chefchaouen to Akchour

Crossing the mountains northeast of Chefchaouen will take trekkers over snowy peaks, through quaint Amazigh (Berber) villages and to the tiny mountain village of Akchour, where God's Bridge and a string of stunning waterfalls are within reach. It's easy to grab a *grand taxi* from Akchour back to Chefchaouen after two days, but for those craving more, it's possible to hike to the *gîte* in Taourarte (p294) before descending to Akchour's waterfalls and then back to Chefchaouen at the end of four days. A five-day hike to Bab Taza is also possible, but you'll need camping gear as there aren't always *gîtes*.

Views are consistently breathtaking. Being close to the Mediterranean, the Rif Mountains are considered the greenest of Morocco's mountains; springtime, with its riot of wildflowers, is one of the most delightful times to walk here.

Despite the mountains, altitude sickness shouldn't be a problem. The Rif Mountains rarely top more than 2500m in height, with most treks only occasionally venturing over 2000m.

Wildlife

The Rif's climate and proximity to Europe endow it with a Mediterranean vibe – the area closely resembles the sierras of southern Spain. Cedars make up a good chunk of the trees, including the rare endemic species *Abies maroccana,* a high-altitude variant of the Spanish cedar. In addition, cork oak, holm pine, wild olive, juniper and carob dot the limestone mountains. The land is thin in nutrients; deforestation is an issue here

TREK AT A GLANCE

Duration Two or four days

Distance 28km or 46km

Difficulty Moderate

Start Chefchaouen

Finish Akchour

Highest Point Sfiha Telj Pass (approximately 1700m)

Accommodation *Gîtes* and camping

Public Transport Grands taxis

Summary The walking here is relatively undemanding but the mountain scenery is spectacular, the tiny Riffian villages worth a detour, and the gorges and weird geology fascinating.

as in other parts of Morocco. Various herbs such as lavender and thyme thrive and are used by the local population for medicine.

Locals may tell you that there are wolves in the mountains, but it's a mistranslation – there are foxes. Wild boars are also native, but have a retiring nature that makes them hard to spot. The Rif's most famous mammals are the Barbary apes (known locally as *mgou*), whose range extends south into the Middle Atlas. Unfortunately, the apes are rarely seen.

You may have better luck with birdlife, though spotting them is also increasingly difficult. Look for raptors wheeling on thermals, including black-shouldered kites, golden eagles and long-legged buzzards. Ravens can sometimes be seen against the limestone cliffs.

Scorpions present a small risk in the Rif, although less so than further south. Be wary of the red scorpion; stings are extremely painful. The venomous *fer à cheval* viper (named for the horseshoe-like mark on its head) is more likely to flee from you than vice versa.

Day 1: Chefchaouen to Afeska

Duration 5½ to 6½ hours

Distance 16.6km

Ascent 990m

Descent 630m

An early-morning start is recommended for the first and most challenging day. Begin on the 4WD track behind Camping Azilane (p285), where a steep ascent climbs through trees to give great views over Chefchaouen's medina. Skirting the southern slopes of **Jebel El Kelaâ** (1616m), the track evens out to follow the stream passing through the hamlet of **Aïn Tissimlane**, before once again rising in an arc to a high pass by the jagged limestone crags of **Sfiha Telj**.

The views here are astounding in both directions, and on a clear day you can see the Mediterranean in the distance. The climb is a killer with a full pack – the hardest of the trek – which explains the necessity for a cool early-morning start.

The track turns east before descending. Stopping regularly to enjoy the fine views, take the right (southern) fork where the track splits – this takes you down in an hour or so to the village of **Azilane**, where there's a *gîte*. If you want to continue a little longer, continue for another hour along a mostly level path to **Afeska**.

English-speaking Shaima provides a warm welcome at **Gîte Afeska** (☎0666212188; Afeska; per person Dh300). Beds are rock hard and the large 31-bed guesthouse can get freezing cold, but the pleasant sunroom provides a warm respite. Breakfast and dinners (included) are scrumptious and Shaina will pack you a lunch to take with you. Vegetarian meals are available on request. There's no wi-fi on the premises and cell reception is unlikely.

Day 2: Afeska to Akchour

Duration 3½ to 4½ hours

Distance 11.7km

Ascent 137m

Descent 850m

From Afeska, the wide *piste* you've been following deteriorates to a smaller track. Heading north, you pass through more oak and pine woods to **Sidi Meftah**, where there's a mausoleum of a *marabout* (saint) and spring, before leaving the woods. Go straight through the valley and ignore the path as it turns left, instead going straight down the hill to the switchbacks that lead to **Imizzar** on the **Oued Farda**.

Once beside the river, turn left (away from the village, northwest), then cross the river below some impressive overhanging cliffs and continue heading northwest. You'll join a well-worn mule track that eventually leads down to **Pont Farda**, an ancient bridge over Oued Farda.

Cross to the west bank of the river and continue north, dwarfed by the surrounding scenery. After an hour, the trail bears left away from the river towards **Ouslaf**, which is overshadowed by a giant rock buttress, but keep on the same path while it bears right, descending to rejoin the river on the outskirts of **Akchour** (398m), which sits on the **Oued Kelaâ**.

Akchour is strung out along the river. As you approach it, you first come to a small cafe with very welcome river-cooled soft drinks, and a dam with a deep pool that seems made for swimming (although the water temperature means short dips only!).

Akchour has a simple *gîte* and the exquisite ecolodge L'Ermitage (p291).

From Akchour, it's easy to get a *grand taxi* (Dh25 per seat) to Chefchaouen along the freshly paved mountain road.

RETURN TO CHEFCHAOUEN

It's possible to trek back to Chefchaouen from Akchour in a day by an alternate route. The route goes via the villages of **Ouslaf**, **Arhermane** and **El Kelaâ**. El Kelaâ is the site of the fascinating **Mosquée Srifi-yenne**, with its strange leaning tower. This route takes six to seven hours and avoids any major climbs or descents.

Chefchaouen to Akchour Trek

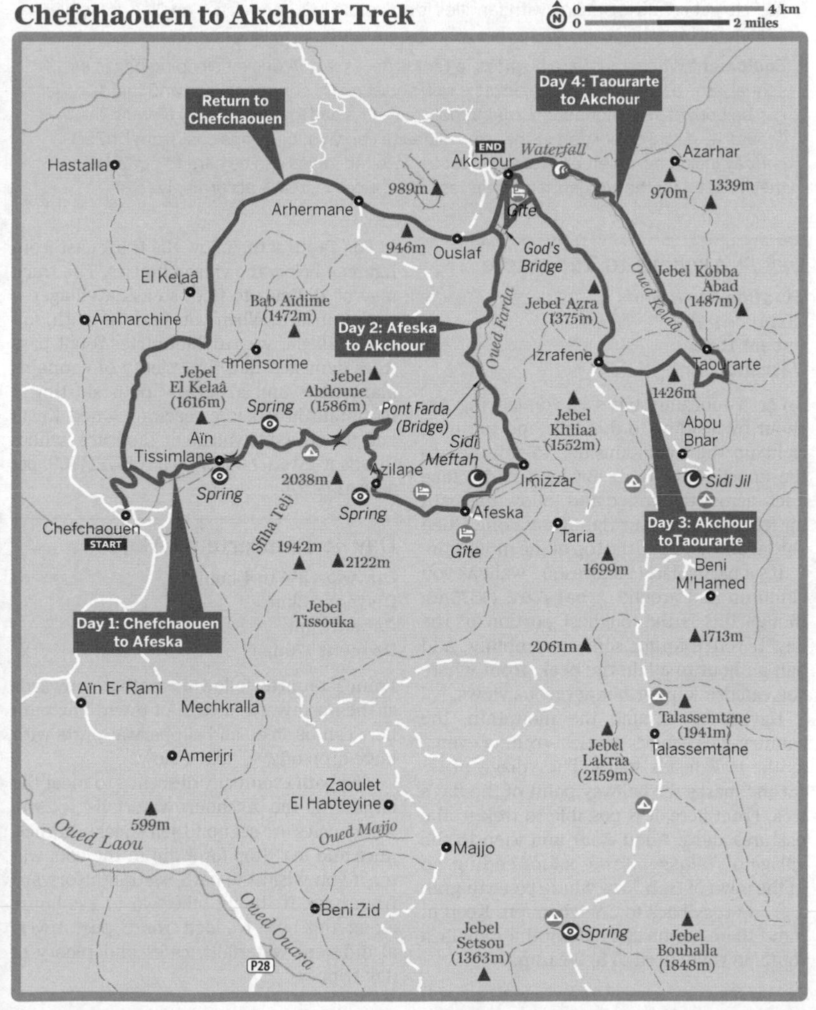

BEFORE YOU GO: CHEFCHAOUEN TO AKCHOUR CHECKLIST

Weather Trekking is possible year-round, though it can be bitterly cold with snow between November and March. There's frequent rain between late September and June. It's fiercely hot in summer, when some water sources dry up.

Guides It can be tough to find a guide to do this particular trek. If you do want one, guides charge Dh400 to Dh500 per day. Chaouen Rural (p283) does a similar trek from Chefchaouen to Afeska, Afeska to Taourarte, and finally from Taourarte to Akchour passing by the waterfalls.

Accommodation Many villages have simple *gîtes* that cost from Dh250 per person including dinner and breakfast. It's also possible to arrange *gîtes* in person during the trek, though there is a risk that the guardian may not be around and the accommodation may be closed – not uncommon.

Camping is not encouraged as local people don't benefit. But in some areas there are no *gîtes*, so it's the only alternative. There are no official campsites en route, so you'll need to get creative. Staying with families is an option in some villages and it is possible to stop for tea with locals and to visit weaving and cheese-making cooperatives.

Equipment Where there are no *gîtes*, a tent is necessary. A decent sleeping bag is essential, as is a light waterproof jacket – rain showers are common. Food and fuel supplies can be bought in Chefchaouen. Hiking poles aren't a bad idea, especially if doing the Taourarte–Akchour portion of the trek. Mules to carry your luggage cost from Dh250 per day including muleteer. From August to October, mules can be hard to organise as they're used for the *kif* (cannabis) harvest, and prices increase accordingly.

Day 3: Akchour to Taourarte

Duration 5 to 6 hours
Distance 9.7km
Ascent 1122m
Descent 381m

An early-morning start sees you leaving Akchour by heading to the dam and taking a right up the mountainside, 45 minutes to the unbelievable God's Bridge (p291). Take a left across the bridge and follow the path up Jebel Azra on your right (not along Oued Farda) and zigzag to the top of the mountain.

It's a particularly picturesque walk as you climb up and around **Jebel Azra** (1375m), though this is the toughest portion of the day. If you're up for some scrambling, add half an hour to attain the peak, from where you can drink in further gorgeous views.

Having cut around the mountain, the countryside becomes gentler – rolling even – as the trail heads south. The village of **Izrafene** marks the halfway point of the day's trek. From here, it is possible to trek to the pastures above **Abou Bnar** and then to the village of **Talassemtane** before ending up in the town of **Bab Taza** where you can grab a *grand taxi* back to Chefchaouen. Keep in mind there are no *gîtes* along the Bab Taza route, so you'll need to free-camp.

For **Taourarte**, follow the track east from Izrafene below the village houses. The track may be difficult to find, so ask a villager if you're unsure. When you find the path, follow it all the way to Taourarte. You'll pass trees damaged in a fire, plenty of cannabis plantations and a narrow path skirting a mountain just before reaching Oued Kelaâ and the riverside village of Taourarte where there's a **gîte** (☎0666758712, 0677214909; per person Dh250).

Day 4: Taourarte to Akchour

Duration 3½ to 4 hours
Distance 8km
Ascent 79m
Descent 770m

From Taourarte, follow the path downwards at the northwestern edge of town. The path here can be steep and slippery at parts with huge drop-offs, so take it slow.

The path eventually descends to meet the largest of the Akchour waterfalls (p290), where cafes are set up to sell snacks, tajines, juice and tea. Stop for a dip in the cool water if you wish; the path is straightforward from here. It should take two to 2½ hours along this well-trodden route past several different waterfalls, cafes and plenty of day-trippers.

You'll end up back in Akchour, where you can either stay the night or head back to Chefchaouen via *grand taxi*. Or you can take the hike back to the blue city through the villages of Ouslaf, Arhermane and El Kelaâ.

MID MEDITERREANEAN COAST

Oued Laou واد لاو

0539 / POP 10,090

A sleepy fishing town for 10 months of the year, Oued Laou *(wed-low)* explodes with sun seekers (mostly Moroccan) in July and August. Freshly constructed bungalows and a few budget hotels accommodate the summer swarms, while a new boardwalk is great for meandering and shopping for a Riffian *djellaba* or a tajine pot. In addition to the rays and friendly beach vibe, many come for the 'Rif-er', as the town is known as a cannabis export hub.

Three buses a day connect Tetouan and Oued Laou (Dh7, two hours). Coming from Tetouan, the Rocade N16 hugs the dramatic coastline for 140km all the way to El Jebha.

Grands taxis run from beside the mosque in Oued Laou to Tetouan (Dh20, one hour) or Chefchaouen (Dh30, one hour). The only way to get to El Jebha or Al Hoceima out of season is via private taxi, but be prepared to pay an obscene Dh500 per carload.

Sleeping & Eating

Seafood is the order of the day here, with corniche restaurants serving up fish fresh (mainly sardines) from the boat, along with the usual selection of tajines.

Hotel Oued Laou GUESTHOUSE €
(0606375929; Blvd Massira; s/d with shared bathroom Dh150/200, d Dh250) Just off the boardwalk, this welcoming hotel (and restaurant in summer) does the trick. Pink hallways lit by Riffian fabric lanterns lead you into each room, which the manager admits are just 'normal'. Lack of frills aside, the manager is extremely hospitable, making this place a worthwhile stay for a night or two in Oued Laou.

Aramar SEAFOOD €
(0622142862; Corniche; mains from Dh30; 6am-11pm) The best of the fish restaurants along the corniche, the Aramar does a tasty platter of *poisson friture* (fried fish) for Dh85. With little to do in Oued Laou, there are far worse ways to spend an afternoon.

Al Hoceima الحسيمة

0539 / POP 55,530

Cream-white buildings overlook the Mediterranean in bustling Al Hoceima *(al ho-see-muh)*. It's easy to spend a day or two here eating fresh fish, soaking in some rays and exploring nearby Al Hoceima National Park.

Founded by the Spanish as Villa Sanjuro, the town was built as a garrison after the Rif Wars in the early 20th century; rebel Abd Al Krim operated nearby. Independence brought the name change to Al Hoceima, but Spanish influence remains strong in language, architecture and business.

In recent years, the city has gone through major renovations, especially on Place Mohammed VI, a wide fountain-lined plaza, and along a sweeping corniche following the coast. Sadly, most of the budget accommodation hasn't kept up; you may need to spend more than you'd like for a decent stay.

Plage Quemado BEACH
Located in a pretty, steep-sided bay, the yellow sand beach below the Mercure Quemado Resort (p297) is a popular hang-out spot in the summer for taking a dip and gawking at the adjacent rock face, which is topped with white city buildings. Pedalos are available to hire in season.

Souq MARKET
(8am-6pm) Stock up on produce, spices, dates and other snacks at Al Hoceima's bustling street market. Fish is freshest in the mornings.

Port PORT
The port is mainly used for a large commercial fishing operation. It's a great place to watch the catch being unloaded, and to find dinner: vendors line up with fresh fish; have your selection grilled at the Club Nautique (p298).

Rif Croisiéres BOATING
(0641599894; www.rifcroisieres.com; 1½hr tour Dh150) The only company to offer boat trips along the coast of the national park, with some great seabird watching, including ospreys if you're lucky. Tours leave from Al Hoceima port as long as the weather is nice enough to sail. Groups of four minimum.

Al Hoceima

Al Hoceima

Sights

1 Plage Quemado D2

Sleeping

2 Hotel Al Khouzama B3
3 Hotel Rif B4
4 Hotel Villa Florido C4
5 Mercure Quemado Resort D1
6 Suites Hotel Mohammed V C1

Eating

7 Basilic B1
8 Boulangerie Patisserie Azir B3
9 Café La Belle Vue B2
10 Espace Miramar C3
11 La Dolce Pizza C3

Drinking & Nightlife

Mercure Quemado Resort .... (see 5)
Suites Hotel Mohammed V .... (see 6)

Shopping

12 Souq C4

South of Al Hoceima

In summer, good options are the three beaches that begin 5km south of town. During the low season they tend to be strewn with rubbish.

Cala Bonita BEACH

Because of its location south of town, Cala Bonita pebble beach manages to avoid some of the crowds, though there are still plenty of umbrellas during summer. The beach is flanked by a cafe, restaurant and a scuba diving club.

A *grand taxi* here should cost about Dh50. Buses leave from beside the Mobil petrol station at the south end of Blvd Mohammed V, stopping on the road (Dh5).

Plage Isri BEACH

This 100m-long grey-sand beach is a good option for soaking in some rays outside of the city bustle. A few food shacks along the beach serve fresh catch during the summer months. It's 5km south of town.

El Peñón de Alhucemas FORT

One of the *plazas de soberanía* (places of sovereignty), this extraordinary white island fortress can be seen a few hundred metres off Plage Sfiha, along with the uninhabited Isla de Mar and Isla de Tierra, which fly the Spanish flag. Spanish rule dates back to 1559, when the Saadi dynasty gave it to Spain in exchange for military assistance. In 1673 the Spanish military established a garrison there and never left.

Today the fort hosts several dozen soldiers and cannot be visited. Spanish sovereignty has been contested by Morocco since independence in 1956.

Plage Sfiha BEACH

A short retreat from the city, wide horseshoe-shaped Plage Sfiha looks out on the Spanish-controlled post-colonial relic, El Peñon de Alhucemas. A couple of other Spanish islands are also visible to the west. The beach is well maintained and lined with umbrella seating and restaurants in summer. Pedalos and jet skis are available for hire.

A private cab here should cost about Dh60. Buses to Ajdir, near Plage Sfiha, leave from beside the Mobil petrol station at the south end of Blvd Mohammed V (Dh7).

Sleeping

Accommodation is in high demand in the summer – book ahead. The streets between Place du Rif and the souq (p295) are packed with cheap, characterless hotels. Most are pretty dingy, so look around before committing.

Hotel Villa Florido HOTEL €

(0539840847; www.florido.alhoceima.com; Place du Rif; s/d/tr Dh350/400/600; wi-fi) This curvaceous art-deco hotel dating from 1920, an island in the Place du Rif, has some nice period charm. Rooms come in different sizes – the triples are huge – and have bathrooms and satellite TV, and most have a balcony. There's a smart cafe downstairs (breakfasts from Dh20). All rooms face the streets, which can be noisy at night.

Hotel Rif HOTEL €

(0539982268; 13 Rue Sultan Moulay Youssef; s/d with shared bathroom Dh60/120, with shower Dh100/150) If your budget is really maxed out, you'll end up in this long hallway lined with simple rooms, which are basic but reasonable for the price tag. In some rooms you get a sink, but bathrooms (squat toilets) are shared. For a handful of extra dirhams you can get a room with a shower.

Hotel Al Khouzama HOTEL €€

(Lavender Hotel; 0539985669; Rue Al Andalous; s/d/tr/q Dh378/496/605/714; wi-fi) Just off Blvd Mohammed V, this rather bland two-star hotel remains popular with business travellers and stands out as one of the best accommodations in the city. The rooms are spacious (though those facing away from the street are a bit dark), and all come with bathrooms and satellite TV. The guys at reception are friendly and helpful.

★Casa Paca B&B €€€

(0673867501, 0539802732; www.casapacamarruecos.com; Plage Sfiha; d/tr/ste Dh750/1050/1530) Approximately 8km south of Al Hoceima overlooking Plage Sfiha and El Peñon de Alhucemas, Casa Paca feels like a home away from home. Half-Spanish, half-Moroccan owner Joaquin and his wife Nabila make delicious dinners on demand (from Dh200) and bready breakfasts on the terrace. Rooms are comfortable, though pricey. In a city dominated by characterless hotels, this B&B is an excellent option.

Free pick-up and drop-off in Al Hoceima is available.

Mercure Quemado Resort RESORT €€€

(0539842200; www.mercure.com; 1 Ave Ibn Tachfine; s/d Dh1515/1640; P wi-fi pool) This holiday-business hotel has been plonked down on Plage Quemado like a cruise ship washed ashore. Rooms are spacious, comfy and well maintained. There's a restaurant with buffet and à la carte options, and a bar where you can have a drink overlooking Plage Quemado. This luxury hotel also features a nightclub, spa and fitness centre.

Suites Hotel Mohammed V HOTEL €€€

(0539982233; Place Mohammed VI; s/d Dh800/950; P wi-fi) A modern but characterless choice. Rooms are spacious and comfortable, with balconies giving truly grand views over the bay, though service is a little lackadaisical. There's a restaurant, a bar and a gym, but no swimming pool.

La Perla HOTEL €€€

(0539984513; Ave Tariq Ibn Zaid; s/d Dh700/850; wi-fi) This modern mirrored-glass high-rise business hotel has recently been upgraded

HIRAK RIF

Tensions flared in Al Hoceima in 2016 and 2017, when the city was the epicentre for Hirak Rif (the Rif Movement). Amazigh (Berber) protesters took to the streets following the death of Mohcine Fikri, a fishmonger who was crushed in a garbage truck after authorities threw out his catch. Protesters demanded an inquiry into Fikri's death, along with better treatment and services, including the construction of a regional cancer hospital. The government refused and initiated a crackdown that led to the arrest of more than 150 activists, including leader Nasser Zefzafi who was sentenced to 20 years in a Casablanca jail.

and comes with comfortable rooms that feature satellite TV and large bathrooms. The location on a busy corner makes it quite noisy if you have rooms on the lower levels. There's a cafe on the ground floor with good breakfasts, and a restaurant upstairs.

Eating & Drinking

Cheap restaurants cluster around Place du Rif, serving up filling tajines, *brochettes* and a bit of seafood from about Dh25 per head. There are also many snack shops around town.

Perhaps it's the seaside holiday air, but Al Hoceima has more good options for having a drink than you might otherwise expect for a town of its size, including several places where you can sit outside.

★Club Nautique SEAFOOD €
(☎0539981461; Gate 2, Port d'Al Hoceima; mains from Dh60; ⊙noon-11pm) This is the main restaurant at the port, and a good one. After 6pm you can buy your fish fresh off the boat and have them grill it for you (alternatively, order straight from the menu). The 2nd floor overlooks the whole port and is a great place to relax and have a beer in the fresh air.

Espace Miramar FAST FOOD €
(☎0531984242; Rue Moulay Ismail; mains from Dh30; ⊙7am-2am) It's hard to go wrong at this 5000 sq m complex with a pizzeria, two cafes, a grill restaurant as well as a children's playground, all perched on the cliffs overlooking the sea, and with occasional live music as well. Moroccan takes on paella are on offer here. It's a series of open-air terraces, so be careful not to get lost.

Café La Belle Vue CAFE €
(131 Blvd Mohammed V; breakfast Dh20; ⊙7am-11pm; 📶) This modern cafe-restaurant gets its name from the terrace at the back overlooking the bay – it really does offer a splendid view. Great for breakfast, coffee, and to take advantage of the wi-fi. There are several similar cafes on this stretch of Mohammed V with great views.

Boulangerie Patisserie Azir PASTRIES €
(☎0531177142; 14 Rue Yousef Ben Tachfine; pastries from Dh4; ⊙5am-8.30pm) This freshly renovated patisserie is the town favourite, with great home-baked bread and tons of different sweets.

La Dolce Pizza ITALIAN €
(☎0531984752; Place du Rif; pizzas Dh35-60; ⊙11am-10pm) The terrace at this cute Italian bistro thrust out into the chaos of Place du Rif is a great place to people watch and have some pizza, shawarma or salad. Service is appallingly slow, menu items are rarely all available and the pizza crust is certainly atypical, but it remains a worthwhile place to grab a non-tajine meal.

Basilic INTERNATIONAL €€
(☎0539980083; 131 Ave Abdelkrim El Khattabi; mains Dh35-90; ⊙7am-midnight) The huge glass-fronted restaurant at the entrance of the Basilic Hotel has a suitably huge menu, which includes 20 different kinds of breakfast, seafood, stir-fries, pizza, pastries, juice cocktails and even cordon bleu. The food tends to be pretty tasty.

Mercure Quemado Resort BAR
(☎0539842200; ⊙4pm-1am) The bar of the Mercure hotel is open to nonguests. It's not the cheapest place to have a drink in Al Hoceima, but it may be the nicest, with a deck overlooking the beach.

Club Nautique BAR
(Gate 2, Port d'Al Hoceima; ⊙noon-11pm) Breathe in the fresh salty sea air with a Moroccan beer atop the Club Nautique fish restaurant. The bar here usually attracts quite a crowd, especially when football is on one of the televisions.

Suites Hotel Mohammed V BAR
(Place Mohammed VI; ⊙10am-11.30pm) The bar is a bit dingy, but the terrace has excellent views over Plage Quemado.

Information

Délégation Provinciale de Tourisme (0539981185; Zanqat Al Hamra, Cala Bonita; 8.30am-4.30pm Mon-Fri) One of the friendliest tourist offices in the region; staff here have good local knowledge and information about boat trips and Al Hoceima National Park.

Getting There & Away

AIR

The small Cherif Al Idrissi Airport, located 12km from town (Dh175 by taxi), has flights to Tangier, Tetouan and Casablanca on Royal Air Maroc. It also serves TUI flights to Brussels and Transavia flights to Rotterdam. The Nador airport 150km east has a wider range of options.

BOAT

Armas (www.navieraarmas.com) offers summer ferries to Motril in Spain. The trip takes about five hours and starts at €33 for a one-way ticket.

BUS

All the bus companies have offices around Place du Rif, including CTM, but all depart from the bus station on the southern edge of town. In summer CTM runs services to **Chefchaouen** (Dh90, 5½ hours, daily) and **Nador** (Dh50, three hours, two daily).

Year-round, CTM has the following departures.

Casablanca Dh200, 10 hours, two daily, via Taza (Dh70, four hours)

Fez Dh125, six hours, two daily

Meknes Dh130, seven hours, two daily

Rabat Dh170, eight hours, two daily

Tangier Dh140, 7½ hours, daily

Tetouan Dh115, seven hours, three daily, via Chefchaouen (Dh90, 5½ hours)

Several small companies also serve the aforementioned destinations. There are at least three buses a day to Tetouan and Tangier (Dh90, 7½ hours). Heading east, there are also a couple of buses a day to Nador (Dh40, 2½ hours) and Oujda (Dh70, five hours).

TAXI

Grands taxis can be found at the bus station. The most popular destinations are Taza (Dh70, 2½ hours) and Nador (Dh60, two hours). For Melilla, change at Nador for the border at Beni Ansar.

Al Hoceima National Park

المنتزه الوطني للحسيمة

Al Hoceima National Park is a seemingly undiscovered stretch of land featuring steep cliffs, Spanish-controlled isles and untouched beaches – perfect for trekking, mountain biking or zipping through the main thoroughfares on a motorbike. The park extends to 485 sq km (including 190 sq km at sea) and is dotted with 37 *douars* (Amazigh settlements) where locals maintain a traditional life. Female cooperatives produce basketwork, essential oils, pottery, weaving and prickly-pear jam procured from local cacti. Because of its isolation, the park has helped preserve several at-risk species, from its thuja forests to an important colony of osprey. If you like your exploration peaceful and your seaside walks uninterrupted, there are few better places to roam.

Little, if anything, is officially organised in the park. There are several well-paved roads, but if you want to go deep you'll need a 4WD. Hiking is the most popular activity, though some opt to explore via mountain bike. A map is available from the tourist bureau in Al Hoceima.

Without your own transport, you'll need to hire a *grand taxi* in Al Hoceima to get to Cala Iris or the park entrance at Beni Boufrah. If there aren't enough people to share with, you may have better luck going to Rouadi and grabbing a taxi from there. Otherwise, expect to pay Dh150 one-way to the park entrance and Dh210 to Cala Iris.

Central Rif Region

Most of the people living in the park are Bokkoya Berbers who live in rural communities centred on fresh water supplies. The women have good knowledge of the medicinal use of local herbs such as the abundant lavender and thyme.

A number of rare trees can be found here, such as wild carob and the endangered thuja, highly prized for its wood. Other plants include wild olive, ilex, pomegranate, ericas, bulbs and orchids. Animals include jackals, wild boar, rabbits and hares.

Coastal Region

This area of the park extends out to sea and is rich in biodiversity. There are 86 species of fish and three types of dolphin. Many species represented here are rare elsewhere in the Mediterranean, such as red coral, various molluscs and algae. Among the 165 bird species, there is a considerable population of osprey *(Pandion haliaetus)*.

There are several remote and scenic beaches, of which the highlight is the fantastic sight of **El Peñón de Vélez de la**

Gomera, one of Spain's *plazas de soberanía* (places of sovereignty).

The park has one *gîte* open year-round and a camping area in Cala Iris. Otherwise, you'll need to drive to Al Hoceima or El Jebha.

Youssef, the owner of cheery **Gîte Jnanate** (☎0666754530; gitejnanate@gmail.com; per person Dh200; 📶) guesthouse in a tiny Amazigh town, is passionate about the park and his guests. The rooms are simple, but the open-air courtyard is bright with Moroccan decorations and birds swoop in past the plants to perch on the light fixtures. Breakfast and dinner, both included, are tasty and have a homemade touch.

Cala Iris & Torres de Alcala كلا ايريس وطوريس القلعة

Cala Iris *(ka-la ir-ees)* is a small fishing port at the western tip of Al Hoceima National Park that floods with tourists when the weather's right (June through September). There's little tourist infrastructure here, save for one restaurant and a campsite. The main attraction is the untrammelled nature, particularly the attractive beaches. East of the port is Isla Cala Iris, a Spanish-owned island that locals walk out to and go fishing when the tide is low enough, although it's not technically legal.

A 10-minute drive or hour-long hike to the east is Torres de Alcala *(toh-res deh-al-ka-la)*, where three semiruined fortifications built in the 16th century stand sentinel over a scruffy village, set back from a shingle beach caught between two rocky headlands.

Shared *grands taxis* to Cala Iris from Al Hoceima cost Dh35 or Dh210 if private.

In Cala Iris there's a **campsite** (☎0539843797; www.amisdecalairis.com; tent/car/lodge/chalet Dh80/85/200/350; 📶) offering breakfast and snacks, and a *gîte* in the park (which has dinner and breakfast). There is also a nameless restaurant behind the Cooperative des Marins Pecheurs that serves fresh seafood, salads and fries.

EAST MEDITERRANEAN COAST

The east Mediterranean coast takes in Nador, the seaside town of Saïdia and the Spanish enclave of Melilla as well as the inland city of Oujda and the Beni-Snassen Mountains.

Melilla مليلية

☎0952 / POP 86,380

Along with Ceuta, Melilla *(meh-lee-yuh,* Arabic: *meh-lee-luh)* is one of two autonomous Spanish cities on the Moroccan coast. The exclave is full of surprises, with a perfectly preserved medieval fortress, magnificent modernist architecture and a wealth of tapas bars – it's a great place to spend the weekend.

At the turn of the 20th century, Melilla was the only centre of trade between Tetouan and the Algerian border. As the city grew, it expressed itself in Modernisme, the architectural style often attributed to Antoni Gaudí, but spearheaded here by Don Enrique Nieto. The result is a living museum of hundreds of striking modernist and art deco buildings.

Many travel here on their way in and out of Morocco via Melilla's airport and ship terminal. Others come out of desperation, namely migrants attempting to reach Europe. Spain has constructed one of the world's most fortified borders to keep the latter group out.

History

Melilla oozes with history. The area has been inhabited for more than 2000 years, but the old city wasn't begun until after Spanish colonial conquest in 1496, then built up in four stages. Up until the end of the 19th century, virtually all of Melilla was contained within a single impregnable fortress. Current borders were fixed by several treaties with Morocco between 1859 and 1894, the last following an unsuccessful siege by Rif Amazigh. The method involved shooting a cannonball and seeing how far it went. More fighting with Amazigh broke out several times in the ensuing years until the Spanish protectorate consolidated its grip in 1927. In 1936 Franco flew here from the Canary Islands to launch the Spanish Civil War. Local politics still tip to the right.

Sights

Melilla La Vieja

Spain's continued presence in Africa is apparent in the well-fortified fortress at the tip of the continent, perhaps better kept today than in centuries past. Wandering its alleyways and plazas is a throwback to medieval

MODERNISME & DON ENRIQUE NIETO

Like many of the movements from which it drew its inspiration (eg the English Arts & Crafts movement), Modernisme was a broad reaction to the material values of an industrial age, which suffused culture with a machinelike spirit. Centred in Barcelona, it was the Catalan version of art nouveau. Modernisme architecture is characterised by the use of curves over straight lines, the frequent use of natural motifs (especially plants), lively decoration and rich detail, asymmetrical forms, a refined aesthetic and dynamism. Its chief proponent was Antoni Gaudí, the architect of Barcelona's famous Sagrada Família cathedral. But in Melilla, Modernisme is synonymous with Don Enrique Nieto.

A student of Antoni Gaudí, Nieto worked on his Casa Milà in Barcelona. Wanting to escape his master's shadow, however, he left for booming Melilla in 1909 and stayed the rest of his life, becoming city architect in 1931. His work included Melilla's main synagogue, the main mosque and several buildings for the Catholic Church, representing the diversity of the city's culture. Perhaps due to the distant location of his canvas, however, this great painter in concrete is not well known outside of Melilla.

times and there's plenty to do, with free museums around every bend and spectacular views over the Mediterranean.

Melilla La Vieja is divided into four precincts, the fourth of which contains the fort Las Victorias, where the cannon fired the shot that set the current boundary of Melilla. This is a prime example of the fortress strongholds that the Spaniards built along the Moroccan littoral during the 16th and 17th centuries, and much of it has been painstakingly restored in recent years. The main entrance is **Puerta de la Marina** (Calle General Macías), from where you ascend to the summit, passing several small museums.

At the northern tip of the fortress is the **Museo Militar** (☎0952685587; 5 Calle Concepión, Melilla La Vieja; ⊙10am-2pm Tue-Sun) FREE, an ode to the city's military campaigns. But the rock that propped up a base for Phoenicians and Romans and later the Spaniards is only the tip of the iceberg. Las Cuevas del Conventico, a three-level network of caves below the fortress, helped Melilla's citizens survive Arab attacks. Above the caves is the 17th-century **Iglesia de la Purísima Concepción** (Parish of the Immaculate Conception; ☎0952681516). Nearby Casa Ibáñez Museum de Arte Contemporáneo has the best collection of Spanish art you'll find in town. And Museo De Historia, Arqueología y Etnográfico delivers fascinating exhibits on Melilla's four distinct cultures: Spanish Catholics, Amazigh (Berber) Muslims, Sephardi Jews and Gitana (Roma).

Cuevas del Conventico HISTORIC BUILDING
(Caves of the Convent; ☎0952680929; Calle Miguel Acosta; ⊙10.30am-2pm & 5-9pm Tue-Sat, 10.30am-2pm Sun Jun-Sep, shorter hours Oct-May) FREE These extensive and well-restored caves were used for storage as well as a refuge during sieges, and pop out at a small beach below the cliffs. The Phoenicians first excavated the tunnels; later occupiers took turns enlarging them and they now extend over three levels. They are meticulously maintained and well lit, which sadly eliminates much of their mystery.

A short film and guided tour (both in Spanish) detail the history of the caves and tunnels that lead to the cliff face. Guided tours run six times daily, three times on Sunday.

Casa Ibáñez Museum De Arte Contemporáneo MUSEUM
(Ibáñez Contemporary Art Museum; ☎0952699232; Plaza de Estopiñán; ⊙10am-2pm & 5-9pm Tue-Sat, 10am-2pm Sun Oct-May, shorter hours Jun-Sep) FREE Melilla's best gallery can be found inside Torre de la Vela, an 18th-century building within the fortress walls. It's worth wandering the six showrooms through the permanent collection of modern and contemporary paintings, sculptures, engravings and a striking documentary photo exhibit. The museum is named after Almería artist Andrés García Ibáñez, who donated much of his work to the city.

Museo de Historia, Arqueología y Etnográfico MUSEUM
(Almacenes de la Peñuelas; ☎0952976572; Plaza de los Aljibes; ⊙10am-2pm & 5-9pm Tue-Sat, 10am-2pm Sun Jun-Sep, shorter hours Oct-May) FREE The fortress' warehouses are now home to two fascinating museums; one

Melilla

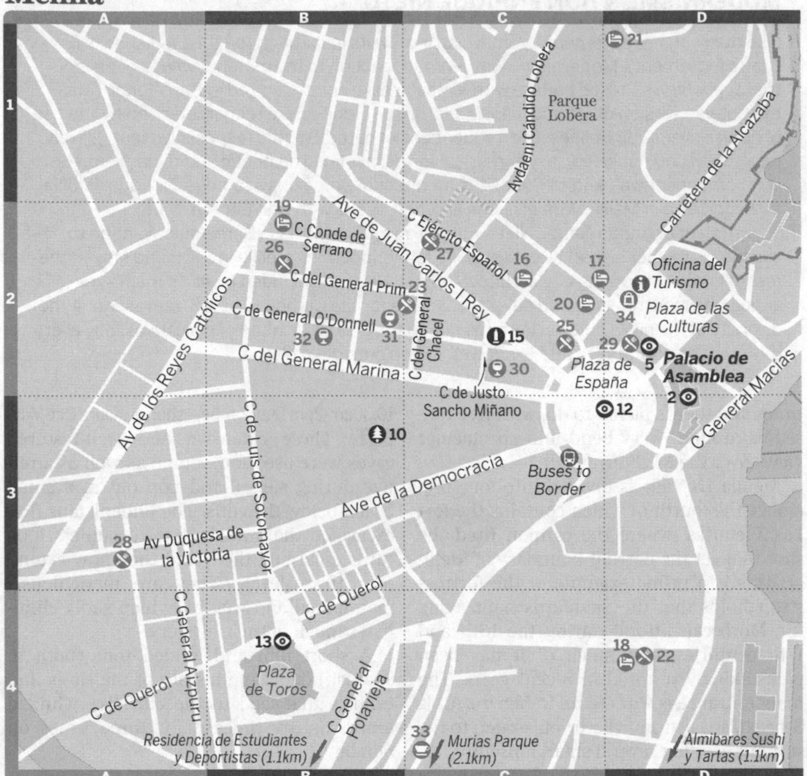

dedicated to the history of the Amazigh (Berber), Sephardic (Jewish) and Gitana (Roma) cultures in Melilla (lower floor), the other tracing the history of prehistoric Melilla to today (top level). The Amazigh exhibit is particularly interesting and is the most thorough anywhere in the region. The Gitana exhibit is the first of its kind in Spain. All signage is in Spanish.

Aljibes de las Peñuelas HISTORIC BUILDING
(Plaza de los Aljibes; 10am-2pm & 5-9pm Tue-Sat, 10am-2pm Sun Jun-Sep, shorter hours Oct-May) FREE Two of the four tiny doors across the courtyard lead into the cavelike, other-worldly cisterns, which once stored as much as 1000 cubic metres of water for the fortress. All that water left Los Aljibes thick with green moss, but Melilla's impeccable restoration effort has the tanks looking stone dry. Don't look down if you're squeamish about heights.

New Town

Construction of the new part of town, west of the fortress, began at the end of the 19th century. Laid out by Gaudí disciple Don Enrique Nieto, Melilla is considered by some to be Spain's 'second modernist city', after Barcelona.

The best way to appreciate this heritage is to stroll through the area to the north of Parque Hernández; it's known as the golden triangle.

★**Palacio de Asamblea** NOTABLE BUILDING
(Plaza de España; 9am-1pm Mon-Fri) Nieto's art-deco Palacio de Asamblea, whose floor plan depicts a ducal crown, is an operating town hall, although the staff at the entrance are willing to show tourists around upon request. Worth seeing are two rooms on the upper floor: Salon Dorado, which contains a large painting of the arrival of Spaniards

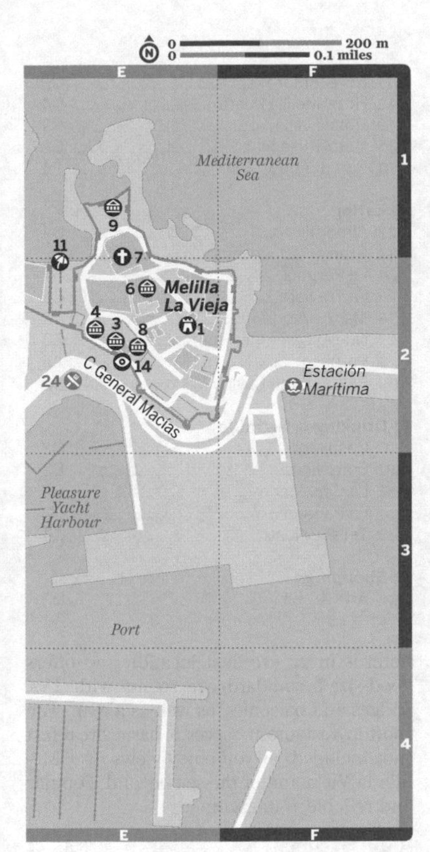

in Melilla in 1497, and the Sala de Plenos, where the local congress meets. Come nightfall, the building lights up a pretty pink.

Plaza de España LANDMARK

Plaza de España is the beating heart of Melilla, with arteries leading to the modernist new town and fortress. It's also where you can catch a bus to the border. At the centre is a central fountain and an art-deco military monument to campaigns in Morocco. Around the roundabout, you'll find Casino Militar, Palacio de Asamblea and Banco de España.

In the distance towards the sea you can spot Melilla's most striking contemporary building, the new **courthouse**, which looks like a flying saucer landed on the roof (closed to visitors).

Casino Militar NOTABLE BUILDING

(Plaza de España; 8am-10pm) The magnificent two-storey building lining Plaza de España holds free temporary art exhibitions in rooms extending from its Enrique Nieto-designed hall. The facade still portrays the Republican coat of arms and the balcony overlooking the plaza feels fit for a dictator – a reminder of how Melilla was one of the first staging grounds for the 1936 Spanish Civil War.

The corner facing Banco de España contains Restaurante Casino Militar (p305), a popular restaurant and tapas bar that pours onto the street at lunchtime.

Parque Hernández PARK

(7am-midnight) FREE The spacious palm-lined park right at the heart of the city is perfect for lounging on a bench with a book or zigzagging through the maze of blue and white ceramic pathways, an ode to the city's modernist design. The northwest corner contains a children's playground.

Statue Grande Libre MONUMENT

(Avenida de Juan Carlos I Rey, New Town) Melilla's role in modern Spanish history isn't forgotten. The Statue Grande Libre marks 7 July 1936, when Franco began the campaign against the government in Madrid. With a soldier and lion backed by a fascist eagle, it feels like a throwback to another, uncomfortable age. Around the statue are colourful ceramic benches, which add to Melilla's Barcelona-like feel.

Plaza de Toros NOTABLE BUILDING

(952699262; 4 Maestro Ángel Pérez García; 9.30am-1.30pm & 5.30-9.30pm) FREE Africa's only active bullfighting ring is operational just once a year for Melilla's Virgen de la Victoria festival. Otherwise, the 8,000-person stadium is open for free 30-minute guided tours explaining the plaza's history and the rules of bullfighting. The tours are a fascinating reflection on a rather gruesome Spanish tradition, without having to witness any bulls die.

Playa de la Ensanada de los Galápagos BEACH

Nestled below cliffs and the towering fortress walls is the secluded beach of Playa de la Ensanada de los Galápagos, open from June to September (with lifeguards on duty), though children can be seen diving into the turquoise water year-round. Find your spot on the picturesque seashell-laden beach by entering through the tunnel across from La Pérgola (p305).

Melilla

Top Sights
1 Melilla La Vieja ... E2
2 Palacio de Asamblea ... D3

Sights
3 Aljibes de las Peñuelas ... E2
4 Casa Ibáñez Museum De Arte Contemporáneo ... E2
5 Casino Militar ... D2
6 Cuevas del Conventico ... E2
7 Iglesia de la Purísima Concepción ... E1
8 Museo de Historia, Arqueología y Etnográfico ... E2
9 Museo Militar ... E1
10 Parque Hernández ... B3
11 Playa de la Ensanada de los Galápagos ... E2
12 Plaza de España ... D3
13 Plaza de Toros ... B4
14 Puerta de la Marina ... E2
15 Statue Grande Libre ... C2

Sleeping
16 Hostal Residencia Rioja ... C2
17 Hotel Anfora ... C2
18 Hotel Melilla Puerto ... D4
19 Hotel Nacional ... B2
20 Hotel Rusadir ... C2
21 Parador de Melilla ... D1

Eating
22 Almoraima ... D4
23 Granier ... C2
24 La Pérgola ... E2
25 La Traviata ... C2
26 Mar de Alborán ... B2
27 Nuevo California ... C2
28 Parnaso ... A3
29 Restaurante Casino Militar ... D2

Drinking & Nightlife
30 Casa Marta ... C2
31 Entrevinos ... B2
32 La Cervecería ... B2
La Pérgola ... (see 24)
33 Tetería Nazarí ... C4

Shopping
34 Arte Ärabè ... D2

Sleeping

There aren't many hotels in Melilla, and the ones that are here tend to be pricey and lack charm. Airbnb isn't much better. Book ahead as everything tends to fill up, even in the quieter months.

Residencia de Estudiantes y Deportistas HOSTEL €
(Residence of Students & Athletes; ☎0952670008; Calle Alfonso X; per person €26; ❄📶) A reasonable budget choice if you don't mind being away from the town centre and like hanging out with students. There are 87 rooms, a cafeteria, a library and a TV lounge. Rooms above the 2nd floor have balconies. A bed comes with free breakfast, lunch (€33) or full board (€39). Take local bus 3, which stops near Plaza España on Calle Marina every 10 minutes, though there are fewer services on weekends. The trip takes 10 to 15 minutes.

Hostal Residencia Rioja HOSTEL €
(☎0956682709; 10 Calle Ejército Español; s/d €22/35; 📶) Don't be put off by the gloomy and uninspiring entrance. Rooms at this rock-bottom pension are a little tired but well kept. All have basins; bathrooms are shared.

Hotel Anfora HOTEL €€
(☎0952683340; www.hotelanfora.net; 12 Calle Pablo Vallescá; s/d €46/73; 📶) This three-star hotel is in an excellent location and offers good-sized, standard-fare rooms with TVs, fridges and balconies, as well as a gym. The rooftop restaurant serves a basic breakfast (not included) as you enjoy views over Melilla la Vieja and of the sea beyond. Popular and reliable, if unexciting.

Hotel Nacional HOTEL €€
(☎0952684540; 10 Calle Conde del Serrano; s/d €40/60; ❄📶) This hotel has mostly compact rooms, with minibars, quaint iron furniture and modern bathrooms. Those facing inside are a bit dark, so get one looking to the street. There's a restaurant on site.

Hotel Rusadir HOTEL €€
(☎0952681240; 5 Calle Pablo Vallescá; s/d €68/80; 📶) This four-star hotel has been completely renovated to excellent effect, including an impressive lobby and design-conscious rooms with TVs, minibars and balconies. The restaurant puts out an impressive breakfast buffet. Good value.

Hotel Melilla Puerto HOTEL €€€
(☎0952695525; tryp.melilla.puerto@melia.com; Explanada de San Lorenzo; s/d €100/€120; 📶) TRYP Melilla Puerto, part of the Melia network of hotels and resorts, is a modern and professional choice. The rooms are spacious, as are the bathrooms, which all have tubs. On the first floor, there's a gym, an ageing

cafe and Almoraima, a gourmet tapas and sushi bar. It's Melilla's classiest option and closest to the clubs and beach.

Parador de Melilla HOTEL €€€
(☎0952684940; www.parador.es; Ave Cándido Lobera; d €100;) You'll want a vehicle to get up the hill to this classy choice with large rooms, a high level of quality furnishings and balconies with great views out to sea. The circular dining room overlooking the city is an elegant touch. Breakfast is included. The adjacent Parque Lobera is great for kids.

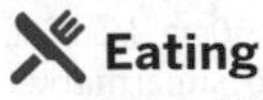

Eating

Many of Melilla's restaurants revolve around tapas, with every drink bought earning you a few bites of a delicious snack. *Raciones* (meal-sized sharable tapas) are also available. You'll find most of Melilla's eating options in the new town.

Granier BAKERY €
(7 Calle General Chacel; sandwiches from €2.50; ⌚10am-2pm & 5-10pm) This cafe and bakery with indoor and outdoor seating is good to grab a quick bite or while away an hour with a book and a coffee. The *bocadillos* are a perfect lunchtime snack, and it does some delicious fruit smoothies.

Restaurante Casino Militar SPANISH €
(☎0952848092; Pasadizo Comandante Emperador; tapas €2.20, mains from €5.50; ⌚8am-midnight;) The restaurant in the corner of Casino Militar and along the alleyway next to Banco de España is the place to be at lunchtime, especially among civil guards. The menu is Mediterranean Spanish with an emphasis on fried fish, or pick from an assortment of quality tapas. Seats outside are coveted and sometimes accompanied by live music.

Parnaso BISTRO €
(☎0952684184; 30 Avenida Duquesa de la Victoria; sandwiches from €3; ⌚7am-1am;) This bistro with outdoor seating has extremely friendly staff and tasty tapas; the spicy chorizo is a standout. For something a little more filling, the pizza is a good bet. Popular during lunch and with the after-work crowd.

Nuevo California INTERNATIONAL €
(☎0952682664; Plaza Menéndez; ⌚7am-1pm & 4-9pm Mon-Sat) This busy cafeteria with a plaza terrace offers a great breakfast, delicious hot chocolate and has friendly waiters eager to help your clumsy Spanish along. In the afternoons, *bocadillos* are best accompanied with a cold *cerveza*.

★**La Pérgola** SEAFOOD €€
(☎0952685628; Calle General Marcías; mains from €12; ⌚noon-midnight Tue-Sun) A waterfront terrace makes this classy spot adjacent to the fortress walls a very pleasant place for a meal or just a late afternoon drink. The speciality is barbecued seafood, and at €12, the *menú del día* (lunch menu) cannot be beat. There's a lively atmosphere in the evening and on Saturday afternoon.

Mar de Alborán SPANISH €€
(☎0656895827; 24 Calle General Prim; set lunch €10; ⌚1-4pm Sun-Fri) It's a challenge to find an empty chair at this jam-packed neighbourhood restaurant within Melilla's modernist golden triangle. *Menu del día* (lunch) specials include a starter, main (often fish), dessert and a beverage. The salads and paella are terrific and there's an excellent selection of fresh catch. Come hungry as there's an extra charge for sharing.

Almibares Sushi y Tartas SUSHI €€
(☎0674737493; 16 Calle Bustamante; 10 pce sushi from €10; ⌚noon-5pm & 9pm-midnight Tue-Sat, noon-5pm Sun;) A considerable walk along the corniche down the beach, this plant-filled sushi restaurant is deservedly trendy. Sushi boats are loaded with creative combinations and the cakes are a hot commodity. Reserve ahead.

Almoraima TAPAS €€
(☎0952695525; Explanada de San Lorenzo, Hotel Melilla Puerto; mains from €12; ⌚1-5pm & 8pm-midnight;) With its small plates and gourmet tapas, the sophisticated resto-bar inside Hotel Melilla Puerto is a scrumptious way to spend an afternoon or evening. The menu is creative, with intriguing takes on couscous, raviolis and stir-fry. Sushi is available Friday to Sunday. The erupting chocolate *coulant* (warm cake) with vanilla ice cream is the stuff dreams are made of.

La Traviata MEDITERRANEAN €€€
(☎0952681925; 5 Calle Ejercito Español; mains from €14; ⌚1-4pm & 9pm-midnight Mon-Sat;) When Melilla's locals have something to celebrate, they come to La Traviata, the fanciest restaurant in town. On the menu are fish caught 500 metres over the border and excellent cuts of meat from the mainland. The wine collection is impressive. Reservations are recommended on Saturdays.

Drinking & Nightlife

Tapas bars are a real treat in Melilla. Puerto Deportivo Noray is Melilla's club zone, with about a dozen different options along the waterfront. Enter through the car park next to the courthouse (the skyscraper with the flying saucer).

★Casa Marta BAR
(Calle Justo Sancho Miñano; ⌚noon-5pm & 8pm-1am) This is a great tapas bar that brims with people of all ages both inside and out: outdoor seating is under a tent in the street. Free tapas are included with drinks (from €2.50); larger plates are available from the menu.

Tetería Nazarí TEAHOUSE
(☎0660125669; 10 Calle Actor Tallaví; ⌚2pm-midnight Tue-Thu & Sun, 2pm-2am Fri & Sat; 📶) Over 100 teas fill the menu of this Moroccan-style teahouse owned by a Spaniard (try his speciality, floral mint tea). To go with your beverage, choose from sweet snacks like crêpes and Moroccan cookies or savoury dishes like hummus and falafel. The candlelight, incense and funky cushions make for a relaxing setting for hanging out in late into the night.

La Cervecería BAR
(☎0952683427; 23 Calle Gral O'Donnell; ⌚noon-4pm & 8pm-midnight; 📶) This Melilla institution has been slinging drinks and tasty tapas (€3) across its long marble bar top since 1991. The decor is an ode to the city's modernist design, with a curvaceous ceramic-laden bench as the focal point below a large marble sundial. Landing a table any night of the week is a feat.

La Pérgola CAFE
(Calle General Marcías; ⌚noon-midnight Tue-Sun; 📶) This cafe-bar on the pleasure-yacht harbour and overlooking estación marítima is an exceedingly pleasant place for a drink in the late afternoon, particularly on Saturday when its wide sunny terrace overflows with chitchatting locals.

Entrevinos BAR
(☎0951086676; 16 Calle Gral O'Donnell; ⌚noon-5pm & 8pm-midnight; 📶) Waiters rarely get a rest at this busy neighbourhood bar. Welcoming staff serve booze to the social clientele along with some of the city's best tapas (€2.50 for beer, €3 for wine). The front terrace is a great place to spend a summer afternoon sipping a glass of *vino*.

Shopping

Arte Ärabè GIFTS & SOUVENIRS
(☎0952684732; Plaza de las Culturas; ⌚9.30am-1.30pm & 5-8.30pm Mon-Fri, 9.30am-1.30pm Sat) Excellent quality (yet pricey) Moroccan gems made by artisans from Tetouan, Marrakesh and Fez are available at this boutique beside the Oficina del Turismo. The selection isn't large, but there are plenty of eye-catching lanterns, bags and cushions, as well as light shirts and dresses.

Murias Parque SHOPPING CENTRE
(☎0951452181; www.parquemelilla.es; Avenida Cuartel de Valenzuela; ⌚10am-10pm Mon-Sat, 11am-9pm Sun) Large mall and supermarket with stores not found in Morocco.

Orientation

Melilla is a semicircle of 12.3 sq km carved out of the Moroccan coastline. The old town, Melilla La Vieja (p301), is a highly complex, multilevel fortress that juts out into the sea. It contains numerous museums, as well as some small residential areas. The port and major beaches lie to the south, with the ferry terminal directly east.

The 'new town' is a broken grid of streets with an attractive commercial centre full of modernist buildings. The heart is the long triangular Parque Hernández (p303), which ends at the circular Plaza de España (p303). Most of the hotels, banks and restaurants are located to the north.

Information

MONEY

Euros are used for all transactions in Melilla. You'll find several banks (with ATMs) around Ave de Juan Carlos I Rey. Most banks will buy or sell dirham at an inferior rate to the Moroccan dealers hanging around the ferry port or the border.

On the Moroccan side of the border, there are a couple of banks where you can change cash.

TELEPHONE

To phone Melilla from outside Spain, dial ☎0034 first.

TIME

Melilla is one hour ahead of Morocco during daylight saving time. Most shops and businesses are closed on Sunday.

TOURIST INFORMATION

Oficina del Turismo (☎0952976189; www.melillaturismo.com; Plaza de las Culturas; ⌚10am-2pm & 4.30-8.30pm Mon-Sat, 10am-2pm Sun) has lots of maps and brochures and friendly, English-speaking staff. It offers special tours of religious sites on Sunday, and the website contains a comprehensive history and architectural tour.

For more history, visit www.melillamonumental.es (Spanish only).

Getting There & Around

AIR

Iberia Regional Air Nostrum (www.airnostrum.com) offers five flights a day between Melilla and Málaga, three daily flights to Madrid, two per week to Barcelona as well as five a week to Almería. Air Europa (www.aireuropa.com) has two flights a day to Málaga. The airport is a 10-minute (€7) taxi ride from town.

BUS

The centre of Melilla is compact and easy to walk around. Buses ply the route between Plaza de España and the border. Call 0952683621 for a local taxi.

FERRY

Trasmediterránea (www.trasmediterranea.es) and Balearia (www.balearia.com) sail from Melilla daily to Málaga and Almería while FRS (www.frs.es) sails six days per week to Motril. Voyages take six to eight hours and start at €35 for foot passengers.

Tickets for ferries to Spain are available online and at the **Estación Marítima** (Ferry Port).

TO & FROM MOROCCO

To get to the border from the airport, you'll need to take a taxi (€7). If in town, catch local bus 2 (marked 'Aforos'), which runs between Plaza de España and the Beni Enzar border post (€0.85, every 15 minutes from 7.30am to 9pm, every 30 minutes to 10pm). The bus drops you 50m from the Spanish border control. From here it's a 200m walk to the Moroccan border.

Before entering Morocco, fill in a white form and get your passport stamped at the booth. Touts may try to sell you a form for €1, but they're free at the booths (get one before you start queueing). If you're driving into Morocco, remember to retain the green customs slip, which you must present when you (and your vehicle) leave the country. Large queues of vehicles entering Morocco are frequent and time-consuming; procedures for foot passengers are quick and easy.

On the Moroccan side of the border, *grands taxis* (Dh6, 15 minutes) to Nador are tucked away in a car park to the right of the crossroads – a 100m walk from the border. If there are no shared taxis leaving for Nador, Vectalia (www.nador.vectalia.ma) bus 20 (Dh4) stops at the crossroads and goes to Nador's bus station (p308) eight times per day. Another option is to get a short cab ride to the Beni Enzar train station (p309) 3km from the border, which also takes you to Nador (Dh16, 18 minutes).

If all else fails, a private cab will cost about Dh80.

When entering Melilla from Morocco, fill in a white form and get your passport stamped. Some nationalities require visas to enter Spain: if they don't stop you here, they will when you try to move onto the mainland. Just make sure to get a stamp within 72 hours to avoid any hassles. Bus 2 goes to Plaza de España (€0.85) or take a taxi (€4).

Nador الناظور

0536 / POP 176,210

A metropolis at the gateway of Morocco just 10km from the Spanish border in Melilla, Nador *(nah-door)* is a coastal city with a pretty corniche by the lagoon to walk on but little else to attract visitors. Most of the hotels are overpriced and uninspired, while the restaurants are nothing special, save for a shockingly good burger joint that may as well be in New York or London.

Perhaps when the new mega development on the outskirts at Marchica is complete, Nador will be more worthwhile. Nador has few attractions, although it does make for a decent transport hub with an international airport, ferry port and a train station that has service to Fez.

Sleeping

Nador's accommodation scene is an ugly combination of high prices and lacklustre service. The very best is Mercure Rif (p308), but you'll pay for it. Cheaper places are found near the bus station, but expect squat toilets and barebones rooms.

Hotel Hassania HOTEL €

(0536605162; 4 Ave des FAR; s/d/tr Dh100/150/200;) With its cheery rooms, rock-bottom prices and convenient location just a 10-minute walk from the bus station, Hotel Hassania is a solid option in a city that's nearly devoid of decent budget accommodation. Rooms are comfortable and the bathrooms are kept clean. The cafe below serves Moroccan breakfast.

Hotel l'Aeroport HOTEL €€

(0536381722; hotelnador@gmail.com; 22 Lot Al Matar; s/d Dh400/616;) A little out of the way, this hotel will be closer to the centre of things when the surrounding developments are finished. In the meantime, it has good, clean and comfortable rooms, although they're a little tight. Breakfast is included. Ask for the swanky Café Select nearby when flagging a taxi.

Hotel Mediterranée HOTEL €€
(☎0536606495; hotel.mediterranee@gmail.com; 2-4 Ave Youssef Ibn Tachfine; s/d Dh490/650; 📶) Mediterranée is clean, pleasant and the best midrange option in the city. Corner rooms have plenty of light, and all have TVs. Views from this hotel have been annihilated by the now-abandoned construction site in front, but it's still only one block back from the corniche.

★ **Mercure Rif Nador** HOTEL €€€
(☎0536328500; www.mercure.com; 1 Ave Youssef Ibn Tachfine; s/d Dh1343/1443; ❄📶🏊) The belle of Nador's accommodation scene, the Mercure stands out on the corniche with its tinted blue glass facade. Rooms are large and with the comfort and amenities you'd expect from this international chain; some have views over the lagoon. The swimming pool on the roof terrace is a neat, pleasant surprise and there's a wonderful in-house spa.

The hotel bar is one of the only places in Nador to score a drink of booze.

Eating & Drinking

There are numerous cheap eats around the bus station, serving up quick *brochettes*, sandwiches and the odd tajine.

Like a lot of smaller Moroccan cities, Nador has a strong cafe culture. Ave Mohammed V is the spot for a lazy coffee.

The bar at the Mercure is the best place to go for a drop of something stronger than mint tea.

★ **Bulls Burger House** BURGERS €
(☎0536603345; 5 Blvd El Farabi; burgers from Dh45; ⏲1.30-11pm) Somehow, one of the best burgers in Morocco has popped up here. Unbelievably soft buns hug perfectly spiced patties dripping with delicious sauces, and it all comes with garlic fries and homemade lemonade on the side. Shut your eyes and you might be in a trendy burger joint in any major city around the world.

Café Pizzeria Antalya CAFE €
(Blvd Prince Héritier Sidi Mohammed; pizzas from Dh50; ⏲8am-10pm) A good option at any time of day is Antalaya, a two-pronged cafe and restaurant that serves pizza, paninis, shawarma and ice cream on one end (Antalaya II) and a smoky cafe with different kinds of breakfasts (from Dh25) on the other. The cafe's corner terrace is a great place to have tea if you've got time to kill.

Restaurant Marhaba SEAFOOD €€
(☎0536603311; Calle Ibn Rochd; mains from Dh50; ⏲noon-11pm) Open since 1975, Marhaba is a local classic and one of the smartest restaurants in town, specialising in fish (done well). The main room is very large, but there's a cosier terrace at the back with fishing nets and plastic lobsters. No alcohol.

Getting There & Away

AIR

Nador International Airport is 23km south of town with connections on Ryanair, Eurowings and Air Arabia to Europe. Royal Air Maroc also flies to Casablanca.

BOAT

Trasmediterranea has 11 sailings a week to Almería (six hours). Naviera Armas sails twice a week to Motril (five hours), while Grandi Navi Veloci has a weekly ferry to Sete in France (29 hours) as well as every six days to Barcelona (24 hours, 30 minutes).

The port of Beni Enzar is 7km from the city but traffic makes it feel much further. The quickest way to get there is by *grand taxi* (Dh6, 15 minutes). Alternatively, you could take Vectalia bus 20 (www.nador.vectalia.ma) from the gare routière to the crossroads near the border (16 trips per day, Dh8). Or, take the train to the station 3km from the border (Dh16, 18 minutes), and take a *petit taxi* from there. If all else fails, a private cab should cost about Dh80.

BUS

From the **bus station** (Rue Genéral Meziane), CTM sends buses to Casablanca, Rabat, Meknes, Fez, Tangier, Larache, Sidi Kacem, Al Hoceima, Chefchaouen and more. In the evening, several slightly cheaper Casablanca-bound coaches run by other companies leave from the same area. CTM also has a **small office** (☎0536600136; Rue Général Meziane; ⏲6.30am-9.30pm) downtown.

The main bus station is southeast of the centre. There are frequent departures:

Al Hoceima Dh40, three hours
Beni Enzar (Melilla border) Dh4, 25 minutes
Fez Dh60, 5½ hours
Oujda Dh35, 2½ hours, via Berkane (Dh20, 1½ hours)
Ras El Maa Dh20, one hour
Rabat Dh100, eight hours
Tetouan Dh120, nine hours, some via Dardara (for Chefchaouen, Dh100, six hours)

CAR & MOTORCYCLE

The Rocade (coastal road) from Nador to Al Hoceima (130km) is a delight to travel. It passes through red cliffs, verdant gorges and, midway, an enormous sculpture of deeply eroded hills.

Within 60km of Nador there are several ramshackle, clifftop cafes that are perfect for a mint tea as you gaze out over the sea. A few of the beaches tucked into coves have restaurants; others are dirty with litter.

TAXI

The huge *grands taxis* lot next to the main bus station serves plenty of destinations.

DESTINATION	COST (DH)	DURATION
Al Hoceima	60	2 hours
Beni Enzar (the Melilla border)	6	15 min
Berkane	35	1 hour
Oujda	60	2 hours
Taza	70	3 hours

TRAIN

Nador Ville train station (Blvd de Tanger) serves the Beni Enzar/Melilla border with a station 3km from the border (Dh16, 18 minutes) as well as Fez (Dh104, six hours, three daily). All of the Fez trains go via Taourirt, where you can change for Casablanca.

Getting Around

In 2018 urban bus company Vectalia (www.nador.vectalia.ma) launched in Nador. Vectalia operates more than a dozen routes around the city and neighbouring regions, including line 20, which travels between Nador's bus station and the crossroads at the Beni Enzar border 16 times per day (Dh4); eight in the morning and eight in the afternoon.

Saïdia السعيدية

0536 / POP 11,700

On the edge of Morocco's northeastern coast, just before the closed Algerian border, lies Saïdia *(say-dee-yuh)*. This sleepy seaside town springs into life in summer, when it throngs with Moroccan holidaymakers, many of them staying in the beach's ample apartment options.

Saïdia's beach is arguably the northeastern coast's finest, with clean golden sand and supple Mediterranean waves. The corniche has plenty of restaurants with attractive beachfront patios and clubs that serve alcohol. Most, though, are closed out of season.

At the beach's western tip, find Saïdia Med, a resort with a golf course and marina. Just beyond is the Unesco Ramsar-protected Moulouya wetlands, home to greater flamingos.

If the Algerian border were open Saïdia would surely be crowded year-round, but for now, it's a hot summer destination well worth the trip, especially with so many budget airlines flying to nearby Oujda-Angad Airport (p316).

Saïdia proper has loungers and umbrellas to hire as well as pedalos – jet skis are banned because of an unfortunate collision.

Saïdia Med has a golf course and a marina with 740 berths. Here you can hire a jet ski (Dh800 per hour), a kayak (Dh40) or a motorboat (Dh1000).

Sleeping & Eating

There are a few hotels in Saïdia proper, while Saïdia Med is reserved for upmarket resorts. However, the vast majority of holidaymakers stay in apartments.

Restaurants serving similar menus of seafood, pizzas, burgers and the like are found all along the corniche (Ave Mohammed V), many of which have gorgeous patios on the sand. There are also some restaurants and snack options along Blvd Hassan II.

Unlike in many places throughout Morocco, drinking is tolerated in Saïdia, as long as it's done indoors. Several clubs on the corniche (most open only during summer) serve alcohol.

Titanic Hotel HOTEL €€

(0536624071; Ave Mohammed V; d Dh350-400;) A cheery blue-and-white hotel on the seafront with decent, breezy rooms, although it's starting to show its age. The balconies host splendid views of the water.

Hotel Atlal HOTEL €€

(0536625021; atlalben@menara.ma; 44 Blvd Hassan II; s/d/ste Dh420/510/1200;) A few blocks off the beach, Atlal has huge bright rooms, fit for the families who tend to visit here. All have balconies. There's a bar and good restaurant down below. However, noise from the basement disco can be a problem.

Iberostar Hotel RESORT €€€

(0536630010; www.iberostar.com; Saïdia Med; r from Dh1100; May-Sep;) If you're simply looking to lie on the beach with everything taken care of, this five-star hotel is the best option when it comes to resorts along Mediterreanéa Saïdia (Saïdia Med). It has extensive grounds and rooms, a spa, sporting facilities, several pools, restaurants and bars. At the beach you can hire a jet ski, a kayak or a motorboat.

Restaurant Boughaz FAST FOOD €

(☎0808503045; Ave Mohammed V; mains from Dh40; ⏰8am-midnight) You can't miss this restaurant shaped like a boat on the Corniche. Boughaz serves burgers, pizzas, tajines and, of course, fish. The terrace out to the sand has tiki umbrellas and white cushions for a relaxing day at the beach.

La Corniche MOROCCAN €€

(Ave Mohammed V; mains Dh20-95; ⏰8am-midnight) This lively family-run seafront restaurant has a terrace that juts out onto the sand, with a fun playground for kids. It can become a real party out there with teenagers bouncing a ball around and families enjoying their lunch. The menu is a mix of Moroccan staples, sandwiches, pasta, pizzas and generous salads.

Getting There & Away

Politics keep the nearby border with Algeria closed.

To get here from Nador, take the Rocade (N16) eastwards to Saïdia, past a mix of salt marsh and sand dunes. You'll also catch good views of the Islas Chafarinas, the last bit of Spain on the northern coast. Arekmane has a new corniche but no further development yet. Ras El Maa, also known as Cap de l'Eau, is faring better. The pedestrianised corniche has a few small restaurants and a nice beach.

AIR

Oujda-Angad Airport (p316) serves Saïdia. Royal Air Maroc has several daily flights to Casablanca and direct flights to Paris Orly. Ryanair operates flights to Paris, Brussels, Marseille and Düsseldorf. TUI has flights to Munich and Düsseldorf. EasyJet, Transavia and Air Arabia all fly to Paris.

Hiring a taxi from Oujda airport to Saïdia costs Dh150 and the journey takes an hour. A seat in a shared taxi from Oujda's bus station is Dh30.

BUS

CTM operates an early-morning bus from Nador (Dh35, two hours), only in summer. Other companies run several buses a day from Oujda to Saïdia (Dh17, one hour) as well as to Berkane.

TAXI

Grands taxis depart from a parking lot on the east end of Saïdia near the kasbah. Shared taxi options include Nador (Dh50, 1¼ hours), Berkane (Dh10, 30 minutes) and Oujda (Dh30, one hour).

Berkane

☎0536 / POP 120,710

Berkane *(behr-kahn)* is a dusty modern town famous for its oranges, and everything in the town is indeed orange, from the taxis and buildings to the wonderful statue of an orange as you enter. It's most useful to travellers as a transit point and a base for exploring the Beni-Snassen Mountains. However, spending a night here isn't too bad thanks to two excellent hotels.

Berkane is easy to navigate as it's stretched along Blvd Mohammed V, which leads from the orange Grande Mosquée in the west to the large roundabout at the other end, dominated by a large orange municipal building. The main bus station is a few minutes drive eastwards along N2 at Boulevard Al Wifak or a 15-minute walk.

CTM and other companies depart from the **main bus station** to Nador (Dh25, 1½ hours), Oujda (Dh18, one hour) and daily in the mornings to Taforalt (Dh10, 30 minutes). Long-distance trips are also available to Fez (Dh130), Rabat (Dh205) and Casablanca (Dh237). There are also buses to Saïdia only during summer.

Grands taxis leave from near the bus station for Oujda (Dh30, one hour), Saïdia (Dh10, 30 minutes) and Nador (Dh60, 1½ hours).

Sleeping & Eating

Surprisingly, tiny Berkane has managed to land not one, but two terrific hotels.

Berkane's eating scene is mostly limited to cafes serving the typical Moroccan snack fare, all of them strung along or near Blvd Mohammed V.

Hotel Rosalina HOTEL €

(☎0536618992; rosalina_hotel@hotmail.fr; 82 Blvd Mohammed V; s/d Dh280/360; ❄📶) This modern hotel is a pleasant option at an affordable price. There's lots of wood panelling, and the rooms are spacious with comfortable beds. The cafe on the ground floor serves a standard Moroccan breakfast, included in the rates.

Ask about private taxis to the Beni-Snassen Mountains if you don't have a vehicle.

★**Canada Inn** HOTEL €€
(☎0536613634; www.hotelcanada.ma; 53 El Bakay Lhbil; s/d/tr/ste Dh350/450/550/650; ❄📶) A top-notch hotel anywhere in the world, the Canada Inn is a high-end option for a midrange price. The rooms are fresh and beautifully designed, with excellent bathrooms that feature dual showerheads. The hotel was opened by a Moroccan who spent time in Canada, hence the name and maple-leaf branding.

The Canada Inn's **restaurant** (mains from Dh30; ⊙7pm-midnight; 📶) is easily one of Berkane's best. You'll find burgers, pasta, tajines, salads and supersweet drinks. The restaurant itself is bright and modern, resembling an airport lounge with muzak to match. A good place to fuel up before heading to the mountains or travelling onwards.

Beni-Snassen Mountains

جبال بني يزناسن

Just outside of Berkane, you'll encounter the Beni-Snassen *(benee sne-seen)* Mountains, where steep limestone cliffs, scenic gorges and lush valleys set the scene for an outdoor playground, without the crowds.

For all intents and purposes a national park, the mountain range is home to tall cacti and almond, fig, olive and juicy apricot-like loquat trees. Sharing the verdant territory are big-horned Barbary sheep and 160 other animal species.

Tiny villages dot the mountainside consisting of just a handful of houses, but all manage to have room to welcome visitors for tea. The largest is Taforalt (Tafoughalt), where you'll find restaurants, accommodation and a charming market. While you might feel as if you've discovered something untouched here, know that you're a tad late to the game. Humans have been visiting Beni-Snassen for at least 80,000 years, judging by remains found at Grotte des Pigeons.

◉ Sights

Taforalt VILLAGE
(Tafoughalt) Taforalt, also known as Tafoughalt, is a somewhat haphazard settlement that arose around a former French military installation. The northern end, which you come upon first if entering from Berkane, contains a small souq with plenty of spices, dates and delicious local almond butter mixed with argan oil. Along the road is a strip of cafes and restaurants.

Grotte des Pigeons ARCHAEOLOGICAL SITE
Follow the throaty pigeon coos up the hill into the oldest known cemetery in North Africa. Traces of 80,000-year-old human remains have been unearthed here, as well as some of the oldest DNA to be extracted on the continent. The cave itself isn't much to look at; leftovers from digs in progress and pigeon feathers call your attention, but the feeling of hanging out in the same spot as early Homo sapiens is an introspective delight.

ROAD-TRIPPING THE BENI-SNASSEN MOUNTAINS

From Berkane, take the national road to Taforalt, a former French military installation, which passes through beautiful mountain scenery. There are cafes and restaurants here, including Club Taforalt (p312) with its terrific pool and backyard garden. You can stay at the nearby Auberge Taforalt (p312) or Riad Oriental (p312), the magnificent French-owned kasbah guesthouse 5km from town.

About 2km back down the national road is a right turn signposted for two *grottes* (caves). Grotte des Pigeons, 1km away, is the site of an active excavation and has revealed human remains from the Pleistocene era, including an ancient burial ground and some early human jewellery (82,000 years old). Keep an eye out for big-horned Barbary sheep, which were recently reintroduced to the area.

Another 5km brings you to Grotte du Chameau (p312), a multistorey cave complex with three entrances that have been closed for years because of flooding damage. Three kilometres further and you'll reach the pretty **Zegzel Gorge** and a beautiful serpentine drive. Don't miss the chance to sample the loquats, a juicy apricot-like fruit that ripens in May and June.

The source of the **Charaâ River** provides a worthwhile detour. Follow signs to the tiny hamlet of **Zegzel**, 2km up a rough side road. At the end there's a popular picnic spot near where the river gushes out of the cliff. Not far from here, a spectacular ridge road cuts east to Oujda. You'll need a 4WD vehicle, a good map and an early start.

Grotte du Chameau CAVE

Named after the camel-shaped mountain above, Grotte du Chameau is an ancient network of limestone and dolomite caves, once used as shelter by early Homo sapiens who hunted in the area. The cave was also a useful source of flint for creating tools and starting fires. Unfortunately, the caves are almost always closed to visitors for safety precautions, but you can still peek through the bars or have a dip outside the cave mouth during summer.

Sleeping & Eating

Accommodation options are limited in the Beni-Snassen Mountains, although you can also base yourself in Berkane to explore the area. Taforalt's market is a great place to stock up on local fruit, dates and nuts before heading down into the mountains. The town also has plenty of restaurants serving tajines and *brochettes*.

Auberge Taforalt GUESTHOUSE €

(0662045119; www.taforaltclub.com; Taforalt; tent/r Dh250/350; Jun-Sep;) This cosy inn has seven rooms and six Berber tents on the roof. It's across the street from Club Taforalt, which has a pool and restaurant.

★ **Riad Oriental** GUESTHOUSE €€

(0600079079; http://hotel-gite-raidoriental.com/en; s/d Dh570/770, chalet s/d Dh490/690; closed Dec-Feb & Ramadan;) Thoughts of paradise are barely avoidable at this gorgeous modern kasbah overlooking the valley and mountains beyond. The rooms and chalets are luxurious, and the breakfast (included) is scrumptious. For some adventure, there's horseback riding, as well as motorbikes and four-wheelers for hire. But you can't be blamed if you simply feel like lounging by the immaculate pool.

A fee (Dh15 per person per night) is added to the bill. A 'Berber tent' chalet for families is also available. The restaurant and pool (adult Dh100, child Dh70) are open to nonguests.

Club Taforalt MOROCCAN €€

(mains Dh60-150; Jun-Sep) This simple restaurant with a huge pool is a fun summer option. Tajines, salads, chips and ice cream are on offer, or you can grab a cold drink to enjoy by the pool (the Dh70 admission includes a beverage). There are no set opening hours, but expect it to be open every day following Ramadan until September.

Getting There & Away

If you don't have your own vehicle, the easiest way to access the park is to take a shared taxi from Berkane (Dh13, 30 minutes). There's also one daily bus (Dh10, 30 minutes) that leaves in the morning from Berkane's main bus station (p310). Alternatively, hire your own taxi; the minimum fare will be in the region of Dh200 for two hours, although not all drivers will be willing to take their vehicles along the poor roads near the hamlet of Zegzel. A cheaper alternative is to take a *grand taxi* to Taforalt and walk down. *Grands taxis* are most frequent on market days (Wednesday and Sunday).

Oujda وجدة

0536 / POP 572,190

Oujda *(woojh-dah)* is the largest city in eastern Morocco, with a millennium of history to draw from. Despite its heritage as a cultural crossroads and a hub for Algerian and Andalusian music, it receives very few foreign travellers. The reason for this is found on the map: it was once the busiest border crossing with Algeria, making it popular with traders and tourists alike. When the border closed in 1995, Oujda became a cul-de-sac and its economy took a major hit. However, recent tourism development along the nearby Mediterranean coast, and the consequent rise in importance of the airport, are having a positive knock-on effect. In addition, Oujda's university remains a mainstay of the economy and the city's intellectual life.

Despite few attractions, Oujda is hassle-free, so you can catch your breath after heading down from the Rif Mountains or before travelling on to Figuig and the Sahara.

History

Oujda lies on the main axis connecting Morocco with the rest of North Africa (the Romans built a road through here). It occupied a key position in controlling the east and was often seen as a vital stepping stone for armies aiming to seize control of the heartland around it.

Founded by the Meghraoua tribe in the 10th century, Oujda remained independent until the Almohads overran it a century later. Under the Merinids, Algerian rulers based in Tlemcen took the town on several occasions, and in the 17th century it fell under the Ottomans in Algiers.

Moulay Ismail put an end to this in 1687, and despite several attacks from Europe, Oujda remained in Moroccan hands until

1907 when French colonial forces in Algeria crossed the frontier and finally occupied the town. The protectorate was still five years away, but the sultan was powerless to stop it.

The French expanded Oujda, adding parks, administrative buildings and its clock tower. Nowadays, Oujda is the burgeoning provincial capital of Morocco's Oriental region.

Sights

Parc Lalla Aicha PARK

(Ave Yacoub Al Mansour; 8am-8pm) Designed in the 1930s by René Maître, the city's chief architect, this beautiful park lined with magnificent trees and bright flowers is worth a stroll. There's a swimming pool (summer only), a cafe, tennis and horse riding.

Medina MEDINA

Oujda's medina is a great slice of tradition and modernity. It isn't large and appeals to local tastes, so don't expect to wade through touts selling carpets, lanterns and cushions. Most shops sell Moroccan clothing, jewellery and housewares. The area near Bab El Wahab, the eastern gate, is chock-full of food stalls selling seasonal produce (Oujda olives are well regarded).

Grande Mosquée MOSQUE

Towering over Oujda's small medina, the oldest mosque in the city, known to followers as Lkebir Jamaa, was built when Merinid ruler Sultan Abou Youssef rebuilt Oujda in the 13th century. Unfortunately, it's difficult to see the minaret from the narrow medina streets.

Clock Tower LANDMARK

Oujda's most recognisable landmark is the 1920s art-deco clock tower that overlooks Place 16 Août. The mosque next to it is arguably more impressive, however.

Banque Al Maghrib NOTABLE BUILDING

The blockish central bank just south of Place 16 Août was built during the colonial French protectorate in the 1920s. It's constructed in the Franco-Moorish style.

Festivals & Events

Oujda is renowned for its music: a cross-cultural mix of Algerian, Andalusian and Moroccan.

Sidi Yahia Moussem CULTURAL

(Ben Younes; Aug & Sep) Patron saint of the city and venerated by Moroccans, Sidi Yahia is also thought to be John the Baptist or perhaps a Castilian rabbi. Thousands of pilgrims flock to the celebrations 6km south of Oujda, which include *tbourida* demonstrations of men on horseback firing rifles. The trees around the shrine (closed to non-Muslims) are festooned with rags, tied to receive blessings – a throwback to pre-Islamic fertility beliefs.

To get to Sidi Yahia, take bus 1 (Dh6) from outside Bab El Ouahab in Oujda, or a *petit taxi* (Dh17).

International Gharnati Festival MUSIC

(dates vary) Gharnati is Algerian music from Andalusia (the name is derived from Granada). The traditional music, played with an ensemble that includes violins and ouds, has been celebrated with an annual festival in Oujda for over a quarter century. Many of the events are held at the Theater Mohammed VI, as well as at several venues across the city.

Oujda International Raï Festival MUSIC

(Jul) Oujda is the Moroccan capital for raï, a music genre developed in Algeria in the 1920s as a form of protest folk. Since 2006 Oujda has organised an eight-day annual festival for raï featuring both classic renditions as well as modern versions from more than a dozen artists. The festival also features rap and *chaabi* folk music artists.

Sleeping

Oujda has a small but decent range of accommodation.

Hôtel Afrah HOTEL €

(0536686533; hotelafrah2017@gmail.com; 15 Rue Tafna; s/d/tr/q Dh100/200/280/380;) Mohammed, the English-speaking owner of this Oujda mainstay, has recently taken over from his father and given Hotel Afrah a much-needed facelift. Renovated rooms are bright with comfortable beds and the bathrooms are clean. More improvements are coming to make the rooftop a chill-out space. It's a simple, carefree budget option in the heart of the city.

Ask about guided tours of the medina.

Hôtel Angad HOTEL €

(0536691451; hotelangad@hotmail.fr; Rue Tafna; s/d Dh182/224, with air-con Dh223/272;) This affordable two-star hotel is an excellent budget option in a convenient location just outside of the medina and down the street from Place 16 Août. It has basic rooms with

Oujda

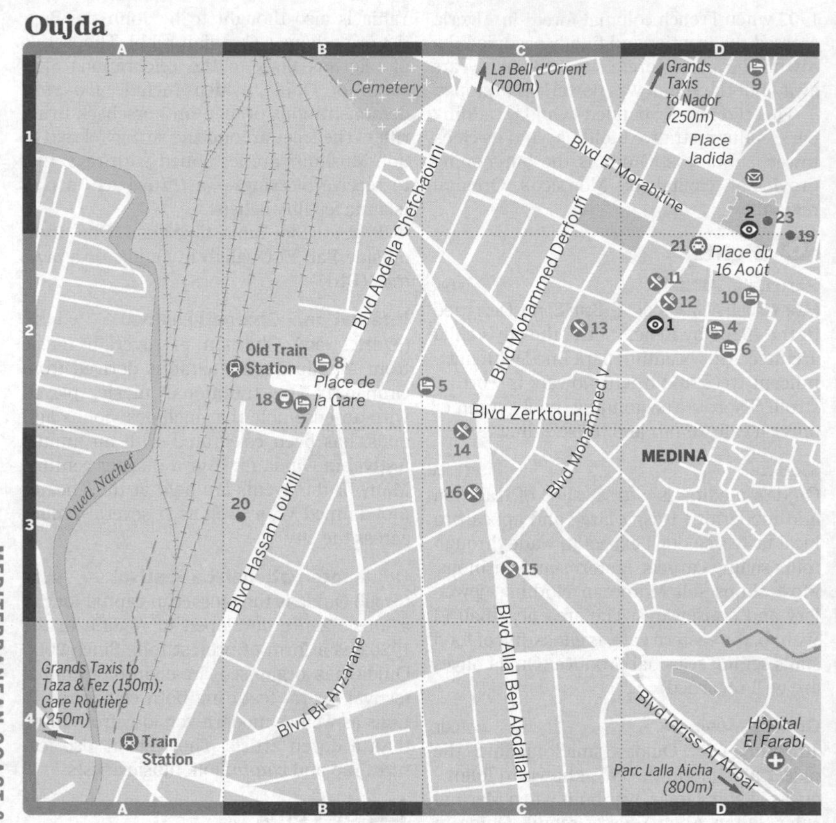

a large bathroom and TV; make sure to get one at the back as the street side can be noisy. The downstairs cafe does breakfast (from Dh12) and pizza.

Hôtel Tlemcen HOTEL €
(☎0536700384; 26 Rue Ramdane El Gadhi; s/d Dh90/180) This welcoming little hotel offers decent value, as long as you don't mind going without wi-fi. It has a grand-looking lobby and small but bright rooms, with private bathrooms and a TV. Find it around the corner from Place 16 Août.

Hotel Jedda HOTEL €€
(☎0536704646; jeddahotel8@gmail.com; 13 Rue Ouartass; s/d Dh300/400; 📶) Largely black marble and glass, the reception at this top midrange option is professional and the rooms are spacious with black leather bed frames. Double rooms are two twins together. There's a cafe next door that serves breakfast (included).

Hotel Al Manar HOTEL €€
(☎0536688855; hotelalmanara@menara.ma; 50 Blvd Zerktouni; s/d Dh360/420; 📶) Centrally located, the Al Manar (meaning 'lighthouse') is suitably towering and has functional and practical decor. Rooms are fine value, although avoid the darker, small-windowed interior rooms.

Hôtel Atlas Orient HOTEL €€€
(☎0536711010; www.hotelsatlas.com; Place de la Gare; s/d Dh1380/1570; ❄📶🏊) The Atlas Orient is a grand hotel in a plaza where the old train station once was. Its rooms are chic with the top-notch service you'd expect for the price. There's a spa, an outdoor pool and guests can pick from three restaurants (Chinese, Moroccan and international). There's also a classy bar, a lounge and a nightclub, which all serve alcohol.

Hôtel Ibis Moussafir HOTEL €€€
(☎0536688202; www.accorhotels.com; Place de la Gare; s/d Dh700/880; 📶🏊) The Ibis has all

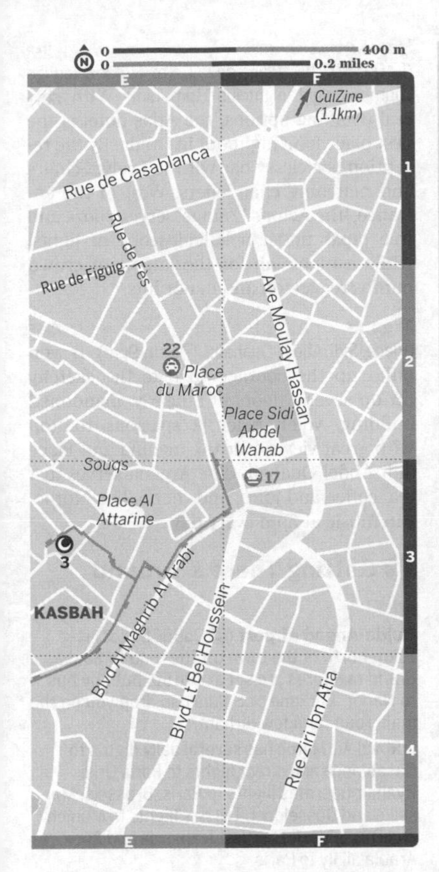

Oujda

Sights
1 Banque Al Maghrib D2
2 Clock Tower D1
3 Grande Mosquée E3

Sleeping
4 Hôtel Afrah D2
5 Hotel Al Manar C2
6 Hôtel Angad D2
7 Hôtel Atlas Orient B2
8 Hôtel Ibis Moussafir B2
9 Hotel Jedda D1
10 Hôtel Tlemcen D2

Eating
11 Café Pâtisserie Colombo D2
12 L'Excellence D2
13 Restaurant Le Comme Chez Soi C2
14 Restaurant Nacional C3
15 Rihab C3
16 Trocadero C3

Drinking & Nightlife
17 Argana F3
18 Hôtel Atlas Orient B2

Transport
19 CTM Office D2
20 Gare d'Oujda B3
21 Petits Taxis D2
22 Petits Taxis E2
23 Trans Ghazala Ticket Office D1

the up-to-the-minute facilities and comfortable rooms you'd expect from this international chain – you could be anywhere in the world. There's a restaurant, a hookah lounge and an outdoor pool that nonguests can use for Dh100 per day. Breakfast is included.

Eating & Drinking

Oujda has plenty of cafes with good Moroccan and international food. The stalls inside Bab El Ouahab offer more traditional fare, including *kefta* (meatballs), bowls of *harira* (soup) and boiled snails.

If you're around during Eid and can get invited into a household, *bekbouka* (meat stew) is a local delicacy.

While Oujda certainly has a strong cafe culture, it's possible to land a glass of wine or bottle of beer at several licensed establishments around town. Hôtel Atlas Orient is the best option, with its classy bar, lounge and nightclub.

★ Restaurant Nacional MOROCCAN €
(☎0536703257; 107 Blvd Allal Ben Abdallah; meals from Dh25; ⏲12.30-11pm) A Oujda institution where people queue for tables at lunchtime (there's a big, packed salon upstairs). Salads are great, and waiters rush with plates of grilled meat, fried fish and tajines. Couscous is available on Friday.

Café Pâtisserie Colombo CAFE €
(☎0536682182; Blvd Mohammed V; croissants Dh2; ⏲5am-10pm; ⓦ) This vintage cafe has been a popular option on Oujda's main strip since the 1940s. Classy waiters in bow ties and brown suit jackets serve delicious pastries, excellent coffee, affordable breakfasts and stacked sundaes for burning hot summer days. Pull up a chair on the terrace and watch the bustle.

CuiZine HEALTH FOOD €
(☎0688608887; 258 Rue de l'Atlas; mains from Dh20; ⏲noon-midnight; ⓦ) Wall-to-wall with wooden crates, trendy CuiZine has a hefty menu of pizzas, loaded potatoes and Moroccan staples. It also has 'fitness' foods

like jam-packed smoothies and 'hyper protein' meals that list the nutritional value in grams. It's a considerable trek from the centre, but worth it for something a little different.

L'Excellence CAFE €

(☎0536712818; 30 Blvd Mohammed V; pizza from Dh35; ⏰8am-10pm) One of the best patisseries in town, L'Excellence specialises in local sweets; try a *makrout* (date-stuffed sweet), *griwech* (fried strips of dough in honey), *kaâk* (bagel-shaped sweet) or *briwate* (triangular puff pastry). The croissants and cakes are tasty too. Upstairs is a pizza restaurant with glass windows that overlook Banque Al Maghrib and Blvd Mohammed V.

Trocadero CAFE €€

(☎0536711100; 71 Blvd Allal Ben Abdellah Al Mahatta; mains Dh22-120; ⏰5am-midnight; 📶) One of a handful of modern black, glass and chrome cafes in Oujda, Trocadero has two floors and a pavement area. The food is good and the menu has more options than most: try the chicken florentina or risotto.

La Belle d'Orient SEAFOOD €€

(☎0536705961; 65 Blvd Ahfir; mains from Dh75; ⏰12.30-11pm) An excellent choice if you're in the mood for fish fresh from the coast. Sardines are grilled on the barbecue outside, there's a fish tajine and a platter of *poisson friture* (various fried fish). Pizzas are also available.

Rihab CAFE €€

(☎0536705151; cnr Blvds Idriss Al Akbar & Allal Ben Abdallah; breakfast from Dh13; ⏰8am-11pm; 📶) This modern cafe on the ground floor of a tall office building serves a variety of decent breakfasts, ice cream and baked goods. As with many Moroccan cafes, men seem to dominate the ground floor while women and families go upstairs. The best feature of Cafe Rihab is the view of the busy roundabout out the windows and from the front patio.

Restaurant Le Comme Chez Soi FRENCH €€

(☎0536686079; 8 Rue Sijilmassa; mains around Dh120; ⏰6.30pm-2am) This licensed restaurant is dimly lit, with white tablecloths and checkered floors. Fish tanks indicate the speciality, but there are also good steaks and salads. There's no physical menu, so get the staff to recite the choices (in French and Arabic). The food is decent and alcohol is a bonus, but the atmosphere is ice cold.

Hôtel Atlas Orient BAR

(☎0536711010; Place de la Gare; ⏰bar & lounge 10pm-midnight, nightclub 11pm-4am) With several drinking options, the Atlas hotel is the best place for a night out in Oujda. By the reception is a classy bar with red velvet chairs and matching chandeliers. West of the entrance, 'the Actor's Lounge' serves booze and free tapas under a kaleidoscope of lights, while a nightclub for the late-night crowd bumps reggaeton and major hits.

Argana CAFE

(Place Sidi Abdel Ouahab; ⏰9am-9pm) If you build up the courage to take the sketchy lift up several floors of a nearly abandoned building, you'll reach a spacious rooftop with great views over the medina and Place Sidi Abdel Ouahab. Cafe Argana serves just tea, coffee and juice, and there's live Moroccan music at 3pm every day.

ℹ Getting There & Around

AIR

Oujda-Angad Airport (☎0536683261) is 15km north of the town off the road to Saïdia. *Grand taxi* fares are set at Dh150, but any bus to Nador, Berkane or Saïdia can drop you on the main road for a few dirham.

Royal Air Maroc has several daily flights to Casablanca and direct flights to Paris Orly. Ryanair operates flights to Paris, Brussels, Marseille and Düsseldorf. TUI has flights to Munich and Düsseldorf. EasyJet, Transavia and Air Arabia all fly to Paris.

BUS

The main bus station sits in the shadow of the huge Mohammed VI Mosque. **CTM** (☎0693079828; Rue Sidi Brahim) has an office just off Place du 16 Août selling tickets to Casablanca (Dh220, nine hours overnight), Taza (Dh85, 3½ hours), Fez (Dh125, five hours), Meknes (Dh150, six hours), Rabat (Dh185, 7½ hours), Figuig (Dh105, six hours) and Tangier (Dh200, 11 hours).

Trans Ghazala runs several daily services to Casablanca via Taza (Dh140), Fez (Dh100), Meknes (Dh120) and Rabat (Dh160). You also can buy tickets for these services at the **Trans Ghazala ticket office** (☎0536685387; Rue Sidi Brahim).

Numerous other companies with ticket offices in the bus station offer frequent departures for Taza, Fez and Meknes, as well as Berkane (Dh18, one hour), Nador (Dh35, three hours) and Al Hoceima (Dh60, six hours). There are two daily buses to Figuig (Dh90, seven hours) and Tangier (Dh150, 14 hours) via Tetouan. Buses to Saïdia (Dh15, one hour) run only during summer.

GRANDS TAXIS

Grands taxis leave regularly from the main bus station to Taza (Dh80, three hours). Change here for onward connections. *Grands taxis* heading north to Nador (Dh60, three hours), Saïdia (Dh30, one hour) and Berkane (Dh30, one hour) congregate north of town near the junction of Rue Ibn Abdelmalek and Blvd Mohammed Derfoufi.

PETITS TAXIS

Red *petits taxis* are plentiful in Oujda. You're unlikely to pay more than Dh10 for any ride. Many line up at Place de 16 Août, near Place du Maroc and outside the bus station.

TRAIN

Oujda is the terminus of the northern branch of the Moroccan train line. There's a brand-new train station to the west of downtown along Blvd Hassan Laoukili. Four trains leave daily for Casablanca (Dh216, 10 hours) and four for Tangier (Dh220, 10 hours). All trains stop at Taza (Dh79, 3½ hours), Fez (Dh116, six hours) and Meknes (Dh137, 6½ hours). Deals are available if purchased online and in advance.

AT A GLANCE

POPULATION

Fez: 1,412,080

WORLD'S OLDEST UNIVERSITY

Kairaouine Mosque & University (p329)

BEST ROOFTOP SUNDOWNER

Cafe Restaurant Place Lahdim (p363)

BEST MEDINA FINE-DINING

La Maison Bleue (p343)

BEST TRANS-ATLANTIC TASTING MENU

Nur (p343)

WHEN TO GO

Apr Perfect spring weather and markets full of orange blossom; wildflowers from Meknes to Volubilis.

Jun Float into Fez for the Festival of World Sacred Music.

Sep Summer's heat has burned off, making for perfect sightseeing conditions.

Volubilis (Oualili; p365)
DEYANDENCHEV/SHUTTERSTOCK

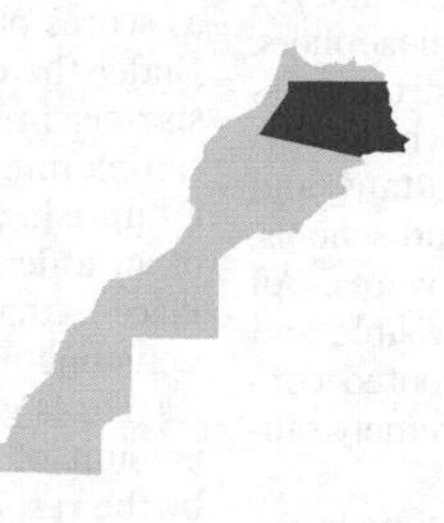

Fez, Meknes & the Middle Atlas

The majestic cities of Fez and Meknes bask in valleys surrounded by fertile plains. The Romans left remains at Volubilis, followed in turn by Muslim dynasties who created the grandest of Morocco's imperial cities.

The intriguing Fez medina is the region's major drawcard. Narrow lanes offer surprises around every corner, from magnificent palaces to mosaic fountains. Meknes presents a more pocket-sized experience, but has some epic relics from Moulay Ismail's reign. Nearby, Moulay Idriss Zerhoun entrances with its mystical ambience.

Beyond rise the Middle Atlas Mountains, where small Amazigh (Berber) villages are surrounded by great cedar forests. To the south, the Middle Atlas segues into the High Atlas and Morocco's distinctive kasbahs begin to make an appearance.

INCLUDES

Fez فاس

0535 / POP 1,412,080

Since it was founded in the 8th century, Fez has attracted scholars and philosophers, mathematicians and lawyers, astronomers and theologians. Craftspeople built hydraulic systems and palaces, sultans and the nobility endowed mosques and schools, and merchants offered exotic wares. All this history and culture is still visible and very much alive today, a deep-rooted context for the residents of this supremely self-confident city.

Most visitors spend all of their time in the medina, the world's largest car-free urban area. Outside of the fringes, where a few bold moped riders persist, the lanes are passable only on foot (human or donkey). Amid the courtyard houses, in various states of repair, are craft workshops large and small. The city offers some exceptionally good courses and craft tours, in which you can meet master artisans, continuing the city's centuries-old legacy of skill and learning.

History

In 789 BCE Idriss I – who founded Morocco's first imperial dynasty – decided that Oualili (Volubilis) was too small and drew up plans for a grand new capital on the east bank of the Oued (River) Fez. He died before the plans were implemented, however, so credit for the founding of Fez is given to his son, Idriss II, who carried out the will of his father, but with a settlement on the west bank.

From the outset, the city grew rapidly. In 818 CE some 8000 Arab families fled a crackdown in Córdoba and settled on the east bank, and a few years later, families who had left Kairouan (Qayrawan) in modern-day Tunisia settled on the west side. These two quarters, now known as Al Andalous and Kairaouine, respectively, developed separately. The Andalusian refugees brought many of the craft and culinary traditions that define the city today, and the Kairaouine elite established its strong tradition of learning.

The Almoravids united the two separate settlements in a single city in 1070, and the succeeding Almohads extended and rebuilt many of the city walls. The city developed a reputation for intellectual clout, as a crossroads of culture between Spain and Senegal; and with the arrival of the Merinid dynasty around 1250, Fez expanded up much of the western hill.

While Fez won and lost status as the political capital of Morocco, it has consistently been considered its spiritual capital, as scores of Muslim saints are buried here. Under the colonial French protectorate, resistance in Fez was particularly strong, with rioting immediately after the treaty in 1912, an uprising in 1944 and finally the signing of an independence agreement in 1956, on Place Batha.

As one of Morocco's most traditional cities, Fez is generally regarded with a certain amount of awe, perhaps tinged with envy, by the rest of the country. Indeed, a disproportionate share of Morocco's intellectual and economic elite hail from here, and it's a widely held belief (especially among Fassis) that anyone born in the Fez medina is more religious, cultured, artistic and refined.

Sights

Fez is a wonderment of fascinating historical monuments and grand buildings. But don't get too consumed with checking attractions off your list – consider them more an excuse to see people going about their everyday lives, in ways unchanged for centuries.

Climb the ridgeline to see Fez's jumbled buildings merge into a palette of white-flecked sandstone, and pick out all the landmark minarets and green tile roofs of the places you've visited.

Medina

Travelling from the Ville Nouvelle of Fez to its medina is like stepping back in time, to an era before motor vehicles, before heavy machinery. Today, more than 150,000 Fassis call this maze of twisting lanes home. There are beautiful buildings and monuments, but the real pleasures come from random exploration and interaction. Follow your nose to a neighbourhood oven or to heaps of freshly cut herbs in the produce markets; follow your ears to a tiny workshop tapping out etched brass trays. Turn a random corner into a kids' football game in a wide spot in the street. Give yourself time and permission to get lost, and when you need to find your way out, ask a shopkeeper for directions or follow a stranger until you're back at a landmark – with a new perspective on how a city can work.

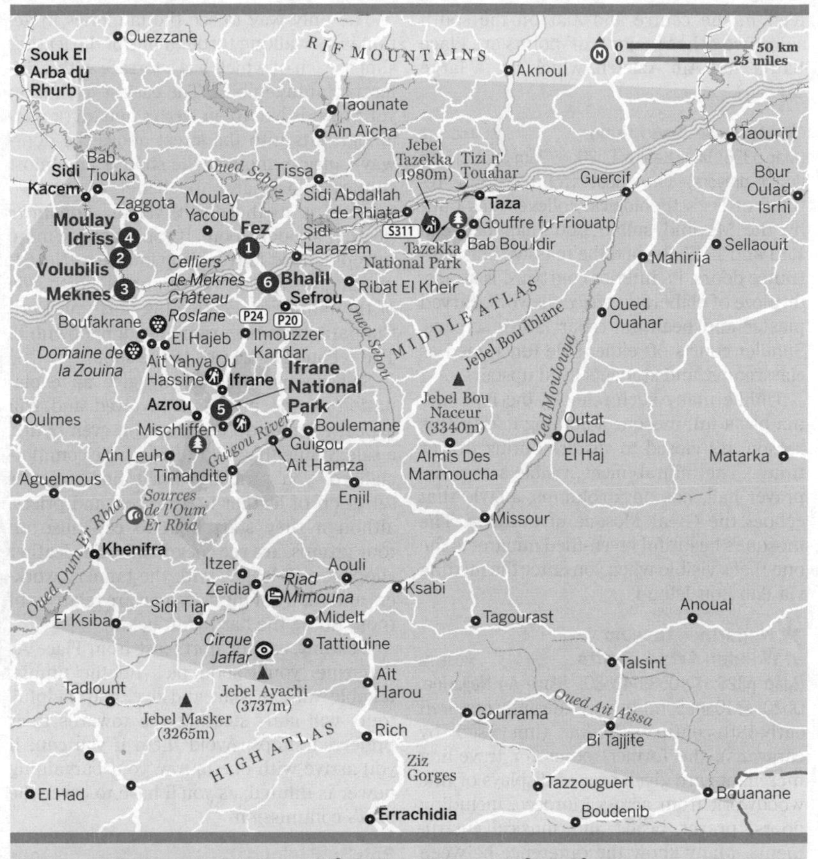

Fez, Meknes & the Middle Atlas Highlights

❶ **Fez** Diving into the warren of this ancient city's medina looking for souqs and souvenirs, and enjoying the sound of the sublime at the Festival of World Sacred Music.

❷ **Volubilis** (p365) Time-travelling through Morocco's finest Roman ruins, strewn with spectacular floor mosaics.

❸ **Meknes** (p354) Exploring the outsized imperial architecture that characterised mighty Moulay Ismail's reign.

❹ **Moulay Idriss Zerhoun** (p368) Spending a day and night to enjoy the atmosphere of this holy town.

❺ **Ifrane National Park** (p373) Hiking in the rolling Middle Atlas mountains around Ifrane and Azrou, perhaps catching sight of a native monkey or two.

❻ **Bhalil** (p353) Making like a troglodyte with a stay in this hillside village famed for its cave dwellers.

The main thoroughfares are Talaa Kebira (Big Slope) and Talaa Seghira (Small Slope), running roughly east from Bab Bou Jeloud, converging near Place An Nejjarine, and continuing to the Kairaouine Mosque. These two streets are lined with most of the historic buildings, major markets and other sightseeing spots.

To navigate, use the medina's setting in a basin. The lowest point is Place R'cif, and if you head downhill, you can get 'out' there. Uphill will lead you, eventually, to a city wall and a major gate.

The gates that most tourists use happen to go in alphabetical order clockwise: Bou Jeloud on the west, Guissa on the north,

R'cif in the centre and Ziat on the south side. Two other major 'exit' points are Place Batha and Ain Azleten, which has a large car park.

★Medersa Bou Inania ISLAMIC SITE

(Map p326; Talaa Kebira; Dh20; ⌚9am-5pm, closed during prayers) The most architecturally refined of Fez's theological colleges was built by the Merinid sultan Bou Inan between 1351 and 1357. Beyond the massive brass entrance doors, its interior courtyard is a masterpiece of elaborate *zellige* tilework, carved plaster and beautiful cedar lattice screens. Smaller courts off either side functioned as classrooms, and students lived upstairs.

Unlike many such schools, the Bou Inania has a full mosque adjoining it. (For this reason, it's closed to visitors during prayer times.) The mihrab niche, visible across the prayer hall, has onyx columns, a style that echoes the Great Mosque of Córdoba. The mosque's beautiful green-tiled minaret is the one that's visible when you enter the medina via Bab Bou Jeloud.

★Nejjarine Museum of Wooden Arts & Crafts MUSEUM

(Map p326; ☎0535740580; Place An Nejjarine; Dh20; ⌚10am-5pm) In a wonderfully restored early-18th-century *funduq* (inn used by caravans), the former rooms for travelling merchants are given over to displays of fine woodwork from across Morocco, including doors, prayer beads and musical instruments. Many show the difference between Amazigh traditional styles and the more Andalusian designs of Fez. A highlight are the worn wooden boards used by Quranic recitation students, patched with copper and adorned with their graduation certificates. The rooftop **cafe** is simple but has great views over the medina.

★Chouara Tannery WORKSHOP

(Dar Dbagh Chouara; Map p326; Derb Chouara, Blida) The largest of the medina's several tanneries, Chouara is one of the city's most iconic sights (and smells). Operating since at least the 16th century, the area was heavily renovated in 2016, but the scene, viewed from the surrounding balconies, remains remarkably medieval. It's striking to see the hard physical labour that goes into the butter-soft, elegant leather goods sold in the surrounding workshops. Try to get here in the morning when the pits are awash with coloured dye.

The only way to see the tanneries in action is by walking through one of the leather shops, each of which has a terrace with a different vantage point. The easiest to find on your own is No. 10 on Derb Chouara (a metal sign juts into the street above the doorway); inside, though, the shop is an almost comical maze, and the better of the two terraces is to the north, via the *babouche* (leather slipper) room. If you're feeling more intrepid, head for the shop known as No. 64, which gives a good view from the north side of the tanneries; keep going north on Derb Chouara, then turn right, heading downhill. The second right leads to the shop.

Salespeople will happily give an explanation of the processes involved and will expect a small tip in return or, even better, a sale. While this might feel a little commercialised, you probably won't find a better selection of leather in Morocco, and prices, although they start high to capitalise on tour groups, are very negotiable. The leather shops are in league with the tannery workers and many of the salesmen are relatives of those doing the hard graft below.

Heading east or northeast from Place As Seffarine, you'll soon pick up the unmistakable waft of skin and dye, and 'helpful' touts will start steering you towards their preferred shops. Avoid them if you can; if you arrive with one in tow, your bargaining power is diluted, as you'll have to cover the tout's commission.

Bab Bou Jeloud GATE

(Blue Gate; Map p326) What's considered the 'front door' of the medina dates only from 1913, when the French punched a hole in the city wall and erected this grand triple-arched gate, decorated with blue tiles on the outer face and green inside. As a modern construction, it abandons the defensive bent entrance of medieval gates in favour of a straight entrance into the street. Outside the walls, the very modest old gate is visible on the left, but now closed off.

Water Clock HISTORIC SITE

(Dar Al Magana; Map p326; opposite Medersa Bou Inania, Talaa Kebira) The only traces of this ingenious medieval device, installed in 1357, are 13 wooden beams jutting from the wall above street level. Each held a brass bowl, into which a metal ball would drop from the window above, to chime the hour. The clockworks were inside the building, powered and regulated by a water cistern that drained at

MEDERSA BOU INANIA: SAIKO3P/SHUTTERSTOCK©

TOP SIGHT
FEZ MEDINA

Fortified walls enclose 220 hectares of homes and businesses, workshops and cornershops, hovels and palaces, all set in a great natural basin. The medina is twice as densely populated as Manhattan, but its sloping narrow pedestrian streets are more serene and intimate than any city in the world.

Medina Logic

The medina has grown up from the banks of the Oued Fez over centuries, and although it might look nonsensical on a map, it follows a certain logic. Its narrow streets provide protection from the harsh sun and insulation against the cold. The biggest streets need only be wide enough for two loaded donkeys, and all the commercial shops, mosques and traders inns that might fuel such traffic are clustered on these wider roads. This leaves residential streets almost silent. Dead-end lanes traditionally served houses inhabited by the same family, and were semi-private; you'll still see people sneaking to the *hanout* (corner store) in a robe.

Upgrades

Designated a Unesco World Heritage site way back in 1981, Fez has undergone a lot of renovation – with an especially big push in the 2010s. Along Talaa Kebira, the souqs are fragrant with cedar, as metal doors have been replaced with more traditional wood. Huge effort has gone into cleaning up the Oued Fez, which had turned into a dumping ground hidden behind high walls. Now it's part of a larger social area that stretches to Place R'cif, a parking-lot-turned-public-square, and a big social scene at night.

TOP TIPS

- ➡ To navigate, use the basin geography. The lowest point is Place R'cif, and if you head downhill, you can get 'out' there. Uphill will lead you to a city wall and a major gate.
- ➡ Fridays are quiet days in the medina: good for taking time to get oriented or admire architecture. Likewise, shopping pressure abates in the late afternoon.

PRACTICALITIES

- ➡ Fez El Bali
- ➡ Map p326

MEDINA LIFE

It's easy to see the Fez medina as medieval, exotic and chaotic. In fact, it's a perfectly modern and functional city – its residents aren't living in the past. Indoor plumbing dates back a millennium; electricity, a century. Houses have satellite TV and high-speed internet. Every house has an address and gets postal delivery. Some buildings are more than 400 years old; parts of Ziat and the eastern medina were built in the last century; some infill is only decades old.

The real key difference is the lack of motor vehicles, which determines the layout of the place. Big produce and meat markets are at the edges of the medina, for easy truck access. Less-perishable goods are carted in to the *hawanit,* the tiny shops that serve residential areas. Trash is collected every day in barrows. Stoves and water are heated with cooking gas, with canisters (and the stove itself, for that matter) delivered by donkey.

As a city, the medina calls for city etiquette. Don't block traffic to take a photo, and be mindful of your backpack, as if you were on a crowded subway. There's even an unwritten rule to foot-traffic flow: keep to the left, like British drivers. This practice may also come from the lack of cars: donkey drivers walk on the left side of their beasts, and hug the wall to give them room. You should give them room too: listen up for those drivers (and cart-pushers too), yelling *Balak!* and *Andak!* to clear the way.

a steady pace. The clock was built along with Medersa Bou Inania (p322) across the road, to track correct prayer times.

Palais Glaoui PALACE

(Map p326; Douh Hamia, Batha; Dh25; ⏲9am-6pm) This is a slightly odd opportunity to tour someone's home and personal art gallery, which also happens to be a deeply dilapidated 18th-century palace, built by a pasha from Marrakesh. The main courtyard, with double-size salons, is the height of Andalusian style and includes a well-preserved early-20th-century bathroom, still in use today. Pass through the dim, enormous kitchen with gigantic cooking pots to reach the smaller harem court in back. Caretaker Abdelkhader's obsessive pointillist paintings fill one major salon.

Musée Belghazi MUSEUM

(Map p326; ☎0535638440; 19 Derb Al Ghorba; admission Dh40, tea Dh25; ⏲10am-6pm Sat-Thu) The dusty displays of silver jewellery are secondary to the experience of finding this mansion, down extra-winding lanes, and relaxing over tea in the glamorously decaying courtyard garden. As it's well signed, it's also a tout-free way to reach the 9th-century Sidi Moussa tannery, Fez's oldest. Across from the museum is a leather shop with a terrace view.

Henna Souq MARKET

(Map p326; Rue Fakharine) One of the medina's oldest marketplaces and also one of its most pleasant, this souq is dominated by a graceful plane tree amid stalls selling pottery and traditional cosmetics, including henna. This is a good place to come if you'd like to be talked through the fascinating array of natural products Moroccans routinely use – stall-holders are friendly and offer little hassle. The *mohtassib* (price controller), now defunct, had his office here, and you can still see his large scales.

At the far end of the square is the restored **Maristane Sidi Frej**, a former psychiatric hospital built by the Merinids in the 13th century. The 15th-century Andalusian scholar and diplomat, Leo Africanus, who wrote *A Description of Africa* in 1526, worked here as a young man. It is now a small *qissaria* (covered market).

Zawiya of Moulay Idriss II ISLAMIC TOMB

(Mausoleum of Moulay Idriss II; Map p326; Derb Moulay Idriss) Although it is in a mosque that's closed to non-Muslims, the tomb of Fez's founder (d. 828) is considered the spiritual heart of the city and is its most-visited spot. It's also a key landmark and worth seeking out, if only to see the towering wood front doors and the profusion of columns and carpets visible from the street. The current structure dates from 1308; a 17th-century expansion added its pyramidal green roof and the medina's tallest minaret.

Chemmaine-Sbitriyine Funduq NOTABLE BUILDING

(Map p326; Sbitriyine; ⏲10am-6pm Sat-Thu, from 3pm Fri) These two adjoining 13th-century *fanadiq* (inns used by caravans) have been thoroughly restored and host a number of

Fez

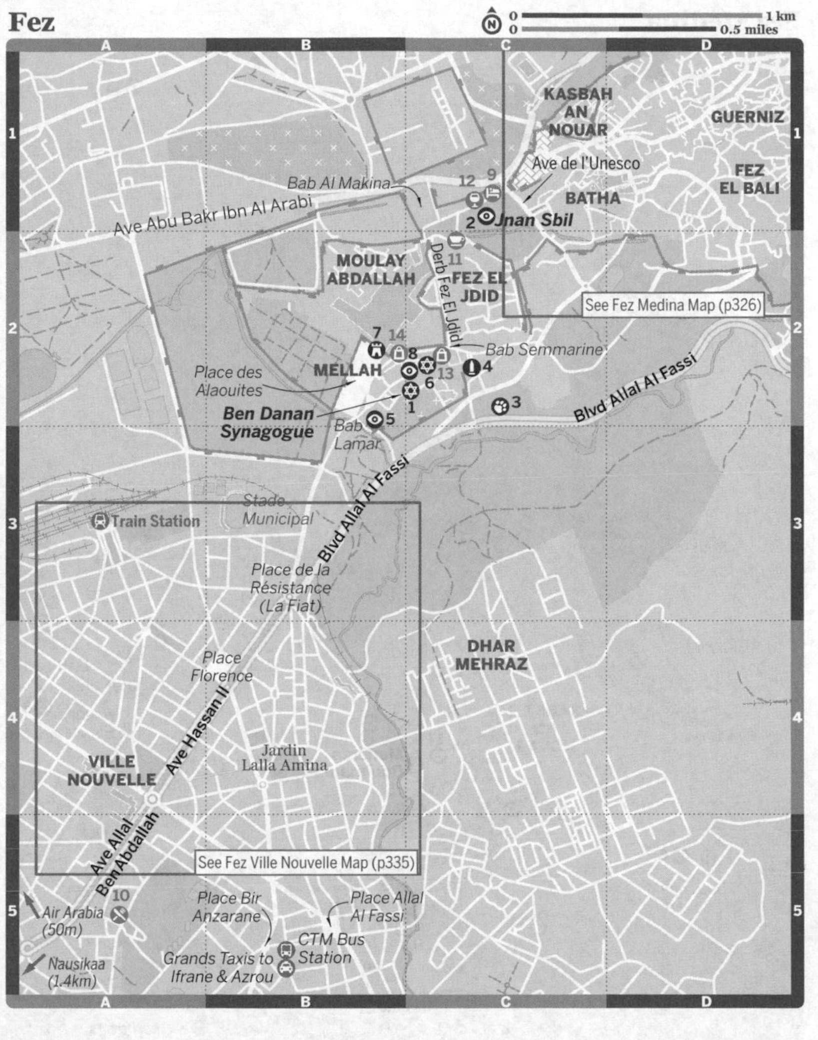

Fez

Top Sights
1 Ben Danan Synagogue C2
2 Jnan Sbil C1

Sights
3 American Fondouk C2
4 Borj Sidi Bounafae C2
5 Jewish Cemetery B2
6 Mellah C2
7 Royal Palace B2
8 Rue des Mérinides C2

Sleeping
9 Hôtel Jnane Sbile C1

Eating
10 MB Restaurant Lounge A5

Drinking & Nightlife
11 Café Restaurant La Noria C2
12 Mezzanine C1

Shopping
13 Gold Shops C2
14 Hasnaoui B2

Fez Medina

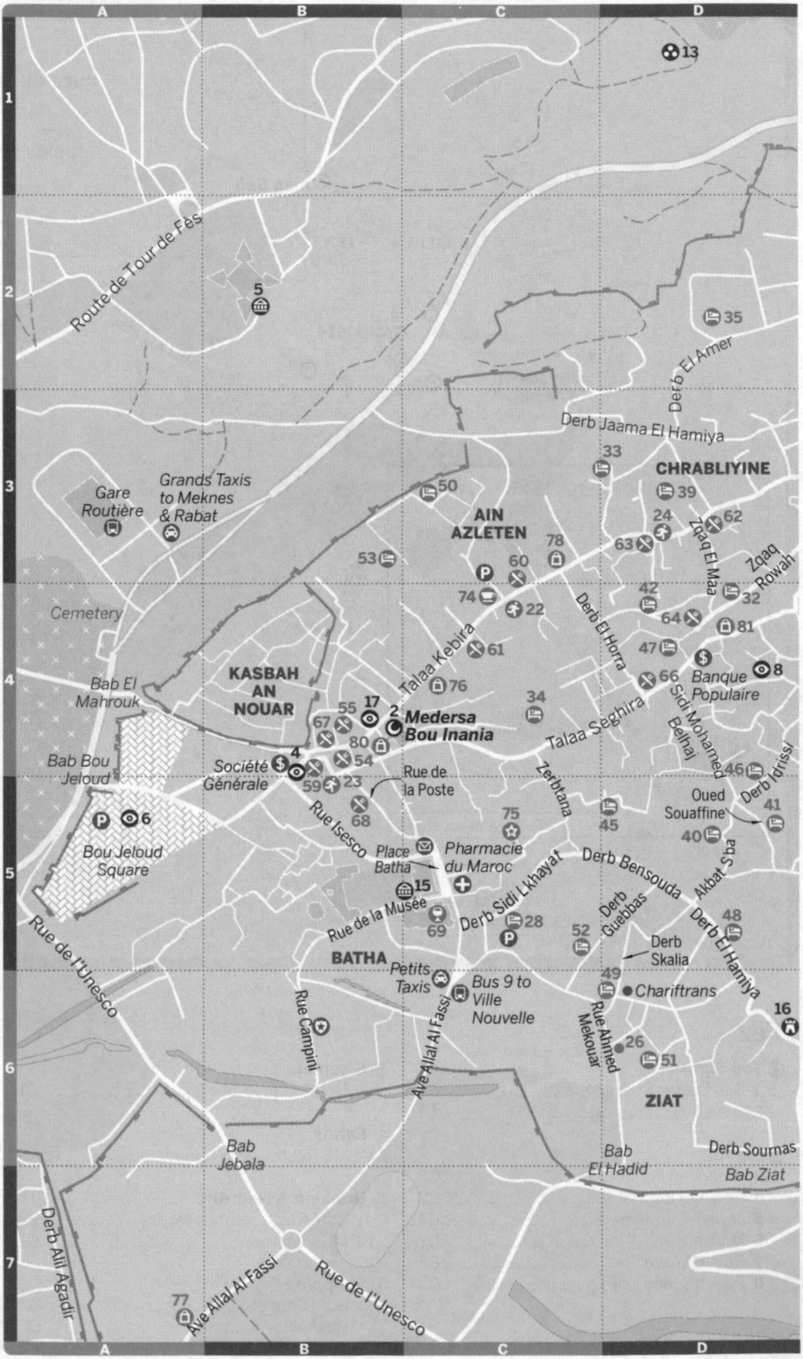

A B C D

1 2 3 4 5 6 7

13
Route de Tour de Fès
5
35
Derb El Amer
Derb Jaama El Hamiya
33
CHRABLIYINE
Gare Routière
Grands Taxis to Meknes & Rabat
50
39
AIN AZLETEN
24
62
53
78
63
60
Zqaq El Maa
Zqaq Rowah
74
42
32
22
Derb El Horra
Cemetery
64
81
61
47
Talaa Kebira
8
Banque Populaire
Bab El Mahrouk
KASBAH AN NOUAR
76
66
17
55
2
Medersa Bou Inania
34
Sidi Mohamed Belhaj
67
80
Talaa Seghira
Bab Bou Jeloud
4
Société Générale
54
46
59
23
Rue de la Poste
Zerbtana
Derb Idrissi
68
Oued Souaffine
41
6
Rue Isesco
75
45
40
Bou Jeloud Square
Place Batha
Pharmacie du Maroc
Derb Bensouda
Akbat Sba
15
Rue de la Musée
Derb Sidi Lkhayat
Derb Guebbas
Derb El Hamiya
69
28
52
48
BATHA
Derb Skalia
Rue de l'Unesco
Petits Taxis
Bus 9 to Ville Nouvelle
49
Chariftrans
Rue Campini
Ave Allal Al Fassi
Rue Ahmed Mekouar
16
26
51
ZIAT
Bab Jebala
Bab El Hadid
Derb Sournas
Bab Ziat
Derb Ain Agadir
77
Ave Allal Al Fassi
Rue de l'Unesco

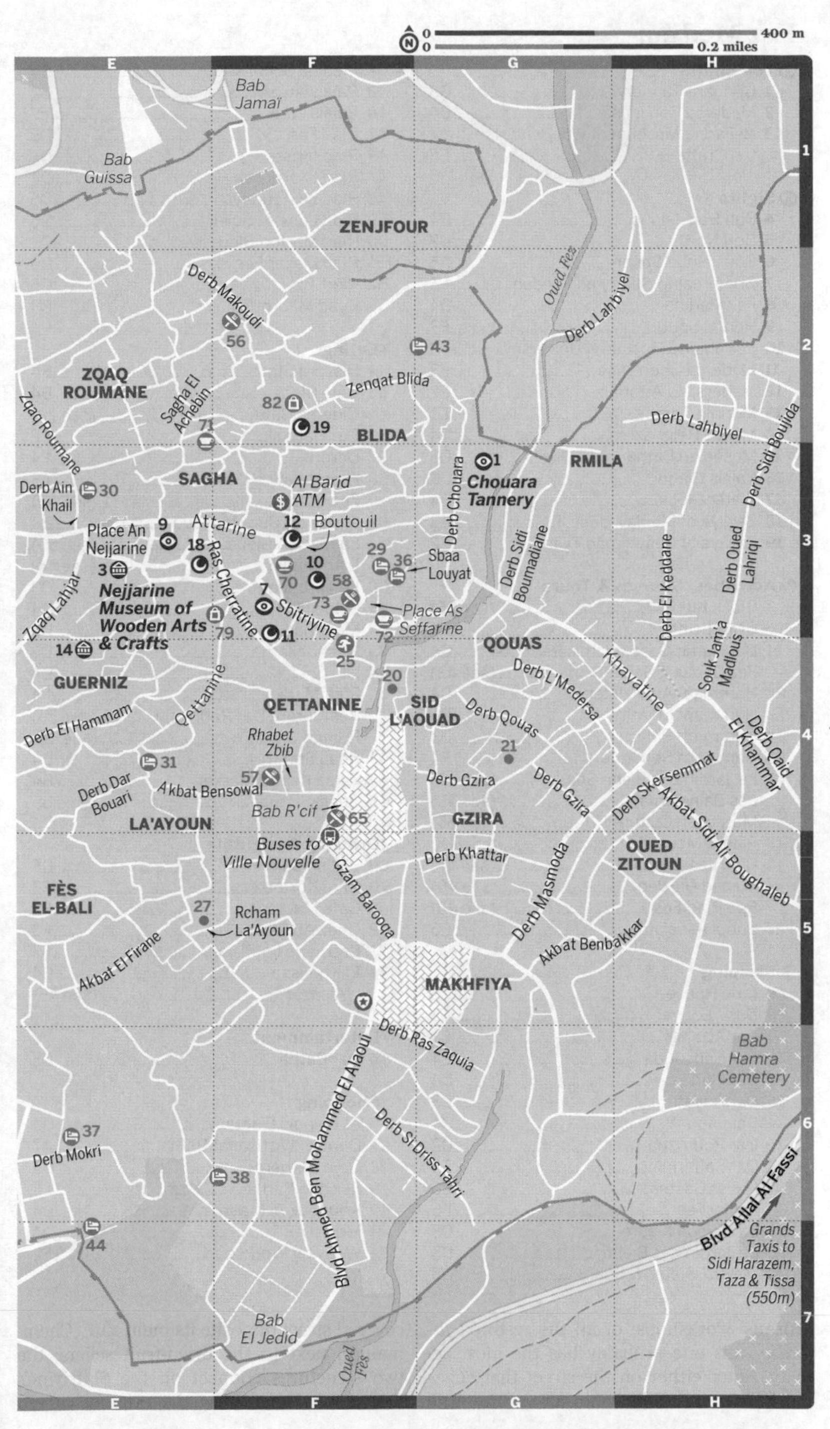
0 400 m
0 0.2 miles
Bab Jamaï
Bab Guissa
ZENJFOUR
Oued Fez
Derb Makoudi
56
43
Derb Lahbiyel
ZQAQ ROUMANE
Zqaq Roumane
Sagha El Achebin
Zenqat Blida
82
19
BLIDA
71
Derb Lahbiyel
Derb Sidi Boujida
1
Chouara Tannery
RMILA
SAGHA
Derb Ain Khail
30
Al Barid ATM
Derb Chouara
Place An Nejjarine
9
Attarine
12
Boutouil
18
Ras Cherratine
10
29
36
Sbaa Louyat
Derb Sidi Boumadiane
Derb El Keddane
Derb Oued Lahriqi
3
Nejjarine Museum of Wooden Arts & Crafts
Zqaq Lahjar
70
58
7
Sbitriyine
73
Place As Seffarine
72
79
11
14
25
QOUAS
Souk Jam'a Madlous
GUERNIZ
20
Derb L'Medersa
Khayatine
QETTANINE
SID L'AOUAD
Qettanine
Derb El Hammam
Derb Qouas
Derb Qaid El Khammar
Rhabet Zbib
21
31
Derb Dar Bouari
57
Akbat Bensowal
Derb Gzira
Derb Gzira
Derb Skersemmat
Akbat Sidi Ali Boughaleb
Bab R'cif
65
LA'AYOUN
GZIRA
Buses to Ville Nouvelle
OUED ZITOUN
Derb Khattar
Derb Masmoda
Gzam Barooqa
FÈS EL-BALI
27
Rcham La'Ayoun
Akbat Benbakkar
Akbat El Firane
MAKHFIYA
Derb Ras Zaquia
Bab Hamra Cemetery
Blvd Ahmed Ben Mohammed El Alaoui
Derb Si Driss Tahri
37
Derb Mokri
38
Blvd Allal Al Fassi
44
Grands Taxis to Sidi Harazem, Taza & Tissa (550m)
Bab El Jedid
Oued Fès

Fez Medina

Top Sights
1 Chouara Tannery ... G3
2 Medersa Bou Inania ... B4
3 Nejjarine Museum of Wooden Arts & Crafts ... E3

Sights
4 Bab Bou Jeloud ... B4
5 Borj Nord ... B2
6 Bou Jeloud Square ... A5
7 Chemmaine-Sbitriyine Funduq ... F3
8 Fez Medina ... D4
9 Henna Souq ... E3
10 Kairaouine Mosque & University ... F3
11 Medersa Cherratine ... F3
12 Medersa El Attarine ... F3
13 Merinid Tombs ... D1
14 Musée Belghazi ... E4
15 Musée du Batha ... C5
16 Palais Glaoui ... D6
17 Water Clock ... B4
18 Zawiya of Moulay Idriss II ... E3
19 Zawiya of Sidi Ahmed Tijani ... F2

Activities, Courses & Tours
Clock Kitchen ... (see 55)
20 Craft Draft ... F4
21 Dar Namir Gastronomic Retreats ... G4
Fez Cooking School ... (see 43)
22 Hammam Ain Azleten ... C4
23 Hammam Mernissi ... B5
24 Hammam Rihab ... D3
25 Hammam Seffarine ... F4
Le Jardin des Biehn Spa ... (see 40)
Les Bains Amani ... (see 43)
Moroccan Culture 101 ... (see 55)
26 Plan-it Morocco ... D6
Riad Laaroussa ... (see 47)
Ruined Garden ... (see 46)
Spa Riad Fès ... (see 45)
27 Subul Assalam ... E5

Sleeping
28 Cine House ... C5
29 Dar 7 Louyat ... F3
30 Dar Attajalli ... E3
31 Dar Bensouda ... E4
32 Dar Finn ... D4
33 Dar Hayati ... D3
34 Dar Jannat ... C4
35 Dar Roumana ... D2
36 Dar Seffarine ... F3
37 Fes et Gestes ... E6
38 Funky Fes ... F6
39 La Maison Maure ... D3
40 Le Jardin des Biehn ... D5
41 Mayfez Suites & Spa ... D5
42 Medina Social Club ... D4
43 Palais Amani ... G2
44 Palais Faraj ... E7
45 Riad Fès ... D5
46 Riad Idrissy ... D4
47 Riad Laaroussa ... D4
48 Riad Les Oudayas ... D5
49 Riad Lune et Soleil ... D6
50 Riad Maison Bleue ... C3
51 Riad Mazar Fes ... D6
52 Riad Tizwa ... C5
53 Ryad Mabrouka ... B3

Eating
54 Bissara Stalls ... B4
55 Café Clock ... B4
Cinema Cafe ... (see 28)
56 Dar Hatim ... F2
57 Darori ... F4
58 Fassi Medina Delice ... F3
Fez Café ... (see 40)
59 Jawharat Bab Boujloud ... B4
La Maison Bleue ... (see 50)
L'Amandier ... (see 44)
60 Le Tarbouche ... C3
61 Made in M ... C4
62 Moi Anan ... D3
63 Nacho Mama ... D3
64 Nur ... D4
65 R'cif Market ... F4
Restaurant Dar Roumana ... (see 35)
Ruined Garden ... (see 46)
66 Snail Stand ... D4
67 Talaa Kebira Market ... B4
68 Veggie Pause ... B5

Drinking & Nightlife
69 British Saloon ... C5
70 Cafe Kortoba ... F3
71 Cafe Maure ... E2
72 Chez Abdellah ... F3
73 Crémerie La Place ... F3
74 El Khmissa ... C4
L'Alcazar ... (see 45)

Entertainment
75 Dar Batha ... C5

Shopping
76 Abdelbaki Elaouni ... C4
77 Centre d'Artisanat Batha ... A7
78 Coin Berbère ... C3
79 Funduq Barka ... F3
80 Kounouz Al Maarifa ... B4
81 Médin'ART ... D4
82 Weaving Workshop ... F2

artisans' workshops; of all the restored *fanadiq,* this one probably has the most activity. Enter either on the street that edges the Kairaouine (Sbitriyine), or on the little covered street opposite its main gate (Chemmaine), next to the dried-fruit sellers; the two structures connect on the Sbitriyine's first floor. Don't miss the original carved cedar beams displayed in the Chemmaine courtyard. On the roof terrace (accessible by lift), you're eye level with the Kairaouine's white minaret and the observation tower of Dar Al Mouaqqit.

Medersa Cherratine ISLAMIC SITE
(Map p326; Ras Cherratine; Dh20; ⌚9am-5pm) It may not be as lavishly ornamented as the Bou Inania or the Attarine, but this 1670 Quranic school has the great benefits of being very large and little visited. It also exists (for now) in a state of mild ruin, unlike more tidied-up Fez spots, and you have the run of the place, through all the old student rooms (former population: 150+) on three floors. With attractive windows opening onto the courtyard, photo ops abound. It even has bathrooms.

Medersa El Attarine ISLAMIC SITE
(Map p326; Rue Attarine, at Derb Smaat Laadoul; Dh20; ⌚9am-5pm) Founded in 1325 in the heart of the medina, this school is a marvel of elegant mosaic tiles, magnificent cut plaster as fine as lace and beautiful original carved cedar. A renovation in 2019 opened the upstairs rooms as well, so you can get a taste of student life – strikingly austere, though each room does have its own letterbox. The institution functioned as a kind of prep school; typically students here advanced to the adjacent Kairaouine University.

Kairaouine Mosque & University MOSQUE
(Al Qarawiyyin; Map p326) Established in 859, the Kairaouine is the spiritual heart of Fez and, arguably, all Morocco. It is also considered the world's oldest university, though it began as a simple *medersa* (school for studying the Quran), funded by Fatima Al Fihria, a member of an elite family who emigrated from the Tunisian city of Kairouan. Expanded over the centuries, the Kairaouine is now very large, with a capacity of 20,000. This is hard to grasp on the ground, though, as shops and houses encircle it, disguising its true shape.

As with all Moroccan mosques, only Muslims may enter. Passersby can glimpse the mosque's courtyard from doors at Chemmaine and on Derb Boutouil, but its scale is best appreciated from above – its minaret and ten rows of green-tiled roofing are visible from almost any rooftop in the medina.

The vast mosque space is also the university. Though it has been state-run since 1963, students still gather as they have for a millennium, in a traditional *halqa,* seated in a circle on the floor around a teacher. Curriculum focuses primarily on classical Arabic language and Islamic studies.

The university library, which is open only to students, holds a vast collection of manuscripts. Visitors with sufficient curiosity and credentials may visit with advance planning – Plan-it Morocco (p334) can make arrangements. The library entrance is on the south side of the complex, on Place Seffarine.

Fez El Jdid

Don't confuse Fez El Jdid (New Fez) with the Ville Nouvelle: this part of the city is 'new' only relative to the medina. It was built in the 13th century by Merinid sultan Abu Yusuf Yacoub, who sought to isolate himself from his subjects, with a buffer of Syrian mercenary guards who lived where Fez El Jdid's mini-medina stands today. Almost half of the area is still given over to the Royal Palace, occasionally visited by Mohammed VI. The area's other main legacy is the Jewish district in the southern half, established in the 15th century. The *mellah*, as it became known, has no remaining Jewish residents but many architectural remnants. In addition to this history, the area is interesting to visit simply as a counterpoint to the old medina. The big gardens on the east side give a breath of fresh air, and there's a lot of non-tourist-oriented life.

★Jnan Sbil GARDENS
(Bou Jeloud Gardens; Map p325; Ave Moulay Hassan; ⌚8am-7pm Tue-Sun) These lush gardens are a breath of fresh air after the intensity of Fez's medina, and a good walking route between Bab Bou Jeloud and the *mellah*. Midday, they can feel a bit dry and empty; they're better at dusk, when locals come in droves to promenade on the shady paths, cool off around the grand central fountains and visit the bird coops, where peacocks and doves are bred. There's a second gate on the east side.

★Ben Danan Synagogue SYNAGOGUE
(Map p325; Derb Djaj, south off Rue des Mérinides; Dh20; ⌚9.30am-6pm) Built in the 17th century to serve the *megorashim* (Jews descended from those expelled from Spain), this synagogue is trimmed in pretty herringbone green tiles, turquoise octagonal pillars and glowing chandeliers. The guardian can point out the main features, including the original deerskin Torah scrolls in an ark built into the wall, and a mikvah (ritual bath) in the basement, filled by an underground water source. B&W photos of other Jewish sites around Morocco are also on display.

The synagogue, which was renovated in 1999, is still used on high holy days. Derb Djaj is roughly midway along Rue des Mérinides; the synagogue can also be reached via Derb Taquriri, near the cemetery.

For navigation purposes and dealing with local would-be guides: about five minutes' walk due east is a second neighbourhood synagogue from the same period, **Al Fassiyine**, built by the local Moroccan Jewish community, but it is not regularly open to the public.

American Fondouk ANIMAL SANCTUARY

(Map p325; 0535931953; www.fondouk.org; Blvd Allal Al Fassi; donations welcome; 8am-noon Mon-Fri) FREE This nonprofit organisation, established in 1927, is dedicated to giving the working donkeys, mules and horses of the Fez medina a better life, with veterinary treatment and also support and education for the often-poor families who depend on the animals for their livelihoods. The group welcomes visitors, and vet volunteers give insightful, ad-hoc tours around the 25 stables and other facilities. Given the possibility of seeing animals with severe injuries, a visit is not recommended for younger children.

Mellah JEWISH SITE

(Map p325) In 1438 Sultan Ar Rashid created Morocco's first official Jewish district, just east of the royal palace. At its peak, some 250,000 Jews lived in the area south of Bab Semmarine. Today, the remaining handful have moved to the Ville Nouvelle, but it's still interesting to see traces of the community in the buildings. The name derives from a salt marsh or the Oued Mellah (Salt River) in the area; now every Jewish quarter in Morocco is called a *mellah*.

Rue des Mérinides, the district's main street, is lined with homes with open balconies. The grandest old homes are in the northwest part of the neighbourhood, but many are in ruins or are now occupied by many poor families. The covered lane along the north edge of the cemetery was once goldsmiths workshops; now the tiny rooms have been repurposed as dwellings. Older doorframes throughout the area still have *mezuzot* (small parchment cases), or small rectangular holes where they used to be.

Next door is the **Jewish Cemetery** (Map p325; Dh10 donation; 8.30am-5pm Mon-Fri, from noon Sun), established in 1883.

Activities

Fez offers a number of ways to enjoy the traditional Moroccan hammam.

Hotel Hammams

This is the easiest option, and good if you want privacy or to go coed. They usually have room for only two or four people, and you must reserve ahead. Many hotels open their hammams to nonguests; Les Bains Amani (p340) and Riad Laaroussa (p339) are two particularly nice choices. Expect to pay about Dh350, plus the same again (or perhaps more) for a massage afterwards. A few places – such as Spa Riad Fès and, more affordably, **Nausikaa** (0535610006; www.nausikaa.ma; Ave Bahnini; hammam Dh100, massage from Dh250; 7am-10.30pm) in the Ville Nouvelle – offer a full spa menu, with various beauty treatments as well.

Spa Riad Fès SPA

(Map p326; 0535947610; www.riadfes.com; 5 Derb Ben Slimane, Zerbtana; hammam/massage from Dh150/595; noon-8pm) If your skin can't

THE FOUNTAINS OF FEZ

You can barely turn a corner in the medina without coming across a public water tap – or at least the beautiful mosaic-trimmed remnants of one. They're just one remnant of an elaborate water system developed mainly in the Almoravid (1061–1147) and Almohad (1147–1248) periods, in which rivers were harnessed and channels dug, so that, like a system of arteries and veins, fresh water flowed into the city and dirty water flowed out. The fountains are the most visible element of this system, usually installed near a hammam and a mosque. The most elaborate ones were endowed by wealthy residents, and one of the finest is the 18th-century Nejjarine fountain, featuring especially elaborate *zellige* tilework and lace-like carved stucco.

Today many of the 60 or so public fountains in the medina have been turned off (locals say it was a government move to force residents to pay for their utilities at home), but a few still have running water. Working or not, shining or chipped or treated more as a public bench or rubbish bin, they remain a meeting point in any neighbourhood. For visitors, they're useful landmarks to navigate by.

FEZ: SIGNPOSTED CITY

A system of self-guided walks leads through the medina, with colour-coded signs mounted above the street. Each route highlights an aspect of traditional Fez, with informative signboards along the way. Attune yourself to the signs, and you can also use them to guide you out of the maze.

Red Artisanal crafts (Bab Bou Jeloud to Place Lalla Yedouna, essentially via Talaa Kebira)

Brown Monuments and souqs (Bab Bou Jeloud to R'cif, mostly along Talaa Seghira, overlapping with the red route near Kairaouine)

Green Palaces and Andalusian gardens (Jnan Sbil to Ain Azleten, through Batha and then following a convenient north–south route)

Blue Knowledge and learning (eastern side of the medina, from Bab Guissa to Al Andalous Mosque)

Purple Fez El Jdid (from Place Moulay Hassan on the north side to Bab Lamar by the Royal Palace)

Orange Walls and ramparts

For an overview, see info boards posted at some gates. There's one just off Talaa Kebira by the Ain Azleten parking, and another by the Royal Palace in Fez El Jdid. Bookshops also carry a printed guide (with a good map), although it's older and the colour-coding differs slightly.

bear another hammam scrub but you still want some pampering, come to this excellent full-service spa. The treatment rooms, overlooking the pool, are somewhat austere – all the lavish luxury comes from the skilled hands of the well-trained staff. One massage aficionado deemed her hour-long Ayurvedic treatment one of the best of her life.

Le Jardin des Biehn Spa HAMMAM
(Map p326; ☎0535741036; www.jardindesbiehn.com; 13 Akbat Sbaa, Douh; 45min hammam/massage Dh350/400; ⏲11am-8pm) Inside one of Fez's quirkiest riads is this cosy spa. Get scrubbed and polished in the mosaic-tiled hammam just big enough for two, under a traditional domed ceiling pierced with starry lights. Afterwards, opt for a relaxing, toning or lymphatic massage with essential oils mixed into sweet almond and argan oils.

Hybrid Hammams

Some public hammams, used regularly by Moroccans, anticipate tourists' needs too. You might pay a bit more than locals do (usually about Dh50 each for entry, exfoliation and massage), but you'll also be provided with all the necessary gear (soap, *kessa*, and so on) and ushered through the process. Hammam Mernissi is the best equipped, with a clean marble-finished public room and a full spa (with private hammam rooms) upstairs. It even has disposable underwear if you show up without an extra pair.

Oher public hammams, **Rihab** (Map p326; 3 Chrabliyine, Talaa Kebira; Dh20; ⏲women 8am-8pm, men 8pm-8am), **Ain Azleten** (Hammam Bou Soueifa; Map p326; Talaa Kebira; entry, scrub, massage each Dh50; ⏲women noon-8.30pm, men 6am-noon & 8.30pm-midnight) and **Hammam Seffarine** (Map p326; Place As Seffarine), are accustomed to tourists and can provide you with gear (but you should bring a change of underwear).

Hammam Mernissi HAMMAM
(Map p326; ☎0535741854; spamernissi@gmail.com; 46 Derb Serrajine, Bab Bou Jeloud; public hammam Dh50, private treatments from Dh250; ⏲women 11am-9pm, men 6-9am & 9pm-midnight) This public hammam is very tourist-friendly, and has a package (Dh200) that covers all your kit (robe, towel, soap, *kessa* glove and so on) and a thorough exfoliation. A 30-minute massage is Dh200 more. Upstairs is a chilled-out spa area (open till 8pm), with four private chambers for hammam and massage.

Neighbourhood Hammams

Every district, even in the Ville Nouvelle, has its own public bath. You'll need to bring your own kit. The easiest way to find them is to ask at shops selling the *kessa*, as it means there's usually one nearby. Expect to pay Dh20, and a bit more for exfoliation or massage. Also expect to attract a lot of friendly attention.

Courses

Arts & Crafts

★ Craft Draft ARTS & CRAFTS
(Map p326; ☎0649894197; www.craftdraft.org; 17 Fondouk Khrashfiyen, R'cif; 4hr workshop per person Dh300; ⊙9am-6pm) In Hamza Fasiki's eyes, everyone is an artisan. In about four hours, he'll turn you into a bookbinder, brass etcher or leather embosser; in two hours, you'll learn the basics of traditional geometric patterns. Hamza learned the skills from his own father, a master craftsperson; in these classes you are able to use wonderful old traditional tools.

Atlas Apothecary ARTS & CRAFTS
(www.atlasapothecary.com; distillation workshop 700Dh) Depending on the season, Miriam's workshops may focus specifically on distillation – you'll make your own rose- or orange-blossom water – or more broadly on Moroccan herbal medicine and even healing cooking. Workshops at her home near R'cif are typically private (you'll need to bring your own group), but she also runs a monthly public workshop (Dh200).

Cooking

Clock Kitchen COOKING
(Map p326; ☎0535637855; www.cafeclock.com; Derb El Magana, Talaa Kebira; baking/cooking course €40/60) Held in Café Clock's (p341) upstairs kitchen, these classes pack a lot into a few hours, thanks to superdynamic teachers. For the half-day cooking class, you start by shopping in the souq, then come back and cook, followed by a massive lunch. For those with a sweet tooth, the baking class covers five biscuit and bread recipes in three hours.

Dar Namir Gastronomic Retreats COOKING
(Courtyard Kitchen; Map p326; www.darnamir.com; 24 Derb Cheikh El Fouki, Al Andalous; full-day class 2-4 people €350) Food writer Tara Stevens, who wrote the Café Clock cookbook, shares her creative approach to tradition in courses at her 450-year-old home, often with her delightful right hand, Rachida. Classes range from a Moroccan wine-and-cheese tasting to a half-day tapas course to a full-day affair, and even an excursion to a goat farm. The house is also available to rent.

Ruined Garden COOKING
(Map p326; ☎0649191410; www.ruinedgarden.com; 13 Derb Idrissi; half-day course Dh550) One of Fez's best dining spots also offers cooking classes: a bread-baking course with a trip to

City Walk
Mazing Medina

START BAB BOU JELOUD
END PLACE R'CIF
LENGTH 3KM; TWO TO THREE HOURS

This route takes you down through the medina to the Kairaouine Mosque and out at R'cif, at the bottom of the hill. It could take a couple of hours or all day, depending on distractions.

The medina's western gate, ❶ **Bab Bou Jeloud**, was built by the French – it once had doors that closed and locked from the outside. For the tour, take the first left after the gate to reach Talaa Kebira, where a market extends up and down the street. To the left is fresh produce; turn right (downhill) and into the scrum of butchers, including one devoted to camel meat. Where the butchers end, you're at ❷ **Medersa Bou Inania** (p322), which represents the Merinid style at its most refined.

Opposite the *medersa* entrance (above eye level) are the remnants of a 14th-century ❸ **water clock** (p322), in turn built atop the former home of Córdoba-born Jewish philosopher Maimonides, who lived here in the mid-12th century.

Continuing downhill on Talaa Kebira, note gates to large courtyards: these are *fanadiq*, inns designed to host merchants and their caravans. Set back a bit on the left, ❹ **Funduq Qaat Smen** has been selling honey and vats of *smen* (aged clarified butter) since it was built in 1336. Just downhill on the right, ❺ **Funduq Tazi** hosts drum makers, as well as potters.

On the left, after Derb Bouhaj, is a ❻ **sheepskin tannery**, noticeable for its stench; Derb Bouhaj leads to the small Ain Azleten tannery. Both historically supplied the district just downhill, Chrabliyine, named for slipper-makers who still work here. After a dogleg to the right, the minaret of the ❼ **Chrabliyine Mosque** rises over the street.

At the bottom of the slope where a building juts into the street, turn right onto Rue Fakhrine (look for a 'Henna Souk and Pottery' sign high on the wall; if you start walking uphill, you've gone too far). Immediately on your left, an open door leads to the ❽ **henna souq** (p324), a pretty

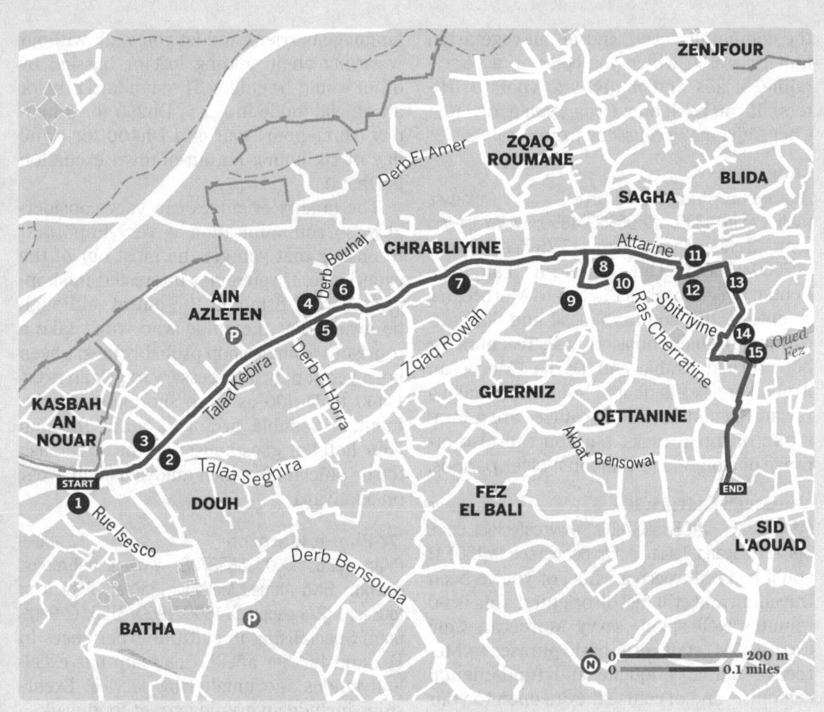

tree-shaded square with friendly dealers in natural cosmetics, pottery and bric-a-brac.

Exiting the henna souq the same way you entered, turn left (south), continuing in Rue Fakhrine. After 50m, the street jogs, and a right turn brings you to Place An Nejjarine, centre of the carpenters district. The carpenters *funduq* is a **9 museum** (p322) dedicated to their craft, and the masterpiece fountain here is trimmed with cedar. In the lanes immediately north, craftspeople build glittering wedding thrones.

Leave the square as you came, turning uphill and taking an immediate left, through an ornate horseshoe arch crossed with a low wooden beam, preventing the passage of loaded mules. At the end of the lane, past stalls selling candles and incense, is the **10 Zawiya of Moulay Idriss II** (p324). Non-Muslims cannot enter but can peer inside. Look up to see an ornate ceiling; the tomb is back and to the right. Left of the entrance is a *mzara,* a spot for 'express' prayers to the Fez founder, with a brass slot for donating alms.

Backtrack along Rue Fakhrine, turning right on Talaa Kebira. Now you are in the *qissariat,* the covered souqs that spread on either side. The street dead-ends at **11 Medersa El Attarine** (p329).

Emerging from the *medersa,* turn left (south). The street passes under two cupolas; the second marks the main entrance to the venerable **12 Kairaouine Mosque & University** (p329). Again, non-Muslims cannot enter. The cupola is part of Dar Mouaqqit, a tower for astronomical observation; it once had its own water clock.

Turn back (noting the Kairaouine's modest white minaret) and take the first street right, to follow the university walls. There's a second, good view into the mosque at Bab Al Werd, on your right, and after the next turn is the restored **13 Funduq Staouniyine**, built for traders from Tetouan.

The sound of metalworkers leads you into pretty **14 Place As Seffarine**, where brass trays and copper pots are made. With the university walls (and the entrance to its library) at your back, you face Medersa As Seffarine, built in 1280 and now in use after a major restoration.

Head out the far right corner of the square. Turn left at the T-junction and pass (on the left) the grander entrance to the Seffarine *medersa.* Then the street leads to the **15 Dyers' Souq**. Climb the bridge to see the river, recently cleaned, then take the next right to exit into Place R'cif, where you can catch a petit taxi.

the community oven, and an all-vegetarian lunch class, in which you cook up a veggie tajine, salads and *maâkouda* (potato fritters). If you book on a Friday, you can watch Chef Najia make couscous from scratch.

Language

Arabic Language Institute LANGUAGE
(ALIF; Map p335; ☎0535624850; www.alif-fes.com; 2 Rue Ahmed Hiba; 3-/6-week course Dh7000/12,000) The American Language Center, which teaches English to Moroccans, is one of the country's best and longest-running Arabic schools as well. Teachers for both formal Arabic and Darija (Moroccan Arabic) are excellent, and homestays make a rewarding add-on. Group courses are a minimum of three weeks, but you can also arrange one-on-one tuition for shorter periods.

Moroccan Culture 101 LANGUAGE
(Map p326; ☎0535637855; www.cafeclock.com; Derb El Magana, Talaa Kebira; per person Dh150) If you'll be in Morocco a while, or you've been travelling and still feel disoriented, this is 90 minutes well spent: savvy Moroccan Café Clock (p341) staff cover basic phrases in Moroccan Arabic, etiquette and fundamental customs – and of course they're open to your FAQs. The course is scheduled on demand, ideally with two or more people.

Subul Assalam LANGUAGE
(Map p326; ☎0535637936, 0663549172; www.sacal-fez.com; 19 Gzem Benameur, R'cif; 3-week group course Dh6000, hourly lessons Dh250) Subul Assalam ('Pathways to Peace') organises language classes, but just as important are the extras: homestays, lectures and excursions, as well as cultural workshops, such as crafts, calligraphy and music. Three-week courses run in Darija (Moroccan Arabic), modern standard Arabic and, notably, Tamazight (Berber). There's also a 10-day intensive option.

Tours

Fez can feel a bit private and closed, so a guided tour here opens many doors. And there are great opportunities to get up close and personal with all kinds of skilled people in the city – whether that's artisans and cooks who've honed their crafts over decades or expert hammam attendants who let no centimetre of skin go unscrubbed.

As well as pointing out incredible architecture and clandestine corners, guides can answer cultural questions, help overcome language barriers, and let you walk without worrying about getting lost or hassled by other would-be guides. The standard rate for an official guide in Fez is Dh250 for a half-day (three-hour) tour and Dh400 for a full day of six hours; an out-of-town excursion is Dh500.

The quality of guides can vary considerably, so communication is very important to ensure that you get the most out of the experience. If you're not interested in shopping, say so firmly at the outset, although be aware that the guide who won't take a tourist to a single shop probably hasn't been born yet. It may be necessary to pay an extra Dh50 to Dh100 as a 'no shopping' supplement. If possible, arrange a guide through your hotel or guesthouse; on the street, ask to see official ID, which guides usually wear on a lanyard.

★Plan-it Morocco TOURS
(Map p326; ☎0535638708; www.plan-it-morocco.com; Blvd Ahmed Mekouar, Batha; 3½hr food tour for 1/2/4 people Dh1600/1950/3150; ⏲9am-6pm) Specialising in cultural experiences in Fez and further afield, this team has excellent guides and unfaltering service. Excursions include an evening street-food walk, a tour of the Jewish quarter, and even a trip to a public hammam. With three months' notice, the team can arrange access to the Kairaouine library (p329). All tours are private; you'll need to arrange your own group.

Culture Vultures CULTURAL
(☎0645223203; www.culturevulturesfez.org; 1-4 people Dh1500) This company's half-day tour, Artisanal Affairs, is a chance to meet and talk to coppersmiths, tanners, tile-makers, cobblers and weavers. Be ready to ask questions; you'll get out of it what you put in. A shorter option (two hours Dh750) is a visit to the **Centre d'Artisanat Batha** (CFQMA; Map p326; ☎0535633016; www.forartisanat.ma; Ave Allal Al Fassi; ⏲9am-4pm Mon-Fri, from 10am Sat & Sun), introducing you to craft students and teachers at this training facility.

There's no shopping involved, and groups are restricted to six.

Photography Walking Tour TOURS
(☎0659661502; www.omarchennafi.com; 3hr tour Dh700) See the medina through the eyes of a local photographer on this laid-back tour, led by professional snapper Omar Chennafi. You'll learn plenty about local Fassi life while you're walking, and Omar strikes a good

Fez Ville Nouvelle

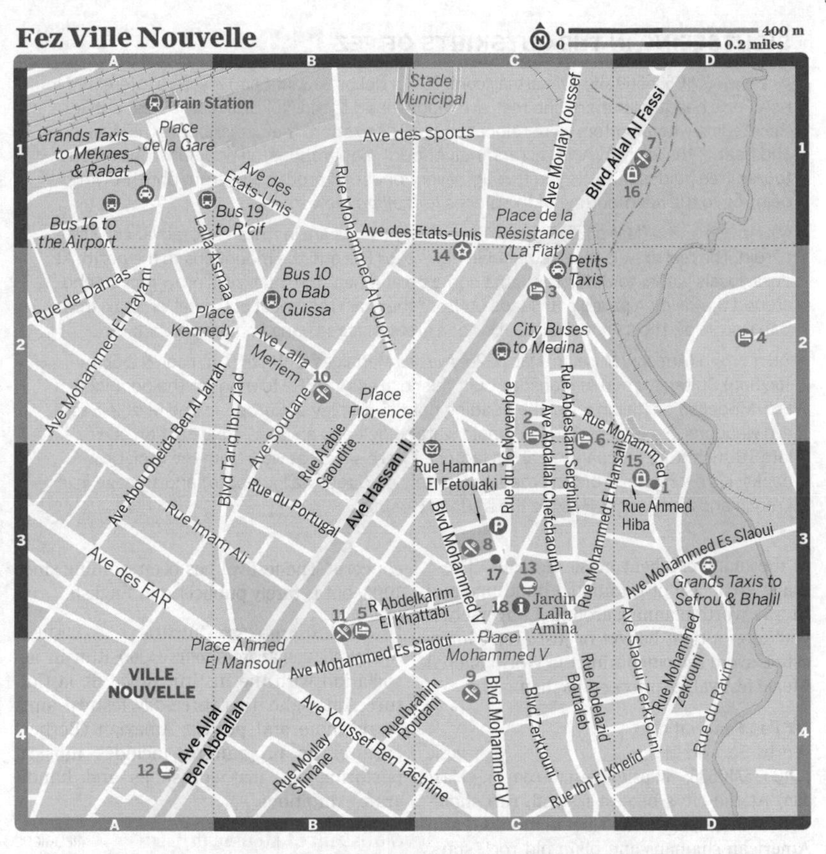

Fez Ville Nouvelle

Activities, Courses & Tours
1 Arabic Language Institute ... D3

Sleeping
2 Across Hotel ... C2
3 Hotel Barceló Fès Medina ... C2
4 Hotel Sahrai ... D2
5 Hôtel Splendid ... B3
6 Youth Hostel ... C2

Eating
7 Carrefour ... D1
8 Central Market ... C3
9 Chez Vittorio ... C4
10 Chicken Mac ... B2
11 Le Jazzy ... B3

Drinking & Nightlife
12 Assouan ... A4
13 Cafe Central Parc ... C3
Jungle Social Club & Tapas ... (see 4)

Entertainment
14 Institut Français ... C2

Shopping
15 ALC/ALIF Bookstore ... D3
16 Borj Fez ... D1

Information
17 Carlson Wagonlit ... C3
18 Délégation Régionale de Tourisme ... C3

balance between technical advice and artistic insights. Tours can be tailored to your interests, focusing on geographical areas or subjects such as architecture or people.

Festivals & Events

On any given night in Fez, there seems to be a band playing in the distance. Sometimes it's just a random party, but sometimes it's one

SIGHTSEEING IN THE OUTSKIRTS OF FEZ

Art Naji (☎0535669166; www.artnaji.com; 20 Ain Nokbi; ⊙8am-6pm) If you're interested in how Fez's beautiful pottery and tiles are made, head to Ain Nokbi, a district just outside the medina where potters were relocated in 2013 to spare their neighbours the dust and heat of the kilns. At Art Naji (and neighbouring operations, all popular stops on bus tours), free guides will take you through every phase of production, from pot-throwing to painting to the hand-cutting of the pieces for *zellige* tilework.

Merinid Tombs (Map p326) These 14th-century tombs are in a dramatic, advanced state of ruin. The real draw is the spectacular views over Fez and the mountains to the north. At dusk, locals gather to watch the lights come on and hear the muezzin's prayer calls echo around the valley. A paved path leads up from the main road west of the hill, or a taxi from Bab Bou Jeloud costs about Dh12. It's not a great place to hang about after dark.

Borj Nord (Armoury Museum; Map p326; Ave des Mérinides; Dh10; ⊙9am-noon & 2-5pm Tue-Sun) Sultan Ahmed Al Mansour built this fortress in 1582 to monitor the populace of Fez. Modelled on Italian forts, the building holds a display of European and Middle Eastern weapons, a model of the Bou Inania water clock and an interesting section on Fez's late-19th-century mechanised arms factory. There's a great view from the roof. Drawbacks: it's a long way from the medina (there's no direct walking path) and signage is in French and Arabic only. Beware the midday closing.

of the many excellent music festivals. These make great use of traditional buildings and they're worth planning around. Conversely, if you're on a tight budget or just aren't interested, avoid the city during the World Sacred Music festival, as prices spike then.

★Fes Festival of World Sacred Music MUSIC
(☎0535740535; https://fesfestival.com; ⊙May/Jun) At the city's biggest festival, rub shoulders with gospel choirs, Tibetan monks, Latin American shamans and plain old rock stars, all in town for a week to contribute to an uncommonly positive and inspirational musical vibe. As eclectic as the artists are the beautiful venues, which include public squares and gardens and restored old palaces.

While big names are a draw (Patti Smith and Youssou N'Dour have played in recent years), equally fascinating are the more intimate concerts held by various *tariqas* (Sufi brotherhoods) from Morocco and around the Muslim world. Fringe events include art exhibitions, films and debates. Some programmes are free, but most shows cost between €15 and €30; tickets and all-access passes (€350) can be purchased on the festival website and at the venues. Accommodation books up far in advance, so organise as far ahead as possible if you plan on attending.

Festival of Andalusian Music MUSIC
(Festival de la Musique Andalouse; ⊙Apr) Orchestras from around Morocco and Spain celebrate their shared musical heritage in classical concerts. The festival has been running since 1995, but is rarely publicised in English.

Festival of Amazigh Culture CULTURAL
(www.festivalamazighfes.com; ⊙Jul) Run in association with the Institut Royal de la Culture Amazighe, this three-day festival aims to promote and protect Amazigh (Berber) culture. Its programme includes musical performances, art workshops and handicraft exhibitions.

Moussem of Moulay Idriss II RELIGIOUS
(⊙last week of Sep) Fez's biggest religious festival honours the city's founder, Moulay Idriss Al Azhar. It kicks off with the delivery of a freshly embroidered cover for the saint's tomb and then artisan guilds make nightly processions on foot and horseback through the medina, with traditional bands and sprays of orange-blossom water. Dates occasionally shift into early October.

Festival of Sufi Culture MUSIC
(www.festivalculturesoufie.com; ⊙Oct) This week-long celebration of mystical Islam includes talks and debates (usually in French only), as well as some spectacular concerts with Sufi musicians from across the world.

Sleeping

Most visitors stay in a traditional guesthouse tucked away in the medina. Standard hotels in the Ville Nouvelle, a petit-taxi ride away, may seem drab in comparison, but they do have more amenities per dirham.

Fez lodging will never fill up entirely, but because each riad has only a few rooms, book ahead for the best selection, especially in spring, fall and during any festivals.

Medina

With hundreds of guesthouses in the medina, you'll almost always find a place to suit your taste and budget. Shoestring travellers used to have only the cheapies near Bab Bou Jeloud, but there are now good riad hostels and excellent homestays with local families – recommended even if you can afford more.

★Medina Social Club HOSTEL €
(Map p326; 0535637839; www.facebook.com/medinasocialclub; Derb El Menia Wosta; dm/d/tr Dh120/550/650;) This large, well-kept riad goes all in on 'social': the place offers tours, classes, Arabic sessions, plus films and music open to the public. Befitting the name, there's plenty of public space to lounge, eat, drink and chat. The private rooms and six-bed dorms are nicely designed (each bed has a light, a locker and plugs); dorms have two showers. The restaurant serves dinner, either a menu at Dh130 or à la carte (*kefta* tajine with eggs Dh70; lamb and dried fruit tajine Dh120).

★Funky Fes HOSTEL €
(Map p326; 0535633196; www.funkyfes.com; 60 Arset Lamdelssi, Bab El Jdid; dm Dh75-100, d Dh335;) Fez's original medina hostel is an amiable, hippie-ish *dar*-turned-crash-pad close to Bab El Jdid. Each of the five dorm rooms has between six and 12 beds, plus a large shower room (ventilation could be better); an en-suite double is up on the plant-covered terrace. There's a communal kitchen and in-house dinners cost Dh40. The staff can arrange tours, activities and cooking classes.

Dar Hayati GUESTHOUSE €
(Map p326; 0535635882, 0612717712; 19darhayati@gmail.com; 19 Derb Bouhaj; d/tr €49/56, d with shared bathroom €39;) Dar Hayati is a simple, good-value guesthouse in a great location off the main shopping street and close to parking at Ain Azleten. What it lacks in fancy mosaics is made up in friendly owners and a great roof terrace with excellent views. Two bedrooms have separate bathrooms and two have shower rooms en suite.

Fes et Gestes GUESTHOUSE €
(Map p326; 0535638532; www.fesetgestes.net; 39 Arsat Al Hamoumi, Ziat; r €50-55) If the Morocco of your imagination is fuelled by 20th-century literati, book one of the three rooms in this guesthouse: each is named after a writer (Karen Blixen, Marguerite Duras and, naturally, Paul Bowles). There's an utterly transporting library, as well as a wild garden inhabited by the French owner's cats. Breakfast is very good too.

Cine House GUESTHOUSE €
(Map p326; 0535638395; cinehouse.19@gmail.com; 8 Sidi Lkhayat, Batha; dm/s/d/q €10/18/30/40;) Opened in 2019, this is a stylish (and tiny) guesthouse with just seven rooms, including a six-bed dorm. What you lose in space, you gain in convenient location and a friendly cafe (p342) downstairs, where an excellent breakfast is just Dh30. The roof terrace is very nice.

Dar Jannat GUESTHOUSE €
(Map p326; 0535636000; www.riadjannat.com; 89 Derb Ahl Tadla, Talaa Seghira; dm €12, d from €32, with shared bathroom €29;) This tranquil place offers traditional splendour at a great price. A couple of the simple, charmingly furnished rooms share a bathroom, and there's a six-bed dorm as well as a larger family room. The helpful owners also run Dar El Yasmine on the same lane. A sign on Talaa Seghira's south side points to the turn north, toward a fountain.

Dar 7 Louyat GUESTHOUSE €€
(House of 7 Turns; Map p326; 0535635604, 0661755401; www.dar7louyat.com; 37 Derb Sbaa Louyat, Seffarine; s/d/tr/q €63/86/95/105;) The tiny alley really does turn seven times before you find this gem, sympathetically restored and dotted with contemporary art. The leafy terrace has a small dipping pool and tremendous views. What distinguishes the place, beyond the six comfortable rooms (some sleep three or four people), is kind staff and exceptionally good food (dinner on request, Dh150 to Dh200); wine is served.

Dar Roumana GUESTHOUSE €€
(Map p326; 0535741637; www.darroumana.com; 30 Derb El Amer, Zqaq Roumane; r €85-145;) Occupying a quiet spot against the northern walls, Dar Roumana is a beautiful restoration job with hard-to-beat views from its roof terrace. Uncommonly, three rooms have bathtubs, and a couple have external windows. The Yasmina suite, with its four-poster bed and balcony, is the pinnacle. A perennial favourite, this place also has one of the medina's better restaurants (p343).

Dar Seffarine GUESTHOUSE €€
(Map p326; ☎0671113528; www.darseffarine.com; 14 Derb Sbaa Louyat, Seffarine; r from €75, ste €110-130;) This house stands on high ground, so it's blessed with external-facing windows, as well as a roof terrace with a mesmerising view down into R'cif. The Iraqi architect owner has applied a light touch to the 14th-century structure, preserving old room layouts – as in the palatial Kobbe Suite, with its domed ceiling. Dinner (Dh200) and alcohol can be served in-house.

La Maison Maure GUESTHOUSE €€
(Map p326; ☎0535740027; www.lamaisonmaure.com; 51 Derb Pacha Baghdadi, Ferrane Couicha, Chrabliyine; d €85, ste €105-125;) The six elegant rooms and suites in this traditional house are furnished with a light, contemporary sensibility, with marble floors, fine antiques and artwork collected by the owner – all kept warm with central heating (a rarity). The roof terrace is the perfect spot for breakfast or a sundowner. An eclectic global restaurant, Le Maure'sk, completes the picture.

Riad Tizwa GUESTHOUSE €€
(Map p326; ☎0658322607; www.riadtizwa.com; 15 Derb Guebbas, Douh; d €70-120, tr €110-150, q €140-180;) This guesthouse offers nine rooms with colour-soaked flair, from a compact double to a large family suite with fireplace. Red Marrakshi rugs festoon the courtyard, which has comfortable seating and a striking wall fountain. There's a salon too. Close to street parking, the riad is in an excellent location for exploring.

Riad Mazar Fes GUESTHOUSE €€
(Map p326; ☎0668073864, 0535741557; www.riadmazarfes.com; 12 Arsat Bennis, Batha; d/ste Dh770/1100;) Parking at the door? A lift? With these rare amenities, you might think you're not in the medina, but the 150-year-old building drips with polished traditional style. The six rooms, with orthopaedic mattresses and decorated in local textiles, edge a courtyard with a fountain, and there are cosy reading nooks upstairs. One weak point: the roof terrace lacks much view.

Dar Finn GUESTHOUSE €€
(Map p326; ☎0655018975; www.darfinn.com; 27 Zqaq Rowah; r €81-110;) Past the dark medina doorway, Dar Finn delivers a better-than-usual surprise: high Fassi style in the main courtyard house, plus an annexe with a walled garden and plunge pool. The multilevel roof has a good view too. Of the seven serene rooms, two family-friendly suites (Rmila and Pacha) have private balconies over the pool; two (Sbaa and Sammarine) lack air-con.

Dar Attajalli GUESTHOUSE €€
(Map p326; ☎0535637728, 0677081192; www.attajalli.com; 2 Derb Qettana, Zqaq Roumane; r Dh640-1115;) Years of patient restoration preserved the integrity of this building, which now has six supremely comfortable, elegant guest rooms. The courtyard is relatively small, which keeps some rooms naturally cool – but also dim. If you prefer light, book La Masria (sleeps four), or the rooftop Menzeh, with the same fine views as the rest of the terrace. Breakfast is bounteous.

Riad Les Oudayas GUESTHOUSE €€
(Map p326; ☎0661198189, 0535636303; www.lesoudayas.com; 5-6 Derb El Hamiya, Ziat; r €90;) More than many guesthouses, this riad feels like a rambling private house, perhaps because the whitewashed rooms and public salon all have fireplaces. Up top is a large roof terrace, but two of the five rooms also have their own terraces. There's an honour bar in the courtyard, next to the tiny, banana-tree-shaded plunge pool, and there's a hammam too.

Riad Lune et Soleil GUESTHOUSE €€
(Map p326; ☎0535634523; www.luneetsoleil.com; 3 Derb Skalia, Batha; r €65-90;) Each room at this French-owned riad is a cornucopia, filled with the evidence of a lifetime of collecting, from old postcards and embroidery to carvings and metalwork. It's not a museum, though; there's plenty of comfort too, such as whirlpool baths. There's also a good kitchen, a rooftop salon for colder weather and parking around the corner (Dh20 per night).

★**Le Jardin des Biehn** BOUTIQUE HOTEL €€€
(Map p326; ☎0535741036; www.jardindesbiehn.com; 13 Akbat Sbaa, Douh; r €150-180, ste €250-450;) This is a place you'll want to stay at again and again, just to try out all the eclectic rooms. Each one conveys its own whimsical story, through superb textiles, vintage finds and objets d'art, collected by Biehn *père,* a French designer and antiquarian. The namesake garden is a veritable forest, with a small pool, plus a great restaurant (p343).

★**Dar Bensouda** GUESTHOUSE €€€
(Map p326; ☎0535638949; www.riaddarbensouda.com; 14 Zqaq Labghal, Qettanine; d/ste

FEZ LODGING: HOW TO CHOOSE

Fez has hundreds of great places to stay, so choosing just one can seem like an overwhelming task. Here are some questions to ask yourself.

Medina or Ville Nouvelle? For most, the atmospheric medina is the obvious choice. But Ville Nouvelle hotels typically have more air and light, and they're easy to find at the end of a long day.

How much luggage? If you have a lot, look for places closer to medina gates and parking areas. Porters wait at parking areas to take your bags on carts.

Do you feel the cold? If yes, make sure your room has air-conditioning; the units function as heaters in winter. Some guesthouses have fireplaces too. Or consider a Ville Nouvelle hotel.

Do you need support? At many small guesthouses, you're left to your own devices and staff disappear after dinner. Bigger places (more than eight rooms, say) will usually have more staff.

Do you want a drink? Not all guesthouses serve alcohol.

What's your style? Some riads wear their history proudly and others are highly polished. If you tend to get overstimulated, places with less-ornate decor can be more restful at the end of the day.

Are you interested in food? Riads that offer meals on request (rather than run full restaurants) can be an opportunity for good home-style cooking and often some surprises beyond the usual Moroccan restaurant menu; simply ask for whatever's in season.

In the end, don't fret too much. Quality is generally high and it's hard to go wrong.

Booking Services

Ziyarates Fes (0620303792, 0535634667; www.ziyaratesfes.com; s/d from Dh150/200) More than 30 families rent rooms in their medina homes; some are more formal B&B situations, with more amenities like private bathrooms, and some are unadorned family life. Either way, it's well organised and you can expect a warm welcome.

Fez Riads (0672513357; www.fez-riads.com) Handles a selection of beautifully restored guesthouses and apartments, with a percentage of proceeds supporting grassroots development projects. Send your dates and preferences and they do the rest.

Lonely Planet (lonelyplanet.com/morocco) Recommendations and bookings.

from Dh1155/1850;) In this 17th-century palace, a warm staff welcomes you into tangible history: floor tiles show centuries of footsteps; worn-smooth wooden doors open on simple, serene rooms. The courtyard view of the sky is mesmerising; then again, the crimson-velvet lounge calls, as does the pool annexe and the multiple roof terraces. The only weak point: slightly bland food.

★ **Riad Laaroussa** GUESTHOUSE €€€
(Map p326; 0674187639; www.riad-laaroussa.com; 3 Derb Bechara, Talaa Seghira; d Dh1200-2200, ste from Dh2700;) A cavernous entrance hall jogs into a dazzling light-filled courtyard, with orange trees and a fountain. Indeed, there's loads of space throughout this 17th-century building, and the joy continues in the eight rooms, decorated with modern art and eclectic furniture; some even have fireplaces. Factor in the outstanding (and large!) pool annexe, and it's one of Fez's best riad experiences.

There's also a **hammam** (hammam/massage Dh350/380; 11am-9pm) and a restaurant (dinner Dh280) serving alcohol.

★ **Ryad Mabrouka** GUESTHOUSE €€€
(Map p326; 0535636345; www.ryadmabrouka.com; 25 Derb El Mitter, Ain Azleten; d/ste Dh1250/1400;) Open since 2003, Mabrouka feels lived-in, in a good way. The large traditional courtyard house is furnished with European antiques and art, and the welcoming staff encourage guests to treat it like home, from the garden and pool up to the roof terrace. The eight rooms have nice extras like bathrobes and olive-oil soap; one small double is only Dh1000.

SLEEPING IN FEZ EL JDID

Given its awkward location midway between the Ville Nouvelle and the medina, but a long walk from both, this area is not ideal as a base, and the lack of sleeping options reflects that. One nice budget place sits on the far edge, close to the medina.

Shiny bright with coloured glass and painted wood, the spotless **Hôtel Jnane Sbile** (Map p325; 0669964326, 0535638635; www.facebook.com/HotelJnaneSbileFes; 22 Kasbat Shems, Bou Jeloud; s/d/tr Dh180/300/370;) offers very reasonably priced rooms, with good-quality beds. The location is convenient if you're driving, or if you want a quiet retreat from the medina: it's just outside the walls and opposite the tranquil gardens for which it's named. There's a great roof terrace.

Riad Idrissy GUESTHOUSE €€€
(Map p326; 0649191410; www.riadidrissy.com; 13 Derb Idrissi; d €85-140;) This magnificently restored townhouse adjoins the excellent Ruined Garden (p342) restaurant, but where the garden is a beautiful shambles, the rooms are fully finished in quirky traditional style. There's informal room service, including a basket of tea and coffee outside your door before 8am, so you can have drinks in bed before easing into the day.

Riad Fès GUESTHOUSE €€€
(Map p326; 0535947610; www.riadfes.com; 5 Derb Ben Slimane, Zerbtana; d/ste from Dh2250/3600;) Blending ancient and modern with impressive panache, this Relais & Chateaux property with 15 rooms has every comfort. The newer quarters wouldn't look out of place in a Parisian boutique hotel yet remain unmistakably Moroccan. Its location is also good: not too far from taxi drop-offs in Place Batha, but also close to Talaa Seghira action. It has a beautiful hammam (p330). If you can't afford to stay here, it's still worth coming for a drink (p344).

Palais Amani HERITAGE HOTEL €€€
(Map p326; 0535633209; www.palaisamani.com; 12 Derb El Mitter, Oued Zhoune, Blida; d/ste from €209/304;) Relatively large for the medina, Palais Amani has 18 rooms, all focused on an expansive garden. Rooms have traditional touches but skew towards modern minimalist. There's a great salon with a fireplace, and lots of services, including a very good seasonal restaurant, a **hammam** (hammam from Dh395; 8am-8pm), **cooking classes** (www.fezcookingschool.com; 2/4hr group class €47/77) and yoga. The British owner and her team are very detail-oriented.

Mayfez Suites & Spa GUESTHOUSE €€€
(Map p326; 0666882024; www.mayfez.com; 36 Oued Souaffine, Douh; d/ste from Dh1500/2400;) Stepping into Mayfez is like stepping into the pages of a glossy magazine. Six palatial suites, each with a private terrace, edge a vast patio and heated pool. The glam decor mixes traditional crafts, gorgeous antiques and even Vuitton-look leather in the lift. Naturally there's a sumptuous spa, as well as a restaurant. You might not need to venture out.

Palais Faraj BOUTIQUE HOTEL €€€
(Map p326; 0535635356; www.palaisfaraj.com; 16-18 Derb Bensouda, Ziat; d from €210; P) A 19th-century palace turned luxe heritage hotel, the Faraj retains some beautiful original features (one suite occupies the old hammam). Classic rooms are just a tiny bit cramped, but the pool is large. Staff is suave, and as it's just outside a quiet medina wall, the atmosphere is calm and open – and it's a cinch to reach by taxi.

Riad Maison Bleue GUESTHOUSE €€€
(Map p326; 0535741873; www.maisonbleue.com; 33 Derb El Mitter, Ain Azleten; d/ste from €190/450;) The El Abbadi family pioneered the luxury riad business in Fez (it also owns La Maison Bleue on Batha). This place is four houses knocked together, for a total of 18 impeccable rooms, scented with orange blossom from the courtyard trees. It also has a spa, the plush Blue Lounge, and a chic terrace restaurant-bar with views to Borj Nord.

Ville Nouvelle

Rooms are in less demand here than in the more popular medina, so much of the time you can get midrange accommodation at budget prices. Naturally, though, hotels are newer and don't show a whole lot of character.

Hôtel Splendid HOTEL €
(Map p335; 0535622148; splendidf@menara.ma; 9 Rue Abdelkarim El Khattabi; s/d Dh353/432; P) 'Splendid' might be overstating it, but this 70-room hotel is good value, with

clean tile floors, big bathtubs and a slight vintage-motel vibe (in a good way); beds can be a bit squishy. The large courtyard pool is nice, though you're on view to surrounding rooms. There's also a restaurant (dinner Dh150). Heat, but no air-con, and wi-fi is lobby-only.

Youth Hostel HOSTEL €
(Map p335; ☎0535624085; www.hihostels.com; 18 Rue Abdeslam Serghini; dm Dh90, d with shared bathroom Dh190; ⏲check-in 9am-9pm, gate open 24hr;) One of the better youth hostels in Morocco, the Fez branch is a leafy little retreat with a traditional tiled salon, and it's often used by Moroccan travellers. Tidy rooms (a few private, several four-bed dorms, and one larger dorm) and the shared facilities are superbly clean, as is the communal kitchen. For the allergic: cats can wander into rooms.

Hotel Sahrai DESIGN HOTEL €€€
(Map p335; ☎0535940332; www.hotelsahrai.com; off Route de l'Hôpital Ghassali, Bab Lghoul, Dhar Mehraz; r/ste from Dh2500/4000; P) On a hill near the Ville Nouvelle, this smart hotel is a world of its own, a retreat with style, space, a spa and restaurants – though you can dip into the medina on the hotel shuttle. Breezy modern architecture is trimmed with beautiful traditional Fassi decorations; understated rooms feature sunken tubs. Only shame: the back view of the mall.

Across Hotel HOTEL €€€
(Map p335; ☎0535940612; www.acrosshotels.com; 76 Ave Abdallah Chefchaouni; s/d Dh1050/1350; P) A sparkling modern hotel in a convenient location, the Across ticks all the boxes. Rooms are clean, with new laminate floors and windows that open; some have balconies. On the roof is a pool and a bar, both with great 360-degree views. The bars and restaurant all have a Portuguese or Brazilian theme, despite French ownership.

Hotel Barceló Fès Medina HOTEL €€€
(Map p335; ☎0535948800; www.barcelo.com; 53 Ave Hassan II; d/ste excl breakfast from €115/165; P) First, to be clear: this Spanish chain hotel is *not* in the medina, but on the east edge of the Ville Nouvelle. The 134 rooms are well designed and spacious, with modern decor; for a small surcharge, you get a distant medina view. There's a spa, restaurant and bar (nonguests welcome). Online discounts can make it upper midrange.

Eating

Fassi cuisine is famed across Morocco for its refinement, although its best dishes are often served only at home. Dinner in a riad – the smaller, the better – is the closest to home cooking you can buy, and the setting is often stunning. Street food abounds in the medina, and the Ville Nouvelle has more non-Moroccan options.

Medina

Many medina guesthouses also have sumptuous restaurants open to non-guests; ideally, reserve ahead. For budget eats, the major snack strips are on the edges of the medina, near the produce markets at Achebine and R'cif, and by Bab Bou Jeloud. The last is the largest, extending to Rue de la Poste, busy with both traditional and modern restaurants.

★**Café Clock** CAFE €
(Map p326; ☎0535637855; www.cafeclock.com; Derb El Magana, Talaa Kebira; mains Dh60-85; ⏲9am-11pm;) With a clientele of foreigners and creative young Fassis and a staff that's cheerful despite the maze of stairs in the multilevel space, Clock is an ideal place to rest and nourish yourself. The menu is a refreshing Moroccan-Euro mix: a signature camel burger, ras el hanout–spiced potato wedges and interesting vegetarian options, among other goodies.

Adding to the cafe is its cultural schedule, mostly free, of storytelling, live music, movies and more – there's something on every night. (It's a good idea to book ahead in the evening, as it can be packed.)

The cafe is at the end of a dark, shoulder-width alley. Look for the small orange-and-blue sign (or a larger one for the Chinese restaurant at the corner) just below the left end of the water clock on Talaa Kebira.

Le Tarbouche MOROCCAN €
(Map p326; ☎0535638466; 43 Talaa Kebira, Haddadine; snacks Dh25-30, mains Dh45-65; ⏲drinks from 10am, meals noon-9.30pm;) This hip little snack joint has a friendly staff and a creative menu. The Moroccan *tabbouleh* (fluffy couscous replaces bulgur) is refreshing, as is the rosemary-mint lemonade. Mains include *merguez* (spicy sausage) pizza, a veggie *bastilla* that's really an ingenious use of a flour tortilla, and even a vaguely Chinese crispy beef dish. Check the cool mural inside.

Made in M MOROCCAN €

(Map p326; ☎0535634116; 246 Talaa Kebira; sandwiches Dh45-60, tajines Dh60-90; ⏰10am-10pm; 📶🖉) With white walls, wicker lampshades and little bistro chairs, Made in M brings an international-coffee-bar aesthetic to the medina – but its food is distinctly Moroccan. It serves breakfast staples (eggs with *khlea,* dried beef) and tasty lunch sandwiches with fresh salads, as well as tajines. Also nice for a juice and a sweet power-snack of a walnut-stuffed date.

Cinema Cafe CAFE €

(Map p326; ☎0535638395; http://cinemacafefez.business.site; 8 Sidi Lkhayat, Batha; mains Dh40-80; ⏰8am-11pm) Wedged in a corner of a building, this little cafe makes the most of its location with a wide-ranging menu that's all fresh and well prepared. The clientele includes both tourists (usually eating the tajines) and young Moroccans (who come for pizza and pasta).

Nacho Mama MEXICAN €

(Map p326; ☎0694277849; www.nachomamaburritohouse.com; 30 Kantarat Bourous, Chrabliyine; mains from Dh60; ⏰10am-9pm Mon-Fri, to 10pm Sat & Sun) You may not have come to Morocco to eat burritos, but it's hard to resist this little place, done up in festive Mexican cut paper. Watch the medina parade from its prime corner, with a cold cucumber-mint drink or a whole meal. It's a side project of Chef Najat Kanaache of Nur, and the staff do hail from Mexico.

Veggie Pause VEGETARIAN €

(Map p326; ☎0535637777; 11 Rue de la Poste; sandwiches Dh35; ⏰1-4pm & 6.30-10pm; 📶🖉) Avocado toast and Buddha bowls come to Fez, along with fresh creative salads, sandwiches and pasta dishes. Everything's vegie, and a lot is vegan too, but really it's a nice spot for anyone looking to add a little variety to their Moroccan travel diet. The place is a tiny box: sit inside or perch at the two tables outside.

Jawharat Bab Boujloud MOROCCAN €

(Map p326; Bab Bou Jeloud; mains from Dh40; ⏰8am-12.30am; 📶) With an enviable spot snuggled up against gate, this is the pick of Bou Jeloud's clamouring pavement cafes. Its tile-and-wood open frontage makes an impression, as do the good-value meals and petite roof terrace – practically close enough to touch the famed blue gate.

Bissara Stalls MOROCCAN €

(Map p326; Talaa Kebira; soup Dh6; ⏰7am-2pm) Don't miss the Fassi speciality of *bissara* (fava-bean soup), served from tiny shops throughout the medina. Our favourites are at the top of Talaa Kebira and in Achebine. Perfect fuel for exploring the city, the soup is served with a hunk of bread and a dash of olive oil; season with salt, cumin and chilli to your taste.

R'cif Market MARKET €

(Map p326; inside Bab R'cif; ⏰8am-8pm Sat-Thu) Those who shop for produce in the medina know that R'cif is the best place to go – its traders always have the freshest fruit, vegetables and meat. It stretches a fairly long way inside the walls west of the main road into Place R'cif; look for several entry gates.

Snail Stand MOROCCAN €

(Map p326; cnr Talaa Seghira & Derb El Horra; small/large portion Dh6/10; ⏰noon-10pm) This permanent stand is a good place to sample a favorite Moroccan comfort food, especially popular in cold weather: a bowl of snails, still in their shells, in a hot aromatic broth seasoned with dozens of spices. You use a safety pin to pluck the meat out of its shell. Look for the bag of shells hanging from the gate.

★ **Ruined Garden** MOROCCAN €€

(Map p326; ☎0649191410; www.ruinedgarden.com; 13 Derb Idrissi; tapas Dh20, mains Dh70-100; ⏰1-9.30pm; 📶🖉) Dine in the wild garden in summer, or by a cosy fire in winter. Lunch has some bargain stews and 'tapas' (Moroccan salads, with some especially good varieties), while dinner has a few more elaborate dishes (including slow-roasted lamb: prebook). Veg dishes are especially good at lunch. An escort is available on request, though it's well signed.

★ **Dar Hatim** MOROCCAN €€

(Map p326; ☎0663266109, 0666525323; darhatim@gmail.com; 19 Derb Ez Zawiya, Funduq Lihoudi; 3-course menus Dh130-250; ⏰11am-3pm & 7-10pm) Husband-wife owners Fouad and Karima have gradually transformed their family home into an elegant restaurant, complete with brocade cushions and painted wood ceilings – but the food remains hearty and home-cooked, and the welcome as warm as if you were visiting relatives. Set menus include kebab and couscous dishes, as well as a special lamb tajine made from a family recipe.

Karima also teaches a morning cooking class, starting with souq shopping and ending with lunch (Dh600 for four people). Book ahead, and Fouad can come collect you so you won't struggle to find the place. If you do walk, look for a covered lane running northwest painted with colourful murals, including one for Dar Hatim; the restaurant is at the end. The couple also run a nearby guesthouse, Riad Al Fassia Palace.

Fassi Medina Delice MOROCCAN €€
(Map p326; Place Seffarine; mains Dh70-80; ⏲11am-8pm Sat-Thu; 📶) This little place just off the north corner of Place Seffarine has the usual menu, but with a few extras (a daily tajine special, plus a *tfaya* option, with caramelized onion and egg) as well as grilled meats and *tanjia* stew, slow-cooked in hammam coals. Everything comes with a salad, which results in a veritable mountain of food.

Darori MOROCCAN €€
(Map p326; ☎0618453738; www.darori.info; 2 Derb Sayour, Place R'habet Zbib, R'cif; two-course menu Dh150, five-course gastronomic menu Dh380; ⏲6-11pm; 🍸) Excellent Moroccan cuisine is served in this sensitively restored house. Book a day ahead to try special dishes such as *tanjia* or *trid* (chewy pastry filled with chicken and onion). There's a vegetarian offering, and wine is available. It's a little out of the way; you can ask to be met at Bab R'cif.

Moi Anan THAI €€
(Map p326; ☎0535635713; www.maisonmoianan.com; 30 Zqaq El Maa, Chrabliyine; mains Dh90-130; ⏲7-11pm Mon-Sat; 📶) Thai food in Fez might seem like a gamble, and while Moi Anan's menu (handily printed on picture cards) is limited, the place is Thai-run and the food is incredibly fresh. Only one waiter works all the tables in the multilevel old house, so go early or be prepared for a leisurely meal. The roof terrace is small but lovely.

Fez Café FRENCH €€
(Le Jardin des Biehn; Map p326; ☎0535635031; www.jardindesbiehn.com; 13 Akbat Sbaa, Douh; mains from Dh80; ⏲noon-3pm & 7.30-10pm; 📶🍸) This charming restaurant is set in the greenery of Le Jardin des Biehn (p338) hotel. Choose a seat under the verandah or inside the quirky brick-red dining room, done up in Arabic calligraphy and Moroccan royal family photos. The food is a seasonal mix of French, Moroccan and Spanish, chalked fresh on a board each day. Alcohol, including cocktails, is served.

Nur GASTRONOMY €€€
(Map p326; ☎0694277849; www.nur.ma; 7 Zqaq El Rouah; 10-course tasting menu Dh800; ⏲6.30-10pm Tue-Sun) Born in Spain of Moroccan parents, chef Najat Kaanache has worked at restaurants such as Noma and travelled extensively in Mexico. Her lovely fine-dining restaurant synthesises her experience into a dazzling, ever-changing tasting menu that highlights transatlantic culinary links (Moroccan mole just makes sense). It's admittedly pricey for Fez, but a bargain next to similarly ambitious global restaurants.

You must book (and pay) ahead; the pre-paid fee includes service but not drinks. If you prefer a shorter menu, choose the 'wine bar' option.

La Maison Bleue MOROCCAN €€€
(Map p326; ☎0535741873; www.maisonbleue.com; 2 Ave de la Liberté, Batha; two/four courses Dh350/550; ⏲8-11pm) The first fine-dining restaurant in the medina, opened in the 1990s, is consistently one of the best. The menu of the usual salads and tajines might not look thrilling, but the execution is absolutely flawless and delicious. The setting, a 1915 mansion, makes it all dreamier, as does the discreet oud player, who alternates with a gnaoua duo.

L'Amandier MOROCCAN €€€
(Map p326; ☎0535635356; www.palaisfaraj.com; 16-18 Derb Bensouda, Bab Ziat; mains Dh180-220; ⏲6.30-11pm; 📶) The elegant Moroccan menu at the Palais Faraj (p340) restaurant includes an especially elaborate array of traditional salads, followed by less common dishes such as chicken stuffed with fruits and couscous. Mediterranean-French and Asian dishes are also an option. On balmy nights, book a table on the terrace, which feels suspended above the medina – you're eye level with the neighbourhood minaret.

The hotel's bar (cocktails Dh150), in another raised wing, is also lovely but can be smoky.

Restaurant Dar Roumana MEDITERRANEAN €€€
(Map p326; ☎0660290404, 0535741637; www.darroumana.com; 30 Derb El Amer, Zqaq Roumane; 2/3 courses Dh275/350; ⏲7-9pm Tue-Sun; 📶🍸) Dining in the lavishly decorated covered courtyard at Dar Roumana is a white-tablecloth affair and a nice change from the full Moroccan food experience. There is some local spicing (zingy *chermoula* sauce), but the general sensibility is French-Italian, with dishes like gnocchi, roast duck and even a bit of ham. Vegetarians should mention their preference when booking. Alcohol is served. Reserving in advance is recommended; when booking, you can ask for an escort to and from the restaurant.

Ville Nouvelle

The Ville Nouvelle is not a dining destination per se, but you won't go hungry – and you might even enjoy a break from the tajine-couscous-*bastilla* cycle. You'll find cheap eats on the streets leading away from the train station (Aves Lalla Asmaa and Lalla Meriem), and a nice little strip on Ave Hassan El Ouazzani, near Jardin Lalla Amina.

Central Market MARKET €

(Marché Municipal; Map p335; Blvd Mohammed V; 8.30am-4pm) In the Ville Nouvelle and in need of fresh fruit and veggies, spices, nuts, olives or dates? Check out the central market, a lovely art nouveau construction where the day's prices are marked on giant chalkboards at the entrance. Enter on the north side (Rue Hammam El Fetouaki) if you want to bypass the butchers. It's liveliest before noon.

Chicken Mac MOROCCAN €

(Map p335; Ave Lalla Meriem; mains Dh25-40; 9am-1am) Several places seem to run together in a busy row of streetside tables and chairs here. Chicken Mac is the last one away from Place Florence, and quickly serves up generous plates of rotisserie chicken, fried fish, couscous and other cheap, filling meals. Takeaway sandwiches are available.

Le Jazzy FRENCH €€

(Map p335; 0666043770, 0535943960; www.facebook.com/lejazzy; 5 Rue Abdelkarim El Khattabi; mains from Dh120; 12.30-11pm) Duck lovers, take note: the foie gras and confit on the menu at this little bistro come from the owner's own poultry farm. There's also a range of fresh homemade pasta and fish dishes, such as a tender prawn and turmeric ravioli. Occasional live music on the weekends.

Chez Vittorio ITALIAN €€

(Map p335; 0535624730; Rue Ibrahim Roudani; mains Dh75-85; noon-3pm & 6-11pm;) Need a break from Moroccan food? Set the time machine for 1967 and head for this lovely place, which serves pizzas and pasta dishes over red tablecloths. Italians might quibble that the food has strayed somewhat, but service and atmosphere are great, and there's a full bar. Good vegetarian dishes too.

Drinking & Nightlife

A stroll in the Ville Nouvelle is a favourite evening pastime. Stop for an ice cream or just sit on a bench and people-watch. Blvd Mohammed V and Ave Hassan II have the greatest concentration of cafes.

Many Ville Nouvelle hotels house bars serving alcohol. The vast majority of licensed venues in the medina serve alcohol only with food.

Medina

The medina is not known for nightlife, but a few places (including the Medina Social Club hostel) have music, and in some cases you can get a beer. Upmarket hotels may have full bars. But for the most part, it's mint tea all day and all night.

★Chez Abdellah CAFE

(Map p326; Rue Lmachatine; 8am-8pm Sat-Thu) Tiled floor to ceiling, this is less a tea shop than a decorative box, a kind of tiny theatre in which Abdellah, a born showman, mixes teas to order from piles of fresh herbs – not just mint, but also wormwood and other traditional digestives. Abdellah swears his secret is the water: it comes from the holy Kairaouine complex (p329). To find him, take the street off Place Seffarine opposite Crémerie La Place. Midway down, a few of Abdellah's seats spill out onto the street.

★L'Alcazar BAR

(Map p326; www.riadfes.com; 5 Derb Ben Slimane, Zerbtana; 10am-midnight) One of the most elegant places for a cocktail (Dh120) in all of Fez, the gorgeous courtyard bar at Riad Fès (p340) drips with atmosphere: the stucco columns catch the light reflected off an ornamental pool, and an oud player strums and sings. It's so alluring, you might consider staying for dinner at the Moroccan restaurant, L'Ambre.

Cafe Maure TEAHOUSE

(Map p326; Place Sagha; 7am-9pm) Head upstairs to this impeccably old cafe, where water for your mint tea is boiled in a copper urn that's set over a wood fire and pumped with bellows (locally made, of course). Sugar is chipped off a large cone with a special hammer. If you're not up for the all-male scene, there's also a nice cafe at street level.

El Khmissa CAFE

(Map p326; Talaa Kebira, Ain Azleten;) A cold beer is hard to come by in the medina, but this four-storey place delivers, along with the requisite mint tea and fresh juices. At ground level it looks dead, but that's because everyone's on the breezy rooftop, or crowded in on the 3rd floor with the gnaoua musicians that play many evenings – a scene popular with young Moroccans.

Crémerie La Place CAFE
(Map p326; Place As Seffarine; ⌚8am-6.30pm) Place As Seffarine is one of the most interesting spots in the medina, and this cafe is a prime place to watch the square's coppersmiths, over juice, tea, coffee and pastries. In summer, afternoon is preferable; there's no shade on outdoor tables in the morning.

Cafe Kortoba CAFE
(Map p326; Derb Boutouil; ⌚9am-6pm Sat-Thu) Up against the wall of the venerable Kairaouine Mosque, this 1940s-look coffee bar, with dapper old waiters in white shirts, seems ever so modern. It's a fun place to sit and nibble an almond pastry and watch the crowds flow by this lively corner.

British Saloon BAR
(Map p326; Place Batha; ⌚10am-2am) Craving a bar scene in the medina? Head for Hotel Batha's two drinking dens. The dark, wood-panelled indoor bar recalls the building's former history as a British consulate with a log fireplace and a giant portrait of Winston Churchill. Outside in the neon-lit back garden (enter via the side street) is a popular hang-out for young Moroccans, with beers from Dh25.

Fez El Jdid

Mezzanine BAR
(Map p325; ☎0535638668; Ave Moulay Hassan; ⌚noon-1am; 📶) Popular with the young Fassi crowd, this multistorey lounge is a nice counterpoint to medina life, just a short walk from Bab Bou Jeloud. The covered roof terrace overlooking Jnan Sbil (p329) is a good place to chill with a beer or cocktail (from Dh60), and there are tapas and larger plates like pastas and burgers (Dh70 to Dh110) if you're peckish.

Café Restaurant La Noria CAFE
(Map p325; off Ave Moulay Hassan, Jnan Sabil; ⌚7am-11.30pm) Set in a tumbledown riad by a splashing fountain, this old-fashioned cafe is a pleasant place for coffee or juice, and convenient to Jnan Sbil and the *mellah*. Outside is its namesake, a waterwheel slowly collapsing into the stream that flows through the park. The entrance is outside the garden on the south side.

Ville Nouvelle

Probably the main reason to come to the Ville Nouvelle is for an alcoholic drink in a modern atmosphere. Most hotels have bars, and there are a few independent operations: some seedy, and a few quite swank, including the bar at **MB** (Maison Blanche; Map p325; ☎0535622727; www.mbrestaurantlounge.com; 12 Rue Ahmed Chaouki; mains Dh170-240; ⌚noon-3pm & 7pm-midnight; 📶). There are also a couple very vintage (mostly male) bars on Ave Mohammed Es Slaoui west of Blvd Mohammed V.

Assouan CAFE
(Map p335; ☎0535625851; Ave Allal Ben Abdallah; ⌚6.30am-1am; 📶) The cafes on the northeast section of Avenue Hassan II are generally for men. After you pass the first roundabout, there's a cluster of more mixed grand cafes, including this one. The tiny Moroccan-style pastries, heavy on the sesame, almonds and coconut, are especially good – pick from the glass case inside before sitting. There's more substantial food, too.

Cafe Central Parc CAFE
(Map p335; Jardin Lalla Amina; ⌚8am-8pm) In a small park, this cafe has a nice breezy upper terrace, along with the usual coffee and tea. Breakfast (from Dh15) is served all day.

Jungle Social Club & Tapas ROOFTOP BAR
(Map p335; ☎0661439522; www.hotelsahrai.com; Hotel Sahrai, Bab Lghoul, Dhar El Mehraz; ⌚5pm-1am Tue-Sun) Dark and full of plants and the occasional giraffe sculpture, Jungle welcomes drinkers with green-velvet seating around a central bar. On the terrace after dark, there's often a DJ. The food is very secondary, as is, at times, the service. You're really here for the views of Fez by night, and of course the chic clientele.

☆ Entertainment

The Fez cultural scene is fairly rich, but the schedule can be erratic. Several cafes have regular live music, both traditional and contemporary, and several annual music festivals help liven the scene.

Institut Français PERFORMING ARTS
(Map p335; ☎0535623921; www.if-maroc.org; 33 Rue Ahmed Loukili, at Ave des Etats-Unis) One of the city's major cultural outlets, scheduling touring and local artists and productions with, *naturellement*, a French bent. Lectures and movies are hosted in the auditorium.

Dar Batha ARTS CENTRE
(Institut Français; Map p326; ☎0535636713; www.if-maroc.org; 15 Derb Salaj, Douh) This restored house is the outpost for Institut Français in the medina. Check the schedule for

interesting dance and musical performances in a beautiful and intimate setting. Turn from Batha into Derb Salaj next to Pharmacie du Maroc; the space is on a short dead-end where the street jogs left.

Shopping

Fez is the artisanal capital of Morocco. The choice of crafts is wide, quality is high and prices are competitive. The main medina routes (principally Talaa Kebira and Talaa Seghira) have most of the shops, but treasures can also be found in out-of-the-way workshops. A craft-oriented tour can take you great places and arm you with info for shopping wisely.

Medina

The main shopping streets are Talaa Kebira and Talaa Seghira, which converge near the bottom of the slope, close to the *qissariat*, the covered market area that stocks more workaday products, such as fabrics and phones. If you see something you like, either buy it or drop a GPS pin so you can find your way back.

Coin Berbère ANTIQUES
(Map p326; ☎0535636946; 67 Talaa Kebira, Haddadine; ⏲10am-8pm) At the corner with Derb El Horra look for this trio of long-established, well-respected shops, all owned by the same family. Together, they stock everything you need to live the Moroccan home dream: antique embroidery, beautiful ceramics, old wooden doors, silver jewellery and, of course, carpets – soothingly arranged by colour.

Weaving Workshop TEXTILES
(Map p326; off Derb Sidi Ahmed Tijani, Blida; ⏲9am-5pm Sun-Thu) Opposite the Zawiya of Sidi Ahmed Tijani, follow the sign for CyberNet, then take an immediate right under an extremely low (fortunately padded) door frame. You'll find yourself inside a cavernous old workshop, alive with the soft click-clack of looms. The men working here make fine scarves, bedspreads and more.

Abdelbaki Elaouni CLOTHING
(Map p326; ☎0668359590; Talaa Kebira; machine-/hand-sewn djellaba from Dh150/300; ⏲10am-6pm Sat-Thu) Look for this recommended *djellaba* tailor just downhill from Cafe Smile. Machine work takes about five days.

Médin'ART ARTS & CRAFTS
(Map p326; ☎0617575079; 19 Zqaq Lhjar, Talaa Seghira; ⏲10.30am-7pm) This shop stocks creative work by Moroccan and French designers, playing on traditional crafts and designs: Mondrian-pattern *babouches*, for instance, monkish tunics trimmed in Moroccan passementerie, or tote bags emblazoned with the Fez taxi logo. Prices are fixed; note it's sometimes closed on Friday.

Funduq Barka ARTS & CRAFTS
(Map p326; Derb Qettanine; ⏲10am-5pm Sat-Thu) This 18th-century traders inn is one of several restored *fanadiq*. This one happens to be reserved primarily for women artisans, including a tarboosh (fez) maker. South along the street on the opposite side is another *funduq*, Kettanine.

Kounouz Al Maarifa BOOKS
(Map p326; ☎0535633303; 11 Talaa Seghira; ⏲10am-8pm Sat-Thu) If you're looking for good reads and don't want to leave the medina for the ALC/ALIF Bookstore in the Ville Nouvelle, this small shop is the next-best

LIFE IN THE LEATHER DISTRICT

For more than a millennium, Fez has produced some of the world's finest leather, particularly a soft, pale-brown goatskin. At the five medina tanneries, little has changed over the years – although the Sidi Moussa tannery does have a giant steel rinsing machine, installed in a 2015 renovation. Otherwise, donkeys still tote the skins to the tanning pits, filled with pigeon poo, salt and lime (which adds the whitish colour). Tanners are organised according to guild principles, with workers typically born into the job. Unfortunately, they also face serious health problems, thanks to being knee-deep in chemicals such as chromium all day.

It's admirable how well the tradition has lasted, but with each passing year, the hard labour of the medina's medieval pits becomes more of a relic preserved only for tourists' cameras. Dozens of modern tanneries in and around the Ville Nouvelle now manage to produce equally sought-after leather, with minimal damage to the environment and the workers' health. But these modern tanneries only export leather – they don't yet make the bags, slippers and other products that are sold around the medina. And the traditional tanneries function as an important reminder that real work goes into their souvenirs.

option, with a decent selection of English- and French-language books, along with maps and postcards.

Fez El Jdid

Derb Fez El Jdid is a locals' destination for caftans and *djellabas*, and also for upholstery, especially the blingy faux-brocade used in modern Moroccan salons. In the *fanadiq* off to the sides of the lane, you can see tailors constructing pillows and bench cushions.

Hasnaoui HOMEWARES
(Map p325; ☎0535622916; 9 Blvd Boukhsissat; ⏰10am-9pm Sat-Thu) If you've been admiring the *zellige*-look ceramic dishes on which your riad breakfast is probably served, you can find them at this friendly shop. Affordable Cocema ceramic, made in Fez, comes in traditional blue-and-white mosaic patterns, as well as green (for Meknes) and red-brown (for Marrakesh) and a dizzying variety of shapes. Prices are fixed.

Gold Shops JEWELLERY
(Map p325; Rue Sekkakine & Blvd Boukhsissat; ⏰Sun-Thu) Historically only Jews were allowed to sell gold jewellery in Fez, and the shops clustered in and just outside Bab El Magana (Clock Gate) are still the primary place to buy it. They have some fine Morocco-specific jewellery, such as filigree Hands of Fatima – or more contemporary glitter-plastic versions on fine gold chains.

Ville Nouvelle

ALC/ALIF Bookstore BOOKS
(Map p335; ☎0535624850; 2 Rue Ahmed Hiba; ⏰9.45am-12.45pm & 2.30-7pm Mon-Sat) On the pleasant little campus of the American Language Center you'll find likely the best English-language bookshop in Morocco, with a huge selection of books about the country, in addition to general reading. Good selection of guides, including photocopied versions of *Fez from Bab to Bab,* the long-out-of-print English edition of an excellent book of medina walking tours.

Borj Fez MALL
(Map p335; www.borjfez.com; Blvd Allal Al Fassi; ⏰10am-9pm) This large, modern mall is a good spot for anything you might have forgotten to pack, as well as fashion with Moroccan flair: blingy accessories at Bigdil and Diamantine, for instance, and cool, full-coverage styles from Marwa. On the top floor is a food court, open till midnight.

MEDINA MAPS

Mobile phones with GPS have transformed medina navigation. Still, you need the right base maps loaded; at last check, both Google and Apple maps were very weak. Instead, try the apps **Here You Go** and **maps.me**. Neither is flawless, but they both fill in many more gaps – and they work offline. It helps to see the big picture, too: the best paper map available is the glossy foldout *Plan de Fès*, sold at many cafes and bookshops for Dh20.

Inside is a **Carrefour** (⏰9am-11pm) hypermarket and adjacent shop (10am to 9.30pm) for beer, wine and liquor.

Orientation

Visitors to Fez will find themselves in three core areas. The medina is called Fez El Bali (Old Fez) and is almost completely encircled by medieval walls. To the west is Fez El Jdid (New Fez), built in the the 1200s as a new walled precinct. It is still distinct, separated from the old medina by some large gardens, schools and hospitals. The westernmost corner of Fez El Jdid just touches the edge of the Ville Nouvelle. The train station and the main CTM bus station are both here; Place Florence, a square and transit hub, is another convenient landmark. Beyond this to the south and east, and in the hills north and south of the medina, are newer-built districts as well.

The eastern Ville Nouvelle is about 3km from Bab Bou Jeloud, a trip commonly made by petit taxi; a solo ride from the medina is Dh10 to Dh15 on the meter, or Dh4 per seat if the taxi is running a fixed route, such as Batha to Place Florence. Buses are also an option, but they can be severely crowded and run erratically. The walk from around Bab Bou Jeloud takes about 45 minutes.

From Bab Bou Jeloud to the north end of Derb Fez El Jdid, via Jnan Sbil, is about a 20-minute walk. You can also take a taxi; the Royal Palace is a good starting point for a walk through, and the ride costs less than Dh10 from almost anywhere.

For buses, not many run through the area, but many go to Bab Jiaf, just down the hill to the east of Bab Semmarine.

Information

ACCESSIBLE TRAVEL

Fez is an extremely challenging destination for travellers with impaired mobility or sight. No transport is wheelchair-accessible, and the medina streets are steep, winding and extremely narrow in parts, with uneven cobbles and lots of debris. One creative solution we've known some intrepid travellers to use: tour the medina on a hired donkey. Discuss it with your hotel (a few of which have lifts).

DANGERS & ANNOYANCES

Fez is generally safe and well policed, but the medina's maze can sometimes make hassle feel more threatening than it is.

➡ At night in the medina, don't walk alone without a clear destination. Ask for an escort from your hotel or restaurant if you're not certain of your way.

➡ Phone snatchings have occurred on broader streets outside the medina (where thieves can easily grab and run, unlike inside the medina).

➡ Young men will often say a street is 'closed'; sometimes it's a dead end, but often they're just steering you out of residential areas and back to shops.

Faux Guides

Faux guides tend to congregate around Bab Bou Jeloud, the main western entrance to the medina, although crackdowns by the authorities have greatly reduced their numbers and hassle. They're a bit more intense in the Jewish quarter, where tourist police don't visit as much.

Shopping

The pressure to buy in Fez can be immense, but the process needn't be a battle – indeed, it's best treated as a game, and mental preparation helps. Carpet sellers especially are masters of their game, and once you sit down to mint tea and suggestions that you might resell one on eBay to fund your trip – well, it might be easier if you just didn't enter the shop at all. It's also worth remembering that street touts, intense as they can be, are just doing the only job they've got. Also, any time you enter a shop with one, your lower threshold for bargaining rises to cover their commission.

On the train to Fez, strangers boarding at Meknes may befriend you. Some are just nice people; others may be touts, who claim to be students or teachers, and just happen to have 'brothers' who have hotels, carpet shops or similar.

Police Stations

Batha (Map p326; Rue de la Musée, Batha) Large and conveniently located near Bab Bou Jeloud.

R'cif (Map p326; Blvd Ahmed ben Mohamed Alaoui) On the main road leading in to Place R'cif.

LGBTIQ+ TRAVELLERS

Fez is generally more conservative than other cities in Morocco and this applies to LGBTIQ+ life as well. There is virtually no visible queer life in the medina, and only a bit in the Ville Nouvelle. Proceed with discretion.

MEDICAL SERVICES

Clinique Al Kawtar (☎0535611900, 0535611881; Ave Mohammed El Fassi, Route d'Imouzzer, New Fez; ⏰24hr) Large modern hospital in the Ville Nouvelle, just off the main road to the airport.

Pharmacie du Maroc (Map p326; Place Batha; ⏰8.30am-12.30pm & 3-7.30pm Nov-Apr, 9am-1pm & 3.30-8pm May-Oct) An easily accessible pharmacy in the medina, with a beautiful interior.

MONEY

In the Ville Nouvelle, banks (with ATMs) are found on Blvd Mohammed V. In the medina, there are several banks at Place R'cif, plus some useful ATMs:

Société Générale (Map p326; Bab Bou Jeloud; ⏰9.15am-5.15pm Mon-Thu, 8.15-11.45am Fri, 9.15am-12.45pm Sat) Just outside Bab Bou Jeloud.

Al Barid At the Batha post office.

Al Barid (Map p326; Derb Smaat Laadoul) Just north of Medersa Attarine, close to the covered souqs.

Banque Populaire (Map p326; Talaa Seghira; ⏰8.15am-3.45pm Mon-Fri) Midway down Talaa Seghira.

POST

The **main post office** (Map p335; cnr Ave Hassan II & Blvd Mohammed V; ⏰8am-4.30pm Mon-Fri) is in the Ville Nouvelle; the one visitors will likely find most convenient is at **Batha** (Map p326; 1 Rue de la Poste; ⏰8am-4pm Mon-Fri), on the edge of the medina. Shops that sell postcards usually sell stamps; many stores can ship large purchases for you.

TOURIST INFORMATION

There is no tourist office in the medina. You can pick up a decent free map of Fez at **Délégation Régionale de Tourisme** (Tourist Information Office; Map p335; ☎0535942492; Ave Mohammed Es Slaoui; ⏰8.30am-4.30pm Mon-Fri) and book official guides. Staff speak English.

Behind the Central Market, **Carlson Wagonlit** (Map p335; ☎0535622958; cnr Place August 20 & Rue El Mokhtar Soussi; ⏰8.30am-12.30pm & 3-7pm Mon-Fri, 9am-noon Sat) is useful for flights and ferries.

TRAVEL WITH CHILDREN

The medina is not easily negotiable by buggy (stroller). If you're travelling with a toddler, you may simply have to carry your tired child – or, in a pinch, hire a porter with a barrow (empty ones wait at parking areas). Some hotels have lifts, but overall they're not common. One perk of the medina is that children don't have to look for car traffic – but do teach them to listen for '*Balak!*' (donkeys coming through). Kids can run around and meet their Moroccan counterparts at Jnan

Sbil (p329) and on the promenade of Ave Hassan II in the Ville Nouvelle. Older animal lovers may like to see the veterinary work at the American Foundouk (p330).

Getting There & Away

AIR

Fes-Saïss Airport (☎ 0535674712), a single beautiful terminal, is 15km south of the city. It has a currency exchange desk and two ATMs (past customs), but no other major services; you cannot buy a SIM card here. Royal Air Maroc (www.royalairmaroc.com) operates daily flights to Casablanca, as well as connections to Europe. **Air Arabia** (☎ 0802000803; www.airarabia.com; Rue Lalla Aicha, Champs des Courses), Ryanair (www.ryanair.com) and **Transavia** (www.transavia.com) fly to various European cities; **TAP** (www.flytap.com) goes to Lisbon. Air Arabia also operates a direct flight to Marrakesh three times a week, and to Agadir and Errachidia twice a week.

BUS

There are two bus stations in Fez. Most visitors will arrive at the main **CTM station** (Map p325; ☎ 0800090030; www.ctm.ma) in the southern Ville Nouvelle.

CTM runs 16 buses a day to Casablanca (Dh95, five hours) via Rabat (Dh80, three hours) between 1.30am and 7.15pm, plus one other premium bus to Rabat only at 9.30pm (Dh100). Buses to Meknes (Dh25, one hour) run 24 hours a day but departure times are irregular. There are six buses a day to Marrakesh (Dh190 to Dh210, eight hours) between 6.30am and 8pm, plus a premium night bus departing at 9.30pm (Dh265). One bus daily goes to Errachidia (Dh130, 7½ hours) via Midelt (Dh85, five hours) at 9.30pm.

Heading north and east, there are seven buses for Tangier (Dh120, six hours); six for Chefchaouen (Dh75, four hours); seven for Tetouan (Dh120, 5½ to seven hours), plus a premium night bus (Dh145); and two for Al Hoceima (Dh115, six hours), one of which is a night bus.

Four buses go to Nador (Dh120 to Dh130, five hours) and six to Oujda (Dh120 to Dh130, 4½ to five hours).

Buy tickets for Chefchaouen in advance because the lack of other transport options means seats always get booked up quickly. Services can be reduced out of season.

The other station, more convenient to the medina and served by a few CTM buses and all other companies, is the **Gare Routière** (Fes Boujloud; Map p326; ☎ 0535636032) outside Bab El Mahrouk. CTM calls this station 'Fes Boujloud'; note that there's no premium service here, and many buses from here take longer on their routes, so for longer trips it can be worth going to the Ville Nouvelle station. Aside from CTM (first desk on the left inside), all other companies are organised by destination around the hall. There are cafes and a left-luggage facility near the back.

The CTM departures from here are:

Agadir (one daily at 7.30pm, Dh280, 13 hours)
Chefchaouen (three daily, Dh75, four to five hours)
Er Rachidia (one daily at 8.30pm, Dh130, 8½ hours)
Marrakesh (two daily at 6am and 7.30pm, Dh170, 10 hours)
Meknes (one daily at 8.30pm, Dh25, two hours)
Midelt (one daily at 8.30pm, Dh85, six hours)
Tangier (one daily at 10.30am, Dh120, eight hours)
Tetouan (three daily, Dh100, six hours)

Other long-distance buses run to:

Casablanca (via Rabat, hourly)
Chefchaouen (four daily)
Marrakesh (five daily)
Midelt and Er Rachidia (12 daily)
Ouarzazate (three daily)
Oujda (10 daily)
Rissani and Erfoud (three daily)
Tangier (13 daily)
Taza (hourly)
Tetouan and Ouezzane (12 daily)

Locally, there are frequent departures to Azrou (Dh25, 1½ hours), Ifrane (Dh25, 1½ hours), Sefrou (Dh11, 45 minutes) and Meknes (frequently).

CAR & MOTORCYCLE

There are several guarded car parks around the medina, and more were being built at last pass. The most convenient are Place Bou Jeloud close to Bab Bou Jeloud; in Batha; north of Talaa Kebira at Ain Azleten; and in the south at Bab El Jdid, on the road in to Place R'cif (you can drive in to Place R'cif, but parking is very limited). In the Ville Nouvelle there's a guarded car park next to the central market.

Chariftrans (Map p326; ☎ 0661326373, 0679552748; 1 Arset Bennis, Douh; ⏲ 9am-1pm & 2-6pm Mon-Sat) is a reliable transport and vehicle-hire company, offering services such as airport pick-ups, day trips from Fez and multiday excursions. **Hamid Essalih** (☎ 0672905008, 0657718700; essalihhamid2020@gmail.com; per day Dh1200) is a recommended taxi driver for scheduled trips in the city and beyond.

If you have a car, you can drive between the Ville Nouvelle and the medina, but taking into consideration navigation, parking and traffic, it's probably simpler to leave your car parked and take taxis.

TAXI

Grand-taxi ranks are dotted around town, organised by destination. **Taxis for Meknes**

(Map p326, Dh25, one hour) and Rabat (Dh80, 2½ hours) leave from in front of the Gare Routière near the medina (near Bab El Mahrouk). The **rank for Sefrou and Bhalil** (Map p335, Dh12, 45 minutes) is located at Slaiki, southeast of Place de la Résistance in the Ville Nouvelle. **Azrou** (Map p325, Dh35, one hour) and Ifrane (Dh30, 45 minutes) taxis leave from in front of the CTM bus station in the Ville Nouvelle.

Grands taxis in front of the train station don't have specific destinations so cannot be shared, but there is a large **taxi lot** (Map p335) just to the west, with cars to Meknes and Rabat, handy if you miss a train.

A few day-trip destinations (Sidi Harazem, Taza and Tissa) are served by *grands taxis* leaving from the suburb of **Sehb El Werd** (Sehb El Ward), a five-minute walk east from Bab Fettouh.

TRAIN

Fez's shiny train station is in the Ville Nouvelle, a 10-minute walk northwest of Place Florence. It has an ATM, shops selling SIM cards, and some snack bars and decent cafes with wi-fi. There's no official left-luggage service, though there's a semiformal one at the Venezia Ice cafe; have a coffee there first, and tip the attendant.

Trains depart almost hourly between 2.50am and 7.40pm to Casablanca (Dh116, four hours), via Rabat (Dh85, three hours) and Meknes (Dh32, 45 minutes). Ten trains go direct to Marrakesh (Dh195, 6½ hours) and four go direct to Tangier (Dh100, 4½ hours), but the hourly service with a transfer to the high-speed line is faster (Dh172, 3½ hours). Of the six daily trains to Taza (Dh39, two hours), three go on to Nador (Dh49, five to six hours) and the other three to Oujda (Dh49, 5½ hours).

 Getting Around

TO & FROM THE AIRPORT

Fes-Saïss Airport Bus 16 (Map p335) runs every 30 minutes, on the hour and half-hour, between the airport (walk out past the car parks to the first traffic circle) and a bus stop next to the train station in the Ville Nouvelle; the fare is Dh4, and the ride takes about an hour.

For a *grand taxi* from the airport to Fez, the set fare, posted on a signboard by the parking area, is Dh120 (up to four people), but in practice any medina destination is Dh150. Transfers organised through your hotel vary in price, but expect to pay around Dh200. Heading out to the airport, the closest place to the medina for a *grand taxi* is the car park in front of the Bab El Mahrouk bus station; the fare is the same, Dh120. You can also get one from the train station, or of course organise one through your hotel. Petits taxis don't run to the airport.

BUS

Fez's bus service can be unreliable and packed like sardine cans; get on as close to an end point as possible and look out for pickpockets. Fare depends on the route, from Dh2.50 to Dh4. Most medina-bound buses stop on **Ave Hassan II** (Map p335).

Bus 9 Bouramana and Place Allal Al Fassi (aka Place Atlas, near the Ville Nouvelle CTM station) via Ave Lalla Meriem and Ave Hassan II to **Place Batha** (Map p326, western medina).

Bus 10 Train station (Map p335, Rue Egypte) via the Gare Routière and Bab Guissa (northern medina) to Bab Sidi Bou Jida (northeastern medina).

Bus 19 Train station (Map p335, Rue Lalla Esmaa) via Ave Lalla Meriem and Ave Hassan II to **Place R'cif** (Map p326, central medina).

TAXI

Drivers of the red *petits taxis* generally use their meters without a fuss, but tourists are often hassled by touts at the train station. Insist on the meter (starting rate of Dh1.40, then Dh0.20/100m, and 50% higher after 8pm), or walk further to hail a taxi. Expect to pay about Dh12 from the train or CTM station to Bab Bou Jeloud, and about Dh15 to Bab R'cif. Rates are 50% higher after 8pm.

Around Place Florence, at Batha and near Bab R'cif, drivers of petits taxis also offer flat fares, typically Dh4 or Dh5 per person; the taxi leaves when all three seats are full, *grand-taxi* style. Listen for drivers yelling destinations. The cars may also roll up to bus stops to collect those tired of waiting.

You'll find taxi ranks outside all the gates of the medina, as well as at **Place Batha** (Map p326). There is a convenient **petits-taxis rank** (Map p335) at Place de la Résistance on the northern edge of the Ville Nouvelle.

Only *grands taxis* go out to the airport. Get them at the lot next to the train station, or in front of the Gare Routière outside the medina's Bab El Mahrouk.

OFF THE BEATEN TRACK

TISSA HORSE FESTIVAL

Each year in September or early October, the prosperous farming town of Tissa is charged by farmers who come from all around to trade their animals and celebrate with exciting *fantasias* (cavalry charges) at **Tissa Horse Festival**. Dates are only set a week or two before. To get there, take a *grand taxi* from Sehb El Werd near Bab Fettouh in Fez (Dh20).

SPA RETREATS FROM FEZ

Moroccan architect Jean-François Zevaco designed **Sidi Harazem** (☎0535690996; P5006, 15km east of Fez; adult Dh50-70, child Dh10-20; ⏲8am-9pm; 🚻), a brutalist thermal bath complex, in the 1960s and it makes a wonderful day out from Fez. There are a number of large single-sex pools and one large mixed pool; note that the water is warm, not hot. Plenty of restaurants and cafes line the gardens.

Sidi Harazem water is high in magnesium and has been valued at least since Roman times. The main entrance is in the south, with sculptural concrete blocks and stairs leading down to a water garden with concrete pergolas. The spring draws crowds at any time of year, and Fassis come to collect water and then enjoy the shady seating areas, market, children's playparks and horse rides. There are three main areas: the Menzah Complex, the Palmiers Complex and the Al Nakhil Complex, each with different admission prices.

The Menzah Complex has a number of family-friendly pools (not all are shaded) as well as a superb circular pool for women only, plus a garden and restaurants. The Palmiers Complex has three shaded pools, one for men, one for women and one for children. The Al Nakhil Complex has two indoor pools (heated to 34°C), one for men and one for women, open from 8am to 6pm October through April (Dh60 per 1½ hours). In this complex, caps are obligatory and can be hired (Dh10).

Expect the resort to be packed with visitors at weekends, during school holidays and in the summer.

Sidi Harazem lies in a valley 15km east of Fez. To get here, take a petit taxi to the suburb Sehb El Werd, southeast of Bab Fettouh. From there, you can take a shared *grand taxi* (15 minutes, Dh6) to Sidi Harazem.

Ultramodern **Vichy Thermalia Spa** (☎0535694064; www.moulay-yacoub-vichy-thermalia-spa-hotel.fr; Moulay Yacoub; indoor pool Dh200, 50min massages from Dh600; ⏲9am-6.30pm) is built around a thermal spring gushing out of the mountainside in the spectacular foothills of the Middle Atlas. Escape the city for a dip in the steamy, sulphurous indoor pool, the water at a comfortable 40°C. Choose from various massages and beauty treatments booked via the website. You'll need private transport for the 20km drive from Fez.

Sefrou صفرو

☎0535 / POP 65,150

Just 40 minutes' drive from Fez, Sefrou *(seff-roo)* is an excellent example of a small Amazigh market town. It was here that Moulay Idriss II lived while overseeing the building of Fez. The town was once home to one of Morocco's largest Jewish communities; all that remains now are the traditional trades of tailoring, button-making and jewellery retailing.

The small medina is worth a wander to see plough-makers and blacksmiths as well as several restored *fanadiq* (ancient inns used by caravans), now artisans workshops. The Sefrou Museum of Multiculturalism is housed in one of them. The best thing to do in Sefrou is wander Haddadine in the medina, then sit in a cafe to watch daily life.

It's an easy day trip from Fez. Time your visit with the Thursday souq, just south of the town centre, to see a real local market without the tourist trappings.

Sights

Medina AREA

The Oued Aggaï flows through the centre of Sefrou's medina, opening the place up and giving it more of an airy feel than that of many old medinas. Although it's still a maze, there's not much to it so navigation is manageable; the best point of entry is the northerly Bab El Maqam. From here the flow of people will take you downhill past pastel-hued souq shops and a local produce market.

Funduq Ghazl WORKSHOP

(Spinners Funduq; Haddadine; ⏲10am-dusk Sat-Thu) This restored *funduq* (ancient caravanserai) now houses textile artisans, including women. There are tailors, thread bobbiners, tassel- and passementerie- makers, and embroiderers. Don't miss the second level. You can walk around and watch them work.

Sefrou Museum of Multiculturalism MUSEUM

(11 Funduq El Kshub, Haddadine; ⏲10am-5pm winter, to 7pm Sat-Thu summer) FREE Located

in the old carpenters *funduq*, this small museum tells the story of Sefrou in an inventive way. It exemplifies the multiculturalism of Morocco, with Sefrou as an example, highlighting the contributions made by Romans, Jews, Arabs and Muslims. It's richly researched and features documentary films and interviews, all curated by resident artist Jess Stephens.

Funduq Fès Jdid WORKSHOP
(Haddadine; 8am-dusk Sat-Thu) This is a beautifully restored *funduq* where weavers work on large looms, alongside slipper makers and tailors. Don't miss the artisans upstairs on the 1st floor.

Jardin Al Kanatir Al Khairia PARK
Skirting the western walls of the medina, Sefrou's public gardens are wedged into a small valley and feel a little like the lost world. Towering tangles of trees tripping down, down, down to the river create a cool retreat beloved by locals. There are peaceful paths and a couple of cafes. Enter off Ave Moulay Hassan or Blvd Mohammed V.

Cascades de Sefrou WATERFALL
It's a leafy 1.5km walk west of town to the Cascades, a modest waterfall. On a hot day, it makes for a pleasant escape. Follow the signs from Ave Moulay Hassan around Al Qala (a semi-fortified village) and along the river's lush valley. At the top, there's a cafe overlooking the waterfall.

WORTH A TRIP

CHERRY FESTIVAL

The annual four-day **Cherry Festival** (Festival des Cerises; 1st week Jun) celebrates the local cherry harvest. There's plenty of folk music, along with displays by local artists, parades, *fantasias* (musket-firing cavalry charges) and the crowning of the Cherry Queen. Sefrou lays claim to the longest-running town festival in Morocco: one hundred years old in 2020, and recognised by Unesco in 2013.

The town produces a programme of events, but it's a moveable feast. The evening concerts usually don't start until at least 10pm, so it's better to stay overnight.

There's a second Amazigh (Berber) stage featuring celebratory *ahidous* music and circular dance. This and the *fantasias* all start in the late afternoon.

Tours

Adil El Ouaddahi WALKING
(0678483865; half-day Dh250) Adil is one of the few English-speaking guides in Sefrou. It's best to avoid the false guides that might approach you. Registered ones have a tag around their neck.

Sleeping & Eating

Accommodation is thin on the ground in Sefrou with just one reasonable option; many people prefer to visit the town as a day trip from Fez. The neighbouring village of Bhalil, a 10-minute drive away, also has a guesthouse, Dar Kamal Chaoui (p354).

There are a few cheap eats with soup, kebabs, rotisserie chicken and tajines in the medina for lunch, but not at night. Some places such as Essaqqaya in the new town are open in the evenings too.

Zubeida's House RIAD €
(0615273469; zubeida.britel@gmail.com; 169/14 Aarssat Dar; d/tr Dh220/280;) This pretty garden with trees and a fountain is home to three pleasant rooms. One of them is upstairs, with a bathroom on the ground floor. Zubeida will cook dinner if you reserve in advance. Bookings through Airbnb only.

Essaqqaya Snack Café Restaurant MOROCCAN €
(0535683089; Blvd Mohammed V; mains Dh30; 8am-11pm Sat-Thu, from 3pm Fri;) This big airy cafe near the sports stadium has an open veranda and comfortable seating inside. It's great for families and women on their own, and in a town that sorely lacks such public facilities, has clean toilets. There are sandwiches, pizzas and gooey cakes. The lasagne (Dh30) comes recommended.

Restaurant Al Farah MOROCCAN €
(Place Haddadine; meals Dh30; 10am-9pm) The best place to eat in Sefrou's medina is the Restaurant Al Farah with simple tables under a shady tree in a slim square. It's easy to find, opposite the knife-grinders and blacksmith with his fiery anvil (Haddadine means ironmongers). There's no menu: go for the feast of spit-roast chicken with *harissa*, chips, beans, bread and salad.

Abdeslam's Teahouse CAFE
(300 Haddadine; 5am-6pm) This tiny hole-in-the-wall serves the best tea in Sefrou. Once you're sitting on one of the wooden stools outside or opposite in one of the larger cafes, you're in the perfect people-watching spot

Sefrou

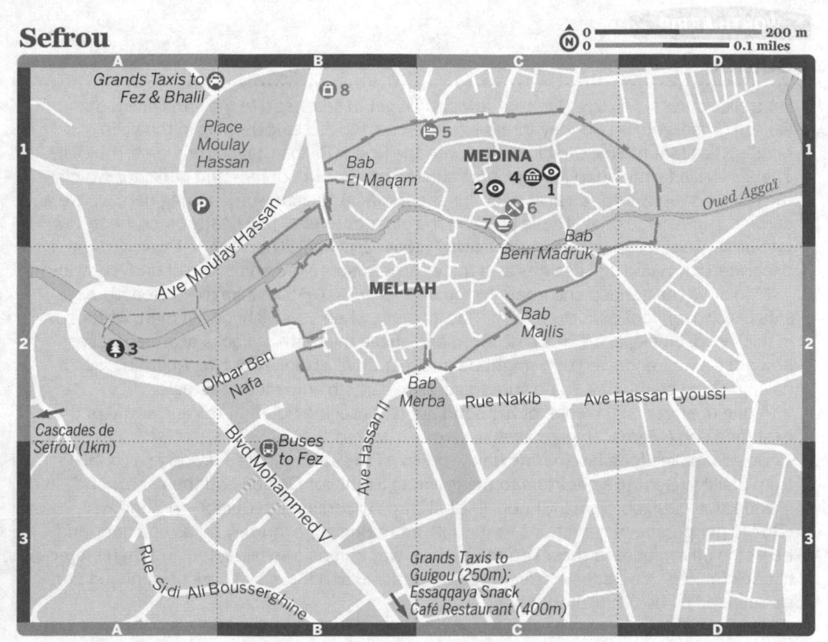

on this busy street through the medina. The barber is next door, then the blacksmith's and the plough-maker.

On the other side of the teahouse, there's a soup shop: it's *bissara* (fava bean and garlic) in the morning and *harira* (tomato and chickpeas) in the afternoon.

Shopping

Ensemble Artisanal ARTS & CRAFTS

(Route de Fès; 9.30am-1pm & 2.30-6.30pm Sat-Thu) Like all state-sponsored Ensembles Artisanaux, this complex features small shops selling a selection of mostly wood and jewellery, plus some rugs. Prices are fixed. It gives you a good idea of what's available in this region. The bowls carved from fruit wood are particularly pleasing.

Getting There & Away

Regular **buses** (Dh10, 40 minutes) and **grands taxis** (Dh12, 30 minutes) run between Sefrou and Slaiki (p350) in Fez in the ville nouvelle. If you'd prefer to get a private *grand-taxi* transfer from your hotel in Fez, expect to pay Dh250 to Dh300 each way. *Grands taxis* to Azrou (Dh30) go via Imouzzer (Dh15) and depart from the same walled *grand-taxi* lot just north of Place Moulay Hassan. *Grands taxis* to Bhalil (Dh4) depart from the same parking lot.

Sefrou

Sights
1 Funduq Fès Jdid C1
2 Funduq Ghazl C1
3 Jardin Al Kanatir Al Khairia A2
4 Sefrou Museum of Multiculturalism C1

Sleeping
5 Zubeida's House C1

Eating
6 Restaurant Al Farah C1

Drinking & Nightlife
7 Abdeslam's Teahouse C1

Shopping
8 Ensemble Artisanal B1

Bhalil البهاليل

0535 / POP 14,000

This curious village is worth a trip for its troglodyte houses built into the picturesque mountainside and picked out in pastel hues of pink, yellow and blue. The cave dwellings date back to the 4th century and for hundreds of years have been inhabited by shepherds to protect against the elements. Some villagers go so far as to use caves for

WORTH A TRIP

GUIGOU

For a slice of rural Amazigh life that few people get to see, head to the small town of Guigou *(ghee-gou)* on Sunday for its weekly souq. Guigou is 1509m up in the scenic Middle Atlas Mountains, lying in a bowl with the Oued (River) Guigou running through it. There's fertile farmland all around, particularly good for the onions and garlic for which the region is renowned. It's also good for sheep, and Amazigh women living here weave carpets, rugs and textiles. These women, the older ones with facial tattoos, come to town on Sunday to sell their wares in the **souq** (5am-2pm Sun). There are flat-weave rugs decorated with Amazigh designs and thick carpets, some red and some of undyed wool.

Men drive their sheep and goats to the **sheep souq** (5am-2pm) on the eastern side of town, on foot or in trucks. This starts early, when several hundred men, wrapped in thick woollen *djellabas*, examine, prod and check the teeth of flocks of sheep, assess how virile a well-endowed ram might be and test-drive a donkey or two. Anything worth having is sold by midday, so be sure to get here early to enjoy the spectacle.

Along the river on the edge of the souq are tents selling hot mint tea and some of the best *msemen* (Moroccan pancakes) we've ever tasted.

Guigou makes for a fascinating day trip. From Fez (90km), take a grand taxi (p350) from Slaiki to Sefrou, a *petit taxi* to the grand taxi rank for Guigou and then another *grand taxi* to Guigou. Kamal Chaoui in Bhalil runs excursions to Guigou on Sunday (Dh770 per person, reservations essential). From Bhalil the journey takes one hour and he'll stop off en route to show you the curious way onions are harvested and then stored in brick tunnels. It's a scenic drive through farmland and forests of cork oak and juniper, surrounded by beautiful mountains.

the primary room of the house. The result is a cool, spacious room, usually used as a salon, while bedrooms and private areas are built above.

The hassle often experienced in larger towns is entirely absent here: people are incredibly friendly, and local women are often found sitting out on the streets making woven buttons for *djellabas* – one of the village's main industries. Bhalil has an excellent local guesthouse and can make a refreshing break from the big-city hustle of Fez.

Sleeping

★ **Dar Kamal Chaoui** GUESTHOUSE €€
(0643032444, 0678838310; www.kamalchaoui.com; 6 Kaf Rhouni; d Dh770;) Kamal Chaoui offers very comfortable accommodation in a traditional village house, and Naima cooks delicious dinners (Dh220). Decorated in local Amazigh style, it has a relaxing roof terrace with sweeping views. Kamal strives for a home-away-from-home atmosphere, and he and Naima join guests at mealtimes. In winter the house is heated via an ingenious wood-fire system to keep things toasty.

Kamal, who speaks excellent English, French and German, is a pillar of the local community and a mine of information on the area. He can arrange mountain hikes, a longer trek to Immouzer El Kandar, plus a variety of other tours, including to Guigou's weekly souq and a visit to troglodyte caves for tea with the inhabitants.

Naima also runs cooking classes (Dh550 per person). Money from tours is funnelled back into the community, helping to clean up the streets and improve conditions for villagers.

Getting There & Away

To get here from Fez, take a *grand taxi* from Slaiki (p350) to Sefrou (p353) (Dh12), then another shared *grand taxi* to Bhalil (Dh4). A private *grand taxi* from Sefrou costs Dh16, and if you give the driver a tip, he'll take you up into the village to drop you near Dar Kamal Chaoui.

Meknes مكناس

0535 / POP 520,430

Quieter and smaller than Fez, Meknes *(meknes)* is overshadowed by its neighbour. If visitors come at all, they usually speed through as part of a day trip to Volubilis. That could all change when its two main attractions – a palace-turned-museum and the mausoleum of Moulay Ismail, one of Morocco's most glorious and notorious sultans – reopen after long renovations. At time of research, though, no date was set for either.

In the meantime, Meknes can be worth a visit if you're in no rush and simply want to relax somewhere with little tourist hassle, a more navigable medina and a pleasant, if slightly shabby, atmosphere. Ordinary Moroccan life thrives among the remnants of Ismail's grandiose city fortifications and in the ville nouvelle, dotted with art deco buildings, an elegant cinema and plenty of bars. Meknes is also a commercial hub for many Amazigh (Berber) villagers, a fact which enlivens its markets.

History

'Meknes of the Olives' was settled by the Miknasa Amazigh tribe some time in the 9th century, and the Almoravids built the first fortress here, in the 11th century. Under the Almohads and the Merinids, the medina was expanded. But all is overshadowed by Moulay Ismail, who became Sultan of Morocco in 1672 and declared Meknes his capital.

In his 55-year reign, Ismail began to build his Dar El Kebira, an imperial city surrounded by 25km of walls, planted with gardens and fed by complex waterworks. He owed his success to two factors. He subdued all dissent in Morocco and kept foreign meddlers at bay with his Black Guard, a fighting force he modelled on Ottoman janissaries by taking sub-Saharan Africans captive, then training them (and, when the time came, their sons) as soldiers. On the construction front, he forced thousands of Christian prisoners, captured when he took territory from Spain, into labour. One of them designed the resplendent Bab El Mansour.

After Ismail's death in 1727, the city lost stature, especially when his grandson Mohammed III (1757–90) moved to Marrakesh. The 1755 earthquake that devastated Lisbon also dealt Meknes a blow. Abandoned monuments were subsequently stripped of their ornamentation for use on buildings elsewhere – which accounts for the stark, austere appearance of some of Ismail's works today.

In 1912 the French made Meknes their military headquarters, and many French farmers settled on the fertile land nearby. After independence most properties were recovered by the Moroccan government and leased to local farmers.

Sights

The heart of the medina is around Place El Hedim and the monumental gateway of Bab El Mansour. On the west and north sides of the square are the commercial parts of the medina; northeast turns more residential. South of Bab El Mansour lies Moulay Ismail's imperial city. Built in the 18th century, a large section is still reserved for royalty today; you can see some of the gardens at the

THE ALMIGHTY MOULAY

Few men dominate the history of a country like the towering figure of Sultan Moulay Ismail (1672–1727). Originating from the sand-blown plains of the Tafilalt region, his family were sharifs (descendants of the Prophet Muhammad) – a pedigree that continues to the current monarchy.

To become sultan, though, required not just good breeding, but also ruthlessness. On inheriting the throne from his brother Moulay Ar Rashid, Moulay Ismail set about diffusing the rival claims of his 83 brothers and half-brothers, celebrating his first day in power by murdering all those who refused to submit to his rule. His politics continued in this bloody vein with military campaigns in the south, the Rif Mountains and Algerian hinterland, bringing most of Morocco under his control. He even brought the Salé corsairs to heel, taxing their piracy handsomely to swell the imperial coffers.

The peace won, Moulay Ismail retired to his capital at Meknes and began building his grandiose imperial city. He plundered the country for the best materials, and pressed into service thousands of European enslaved people captured by Barbary pirates. Ismail is renowned for his cruelty and vengefulness, but he is also remembered as a great builder, who helmed Morocco's last great golden age.

Moulay Ismail also considered himself a lover. Although he sought (but failed to receive) the hand in marriage of Louis XIV of France's daughter, he still fathered hundreds of children. Rather foolishly, however, he did nothing to secure his succession. When he died the sultanate was rocked by a series of internecine power struggles, from which the Alaouites never fully recovered.

Nevertheless, his legacy was to be the foundation of modern Morocco. He liberated Tangier from the British, subdued the Amazigh tribes and relieved the Spanish of much of their Moroccan territory. Moulay Ismail sowed the seeds of the current monarchy, and beneath his strong-arm rule the coherent entity of modern Morocco was first glimpsed.

golf club, across the street from Koubbat As Sufara. The narrow streets of the old *mellah* are in the west of the medina – look for the distinctive balconied houses.

The ville nouvelle, which locals call the Hamria, is about a 30-minute walk to the east, across the gully of a now-dry river.

Medina

Place El Hedim SQUARE
(Map p358) Cleared by Moulay Ismail so his populace could better admire Bab El Mansour, this square is the social heart of the medina, and it really livens up at night. Families come out to stroll, snack at the cafes, play football and listen to musicians. Kids zip around in battery-powered cars and occasionally (and somewhat unfortunately) a monkey or an ostrich is dragged in for photo ops. Park yourself at a snack stand or a nearby rooftop to watch the show.

Dar Jamaï Museum MUSEUM
(Map p358; 0555530863; Place El Hedim) On the north side of Place El Hedim, this museum was under renovation at last visit. Built in 1882 by the powerful Jamaï family, two of whom were viziers to Sultan Moulay Al Hassan I, the palace building has been a museum since 1920. Its collection includes traditional ceramics, jewellery, textiles and cedar-wood craft. The Andalusian garden and courtyard are shady, peaceful spots dotted with orange trees.

Medersa Bou Inania ISLAMIC SITE
(Map p358; Rue Nejjarine; Dh60; 10am-6pm) Opposite the Grande Mosquée, this religious school, completed in 1358, is typical of the exquisite Merinid interior design. Although it is not as lavish as its counterpart of the same name in Fez, it does display the classic *zellige* tile, delicate stucco and carved cedar-wood ceiling. You can explore the student rooms, the roof and even the school's hammam (down a hall to the left, opposite the ticket desk).

Musée de Meknès MUSEUM
(Map p358; Rue Dar Smen; Dh10; 9am-6pm Tue-Sun) Housed in the peeling old tribunal building in the imperial city walls, this small museum is long overdue for a refresh, but while the larger Dar Jamaï museum is closed, it's the only real option for seeing Meknes craft culture and history. Look out for the remarkable set of leather armour encrusted with coral beads, turquoise studs and coins. Information is in French only.

Mausoleum of Sidi Ben Aïssa MAUSOLEUM
(Map p358) Known as Cheikh El Kamel for his perfection in learning, Sidi Ben Aïssa (1465–1526) inspired the Aïssawa Sufi brotherhood, widely followed in North Africa. Once notorious for self-mutilation, adherents are now better known for their intense, trance-inducing music and their ecstatic emotional response. The tomb (closed to non-Muslims) is a year-round pilgrimage site, but especially lively during the annual moussem (p359).

Imperial City

★**Bab El Mansour** GATE
(Map p358) The focus of Place El Hedim is this huge gate, perhaps the grandest of all imperial Moroccan gateways. The gate is well preserved, if a bit dulled by soot, with intricate mosaic tilework and inscriptions across the top. It was completed by Moulay Ismail's son, Moulay Abdallah, in 1732. You can't actually pass through, though the front door is sometimes open to host exhibitions. Otherwise, there's a little foot passage through the wall to the left of the gate.

The two white columns either side of the gate are marble, thought to have been originally installed at Volubilis (p365), given their Italian source. Along the top of the gate, the Arabic inscription is a boasting poem in the voice of the gate itself, praising its own beauty and, by extension, the might of Moulay Abdallah.

Place Lalla Aouda SQUARE
(Mechouar; Map p358) South of Bab El Mansour lies this public garden and car park that's a popular place with local families in the evening – less raucous than Place El Hedim, and with more places to sit. In the past it was the parade ground where Moulay Ismail once inspected his famed Black Guard, which started with some 16,000 enslaved men from sub-Saharan Africa. By the time of his death, the guard had expanded tenfold and had chased out both European and Ottoman troops.

Mausoleum of Moulay Ismail MAUSOLEUM
(Map p358) Closed since 2016 for a massive renovation, the final resting place of the sultan who made Meknes his capital in the 17th century is ordinarily a must-see for anyone travelling through town. Before the closure, non-Muslim visitors were allowed into the entry hall and the front courtyards; this may still be the case when it reopens.

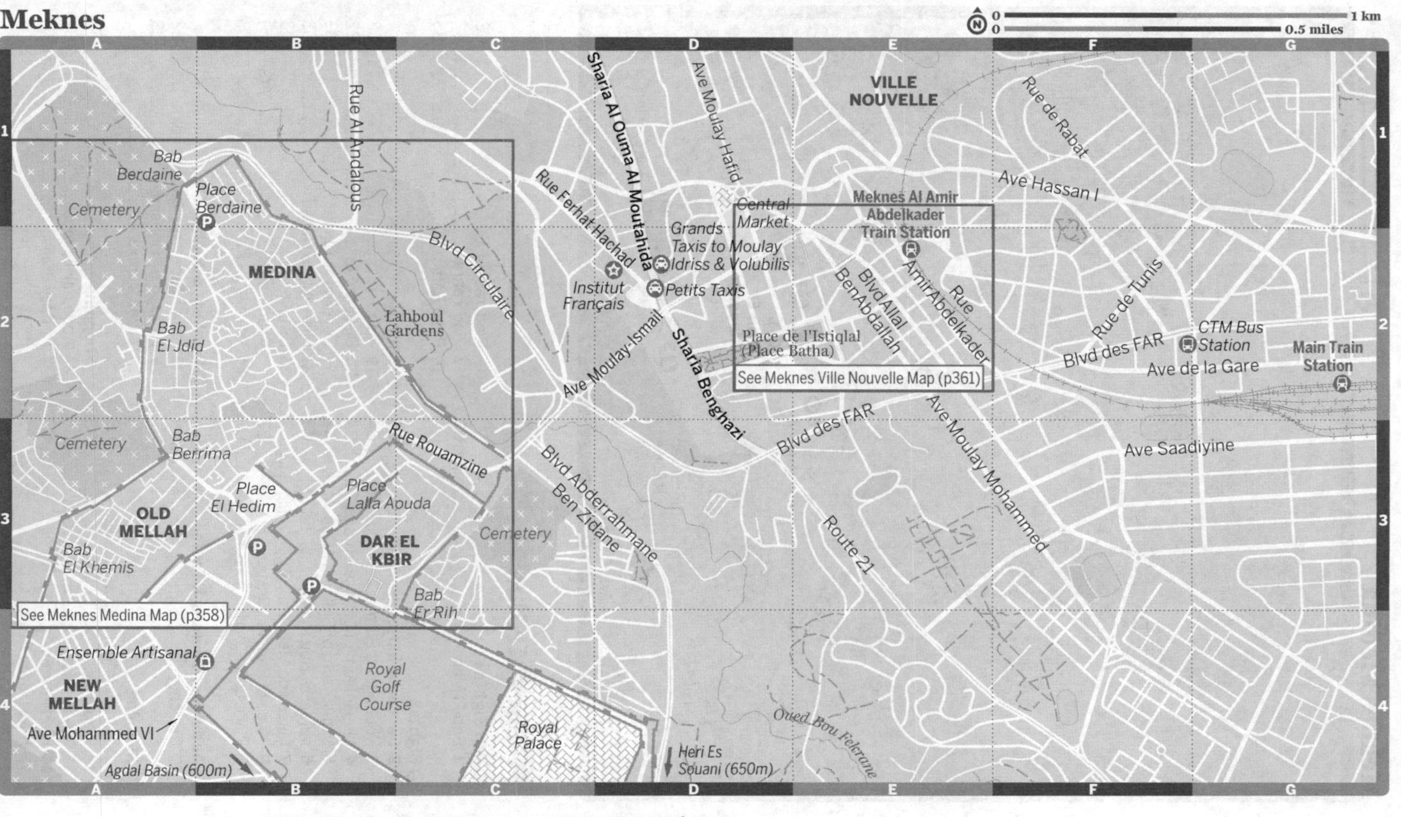

Meknes
0
0
1 km
0.5 miles
VILLE NOUVELLE
Rue Al Andalous
Sharia Al Ouma Al Moutahida
Ave Moulay Hafid
Rue de Rabat
Ave Hassan I
Bab Berdaine
Place Berdaine
Cemetery
MEDINA
Blvd Circulaire
Rue Ferhat Hachad
Grands Taxis to Moulay Idriss & Volubilis
Central Market
Meknes Al Amir Abdelkader Train Station
Institut Français
Petits Taxis
Lahboul Gardens
Bab El Jdid
Blvd Allal BenAbdallah
Rue AmirAbdelkader
Rue de Tunis
Place de l'Istiqlal (Place Batha)
CTM Bus Station
Blvd des FAR
Ave de la Gare
Main Train Station
Ave Moulay-Ismail
Sharia Benghazi
See Meknes Ville Nouvelle Map (p361)
Cemetery
Bab Berrima
Rue Rouamzine
Blvd des FAR
Ave Moulay Mohammed
Ave Saadiyine
Place El Hedim
Place Lalla Aouda
Blvd Abderrahmane Ben Zidane
OLD MELLAH
Cemetery
Route 21
Bab El Khemis
DAR EL KBIR
Bab Er Rih
See Meknes Medina Map (p358)
Ensemble Artisanal
Royal Golf Course
NEW MELLAH
Ave Mohammed VI
Royal Palace
Heri Es Souani (650m)
Oued Bou Fekrane
Agdal Basin (600m)

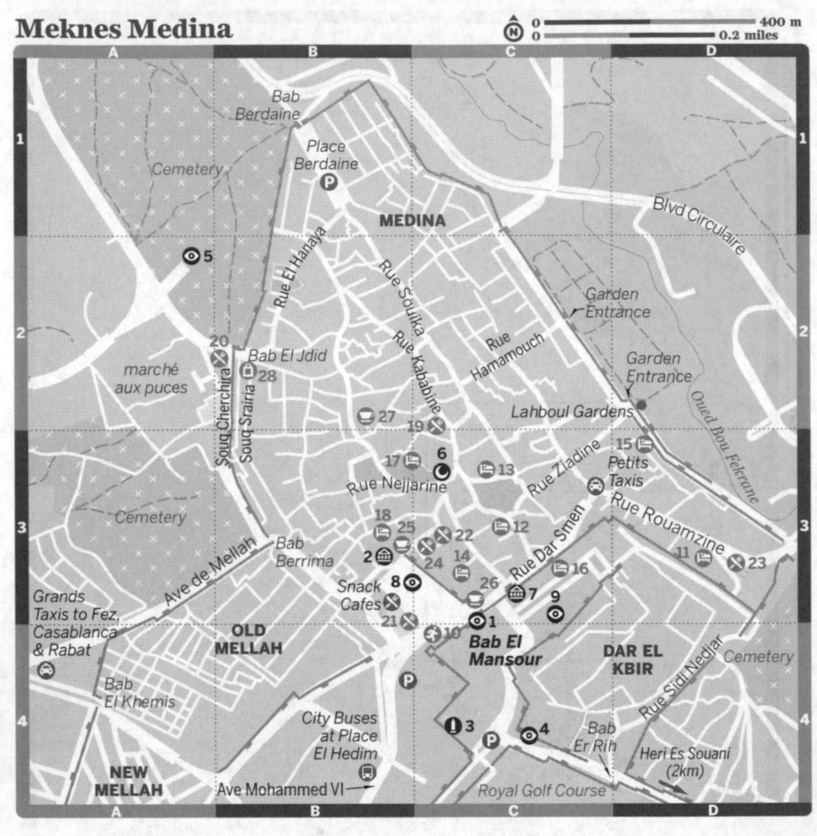

Meknes Medina

Top Sights
1 Bab El Mansour C3

Sights
2 Dar Jamaï Museum B3
3 Koubbat As Sufara C4
4 Mausoleum of Moulay Ismail C4
5 Mausoleum of Sidi Ben Aïssa A2
6 Medersa Bou Inania C3
7 Musée de Meknes C3
8 Place El Hedim B3
9 Place Lalla Aouda C3

Activities, Courses & Tours
10 Calèches C4

Sleeping
11 Maroc Hotel D3
12 Riad d'Or C3
13 Riad El Ma C3
14 Riad Felloussia C3
15 Riad Lahboul D3
16 Riad Yacout C3
17 Riad Zahraa B3
18 Ryad Bahia B3

Eating
19 Aisha C2
20 Bissara Stalls B2
21 Covered Market B3
22 Mille et Une Nuits C3
23 Omnia D3
Ryad Bahia .... (see 18)
24 Ya Hala C3

Drinking & Nightlife
25 Cafe Restaurant Place Lahdim B3
26 Pavillon des Idrissides C3
27 Zazen Centre B2

Shopping
28 Abdelhak Ezzouak B2
Pottery Stalls .... (see 21)

Koubbat As Sufara MONUMENT
(Kara Prison; Map p358; Dh60; ⌚10am-6pm Apr-Sep, to 5pm Oct-Mar) Moulay Ismail's reception hall for foreign ambassadors is a lovely show of *zellige* (patterned tile) work. It's here that Unesco officially inscribed Meknes in the World Heritage Site registry in 1996. In front of the building, small windows provide light for a 40-hectare crypt below. Descend via stairs to the right of the reception hall; the entrance fee covers both.

Heri Es Souani RUINS
(Royal Stables and Granary; Dh70; ⌚9am-5pm) Moulay Ismail considered this early-18th-century complex one of his finest architectural projects, and on paper it's a marvel. The massive, thick-walled, barrel-vaulted granaries (tribes paid taxes in grain) were kept cool through a system of underfloor water channels, drawing from a cistern below. Outside to the west are the remains of stables for a supposed 12,000 horses. In practice, unless you're particularly interested in water engineering, there is not much to see, considering the rather steep admission price.

Agdal Basin LAKE
(Sahrij Souani) Adjacent to the Heri Es Souani lies an enormous stone-lined lake, the Agdal Basin, built in the 18th century as both a reservoir for Moulay Ismail's gardens and a pleasure lake. Originally it was surrounded by high walls and fed by a complex system of wells and aqueducts. Today the water is stagnant, but it's still a pleasant place for photos, perhaps by the Giacometti-like statue of a traditional water-seller that sits at one corner.

Outside the Centre

Palais Al Mansour PALACE
(⌚9am-5pm) FREE Moulay Ismail's summer palace, built in the countryside in the 17th century, now sits in the middle of the urban fabric of Meknes – there's even a neighbourhood playground out front. It has undergone a massive restoration, although at last visit, only the round, domed storage room was open to visitors. It's far south from the centre, so only worth a visit if you're travelling by car or if you just want an excuse to witness ordinary life in a regular city district.

Tours

Compared with Fez or Marrakesh, the Meknes medina is small and fairly easy to navigate. Still, an official guide can point out details you'd otherwise miss. Rates per half-/full day are Dh300/500; book through your hotel, or go to the **tourism delegation** (Map p361; ☎0535525538; Rue de l'Union Africaine; ⌚8am-4.30pm Mon-Fri).

Calèche (Map p358; Place El Hedim) (horse-drawn carriage) rides of the imperial city with a guide are easy to pick up around Place El Hedim and in Place Lalla Aouda.

Club Farah HORSE RIDING
(☎0535548844; www.clubfarah.com; hour/half-day/full-day rides Dh120/350/600) Experienced riders should look into an adventure with this Swiss-Moroccan company, which runs trips around the country, such as an eight-day Imperial Cities ride or a two-week trek through the desert. You can also take short courses and day rides at the horse farm outside Meknes; contact for reservations and directions.

Festivals & Events

Moussem of Sidi Ben Aïssa RELIGIOUS
(⌚Oct) The Aïssawa Sufi brotherhood leads this week-long festival at the Mausoleum of Sidi Ben Aïssa (p356), when tens of thousands attend for *fantasias* (musket-firing cavalry charges), singing, and dancing to the Aïssawas' distinctive brand of trance-inducing music. It starts on the eve of the Prophet Muhammad's birthday, on the Islamic lunar calendar, so it shifts back a bit each year.

Notoriously, the Aïssawas titillated European onlookers in the 19th century with their bloody rituals of self-flagellation and glass eating. Their practice today is far less extreme, but dancers do still speak in tongues, impersonate animals and collapse with emotion. Festival attendees typically do not wear red or black, as this is thought to upset the entranced people in the procession.

Sleeping

Meknes' medina has dozens of lovely riads and relatively few guests, so rates can be very reasonable. The cheapest hotels, along Rue Dar Smen and Rue Rouamzine, are exceedingly basic and fill quickly if there's any festival on. In the ville nouvelle, some excellent-value places have retro style – but pervasive cigarette smoke is always a risk.

Medina

Riad Zahraa GUESTHOUSE €
(Map p358; ☎0667768302; azizahimmich@gmail.com; 5 Sidi Abdallah El Kassri, Medina; d/tr/apt from €25/30/60; ❄📶⛱) This homey, welcoming place gives budget travellers a slice of the good riad life, complete with a roof

terrace and a small pool. There's a room configuration for nearly everyone, from snug doubles to expansive family rooms to a couple of multibedroom apartments. Breakfasts are bountiful too.

Maroc Hotel HOTEL €
(Map p358; ☎0535530075; 7 Rue Rouamzine; r with shared bathroom per person Dh100, roof terrace Dh50) The shoestring Maroc is a five-minute walk from Bab El Mansour. Up a set of stairs off Rue Rouamzine, it's quiet, with simple rooms (with sinks). Shared bathrooms are clean. You can also opt for a mattress on the roof terrace. At last pass, the hotel was for sale, so this could mean quality will be affected.

★ **Ryad Bahia** GUESTHOUSE €€
(Map p358; ☎0535554541, 0662082864; www.ryad-bahia.com; 13 Tiberbarine, Medina; d from €60; 📶) This converted family home is a short walk from Place El Hedim. The main entrance opens onto a leafy courtyard, which also hosts a great restaurant (p363). Rooms are pretty and carefully restored, and owners Bouchra and Abdellatif, keen travellers themselves, are eager to swap travel stories as well as advise guests; Bouchra is even a licensed guide. The riad opens its doors to nonguests for drinks and pastries each afternoon. If you prefer more space to spread out, ask about the owners' other property, Les Jardins de Ryad Bahia, a lovely private house on the outskirts of Meknes – convenient if you're driving.

Riad Felloussia GUESTHOUSE €€
(Map p358; ☎0535530840, 0676987717; www.riadfelloussia.com; 23 Derb Hammam Jdid, Medina; r €80-120; 📶) Down several turns off Rue Dar Smen, Felloussia reveals a fine view of Place El Hedim from its roof terrace. Five meticulously restored rooms are set around a small inner courtyard. The large Toubkal suite has a bed upstairs – a love-it-or-hate-it situation – and the snug Mouzda has luxe atmosphere at a budget rate (€60 max). Deep discounts via the hotel website.

Riad Yacout BOUTIQUE HOTEL €€
(Map p358; ☎0535533110; www.riad-yacout-meknes.com; 22 Place Lalla Aouda, Medina; d from Dh530, ste from Dh780; P📶🏊) Traditional style meets all the modern comforts at Riad Yacout. Rooms have extras like hairdryers and lockboxes, bathrooms are a bit shinier than most, and the staff work hard on service. There's a dip pool on the roof, where tables are set out for meals. The location, built into the imperial city walls, is handy for parking and taxi drop-offs.

Riad El Ma GUESTHOUSE €€
(Map p358; ☎0661514824; www.riad-el-ma.com; 4 Derb Sidi Besri, Medina; r Dh550-650, ste Dh850; 📶🏊) This pretty, traditional riad has a well-restored courtyard and a multilevel roof terrace with plunge pool and bird's-eye view of the Medersa Bou Inania. The standard rooms are better value than the larger ones, as the size difference is minimal. A set-menu dinner is available for Dh150. El Ma is French-owned but run by two welcoming local women.

Riad Lahboul GUESTHOUSE €€
(Map p358; ☎0535559878, 0675716917; www.riadlahboul.com; 6 Derb Ain Sefli, Rouamzine; d €60-70, f from €100; 📶) This cosy riad has six ornate rooms, including a large family room and others that can be combined to create petite apartments. Its *table d'hôte* (set menu Dh200) is a good option as the food gets rave reviews (nonguests welcome; book a day ahead). The leafy roof terrace is lovely, with a view over the medina walls.

Riad d'Or GUESTHOUSE €€
(Map p358; ☎0535533871, 0641078625; 17 Derb Ain El Anboub, Medina; r/ste €50/90; 📶🏊) This guesthouse occupies three buildings, with rooms accessible by odd staircases and opening onto unexpected courtyards. It's a bit of a sprawling shambles (maintenance is needed), but the staff is welcoming, some of the large rooms can sleep four or more, and there's a decent-size swimming pool. Allergy sufferers note: cats live here.

Ville Nouvelle

Hôtel Palace HOTEL €
(Map p361; ☎0535400468; www.hotelpalacemeknes.com; 11 Rue Mohammed El Meknassi, Ville Nouvelle; s/d Dh350/400; P📶) The 40-room Palace offers modern style that's minimalist by Moroccan standards. The rooms are large and airy, and many come with a teeny balcony, part of the nice art deco facade. On the ground floor is a restaurant and bar (open till 11pm).

Hôtel Majestic HOTEL €
(Map p361; ☎0535522035; www.hotelmajesticmeknes.ma; 19 Ave Mohammed V, Ville Nouvelle; s/d Dh287/374; 📶) Open since 1936, the Majestic is a fine deco building not far from the train station, but it does show its age. Aficionados of old-time hotels can overlook some dilapidation to enjoy snug rooms with tile floors, a

Meknes Ville Nouvelle

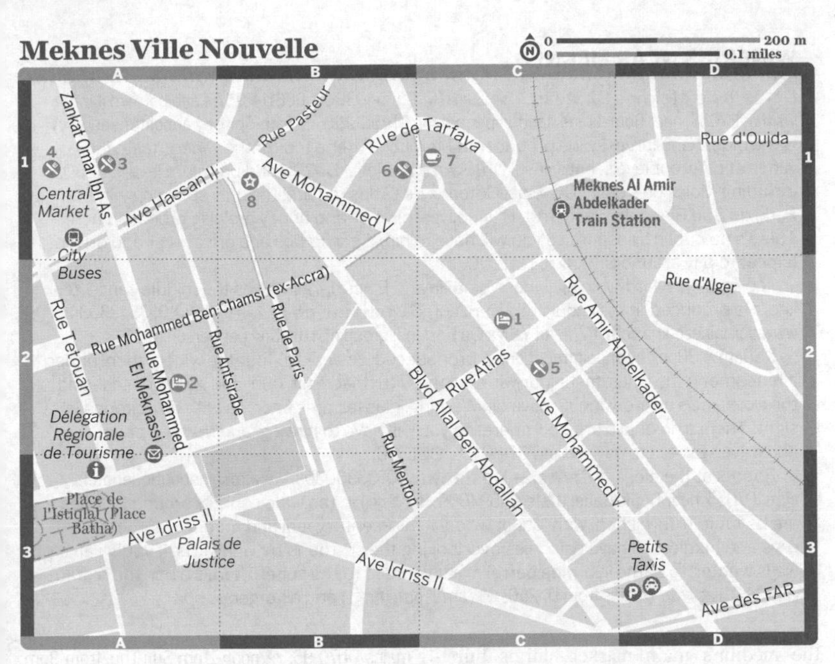

quiet courtyard and a pleasant roof terrace. But if your top criterion for lodging is cleanliness, look elsewhere.

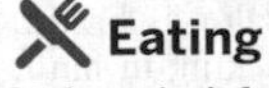

Eating

Meknes isn't known as a foodie destination. Rue Rouamzine has a string of fried-fish snack joints and drinks come with snacks in the ville nouvelle. In the medina, a few of the riads serve nonguests if you book ahead, but with a couple of exceptions, cheap eats are the way to go.

Promenade Palace INTERNATIONAL €

(Map p361; ☎0535523420; cnr Rue de Tarfaya & Sahat Lahri, Ville Nouvelle; mains from Dh40; ⏲6am-1am; 📶) Set over two floors as well as the pavement, this cafe-restaurant is shiny, bright and frequented by men and women (even solo). Its Moroccan menu is fine (Friday has a veg couscous special for Dh38), but in the evening most people are here for coffee and cakes.

Bissara Stalls STREET FOOD €

(Map p358; dishes from Dh4) Just outside the medina's Bab El Jdid (noted for its musical-instrument sellers) is a clutch of very busy, very popular shops selling *bissara* (fava-bean soup) as well as all the other major street-food groups, including varied sandwiches.

Meknes Ville Nouvelle

Sleeping

1 Hôtel Majestic C2
2 Hôtel Palace A2

Eating

3 Gambrinus A1
4 Marché Municipal A1
5 Marhaba Restaurant C2
6 Promenade Palace B1

Drinking & Nightlife

7 La Tulipe C1

Entertainment

8 Cinema Camera B1

Marhaba Restaurant MOROCCAN €

(Map p361; 23 Ave Mohammed V, Ville Nouvelle; dishes from Dh10; ⏲noon-10pm; 📶) The essence of cheap and cheerful, this canteen-style place has been dishing up affordable, simple food since 1983. At lunchtime, go for the freshly grilled meats. After 4pm do as everyone else does and fill up on a bowl of *harira* and a plate of *maâkouda* (potato fritters) with bread and hard-boiled eggs – all miraculously priced at only Dh10.

Covered Market MARKET €

(Map p358; Place El Hedim, Medina; ⏲8.30am-10pm) Virtually a tourist attraction in itself,

WINERIES NEAR MEKNES

Celliers de Meknes Château Roslane (☎0535403008, 0661143157; f.aabibou@roslane-ws.ma; P7055, near Boufekrane; tasting per person Dh150-250; ⏲9am-5pm, by appointment only) is the oldest and largest wine producer in Morocco. After a tour of the winery, taste four wines at different levels: entry level Dh150, middle level Dh200 and premium level Dh250, including Morocco's only AOC wine, Côteaux de l'Atlas red and the only sparkling wine, La Perle du Sud Blanc de Blanc Brut. Fruit, olives, olive oil and honey are also produced here. There's no public transport, so you will have to hire a *grand taxi* or a private car and driver. Expect to pay around Dh600 to Dh1200.

Top quality, award-winning wines Volubilia and Epicuria, as well as the middle-range Zellige, are produced at the exquisitely manicured **Domaine de la Zouina** (☎0535433034; www.domainezouina.com; R712, Ait Yahya Ou Hassine; group of 4, tasting per person Dh300; ⏲8.30am-4.30pm, by appointment only), pronounced '*zween*-ah'. Tour the winery then, under a tent among the vines, taste four wines along with dried fruit, nuts and goat's cheese and the Domaine's award-winning olive oil. Warning: glasses are generous with no spitoons in sight! There's no public transport here, so you will have to hire a *grand taxi* or a private car and driver. Expect to pay around Dh600 to Dh1200.

Rooms at the elegant **Château Roslane** (☎0535300303; www.roslaneboutiquehotel.com; P7055, near Boufekrane; d/ste €459/609; P 📶 🏊) in the wine country around Meknes are beautifully furnished, with lots of wood, a mid-century feel and modern Moroccan rugs and textiles. All have balconies overlooking the surrounding vineyards. If you've always wanted to bathe in a wine barrel, treat yourself to the suite! There's a bar, the restaurant **L'Oliveraie** (mains from Dh250; ⏲7am-11pm; P 📶) and a gorgeous spa.

the medina's main market hall is bursting with beautifully arranged pyramids of sugary sweet delicacies, baskets of dried fruits and olives in glistening piles. The faint-hearted may want to avoid the butchers and the automated chicken-plucking machines on the west side.

Gambrinus MOROCCAN €

(Map p361; ☎0535520258; Zankat Omar Ibn As, Ville Nouvelle; mains Dh50-70, set menu Dh77; ⏲8am-10pm) This elegant old restaurant-cafe doesn't look like it has changed much since the first Gambrinus rolled into town from Czechoslovakia in 1914 – although the menu is now firmly Moroccan. It's popular with locals of a certain age, who come for coffee or, on the restaurant side, rabbit tajines, grilled lamb and steaks.

Aisha MOROCCAN €€

(Map p358; ☎0620574730; Rue Kababine, Medina; mains from Dh70; ⏲9am-11pm; 🌶) This tiled box of a room has a maximum capacity of 10, so while you may want to lounge after your delectable home-style meal, it's only polite to roll out and make room for more of Aisha's many fans. She takes special pride in *rfissa*, spiced chicken on a bed of bread scraps. Vegetarians and vegans warmly welcomed.

Ya Hala MOROCCAN €€

(Map p358; ☎0649988816; restaurant.yahala@gmail.com; 10 Rue Sidi Amar Bou Aouda, Medina; mains Dh70-95; ⏲noon-11pm Sun-Thu, from 3pm Fri; 📶) There's a nice atmosphere at this petite restaurant, with chatter from the family kitchen upstairs and the chef's son bustling about at the tables downstairs. Everything in the white plaster dining salon is bright, clean and modern, though lacking in natural light. Dishes are cooked fresh to order – allow plenty of time.

Omnia MOROCCAN €€

(Map p358; ☎0535533938, 0694226437; 8 Derb Ain Fouki, Rouamzine; set menu Dh110; ⏲noon-10.30pm) This low-key restaurant – really a few salons in a family home – is a relaxing spot with a varied menu, including the local speciality *kamama* (beef or chicken with tomatoes and honey) and *kababe mardoure* (beef kebab with egg). You can order à la carte, but the default is with salads, plus tea and cookies. Beer and wine available.

The entrance is up some stairs off Rouamzine, and set back a bit on the left – don't be deterred by the shuttered shop fronts.

Mille et Une Nuits MOROCCAN €€

(Map p358; ☎0535559002; off Rue Sidi Amar Bou Aouda, Medina; mains Dh75-95; ⏲noon-10pm) If this friendly restaurant feels a little like somebody's home glamorously made over as a Moroccan palace, that's because it is just that. It's a bit dark inside and ever so slightly shabby, but the traditional salon seating makes for a comfy lunch spot, and the

Moroccan fare on offer is very tasty. Allow time; meals are cooked to order.

Ryad Bahia MOROCCAN €€

(Map p358; ☎0535554541; 13 Tiberbarine, Medina; mains from Dh90, set menus Dh160-190; ⊙noon-3pm & 7-10pm;) This guesthouse restaurant has candlelit tables around its courtyard. If you're not also staying at the riad, call to reserve a day (or at least a few hours) ahead, to give the staff a chance to shop and prepare – all the traditional Moroccan food is cooked to order and presented beautifully.

Drinking & Nightlife

It's a popular adage that Meknes has more bars than any other Moroccan city. However, it's still difficult to find a place to drink alcohol in the medina, where there are no bars. Omnia serves beers and local wines with meals.

Many ville nouvelle hotels have bars and a few even house nightclubs (generally midnight to 3am).

Zazen Centre CAFE

(Map p358; ☎0660046096; www.instagram.com/zazencentre; 10 Derb Laktout, Medina; ⊙9am-10pm) At the end of a skinny lane, this little courtyard house is a social hub for creative young Meknassis, hosting acoustic music and art workshops. It's open all day, so check for events on the Instagram account, or just pop in for coffee or a snack (starting with breakfast, Dh30) and admire the cool decor.

Cafe Restaurant Place Lahdim CAFE

(Map p358; cnr Place El Hedim & Sidi Amar Bouaouda, Medina; ⊙10am-10.30pm) Come dusk, this succession of roof terraces is where young locals settle in for a sundowner coffee. The best tables are at the top, where you can watch the sun brush the Imperial City walls and Bab El Mansour with gold. Service is slow at peak times. It also does breakfast (from Dh25). The door is just inside the medina gate.

La Tulipe CAFE

(Map p361; ☎0535511094; Rue de Tarfaya, Ville Nouvelle; ⊙5.30am-11pm;) A modern Moroccan cafe, with a large terrace and very decent coffee. Set on a quiet cul-de-sac, it's a pleasant spot to kill an hour or two, and the patisseries (sweet and savoury) are delicious. Pick from the sweets counter, then order drinks and pay at the till. It's female-friendly.

Pavillon des Idrissides CAFE

(Map p358; 147 Rue Dar Smen, Medina; ⊙9am-11pm;) Enter through the horseshoe arch on the corner of Place El Hedim to reach this rooftop cafe-restaurant with a coveted view overlooking the square and Bab El Mansour. Come for a coffee or fresh juice at sunset; food is bland at best.

Entertainment

Cinema Camera CINEMA

(Map p361; Ave Hassan II, Ville Nouvelle) Swing by this grand old cinema, built in 1938, even if you don't have time for a feature film – the sweeping mural along the staircase is a masterpiece art deco work. The adjacent pedestrian street is lively at night.

Institut Français PERFORMING ARTS

(Map p357; ☎0535524071; www.if-maroc.org; Rue Ferhat Hachad; ⊙9am-12.15pm & 2-6pm Mon-Sat, plus evening events) A major centre for Meknes cultural life, this massive complex has a busy schedule of films, plays, concerts and exhibitions. There's also a garden cafe. If you're in town for a night or two, check the schedule to see what's on.

Shopping

The Meknes souqs pale in comparison to those in Fez or Marrakesh, but there is a relative lack of hassle here. Unique to Meknes is the craft of damascene, black steel inlaid with intricate silver wire. There's a handful of good-value carpet shops opposite the Mausoleum of Moulay Ismail.

Abdelhak Ezzouak ARTS & CRAFTS

(L'Art de Damaskini; Map p358; 86 Souq Srairia, Medina; ⊙10am-6pm Sat-Thu) Mr Ezzouak's

SHOPPING IN THE SOUQS & QISSARIAT

The lane just left of Dar Jamaï leads directly into the souqs, selling a mix of souvenirs and functional goods for locals. Off either side of the northbound lane (as well as east along Rue Nejjarine, past the Grande Mosquée) are *qissariat*, covered markets with stalls, many devoted to textiles and carpets. Friday to Sunday, look out for dealers from Amazigh villages auctioning fine wares to shop owners, or city dealers auctioning secondhand clothes to village women. Outside the western city wall, heading north from Bab Berrima, is a colourful souq selling spices, herbs and nuts, and street vendors selling new clothes. Near Bab El Jdid, bear left into a lively *marché aux puces* (flea market).

little damascene metalwork shop is the northernmost of several in this strip, interspersed with more functional metal crafts such as bike repair. He can show how the silver wires are tapped into the oxidised steel and fired again, and he has assorted decorative pieces and jewellery for sale.

Pottery Stalls ARTS & CRAFTS

(Map p358; Place El Hedim; ⌚9am-10pm) In front of the covered market, pottery dealers present literal piles of wares. It's a no-pressure place to browse for functional pottery such as simple terracotta tajines.

Ensemble Artisanal ARTS & CRAFTS

(Map p357; Ave Mohammed VI; ⌚10am-1pm & 3-7pm Mon-Sat) This is the place to go if you want to get an idea of what to look for and how much to spend. Quality is high and prices are fixed.

ℹ Information

The **central post office** (Map p361; Rue de l'Union Africaine; ⌚8am-4.30pm Mon-Fri) is a massive building in the ville nouvelle. There are plenty of banks with ATMs in both the ville nouvelle (mainly on Ave Hassan II and Ave Mohammed V) and the medina (Rue Rouamzine, plus a BMCI on the north side of Place El Hedim).

ℹ Getting There & Away

BUS

The **CTM bus station** (Map p357; ☎0522438282; www.ctm.ma; Ave des FAR) is east of the ville nouvelle, a few long blocks west of the main train station. Prices are for Comfort class; Comfort Plus buses cost a bit more.

CTM departures include Casablanca (Dh90, 3½ to four hours, seven daily), Rabat (Dh55, two hours, 11 daily), Fez (Dh25, one hour, hourly), Marrakesh (Dh180, seven to eight hours, two daily), Tangier (Dh95, five hours, four daily), Oujda (Dh145, five to seven hours, three daily), Taza (Dh70, three hours, eight daily), Errachidia (Dh110 to Dh120, six to seven hours, three daily) and Nador (Dh125, 6½ hours, three daily).

Other buses depart from the Gare Routière, west of the medina, outside Bab El Khemis. These buses are cheaper and serve some destinations that CTM doesn't; they can be less reliable, however. The station has left-luggage and snack stands. Buses to Fez run hourly from 5am to 10pm and cost Dh15.

Tickets are purchased from the numbered windows:

Window 1 Fez (Dh15, nine daily), Ouarzazate (Dh170, one daily), Errachidia (Dh110, four daily)

Window 2 Rabat (Dh40, hourly) and Casablanca (Dh60, hourly), Sidi Kacem (Dh15, two daily)

Window 3 Tetouan (Dh75, eight daily), Chefchaouen (Dh50, four daily), Ouezzane (Dh35, two daily) and Tangier (Dh70, seven daily)

Window 4 Sefrou (Dh20, two daily), Taza (Dh50, four daily), Nador (Dh100, seven daily) and Oujda (Dh100, nine daily)

Window 5 Khenifra (Dh47, four daily) and Marrakesh (Dh120, six daily)

For Moulay Idriss (Dh7), city bus 15 runs from the stop south of **Place El Hedim** (Map p358); it also passes near the Gare Routière.

TAXI

Most *grands taxis* convene near the Gare Routière, outside the medina's Bab El Khemis.

In the lot in front, you'll find cars to Ifrane, Azrou, Midelt, Chefchaouen and Ouezzane. You can also go to Moulay Idriss (Dh10, 20 minutes), but for this you may find a smaller rank in the ville nouvelle more convenient. Look for it opposite the entrance to the Institut Français. In both cases, you can also arrange a car to add on Volubilis, for a fixed half-day rate of Dh400 for the whole car, but note that you can also get a far cheaper taxi to Volubilis after you arrive in Moulay Idriss.

From the triangular lot across the road from the Gare Routière, taxis go to Fez (Dh25, one hour), Rabat (Dh50, two hours) and Casablanca (Dh80, three hours).

Taxis run to Fes-Saïss Airport at a day/night fixed rate of Dh400/Dh500 or to Casablanca Airport for Dh1400.

TRAIN

Of Meknes' two train stations, the more convenient is Meknes Al Amir Abdelkader, on the east edge of the ville nouvelle. (The main train station, further east, is better connected with city buses, but otherwise remote from the medina.) There are trains to Fez (Dh32, 45 minutes, hourly), Taza (Dh54, 3½ hours, six daily), Nador (Dh108, 6½ hours, three daily) and Oujda (Dh124, 6½ hours, three daily). Trains also go to Casablanca (Dh114, three hours, hourly) via Rabat (Dh84, two hours), as well as to Marrakesh (Dh216, six hours, nine daily). For Tangier, there are four direct trains a day (Dh98, 3½ hours), but the route with a transfer to the high-speed line in Kenitra is faster, if pricier (Dh156, 2¾ hours, hourly).

ℹ Getting Around

BUS

Red-and-blue city buses connect the medina and the ville nouvelle, although some take a circuitous route, so it's more efficient to take a taxi or walk. The most useful may be bus 14, from the CTM bus station to Bab Bou Ameir, at the east edge of the medina. Buses 10 and 24 run from the main (eastern) train station, through the ville nouvelle on Ave Mohammed V and past a major **bus stop** (Map p361; Ave Hassan II) on Ave Hassan II, in front of the central market, continuing to the major medina bus stop, just south of Place El Hedim. From near Place El Hedim, nearly all buses go to the Gare Routière. Tickets are Dh3.

TAXI

The fare for pale-blue petits taxis from the ville nouvelle to the medina is between Dh7 to Dh15 (starting rate of Dh1.40, then Dh0.20/100m, and 50% higher after 8pm). Some also operate grand-taxi style, with a per-seat fare of Dh2.50; look for them where Ave Hassan II runs into Ave Moulay Ismail. In the medina, they congregate where Rue Dar Smen intersects with **Rue Rouamzine** (Map p358).

Arriving at Al Amir Abdelkader train station, you may have to dodge opportunists who'd prefer not to use the meter. If in doubt, walk south on Ave Mohammed V to the taxi rank at **Ave des FAR** (Map p361).

Volubilis (Oualili) وليلي

Excavations indicate that the site of Volubilis *(vol-oo-bill-iss)* was originally settled by Carthaginian traders in the 3rd century BCE, although less than half of the site has been excavated so far. One of the Roman Empire's most remote outposts, Volubilis was annexed in 25 BCE. According to some historians, Rome imposed strict controls on what could and could not be produced in its North African possessions, according to the needs of the empire. One result was massive deforestation and the large-scale planting of wheat around Volubilis. At its peak, it is estimated that the city was home to up to 20,000 people. The site's most impressive monuments were built in the 2nd and 3rd centuries CE, including the triumphal arch, capitol, baths and basilica.

The Romans installed Amazigh aristocrat Juba II of Mauretania (50 BCE–24 CE) as king of Volubilis. Educated in Rome, Juba II was married to the daughter of Mark Anthony and Cleopatra. His handsome bronze bust is in the Museum of History & Civilisation (p204) in Rabat.

After the neighbouring Amazigh tribes began to reassert themselves, the Romans abandoned Volubilis around 280 CE. Nevertheless, the city's population of Amazigh, Greeks, Jews and Syrians continued to speak Latin right up until the arrival of Islam. Moulay Idriss found sanctuary here in the 8th century, before moving his capital to Fez. Volubilis continued to be inhabited until the 18th century, when its marble was plundered for Moulay Ismail's palaces in Meknes, and its buildings were finally felled by the Lisbon earthquake of 1755.

★ **Volubilis** RUINS

(adult/child Dh70/30; ⌚8.30am-sunset) Sitting in the middle of a fertile plain, the ruined Roman city of Volubilis is the best-preserved archaeological site in Morocco. Its most amazing features are the many beautiful mosaics preserved in situ, and it was declared a Unesco World Heritage site in 1997. Volubilis is about 33km north of Meknes and can easily be combined with nearby Moulay Idriss Zerhoun to make a fantastic day trip from Meknes or Fez.

Only about half of the 40-hectare site at Volubilis has been excavated. The better-known monuments are in the northern part of the site, furthest from the entrance in the south.

In the heat of a summer day, the sun can be incredibly fierce, so bring a hat and plenty of water. Spring is the ideal season, when wildflowers blossom amid the abandoned stones, and the surrounding fields are at their greenest. The best time to visit is either first thing in the morning or late afternoon; at dusk, when the last rays of the sun light the ancient columns, Volubilis is at its most magical.

Although parts of certain buildings are roped off, you are free to wander the site at will. Just beyond the entrance gate lies a small on-site **museum**, which displays the ancient city's most celebrated finds and includes some of the prized discoveries, such as some fine bronzes, although many remain in the Archaeology Museum in Rabat.

➡ **Hiring a guide**

Information boards are much improved and explain in English, French and Arabic what you're actually seeing. It's well worth hiring a guide, especially if you're pressed for time. Official guides hang about at the entrance to the site and conduct good one-hour tours for Dh250. Between them, the guides speak virtually every language under the sun. To get the most out of your tour, insist on getting one that speaks your language fluently.

If you prefer to wander on your own, allow at least two hours to see the essentials.

➡ **Ancient Volubilis**

Although the least remarkable part of the site, the **olive presses** here indicate the economic basis of ancient Volubilis, much as the plentiful olive groves in the surrounding

Volubilis

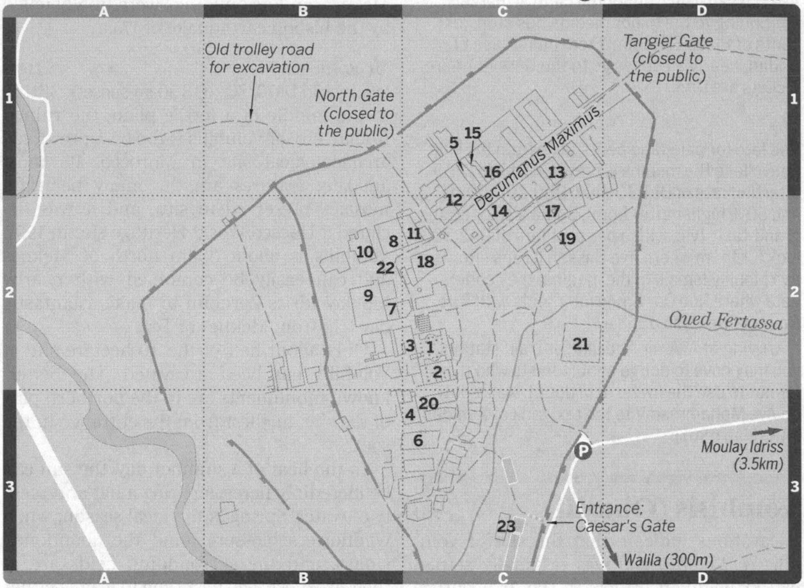

Volubilis

Sights

1	Basilica	C2
2	Capitol	C2
3	Forum	C2
4	Galen's Thermal Baths	C3
5	House of Dionysus & the Four Seasons	C1
6	House of Orpheus	C3
7	House of the Acrobat	B2
8	House of the Columns	B2
9	House of the Dog	B2
10	House of the Ephebus	B2
11	House of the Knight	C2
12	House of the Labours of Hercules	C2
13	House of the Marble Bacchus	C1
14	House of the Nereids	C2
15	House of the Nymphs Bathing	C1
16	House of the Wild Beasts	C1
17	House of Venus	C2
18	North Baths	C2
19	Olive Press	C2
20	Restored Olive Press	C3
21	Temple of Saturn	C2
22	Triumphal Arch	B2
23	Visitor Centre & Museum	C3

area do today – look for the flat presses and stone storage vats dotted about the site. Wealthy homeowners had private olive presses.

➡ Buildings

Next to the House of Orpheus are the remains of **Galen's Thermal Baths**. Although largely broken, they clearly show the highly developed underfloor heating in this Roman hammam (look for the low arches). Opposite the steam room are the communal toilets – where citizens could go about their business and have a chat at the same time.

The **Capitol**, **Basilica** and 1300-sq-metre **Forum** are, typically, built on a high point. The Capitol, dedicated to the Triad of Jupiter, Juno and Minerva, dates back to 218 CE; the Basilica and Forum lie to its north. The reconstructed columns of the Basilica are usually topped with storks' nests – an iconic Volubilis image if the birds are nesting at the time of your visit. Around the Forum is a series of plinths carved with Latin inscriptions that would have supported statues of the great and good. Keep your eyes out for the carved stone drain-hole cover – an understated example of Roman civil engineering.

The marble **Triumphal Arch** was built in 217 in honour of Emperor Caracalla and his mother, Julia Domna. The arch, which was originally topped with a bronze chariot, was reconstructed in the 1930s, and the mistakes made then were rectified in the 1960s. The hillock to the east provides a splendid view over the entire site.

➡ Houses with Mosaics

The **House of Orpheus** is the finest and largest home, containing a mosaic of Orpheus charming animals by playing the lute, and a dolphin mosaic in the dining room. Note the private hammam has a caldarium (hot room) with visible steam pipes, a tepidarium (warm room) and a frigidarium (cold room), as well as a solarium.

On the left just before the triumphal arch are a couple more roped-off mosaics. One, in the **House of the Acrobat**, depicts an athlete being presented with a trophy for winning a desultory race, a competition in which the rider had to dismount and jump back on his horse as it raced along. To the west of here is the **House of the Dog**, famed not for its mosaics but a lonesome rock plinth with a giant phallus carved into the top of it – this establishment was once a brothel for weary warriors who would stop off here after making it back to the triumphal arch after battle.

From the arch, the ceremonial road, Decumanus Maximus, stretches up the slope to the northeast. The houses lining it on either side contain the best mosaics on the site. The first on the far side of the arch is known as the **House of the Ephebus** and contains a now-incomplete mosaic of Bacchus in a chariot drawn by panthers.

Next along, the **House of the Columns** is so named because of the columns arranged in a circle around the interior court – note their differing styles, which include spirals. Adjacent to this is the **House of the Knight**, also called House of the Cavalier/Rider with its incomplete mosaic of Bacchus and Ariadne. The naked Ariadne has suffered somewhat from the attentions of admirers.

The next four houses are named for their excellent mosaics: the **House of the Labours of Hercules**, the **House of Dionysus and the Four Seasons**, the **House of the Nymphs Bathing**, though the nymph mosaics are heavily damaged, and the **House of the Wild Beasts**. The first is almost a circular comic strip, recounting the Twelve Labours. Several of Hercules' heroic feats were reputed to have occurred in Morocco, making him a popular figure at the time.

Some of the best mosaics are saved until last. Cross the Decumanus Maximus and head for the lone cypress tree, which marks the **House of Venus**, home of King Juba II. There are two particularly fine mosaics here, appropriately with semi-romantic themes. The first is the *Abduction of Hylas by the Nymphs*, an erotic composition showing Hercules' lover Hylas being lured away from his duty by two beautiful nymphs. The second mosaic is *Diana Bathing*. The virgin goddess was glimpsed in her bath by the hunter Acteon, whom she turned into a stag as punishment. Acteon can be seen sprouting horns, about to be chased and devoured by his own pack of hounds – the fate of mythical peeping toms everywhere.

Sleeping & Eating

Hotel Volubilis HOTEL €€

(☎0679052126; volu.mus@hotmail.com; Route de Meknes; s/d/tr Dh400/540/640; P) The best feature of this large four-star hotel on a rise above Volubilis is its expansive views over the Roman ruins and surrounding countryside, which make up for the general lack of atmosphere. All rooms have a TV and fridge, and benefit from the views – as do the terraces, pool, panoramic bar and restaurant (menu Dh80 to Dh100).

Café La Corbeille Fleurie MOROCCAN €

(Volubilis; salads Dh25-40, tajines Dh40; ⏲8.30am-sunset) When you need a breather after clambering over all those Roman ruins, this cafe overlooking Volubilis is perfect. There's plenty of shade, cold drinks and ice cream. Salads and tajines are on offer too.

Walila MOROCCAN €€€

(☎0652096373, 0661777670; azayr@hotmail.com; adjacent to Volubilis; lunch Dh200; ⏲12pm-3pm; P) Once the childhood home of a French minister, this 1920s farmstead is in a tranquil farm setting a five-minute walk from Volubilis. The affable owner Azzeddine used to be a chef in Holland – guests enjoy his organic modern Moroccan lunches. It's the perfect shady spot after exploring the ruins. Donkeys, chickens and peacocks roam under the trees. Advance booking is essential.

The original house offers three cosy but somewhat musty rooms (r from Dh550), mixing Berber textiles with French antiques and open fires. There's one bathroom between them. The barn has a large restaurant catering for groups, and another bedroom with bathroom upstairs. There's no wi-fi.

Getting There & Away

The simplest and quickest way to get to Volubilis is to hire a *grand taxi* for the return trip. A half-day outing from Meknes should cost Dh350, with a couple of hours at the site and a stop at

Moulay Idriss Zerhoun (worth an overnight stay in itself). The same trip from Fez (about twice the distance) will cost about Dh1000.

A cheaper alternative is to take a shared *grand taxi* from Meknes to Moulay Idriss Zerhoun (Dh10; ask for Zerhoun), and then hire a *grand taxi* to take you to Volubilis (Dh30 complete hire, one way). If the taxi waits for you and takes you back to Meknes, the cost is Dh120. If you don't arrange in advance to be taken back, simply ask the guardian at Volubilis car park to find you a taxi. Note that shared *grands taxis* to Moulay Idriss only run from near the Meknes Institut Français.

If the weather isn't too hot, it's a lovely one-hour walk (one way) between Moulay Idriss Zerhoun and Volubilis. Alternatively, trot down on a donkey arranged through Dar Zerhoune (p370) in Moulay Idriss Zerhoun (Dh150, one hour), and take a taxi back.

Moulay Idriss Zerhoun

مولاي ادريس

0535 / POP 11,620

The whitewashed town of Moulay Idriss Zerhoun *(moo-lay id-riss zer-hoon)* is perched prettily astride two green hills in a cradle of mountains. It is one of the country's most important pilgrimage sites, as the mausoleum of Morocco's first Islamic leader, Moulay Idriss, lies at its heart. Given its picturesque setting, history and national importance, it's a mystery why so many tourists don't stay more than an hour or two.

Moulay Idriss Zerhoun's holy status kept it closed to non-Muslims until 1912, and it wasn't until 2005 that non-Muslims were allowed to stay overnight in the town. Its previous inaccessibility has helped protect the town's peaceful way of life and mystical ambience; those who do stay are invariably charmed. Appealing local guesthouses cater to visitors and it's still a relaxed place with a centre free of carpet shops. Pull up a chair at a cafe and get hooked on local life.

History

The town is named for Moulay Idriss, a great-grandson of the Prophet Muhammad, the founder of the country's first real dynasty, Morocco's first Islamic leader and its most revered saint. His tomb is in the centre of the town, and is the focus of the country's largest *moussem* every August.

Moulay Idriss fled Mecca in the late 8th century in the face of persecution at the hands of the recently installed Abbasid caliphate, which was based in Baghdad. Idriss settled at Volubilis, where he converted the locals to Islam and made himself their leader, establishing the Idrissid dynasty.

Sights

Haroune Aqueduct LANDMARK

(east of Moulay Idriss Zerhoun) Also known as the Roman aqueduct (though it's not that old), this is a remarkable structure probably built to provide water to Moulay Idriss.

Mausoleum of Moulay Idriss MAUSOLEUM

(Place Mohammed VI) The Mausoleum of Moulay Idriss is Morocco's most important pilgrimage site, and the town is swamped every August during the annual moussem (p370) to venerate it; it's said locally that five pilgrimages to Moulay Idriss during the *moussem* equals one hajj to Mecca. The entrance is located at the top of the town's main square, via a three-arched gateway surrounded by shops selling religious trinkets – non-Muslims cannot enter beyond the inner barrier, but it's worth a peak inside the grand entrance.

Roman Baths RUINS

(east of Moulay Idriss Zerhoun) The Roman Baths have a small circular pool that sometimes has water in it. When it does, it's often full of boys and young men, and women visitors might not feel comfortable having a dip. The baths do make a great destination for a walk, though, especially coupled with the Haroune aqueduct (a one-hour loop from Moulay Idriss Zerhoun).

Cylindrical Minaret MOSQUE

(Rue Khibar) The only cylindrical minaret in Morocco is found at the Sentissi Mosque. Built in 1939, it is covered in pretty green *zellige* and white Kufi script. Find it by climbing steps into the medina next to two cafes side by side: **Benanni** and **Le Minaret Cylindrique**.

Grande & Petite Terrasses VIEWPOINT

These lofty medina vantage points provide stunning views over Moulay Idriss and the green-roofed mausoleum. The Grande Terrasse is broader and better for capturing panoramic vistas of the hilltop town and surrounding landscape on camera. Both terraces are difficult to find on your own; keep heading uphill and you'll get near, but you may have to ask a local to help you get to the exact spots. Dar Zerhoune has a handy map. It's not essential to have a guide take you up the steep steps to the panoramic viewpoint at the top, but you'll probably be

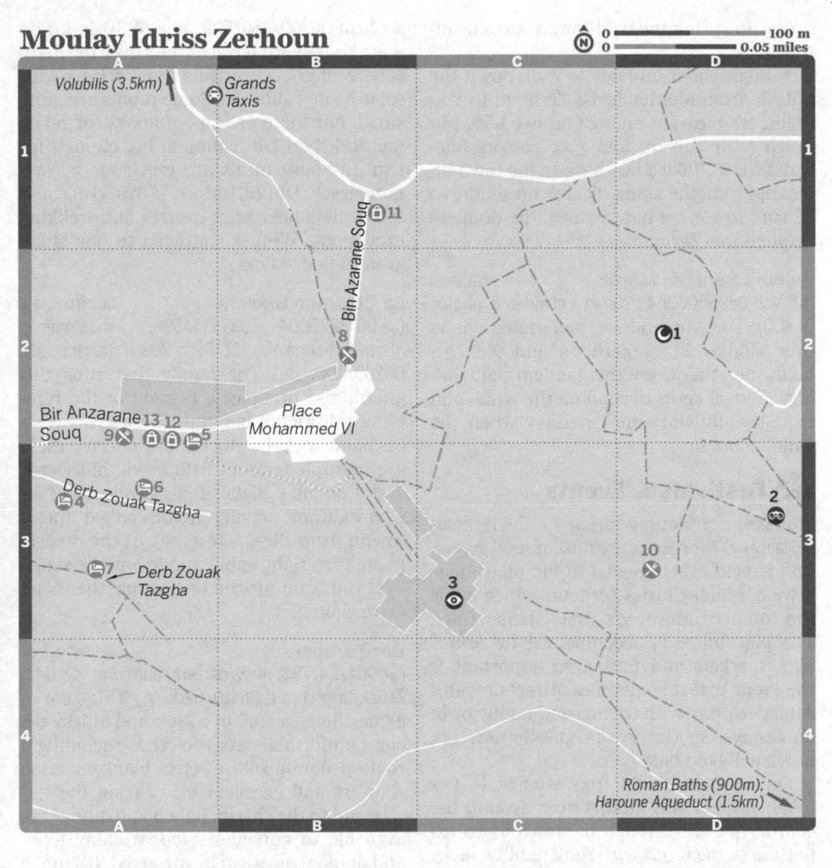

Moulay Idriss Zerhoun

Sights
1 Cylindrical Minaret D2
2 Grande & Petite Terrasses D3
3 Mausoleum of Moulay Idriss C3

Activities, Courses & Tours
Hajiba Dahik .... (see 6)

Sleeping
4 Dar Al Andaloussiya Diyafa A3
5 Dar Ines A2
6 Dar Zerhoune A3
7 La Colombe Blanche A3

Eating
Dar Zerhoune .... (see 6)
8 Grillade Albanna B2
9 Restaurant Boukhrissa A2
10 Scorpion House D3

Shopping
11 Basketware Shop B1
12 Brassware Shop A2
13 Olive Shop A2

approached by one of the young men who hang around at the mausoleum, hoping to earn Dh20 or so. If you'd like a bit more insight into life in the medina, there are a couple of interesting tours from **Hajiba Dahik** (☎0642247793; www.darzerhoune.com; Dar Zerhoune; 1-4 people Dh300) and **Mourit El Khoumsi** (☎0660385289; per 2hr Dh200).

Activities

The hills around Moulay Idriss Zerhoun are perfect for walking, with tree-shaded paths and fantastic views across the countryside. Roman baths and an aqueduct are worthwhile destinations, and you'll come across donkeys grazing and shepherds with their flocks. In spring the wildflowers are a beautiful sight.

It takes about an hour to walk down the hillside from Moulay Idriss Zerhoun to Volubilis. It's pleasant enough on two legs, but much more fun on four (per person, one-way Dh150). Take a taxi back to the town after exploring the ruins. There's no shade, so be sure to wear a hat. Arrange the donkeys through Dar Zerhoune.

Séjours Sportifs Maroc PARAGLIDING
(Jilali 0696606044; 20min incl video & photos Dh800) For stupendous panoramic views over Moulay Idriss Zerhoun and the Zerhoun mountains, try this tandem paragliding. Take-off spots depend on the wind, and trips usually start after midday when the wind comes up.

Festivals & Events

Moussem of Moulay Idriss RELIGIOUS
(late Aug) Morocco's greatest annual *moussem* is held every August in the pilgrimage town of Moulay Idriss Zerhoun, which holds the tomb of Morocco's first Islamic ruler. The pilgrimage is accompanied by *fantasias,* markets and music; so important is the event that it sometimes attracts royalty. Attendees stay with friends and family or in homestays, so the town's guesthouses are not usually too busy.

On Thursday night from August to October, various Sufi groups from around the country parade through the town as an extension of the *moussem*. You might be lucky enough to catch them singing prayers in the mausoleum in the evenings – a truly magical experience.

Donkey Day CULTURAL
(Dar Zerhoune Donkey Project; 0642247793; www.darzerhoune.com/donkeys; car park opp Red Crescent; 10am-12.30pm Sun, once per month) Here's a fascinating insight into the importance of donkeys in medina life. A monthly Donkey Day is organised by Kiwi Rose Button in collaboration with the American Fondouk (p330) in Fez, when local owners bring their animals to be treated for free by the visiting veterinarians.

Sleeping

There are a number of budget and midrange guesthouses in Moulay Idriss.

Dar Ines GUESTHOUSE €
(0535544907, 0667156795; www.darinesmoulaydriss.com; 57 Hay Tazga, Derb Amjout; s/d/ste from Dh300/350/500;) This grand guesthouse with terrace views over the main square offers seven traditional rooms with solar-heated showers. Some rooms are quite small, but there are lots of nooks for relaxing and there's a hammam big enough for two. In-house meals are excellent (guests/nonguests Dh120/Dh140 – reserve), and the owners offer craft courses and trekking excursions. Wi-fi is restricted to one small ground-floor salon.

La Colombe Blanche GUESTHOUSE €
(0678225004, 0535544596; www.maisondhote-zerhoune.ma; 21 Derb Zouak Tazgha; s/d Dh250/400;) The family that runs this guesthouse occupies a portion of the rambling traditional building so they're always on hand to help. Rooms are decent, there are multiple terraces with lovely hill views, and Colombe Blanche also bills itself as a restaurant serving home-cooked meals (menu from Dh95 – reserve). At the mausoleum, turn right uphill and follow the signs.

If you want air-con or heating, there's an extra charge.

Dar Zerhoune GUESTHOUSE €€
(0642247793; www.darzerhoune.com; 42 Derb Zouak Tazgha; s/d Dh410/620;) This gem of a guesthouse is full of colour and quirky decor. Comfortable areas to relax (including a rooftop hammock), electric blankets, good showers and excellent views from the terrace add to the charm. Lunch and dinner are available to non-guests too. Walking tours and donkey rides can be arranged. It's to the right uphill from the mausoleum.

Dar Al Andaloussiya Diyafa GUESTHOUSE €€
(0661253462; Zouak Tazgha; d Dh418;) This colourful guesthouse has 10 rooms. Most have a window to the outside, but bathrooms are on the small side. There are great views from the roof terrace, and dinner is available (menu Dh120).

Eating

Moulay Idriss Zerhoun is known for its delicious *kefta* (grilled meatballs). You'll find these and other offerings at the numerous inexpensive restaurants around the main square.

Restaurant Boukhrissa KEBAB €
(0643158896; Bir Anzarane Souq; kefta per 300g Dh40; 11am-9pm) The *kefta* here are some of the best in town. They come with tomatoes and onions, bread, chips, Moroccan salad and olives at Dh40 for two.

Grillade Albanna KEBAB €
(☎0666201370; off Place Mohammed VI; kefta Dh30; ⊙11am-9pm) Moulay Idriss is known for its *kefta*, and this simple grillhouse just off the town's main square is a local favourite. Take a people-watching seat while you wait for your meat to be grilled to order; the *kefta* (meatballs) is fresh, packed with flavour and served simply with grilled tomatoes, fresh bread and ground chilli.

★ **Scorpion House** MEDITERRANEAN €€€
(☎0535544729; www.scorpionhouse.com; 54 Drouj El Hafa; per person incl tip Dh800; ⊙noon-2.30pm;) A delicious, freshly made feast is served at this fabulous house high up on the mountainside. Expect a bountiful buffet of locally sourced, creative salads and treats cooked on the *shwaya* (traditional charcoal grill), with a Mediterranean twist. The setting is a feast, too, with spectacular views across the mountains, all the way down to Volubilis. Reserve ahead; payment is made on booking.

Dar Zerhoune MOROCCAN €€€
(☎0642247793; www.darzerhoune.com; 42 Derb Zouak Tazgha; meals Dh150-200; ⊙noon-2.30pm & 6-10pm;) Lunch or dinner on the Dar Zerhoune terrace is a treat with its inspiring views over the town and surrounding mountains. Choose a traditional three-course menu or a 'Taste of Moulay Idriss' with fresh sardines, *kefta* (meatballs) and grilled chicken. There's a vegetarian option and other dietary needs can be accommodated. Bookings preferred, but not essential.

Shopping

Olive Shop FOOD
(Abderrahim El Ghrissi; Bir Anzarane Souq; olives per kilo Dh20; ⊙10am-7pm Sat-Thu) Indulge in local produce at Abderrahim's shop with its glistening array of the best olives from the region: green ones with garlic or preserved lemon, shrivelled semidried black ones, or plump dark pink ones. There are tubs of dried figs, almonds, preserved lemons and carob, as well as plastic bottles of the distinctively flavoured local olive oil.

Brassware Shop ANTIQUES
(Driss Belfekih; Bir Anzarane Souq; ⊙noon-8pm Sat-Thu) Delve into this treasure trove of brass antiques left over from colonial French Protectorate times – lamps, kettles, jugs, trays, candlesticks and all sorts of weird and wonderful knick-knacks. There are a few new items, too, such as heavy mortars and pestles.

Basketware Shop ARTS & CRAFTS
(Bin Azarane Souq; ⊙9am-7pm Sat-Thu) This tiny hole-in-the-wall shop sells well-made flat baskets of all sizes, mats for the terrace, table mats and hats.

Getting There & Away

Grands taxis (Dh10, 20 minutes) to Moulay Idriss Zerhoun leave Meknes from outside the Institut Français (ask for 'Zerhoun').

The red city bus (No. 15) runs from Bab El Mansour in Meknes to Moulay Idriss (Dh7) throughout the day but makes multiple stops and takes an hour.

For onward travel by train to Tangier, Rabat, Casablanca and Marrakesh, it's more efficient to take a *grand taxi* to Sidi Kacem (Dh17) rather than Meknes.

A taxi to Volubilis costs Dh30 each way, or Dh120 if the driver waits while you visit the site. Alternatively, ride a donkey down to Volubilis and take a taxi back.

Grands taxis leave Moulay Idriss Zerhoun from the stand at the bottom of town on the main road. If you want to get to Fez, you'll have to go via Meknes.

From Meknes, a half-day tour to Volubilis and Moulay Idriss Zerhoun costs about Dh350.

Local taxi driver **Hamid El Bouzidi** (☎0663292629) offers private transfers to Fez (Dh350), Fez airport (Dh400), Meknes or Sidi Kacem (Dh150), Rabat (Dh600) and Chefchaouen (Dh800).

MIDDLE ATLAS

South of Fez and Meknes, the low-rise Middle Atlas mountains come into play. Oak and cedar forests create refreshing pockets of woodland and easy hiking terrain, connecting the dots between Berber hill towns and villages. Further south, towards Midelt, the forests give way to dramatic barren slopes as the desert calls.

Ifrane إفران

☎0535 / POP 73,790 / ELEV 1664M

As foreign tourists head to the medinas for a taste of the 'real' Morocco, Moroccan tourists find more favour with places such as Ifrane *(if-ran)*. Tidy, ordered and modern, it feels more like Switzerland relocated to the Middle Atlas than North Africa. Its clean air, scrubbed streets and leafy outlook make it popular with tour groups.

The French built Ifrane in the 1930s, deliberately trying to recreate an alpine-style resort. It has neat red-roofed houses, blooming flower beds and lake-studded parks. It is a popular summer day trip for picnickers; in winter the affluent flock here for nearby skiing, and the hoi polloi come for the pure fun of throwing snowballs. The young Moroccan elite study at Al Akhawayn University.

Sleeping & Eating

Hotel prices in Ifrane reflect the town's affluence, and its year-round popularity means demand for rooms runs high – particularly with tour groups. If you're on a budget, you'd be better off staying in Azrou. Hotels here rarely have air-conditioning but all feature central heating.

Most of the cafes and hotels are clustered in the centre along Rue de la Cascade and Ave de la Poste, close to the stone lion statue. The glass-and-chrome modern cafes offer sandwiches and pizzas as well as main meals. Most hotels have a restaurant too. Those on a budget will find the food in Ifrane pricey.

Hôtel Chamonix HOTEL €€
(0535566028; www.lechamonix.com; Ave de la Marche Verte; s/d Dh628/702;) Right across the street from Ifrane's stone lion, this three-star place is well maintained and centrally located. Rooms are bright and spacious, if a little bland, with attached bathrooms and central heating. There's also a decent restaurant and bar. During the snow season, expect price hikes of 15% to 20%.

Hotel Les Tilleuls HOTEL €€
(0535566658, 0661161186; hoteltilleuls@gmail.com; cnr Ave des Tilluels & Rue de la Cascade; s/d excl breakfast Dh300/400) The cheapest hotel in Ifrane has been welcoming guests since 1935. The entrance and bar as well as two floors of rooms have been renovated, but there's still a way to go. In the meantime its selling points are large, en-suite rooms and its convenient location on the corner of Ifrane's main square.

FINE DINING NEAR IFRANE

Built by the French in 1929, the atmospheric old Hotel Les Truites now operates as **Restaurant Les Truites** (0535663002; www.lestruites.com; N8, Immouzer El Kandar; mains from Dh105; 9am-8pm). It specialises in delicious local trout (hence the name), as well as rabbit, venison and wild boar. The sautéed potatoes are legendary. Simple gingham tablecloths, smiley waiters, a roaring fire in winter and a glass of wine with your fresh trout make this very special.

★ **Hôtel L'Empreinte** HOTEL €€€
(0535566184; lempreintedifrane@gmail.com; cnr Rue des Lilas & Rue des Erables; s/d Dh750/850, ste Dh1500;) One of the better options in Ifrane and bang in the centre, L'Empreinte occupies a large corner site with a cafe and restaurant. The rooms are a good size and feature lots of wood and local art. There's no air-conditioning, but good heating.

Michlifen Ifrane HOTEL €€€
(0535864000, 0535864041; www.michlifen.com; off Ave Hassan II; excl breakfast r/ste from Dh2300/3550;) Overlooking Ifrane from the north, this oversized ski-lodge-style hotel is one of Morocco's most luxurious. Local cedar and stone is evident throughout the rather dark interior, with rooms echoing a luxury chalet. The view from the pool is sublime and you can even fish in the river that runs through the hotel grounds. There's a sumptuous bar and a restaurant.

Hôtel Perce-Neige HOTEL €€€
(0535566350; hperceneige@gmail.com; Rue des Asphodelles; s/d Dh650/810, ste Dh1200-1350;) Hôtel Perce-Neige is a pretty establishment down a leafy street about 200m southeast of the centre. The rooms could be a bit bigger, and some are a little faded for the price, but they're very comfortable and come with satellite TV and bathrooms. Those at the front can be a bit noisy, but they have large balconies.

L'Adresse CAFE €€
(0535567248; Ave de la Marche Verte; breakfast Dh28-35, mains Dh65-145; 7am-11.30pm) Like so many of Ifrane's cafes, L'Adresse is all modern glass and chrome and sits on a corner, so perfect for people-watching. Have breakfast here, afternoon tea or a full meal.

Forest Restaurant CAFE €€
(cnr Ave del Porte & Rue de la Cascade; mains Dh79-149; 7.30am-11pm Mon-Fri, to midnight Sat & Sun;) This chilled-out cafe attracts Ifrane's wealthy university students. It's a little on the pricey side, but if you're craving some decent international food, Forest is a treat. Start the day with eggs or croissants, or come later for burgers, excellent pasta and pizzas. Finish off with a warming dessert such as apple crumble.

La Paix CAFE €€

(☎0535566675; Ave de la Marche Verte; coffee and croissant Dh35; ⏰9am-10pm; 📶) Go ahead and rub your eyes, because you won't believe you're in Morocco once you've crossed the threshold of this upmarket cafe-patisserie. First there's the astroturfed outdoor patio with garden furniture; then there's the wide glass frontage and minimalist white interior to behold. La Paix is situated next door to Café L'Adresse – come for a breakfast of croissant and coffee.

There's an impressive menu that includes rabbit tajine (Dh80), trout (Dh150 to Dh180) and salads, but not everything listed is available. Service can be surly.

ℹ Getting There & Away

The Gare Routière is south of town and services both CTM and local buses. The station has a cafe and shop for snacks.

Each morning and evening, CTM buses leave for Marrakesh (Dh155, 10½ hours) via Beni Mellal. There's a daily 1pm departure for Casablanca (Dh125, five hours), two for Meknes (Dh25, one hour) and one to Rabat (Dh95, 2½ hours).

There are frequent daily non-CTM bus departures to Fez, Azrou and Khenifra, as well as four daily to Marrakesh, five daily to Rabat and one daily to Casablanca.

Grands taxis also congregate at the bus station; they go to Fez or Meknes (Dh30) and Azrou (Dh9). *Grands taxis* to Dayet Aoua can be hired privately for Dh250, or it'll cost Dh600 for a full day trip of the Lake Circuit. To go to Oum Er Rbia (p374), expect to pay about Dh1000 for a full day.

Ifrane National Park

Easy hiking trails through magnificent mountains, cedar and oak forests studded with waterfalls and lakes, and remote Amazigh villages all await in the little-known Ifrane National Park.

The 1250 sq km reserve is an accessible one-hour drive from Fez or Meknes. But linger awhile to discover what it has to offer: Ramsar wetland sites with their rich flora and fauna, exceptional bird life, rare plants, and a variety of wildlife. By far the most famous animal is the endangered Barbary macaque; the forests provide sanctuary for numerous troops and they are relatively easy to see in the wild. Other mammals include the wild boar and Atlas golden wolf. Nomads build temporary accommodation or pitch tents to graze their flocks during the summer.

LOCAL KNOWLEDGE

FESTIVAL INTERNATIONAL D'IFRANE

Held over seven days in late July, **Festival International d'Ifrane** (www.festivalifrane.com; ⏰Jul) aims to show off local cultural heritage and features the latest Moroccan music stars as well as plenty of traditional music, including *ahidous* (a celebratory circle dance with musicians in the middle). Sporting events such as cross-country races, fishing and shooting competitions, football and basketball as well as cinema and a conference complete the picture.

The towns of Azrou and Ifrane are gateways to the park, while small villages such as Ain Leuh provide a glimpse into rural Amazigh life.

Around Ifrane

Dayet Aoua LAKE

Dayet Aoua is surrounded by woodlands in an area notably rich in bird life. The lake is a popular picnic destination for families on weekends, but during the week you'll get it largely to yourself. In summer the water all but dries up, and locals trot around the lake bed on horseback. At other times you can rent pedalos here, and year-round it makes a good bike circuit. From Ifrane, a one-way taxi costs about Dh250.

The lake attracts significant numbers of ducks and waders, including crested coot, woodpeckers, tree creepers and nuthatches, which flit among the trees around the south-eastern end of the lake. Also keep an eye out for raptors, including booted eagles, black and red kites, and harriers.

Lake Circuit SCENIC DRIVE

A pretty diversion north of Ifrane is the lake circuit around Dayet Aoua. Signposted off the main Fez road 17km north of Ifrane, the route winds for 60km through the lake country between the P24 and P20. If you don't have your own vehicle, hiring a *grand taxi* in Ifrane for a day trip should cost about Dh600.

Beyond Dayet Aoua, the road loops east and then south, skirting past small Dayet Hachlaf and then Dayet Ifrah. Although this trip is billed as a scenic drive, the joy of the area is to get out and walk along the lake shore and enjoy the tranquillity of the

SKIING IN IFRANE

There's usually enough snow between November and March for skiing at **Michlifen**. This volcanic crater is a perfect bowl, surrounded by majestic cedar trees, and has a new drag lift for each of its two gentle slopes. Equipment can be hired on site. A *grand taxi* from Ifrane or Azrou costs Dh300 for a round trip.

scenery. This is an area made for hikers, mountain bikers and birdwatchers. Note that the road is paved but a bit scarred in some parts, and liable to be snowbound in winter. Unfortunately, the lakes can dry up completely in summer, making it less attractive.

If you want to linger longer, there's a good sleeping option at Dayet Aoua, the delightfully rustic **Le Gîte Dayet Aoua** (☎0661351257, 0535610575; www.gitedayetaoua.com; Dayet Aoua; d/superior Dh400/500; P ❄).

Oued Tizguit BIRD SANCTUARY

One of the Ramsar sites in the national park, this wetland southeast of Ifrane is home to rare insects (caddisfly and stonefly) and plants (Atlas daisy). There are lots of birds including the common pochard, plus amphibians, common otters and over 200 aquatic plants.

Around Azrou

Agdal Plateau & Kherzouza Cliffs HIKING

This leisurely day hike starts from the forests at Moudmame just outside Azrou, climbing steadily through crops of oak trees that morph into fragrant cedar at about 1800m. You'll then strike out over the broad Agdal plateau, inhabited by Amazigh shepherds and honey farms, before dipping back into the forests and eventually emerging at the craggy Kherzouza cliffs, with spectacular views over Azrou.

Signposting for this walk is poor, and if you don't have a good map or GPS, it's advisable to book a mountain guide such as Saleh Boudaoud or Abdellah Lahrizi. The walk is about 10km from Moudmame, though you can start from Azrou if you fancy the extra 8km walk to get to Moudmame from the town.

Oum Er Rbia Springs RIVER

(Sources Oum Er Rbia; parking Dh10, cave Dh10) Several dozen fresh- and salt-water (brine) springs emerge from the rocks to form a series of waterfalls at Oum Er Rbia, and the river cascades down the mountainside. Along the banks are simple bamboo cabins with cushions and tables that you can rent (per day Dh100). Above them are makeshift cafes that supply mint tea and tajines to order. It's too dangerous to swim, but locals love to spend the day here, relaxing in the cabins surrounded by magnificent scenery.

★ **Les Jardins d'Azrou** FARMSTAY €€

(☎0662190889, 0663772687; www.lesjardinsdazrou.com; Route d'Ifrane, 3km from Azrou; s/d/tr Dh400/550/650; P 📶) Outside Azrou with lovely mountain views, this farm produces organic fruit juice, jams and honey. The five pretty rooms are comfortable with double-glazed windows, central geothermal heating and solar-powered hot water, perfect for snowy winters. Meals cost from Dh125 to Dh300 and the menu is inventive, including Swiss fondu, local mushrooms and trout. Vegetarians are well catered for.

Owner Abdellah can arrange walks, longer hikes over several days, mountain bikes and horseriding.

Ain Leuh & Around

This pretty village within the Ifrane National Park is an excellent example of a rural Amazigh (Berber) settlement. It's crowned by a small 17th-century kasbah used to control the local population during Moulay Ismail's time. The surrounding farmland produces fruit, especially cherries, and is also used for raising livestock. Ain Leuh *(ain li-oo)* makes a pleasant stop for mint tea while exploring the park and has some interesting places to visit.

A major **souq** (Taberghazit, 3km north of Ain Leuh; ⏲4am-2pm Wed) held just outside town on Wednesday attracts people from all over the region. A small souq for clothing is also held on Wednesday in the centre of town.

A shared *grand taxi* from Azrou costs Dh15 and stops on the only street, Blvd Hassan II. These are easiest to find on a Wednesday when lots of people head for the weekly souq. A private taxi from Azrou will cost Dh500.

Various excellent walks start in Ain Leuh, ranging from four hours to three days. Spectacular scenery, waterfalls, Amazigh villages, and superb birding at Ramsar sites make these worthwhile.

Ouiouane Lake BIRD SANCTUARY

Set in the Ifrane National Park, this Ramsar site is a five-hour walk or 35-minute drive south of Ain Leuh.

Afenourir Lake WALKING

This four-hour walk from Ain Leuh takes you to the volcanic lake. It's a Ramsar site, so birdwatching is prime here, as is the spectacular scenery.

Oum Er Rbia Springs WALKING

A three-day hike from Ain Leuh to Oum Er Rbia Springs takes in Zaouia Ifrane and another Ramsar site, Ouiouane Lake. There are mountain *gîtes* to stay in, or you can take camping equipment.

Zaouia Ifrane WALKING

This is a six-hour trek into the Ifrane National Park, beginning in Ain Leuh and passing several Amazigh villages and a waterfall. It's fairly strenuous, but the views make it worthwhile. Zaouia Ifrane is a tiny village surrounded by waterfalls and mountains.

Tours

Official Middle Atlas mountain guides work for set rates. It's Dh300/Dh200 per person per full/half-day, not including lunch or transport. With food and transport, expect to pay about Dh1000 per day for one to two people.

Multiday treks, including mule, accommodation, food and guide, cost Dh800 to Dh1200 per day, depending on the number of hikers.

Saleh Boudaoud (0632361990; www.boudaoudtrekking.jimdo.com; half/full day per person from Dh200/300) is an excellent English-speaking guide who has worked extensively on the Barbary macaques and is also knowledgeable about birds.

Abdellah Lahrizi is an official guide and owner of the rural guesthouse Les Jardins d'Azrou.

Horse riding (Dh200 per hour) and mountain biking (Dh700 per day) are popular here, but you may have to hire a guide to facilitate these excursions. For horse riding, note that the costs don't include professional guides or equipment; you'll either be led around by the rein or left completely to your own devices, which may not live up to your expectations.

Azrou أزرو

0535 / POP 48,250 / ELEVATION 1250M

Monkeys and fragrant cedar forest trails draw visitors to Azrou *(az-roo)*, and the town itself is a thoroughly unhurried, relaxing spot in which to wind down if you're feeling frazzled after too many big cities. It's an important Amazigh market centre deep in the Middle Atlas, with a shaggy mane of woods and high meadows that burst into flower every spring.

Azrou

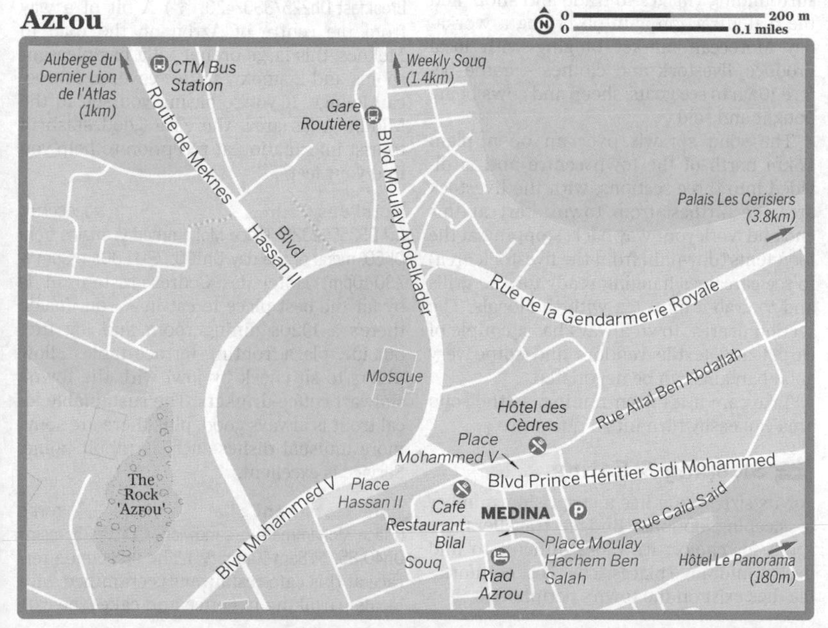

Azrou (Great Rock) takes its name from the isolated outcrop marking the town's western boundary. The big Ennour mosque, beautifully finished with local cedar, provides another handy landmark. Azrou's petite medina is most easily accessible from the south side of Place Mohammed V and is a refreshing place to wander without hassle, particularly if you're on the lookout for a carpet, for which the town and surrounding region are famous. Tuesday's souq provides a fascinating insight into rural Amazigh culture.

Sights

Trails into the hills southeast of town can be reached on foot. From the centre of Azrou, ask for directions to the Sbab hammam, south of the medina. From here, take the road to the left of the hammam (alongside the men's entrance) and follow your nose uphill to the cemetery, which you should find on your left. The road will eventually peter out and be replaced by a pathway that follows the river and ascends into the mountains.

★Souq MARKET

(sunrise-sunset Tue; P) Azrou's weekly souq is one of the largest in the Middle Atlas and truly a sight to behold, but it's not a souvenir-fest: mountain people come from surrounding villages to trade and shop, and the real attraction is in observing a workaday Moroccan market bulging with local produce, livestock and clothes – come before 10am to see goats, sheep and cows being bought and sold.

The souq sprawls over an open plain 1.5km north of the town centre and is divided into three sections, with the livestock area the furthest from town. Start at this end and work your way back, stopping at the food tents (downhill from the livestock area) to see carcasses hanging ready for the grills and to grab a mint tea with the locals. The section nearest town always has a couple of carpet and textile vendors and some very good bargains can be negotiated.

Take care if it's been raining, as the souq area can easily turn into a quagmire.

Sleeping & Eating

For its size, Azrou has a surprising number of sleeping options. Budget travellers are spoilt for choice; it's more difficult to find decent midrange places. The most comfortable digs exist on the town's peripheries.

The best cheap eats are found in three main areas – strung along Blvd Moulay Abdelkader south of the bus station, and clustered around Place Hassan II and Place Moulay Hachem Ben Salah. You can find all the trusty favourites here – rotisserie chicken, *brochettes* and steaming bowls of *harira*.

If you're looking for an alcoholic drink in Azrou, **Hôtel Le Panorama** (0535563649; Rue al Hancali; s/d excl breakfast Dh283/348;) has two bars to choose from. **Palais des Cerisiers** (0535563830; www.lepalaisdescerisiers.com; Route du Cèdre de Gouraud, btwn Azrou & Ifrane; s/d Dh950/1102, apts for 4 Dh1222-1404; P) offers a more upmarket setting for a drink, but you'll need a car to get there.

★Riad Azrou GUESTHOUSE €

(0535364394, 0661064242; www.riadazrou.com; Place Moulay Hachem Ben Saleh; s/d/f Dh250/350/580;) This pretty, traditional house is Azrou's best value riad, offering a greater level of comfort and more amenities than its neighbours (reflected in the prices). Rooms are large with decent bathrooms and traditional Berber furnishings. Enjoy breakfast on the terrace with beautiful views.

Auberge du Dernier Lion de l'Atlas GUESTHOUSE €

(0535561868, 0662156488; www.dernierlionatlas.ma; 16 Route de Meknes; dm Dh75, s/d/tr excl breakfast Dh225/330/420;) A bit of a way from the centre of Azrou on the road to Meknes, this large orange villa has pleasant rooms and a smoky, *zellige*-covered Moroccan lounge. If you're basing yourself in the Middle Atlas area, there's a good stash of tourist information at reception to help you find your feet.

Hôtel des Cèdres MOROCCAN €

(0535562326; Place Mohammed V; mains from Dh60, menu of the day Dh100; 11.30am-3pm & 7.30-10pm) Hôtel des Cèdres' restaurant is by far the best place to eat in Azrou. Inside there's a 1920s dining room and log fire; outside, plaza-fronting terrace tables allow diners to sit cheek by jowl with the town's stalwart coffee-drinkers. The sustainable local trout is always good, plus there are some more unusual dishes such as rabbit tajine. Service is excellent.

Café Restaurant Bilal CAFE €

(Place Mohammed V; sandwiches Dh15-25, mains Dh40-85; 8am-10pm;) The streetside terrace at this cafe-restaurant is crammed with locals partaking in coffee and cake (the cafe doubles as a patisserie), but upstairs there's a quiet dining room that makes a good base for checking emails over a sandwich, tajine, pizza or the local speciality, trout. Service is slow but friendly.

Getting There & Away

Azrou sits at a crossroads, with one axis heading northwest to southeast from Meknes to Errachidia, and the other northeast to Fez and southwest to Marrakesh. Its location makes it a transport hub for the region, and buses heading all over Morocco pass through here. There's no railway line.

CTM (Blvd Hassan II) offers daily departures from its bus station on Blvd Hassan II to Casablanca (Dh140, five hours), Fez (Dh35, 1½ hours), Marrakesh (Dh150, eight hours) and Meknes (Dh35, 1¾ hours).

Other cheaper companies leave from the **Gare Routière** (Blvd Moulay Abdelkader) on Blvd Moulay Abdelkader. There are frequent daily departures to Fez (Dh20), Meknes (Dh20), Ifrane (Dh10), Marrakesh (Dh120), Midelt (Dh50) and Errachidia (Dh85). Three buses a day run to Casablanca (Dh75 to Dh85).

The grand-taxi lot is up a stepped path above the Gare Routière. Taxis go to Fez (Dh35, one hour), Meknes (Dh35, one hour), Khenifra (Dh35, one hour) and Ifrane (Dh9, 10 minutes), and less frequently to Midelt (Dh60, two hours). Those for Ain Leuh (Dh15, 30 minutes) wait beside the Shell petrol station on the main road out to the southwest by the commissariat (police station).

If you want a private taxi out of town, head to the grand-taxi rank behind the mosque, on Blvd Moulay Abdelkader.

Midelt ميدلت

0535 / POP 45,160 / ELEV 1508M

Midelt *(mi-delt)* sits in apple country between the Middle and the High Atlas and makes a handy break between Fez and the desert. Coming from the north, in particular, the landscape offers some breathtaking views, especially of the eastern High Atlas, which seem to rise out of nowhere.

Midelt consists of little more than one main street (Ave Mohammed V in the north, which becomes Ave Hassan II to the south), a modest souq and a number of oversized hotel-restaurants on the outskirts, which cater to the tourist buses whistling through to or from the desert. The town itself is of little interest to tourists, but it makes a good base for some off-*piste* exploring of the Jebel Ayachi region.

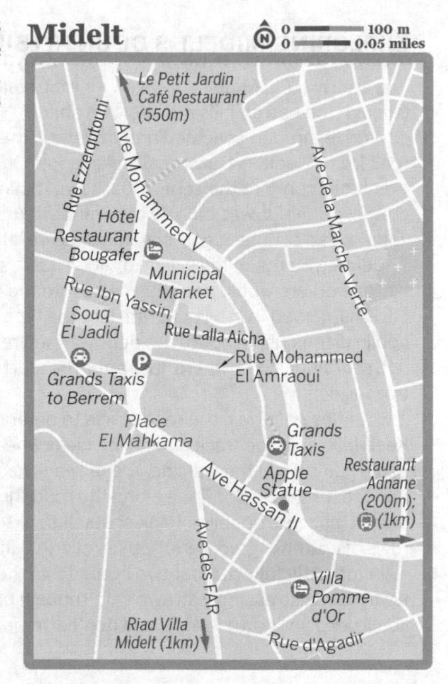

Sleeping & Eating

Central Midelt has a couple of lovely villa guesthouses, and some enormous 'kasbah' hotels slightly further out of town. However, most visitors use Midelt as a stopover to break up the long journey to and from the desert.

Because many of the hotels in and around Midelt are in suburban locations, in-house restaurants are usually your best bet for dinner.

Hôtel Restaurant Bougafer HOTEL €
(0626338687; hamidbougafer@gmail.com; 7 Blvd Mohammed VI; d Dh150-300) This is a clean, modern option in a central location with the added benefit of a restaurant on the ground floor (mains from Dh70). Cheaper rooms have shared bathrooms and/or toilets.

Riad Villa Midelt GUESTHOUSE €€
(0535360851; villamidelt@yahoo.fr; Ave El Farabi; s/d Dh400/500, d half-board Dh700; P) In a garden setting, this large 10-room suburban house offers spacious rooms, some with balconies. There are also suites for four people at Dh700. The biggest surprise is the lovely pool in a walled garden. The amiable staff can whip up dinner for Dh150. The villa is well signposted from central Midelt, and a petit taxi to/from the bus station costs Dh10.

EXPLORING MIDELT'S COUNTRYSIDE

The area around Midelt is heaven for mountain bikers, as well as ideal hiking country (though the barren hills are short on shade).

A drive through spectacular **Gorges d'Aouli**, following the river along a badly degraded road from Midelt, is truly breathtaking. Past the first abandoned village of Mibladene, you'll eventually come to the eerie ghost-town mining village of Aouli *(ow-li)* and the dramatic crevasse it fills. It was built by the French in the 1930s and at its peak housed 6000 workers. Today just a couple of guardian families are left. It's a scenic 30km drive northeast of Midelt.

Before you reach the village of Aouli itself, stop off at *les galleries* – one of the locations where workers would have burrowed into the hills for lead, copper and silver. The domed caverns, carved into hillocks, are just the type of place where you might expect to hear goblin drums rising out of the depths. They're difficult to find; look for a dirt track on your left, seemingly to nowhere, just after the start of the only village along the S317 coming from Midelt.

After *les galleries,* the road starts to deteriorate in places as you get deeper into the hills. Keep following the track and it'll be clear when you reach Aouli itself – note the open shafts, some halfway up the cliffside, the railway line that disappears 20km into the mountainside, and the furnaces. Continue along the road through the village and the road will eventually start to ascend, doubling back on itself to reach an abandoned mosque and hundreds of rows of crumbling workers' houses overlooking the gorge.

In total, it'll take at least two hours to get here and back from Midelt. You leave Midelt via a plain distressingly strewn with rubbish blown across from the unsecured town dump. You'll need your own vehicle and don't attempt the drive when the river is high. Alternatively,

★ **Villa Pomme d'Or** GUESTHOUSE €€€
(☎0535583977; villapommedor@gmail.com; Rue Tanger; s/d Dh700/850; P 🛜 ≋) This elegant 1940s villa in central Midelt overlooks a park and has a lovely garden and large pool. It's beautifully furnished with very comfortable beds. Rooms have a fridge, TV, central heating and enormous bathrooms. The sumptuous dining room is open from 7pm (menu Dh145) and breakfast is served on the veranda in good weather. Red wine is available.

Le Petit Jardin Café Restaurant MOROCCAN €
(☎0535360714, 0649766911; nasiri_abdelhai@hotmail.com; Ave Mohamed V/Route de Meknes; mains Dh65-80; ⏲8am-10pm) You can sit out the front and watch the traffic on the outskirts of town, or discover the pretty garden at the back. Abdelhai serves breakfast (Dh30) and the usual array of pizzas, tajines and *brochettes*.

Restaurant Adnane MOROCCAN €
(☎0661077061; Ave Hassan II; menu Dh70; ⏲8am-11pm; 🛜) The leafy corner terrace at Adnane is a perfect spot for watching the world go by while you wait for a delicious plateful of rotisserie chicken. Here it's served with bread and olives, lentils, fragrant rice, herby tomato salad and tasty chicken gravy: possibly the best spread you'll find in any similar joint across Morocco.

ℹ Getting There & Away

The Gare Routière is 2km east of central Midelt, and CTM buses run from here (mostly at night). There's an evening departure to Casablanca (Dh175, seven hours) via Rabat (Dh145, five hours), and to Rissani (Dh95, four hours) via Errachidia (Dh50, two hours) and Erfoud (Dh80, 3½ hours). There are also night-time services for Azrou (Dh55, two hours), Meknes (Dh80, three hours) and Fez (Dh90, five hours).

Other buses cover the same routes at more sociable hours – Fez (Dh65, five hours) is serviced by four departures through the day.

Grands taxis to Azrou (Dh75, two hours), Errachidia (Dh55, two hours), Meknes (Dh85, three hours) and Fez (Dh110, three hours) depart from a lot near the central Apple Statue off Ave Hassan II; grands taxis to Berrem (Dh18) depart from a different square off Ave Hassan II.

Taza تازة

☎0535 / POP 141,890

Taza fulfils all the criteria of a sleepy provincial centre, and if it weren't for the deep caves and empty trails on its doorstep, it probably wouldn't be worth stopping by. In town, climb the impressive restored fortifications up to Taza Haute, the walled medina, for panoramic views of the Rif to the north and the Middle Atlas to the south. Afterwards, head out to explore the eastern

Ksar Timnay Inter-Cultures offers this circuit as a day tour (4x4 vehicle, seven hours, including picnic lunch for up to four people, Dh1200).

The village of Berrem is also known as the Kasbah des Noyers for its ancient walnut trees and makes a good starting point for a gentle 30-minute walk to the **Gorges des Berrem** (Kasbah des Noyers) overlook. Head to the village mosque and cross the bridge to join the trail. There's no shade. It's 6km west of Midelt and a Dh6 shared grand taxi ride.

The **Cirque Jaffar** winds through the foothills of Jebel Ayachi, 26km southwest of Midelt. It's a rough 50km *piste* from town that takes 1½ hours each way. Regular cars will grumble on the route in all seasons, but the dramatic crests of the Atlas are otherworldly driving companions. Once the road becomes too steep to drive, continue on foot: it's an incredible walk through the Jaffar gorge.

Twenty kilometres north of Midelt, **Ksar Timnay Inter-Cultures** (☎0535360188, 0678975355; www.ksar-timnay.com; RN13, 9km south of Zaida; s/d Dh390/470, Riad Mimouna s/d Dh490/650; P 📶 🏊) sits in large leafy grounds and offers a wide range of accommodation from rooms to family apartments, as well as camping and caravanning. Rooms are large and comfortable enough; those in fancier Riad Mimouna are a bit smarter than the standard rooms. It makes a reasonably priced stop-off point en route to the desert. Dinner is Dh120 in the licensed restaurant.

The owners are passionate about the region and offer a number of excursions, including trekking to Jebel Masker (3265m) and Jebel Ayachi (3737m), and full-day 4x4 drives to Cirque Jaffar or Gorges d'Aouli (per vehicle for up to four people Dh1200, including lunch). The birdwatching walk around the ecological lake is free (Dh80 for a picnic lunch).

Middle Atlas, including Gouffre du Friouato (one of the most incredible open caverns in the world) and Tazekka National Park.

History

The fortified citadel of Taza is built on the edge of an escarpment overlooking the only feasible pass between the Rif Mountains and the Middle Atlas. It has been important throughout Morocco's history as a garrison town from which to exert control over the country's eastern extremities.

Tizi n'Touahar, as the pass is known, was the traditional invasion route for armies moving west from Tunisia and Algeria. This is, in fact, where the Romans and the Arabs entered Morocco. The town itself was the base from which the Almohads, Merinids and Alaouites swept to conquer lowland Morocco and establish their dynasties.

All Moroccan sultans had a hand in fortifying Taza. Nevertheless, their control over the area was always tenuous because the fiercely independent and rebellious local tribes continually exploited any weakness in the central power in order to overrun the city. Never was this more so than in the first years of the 20th century, when 'El Rogui' (Pretender to the Sultan's Throne) Bou Hamra held sway over most of northeastern Morocco.

The French occupied Taza in 1914 and made it the main base from which they fought the prolonged rebellion by the tribes of the Rif Mountains and Middle Atlas.

Sights & Activities

Taza is divided neatly in two: the ville nouvelle (also called Taza Bas, or Lower Taza), centred on Place de l'Indépendance, and the walled medina (Taza Haute), occupying the hill 2km to the south. The unremarkable ville nouvelle is of little interest to visitors, but this is where most of the accommodation is, along with the bus and train stations.

The majestic restored medina walls, around 3km in circumference, are a legacy from when Taza served briefly as the Almohad capital in the 12th century. The two most interesting sections are the crumbling **bastion** (Map p380), now used as a grain store, and the **Bab Er Rih** (Gate of the Wind; Map p380), for its spectacular views. The outer road that leads to Bab Er Rih is also interesting for its richly decorated doorways and windows high up in the walls, guarded by old, carved cedar screens.

Not far from Bab Er Rih, and visible over the top of the houses, is the **Grande Mosquée** (Map p380), which the Almohads began building in 1135. Just off Place Aharrach, around the back of the Hotel de l'Etoile, is a small local **hammam** (Map p380;

Taza Haute

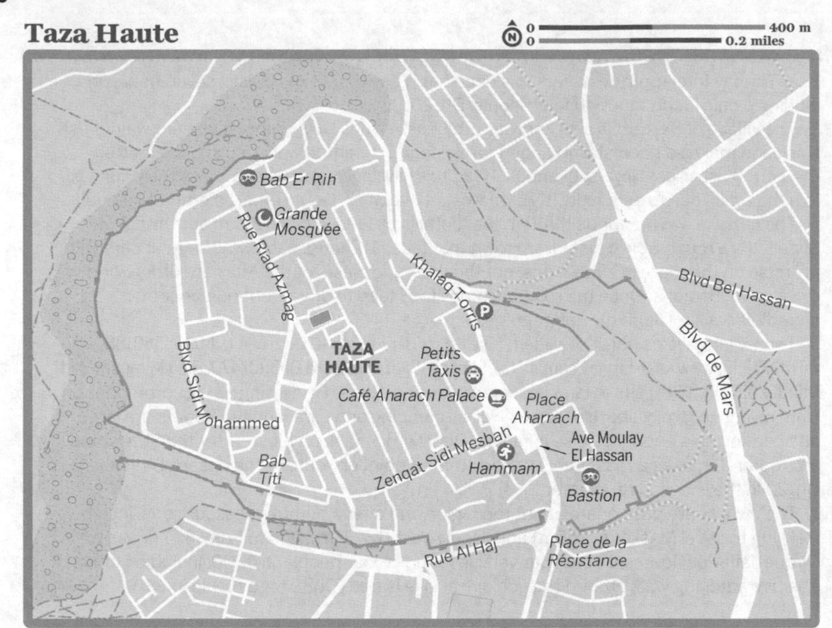

off Zenqat Sidi Mesbah; Dh12.50; ⏲ men 5am-noon & 7pm-midnight, women noon-7pm).

Sleeping

Taza has only a handful of hotels, mostly in the ville nouvelle.

Hôtel de la Gare HOTEL €
(☎0535672448; Ave Mohammed VI; s/d excl breakfast Dh200/300, r with shared bathroom Dh130; 📶) Clean, comfortable (if somewhat brown) rooms surround an inner courtyard in this good-value choice. It's convenient for the train and bus stations. Cheaper rooms have no air-con.

Grand Hôtel du Dauphiné HOTEL €
(Map p381; ☎0535673567; dauphinehotel 2019@gmail.com; Place de l'Indépendance; s/d Dh185/290) Ideally located on the ville nouvelle's main square, the Dauphiné is good value in the budget category but suffers from noisy plumbing and a noisy downstairs bar. Rooms are sorely in need of a revamp, but all benefit from small balconies. On the ground floor there's also a **restaurant** (mains Dh60-80; ⏲8am-3pm & 7-10pm). A fair option if you decide to stay in the ville nouvelle.

Hôtel La Tour Eiffel HOTEL €€
(☎0535671562; www.hotellatoureiffel-taza.com; Blvd Bir Anzarane; s/d excl breakfast Dh308/385; 📶) Stuck on the road out of town heading towards Oujda, the Tour Eiffel is named for its high aspirations. Past the cramped lobby, a lift swishes you up to well-sized, fairly comfy rooms with TVs and fridges, many with great views out towards the mountains. Breakfast is an extra Dh39, and there's an in-house restaurant.

Eating & Drinking

Taza Haute has the usual selection of kebab-touting snack stalls and cafes around the main square, Place Aharrach. In the ville nouvelle, the streets fanning out from Place de l'Indépendance (particularly Ave Mohammed V and Ave Moulay Youssef) are lined with patisseries and restaurants serving fast food. Taza has plenty of modern cafes in the new city and around the medina's main square, Place Aharrach.

There's a hopping bar attached to the Grand Hôtel du Dauphiné in the ville nouvelle. Look for the terrace cafe with mirrored windows.

Yocool MOROCCAN €
(Map p381; ☎0770720480; Rue Oujda; mains Dh30-45; ⏲4pm-midnight summer, noon-7pm winter) Very cool indeed, this place is all red brick with black accents, good music and a great vibe. It specialises in *pasticcio*, which

in Morocco is fries in a white sauce topped with lots of cheese and grilled (Dh30). Pizzas and tacos are also on offer.

Moulin à Paris BAKERY €
(Map p381; Place de l'Indépendance; croissants Dh1.50; ⏰6am-10pm) Just the place for breakfast – grab some yoghurt along with a pastry or some biscuits and head to one of the cafes on either side for coffee.

La Casa MOROCCAN €
(Map p381; Ave Mohammed V; sandwiches from Dh20; ⏰5am-10pm; 📶) One of a rash of modern places that look quite out of place in sleepy Taza; there's a cafe at the front with pavement seating and a dimly lit restaurant at the back. It does the usual paninis and shawarma, as well as unexpectedly delicious pizzas. Breakfast and ice cream are also served.

Mou Mou MOROCCAN €
(Map p381; Ave Moulay Youssef; mains from Dh30; ⏰11.30am-midnight) Come night-time, happy customers – including lots of families and women – spill out the door of this packed corner joint with Moroccan music joyously blaring out. Tasty food is the order of the day here: kebabs, paninis and pizzas, including one topped with *merguez* (spicy sausages). Juices are also good.

Café Aharach Palace CAFE
(Map p380; Place Aharach, Taza Haute; ⏰7am-10pm) This modern place has a prime position on Place Aharach, and is perfect for watching the world go by over a *nus-nus* (half-half coffee with milk). It might call itself a *glacier*, but it doesn't serve ice cream.

ℹ Getting There & Around

Sky-blue *petits taxis* (Dh8) run regularly between the **ville nouvelle** (Map p381; Place de l'Indépendance) and **Taza Haute** (Map p380; Place Aharrach). Few buses actually originate in Taza, but plenty pass through on their way between Oujda and points west of Taza such as Fez, Tangier and Casablanca, as well as to the coast.

The **CTM office** (Map p381; ☎0535282007; Place de l'Indépendance; ⏰24hr), which doubles as the bus stop, is located in the ville nouvelle. Buses run to Casablanca (Dh155 to Dh170, 6½ hours), Fez (Dh50 to Dh55, 1½ hours), Meknes (Dh70, 3½ to five hours), Rabat (Dh140, 4½ to five hours), Oujda (Dh80, 2½ hours) and Nador (Dh80, four hours).

The Gare Routière is on Blvd Bir Anzarane near the train station, but frequent CTM and train services to/from Taza mean you're unlikely to need it.

Grands taxis depart from a lot in front of the train station (Fez Dh45, Meknes Dh75).

Taza's train station is off Blvd Bir Anzarane in the north of town. Taza's location on the train line makes rail the best transport option. Six trains a day run to Fez (Dh59, two hours), Rabat (Dh174, five to six hours), Casablanca (Dh220, six to seven hours) and Meknes (Dh87, three to four hours). There are two direct trains to Tangier (Dh224, seven hours), and one changing at Kenitra for El Boraq, the high-speed train (six hours). Several of the other trains noted here also involve a change in Fez (check online for details; www.oncf-voyages.ma). In the opposite direction, three trains go to Oujda (Dh117, three to 3½ hours).

Note there is no place to buy water at the train station, but there is a large supermarket, Marjane, in front of the station.

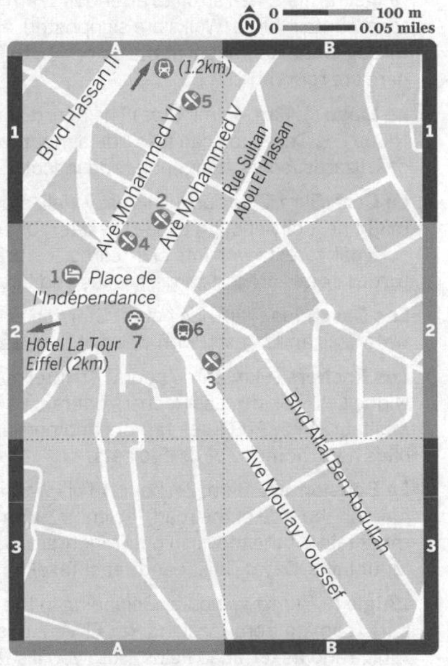

Taza Ville Nouvelle

Sleeping
1 Grand Hôtel du Dauphiné A2

Eating
Grand Hôtel du Dauphiné .... (see 1)
2 La Casa A1
3 Mou Mou A2
4 Moulin à Paris A2
5 Yocool A1

Transport
6 CTM Office A2
7 Petits Taxis A2

Tazekka National Park منتزه تاركة الوطني

Majestic cedars, stands of holm oak and gently rising hills make the terrain of Tazzeka National Park a joy to hike through, yet it flies under the radar of most visitors to Morocco. The small park unfurls for 137 sq km southwest of Taza, and was created to protect the cedar trees.

A wonderful circuit road runs through the park for 78km, providing magnificent vistas and passing the Gouffre de Friouato, an extensive cave system, the depression of **Dayet Chiker** with its small farming villages, and the waterfalls at Ras El Ma.

In addition to the cedars and oaks, there are juniper, thuja and the rare common yew. North African Barbary deer were introduced to the park 20 years ago with great success, and other fauna such as mouflons, wild pigs,

WALKING ROUTES IN TAZEKKA

The park's competent **Tourist Information Office** (Aziz Rahmouni 0661613929; www.tazekka.com; Bab Bou-Idir; 9am-7pm Sat & Sun Jul & Aug, 10am-6pm Sat & Sun Sep-Jun), at Bab Bou-Idir, promotes several hikes through information boards and maps; walks range from a 1.4km stroll to a serious 17km day trek. A couple of the routes are suitable for mountain bikes. Walks are signposted, and if you want a guide, you can arrange one through Aziz Rahmouni at the office (up to four people from Dh200). All distances listed here are round-trip.

Le Liège (1.4km, 45 minutes) The shortest and easiest walk begins at the Aire de Pique-Nique Les Cerfs. You can also ride a mountain bike along this path. Expect to see cork oak, lizards, boars, hedgehogs and insects.

Le Cerf (5km, 2¼ hours) This easy walk starts at Aire de Pique-Nique Les Cerfs; you might be lucky enough to see the deer for which the trail is named. It passes through cork oak forests with lots of streams, log bridges and the lookout point, El Ghenaj. River turtles, toads, frogs, lizards, snakes and birds abound on this route.

Les Cascades (7km, 2¼ hours) Starting at Ras El Ma, this is another easy walk to see waterfalls and forests, with views of the Ras El Ma gorge.

Les Rochers (9km, three hours) An intermediate walk that starts at Aire de Pique-Nique Les Oiseaux, Les Rochers offers tremendous views over Dayet Chiker and the Sidi Majbeur Valley. You'll see raptors and perhaps boars too. There are lots of caves in the cliffs here, home to birds and bats.

Le Bouslama (2.3km, 2¾ hours) This walk starts 3km from Bab Bou-Idir, where you can park on the side of the road. It climbs 190m through thick holm oak forest on Bouslama mountain. At the top is an old French-era lookout with sweeping views of Taza, the Rif Mountains, Dayat Chiker and Jebel Tazekka.

L'Aigle (2.3km, two hours) Beginning in the village of Sidi Majbeur at the entrance to the park (coming from Taza and Ras El Ma), this walk climbs 230m and has views over the village and its terraced fields. Here you'll see raptors such as eagles and kestrels.

Le Bouhadli (4.5km, 1¾ hours) Described as difficult, this walk starts at Bab Bou-Idir Holiday Village and zigzags 265m up Bou'Adli (1835m). Views over the Rif and Middle Atlas Mountains are worth the effort.

Le Chêne Zeen (4.6km, 4½ hours) A difficult walk that climbs 500m, this one starts at Bab Bou-Idir car park. Pass through forests of Portuguese oak, a very old species, and the River Lakhal gorge where you'll see the village of Beni Senane and its mill. The rewards are views over the gorge and Jebel Tazekka. On the way, you might spot nightingales, pigeons, nuthatches, hedgehogs, reptiles and foxes.

La Cedraie (17.3km, five hours) This is the best-known walk and is also suitable for mountain bikes. It 's rated difficult and climbs almost 500m. Starting 6km from Bab Bou-Idir on the road to Bab Azhar, you pass through cedar forests, with views over the Rif and Middle Atlas Mountains and surrounding valleys. Look out for birds, lizards, boars, hedgehogs and numerous insects.

Barbary squirrels and bats proliferate here, as well as dozens of bird species, including Bonelli's eagle.

The 'circular' route begins south of Taza at Ras El Ma, though you can join it anywhere you enter the park. Follow the road P5420 past waterfalls, caves, the information office, forests and small villages.

Roads are sealed but not always in good condition.

Sights & Activities

★Gouffre de Friouato — CAVE

(☎0668576194, 0666014790; Dh5, guide Dh200, protective clothing & headlamp Dh50; ⊙8am-6pm) More than 20m wide and 230m deep, the Gouffre de Friouato is said to be the deepest cavern in North Africa, and the cave system is possibly the most extensive. It was first investigated in 1935, and access leads down 520 precipitous steps (with handrails) to the floor of the cavern.

A return *grand taxi* from Taza Haute costs Dh300 and up, depending on how much time you want to spend here.

Once you reach the bottom of the stairs, you can squeeze through a hole to start exploring the fascinating chambers that are found 200 more steps below. It's dark and eerily beautiful: wear clothes you don't mind dirtying, but be prepared for a strenuous climb back up.

The most spectacular chambers, full of extraordinary formations, are the Salle de Lixus and the Salle de Draperies. They do indeed resemble thin sheets of curtains, frozen and calcified. Allow at least three hours there and back. Speleologists have explored to a depth of 300m, and they believe there are more rooms another 500m below.

The admission fee allows you to enter the cavern mouth at a depth of 160m. Beyond that, a guide (hire at the entrance) is needed to go further underground to the grandest chambers. Bank on the occasional scramble, and be prepared to squeeze through narrow sections; it's not recommended for claustrophobes. Overalls, nonslip overshoes and a helmet with lamp must be rented. Take the protective gear seriously – people have been killed here by falling rocks.

Gouffre de Friouato is well signposted, up a very steep road 25km from Taza. There's a small cafe close to the entrance.

Ras El Ma — WATERFALL

(R507) Climbing out of Taza into the mountains as you travel south on the R507 affords wonderful views. The waterfalls, just outside the park, are at their best from November to May. They emanate from a spring surrounded by ash, cherry and olive trees. There are a few small restaurants along the road here, serving drinks and tajines.

Sleeping & Eating

At major sites such as Ras El Ma and Gouffre de Friouato are small, somewhat makeshift cafes selling biscuits, drinks and tajines. While they are usually open out of season, the owners might not be cooking. It's a good idea to take a picnic.

★Auberge Ain Sahla — LODGE €€

(☎0661893587; www.ainsahla.com; off P5420, Bouchfaa; d/f Dh700/1300; P ☜ ≋) The Auberge is a large complex set in magnificent gardens with citrus trees, pomegranates, date palms, running water and pergolas dripping with bunches of grapes. The red pisé buildings hide a veritable warren of rooms of various sizes, all with magnificent views across the mountains to the peak of Jebel Tazekka. Eat outside around the pool or in the large restaurant with its grand piano.

Getting There & Around

Hiring a private *grand taxi* for the day from Taza will cost in the region of Dh500. From Fez, expect to pay about Dh1000 for a day trip.

There are several access points into the park, and as there are no boundary fences, you're free to enter anywhere to follow the narrow, twisty mountainous roads. There is no public transport in the park, however.

In the west, off the A2 highway between Fez and Taza, you can take the P5407 to the village of Tahala and join the P5426 in the park. This will take you along the northern shores of the large dam, Bab Louta. Another popular route into the park is to take the the Oued Amlil exit of the A2 onto the P5420. The R507 from Taza enters the park just south of Ras El Ma.

AT A GLANCE

POPULATION
Agadir: 421,844

APPROXIMATE COASTLINE OF MOROCCO
1835km

BEST HISTORIC KASBAH HOTEL
Tizourgane Kasbah (p410)

BEST BEACHFRONT LUXURY KASBAH
Ksar Massa (p395)

BEST KITESURFING CAMP
Dakhla Attitude (p437)

WHEN TO GO

Feb Trek the Anti Atlas and hit the Atlantic Coast for winter sun and surf.

Mar Celebrate the harvest under almond tree blossoms alongside Tafraoute's locals.

Nov Catch Taliouine's saffron festival and Imouzzer des Ida Outanane's olive harvest.

Paradise Valley (p399)

Southern Morocco & Western Sahara

The Souss Valley, where goats climb argan trees beneath weird rock formations in the Anti Atlas, draws a line across Morocco. South of this fertile valley, the pace of life in mountain villages and Saharan gateways is seductively slow.

A sense of somewhere fresh gusts through the region like the spring winds. On rugged seafronts, sip a mint tea and gaze at the wild Atlantic Coast. When trekking, mountain biking or driving through wrinkled Anti Atlas foothills, stop before the next oasis village and appreciate the silence.

Continue further south to Dakhla, an emerging scene for outdoor activities and desert exploration, and some of the world's best kitesurfing.

INCLUDES

Climate

Southern Morocco has three distinct geographical areas, each with its own microclimate. The semitropical, verdant Souss Valley is hot and humid, with temperatures ranging between 22°C and a steamy 38°C, when water vapour rises like a mist from the huge citrus groves that fill the valley. The valley is also prone to heavy winds in spring. The climate of the barren Anti Atlas veers between freezing winters and hot, dry summers. The deep southern coast enjoys a more constant year-round sunny climate.

Language

Arabic remains the lingua franca of major cities in the south. The Chleuh tribes who dominate the Souss speak Tashelhit, a Tamazight dialect, most noticeable in the Anti Atlas. French is widely spoken and Spanish is still heard in some of Spain's former territories.

SOUSS VALLEY

Rending its way between the High Atlas and the Anti Atlas, the fertile Souss Valley supports farms that the region, from Agadir city folk to rural shepherds, rely on. The valley is home to Southern Morocco's most cosmopolitan cities, from the all-inclusive beach resorts of Agadir to boutique design hotels in Taroudant, a more chill, but just as sophisticated, alternative to Marrakesh. Outdoor enthusiasts are also well catered to here: world-class waves draws surfers to Taghazout, while rare bird and mammal species in Souss-Massa National Park keep animal lovers happy.

The region is justifiably famous for its frizzy argan trees, beloved of local goats and cosmetologists everywhere. While driving in the mountains, pull over for a picnic among frolicking kids, and keep your camera at the ready: the classic Souss shot is a goat casually balanced on an argan treetop, munching sun-ripe argan nuts.

Cities in the Souss are well-serviced by buses and taxis, with Agadir as a hub. But for exploring the hinterland – especially where the argan tree goats can be seen – it's best to have your own transport. If you're driving from Marrakesh, the Tizi n'Test road crosses one of the most spectacular and perilous passes in the country, over the High Atlas.

Agadir اكادير

☎ 548 / POP 421,844

With a busy port and beach resort sprawling beneath its kasbah, Agadir (*ah-gah-deer*) was completely rebuilt following a devastating earthquake in 1960. It is now the country's premier destination for all-inclusive beaches and clubs aimed at holidaymaking Europeans. Laid out as a large grid of downtown streets, surrounded by spacious residential suburbs, Agadir's concrete-covered inland quarters are ugly and sterile. However, the city hits its stride on the beachfront promenade and the massive souq, where Moroccan street life comes with a refreshing sense of space. Arching south of the shiny white marina, the sandy beach offers clean water and 300 sunny days a year.

Agadir caters mainly to package-tour holidaymakers and will appeal less to independent travellers. Families will enjoy relaxing on the beach and wandering around the handful of sights. If you do not have children in tow, we recommend heading elsewhere.

History

Named after the *agadir* (fortified granary) of the Irir tribe, Agadir has a long history of boom and bust. It was founded in the 15th century by Portuguese merchants wanting to develop trade links with the Saharan caravans. From the mid-16th century, as the Saadian empire expanded, the port became prosperous from the export of local sugar, cotton and saltpetre, and products from Saharan trade, which the Moroccans then controlled. But this prosperity ended in the 1760s, when the Alaouite Sultan Sidi Mohammed Ben Abdallah diverted the trade to Essaouira.

The French colonists went some way towards redeveloping Agadir in the 20th century, but the earthquake on 29 February 1960 completely destroyed the city. As many as 18,000 people perished, around half of the population. The authorities, unable to cope with the apocalyptic aftermath of death and disease, sprayed the area with lime and DDT, and left the dead where they had been buried, in the collapsed city. The mound this created is now known as Ancienne Talborjt.

Since its reconstruction, Agadir has developed into an important port, with a large fishing fleet helping to make Morocco the world's largest exporter of tinned sardines. Agadir has also become Morocco's top beach resort, and the luxury marina complex signals ambitions to move upmarket.

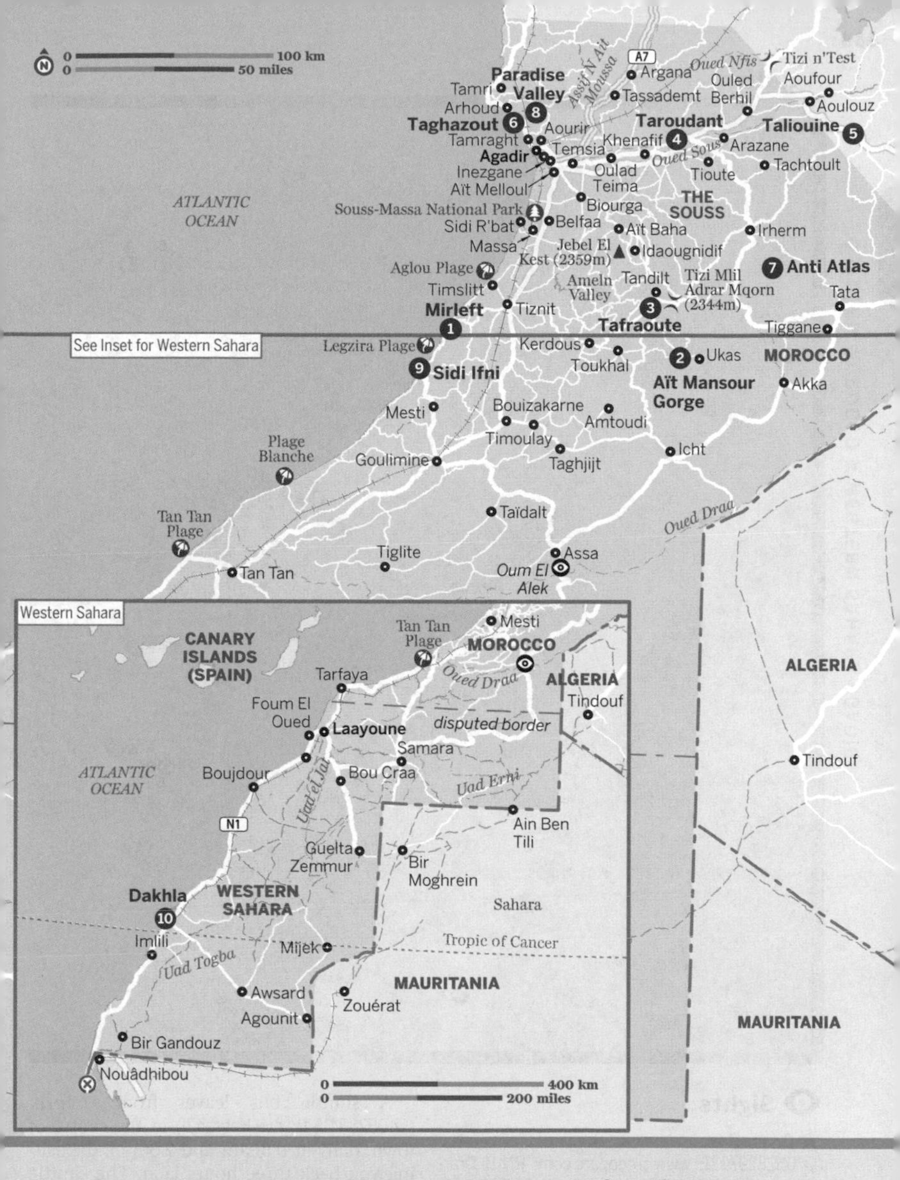

Southern Morocco & Western Sahara Highlights

1. **Mirleft** (p421) Shredding gnarly waves at this super chill hippie hangout.
2. **Aït Mansour Gorge** (p411) Exploring green *palmeraies* (palm groves) beneath ochre cliffs.
3. **Tafraoute** (p407) Visiting Amazigh (Berber) houses and cycling between blue boulders.
4. **Taroudant** (p400) Hitting the medina market in this bustling trading centre.
5. **Taliouine** (p405) Tasting rich saffron and argan oil.
6. **Taghazout** (p397) Working on your om at Morocco's premier yoga-and-surf getaway.
7. **Anti Atlas** (p405) Trekking, driving or cycling through the concertinaed foothills.
8. **Paradise Valley** (p399) Splashing through rock pools in olive groves.
9. **Sidi Ifni** (p424) Strolling past art-deco relics under swaying palms in this seaside town.
10. **Dakhla** (p435) Sailing, windsurfing or kiteboarding on the expansive lagoon.

Agadir

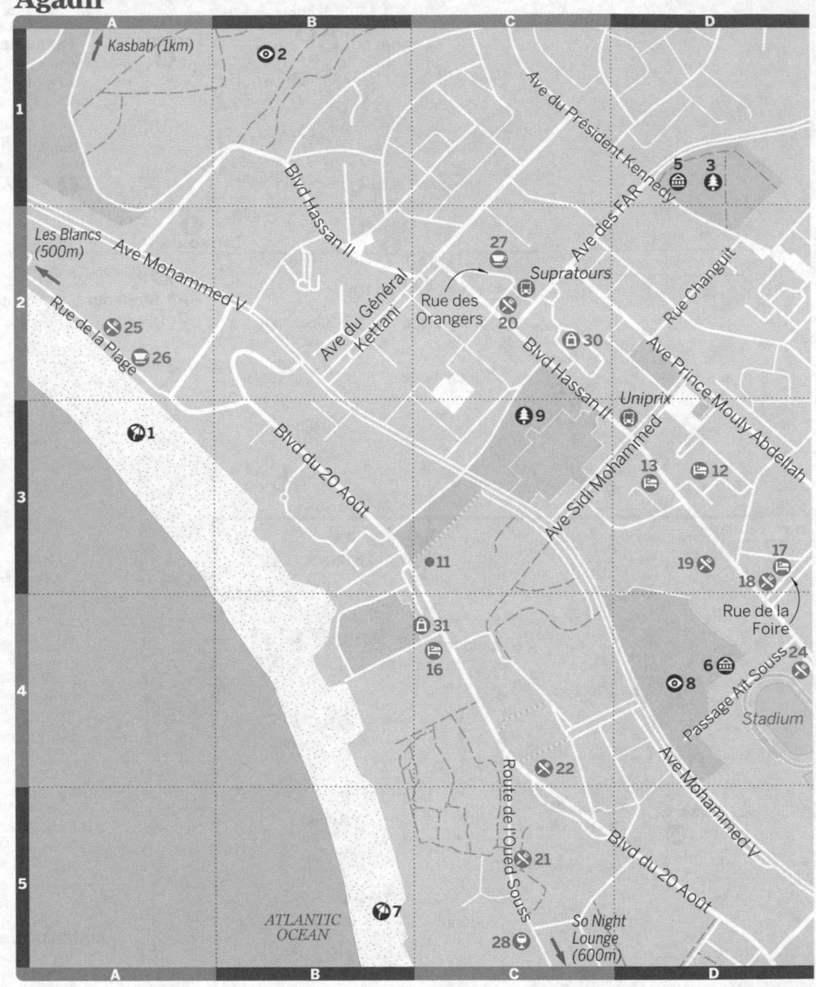

Sights

★CrocoParc ZOO

(☎0528297931; www.crocoparc.com; RN 8, Drarga; adult/child Dh75/45, with shuttle Dh200/120; ⏲10am-6.30pm; P) If anyone in your party is partial to a reptile, it's almost worth making a special trip to Agadir to visit this park, absolutely teeming with Nile crocs swimming and sunning around a pond (although the green dye in the water is a little too obvious). There are also iguanas, massive snakes and tiny monkeys. For the flora fans, gardens feature rare trees, cacti, flowers and several lily ponds.

A shuttle bus leaves from **Uniprix** (☎0528841841; Ave Hassan II) in the centre of town, daily at 9.30am and 2.30pm, depositing you back three hours later. The shuttle will also collect you from your hotel with advance notice. The fee for the shuttle bus and park admission is combined and includes a glass of tea and guided tour.

Kasbah HISTORIC SITE

(off Ave Al Moun) Offering superb views, the hilltop kasbah 7km northwest of the centre is a rare survivor of the 1960 earthquake. Built in 1541 and restored in the 1740s, the area once housed 300 people. All that remains is

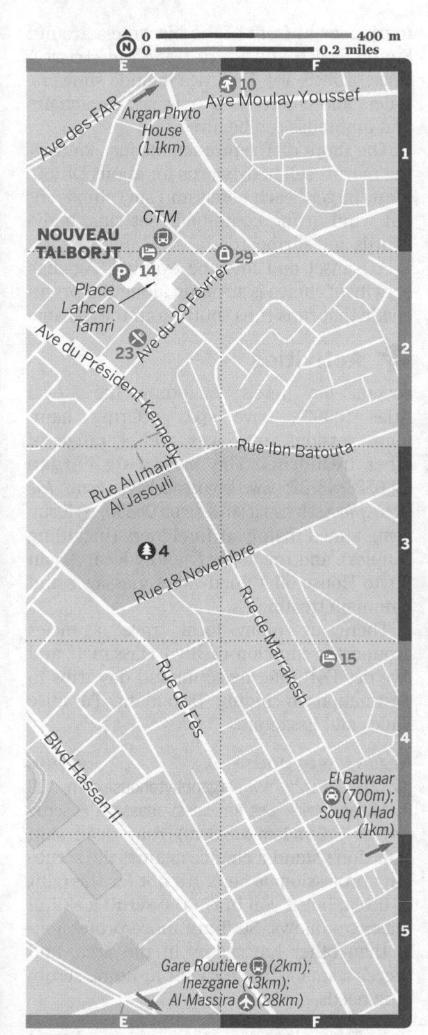

Agadir

Sights

1	Agadir Beach	A3
2	Ancienne Talborjt	B1
3	Jardin de Olhão	D1
4	Jardin Ibn Zaidoun	E3
5	Mémoire d'Agadir	D1
6	Musée du Patrimoine Amazigh	D4
7	Palm Beach	B5
8	Théâtre en Plein Air	D4
9	Vallée des Oiseaux	C3

Activities, Courses & Tours

10	Musée de l'Argan	F1
11	Petit Train d'Agadir	C3

Sleeping

12	Atlantic Hôtel	D3
13	Hôtel Kamal	D3
14	Hôtel Sindibad	E2
15	Riad Les Chtis D'Agadir	F4
16	Royal Atlas	C4
17	Studiotel Afoud	D3

Eating

18	Café Tafarnout	D3
19	Côté Court	D3
20	Daffy	C2
21	La Scala	C5
	L'Anice	(see 17)
22	Le Jardin d'Eau	C4
23	Majistic	E2
24	Mezzo Mezzo	D4
25	Pistachios	A2

Drinking & Nightlife

26	Jour et Nuit	A2
27	Orange Café	C2
28	Papagayo	C5

Shopping

29	Ensemble Artisanal	F2
30	Marché Central	C2
31	Tafoukt Souq	C4

the outer wall, though traces of the dwellings can still be made out. The inscription over the entry arch in Dutch and Arabic ('Believe in God and respect the King') is a reminder of the beginning of trade with the Low Countries.

The walk up to the kasbah is long, hot and uncomfortable: get a taxi (about Dh30) and walk back down.

Ancienne Talborjt HISTORIC SITE

(off Ave Al Moun) The grassy area below the kasbah covers the remains of old Agadir town and constitutes a mass grave for all those who died in the 1960 earthquake.

Jardin Ibn Zaidoun PARK

(Rue 18 Novembre; 24hr) This pleasant green oasis in the urban melee is home to dozens of trees towering over families picnicking with their portable shishas. The eucalyptus lining the park imbue the area with a lovely health-giving aroma, surely appreciated by the young men perennially doing press-ups in the adjacent dirt yard. It makes for a restorative stroll or reading break.

Théâtre en Plein Air THEATRE

(Passage Aït Souss; 24hr) FREE This large open-air theatre-in-the-round is for the design-heads. Hemmed in by large magnolia trees and some bougainvillea doing the best it can, the theatre was constructed in the

Brutalist style after the 1960 earthquake; it's a paean to mid-century design. The approach is dramatic, along the Passage Aït Souss.

Marina AREA
(☎0661215746; off Ave Mohammed V) The city's most modern attraction is a billion-dirham Dubai-esque pleasure port between the beach and commercial port. As well as mooring for your floating gin palace, the complex of white neo-kasbahs has holiday apartments, cafes, restaurants and boat trips for groups (including a faux pirate ship called the *Jack Sparrow*).

Mémoire d'Agadir MUSEUM
(cnr Ave du Président Kennedy & Ave des FAR; adult/child Dh20/10; 9am-12.30pm & 3-6pm Mon-Sat) This small museum in the southwest corner of Jardin de Olhão, entered from outside the park, is dedicated to the 1960 earthquake. Displays include interesting photos of Agadir since the 1920s, while others show the effects of the quake.

Jardin de Olhão PARK
(Ave du Président Kennedy; 2-6pm Tue-Sun) A cool, relaxing garden created in 1992 to mark the twinning of Agadir with the Portuguese town of Olhão. Good for retreating for a cool drink or to plan your next move.

Musée du Patrimoine Amazigh MUSEUM
(☎0528821632; Passage Aït Souss; adult/child Dh10/5; 9.30am-12.30pm & 2-5.30pm Mon-Sat) With an excellent display of photographs and Berber artefacts, especially jewellery and daggers, the museum is a great place to learn about the traditional life and culture of the region's Amazigh (Berber) people.

Vallée des Oiseaux PARK
(Valley of the Birds; 11am-6pm) FREE This leafy city-centre retreat in the dry riverbed running down from Blvd Hassan II to Blvd du 20 Août is a handy – and more scenic – way to walk to the beach area from the centre of town. There's a shaded children's playground.

Beaches

Agadir's glory is its **crescent beach**, which usually remains unruffled when the Atlantic winds are blustering elsewhere. It's clean and well maintained, spotlit at night and patrolled by lifeguards and police during peak periods (mid-June to mid-September). There is a strong undertow.

The beach is mostly hassle-free, but single females or families will have a more relaxed time at one of the private beaches near the marina, or in front of the big hotels around Sunset Beach and **Palm Beach** (deckchair & umbrella Dh30;). Facilities include showers, toilets and children's play areas; deckchairs and umbrellas can be hired.

The shops on the promenade just south of the marina sell bodyboards for about Dh150. Many larger beach hotels and surf clubs rent out windsurfing equipment, jet skis, bodyboards and surfboards.

At sunset and into the evening, Agadir's activity of choice is strolling along the promenade that runs runs south from the marina.

Activities

Several big hotels, including the Royal Atlas (p392), have spas offering hammam sessions, massages and a range of other treatments. The **Musée de l'Argan** (☎0528848782; www.lemuseedelargan.com; Ave Moulay Youssef; hammam & scrub Dh350; 10am-9pm), aimed mainly at foreigners (including couples), and the super friendly local Argan Phyto House offer good-value massages and hammam treatments.

There are many local travel agencies around the junction of Blvd Hassan II and Ave des FAR offering tours and day trips to destinations including Taroudant, Paradise Valley and Essaouira.

Argan Phyto House HAMMAM
(☎0528221272; www.arganphytohouse.com; 19 Rue Imam Malek, Les Amicales; massage & scrub Dh400; 9am-1pm & 3-8pm) Your dead skin cells don't stand a chance against the scrubbing professionals here. It's not for the faint of heart, but if you brave the scrub a skilful massage follows. Staff are more professional than other hammams in the area, and there's a small store for your at-home scrubbing needs.

Petit Train d'Agadir TOURS
(Blvd du 20 Août; adult/child Dh18/12; every 40min from 9.15am) This chain of buggies snakes around the city centre and along the beach for 35-minute rides. Sitting back and watching Agadir float past at sunset is a pleasant way to see the city.

Festivals & Events

Festival Timitar MUSIC
(www.festivaltimitar.ma; Jul) Festival Timitar attracts Moroccan and international musicians and DJs to Agadir every July, drawing about half a million attendees reveling in Amazigh (Berber) culture. Expect lots of visiting acts from other parts of Africa.

Concert for Tolerance MUSIC
(Oct) Agadir's annual Concert for Tolerance takes place on the northern end of the beach in October. The concert's diverse programme of DJs, dance music and local rap is wildly popular with Agadir's younger residents. If you're in town and fancy a locals-only groove, the concert is definitely worth a visit.

Sleeping

Agadir targets midrange and top-end visitors, but away from the beach are more affordable options. Booking ahead is recommended for Easter, summer and Christmas to New Year. Luxury beachfront hotels and resorts run south of the centre on Rue Oued Souss and Chemin des Dunes, and riads and kasbahs are found inland or to the south en route to Inezgane.

The best area for budget options is away from the ocean in Nouveau Talborjt, where there are three budget hotels on Place Lahcen Tamri. The all-night bus activity ensures that most hotel receptions here are open 24 hours; by night the area is a little seedy.

Riad Les Chtis D'Agadir GUESTHOUSE €
(0528821996; www.riadleschtisdagadir.com; 27 Rue Houmane El Fetouaki; r from €35;) Located in a residential neighbourhood, this family-owned guesthouse has beautifully tiled, compact rooms opening onto a central courtyard. The Francophone owners are friendly and eager to please (and speak a little English too). Breakfast is taken at a shared table with other guests. A cosy spot, it's a refreshing alternative to Agadir's lookalike hotels.

Hôtel Kamal HOTEL €
(0528842817; www.hotel-kamal.com; Blvd Hassan II; s/d Dh350/375;) A popular, well-run hotel with a vintage feel, the Kamal's airy foyer features nice rugs and inlaid mirrors. The massive pool is fringed with palms and cacti and has tiled lanes for lap swimming. Rooms are a bit of a letdown, especially the bedding, but they do include sweet hand-painted touches and pleasant bathrooms with tile and marble. Great value.

Hôtel Sindibad HOTEL €
(0528823477; sinhot@menara.ma; Place Lahcen Tamri; s/d Dh250/300;) This blue-and-white hotel packs more character than you'd expect from its compact rooms and slightly dingy locale. Rooms feature tiny, sweet balconies with window box geraniums, and hallways are adorned with photographs of Morocco, including a photoshopped Angelina Jolie with Amazigh (Berber) face tattoos. The star attraction is the hotel's rooftop pool and succulent-strewn terrace.

Studiotel Afoud APARTMENT €€
(0528843999; www.studiotel-afoud.com; Rue de la Foire; apt from Dh850;) These studios are simple but pleasant, each featuring a kitchen with hotplate and fridge, and a balcony overlooking the peeling neighbouring buildings. There's a pyramid-shaped pool on the 2nd floor, and cots are available. On the ground floor there's a lovely cafe, a grocery booth and a bookcase of paperback novels. It's a 10-minute walk from the beach.

Atlantic Hôtel HOTEL €€€
(0528843661; www.atlantichotelagadir.com; off Blvd Hassan II; s/d Dh900/1200;) The jewel in the Atlantic's crown is its stunning pool, hemmed in by billows of colourful bougainvillea, lanterns, palm trees and a wall of beautiful brick and tile work. If you can tear yourself away, there's a small business centre,

OFF THE BEATEN TRACK

RURAL AGADIR ESCAPES

Located on a spectacular hilltop 15km inland from Agadir, the 30+ rooms and suites in **Atlas Kasbah** (0661488504; www.atlaskasbah.com; Route d'Azrarag, Tighanimine El Baz; r from Dh800;) are the ideal overnight haven after partaking in Atlas Kasbah's busy menu of ecofriendly and cultural activities. Guests can indulge in hammam and massage treatments, learn about Moroccan cuisine and crafts, or go hiking or donkey riding to nearby Amazigh villages. The team behind Atlas Kasbah is strongly focused on sustainable practices and has won awards for its responsible approach to tourism.

Located in pleasant rural surroundings around 20km from Agadir, **Paradis Nomade** (0671121535; www.paradis-nomade.com; Douar Azarag; s/d from Dh400/500, tent per person Dh150;) combines impressive suites, smaller but still comfortable rooms, and the option of staying in Amazigh-style tents. An Amazigh ambience is also carried through to the best of the rooms, and the garden surroundings are enlivened with a compact swimming pool and a spacious restaurant and bar area.

as well as a wading pool and a snack bar with cocktail specials. Rooms are basic but clean and comfortable.

Royal Atlas HOTEL €€€
(☎0528294040; www.hotelsatlas.com; Blvd du 20 Août; r from Dh1557;) This beachfront colossus ticks all the five-star boxes with a Moroccan flourish. Carpets, statues and lanterns dot the tiled floors leading to the bar and pool, and sleek, relaxing rooms and suites in ash-blonde wood and beige upholstery. Facilities include a nightclub, gym, Daniel Jouvance spa, private beach, two restaurants and all the extras you would expect.

Eating

There's a great choice of cafes and patisseries, where you can start the day or recover from the rigours of the beach. Some restaurants in Agadir are licensed, and the city's beachfront promenade is packed with touristy restaurants serving everything from burgers to Indian and Spanish cuisine.

Daffy MOROCCAN €
(Rue des Orangers; tajines Dh50; 11am-11pm) The orange trees that look dusty and sad from across the square are much more pleasant from under Daffy's thatch lanterns. Matching raffia chairs, patterned tablecloths and a warm taupe fresco-esque paint job give everything a pleasant rural aesthetic. Moroccan favourites are on offer, including tajines, soup, couscous (on Friday) and salads.

Café Tafarnout CAFE €
(☎0528844450; Blvd Hassan II; snacks Dh35; 5.30am-11pm) Agadir's smartest and most popular cafe, with indoor and outdoor seating and a comprehensive menu of salads, pizza, panini, pastas and burgers. The cactus-filled patio on the street makes for pleasant people-watching. For dessert (or breakfast) there's a wide range of gâteaux, tarts, croissants, milkshakes and crêpes.

L'Anice CAFE €
(☎0528848164; Rue de la Foire; breakfast from Dh30; 7am-midnight;) Cool and comfortable, this smart cafe under the Studiotel Afoud features blue-sofa lounge seating and plenty of plants on its terrace overlooking the sedate street. The menu features lots of breakfast options, as well as fresh salads (from Dh30), tajines (from Dh50) and couscous on Fridays.

Pistachios ICE CREAM €
(Rue la Plage; ice cream from Dh10; 10am-10pm) Outdoor tables and energetic English-speaking staff are standouts at this modern cafe with some of the best ice cream in town. Cool down with the lemon, melon or orange flavours, or linger over breakfast and coffee as you take in the views of Agadir's beachfront promenade.

★ Le Jardin d'Eau MOROCCAN €€
(☎0528840195; www.jardindeau-agadir.com; Blvd de 20 Août; tajines from Dh70; 11.30am-2.30am) By far the best restaurant on the Blvd de 20 Août touristS strip, the Jardin d'Eau slings fragrant, flavoursome tajines, salads and meat-based mains sourced from a collective farm south of the city, as well as freshly caught seafood. Service is subtly attentive, and the decor is warmly exotic, with lanterns, wood carvings and an atrium bursting with plants. Live music nightly.

Côté Court FUSION €€
(☎0528826533; off Blvd Hassan II; mains Dh85-160; noon-3pm & 7-11pm, wine bar 6pm-2am) This restaurant at the Royal Tennis Club occupies a lovely outdoor area presided over by a glamorous French patron. The garden and grounds feature up-lit trees, basket lamps and the pizza oven flickering away. Service is attentive, and the menu incorporates a range of Asian, Mediterranean and Spanish influences. Specials change daily.

There's a wine bar on the property, featuring an extensive selection of wines by the glass from Europe and the US (from Dh50).

Mezzo Mezzo ITALIAN €€
(☎0528848819; www.facebook.com/MezzoMezzo-Agadir; Blvd Hassan II; pizza Dh70-130; 7pm-1am;) A shining beacon among Agadir's many pizzerias, Mezzo Mezzo offers a good range of pizzas and wines by the glass. The kitchen also turns out pasta and fish dishes for the small dining room (presided over by an oversized painting of a zebra) and sidewalk tables.

La Scala SEAFOOD €€€
(☎0528846773; Rue Oued Souss; meals Dh140-300) One of Agadir's best fish restaurants, with two pages of the menu devoted to seafood. Pasta and meat dishes are also available, and the food is generally elegant, fresh and beautifully presented.

Marina

The upmarket marina at the northern end of the seafront promenade has a concentration of midrange and top-end restaurants and cafes, where you can dine in style on international food.

Les Blancs SEAFOOD €€

(☎0528828368; mains Dh130-190; ⏰11am-midnight) Occupying a series of elegant white blocks by the beach at the entrance to the marina, Les Blancs' claim to fame is its paella, the house speciality (two people minimum). In season, book ahead to score an outside table. For a sunset snack, pizza (Dh90) is served in the terrace bar.

Pure Passion INTERNATIONAL €€€

(☎0528840120; www.purepassion.ma; Agadir Marina; mains Dh150-240; ⏰noon-11pm) A black-and-purple colour scheme and Victorian light fixtures reinforce the Gothic chic at this restaurant, considered one of Agadir's best. Score a table on the terrace for marina views, and sample *crevettes pil pil* (prawns in a garlic sauce), fresh Dakhla oysters and good vegetarian options. The wine, beer and cocktail list runs across multiple pages, and the three-course lunch menu (Dh180) is excellent value.

Drinking & Nightlife

Blvd du 20 Août and Rue Oued Souss are good for bars and nightclubs. At the marina and along the promenade there are also plenty of cafes and bars. Beers are typically Dh5 to Dh10 more expensive at night, but many bars extend their daytime prices during early-evening happy hours. Many also offer the dubious pleasure of karaoke or crooning entertainers.

You'll find a crooner at Le Jardin d'Eau and the occasional showgirl performance at the nightclubs. Otherwise, entertainment is best sought in other Moroccan cities.

So Night Lounge CLUB

(Sofitel Royal Bay, Chemin des Dunes; ⏰6pm-late) The hippest club in Agadir and one of the most expensive, laid out on several levels with features like champagne and vodka bars, a live-music stage and a restaurant, all held up by massive columns. Local players save this one for the climax of the evening's entertainment.

Papagayo CLUB

(Chemin des Dunes, Hotel Riu Tikida Beach; cover Dh200; ⏰6pm-late) One of Agadir's most popular nightclubs, attracting international DJs and the party set (you saw them sleeping it off by the pool earlier). If you're up for a fist pump or two, join the fun: dance the night away on Papagayo's spacious dance floor, and take a break from the beat right on the beach.

TOP CHEAP EATS

Souq Al Had (p394) At lunchtime, tajines bubble away outside the many cheap snack stalls.

Nouveau Talborjt One of several popular restaurants collectively known as La Soupe, **Majistic** (Ave du 29 Février; soup Dh15; ⏰7am-midnight) trades in *harira* soup and mint tea. Budget cafes and restaurants have seats on nearby Place Lahcen Tamri.

Port At the entrance to the port, off Ave Mohammed V, you can pick up an ultra-fresh, no-nonsense fish meal from around Dh70. Check costs before ordering; the various catches differ greatly in price (seafood such as crab is about Dh300 per 1kg). The **stalls** (meals around Dh50; ⏰11.30am-10pm) close in the early evening during the winter.

Jour et Nuit CAFE

(Rue la Plage; ⏰24hr) A popular spot for a seafront sundowner. The newer of the two neighbouring branches has a panoramic terrace with brilliant views of the beach.

Orange Café CAFE

(Rue des Orangers; ⏰10am-8pm; 📶) This cool little courtyard cafe, with chilled Arabic electronica on the stereo and a fountain gurgling away, serves coffee and light meals (Dh25 to Dh35).

Shopping

Souvenirs are often trucked into Agadir from other parts of Morocco and tend to be of low quality, although Marrakshi vendors have started to outsource production here. Marché Central is the most atmospheric and hassle-free option in the city centre, but head to Souq Al Had (p394) for a real Moroccan vibe.

Marché Central ARTS & CRAFTS

(off Blvd Hassan II; ⏰8am-4pm Mon-Sat) This covered, breezy market will appeal to fans of Brutalist architecture; it's all concrete and corrugated metal. Inside, it's a mix of leather tailors at work and vendors insisting there will be 'no hassle' if only you step into their shops. There are some great finds here though, including Tuareg jewellery, pottery and all manner of *djellabas* (full-length hooded garment with long sleeves) and caftans.

WORTH A TRIP

SOUQ AL-HAD

Leave the seafront to shop with the locals at the **Souq Al Had** (Blvd Abderrahim Bouabid; ⌚7am-11pm Tue-Sat), which slaps a big, messy dollop of Moroccan atmosphere onto concrete Agadir. Stalls sell everything from *djellabas* to fish and include some good handicrafts, leatherwork and lanterns. Among the lines of fresh produce from the Souss Valley, look out for Berber apothecaries selling herbal incense, lipstick and potions that have all sorts of effects on the bowels.

Ensemble Artisanal ARTS & CRAFTS
(☎0528823872; Ave du 29 Février; ⌚10am-12.30pm & 2.30-5pm Mon-Sat) Over a dozen vendors, spread out over two large blue-and-white Brutalist souqs, sell some of the finest crafts in Agadir. Fine leatherwork (everything from jackets to card holders), pottery, Amazigh (Berber) jewellery, carved wooden pieces and daggers are all on offer here. After shopping, you can drop into a shaded chair in the central courtyard and plan your next move.

Tafoukt Souq GIFTS & SOUVENIRS
(Blvd du 20 Août; ⌚9.30am-12.30pm & 2-6pm) A touristy but well-located blue-and-white bazaar with everything from pottery to football tops and pool toys. In the centre are some surprisingly attractive green-tiled planters. There's also a handy mini-supermarket selling snacks, souvenirs and beer and liquor.

Getting There & Away

AIR

Al Massira Airport (☎0801000224; www.onda.ma; N10), mainly served by Royal Air Maroc, European charter flights and budget airlines, is 25km southeast of Agadir en route to Taroudant. Facilities include a post office, bag-wrap service, cafes, SIM vendors, souvenir shops and wi-fi.

BUS

Although a good number of buses serve Agadir, it is quite possible you'll end up in Inezgane, 13km south, the regional transport hub. Check before you buy your ticket. Plenty of grands taxis (Dh7) and local buses (Dh10) shuttle between there and Agadir.

All the major bus companies, and plenty of smaller companies, serve the massive circular **Gare Routière** (Blvd Abderrahim Bouabid), past Souq Al Had. If you want to travel on a specific bus, it is worth booking ahead.

CTM (☎0528825341; www.ctm.ma), which has a Nouveau Talborjt ticket office off Place Lahcen Tamri, has several daily departures to destinations including Casablanca (Dh275, 10 hours), Dakhla (Dh410, 20 hours), Essaouira (Dh65, 3½ hours), Laayoune (Dh250, 11½ hours), Marrakesh (Dh115, 3½ hours), Rabat (Dh250, 7½ hours), Tangier (Dh345, 12½ hours), Taroudant (Dh35, two hours) and Tiznit (Dh40, 1¾ hours).

Supratours (☎0528841207; www.supratours.ma), which has a city-centre ticket office on Rue des Oranges, offers similar services.

Catch bus 32 for Tamraght and Taghazout.

CAR & MOTORCYCLE

The distances involved in touring southern Morocco make it worth considering hiring a car.

Local agencies charge from about Dh300 for a small car for one day, though there's usually room for haggling. Note that you'll need to stump up an additional cost to reduce your insurance excess.

Local agencies are clustered in the arcade across Ave du Prince Moulay Abdallah from the bottom of Ave du 29 Février, around the junction of Ave des FAR and Blvd Hassan II, and the corner of Ave Mohammed V and Ave du Général Kettani.

Avis, Budget, Europcar and Hertz have offices both in the latter location and at the airport, where Thrifty and Sixt also have desks. Most accommodation options can also arrange car hire. Scooters and motorbikes are also available, but check the state of the machines carefully.

TAXI

The main grand-taxi rank, known as **El Batwaar** (Rue Mohamed Iqbal), is located at the north end of Souq Al Had. Destinations include Essaouira (Dh120), Inezgane (Dh15) and Taroudant (Dh50).

Getting Around

TO & FROM THE AIRPORT

You can catch a taxi straight from Al Massira Airport to numerous destinations. Tariffs for private hire are displayed at the airport information booth, and include the following destinations: Agadir or Inezgane (Dh200), Essaouira or Goulimime (Dh1000), Mirleft (Dh700), Tafraoute (Dh900), Taghazout (Dh300), Taroudant or Tiznit (Dh450).

Bus 37 runs from outside the airport (about 500m straight out on the road) to Inezgane (Dh10, 6.45am to 10.15pm), from where you can continue to Agadir and destinations throughout southern Morocco.

BUS

Journeys within Agadir cost Dh5, and you can buy tickets on the bus. Buses run along Ave Mohammed V between the port and Inezgane.

TAXI

Orange *petits taxis* run around Agadir. Prices are worked out by meter; ask for it to be switched on. It shouldn't cost more than Dh20 to cross town.

Souss-Massa National Park منتزه سوس ماسّة الوطني

One of Morocco's most significant national parks and bird reserves, Souss-Massa is a spectacular and wild place of cliffs, sand dunes, fertile valleys, coastal steppes and forests. It is also one of the last North African refuges for several rare bird and animal species, including the northern bald ibis, several gazelle species, red-necked ostriches and scimitar-horned oryx.

You'll find two accommodation options in the tiny village of Sidi R'bat within the park, which also has two claims to fame. According to locals, this is where the biblical Jonah was vomited up by a whale. It was also here, allegedly, that 7th-century Arab conqueror of Morocco Uqba Bin Nafi rode his horse triumphantly into the Atlantic and called on God to witness that he could find no land left to conquer.

Activities

Birdwatching

The Souss estuary, at the northern end of the park, and the Massa coastal lagoon, near the southern end, are ideal for birdwatching, best from March to April and October to November. Birds found here include ospreys, marbled ducks, cormorants, greater flamingos, flocks of sandgrouse and warblers. But the biggest attraction is the northern bald ibis. These birds, revered in ancient Egypt and once widespread in central Europe, North Africa and the Middle East, are an endangered species, with the world's only sizeable population found on this stretch of coast. Tourism development is an ongoing threat to the four local breeding grounds, which remain off-limits, but you can spot ibises around Oued Massa or at the mouth of the Tamri River.

Walking

The park is a great place for walking. Animals such as jackals, red foxes, wild cats, genets and Eurasian wild boars are found here, while a large fenced area in the north of the park contains species that have disappeared from the south, including Dorcas and dama gazelles, addaxes, red-necked ostriches and scimitar-horned oryxes.

Guides can be arranged in the village of Massa, some 60km south of Agadir (signposted from the N1). From there, a track leads along the river to the estuary mouth (5km) and a tarred road leads to Sidi R'bat (8km). Guides aren't required, but engaging one will greatly increase your chances of finding animals.

Sleeping & Eating

Outside the town of Massa, where you can find simple snack stands, your eating options will be limited to the restaurants at La Dune or Ksar Massa.

La Dune GUESTHOUSE €€
(☎0666807824; www.ladune.de; Sidi R'bat; s/d Dh350/400, tents from Dh250; P) La Dune has basic two- and four-person Amazigh (Berber) tents, a pleasantly cool tented restaurant (dinner Dh70) and African-themed, occasionally garish rooms with balconies overlooking the surf. The massive wild beach is easily accessible via a downhill path through the dunes. This is the best midrange option if you want to sleep in the park.

Ksar Massa HOTEL €€€
(☎0661280319; Sidi R'bat; s/d Dh1300/1500; P) Spectacularly located on the never-ending Sidi R'bat beach, Ksar Massa is a fantastical destination in itself. The contemporary kasbah (in a rather strange colour scheme) is a wonderful place to unwind, with hazy ocean views from its perch above the pale sands. Luxuriously spacious rooms and suites are subtly elegant, and meals (lunch/dinner Dh170/300) are sumptuous affairs with multiple dishes.

Getting There & Away

From Agadir and Inezgane, Tiznit-bound local buses and grands taxis will drop you in Belfaa or Massa (about Dh25). From either, a grand taxi to Sidi R'bat costs about Dh200.

Accommodation options in Sidi R'bat also offer transfers to/from Agadir airport (about Dh450). From Massa, it is about an hour's walk to the Massa river mouth; 4WDs also head into the park, but both Oued Massa and Oued Souss are usually accessible by 2WD (or grand taxi).

Travel agencies in Agadir also offer convenient day trips to the area.

Tamraght & Aourir

Ten kilometres south of Taghazout lie Aourir (*aw-reer*) and Tamraght (*tahm-ragt*), tiny coastal towns you might mistake for sleepy until you head off the highway down to the wide, soft sand beaches. Here, blissed-out Moroccans and foreigners stay busy in search of the ultimate surfing rush beneath perpetually sunny skies. The area's many breaks vary in terms of seclusion and skill level, and lessons and rentals are widely available.

The scene here is more relaxed (and inexpensive) than increasingly glamorous Taghazout, but yoga and green juice are slowly making inroads here too. One important constant is the ubiquity of locally grown bananas available for sale on the roadside through Aourir, as well as crafts, spices and other market goods in its small but busy souq.

Tamraght and Aourir can be reached on local bus 32 from Agadir (Dh5).

Activities

Surf Maroc SURFING

(https://surfmaroc.com; surfboard/bodyboard/paddleboard rental from Dh70/35/100, surf lessons from Dh400) This British-owned surf academy was the first in the region to offer lessons, accommodation and meals for would-be wave shredders. From its oceanside base on Imourane Beach, Surf Maroc offers lessons and board and wetsuit rental.

Sleeping

Accommodation includes simple hotels, yoga- and surf-focused options and a luxury riad concealed in the sleepy lanes of Tamraght.

Lunar Surf House GUESTHOUSE €

(0679535049; www.thelunarsurfhouse.com; dm/d from €14/34; P) Lunar Surf House is an excellent place to stay even if you're not into surfing. Surfboard hire and lessons are available, but the colourfully decorated rooms and dorms are also the perfect base for trips to Paradise Valley or yoga on the roof. Delicious meals are taken on the rooftop terrace and feature *amlou* (argan-nut butter) made in-house.

Filtered drinking water is provided. There's a two-night minimum. Day trips to Paradise Valley (€32) or longer desert excursions (from €280) are available.

Hotel Littoral HOTEL €

(0528314726; www.hotellittoral.com; Route d'Essaouira, Aourir; s/d Dh250/350;) The kitschy Hotel Littoral is basic but comfortable, with a bar-restaurant, swimming pool and well-equipped rooms. The bathrooms are a little dingy, but it's handily located for transport options north to Essaouira or south to Agadir, and there's a pleasant terrace restaurant facing the main road. It's a perfectly serviceable option for DIY surfers on a budget.

Villa Mandala GUESTHOUSE €€

(0528314773; https://surfmaroc.com; Aourir; r per week incl full-board Dh9000;) This beachfront villa at the southern end of Banana Beach is run by Surf Maroc and can be booked for yoga-focused stays of one or two weeks. The decor mixes traditional and contemporary with a pool terrace and a plush interior dotted with light-coloured textiles. Prices include all meals at a communal shared table. Surfing is also available.

★ **Riad Dar Haven** RIAD €€€

(0528315434; www.riad-dar-haven.com; Hay Ait Soual, Tamraght; r/ste from Dh840/900;) Concealed behind a simple door in a nondescript Tamraght street, this lovely riad features nine rooms and suites with tiled floors and thoughtful design touches, arrayed around a swimming pool and shaded courtyard. A stunning hammam and spa are available, and an adherence to sustainable practices has earned the property Green Key status. Excellent lunches and dinners are also available.

Nonguests are welcome for meals (Dh190 per person), but priority is given to in-house guests, so phone ahead to check availability and make bookings. There is a room on the ground floor for those with limited mobility.

Eating

There are beachy restaurants with good seafood, and Tamraght and Aourir both have good cafes and simple Moroccan restaurants.

Let's Be Healing Food CAFE €

(0623535194; Tamraght; breakfasts from Dh50, tacos from Dh75; 10am-11pm;) Bursting with plants, antiques and busy paisley prints on everything from umbrellas to upholstery, this new addition to the tiny Tamraght scene cannily trades in deliciously executed millennial favourites like green juice, avocado toast, tacos and smoothie

BEYOND THE GLITTER

Amazigh (Berber) jewellery serves a wider purpose than simple adornment. A woman's jewellery identifies her as a member of a clan or tribe, it is a sign of her wealth, it reflects cultural traditions, and it has power beyond the visual – to protect her from the evil eye.

A woman will receive jewellery from her mother until she marries. For her marriage, her future husband will commission his mother or sister to provide jewellery. These pieces will be kept by her as a dowry and added to throughout her life; they will always be made of silver, as gold is considered evil.

Necklaces are important; the traditional assemblage in the southern oasis valleys sometimes features talismans of silver, pink coral, amazonite, amber, Czech glass and West African ebony beads. Women will also own bracelets, *fibules* (elaborate brooches, often triangular, used for fastening garments), anklets, earrings and headdresses. Some jewellery will be worn every day, while the finest pieces will be saved for occasions such as festivals, pilgrimages and funerals.

Jewellery's protective, medicinal and magical properties are extremely important. The necklaces contain charms bought from magicians or holy men, offering protection against the evil eye, disease, accidents and difficulties in childbirth. Silver is believed to cure rheumatism; coral symbolises fertility and is thought to have curative powers; amber is worn as a symbol of wealth and to protect against sorcery (it's also considered an aphrodisiac and a cure for colds); amazonite and carnelian stones are used in divining fortunes; and shells traded from East Africa symbolise fertility.

Talismans feature stylised motifs of animals, the sun, moon and stars, which are all believed to have supernatural powers. A common symbol to ward off the evil eye is the hand of Fatima, daughter of the Prophet Muhammad. Any depiction of the hand (which represents human creative power and dominance), or of the number five, is believed to have the same effect as metaphorically poking your fingers into the evil eye with the words *khamsa fi ainek* (five in your eye).

bowls. Omnivores will be limited to fish options. The clientele look like extras from *Eat Pray Love.*

Babakoul CAFE €

(☎0611147625; Tamraght; breakfast from Dh30, mains Dh20-50; ⏰8am-11pm) With a breezy outdoor patio and a crazy mosaic of tiles on the floor, this cool little cafe is a relaxing spot to hang out in after a day's swimming or surfing. The versatile menu veers from crêpes to grills and pizza; the fresh fruit juices and smoothies are also good. Tajines, couscous and *bastilla* (savoury-sweet pies) are available with advance notice.

Banana Beach SEAFOOD €€

(mains Dh70; ⏰8am-4pm) At the northern end of the beach, Banana Beach is a great spot to while away a few hours, offering sunloungers on the sand and seafood, omelettes, sandwiches and cold beer.

Chez Brahim SEAFOOD €€

(Rocher du Diable; mains Dh90-280; ⏰noon-10pm) A basic, chilled beachside cafe in teal and orange, with a terrace from which you can watch the wipeouts of beginner surfers. Fish is the name of the game here, and it's all fresh and simply prepared. Unlicensed.

Taghazout تغازوت

☎0528 / POP 5233

The laid-back fishing village of Taghazout (*tag-ah-zoot*), once famous for calamari and hippies, is now considered one of Morocco's premier surfing destinations for learners and pros. The formerly scruffy beachside village is glamming itself up for more guests than ever before.

All inclusive surf-and-yoga packages have become big business here, and each new guesthouse seems even more perfectly tailored to the Instagram aesthetic of succulents, straw *objets* artfully strewn everywhere and boldly painted walls inviting you to pose for a selfie.

But the emphasis on surf culture, rather than Moroccan or Amazigh (Berber) culture, means less culture shock on a short holiday. Grab an açai bowl and a flat white on your way to yoga class, if that's what you're into: we don't judge here. And given the influx of foreign tourists, and Moroccans, a lot of people are into it: the main Taghazout drag can be overwhelmingly busy during the summer holidays.

MOROCCAN NUTELLA

Amlou, a delicious paste of ground argan nuts, honey, argan oil and almonds, is as common in this region as the argan trees that dot the hillsides, and for our money is far more delicious than Nutella. A Moroccan breakfast staple, it's most often served as a topping for pancakes, crepes or rolls, but it's also delicious as a topping for oatmeal, or – real talk – straight from the jar. It's sold at roadside stalls throughout the region; keep a particular eye out at the hotel restaurants in Immouzer des Ida Outanane. The kitchen at Lunar Surf House (p396) also turns out a delicious version by the jar.

Activities

Surf breaks such as Hash Point, Panorama, Anchor Point, La Source, Killer Point and Mysteries surround the village, and the surf is most reliable from October to April. Breaks are populated most of the winter with newbies, though, so DIY surf heads may want to head elsewhere down the coast (Mirleft is a great option).

The leading operator for lessons, board hire and accommodation packages is British-owned Surf Maroc, but numerous locals have followed in its wake, offering accommodation and surf packages. Board and wetsuit hire is available from many places in town.

★Surf Maroc SURFING

(0528200230; https://surfmaroc.com) Run by a group of passionate British surfers, Surf Maroc offers surfing lessons, board hire and yoga, and also operates a good cafe and interesting accommodation options around Taghazout and in Aourir. All-inclusive surfing packages, including lessons, board hire, meals and accommodation, begin at Dh5600 per week, and accommodation only is also available on a per-night basis.

Check the Surf Maroc website for more information on its diverse range of accommodation and activities.

Sleeping

Taghazout has a good range of accommodation, from simple *auberges* to a very comfortable luxury designer guesthouse. Locals also rent out apartments and rooms, which may be your only option in summer if you haven't booked ahead.

L'Auberge GUESTHOUSE €

(0528200272; https://surfmaroc.com; r per person from Dh300;) This whitewashed beachfront building was actually Taghazout's first guesthouse, and it's still a great place to stay with simple but stylish rooms giving front row access to the village's compact town beach and a few cafes.

Dfrost Al Mugar HOSTEL €€

(0662110300; www.dfrostsurfandyoga.com; Route d'Essaouira; dm/r €39/50;) This new surf-and-stay hostel is giving the Surf Maroc monopoly a run for its money. Rooms are pleasant, the right-on-the-beach location is killer, tons of activities (like yoga and stand-up paddleboarding) are available, and the hot tub and fireplace are icing on the cake. Best of all, there's a cosy beachside platform and bar that are open to nonguests.

Taghazout Villa GUESTHOUSE €€

(0528200230; https://surfmaroc.com; dm/s/d Dh300/700/900;) Taghazout Villa is Surf Maroc's good-value option for guests keen for a longer stay to learn how to surf. Nine rooms have a beachy ambience, and there's oodles of breezy, colourful communal areas and a bar. It's a social scene with great views out to sea.

Nearby self-contained apartments are also available for independent surfers keen to explore the breaks around Taghazout.

Yalah Surf Hostel HOSTEL €€

(0676069495; www.yalahsurf.com; behind West Coast restaurant; r from Dh400;) Run by the friendly Yassine, this accommodation has basic double, twin and quadruple rooms with shared bathrooms. It's a very friendly hostel vibe, with a social rooftop with guitar and card games. Surf lessons and gear hire also available.

★Amouage BOUTIQUE HOTEL €€€

(0528200230; https://surfmaroc.com; full-board incl surf lessons from Dh1250;) Effortlessly raising the bar in Taghazout is Surf Maroc's super-stylish 'designer guesthouse'. Brilliant local art and photography fill the airy public spaces, an infinity pool with day beds segues to the Atlantic's horizon, and a hammam and massage centre is ideal after days spent surfing or exploring. There's also a restaurant and bar open to nonguests for lunch and dinner.

Nonguests can sign up for twice-daily yoga classes (Dh120) or events including movie nights and barbecues.

★Munga Guesthouse HOTEL €€€

(☎0698680680; www.mungaguesthouse.com; Rue Iwlit; dm/d/ste €40/130/190;) The spacious rooms at this stylish spot are creatively designed with driftwood, which shows up in the most surprising places, such as the floor-to-ceiling bed frames. Communal spaces are decorated in a safari theme, with photographs of lions, animal-skin furniture and carved wooden masks; the azure-tiled rooftop pool rounds things out.

World of Waves HOTEL €€€

(☎0528200037; www.wow-surfhouse.com; Front de Mer, Villa Tizniti; s/d €75/95;) Opened in 2019, this Taghazout sleeping option falls in line with the town's familiar hotel aesthetic: whitewashed walls, weathered wood furniture, colourful textiles and tons of cacti. Surf and yoga packages are available here too. What makes WOW stand out is its location, right on the promenade overlooking the waves, fronted by a creative cafe.

Eating & Drinking

There are restaurants and snack bars (all unlicensed) on the main road. At the foot of the lanes leading to the beach, funky cafes serve Moroccan and international food, including recommended fruit juices and smoothies.

The cafes near the main beach are good for coffee and juices, while Cafe Mouja has occasional music and cinema nights. There's a licensed bar at Amouage, which is only open to guests.

Dar Jospehine INTERNATIONAL €

(☎0674776018; mains Dh60-70; ⌚8.30am-11pm) The best of the cafes along Taghazout's main street, Dar Josephine features shaded tables under a grape arbour and a pride of friendly local cats. The three-course menu (Dh100) is good value and options for mains include catch-of-the-day *pil pil* and a robust *kefta* (meatball) tajine. International influences creep in with zingy tzatziki and a hearty lasagna.

Fish Stalls SEAFOOD €

(fish from Dh40; ⌚10am-10pm) Grab a plastic chair and join Tagazhout locals chowing down on the catch of the day. Grill-masters fan the fish sizzling on the roadside barbecues; delicious cooking smells are all the marketing these places need. Possibly the cheapest and most-atmospheric meal in town.

Cafe Mouja CAFE €€

(https://surfmaroc.com; snacks & mains Dh40-100; ⌚8am-11pm;) Expansive windows with brilliant Atlantic Ocean views and chunky wooden furniture both feature at this coolly hip cafe behind Surf Maroc's shop. The menu straddles Moroccan favourites and western comfort food – chicken baguettes, beetroot-and-lentil salad – plus good smoothies, homemade ginger beer and vegetarian offerings. Music and movie nights are regular events.

L'Auberge Resto INTERNATIONAL €€

(mains Dh60-80; ⌚8am-11pm) The cafe at L'Auberge is a funky hangout serving Moroccan and international food. Comfort food options include nachos, a shared antipasto plate, and excellent salads and curries. Named after a nearby surf break, the Killers burger combines cheese, avocado and caramelised onions. Moroccan options include tajines and a great Moroccan chicken stew. The patio setting is quite romantic.

Panorama Bar CAFE

(☎0528200126; ⌚11am-10pm) Featuring a 180-degree view of the beach and breakers, the Panorama is a perfect place to take a juice break while exploring the town. Simple meals are available, including pizza and fish.

Information

There are no ATMs in Taghazout; the nearest one is in Aourir.

Getting There & Around

Bus number 32 runs along Ave Mohammed V in Agadir before heading to Taghazout (Dh5), with stops in Aouriri and Tamraght. *Grands taxis* from Agadir cost Dh10. The town's main strip is eminently walkable, even if you've had too much sun and surf.

Imouzzer Ida Ou Tanane & Paradise Valley

إيموزار إداوتنان و وادي الجنة

If you brave the winding mountain road to get to Paradise Valley you'll be richly rewarded with this hidden gorge, bursting with oleander and palms and studded with jewel-like ponds perfect for swimming. Local producers have formed a *route du miel* (honey route), and stalls sell the sweet stuff as well as argan oil and *amlou*. Signs by the road point to walking trails. Push on to the village of Imouzzer des Ida Outanane (*im-oo-zehr des ee-dah oot-ah-nahn*) for lunch with a breathtaking view over the Anti Atlas.

DON'T MISS

CASCADES D'IMOUZZER

One of North Africa's most storied waterfalls, unfortunately the **Cascades d'Imouzzer** are only intermittently running these days depending on rainfall. Whether or not they're 'on', the steep 4km walk down to the falls can be pleasant (once you say plenty of *non mercis* to the *faux guides* toward the start of the trail). You'll have the most chance of seeing the falls in action from February to August.

When it's flowing, water falls off the edge of the plateau in several chutes, running down one cliff face known as the Bride's Veil. The path to the foot of the falls finishes at an iridescent blue plunge pool with overhanging rocks and foliage; sadly we can't recommend the water for swimming. If you can cross the river here, you can climb to a plateau and see the top plunge pool, and caves once inhabited by hippies.

There are trails down to the falls signed from the village, and from the garden at Hôtel des Cascades.

The area turns white in February and March when the almond trees blossom. There is a honey harvest and festival in July and August, and around late November you may be lucky enough to witness the olive harvest. Locals climb into the trees to shake olives from the branches and oil is pressed in the village. Thursday is souq day.

Sleeping & Eating

The hotels in Paradise Valley, on the road to Imouzzer, are very similar: all have pools, tiled restaurants, nice views of the gorge and simple rooms with wet en-suite bathrooms. **Auberge Bab Imouzer** (0670131006; www.aubergebabimouzer.com; Route d'Immouzer, Paradise Valley; s/d Dh200/300 excl breakfast;) has the best pool and nicest view, **Hotel Tifrit** (0528216708; www.hotel-tifrit.net; Route d'Immouzer, Paradise Valley; r from Dh500 excl breakfast;) has the best rooms, and **Auberge Le Panoramic** (0661623779; Route d'Immouzer, Paradise Valley; s/d incl half-board Dh280/500;) has the nicest staff. The best option close to the falls is Hôtel des Cascades.

There are basic cafes at the bottom of the path to the falls and on the way up. Along the road to Paradise Valley are some snack spots with tables in the river for cooling your toes. Accommodation options around Paradise Valley all have cafes featuring Moroccan standards; Hôtel des Cascades offers the most upscale, French-influenced menu. Try the local honey.

Hôtel des Cascades HOTEL €€
(0528218808; www.cascades-hotel.net; Imouzzer Ida Ou Tanane; s/d excl breakfast Dh462/562;) In a wonderful location perched above the Cascades d'Imouzzer, this hotel is set in a riotous succulent garden with tennis courts. Most of the slightly stuffy rooms have balconies or private terraces, but bathrooms could use some modernising. There's a whiff of the institutional about the place, made up for by the verdant setting.

There's a licensed restaurant (well-portioned mains Dh80). Tour groups arrive at the restaurant around 12.30pm, so try and time a lunch visit before or after. Paths descend 4km from the garden to the cascades. Breakfast is Dh40.

Getting There & Away

Buses and grands taxis run between Aourir and Imouzzer (Dh35) until about 4pm. From Agadir, it's hard to visit the falls in a day by public transport; you can visit on a tour – Lunar Surf House (p396) offers one – or hire a grand taxi. Thursday, when Imouzzer's weekly market takes place, is a good day to find a taxi, but a bad time to drive as the narrow road is busy. Between October and May, the river sometimes destroys the road.

Taroudant تارودانت

0528 / POP 80,149

Taroudant (*tahr-oo-dahnt*) is sometimes called 'Little Marrakesh', but that description doesn't do the Souss Valley trading centre justice. Hidden by magnificent red-mud walls, and with the snowcapped peaks of the High Atlas beckoning beyond, Taroudant's souqs and squares have a healthy sprinkling of Maghrebi mystique. Yet it is also a practical place, a market town where Imazighen (Berbers) trade the produce of the rich and fertile Souss Valley.

There aren't any must-see sights. Instead, the medina is a place to stroll and linger. The two souqs are well worth a browse, more laid-back than Marrakesh, but with a sense of historical inheritance missing in Agadir. With the little-explored western High Atlas, the Anti Atlas and the coast all nearby, the town makes a good base for trekking and activities. Sixty-five kilometres inland from Al Massira Airport, it's a more atmospheric staging post to/from the airport than Agadir.

History

Taroudant was one of the early bases of the Almoravids, who established themselves here in 1056 CE, at the beginning of their conquest of Morocco. In the 16th century, the emerging Saadians made it their capital for about 20 years. By the time they moved on to Marrakesh, they had turned the Souss Valley, in which the city stands, into the country's most important producer of sugar cane, cotton, rice and indigo; all valuable trade items on the trans-Saharan trade routes the dynasty was keen to control. The Saadians constructed the old part of town and the kasbah, though most of it was destroyed and the inhabitants massacred in 1687 by Moulay Ismail, as punishment for opposing him. Only the ramparts survived. Most of what stands inside them dates from the 18th century.

Taroudant continued to be a centre of intrigue and sedition against the central government well into the 20th century, and indeed played host to El Hiba, a southern chief who opposed the Treaty of Fez, the 1912 agreement that created the colonial French Protectorate.

Sights & Activities

Taroudant is a great base for trekking in the western High Atlas region, including the secluded **Tichka Plateau**, a delightful area of highland meadows and hidden gorges (two-day minimum). The **Afensou** and **Tizi n'Test** areas are ideal for day walks. Agencies in town offer treks, as do many guesthouses; insist on travelling with a qualified guide. Charges start at about Dh600 per person per day, including transport and picnic.

★Palais Musée Claudio Bravo HOUSE
(0528216078; www.palaisclaudiobravo.com/en; Route de Tamaloukt; incl tea Dh200; by appointment) This particular *palais* defies categorisation: it's a hotel, a museum and the former residence of deceased Chilean painter Claudio Bravo, who selected the countryside outside Taroudant as the ideal base for his dream home. The architecture of his house is noteworthy, as are its amazing contents, including paintings by Bravo and Francis Bacon, as well as dinosaur fossils, priceless antiques from Mali, India, Japan and Morocco as well as wonderful gardens. His devoted staff keep up the place and run tours.

Ramparts HISTORIC SITE
The 7.5km of ramparts surrounding Taroudant are among the best-preserved rammed-earth walls in Morocco. Their colour changes from golden brown to deepest red depending on the time of day. They can easily be explored on foot (two hours), preferably in the late afternoon; or take a bike or *calèche* (horse-drawn carriage) and see the walls by moonlight.

Some horses look very fit; others not so much. Don't patronise a *calèche* driver who doesn't look after his animals.

Place Al Alaouyine SQUARE
(Place Assarag) During Moroccan holidays, Place Al Alaouyine is like Marrakesh's Djemaa El Fna in miniature, with storytellers, snake charmers, escapologists and performers working the crowds.

Bab El Kasbah NOTABLE BUILDING
Built in the 16th and 17th centuries, a string of mighty defensive towers serve as the city gates. Considered the main gate, the triple-arched Bab El Kasbah (also known as Bab Essalsla) is approached via an avenue of orange trees. Steps lead to the top of the tower, where you can walk along the ramparts.

Kasbah AREA
The old kasbah quarter, originally a fortress built by Moulay Ismail, is today a poor but safe residential area, where winding lanes and low archways lead to tiny squares and dead ends. The governor's palace, on the eastern side of the kasbah, now forms part of Hôtel Palais Salam (p404). It's nice for getting a taste of a workaday Taroudant neighbourhood.

Tours

La Maison Anglaise CULTURAL
(0661236627; www.cecu.co.uk; 422 Derb Afferdou; half-/full-day excursions excl lunch from Dh260/300) Excellent guides and activities including mountain treks, Amazigh village visits, birdwatching trips, cookery lessons and even survival lessons in Moroccan Arabic. All trips are either half- or full-day excursions; no overnight trips are offered. The excursion to the valley at Afensou in the High Atlas involves walking through olive groves to a swimming hole.

Packed lunches are available for an extra Dh50; lunch in an Amazigh (Berber) village costs Dh80. Prices assume a minimum of four people; otherwise, the cost can be shared among a smaller number of participants.

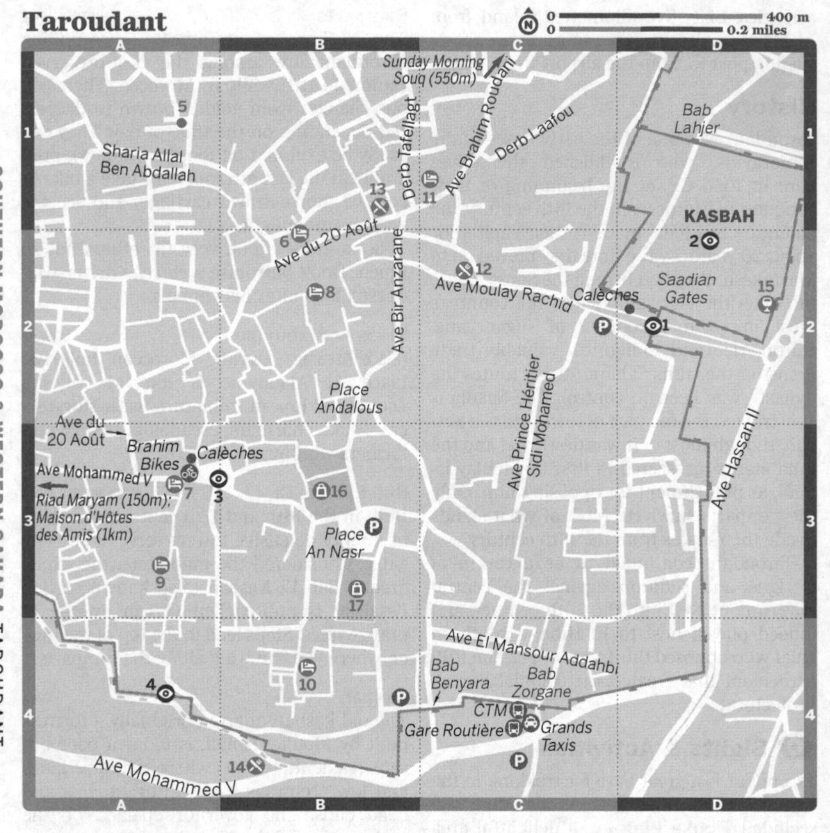

Taroudant

Sights
1 Bab El Kasbah ... D2
2 Kasbah ... D2
3 Place Al Alaouyine ... A3
4 Ramparts ... A4

Activities, Courses & Tours
5 La Maison Anglaise ... A1

Sleeping
6 Dar Zahia ... B2
7 Hôtel Taroudant ... A3
8 Palais Oumensour ... B2
9 Riad Dar Dzahra ... A3
10 Riad Taroudant ... B4
11 Ryad Tafilag ... C1

Eating
12 Chez Nada ... C2
13 Fruit & Vegetable Market ... B1
14 Jnane Soussia ... B4

Drinking & Nightlife
15 Hôtel Palais Salam ... D2

Shopping
16 Souq Arabe ... B3
17 Souq Berbère ... B3

Sleeping

Because there's not much to do here aside from wander the souqs, you'll want to pay special attention to your sleeping arrangements. There are a few budget options, but Taroudant really excels in midrange riads, with one very special top-end property: Palais Musée Claudio Bravo (p404). Many midrange hotels offer pick-ups from Agadir Al Massira Airport (Dh500) and can organise activities.

Maison d'Hôtes des Amis GUESTHOUSE €
(☎ 0667601686; www.chambresdesamis.com; Sidi Belkas; r from Dh160;) This budget guesthouse has aged but sizeable rooms, basic bathrooms with intermittent hot water, a couple of salons, and a roof terrace for breakfast. It's 800m west of Bab Taghount (on the west side of the ramparts) at the beginning of the open countryside, although street noise and the nearby mosque overwhelm any suburban tranquility.

The friendly and responsive proprietor, Said Dayfollah, offers bike hire, trekking and activities, pick-ups from Al Massira Airport (Dh300) and meals on request (Dh70).

Hôtel Taroudant HOTEL €
(☎ 0528852416; Ave Mohammed V, Place Al Alaouyine; s/d excl breakfast from Dh160/200) In this central budget option, tiled corridors lead past a dark foyer restaurant and through a courtyard featuring birds singing in huge magnolia and jacaranda trees, to simple, small rooms with wet bathrooms. Busy tiles lend character. No breakfast is provided, but you can pop across the street to Café Oasis.

Staff don't always answer the phone, but this place is rarely fully booked.

Riad Dar Dzahra RIAD €€
(☎ 0528851085; www.dzahra.com; Place Assarag; s/d/ste Dh400/540/770;) The life's work of Frenchman Yves, Dzahra is the only clay riad in Taroudant. Ten spacious rooms are centred around several courtyards and a lovely pool, shaded by palms and bougainvillea. Family rooms feature sleeping alcoves that will delight tots, and French films are screened on the roof terrace. Yves is very knowledgeable about the area and is happy to offer opinions and recommendations. Bicycles are available (€5 for three hours) as well as dinner (Dh130) and beer.

Ryad Tafilag BOUTIQUE HOTEL €€
(☎ 0528850607; www.riad-tafilag.com; Ave Brahim Roudani, Derb Tafellagt; r from €50;) Consisting of adjoining medina houses, this colourful hotel is a warren of staircases, terraces, lounges and a hammam. The nine rooms and suites, three of which have private terraces, are unfussily artistic. Free bikes are offered to guests, and meals are served in elegant common areas. There are two plunge pool concealed amid the Moroccan design wizardry.

Palais Oumensour BOUTIQUE HOTEL €€
(☎ 0528550215; www.palaisoumensour.com; Al Mansour Borj Oumensour Tadjount; s/d €65/70;) Tasteful and tranquil, Palais Oumensour hides away on a medina lane by the Catholic church garden. Above the central courtyard with its jade pool, the 10 understated rooms combine modern comforts and traditional materials, with prints from French painter Georges Braque and *tadelakt* (waterproof plaster) walls. Elegant public spaces include a hammam, a massage room, a roof terrace with High Atlas views and a bar.

Riad Taroudant RIAD €€
(☎ 0700863884; 243 Ave Al Quds, Derb J'did; s/d Dh300/400;) In a residential neighbourhood near the medina's southern entrance, the highlight of Riad Taroudant is the rooftop terrace with cactus garden and resident blind cat. Downstairs, a compact pool provides a haven from the Moroccan heat. Rooms are simply furnished but comfortable; the restaurant was undergoing renovations when we dropped in.

Air-con is available but is subject to a small additional charge.

★ **Dar Al Hossoun** BOUTIQUE HOTEL €€€
(☎ 0528853476; www.alhossoun.com; s/d Dh1050/1300;) This hotel is on a huge plot of land around 5km west of Taroudant, but its gardens are designed so that every space feels intimate, including two pools, plenty of serene common areas and seemingly infinite succulents. Rooms are tastefully appointed, as are common areas. Peacocks and 36 cats roam the grounds, resulting in amusing animal kingdom hijinks. Everything is utterly lush.

The pools are available to nonguests (Dh60). Taxi out for the afternoon and stay for drinks and dinner (prix-fixe Dh220) under the soaring cacti. Or, if self-driving, take P1708 5km west of town to the village of Al Nowayle. From here, follow signs leading about two kilometres north of the village.

OFF THE BEATEN TRACK

TIOUTE KASBAH

Southwest of Taroudant, Tioute Kasbah was once used as a location for a 1954 French production of Ali Baba and the Forty Thieves. The stone kasbah overlooks a *palmeraie* (palm grove) and a couple of restaurants, with the High Atlas and Anti Atlas in the distance. Visit early to ensure you find a grand taxi (Dh15, 30 minutes) there and back, and to beat the tour groups.

★ **Dar Zahia** RIAD €€€

(☎0528850801; www.darzahia.com; 175 Derb Chrif; r €85) This gorgeous property belonged to a French couple for years before it welcomed guests, and it still retains the feel of a private home – albeit that of a fabulously chic couple. Four rooms are clustered around a patio with soaring silk floss and banana trees, and bougainvillea blossoms flutter down into the plunge pool.

Objets from the souq adorn public spaces where breakfast and dinner (€20) are taken. Everything is so quietly elegant you'll have trouble tearing yourself away to visit shops personally recommended by Zahia, the owner and namesake.

Palais Musée Claudio Bravo DESIGN HOTEL €€€

(☎0528216078; www.palaisclaudiobravo.com/en; Route de Tamaloukt; s/d €80/100; P 🛜 🏊) Ten kilometres north of Taroudant stands this extraordinary property: the home, museum and studio of Chilean painter Claudio Bravo. Rooms are furnished with wonderful antiques, but pale in comparison to common spaces: for example, pool furniture is made from the same Makrana marble as the Taj Mahal.

You can sleep in the same suite that once hosted Jacques Chirac (€300 per night). Or just come here to gawp on a tour (p401).

Eating & Drinking

The hotel cafes and touristy restaurants on Place Al Alaouyine are fine for breakfast, and serve tajines and simple grills later in the day. The best place to look for cheap eats is around Place An Nasr and north along Ave Bir Zaran. With a few exceptions, your riad's kitchen may be your only option in the evening. Plan accordingly.

There aren't many places to wet your whistle with anything stronger than juice, but Hôtel Palais Salam has a poolside bar. Most riads allow guests to bring their own alcohol.

Chez Nada MOROCCAN €

(☎0528851726; Ave Moulay Rachid; mains Dh50-60, set menu Dh80; ⊙7am-11pm) This 60-year-old restaurant specialises in tajines, including one with pigeon (or chicken), prunes and grilled almonds. Above the male-dominated ground-floor cafe and elegant white 1st-floor dining room, the roof terrace has views over leafy public gardens. *Bastilla* and royal couscous should be ordered two hours ahead. In a town with limited evening dining options outside the riads, this is a handy option.

Fruit & Vegetable Market MARKET €

(Ave 20 Août; ⊙7am-4pm) A good option for putting together a picnic.

Riad Maryam MOROCCAN €€

(☎0666127285; www.riadmaryam.com; Ave Mohammed V; menu Dh200; ⊙7-10pm) The first Taroudant riad to open as accommodation, Riad Maryam has been overtaken by other flasher options, but it's still a wonderful location for an evening meal. Multicourse menus, including soup, salad and dessert, are served in the verdant inner courtyard. Prior booking is essential, so follow the signs and visit in the morning to book for the evening.

The family owners speak French but little English. The riad isn't always open for guests; it's best to call ahead.

Jnane Soussia MOROCCAN €€

(☎0528854980; Ave Mohammed V; mains Dh70-100; ⊙10am-11pm) This garden restaurant has tented seating areas set around a large swimming pool adjacent to the city ramparts. The house specialities, which include *mechoui* (whole roast lamb) and pigeon *bastillas*, have to be ordered in advance, but the chicken tajine with lemon and olives is good for a light lunch, and everything is decent.

Hôtel Palais Salam BAR

(Ave Moulay Ismail; ⊙2-11pm) Tucked away poolside in the lush, expansive gardens of the Hotel Palais Salam, this is the best (only!) place to relax over a cold beer away from the hubbub of the medina. Jutted up against the city ramparts, the crumbling decadence of the grounds are a throwback to a bygone era. The scruffiness only adds to the romance.

Shopping

Taroudant is the central Chleuh city of the Souss. As such it's a good place to look for the quality silver jewellery for which this Amazigh (Berber) group is renowned. The jewellery is influenced both by Saharan tribes and by Jewish silversmiths, who formed a significant part of the community until the late 1960s, when the majority emigrated to Israel.

★ **Souq Arabe** MARKET

(⊙10am-11pm) The main souq, also known as the grand souq, has wonderful antique leather goods, textiles and jewellery shops hidden in the quiet streets. It's slightly more high-pressure than the Souq Berbère, but this is still Taroudant: everything is pretty chill.

Sunday Morning Souq MARKET
(⏲7am-1pm) This large market, held outside Bab El Khemis north of the kasbah, brings in people from the whole region. It's worth a visit for local flavour, and to pick up produce for self-catering or long transits.

Souq Berbère MARKET
(Marché Municipal Jnan Jamaa; ⏲10am-11pm) Also known as the *marché municipal* (central market), this souq, on the south side of Place An Nasr, serves as the shopping centre for workaday Taroudant: trainers, mobile phone accessories, exercise gear, pots, pans and so on. It's a great window into local life, and who knows, maybe you'll find a colander you love.

Getting There & Away

Buses depart from the station outside Bab Zorgane. **CTM** (☎0528853858; www.ctm.ma; Bab Zorgane) has the most reliable buses, with at least one daily service to each of the following destinations: Agadir (Dh35, two hours), Casablanca (Dh210, seven hours overnight), Marrakesh (Dh115, four hours overnight) and Ouarzazate (Dh115, five hours).

Other companies serve Agadir and Inezgane (Dh30, 1½ hours, hourly), Taliouine (Dh80, 1½ hours, daily) and Tata (Dh90, five hours, daily).

Grands taxis gather just outside Bab Zorgane. Destinations include Agadir (Dh40), Inezgane (Dh35) – where you can change for more frequent, services to Agadir – and Marrakesh (Dh140). To travel via the mountainous and spectacular Tizi n'Test, you will need to hire the entire taxi (around Dh1300).

Accommodation providers can organise pick-ups from Agadir's Al Massira Airport (p394) (around Dh500).

Getting Around

Taroudant is a great place to cycle; bikes can be hired at **Brahim Bikes** (☎0662741091; Place Al Alaouyine; per hr/day Dh10/60) on the main square. Petits taxis charge Dh8 per trip (Dh10 after 8pm).

You can tour the ramparts in a *calèche*. The horse-drawn carriages gather just inside Bab El Kasbah, on Place Alaouyine and at other prominent spots. A one-way trip across town should cost roughly the same as by petit taxi, although the driver may disagree; the going rate is Dh15.

A one-hour tour, including the medina, a circuit of the ramparts and a small tannery should cost Dh100. As always, pay attention to whether the horse looks healthy; don't patronise drivers who don't look after their animals properly.

ANTI ATLAS MOUNTAINS

The Anti Atlas remains one of the least-visited parts of Morocco's mountains, which is surprising, given its stark beauty and proximity to Agadir. Bizarre, bulbous rock formations soar over centuries-old Chleuh settlements and high-altitude farms, clustered around palm-ringed oases. Given the diversity of mountainscapes, from granite boulders to red-lava flows, it's small wonder this region is becoming a paradise for trekking, climbing and bouldering aficionados.

Taliouine تالوين

☎0528 / POP 5844

The dusty, scraggly village of Taliouine (*tah-lee-oo-ween*) is dominated by surrounding hills topped with crumbling *igherm* (collective granaries) and the impressive Glaoui kasbah. Numerous agencies run treks using Taliouine as a base, but it's not a well-trafficked area. Anti Atlas hikers setting off on treks from here usually only encounter Amazigh (Berber) goat herds, goats and the occasional reptile on the trail.

Taliouine is also the African centre of *l'or rouge* (red gold) – saffron, the world's most expensive spice. The purple *Crocus sativus* flower, from which the spice comes, grows only above 1200m. It flowers between mid-October and mid-November, when you can see locals picking the flowers around villages 12km east of Taliouine. Around the first weekend in November, a saffron festival breathes life into this sleepy town, usually featuring nightly concerts from some of Amazigh music's biggest names. Villagers dance en masse to the beat of bendirs (traditional hand drums).

Sights

★**Calligraphie Tifinaghe** ARTS CENTRE
(☎0601353151; www.molidaz.blogspot.com; ⏲8.30am-12.30pm & 2-6.30pm) Poet and calligrapher Moulid Nidouissadan paints Amazigh (Berber) proverbs and colourful compositions from natural inks. Free to every visitor is a rendition of their name in Tamazight – crafted via a combination of saffron ink and a blowtorch. Other well-priced souvenirs include T-shirts and tote bags. Moulid speaks French and a smidgen of English.

Dar Azaafaran MUSEUM
(☎0528534413; ⏲8am-7pm) FREE This modern information centre is devoted to *l'or rouge* – red gold, the nickname for saffron –

with a small museum, saffron for sale by local cooperatives and a display of the current going rate. There are also a few saffron agricultural tools strewn about. Displays are in French. Opening hours are not strictly adhered to.

Glaoui Kasbah HISTORIC SITE
Gazing at the brown hills, the kasbah is mostly disintegrating, but it makes a pleasant sunset stroll. It's best experienced by spending the night at Escale Rando.

Monday Souq MARKET
(7am-1pm Mon) The village comes to life during the Monday souq, near Auberge Le Safran.

Tours

Talioujne is a popular trekking centre for nearby Jebel Siroua, which offers some of the finest walking in the Anti Atlas. Trekking guides can be arranged through accommodation or local operators.

Auberge Le Safran TREKKING
(0668394223; www.auberge-safran-taliouine-sud-maroc.com; 1-day trek per person from Dh500) Mahfoud and his brother are licensed guides, leading treks from one to 15 days into the Anti Atlas. During saffron harvesting season, you can watch locals pick the precious flowers; otherwise, treks lead to mountain rock pools, oases and argan orchards. English and French is spoken at this professional outfit, well-suited to hard-core trekkers.

Zafrani CULTURAL
(0613880526; www.zafrani.ch) This Swiss-Moroccan company can organise a great variety of personalised tours from trekking to stargazing and skiing to meditation, catering to individuals and families. Trekking and cultural trips normally incorporate the region's saffron and argan heritage. Accommodation can also be arranged, as well as treks in other parts of Morocco.

Festivals & Events

Festival du Safran FOOD & DRINK
(Nov) At the beginning of November (usually the first weekend) the town draws all comers for a celebration of spice, with nightly concerts from well-regarded Amazigh (Berber) musicians, which works townsfolk into a frenzy of *ahouach* (celebratory dancing) to the beat of bendirs. Book accommodation well ahead.

Sleeping & Eating

The best of Taliouine's accommodation is slightly out of town in more rural surroundings, often with views of the atmospheric kasbah. There are also cheap hotels on the main street.

For dinner, ask for half-board at your accommodation or try Auberge Le Safran or Souktana. At the west end of the main drag near the Gare Routière, grills smoke away; you can also get a tajine made with saffron (around Dh50) at Auberge Siroua.

★ Escale Rando GUESTHOUSE €
(0662547828, 0528534600; www.escalerando.fr; Kasbah de Taliouine; r incl half-board from Dh300;) Abutting the kasbah, Escale Rando is a romantic little spot centred on a courtyard with gardens, lights, fountains and 26 tortoises. There are four high-ceilinged rooms, a fully equipped kitchen and, for hot nights, a terrace where guests can sleep alongside the kasbah battlements. Dinners are exceptional. Some English is spoken.

Auberge Le Safran HOTEL €
(0668394223; www.auberge-safran-taliouine-sud-maroc.com; s/d Dh200/250;) Le Safran has basic, colourful en-suite rooms, with two doubles on the roof terrace and a spacious four-person suite. The 1st-floor salon looks across the fields at the kasbah and mountains beyond. The hotel harvests its own saffron, which it sells on site and uses in the delicious meals. There's also a hammam and huge pool with saffron flower mural (it's a one-horse town after all). Ask for a room at the back to minimise road noise.

Chez Souad GUESTHOUSE €
(0671056846; moradchoukri@yahoo.fr; s/d Dh70/150) Overlooking a dusty football pitch, this sprawling family home has a rooftop terrace with views of the kasbah and town. There are eight rooms accommodating up to four people each, three with private bathroom. Half-board is available (Dh160 per person), and Souad's brother, Morad Choukri, is a trekking guide.

Auberge Tobkal HOTEL €
(0528534343; aubergetoubkal@yahoo.fr; s/d Dh200/250;) At this trekking-orientated inn, guests consult maps in the relaxing communal area, and owner Ahmed can offer advice and arrange guides. Rooms are simple but serviceable, largely the same save for the rather garish colours. It's east of the village, along the N10 toward Tata. Half-board is Dh200.

Auberge Souktana GUESTHOUSE €
(☎0528534075; souktana@menara.ma; N10; tent site Dh50, bungalow s/d Dh100/160, rooms s/d Dh180/220; P 📶) This cosy spot, on the main road 500m before the turn-off for the kasbah coming from Taliouine, features a wide range of accommodation. Rooms are centred around a sweet indoor hearth, and bungalows with shared bathrooms offer great value. There are fruit trees and nice views of the mountains out back. Meals are taken in a slightly institutional communal room.

Shopping

Taliouine is a great place to pick up some saffron. Numerous shops and boutiques sell it here for around Dh40 per gram: try Dar Azaafaran or **Coopérative Souktana du Safran** (☎0528534452; ⏲8.30am-6.30pm). But beware 'counterfeit saffron'; the genuine article should stain your fingers yellow (rather than red), taste bitter (rather than sweet) and carry a spicy price tag.

Getting There & Away

The N10 east of Taliouine crosses a beautiful and immense landscape, before joining the N9 (the main Marrakesh–Ouarzazate road) near the turn-off to Aït Ben Haddou.

Taliouine has a small bus station. There are not always seats available on the buses passing through town, so *grands taxis*, also found at the bus station, are a better option.

Grands taxis run from Taliouine to Ouarzazate, but direct taxis are rare, and you will normally have to change at Tazenakht (Dh37). For Taroudant there are relatively frequent direct taxis, but it is often quicker to change at Ouled Berhil (Dh35).

Tafraoute تافراوت

☎0528 / POP 4931

Occupying pride of place in the gorgeous Ameln Valley, the village of Tafraoute (*tahfrah-oot*) is surrounded on all sides by red granite and quartzite mountains, as well as smooth rocks ranging in size from marbles to apartment blocks. These, and the fact that they're well off the tourist track, delights climbers and trekkers. Its creature comforts (including one bar and one licensed restaurant) make Tafraoute a logical base to rest up before or after a mountain sojourn.

Sights

Le Châpeau de Napoléon NATURAL FEATURE
(Napoleon's Hat; Aguerd-Oudad) These rocks don't look much like Napoleon's hat, to be frank, but they're still weird and impressively massive, soaring above the little town of Aguerd-Oudad. It's possible to climb to the top; the views over the boulder-strewn landscape are exceptional. Aguerd-Oudad makes for a nice stroll or bike ride. From the roundabout by the Afriquia petrol station in Tafraoute, take the R107 toward Tizi Amanouz.

Maison Berbère Traditionnelle NOTABLE BUILDING
(☎0673829054; maisonberbere30@yahoo.fr; adult Dh15; ⏲8am-6pm) Maison Traditionnelle stands in the largely uninhabited hilltop village of Tazekka, where bulbous boulders have been incorporated into the *pisé* (rammed earth) walls of the centuries-old houses. You can visit the Carved Gazelle as part of a tour of the four-floor dwelling, where the knowledgeable proprietor Mahfoud's family once lived. It's possible to stay the night here (Dh150/230 per person including breakfast/half-board). Mahfoud, a trekking guide, offers Amazigh (Berber) music soirées and tea ceremonies.

Pierres Bleues PUBLIC ART
(Painted Rocks) The bizarrely beautiful Pierres Bleues are the work of Belgian artist Jean Verame, who spray-painted the smooth, rounded boulders in shades of blue, red, purple and black in 1984. Decades later, they remain vivid against the red desert. Visitors disagree over whether it's art or a blight on the landscape, but villagers give the rocks a fresh coat of paint every year to keep the controversy fresh. You'll find them some 7km south of Tafraoute, 500m past the turnoff for Aït Mansour; a piste leads uphill to the right.

Carved Gazelles ROCK ART
The most easily accessible examples of prehistoric rock engravings found in the Tafraoute area are the Carved Gazelles, 2km away in the village of Tazekka. There are actually two gazelles: one on the upturned face of a fallen boulder, and another on a larger boulder above eye height. They're prominent and quite elegant. It's a pleasant mountain-bike ride or walk 2km from central Tafraoute. The easiest way to find it is to walk along Route de Tazekka to Camping Tazka on the Tiznit road (R104), and ask the jovial Anglophone Mohamed for directions once you arrive.

Activities

The best way to see the beautiful surrounding countryside is by walking or cycling, and several companies and guides offer mountain-biking and trekking trips. Operators have booths near Hôtel Salama.

Tafraoute

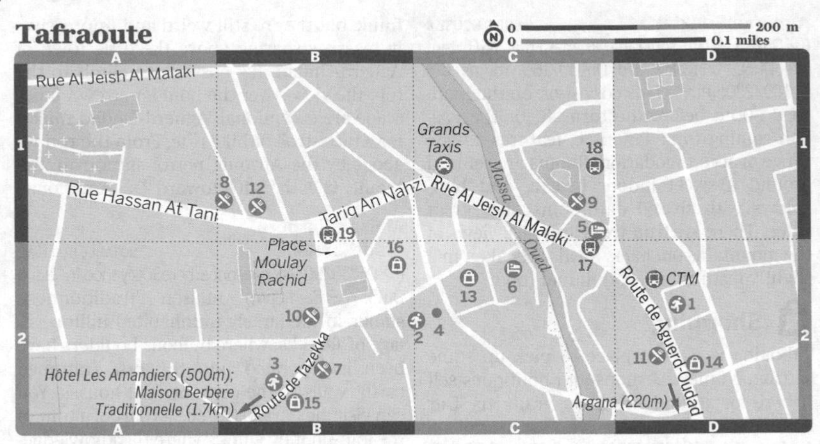

Tafraoute

Activities, Courses & Tours

- Au Coin des Nomades .... (see 13)
- 1 Maison de Vacances D2
- New Hammam .... (see 5)
- 2 Old Hammam C2
- 3 Tafraoute VTT B2
- 4 Tawada C2

Sleeping

- 5 Auberge Les Amis C1
- 6 Hôtel Salama C2

Eating

- 7 Café-Restaurant Atlas B2
- 8 Cafe-Restaurant Panorama B1
- 9 Fruit & Vegetable Market C1
- 10 L'Étoile d'Agadir B2
- 11 Restaurant La Kasbah D2
- 12 Restaurant L'Étoile du Sud B1

Shopping

- 13 Au Coin des Nomades C2
- 14 Maison du Troc D2
- 15 Maison Tuareg B2
- 16 Souq B2

Transport

- 17 Buses to Aït-Mansour Gorge C2
- 18 Buses to Ameln Valley C1
- 19 Buses to Tiznit B1

Cycling

The stunning, palm-filled Aït Mansour Gorge (p411) and the Pierres Bleues (p407) are great cycling destinations. Several places hire out bikes of varying quality; expect to pay about Dh50/300 per day for a road/mountain bike with helmet, pump and puncture-repair kit.

Maison de Vacances CYCLING
(0528800197; www.tafraout.info; bike hire per day Dh60-120; 8.30am-10pm) A decent place to rent a mountain bike, conveniently located on the road toward good biking destinations like Le Châpeau de Napoléon, the Pierres Bleues and the Carved Gazelle.

Tafraoute VTT CYCLING
(0670409384; www.tafraout-vtt.cla.fr; bike hire per day from Dh60, rack hire Dh70-100) This is the only place in town to rent bike racks for cars – useful for a drive-and-cycle trip to Aït Mansour.

Trekking & Climbing

Tafraoute and the Anti Atlas offer numerous climbing routes and trekking possibilities. Most of the walks are strenuous and require some route-finding skills. David Wood's *Walks and Scrambles in the Moroccan Anti Atlas* (Ciccerone 2018) is an excellent resource for coming to grips with the myriad options for getting outdoors around Tafraoute. Online, www.climb-tafraout.com and www.climbmorocco.com are good resources for climbers.

Tawada HIKING
(0661822677) If you're counting dirhams, accredited English-speaking guide Brahim Bahou might agree to a lower rate than if you go through the main players. He offers information and guided treks lasting for one day or more, and can organise mules.

Au Coin des Nomades CLIMBING
(0661627921; tafraoutdesert@gmail.com) Houssine Laroussi, a respected climber, is a good

source of trekking and climbing information, including guides, books and topographical maps. He can also organise village homestays and advise on buses to get to lesser-visited areas like Aït Mansour. Located near the entrance of Hôtel Salama.

Hammams

Tafraoute is a good place for a throwback hammam experience; some houses here still lack water. There are three in town; massages are available at the **new hammam** (Dh12; men 7am-10pm, women to 7pm) behind Auberge Les Amis, although the male-only **old hammam** (Dh12; men 7am-10pm), just behind the market, is more authentic.

Festivals & Events

Almond Blossom Festival CULTURAL
(Feb) The Tafraoute area celebrates its almond harvest, the largest in Morocco, at this festival. It features traditional song, dance, food stalls and folklore (but you'll have to brush up your Tamazight to fully appreciate the latter). Even if you can't grasp the tall tales, the festival puts locals in a great mood that is well worth enjoying.

Sleeping

Accommodation options in town are numerous and good value; staying in the nearby Ameln Valley is also an option. There are two campgrounds 1km west of town on the Tiznit road (R104).

Hôtel Salama HOTEL €
(0528800026; R104; s/d Dh200/300;) Neat as a pin, the good-sized rooms at the Salama are the best value in Tafraoute. Doubles feature balconies overlooking the sweet square and cafe below; every room has TV and air-con, as well as comfy chairs and a writing desk. Communal spaces include a comfortable atrium and a massive roof terrace with great views of the rock formations beyond the town.

Argana HOSTEL €
(0528801496; www.argana-tafraout.com; R107; s/d with shared bathroom Dh150/200;) Argana has the most comfortable hostel rooms in town. Also on offer are a laundry service, good breakfasts, a lounge, terraces and advice from the helpful owner Mustapha, an English-speaking trekking aficionado. There are free bicycles for guest use.

Auberge Les Amis HOTEL €
(0528801921; auberge.lesamis@yahoo.fr; Place Moulay Rachid; r from Dh200;) Overlooking Place Moulay Rachid, Les Amis has nine rooms across three floors and a welcoming team at reception eager to help you however they can. Good English is spoken, and rooms are tidy with big windows. There's a cute terrace overlooking the street action below. Breakfast is Dh20.

★ **El Malara** BOUTIQUE HOTEL €€
(0658181836; www.elmalara.com; s/d Dh560/650;) Located above a mountain valley, expat French owners Bernardette and Jean have crafted a beautiful Moroccan guesthouse with six stylish rooms. Shared public spaces include a salon, lounge, pool and bar, and a fine attention to detail and traditional decor flows throughout the property. Rooms here represent excellent value.

El Malara is located around 15km from Tafraoute down a piste road via the Painted Rocks, best visited with your own transport.

Hôtel Les Amandiers HOTEL €€
(0528800088; www.lesamandiers-hotel.com; s/d Dh385/496;) This hilltop pile has slightly tired rooms with small balconies taking in incredible views of the rock formations ringing Tafraoute. The pool and restaurant share the views, but the bar is tucked away inside without any views. You may have the place to yourself, which will be either nice or creepy depending on how recently you've seen *The Shining*.

Eating & Drinking

Tafraoute has several cafes on the main squares, perfect for people-watching. For a sunset beer, head to the panoramic terrace at Hôtel Les Amandiers. Beer and wine is also available at Restaurant La Kasbah.

Café-Restaurant Atlas CAFE €
(mains Dh40; 8am-10pm) The covered terrace at Atlas is a popular hangout, with cheese omelettes, *brochettes* (kebabs), tajines and sandwiches on the broad menu. The sidewalk seating is a good place to keep tabs on traffic, just like the rest of the gossiping patrons.

L'Étoile d'Agadir CAFE €
(breakfast Dh30; 8am-6pm) Facing the Atlas, this is Tafraoute's favourite cafe for a continental breakfast in the morning sun. After serving breakfast, L'Etoile remains open for drinks throughout the day.

Fruit & Vegetable Market MARKET €
(7am-4pm) Located in the lanes near Place Moulay Rachid, this is a good place to grab fibrous produce for a picnic.

WORTH A TRIP

TIZOURGANE KASBAH

Overlooking the main road, roughly 65km from Tafraoute and 100km from Agadir, is the stunningly renovated 13th-century **Tizourgane Kasbah** (0661941350; www.tizourgane-kasbah.com; Route d'Agadir, Idaougnidif; r per person incl half-board Dh350;). Rooms are simply decorated, with carpets, stripy bedspreads, fans and shared bathrooms, but derive extra romance from the setting. There's a hammam, and a terrace restaurant surveys the wrinkled hillsides, scattered villages and Jebel El Kest.

The kasbah was essentially a fortified town, enclosing 25 houses, a mosque, a granary and a prison, and thick stone walls tower above the passages around the ancient structure. If you're just passing, you can tour the kasbah for Dh10. Buses on the Aït Baha route to Agadir can drop you here.

★**Restaurant La Kasbah** MOROCCAN €€
(0672303909; tajines from Dh65; noon-9pm) Decorated with rugs, lanterns and jewellery, this licensed restaurant serves dishes including a wonderful beef-and-prune tajine, *harira* (lentil soup) and the house speciality, nomad tortilla: *kalia* (minced meat with tomato, peppers, egg, onion and 44 spices served in a tajine). Argan oil and spices abound in all the dishes.

Restaurant L'Étoile du Sud MOROCCAN €€
(0528800038; set menu Dh90; noon-3pm & 6pm-late) L'Étoile du Sud serves a good set menu in a rather kitsch Bedouin-style tent. You may have to share the place with tour groups, particularly at lunchtime, but the service is professional and on warm nights it's one of the best places to eat.

Cafe-Restaurant Panorama CAFE €€
(mains Dh70; 11am-10pm;) This casual restaurant dishes up tajines, omelettes and large glasses of fruit juice. It offers what it says on the tin: panoramic views.

Hôtel Les Amandiers BAR
(4-11pm) Order a Flag Special or Heineken from the inside bar and then retire to the outside deck for great views. Just the ticket if you've been mountain biking or hiking amid Tafraoute's quirky landscapes (or even if you haven't!). Note it's around 1km southwest of the centre of town; the last bit is uphill.

Shopping

Several slipper shops around the market area sell the traditional leather slippers (yellow for men, red for women). Look out for people selling local argan and olive oil. Numerous shops around the post-office square sell Berber jewellery, argan products and souvenirs. There's less pressure shopping here than in the cities.

Au Coin des Nomades GIFTS & SOUVENIRS
Amazigh (Berber) handiwork and local souvenirs at reasonable prices. Hours are sporadic, but adjacent shopkeepers usually phone owner Houssine Laroussi if he is not around.

Maison du Troc ARTS & CRAFTS
(0528800035; Route Imiane; 9am-9pm) A good range of Amazigh (Berber) and Tuareg products, including pottery, jewellery, blankets and camel-wool kilims (carpets). Products are sourced from across the Anti Atlas region, not just locally. Proprietor Mohamed is a great source of knowledge on the area, and stocks a range of hiking and climbing books and area maps (from Dh150).

Souq ARTS & CRAFTS
(Tue & Wed) A lively weekly souq takes place near Hôtel Salama. Small dealers sometimes sell Berber carpets here.

Maison Tuareg ARTS & CRAFTS
(0670409384; Ave Mohammed V; 9am-12.30pm & 2.30-6pm Mon-Sat & by appointment) Stocks Berber and Tuareg carpets, jewellery and souvenirs from the Atlas, Rif and Sahara. Shopkeep Saïd is a shrewd salesman: we dare you to leave his shop empty-handed.

Information

There are numerous banks with ATMs and exchange facilities in the centre.

For tourist information and local events, visit www.pays-tafraout.ma.

Getting There & Away

Buses for regional destinations depart from outside the various company offices, mostly on Rue Al Jeish Al Malaki. **CTM** (0528801789; www.ctm.ma; Route Aguerd-Oudad) has departures to Tiznit (Dh40, 2½ hours) and Agadir (Dh60, 6¾ hours).

Local buses to the Ameln Valley (Dh5) leave from outside Cafe Paris every half-hour, stopping on request at different villages. Lux bus 20 to Tiznit (Dh30) leaves from a stop near Place Mohammed V.

Four buses from noon Monday to Saturday travel to Aït Mansour (Dh25) from outside the Auberge Les Amis. This service can be infrequent so check with Houssine Laroussi at Au Coin des Nomades (p408) to make sure it is still running.

Station wagons and Land Rovers do the rounds of various villages in the area, mostly on market days (Dh8). They hang around the post office square, and on Rue al Jeish Al Malaki by the Afriquia petrol station at the bottom of Tariq An Nahzi. Grands taxis leave for Tiznit (Dh40) in the morning from the latter location.

Aït Mansour Gorge

The Aït Mansour Gorge (*ah-yeet mahnsoor*) is as green and verdant as the surrounding desert is red, rocky and dry. As you crest the ridge and slowly wind your way into the valley below, you begin to hear the trickle of water and the temperature drops perceptibly, along with your blood pressure (smiling and waving locals going about their business help as well). A paradise of green vegetation and animal life, including birds, fish and frogs, at the bottom of red granite cliffs hundreds of metres high, this is a place for strolling, picnicking in the sun-dappled shade of palm trees and cooling off from the heat of the day in the time-honoured nomadic tradition.

The quiet oases of Aït Mansour are best enjoyed by walking or cycling, so you can greet locals and pull off the asphalt to explore the palm groves and pools.

Sleeping & Eating

There is simple accommodation in Aït Mansour and Tiouadou. Contact Houssine at Au Coin des Nomades (p408) or Mohamed at Maison du Troc in Tafraoute to book accommodation in these areas.

Auberge Aït Mansour GUESTHOUSE €
(0676735198; Aït Mansour; r per person Dh80) In the village of Aït Mansour at the beginning of the oasis, Auberge Aït Mansour offers mattresses on the floor and new flush toilets. Owner Abdou can guide you to the old village nearby for oasis views and cooks a mean Berber omelette.

Auberge Sahnoun GUESTHOUSE €
(0528218365, 0667095376; maisonsahnoun@gmail.com; Tiouadou; r per person incl half-board Dh150) A T-intersection at Afella Ighir leads 5km northeast to the village of Tiouadou, where the family-run Auberge Sahnoun is on the edge of a *palmeraie*. It has three basic rooms, with mattresses on the floor and a shared bathroom with hot water, and a roof terrace. The auberge's late owner, Mohamed Sahnoun, was involved in village development projects.

Chez Messaoud MOROCCAN €
(0670793567; tajines Dh30; 10am-7pm) Messaoud and his family dish up simple Moroccan fare, like tajines and omelettes, as well as a wide variety of cold sodas and juices. You can eat on a little dirt patio or at plastic tables by the roadside (surprisingly the more verdant option). Chez Messaoud is located in the middle of the gorge, about 25km from the turnoff from R107 in the settlement of Aït Mansour proper.

Getting There & Away

It's a gorgeous drive from Tafraoute. Twisting mountain roads will either delight or terrify, or maybe both. If you're self-driving, take all the necessary precaution (beep your horn at blind corners and drive slowly enough to veer off the one-lane road if a truck comes suddenly speeding around the corner).

BICYCLE

Cycling the gorge is a wonderful way to experience its slow pace. But unless you're in extremely good shape, cycling from Tafraoute would be an ambitious undertaking. Pick up a bike and bike rack from Tafraoute VTT (p408) for a more relaxed day trip.

BUS

A bus operates on an irregular basis, and schedules are subject to change. Contact the good folks at Au Coin des Nomades (p408) or Maison du Troc in Tafraoute for the latest information.

CAR & MOTORCYCLE

Leave Tafraoute on R107 to Aguerd-Oudad. Just after passing the town of Aousift there's a sign for Aït Mansour at a fork in the road. Take the left fork, and wind your way up a nerve-rattling, narrow road with plenty of blind corners and far too few guard rails. From the intersection it's 25km to the oasis of Aït Mansour; the views are spectacular the whole way.

From Aït Mansour, it's another 10km to a T-intersection at Afella Ighir. If you're driving a normal car, turn around here; if you're in a 4x4, feeling adventurous and it hasn't rained you can turn left here toward the town of Tiouadou, and carry on through the Timguilcht Gorge via the towns of Tizerkine and Taghaout (27km), rejoining the road back to Tafraoute at Taloust.

Alternatively, hire a 4x4 and driver from Maison du Troc in Tafraoute. Expect to pay around Dh1200.

Ameln Valley & Jebel El Kest وادي املين وجبل لكست

Nestled in a valley dramatically set beneath soaring, craggy red rock cliffs culminating in **Jebel El Kest** (2359m), the picturesque Amazigh villages surrounding Tafraoute seem to reflect the colour of the rocks around them: in the morning the town glows yellow-gold, slowly changing throughout the day to ruddy rose as the sun sets. If watching (or photographing) the gorgeous light on weird rock formations isn't enough for you, the mountains surrounding also offer myriad trekking and climbing opportunities.

Sights

★Maison Traditionnelle MUSEUM
(0666918145; Oumesnate; Dh10; 8am-sunset) The 3-storey granite, palm and argan house, some 400 years old, was inhabited by 20 family members – three generations – until 1982. The owner, Mohammed, is friendly, knowledgeable and multilingual, and obviously takes great pleasure in sharing tales of traditional life. On the tour you'll wind your way through the central kitchen, storehouse, bedrooms and, finally, the salon reserved for formal guests (you!). Highly recommended.

At Oumesnate, 6km from Tafraoute, follow the signs through the village and then the footpath to this museum house.

Rock Engravings ARCHAEOLOGICAL SITE
(Tirnmatmat) The village of Tirnmatmat is the furthest from Tafraoute of the Ameln Valley's 26 villages, and features interesting rock engravings of various animals and hunters. The carvings are undated, but archaeologists think they may be prehistoric. The drive up to the village, through the dramatic rocky valley, is just as nice as the engravings.

To find the rock engravings at Tirnmatmat, take the Tiznit road (R104), then after 14km turn north at Tahala towards Aït Omar. Just before the village, an unmarked track leads to Tirnmatmat, where you will find the engravings along the riverbed (the local kids will lead you there, or you can engage a guide from Tafraoute). The village sits in a lovely spot and there are excellent walks in all directions.

Sleeping & Eating

The villages have numerous basic *gîtes* (trekkers' hostels), *maisons d'hôtes* (small hotels) and homestays; Au Coin des Nomades (p408) or Maison du Troc (p410) can organise a stay.

L'Arganier d'Ammelne HOTEL €
(0528800069; www.arganierammelne.com; Route d'Agadir, Tandilt; s/d incl half-board Dh280/380;) L'Arganier d'Ammelne's pink, yellow and *pisé* rooms open onto a flowery garden. The terrace restaurant (meals/menu Dh40/80) serves dishes including local specialities and a delicious beef tajine with apricots, almonds and prunes. Five new rooms and a new swimming pool are evidence the owners are keen to make sure their accommodation remains one of the friendliest around.

Yamina GUESTHOUSE €
(0670523883, 0528216621; www.yamina-tafraout.com; Tandilt; r per person incl half-board Dh250;) At the top of the village, Yamina is run by an Amazigh (Berber) woman and her French husband, who have created a unique cross between a comfortable guesthouse and a *maison traditionnelle* (traditional house). Reached along terraces, courtyards and earthen walkways with low ceilings, the simple rooms are beautifully decorated with cheery paintwork on the walls and beams.

Oumesnate Maison d'Hôte GUESTHOUSE €
(0661513793; Oumesnate; per person incl half-board Dh250;) Staying in the guesthouse next to Oumesnate's Maison Traditionnelle – run by the same family – is a wonderful way to get an insight into Amazigh (Berber) village life. Rooms have en suites, and meals (Dh70) are available with notice. Trekking, 4WD and bike tours can be arranged.

Chez Amaliya HOTEL €€
(0528800065; www.chezamaliya.com; Tazoulte; s/d from Dh330/500; closed Jun;) A few hundred metres past the turning for Tandilt, Oumesnate and Agadir, this hotel is one of the valley's grandest options. A nomad-style tent and Jebel El Kest's lion face rise dramatically beyond the pool, and paintings and local maps decorate the foyer. Rooms are comfortable, and there are three spacious rooftop apartments (Dh1000) good for groups and families.

Chez Amaliya has the most well-stocked bar for many a mountain valley, and the smart restaurant (menu Dh100) is open from noon to 9pm and accepts nonguests. The chicken *bastilla* is recommended, but you'll need to give the kitchen at least two hours' notice.

Bio Beldi MOROCCAN €
(0697820288; restaurantbiobeldi@gmail.com; Aït Omgas; 9am-11.30pm; tajines from Dh30)

Friendly proprietor Yassine has done an excellent job converting the family home into a welcoming restaurant, the only one of its kind in the Ameln Valley, complete with a back garden. Tajines and couscous are great value and tasty, especially the gratis homemade goat cheese and crudités that begin every meal here.

To get there, head north from Tafraoute on R105, then turn left toward Chez Amaliya. Bio Beldi is just under four kilometres into the valley once you make the turn, in the tiny settlement of Aït Oumgas.

Getting There & Away

Grands taxis (Dh8) head along the main road between the villages, and Tafraoute has regular bus services (Dh5). Note these buses also double as the school bus and only run during the day.

Tata طاطا

0528 / POP 18,611

Situated on the Saharan plain at the foot of Jebel Bani, Tata seems a long way from anywhere. An oasis settlement that sprung up on trade routes from West Africa, Tata roughly means 'take a break' in Tashelhit (a Tamazight dialect). Today, the town's remoteness and the turban-wrapped men sipping tea in the shade recall those caravan days of yore. Close to the Algerian border, the small town has a garrison feel, and with four types of police and military stationed here you may be questioned on your way into town.

The town's *palmeraie* is well worth exploring. You can drive a 7km circuit of it, or catch a local bus (Dh5). Above the village at the far end of the *palmeraie* is a white hilltop *marabout* (saint's tomb), which you can see from Tata.

Tours

Tata is best as a base for off-the-beaten-track excursions, such as desert camping. The oasis, kasbah and *agadir* (fortified granary) at the nearby village of Akka, as well as the the rock engravings in the area, are all among the finest in Morocco. The rock carvings aren't easy to find: you'll need to hire a guide.

Maison du Patrimoine OUTDOORS
(0613241312; issam3599@hotmail.com; Ave Mohammed V; 10am-4pm) Helpful multilingual Amazigh (Berber) guide Isam, based at souvenir shop Maison du Patrimoine, charges about Dh350 per day for one or two people (Dh900 including 4WD). Opening hours are very flexible; it's best to contact him by email or phone before arriving in Tata.

Sleeping & Eating

Accommodation options include basic hotels around the souq, more comfortable options with private bathrooms, and a special authentic kasbah experience.

The only option for a cold beer is the bar at the Hotel Les Relais des Sables. The ambience inside is a tad smokey and blokey; it's far more enjoyable having a Moroccan dust-dousing beer outside, sitting by the pool.

Hôtel La Renaissance HOTEL €
(0528802225; larenaissance1982@gmail.com; Ave des FAR; s/d Dh150/200; wi-fi) This central stalwart with *palmeraie* views has small but spotless rooms and a pleasant lounge and breakfast terrace. The only downsides are the cramped bathrooms and the somewhat gloomy downstairs bar, without a woman in sight. Breakfast is a little expensive at Dh50.

Municipal Campsite CAMPGROUND €
(Ave Mohammed V; per tent incl shower from Dh30) Next to the dry river, with a reasonable ablutions block that has flush toilets. It's the only option in town for DIY campers.

Oasis Dar Ouanou GUESTHOUSE €€
(0660232538; www.dar-wanou.e-monsite.com; Akka Izankad; r from Dh500; wi-fi) By the N12 3km southwest of Tata, this ramshackle but clean building has cool rooms, a courtyard with fountains and palms, and oasis and mountain views from the roof terrace. Highly recommended if you have your own transport.

Dar Infiane GUESTHOUSE €€
(0661610170, 0528802104; www.darinfiane.com; Infiane; r per person from Dh570; pool) Tata's old kasbah, perched above the *palmeraie*, has been turned into a Green Key guesthouse. The 10 rooms are decorated with wonderful, authentic details, including original eccentricities like low beams. There's a roof terrace for sunning and a tiny plunge pool for cooling off. Some guests rave about magical evenings in the still of the Sahara night, but others have found fault with the service.

Hotel Les Relais des Sables HOTEL €€
(0528802301; www.hotelrelaisdessables.com; Ave des FAR; s/d from Dh360/460; wi-fi pool) The pool, bar, restaurant and gardens are more impressive than the small en-suite rooms

in stuffy bungalows. It's popular with tour groups and overlanders, and a new renovation will spiff up communal areas even more.

Even if you're not staying here it's worth popping in for a frosty Flag Special – it's the only place you'll get a cold beer for many a dusty kilometre.

Oasis de Rêve MOROCCAN €
(Ave Mohammed V; mains Dh30-40; ⏲8am-11pm) Located on the edge of the souq at the southern end of Tata's main drag, Oasis de Rêve has a friendly, welcoming owner with a smidgen of English and the ability to rustle up something good most times of the day. How does chicken *brochettes*, chips and salad for around Dh40 sound?

ℹ Getting There & Away

Tata's Gare Routière is located just south of the centre of town. CTM and Supratours do not serve Tata, but **Satas** (☎0672311843; Gare Routière; ⏲8.30am-12.30pm & 2-6pm Mon-Sat) has daily departures to Agadir (Dh100, eight hours), Goulimime (Dh102, five hours), Marrakesh (Dh170, 10 hours), Taroudant (Dh60, five hours), Tiznit (Dh80, 6½ hours) and Zagora (Dh92, eight hours).

Grands taxis leave from Place de la Marche Verte to Akka-Irhen for Taliouine (Dh30), Agadir (Dh100), Bouizakarne for Tiznit (Dh100), Goulimime (Dh80), Igherm for Tafraoute (Dh50), Ouarzazate (Dh140) and Taroudant (Dh80).

Trekking in the Anti Atlas

The arid, pink- and ochre-coloured Anti Atlas, the last significant mountains before the Sahara, are little visited despite the wonderful outdoor opportunities. Taliouine is well set up for trekking, and Tafraoute is the centre of a burgeoning climbing scene. The quartzite massif of **Jebel El Kest** (2359m), the 'amethyst mountain', lies about 10km north of Tafraoute, and the twin peaks of **Adrar Mqorn** (2344m) are 10km southeast. Beneath the jagged mass of these peaks lie lush irrigated valleys and a string of oases.

At the eastern end of the Anti Atlas near Taliouine, **Jebel Siroua** (3305m) rises starkly above the landscape. This dramatic volcano makes an excellent centrepiece for varied long-distance treks.

For further advice, and to arrange guides, mules and gear, contact operators in Tafraoute, Taliouine and Taroudant.

Around Tafraoute

Morocco has such a wealth of trekking options that perhaps it is not surprising that an area with the potential of Tafraoute has not yet been fully exploited. The adventurous trekker will find here, as elsewhere in the Moroccan south, many challenging and rewarding routes. Because of local depopulation caused by movement to the cities and the decline in the use of mules for agriculture, many paths are partially abandoned, and nature is particularly wild here. Trekkers might spot Cuvier's gazelles, wild boars, Barbary sheep and rich endemic vegetation.

This is a tougher area than the M'Goun Massif or Tichka Plateau, and visitors will need to cope with a lack of facilities and the harsh climate. This close to the Sahara, summer (June until mid-September) is blisteringly hot, and winter sees the occasional snowfall on the high passes and peaks, so the region is best tackled at the end of winter. Late February is ideal. Daytime temperatures may be 20°C, but at night it can drop below freezing.

Other than the odd small shop, you won't find many supplies in the area, so the great challenge is carrying enough food and water to keep you going. As with other remote Moroccan areas, it is often possible to stay in village houses, but you must still be prepared to camp and to carry food and water.

The best way of doing this is by hiring a guide and mules; there are trekking guides – and *faux guides* (unofficial guides) – in Tafraoute. As ever, insist on seeing a guide's ID card before you start discussing possibilities. As a rule, trained mountain guides do not tout for business in the street. Mules are rarely found around Tafraoute, but you may be able to arrange this through your guide.

Jebel El Kest and the approaches from Tafraoute are covered by the 1:50,000 map sheets *Had Tahala* and *Tanalt,* while the whole area is covered by 1:100,000 sheets *Annzi, Tafrawt, Foum Al Hisn* and *Taghjijt*. David Wood's book *Walks and Scrambles in the Anti-Atlas* (Ciccerone 2018) is also a wonderful reference. You should be able to find these resources with super-helpful Mohammed in Maison du Troc (p410), in specialist bookshops or in good big-city bookshops in Morocco.

This part of the Atlas is not well developed for tourism, and transport is an issue throughout. *Camionettes* (pick-up trucks) and minibuses provide a reliable though infrequent service to some villages and grands

Around Tafraoute

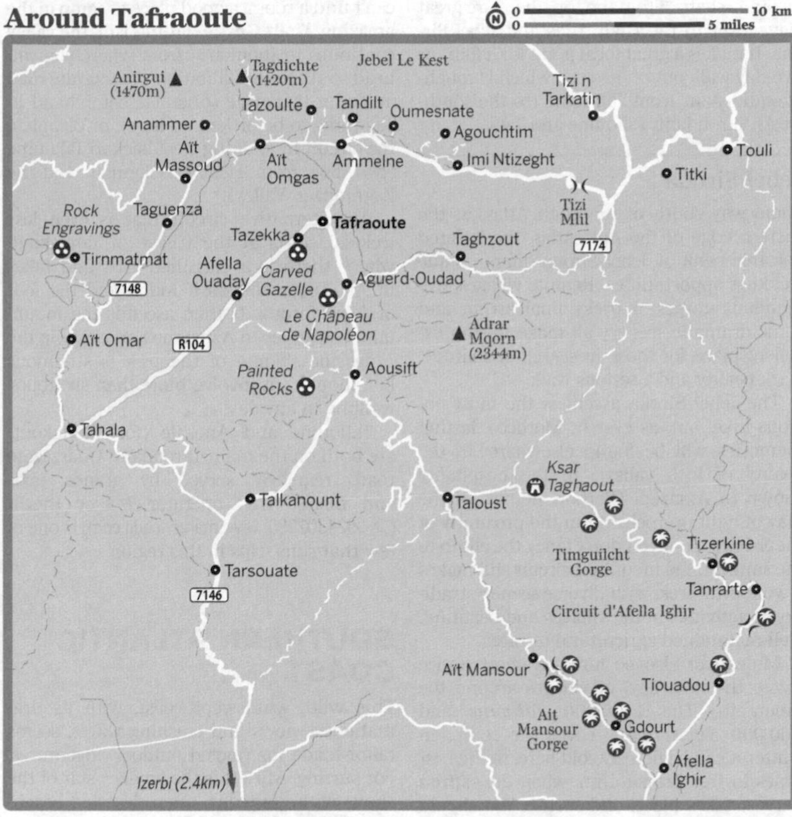

taxis run on souq days, but at other times you may need to hire one to get to trailheads. As always, we don't recommend hitching.

Adrar Mqorn & Around

Southeast of Tafraoute the possibilities are exciting. The scramble up Adrar Mqorn (2344m) is hard but worthwhile. Due south of its twin peaks are the palm-filled oasis gorges of **Aït Mansour** and **Timguilcht**.

Ameln Valley

There are some 26 villages neatly spaced out through the Ameln Valley, which runs along the south side of Jebel El Kest, and they make for a great walk. You'd need weeks to do a full circuit, but a stunningly beautiful and suitably stretching five-day walk would start in **Oumesnate**, take in several villages and head up to Tagdichte for an ascent of Jebel El Kest. Alternatively, the ascent could be tackled as part of a gentle trek east through the valley from, say, **Tirnmatmat** to Oumesnate, both just off the road. You could also base yourself at Oumesnate Maison d'Hôte (p412) and go on treks from there.

Jebel El Kest

The area's star attraction is this massive quartzite ridge that stretches away northwest of Tafraoute. Despite the harshness of the landscape, the Imazighen (Berbers) who live in local villages manage to grow the mountain staples of wheat, barley, olives, figs and almonds. The village of **Tagdichte** is the launching point for a day ascent of Jebel El Kest (2359m). Tagdichte can be accessed by minibus or taxi, and homestay accommodation can be arranged there.

Jebel Aklim

Jebel Aklim (2531m) sits in an even remoter area than Jebel El Kest, yet is surrounded by Amazigh (Berber) villages in valleys guarded by old kasbahs. From the top, there are great views over to the High Atlas and Jebel Siroua. It makes a great focal point for a four- or five-day walk out of **Igherm**, which is roughly equidistant from Tafraoute (to the southwest), Taroudant, Taliouine and Tata.

Jebel Siroua

Some way south of the High Atlas, at the eastern edge of the Anti Atlas, the isolated volcanic peak of Jebel Siroua offers unique trekking opportunities. Remote villages, tremendous gorges, a tricky final ascent and some dramatic scenery all make this an excellent place for those in search of solitude, stark beauty and a serious walk.

The Jebel Siroua ascent is the most obvious hike, but, as ever in Morocco, lasting memories will be found elsewhere: in the beauty of lush valleys, in the hospitality shown in Amazigh (Berber) homes, in the play of light on rock and in the proximity of the Sahara. So if you don't fancy the climb to the summit, the mountain circuit still makes a wonderful trek, with diverse scenery, traditional activities in the villages and beautiful, well-maintained agricultural terraces.

Mules can also be hired at short notice (often the next day) at villages around the mountain. The 1:100,000 *Taliwine* and 1:50,000 *Sirwa* maps cover the route. In winter it can be fiercely cold here, so the best times to trek are autumn, when the saffron harvest takes place, and spring. You should be able to find these maps in Maison du Troc (p410), in specialist bookshops or in good big-city bookshops in Morocco.

If you need supplies, there are small stores in Taliouine and Tazenart, and weekly markets take place in Taliouine, Aoulouz, Askaoun, Tazenakht and Igli.

ROUTES

There's a challenging, week-long trek that allows you to walk out of Taliouine along a gentle dirt trail, which heads eastward up the **Zagmouzen Valley** to **Tagmout**. The route then heads northeast through **Atougha**, from where the summit of Jebel Siroua is best reached in two days, with a night at **Tegragra**. Walking at a regular pace, you'll ascend the summit on the morning of the fourth day.

After descending into the gorges, you'll reach the extraordinary cliff village of **Tizgui**, where you can spend the night, before continuing to **Tagouyamt** on the fifth day. The village has limited supplies and, in case you can't find a room, a good place to camp in the amazing **Tislit Gorge**. From Tislit, the valley continues to Ihoukarn, from where you can head south to the Taliouine–Ouarzazate road at Tizi n'Taghatine (organise beforehand in Taliouine to be picked up here); or complete the circuit by walking west back to Taliouine (two days from Tislit via Tagmout and the Zagmouzen Valley).

An alternative circuit that is even less trekked starts at the village of Tamlakout, where there is a classified *gîte*, and takes in Aït Tigga, the Assif Mdist and the foot of Jebel Siroua. It then ascends the mountain, continues to Aziouane and exits via the Amassines. Some of the trek is strenuous but should not involve more than six hours' walking in any day.

Taliouine and Anezale (for Tamlakout) are both on the main Taroudant–Ouarzazate road, regularly served by grands taxis and buses. Trek operator **Maroc Inédit** (☎0524302985; www.maroc-inedit.com) is one of few that runs trips in this region.

SOUTHERN ATLANTIC COAST

This wild, windswept coast, with its dramatic sea views and crashing waves, seems tailor-made for rugged outdoor adventures. For surfing, Mirleft is the low-key star of the show, with gorgeous, often deserted beaches offering a variety of waves. The Spanish art-deco colonial gardens and buildings of Sidi Ifni offer a more genteel experience.

Inland, hillsides bursting with cacti and argan trees give way to the northwest reaches of the Sahara and its dunes, bizarre rock formations and oases. Tiznit, a regional centre of Islamic learning with an architecturally important mosque and labyrinthine silver souq, is as cosmopolitan as it gets around here. In other population centres, like Goulimime and Tan Tan, time slips sleepily by until the weekly souq, where locals from around the region trade camels and other desert essentials.

Tiznit تزنيت

☎0528 / POP 74,699

Tiznit (*tihz-niht*) is a walled medina town with a serious sense of hometown pride. One of the largest cities in the south, it's more cosmopolitan than other places in this dusty region: as a capital of Islamic scholarship, imams come here to study from throughout Morocco and even the Sahel. Tiznit's central mosque is of architectural note, featuring protruding wooden poles that echo the famous religious centre in Timbuktu. The city also has a significant Jewish footprint, including a historic Jewish quarter where silversmiths forged jewellery and other raiment.

The central souq remains a wonderful place to shop for Berber silver, both traditional and modern, especially after locals emerge from their heat-of-the-day siesta to catch up on the afternoon's gossip. It's a conservative but friendly place, and excellent dining and accommodation options make Tiznit a natural stopover between the Anti Atlas and the coast.

History

In 1881 Sultan Moulay Al Hassan (1873–94) founded Tiznit as a base from which to assert his authority over the rebellious Amazigh (Berber) tribes of the south. To do this, he built the town's perimeter walls. Jewish silversmiths were moved into the town and gave it a reputation for silver workmanship.

However, Tiznit remained embroiled in local sedition and was a centre of dissent against the 1912 treaty that turned Morocco into a French and Spanish protectorate. This resistance movement was led by El Hiba, the so-called Blue Sultan from the Western Sahara, who earned his nickname for always wearing his Sahrawi veil.

Following Sultan Moulay Hafid's capitulation to the French at the Treaty of Fez, El Hiba proclaimed himself sultan here in 1912. The notoriously fierce southern tribes rose to support him, and El Hiba marched north at the head of an army of men from the Tuareg and Anti Atlas tribes. They were welcomed as liberators in Marrakesh, but much of the army was slaughtered by the French as it moved towards Fez. El Hiba retreated to Taroudant and then Tiznit and then up into the Anti Atlas, where he pursued a campaign of resistance against the French until his death in 1919.

Sights

Grande Mosquée MOSQUE

The minaret of the Grande Mosquée (closed to non-Muslims) is studded with jutting wooden sticks, in the style of Sahel mosques including the famous Djinguereber Mosque in Timbuktu, Mali. Local legend suggests this is where the souls of the dead congregate. More likely, these were left in place by the masons who built the minaret to help them climb up and replaster. There's a very atmospheric single palm standing in the small square at the mosque's entrance.

Tiznit City Walls HISTORIC SITE

Built in 1886 by Sultan Hassan I, the 5km of plaster walls signify the inauguration of Tiznit as an official city. It's possible to climb onto sections of the walls, which have some 30 towers and nine gates. On the northern side of the medina, **Bab Targua** overlooks a *palmeraie* with a natural spring, used as a laundry by local women.

Source Bleue SPRING

The original town spring is now a shallow, stagnant pool, and green rather than blue. Legend claims a woman of ill repute, Lalla Zninia, stopped to rest here at what was then plain desert. She spent the next three days repenting her wicked ways, and God was so impressed that he showed forgiveness by having a spring gush beneath her feet.

Her name was thus given to the village that preceded Sultan Moulay Al Hassan's 19th-century fortress town. The adjacent citadel is undergoing careful restoration and is also worthy of a quick stroll. Nearby are more jewellery and Berber crafts shops.

Sleeping

Hotels are gathered around the large roundabout to the southeast of Bab Aït Jarrar, with a few options in the medina.

Bab El Maader GUESTHOUSE €

(☎0673907314; ym@bab-el-maader.com; 132 Rue El Haj Ali; r €30; ⊗Oct-Jun) This traditional house in the medina is one of Tiznit's best addresses, a five-room guesthouse with a courtyard, plenty of great decorative touches and good use of Moroccan fabrics and materials. Staff can also arrange trips in

OFF THE BEATEN TRACK

AGLOU PLAGE

At the south end of Aglou beach is **Le Chant du Chameau** (☎0667904991; www.chantduchameau.com; per person incl half-board €35), a delightful French-Moroccan guesthouse. Apart from a rust-red house, some fantasy tents and a dramatic view of the beach and sea, it also offers excursions in the area and a week-long course in *tadelakt* (Moroccan plaster works).

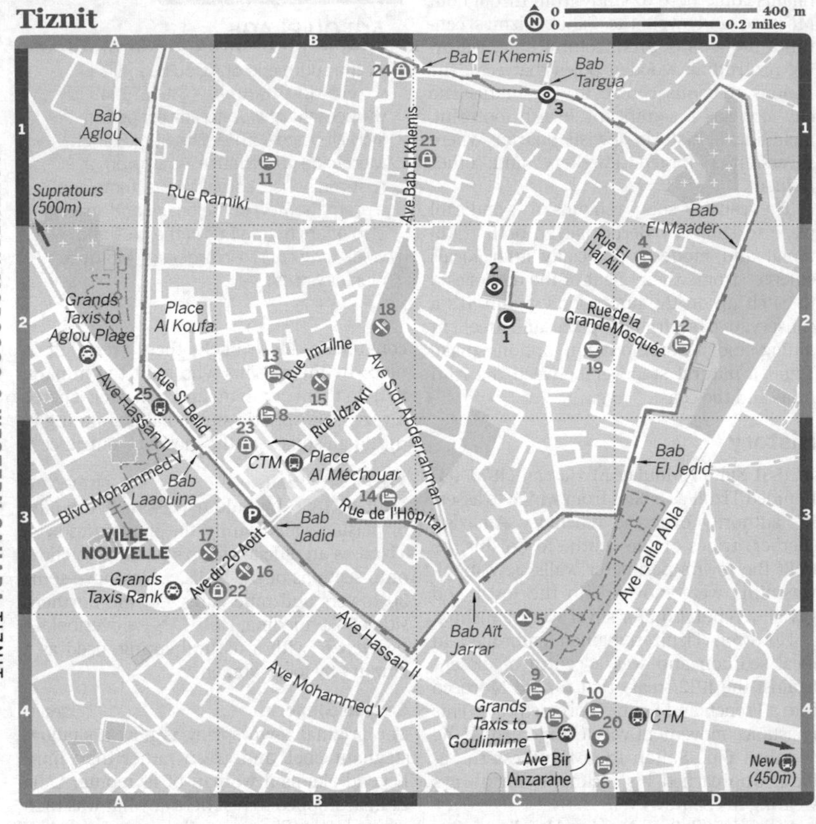

Tiznit

Sights
1 Grande Mosquée C2
2 Source Bleue C2
3 Tiznit City Walls C1

Sleeping
4 Bab El Maader D2
5 Camping Municipal C4
6 Hôtel Al Amal C4
7 Hôtel de Paris C4
8 Hôtel des Touristes B2
9 Hôtel Idou Tiznit C4
10 Hôtel Tiznit C4
11 Maison Du Soleil B1
12 Riad Janoub D2
13 Riad Le Lieu B2
14 Tigmi Kenza B3

Eating
15 À l'Ombre du Figuier B2
16 Food Market B3
17 La Ville Nouvelle A3
Restaurant Al Amal (see 6)
Riad Le Lieu (see 13)
18 Snack Stands B2

Drinking & Nightlife
19 Espace Asrir C2
20 Hotel Mauritania C4

Shopping
21 Bijouterie Bab Alkhmis C1
22 Ensemble Artisanal B3
23 Jewellery Souq B3
24 Trésor du Sud B1

Transport
25 Bus Stop for Sidi Ifni and Mirleft A2

the region. Be sure to email in advance; in the off-season or shoulder season, the hosts might not be receiving guests.

Hôtel des Touristes HOTEL €
(☎0528862018; Place Al Méchouar; s/d from Dh60/105; 📶) This welcoming 1st-floor hotel is a dependable, central budget option. Rooms are entered from a quiet, cheerful communal area with a book exchange; those overlooking Place Al Méchouar have small balconies, but all lack fans (and much privacy). The room next to the flush toilet is particularly hot and noisy.

Hôtel de Paris HOTEL €
(☎0528862865; Ave Hassan II; s/d Dh120/160; 📶) The simple rooms with en suites are clean and bright, and a handy cafe-restaurant downstairs makes Hôtel de Paris a good choice if you're just overnighting between buses.

Hôtel Tiznit HOTEL €
(☎0528862411; tiznit-hotel@menara.ma; Ave Bir Anzarane; s/d Dh250/310; P📶🏊) Set in leafy grounds with a large pool, Tiznit is a little retro, with ashtrays outside each room and pink frilly upholstery. Rooms are reasonably spacious, though, and it's behind a secure gate. Women travellers may prefer this hotel to the other budget options in town, as there is no attached cafe filled with staring men.

Camping Municipal CAMPGROUND €
(☎0528601354; Bab Aït Jarrar; per person Dh36) The municipal campground, next to the old walls, is a serviceable choice if you're doing DIY accomms. Don't expect atmosphere.

★ **Riad Janoub** GUESTHOUSE €€
(☎0528602726, 0679005510; www.riadjanoub.com; 193 Rue de la Grande Mosquée; r from €70; 📶🏊) Polyglot owners Priya and Aby are attentive hosts in this modern riad, which has Moroccan and European salons, a massage room and a roof terrace, all overlooking the restful pool and garden of palms and cacti. The seven comfortable rooms, including a wheelchair-accessible option, have soft colour schemes, rugs and traditional trimmings. Aby is a wealth of knowledge about Tiznit. Poolside dinners at the riad are exceptional, including a unique Indian-Moroccan fusion menu. Breakfast included.

Tigmi Kenza RIAD €€
(☎0528600362; www.tigmi-kenza.com; 30 Rue Al Mourabitine; r from Dh650) Kenza's six elegantly simple rooms are centred around a petite, tiled courtyard with a marble fountain. Look out for the traditional carved doors and wooden ceilings. Bathrooms are huge and gorgeously tiled in blue.

Maison Du Soleil GUESTHOUSE €€
(☎0672311353; www.facebook.com/maisondusoleiltiznit; 470 Rue Tafoukt; r from €45; 📶) The 'House of the Sun' fulfills its name on the rooftop terrace, bursting with a variety of plants, and the two spacious en-suite rooms adjoining it. The rooms with shared bathrooms downstairs are more prosaic, but host Mohamed is friendly and super-organised. The bright interior decor is a colourful surprise just metres from the medina's neutral walls. Rates are negotiable.

Hôtel Al Amal HOTEL €€
(☎0528862462; 465 Ave Bir Anzarane; s/d Dh320/420; P📶) Majid is the garrulous proprietor of this hotel, and he's *very* proud of the smart TVs in each of his 12 spotless, modern rooms. There's also a big Moroccan-style salon in the basement, a varied breakfast menu at the good cafe and protected parking for overlanders. He's got big plans for the roof terrace, which already has sweeping views.

Riad Le Lieu GUESTHOUSE €€
(☎0528600019; riadlelieu@hotmail.fr; 273 Impasse Issaoui; s/d Dh220/525; 📶) Five double rooms and suites share this former courthouse with the restaurant of the same name. One suite has a private shower, but otherwise the rooms all share bathrooms. The interior is colourful but otherwise nothing special; it's the warm welcome and copious breakfast (Dh30) that make this a relaxing haven in the medina.

Hôtel Idou Tiznit BUSINESS HOTEL €€
(☎0528600333; Ave Hassan II; r from Dh500; P🏊) Modern business rooms surround a big, bright pool that no one ever seems to swim in. If you're travelling for work, this is a comfortable option just on the town's central roundabout. You can even get a beer at the downstairs bar.

Eating & Drinking

Tiznit punches above its weight in terms of eating options, including atmospheric riads, Moroccan-Indian fusion and a stylish and innovative restaurant in a hidden medina courtyard.

Restaurant Al Amal MOROCCAN €
(☎0528862462; 465 Ave Bir Anzarane; mains Dh30-50; ⏰8am-11pm; 📶) The welcoming Al Amal Hotel hosts a couple of good eating

options pitched at a higher level than most of the city's other cafes and restaurants. Seafood, tajines and good pasta are the standouts; the downstairs cafe is known for good breakfasts.

La Ville Nouvelle CAFE €
(17 Ave du 20 Août; mains Dh30-66; ⏲7am-9pm; 📶) At this popular multistorey cafe, brisk waiters serve the classic salads, *brochettes*, tajines and *kefta* (meatballs). It's also a top spot for coffee and Tiznit's best French-style baked goods. There's even a special non-smoking floor.

Snack Stands FAST FOOD €
(snacks from Dh5; ⏲11am-10pm) Along Ave Sidi Abderhman, the main road through the medina, these stalls are good for a cheap, fast feed.

Food Market MARKET €
(Ave du 20 Août; ⏲9am-4pm Mon-Sat) Good option for picnic supplies – especially the incredible varieties of dates – and for atmospheric wandering.

★ **À l'Ombre du Figuier** MOROCCAN €€
(☎0528861204; www.facebook.com/ombredufiguier; 22 Passage Akchouch, Quartier Idzakri; mains Dh60-75; ⏲11.30am-11.30pm Tue-Sun) Follow the signs through alleyways and under low doorways to one of southern Morocco's best restaurants. Colourful tables are arrayed under the dappled shade of a sprawling fig tree. The menu is meat-heavy, with lamb, beef and turkey, but there's often a seafood *plat du jour*. Side dishes include a delicious cucumber and melon soup or Moroccan salad. For dessert, refresh the palate with chilled pineapple gazpacho.

Riad Le Lieu MOROCCAN €€
(☎0528600019; 273 Impasse Issaoui; mains Dh35-75; ⏲8am-10pm; 📶) The charming Aïcha attracts locals and tourists alike with her daily specials, which typically include tomato and goat-cheese salad, *bastilla* and camel, beef or sardine tajines. The intimate setting is a yellow courtyard with foliage and lanterns overhead. There are just four tables, so it pays to drop by and book ahead.

Espace Asrir CAFE
(☎0662767904; 133 Rue Id Ali Oubihi; ⏲10am-11pm; 📶) Housed in a heritage courtyard house, Asrir is a surprising find amid the winding alleyways of Tiznit's medina. Tasty juices and coffee are served to a soundtrack of delicate birdsong, and old radios and a piano fill nooks and crannies perfect for escaping the Moroccan sun. Tiznit's younger residents come to chat over shisha, mint tea and light snacks.

Hotel Mauritania BAR
(Ave Bir Anzarane; ⏲10am-10pm) One of the only places in town to get a cold beer, the back bar at the Hotel Mauritania dispenses icy Heineken and Flag Special, making it a favourite watering hole of visiting motorcycle riders and 4WD desert-bashing enthusiasts. It's a little dismal, but you probably won't care after a few rounds.

Shopping

Tiznit medina makes for a fun wander, especially around spots such as the jewellery souq and Rue Imzilne, a street of leather-sandal shops. Things come alive in the cool of the evening, with folks out gossiping and watching passersby. The Amazigh (Berber) traders here are tough salesmen, but it is still worth trying to strike a bargain. Things liven up considerably on Thursday, which is market day.

Bijouterie Bab Alkhmis JEWELLERY
(☎0667306664; Ave Bab El Khemis; ⏲8am-8pm) A good selection for traditional silver and Berber handicrafts. Proprietor Mohammed has good knowledge of tribal jewellery variations and a sly sense of humour. Bring your bargaining skills, but don't forget you're also paying for the fun experience of chatting with him.

Trésor du Sud JEWELLERY
(Ave Bab El Khemis, Ave Sidi Abderhman; ⏲9am-noon & 3-5pm Mon-Sat, also by appointment) Jewellery shops are found along Ave Sidi Abderhman, the main road through the medina. At the top, Trésor du Sud is not the cheapest, but the work is good and it deals in hallmarked solid silver.

Jewellery Souq JEWELLERY
(⏲8.30am-8pm Mon-Sat) With its long history of silversmiths, the jewellery souq has some of southern Morocco's best work. It's a pleasant place to wander, with blue-doored shops and windows full of silverware. Some of the jewellery is made in Tiznit and some from Saharan tribes to the south. You'll need time to look around and bargain to get the best prices.

Ensemble Artisanal JEWELLERY
(Ave du 20 Août; ⏲9am-12.30pm & 2.30-8pm Mon-Sat) If you're after more modern-looking silver jewellery, the artisans assembled at this

neo-souq ply their shiny wares in brightly lit display cases. There's a lot to choose from and there's little pressure to buy.

Getting There & Around

BUS

Inter-city buses will eventually leave from the new bus station just off the Tafraoute road, but at the time of writing this new departure point was still not open. CTM has an office closer to the centre on the same road, and also one on Place Al Méchouar in the medina. CTM serves Agadir (Dh40, two hours), Dakhla (Dh370, 20 hours), Goulimime (Dh45, 2½ hours), Laayoune (Dh210, nine hours), Tafraoute (Dh40, 2½ hours) and Tan Tan (Dh95, 4½ hours). **Supratours** (www.supratours.ma) has similar services from its office northwest of the medina.

Cheaper bus offices are clustered on Ave Lalla Abla, just northeast of the roundabout near Bab Aït Jarrar.

Green Lux buses leave from a stand near Bab Laaouina on the western edge of the medina. Bus 18 travels to Sidi Ifni (Dh20, two hours) via Mirleft (Dh10, one hour).

GRANDS TAXIS

Taxis leave from the main grand-taxi rank, opposite the main post office in the western part of town, serving Agadir (Dh35), Inezgane (Dh30), Mirleft (Dh15), Sidi Ifni (Dh27) and Tafraoute (Dh40).

Taxis for Aglou Plage (Dh6) leave from a stand on Ave Hassan II, and for Goulimime (Dh35) from a stand just south of the roundabout near Bab Oulad Jarrar (across Route de Goulimime from the Total garage).

PETITS TAXIS

Red petits taxis charge Dh7 for a journey (Dh10 after 7.30pm), maximum three occupants.

Mirleft ميرلفت

0528 / POP 7026

Sleepy Mirleft (*meer-left*) is the unassuming, yet undisputed, star of Morocco's southern-beach scene. Some of the best surf and sand in the country stretch out a few minutes' drive from a dusty main drag, painted atmospherically in pink and purple. Despite punching above its weight in terms of hotels, hostels and charming cafes, this town remains sleepily Moroccan; in the streets sides of goat hang next to surfboards, alongside straw bags, stacks of cleaning supplies and the odd caftan.

Aside from having hosted a few artists, water-sport enthusiasts and a handsome guitar player you may have heard of named Jimi Hendrix, Mirleft has mostly flown under the radar of western tourists. However, the town is hugely popular in July and August with northern Moroccans, so much so that at weekends a bed can be hard to come by. At other times, though, you might have a whole perfect beach to yourself.

Sights & Activities

Stroll down the arcaded main street, which resembles the set of a cowboy film. Under the pink-and-blue arches you will find arts and crafts, argan products, souvenirs, carpets, surfboards, beach-tennis sets and two small vegetable markets.

If at first the scruffy village seems uninspiring, the gentle bustle soon becomes contagious. A social morning coffee is followed by a trip to the beach – choose from **Mirleft Beach** (Imin Tourga Beach), **Aftas Beach**, **Plage Sauvage** and **Marabou Beach** (Sheikh Beach). The first is the longest, while the last is the most dramatic, with its *marabout's* tomb and savage-looking rocks.

There are plenty of activities to keep you busy, with several surf schools, mostly located on Ave Legzira or the road to Mirleft Beach. The beach is good for surf casting (fishing), and hotels and guides can organise trips from trekking to desert excursions.

Spot-M SURFING
(0661441933; www.surfingholidaysmorocco.com; half-day lesson incl rentals Dh150) British-owned surf specialist with a fully equipped surf shop in the middle of town and accommodation in a house on Mirleft Beach. Beginner and intermediate surfers are welcome, and one- to five-night trips exploring remote Saharan waves are also offered. Spot-M is an excellent steward for both the beaches and the surfer community: instructors' annual end-of-summer volunteer beach clean-up goes a long way to keeping Mirleft pristine.

Morliv SURFING
(0659214049; aalaoui_karim@live.fr) Karim's surf school had just launched when we passed through. His energy, fun attitude, and low prices make it a great option for shredding class in Mirleft.

Biscou Surf School SURFING
(board & wetsuit rental Dh100; vary) Rachid is the skilled instructor and all-around chill dude at this new surf school. He rents out quality boards and suits for DIYers and leads lessons at Plage Sauvage and other hidden

SURFING THE SOUTHERN ATLANTIC COAST

Morocco's beaches have been lashed by Atlantic waves since time immemorial, but it wasn't until Western hippies started coming around in the 1960s that people started riding them. Since then, buoyed by an increasing number of Moroccan surfers and instructors, surfing has become big business in this part of Morocco. The scene peaked when celebrity surfer Kelly Slater visited in 2014 – he picked Taghazout as his shredding headquarters.

Mondo Barneys

So you're a brand-new surfer? No worries: so are most of the folks dipping their toes into the water these days. Surf coaching outfits abound up and down the coast, but if you want to try just one or two lessons to see how you get on, Mirleft (p421) or Sidi Ifni (p424) are preferable to Taghazout, where outfits usually require a few days' commitment. In Mirleft, Morliv (p421) or Surf en Marruecos are good for absolute beginners; Ifni Surf (p424) in Sidi Ifni is also reliably good.

Surf-and-Yoga Packages

Surf-and-yoga holidays are trending on the southern coast, drawing Europeans and even Americans escaping frigid northern winters. There are tons of all-inclusive options; while they often require a minimum stay (usually four days), there's no simpler option if you want to maximise your time in the water and minimise faff. Taghazout (p397) is ground zero for these package holidays, which can include posh cocktails and private accommodation at Amouage (p398), or cheap-and-cheerful hostel vibes at Yalah Surf Hostel (p398).

DIY Surfers

For those who want to surf but don't want to commit to four days eating at the same dinner table, there are plenty of independent surfing outfits that rent gear and provide lessons à la carte. Tamraght (p396), 10 kilometres south of Taghazout, is a less-developed, more chilled-out version of its northerly sibling. Here, Lunar Surf House (p396) can sort you out with gear rentals, lessons, yoga, meals and even desert excursions, but you only pay for what you want. A few kilometres south of Tamraght is sleepier-still Aourir (p396), where you can surf and sleep and eat, but nowhere organises all three. But super-tasty Aourir bananas sweeten the deal.

Surf Guiding

If you already know your barrels from their backsides, you might go for surf guiding services offered by many surf outfits along the coast. This usually includes transportation to and from locals-only surf breaks, and sometimes a packed lunch. Surf Maroc (p398) in Taghazout, and Spot-M (p421) in Mirleft are both super knowledgeable about the breaks along their stretches of coast, and can steer you to waves suitable for your level. These outfits can also hook you up with car rentals if you want to strike out on a solo surfing safari.

spots. He and his team get raves from beginners and advanced surfers alike.

Chasseurs de Vagues SURFING
(☎0670729583; Aftas Beach; half-day lesson Dh150) Najib and his team will whip your shredding right into shape at this surf school on Aftas Beach. Note that he doesn't rent equipment if you're not taking a lesson.

Surf en Marruecos SURFING
(Mirleft Surf Shop; ☎0615990470; www.surfenmarruecos.com; full-day lesson incl rental Dh200) This Spanish-owned surf school spearheaded Mirleft's development as a surf destination, and organises an international longboard competition here every August. Book ahead for surf camp packages including accommodation and meals. Otherwise just drop by their shop, on the road to Mirleft Beach, and ask for Mohamed.

Le Nid d'Aigle PARAGLIDING
(☎0658458223; www.nidaigle.com; Route de Mirleft) Le Nid d'Aigle is surely the region's most picturesque paragliding camp, on top of an appropriately windy ridge. Tandem paragliding flights begin at €50 and accommodation, including half-board, is €45 per night.

Le Jardin d'Orient HAMMAM
(☎0652241020; 1hr treatment Dh200; ⊙by appointment) Look for the blue door behind the fish market to discover this stylish combination of massage and hammam. Masseuses are skilled and professional, and waxing and facials are also available. Don't miss the biggest cactus you've ever seen reclining in the front garden.

Sleeping

Mirleft is home to a raft of wonderful accommodations at every price range, from beachside hostels to a wonderfully unique mountaintop boutique hotel.

★**Aftas Beach House** HOSTEL €
(☎0675164271; www.aftasmirleft.com; Aftas Beach; r from Dh200/300; 📶) This whitewashed house overlooking the rocky cove of Aftas Beach is one of the best hostels in southern Morocco, not for its simple rooms and shared bathrooms, but for its perfect location that lets you fall asleep to crashing Atlantic waves. Thoughtful staff and several beachfront cafes next door mean you never have to leave if you don't want to.

If you've got time, patience, a good attitude and think you'll be hungry in a few hours, head next door to the unnamed Jamaican-themed cafe, where Hassan can whip up one of the best tajines you've ever had (if he feels like it), from Dh50.

Hôtel Abertih HOTEL €
(☎0528719304; www.abertih.com; r incl half-board from Dh300; 📶) Looking like it popped out of a Cubist painting, pink-and-purple Abertih is equally colourful inside, where terraced courtyards bursting with succulents lead to 11 rooms above the licensed ground-floor restaurant popular with local punters. The hotel offers half-board and hire-car packages.

Mirleft Soul Hostel HOSTEL €
(☎0528719149; www.mirleftsoulhostel.com; dm Dh90, r w shared bathroom Dh150; 📶) Even the 10-bed dorm manages to feel light and airy in this new addition to Mirleft's budget accommodation scene, a short walk down the hill behind the main road. The welcome is warm, views over the garden valley are lovely, breakfast is included and mint tea is free all day. Not bad for the cheapest beds in town.

Sally's B&B B&B €€
(☎0528719402; www.sallymirleft.com; Les Amicales; r Dh600-1300; 📶) Created by Sally the horse-loving aesthete, this gorgeous cliff-top villa above Mirleft Beach (p421) has breathtaking views up the coast. With six en-suite rooms and antiques decorating the lounge, it's a stylish and comfortable hideaway.

Aftas Trip GUESTHOUSE €€
(☎0666026537; www.aftas-trip.com; d from Dh550; 📶) Superb Atlantic views and a versatile range of accommodation combines at this hilltop destination around 5km north of Mirleft town. Rooms range from family-friendly mini-apartments to more prosaic Amazigh-style tents, and the English-speaking Aftas Trip team can arrange surfing, paddleboarding, fishing and desert explorations by trekking or 4WD. Meals (from Dh85) are served in a large Amazigh tent in the pretty garden. Breakfast is Dh50.

★**Les 3 Chameaux** GUESTHOUSE €€€
(☎0528719187; www.3chameaux.com; ste from Dh1100; P📶🏊) High on the hill in a renovated 1930s military fort, Mirleft's best address is a lovely guesthouse with views over the village, sea and cactus-covered hills. It's an all-suite property, and rooms and common spaces are tastefully decorated with museum-quality antiques, textiles and vintage travel posters. Oscar the huge golden Labrador presides over the pool (heated in winter) and tennis court.

The licensed restaurant (dinner Dh240) has gorgeous views over the ruined hilltop kasbah, which you can easily walk to. Breakfast is Dh70.

Dar Najmat BOUTIQUE HOTEL €€€
(☎0528719056; www.darnajmat.com; r incl half-board from €137; 📶🏊) With its infinity pool seeming to melt into Marabou Beach, Dar Najmat's view is one of the best on the Moroccan coast. You'll want to start taking photos as soon as you pull off the road, 2km south of Mirleft. The decor in the seven rooms and two-bedroom apartment is perfect, with Moroccan materials achieving a contemporary and harmonious ambience.

Eating & Drinking

The best eating in town is at restaurants attached to a couple of the main-street hotels.

The highly convivial bar at the Hôtel Abertih serves decent wine and exceptionally cold San Miguel lager. Otherwise, you're dry until Sidi Ifni.

Tifawin Cafe CAFE €
(☎0611908323; www.facebook.com/TifawinCafe; mains Dh20-30; ⊙7.30am-10pm; 📶) Tifawin's laid-back cosmopolitan style includes

excellent juices and smoothies – especially anything incorporating creamy avocado – and Moroccan pancakes with honey or *amlou* (a winning combination of argan-nut butter with honey and almonds). Comfort food for hungry surfers includes muesli, omelettes and toasted sandwiches, and Tifawin's bright blue-and-yellow decor adds a colourful touch to Mirfelt's arcaded main drag.

Zan Zan Cafe CAFE €

(0671471736; 9am-10pm) When you tire of tajine, the friendly folk at Zan Zan will dish you up decent pasta, coffee and smoothies in a cosy yet tasteful setting overlooking the dusty main road of Mirleft. There's a lending library with lots to read (in French), and the owners are welcoming and fun.

Cafe Aftas CAFE €

(0670729583; Aftas Beach; snacks Dh20-30; 8am-10pm;) Mint tea, coffee and omelettes combine with up close and personal views of Aftas Beach at this fun spot with a funky beach-shack ambience. Colourful murals and the easygoing vibe of owner Najib create one of Morocco's most laid-back cafes. He can also hook you up with surfing lessons through his Chasseurs de Vagues (p422) surf school.

Restaurant Ayour MOROCCAN €€

(0528719171; meals Dh70; noon-10pm) Cosy Ayour is one of Mirleft's better standalone restaurants. Prices are a little inflated, but the tajines, fish and other meals here are a smidge better than their competitors along the strip.

Hôtel Abertih MOROCCAN €€

(0528719304; mains Dh60-120; 7pm-late) The restaurant and bar at the Hôtel Abertih puts a social after-dark spin on Mirleft. Round tables host diners for an ever-changing menu of seafood and meat dishes, and after grilled sole or couscous with chicken, leave room for dessert with one of coastal Morocco's better crème caramels. There's also a compact wine list and lots of cold beer.

Book ahead if you can, but French owner Didier usually finds room for additional diners on the 1st floor.

Getting There & Away

Lux bus 18 links Mirleft to Tiznit (Dh10, one hour) and Sidi Ifni (Dh10, 45 minutes). Grands taxis also run to Sidi Ifni (Dh13) and Tiznit (Dh15) from Mirleft.

Sidi Ifni سيدي إفني

0528 / POP 20,051

Only recovered from the Spanish in 1969, Sidi Ifni (*sih-dee if-nee*) retains a sleepy Iberian flair, and the eerily deserted art-deco buildings are a reminder of Spain's colonial ambitions. At the heart of what was the Spanish Sahara, Ifni was once a base for slave-trading operations and later a large exporter of fish to the Spanish mainland. When the sun sets on the ocean esplanade and dilapidated streets, and the Atlantic rolls in, Ifni seems an almost spooky outpost.

The locals have painted the town blue and white, reflecting the colour scheme of their turbans and robes. They support Spanish football teams, take siestas and are more likely to greet travellers with *hola* than *bonjour*. You might hear Spanish beats blaring from a cafe, and the expats and local cafe crowd are laid-back even by Moroccan standards. Equally easygoing are visiting surfers, seeking out excellent Atlantic waves on nearby beaches.

Sights & Activities

There's some excellent surfing around Ifni, and paddleboarding is also becoming popular.

Beach BEACH

The beach is big and rarely busy. While frequently rough waves make swimming inadvisable, its position beneath dramatic cliffs – as well as its significant length – invites sunset strolls. The odd construction just offshore is the remains of an old land-sea conveyor, which was used to take cargo from ships to the old Spanish port.

Ifni Surf SURFING

(0662533717; www.ifnisurf.com; Blvd Moulay Youssef; board & wetsuit hire per day Dh150, 2hr lesson incl equipment Dh200, kayak & wetsuit hire per hr Dh60) Ifni's first surf instruction company also offers kayaking at Legzira Plage, quad bike and 4WD desert excursions, and market visits and cooking classes. Book well ahead, and don't expect much help in the off-season or if they are busy.

Sleeping

New guesthouses courtesy of a few pioneering European expats has seen Ifni's accommodation options improve in recent years.

Sidi Ifni

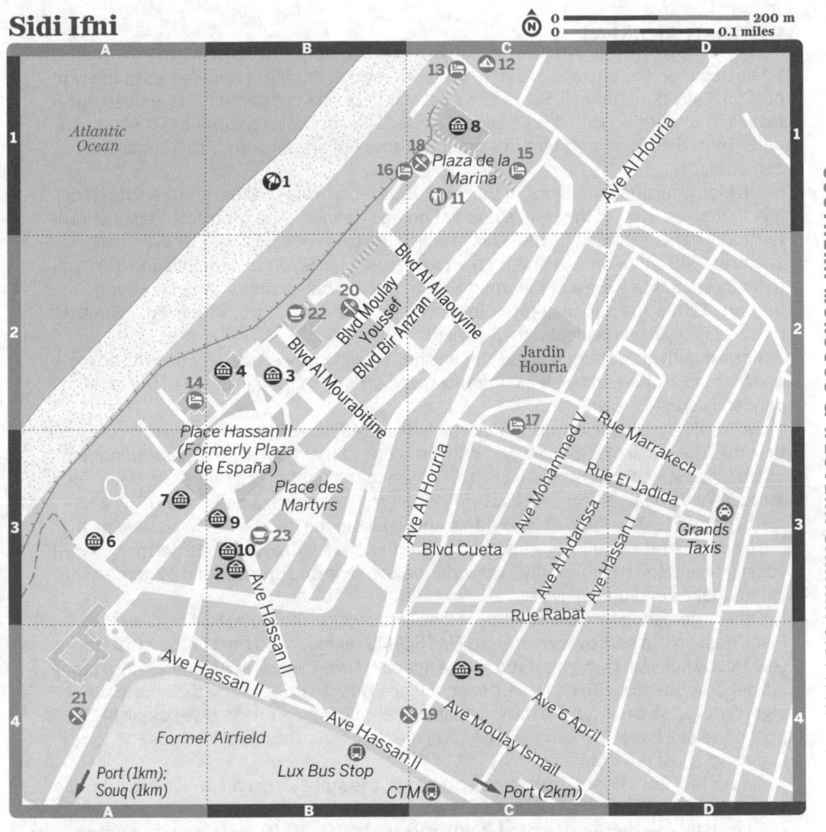

Sidi Ifni

Sights

1	Beach	B1
2	Cine Avenida	B3
3	Former Spanish Consulate	B2
4	Law Courts (Former Church)	B2
5	Letterbox	C4
6	Lighthouse	A3
7	Royal Palace	A3
8	Ship House	C1
9	Town Hall	B3
10	Twist Club	B3

Activities, Courses & Tours

11	Ifni Surf	C1

Sleeping

12	Camping Sidi Ifni	C1
13	Hôtel Ait Baamrane	C1
14	Hôtel Bellevue	A2
15	Hôtel Suerte Loca	C1
16	Logis La Marine	B1
17	Xanadu	C2

Eating

18	Café Miramar	C1
	Hôtel Suerte Loca	(see 15)
19	Municipal Market	C4
20	Nomad	B2
21	Supermarché Marina	A4

Drinking & Nightlife

22	Café Tagoute	B2
23	Eddib	B3
	Hôtel Bellevue	(see 14)

Hôtel Suerte Loca HOTEL €
(☎0528875350; Blvd Moulay Youssef; r from Dh170, with shared bathroom Dh100; 📶) Simple rooms, some with balconies overlooking Ifni's beach, feature at this friendly hotel adorned with mosaics and cactus. The friendly, English-speaking owner also presides over a lively cafe and bead shop on the ground

SPANISH SIDI IFNI

Spain acquired the enclave of Sidi Ifni after defeating the Moroccan forces in the war of 1859. They christened it Santa Cruz del Mar Pequeña but seem to have been uncertain as to what to do with it, as they did not take full possession until 1934. Most of Ifni dates from the 1930s and features an eclectic mix of art deco and traditional Moroccan styles.

On Moroccan independence in the late 1950s, Spain refused to withdraw, citing the fact that some 60% of the town's population was Spanish. The protracted dispute over territorial rights included the Ifni War, in which the town was besieged. It eventually ended in 1969 when the UN brokered an agreement for Spain to cede the enclave back to Morocco. Santa Cruz was renamed Sidi Ifni, after a holy man buried in the town in the early 1900s. Ifni still celebrates 'Independence Day' (30 June) with a small Amazigh (Berber) festival on the abandoned airfield.

Ifni is mostly a contented place, but clashes occasionally erupt between the police and townsfolk, sparked by high unemployment and the marginalisation of the independently spirited town.

Sidi Ifni has a unique atmosphere, which has lured more than a few passing foreigners to settle. The small old Spanish part of town is one of the main attractions, but not so much for its specific sights – which aren't open to the public – as for its laid-back retro attitude. At its heart is **Place Hassan II** (often still called Plaza de España), the colonial centrepiece. The large square with a small park in the middle is surrounded by the main administrative buildings: law courts (former church), royal palace, former Spanish consulate and town hall, mostly in grand art-deco style and surrounded by gardens of cactus, palms and bougainvillea.

Other interesting remnants of the colonial era include the Hôtel Bellevue, also on Place Hassan II, a nearby **lighthouse** (Ave Sidi Mohammed) and the clifftop **ship house** (Ave Moulay Abdellah), which served as the Spanish Naval Secretariat. There's also some art-deco architecture in the streets east of Place Hassan II, including the shuttered nightclub **Twist Club** (off Ave Hassan II) and cinema **Cine Avenida** (Ave Hassan II). The post office still has a **letterbox** (Ave Mohammed V) outside marked 'Correos – Avion/Ordinario' (Post – Air Mail/Ordinary).

One of Sidi Ifni's finest Spanish-era buildings, the stately **Town Hall** or *hôtel de ville* stands in a garden of cactus and plumbago, facing Place Hassan II. It's washed in white paint with blue vertical stripes imitating art-deco columns. You can't go in, but if the gates are unlocked it's worth peeking into the grounds for a closer look.

Trimmed by palm trees, the imposing **Royal Palace** is adjacent to the relaxed Place Hassan II (formerly Plaza de España). This building in particular, with its high gates, manicured garden and out-of-context pretension, hearkens back to the days of when the Spanish colonial military was garrisoned here.

floor, and surf lessons can be arranged. If you want to stick around for a while, there's an apartment available to rent for €140 per week.

Camping Sidi Ifni CAMPGROUND €
(0658019813; off Ave Al Hourria; tent/caravan/r Dh30/70/120) Next to the outdoor swimming pool at the north end of the beach, with fabulous views of the roaring surf, this is a picture-perfect option for those who travel with their homes on their backs. It's beloved by European vanlife types.

Hôtel Bellevue HOTEL €
(0528875272; Place Hassan II; s/d Dh170/200, with shared bathroom Dh105/130) The art-deco charms of the Bellevue's exterior are less awe-inspiring inside, where you'll find just a few lampshades and stained-glass windows. But ship-shape rooms and coastal views from the bar-restaurant and balconies make this a pleasant budget choice. Request an en-suite room upstairs; those downstairs are darker and the shared shower is a frugal rooftop affair.

Hôtel Ait Baamrane HOTEL €
(Rue des Plages; s/d Dh150/180) It's fewer than 100 steps from the door of your room to the water's edge at this beachfront pile of bricks, which is the main reason to stay here. Otherwise it's extremely basic, but the reasonably clean rooms are available for a pittance.

There's an attached bar and restaurant overlooking the waves.

Staff take a laissez-faire approach to most everything, which is fitting because there's no phone, website or way to prebook. However, you shouldn't have a problem finding a room here unless it's a summer weekend.

Logis La Marine B&B €€
(☎0641766096; www.logislamarine.com; 1 Ave Moulay Abdellah; s/d/q €55/60/105, d with balcony €80; 📶) Formerly the headquarters of the Spanish navy, this art-deco clifftop mansion has superb views of the Atlantic. Charming owners Benoit and Dominique have adorned many rooms with heritage art-deco furniture and local art, and shared breakfasts (included) and dinners (€15) are enjoyed in a shaded garden populated by a posse of tortoises. Bathrooms are relatively compact.

Ask Dominique about looking through the photo albums crammed with poignant images of Sidi Ifni's relatively recent Spanish heritage.

Xanadu GUESTHOUSE €€
(☎0528876718; www.maisonxanadu.com; 5 Rue El Jadida; s/d Dh360/550; 📶) Tucked away off Ave Mohammed V, this restored house offers a contemporary take on the Ifni aesthetic, with soothing colours in each of the five rooms. Good breakfast is served on the roof and the book-filled lounge is ideal for whiling away an evening. Book ahead if you want to stay here; the host isn't always in town.

Eating & Drinking

Cafes line Ave Hassan II, with views of Place Hassan II, and other restaurants have views of the wild Atlantic.

As with most Moroccan towns this size, there aren't many choices for a drink. An exception of particular note is the roof terrace at the Hôtel Bellevue, a top spot to combine a Casablanca lager and an Atlantic sunset. Beer is also available at the beachfront bar at Hôtel Ait Baamrane.

Café Miramar MOROCCAN €
(☎0528876637; R104; tajines from Dh40; 🕗8am-midnight; 📶) This cliffside family-run cafe dishes up the usual suspects (tajines, *brochettes*, Friday couscous) with cheery flair and gorgeous ocean views. Bouquets of flowers, while faux, liven up what would otherwise be a rather institutional room. The owners are detail oriented and friendly.

Hôtel Suerte Loca MOROCCAN €
(☎0528875350; Blvd Moulay Youssef; omelettes from Dh15; 🕗9am-2pm & 6-11pm) It's an easy-going vibe at this cafe, beloved by surfers and other mega-chilled folks. The English-speaking owner serves good breakfasts, juice, coffee and a date-almond milkshake. At night, occasional live music creates a gentle buzz.

Municipal Market MARKET €
(cnr Ave Mohammed V & Ave Hassan II; mains Dh15-40; 🕗10am-10pm) In addition to the fish market, produce market and surrounding cafes, look out for the courtyard of smoking grills. In this atmospheric outdoor spot, where cooks fan the coals and call out to customers, you can get grilled seafood – including sardines, fish and prawns – served with salad and bread.

Supermarché Marina SUPERMARKET €
(Blvd Le Caire; 🕗8am-6pm) This well-stocked supermarket is a good place to re-up on toiletries and snacks, or to snag an ice cream bar to take the edge off the Ifni sun.

★Nomad SEAFOOD €€
(☎0662173308; 5 Blvd Moulay Youssef; mains Dh70-100; 🕗noon-10.30pm Tue-Sun) The best restaurant in Sidi Ifni serves excellent grills and seafood, often to a soundtrack of Western music – English-speaking owner Abdellah is a big fan of the blues – amid an elegant Moorish-style interior. Service is super friendly, and everything is fresh and thoughtfully prepared, especially the plate-covering Pariada of the Sea, a mixed grill of fish, calamari and octopus.

Café Tagoute CAFE
(☎0672769520; Blvd Moulay Abdellah; 🕗7am-11pm) Pull up a chair, order a Coca Cola and join the dozens of young men shooting the breeze at this cafe, one of several on the cliff-hugging corniche overlooking the waves breaking on Ifni beach. Breakfasts available too, from Dh15.

Eddib CAFE
(Ave Hassan II; 🕗8am-late) Our favourite of the laid-back cafes lining Ave Hassan II. Order up a robust black coffee, tune in to the bouncy 1960s Spanish pop music and take in views across the street of the cool art-deco profile of the Cine Avenida. The friendly owner speaks English.

Hôtel Bellevue BAR
(Place Hassan II; 🕗11am-11pm) Perched on a cliff above the beach, the bar at Hôtel

WORTH A TRIP

MESTI

Tucked into the cactus-covered hills 20km above Ifni is the little town of Mesti (also known as Arbâa Mesti). There's not much to see at first glance – you might be tempted to zoom straight through on your way from Goulimime or Tiznit – but you'd be missing a great opportunity to snag some one-of-a-kind souvenirs. Locals in Mesti have cannily made use of their agricultural prowess to establish two wonderful agricultural cooperatives that are well worth a stop. **Miel Afoulki** (0661472433; www.cooperativeafoulki.net; Mesti) sells jars of unique flavours of honey from local bees, feeding on flowers from euphorbia and orange trees. Down the street, the women at **Tafyoucht Cooperative** (0528218416; Mesti) trade in oil and cosmetics made from rich argan oil and nuts. Neither collective keeps regular hours; you're most likely to find someone there in the afternoon.

Bellevue (p426) is a wonderful spot for a sundowner. Order a Casablanca lager and watch the breakers roll into the beach below. Simple food is available (tajines from Dh30).

Getting There & Away

CTM (0528780050; www.ctm.ma; Ave Hassan II) has daily departures to destinations including Casablanca (Dh270, 12 hours), Marrakesh (Dh180, 7½ hours), Agadir (Dh75, four hours) and Laayoune (Dh185, eight hours). Lux bus 18 travels via Mirleft (Dh10, 45 minutes) to Tiznit (Dh20, 1½ hours).

The grand-taxi station is on the east side of town. Taxis serve Goulimime (Dh30), Legzira Plage (Dh13), Mirleft (Dh13), Tiznit (Dh27) and Agadir (Dh60).

Legzira Plage شاطئ الكزيرة

El Gzira, usually called Legzira Plage, is a superb secluded bay, with excellent sand and a dramatic natural stone arch reaching over the sea. There were actually two arches up until recently, but the smaller one collapsed in the dark of night in 2016. The arch that remains standing is the more spectacular of the two, and the beach is still worth visiting.

It's accessible from Route 104, but more atmospherically reached by walking along the beaches and cliffs. This is only possible at low tide, so check tide times before you start walking. Tourism development is slowly spreading down the access road from Route 104, but the beach itself remains pristine and largely undeveloped.

Grands taxis stop on Route 104 between Sidi Ifni (Dh15) and Mirleft (Dh20). Buses also run from Sidi Ifni (Dh10) and Mirleft (Dh15).

Sleeping & Eating

Simple hotels and guesthouses face the beach near the main access road. Half-board is around Dh300 per person per night.

Beachfront cafes charge around Dh50 for mains and the seafood is always good.

Beach Club PENSION €

(0670522800; s/d from Dh200/300) Beach Club has nice, all-white rooms along Legzira Plage, some with shared sea-facing balconies. There's a restaurant with decent tajines from Dh50. You'll find the accommodation at the quieter northern end of the beach.

Sables d'Or PENSION €

(0661302495; eddibmohamed2@yahoo.se; s/d from Dh200/300) Sables d'Or has small but comfortable rooms, opening onto terraces with sea views. The restaurant, adorned with colourful Berber carpets and wall hangings, does basic tajines from Dh50.

Goulimime كلميم

0528 / POP 118,318

Once the 'Gateway of the Sahara', bland and dusty Goulimime (or Guelmim, both pronounced *gool-imeem*) sprang up as a border town where farmers from the fertile Souss traded with nomads from the south. If you have come from the north, you will still recognise Goulimime as a liminal place: for the first time, you will see Sahrawi (Arab-Amazigh nomads from the Sahara) in the majority.

Six days out of seven, you'll want to blow straight through town. But on Saturday mornings, a souq including a fun camel market brings the town to life. A week-long *moussem* (festival) and camel fair is held here around the end of July.

Festivals & Events

Camel Festival FAIR

As a historic trading town for Amazigh tribes in the Sahara and farmers from the adjacent fertile plains, camels have been big business in Goulimime for millennia. These days the best camels get to ride in the back of Tuareg pick-up trucks, but for one atmospheric week at the end of July, the basic gist is still the same. Bring your camera.

Sleeping & Eating

If you're transiting, there are cheapies close to the *grand-taxi* station, but many Goulimime hotels may not appeal to women. If you have transport, there is better accommodation outside town at the Oasis Palm Hotel.

Around the bus station and north of the post office are good areas for cafes and restaurants.

Maison d'Hôtes Nomades GUESTHOUSE €
(0667909642; off Route d'Asrir; s/d Dh200/350) This *pisé* house right in the oasis has camels in the stables and argan and cactus products for sale. Rooms have en-suite bathrooms and the views from the roof terrace are wonderfully evocative. Much of the guesthouse's food – including organic honey, butter and vegetables – comes from its own gardens and animals, and one- to seven-night desert journeys are also available.

Hôtel Hamza HOTEL €
(0528873975; off Route d'Agadir; s/d Dh250/350;) In this quiet and welcoming caravanserai near the tourist office, expansive corridors lead to spacious rooms with bathrooms of varying quality.

Hôtel Ijdiguen HOTEL €
(0661700303; Blvd Ibnou Battouta; s/d Dh75/150) Conveniently across the road from the *grand-taxi* station, Ijdiguen (Ichdigen) is clean and welcoming, with tiled corridors, reasonable rooms and shared showers. Rooms can get noisy at night, as the bus station is so close. The neighbourhood might not be comfortable for women travelling alone.

Oasis Palm Hotel HOTEL €€
(0528779300; www.oasispalmhotel.com; Route d'Agadir RN1; r from €60; P) Goulimime's most attractive hotel has more than 100 comfortable rooms arrayed around pleasant palm-fringed patios and an expansive swimming pool. Yet all of these, as well as the lobby, three restaurants and other facilities stand eerily empty. Staff seem alarmed by the possibility that guests might arrive at any moment. It's 10km northeast of the city near the airport.

Le Petit Marin MOROCCAN €
(Ziz Garage, Route d'Agadir; meals Dh50-80; 8am-10pm) Near Place Bir Anzarane, this Westernised snack bar serves dishes ranging from pizzas, burgers and spaghetti to tajines and pil-pil prawns with olive oil, garlic and chilli. Things get lively on Fridays, when folks gather here after attending mosque across the road.

Shopping

Unless you're in the market for tupperware or a camel, you probably won't find anything of use at Goulimime's Saturday souq. But, as the biggest market in the area, it's a fascinating window into the modern necessities of Amazigh (Berber) life. It's definitely worth a wander if you're passing through on a Saturday, although probably doesn't merit a special trip..

Getting There & Away

Royal Air Maroc Express (www.royalairmaroc.com) links Goulimime Airport to Casablanca, Tan Tan and Laayoune.

The bus station is a 10-minute walk north of Place Bir Anazarane. **CTM** (www.ctm.ma; Blvd Ibnou Battouta) and **Supratours** (www.supratours.ma) have regular departures to Agadir (Dh90, five hours), Casablanca (Dh300, 12 hours), Dakhla (Dh350, 16 hours), Laayoune (Dh180, 7½ hours), Marrakesh (Dh190, 7½ hours), Rabat (Dh330, 13½ hours), Tan Tan (Dh50, two hours) and Tiznit (Dh45, 2¾ hours). Daily **Satas** (0528872213; Gare Routière) buses are a slightly cheaper option for most of these destinations.

You can catch grands taxis from behind the bus station to Inezgane (Dh75), Laayoune (Dh275), Sidi Ifni (Dh30), Tan Tan (Dh50) and Tiznit (Dh35).

OFF THE BEATEN TRACK

FORT BOU-JERIF RESORT

Run by French expat Pierre, **Fort Bou-Jerif Resort** (0672130017; www.boujerif.com; campsites from Dh45, incl half-board s/d/tent from Dh440/880/315;) is a wonderful oasis of civilisation in the desert about 40km northwest of Goulimime (the last 9km is a rough dirt track). Built near a ruined French Foreign Legion fort, this compound has a range of sleeping options, from rooms in a motel and a hotel to nomad tents and campsites.

There is an excellent restaurant (menu Dh200), where you can try a camel tajine. It also offers 4WD trips to Plage Blanche, a little-visited and unspoiled stretch of beach 40km west of Bou-Jerif.

Tan Tan & Tan Tan Plage طانطان وشاطئ طانطان

El Ouatia, also known as Tan Tan Plage, is a dilapidated seaside resort overlooking a long, windswept beach with impressive breakers: only the very hardy or very foolish would want to swim or surf here. The resort is 25km west of its sister Tan Tan. Both towns briefly come to life during the Moroccan summer holiday; otherwise, you'll have the promenade, cafes and dinky hotels all to yourself. After 130km of bleak desert highway, the remoteness can feel either delicious or a little spooky.

Festivals & Events

Tan Tan Moussem CULTURAL
(early Dec) A Unesco-protected *moussem* (festival) takes place in December. It's an important fixture in the Amazigh (Berber) social calendar, drawing tribes from all over the region. Festivities include horse racing, camel trading and traditional music.

Sleeping & Eating

There are seafront hotels and campgrounds on the port road at Tan Tan Plage. Tan Tan has a couple of OK accommodation options near to good cafes if you need to overnight.

In Tan Tan, there are cheap eateries on Ave Hassan II, Ave Mohammed V and around the bus station. Hôtel Sable d'Or is a popular choice.

Fresh seafood is a standout in the cafes of Tan Tan Plage. The town's main square has everything from bakeries to grill restaurants specialising in meaty cuts of camel and lamb from adjacent butcheries.

Ksar Tafnidilt GUESTHOUSE €
(0663233115; www.tafnidilt.com; r per person incl half-board from Dh450; P) It's a dusty six kilometres from the RN1 between Tan Tan and Goulimime, but catching first sight of this guesthouse is worth any minor dings on your car. It's an imposing faux kasbah on a hilltop, facing a ruined real kasbah on the next hilltop, with a swimming pool, good restaurant, boutique and calm interior courtyard decorated with palm trees and whale vertebrae.

The track from the highway is sometimes covered in sand drifts, but may be passable in a normal car with a reasonably sporty driver. Contact Magali in advance to get an update on the piste (French only).

Riad Essadia GUESTHOUSE €
(0528879214; riad.essadia@gmail.com; Ave Mohammed V, Tan Tan Plage; r from Dh320;) The best place to stay in either Tan Tan or Tan Tan Plage, Riad Essadia has eight rooms opening onto a spacious central courtyard in mosaic tile, which flows out onto the beach promenade. Rooms are charming, but some lack external windows so natural light can be limited. However, the characterful shared spaces easily offset this. Breakfast and other meals are enjoyed with Atlantic views.

Hôtel La Belle Vue HOTEL €
(0675653417; Ave Mohammed V, Tan Tan Plage; s/d excl breakfast Dh300/400;) This appropriately named, family-run seafront hotel has basic en-suite rooms, the best with views over the promenade and crashing surf beyond. The cafe-restaurant (breakfast and meals Dh25 to Dh90) is one of Tan Tan Plage's best, serving tajines, omelettes, sardines and calamari.

Hôtel Sable d'Or HOTEL €
(0528878069; Ave Hassan II, Tan Tan; s/d Dh150/200;) Next to the banks on the main road, this super-friendly, family-run hotel has comfortable en-suite rooms with flat-screen TV. Ask for a room at the rear, away from the main road. There's a cafe-restaurant with a pool table.

La Scala SEAFOOD €
(Chez Abdellah; 0528879324; Tan Tan Plage; mains Dh45-80; 11am-midnight) A short walk from Tan Tan Plage's main square, La Scala is one of the town's best seafood restaurants. The friendly owner Abdellah is eager to please visitors who've made the big trek south, and plates of octopus salad, grilled calamari and sole are very generous servings. Italian and Spanish influences also feature, with paella and pizza on the menu.

Getting There & Away

Royal Air Maroc (www.royalairmaroc.com) flies between **Tan Tan Airport** and Casablanca.

In Tan Tan, **CTM** (0528765886; www.ctm.ma; Ave Hassan II, Tan Tan) has daily departures to Agadir (Dh130, six hours), Dakhla (Dh320, 14 hours), Goulimime (Dh50, 1½ hours), Laayoune (Dh140, five hours) and Tiznit (Dh95, 3½ hours).

Supratours (0528877795, Tan Tan Plage 0528879665; www.supratours.ma; Ave Hassan II, Tan Tan), which stops in Tan Tan and also at its office in Tan Tan Plage, opposite the Dubai Hotel, operates similar services at slightly higher prices.

Other, cheaper (and less comfortable) companies, all serving the same destinations, use Tan Tan **Gare Routière** (Place de la Marche Verte, Tan Tan), off Ave Mohammed V, about 1km south of Ave Hassan II.

From Tan Tan's Gare Routière, grands taxis head to Agadir (Dh110), Goulimime (Dh50), Inezgane (Dh110), Laayoune (Dh150), Tan Tan Plage (Dh15), Tarfaya (Dh160) and Tiznit (Dh80).

Grands taxis to Tan Tan Plage also leave from the top of Blvd El Amir Moulay Abdallah, a few hundred metres south of Ave Hassan II.

Tarfaya طرفاية

☎0528 / POP 8027

Seductively remote, the working port town of Tarfaya (*tar-fah-yah*) was the centre of the Spanish Protectorate of Cap Juby, now known as the Tarfaya Strip. Tarfaya also trades on its history as a stopover station on the French Aéropostale mail service, connecting France with its colonies in Africa. The French writer Antoine de Saint-Exupéry, who would later go on to write *Le Petit Prince,* was station chief here for 18 months beginning in 1927. It was here that Exupéry wrote his first novel, *Southern Mail.*

The town is now home to a new commercial port, which aims to relaunch ferry connections with the Canary Islands in the near future. The beachfront promenade is a relaxing spot. Tarfaya's charm, however, is primarily in the crumbling colonial relics that appear within the shifting sands.

Sights & Activities

There are some good fishing, surfing and kitesurfing spots around Tarfaya. Ask your accommodation or Les Amis de Tarfaya about organising an expedition.

Musée Saint-Exupéry MUSEUM

(☎0661079488; Dh10; ⌚vary) Tarfaya's main claim to fame is its association with the French pilot and writer Antoine de Saint-Exupéry. In 1926 he began flying in the airmail service between France and Senegal, and Cap Juby (as Tarfaya was known at the time) was one of the stops. This museum tells the stories (in French) of Saint-Exupéry, the airmail service's founder, Pierre-Georges Latécoère, and the service itself, which eventually became part of Air France. If you want to visit, call ahead.

In 1927 Saint-Exupéry was appointed station manager for Cap Juby, and he spent over a year here. During that time he wrote his first novel *Courrier Sud* (Southern Mail), in which an airmail pilot dies south of Boujdour in the desert of Rio de Oro. He also picked up inspiration for his most famous story, *Le Petit Prince* (The Little Prince), which features a pilot lost in the desert.

Monument MONUMENT

At the north end of the beach, a monument honours Saint-Exupéry's memory: a dinky green Bréguet 14 biplane, the sort he used to fly. This will be of interest to aviation enthusiasts; for others it's a pleasant walk on the beach.

Assalama Ferry Wreck HISTORIC SITE

The wrecked Armas ferry, *Assalama,* 2km south of town, worked the short-lived route between Tarfaya and Fuerteventura when it went down in 2008. Its rusted shell is visible just offshore, and is fascinating in an apocalyptic Mad Max kind of way.

Casa Mar HISTORIC SITE

Numerous romantically dilapidated colonial-era buildings date from the days when Saint-Exupéry touched down here. The Casa Mar is abandoned but still standing and can be easily reached at low tide. This is the most atmospheric sight in town.

Sleeping & Eating

Cafes on the main street serve cheap dishes such as grilled fish and pizza. Don't expect anything fancy.

Casa Mar HOTEL €

(☎0528895326; s/d Dh200/250) Just outside the port entrance, the Casa Mar offers predictably basic rooms (breakfast included). Staff is helpful and friendly, and some rooms look out over the port. The **cafe-restaurant** (mains Dh30-70; ⌚10am-9pm; 📶) serves whatever's fresh from the fish market, from sole to calamari and octopus. The cafe, a popular meeting point, is a good place to check your emails and watch local characters stroll in

Hotel Tarfaya HOTEL €

(Aoudate; ☎0528895868; Ave Ahmed Haidar; r per person from Dh200; 📶) Available with or without balcony and private bathroom, the Tarfaya's 35 basic rooms feature checkered bedding, satellite TV and sea views from the upper floors. Check out a few before you commit. The ground-floor cafe is a favourite of locals watching Spanish football, and features views of the truck stop beyond.

Restaurant Canalina SPANISH €
(☎ 0641785521; www.tarfayahotelcanalina.com; Ave Mohamed V; mains Dh40; ⏲ vary) The Canalina, when it's open, is likely the best restaurant in town, featuring seafood, tortillas and other Iberian fare. Unfortunately, hours are irregular. The Canalina also rents out spacious mini-apartments, all with compact kitchens, which make a good accommodation solution if you're in town for a few days.

ℹ Information

Information is available from the English-speaking Sadat at **Les Amis de Tarfaya** (☎ 0661079488; sadat@yours.com; Musée Saint-Exupéry), a local tourism association based at the Musée Saint-Exupéry, but the museum's opening hours are extremely flexible. Better to email ahead if you need guidance.

ℹ Getting There & Away

Bus companies, including CTM, stop in Tarfaya, but **Supratours** (☎ 0528895284; www.supratours.ma; Route du Port) has the only reliable office. Daily Supratours departures head for Agadir (Dh200, 10½ hours), Dakhla (Dh230, nine hours), Goulimime (Dh130, six hours), Laayoune (Dh50, two hours), Marrakesh (Dh280, 13 hours), Tan Tan (Dh90, three hours) and Tiznit (Dh170, eight hours).

Grands taxis go to Laayoune (Dh55, two hours) and Tan Tan (Dh95, three hours).

WESTERN SAHARA

After crossing the forlorn expanses of the *hamada* (stony desert) south from Tarfaya, the Western Saharan city of Dakhla makes for a relaxed destination. A constant feature is the cobalt intensity of the Atlantic, softened by palm trees, an oceanfront esplanade and a shallow island-studded lagoon.

The region's Spanish past echoes languidly in cafes, while one of the world's best kiteboarding scenes attracts international visitors seeking a more energetic experience.

Despite what is indicated by the Moroccan flags snapping in tropical breezes, this is still a disputed region. The Polisario Front, comprised of Sahrawi separatists, continues to agitate for the establishment of a Sahrawi state in Western Sahara, although armed conflict ended in 1991. Tensions now are low, especially as Sahrawi and Moroccan businesses see huge profits from regional development.

Against this background of low-key contention, pioneering expats, Sahrawi and Moroccans are developing eco-aware tours exploring the lagoon and surrounding desert.

Beyond the foothills of the Anti Atlas lies a parched hinterland starved of moisture. Here temperatures can exceed 45°C during the day and plunge to 0°C at night, while an annual rainfall of less than 125mm gives a suffocating aridity hovering between 5% and 30% – dry enough to mummify corpses. The desert wind, known locally as the *chergui, irifi* or *sirocco,* adds to the harsh conditions. In March and April, sandstorms also plague the desert, making driving inadvisable.

If you're venturing into the backcountry, it's important to carry a good supply of water, as well as reserve water in case you get stuck. In winter it is also essential to carry a warm sleeping bag and some warm clothing, as desert nights can be bitterly cold.

History

Despite its windswept desolation, the Western Sahara has a long and fraught history. Ask most Moroccans about the status of the Western Sahara and they will insist it belongs to their country, yet Saharawi groups (and the UN) maintain it is under dispute. The way the border is drawn is a particular matter of contention: until recently, bringing a map to Morocco that showed a firmly demarcated border with the Western Sahara could land you in police interrogation.

Islamic armies started to spread Islam among the Zenata and Sanhaja Berber tribes here in the 7th century. A second wave of Arab settlers, the Maqil from Yemen, migrated to the desert in the 13th century, and the whole region became predominantly Arab.

In the 19th century, the Spanish grabbed the Western Sahara and renamed it Rio de Oro. In reality, Sheikh Ma El Ainin and his son El Hiba controlled the desert and the nomadic tribes well into the 20th century. From the 1930s, an uneasy colonial peace prevailed until Moroccan independence in the late 1950s, when new nationalist fervour saw the genesis of the Polisario Front and a guerrilla war against the Spanish.

When it was abandoned by Spain in 1975, Morocco and Mauritania both raised claims to the desert region, but Mauritania soon bailed out. In November 1975 King Hassan II orchestrated the Green March – 350,000 Moroccans marched south to stake Morocco's historical claim to the Western Sahara.

Over the following years, Rabat poured in 100,000 troops to stamp out resistance and gained the upper hand. The UN brokered a ceasefire in 1991, but the promised referendum, in which the indigenous Sahrawi could choose between independence and integration with Morocco, has yet to materialise.

Ever since, Morocco has strengthened its hold on the territory, pouring money into infrastructure projects, particularly offshore oil exploration, and attracting Moroccans from the north to live here tax-free. Until late 2010, the troubled area seemed to be lying dormant, with the dispute largely forgotten by the world beyond this remote region. However, on 8 November 2010, Moroccan security forces stormed the Gadaym Izik camp near Laayoune in an attempt to break up the 15,000-strong protest camp. Both sides incurred fatalities in the ensuing clashes, which turned into riots and engulfed the city, with 700-plus Sahrawi injuries and scenes of fire and destruction in the international media. The region has seen several clashes and riots since then, most recently in 2014 in Laayoune, and Africa's longest-running territorial dispute continues.

Since 2014, the Moroccan government has further advanced activities to solidify its hold on the region, including ongoing migration of Moroccans to the cities and the establishment of smaller communities along the coast, and in November 2015 the Moroccan King Mohammed VI visited to announce multimillion-dollar investments aimed at promoting economic development in the region. In December 2013, a four-year deal signed between Morocco and the European Union to allow European vessels to fish off the Moroccan coast also included the disputed waters off Western Sahara.

Phosphate is also big business in Western Sahara: Morocco holds more than 72% of the world's supply of this finite resource, which is necessary for production of synthetic fertiliser, and hence the world food supply. Bou Craa, the phosphate mine outside Laayoune, is the largest and most profitable phosphate mine in the world.

Dakhla locals report of a cautious rapprochement between the Moroccan and Sahrawi communities – including marriages between the two groups – but the referendum promised back in 1991 still shows no sign of being scheduled. If and when it does take place, the ongoing economic and social expansion of Morocco in the area means that probably only restricted autonomy and not full independence will be on the table for the Sahrawi.

For the most up-to-date information on the Western Sahara, or the Sahrawi Arab Democratic Republic (as the separatist government calls the occupied territory), check these resources:

- ARSO (www.arso.org)
- BBC (www.bbc.co.uk)
- CIA World Factbook (www.cia.gov)
- Global Voices (www.globalvoicesonline.org)
- UN (www.un.org)
- Crisis Group (www.crisisgroup.org)

LANGUAGES OF THE WESTERN SAHARA

In the Western Sahara, Arabic and French are spoken almost universally. As a previous Spanish Protectorate, the more common second language was, until recently, Spanish, a habit that lingers in the older generation. English is also spoken, due to the UN presence.

Dangers & Annoyances

Despite ongoing tensions in the Western Sahara, travel in much of the west of this region is still considered safe by most government travel advisories. Flying in and out of Dakhla from Casablanca or Agadir is straightforward and safe.

Spain has been most critical of Morocco's presence in the Western Sahara, so Spanish travellers are most likely to field questions from Moroccan officials. Occupations likely to ring alarm bells at police posts are journalist or aid worker. If police confirm that you work in an occupation of that nature, you could be followed, detained, sent back to Morocco proper or even deported. Authorities tend to be more wary of travellers visiting Laayoune than Dakhla.

That said, Spanish and other nationalities visiting for legitimate purposes of tourism are likely to have no problems at all.

Travelling overland, and approaching the Western Sahara through towns such as Tarfaya, Tan Tan, Goulimime and Tata, you should also be prepared for the regular occurrence of police checkpoints. Foreigners are invariably asked about their occupation, reason for visiting, and next destination, and passports are requested so details can be recorded.

For most people, exchanges between police and travellers at checkpoints usually dissolve quickly into the relative merits of the Barcelona and Real Madrid football teams. However, everyone should treat the checkpoint stops seriously, tedious though they are, as there is a small risk of travellers being mistaken for a journalist or Polisario sympathiser.

In the Western Sahara, your passport and visa details will be noted down, along with your vehicle details if you are driving. If you're on a bus, you can usually stay in your seat while the police take your ID and write down your particulars. To streamline these encounters, it's a good tactic to have multiple photocopies of the identification pages from your passport to hand over, rather than the actual document.

Once in both Laayoune (especially) and Dakhla, you will be aware of the military and police, both of whom are sensitive to photography around military installations.

Laayoune العيون

☎0528 / POP 217,732

The Spanish created Laayoune (*la-ah-yoon*) as an outpost from which to administer the nearby Bou Craa phosphate mines. The Moroccans had bigger ambitions and spent more than US$1 billion turning it into the Western Sahara's principal city. Now neither Sahrawi nor Spanish, its population is mostly Moroccans, lured from the north by the promise of healthy wages and tax-free goods. As a result, the town is much less laid-back than others in Southern Morocco.

A government centre and military garrison with UN Land Cruisers drifting along its drab and dusty avenues, Laayoune is not worth a visit for its own sake, especially given lingering tensions between Moroccans and Sahrawi. Unless you're travelling overland to Dakhla, your time in Morocco is better spent elsewhere.

Sights

St Francis of Assisi Cathedral CHURCH

(Église Espanole; Ave Hassan II) Notable for its mid-century Spanish architectural style, this cathedral was designed by the architect Diego Méndez, famous for having worked on the *Valle de los Caídos* (Valley of the Fallen) outside Madrid, where Franco was buried until 2019. When open, it's a respite from the heat and sun, and the priests are knowledgeable about the area and happy to chat. Masses are given Saturday 7pm and Sunday 11am. It's opposite a pleasant garden park.

Sleeping & Eating

Unsurprisingly due to the UN presence, accommodation in this desert outpost is expensive by Moroccan standards.

If you came to Laayoune expecting an interesting culinary scene, you'll be disappointed. There are simple restaurants around Place Dchira, including a McDonald's that comes recommended by locals. Otherwise, wander down Blvd de Mekka for smoky cafes filled with loitering men, or head to a hotel restaurant. The best place for a leisurely coffee or mint tea are the cafes around Place Dchira. Beer and wine aren't readily available.

Hôtel Jodesa HOTEL €

(☎0528992064; 223 Blvd de Mekka; s/d Dh120/190, with shower Dh170/220; 📶) Behind its dilapidated two-tone facade and a cafe full of loitering men, this central cheapie has basic but reasonably spacious rooms. If you're a light sleeper, ask for a room at the back of the building.

Sahara Line Hotel HOTEL €€

(☎0528995454; Blvd El Kairaouane; s/d Dh390/490; 📶) A UN favourite, the Sahara Line has carpeted, comfortable rooms in blonde wood with fridge, bathroom and TV. There's a restaurant on the top floor, and staff speak good English.

Hôtel Nagjir HOTEL €€

(☎0528894168; Place de la Résistance; s/d from Dh418/636; 📶) Beyond its grand reception in mosaic tile, the four-star Nagjir has a restaurant and scruffy rooms. If you're in a kitsch mood there is also a suite with a pleather and diamanté queen bed with views over the dusty plaza below. It has another '70s-style hotel, Nagjir Plage, by the sandy beach at Foum El Oued, 22km from town.

Hôtel Al Massira HOTEL €€€

(☎0528994848; Blvd de Mekka; s/d from Dh775/955; 📶) If you find yourself stuck in Laayoune and in need of some peace and quiet, you could do worse than the Massira's calm, spacious rooms, set above an expansive foyer and palm-filled courtyard. Because most guests have expense accounts, things are a little overpriced.

Hôtel Parador HOTEL €€€

(☎0528892814; Ave de l'Islam; s/d Dh1800/2200; 📶) This survivor from Spanish days, built in hacienda style around gardens and a pretty fountain, has a faintly colonial bar and a decent restaurant. The rooms are done up in muted mauves, and some open onto a pleasant courtyard. Check a few before committing, as cleanliness is sometimes an issue. It's a serene spot, but wildly overpriced.

Pizzeria La Madone PIZZA €

(☎0528993252; 141 Ave Chahid Bouchraya; pizzas from Dh50; ⏰11am-midnight) A popular place with families, the Madone specialises in thin-crust pizzas with a variety of bizarre topping combinations, like calamari and turkey. Tajine, pasta and panini are available as well.

Getting There & Around

AIR

Hassan I Airport (0528893791; www.onda.ma) is 1.5km southwest of Laayoune. Flights from Agadir to Dakhla sometimes transit here.

Binter Canarias (www.bintercanarias.com) flies to/from various destinations in the Canary Islands, and Royal Air Maroc (www.royalairmaroc.com) has flights to/from Casablanca and Agadir. RAM also runs a flight from Dahkla four times per week.

BUS

Buses mostly leave from the offices towards the southern end of Blvd de Mekka; however, a new bus station located to the west of central Laayoune was awaiting completion at the time of research.

Book ahead for daily **CTM** (www.ctm.ma; Blvd de Mekka) departures to Agadir (Dh250, 11 hours), Dakhla (Dh180, eight hours), Goulimime (Dh180, seven hours), Marrakesh (Dh360, 14 hours), Tan Tan (Dh140, five hours) and Tiznit (Dh210, nine hours). **Supratours** (www.supratours.ma; Place Oum Saad) services cost slightly more than CTM's; **SATAS** (Blvd de Mekka) services cost the same or marginally less, but there's minimal difference in service between the three companies.

GRANDS TAXIS

Grand taxi services include Tarfaya (Dh50), Tan Tan (Dh150), Goulimime (Dh250), Inezgane (for Agadir, Dh220) and Dakhla (Dh200).

PETITS TAXIS

Red-and-white petits taxis charge about Dh5 to take you across town (Dh10 at night), including to the main grand-taxi station, located about 2km east of the centre along Blvds Prince Moulay Abdallah and Abou Bakr Seddik.

Dakhla الداخلة

0528 / POP 106,277

Established by the Spanish in 1844 and formerly called Villa Cisneros, Dakhla (*dakh-lah*) lies just north of the Tropic of Cancer on a sandy peninsula stretching 40km from the main coastline. It's a lonely 500km drive from Laayoune, and more than 1000km from Agadir, through endless desert; Dakhla is actually closer to Nouâdhibou (Mauritania) than any Moroccan city.

But Dakhla feels more prosperous than most southern towns, with an emerging tourism scene driven by kitesurfing. North of town, there are plenty of luxury resorts offering all-inclusive kitesurfing packages aimed at Europeans, as well as tented camps for DIYers.

Although Western Saharan tensions do still linger under the sea-breeze surface, investment by the Moroccan government and developers continues, and the population continues to grow with new arrivals from the north. New apartment blocks stretch the town boundaries and Dakhla's port is home to Morocco's largest fishing fleet.

Activities & Tours

Kitesurfing is the biggest game in town, with strong winds and the calm waters of the lagoon providing year-round access to some of the best conditions on the planet. When the Moroccan royal family holidayed and kitesurfed here in 2016, the profile of Dakhla for Moroccan visitors from the northern cities surged overnight.

Kayaking and SUP are also popular if the wind is not quite right, and resorts offer desert trips and surfing to their guests. Sailing on the lagoon and exploring Dakhla's desert hinterland is also possible, and fishing excursions can be booked through the better hotels.

★Dakhla Rovers TOURS

(0636808515, 0636808514; www.dakhla-rovers.com) Italian couple Nico and Martina incorporate all their experience as adventurers, marine biologists and diving instructors in providing a range of experiences exploring the natural diversity around Dakhla and the Western Sahara. Options include birdwatching in Dakhla's Ramsar zone, 4WD desert trips from two to four days and customised excursions taking in local wildlife such as the big-eared Saharan fennec fox.

Dakhla Rovers is very focused on ensuring the travellers' scene in Dakhla develops with good adherence to sustainable and ecologically sound practices.

★Sahara Sailing BOATING

(0619250454; 1hr Dh400, half-/full-day Dh700/1300) British expats Neil and Jackie Hutchinson are joined by local sailors as they navigate their catamaran around the lagoon. Excursions incorporate lunch – including terrific carrot cake – and guests are encouraged to be as active or relaxed as they wish in sailing the boat. Helping the crew hoist sails is a good way to earn another slice of cake.

Dakhla

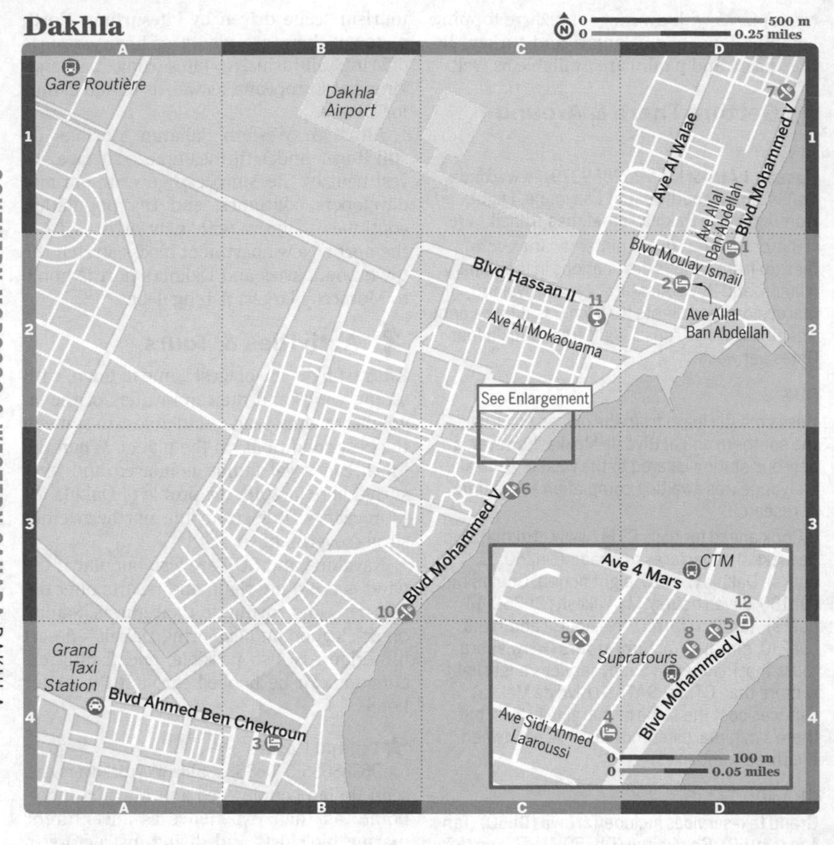

Dakhla

Sleeping

1 Dar Rio Oro D2
2 Hotel Al Baraka D2
3 Hôtel Erraha B4
4 Hôtel Sahara C4

Eating

5 Café Bahia D4
6 Café Restaurant Samarkand C3
7 Casa Lola D1
8 Casa Luis D4
9 Gladys C4
10 Le Palais Rhoul B3

Drinking & Nightlife

11 Hassan Fruits C2

Shopping

12 Complexe d'Artisanat de Dakhla D3

Sleeping

Downtown Dakhla has scruffy budget options, and a few higher-end places. Twenty kilometres north of town, there's a cluster of kitesurfing camps and luxury resorts, all of which include airport transfers in their rates.

Camping Vignt-Cinq TENTED CAMP **€**

(☎0515374934; Km 27, Lagoon; tent Dh200) It's the chillest vibe imaginable at this tented camp, well-suited to that rare animal: the kitesurfer on a budget. Proprietor Sidatee and his family hang out in their tent while campers live the dream riding waves or – you guessed it – chilling out on the beach. It's best suited for the self-sufficient, with their own kitesurfing gear and meal-prep kit.

Turn right onto a dirt road just before the police checkpoint at the lagoon.

Hôtel Sahara HOTEL €
(☎0528897773; Ave Sidi Ahmed Laaroussi; s/d from Dh65/80) The Sahara's dingy rooms have little balconies overlooking men milling about and sitting in cafes (women will attract a lot of attention here). The basic options share showers and squat toilets; the better-value en-suite rooms have sit-down toilets and TVs.

Dar Rio Oro GUESTHOUSE €€
(☎0655821260; dar.rio.oro@gmail.com; Ave Mohammed V; s/d from Dh630/690; 📶) This multi-storey townhouse a short walk north of Dakha's waterfront has a variety of comfortable and stylish rooms and mini-apartments with kitchen facilities. Some rooms share bathrooms, but only ever with one other guest room. The decor incorporates traditional Berber motifs and the rooftop terrace provides great views, especially at sunset. Excursions and rental cars can be arranged.

Hotel Al Baraka HOTEL €€
(☎0528934744; hotelalbarakadakhla@gmail.com; Ave Allal Ben Abdellah; s/d Dh550/759, ste Dh850-1000; 📶) Located a short walk from good restaurants, the rooms at the Al Baraka still retain that minty-fresh just-opened ambience. Big-screen TVs provide access to a planet's worth of satellite services and rooms on the top floor have a glimmer of ocean view. Hotel manager Abdo is very responsive, but other staff can struggle with simple requests.

Hôtel Erraha HOTEL €€
(☎0528898811; Ave Banchekroune; s/d Dh200/400; 📶) The Erraha's spacious rooms are decorated in a chintzy fashion you might associate with a matronly relative, and the space adjoins a mosque that draws the devout. Bathrooms are a grim affair, with broken appliances and peeling paint. Despite welcoming staff, unless you arrive late into the nearby grand-taxi station there are better options in town.

★**Ocean Vagabond** RESORT €€€
(☎0613037861; www.oceanvagabond.com; Km 28, Lagoon; r incl full-board from €115; P📶) 🍃 Ocean Vagabond draws Euro yuppies with brilliant ocean views, a beach bar, yoga, massage pavilions and a pleasing Instagram vibe. Villas and bungalows are stylish, and the focus on providing a brilliant kitesurfing experience is maximised with a well-stocked gear shop and lessons from world champion kitesurfers.

Ocean Vagabond has also been awarded Green Key status for sustainable tourism practices, including solar electricity, filtered water and a massive tree-planting programme.

Dakhla Attitude RESORT €€€
(☎0661835010; www.dakhla-attitude.ma; Km 30, Dakhla Lagoon; s/d incl full-board from Dh825/1155; 📶) The first of Dakhla's kitesurfing camps has now evolved into an expansive and very comfortable resort with breezy hillside bungalows, an excellent restaurant and a sandy beachfront bar attended by quite possibly the most laid-back dogs in all Morocco. It's a true destination resort with yoga, massage and activities for children, and has a prime location right on the lagoon.

If you're self-driving, know that the road to get here is difficult to navigate in a normal car, due to drifting dunes. Four-by-four transfers are included in all bookings.

Zenith Dakhla RESORT €€€
(☎0661233948; www.zenith-dakhla.com; Km 27, Lagoon; r incl full-board from €118; 📶🏊) Located across the road from the lagoon, this German-owned kitesurfing resort wows with elegant design features, including a swimming pool, a restaurant with soaring ceilings and furniture crafted from recycled timber. The chic design continues to the rooms and villas with rainforest outdoor showers, cooling tones and classy bathrooms.

Significant discounts can often be negotiated if you drop by.

Eating & Drinking

Spanish cuisine provides a pleasant respite from tajines here, with several restaurants dishing up tapas, paella and tortilla. The restaurants in the luxury resorts north of town are generally top notch, but they're difficult to access without your own transport.

Options for a casual drink include Casa Luis and Casa Lola. Things are more open at the top-end Le Palais Rhoul and at the beachside bars in the luxury kitesurfing resorts.

Café Restaurant Samarkand SEAFOOD €
(☎0528898316; Ave Mohammed V; mains Dh50-70; ⏰8am-11pm) This waterfront cafe commands stupendous views across the narrow Dakhla Bay. The bougainvillea-kissed pavilions are a great escape from Dakhla's dusty streets, and Samarkand is one of the town's only cafes where the clientele regularly includes both men and women. The menu features fish and other dishes; order in advance for couscous or fish *bastilla*.

Gladys MOROCCAN €
(mains Dh20-30; ⏰6-10pm) Located on a busy shopping street, Gladys serves up well-priced tajines to a loyal band of locals. Aside from the food, it's a great place to check out

neo-Tuareg dress sense (think blue robes over Adidas trackies). The kitchen is helmed by female members of a single family, and no, we don't know why it is called Gladys.

Café Bahia SEAFOOD €
(☎0528930062; 16 Ave Mohammed V; mains Dh50-70; ⊙noon-10pm) What's on the menu here? There is no menu. But there's fish and Coca Cola, and rumour has it you can get a beer disguised in a teacup if you ask nicely. Scruffy but serviceable rooms (Dh100 per person) are available upstairs if you overdo it on octopus and teacup beer.

★**Casa Lola** SPANISH €€
(☎0528930692; Ave Al Wallae; tapas Dh40-120; ⊙1-3.30pm Mon-Fri, 8.30pm-midnight daily) This stylish restaurant celebrates the region's recent Spanish heritage with hot and cold tapas – the shrimp croquettes and the calamari are both very good – while local octopus and grilled whiting are popular menu items. The namesake Lola keeps regular business visitors from the Canary Islands very happy, dispensing both good humour and complimentary aperitivo shots. Beer and wine are also served.

Casa Luis SEAFOOD €€
(☎0528898193; Ave Mohammed V; mains Dh70-120; ⊙8.30am-11pm) Spanish flavours and seafood come together at this long-established local favourite. Tuck into tortilla, paella and grilled catch of the day (which sometimes include lobster). Chicken and grilled beef also feature, and beer and wine are served.

Le Palais Rhoul MOROCCAN €€€
(☎0673224110; 100 Ave Mohammed V; mains Dh130-180; ⊙7-11pm) Trimmed with Asian design cues, this elegant lounge and bar would be more at home in cosmopolitan Casablanca. Blackboard menus highlight fragrant tajines and an excellent seafood *bastilla*, and the wine list with French, Spanish and Moroccan varietals is the best in town. The dining room segues to exterior terraces with ocean views, a great spot to share a shisha.

Hassan Fruits JUICE BAR
(Ave Al Walae; juices from Dh15; ⊙6pm-late) Across the pedestrian crossing from the Dakhla peninsula monument, this is popular for a slice of cake and a fruit cocktail. Look for the fluorescent plastic chairs out front.

Shopping

A pedestrianised shopping lane runs north from Ave Sidi Ahmed Laaroussi between Hôtel Sahara and Hôtel Aigue. Vendors here sell goods ranging from argan oil to bright *melhaf* (colourful Berber fabrics).

Complexe d'Artisanat de Dakhla ARTS & CRAFTS
(cnr Ave Mohammed V & Blvd 4 Mars; ⊙noon-10pm) This is less a complex and more a few dusty floors under continuous construction overseen by a bored security guard. At time of writing there was one brightly lit jewelry store and one carpet shop, and several dozen shops waiting to be rented. The structure itself is quite grand, and is the most interesting thing about the place.

Getting There & Around

AIR

As the distances in Western Sahara are so great, flying direct from Agadir and Casablanca is recommended.

Dakhla Airport (☎0528930630; www.onda.ma) is a 2.5km drive north of the waterfront. Royal Air Maroc (www.royalairmaroc.com) has regular flights to/from Casablanca and Agadir, and to Las Palmas on Gran Canaria (Tuesday only). RAM also runs flights to Laayoune four times per week. A shared taxi from the airport to central hotels costs Dh15.

BUS

CTM (☎0528898166; Blvd 4 Mars) and **Supratours** (Ave Mohammed V) both have offices in the centre, but buses depart from the Gare Routière, on the western edge of town. Bus companies also have offices on and around Ave Banchekroune, between the grand-taxi station and the Edderhem Mosque. Opening hours can be flexible at the offices, so if you have to have a ticket on a certain bus it's worth schlepping to the Gare Routière or asking your hotel to book for you.

Book ahead for popular daily CTM services to Agadir (Dh410, 20 hours), Laayoune (Dh180, 8½ hours), Marrakesh (Dh500, 23 hours) and Tan Tan (Dh320, 13½ hours).

For onward travel to Nouâdhibou and Nouakchatt in Mauritania, Supratours has an arrangement with a Mauritanian bus company for cross-border buses. Enquire at the Supratours office for details, but only after careful review of FCO security guidelines for Mauritania.

GRANDS TAXIS

The grand-taxi station is in Al Messira, southwest of the centre. Destinations include Inezgane (for Agadir, Dh420) and Laayoune (Dh200).

PETITS TAXIS

White-and-cerulean petits taxis whiz around town (average trip day/night Dh5/6).

Understand Morocco

History

Morocco is an old nation. The current king, Mohammed VI, is part of the Alaouite dynasty that's ruled the country since the 17th century. Before that, the Imazighen – the free, unconquered people – inhabited Morocco since prehistoric times, long before empires and invaders left their mark, from the Romans to the Arabs, who brought Islam. Morocco's ties across the Mediterranean to Europe and across the Sahara have given rise to a unique nation with a singular history.

The Imazighen Meet the Romans

Morocco's earliest inhabitants were ancestors of Morocco's Amazigh (plural Imazighen, loosely translated as 'free born'), who may have been distant cousins of the ancient Egyptians. They were joined by Mediterranean anglers and Saharan horse-breeders around 2500 BCE, with Phoenicians showing up fashionably late around 800 BCE and East Africans around 500 BCE.

When the Romans took control around 40 CE, they didn't know quite what to make of this multicultural milieu. The Romans called the expanse of Morocco and Western Algeria 'Mauretania' and the indigenous people 'Berbers', meaning 'barbarians'. The term has recently been reclaimed and redeemed by the Berber Pride movement, but at the time it was taken as a slur.

The ensuing centuries were one long lesson for the Romans in minding their manners. First the Imazighen backed Hannibal and the Carthaginians against Rome in a protracted spat over Sicily known as the Punic Wars (264–202 BCE). Fed up with the 'unruly' Imazighen, the new Roman Emperor Caligula finally declared the end of Amazigh autonomy in the Maghreb (northwest Africa) in 40 CE.

Defying Orders under Roman Noses

True to his ruthless reputation, Roman emperor Caligula divided relatively egalitarian Imazighen clans into subservient classes of enslaved people, peasants, soldiers and Romanised aristocrats. This strategy worked with Vandals and Byzantines, but Imazighen in the Rif and Atlas mountains fought back and drove out the Romans. Many Imazighen

TIMELINE

Origin

According to Amazigh (Berber) folklore, the earth's first couple birthed 100 babies and left them to finish the job of populating the planet.

248,000–73,000 BCE

Precocious 'pebble people' begin fashioning stone tools far ahead of the European Stone Age technology curve.

5000–2500 BCE

Once the Ice Age melts away, the Maghreb becomes a melting pot of Saharan, Mediterranean and indigenous people. They meet, mingle and merge into a diverse people: the Imazighen (Berbers).

refused to worship Roman gods, and some practised the new renegade religion of Christianity in open defiance of Roman rule. Christianity took root across North Africa; St Augustine was a Amazigh convert.

Ultimately Rome was only able to gain a sure foothold in the region by crowning local favourite Juba II king of Mauretania. The enterprising young king married the daughter of Mark Antony and Cleopatra, supported scientific research and performing arts, and helped foster Moroccan industries still vital today: olive oil production from the region of Volubilis (near Meknes), fishing along the coasts, and vineyards on the Atlantic plains.

The Roman foothold in Mauretania slipped in the centuries after Juba II died because of increasingly organised Amazigh uprisings inland and attacks on the Atlantic and Mediterranean coasts by the Vandals, Byzantines and Visigoths. But this new crop of marauding Europeans couldn't manage Mauretania, and neither could Byzantine Emperor Justinian. Justinian's attempt to extend his Holy Roman Empire turned out to be an unholy mess of treaties with various Amazigh kingdoms, who played their imperial Byzantine connections like face cards in high-stakes games. The history of Morocco would be defined by such strategic gamesmanship among the Imazighen, whose savvy, competing alliances helped make foreign dominion over Morocco a near-impossible enterprise for more than a millennium.

Islam Arrives in Morocco

By the early 7th century, the Imazighen were mostly worshipping their own indigenous deities, alongside a smattering of local Jewish and Christian converts. History might have continued thus but for a middle-aged man thousands of kilometres away who'd had the good fortune to marry a wealthy widow and yet found himself increasingly at odds with the elites of his Arabian Peninsula town of Mecca. Muhammad Bin Abu Talib was his given name, but he would soon be recognised as the Prophet Muhammad for his revelation that there was only one God and that believers shared a common duty to submit to God's will. The polytheist ruling class of Mecca did not take kindly to this new religion, which assigned them shared responsibilities and took away their minor-deity status, and kicked the Prophet out of town in 622.

This exile only served to spread the Prophet Muhammad's message more widely. By the Prophet's death in 632, Arab caliphs – religious leaders inspired by his teachings – were carrying Islam east to Central Asia and west to North Africa. But infighting limited their reach in North Africa, and it took Umayyad leader Uqba Bin Nafi until 682 to reach the Atlantic shores of Morocco. According to legend, Uqba announced he would charge into the ocean if God would only give him the signal. But the legendary Algerian Amazigh warrior Queen Al Kahina would have none of Uqba's grandstanding, and with her warriors soon forced Uqba to retreat back to Tunisia.

Pre-Islamic Sites

Carved Gazelles, Tafraoute

Roman Diana mosaics at Volubilis

Phoenician/Roman ruins at Lixus

Prehistoric petroglyphs, Oukaimeden

Chellah, Rabat

1600 BCE

Bronze Age petroglyphs in the High Atlas depict fishing, hunting and horseback riding – a versatile combination of skills and cultures that would define the adaptable, resilient Imazighen.

950 BCE

The Imazighen rebuff Rome and its calendar year, and start tracking their history on their own calendar on 13 January; it's maintained for centuries after the Muslim Hejira calendar is introduced.

800–500 BCE

The Maghreb gets even more multicultural as Phoenicians and East Africans join the Imazighen.

4th–1st century BCE

Romans arrive to annex Mauretania, and 250 years later they're still trying, with limited success and some Punic Wars to show for their troubles.

Key Islamic Sites Open to Non-Muslims

- *Tin Mal Mosque, Ijoukak*
- *Medersa Bou Inania, Fez*
- *Zawiya Nassiriyya, Tamegroute*
- *Hassan II Mosque, Casablanca*

Although an armed force failed to win the Imazighen over to Islam, force of conviction gradually began to succeed. The egalitarian premise of Islam and its emphasis on duty, courage and the greater good were compatible with many Amazigh beliefs, including clan loyalty broadly defined to include almost anyone descended from the Amazigh equivalent of Adam and Eve. Many Imazighen willingly converted to Islam – and not incidentally, reaped the benefits of Umayyad overland trading routes that brought business their way. So although Uqba was killed by his Amazigh foes before he was able to establish a solid base in Morocco, by the 8th century his successors were able to pull off this feat largely through diplomatic means.

Islam Stays, but Umayyads Must Go

The admiration between the Amazigh and the Arab Umayyads was not always mutual, however. While the Umayyads respected Jews and Christians as fellow believers in the word of a singular God, they had no compunction about compelling the polytheist Imazighen to pay special taxes and serve as infantry, aka cannon fodder. The Umayyads greatly admired Amazigh women for their beauty, but this wasn't necessarily advantageous; many were conscripted into Umayyad harems.

Even the Imazighen who converted to Islam were forced to pay tribute to their Arab overlords. A dissident school of Islamic thought called Kharijism critiqued the abuses of power of the Umayyads as a corruption of the faith, and called for a new moral leadership. In the mid-8th century, insurrections erupted across North Africa. Armed only with slings, a special force of Imazighen defeated the elite Umayyad guard. The Umayyads were soon cut off from Spain and Morocco, and local leaders took over an increasingly lucrative trade in silver from the Western Sahara, gold from Ghana and enslaved people from West Africa.

Key Moroccan Dynasties

- *Idrissid (8th–10th century)*
- *Almoravid (11th–12th century)*
- *Almohad (12th–13th century)*
- *Merinid (13th–15th century)*
- *Saadian (16th–17th century)*
- *Alaouite (17th century–present)*

A Death-Defying Dynasty: The Idrissids

Looking back on early Amazigh kingdoms, the 14th-century historian Ibn Khaldun noted a pattern that would repeat throughout Moroccan dynastic history. A new leadership would arise determined to do right, make contributions to society as a whole and fill the royal coffers. When the pursuit of power and royal comforts began to eclipse loftier aspirations, the powers that be would forfeit their claim to moral authority. A new leadership would arise determined to do right, and the cycle would begin all over again.

So it was with the Idrissids, Morocco's first great dynasty. A descendant of the Prophet Muhammad's daughter Fatima, Idriss I fled Arabia for Morocco in 786 CE after discovering ambitious Caliph Harun Al Rashid's plan to murder his entire family. But Idriss didn't exactly keep a low profile. After being proclaimed an imam (religious leader) by the local

49 BCE
North African King Juba I supports Pompey's ill-fated power play against Julius Caesar. Rome is outraged, but senators pick up where Pompey left off and assassinate Caesar.

25 BCE–23 CE
Rome gets a toehold in Mauretania with farms, cities and art, thanks to Juba II. He expands Volubilis into a metropolis of 20,000 residents, including a sizeable Jewish community.

200–429
Vandals and Visigoths take turns forcing one another out of Spain and onto the shores of Morocco, until local warriors from the Rif Mountains convince them to bother the Algerians instead.

533
Justinian ousts the last Vandals from Morocco, but his grand plans to extend the Holy Roman Empire are soon reduced to a modest presence in Essaouira, Tangier and Salé.

Imazighen, he unified much of northern Morocco in the name of Islam. Just a few days after he'd finally settled into his new capital at Fez in 792, Rashid's minions finally tracked down and poisoned Idriss I. Yet death only increased Idriss I's influence; his body was discovered to be miraculously intact five centuries later, and his tomb in the hillside town of Moulay Idriss Zerhoun remains one of the holiest pilgrimage sites in Morocco.

His son Idriss II escaped Rashid's assassins and extended Idrissid control across northern Morocco and well into Europe. In perhaps the first (but certainly not the last) approximation of democracy in Morocco, Idriss II's 13 sons shared power after their father's death. Together they expanded Idrissid principates into Spain and built the glorious mosques of Fez: the Kairaouine and the Andalous.

Warriors Unveiled: The Almoravids

With religious leaders and scholars to help regulate trade, northern Morocco began to take shape as an economic entity under the Idrissids. But the south was another story. A dissident prophet emerged near Salé brandishing an Amazigh version of the Quran, and established an apocryphal Islam called Barghawata that continued to be practised in the region for centuries. The military strongmen who were left in control of trading outposts in the Atlas Mountains and the Sahara demanded what they called 'alms' – bogus religious nomenclature that didn't fool anyone, and stirred up resentments among the faithful.

From this desert discontent arose the Sanhaja, the pious Saharan Amazigh tribe that founded the Almoravid dynasty. While the Idrissid princes were distracted by disputes over Spain and Mediterranean Morocco, the Sanhaja swept into the south of Morocco from what is today Senegal and Mauritania. Tough doesn't do justice to the Sanhaja; they lived on camel meat and milk instead of bread, wore wool in the scorching desert and abstained from wine and music. Their habit of wearing dark veils is still practised today by the few remaining Tuareg, the legendary 'Blue Men' of the desert (and the many tourists who imitate them in camel-riding photo-ops). When these intimidating shrouded men rode into Shiite and Barghawata outposts under the command of Yahya Ibn Umar and his brother Abu Bakr, they demolished brothels and musical instruments as well as their opponents.

From Marrakesh to Barcelona, the Ultimate Power Couple

After Umar was killed and Abu Bakr was recalled to the Sahara to settle Sanhaja disputes in 1061, their cousin Youssef Ben Tachfine was left to run military operations from a campsite that would become Marrakesh the magnificent. To spare his wife the hardships of life in the Sahara, Abu Bakr divorced brilliant Amazigh heiress Zeinab En Nafzawiyyat and

An incisive look at religious life on opposite ends of the Muslim world, anthropologist Clifford Geertz's groundbreaking *Islam Observed: Religious Development in Morocco and Indonesia* reveals complex variations within the vast mosaic of Islam.

662–682

Arabs invade the Maghreb under Umayyad leader Uqba Bin Nafi, introducing Islam to the area. Amazigh warriors eventually boot out the Umayyads but decide to keep the Quran.

711

Northern Morocco and most of Spain come under Umayyad control, and the Imazighen are strategically settled throughout Andalusia.

788–829

Islam takes root in Morocco under Idriss I and Idriss II, who make Fez the epitome of Islamic art, architecture and scholarship and the capital of their Idrissid empire.

8th century

Through shared convictions and prudent alliances, Arab caliphates control an area that extends across the Mediterranean and well into Europe, just 320km shy of Paris.

arranged her remarriage to his cousin. Though an odd romantic gesture by today's standards, it was an inspired match. It would be Zeinab's third marriage: before marrying Abu Bakr, she was the widow of one of the leading citizens of Aghmat and had considerable fortune and political experience at her command. Between Tachfine's initiative and Zeinab's financing and strategic counsel, the Almoravids were unstoppable.

Amazigh Queen Al Kahina had one distinct advantage over the Umayyads: clairvoyance. The downside? She foretold her own death at the hands of her enemy.

The Almoravids took a while to warm up to their new capital of Marrakesh – too many mountains and rival Imazighen around, and too few palm trees. To make themselves more at home, the Almoravids built a mud wall around the city, 8m high and 19km long, and set up the ingenious *khettara* (underground irrigation system) that still supports the *palmeraie* – a vast palm grove outside Marrakesh now dotted with luxury villas and hotels. The Jewish and Andalusian communities in Fez thrived under Tachfine, a soft-spoken diplomat and, like his wife, a brilliant military strategist. His Spanish Muslim allies urged him to intercede against Christian and Muslim princes in Spain, complaining bitterly of extortion, attacks and debauchery. At the age of almost 80, Tachfine launched successful campaigns securing Almoravid control of Andalusia right up to the Barcelona city limits.

Sticks & Stones: The Almohads

Tachfine was a tough act to follow. Ali was his son by a Christian woman, and he shared his father's commitments to prayer and urban planning. But while the reclusive young idealist Ali was diligently working wonders with architecture and irrigation in Marrakesh, a new force beyond the city walls was gathering the strength of an Atlas thunderstorm: the Almohads.

Almohad historians would later fault Ali for two supposedly dangerous acts: leaving the women in charge and allowing Christians near drink. While the former was hardly a shortcoming – after all, his stepmother's counsel had proved instrumental to the Almoravids – there may be some merit in the latter. While Ali was in seclusion praying and fasting, court and military officials were left to carry on, and carry on they did. Apparently, Almoravid Christian troops were all too conveniently stationed near the wine merchants of Marrakesh.

The Hard Knocks of Ibn Tumart

None of this sat well with Mohammed Ibn Tumart, the Almohad spiritual leader from the Atlas who'd earned a reputation in Meknes and Salé as a religious vigilante, using his walking stick to shatter wine jars, smash musical instruments and smack men and women with the audacity to walk down the street together. Ibn Tumart finally got himself banished from Marrakesh in the 1120s for knocking Ali's royal sister off her horse with his stick.

1062

With the savvy Zeinab as his wife and chief counsel, Amazigh leader Youssef Ben Tachfine founds Marrakesh as a launching pad for Almoravid conquests of North Africa and Europe.

1069

The Almoravids take Fez by force and promptly begin installing mills and lush gardens and cleaning up the city with running water and hammams.

1082

Almoravid control stretches south to Ghana and Timbuktu, east to Algiers, and north from Lisbon to Spain's Ebro River, near Barcelona.

1121–30

Almohad spiritual leader Mohammed Ibn Tumart loudly condemns Almoravid indulgence in music and wine, and champions scientific reasoning and political organisation based on a written constitution.

But though Ibn Tumart died soon after, there was no keeping out the Almohads. They took over Fez after a nine-month siege in 1145, but reserved their righteous fury for Marrakesh two years later, razing the place to the ground and killing what was left of Ali's court (Ali died as he lived, quietly, in 1144). Their first projects included rebuilding the Koutoubia Mosque – which Almoravid architects, not up on their algebra, had misaligned with Mecca – and adding the soaring, sublime stone minaret that became the template for Andalusian Islamic architecture. The Tin Mal Mosque was constructed in the High Atlas to honour Ibn Tumart in 1156, and it remains a wonder of austere graces and unshakeable foundations.

Almohad Demolition & Construction Crews

A bloody power struggle ensued between the sons of Ibn Tumart and the sons of his generals that wouldn't be settled definitively until 1185, when Abu Yusuf Yacoub, the young son of the Muslim governor of Seville and Valencia, rode south into Morocco and drove his foes into the desert. But he also kept and expanded his power base in Spain, winning so many victories against the princes of Spain that he earned the moniker Al Mansour, 'the Victorious'. He modelled Seville's famous La Giralda after Marrakesh's Koutoubia minaret and reinvented Marrakesh as an Almohad capital and learning centre to rival Fez.

Yacoub Al Mansour's urban-planning prowess also made Fez arguably the most squeaky-clean city of medieval times, with 93 hammams, 47 soap factories and 785 mosques complete with ablutions facilities. Mansour was also a patron of great thinkers, including Aristotle scholar Ibn Rashid – whose commentary would help spark a Renaissance among Italian philosophers – and Sufi master Sidi Bel Abbes. However, Mansour's enlightenment and admiration of architecture was apparently not all-encompassing; several synagogues were demolished under his rule.

The most comprehensive Amazigh history in English is *The Berbers*, by Michael Brett and Elizabeth Fentress. The authors leave no stone carving unturned, providing archaeological evidence to back up their historical insights.

Defeated by Bulls & Betrayal

Similar thinking (or lack thereof) prevailed in 12th-century Europe, where a hunt for heretics turned to officially sanctioned torture under papal bulls of the egregiously misnamed Pope Innocent IV. Bishop Bernard of Toledo, Spain, seized Toledo's mosque and rallied Spain's Castilian Christian kings in a crusade against their Muslim rulers.

The Almohads were in no condition to fight back. When Mansour's 16-year-old son was named caliph, he wasn't up to the religious responsibilities that came with the title. Instead, he was obsessed with bullfighting and was soon gored to death. Mansour must have done pirouettes in his grave around 1230 when his next son tapped as caliph, Al Mamun, allied with his Christian persecutors and turned on his fellow Almohads in a desperate attempt to hang onto his father's empire. This short-lived caliph added the ultimate insult to Almohad injury when he climbed the

1147

The Almohads finally defeat the Almoravids and destroy Marrakesh after a two-year siege, paving the way for Yacoub El Mansour and his architects to outdo the Almoravids with an all-new Marrakesh.

1199

A vast swath of prime Mediterranean commercial real estate from Tripoli to Spain is consolidated under Almohad control.

1276

Winds of change blow in from the Atlas with the Zenata Imazighen, who oust the Almohads and establish the Merinid dynasty with strategic military manoeuvres and even more strategic marriages.

1324–52

Tangier-born adventurer Ibn Battuta picks up where Marco Polo left off, travelling from Mali to Sumatra and Mongolia and publishing *Rihla* – an inspired though not entirely reliable travel guide.

Koutoubia Mosque's minbar (pulpit) and announced that Ibn Tumart wasn't a true Mahdi (leader) of the faithful. That title, he claimed, rightfully belonged to Jesus.

By Marriage or Murder: The Merinids

When the Zenata Imazighen from the Anti Atlas Mountains invaded the Almohad capital of Marrakesh in 1269, the Almohad defeat was complete. The Zenata had already ousted the Almohads in Meknes, Salé and Fez and along most of the Atlantic Coast. To win over the devout, they promised moral leadership under their new Merinid dynasty. Making good on the promise, the Merinids undertook construction of a *medersa* (school for studying the Quran) in every major city they conquered, levying special taxes on Christian and Jewish communities for the purpose. In exchange, they allowed these communities to practice key trades, and hired Christian mercenaries and Jewish policy advisers to help conduct the business of the Merinid state.

But this time the new rulers faced a tough crowd not easily convinced by promises of piety. Fez revolted, and the Castilian Christians held sway in Salé. To shore up their Spanish interests, the Merinids allied with the Castilian princes against the Muslim rulers of Granada. Once again, this proved a losing strategy. By the 14th century, Muslim Spain was lost to the Christians, and the Strait of Gibraltar was forfeited. The Merinids also didn't expect the Spanish Inquisition, when more than one million Muslims and Jews would be terrorised and forcibly expelled from Spain.

Without military might or religious right to back their imperial claims, the Merinids chose another time-tested method: marriage. In the 14th century, Merinid leaders cleverly co-opted their foes by marrying princesses from Granada and Tunis, and claimed Algiers, Tripoli and the strategic Mediterranean port of Ceuta.

The symbol on the Amazigh (Berber) flag is the Tifinagh letter 'yaz' and symbolises a free person, the meaning of *amazigh*.

Death by Plague & Office Politics

But the bonds of royal marriage were not rat-proof, and the Merinid empire was devastated by plague. Abu Inan, son of the Merinid leader Abu Hassan, glimpsed opportunity in the Black Death and proclaimed himself the new ruler despite one minor glitch: his father was still alive. Abu Hassan hurried back from Tripoli to wrest control from his treacherous son in Fez, but to no avail. Abu Inan buried his father in the royal Merinid necropolis outside Rabat in 1351, but he too was laid to rest nearby after he was strangled by one of his own advisers in 1358.

The Merinids had an unfortunate knack for hiring homicidal bureaucrats. To cover his tracks, Abu Inan's killer went on a royal killing spree, until Merinid Abu Salim Ibrahim returned from Spain and terminated this rampaging employee. Abu Salim's adviser sucked up to his boss by offering his sister in marriage, only to lop off Abu Salim's head after the

1348

Bubonic plague strikes Mediterranean North Africa; Merinid alliances and kingdoms crumble. Rule of law is left to survivors and opportunists to enforce, with disastrous consequences.

1377

At Kairaouine University in Fez, Ibn Khaldun examines Middle Eastern history in his groundbreaking *Muqaddimah*, explaining how religious propaganda, taxation and revisionist history make and break states.

1415

In search of gold and the fabled kingdom of Prester John (location of the Fountain of Youth) Portuguese Prince Henry the Navigator begins his conquests of Moroccan seaports.

1480–92

Ferdinand and Isabella conquer Spain, and the persecution of Muslims and Jews escalates.

wedding. He replaced Abu Salim with a Merinid patsy before thinking better of it and strangling the new sultan too. This slippery adviser was assassinated by another Merinid, who was deposed a scant few years later by yet another Merinid – and so it continued for 40 years, with new Merinid rulers and advisers offing the incumbents every few years. While the Merinids were preoccupied with murderous office politics in Meknes and Fez, the Portuguese seized control of coastal Morocco.

Historic Moroccan Jewish Quarters

- Tamnougalt
- Demnate
- Fez
- Zagora
- Essaouira
- Marrakesh

Victory is Sweet: The Saadians

Much of Portugal (including Lisbon) had been under Muslim rule during the 12th century, and now the Portuguese were ready for payback – literally. The tiny, rugged kingdom needed steady supplies of food for its people and gold to fortify its growing empire, but Morocco stood in the way. No nation could wrest overland Saharan trade routes from the savvy Imazighen warriors who'd controlled key oases and mountain passes for centuries. Instead, the Portuguese went with tactics where they had clear technical advantages: naval warfare and advanced firearms. By systematically capturing Moroccan ports along the Mediterranean and Atlantic coasts, Portuguese gunships bypassed Amazigh middlemen inland and headed directly to West Africa for gold and enslaved people.

Sugar Caravans

Once trade in the Sahara began to dry up, something had to be done. Entire inland communities were decimated, and formerly flush Marrakesh was wracked with famine. The Beni Saad Imazighen – now known to history as the Saadians – from the Draa Valley took up the fight against the Portuguese. With successive wins against European, Amazigh and Ottoman rivals, the Saadians were able to reinstate inland trade. Soon the Saadians were in control of such sought-after commodities as gold, enslaved people, ivory, ostrich feathers and the must-have luxury for trendy European royals: sugar.

The Saadians satisfied European sugar cravings at prices that make today's oil companies and cocaine cartels look like rank amateurs. With threats of full-scale invasion, the Saadians had no problem scaring up customers and suppliers. The most dangerous sugar-dealer of all was Saadian Sultan Ahmed Al Mansour Ed Dahbi, who earned his names Al Mansour (the Victorious) for defeating foes from Portugal to the Sudan, and Ed Dahbi (the Golden) for his success in bilking them. This Marrakshi Midas used the proceeds to line his Badia Palace in Marrakesh from floor to ceiling with gold and gems. But after the sultan died, his short-lived successor stripped the palace down to its mud-brick foundations, as it remains today. The Saadian legacy is most visible in the Saadian Tombs, decked out for a decadent afterlife with painted Carrara marble and gold leaf. The Saadians died as they lived: dazzling beyond belief and a touch too rich for most tastes.

1497–1505

Moroccan ports are occupied by English, Portuguese and Spanish forces and sundry pirates, from Mediterranean Melilla to Agadir on the Atlantic coast.

1498

Church Inquisitors present European Muslims and Jews with a choice: conversion and persecution; or torture and death. Many choose neither of these and escape to Morocco.

1525

Like a blast of scorching desert wind, the Beni Saad Imazighen blow back European and Ottoman encroachment in Morocco, and establish a new Saadian dynasty in Marrakesh.

1578

The Saadians fight both alongside and against Portugal at the Battle of Three Kings, ending with 8000 dead, a scant 100 survivors and the decimation of Portugal's ruling class.

The Rise of Mellahs

Under the Saadians, Jewish communities also took up crucial roles as dealers of salt and sugar. When European Jews faced the Inquisition, forced conversions and summary executions, the comparatively tolerant Saadian dynasty provided these communities with some security, setting aside a section of Marrakesh next to the royal kasbah as a Jewish quarter, or *mellah* – a name derived from the Arabic word for salt. This protection was repaid many times over in taxes levied on Jewish and Christian businesses, and the royally flush Saadians clearly got the sweet end of the deal. Yet several Jewish Moroccans rose to prominence as royal advisers, and in the Saadian Tombs of Marrakesh, trusted Jewish confidantes are buried closer to kings than royal wives.

Amazigh (Berber) Languages in Morocco

Tamazight, Middle Atlas

Tashelhit, Central Morocco

Tarifit, Rif

Tamashek, Sahara

By day, Jewish merchants traded alongside Christian and Muslim merchants, and were entrusted with precious salt, sugar and gold brought across the Sahara; by night they were under official guard in their quarters. Once the Jewish quarters of Fez and Marrakesh became overcrowded with European arrivals, other notable districts were founded in Essaouira, Safi, Rabat and Meknes, and the traditions of skilled handicrafts that flourished there continue to this day. The influence of the *mellahs* spread throughout Morocco, especially in tangy dishes with the signature salted, pickled ingredients of Moroccan Jewish cuisine.

Pirates & Politics: The Early Alaouites

The Saadian empire dissolved in the 17th century like a sugar cube in Moroccan mint tea, and civil war prevailed until the Alaouites came along. With illustrious ancestors from the Prophet Muhammad's family and descendants extending to the current King Mohammed VI, the Alaouites were quite a change from the free-wheeling Saadians and their anarchic legacy. But many Moroccans might have preferred anarchy to the second Alaouite ruler, the dreaded Moulay Ismail (1672–1727).

A despot whose idea of a good time included public disembowelments and amateur dentistry, Moulay Ismail was also a scholar, father to hundreds of children and Mr Popularity among his royal European peers. European nobles gushed about lavish dinner parties at Moulay Ismail's palace in Meknes, built by Christian enslaved people who were routinely forced to convert to Islam and subjected to abuse. Rumour has it that when these decidedly non-union construction workers finished the job, some were walled in alive. The European royal party tab wasn't cheap, either, but Moulay Ismail wasn't worried: piracy would cover it.

In Her Majesty's Not-So-Secret Service: Barbary Pirates

England's Queen Elizabeth I kicked off the Atlantic pirate trade, allying against her arch-nemesis King Phillip II of Spain with the Saadians

1591

With 4000 European mercenaries, Ahmed Al Mansour Ed Dahbi crosses the Sahara and defeats a 40,000-strong army for control of the fabled desert caravan destination of Timbuktu.

1610–14

Oxford graduate and erstwhile lawyer Henry Mainwaring founds the Masmouda Pirates Republic near Rabat, pillaging Canadian cod, French salt-fish and Portuguese wine. He is later elected to Britain's parliament.

1659–66

The Alaouites end years of civil war and strike an uneasy peace with the Barbary pirates controlling Rabati ports.

1662

Portugal gives Tangier to the British as a wedding present for Charles II. After a lengthy siege, it is eventually returned to Moroccan control in 1684.

2000 YEARS OF MOROCCAN JEWISH HISTORY

By the 1st century CE, Jewish communities that were already well established in Morocco included farmers, metalworkers, dyers, glassblowers and bookbinders. The Merinids established the first official Jewish quarter in Fez, where Jewish entrepreneurs excluded from trades and guilds in medieval Europe were able to conduct business. Jewish Moroccans were taxed when business boomed for the ruling dynasty and sometimes blamed when it didn't, yet they managed to flourish under the Merinids and Saadians, while European Jews faced the Inquisition and persecution.

Under Alaouite rule in the 17th to 19th centuries, the official policy toward Jewish Moroccans was one of give and take: on one hand they had opportunities as tradespeople, business leaders and ambassadors to England, the Netherlands and Denmark in the 19th century; on the other hand they were subjected to taxes, surveillance and periodic scapegoating. But in good times and bad, Jewish Moroccans remained a continuous presence.

By 1948, some 300,000 Jewish Moroccans lived in Morocco. Many left after the founding of the states of Morocco and Israel, and today only an estimated 3000 to 8000 remain, mostly in Casablanca. A Jewish community centre in Casablanca was a bombing target in 2003, and though no one was harmed at the community centre, blasts at the trade centre killed 33 and wounded 100. Yet the Casablanca community remains intact, and the city is home to the Museum of Moroccan Judaism, the only museum in the Arab world devoted to Judaism.

Under the current king, Jewish schools now receive state funding, and a few Jewish expatriates have responded to a royal invitation to return. Ancient synagogues are being restored, such as the Simon Attias Synagogue in Essaouira. Yet the everyday champions of Jewish heritage in Morocco remain ordinary Moroccans, the one million people worldwide of Moroccan Jewish heritage and culturally engaged travellers, who together ensure Moroccan Jewish customs, festivals and landmarks get the attention they deserve.

and specially licensed pirates known as privateers. The most notoriously effective hires were the Barbary pirates, Moriscos (Spanish Muslims) who'd been forcibly converted and persecuted in Spain and hence had an added motivation to shake down Spaniards. James I outlawed English privateering in 1603, but he didn't seem to mind when his buddy Moulay Ismail aided and abetted the many British and Barbary pirates who harboured in the royal ports at Rabat and Salé – for a price.

But pirate loyalties being notoriously fickle, Barbary pirates attacked Ireland, Wales, Iceland and even Newfoundland in the 17th century. Barbary pirates also took prisoners, who were usually held for ransom and freed after a period of servitude, including one-time English allies. Captives were arguably better off with Barbary pirates than French profiteers, who typically forced prisoners to ply the oars of slave galleys until death. Nevertheless, after pressure from England secured their release in 1684, a number of English captives were quite put out about the whole

1672

The Alaouite Moulay Ismail takes the throne. One of the greatest Moroccan sultans, he rules for 55 years, and the Alaouite succession lasts to the present day.

18th century

The Alaouites rebuild the ancient desert trading outpost of Sijilmassa, only to lose control of it to Aït Atta Imazighen warriors, who raze the town. Only two not-so-triumphal arches remain.

1757–90

Sidi Mohammed III makes a strategic move to the coast, to rebuild Essaouira and regain control over Atlantic ports. Inland imperial cities of Fez and Meknes slip into decline.

1767–1836

Cash-strapped Morocco makes extraordinary concessions to trading partners, granting Denmark trade monopolies in Agadir and Safi, and France and the US license to trade in Morocco for a nominal fee.

experience and burned the port of Tangier behind them. But other English saw upsides to piracy and kidnapping: when the Portuguese were forced out of Essaouira in the 17th century, a freed British prisoner who'd converted to Islam joined a French profiteer to rebuild the city for the sultan, using free labour provided by European captives.

Whatever happened to Barbary pirates? How did Islam mesh with Amazigh (Berber) beliefs? And why was Morocco the exception to Ottoman rule? Jamil Abun-Nasr unravels these and other Moroccan mysteries in *A History of the Maghreb in the Islamic Period*.

Troubled Waters for Alaouites

After Moulay Ismail's death, his elite force of 50,000 to 70,000 Abid, or 'Black Guard', ran amok, and not one of his many children was able to succeed him. The Alaouite dynasty would struggle on into the 20th century, but the country often lapsed into lawlessness when rulers overstepped their bounds. Piracy and politics became key ways to get ahead in the 18th and 19th centuries – and the two were by no means mutually exclusive. By controlling key Moroccan seaports and playing European colonial powers against one another, officials and outlaws alike found they could demand a cut of whatever goods were shipped through the Strait of Gibraltar and along the Atlantic coast.

In the late 18th century, when Sidi Mohammed Ben Abdullah ended the officially condoned piracy of his predecessors and nixed shady side deals with foreign powers, the financial results were disastrous. With added troubles of plague and drought, Morocco's straits were truly dire.

European Encroachment

For all their successful European politicking, the early Alaouites had apparently forgotten a cardinal rule of Moroccan diplomacy: never neglect Amazigh alliances. Sultan Moulay Hassan tried to rally support among the Imazighen of the High Atlas in the late 19th century, but by then it was too late. France began to take an active interest in Morocco around 1830 and allied with Imazighen across North Africa to fend off the Ottomans. After centuries of practice fighting Moroccans, Spain took control of areas of northern Morocco in 1860 and generated lasting resentment for desecrating graveyards, mosques and other sacred sites in Melilla and Tetouan. While the UK's wily Queen Victoria entertained Moroccan dignitaries and pressed for Moroccan legal reforms, her emissaries were busy brokering deals with France and Spain.

Footloose & Duty-Free in Tangier

Order became increasingly difficult to maintain in Moroccan cities and in Amazigh mountain strongholds, and Moulay Hassan employed powerful Amazigh leaders to regain control – but accurately predicting Moulay Hassan's demise, some Imazighen cut deals of their own with the Europeans. By the time Moulay Hassan's teenage successor Sultan Moulay Abdelaziz pushed through historic antidiscrimination laws to impress Morocco's erstwhile allies, the Europeans had reached an

1777

A century after the English leave Tangier a royal wreck, Morocco gets revenge and becomes the first country to recognise the breakaway British colony calling itself the United States of America.

1830

France seizes the Algerian coast, increasing pressure on the Moroccan sultan to cede power in exchange for mafia-style protection along Morocco's coasts from the advancing Ottomans.

1860

If at first you don't succeed, try for seven centuries: Spain takes control of a swath of northern Morocco reaching into the Rif Mountains.

1880

France, Britain, Spain and the US meet in Madrid and agree that Morocco can retain nominal control over its territory – after granting themselves tax-free business licenses and duty-free shopping.

understanding: while reforms were nice and all, what they really wanted were cheap goods. By 1880, Europeans and Americans had set up their own duty-free shop in Tangier, declaring it an 'international zone' where they were above the law and beyond tax collectors' reaches.

But the lure of prime North African real estate proved irresistible. By 1906 Britain had snapped up strategic waterfront property in Egypt and the Suez; France took the prize for sheer acreage from Algeria to West Africa; Italy landed Libya; Spain drew the short stick with the unruly Rif Mountains and a whole lot of desert. Germany was incensed at being left out of this arrangement and announced support for Morocco's independence, further inflaming tensions between Germany and other European powers in the years leading up to WWI.

The Protectorate

Whatever illusions of control Morocco's sultanate might've been clutching slipped away at the 1906 Conference of Algeciras, when control of Morocco's banks, customs and police force was handed over to France for 'protection'. The 1912 Treaty of Fez establishing Morocco as a French protectorate made colonisation official, and the French hand-picked a new sultan with all the backbone of a sock puppet. More than 100,000 French administrators, outcasts and opportunists arrived in cities across Morocco to take up residence in French *villes nouvelles* (new towns).

Resident-General Louis Lyautey saw to it that these new French suburbs were kitted out with all the mod cons: electricity, trains, roads and running water. *Villes nouvelles* were designed to be worlds apart from adjacent Moroccan medinas (historic city centres), with French schools, churches, villas and grand boulevards named after French generals. No expense or effort was spared to make the new arrivals feel right at home – which made their presence all the more galling for Moroccans footing the bill through taxes, shouldering most of the labour and still living in crowded, poorly serviced medinas. Lyautey had already set up French colonial enterprises in Vietnam, Madagascar and Algeria, so he arrived in Morocco with the confidence of a CEO and a clear plan of action: break up the Imazighen, ally with the Spanish when needed and keep business running by all available means.

A Traveller's History of North Africa, by Barnaby Rogerson, is a handy and accessible guide that puts Morocco amid the wider currents of regional history.

Nationalist Resistance

Once French-backed Sultan Yusuf died and his French-educated 18-year-old son Mohammed V became sultan, Lyautey expected that French business in Morocco would carry on as usual. He hadn't counted on a fiery young nationalist as sultan or the staunch independence of ordinary Moroccans. Mining strikes and union organising interfered with France's most profitable colonial businesses, and military attention was diverted to force Moroccans back into the mines. Imazighen had never accepted foreign dominion without a fight, and they were not about to

1906

The controversial Act of Algeciras divvies up North Africa among European powers, but Germany isn't invited – a slight that exacerbates tensions north of the Mediterranean.

1912

The Treaty of Fez hands Morocco to the French protectorate, which mostly protects French business interests at Moroccan taxpayer expense with the ruthless assistance of Amazigh warlord Pasha El Glaoui.

1921–26

Under the command of Abd El Krim, Amazigh leaders rebel against Spanish rule of the Rif Mountains, and Spain loses its foothold in the mountains.

1942

In defiance of Vichy France, Casablanca hosts American forces staging the Allied North African campaign. This move yields US support for Moroccan independence and the classic Humphrey Bogart film *Casablanca.*

make an exception for the French. By 1921 the Rif was up in arms against the Spanish and French under the leadership of Ibn Abd Al Krim Al Khattabi. It took five years, 300,000 Spanish and French forces and two budding Fascists (Francisco Franco and Marshal Pétain) to capture Ibn Abd Al Krim and force him into exile.

Moulay Ismail was a pen pal of England's James II and Louis XIV of France, and tried to convert the Sun King to Islam by mail.

The French won a powerful ally when they named Amazigh warlord Thami El Glaoui pasha of Marrakesh, but they also made a lot of enemies. The title gave the pasha implicit license to do as he pleased, which included mafia-style executions and extortion schemes, kidnapping women and children who struck his fancy, and friendly games of golf at his Royal Golf Club with US president Dwight D Eisenhower and British prime minister Winston Churchill. The pasha forbade talk of independence under penalty of death, and conspired to exile Mohammed V from Morocco in 1953 – but Glaoui would end his days powerless, wracked with illness and grovelling on his knees for King Mohammed V's forgiveness.

Although the colonial French protectorate of Morocco was nominally an ally of Vichy France and Germany in WWII, independent-minded Casablanca provided crucial ground support for the Allied North African campaign. When Morocco's Istiqlal (Independence) party demanded freedom from French rule in 1944, the US and Britain were finally inclined to agree. Under increasing pressure from Moroccans and the Allies, France allowed Mohammed V to return from exile in 1955. Morocco successfully negotiated its independence from France and Spain between 1956 and 1958.

A Rough Start: After Independence

When Mohammed V died suddenly of heart failure in 1961, King Hassan II became the leader of the new nation. Faced with a shaky power base, an unstable economy and elections that revealed divides even among nationalists, Hassan II consolidated power by cracking down on dissent and suspending parliament for a decade. With heavy borrowing to finance dam-building, urban development and an ever-expanding bureaucracy, Morocco was deep in debt by the 1970s. Attempts to assassinate the king underscored the need to do something, quickly, to turn things around – and then in 1973, the phosphate industry in the Spanish-controlled Western Sahara started to boom. Morocco staked its claim to the area and its lucrative phosphate reserves with the Green March, settling the area with Moroccans while greatly unsettling indigenous Saharawi people agitating for self-determination.

Western Sahara

Talk of 'Greater Morocco' began in the 1950s, but in the 1970s it became the official explanation for Morocco's annexation of phosphate-rich Spanish Sahara. There was a snag: the Popular Front for the Liberation of the Sagui Al Hamra and the Rio di Oro (Polisario, a Saharawi pro-independence

1943–45

When the Allies struggle in Italy, US General Patton calls in the Goums, Morocco's elite force of mountain warriors. With daggers and night-time attacks, they advance the Allies in Tuscany.

1944–53

Moroccan nationalists demand independence from France with increasing impatience. Sultan Mohammed V is inclined to agree and is exiled to Madagascar by the protectorate for the crime of independent thought.

1955–56

Morocco successfully negotiates its independence from France, Spain cedes control over most of its colonial claims within Morocco and exiled nationalist Mohammed V returns as king of independent Morocco.

1961

When Mohammed V dies suddenly, Hassan II becomes king. He transforms Morocco into a constitutional monarchy in 1962, but the 'Years of Lead' deal heavy punishments for dissent.

AMAZIGH PRIDE & PREJUDICE

Despite a rich tradition of poetry, petroglyphs, music and art dating as far back as 5000 BCE, the Amazigh were often misconstrued as uneducated by outsiders because no standard written system had been consistently applied to their many distinct languages. The Romans tried for 250 years to take over Amazigh territory and institute Roman customs, and when that failed, they bad-mouthed their adversaries, calling them 'Berbers', or barbarians. The name stuck, and so did anti-Amazigh prejudice.

The protectorate established French as the official language of Morocco to make it easier to conduct (and hence control) business transactions and affairs of state. Complex Amazigh artistic symbolism and traditional medicine were dismissed as charming but irrelevant superstition by those not privy to the oral traditions accompanying them, and the educated classes were encouraged to distance themselves from their roots. But Amazigh languages and traditions have persisted in Morocco, and the Berber Pride movement has recently reclaimed 'Berber' as a unifying term.

After independence in 1956, Arabic was adopted as the official language, though French continues to be widely spoken, particularly in government and business, and Darija is the commonly understood Moroccan Arabic dialect. As recently as the 1980s, the use of Amazigh script was subject to censure in Morocco. But with the backing of King Mohammed VI – who is part Amazigh himself – the ancient Tifinagh alphabet that first emerged around the time of Egyptian hieroglyphics was revived in 2003, and a modernised version is now being taught in many state schools as a standardised written language. In 2011, Tamazight became an official state language.

More than 60% of Moroccans now call themselves Amazigh or Berber, and Amazigh languages are currently spoken by some 8.5 to 10 million Moroccans. Berber Pride is now mainstream in Morocco, with the introduction of the official Moroccan broadcaster La Chaîne Tamazight, offering TV and radio programmes in three Amazigh languages. Yet Human Rights Watch reported that in 2010, parents who gave their children Amazigh names were told the names were rejected by state bureaucrats as 'not recognisably Moroccan'. After a public outcry, the policy was reversed, so babies, too, can show Berber Pride in Morocco.

Today, Amazigh activists are campaigning for Yennayer, the Amazigh New Year's Day on 12 January, to become a national holiday.

militia) declared the region independent. Putting his French legal training to work, Hassan II took the matter up with the International Court of Justice (ICJ) in The Hague in 1975, expecting the court would provide a resounding third-party endorsement for Morocco's claims. Instead, the ICJ considered a counter-claim for independence from the Polisario and dispatched a fact-finding mission to Spanish Sahara.

The ICJ concluded that ties to Morocco weren't strong enough to support Moroccan sovereignty over the region, and Western Sahara was entitled to self-determination. In a highly creative interpretation of this court judgement, Hassan II declared that Morocco had won its case and

1975
The UN concludes that the Western Sahara is independent, but Hassan II concludes otherwise, ordering the Green March to enforce Morocco's claims to the region and its phosphate reserves.

1981
After the Casablanca Uprising, the military rounds up dissenters and unionists nationwide. But demands for political reforms increase, and many political prisoners are later exonerated.

1984
Morocco leaves the Organisation of African States (now the African Union) in protest against the admission of Saharawi representatives.

1994
Years of poor relations between Morocco and Algeria, primarily over the Western Sahara issue, lead to the closure of the border between the two countries.

ordered a celebratory 'peace march' of more than 350,000 Moroccans from Marrakesh into Western Sahara in 1975 – some never to return. This unarmed 'Green March' was soon fortified by military personnel and land mines, and was vehemently resisted by armed Polisario fighters.

While still a national holiday, the Green March is no longer the symbol of national pride it once was; Green March murals that once defined desert-cafe decor have been painted over with apolitical dune-scapes, and images of the march have been removed from the Dh100 note.

In 1991, a truce was brokered between Morocco and Polisario, and continues to be monitored by UN peacekeepers. As part of the deal a referendum on independence was promised, but Morocco has never allowed it to be held. At best, Rabat maintains that it will grant Western Sahara autonomous status. In January 2017, Morocco rejoined the African Union, which recognises the self-declared Sahrawi Arab Democratic Republic, and in December 2017, negotiations between the Moroccan government and the Polisario were held for the first time in six years, in an effort to initiate a resolution to the conflict. But today, the status of Western Sahara still remains unresolved in international law, a rallying cry for many Saharawi, a political taboo in the national conversation and an awkward nonstarter for many deeply ambivalent Moroccan taxpayers.

Read first-hand accounts of Morocco's independence movement from Moroccan women who rebelled against colonial control, rallied and fought alongside men in Alison Baker's *Voice of Resistance: Oral Histories of Moroccan Women.*

Years of Lead

Along with the growing gap between the rich and the poor and a mounting tax bill to cover Morocco's military spending in Western Sahara, King Hassan II's suppression of dissent fuelled further resentment among his subjects. By the 1980s, the critics of the king included journalists, trade unionists, women's rights activists, Marxists, Islamists, Imazighen advocating recognition of their culture and language, and the working poor – in other words, a broad cross-section of Moroccan society.

The last straw for many came in 1981, when official Moroccan newspapers casually announced that the government had conceded to the International Monetary Fund to hike prices for staple foods. For the many Moroccans subsisting on the minimum wage, these increases meant that two-thirds of their income would be spent on a meagre diet of sardines, bread and tea. When trade unions organised protests against the measure, government reprisals were swift and brutal. Tanks rolled down the streets of Casablanca, and hundreds were killed, at least 1000 wounded and an estimated 5000 protesters arrested in a nationwide roundup.

Far from dissuading dissent, the Casablanca Uprising galvanised support for government reform. Sustained pressure from human rights activists throughout the 1980s achieved unprecedented results in 1991, when Hassan II founded the Equity and Reconciliation Commission to investigate human rights abuses that occurred during his own reign. In his first public statement as king upon his father's death in 1999, Mohammed VI

1999

Soon after initiating a commission to investigate abuses of power under his own rule, Hassan II dies. All hail Mohammed VI and hope for a constitutional monarchy.

2001

The Royal Institute of Amazigh Culture (IRCAM) is founded on October 17 by the king.

2002–07

Historic reforms initiated under Mohammed VI include regular parliamentary and municipal elections across Morocco, plus the Mudawanna legal code offering unprecedented protection for women.

2004–05

The Equity and Reconciliation Commission televises testimonies of the victims of Moroccan human-rights abuses during the 'Years of Lead' and becomes the most watched event in Moroccan TV history.

vowed to right the wrongs of the era known to Moroccans as the Years of Lead. The commission has since helped cement human rights advances, awarding reparations to 9280 victims of the Years of Lead by 2006.

New Regime, New Hopes

As locals will surely tell you, there's still room for improvement in today's Morocco. The parliament elected in 2002 set aside 30 seats for female members of parliament and implemented some promising reforms: Morocco's first-ever municipal elections, employment non-discrimination laws, the chance to study the Tamazight language in state schools, and the Mudawanna, a legal code protecting women's rights to divorce and custody. But tactics from the Years of Lead were revived after the 2003 Casablanca trade centre bombings and a 2010 military raid of a Western Sahara protest camp, when suspects were rounded up – in 2010, Human Rights Watch reported that many of them had been subjected to abuse and detention without legal counsel. Civil society is outpacing state reforms, as Moroccans take the initiative to address poverty and illiteracy through enterprising village associations and non-governmental organisations.

Morocco's Arab Spring

In early 2011 Morocco was rocked by the Arab Spring protests that were sweeping across the Middle East and North Africa. Protesters demanded more devolution of power and political accountability. Mohammed VI reacted with a deftness that eluded many other leaders and announced a series of constitutional reforms, which included giving more power to parliament and making Tamazight an official state language. The reforms were quickly passed in a national referendum. Although some demonstrators have continued to call for deeper reforms, Morocco's stability continues be a valued prize for most of its citizens.

According to the 2020 Human Development Index, the annual gross national income in Morocco is US$7368 per capita, but 5% of its working population live on US$3.20 a day.

Morocco Today

Morocco in the 21st century is a confident country, increasingly sure of its role as a stable link between Europe, Africa and the Arab world, and a place that welcomes tourists and investors alike. It sailed through the Arab Spring unscathed, and while the perennial question of Western Sahara shows no sign of resolution, the nation is taking big steps to cement its role as a regional player, and a leader in renewable energy and responses to climate change.

Regional Ambitions

On the geopolitical front, the unresolved conflict in Western Sahara has continued to make headlines. Morocco briefly threatened to expel the UN peacekeeping mission there after the UN secretary general used the word 'occupation' in relation to Morocco's presence in the disputed territory.

2004

Morocco signs free-trade agreements with the EU and the US, and gains status as a non-NATO ally.

2006

Morocco proposes 'special autonomy' for the Western Sahara and holds the first direct talks with Polisario in seven years, which end in a stalemate.

2011

Pro-democracy revolutions in Tunisia and Egypt inspire Morocco's February 20 Movement; in response, the king announces limited constitutional reform, passed by national referendum.

2011

The revised Moroccan constitution establishes Tamazight and Amazigh (Berber) culture as a national language and a national heritage, respectively.

Tensions flared further in 2016 when Morocco deployed new troops to the border with Mauritania, ostensibly to crack down on smuggling but raising protests from Saharawis. Despite this, Western Sahara may no longer be the stumbling block to Morocco's regional ambitions that it once was. In 2017, Morocco rejoined the African Union, the regional body it had left in protest in 1984 when the Western Saharan government-in-exile was admitted. This move reflected Morocco's desire to flex its economic muscles in the region and build on its growing economic influence in West Africa.

Part of Morocco's economic plan is to become Africa's flagship for green energy. The government has invested heavily in renewable energy, and Morocco has both the continent's largest wind farm and solar power plant, powered by Atlantic breezes and Saharan sun. These credentials were at the forefront when Marrakesh hosted the UN climate change conference in 2016, and in 2018 it ranked second in that year's Climate Change Performance Index.

Speeding Ahead?

The construction of the high-speed train line between Tangier and Casablanca, cutting the journey time from five to two hours, has been Morocco's flagship infrastructure project, with the first trains rolled out in late 2018. This building boom has seen major towns and cities receive much-needed facelifts, alongside state-of-the-art theatres designed by world-class architects. Most Moroccans hail the train as a boon to business and a way for people to see more of their country, while some have criticised the grand projects as an extravagance when a sizeable proportion of the population scrape along near the poverty line with poor access to education and healthcare.

Youth unemployment has decreased and currently hovers around 22%. There have been modest improvements on free speech issues, but social and human rights organisations have faced continued hurdles to operate without restriction, and direct political criticism of the monarchy remains a deep taboo. As Morocco's economy has slowed, in part owing to the decline of agriculture, the statistic that around 40% of Moroccans – mostly women – would emigrate if they were given the chance, continues to sting. Morocco will continue to redefine itself for the 21st century, and the challenges, as well as opportunities, are myriad.

Breathing New Life into Ancient Medinas

Morocco is on a mission to create new opportunities for its ancient medinas. In October 2018, the King Mohammed VI announced a Dh2.35 billion fund to be distributed between five cities – Marrakesh, Meknes, Salé, Tetouan and Essaouira – for the sustainable renovation and development of their old cities. As well as preserving their rich historical and architectural heritage, the programme aims to better the living conditions of medina dwellers, with improved infrastructure and new public spaces.

2013

For the first time ever, 10 million tourists visit Morocco in a single year, despite the ongoing effects of Arab Spring protests in surrounding North African countries.

2016

Elections see the ruling moderate Islamist Justice and Development Party (PJD) increase their representation in parliament as well as providing Morocco's prime minister.

2016

The first stage of the Noor Power Station, the world's largest concentrated solar power plant, is connected to the country's power grid.

2017

The African Union readmits Morocco after a 33-year absence, leaving the question of the disputed Western Sahara open.

Another objective is generating revenue and creating jobs, with a focus on handicrafts and vocational training for both young people and women.

In Marrakesh, plans include the restoration of six *fanadiq* (inns once used by caravans), historical monuments and gardens, the redevelopment of the Djemaa El Fna square, and the creation of new routes for visitors, as well as interactive information platforms.

This all follows on from Fez. At the request of the king, a government office called ADER Fès was set up in 1989 to oversee the ambitious restoration of its 9th-century medina, working only with contractors who use traditional building methods. By the end of 2017, more than 3000 buildings in danger of collapse had been made safe, including 26 historic monuments. One of the most famous of which is the Kairaouine Library, believed to be the world's oldest working library.

Four of the city's many crumbling *fanadiq* – including the 13th-century Chemmaine-Sbitriyine Funduq – were restored with help from the Millennium Challenge Corporation and have become spaces for artisans to sell their wares. Another flagship architectural project is the striking Place Lalla Yeddouna, which has created a new route across the Bou Khrarab river and through the medina, along with workshops for craftspeople.

Global Voices Morocco provides a roundup of Moroccan news and opinion online, including English translations of bloggers' responses to Moroccan news at www.globalvoicesonline.org/-/world/middle-east-north-africa/morocco.

COVID-19 Response in Morocco

As of the end of 2020, the Moroccan government reported 439,193 cases of the novel coronavirus and 7,388 deaths. The first case in the country was reported on March 2nd, imported by a Moroccan man who returned to the country from Europe in late February. Within weeks cases began to quickly rise, resulting in a suspension of all international flights by March 15th and closures of public gathering spaces such as schools, mosques, restaurants, and more the following day; followed by the declaration of a state of emergency on March 19th. As the government continued to implement increasingly strict measures to prevent the spread of the virus, the private sector and international donors announced projects to provide financial aid, food aid, and shelter to various at-risk communities across the country as well as economic relief to affected businesses.

Health officials in Morocco blame the continuing spread of the virus through summer 2020 to inter-familial transmission and significant violations of the state of emergency, including small-scale clashes with patrol units enforcing lockdown measures. Cases continued to rise to a peak of 49,800 active cases on November 15th after relaxing control measures from June on account of economic considerations appears to have contributed to a faster spread of the disease.

From September border restrictions begin to relax and some tourists are allowed to enter, though mandatory curfews and business closures continue through the end of 2020 and movement between regions of the country is at times restricted.

2018

Two European women are murdered in the mountains below Jebel Toubkal by a group of men claiming allegiance to ISIS, raising the spectre of terrorism in Morocco for the first time in nearly a decade.

2019

Compulsory one-year military service for Moroccan citizens is reintroduced after a 13-year hiatus, despite popular outcry against the decision.

2020

Marrakesh becomes Africa's first City of Culture, with a pan-African programme of art and culture events planned throughout the year.

2021

In exchange for a resumption of diplomatic relations between Morocco and Israel (suspended since 2000), the USA breaks ground on a consulate in Western Sahara – acknowledging Morocco's authority over the region.

Daily Life in Morocco

For travellers, Morocco can be about haggling for carpets, sunsets over the Sahara, dodging snake charmers in Djemaa El Fna and going in search of the Beat-generation writers in Tangier. It certainly makes for an exciting picture, but what is it like for Moroccans? Taking some time to explore the major themes in Moroccan society and daily life will enhance anyone's visit to this culturally rich country.

Language & Identity

Morocco's original inhabitants were the Imazighen (Berbers), but the arrival of Arabs and the introduction of Islam has over the centuries mixed and remixed the two populations to a point where the line between Arab and Amazigh is often blurred. But culturally there's frequently been a clear demarcation between speakers of Moroccan Arabic (called Darija) and Amazigh languages known as Tamazight.

Arabic speakers, personified in the Alaouite dynasty that has ruled Morocco since the 17th century, have traditionally held the upper hand, despite speakers of Amazigh languages often holding a demographic majority. This position was institutionalised by the French in the 1930s when they passed laws to discriminate against Imazighen. For much of the 20th century it was illegal to even register many traditional Amazigh names at birth, and Amazigh education was banned.

For a millennia-old civilisation, Morocco looks young. Around half the population is under 25, almost a third is under 15, and just 7% is over 65. As of 2020, the median age in Morocco is 30.

In 21st-century Morocco, Amazigh culture is having something of a renaissance. In 2011 the constitution was revised to make Tamazight an official national language. The effects of this are most immediately visible by the new Tamazight signage that adorns government buildings (and, increasingly, road signs) along with Arabic and French. Amazigh education, now formally encouraged, still lags behind in quality because of poor training and facilities, although it's still early days in a renaissance in national identity for a culture whose roots are so deep in Moroccan culture.

The rise of Tamazight is reflected in the relative fall from grace of French, the language of Morocco's colonial past. French is no longer listed as an official state language, though it remains a language of much business, and the ability to speak it is frequently perceived as a marker of social status. In higher education today, however, many lessons are taught in English; some argue that French should ultimately be done away with altogether, and English tuition encouraged to increase Morocco's competitiveness in a global economy.

Social Norms

Family Values

Family remains at the heart of much of Moroccan life, and while individuals may have ambitions and ideas of their own, their aspirations are often tied in some way to family – a much-admired trait in Morocco. Success for the individual is seen as success for the family as a whole. Even major status symbols such as cars or satellite TVs may be valued less as prized possessions than as commodities benefiting the entire family.

This is beginning to change, as the emerging middle class represents moves out of large family homes and into smaller apartments in the suburbs, where common property is not such a given. But family connections remain paramount. Even as Morocco's economy has grown, remittances from Moroccans living in Spain and France to family back home represent 6.2% of national GDP.

Since family is a focal point for Moroccans, expect related questions to come up in the course of conversation: Where is your family? (The idea of holidaying without your family can be anathema.) Are you married, and do you have children? If not, why not? These lines of inquiry can seem a little forward, but they are a roundabout way of finding out who you are and what interests you. Questions about where you work or what you do in your spare time are odd ice-breakers since what you do for a living or a hobby says less about you than your family.

Morocco, 1980–2010

Life expectancy increased by eight years.

Primary school enrolment increased by 22%.

GNI per capita increased by 11%.

Education & Economy

One of the most important indicators of social status in Morocco is education. As a whole, the country has an adult literacy rate of 74%, with slightly more men than women being literate. The disparity is heightened in poorer rural areas. Here, three-quarters of women cannot read or write, and less than 50% of first-graders complete primary school. Schooling to age 14 is now officially mandated, and local initiatives are slowly improving opportunities for education in the Moroccan countryside.

For vulnerable rural families, just getting the children fed can be difficult, let alone getting them to school. Around a quarter of Moroccans are judged to live in near or absolute poverty, and suffer from food insecurity (living in fear of hunger). Under-employment often means that a steady income is a rarity, and 35% of the average Moroccan income covers basic foodstuffs. Only 10% of Moroccans can afford imported foods at the supermarket, let alone eating at restaurants. Although the Moroccan economy has grown well in the 21st century, and Morocco has a burgeoning middle class, its benefits have not always been spread equally: improvements are needed in education to match the growth of Morocco's service industry, which in recent years has even overtaken agriculture for its contribution to GDP.

Frustratingly for many Moroccans, getting ahead can still be a case of who you know as much as what you know. Morocco rates low on Transparency International's corruption perception index, and most Moroccan

THE FOREIGNERS NEXT DOOR

With an attractive climate and exchange rate, Morocco has around 85,000 foreign residents – and counting. Many Moroccan emigrants from Europe and the US are returning to Morocco to live, retire or start businesses, creating a new upper-middle class. The carefree spending of returnees is a source of revenue and of a certain amount of resentment for Moroccans, who grumble openly about returnees driving up costs and importing a culture of conspicuous consumption that's unattainable and shallow.

An international vogue for riads has seen many Europeans buying and restoring historic buildings – and sometimes pricing Moroccans out of the housing market and leaving medina neighbourhoods strangely empty and lifeless off-season. It's a double-edged sword: maintenance and restoration of centuries-old medina houses is often beyond the reach of the families who live in them and who grab with both hands the chance to upgrade to homes with modern amenities in the *villes nouvelles* (new cities). At the same time, others grumble that the European influx brings to mind colonial-era enclaves.

Travellers can make the exchange more equitable by venturing beyond riad walls to explore Moroccan culture, meet Moroccans on their own turf and ensure Moroccans benefit from tourism.

families at some time will have butted up against the concept of *wasta*, the need to have a well-connected middleman to get a job or access a service. This is particularly frustrating for an increasingly educated youth suffering high levels of unemployment, who demand a more meritocratic society.

Shifting Gender Roles

Morocco is a male-dominated society, particularly in the public sphere. Take one look at the people nursing a coffee all afternoon in a pavement cafe and you might even ask, where are all the women? However, significant progress is being made on women's rights, and the push for change has been led from the ground up, with women's groups creating a singular brand of Islamic feminism to affect change.

The Majlis, Morocco's lower parliament, has 60 seats (of 395) reserved for women. On regional councils (directly elected), one-third of seats are reserved for women.

Two decades ago most of the people you'd see out and about, going to school, socialising and conducting business in Morocco would have been men. Women were occupied with less high-profile work, particularly in rural areas, such as animal husbandry, farming, childcare, and fetching water and firewood. Initiatives to eliminate female illiteracy have given girls a better start in life, and positive social pressure has greatly reduced the once-common practice of hiring girls under 14 years of age as domestic workers. Women now represent nearly a third of Morocco's formal workforce, forming their own industrial unions, agricultural cooperatives and artisans' collectives. More than 40% of university graduates today are women.

A major societal change came in 2004, with the overhaul of Morocco's Mudawanna legal code. Revising these laws guaranteed women crucial rights with regard to custody, divorce, property ownership and child support, among other protections. The direction of travel hasn't been universally smooth, however. In 2012, Moroccan society was shocked by the case of a 16-year-old girl who committed suicide after being forced to marry her rapist, drawing attention to a clause in the law that allowed a man to be 'forgiven' his crime by marrying his victim. The law was amended after a public outcry. Although the legal age of marriage remains 18 years, child marriages may still be allowed if a special dispensation is given by an Islamic judge.

The modern Moroccan woman's outlook extends far beyond her front door, and female visitors will meet Moroccan women eager to chat, compare life experiences and share perspectives on world events. Male-female interactions are still sometimes stilted by social convention, though you're bound to spot couples meeting in parks and cafes, but

DRESSING TO IMPRESS IN MOROCCO

Many travellers to Morocco wonder what is the best way to dress when visiting the country.

Women aren't expected to cover their head in Morocco. Some Moroccan women do and some don't wear a hijab (headscarf). Some wear it for religious, cultural, practical or personal reasons, or alternate, wearing a head covering in the streets but taking it off at home and work. A full face-covering veil is unusual in cities, and even rarer among rural women working in the fields. Context is important. Likewise, that chic knee-length skirt you see a Moroccan woman wearing in a Marrakesh restaurant is likely to be swapped for more conservative *djellaba* (full-length hooded garment with long sleeves) while visiting the medina.

That said, your choice of attire may be perceived as a sign of respect for yourself and Moroccans alike. For both men and women, this means not wearing shorts, sleeveless tops or revealing clothing. If you do, some people will be embarrassed for you and the family that raised you and avoid eye contact. So if you don't want to miss out on some excellent company – especially among older Moroccans – dress modestly.

MOROCCAN SOCIAL GRACES

Many visitors are surprised at how quickly friendships can be formed in Morocco, and are often a little suspicious. True, carpet dealers aren't after your friendship when they offer you mint tea, but notice how Moroccans behave with one another, and you'll see that friendly overtures are more than a mere contrivance.

People you meet in passing are likely to remember you and greet you warmly the next day, and it's considered polite to stop and ask how they're doing. Greetings among friends can last 10 minutes as each person enquires after the other's happiness, wellbeing and family. Moroccans are generous with their time and extend courtesies that might seem to you like impositions, from walking you to your next destination to inviting you home for lunch. To show your appreciation, stop by the next day to say hello and be sure to compliment the cook.

conversations about hijab that obsess the media in some parts of the world seem less relevant here, where you'll see a devout young woman covering her hair walking with a friend with free-flowing hair and another wrapped up in a headscarf worn purely as a fashion statement. These are young Moroccan women on the move, commuting to work on motor scooters, taking over pavements on arm-in-arm evening strolls and running for key government positions.

Social Behaviour

At times it can feel as if there is one rule for behaviour in public and another for private. The key word is discretion. A decade ago, Morocco's gay community was beginning to seek tentative public approbation, but a conservative shift has seen a number of high-profile prosecutions (some including foreigners) and a shutting of the closet door. Morocco's relationship with alcohol can feel similarly complicated: despite the popularity of bars and a burgeoning brewing industry aimed almost entirely at a domestic market, a traveller who accidentally clinks his bottles together while getting in a petit taxi to go to a medina is liable to be asked to get out, as medinas are seen as more socially and religiously conservative. Yet with proper discretion, there is plenty of latitude when it comes to socially acceptable behaviour.

Religion

Morocco is 99% Muslim. Christian and Jewish communities have existed here for centuries, although in recent years their numbers have dwindled.

The Five Pillars of Islam

Soaring minarets, shimmering mosaics, intricate calligraphy, the muezzin's call to prayer: much of what thrills visitors in Morocco today is inspired by a deep faith in Islam. Islam is built on five pillars: *shahada*, the affirmation of faith in Allah and Allah's word entrusted to the Prophet Muhammad; *salat* (prayer), ideally performed five times daily; *zakat* (charity), a moral obligation to give to those in need; *sawn*, the daytime fasting practised during the month of Ramadan; and *hajj*, the pilgrimage to Mecca that is the culmination of lifelong faith for Muslims.

Best-selling Moroccan feminist writer Fatima Mernissi exposes telling differences and uncanny similarities in the ideals of women in Europe and the Middle East in *Scheherazade Goes West: Different Cultures, Different Harems*.

Moroccan Islam

While all Muslims agree on these basic tenets received by the Prophet Muhammad, doctrinal disagreements ensued after his death. The Umayyads challenged his son-in-law Ali's claim to the title of caliph, or leader of the faithful. Some Muslims continued to recognise only successors of Ali; today they are known as Shiites. But in numerical terms, the Umayyad caliphate's Sunni Muslim practice is more common today.

It was the Umayyads who brought Islam to Morocco at the end of the 7th century and, hence, Morocco today is almost entirely Sunni. Morocco's ruling Alaouite dynasty claims descent from the Prophet Muhammad, and King Mohammed VI holds the unusual position of *Amir Al Mumineen*, meaning Commander of the Faithful, making him the spiritual leader of the country as well as head of state.

French Resident-General Lyautey banned non-Muslims from mosques in Morocco, perhaps to avoid conflict. Moroccans appreciated the privacy so much that they ousted the French from Morocco and kept the ban.

Morocco follows the Maliki school of Sunni thought. Historically this school has been less strict, with Maliki *qaids* (chiefs) applying Sharia law according to local custom instead of absolutist rule of law. This applies mainly in the case of family law (*mudawanna*) such as marriage and inheritance.

Marabouts & Zawiyas

An important Moroccan tradition is the custom of venerating *marabouts* (saints). *Marabouts* are devout Muslims whose acts of devotion and professions of faith are so profound, their very presence is considered to confer *baraka*, or grace, even after their death.

This practice of honouring *marabouts* is more in line with ancient Amazigh (Berber) beliefs and Sufi mysticism than orthodox Islam, which generally discourages anything resembling idol worship. Visits to *zawiyas* (shrines) are side trips for the many devout Moroccans who spend a lifetime preparing and planning for the hajj.

Sufism in Morocco

It's often commented that Morocco follows one of the most moderate forms of Islam. One reason for this is the strong roots that Sufism has in the country. Sufism is the mystical strand of Islam, where adherents seek perfection of worship in their quest to encounter the divine. This often involves the use of music and *dhikr* (repetitive prayer) to help gain spiritual enlightenment.

Sufism revolves around orders or brotherhoods known as *tariqa*, founded by a spiritual leader. The most famous worldwide are the Mevlevis, followers of the Sufi poet Rumi, also known as the whirling dervishes of Turkey. In Morocco, two of the most important *tariqa* are the Tijaniyya and the Boutchichiyya. Tijaniyya was founded in the late 18th century by Al Tijani, who is buried in Fez. The Boutchichiyya was founded around the same time, and today many in the order hold high-ranking positions in the Moroccan government.

Many observers cite the continued influence of Sufism in Morocco as an important bulwark against the rise of more religiously conservative and politically radical forms of Islam such as Salafism.

Music

Any trip to Morocco comes with its own syncopated soundtrack: the early-evening *adhan* (call to prayer) and the ubiquitous donkey-cart-drivers' chants of *Balek!* (watch out!) – fair warning that since donkeys don't yield, you'd better, and quick. Adding to the musical mayhem are beats booming out of taxis, ham radios and roadside stalls, and live-music performances at restaurants and weddings, on street corners and headlining at festivals year-round. There are plenty of Maghrebi beats to tune into.

Classical Arab-Andalucian Music

Leaving aside the thorny question of where it actually originated (you don't want to be the cause of the next centuries-long Spain–Morocco conflict, do you?), this music combines the flamenco-style strumming and heart-string-plucking drama of Spanish folk music with the finely calibrated stringed instruments, complex percussion and haunting half-tones of classical Arab music.

You'll hear two major styles of Arab-Andalusian music in Morocco: Al Aala (primarily in Fez, Tetouan and Salé) and Gharnati (mostly Oujda). The area of musical overlap is Rabat, where you can hear both styles. Keep an eye out for concerts, musical evenings at upscale restaurants in Casablanca and Fez, and Essaouira playing host to the annual **Festival des Andalousies Atlantiques** (www.facebook.com/FestivalDesAndalousiesAtlantiques; ⌚late Oct).

Look for performances by Gharnati vocalist Amina Alaoui, Fatiha El Hadri Badraï and her traditional all-female orchestras from Tetouan, and Fes Festival of World Sacred Music headliner Mohamed Amin El Akrami and his orchestra.

Gnaoua

Joyously bluesy, with a rhythm you can't refuse, gnaoua began among freed enslaved people as a ritual of deliverance from slavery and into God's graces. Don't be surprised if the beat sends you into a trance – that's what it's meant to do. A true gnaoua *lila* (spiritual jam session) may last all night, with musicians erupting into leaps of joy as they enter trance-like states of ecstasy.

Join the crowds watching in Marrakesh's Djemaa El Fna or at the annual **Gnaoua World Music Festival** (www.festival-gnaoua.net; ⌚late Jun) in Essaouira, and hear Gnaoua on Peter Gabriel's Real World music label. Gnaoua *mâalems* (master musicians) include perennial festival favourites Abdeslam Alikkane and his Tyour gnaoua, crossover fusion superstar Hassan Hakmoun, Saïd Boulhimas and his deeply funky Band of Gnawas, Indian-inflected Nass Marrakech and reggae-inspired Omar Hayat. Since Gnaoua are historically a brotherhood, most renowned gnaoua musicians have been men – but the all-women Sufi group Haddarates plays gnaoua trances traditionally reserved for women, and family acts include Brahim Elbelkani and La Famille Backbou.

No, that's not a musical rugby scrum: the *haidous* is a complex circle dance with musicians in the middle, often performed in celebration of the harvest.

MOROCCAN MUSIC FESTIVALS

March Beat Hotel (p92) in Marrakesh

April Printemps Musical des Alizés (p237) in Essaouira, Sahara Music Festival (p158) at Erg Chigaga

June Fes Festival of World Sacred Music (p336), Gnaoua World Music Festival (p237) in Essaouira, Festival Mawazine (p205) in Rabat

July National Festival of Popular Arts (p92) in Marrakesh, Voix de Femmes (p277) in Tetouan, Festival Timitar (p390) in Agadir, Jazzablanca (p190) in Casablanca

August Atlas Electronic (https://atlas-electronic.com) in Marrakesh

September TANJAzz (p255) in Tangier, Jazz au Chellah (p28) in Rabat, L'Boulevard Festival of Casablanca (p190), Oasis Festival (http://theoasisfest.com) in Marrakesh

October Festival of Sufi Culture (p336) in Fez, Festival des Andalousies Atlantiques (p238) and MOGA (p237) in Essaouira

November Visa for Music (p206) in Rabat

Amazigh Folk Music

There's plenty of other indigenous Moroccan music besides gnaoua, thanks to the ancient Amazigh (Berber) tradition of passing along songs and poetry from one generation to the next. You can't miss Amazigh music at village *moussems* (festivals), Agadir's **Festival Timitar** (www.festivaltimitar.ma; ⌚Jul) of Amazigh music, the **National Festival of Popular Arts** (⌚Jul) in Marrakesh and Imilchil's **Marriage Moussem** (Imilchil; ⌚Sep), as well as weddings and other family celebrations.

The most renowned Amazigh folk group is the Master Musicians of Joujouka, who famously inspired the Rolling Stones, Led Zeppelin and William S Burroughs, and collaborated with the Stones' Brian Jones on experimental music with lots of clanging and crashing involved. Lately the big names are women's, including the all-woman group B'net Marrakech and the bold Najat Aatabou, who sings protest songs against restrictive traditional roles.

From Marock to Hibhub

Like the rest of the Arab world, Moroccans listen to a lot of Egyptian music, but Moroccopop is gaining ground. A generation of local DJs with cheeky names such as Ramadan Special and DJ Al Intifada have mastered the art of the unlikely mashup. And so have some of the more intriguing talents to emerge in recent years: Hoba Hoba Spirit, whose controversy-causing, pop-punk 'Blad Skizo' (Schizophrenic Country) addresses the contradictions of modern Morocco head on; Moroccan singer-songwriter Hindi Zahra, Morocco's answer to Tori Amos, with bluesy acoustic-guitar backing; Darga, a group that blends ska, Darija rap and a horn section into Moroccan surf anthems; and the bluntly named Ganga Fusion and Kif Samba, who both pound out a danceable mix of funk, Amazigh (Berber) folk music, reggae and jazz. Algerian influences are heard in Morocco's raï scene, most notably Cheb Khader, Cheb Mimoun and Cheb Jellal.

But ask any guy on the street with baggy cargo shorts and a T-shirt with the slogan MJM (*Maroc Jusqu'al Mort* – Morocco till Death) about Moroccan pop, and you'll get a crash course in *hibhub* (Darija for 'hip hop'). Meknes' H-Kayne raps gangsta-style, while Tangier's MC Muslim raps with a death-metal growl, and Fez City Clan features a talented rapper and an Arabic string section.

Marock on Film

This Is Maroc (2010) Hat Trick Brothers' road trip

I Love Hip Hop in Morocco (2007) H-Kayne, DJ Key, Bigg and other hip-hop groups struggle to get gigs

The acts that consistently get festival crowds bouncing are Agadir's DJ Key, who remixes hip-hop standards with manic scratching and beat-boxing, and Marrakesh's Fnaire, mixing traditional Moroccan sounds with staccato vocal stylings. Rivalling 'Blad Skizo' for youth anthem of the decade is Fnaire's 'Ma Tkich Bladi' (Don't Touch My Country), an irresistibly catchy anthem against neocolonialism with a viral YouTube video. Popular female rappers include Manal and ILY.

International musicians find themselves increasingly attracted to Morocco. The **Fes Festival of World Sacred Music** (0535740535; https://fesfestival.com; May/Jun) attracts an ever-more diverse range of headline acts, from Björk to Patti Smith, while Rabat's **Festival Mawazine** (Rythmes du Monde; www.festivalmawazine.ma; Jun) brings in the pop mainstream from Beyoncé to Elton John.

The latter highlighted the sometimes delicate nature of the position of music in Morocco – while the government defended Elton John's homosexuality against Islamist criticism, Moroccan musicians have to tread a finer line, especially if commenting on social issues. In 2012, following the the Arab Spring, rapper El Haked was imprisoned for a year for 'undermining the honour' of public servants when the video for his song 'Klab Ed Dawla' (Dogs of the State) pictured corrupt police wearing the heads of donkeys. El Haked had previously been jailed for criticising the monarchy.

To explore Amazigh music in a variety of styles, languages and regions, check out samples and musician bios from basic bluesy Tartit to '70s-funky Tinariwen at www.agraw.com.

Literature & Cinema

Morocco's rich oral tradition has kept shared stories and histories alive. Watch singers in Marrakesh's Djemaa El Fna or listen in on a weekly session of *hikayat* (storytelling) at Cafe Clock with the square's last traditional storyteller, and you'll understand how the country's literary tradition has remained so vital and irrepressible, despite press censorship. More recently, novelists such as Tahar Ben Jelloun and Laila Lalami have brought their rich prose to bear on the national experience. Moroccan cinema is younger still, but the country is actively moving beyond being a glitzy film location to being a producer in its own right.

Literature

A Different Beat

The international spotlight first turned on Morocco's literary scene in the 1950s and '60s, when Beat Generation authors Paul and Jane Bowles took up residence in Tangier and began recording the stories of Moroccans they knew, and William S Burroughs penned *Naked Lunch* at the Hotel El Muniria. *The Sheltering Sky* is Paul Bowles' most celebrated Morocco-based novel, while the nonfiction *Their Heads Are Green and Their Hands are Blue* is a valuable travelogue. Following exposure from the Beats, local writers broke onto the writing scene. Check out Larbi Layachi's *A Life Full of Holes* (written under the pseudonym Driss Ben Hamed Charhadi), Mohammed Mrabet's *Love With a Few Hairs* and Mohamed Choukri's *For Bread Alone.* Like a lot of Beat literature, these books are packed with sex, drugs and unexpected poetry – but if anything, they're more streetwise, humorous and heartbreaking.

Grab a copy of Richard Hamilton's *Tangier: From the Romans to the Rolling Stones* or Josh Shoemake's *Tangier: A Literary Guide for Travellers* for a tour of this most storied of Moroccan cities, with appearances by everyone from William Burroughs to Mohamed Choukri and Mick Jagger.

Coming Up for Air

Encouraged by the outspoken Tanjaoui authors, Moroccan poet Abdellatif Laâbi founded the free-form, free-thinking poetry magazine *Anfas/Souffles* (Breath) in 1966, not in the anything-goes international zone of Tangier, but in the royal capital of Rabat. What began as a journal became a movement of writers, painters and filmmakers all heeding Laâbi's editorial outcry against government censorship. *Anfas/Souffles* published another 21 daring issues, until the censors shut it down in 1972 and sent Laâbi to prison for eight years for 'crimes of opinion'.

The literary expression Laâbi equated to breathing has continued unabated. In 1975 *Anfas/Souffles* cofounder and self-proclaimed 'linguistic guerrilla' Mohammed Khaïr-Eddine published his confrontational *Ce Maroc!,* an anthology of revolutionary writings. A Souss Amazigh (Berber) himself, Khaïr-Eddine called for the recognition of Amazigh identity and culture in his 1984 *Legend and Life of Agoun'chich,* which served as a rallying cry for today's Berber Pride movement.

Living to Tell

Still more daring and distinctive Moroccan voices have found their way into print over the past two decades, both at home and abroad. Among the most famous works to be published by a Moroccan author are *Dreams of Trespass: Tales of a Harem Girlhood* and *The Veil and the Male Elite: A Feminist Interpretation of Women's Rights in Islam,* both by Fatima Mernissi, an outspoken feminist and professor at the University of Rabat. In Rabat author Leila Abouzeid's *Year of the Elephant* and *The Director and Other Stories from Morocco,* tales of Moroccan women trying to reinvent their lives on their own terms become parables for Morocco's search for independence after colonialism.

The past several years have brought increased acclaim for Moroccan writers, who have continued to address highly charged topics despite repeated press crackdowns. Inspired by *Anfas/Souffles,* Fez-born expatriate author Tahar Ben Jelloun combined poetic devices and his training as a psychotherapist in his celebrated novel *The Sand Child,* the story of a girl raised as a boy by her father in Marrakesh, and its sequel *The Sacred Night,* which won France's Prix Goncourt. In *The Polymath,* 2009 Naguib Mahfouz Prize–winner Bensalem Himmich reads between the lines of 14th-century scholar and political exile Ibn Khaldun, as he tries to stop wars and prevent his own isolation. Several recent Moroccan novels have explored the promise and trauma of emigration, notably Mahi Binebine's harrowing *Welcome to Paradise,* Tahar Ben Jelloun's *Leaving Tangier,* and Laila Lalami's celebrated *Hope and Other Dangerous Pursuits.* In 2016 Leila Slimani won the Prix Goncourt, France's top literary prize, for her novel *Chanson Douce.*

In *Moroccan Folk Tales,* Jilali El Koudia presents 31 classic legends ranging from a Amazigh (Berber) version of *Snow White* to the tale of a woman who cross-dresses as a Muslim scholar.

Cinema

On Location in Morocco

Until recently Morocco had been seen mostly as a stunning movie backdrop, easily stealing scenes in such dubious cinematic achievements as *Sex and the City 2, Prince of Persia, Alexander* and *Sahara.* But while there's much to cringe about in Morocco's filmography, the country has had golden moments on the silver screen in Hitchcock's *The Man Who Knew Too Much,* Orson Welles' *Othello* and David Lean's *Lawrence of Arabia.*

Morocco has certainly proved its versatility: it stunt-doubled for Somalia in Ridley Scott's *Black Hawk Down,* Tibet in Martin Scorsese's *Kundun,* Lebanon in Stephen Gaghan's *Syriana,* and Iraq in Clint Eastwood's *American Sniper.* Morocco also stole the show right out from under John Malkovich by playing itself in Bernardo Bertolucci's *The Sheltering Sky,* and untrained local actors Mohamed Akhzam and Boubker Aït El Caid held their own with Cate Blanchett and Brad Pitt in the 2006 Oscar-nominated *Babel,* and the country played host to 007 in the 2015 Bond film, *Spectre.*

None of the 1942 classic *Casablanca* was actually shot in its namesake city, but the Hollywood set of Rick's Café Américain was reportedly based on the historic El Minzah hotel in Tangier.

Morocco's Directorial Breakthrough

Historically, Morocco has imported its blockbusters from Bollywood, Hollywood and Egypt, but today Moroccans are getting greater opportunities to see films shot in Morocco that are actually by Moroccans and about Morocco. In 2015 half of the top 10 box office hits in Morocco were locally made.

Moroccan filmmakers are putting decades of 'Ouallywood' (aka the iconic film studio in Ouarzazate) filmmaking craft and centuries of local storytelling tradition to work telling epic modern tales, often with a *cinéma vérité* edge. Morocco's 2010 Best Foreign Film Oscar contender was Nour-Eddine Lakhmari's *Casanegra,* about Casablanca youth thinking fast and growing up faster as they confront the darker aspects of life in the White City. Other hits include Latif Lahlou's *La Grande Villa* (2010), tracking one couple's cultural and personal adjustments after relocating from Paris to Casablanca.

MOROCCO'S LANDMARK CINEMA REVIVAL

Despite Morocco's creative boom, cinephiles fear for Morocco's movie palaces since ticket prices can't compete with pirated DVDs and video streaming. Thirty years ago, Morocco had 250 cinemas; today there are around 30.

While it may be too late for some historic cinemas, Moroccan theatre buffs have rallied to preserve and promote other architectural wonders. Tangier's 1930s **Cinema Rif** (Cinematheque de Tanger; 0539934683; www.cinemathequedetanger.com; Grand Socco; 9am-10pm Tue-Sun;) has reopened as a nonprofit cinema featuring international independent films and documentaries. **Cinéma Camera** (Ave Hassan II, Ville Nouvelle) in Meknes – possibly Morocco's most glorious art deco cinema – continues to thrive on mainstream Egyptian, Hollywood and Bollywood fare (check out its fabulous 'Golden Era Hollywood' mural). Casablanca's 1930s **Cinéma Rialto** (0522262632; www.facebook.com/cinemarialto; Rue Mohammed El Qory; 2-8pm; Marché Central) has been restored and reinvented as both a cinema and popular concert venue, while the art deco **Cinéma Renaissance** (0537722168; www.renaissance.ma; 360 Ave Mohammed V; adult/student Dh50/30; Medina Rabat) in Rabat has been transformed from a theatre to a cinema, cultural space and cafe.

Euro-Moroccan films have already become mainstays of the international festival circuit, notably Faouzi Bensaïdi's family-history epic *A Thousand Months,* winner of the 2003 Cannes Film Festival Le Premier Regard, and Laïla Marrakchi's *Marock,* about a Muslim girl and Jewish boy who fall in love, which screened at Cannes in 2005. With their stylish handling of colliding personal crises in *Heaven's Doors* (2006), Spanish-Moroccan directors Swel and Imad Noury hit the festival circuit with *The Man Who Sold the World,* a Dostoyevsky-existentialist fable set in Casablanca.

How big is Bollywood in Morocco? Around a third of all films shown in Morocco originate in Bollywood, and stars from Shah Rukh Khan to Amitabh Bachchan make regular appearances at the Marrakesh International Film Festival.

Thanks to critical acclaim and government support, new voices and new formats are emerging in Moroccan cinema. Young directors are finding their voices through a new film school in Marrakesh and short-film showcases, including back-to-back short-film festivals in Rabat and Tangier in October. Women directors have stepped into the spotlight, from Farida Benlyazid's 2005 hit *The Dog's Life of Juanita Narboni,* a Spanish expat's chronicle of Tangier from the 1930s to the 1960s, to star Mahassine El Hachadi, who won the short-film prize at the 2010 Marrakesh International Film Festival while still in film school.

Leila Kilani's *Les Yeux Secs* (Cry No More; 2003) broke further ground by not only being filmed in an Amazigh (Berber) language rather than Arabic, but tackling hard subjects such as female trafficking and prostitution. The use of social critique hasn't been without criticism, but filmmakers have been unafraid to push back in the name of artistic freedom. Star director Nabil Ayouch's *Much Loved* (2014) was banned for discussing prostitution, but *Behind Closed Doors,* directed the same year by Mohammed Ahed Bensouda, focused on workplace sexual harassment of women and led to a national discussion on changing Moroccan laws. In 2018, Faouzi Bensaïdi's *Volubilis,* a tale of love in a world of despair, won acclaim at home and abroad.

Arts & Crafts

The usual arts and crafts hierarchy is reversed in Morocco, where the craft tradition is ancient and revered, and visual art is a more recent development. Ornament is meant to be spiritually uplifting, while nonfunctional objects and representational images have traditionally been viewed as pointless – or worse, vanity verging on idolatry. While Morocco's contemporary visual arts scene is growing, its many beautiful crafts – from carpets and leather to pottery and metalwork – make the quintessential souvenir of any trip.

Visual Arts

Perhaps because it has been relegated to a marginal position, Moroccan contemporary art has particular poignancy and a sense of urgency, expressing aspirations and frustrations that can be understood instinctively – while eluding media censorship.

The new artworks emerging from Morocco are not kitschy paintings of eyelash-batting veiled women and scowling turbaned warriors, though you'll still find these in tourist showrooms. These form a 19th-century French Orientalist tradition made largely for export, and contemporary Moroccan artists such as Hassan Hajjaj are cleverly tweaking it. Hajjaj's provocative full-colour photographs of veiled women are not what you'd expect: one tough lady flashing the peace sign wears a rapper-style Nike-logo veil, emblazoned with the slogan 'Just Do It' across her mouth, while his 'Kesh Angels' series showed women bikers on the streets of Marrakesh.

Artists to look out for include Larbi Cherkaoui, who creates a hybrid of fine art and Arabic calligraphy on goatskin; filmmaker and designer Hassan Hajjaj, best known for his colourful, subversive photography that mixes up Moroccan heritage and contemporary society; and Hicham Benohoud, whose paintings, videos and installations question identity.

Morocco's visual-art scene put down roots in the 1950s and '60s, when folk artists in Essaouira and Tangier made painting and sculpture their own by incorporating Amazigh (Berber) symbols and locally scavenged materials. Landscape painting became a popular way to express pride of place in Essaouira and Asilah, and abstract painting became an important means of poetic expression in Rabat and Casablanca.

Marrakesh's art scene combines elemental forms with organic, traditional materials, helping to ground abstract art in Morocco as an indigenous art form. The scene has taken off in the past decade, first with the **Marrakech Biennale** (www.marrakechbiennale.org) that launched in 2005, and now the annual **1-54 Contemporary African Art Fair** (Contemporary African Art Fair; www.1-54.com; La Mamounia; ⏲Feb), an international showcase of emerging and established artists.

Calligraphy

Calligraphy remains Morocco's most esteemed visual art form, practiced and perfected in Moroccan *medersas* (schools for studying the Quran) over the last 1000 years. In Morocco, calligraphy isn't just in the Quran: it's on tiled walls, inside stucco arches, and literally coming out of the woodwork. Look carefully, and you'll notice that the same text can have an incredibly different effect in another calligraphic style. One calligrapher might take up a whole page with a single word, while another might turn it into a flower, or fold and twist the letters origami-style into graphic patterns.

To find out more about where those sinuous traditional designs originated and trace a few yourself, check out *The Splendour of Islamic Calligraphy* by Abdelkebir Khatibi and Mohammed Sijelmassi. You can also take a class at Cafe Clock in Fez, Marrakesh or Chefchaouen.

The style most commonly used for Qurans is Naskh, a slanting cursive script, while high-impact graphic lettering is the Kufic style. Cursive letters ingeniously interlaced to form a shape or dense design are hallmarks of the Thuluth style. You'll see three main kinds of Kufic calligraphy in Morocco: angular, geometric letters are square Kufic; those bursting into bloom are foliate Kufic; and letters that look like they've been tied by sailors are knotted Kufic.

Lately, contemporary artists have reinvented calligraphy as a purely expressive art form, combining the elegant gestures of ancient scripts with the urgency of urban graffiti. Farid Belkahia's enigmatic symbols in henna and Larbi Cherkaoui's high-impact graphic swoops show that even freed of literal meanings, calligraphy can retain its poetry.

Crafts

For instant relief from homogenised homeware, head to your nearest Moroccan souq to admire the inspired handiwork of local artisans. Most of Morocco's design wonders are created without computer models or even an electrical outlet, relying instead on imagination, an eye for colour and form, and steady hands.

All this takes experience. In Fez, the minimum training for a ceramic *mâalem* (master craftsman) is 10 years, and it takes a *zellige* (geometric tile) mosaic-maker three to four months to master a single shape – and with 360 shapes to learn, mastery is a lifelong commitment. When you watch a *mâalem* at work, it's the confidence of the hand movements, not the speed, that indicates a masterwork is in the making. Techniques and tools are handed down from one generation to the next, and friendly competition among neighbours propels innovation.

Instead of sprawling factory showrooms, *mâalems* work wonders in wardrobe-sized workshops lining the souqs, each specialising in a traditional trade. But artisans in rural areas are not to be outdone: many Moroccan villages are known for a style of embroidery or a signature rug design. Most of the artisans you'll see in the souqs are men, but you're likely to glimpse women *mâalems* working behind the scenes knotting carpets in Anti Atlas and Middle Atlas villages, weaving textiles along the southern coast and painting ceramics in Fez, Tamegroute and Safi.

Carpets

If you manage to return from Morocco without a carpet, congratulate yourself on being one of few travellers to have outsmarted the wiliest salespeople on the planet.

Fair-Trade Carpets

- *Women's Cooperative of Aït Bououli*
- *Coopérative de Tissage, Ouarzazate*
- *Ensemble Artisanals in cities nationwide*
- *Anou (www.theanou.com)*

Travellers are hooked because there's a carpet out there for almost everyone. Women in rural Morocco traditionally created carpets as part of their dowries, expressing their own personalities in exuberant colours and patterns, and weaving in symbols of their hopes for health and married life. Now carpets are mostly made as a way to supplement household income, but in the hands of a true *mâalem,* a hand-woven carpet brings so much personality and *baraka* (grace) underfoot, it could never be mistaken for a mere doormat.

Carpets you see in the souqs may already have been bought and sold three or four times, with the final price representing a hefty mark-up over what the weaver was paid for her work. Consider buying directly from a village association instead: the producer is more likely to get her fair share of the proceeds, you'll get a better deal without extensive bargaining and you may meet the artisan who created your new rug.

Another feel-good option is **Anou** (www.theanou.com), an online community of artisans set up by Peace Corps volunteer Dan Driscoll. The often-illiterate artisans are trained in the technology needed to set up

TOP CARPET-BUYING TIPS

➡ Know your limits, namely how much blank wall and floor space you actually have, your airline's luggage weight limit, the cost of shipping and duty, and what you're willing to pay.

➡ Tread cautiously with antique rugs. Precious few genuine antique rugs are left in Morocco. New rugs are aged by being taken out back and stomped on, bleached by the sun or otherwise treated.

➡ Inspect the knots. You'll be asked to pay more for carpets with a higher number of knots per sq cm, which you'll begin to discern by examining the back of carpets to look for gaps between knots. Some carpets are washed in hot water to bind the wool together more tightly, but you can often distinguish these shrunken rugs by their irregular borders.

➡ Get plenty of vegetables. Prices are often higher for carpets whose wool is coloured using vegetable dyes (which tend to fade faster) instead of synthetics; you can usually tell these by their muted tones, and the carpet seller may be able to tell you what plant was used to make the dye.

➡ There's no set price, so enjoy the transaction. Banter before you bargain, keep your sense of humour, come back tomorrow, and knock back plenty of mint tea. Besides fond memories, at the end of it all you should have a carpet that suits you.

their own selling space and in how to promote and ship their products, cutting out the middle man. They sell homewares, jewellery and accessories.

Textiles

Hand-stitched, woven and embroidered – there's a long tradition of female artisans producing beautiful textiles; more recently it's helped attract international designers, as well as global clothing brands, to Morocco. One-third of women are employed in the industrial garment industry, but for meticulous handiwork with individual flair, check out traditional textiles.

Embroidery

Moroccan stitchery ranges from simple Amazigh (Berber) designs to minutely detailed *terz Fassi*, the elaborate nature-inspired patterns that are stitched in blue upon white linen and that women in Fez traditionally spend years mastering for their dowries. Rabati embroidery is a riot of colour, with bold, graphic flowers in one or two colours of silk thread that almost completely obscures the plain-cotton backing. But the ladies of Salé also deserve their due for their striking embroidery in one or two bold colours along the borders of crisp white linen.

The most reliable resource in English on Moroccan carpets is the (aptly named) *Moroccan Carpets*, by Brooke Pickering, W Russell Pickering and Ralph S Yohe. It's packed with photos to help pinpoint the origins and style of any carpet that mysteriously followed you home.

Passementerie

What's that line of fine silk thread down a medina side alleyway? That would be a *passementerie* (decorative trimming) artisan at work, spinning thread from a nail stuck in the wall, until it's the perfect width and length to make into silken tassels and the ornate trims that adorn *djellabas* (full-length hooded garments with long sleeves). In a cupboard-sized Moroccan *passementerie* shop, you'll find enough gold braid to decorate an army of generals and more tassels than a burlesque troupe could spin in a lifetime – but you'll also find a jackpot of small, portable gifts.

Felt

Handmade felt hats, slippers, coats, pillows, bags or floor coverings really put wool through the wringer: it's dyed, boiled and literally beaten to a pulp. Instead of being woven or sewn, felt is usually pounded with *savon noir* (natural palm soap), formed into the intended shape on a mould and allowed to dry gradually to hold its shape. Felt makers are usually found in the wool souq in major cities.

Weaving

Beyond the sea of imported harem pants and splashy synthetic *djellabas* in the souqs, hand-woven Moroccan fabrics with exceptional sheen and texture may catch your eye: nubby organic cotton from the Rif, shiny 'cactus silk' (actually rayon) woven with cotton, sleek Marrakesh table linens and whisper-soft High Atlas woollen blankets. Some lesser-quality knock-offs are industrially produced, but connoisseurs seek out the plusher nap, tighter weave and elegant drape of hand-woven Moroccan fabrics.

Answers to your every 'how'd they do that?' are on display at state-run Ensemble Artisanales, where you can watch artisans at work and purchase their handiwork at fixed, if somewhat higher, prices.

In souqs, village cooperatives and Ensemble Artisanal showrooms, you might glimpse two to four women at a time on a loom, working on a single piece. Men work larger looms for *djellaba* fabric, pushing the shuttle with their arms as they pound pedals with their feet – producing 1m of fabric this way is a workout equivalent to running several miles while dribbling a basketball. You can buy linens and clothing ready-made or get hand-woven fabric by the bolt or metre, and have Moroccan decor and couture custom-made to your specifications. Tailors can be found in every major city, but be sure to leave enough time for the initial consultation plus two fittings for clothing.

Leatherwork

Now that there's not much call for camel saddles, Moroccan leather artisans keep busy fashioning embossed leather book covers and next season's must-have handbags with what look like medieval dentistry tools. Down dingy *derbs* (alleyways), you'll discover freshly tanned and dyed leather being sculpted into pointy *babouches* (slippers) and fashion-forward pouffes. Along these leather souqs, you might spot artisans

CARPET CATEGORIES

Beni Ourain Woven by 17 different Amazigh (Berber) tribes in the Middle Atlas, traditional patterns are black or brown lines and abstract and geometric shapes on a shaggy cream wool background. They often feature symbols to bring luck and help ward off the evil eye.

Kilims These flat-woven rugs make up for their lack of pile with character. Some include Tamazight (Berber language) letters and auspicious symbols such as the Southern Cross and *fibule* (brooch) in their weave. Ask the seller to explain them for you – whether it's genuine or faux folklore, the carpet-seller's interpretation all adds to the experience.

Azilal Soft and lustrous, these High Atlas rugs are only limited by the imagination of the weaver. Expect vivid colours and intense geometric designs. Less rug, more floor art.

Boucharouite Upcycling at its finest, these rag rugs are riots of colour, woven by women from scraps of cloth and wool. Traditionally, they were put rag-side down to hold the heat in winter, but you'll want to show off their exuberant patterns.

Rabati Highly prized, plush pile carpets in deep jewel tones, featuring an ornate central motif balanced by fine detail along the borders. Many of the patterns may remind you of a formal garden, but you may see newer animal motifs and splashy modern abstract designs.

Zanafi Kilims and shag carpeting, together at last. Opposites attract in these rugs, where sections of fluffy pile alternate with flat-woven stripes or borders.

Chichaoua Simple and striking, with spare zigzags, asterisks and enigmatic symbols on a variegated red or purple background.

dabbing henna onto stretched goatskin to make 'tattooed' leather candle-holders, lampshades or standalone artworks. If you're around for a couple of days, you can even commission a custom-made bag or butter-soft leather jacket.

Traditionally, men's *babouches* are canary yellow; women's *babouches* come in a wider range of colours and designs – pointy, round, plain, embroidered or even scattered with sequins.

Never let it be said that Moroccan leatherwork can't keep up with modern trends: look out for the traditional *babouches* (leather slippers) branded with English and Spanish football club logos, along with Raja Casablanca and MAS Fes for the domestic tourism market.

Ceramics

Moroccan ceramics are a delight, and different regions have their own designs. Fine Fassi pottery is blue and white, Meknes ceramics tend to be green and black, Tamegroute pottery has a distinctive green glaze, and Safi is all bright colours and geometric patterns, while Marrakesh specialises in monochrome ceramics in red, graphite or orange. Many rural areas specialise in plain terracotta pots, often adorned with Amazigh (Berber) good-luck symbols painted in henna. If you want to read up on Moroccan ceramics, try *The Earth Has Three Colors* (2019) by David Packer.

Zellige

To make a Moroccan fountain, grab your hammer and chisel, and carefully chip a glazed tile into a geometrically correct shape. Good job – now only 6000 more to go. Then again, you might leave it to the Moroccan mosaic masters to decorate your riad courtyard with dazzling *zellige* (colourful geometric mosaic tiles). Fez has a reputation for the most intricate, high-lustre *zellige*, and the historic fountains around town dating from the Middle Ages are convincing advertisements for Fassi masterworks.

Brass, Copper & Silver

Tea is a performance art in Morocco, requiring just the right props. As if tea poured from a great height wasn't dramatic enough, gleaming brass teapots and copper tea trays are hammered by hand to catch the light and engraved with calligraphy to convey *baraka* on all who partake. Pierced brass lamps and recycled tin lanterns add instant atmosphere – and if all else fails to impress, serve your guests a sliver of cake with an inlaid knife from Morocco's dagger capital, Kalaat M'Gouna.

Most 'silver' tea services are actually nickel silver, and should cost accordingly – about Dh50 to Dh250 for the teapot, and usually more for the tray, depending on size and design.

Jewellery

Not all that glitters is gold in Morocco, since many Amazigh (Berbers) traditionally believe gold to be a source of evil. You may see some jewellers with magnifying glasses working a tricky bit of gold filigree, but most gold you see in the souqs is imported from India and Bali.

Sterling silver will be marked with 925 and is often sold by weight rather than design. Morocco's mining operations are more concerned with phosphates and fossils than with precious gems, but you will see outsized folkloric necklaces and headdresses inset with semiprecious stones, including coral, agate, cornelian and amber.

But Moroccan artisans don't need precious materials to create a thing of beauty. Ancient ammonite and trilobite fossils from Alnif make fascinating prehistoric amulets, and striking Amazigh *fibules* (brooches) are one of Tiznit's specialities. Layered wood, nickel silver and brightly coloured enamel make groovy cocktail rings in Marrakesh, and desert Tuareg talismans in leather and silver are fitting gifts for international men of mystery.

In *Women Artisans of Morocco: Their Stories, Their Lives* (2018) author Susan Schaefer Davis talks to 25 women around Morocco who produce crafts in the age-old way.

BUYING SUSTAINABLE SOUVENIRS

Argan Oil

Traditionally orange-tinted and rich in vitamin E, argan oil is pressed from olive-like fruit handpicked from the tree. It's arduous work, and buying from a collective is the best way to ensure that the women workers are paid fairly. Some of the argan oil sold in medinas is watered down with other less expensive oils. Some goats have learned to climb low-hanging argan trees to eat the nuts, and others are tethered to the trees as a photo op, which shouldn't be encouraged.

Carpets & Blankets

Berber blankets are often made with wool so natural that you can feel the lanolin on them. Most weavers use a combination of natural and artificial dyes to achieve the desired brilliance and lightfastness. Some cooperatives card and dye their own wool for natural colours, but for bright colours it's better that they source their wool from reputable dyers instead of handling and disposing of chemical dyes themselves. For associations advancing best environmental practices and paying women weavers fairly, visit the cooperatives at Aïn Leuh (p373) in the Middle Atlas, **Women's Cooperative of Aït Bououli** (0616247899, 0671419106; 9am-5pm) and **Association Gorge du Dadès** (0666396949, 0677909670; Km 24, Aït Oudinar; 2-5pm Mon-Sat).

Thuja Wood

Essaouira is famous for its woodworking, and particularly for products made from fragrant thuja wood, a medium to dark reddish-brown wood with plenty of knots. While it's not an endangered species, buying anything made from thuja increases demand and therefore encourages illegal logging; if you do buy, make sure it's from a cooperative, such as the **Coopérative Artisanale des Marqueteurs** (0671737399; 6 Rue Khalid Ibn Oualid, Medina; 10am-9pm) in Essaouira and the **Cooperative Artisanale des Femmes de Marrakesh** (0662322630; 67 Souq Kchachbia; 10am-7pm).

Tyre Tread Upcycling

Used tyres don't biodegrade and burning them produces toxic fumes, but when cleverly repurposed by Moroccan artisans, they make fabulous home furnishings. Tyre-tread mirrors make any entryway look dashingly well-travelled, and inner-tube tea trays are ideal for entertaining. For the best selection, visit the artisans upcycling tyres that line the south end of Rue Riad Zitoun El Kedim in Marrakesh.

Woodwork

The most fragrant part of the souq is the woodworkers' area, aromatic from the curls of wood carpeting the floors of master-carvers' workshops. These are the artisans responsible for the ancient carved, brass-studded cedar doors and those carved cedar *muqarnas* (honeycomb-carved) domes that cause wonderment in Moroccan palaces. Tetouan, Meknes and Fez have the best reputations for carved wood ornaments, but you'll see impressive woodwork in most Moroccan medinas.

For the gourmets on your gift list, hand-carved orangewood *harira* (lentil soup) spoons are small ladles with long handles that make ideal tasting utensils. Cedar is used for ornate jewellery boxes and hefty chip-carved chests are sure to keep the moths at bay. The most prized wood is thuja wood, knotty burl from the roots of trees indigenous to the Essaouira region. Buy from artisans' associations that practise responsible tree management and harvesting.

Architecture

Stubbed toes come with the territory in Morocco: with so much intriguing architecture to gawp at, you can't always watch where you're going. Some buildings are more memorable than others – as in any developing country there's makeshift housing and cheap concrete – but it's the striking variation in architecture that keeps you wondering what's behind that wall or beyond the wrought-iron window grill. Here are some Moroccan landmarks likely to leave your jaw on tiled floors and your toes in jeopardy.

Art Deco Villas

When Morocco came under French colonial control, *villes nouvelles* (new towns) were built outside the walls of the medina, with street grids and modern architecture imposing strict order.

But one style that seemed to bridge local Islamic geometry and streamlined European modernism was art deco. In 1924, painter Jacques Majorelle coloured his art deco villa, Jardin Majorelle, a deep blue – now known as Majorelle blue – with touches of vivid yellow.

In the 1930s, Casablanca cleverly grafted Moroccan geometric detail onto whitewashed European edifices, adding a signature neo-Moorish look to villas, theatres and hotels, notably Marius Boyer's **Cinéma Rialto** (0522262632; www.facebook.com/cinemarialto; Rue Mohammed El Qory; 2-8pm; Marché Central), which is still a working cinema and concert hall.

Tangier rivalled Casablanca for neo-Moorish decadence, with its 1940s **Cinema Rif** (Cinematheque de Tanger; 0539934683; www.cinemathequedetanger.com; Grand Socco; 9am-10pm Tue-Sun;) and 1930s **El Minzah hotel** (0539333444; www.leroyal.com; 85 Rue de la Liberté; d/ste from Dh2000/3500;) – allegedly the architectural model for Rick's Café Américain in the 1942 classic *Casablanca*.

Top Art Deco

Villa des Arts, Casablanca

Jardin Majorelle, Marrakesh

Cinema Rif, Tangier

El Minzah hotel, Tangier

Fanadiq

Since medieval times, *fanadiq* (inns for travelling caravans, plural of *funduq*) featured ground-floor stables or artisans' workshops, and rented rooms upstairs. From the nonstop flux of artisans and traders emerged cosmopolitan ideas and new inventions. *Fanadiq* once dotted caravan routes, but as trading communities became more stable and affluent, most *fanadiq* were gradually replaced with private homes and storehouses.

Around 140 *fanadiq* remain in Marrakesh alone, including historic structures near Place Bab Fteuh, several lining Rue Dar El Bacha and one on Rue El Mouassine featured in the film *Hideous Kinky*. In Fez, an exemplary *funduq* dating from 1711 underwent a six-year renovation to become the spiffy **Nejjarine Museum of Wooden Arts & Crafts** (0535740580; Place An Nejjarine; Dh20; 10am-5pm).

Hammams

These domed buildings have been part of the Moroccan urban landscape since the Almohads, and every village aspires to a hammam of its own – often the only local source of hot water. Traditionally they are built of mudbrick, lined with *tadelakt* (satiny hand-polished limestone plaster that traps moisture) and capped with a dome that has star-shaped vents to let steam escape. The domed main room is the coolest area, with side rooms offering increasing levels of heat.

The boldly elemental forms of traditional hammams may strike you as incredibly modern, but actually it's the other way around. The hammam is a recurring feature of landscapes by modernist masters Henri Matisse and Paul Klee, and Le Corbusier's International Style modernism was inspired by the interior volumes and filtered light of these iconic domed North African structures.

Tadelakt has become a sought-after surface treatment for pools and walls in stylish homes, and pierced domes incorporated into the 'Moroccan Modern' style feature in umpteen coffee-table books. To see these architectural features in their original context, pay a visit to your friendly neighbourhood hammam – there's probably one near the local mosque, since hammams traditionally share a water source with ablutions fountains.

Historic Hammams

Hammam Bab Doukkala, Marrakesh

Hammam Seffarine, Fez

Hammams of the Hassan II Mosque, Casablanca

Kasbahs

Wherever there were once commercial interests worth protecting in Morocco – salt, sugar, gold, enslaved people – you'll find a kasbah. These fortified quarters housed the head family, its guards and all the necessities for living in case of a siege. The *mellah* (Jewish quarter) was often positioned within reach of the kasbah guard and the ruling power's watchful eye. One of the largest remaining kasbahs is Marrakesh's 11th-century kasbah, which still houses a royal palace and acres of gardens, and flanks Marrakesh's *mellah*. Among the most photogenic northern kasbahs are the red kasbah overlooking all-blue Chefchaouen and Rabat's whitewashed seaside kasbah with its elegantly carved gate, Bab Oudaïa.

Unesco World Heritage designations saved **Taourirt Kasbah** (Ave Mohammed V; Dh20; ⌚8.30am-6pm) in Ouarzazate and the rose-coloured mud-brick Aït Ben Haddou (p142), both restored and frequently used as film backdrops. To see a fine example of a southern kasbah, head to **Kasbah Amridil** (☎0524852387; with/without guide Dh60/10; ⌚8am-7pm) in Skoura.

Medinas: Morocco's Hidden Cities explores the shadows of ancient Moroccan walled cities, with painterly images by French photographer Jean-Marc Tingaud and illuminating commentary by Tahar Ben Jelloun.

Ksour

The location of *ksour* (fortified villages, plural of *ksar*) in southern Morocco are spectacularly formidable: atop a rocky crag, against a rocky cliff or rising above a palm oasis. Towers made of metres-thick, straw-reinforced mudbrick are elegantly tapered at the top to distribute the weight, and capped by zigzag merlon (the solid part between two crenels). Like a desert mirage, a *ksar* will play tricks with your sense of scale and distance with its odd combination of grandeur and earthy intimacy. From these watchtowers, Timbuktu seems much closer than 52 days

ENDANGERED MONUMENTS: GLAOUI KASBAHS

The once-spectacular Glaoui kasbahs at **Taliouine**, **Tamdakhte** (tip Dh15) and especially **Telouet** (Dh20; ⌚9am-5pm) have been largely abandoned to the elements – go and see them now before they're gone. These are deeply ambivalent monuments: they represent the finest Moroccan artistry (no one dared displease the Glaoui despots) but also the betrayal of the Alaouites by Amazigh (Berber) warlord Pasha El Glaoui, who collaborated with French colonists to suppress his fellow Moroccans. But locals argue Glaoui kasbahs should be preserved, as visible reminders that even the grandest fortifications were no match for independent-minded Moroccans.

away by camel, and in fact the elegant mud-brick architecture of Mali and Senegal is a near relative of Morocco's *ksour*.

To get the full effect of this architecture in splendid oasis settings, visit the *ksour*-packed Dadès and Draa valleys, including Amezrou's part-crumbling *ksar* with its fascinating mix of cultures, and the recently restored **Ksar El Khorbat** (☎0535880355; www.elkhorbat.com) in Tinejdad. This sustainable, community-run project includes a museum, a guesthouse, a restaurant and a women's craft workshop. Residents will show you around the still-inhabited *ksar*.

Caravan stops are packed with well-fortified *ksour*, where merchants brought fortunes in gold, sugar and spices for safekeeping after 52-day trans-Saharan journeys. In Rissani, a half-hour circuit will lead you past half a dozen crumbling *ksour*, some of which are slated for restoration. Along caravan routes heading north through the High Atlas toward Fez, you'll spot spectacular *ksour* rising between snowcapped mountain peaks, including a fine hilltop tower that once housed the entire 300-person community of Zaouiat Ahansal.

Morocco is giving its medinas a makeover. As part of an ambitious multimillion-dollar project, and following on from Rabat and Fez, the ancient cities of Marrakesh, Essaouira, Salé, Meknes and Tetouan will be revitalised, with the work expected to wrap up in 2022.

Medersas

More than schools of rote religious instruction, Moroccan *medersa* have been vibrant centres of learning for law, philosophy and astronomy since the Merinid dynasty. For enough splendour to lift the soul and distract all but the most devoted students, visit the 14th-century **Medersa Bou Inania** (Talaa Kebira; Dh20; ⌚9am-5pm, closed during prayers) in Fez, bedecked in *zellige* (colourful geometric mosaic tilework). Now open as a museum, this *medersa* gives some idea of the austere lives students led in sublime surroundings, with long hours of study, several roommates, dinner on a hotplate, sleeping mats for comfort and one communal bathroom for up to 900 students.

Mosques

Even small villages may have more than one mosque, built on prime real estate in town centres with one wall facing Mecca. Mosques provide moments of sublime serenity in chaotic cities and busy village market days. Towering minarets not only aid the acoustics of the call to prayer, but also provide a visible reminder of Allah and community that puts everything else – minor spats, dirty dishes, office politics – back in perspective.

Mosques in Morocco are closed to non-Muslims, with two exceptions that couldn't be more different: Casablanca's vast and ornate **Hassan II Mosque** (Blvd Sidi Mohammed Ben Abdallah; guided tours adult/child 4-12yr Dh120/30; ⌚tours 9am, 10am, 11am & 3pm) and the roofless and austere **Tin Mal Mosque** (☎0618126514; suggested tip Dh10-20; ⌚9am-5pm) nestled in a High Atlas valley. The Hassan II Mosque was completed in 1993 by French architect Michel Pinseau with great fanfare and considerable controversy: with room for 25,000 worshippers under a retractable roof and a 210m-high laser-equipped minaret, the total cost has been estimated at €585 million, not including maintenance or restitution to low-income former residents moved to accommodate the structure. At the other end of the aesthetic spectrum is the elegant simplicity of Tin Mal Mosque, built in 1156 to honour the Almohads' strict spiritual leader, Mohammed Ibn Tumart, with soaring arches that lift the eye and the spirits ever upward.

Eight of the world's leading Islamic architectural scholars give you their best explanations in *Architecture of the Islamic World: Its History and Social Meaning*, by Oleg Grabar et al.

Muslims assert that no Moroccan architecture surpasses buildings built for the glory of Allah, especially mosques in the ancient Islamic spiritual centre of Fez. With walls and ablutions fountains covered in lustrous green and white Fassi *zellige* and mihrabs (niches indicating

Pick up a copy of Tahir Shah's *The Caliph's House* for a rollicking account of his project to restore an old Casablanca mansion, starting with exorcising the resident *jinns* (genies) before the builders would start work.

the direction of Mecca) swathed in stucco and marble, Fez mosques are purpose-built for spiritual glory. When vast portals are open between prayers, visitors can glimpse (no photos allowed) Fez's crowning glory: **Kairaouine Mosque and University** (Al Qarawiyyin), founded in the 8th century by a trailblazing heiress, Fatima Al Fihri. Non-Muslims can also see Morocco's most historic minbar (pulpit): the 12th-century Koutoubia minbar, inlaid with silver, ivory and marquetry by Cordoba's finest artisans, and housed in Marrakesh's **Badia Palace** (behind Place des Ferblantiers; adult/child Dh70/30; ⊙9am-5pm).

Ramparts

Dramatic form follows defensive function in many of Morocco's trading posts and ports. The Almoravids took no chances with their trading capital and wrapped Marrakesh in 19km of pink *pisé* (rammed earth reinforced with clay and chalk) walls, 2m thick. Old Fez is similarly surrounded. Coastal towns like Essaouira and Asilah have witnessed centuries of piracy and fierce Portuguese–Moroccan trading rivalries – hence the heavy stone walls dotted with cannons, and crenellated ramparts that look like medieval European castle walls.

Riads

Near palaces in Morocco's major cities are grand riads, mansions built around courtyard gardens, where families of royal relatives, advisers and rich merchants whiled away idle hours gossiping in *bhous* (seating nooks) paved with *zellige* and filled with songbirds twittering in fruit trees. Not a bad setup really, and one you can enjoy today in one of the many converted riad guesthouses in Marrakesh, Fez and other medinas around Morocco.

So many riads have become B&Bs over the past decade that 'riad' has become a synonym for 'guesthouse' – but technically, an authentic riad has a courtyard garden divided into four parts, with a fountain in the centre. A riad is also not to be confused with a *dar,* which is a simpler, smaller house constructed around a central light well, perfect for cramming into a medina and a more practical structure for hot desert locales and chilly coastal towns. With several hundred riads, including extant examples from the 15th century, Marrakesh is the riad capital of North Africa.

From outside those austere, metre-thick walls, you'd never guess what splendours await beyond brass-studded doors: painted cedarwood ceilings, ironwork balconies and archways dripping with stucco. Upkeep isn't easy, and modernising ancient structures with plumbing and electricity without destabilising the foundations is especially tricky. Built in clay or mudbrick with a thick lime plaster covering, their walls insulate against street sound, keep cool in summer and warm in winter, and wick away humidity instead of trapping it like mouldy old concrete – building materials of the future, as well as the past.

Top Souqs

- *Souq Haddadine, Marrakesh*
- *Henna Souq, Fez*
- *Souq El Ghezel, Salé*
- *Fish Souq, Essaouira*

Souqs

In Morocco, souqs – the market streets of a medina – covered with wooden grilles for shade and shelter, are known as *quissariat* (covered markets). They're criss-crossed with smaller, no-name streets lined with food stalls, storerooms and wardrobe-sized workshops carved into thick earthen walls. When (not if) you get lost among them, keep heading onward until you intersect with the next souq or buy a carpet, whichever happens first.

LOST IN THE MEDINA MAZE? FOLLOW SOUQ LOGIC

In labyrinthine Moroccan medinas, winding souqs hardly seem linear, but they do adhere to a certain logic. Centuries ago, market streets were organised by trade so that medieval shoppers would know where to head for pickles or camel saddles. More than other medinas, Fez souqs maintain their original medieval organisation: kiosks selling silver-braided trim are right off the caftan souq, just down the street from stalls selling hand-woven white cotton for men's *djellabas*.

What about wool? That's in a different souq, near stalls selling hand-carved horn combs for carding wool. The smelliest, messiest trades were pushed to the peripheries, so you'll know you're near the edge of the medina when you arrive at tanneries or livestock markets. In Marrakesh, the saddle-making souq is at the northeast end of the souq, not far from the tanneries.

Zawiyas

Don't be fooled by modest appearances or remote locations in Morocco: even a tiny village teetering off the edge of a cliff may be a major draw because of its *zawiya* (shrine to a *marabout*, or saint). Just being in the vicinity of a *marabout* is said to confer *baraka* (grace). **Zawiya Nassiriyya** (suggested donation Dh20; ⏲morning & late afternoon Sat-Thu) in Tamegroute is reputed to cure the ill and eliminate stress, and the **Zawiya of Sidi Moussa** in the Aït Bougmez Valley is said to increase the fertility of female visitors.

To boost your *baraka*, you can visit these shrines as well as the **Zawiya of Moulay Ali Ash Sharif** (⏲8am-6pm) in Rissani, which is now open to non-Muslims. Most *zawiyas* are closed to non-Muslims – including the famous **Zawiya of Moulay Idriss II** (Mausoleum of Moulay Idriss II; Derb Moulay Idriss) in Fez, and all seven of Marrakesh's *zawiyas* – but you can often recognise a *zawiya* by its ceramic green-tiled roof. In rural areas, a *marabout*'s shrine (often confusingly referred to as a *marabout* rather than *zawiya*) is typically a simple mud-brick base topped with a whitewashed dome, though in the Ourika Valley village of Tafza you can see a rare red-stone example.

Landscapes & Wildlife

A day's journey in Morocco can take you from Atlantic beaches through rich farmland and over high mountain passes to the Sahara itself. The human landscape is no less fascinating – almost half of all Moroccans still live in rural areas, and everywhere you'll spot people working this extraordinary land, harvesting barley on tiny stone-walled terraces, tending to olive and argan groves, taking donkey-cart loads of alfalfa to market or leading their flocks of sheep to mountain pastures.

Coastline

When the Umayyads arrived in Morocco, they rode their horses onto Atlantic beaches and dubbed the country *Al Maghreb* (where the sun sets), knowing that the sea marked the westernmost limit of their conquests. The coast has played a central role in Moroccan history, from the Barbary pirates to the Allied landings of WWII; today the country is developing stretches of both its Atlantic and Mediterranean coastlines into shiny new tourist hubs complete with villas and resorts. Luckily for nature lovers, there's still pristine coastline in between, with rare shorebirds and cliff-edge vistas.

If you're going for a dip, be aware that the Atlantic rollers can hide some fearsome riptides, and once you're in the water, there's nothing between you and the Americas – or at best, the Canary Islands.

Fishing and international trade have defined the Atlantic coast's economy ever since the ancient Phoenicians and Romans established their port at Lixus. But the Atlantic also has its wild side, with raw, rocky beaches around whitewashed Asilah, and wetland habitats, such as the lagoon of Merja Zerga National Park in Moulay Bousselham, attracting flamingos and rare African wildfowl. South of Casablanca are the ports of Oualidia and Essaouira, former pirates' coves where rare wildlife still flourishes and Morocco's best seafood is served port-side. South of the commercialised boardwalks of Agadir, resort beaches empty into great sandy expanses stretching through Western Sahara to Mauritania.

By contrast, the craggy Mediterranean coast has remained relatively undeveloped until recently, despite a spectacular coastline of sheltered coves and plunging cliffs. Tangier and the Spanish enclave port towns of Ceuta and Melilla make the best of their advantageous positions, with scenic overlooks and splendid coastal villas. The major barrier to the east is the Rif Mountains, rugged terrain inhabited by staunchly independent Amazigh (Berbers), but motorways that skirt along the Rif to Saïdia and Oujda have made this stretch of coast accessible as never before.

Mountains

Three mountain ranges ripple diagonally across Morocco: the Rif in the north, the Middle Atlas (south of Fez) and the High Atlas (south and northeast of Marrakesh), with the southern sub-chain of the Anti Atlas slumping into the desert. The monumental force of plate tectonics brought these ranges into existence. Around 60 million years ago, a dramatic collision of the Africa and Eurasia plates lifted up the High Atlas, while closing the Strait of Gibraltar and raising the Alps and Pyrenees.

More recently, the mountains have provided shelter for self-sufficient Imazighen (Berbers), a safe haven for those fleeing invaders and a strategic retreat for organising resistance against would-be colonisers.

In the north, the low Rif Mountains form a green, fertile arc that serves as a natural coastal barrier. Even the Vandals and Visigoths were no match for the independent-minded Riffian Imazighen, who for millennia successfully used their marginal position to resist incursions from Europe and Africa alike. The Rif has remained politically marginalised, which has had one highly debatable advantage until now: kif (hashish) is widely grown in the region east of Tetouan. It's taken huge government investment to improve access to the region via new infrastructure. Well-graded roads make exploring the Rif more possible than ever.

When hiking in the Rif, try not to step on the kif. Morocco is the one of the world's largest producers of hashish, most of it destined for markets in western Europe.

The Middle Atlas is the Moroccan heartland, a patchwork of farmland that runs from Volubilis to Fez and gradually rises to mountain peaks covered with fragrant forests of juniper, thuja and cedar. This sublime trekking country is also home to the Barbary monkeys, Morocco's only (nonhuman) primate. Running northeast to southwest from the Rif, the range soars to 3340m at its highest point.

But the real drama begins east of Agadir, where foothills suddenly rise from their crouched position to form the gloriously precipitous High Atlas Mountains. South of Marrakesh, the High Atlas reach dizzy heights at Jebel Toubkal, North Africa's highest summit (4167m). On the lower flanks, the mountains are ingeniously terraced with orchards of walnuts, cherries, almonds and apples, which erupt into bloom in spring. The High Atlas hunkers down on to the southeast into the Anti Atlas range, which protects the Souss Valley from the hot winds of the rising Sahara desert.

Desert

No landscape is more iconic in Morocco than the desert, with rolling dunes and mud-brick *ksour* (fortified villages, plural of *ksar*) rising majestically from hidden palm oases. But most of the desert is neither oasis nor dune, and it's virtually uninhabitable. Vast tracts of barren, sun-bleached *hamada* (stony desert) are interrupted by rocky gorges, baked over millions of years by the desert's ovenlike heat until the blackened surface turns glassy. The desert forms still-disputed borders east and south to Algeria and Mauritania. South of the Anti Atlas Mountains, the barren slopes trail off into the stony, almost trackless desert of Western Sahara.

Even today, the sight of an oasis on this desolate desert horizon brings a rush of elation and wonder – but when ancient caravans emerged after a gruelling 52-day trans-Saharan journey with final stretches of dunes at Erg Chigaga and Tinfou, the glimpse of green on the horizon at Zagora was nothing short of life-saving. From Zagora, caravans heading to

DUST-UP IN THE DESERT

To see the desert the way nature intended, take a dromedary instead of an all-terrain vehicle. The 4WDs break up the surface of the desert, which is then scattered into the air by strong winds. By one estimate, the annual generation of dust has increased by 1000% in North Africa in the last 50 years – a major contributor to drought, as dust clouds shield the earth's surface from sunlight and hinder cloud formation. What happens in the desert has far-reaching consequences: dust from the Sahara has reached as far away as Greenland. If you travel by dromedary instead, desert wildlife won't be scared off by the vibrations, and you're much more likely to spot small, sensitive and adorable, big-eared desert creatures like the fennec fox, jerboa and desert hedgehog.

Middle Atlas laden with gold proceeded warily through the Draa Valley from one well-fortified *ksar* to the next, finally unloading the camels and packing up mules at Skoura.

Some caravans passed through the ancient desert gates of Sijilmassa (now decidedly in ruins near Rissani), though there was no easy route: one approach was via the rose-gold dunes of Erg Chebbi at Merzouga, while the other led past formidable Jebel Saghro, inhabited by equally formidable seminomadic Aït Atta warriors. Today the mood in oases is considerably more relaxed, with a slow pace in the daytime heat and sociable evenings as visitors and locals gather around a warming fire.

You might occasionally see live hedgehogs for sale in Moroccan souqs. While they can be eaten for food, they're also used as remedies against witchcraft and the evil eye.

Wildlife

Even after millennia of being inhabited, farmed and grazed, Morocco still teems with wildlife – a testament to sustainable traditional practices and careful resource management handed down through generations. Today Morocco's 40 different ecosystems provide a habitat for many endemic species. Industrialisation has put considerable pressure on Morocco's delicately balanced natural environments, and while steps are being taken to create wildlife reserves for Morocco's endangered species, visitors can do their part to preserve natural habitats by staying on marked *pistes* (unsealed tracks) and taking rubbish away with them.

Coastal Species

Away from the urban sprawl of port cities and resort complexes are long stretches of rugged Moroccan coastline, where people are far outnumbered by abundant bird populations and marine mammals such as dolphins and porpoises. Along beaches, you'll spot white-eyed gulls, Moroccan cormorants and sandwich terns. Seabirds and freshwater birds thrive in preserves such as Souss-Massa National Park, where you might spy endangered Northern bald ibis along with the ducks and waders who migrate from Europe for the winter.

Sahara: A Natural History, by Marq de Villiers and Sheila Hirtle, is a highly readable account of the Sahara's wildlife, its people and geographical history.

Desert Habitats

The Sahara may seem like a harsh place, but it's home to numerous creatures, including several furry ones: several varieties of gerbils; long-eared, spindly-legged, cartoonish jerboas; and the desert hedgehog, the world's tiniest hedgehog, which weights between 300g and 500g. The delightful fennec fox has fur-soled feet and huge batlike ears to dissipate the desert heat; pups look like chihuahuas, only fuzzier. This desert fox is stealthy and nocturnal, but if you're travelling by dromedary and staying overnight in the desert, you might catch a brief glimpse or even spot an elusive sand cat, the only feline native to the deserts of Africa and Asia.

While the heat makes most humans sluggish, many desert creatures are elegant and swift. Dorcas gazelles are common, and you might also catch a glimpse of a rare, reddish Cuvier's gazelle. Lizards darting through the desert include skinks and spiny-tailed lizards, and you might catch sight of the devilish-looking (though not especially poisonous) horned

SOLAR SAHARA

One thing the desert has in copious amounts (apart from sand) is sunshine, and Noor Ouarzazate, covering an area of 3000 hectares, produces enough electricity to power a city twice the size of Marrakesh. The solar plant is helping Morocco meet its 2030 goal of being more than 50% powered by renewables, with 35% of the country's energy coming from renewables in 2019.

THE BARBARY MACAQUE: MYTHS & REALITIES

Legend has it that Azrou's Barbary macaques are descended from an impish family who disrespected their hosts. One day the family went walking in the cedar forests, got lost and ran out of food. A charitable family invited them in to share their meal and, it being the day of prayers (Friday), it was couscous on the table. When the family had gorged themselves, they started to play with their food by rolling the couscous into balls to throw at each other. God was not happy and punished them by turning them into monkeys to run wild in the forests forever.

The biggest concentration of Barbary macaques is in this region of the Middle Atlas, where food and water are abundant. There are dozens of monkey troops around, but there's virtually nothing in the way of organised tourism to observe the monkeys in a responsible manner. Most guides and drivers are not educated in how to view the monkeys in the wild in the most ethical way.

Most tourists head to two well-trodden spots just outside Azrou – **Moudmame** (parking Dh5, toilets Dh4) and **Cèdre de Gouraud** (8km east of Azrou; parking Dh5, toilets Dh4) – where monkey sightings can be guaranteed, and where peanuts are for sale. The two troops that hang out here do so because they have become habituated to being fed by visitors who claim not to know any better. Young monkeys are being taught to head to these areas rather than learning to fend for themselves.

Feeding the macaques causes health problems such as obesity, because the foods being offered are not suitable for their stomachs. Being around humans increases stress, and several are killed each year by cars due to begging on the road (though there are reduced speed limits in the park to prevent this from happening). Diseases such as hepatitis A, herpes B, monkey pox, tuberculosis and rabies can be transferred to humans – especially if people feed the monkeys straight from their hand or try to touch them. If you're bit by an agressive monkey, be sure to go straight to the hospital. Feeding also makes young monkeys more vulnerable to poaching.

The Barbary macaque is now close to extinction. There are only about 10,000 of these monkeys living in the wild in Morocco and Algeria. This represents a decline of more than 50% since 1977, largely a result of poaching (for pets) and habitat destruction. For more information on the macaques, visit the website www.ifaw.org.

viper. Golden jackals are the most common predator in the Sahara, though in the more remote parts of Western Sahara, a few desert-adapted cheetahs may yet survive.

> One less-than-charming fact about snake charming: to prevent them from biting handlers, snakes' mouths are sometimes stitched closed. This often causes fatal mouth infections and leaves snakes unable to feed. To discourage this practice, don't pose with or tip snake charmers handling snakes whose mouths are stitched shut.

Mountain Wildlife

Forested mountain slopes are Morocco's richest wildlife habitats, where it's easy to spot sociable Barbary macaques in the Rif and Middle Atlas, especially around Azrou. Less easy to track are mountain gazelles, lynx and the endangered mouflon (Barbary sheep). The mouflon are now protected in a High Atlas preserve near the Tizi n'Test, where its only predator is the critically endangered Barbary leopard – the last population of leopards in North Africa.

Golden eagles soar in Atlas Mountain updrafts, and High Atlas hikes might introduce you to red crossbills, horned larks, acrobatic booted eagles, Egyptian vultures, and both black and red kites. In springtime, butterflies abound in the mountains, including the scarlet cardinal and bright yellow Cleopatra.

National Parks

With cities encroaching on natural habitats, the Moroccan government is setting aside protected areas to prevent the further disappearance of rare plant and animal species. Toubkal National Park (p116) in the High Atlas Mountains was the first to be created, in 1942. After the vast Souss-Massa National Park (p395) was founded in 1991 outside Agadir,

THE BARBARY LION – BACK FROM THE DEAD?

When Morocco's national football team – the Atlas Lions – takes to the pitch, it's honouring one of the country's most iconic animals, albeit one that has long been on the extinct species list.

The Barbary lion was once North Africa's top predator. It was the largest and heaviest of all lion subspecies, and males were famed for their thick black manes. They were hunted by the Romans to provide sport for the gladiatorial combats of the Colosseum, while later Moroccan sultans gave them as diplomatic gifts. Slowly exterminated across the region through hunting and habitat loss, the lions persisted in heavily forested parts of Morocco's Atlas and Rif mountains well into the 20th century. The last wild lion is thought to have been shot in 1942, although recent research suggests that populations survived into the 1960s – no doubt aided by their naturally solitary behaviour, rather than living in prides as lions do in sub-Saharan Africa.

Remnant lion populations of mixed heritage survived in zoos across the world, including the personal zoo of the king of Morocco. In recent years a captive breeding programme, coupled with the latest genetic fingerprinting techniques, has been attempting to re-create a genetically pure and viable population of the big cats. The ultimate aim of the International Barbary Lion Project is to establish a protected reserve in the Atlas Mountains large enough to allow a limited reintroduction programme. While this is a long way off – and the willingness of locals to share land with a top predator remains unknown – perhaps the last roar of this magnificent animal is yet to be heard.

Morocco created four new national parks in 2004: Talassemtane (p290) in the Rif; Al Hoceima (p299) in the Mediterranean, with outstanding coastal and marine habitats along the Mediterranean that include one of the last outposts of osprey; Ifrane National Park (p373) in the Middle Atlas, with dense cedar forests and Barbary macaques; and the Eastern High Atlas National Park.

Morocco's 11 national parks and 35 nature reserves, forest sanctuaries and other protected areas overseen by Morocco's Direction des Eaux et Forêts are conserving species and advancing natural sciences. The park staff are tracking the region's biodiversity through botanical inventories, bird censuses, primate studies and sediment analyses. These studies are critical to understanding the broader causes of habitat loss in Morocco and beyond; the Spanish and US park services have studied Morocco's parklands to better understand biodiversity concerns.

The Sahara Conservation Fund (www.saharaconservation.org) is an international NGO dedicated to preserving the wild creatures of the Sahara that provides a preview of wildlife you might spot in this vibrant desert ecosystem.

Parks have proven a boon to local wildlife but a mixed blessing for human residents. While national parks protect local ecosystems and attract tourist revenue, access for local communities to water, grazing land and wild plants harvested for food and medicine has been limited or cut off entirely. But by conserving parkland, the Ministries of Tourism and Agriculture aim to help local ecosystems flourish, gradually restore arable land and ultimately benefit local communities with ecotourism that provides a profitable alternative to kif cultivation. In the near future, fees for park admission may be instituted to support the parks' conservation, scientific and community missions. Meanwhile, the best sights in Morocco are still free, and visitors can show their appreciation to local communities by supporting local NGOs along their route.

Creative Conservation

The only thing more natural than the wonders of Morocco is the impulse to preserve them. Morocco is in a fortunate position: to envision a more sustainable future, it can look to its recent past. Ancient *khettara* (underground irrigation systems), still in use, transport water from natural springs to fields and gardens in underground channels, without losing precious water to evaporation. Although certification is still a novel concept, most small-scale Moroccan farming practices are organic by default, since chemical fertilisers are costly and donkey dung pretty much comes with the territory.

Community hammams use power and water for steamy saunas more efficiently than individual showers or baths. Locally made, detergent-free *savon noir* ('black soap' made from natural palm and olive oils) is gentle enough for a shave and effective as laundry soap, without polluting runoff – and leftover 'grey water' can be used for gardens and courtyard fountains. With Morocco's traditional mud-brick architecture, metre-thick walls provide natural insulation against heat in summer and chill in winter, eliminating most street noise and the need for air-con and central heating.

Morocco is also thinking fast on its feet, becoming an early adopter of resource-saving new technologies. The pioneering nation already has one of Africa's biggest wind farms at Tarfaya, while Ouarzazate is home to the world's largest concentrated solar power plant, and the aim is that by 2030, more than half of Morocco's energy will be provided by renewables.

To tackle challenges still ahead, Morocco will need all the resourcefulness it can muster. Because of the demands of city dwellers and tourist complexes, many villages around Marrakesh now lack a reliable source of potable water. Damming to create reservoirs frequently strips downstream water of valuable silt needed to sustain farms and coastal wetlands. Forests are also under threat, with an average of 8 sq km lost

NOTABLE NATIONAL PARKS

NATIONAL PARK	LOCATION	FEATURES	ACTIVITIES	BEST TIME TO VISIT
Al Hoceima National Park	Al Hoceima	thuja forest, limestone escarpments, fish eagles	hiking, birdwatching	May-Oct
Ifrane National Park	Middle Atlas	Amazigh (Berber) villages, cedar forests and monkeys	hiking, culture, wildlife-watching	May-Sep
Iriqui National Park	near Foum Zguid	arid savanna and ephemeral wetlands, sand dunes, acacia and tamarisk trees, migratory birds including flamingo	birdwatching, wildlife-watching	Oct-Apr
Merja Zerga National Park	Moulay Bousselham	lagoon habitats; 190 species of waterfowl including African marsh owl, Andouin's gull, flamingo and crested coot	wildlife-watching	Dec-Jan
Souss-Massa National Park	south of Agadir	coastal estuaries and forests, 275 species of birds including endangered bald ibis as well as mammals and endangered species	hiking, wildlife-watching, birdwatching	Mar-Oct
Talassemtane National Park	Chefchaouen	cedar and fir forests; Barbary macaque, fox, jackal and bats	wildlife-watching, hiking	May-Sep
Tazekka National Park	near Taza	oak forests and waterfalls	hiking	Jun-Sep
Toubkal National Park	near Marrakesh	highest peak in North Africa	hiking, climbing	May-Jun

each year, including Moroccan pine, thuja and Atlas cedar. Pollution is a weighty concern, literally: Morocco generates more than 5 million tonnes of solid waste each year.

Mosques in Morocco are being converted into showcases for green living, with LED lighting, solar thermal water heaters and photovoltaic electrical systems. The aim is to cover around 15,000 state-funded mosques around the country to inform people of the benefits of going green.

Everywhere you travel in the country, you'll notice minor modifications that collectively make major savings in scarce resources. Plastic bags were banned in 2016, and a law passed in 2019 prohibits the manufacture, import, export and marketing of plastic bags. Solar water heaters provide instant hot water for showers in the afternoon and evening, so taking showers at those times saves water that might otherwise be wasted by running the tap while gas heaters warm up. Reforestation programmes are helping prevent erosion, and you can help by staying on marked mountain paths and supporting local NGO reforestation initiatives. Organic gardens provide fresh ingredients for meals, reducing the dependence on food transported over long distances – and ordering local, seasonal specialities provides positive reinforcement for local food sourcing. The Clef Verte (Green Key) programme also certifies hotels and guesthouses that institute a range of resource-conserving measures, from low-flow toilets to environmentally friendly cleaning products, although it has received criticism from some for granting certificates to hotels with distinctly high-impact facilities such as swimming pools.

Add these traditional, national and local resource-saving practices together, and Morocco is poised not only to make the switch to sustainable tourism, but to show Europe how it's done.

Survival Guide

Safe Travel

DANGERS & ANNOYANCES

Morocco is a pretty safe country that can be navigated with a bit of common sense, but there are a few things to be aware of.

Getting Lost

For years, there's been a slow process of replacing old French, Spanish and Amazigh (Berber) names with Arabic ones. The result so far is that, depending on whom you talk to, what map you use or which part of the street you are on, you're likely to see up to three different names.

The general Arabic word for street is *sharia* or *derb* in medinas (*zankat* for smaller ones). The French avenue, boulevard and *rue* are still common. In the north and far south you'll still find the Spanish *calle* and *avenida*.

Street names won't help much in the labyrinthine medinas. If you feel you're getting lost, stick to the main paths (which generally have a fair flow of people going either way), and you'll soon reach a landmark or exit. Ask a shopkeeper for directions if you're completely lost and carry your accommodation's business card or address with you.

Theft

On the whole, theft is not a huge problem in Morocco. Travellers can minimise risk by being careful in major cities and taking some basic precautions. When wandering the streets, keep valuables you carry to a minimum and keep what you must carry well hidden.

Be vigilant when withdrawing money from ATMs. External money pouches attract attention, so opt for pouches or money belts worn under your clothes. They are better places to keep your money, passport and other important documents, but keep a small amount of everyday cash easily accessible to avoid having to flash your stash.

If you prefer to keep things in your room (preferably locked inside your suitcase), nine times out of 10 you'll have no trouble. Rooms in top-end hotels often have safes. Other hotels sometimes have a safe at reception, where you could stow valuables.

Leaving anything in a car, even out of sight, is asking for trouble.

Treat the medinas with particular caution at night. The medinas in Marrakesh, Casablanca and Tangier have a reputation for petty theft. A common tactic is for one person to distract you while another cleans out your pockets. Late-night knife crime occasionally occurs.

Guides & Faux Guides

Morocco's notorious hustlers and *faux guides* (unofficial guides) remain an unavoidable part of the Moroccan experience. *Brigades touristiques* (tourist police) have been set up in the principal tourist centres, and anyone suspected of trying to operate as an unofficial guide could face jail and/or a huge fine. This has greatly reduced, if not eliminated, the problem.

You'll generally find *faux guides* hanging around the entrances to the big cities' medinas and outside bus, train and ferry stations. Although high unemployment rates drive their numbers, not all are complete imposters; some are very experienced and speak several languages. Often their main interest is the commission gained from your souq shopping. Brush them off with a firm '*la shukran*' (no thanks).

To dig deeper in to your destination, most hotels and guesthouses can arrange licensed guides.

Dealing with Guides

Agree on a price before setting off on a tour. Set some parameters on what you expect to see and the number of shops you're taken to. If you don't want a shopping expedition included in your tour, make this clear beforehand.

Unofficial guides charge around Dh50 to Dh100 per day. Rates should always be per guide, not per person.

A few dirham will suffice if you want to be guided to a specific location, such as a medina exit.

Whatever you give, you'll often get the 'you can't possibly be serious' look. The best reply is the 'I've just paid you well over the odds' look.

Maintain your good humour and, after a couple of days in a place, the hassle tends to lessen considerably.

Official guides can be engaged through tourist offices and some hotels at the fixed price of around Dh250/300 per day (plus tip) for a local/national guide.

It's well worth taking a guide when exploring Fez and Marrakesh medinas. The guide can help you find interesting sights and shops in the melee, stop you from getting lost and save you from being hassled by other would-be guides.

Driving & Transport

Drivers should note that motorised hustlers operate on the approach roads to Fez and Marrakesh. These motorcycle nuisances are keen to find you accommodation and so on, and can be just as persistent as their counterparts on foot.

Travellers disembarking from (and embarking on) the ferry in Tangier may receive some hassle from touts and hustlers.

Arriving by train in cities like Fez and Marrakesh, you may run into 'students' or similar, with the uncanny knowledge that your preferred hotel is closed or full, but they just happen to know this great little place run by their cousin.

Thanks But No Thanks

Faux guides abound in tourist hot-spots, hustling to 'help' you and earn some commission from souvenir shops. The following are useful tactics for dealing with unwanted attention:

- Politely decline all offers of help you don't want, with '*la shukran*' (no thanks), but don't shake hands or get involved in any lengthy conversation.
- Give the impression that you know exactly where you're going, or explain that you employed a guide on your first day and now you'd like to explore on your own.
- Wear dark sunglasses and retreat to a cafe, restaurant or taxi if you're beginning to lose your cool.
- In extreme situations, use the word 'police' (*shurta* or *ibulees*) and look like you mean it.

GOVERNMENT TRAVEL ADVICE

For the latest travel advice refer to the following websites:

Australian Department of Foreign Affairs (www.smartraveller.gov.au)

Canadian Consular Services Bureau (www.voyage.gc.ca)

Dutch Ministry of Foreign Affairs (www.nederlandwereldwijd.nl)

German Ministry of Foreign Affairs (www.auswaertiges-amt.de)

Japanese Ministry of Foreign Affairs (www.mofa.go.jp)

New Zealand Ministry of Foreign Affairs and Trade (www.safetravel.govt.nz)

UK Foreign & Commonwealth Office (www.gov.uk/foreign-travel-advice)

US State Department (www.travel.state.gov)

Drugs

Morocco's era as a hippie paradise, riding the Marrakesh Express and all that, has been consigned to history. Hashish (known as kif) is widely grown in the Rif Mountains. It's illegal to buy, sell or consume hashish in Morocco. If you're going to smoke kif, don't do it in public and be extremely circumspect about who you buy it from.

If caught with hashish, you may be looking at a fine and, in the worst case, a prison sentence. Although some locals smoke as a recreational pastime, as a tourist you're more vulnerable.

Scams & Hassle

Many stories of extortion and ripoffs in Morocco are drug-related. Recent legislation and a hard government line may have forced dealers to give up their more aggressive tactics, but the hassle has not disappeared.

A traditional ploy is to get you stoned, force you to buy a piece of hash the size of a brick and then turn you over to the police (or at least threaten to). Once you've purchased hash, or even just smoked some, you're unlikely to call the cops, and the hustlers know it.

Hot Spots

New arrivals should ignore late-night offers of hashish. These dealers have a sixth sense for greenness and won't miss an opportunity to squeeze large amounts of money out of the uninitiated.

The town of Issaguen (also known as Ketama) and the Rif Mountains are Morocco's kif-growing heartland. Issaguen in particular can be a bag-load of trouble, and is best avoided unless you're accompanied by a reliable guide.

Majoun

You may occasionally be offered *majoun*, a traditional sticky fudge made of butter, dried fruits, seeds, spices and cannabis resin. A small ball of *majoun* can send you reeling.

Anyone with a slight tendency to paranoia when smoking weed should be aware that this is a common reaction among first-time *majoun* munchers.

Spanish Customs

Although the Spanish police have a relaxed attitude towards small amounts of hash for private use, Spanish customs will come down hard on people entering the country from Morocco in possession of the drug, and you could be done for trafficking. If you're taking a car across, the chances that it will be searched are high. Never carry parcels or drive vehicles across borders for other people.

SOLO TRAVELLERS

Morocco has a well-established tourist trail, and solo travel here is safe and relatively easy, though it's not as common as in some other parts of the world. Solo travellers will often find themselves befriended by locals, and you will usually receive less hassle than groups.

Food portions in tourist restaurants are large, with meals designed to share; eating at cheap local grill stands can be a better option for solo travellers with small appetites.

Accommodation options can be a hindrance, as not many riads offer single rooms or discounts for solo travellers. The country's main tourist hotspots – Marrakesh, Fez, Essaouira, Tangier and Chefchaouen – all have decent hostel options, but elsewhere quality is poor, and choice is limited.

Similarly, transport is a cinch if you stick to the well-trodden tourist path as bus departures are plentiful, but it can be extremely expensive for solo travellers to access less touristed attractions and destinations – often the only option is to hire a grand taxi for a private trip for a grand old sum. Always ask if there is a local *collective* (shared) grand taxi departure to your destination before hiring one privately.

Morocco's northern Atlantic coast is recommended for solo travellers because of its relaxed atmosphere, good bus network, range of tours and activities, and good-value accommodation.

Marrakesh is perennially popular because it has the country's best hostels, and it's easy to latch onto group tour departures to other areas of the country, such as High Atlas trekking days, cycling tours, Essaouira jaunts and multiday Sahara desert trips.

Destinations that are known for one particular activity, such as Zaouiat Ahansal for rock climbing, Taghazout for surfing, also usually have a welcoming community vibe.

One downside of travelling alone is that several of Morocco's best speciality city tours are only offered as private tours, which become cheaper the bigger your group is. Expect hefty single supplements if you want to do anything out of the ordinary.

WOMEN TRAVELLERS

One of the big benefits of travelling in Morocco as a woman is that you will have the opportunity to interact with local women (which male travellers won't). The country has an unfortunate reputation for hassle among foreign women, and although Moroccan men in popular tourist towns are now used to seeing female tourists, it's still a fact of travel in Morocco that women are likely to receive some unwanted attention.

Know, though, that the problem is not isolated to foreigners – local women get hassled too. Before marriage, many Moroccan men have little opportunity to meet and get to know women outside their family – a major reason why Western women receive so much attention. This can come as something of a shock to first-time visitors, and some travellers find the constant attention extremely wearing.

In September 2018, the Hakkaoui law was passed in Morocco, promising tougher penalties for sexual harassment, including unsolicited acts and signals in public, and violence against women. However, it's worth noting that unwanted attention towards foreign women rarely escalates beyond unprompted conversation and catcalling. Teenage boys are the worst offenders for unwanted physical contact, which in itself is also rare.

Two Scandinavian women were murdered in December 2018 while hiking unescorted in a remote area of the High Atlas Mountains, after being warned by local guides not to camp alone. It was an unprecedented act committed by extremists linked to the Islamic State, which sent shockwaves through the tourism industry. Morocco is a safe country for female travellers, but always heed local advice.

Dress

Clothes that cover your shoulders and knees are culturally appropriate for Morocco. Dress equally modestly and you're more likely to be treated with respect by the locals.

Women who look physically different to the Moroccan norm – for example, if you have tattoos, multiple piercings or dreadlocks – are likely to experience a much greater level of harassment and possibly be offered sex or drugs.

Bikinis are acceptable on private beaches, but play things by ear in hotel pools: some are fine; at others, it will attract unwanted attention.

Sunbathing topless on the beach is never appropriate in Morocco.

Tips & Advice

- As a general rule, Moroccan life is more traditional in the city medinas, and attitudes towards women are more progressive in the *villes nouvelles* (new towns), so foreign women receive less unwanted attention in the latter.
- Hammams are wonderful female-only environments where women travellers can interact with local women.
- Late afternoon and early evening are the times when many local women come out to shop and catch up with friends on the streets, which can make it a great time to wander in the company of other women. This is also a good time for travelling mothers to meet Moroccan mums and their kids.
- Hotel and public swimming pools usually attract groups of men, whether they be swimming or drinking at a poolside bar.
- Be aware that some budget hotels double as brothels; any cheap hotel above a popular locals' bar is a likely contender.
- If you want an alcoholic drink, head to a large hotel or restaurant serving alcohol rather than braving a bar, as these are generally male-dominated establishments. Local women who frequent watering holes (even the posher ones) are generally prostitutes.

Male Travelling Companions

Women travelling with male companions are less likely to experience much of the hassle that solo women might encounter. Note that the concept of male/female friends travelling together is not one that Moroccans are likely to understand.

There is no issue for unmarried foreign couples to book double rooms in Moroccan hotels. However, if your partner is thought to be Muslim and you're not married, you may meet with some uncomfortable situations at hotel reception desks. Many hotels will refuse to accommodate you because premarital sex for Muslims is forbidden, and Morocco has a stern attitude to sex work.

If you are a Moroccan woman (or Moroccan in appearance), travelling with your non-Moroccan spouse, it is advisable to carry a copy of your marriage certificate.

Transport

It is perfectly safe for women to take public transport, and there are just as many local women as men on buses and in *grands taxis*. Try to sit next to other women, especially in *grands taxis* where you're squeezed in closely, and on trains, where you could potentially be trapped inside a compartment.

Most women travel in *grands taxis* without problems, regardless of where they sit, but you could pay for two seats to get a ride by yourself in the front. Riders are often piled into the back with little regard to personal space.

Hitchhiking isn't recommended.

Safety Precautions

Women are less visible on the streets of Morocco after dark. In some neighbourhoods and towns, it may not be considered safe to wander around alone at night, but it's also perfectly fine in many places – ask locals for their advice. In big cities such as Marrakesh and Fez, some medina restaurants will offer to walk women back to their hotel; ask when booking. Avoid walking alone in remote areas such as isolated beaches, mountains, forests and sand dunes.

A simple, repeated *non merci* or *la shukran* (no thank you) is much more effective than reacting with aggression if you're subject to persistent attention.

The key concept is 'respect', something that most Moroccans hold dear. *Hashouma!* (shame!) can also be used to embarrass would-be harassers.

Wearing a wedding ring may help you avoid unwanted attention, but it's debatable whether it really makes much of a difference.

Take extra care at music festivals (and other large gatherings) as complaints have been made of physical harassment.

Directory A–Z

Accessible Travel

Morocco has few accessible facilities, but the country is not necessarily out of bounds for travellers with a physical disability and a sense of adventure. Some factors to be aware of:

- Narrow medina streets and rutted pavements can make mobility challenging.
- Not all hotels (almost none of the cheaper ones) have lifts, so booking ground-floor hotel rooms ahead of time is essential. Riads invariably have steep, narrow and twisting stairs.
- Only a handful of the very top-end hotels have accessible rooms.
- Travelling by car is probably the best option, though you'll be able to get assistance in bus and train stations (a tip will be required).
- Many tour operators can tailor trips to suit your requirements.
- Vision- or hearing-impaired travellers are poorly catered for. Hearing loops, Braille signs and talking pedestrian crossings are nonexistent.

Organisations with information, advice and assistance on world travel for the mobility impaired include the following:

Morocco Accessible Travel (http://moroccoaccessibletravel.com) This outfit organises tours around Morocco, including the first-ever accessible camel saddle.

Disabled Travelers Guide (www.disabledtravelersguide.com) A general guide for travellers with disabilities.

Mobility International USA (www.miusa.org) Promoting the inclusion of people with disabilities in international programmes, with a page of air-travel tips.

Society for Accessible Travel & Hospitality (www.sath.org) Has news, tips and members' articles and blogs.

Download Lonely Planet's free *Accessible Travel* guide from https://shop.lonelyplanet.com/categories/accessible-travel.com.

PRACTICALITIES

Internet Access Many cafes and restaurants and most hotels and riads offer free wi-fi although speeds can vary. In cheaper accommodation, it might only be available in public areas.

Smoking A national pastime in Morocco. Nonsmoking restaurants and hotels are rare, but most popular eateries and cafes have outdoor seating. Most riads and midrange hotels and higher allow smoking only in open areas.

Tourist Information Some cities and larger towns have tourist offices run by the Moroccan National Tourist Office (www.visitmorocco.com) but are often just brochure depositories. Hotel staff are usually more helpful.

Weights & Measures Morocco uses the metric system.

Customs Regulations

Importing or exporting dirhams is forbidden although checks are rare, so don't worry about any loose change. Forbidden items include arms, controlled drugs, and printed, audio or video media containing material that's 'immoral, sexual or offensive'.

Duty-free allowances:

- up to 200 cigarettes, 50 cigars or 400g of tobacco
- 1L of spirits and 1L of wine
- 150ml of perfume and 250ml of eau de toilette

Electricity

Electricity is reliable, but bring a torch for off-the-beaten-track destinations in the mountains and desert.

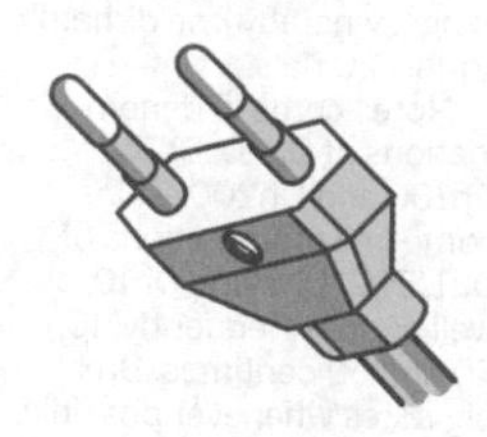

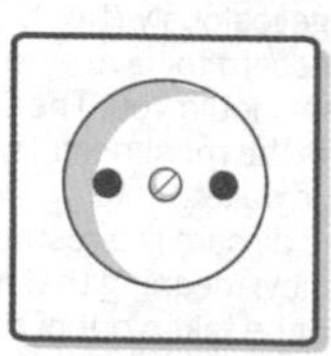

Type C
220V/50Hz

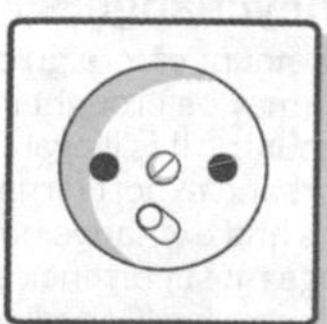

Type E
220V/50Hz

EMERGENCY & IMPORTANT NUMBERS

Always dial the local four-digit area code even if you are dialling from the same town or code area.

Ambulance	☎15
Fire	☎15
Police (city)	☎19
Gendarmerie (police outside cities)	☎177

Legal Matters

Moroccan law prohibits the possession, offer, sale, purchase, distribution and transportation of hashish (known locally as kif). The penalties for possessing even small amounts of drugs are severe and include up to 10 years' imprisonment, heavy fines and confiscation of your vehicle or vessel. Acquittals in drugs cases are rare.

If you get into trouble, your first call should be to your embassy or consulate; it's not unknown for local police to be in on scams. The **London-based Fair Trials International** (www.fairtrials.net) provides legal assistance and advocacy to individuals facing criminal charges in a foreign country.

If you get arrested by the Moroccan police, you won't have much of a legal leg to stand on. It's unlikely that any interpreter on hand will be of sufficient standard to translate an accurate statement that will, nonetheless, play a vital part in subsequent judicial proceedings. According to some human rights groups, physical abuse while in custody is not unknown.

LGBTIQ+ Travellers

Male-male sexual behaviour (including kissing) are illegal in Morocco and carry a potential jail term of up to three years and/or a fine. The authorities have recently shown an increased tendency to prosecute locals, and within Moroccan society, homophobia is still prevalent.

For travellers, some cities are more gay-friendly than others, with Marrakesh taking the top spot, followed by Tangier. However, there are no dedicated gay destinations, and nightlife has become increasingly low-key in recent years.

Same-sex couples usually have no problem when requesting a double bed in midrange and luxury accommodation in Marrakesh, but discretion is recommended. Hotels are required by law to provide two single beds for men sleeping in the same room who aren't related.

Solo gay travellers should be aware that because of poverty, a distinctly unpleasant but very real element of the gay scene is the number of young male prostitutes. This has led authorities to crack down on mixed foreigner-Moroccan gay couples in recent years. Solo gay travellers should also be wary of using social media apps to attempt to access the local scene. There have been several cases of foreigners being robbed and physically assaulted after having used the apps to meet up. It's best to only meet contacts in a public place, and inform others where you are going and who you are meeting.

Lesbian travellers are far less likely to encounter any problems. Transgender travellers, on the other hand, may be subject to abusive behaviour, particularly transgender women. The transgender community does not have a high profile, and sex reassignment surgery is not available in Morocco, so education is lacking.

USEFUL NUMBERS

Morocco country code	212
International access code from Morocco	00
Directory enquiries	160
Spain country code (including Melilla and Ceuta)	34

Maps

Few decent maps of Morocco are available in the country itself, so if you're going off-the-grid, get one before leaving home. Michelin's No 742 countrywide map is arguably the best.

Google Maps has good coverage but struggles with the tangle of medina alleyways; Maps.me fares better. Download maps offline so you have them when roaming isn't available.

Money

ATMs

Guichets automatiques (ATMs) are the easiest way to access your money in Morocco. A common sight even in the smallest towns, virtually all ATMs accept Visa, MasterCard, Electron, Cirrus, Maestro and InterBank cards. Most banks charge you for withdrawing money from foreign cash machines (check before travelling), and some ATMs issue a charge on top of this.

BMCE (Banque marocaine du commerce extérieur), Banque Populaire, BMCI (Banque marocaine pour le commerce et l'industrie), Société Générale and Attijariwafa Bank offer reliable service.

The amount of money you can withdraw from an ATM generally depends on the conditions attached to your card; machines will dispense no more than Dh2000 at a time.

Black Market

The easy convertibility of the dirham leaves little room for a black market, but you'll find people in the streets asking if you want to exchange money, especially in Tangier, Casablanca and on the borders of (and just inside) the enclaves of Ceuta and Melilla. Avoid these characters; there's no monetary benefit to be had from such transactions, and scams are common.

Cash

You'll need to carry some cash with you. Many riads will also accept payment in euros but often at less preferential rates than you can get at the bank.

Keep a handful of small denomination notes in your wallet for day-to-day transactions. Put the rest in a money belt or another safe place.

If you're travelling to out-of-the-way places, make sure you have enough cash to last until you get to a decent-sized town. Keep a small stash of euros in case of emergency.

The endless supply of small coins may be annoying, but they're handy for taxis, tips and guides.

Credit Cards

Major credit cards are widely accepted in the main tourist centres. They often attract a surcharge of up to 5%.

The main credit cards are MasterCard and Visa; if you plan to rely on plastic, the best bet is to take one of each. Many large bank branches will give you cash advances on Visa and MasterCard. Take your passport with you.

Currency

The Moroccan currency is the dirham (Dh), which is divided into 100 centimes. You might also occasionally hear older people give prices in rials – an old unofficial usage, whereby one dirham equals 20 rials.

Notes come in denominations of Dh20, Dh50, Dh100 and Dh200. Coins come in denominations of Dh1, Dh2, Dh5 and Dh10, as well as, less frequently, 10, 20 and 50 centimes. Break big notes whenever possible. Moroccans guard their small change jealously (taxi drivers never seem to have any), and so should you. The Dh20 note is the most useful note in your wallet.

The dirham is a restricted currency, meaning that it cannot be taken out of the country and is not available abroad. The dirham is fairly stable, with no major fluctuations in exchange rates. Euros, US dollars and British pounds are the most easily exchanged currencies.

In the Spanish enclaves of Ceuta and Melilla, the currency is the euro. The Moroccan banks on the enclaves' borders exchange cash only. Banks in Ceuta and Melilla deal in dirham but at rates inferior to those in Morocco.

Moneychangers

Any amount of foreign currency may be brought into the country. It is illegal to import and export dirham. Banks and exchange bureaus change most currencies, but Australian, Canadian and New Zealand dollars are often not accepted. You'll occasionally be asked for ID when changing money.

Moroccan banking services are reasonably quick and efficient. Rates vary little from bank to bank, but it doesn't hurt to look around.

Hang on to all exchange receipts. They show you changed money legally, and you'll need them to convert leftover dirham at most Moroccan banks and bureaux de change.

Taxes & Refunds

A city tax on accommodation is levied in some places, including Marrakesh. Many accommodations include this in their quoted rates, but ask guests to pay it separately in local currency upon arrival.

It is possible for visitors to claim a 20% VAT refund on some purchased goods (minimum spend of Dh2000) on departure from Marrakesh or Casablanca.

Opening Hours

Although it's a Muslim country, Morocco follows the Monday to Friday working week for business purposes. Friday is the main prayer day, so many businesses take an extended lunch break on Friday afternoon or don't open at all. During Ramadan the rhythm of the country changes, and office hours shift to around 10am to 3pm or 4pm.

Banks 8.30am–6.30pm Monday to Friday

Post offices 8.30am–4.30pm Monday to Friday

Government offices 8.30am–6.30pm Monday to Friday

Restaurants noon–3pm and 7pm–10pm (cafes generally open earlier and close later)

Bars 6pm until late

Shops 10am–7pm Monday to Saturday

Post

Offices of Poste Maroc (www.poste.ma) are distinguished by a yellow 'PTT' sign or the 'La Poste' logo. *Tabacs*, the small tobacco and newspaper kiosks scattered about city centres, often sell stamps and have shorter queues. The postal system is reasonably reliable, if not terribly fast.

It takes at least a week for letters to reach European destinations and two weeks to get to Australia and North America. Sending post from a city normally gives it a head start. Worldwide postcards cost around Dh25 to send.

Public Holidays

Banks, post offices and most shops close on the main public holidays, but transport still runs.

New Year's Day (1 January)

Independence Manifesto (11 January) Commemorates the publication in Fez of the Moroccan nationalist manifesto for independence.

Labour Day (1 May)

Feast of the Throne (30 July) Commemorates King Mohammed VI's accession to the throne.

Allegiance of Oued Eddahab (14 August) Celebrates the 'return to the fatherland' of the Oued Eddahab region in the far south.

MAJOR ISLAMIC HOLIDAYS

The rhythms of Islamic practice are tied to the lunar calendar; each year the Islamic calendar begins about 11 days earlier than the previous year. Dates are approximate as they rely on the sighting of the new moon.

The following principal religious holidays are celebrated countrywide, with interruptions and time changes to many local bus services and increased pressure on transport in general. Apart from on the first day of Ramadan, offices and businesses close.

Moulid An Nabi celebrates the birth of the Prophet Muhammad. Children are often given presents.

Eid Al Fitr (Feast of the Breaking of the Fast), also known as Eid As Sagheer (the Small Feast), is the end of Ramadan. The four-day celebration begins with a meal of *harira* (lentil soup), dates and honey cakes, and the country grinds to a halt during this family-focused period.

Eid Al Adha (Feast of the Sacrifice) sees sheep traded for the ritual sacrifices that take place throughout the Muslim world during this three-day celebration. Also known as the Eid Al Kabeer (Grand Feast), it commemorates Ibrahim's sacrifice. The sheep sacrifice is often a very public event – be prepared for the possibility of seeing blood running in the gutters, and sheep heads being flamed over fires in the street.

HOLIDAY	2021	2022	2023	2024
Ramadan begins	13 Apr	3 Apr	22 Mar	10 Mar
Eid Al Fitr	13 May	3 May	21 Apr	9 Apr
Eid Al Adha	20 Jul	10 Jul	28 Jun	16 Jun
Islamic New Year	8 Aug	28 Jul	18 Jul	7 Jul
Moulid An Nabi	18 Oct	8 Oct	26 Sep	15 Sep

TRAVELLING DURING RAMADAN

Ramadan Mubarak! (Happy Ramadan!) Ramadan is a lunar month dedicated to *sawm* (fasting) – from sun-up to sundown, the faithful abstain from food, drink, tobacco and sex to concentrate on spiritual renewal – and *zakat* (charity).

Many businesses operate with limited hours and staff, so try to book accommodation, transport and tours in advance. Call offices to ensure someone will be there. Most restaurants are closed during the day, so pack lunches or reserve at tourist restaurants. Shops often close in the afternoon, and bargaining is better before thirst is felt in the midday heat. When Ramadan falls in the summer, be prepared for long, hot days.

At sunset, streets fill with Ramadan light displays, music, tantalising aromas and offers of sweets. After an *iftar* (meal that breaks the fast) of dates, soup or savoury snacks, people gobble sweets until the late-night feast. More visits and sweets follow and then sleep before an early rise for the *suhoor* (meal before sunrise).

Tourists are exempt from fasting, but you should avoid eating, drinking or smoking in public.

When a new friend offers you sweets or invites you to a feast, you honour by accepting. You're not obliged to return the favour or eat the sweets; consider reciprocating the *zakat* by giving to a local charity.

Anniversary of the King's and People's Revolution (20 August) Commemorates the exile of Mohammed V by the French in 1953.

Young People's Day (21 August) Celebrates the king's birthday.

Anniversary of the Green March (6 November) Commemorates the Green March 'reclaiming' the Western Sahara in 1975.

Independence Day (18 November) Commemorates independence from France.

Telephone

Within Morocco, always dial the local four-digit area code even if you are calling from the same town or code area. Moroccan landline numbers start with 05, and mobile numbers begin with 06.

Mobile Phones

If you have an unlocked mobile phone, you can buy a prepaid Moroccan mobile SIM card. Morocco's GSM mobile phone networks include Maroc Telecom (www.iam.ma), Orange (www.orange.ma) and Inwi (www.inwi.ma). Coverage is generally good, apart from thick-walled kasbah hotels, in the mountains and deserts. Travellers will be able to access 4G in most cities and many towns.

SIM cards are available at many airports on arrival, at any of the mobile network provider stores and also from roving vendors wearing the branded clothing of the mobile network who hang out near the network stores in larger cities. Phone company representatives at the airports often offer basic SIMs for free to arriving tourists. You'll usually need your passport, either to buy the SIM or to activate it.

Prepaid packages vary; for Dh100, you can get 200 call minutes plus 10GB data. Many packages do not offer international SMS.

Scratch cards to top up your credit can be bought at *téléboutiques* (private phone offices) and newsstands.

Time

Morocco is on Western European Time (GMT/UTC plus one hour). Morocco does not observe daylight saving time. If you're travelling to/from Spain (including Ceuta and Melilla), note that Spanish clocks run on GMT+2 in summer, so double-check your times if catching a ferry.

When it's noon in Morocco, the time elsewhere is as follows:

CITY	TIME
Auckland	midnight
London	noon
Los Angeles	3am
New York	6am
Paris & Rome	1pm
Perth & Hong Kong	7pm
Sydney	10pm

Toilets

Flush toilets can be a luxury in a country struggling with water shortages. Outside midrange and top-end hotels and restaurants, toilets are mostly of the squat variety. Squat toilets feature a tap, hose or container of water for sluicing – the idea being to wash yourself (with your left hand) after performing.

There's often no *papier hygiénique* (toilet paper), so keep a supply with you. Don't throw the paper into the toilet as the plumbing is often dodgy; discard it in the bin provided.

Public toilets are rare outside the major cities. If you find a public toilet, you'll need to bring a tip for the attendant, stout-soled shoes and very often a nose clip.

Travel Insurance

A travel-insurance policy to cover theft, loss and, in particular, medical problems is strongly recommended for all visitors to Morocco. Some policies specifically exclude 'dangerous activities', which can include scuba diving, motorcycling, skiing and even trekking, so ensure your policy covers these if needed. Make sure you have adequate travel medical insurance and any relevant car insurance if you're driving.

Worldwide travel insurance is available at www.lonelyplanet.com/insurance. You can buy, extend and claim online any time – even if you're already on the road.

Visas

Nationals of 68 countries can enter Morocco visa-free for up to 90 days. Passport holders from other countries must apply in advance for a three-month visa (single/double entry about US$25/35). Applications can take up to two weeks, and you need three passport photos.

Visa Extensions

Travellers requiring a visa extension find it easiest to head to mainland Spain or one of the Spanish enclaves in Morocco, and re-enter after a few days.

Although doing a visa run generally presents few problems other than travel costs, it leaves you at the mercy of individual immigration officers on re-entry. Travellers have occasionally come unstuck this way.

An alternative is to apply for a visa extension, issued by the Directorate General of National Security. In practice, these are unobtainable.

Residence (*carte de sejour*) is also available, but it is difficult to get and requires proof of employment.

Go to the nearest police headquarters (*préfecture de police*) to check what documents they require. If possible, take a Moroccan friend to help you deal with the bureaucracy.

Volunteering

There are many international and local organisations that arrange voluntary work on regional development projects in Morocco. They generally pay nothing, sometimes not even providing lodging, and are aimed at young people looking for something different to do for a few weeks over the summer.

Some of these organisations are really just summer camps and international exchange programmes. Always ask of the organisation 'who benefits?' Good volunteering projects should be aimed at providing outcomes for beneficiaries, not the volunteer.

A good starting point is Lonely Planet's *The Big Trip*, a guide to gap years and overseas adventures that includes a chapter on volunteering and working overseas, as well as a directory of resources.

Women Travellers

See the Safe Travel (p488) and Health (p507) chapters for information.

Work

With more than 20% youth unemployment, Morocco isn't fertile ground for job opportunities. A good command of French is a prerequisite, and some Arabic would help. There are more volunteering opportunities.

If you secure a position, your employer will have to help you get a work permit and arrange residency, which can be a long process.

There are a few possibilities for teaching English as a foreign language although they are not terribly well paid. Rabat is one of the best places to start looking.

The best times to try are around September and October (the beginning of the academic year) and, to a lesser extent, early January. Having a TEFL (Teaching English as a Foreign Language) qualification will be useful.

Transport

GETTING THERE & AWAY

Transport reform has encouraged an explosion of visitor numbers to Morocco. The government's 'open skies' policy means an ever-increasing number of European budget airlines fly to the country.

Ferry services from Europe provide a more-romantic and lower-carbon option than flying.

Flights, cars and tours can be booked online at www.lonelyplanet.com/bookings.

Entering Morocco

Border formalities are fairly quick and straightforward. Regardless of where you enter, your passport must be valid for at least six months from your date of entry.

International Health Certificate

An international certificate of vaccination (or yellow fever certificate) is no longer required for entry into Morocco, even if coming from a country where yellow fever is endemic.

We recommend, however, that travellers carry a certificate if they have been in an infected country during the previous month to avoid any possible difficulties with immigration.

There is always the possibility that a traveller without an up-to-date certificate will be vaccinated and detained in isolation at the port of arrival for up to 10 days, or possibly repatriated.

Air

Direct flights are available from cities across Europe, the Middle East, West Africa and North America.

Airports & Airlines

Royal Air Maroc (www.royalairmaroc.com) is Morocco's national carrier. Casablanca's **Mohammed V International Airport** (0522435858; www.casablanca-airport.com) is the country's main gateway, followed by **Marrakech Menara Airport** (0524447910; www.marrakesh-airport.com;). Other important airports include **Fes-Saïss** (0535674712) (Fez) and **Ibn Batouta International** (0539393720) in Tangier. Smaller airports are dotted across the country.

Air Arabia (www.airarabia.com) is a budget-friendly airline with international and domestic flights. For information about Moroccan airports, visit the website of Office National des Aéroports (www.onda.ma).

Land

You can cross to mainland Spain via the Spanish enclaves of Ceuta and Melilla in northern Morocco.

Morocco's border with Algeria remains closed. Algeria is reluctant to reopen it until the status of the Western Sahara is resolved – don't hold your breath.

Most Western governments advise against travel to Mauritania.

Sea

There are extensive ferry links between northern Morocco and southern Europe, the most popular of which is Algeciras (Spain) to Tanger Med, 48km east of Tangier. A fast catamaran travels from Tarifa, Spain, to Tangier Port in the city.

➡ Book in advance during peak periods (particularly Easter, the last week in August and the last week in October), allow an hour before departure to get tickets and navigate passport control. If you're arriving in Morocco, remember to get your

> **DEPARTURE TAX**
>
> Departure tax is included in the price of a ticket.

Ferry Routes

passport stamped on the ferry.

➡ Remember the time difference with Spain (Morocco is one hour behind during daylight saving time, April to November).

➡ In Tangier and Algeciras, avoid touts who try to guide you to travel agencies for commission.

➡ Discounts for students and young people with an ISIC card or similar, and InterRail or Eurail passholders are common. Children between two and 12 years often travel for half the fare, those aged under two travel free, and over-60s can often get reductions.

➡ Vehicles can be taken on most ferries for an extra fee; bicycles are normally free.

Ferry Companies & Routes

Direct Ferries (www.directferries.com) sells tickets for most of the following. The Europe-wide service has sites in most European languages.

Trasmediterranea (www.trasmediterranea.es) Almería–Melilla, Almería–Nador, Algeciras–Ceuta, Algeciras–Tanger Med, Málaga–Melilla.

Balеària (www.balearia.com) Algeciras–Ceuta, Algeciras–Tanger Med, Algeciras-Melilla, Motril-Melilla.

FRS (www.frs.es) Algeciras–Ceuta, Algeciras–Tanger Med, Gibraltar–Tanger Med, Tarifa–Tangier Port.

Grandi Navi Veloci (www.gnv.it) Barcelona–Tanger Med, Barcelona–Nador, Genoa–Tanger Med, Sète–Tanger Med, Sète–Nador.

Grimaldi Lines (www.grimaldi-lines.com) Savona–Tanger Med, Barcelona–Tanger Med.

France

The journey from Sète (two hours by train from Marseilles) to Tangier takes 36 hours and to Nador takes 28 hours.

There are three sailings weekly to Tangier and one to Nador.

Gibraltar

There's one ferry a week from Tanger Med. The trip takes a similar length of time to sailings to/from Algeciras (90 minutes), and tickets cost the same.

Algeciras is a better option as it's a busier port with more choice.

Italy

Two ferry companies sail from Italy to Tanger Med. Grandi Navi Veloci has a thrice-weekly service from Genoa, and there's a weekly service on Grimaldi Lines from Savona; both take just over 48 hours.

Spain

Ferries from Spain to Morocco are plentiful. Tickets start at about €30, depending on the season.

Hydrofoils and catamarans (also referred to as fast ferries) are used extensively.

Spanish passport control is uncomplicated, but non-EU citizens and Schengen visa-holders should make sure they get an exit stamp before boarding the ferry.

You need to fill in an embarkation form on board, and get your passport stamped before disembarking.

ALGECIRAS TO TANGER MED

The busiest crossing between Europe and Morocco. Ferries run at least every 1½ hours, hourly in summer. The crossing usually takes an hour.

Services typically run from 7am (or 6am in summer) until 10pm, but during peak demand in August 24-hour services aren't unknown.

ALGECIRAS TO CEUTA

Several daily high-speed ferries (30 minutes to one hour) leave in both directions.

CLIMATE CHANGE & TRAVEL

Every form of transport that relies on carbon-based fuel generates CO_2, the main cause of human-induced climate change. Modern travel is dependent on aeroplanes, which might use less fuel per kilometre per person than most cars but travel much greater distances. The altitude at which aircraft emit gases (including CO_2) and particles also contributes to their climate change impact. Many websites offer 'carbon calculators' that allow people to estimate the carbon emissions generated by their journey and, for those who wish to do so, to offset the impact of the greenhouse gases emitted with contributions to portfolios of climate-friendly initiatives throughout the world. Lonely Planet offsets the carbon footprint of all staff and author travel.

ALMERÍA TO MELILLA

Around eight sailings a week, with crossings taking up to eight hours.

ALMERÍA TO NADOR

Daily departures in either direction, taking six/eight hours to Almería/Nador.

BARCELONA TO TANGIER

Two companies offer this route to Tangier, one stopping in Barcelona en route from Genoa (Italy). The three weekly sailings take about 30 hours.

MÁLAGA TO MELILLA

The daily service is normally an afternoon/night ferry between Málaga and Melilla. It takes up to seven hours.

TARIFA TO TANGIER

Catamarans leave every hour or so and cross the strait in 40 minutes, making this the fastest and most practical route.

The fare includes a free bus transfer to Algeciras on presentation of your ferry ticket.

The transfer takes 50 minutes, and making the trip via Tarifa is a faster way to get to Algeciras than the slower direct ferries.

MOTRIL TO AL HOCEIMA & NADOR

Naviera Armas has summer services from Motril to Al Hoceima and Nador. Sailings are every Saturday.

GETTING AROUND

Air

National carrier **Royal Air Maroc** (www.royalairmaroc.com) is the main domestic airline. All flights are via its hub at **Mohammed V International Airport** (☐0522435858; www.casablanca-airport.com) in Casablanca. Royal Air Maroc serves Tangier, Nador, Oujda, Fez, Errachidia, Marrakesh, Essaouira, Agadir, Laayoune and Dakhla.

Flying is relatively expensive but may be worth it if you are pushed for time. The 2¼-hour flight from Casablanca to Dakhla costs from Dh980, compared with Dh600 for a 1st-class seat on the 32-hour CTM bus journey.

A cheaper option is **Air Arabia** (www.airarabia.com), which covers 10 Moroccan cities, including Agadir, Casablanca, Rabat and Zagora. Fly between Marrakesh and Fez from Dh291 in just one hour, compared to an eight-hour bus journey for around Dh190.

Bicycle

Mountain biking can be a great way of travelling around Morocco. There are plenty of opportunities for getting off the beaten track, with thousands of kilometres of remote *pistes* (dirt tracks) to be explored.

Hazards

Surfaced roads are generally well-maintained once completed, but they tend to be narrow and in less-frequented areas may have jagged edges, which can be hairy given the kamikaze drivers. Beware of stone-throwing children in remote areas.

Hire

You'll find bicycles for hire in places such as Marrakesh, Essaouira and Taroudant, but don't expect to find the latest models of mountain bike.

Transport

Bus companies will generally carry bicycles as luggage for an extra fee. Likewise on trains, although it's generally only possible to transport bikes in the goods wagon.

Boat

There are no public boats around Morocco. If you're lucky to have your own boat, there are several marinas along the Atlantic coast, including in Tangier, Casablanca, Salé and Agadir.

Bus

The cheapest and most efficient way to travel around the country, buses are generally safe, although drivers sometimes leave a little to be desired.

Many buses have meagre curtains, so to avoid melting in the sun, pay attention to where you sit. Heading from north to south, sit on the right in the morning and the left in the afternoon; east to west, sit on the right, or on the left if travelling from west to east. You will often be assigned a seat when you purchase your ticket, but you can ask to choose a place.

Operating on many intercity routes, night buses can be both quicker and cooler, although risks from other road users are considerably heightened.

Bus trips longer than three hours incorporate a scheduled stop to stretch your legs and grab a snack. Buses are sometimes delayed at police checkpoints for about 10 minutes – longer than *grands taxis*, whose local drivers usually know the police.

Bus Stations

Some Moroccan bus stations are like madhouses, with touts running around calling any number of destinations of buses about to depart. Most cities and towns have a single central bus station (*gare routière*), but the bus companies Supratours and CTM often maintain separate terminals and usually have offices outside the station. Occasionally, there are secondary stations for a limited number of local destinations.

LUGGAGE

Bus stations in the main cities often have left-luggage depots (*consigne*), sometimes open 24 hours. Charges are around Dh10 per day; padlock your bags.

TOUTS

Touts will happily guide you to a ticket booth (and take a small commission from the company). Always double-check that their recommended service really is the most comfortable, direct and convenient option.

Bus Operators

Where possible, and especially if services are infrequent or do not originate in the place you want to leave, book ahead for CTM and Supratours buses. Particularly busy routes are Marrakesh–Essaouira and Casablanca–Marrakesh, where you may need to reserve seats two days in advance in high season.

CTM

With the most comprehensive nationwide network, CTM (www.ctm.ma) serves most destinations of interest to travellers. Established in 1919, it is Morocco's oldest bus company.

On CTM buses, children four years and older pay full fare, which tends to be 15% to 30% more expensive than most other lines – comparable to 2nd-class fares on normal trains. Tickets can normally be purchased in advance; check departures with the online timetable.

CTM coaches are modern and comfortable, with air-conditioning and heating (they sometimes overdo both).

Some routes between major cities offer a premium service, with comfier seats, more legroom and free wi-fi. Fares are around 40% higher than the regular service.

Carry-on baggage can weigh a maximum of 5kg; hold baggage is charged by weight.

SUPRATOURS

The ONCF train company runs Supratours (www.supratours.ma) to complement its rail network. For example, train passengers continuing south from Marrakesh link up at the station with coaches to destinations including Agadir and Ouarzazate. Supratours also runs the busy Marrakesh–Essaouira coach service.

At train ticket offices, it's possible to buy a ticket covering a complete trip with both rail and bus components.

On trains, travellers with tickets for connecting buses have priority.

Supratours is similar to CTM in terms of both its fares and the comfort of its buses, and you can check departures online.

OTHER COMPANIES

In the south, SATAS is a reasonably good second-tier option, as is Trans Ghazala (www.transghazala.ma) in the north.

At the bottom end of the price range, and on shorter routes, there are a fair number of operators with one or two well-worn buses. These services depart when sufficiently full and frequently stop to pick up more passengers.

Car & Motorcycle

Morocco is a country made for driving and offers freedom to explore the more unusual routes in your own time.

Daylight driving is generally no problem and not too stressful outside of big cities, though Moroccan drivers often need to be treated with caution and safe distances.

The roads connecting Morocco's main centres are generally good, and there's an expanding motorway network, which comes with small toll fees. The main routes include the following:

- Tangier down the Atlantic coast to Safi (via Casablanca and Rabat)
- Rabat inland to Oujda via Meknes and Fez
- Casablanca south to Agadir via Marrakesh
- Tangier to Oujda via Tetouan and Nador

Bringing Your Own Vehicle

Every vehicle should display the nationality plate of its country of registration, and you must always carry proof of ownership of a private vehicle. Moroccan law requires a 'green card' (*carte verte*, or International Motor Insurance Card) as proof of insurance. A warning triangle (to be used in case of breakdown) is compulsory.

Obtain a green card from your insurer before leaving home; otherwise, local insurance (*assurance frontiere*), costing about Dh650 for 10 days, must be purchased at the ferry port or a nearby broker (*bureau d'assurance*).

Ask for the optional *constat amiable* form, which both parties fill out in the event of a minor road accident. They can also be purchased at *tabacs* in cities.

At the port, or on the ferry on longer crossings, you must also fill in the TVIP form (temporary vehicle importation declaration – *declaration d'admission temporaire de moyens de transport*), valid for six months or until you and the vehicle leave the country.

There is no need for a *carnet de passage en douane* for temporarily importing your vehicle to Morocco.

Driving Licence

International driving permits are recommended for Morocco by most auto organisations, but many foreign (including EU) licences are accepted as long as they have your photograph.

You must carry your licence or permit as well as your passport when driving.

Fuel & Spare Parts

The country is well served with petrol stations, although they're fewer and further between in the Western Sahara. If you're travelling off the beaten track, refuel at every opportunity. Keep a close eye on the gauge in the southern desert and fill up wherever you get a chance, as stations don't always have supplies of fuel.

Leaded and less-common unleaded (*sans plomb*) petrol costs around Dh11 per litre, and diesel (*gasoil*) is around Dh10. In the Western Sahara, tax-free petrol is about 30% cheaper. Fuel in the Spanish enclaves of Ceuta and Melilla is comparably priced to Morocco.

Moroccan mechanics are generally good, and decent-sized towns should have at least one garage.

Hire

Hiring a car costs about Dh300 per day with unlimited mileage. For longer rentals, lower daily rates are sometimes available. Prebooking gives the cheapest deals. Most companies demand a (returnable) cash deposit (Dh3000 to Dh5000) or take an impression of your credit card.

With international firms such as Hertz, Budget, Europcar, National and Avis, you can prebook online. There are also numerous local agencies.

Make sure you understand what is included in the price and what your liabilities are. Always check the car's condition before signing up and make sure it comes with a spare tyre, tool kit and full documentation, including insurance cover. Keep the car's documents and your licence with you, rather than in the car, as you'll need them if the car is stolen or damaged. Keep receipts for oil changes or mechanical repairs; these costs should be reimbursed.

Insurance must, by law, be sold along with all rental agreements. Make sure that prices include collision damage, insurance and tax (20%). You should also take out Collision Damage Waiver insurance, typically about Dh35 to Dh60 a day (often with an excess of up to Dh5000). Super Collision Damage Waiver, which eliminates or minimises the excess, may be available for an extra Dh60 or so a day.

Unless you hire a 4WD, your rental agreement will probably not allow off-road (*piste*) driving.

Motorcycle

Motorcycle touring is popular, but many bikes are unfamiliar to mechanics in Morocco, particularly those with larger capacity engines, so repairs can be tricky. Carry a good toolkit and all necessary spares, including cables and levers, inner tubes, puncture repair kit, tyre levers, pump, fuses, chain, washable air filter and cable ties.

Some insurance policies do not allow foreign motorcycle licences to be used in Morocco. See **Horizons Unlimited** (www.horizonsunlimited.com) for detailed advice on motorbiking in the region.

Parking

Parking zones are often watched by *gardiens de voitures* (car park attendants). Payment of a few dirhams gives a trouble-free parking experience.

In the big city centres, parking tickets are issued from kerbside machines (Dh3 per hour for a maximum stay of two hours). Parking is free on Sundays, although there's sure to be a car park attendant hanging around to take your Dh3.

Parking is not allowed at kerbsides painted in red-and-white stripes. Stopping is not allowed on green-and-white stripes. Fines for illegally parked cars can reach Dh1500.

Roadblocks

Police control points are common on main roads in and out of most sizeable towns. Foreigners are unlikely to be stopped, but it's still a good idea to slow down and put on your best smile.

Roadblocks are also common in sensitive areas like the Western Sahara, the Rif Mountains around the hashish-producing region of Ketama and the road to Figuig near the Algerian border.

Police are more vigilant in these areas, but at most, you'll be asked to show your passport, driving licence and the vehicle's papers, and asked the purpose of your visit and destination.

Road Hazards

Road accidents are as common in Morocco as an offer of mint tea. Treat all vehicles as ready to veer out and cut you off at inopportune moments.

Cyclists and pedestrians often have poor traffic awareness. Roads are often busy with people (including groups of schoolchildren), bicycles, horses and carts, donkeys and so on.

In the *hamada* (stony desert), tar roads sometimes disappear without warning, replaced by stretches of sand, gravel and potholes. If a strong *chergui* (dry, easterly desert wind) is blowing and carrying a lot of dust, you'll have to wait until it eases off if you don't want to do your car considerable damage.

High Atlas and Middle Atlas passes are often closed because of snow in winter. Seek local advice before travelling or check the road signs along the routes.

Entering cities and towns, park outside the medina or find out if the route to your accommodation is easily drivable – narrow medina streets weren't designed for cars.

Driving at night is particularly hazardous: it's legal (and very common) for vehicles travelling under 20km/h to drive without lights.

Road Rules

Drive on the right-hand side of the road. Give way to traffic entering a roundabout from the right when you're already on one.

The fine for missing a red stop sign is Dh400 if you pay on the spot and Dh700 if you don't.

The speed limit in built-up areas is 40km/h, between 60km/h and 100km/h on national routes, and 120km/h on motorways. Police with radar guns are common, so watch your speed.It's the law to wear a seatbelt.

Tolls apply on motorways – for example, Rabat to Tangier is about Dh80 and Rabat to Casablanca is Dh25. You take a ticket upon entering the motorway and pay at the end.

In the event of an accident, especially involving injuries, drivers are officially required to remain at the scene. Vehicles cannot be moved until the police have arrived – this may take hours.

Pick up a *constat amiable* form from your insurer in case you have an accident; they can be purchased at *tabacs* (corner shops) in cities.

Local Transport

Grand Taxi

The Mercedes saloons you'll see on Moroccan roads and gathered near bus stations are shared taxis (*grands taxis* in French or *taxiat kebira* in Arabic). On many routes the older cars are being replaced with newer people carriers.

The Ziz and Draa valleys, the Tizi n'Test mountain pass and the Rif Mountains, all scenic areas not well-served by buses, are good to visit in a taxi.

Grands taxis link towns to their neighbours, often in a relay system that may necessitate changing a few times on longer journeys. *Grands taxis* sometimes ply longer routes, but these services are rarer and usually leave first thing in the morning.

Grands taxis take six cramped passengers (two in the front, four in the back) and leave when full. It can often be advantageous to pay for two seats to get the taxi going earlier and give yourself more space. This is particularly useful for solo women, as you should get the front seat to yourself – you might even get a seatbelt, a rarity in the back.

The fixed-rate fares are a little higher than bus fares, but still very reasonable. Make it clear you want to pay for *une place* (one spot) in a *taxi collectif* (shared taxi). Another expression that helps explain that you don't want the taxi to yourself is *maa an nas* (with other people). If you've got particularly heavy/bulky luggage, there might be a surcharge.

Hiring an entire taxi is sometimes a good option – especially if you're travelling with a small group, or you

TRAVELLER ETIQUETTE

When travelling on public transport, it's considered both selfish and bad manners to eat while those around you go without. Always buy a little extra to offer to your neighbours.

Next comes the ritual. If you offer food, etiquette dictates that your fellow passengers should decline it. It should be offered a second time, a little more persuasively, but again it will be turned down. On a third, more insistent offer, your neighbours are free to accept the gift if they wish to.

If you are offered food, but you don't want it, it's good manners to accept a small piece anyway, and to pat your stomach contentedly to indicate that you are full. In return for participating in this ritual, you should be accorded great respect, offered protection and cared for like a friend.

want to travel along an unpopular route without waiting hours for other passengers. The fare should be six times the cost for one place. If you'll be travelling through a scenic area, make sure plans for stopping en route are clear.

Grand taxi drivers often have a boy-racer mentality. Overtaking on blind corners can be a badge of honour, and speed limits are only adhered to when there's a police roadblock in sight. Night-time journeys are best avoided.

Local Buses

The bigger cities have public bus services. Tickets are typically Dh5. Buses can be ludicrously overcrowded, and routes often hard to discern. *Petits taxis* are often an easier and faster option.

Petit Taxi

Cities and bigger towns have local *petits taxis* that are a different colour in every city. *Petits taxis* are licensed to carry up to three passengers, but are not permitted to go beyond the city limits.

Petits taxis are metered in cities, less commonly so in smaller towns. To ask in French for the meter to be switched on, say *'tourne le conteur, si'l vous plaît'*. Where taxis are not metered, agree on a price beforehand.

If the driver refuses to use the meter and won't give you a price, ask to stop and get out. Most *petit taxi* drivers are honest, but some in Marrakesh and Casablanca are notoriously greedy with tourists.

Multiple hire is common. The price should be the same whether you hail an empty taxi and pick up other passengers en route, or there are already others in a taxi you wave down, or you travel alone.

From 8pm (often 9pm in summer) there is normally a 50% surcharge.

While Uber no longer operates in Casablanca, the app-based ride-sharing service Careem (www.careem.com) is available in both Casablanca and Rabat. Prices tend to be higher and waiting times longer.

Pick-up Truck & 4WD

In more remote areas, especially the Atlas Mountains, locals travel between towns and villages in *camionettes* (pick-up trucks), old vans or the back of trucks.

The best time to find a lift is early on market days (generally once or twice a week). Waits for departures can be considerable.

On remote *pistes* (dirt tracks) that would destroy normal taxis, 4WD taxis operate.

Tram

Casablanca and Rabat both have new and modern tram networks, which are an excellent and cheap way to explore those cities.

Tours

Whether it's your first or your fifth time in Morocco, taking a tour is great for speeding you around the highlights if you're short of time, giving you behind-the-scenes access to people and places, and getting you off the beaten track.

Authentic Morocco (www.authentic-morocco.com) This reliable company supports local communities and practices low-impact tourism, offering itineraries from camel treks to tours of Roman ruins.

Desert Majesty (www.desertmajesty.com) A highly recommended local agency offering trips to the High Atlas and the desert at competitive prices.

Inside Morocco Travel (www.insidemoroccotravel.com) This well-run company specialises in trekking trips to the High Atlas from Marrakesh, but it can put together just about any trip you want.

Journey Beyond Travel (www.journeybeyondtravel.com) The experienced team at this highly regarded Ifrane-based company puts together tailor-made private tours to anywhere in the country.

Nature Trekking Maroc (www.berberemaroctrekking.com) Off-the-beaten-track trekking, horse riding, mountain biking, skiing and 4WD trips.

Plan-it Morocco (http://plan-it-morocco.com) This highly recommended, female-owned agency offers creative insider-access tours, perhaps meeting artists in their Marrakesh ateliers, a literary tour of Tangier or street food in Fez.

Sahara Experience (http://sahara-experience.com) This professional outfit organises a host of memorable tours, from day trips to overnights and multiday circuits (both guided and self-drive) to get you off the beaten track.

Toubkal Guide (https://toubkalguide.com) Trekking tours led by local guides and muleteers in Toubkal National Park and the rest of the High Atlas.

Wild Morocco (https://wildmorocco.com) This superb outfit offers well-planned, multiday desert treks as well as overnights at their desert camp in the shadow of Erg Chigaga. Longer excursions combining trekking in the Atlas Mountains are also possible.

Wildcat Adventures (www.wildcat-bike-tours.co.uk) This UK-based outfit offers road- and mountain-bike tours in the High Atlas and Anti Atlas, plus a bike-trek-camel itinerary.

Train

Run by ONCF (Office National des Chemins de Fer; www.oncf.ma), Morocco's train network is one of Africa's best, linking most of the major cities. In general, trains are reasonably priced and comfortable, but they don't always run to their timetables.

There have been a number of train accidents, including

Supratours & Train Network

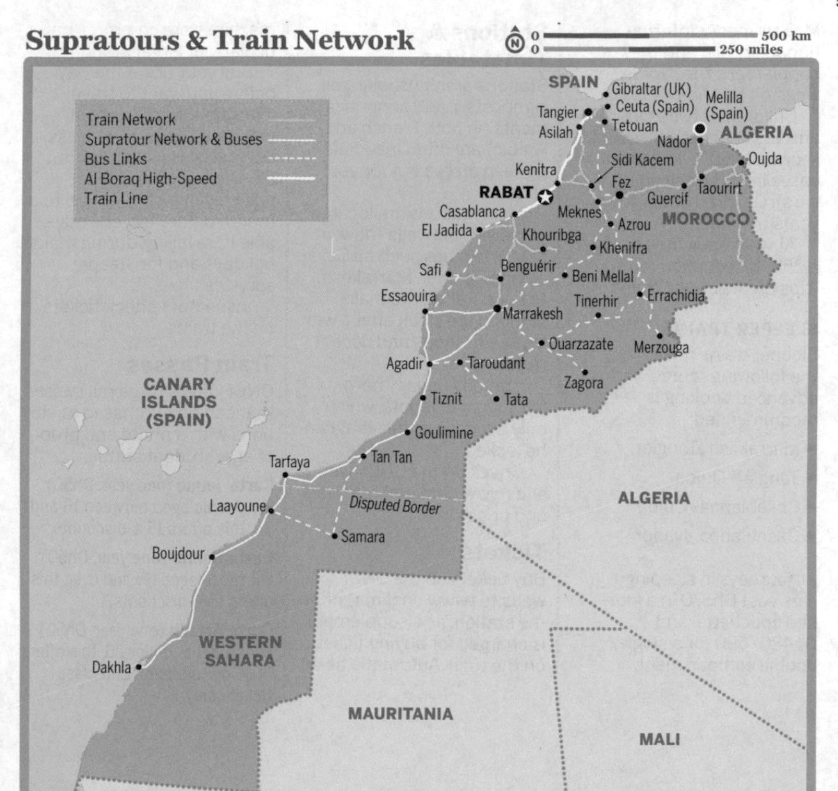

fatalities, over the years, most recently in 2018 in Bouknadel. While investment has been poured into glossy train stations in Rabat and Casablanca, less has been spent on rolling stock.

However, the shiny new Al Boraq, Africa's first high-speed train linking Tangier, Rabat and Casablanca launched in late 2018, reducing the travel time between Tangier and Casablanca from five hours to just over two, with top speeds of 320km/h on the Tangier–Kenitra stretch.

There are two main lines: Tangier to Marrakesh via Rabat and Casablanca; and Oujda or Nador in the north-east down to Marrakesh, passing Fez and Meknes before joining the line from Tangier at Sidi Kacem.

Also operated by ONCF, Supratours buses link many destinations to the train network.

Trains are particularly convenient around Casablanca and Rabat, with services leaving every 30 minutes between the two cities.

There are also four overnight trains with sleeper cars, including Tangier–Marrakesh and Casablanca–Oujda.

Classes & Costs

There are three types of train; the main difference between the two standard trains is comfort:

- *Al Boraq* – the high-speed train between Tangier and Casablanca, with stops in Kenitra and Rabat.
- *Rapide* (Train Rapide Climatisé, TCR) – standard for intercity services.
- *Ordinaire* (Train Navette Rapide, TNR) – less comfortable, without air-conditioning, apart from the double-decker Rabat–Casablanca shuttle. Mostly late-night and local services.

First- and 2nd-class fares are available, with six seats in 1st-class compartments and eight in 2nd class. First-class tickets include a reserved seat, while in 2nd class you just sit in any empty seat. Second class is more than adequate on short journeys. For longer trips, the extra for 1st class is worth paying.

Shuttle services operate regularly between Kenitra, Rabat, Casablanca and

Mohammed V International Airport, and they supplement the *rapide* services on this line.

Children between four and 12 years get a discount (normally 50%, less in a few cases including sleeping cars). Children under four years travel free.

At weekends travellers get a 25% discount on return trips on major-line trains.

SLEEPER TRAINS

Sleeper trains run along the following routes, and advanced booking is recommended:

- Marrakesh–Tangier
- Tangier–Oujda
- Casablanca–Oujda
- Casablanca–Nador

All journeys in sleeping cars cost Dh370 in a four-bed couchette, and Dh480/690 for a single/double compartment.

Stations & Timetables

Stations aren't usually well signposted, and announcements (in both French and Arabic) are often inaudible, so keep an eye out for your stop.

Most stations are located in the ville nouvelle (new town). In cities such as Casablanca, Tangier, Marrakesh, Fez and Rabat, the main stations are sleek affairs with free wi-fi, shops and decent restaurants.

Stations usually have left-luggage depots, which only accept luggage that can be locked.

Check on the ONCF website (www.oncf.ma) for times and prices.

Tickets

Buy tickets on the ONCF website (www.oncf.ma) or at the station, as a supplement is charged for buying tickets on the train. Automatic ticket machines are common, particularly at larger stations.

Buy your ticket the day before you want to travel if possible, particularly if you want to travel 1st class. Second-class seats cannot be reserved. First-class tickets can be bought up to a month before travel – advisable if travelling during major holidays and for sleeper services.

Inspectors check tickets on the trains.

Train Passes

ONCF offers three rail passes that can be purchased at stations with a photo and proof of age/student status.

Carte Jeune (one year, Dh50) For people aged between 16 and 30, this offers 15% discounts.

Carte Senior (one year, Dh50) For those aged 60 and over, this offers 15% discounts.

Carte Attalib (one year, Dh50) For students under 26, this offers 30% discounts on 2nd-class tickets only.

Health

Prevention is the key to staying healthy in Morocco, and a little planning before departure will save you trouble later. With luck, your worst complaint on your trip will be a bad stomach, which can be avoided with a few precautions. Car accidents are a common reason for travellers to need medical help. Medical facilities can be excellent in large cities but basic in more remote areas.

For information on the COVID-19 pandemic, see p3 and p23.

BEFORE YOU GO

Insurance

Adequate health insurance is vital when travelling to Morocco. The national health service isn't always great, and the few good private hospitals are expensive.

You may prefer a policy that pays the medical facility directly rather than you having to pay on the spot and claim later, although in practice most Moroccan doctors and hospitals insist on payment up front. If you have to claim later, make sure you keep all documentation. Carry proof of your insurance with you; this can be vital for avoiding any delays to treatment in emergency situations.

Some policies ask you to call a centre in your home country, which makes an immediate assessment of your problem; keep your insurer's emergency telephone number on you.

Find out which private medical service your insurer uses in Morocco so that you can call them direct in the event of an emergency. Your policy should ideally cover emergency air evacuation home or transport by plane or ambulance to a hospital in a major city.

Medical Checklist

Consider packing the following items in your medical kit:

- antibiotics (if travelling off the beaten track)
- antibacterial hand gel
- antidiarrhoeal drugs (eg loperamide)
- paracetamol or aspirin
- anti-inflammatory drugs (eg ibuprofen)
- antihistamines (for hay fever and allergic reactions)
- antibacterial ointment (eg Bactroban) for cuts and abrasions
- steroid cream or cortisone (for allergic rashes)
- bandages, gauze and gauze rolls
- adhesive or paper tape
- scissors, safety pins and tweezers
- thermometer
- pocket knife
- DEET-containing insect repellent
- insect spray for clothing, tents and mosquito nets
- sun block
- oral rehydration salts (eg Dioralyte)
- iodine or other water-purification tablets

Bring medications in their original, clearly labelled containers. A signed and dated letter from your physician describing your medical conditions and medications, including generic names, is also helpful. See your dentist before a long trip; carry a spare pair of contact lenses and glasses (and take your optical prescription with you).

Websites

Useful resources to consult before departure:

NHS (www.fitfortravel.nhs.uk) UK government website.

CDC (wwwnc.cdc.gov/travel) US government website.

Health Canada (www.canada.ca/en/health-canada/services/healthy-living/travel-health.html) Canadian government website.

International Association for Medical Advice to Travellers (www.iamat.org) Gives access to its online database of doctors with recognised training.

Smartraveller (www.smartraveller.gov.au) Australian government website.

WHO (www.who.int/ith) Information from the World Health Organisation.

RECOMMENDED VACCINATIONS

Although no specific vaccinations are required for Morocco, the US Centers for Disease Control and Prevention (CDC) suggests the following as routine:

- diphtheria
- tetanus
- measles
- mumps
- rubella
- polio

The CDC also suggests the following for Morocco:

- hepatitis A and B
- typhoid
- rabies

Don't leave health matters until the last minute: some vaccines don't ensure immunity for two weeks, so visit a doctor four to eight weeks before departure.

Before leaving home, ensure that all your routine vaccination cover is complete. Ask your doctor for an international certificate of vaccination, listing all the vaccinations you've received.

IN MOROCCO

Availability & Cost of Health Care

Primary medical care is not always readily available outside major cities and towns. Your accommodation may be able to recommend the nearest source of medical help, and embassy websites sometimes list doctors and clinics. In an emergency, contact your embassy or consulate.

Pharmacies These are generally well stocked, and pharmacists can provide advice (usually in French) covering common travellers' complaints. They can sell over-the-counter medication, often including drugs only available on prescription at home, and advise when more specialised help is needed. Double-check any unfamiliar purchases; readers have reported receiving incorrect and potentially dangerous medication for their conditions.

Doctors and clinics If you are being treated by a doctor or at a clinic, particularly outside the major cities, you will often be expected to purchase medical supplies on the spot – even including sterile dressings or intravenous fluids.

Dental care Standards are variable – Marrakshi street dentists around Djemaa El Fna aren't recommended! Travel insurance doesn't usually cover dental work other than emergency treatment.

Infectious Diseases

Hepatitis A

Spreads Through contaminated food (particularly shellfish) and water.

Symptoms and effects Jaundice, dark urine, a yellow colour to the whites of the eyes, fever and abdominal pain. Although rarely fatal, it can cause prolonged lethargy and delayed recovery.

Prevention Vaccine (Avaxim, VAQTA, Havrix) is given as an injection, with a booster extending the protection offered. Hepatitis A and typhoid vaccines can also be given as a combined single-dose vaccine (hepatyrix or viatim).

Hepatitis B

Spreads Through infected blood, contaminated needles and sexual intercourse.

Symptoms and effects Jaundice and liver problems (occasionally failure).

Prevention Travellers should make this a routine vaccination, although Morocco gives hepatitis B vaccination as part of routine childhood vaccination. It is given singly, or at the same time as hepatitis A.

HIV & AIDS

Morocco has an HIV infection rate of 0.1%, primarily among intravenous drug users, men who have sex with men and sex workers.

Spreads Through infected blood and blood products; sexual intercourse with an infected partner; 'blood to blood' contacts, such as through contaminated instruments during medical, dental, acupuncture and other body-piercing procedures, or sharing used intravenous needles.

Leishmaniasis

Spreads Through the bite of an infected sandfly or dog. It may be found in rural areas in the Atlas Mountains, where sandflies are more prevalent between June and October.

Symptoms and effects Slowly growing skin lump or sores. It may develop into a serious, life-threatening fever, usually accompanied by anaemia and weight loss.

Prevention and treatment Avoid sandfly bites. There is no vaccine, but treatment with an antimonial drug such as Glucantime or Pentostam is straightforward, usually involving an injection.

Rabies

Spreads Through bites or licks on broken skin from an infected animal. Rabies is endemic to Morocco.

Symptoms and effects Initial symptoms are pain or tingling at the site of the bite with fever, loss of appetite and headache. If untreated, both 'furious' and less-common 'dumb' rabies are fatal.

Prevention and treatment People travelling to remote areas, where a reliable source of post-bite vaccine is not available within 24 hours, should be vaccinated. Any bite, scratch or lick from a warm-blooded, furry animal should immediately be thoroughly cleaned. If you have not been vaccinated and you get bitten, you will need a course of injections starting as soon as possible after the injury. Vaccination does not provide immunity; it merely buys you more time to seek medical help.

Tuberculosis

Spreads Through close respiratory contact and, occasionally, infected milk or milk products.

Symptoms and effects Can be asymptomatic, although symptoms can include a cough, weight loss or fever months or even years after exposure. An x-ray is the best way to confirm if you have tuberculosis.

Prevention BCG vaccine is recommended for those mixing closely with the local population, whether visiting family, planning a long stay, or working as a teacher or health-care worker. As it's a live vaccine it should not be given to pregnant women or immuno-compromised individuals.

Typhoid

Spreads Through food or water that has been contaminated by infected human faeces.

Symptoms and effects Initially, usually fever or a pink rash on the abdomen. Septicaemia (blood poisoning) may also occur.

Prevention Typhim Vi or Typherix vaccine. In some countries, the oral vaccine Vivotif is also available.

Traveller's Diarrhoea

Causes Strains of travel – unfamiliar food, heat, long days and erratic sleeping patterns – can all make your body more susceptible to an upset stomach.

Prevention Water is generally safe to drink in cities, but elsewhere you should only drink filtered water. Eat fresh fruits or vegetables only if they are cooked or if you have washed or peeled them yourself. Buffet meals, which may have been sitting out for some time, can be risky; food should be piping hot. Meals freshly cooked in front of you (like most street food) or served in a busy restaurant are more likely to be safe. Be sensible but not paranoid: food is one of the treats of visiting Morocco, so don't miss out.

Hygiene Pay close attention to personal hygiene. Many Moroccan meals are eaten with the hand, so always wash before eating and after using the toilet. Even the smallest restaurant will have a sink, but soap is less common, especially at cheap hotels. Antibacterial hand gel, which cleans without needing water, is useful.

Treatment Drink plenty of fluids and preferably an oral rehydration solution; pharmacies stock these inexpensive *sels de réhydration orale*. Avoid fatty food and dairy products. A few loose stools don't require treatment, but if you start having more than four or five a day, take an antibiotic (usually a quinolone drug) and an antidiarrhoeal agent (such as loperamide). If diarrhoea is bloody, persists for more than 72 hours, and is accompanied by fever, shaking chills or severe abdominal pain, seek medical attention.

Environmental Hazards

Altitude Sickness

Causes Lack of oxygen at high altitudes (more than 2500m) affects most people to some extent. The effect may be mild or severe and occurs because less oxygen reaches the muscles and brain at high altitudes, requiring the heart and lungs to compensate by working harder. There is no hard-and-fast rule as to what is too high: Acute Mountain Sickness (AMS) has been fatal at 3000m, although 3500m to 4500m is the usual range.

Symptoms and effects Symptoms of AMS usually (but not always) develop during the first 24 hours at altitude. Mild symptoms include headache, lethargy, dizziness, difficulty sleeping and loss of appetite. Potentially fatal, AMS may become more severe without warning. Severe symptoms include breathlessness; a dry, irritative cough (which may progress to the production of pink, frothy sputum); severe headache; lack of coordination;

TAP WATER IN MOROCCO

Tap water is chlorinated in Morocco's cities and is generally safe to drink – certainly to clean your teeth with. Elsewhere, stick to treated water, or filter or purify it yourself.

Bottled water is available everywhere although there is an environmental cost of the mountains of discarded (and unrecycled) plastic bottles. LifeStraw (www.lifestraw.com) and Steripen (www.steripen.com) make environmentally friendly alternatives.

Off the beaten track, water drawn from wells or pumped from boreholes should be safe, but never drink water from rivers or lakes because this may contain bacteria or viruses that can cause diarrhoea or vomiting.

FURTHER READING

International Travel Health Guide by Stuart Rose MD

The Travellers' Good Health Guide by Ted Lankester

Travellers' Health by Dr Richard Dawood

confusion; irrational behaviour; vomiting; drowsiness and unconsciousness.

Prevention If trekking, build time into your schedule to acclimatise and ensure your guide knows how to recognise and deal with altitude sickness. Morocco's most popular trek, to Jebel Toubkal, reaches the 4167m summit relatively quickly, so many people may suffer even mildly. The longer treks in the M'Goun Massif also reach heights of around 4000m. Treks in the Rif Mountains and Jebel Saghro are considerably lower, so don't carry the same risks.

Treatment Treat mild symptoms by resting at the same altitude until recovery or preferably descend – even 500m can help. Take paracetamol or aspirin for headaches. If symptoms persist or become worse, immediate descent is necessary. Drug treatments should never be used to avoid descent or to enable further ascent. Diamox (acetazolamide) reduces the headache of AMS and helps the body acclimatise to the lack of oxygen. It is only available on prescription, and those who are allergic to sulfonamide antibiotics may also be allergic to Diamox.

Heat Illness

Causes Occurs following heavy sweating and excessive fluid loss with inadequate replacement of fluids and salt. This is particularly common in hot climates when taking unaccustomed exercise before full acclimatisation.

Symptoms and effects Headache, dizziness and tiredness.

Prevention Dehydration is already happening by the time you feel thirsty – drink sufficient water to produce pale, diluted urine. Morocco's sun can be fierce, so bring a hat.

Treatment Consists of fluid replacement with water, fruit juice or both and cooling by cold water and fans. Treating salt loss consists of consuming salty fluids such as soup or broth, and adding a little more table salt to foods than usual.

Heatstroke

Causes Extreme heat, high humidity, physical exertion or use of drugs or alcohol in the sun and dehydration. Occurs when the body's heat-regulating mechanism breaks down.

Symptoms and effects An excessive rise in body temperature leads to the cessation of sweating, irrational and hyperactive behaviour, and eventually loss of consciousness and death.

Treatment Rapid cooling by spraying the body with water and fanning is ideal. Emergency fluid and electrolyte replacement by intravenous drip is usually also required.

Insect Bites & Stings

Causes Mosquitoes, sandflies (found around the Mediterranean beaches), scorpions (common in southern Morocco), bees, wasps, bedbugs and scabies (both found in cheaper accommodation).

Symptoms and effects More likely to be an irritant than a health risk. Sandflies have a nasty, itchy bite and can carry the rare skin disorder leishmaniasis. Scorpions have a painful sting, but it's rarely life-threatening. Bedbugs lead to very itchy, lumpy bites. Tiny scabies mites live in the skin, particularly between the fingers, and cause an intensely itchy rash.

Prevention and treatment DEET-based insect repellents. Spraying a mattress with an appropriate insect killer will do a good job of getting rid of bedbugs. Scabies is easily treated with lotion available from pharmacies; people you come into contact with also need treatment to avoid spreading scabies between asymptomatic carriers.

Snake Bites

The chances of seeing a snake in Morocco, let alone being bitten by one, are slim. Nevertheless, there are a few venomous species, such as the horned viper, found in the southern desert areas. Snakes like to bask on rocks and sand, retreating during the heat of the day.

Prevention Do not walk barefoot or stick your hand into holes or cracks.

Treatment If bitten, do not panic. Half of those bitten by venomous snakes are not actually injected with venom (envenomed). Immobilise the bitten limb with a splint (eg a stick) and apply a bandage over the site, with firm pressure, similar to applying a bandage over a sprain. Do not apply a tourniquet, or cut or suck the bite. Get to medical help as soon as possible so that antivenom can be given if necessary.

Women's Health

Tampons can be hard to buy in Morocco. Carrefour is the only dependable supermarket to stock them, and even then offers limited choice. Reusable menstruation products are even harder to find – if you use one, bring it with you. Sanitary pads are readily available in pharmacies, which are abundant in all Moroccan towns and cities. Do not flush tampons or pads down the toilet, as the plumbing can't cope.

Language

The official language in Morocco is Arabic, which is used throughout the country. Tamazight/Berber is spoken in the Rif and Atlas Mountains. Most Berbers or Amazigh also speak at least some Arabic. French is still regularly used in the cities, but much less so among rural Amazighs.

MOROCCAN ARABIC

Moroccan Arabic (Darija) is a descendant both classical and Modern Standard Arabic (MSA) that has undergone a lot of linguistic change due to the free borrowing and loan blends from several languages, especially Frehnch. This is the everyday spoken language you'll hear when in Morocco.

All publications and signs, however, are written in MSA, which is the common written form in all Arabic-speaking countries. Note though that in Morocco, standard Western numeric symbols are used rather than those normally used in Arabic.

In this language guide we've represented the Arabic phrases with the Roman alphabet using a simplified pronunciation system. The vowels are:

a	as in 'had'
aa	like the 'a' in 'father'
ai	as in 'aisle'
ay	as in 'day'
e	as in 'bet'
ee	as in 'beer', only softer
i	as in 'hit'
o	as in 'note'
oo	as in 'food'
ow	as in 'how'
u	as in 'put'

WANT MORE?

For in-depth language information and handy phrases, check out Lonely Planet's *Moroccan Arabic Phrasebook*. You'll find it at **shop.lonelyplanet.com**, or you can buy Lonely Planet's iPhone phrasebooks at the Apple App Store.

Note that when double consonants occur in the pronunciation guides, each consonant is pronounced. For example, hammam (bath) is pronounced 'ham-mam'. The apostrophe (') represents the glottal stop (like the closing of the throat before saying 'Oh-oh!'). Other consonant sounds to keep in mind are:

dh	like the 'th' in 'this'
gh	a throaty sound like the French 'r'
h	a strongly whispered 'h'
kh	as the 'ch' in the Scottish loch
q	a strong, throaty 'k' sound

Basics

When addressing a man, the polite term more or less equivalent to 'Mr' is aseedee (shortened to see before a name); for women it's lalla, followed by the first name. To attract the attention of someone in the street or a waiter in a cafe, the word shreef is used.

The abbreviations 'm/f/pl' (male/female/plural) are used where applicable.

Hi.	labaas (informal) bikheer (response)
Hello.	assalaamu alaykum (polite) wa alaykum ssalaam (response)
Goodbye.	bsslaama/ma'a ssalaam
Please.	'afak/'afaki/'afakum (said to m/f/pl)
Thank you.	shukran
You're welcome.	la shukran 'ala waajib
Excuse me.	smeh/semhee/semhu leeya
Yes./No.	eeyeh/la
How are you?	ash khbaarek?
Fine, thank you.	bekheer, lhamdoo llaah

What's your name?	asmeetek?
My name is ...	smeetee ...
Do you speak English?	wash kat'ref negleezeeya?
I don't understand.	mafhemtsh

Accommodation

Where is a ...?	feen kayn ...?
campsite	shee mukheyyem
hotel	shee ootayl
youth hostel	daar shshabab

Is there a room available?
wash kayn shee beet khaweeya?

Can I see the room?
wash yemkenlee nshoof lbeet?

How much is a room for one day?
bash hal kayn gbayt l wahed nhar?

I'd like a room ...	bgheet shee beet ...
for one person	dyal wahed
for two people	dyal jooj
with a bathroom	belhammam

air-conditioning	klimatizur/mukayyif
bed	namooseeya
blanket	bttaaneeya
hot water	lma skhoon
key	saroot
sheet	eezar
shower	doosh
toilet	beet lma

Directions

Where is the ...?
feen kayn ...?

What is the address?
ashnoo hoowa l'unwan?

Please write down the address.
kteb l'unwan 'afek

Please show me on the map.
werri liya men l kharita 'afak

How far?
bshhal b'ayd?

Go straight ahead.
seer neeshan

Turn ...	dor ...
at the corner	felqent
at the traffic lights	fedo elhmer
left/right	'al leeser/leemen

Question Words – Arabic

How?	keefash?
What?	ash?
When?	eemta?
Where?	feen?
Which?	ashmen?
Who?	shkoon?
Why?	'lash?

behind	men lluur
here	hna
next to	hda
opposite	'eks
there	temma

north	shamel
south	janoob
east	sherq
west	gherb

Eating & Drinking

A table for..., please.
tabla dyal ... 'afak

Can I see the menu, please?
naqdar na'raf lmaakla lli 'andkum?

What do you recommend?
shnoo tansahni nakul?

I'll try what she/he is having.
gha nzharrab shnoo kaatakul hiyya/huwwa

I'm a vegetarian.
makanakoolsh llehem

I'd like something to drink.
bgheet shi haazha nashrubha

Please bring me ...	llaa ykhalleek zheeb li ...
a beer	birra
a glass/bottle of red/white/ rose wine	kaas/qar'a dyal hmar/byad/ roozi shshrab
a napkin	mandeel
some bread	shwiyya dyaal lkhoobz
some pepper	shwiyya dyaal lebzaar
some salt	shwiyya dyaal lmelha
some water	shwiyya dyaal lmaa

I didn't order this.	tlabtsh had shshi
Without ..., please.	bla ... 'afak
This is excellent!	had shshi ldeed bezzef!
Cheers!	bsaha!
The bill, please.	lahsaab, 'afak

Meat & Fish

anchovies	shton
beef	baqree
camel	lehem jemil
chicken	farooj/dujaj
cod	lamoori
fish	hut
kidneys	kelawwi
lamb	lehem ghenmee
liver	kebda
lobster	laangos
meat	lehem
sardines	serdeen
shrimp	qaimroon
sole	sol
tuna	ton
whiting	merla

Fruit & Vegetables

apple	teffah
apricot	meshmash
artichoke	qooq
aubergine	lbdanzhaal
banana	banan/moz
cucumber	khiyaar
dates	tmer
figs	kermoos
fruit	fakiya
garlic	tooma
grapes	'eineb
green beans	loobeeya
lentils	'aads
lettuce	khess
mushroom	fegg'a
olives	zeetoun
onion	besla
orange	limoon
peas	zelbana bisila
pomegranate	reman
potatoes	batatas
tomato	mataisha tamatim
vegetables	khoodar
watermelon	dellah
white beans	fasooliya

Other

bread	khoobz
butter	zebda
cheese	fromaj/jiben
chips	ships
eggs	bayd
oil	zit
pepper	filfil/lebzaar
salt	melha
soup	shorba
sugar	sukur
yoghurt	zabadee/laban/danoon

Emergencies

Help!	'teqnee!
Help me, please!	'awennee 'afak!
Go away!	seer fhalek!
I'm lost.	tweddert
Thief!	sheffar!
I've been robbed.	tsreqt
Call the police!	'ayyet 'la lbùlees!
Call a doctor!	'ayyet 'la shee tbeeb!
There's been an accident!	uq'at kseeda!
Where's the toilet?	feen kayn lbeet lma?

Numbers – Arabic

1	wahed
2	jooj
3	tlata
4	reb'a
5	khamsa
6	setta
7	seb'a
8	tmenya
9	tes'ood
10	'ashra
20	'ashreen
30	tlateen
40	reb'een
50	khamseen
60	setteen
70	seb'een
80	tmaneen
90	tes'een
100	mya
200	myatayn
1000	alf
2000	alfayn

I'm sick.	ana mreed
It hurts here.	kaydernee henna
I'm allergic to (penicillin).	'andee lhsaseeya m'a (lbeenseleen)

Shopping & Services

Where is the ...?	feen kayn ...?
bank	shee baanka
barber	shee hellaq
chemist/pharmacy	farmasyan
... embassy	ssifaara dyal ...
market	souk
police station	lkoomeesareeya
post office	lboostaa
restaurant	ristura/mat'am
souvenir shop	baazaar
travel agency	wekaalet el aasfaar

I want to change ...	bgheet nserref ...
some money	shee floos
travellers cheques	shek seeyahee

I'd like to buy ...	bgheet nshree ...
I'm only looking.	gheer kanshoof
Can I look at it?	wakhkha nshoofha?
I don't like it.	ma'jebatneesh
How much is it?	bshhal?
That's very expensive.	ghalee bezzaf
Can I pay by credit card?	wash nkder nkhelles bel kart kredee?

big	kabeer
small	sagheer
open	mehlool
closed	masdood

Time & Dates

What time is it?	shal fessa'a?

yesterday	lbareh
today	lyoom
tomorrow	ghedda

morning	fessbah
afternoon	fel'sheeya
evening	'sheeya

day	nhar
week	l'usbu'
month	shshhar
year	l'am

early/late	bekree/m'ettel
quickly/slowly	dgheeya/beshweeya

Monday	nhar letneen
Tuesday	nhar ttlat
Wednesday	nhar larb'
Thursday	nhar lekhmees
Friday	nhar jjem'a
Saturday	nhar ssebt
Sunday	nhar lhedd

January	yanaayir
February	fibraayir
March	maaris
April	abreel
May	maayu
June	yunyu
July	yulyu
August	aghustus/ghusht
September	sibtimbir/shebtenber
October	uktoobir
November	nufimbir/nu'enbir
December	disimbir/dijenbir

Transport

Public Transport

When does the ... leave/arrive?	wufuqash kaykhrej/kaywsul ...?
boat	lbaboor
city/intercity bus	ttubees/lkar
train	tran
plane	ttayyyaara

I'd like a ... ticket.	'afak bgheet wahed lwarka l ddar lbayda ...
return	bash nemshee oo njee
1st/2nd class	ddaraja lloola/ttaneeya

Where is the ...?	feen kayn ...?
airport	mataar
bus station	mhetta dyal ttobeesat
bus stop	blasa dyal ttobeesat
ticket office	maktab lwerqa
train station	lagaar

What's the fare?
shhal taman lwarka?

Please tell me when we get to ...
'afak eela wselna l ... goolhaleeya

I want to pay for one place only.
bgheet nkhelles blaasaawaheda

Stop here, please.
wqef henna 'afak

Please wait for me.
tsennanee 'afak

Driving & Cycling

Where can I hire a ...?	feen yimkin li nkri ...?
bicycle	bshklit
camel	jmel
car	tumubeel
donkey	hmar
horse	'awd

Can I park here?
wash nqder nwakef hna?

How long can I park here?
sh-hal men waket neqder nstatiun hna?

How do I get to ...?
keefesh ghaadee nuwsul l ...?

Where's the next petrol station?
fin kayna shi bumba dyal lisans griba?

I'd like ... litres.
bgheet ... itru 'afak

Please check the oil/water.
'afak shuf zzit/lma

We need a mechanic.
khesna wahed lmikanisyan

The car has broken down at ...
tumubeel khasra f ...

I have a flat tyre.
'ndi pyasa fruida

TAMAZIGHT LANGUAGE

There are three main dialects among Tamazight speakers, which in a certain sense also serve as loose lines of ethnic demarcation.

In the north, in the area centred on the Rif, the locals speak a dialect that has been called Riffian and is spoken as far south as Figuig on the Algerian border. The dialect that predominates in the Middle and High Atlas and the valleys leading into the Sahara goes by various names, including Berber or Tamazight.

More settled tribes of the High Atlas, Anti Atlas, Souss Valley and southwestern oases generally speak Tashelhit or Chleuh, also referred to as Tassousit. The following phrases are a selection from the Tashelhit dialect, the one visitors are likely to find most useful.

Basics

Hello.	la bes darik/darim (m/f)
Hello. (response)	la bes
Goodbye.	akayaoon arbee
See you later.	akranwes daghr
Please.	barakalaufik
Thank you.	barakalaufik
Yes.	yah
No.	oho
Excuse me.	samhiy
How are you?	meneek antgeet?
Fine, thank you.	la bes, lhamdulah
Good.	eefulkee/eeshwa
Bad.	(khaib) eeghshne

Practicalities

food	teeremt
mule	aserdon
somewhere to sleep	kra lblast mahengane
water	arman
Is there ...?	ees eela ...?
Do you have ...?	ees daroon ...?
How much is it?	minshk aysker?
Give me ...	fky ...
I want ...	reegh ...
a little/lot	eemeek/bzef
no good	oor eefulkee
too expensive	eeghla
I want to go to ...	addowghs ...
Where is (the) ...?	mani gheela ...?
Is it near/far?	ees eeqareb/yagoog?
straight	neeshan
to the left	fozelmad
to the right	fofasee
mountain	adrar
river	aseef
the pass	tizee
village	doorwar
yesterday	eedgam
today	(zig sbah) rass
tomorrow	(ghasad) aska

GLOSSARY

This glossary is a list of Arabic (A), French (F), Spanish (S) and Tamazight (T) terms that are used throughout this guide. For a list of trekking terms, see p59.

agadir (T) – fortified communal granary
'ain (A) – water source, spring
aït (T) – family (of), often precedes tribal and town names
Alawite – hereditary dynasty that has ruled Morocco since the late 17th century
Allah (A) – God
Almohads – puritanical Muslim group (1147–1269), originally Berber, that arose in response to the corrupt Almoravid dynasty
Almoravids – Muslim group (1054–1147) that ruled Spain and the Maghreb
Amazighs (or Berbers) – indigenous inhabitants of North Africa

bab (A) – gate
babouches (F) – traditional leather slippers
banu (A) – see *beni*
baraka (A) – divine blessing or favour
Barbary – European term used to describe the North African coast from the 16th to the 19th centuries
ben (A) – (or *ibn*) son of
beni (A) – 'sons of', often precedes tribal name (also *banu*)
Berbers (or Amazighs) – indigenous inhabitants of North Africa
borj (A) – fort (literally 'tower')
brigade touristique (F) – tourist police
bureau des guides (F) – guides' office

caid/caliph – town official
calèche – horse-drawn carriage
calle (S) – street
camionette (F) – minivan or pick-up truck
capitol – main temple of Roman town, usually situated in the forum
caravanserai – large merchants' inn enclosing a courtyard, providing accommodation and a marketplace (see also *funduq*)
chergui (A) – dry, easterly desert wind
Compagnie de Transports Marocaine – CTM; national bus company
corniche (F) – coastal road
corsair – 18th-century pirate based at Salé

dar (A) – traditional town house with internal courtyard
Délégation Régionale du Tourisme – tourist office; see also ONMT
derb (A) – lane or narrow street
djemaa (A) – Friday mosque (also *jami'*, *jemaa* and *jamaa*)
douar (A) – generally used for 'village' in the High Atlas

Eaux et Forêts – government ministry responsible for national parks
eid (A) – religious festival or national holiday
Ensemble Artisanal – government handicraft shop
erg (A) – sand dunes

fantasia (S) – military exercise featuring a cavalry charge often seen at culture events
faux guides (F) – unofficial or informal guides
foum (A) – usually the mouth of a river or valley (from Arabic for 'mouth')
funduq (A) – *caravanserai* (often used to mean 'hotel')

gardiens de voitures (F) – car-park attendants
gare routière (F) – bus station
gîte, gîte d'étape (F) – trekkers' hostel, sometimes a homestay
Gnaoua – bluesy Moroccan musical form that began with freed enslaved people in Marrakesh and Essaouira
grand taxi (F) – (long-distance) shared taxi

haj (A) – pilgrimage to Mecca, hence *haji* or *hajia*, a male or female who has made the pilgrimage
halqa (A) – street theatre
hammada (A) – stony desert
hammam (A) – Turkish-style bathhouse with sauna and massage
hanbel (A) – see *kilim*
haram (A) – literally 'forbidden', the word is sometimes used to denote a sacred or forbidden area, such as the prayer room of a mosque
Hejira – flight of the Prophet from Mecca to Medina in AD 622; the first year of the Islamic calendar

ibn (A) – son of (see also *ben*)
Idrissids – Moroccan dynasty that established a stable state in northern Morocco in the 9th century
iftar (A) – breaking of the fast at sundown during Ramadan; breakfast (also *ftur*)
imam (A) – Muslim cleric
Interzone – name coined by author William Burroughs for the period 1923–56, when Tangier was controlled by nine countries

jebel (A) – hill, mountain (sometimes *djebel* in former French possessions)
jedid (A) – new (sometimes spelled *jdid*)
jellaba (A) – popular flowing garment; men's *jellabas* are usually made from cotton or wool, while women's come in light synthetic fabrics

kasbah (A) – fort, citadel; often also the administrative centre (also *qasba*)
kif (A) – marijuana
kilim (A) – flat-woven blankets or floor coverings (also *hanbel*)
koubba (A) – sanctuary or shrine (see also *marabout*)
ksar (A) – fort or fortified stronghold (plural *ksour*)

mâalem – master artisan
Maghreb (A) – (literally 'west') area covered by Morocco, Algeria, Tunisia and Libya
maison d'hôte (F) – guesthouse, often a restored traditional Moroccan house

majoun (A) – sticky paste made of crushed seeds of the marijuana plant
marabout – holy man or saint; also often used to describe the mausoleums of these men
mechouar (A) – royal assembly place
medersa (A) – college for teaching theology, law, Arabic literature and grammar (also called *madrassa*)
medina (A) – old city; used to describe the old Arab parts of modern towns and cities
mellah (A) – Jewish quarter of the medina
Merenids (A) – Moroccan dynasty (1269–1465), responsible for the construction of many of Morocco's *medersas*
mihrab (A) – prayer niche in the wall of a mosque indicating the direction of Mecca (the *qibla*)
minbar (A) – pulpit in mosque; the *imam* delivers the sermon from one of the lower steps because the Prophet preached from the top step
moulay (A) – ruler
Mouloud – Islamic festival celebrating the birth of the Prophet
moussem (A) – pilgrimage to *marabout* tomb; festival in honour of a *marabout*
muezzin (A) – mosque official who sings the call to prayer from the minaret
muqarna (A) – decorative plasterwork
musée (F) – museum

ONMT – Office National Marocain du Tourisme, national tourist body, sometimes called Délégation Régionale du Tourisme
ordinaire (F) – less comfortable train, slightly slower than a *rapide*
oued (A) – river or stream, including dry riverbeds (sometimes *wad* or *wadi*)
oulad (A) – sons (of), often precedes tribal or town name

palmeraie (F) – palm grove
pastilla – a rich, savoury-sweet chicken or pigeon pie made with fine pastry; a dish of layered pastry with cinnamon and almonds served as dessert at banquets
pasha – high official in Ottoman Empire (also *pacha*)
pensióne (S) – guesthouse
petit taxi (F) – local taxi
pisé (F) – building material made of sundried clay or mud
piste (F) – unsealed tracks, often requiring 4WD vehicles
place (F) – square, plaza
plage (F) – beach
plazas de soberanía (S) – 'Places of sovereignty', the name given to the Spanish possessions in North Africa
Prophet (Mohammed), the – founder of Islam, who lived between AD 570 and AD 632

qissaria (A) – covered market sometimes forming the commercial centre of a medina
Quran – sacred book of Islam

Ramadan (A) – ninth month of the Muslim year, a period of fasting
rapide (F) – type of train more comfortable and slightly faster than an *ordinaire*
refuge (F) – mountain hut, basic hikers' shelter
riad (A) – traditional town house set around an internal garden
ribat (A) – combined monastery and fort

Saadians – Moroccan dynasty that ruled in the 16th century
sharia (A) – street
sherif (A) – descendant of the Prophet
Shiites – one of two main Islamic sects, formed by those who believed the true *imams* were descended from the Prophet's son-in-law Ali (see also *Sunnis*)
sidi (A) – honorific (equivalent to 'Mr'; also *si*)
souq (A) – market
Sufism – mystical strand of Islam that emphasises communion with Allah through inner attitude
Sunnis – one of two main Islamic sects, derived from followers of the Umayyadcaliphate (see also *Shiites*)
Syndicat d'Initiative (F) – government-run tourist office

tabac (F) – tobacconist and newsagency
tadelakt (A) – waterproof lime plaster mixed with pigments and polished with a stone to give it a smooth, lustrous finish, originally used for the walls of *hammams* but now a favourite of interior designers
tariq (A) – road, avenue
téléboutique (F) – privately operated telephone service
tizi (T) – mountain pass
Tuareg – nomadic Berbers of the Sahara, also known as the Blue Men because of their indigo-dyed robes

ville nouvelle (F) – new city; town built by the French alongside existing towns
vizier – another term for a provincial governor in the Ottoman Empire, or adviser to the sultan in Morocco

zawiya (A) – religious fraternity based around a *marabout*; location of the fraternity (also *zaouia*)
zellij (A) – ceramic

Behind the Scenes

SEND US YOUR FEEDBACK

We love to hear from travellers – your comments keep us on our toes and help make our books better. Our well-travelled team reads every word on what you loved or loathed about this book. Although we cannot reply individually to your submissions, we always guarantee that your feedback goes straight to the appropriate authors, in time for the next edition. Each person who sends us information is thanked in the next edition – the most useful submissions are rewarded with a selection of digital PDF chapters.

Visit **lonelyplanet.com/contact** to submit your updates and suggestions or to ask for help. Our award-winning website also features inspirational travel stories, news and discussions.

Note: We may edit, reproduce and incorporate your comments in Lonely Planet products such as guidebooks, websites and digital products, so let us know if you don't want your comments reproduced or your name acknowledged. For a copy of our privacy policy visit lonelyplanet.com/privacy.

OUR READERS

Many thanks to the travellers who used the last edition and wrote to us with helpful hints, useful advice and interesting anecdotes: Claire Washington, David Adair, Davide Mantiero, Dawn Smith, Donnie Ebbs, Elke Ganter, Esin Namer, Frank Schoenhoeffer, Gianpiero Caltagirone, Grethe Hoel, Johan Bos, Johanna Köllner, Jon Giddings, Jonathan Gelfand, Jürgen Husch, Kari Brawn, Kendra Litke, Linde Barrera, Marion Doise, Mizio Matteucci, Nancy Matela, Oujil Achraf, Sara Braden, Tom Denman, Will Goddard, Yaqin Wang

WRITER THANKS

Stephen Lioy

Many thanks to: Lauren for the trust; Niko, Cynthia and Joao for the inspiration; Brahim and Hamid for the experience; Alannah, Amanda, Debbie and John for the mountain company; all the Amazigh of the High Atlas for the many teas and talks along the way; and Gulmira and Gerda, as ever, for putting up with long absences in the name of work and adventure. One of these days I'm going to hire you two as my assistants.

Joel Balsam

Forever thanks to my partner, Stephanie Foden, for coming along with me on this hectic yet rewarding adventure – one of many. Team Lee. I'd also like to thank Carrie Rohrer, Mey Zniber, Abdeslam Mouden, Rhani Abdelghani, Yassine Bernaoui and Rachel Pearsey for their help with last-minute clarifications. And thanks to brothers Ossama and Tarek for arriving out of nowhere when we were stranded in the rain and driving us to Al Hoceima. Much appreciated.

Stephanie d'Arc Taylor

Didier and Caroline in Agadir; Sophie, Veronica and Larby in Tamraght; Mohammed and sweet family in Oumesnate; Aby in Tiznit; Lilith, Justus, Hassan and Hussein in Mirleft; Nico and Martina in Dakhla. Silke and Javid for graciously hosting me in Rabat. My LP family: Lauren Keith, Rebecca Milner, Vicky Smith, Elly Jones. My actual family: Xtine, John, Cathy. My chosen family: Maya, Alice, A&E, Loveday.

Sarah Gilbert

A thousand and one thanks to everyone who was so kind, hospitable and generous with their time on my travels around Morocco. Particular thanks go to Emma Wilson in Essaouira, Michele Reeves in Marrakesh, Emily Burrows in Zagora, Kamil Sellami and Lahbib El Moumni, both in Casablanca, Jan Godfrey in Salé, Caroline Vanthuyne in Asilah, Abdellah Hajja in M'Hamid and my Fassi friend Amine Sebbane.

Zora O'Neill

A big thank you from the heart to Mrs Bennett, the MDG, Paul Clammer, Robyn Kerrison, the lovely Rachida, Heather Harris, David Amster, Helen Ranger, and Hanae, who will be a star someday.

Lorna Parkes

A massive *shukran* to the welcoming people of Marrakesh, the shop owners who asked after my family, the local women who led me by the hand when I got lost, and the expats who joined me for city updates over mint tea. Particular thanks goes to Mohamed Nour and Mandy Sinclair for being generous with their time, and to my family back home – especially Rob – who held the fort while I was away.

Helen Ranger

Rediscovering the rural Middle Atlas with its small towns and glorious countryside has been delightful. Special thanks to drivers Nabil Ben Hssin and Hamid El Bouzidi. Specialist guide Saleh Boudaoud in Ifrane National Park provided invaluable help and information on the flora and fauna. For company on the road, I thank Rose Button, Mike Richardson, Pauline Möller and James Kindell. And at last I got to meet fellow writer Zora O'Neill in Fez.

ACKNOWLEDGEMENTS

Climate map data adapted from Peel MC, Finlayson BL & McMahon TA (2007) 'Updated World Map of the Köppen-Geiger Climate Classification', *Hydrology and Earth System Sciences*, 11, 1633–44.

Cover photograph: Aït Ben Haddou; Jan Wlodarczyk/Alamy Stock Photo ©

This Book

This 13th edition of Lonely Planet's *Morocco* guidebook was researched and written by Stephen Lioy, Joel Balsam, Stephanie d'Arc Taylor, Sarah Gilbert, Zora O'Neill, Lorna Parkes and Helen Ranger. The previous edition was written by Jessica Lee, Brett Atkinson, Paul Clammer, Virginia Maxwell, Lorna and Regis St Louis. This guidebook was produced by the following:

Destination Editor Lauren Keith

Senior Product Editors Elizabeth Jones, Fergus O'Shea, Victoria Smith

Regional Senior Cartographer Valentina Kremenchutskaya

Product Editors Ronan Abayawickrema, Carolyn Boicos, Anne Hayden

Book Designers Lauren Egan, Michael Weldon

Assisting Editors Judith Bamber, Melanie Dankel, Christopher Pitts, Sarah Stewart, Sam Wheeler

Cartographer Rachel Imeson

Cover Researcher Naomi Parker

Thanks to Daniel Bolger, Taoufik El Ayachi, Victoria Harrison, Karen Henderson, Sandie Kestell, Amy Lynch, Charlotte Orr, Genna Patterson, Martine Power, Kirsten Rawlings, Claire Rourke, Kathryn Rowan, Angela Tinson

Index

Map Pages **000**
Photo Pages **000**

Map Pages **000**
Photo Pages **000**

N

O

P

Map Pages **000**
Photo Pages **000**

Map Legend

Sights

- Beach
- Bird Sanctuary
- Buddhist
- Castle/Palace
- Christian
- Confucian
- Hindu
- Islamic
- Jain
- Jewish
- Monument
- Museum/Gallery/Historic Building
- Ruin
- Shinto
- Sikh
- Taoist
- Winery/Vineyard
- Zoo/Wildlife Sanctuary
- Other Sight

Activities, Courses & Tours

- Bodysurfing
- Diving
- Canoeing/Kayaking
- Course/Tour
- Sento Hot Baths/Onsen
- Skiing
- Snorkelling
- Surfing
- Swimming/Pool
- Walking
- Windsurfing
- Other Activity

Sleeping

- Sleeping
- Camping
- Hut/Shelter

Eating

- Eating

Drinking & Nightlife

- Drinking & Nightlife
- Cafe

Entertainment

- Entertainment

Shopping

- Shopping

Information

- Bank
- Embassy/Consulate
- Hospital/Medical
- Internet
- Police
- Post Office
- Telephone
- Toilet
- Tourist Information
- Other Information

Geographic

- Beach
- Gate
- Hut/Shelter
- Lighthouse
- Lookout
- Mountain/Volcano
- Oasis
- Park
- Pass
- Picnic Area
- Waterfall

Population

- Capital (National)
- Capital (State/Province)
- City/Large Town
- Town/Village

Transport

- Airport
- Border crossing
- Bus
- Cable car/Funicular
- Cycling
- Ferry
- Metro station
- Monorail
- Parking
- Petrol station
- Subway station
- Taxi
- Train station/Railway
- Tram
- Underground station
- Other Transport

Routes

- Tollway
- Freeway
- Primary
- Secondary
- Tertiary
- Lane
- Unsealed road
- Road under construction
- Plaza/Mall
- Steps
- Tunnel
- Pedestrian overpass
- Walking Tour
- Walking Tour detour
- Path/Walking Trail

Boundaries

- International
- State/Province
- Disputed
- Regional/Suburb
- Marine Park
- Cliff
- Wall

Hydrography

- River, Creek
- Intermittent River
- Canal
- Water
- Dry/Salt/Intermittent Lake
- Reef

Areas

- Airport/Runway
- Beach/Desert
- Cemetery (Christian)
- Cemetery (Other)
- Glacier
- Mudflat
- Park/Forest
- Sight (Building)
- Sportsground
- Swamp/Mangrove

Note: Not all symbols displayed above appear on the maps in this book

Sarah Gilbert
Central Morocco, Northern Atlantic Coast Sarah is an award-winning, globe-trotting freelance writer and photographer. Based in London – occasionally – she writes about everything from sustainable tourism, wildlife and conservation to art and culture and food and drink for numerous magazines, newspapers and websites. Since 2014, she has covered a host of diverse destinations for Lonely Planet, including Morocco, Puerto Rico, Switzerland, Thailand, Bolivia and Uruguay. Sarah has travelled to 75 countries and counting, and feels equally at home in a city guesthouse, remote safari lodge or a wooden hut in the Amazon rainforest. Sarah also wrote the Plan Your Trip, Understand and Survival Guide chapters.

Zora O'Neill
Fez, Meknes & the Middle Atlas Zora visited Morocco for the first time in 2000, 28 years after her mother named her for a friend in Tangier. A writer for Lonely Planet since 2005, she is also the author of *All Strangers Are Kin*, a travel memoir about studying Arabic across the Middle East and in Morocco. She lives in Queens, New York, where she hears Arabic spoken every day. Find out more at zoraoneill.com.

Lorna Parkes
Marrakesh A Londoner by birth, Melburnian by palate and an ex-Lonely Planet staffer in both cities, Lorna has contributed to numerous Lonely Planet books and magazines. She's discovered she writes best on planes, and is most content when researching food and booze. Wineries and the tropics (not at the same time!) are her go-to happy places, but Yorkshire will always be special to her. Follow her at @Lorna_Explorer. Lorna also contributed to the Directory chapter.

Helen Ranger
Fez, Meknes & the Middle Atlas Although born in the UK, Helen left in her early 20s to explore other shores. Cape Town became her home for many years – there's something about that mountain that's magnetic. Swapping 34 degrees south for 34 degrees north 15 years ago, Helen now lives in the medieval medina of Fez in Morocco, where she restored a traditional courtyard house. When not researching for Lonely Planet, Helen runs a bespoke travel consultancy in Morocco and translates art books from French to English. Travelling and writing are passions. For Lonely Planet, she concentrates on African destinations, contributing to books about Morocco and Fez, South Africa and Cape Town, Equatorial Guinea, Gabon and Madagascar. All things food-related are another passion and she enjoys contributing to Lonely Planet books on food and wine.

OUR STORY

A beat-up old car, a few dollars in the pocket and a sense of adventure. In 1972 that's all Tony and Maureen Wheeler needed for the trip of a lifetime – across Europe and Asia overland to Australia. It took several months, and at the end – broke but inspired – they sat at their kitchen table writing and stapling together their first travel guide, *Across Asia on the Cheap*. Within a week they'd sold 1500 copies. Lonely Planet was born.

Today, Lonely Planet has offices in Tennessee, Dublin and Beijing, with a network of over 2000 contributors in every corner of the globe. We share Tony's belief that 'a great guidebook should do three things: inform, educate and amuse'.

OUR WRITERS

Stephen Lioy

Central Morocco Stephen is a photographer, writer, hiker and travel blogger based in Central Asia. A 'once in a lifetime' Euro trip and post-university move to China set the stage for what would eventually become a semi-nomadic lifestyle based on sharing his experiences with would-be travellers and helping provide that initial push out of comfort zones and into all that the planet has to offer. When Stephen isn't at home in Kyrgyzstan, he can usually be found leading very large tour groups of very small children through all the favourite capital cities of the world or, in between work periods, out in the mountains sleeping in a tent and eating the sort of things your stomach warns you about. Follow Stephen's travels at www.monkboughtlunch.com and see his photography at www.stephenlioy.com. Stephen also wrote the Trekking in Morocco chapter.

Joel Balsam

Mediterranean Coast & the Rif Mountains Who's the man behind the flower beard? Joel is a Canadian freelance journalist, backpacker and nomad who has been travelling the world pretty much non-stop since 2015 (50 countries and counting). His work has appeared in *National Geographic Travel, Time,* the *Guardian, Travel + Leisure, ESPN* and *Vice*. For Lonely Planet, he's worked on two guidebooks so far: *Georgia, Armenia and Azerbaijan* and *Morocco*. Travel writing has always been a dream for Joel, well, since becoming an NHL goalie didn't work out (he's Canadian after all). His favourite moments out there in the world occur when he's hopping around from food stand to food cart in a busy market, trying whatever he can get his hands on. If he has one goal, it's to show people that there's so much more to life than their own little neighbourhood or city.

Stephanie d'Arc Taylor

Southern Morocco & Western Sahara A native Angeleno, Stephanie grew up with the west LA weekend ritual of going for Iranian sweets after ten zaru soba in Little Osaka. Later, she quit her PhD to move to Beirut and become a writer. Since then, Stephanie has published work with the *New York Times*, the *Guardian, Roads & Kingdoms*, and *Kinfolk* magazine (among others), and co-founded Jaleesa, a venture-capital-funded social-impact business in Beirut. She was lucky enough to become a Lonely Planet writer in 2018, and to have the opportunity to see whether it's possible to drink too many coconuts in the Caribbean. There is proof on Instagram @zerodarctaylor.

OVER PAGE MORE WRITERS

Published by Lonely Planet Global Limited
CRN 554153
13th edition – September 2021
ISBN 9781787015920

10 9 8 7 6 5 4 3 2 1
Printed in China